T0301288

QUANTITATIVE INVESTMENT ANALYSIS

CFA Institute is the premier association for investment professionals around the world, with over 160,000 members in 165 countries and territories. Since 1963 the organization has developed and administered the renowned Chartered Financial Analyst® Program. With a rich history of leading the investment profession, CFA Institute has set the highest standards in ethics, education, and professional excellence within the global investment community and is the foremost authority on investment profession conduct and practice. Each book in the CFA Institute Investment Series is geared toward industry practitioners along with graduate-level finance students and covers the most important topics in the industry. The authors of these cutting-edge books are themselves industry professionals and academics and bring their wealth of knowledge and expertise to this series.

QUANTITATIVE INVESTMENT ANALYSIS

Fourth Edition

Richard A. DeFusco, CFA

Dennis W. McLeavey, CFA

Jerald E. Pinto, CFA

David E. Runkle, CFA

WILEY

Cover image: © r.nagy/Shutterstock
Cover design: Wiley

Copyright © 2004, 2007, 2015 by CFA Institute. All rights reserved.

Published by John Wiley & Sons, Inc., Hoboken, New Jersey.
Published simultaneously in Canada.

No part of this publication may be reproduced, stored in a retrieval system, or transmitted in any form or by any means, electronic, mechanical, photocopying, recording, scanning, or otherwise, except as permitted under Section 107 or 108 of the 1976 United States Copyright Act, without either the prior written permission of the Publisher, or authorization through payment of the appropriate per-copy fee to the Copyright Clearance Center, Inc., 222 Rosewood Drive, Danvers, MA 01923, (978) 750-8400, fax (978) 646-8600, or on the Web at www.copyright. com. Requests to the Publisher for permission should be addressed to the Permissions Department, John Wiley & Sons, Inc., 111 River Street, Hoboken, NJ 07030, (201) 748-6011, fax (201) 748-6008, or online at http://www. wiley.com/go/permissions.

Limit of Liability/Disclaimer of Warranty: While the publisher and author have used their best efforts in preparing this book, they make no representations or warranties with respect to the accuracy or completeness of the contents of this book and specifically disclaim any implied warranties of merchantability or fitness for a particular purpose. No warranty may be created or extended by sales representatives or written sales materials. The advice and strategies contained herein may not be suitable for your situation. You should consult with a professional where appropriate. Neither the publisher nor author shall be liable for any loss of profit or any other commercial damages, including but not limited to special, incidental, consequential, or other damages.

For general information on our other products and services or for technical support, please contact our Customer Care Department within the United States at (800) 762-2974, outside the United States at (317) 572-3993, or fax (317) 572-4002.

Wiley publishes in a variety of print and electronic formats and by print-on-demand. Some material included with standard print versions of this book may not be included in e-books or in print-on-demand. If this book refers to media such as a CD or DVD that is not included in the version you purchased, you may download this material at http://booksupport.wiley.com. For more information about Wiley products, visit www.wiley.com.

ISBN 978-1-119-74362-0 (Hardcover)
ISBN 978-1-119-74365-1 (ePDF)
ISBN 978-1-119-74364-4 (ePub)

Printed in the United States of America.
SKY10029847_091521

CONTENTS

CHAPTER 2
Organizing, Visualizing, and Describing Data

CHAPTER 10
Machine Learning

PREFACE

We are pleased to bring you *Quantitative Investment Analysis, Fourth Edition*, which focuses on key tools that are needed for today's professional investor. In addition to classic areas such as the time value of money and probability and statistics, the text covers advanced concepts in regression, time series, machine learning, and big data projects. The text teaches critical skills that challenge many professionals, and shows how these techniques can be applied to areas such as factor modeling, risk management, and backtesting and simulation.

The content was developed in partnership by a team of distinguished academics and practitioners, chosen for their acknowledged expertise in the field, and guided by CFA Institute. It is written specifically with the investment practitioner in mind and is replete with examples and practice problems that reinforce the learning outcomes and demonstrate real-world applicability.

The CFA Program Curriculum, from which the content of this book was drawn, is subjected to a rigorous review process to assure that it is:

- Faithful to the findings of our ongoing industry practice analysis
- Valuable to members, employers, and investors
- Globally relevant
- Generalist (as opposed to specialist) in nature
- Replete with sufficient examples and practice opportunities
- Pedagogically sound

The accompanying workbook is a useful reference that provides Learning Outcome Statements that describe exactly what readers will learn and be able to demonstrate after mastering the accompanying material. Additionally, the workbook has summary overviews and practice problems for each chapter.

We are confident that you will find this and other books in the CFA Institute Investment Series helpful in your efforts to grow your investment knowledge, whether you are a relatively new entrant or an experienced veteran striving to keep up to date in the ever-changing market environment. CFA Institute, as a long-term committed participant in the investment profession and a not-for-profit global membership association, is pleased to provide you with this opportunity.

ACKNOWLEDGMENTS

Special thanks to all the reviewers, advisors, and question writers who helped to ensure high practical relevance, technical correctness, and understandability of the material presented here.

We would like to thank the many others who played a role in the conception and production of this book: the Curriculum and Learning Experience team at CFA Institute, with special thanks to the curriculum directors, past and present, who worked with the authors and reviewers to produce the chapters in this book; the Practice Analysis team at CFA Institute; and the Publishing and Technology team for bringing this book to production.

ABOUT THE CFA INSTITUTE INVESTMENT SERIES

CFA Institute is pleased to provide the CFA Institute Investment Series, which covers major areas in the field of investments. We provide this best-in-class series for the same reason we have been chartering investment professionals for more than 45 years: to lead the investment profession globally by setting the highest standards of ethics, education, and professional excellence.

The books in the CFA Institute Investment Series contain practical, globally relevant material. They are intended both for those contemplating entry into the extremely competitive field of investment management as well as for those seeking a means of keeping their knowledge fresh and up to date. This series was designed to be user friendly and highly relevant.

We hope you find this series helpful in your efforts to grow your investment knowledge, whether you are a relatively new entrant or an experienced veteran ethically bound to keep up to date in the ever-changing market environment. As a long-term, committed participant in the investment profession and a not-for-profit global membership association, CFA Institute is pleased to provide you with this opportunity.

THE TEXTS

Corporate Finance: A Practical Approach is a solid foundation for those looking to achieve lasting business growth. In today's competitive business environment, companies must find innovative ways to enable rapid and sustainable growth. This text equips readers with the foundational knowledge and tools for making smart business decisions and formulating strategies to maximize company value. It covers everything from managing relationships between stakeholders to evaluating merger and acquisition bids, as well as the companies behind them. Through extensive use of real-world examples, readers will gain critical perspective into interpreting corporate financial data, evaluating projects, and allocating funds in ways that increase corporate value. Readers will gain insights into the tools and strategies used in modern corporate financial management.

Equity Asset Valuation is a particularly cogent and important resource for anyone involved in estimating the value of securities and understanding security pricing. A well-informed professional knows that the common forms of equity valuation—dividend discount modeling, free cash flow modeling, price/earnings modeling, and residual income modeling—can all be reconciled with one another under certain assumptions. With a deep understanding of the underlying assumptions, the professional investor can better understand what other investors assume when calculating their valuation estimates. This text has a global orientation, including emerging markets.

Fixed Income Analysis has been at the forefront of new concepts in recent years, and this particular text offers some of the most recent material for the seasoned professional who is not a fixed-income specialist. The application of option and derivative technology to the once staid province of fixed income has helped contribute to an explosion of thought in this area. Professionals have been challenged to stay up to speed with credit derivatives, swaptions, collateralized mortgage securities, mortgage-backed securities, and other vehicles, and this explosion of products has strained the world's financial markets and tested central banks to provide sufficient oversight. Armed with a thorough grasp of the new exposures, the professional investor is much better able to anticipate and understand the challenges our central bankers and markets face.

International Financial Statement Analysis is designed to address the ever-increasing need for investment professionals and students to think about financial statement analysis from a global perspective. The text is a practically oriented introduction to financial statement analysis that is distinguished by its combination of a true international orientation, a structured presentation style, and abundant illustrations and tools covering concepts as they are introduced in the text. The authors cover this discipline comprehensively and with an eye to ensuring the reader's success at all levels in the complex world of financial statement analysis.

Investments: Principles of Portfolio and Equity Analysis provides an accessible yet rigorous introduction to portfolio and equity analysis. Portfolio planning and portfolio management are presented within a context of up-to-date, global coverage of security markets, trading, and market-related concepts and products. The essentials of equity analysis and valuation are explained in detail and profusely illustrated. The book includes coverage of practitioner-important but often neglected topics, such as industry analysis. Throughout, the focus is on the practical application of key concepts with examples drawn from both emerging and developed markets. Each chapter affords the reader many opportunities to self-check his or her understanding of topics.

All books in the CFA Institute Investment Series are available through all major booksellers. And, all titles are available on the Wiley Custom Select platform at http://customselect. wiley.com/ where individual chapters for all the books may be mixed and matched to create custom textbooks for the classroom.

CHAPTER 1

THE TIME VALUE OF MONEY

Richard A. DeFusco, PhD, CFA
Dennis W. McLeavey, DBA, CFA
Jerald E. Pinto, PhD, CFA
David E. Runkle, PhD, CFA

LEARNING OUTCOMES

The candidate should be able to:

- interpret interest rates as required rates of return, discount rates, or opportunity costs;
- explain an interest rate as the sum of a real risk-free rate and premiums that compensate investors for bearing distinct types of risk;
- calculate and interpret the effective annual rate, given the stated annual interest rate and the frequency of compounding;
- solve time value of money problems for different frequencies of compounding;
- calculate and interpret the future value (FV) and present value (PV) of a single sum of money, an ordinary annuity, an annuity due, a perpetuity (PV only), and a series of unequal cash flows;
- demonstrate the use of a time line in modeling and solving time value of money problems.

1. INTRODUCTION

As individuals, we often face decisions that involve saving money for a future use, or borrowing money for current consumption. We then need to determine the amount we need to invest, if we are saving, or the cost of borrowing, if we are shopping for a loan. As investment analysts, much of our work also involves evaluating transactions with present and future cash flows. When we place a value on any security, for example, we are attempting to determine the worth of a stream of future cash flows. To carry out all the above tasks

---

Quantitative Methods for Investment Analysis, Second Edition, by Richard A. DeFusco, PhD, CFA, Dennis W. McLeavey, DBA, CFA, Jerald E. Pinto, PhD, CFA, David E. Runkle, PhD, CFA. Copyright © 2019 by CFA Institute.

accurately, we must understand the mathematics of time value of money problems. Money has time value in that individuals value a given amount of money more highly the earlier it is received. Therefore, a smaller amount of money now may be equivalent in value to a larger amount received at a future date. The **time value of money** as a topic in investment mathematics deals with equivalence relationships between cash flows with different dates. Mastery of time value of money concepts and techniques is essential for investment analysts.

The chapter[1] is organized as follows: Section 2 introduces some terminology used throughout the chapter and supplies some economic intuition for the variables we will discuss. Section 3 tackles the problem of determining the worth at a future point in time of an amount invested today. Section 4 addresses the future worth of a series of cash flows. These two sections provide the tools for calculating the equivalent value at a future date of a single cash flow or series of cash flows. Sections 5 and 6 discuss the equivalent value today of a single future cash flow and a series of future cash flows, respectively. In Section 7, we explore how to determine other quantities of interest in time value of money problems.

2. INTEREST RATES: INTERPRETATION

In this chapter, we will continually refer to interest rates. In some cases, we assume a particular value for the interest rate; in other cases, the interest rate will be the unknown quantity we seek to determine. Before turning to the mechanics of time value of money problems, we must illustrate the underlying economic concepts. In this section, we briefly explain the meaning and interpretation of interest rates.

Time value of money concerns equivalence relationships between cash flows occurring on different dates. The idea of equivalence relationships is relatively simple. Consider the following exchange: You pay $10,000 today and in return receive $9,500 today. Would you accept this arrangement? Not likely. But what if you received the $9,500 today and paid the $10,000 one year from now? Can these amounts be considered equivalent? Possibly, because a payment of $10,000 a year from now would probably be worth less to you than a payment of $10,000 today. It would be fair, therefore, to **discount** the $10,000 received in one year; that is, to cut its value based on how much time passes before the money is paid. An **interest rate**, denoted r, is a rate of return that reflects the relationship between differently dated cash flows. If $9,500 today and $10,000 in one year are equivalent in value, then $10,000 − $9,500 = $500 is the required compensation for receiving $10,000 in one year rather than now. The interest rate—the required compensation stated as a rate of return—is $500/ $9,500 = 0.0526 or 5.26 percent.

Interest rates can be thought of in three ways. First, they can be considered required rates of return—that is, the minimum rate of return an investor must receive in order to accept the investment. Second, interest rates can be considered discount rates. In the example above, 5.26 percent is that rate at which we discounted the $10,000 future amount to find its value today. Thus, we use the terms "interest rate" and "discount rate" almost interchangeably. Third, interest rates can be considered opportunity costs. An **opportunity cost** is the value that investors forgo by choosing a particular course of action. In the example, if the party who supplied $9,500 had instead decided to spend it today, he would have forgone earning

---

[1]Examples in this, and other chapters, in the text were updated by Professor Sanjiv Sabherwal of the University of Texas, Arlington.

5.26 percent on the money. So we can view 5.26 percent as the opportunity cost of current consumption.

Economics tells us that interest rates are set in the marketplace by the forces of supply and demand, where investors are suppliers of funds and borrowers are demanders of funds. Taking the perspective of investors in analyzing market-determined interest rates, we can view an interest rate r as being composed of a real risk-free interest rate plus a set of four premiums that are required returns or compensation for bearing distinct types of risk:

r = Real risk-free interest rate + Inflation premium + Default risk premium + Liquidity premium + Maturity premium

- The **real risk-free interest rate** is the single-period interest rate for a completely risk-free security if no inflation were expected. In economic theory, the real risk-free rate reflects the time preferences of individuals for current versus future real consumption.
- The **inflation premium** compensates investors for expected inflation and reflects the average inflation rate expected over the maturity of the debt. Inflation reduces the purchasing power of a unit of currency—the amount of goods and services one can buy with it. The sum of the real risk-free interest rate and the inflation premium is the **nominal risk-free interest rate**.[2] Many countries have governmental short-term debt whose interest rate can be considered to represent the nominal risk-free interest rate in that country. The interest rate on a 90-day US Treasury bill (T-bill), for example, represents the nominal risk-free interest rate over that time horizon.[3] US T-bills can be bought and sold in large quantities with minimal transaction costs and are backed by the full faith and credit of the US government.
- The **default risk premium** compensates investors for the possibility that the borrower will fail to make a promised payment at the contracted time and in the contracted amount.
- The **liquidity premium** compensates investors for the risk of loss relative to an investment's fair value if the investment needs to be converted to cash quickly. US T-bills, for example, do not bear a liquidity premium because large amounts can be bought and sold without affecting their market price. Many bonds of small issuers, by contrast, trade infrequently after they are issued; the interest rate on such bonds includes a liquidity premium reflecting the relatively high costs (including the impact on price) of selling a position.
- The **maturity premium** compensates investors for the increased sensitivity of the market value of debt to a change in market interest rates as maturity is extended, in general (holding all else equal). The difference between the interest rate on longer-maturity, liquid Treasury debt and that on short-term Treasury debt reflects a positive maturity premium for the longer-term debt (and possibly different inflation premiums as well).

---

[2]Technically, 1 plus the nominal rate equals the product of 1 plus the real rate and 1 plus the inflation rate. As a quick approximation, however, the nominal rate is equal to the real rate plus an inflation premium. In this discussion we focus on approximate additive relationships to highlight the underlying concepts.

[3]Other developed countries issue securities similar to US Treasury bills. The French government issues BTFs or negotiable fixed-rate discount Treasury bills (*Bons du Trésor àtaux fixe et à intérêts précomptés*) with maturities of up to one year. The Japanese government issues a short-term Treasury bill with maturities of 6 and 12 months. The German government issues at discount both Treasury financing paper (*Finanzierungsschätze des Bundes* or, for short, *Schätze*) and Treasury discount paper (*Bubills*) with maturities up to 24 months. In the United Kingdom, the British government issues gilt-edged Treasury bills with maturities ranging from 1 to 364 days. The Canadian government bond market is closely related to the US market; Canadian Treasury bills have maturities of 3, 6, and 12 months.

Using this insight into the economic meaning of interest rates, we now turn to a discussion of solving time value of money problems, starting with the future value of a single cash flow.

3. THE FUTURE VALUE OF A SINGLE CASH FLOW

In this section, we introduce time value associated with a single cash flow or lump-sum investment. We describe the relationship between an initial investment or **present value (PV)**, which earns a rate of return (the interest rate per period) denoted as r, and its **future value (FV)**, which will be received N years or periods from today.

The following example illustrates this concept. Suppose you invest $100 (PV = $100) in an interest-bearing bank account paying 5 percent annually. At the end of the first year, you will have the $100 plus the interest earned, $0.05 \times \$100 = \$5$, for a total of $105. To formalize this one-period example, we define the following terms:

PV = present value of the investment
FV_N = future value of the investment N periods from today
r = rate of interest per period

For $N = 1$, the expression for the future value of amount PV is

$$FV_1 = PV(1 + r) \tag{1}$$

For this example, we calculate the future value one year from today as $FV_1 = \$100(1.05) = \$105$.

Now suppose you decide to invest the initial $100 for two years with interest earned and credited to your account annually (annual compounding). At the end of the first year (the beginning of the second year), your account will have $105, which you will leave in the bank for another year. Thus, with a beginning amount of $105 (PV = $105), the amount at the end of the second year will be $105(1.05) = \$110.25$. Note that the $5.25 interest earned during the second year is 5 percent of the amount invested at the beginning of Year 2.

Another way to understand this example is to note that the amount invested at the beginning of Year 2 is composed of the original $100 that you invested plus the $5 interest earned during the first year. During the second year, the original principal again earns interest, as does the interest that was earned during Year 1. You can see how the original investment grows: The $5 interest that you earned each period on the $100 original investment is known as **simple interest** (the interest rate times the principal). **Principal** is the amount of funds originally

Original investment	$100.00
Interest for the first year ($100 × 0.05)	5.00
Interest for the second year based on original investment ($100 × 0.05)	5.00
Interest for the second year based on interest earned in the first year (0.05 × $5.00 interest on interest)	0.25
Total	$110.25

invested. During the two-year period, you earn $10 of simple interest. The extra $0.25 that you have at the end of Year 2 is the interest you earned on the Year 1 interest of $5 that you reinvested.

The interest earned on interest provides the first glimpse of the phenomenon known as **compounding**. Although the interest earned on the initial investment is important, for a given interest rate it is fixed in size from period to period. The compounded interest earned on reinvested interest is a far more powerful force because, for a given interest rate, it grows in size each period. The importance of compounding increases with the magnitude of the interest rate. For example, $100 invested today would be worth about $13,150 after 100 years if compounded annually at 5 percent, but worth more than $20 million if compounded annually over the same time period at a rate of 13 percent.

To verify the $20 million figure, we need a general formula to handle compounding for any number of periods. The following general formula relates the present value of an initial investment to its future value after N periods:

$$FV_N = PV(1 + r)^N \tag{2}$$

where r is the stated interest rate per period and N is the number of compounding periods. In the bank example, $FV_2 = \$100(1 + 0.05)^2 = \$110.25$. In the 13 percent investment example, $FV_{100} = \$100(1.13)^{100} = \$20,316,287.42$.

The most important point to remember about using the future value equation is that the stated interest rate, r, and the number of compounding periods, N, must be compatible. Both variables must be defined in the same time units. For example, if N is stated in months, then r should be the one-month interest rate, unannualized.

A time line helps us to keep track of the compatibility of time units and the interest rate per time period. In the time line, we use the time index t to represent a point in time a stated number of periods from today. Thus the present value is the amount available for investment today, indexed as $t = 0$. We can now refer to a time N periods from today as $t = N$. The time line in Figure 1 shows this relationship. In Figure 1, we have positioned the initial investment, PV, at $t = 0$. Using Equation 2, we move the present value, PV, forward to $t = N$ by the factor $(1 + r)^N$. This factor is called a future value factor. We denote the future value on the time line as FV and position it at $t = N$. Suppose the future value is to be received exactly 10 periods from today's date ($N = 10$). The present value, PV, and the future value, FV, are separated in time through the factor $(1 + r)^{10}$.

The fact that the present value and the future value are separated in time has important consequences:

FIGURE 1   The Relationship between an Initial Investment, PV, and Its Future Value, FV

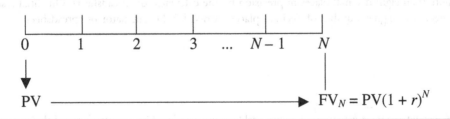

- We can add amounts of money only if they are indexed at the same point in time.
- For a given interest rate, the future value increases with the number of periods.
- For a given number of periods, the future value increases with the interest rate.

To better understand these concepts, consider three examples that illustrate how to apply the future value formula.

EXAMPLE 1   The Future Value of a Lump Sum with Interim Cash Reinvested at the Same Rate

You are the lucky winner of your state's lottery of $5 million after taxes. You invest your winnings in a five-year certificate of deposit (CD) at a local financial institution. The CD promises to pay 7 percent per year compounded annually. This institution also lets you reinvest the interest at that rate for the duration of the CD. How much will you have at the end of five years if your money remains invested at 7 percent for five years with no withdrawals?

Solution: To solve this problem, compute the future value of the $5 million investment using the following values in Equation 2:

$$PV = \$5,000,000$$
$$r = 7\% = 0.07$$
$$N = 5$$
$$FV_N = PV(1 + r)^N$$
$$= \$5,000,000(1.07)^5$$
$$= \$5,000,000(1.402552)$$
$$= \$7,012,758.65$$

At the end of five years, you will have $7,012,758.65 if your money remains invested at 7 percent with no withdrawals.

Note that in this and most examples in this chapter, the factors are reported at six decimal places but the calculations may actually reflect greater precision. For example, the reported 1.402552 has been rounded up from 1.40255173 (the calculation is actually carried out with more than eight decimal places of precision by the calculator or spreadsheet). Our final result reflects the higher number of decimal places carried by the calculator or spreadsheet.[4]

---

[4]We could also solve time value of money problems using tables of interest rate factors. Solutions using tabled values of interest rate factors are generally less accurate than solutions obtained using calculators or spreadsheets, so practitioners prefer calculators or spreadsheets.

EXAMPLE 2   The Future Value of a Lump Sum with No Interim Cash

An institution offers you the following terms for a contract: For an investment of ¥2,500,000, the institution promises to pay you a lump sum six years from now at an 8 percent annual interest rate. What future amount can you expect?

Solution: Use the following data in Equation 2 to find the future value:

$$PV = ¥2,500,000$$
$$r = 8\% = 0.08$$
$$N = 6$$
$$FV_N = PV(1 + r)^N$$
$$= ¥2,500,000(1.08)^6$$
$$= ¥2,500,000(1.586874)$$
$$= ¥3,967,186$$

You can expect to receive ¥3,967,186 six years from now.

Our third example is a more complicated future value problem that illustrates the importance of keeping track of actual calendar time.

EXAMPLE 3   The Future Value of a Lump Sum

A pension fund manager estimates that his corporate sponsor will make a $10 million contribution five years from now. The rate of return on plan assets has been estimated at 9 percent per year. The pension fund manager wants to calculate the future value of this contribution 15 years from now, which is the date at which the funds will be distributed to retirees. What is that future value?

Solution: By positioning the initial investment, PV, at $t = 5$, we can calculate the future value of the contribution using the following data in Equation 2:

$$PV = \$10 \text{ million}$$
$$r = 9\% = 0.09$$
$$N = 10$$
$$FV_N = PV(1 + r)^N$$
$$= \$10,000,000(1.09)^{10}$$
$$= \$10,000,000(2.367364)$$
$$= \$23,673,636.75$$

This problem looks much like the previous two, but it differs in one important respect: its timing. From the standpoint of today ($t = 0$), the future amount of $23,673,636.75 is 15 years into the future. Although the future value is 10 years from

FIGURE 2   The Future Value of a Lump Sum, Initial Investment Not at $t = 0$

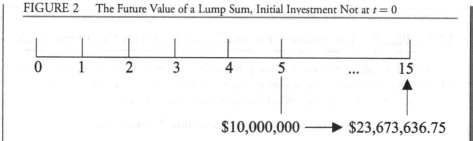

its present value, the present value of $10 million will not be received for another five years.

As Figure 2 shows, we have followed the convention of indexing today as $t = 0$ and indexing subsequent times by adding 1 for each period. The additional contribution of $10 million is to be received in five years, so it is indexed as $t = 5$ and appears as such in the figure. The future value of the investment in 10 years is then indexed at $t = 15$; that is, 10 years following the receipt of the $10 million contribution at $t = 5$. Time lines like this one can be extremely useful when dealing with more-complicated problems, especially those involving more than one cash flow.

In a later section of this chapter, we will discuss how to calculate the value today of the $10 million to be received five years from now. For the moment, we can use Equation 2. Suppose the pension fund manager in **Example 3** above were to receive $6,499,313.86 today from the corporate sponsor. How much will that sum be worth at the end of five years? How much will it be worth at the end of 15 years?

$$PV = \$6,499,313.86$$
$$r = 9\% = 0.09$$
$$N = 5$$
$$FV_N = PV(1 + r)^N$$
$$= \$6,499,313.86(1.09)^5$$
$$= \$6,499,313.86(1.538624)$$
$$= \$10,000,000 \text{ at the five-year mark}$$

and

$$PV = \$6,499,313.86$$
$$r = 9\% = 0.09$$
$$N = 15$$

$$FV_N = PV(1 + r)^N$$
$$= \$6,499,313.86(1.09)^{15}$$
$$= \$6,499,313.86(3.642482)$$
$$= \$23,673,636.74 \text{ at the 15-year mark}$$

These results show that today's present value of about $6.5 million becomes $10 million after five years and $23.67 million after 15 years.

3.1. The Frequency of Compounding

In this section, we examine investments paying interest more than once a year. For instance, many banks offer a monthly interest rate that compounds 12 times a year. In such an arrangement, they pay interest on interest every month. Rather than quote the periodic monthly interest rate, financial institutions often quote an annual interest rate that we refer to as the **stated annual interest rate** or **quoted interest rate**. We denote the stated annual interest rate by r_s. For instance, your bank might state that a particular CD pays 8 percent compounded monthly. The stated annual interest rate equals the monthly interest rate multiplied by 12. In this example, the monthly interest rate is $0.08/12 = 0.0067$ or 0.67 percent.[5] This rate is strictly a quoting convention because $(1 + 0.0067)^{12} = 1.083$, not 1.08; the term $(1 + r_s)$ is not meant to be a future value factor when compounding is more frequent than annual.

With more than one compounding period per year, the future value formula can be expressed as

$$FV_N = PV\left(1 + \frac{r_s}{m}\right)^{mN} \tag{3}$$

where r_s is the stated annual interest rate, m is the number of compounding periods per year, and N now stands for the number of years. Note the compatibility here between the interest rate used, r_s/m, and the number of compounding periods, mN. The periodic rate, r_s/m, is the stated annual interest rate divided by the number of compounding periods per year. The number of compounding periods, mN, is the number of compounding periods in one year multiplied by the number of years. The periodic rate, r_s/m, and the number of compounding periods, mN, must be compatible.

EXAMPLE 4   The Future Value of a Lump Sum with Quarterly Compounding

Continuing with the CD example, suppose your bank offers you a CD with a two-year maturity, a stated annual interest rate of 8 percent compounded quarterly, and a feature

---

[5]To avoid rounding errors when using a financial calculator, divide 8 by 12 and then press the %*i* key, rather than simply entering 0.67 for %*i*, so we have $(1 + 0.08/12)^{12} = 1.083000$.

allowing reinvestment of the interest at the same interest rate. You decide to invest $10,000. What will the CD be worth at maturity?

Solution: Compute the future value with Equation 3 as follows:

$$PV = \$10,000$$
$$r_s = 8\% = 0.08$$
$$m = 4$$
$$r_s/m = 0.08/4 = 0.02$$
$$N = 2$$
$$mN = 4(2) = 8 \text{ interest periods}$$
$$FV_N = PV\left(1 + \frac{r_s}{m}\right)^{mN}$$
$$= \$10,000(1.02)^8$$
$$= \$10,000(1.171659)$$
$$= \$11,716.59$$

At maturity, the CD will be worth $11,716.59.

The future value formula in Equation 3 does not differ from the one in Equation 2. Simply keep in mind that the interest rate to use is the rate per period and the exponent is the number of interest, or compounding, periods.

EXAMPLE 5   The Future Value of a Lump Sum with Monthly Compounding

An Australian bank offers to pay you 6 percent compounded monthly. You decide to invest A$1 million for one year. What is the future value of your investment if interest payments are reinvested at 6 percent?

Solution: Use Equation 3 to find the future value of the one-year investment as follows:

$$PV = A\$1,000,000$$
$$r_s = 6\% = 0.06$$
$$m = 12$$
$$r_s/m = 0.06/12 = 0.0050$$
$$N = 1$$
$$mN = 12(1) = 12 \text{ interest periods}$$
$$FV_N = PV\left(1 + \frac{r_s}{m}\right)^{mN}$$
$$= A\$1,000,000(1.005)^{12}$$

$$= \text{A\$1,000,000}(1.061678)$$
$$= \text{A\$1,061,677.81}$$

If you had been paid 6 percent with annual compounding, the future amount would be only A\$1,000,000(1.06) = A\$1,060,000 instead of A\$1,061,677.81 with monthly compounding.

3.2. Continuous Compounding

The preceding discussion on compounding periods illustrates discrete compounding, which credits interest after a discrete amount of time has elapsed. If the number of compounding periods per year becomes infinite, then interest is said to compound continuously. If we want to use the future value formula with continuous compounding, we need to find the limiting value of the future value factor for $m \rightarrow \infty$ (infinitely many compounding periods per year) in Equation 3. The expression for the future value of a sum in N years with continuous compounding is

$$\text{FV}_N = \text{PV}e^{r_s N} \tag{4}$$

The term $e^{r_s N}$ is the transcendental number $e \approx 2.7182818$ raised to the power $r_s N$. Most financial calculators have the function e^x.

EXAMPLE 6   The Future Value of a Lump Sum with Continuous Compounding

---

Suppose a \$10,000 investment will earn 8 percent compounded continuously for two years. We can compute the future value with Equation 4 as follows:

$$\text{PV} = \$10,000$$
$$r_s = 8\% = 0.08$$
$$N = 2$$
$$\text{FV}_N = \text{PV}e^{r_s N}$$
$$= \$10,000e^{0.08(2)}$$
$$= \$10,000(1.173511)$$
$$= \$11,735.11$$

With the same interest rate but using continuous compounding, the \$10,000 investment will grow to \$11,735.11 in two years, compared with \$11,716.59 using quarterly compounding as shown in **Example 4**.

TABLE 1   The Effect of Compounding Frequency on Future Value

Frequency	r_s/m	mN	Future Value of $1
Annual	8%/1 = 8%	1 × 1 = 1	$1.00(1.08) = $1.08
Semiannual	8%/2 = 4%	2 × 1 = 2	$1.00(1.04)^2 = $1.081600
Quarterly	8%/4 = 2%	4 × 1 = 4	$1.00(1.02)^4 = $1.082432
Monthly	8%/12 = 0.6667%	12 × 1 = 12	$1.00(1.006667)^{12} = $1.083000
Daily	8%/365 = 0.0219%	365 × 1 = 365	$1.00(1.000219)^{365} = $1.083278
Continuous			$1.00e^{0.08(1)} = $1.083287

Table 1 shows how a stated annual interest rate of 8 percent generates different ending dollar amounts with annual, semiannual, quarterly, monthly, daily, and continuous compounding for an initial investment of $1 (carried out to six decimal places).

As Table 1 shows, all six cases have the same stated annual interest rate of 8 percent; they have different ending dollar amounts, however, because of differences in the frequency of compounding. With annual compounding, the ending amount is $1.08. More frequent compounding results in larger ending amounts. The ending dollar amount with continuous compounding is the maximum amount that can be earned with a stated annual rate of 8 percent.

Table 1 also shows that a $1 investment earning 8.16 percent compounded annually grows to the same future value at the end of one year as a $1 investment earning 8 percent compounded semiannually. This result leads us to a distinction between the stated annual interest rate and the **effective annual rate** (EAR).[6] For an 8 percent stated annual interest rate with semiannual compounding, the EAR is 8.16 percent.

3.3. Stated and Effective Rates

The stated annual interest rate does not give a future value directly, so we need a formula for the EAR. With an annual interest rate of 8 percent compounded semiannually, we receive a periodic rate of 4 percent. During the course of a year, an investment of $1 would grow to $1(1.04)^2 = $1.0816, as illustrated in Table 1. The interest earned on the $1 investment is $0.0816 and represents an effective annual rate of interest of 8.16 percent. The effective annual rate is calculated as follows:

$$EAR = (1 + \text{Periodic interest rate})^m - 1 \tag{5}$$

[6]Among the terms used for the effective annual return on interest-bearing bank deposits are annual percentage yield (APY) in the United States and equivalent annual rate (EAR) in the United Kingdom. By contrast, the **annual percentage rate** (APR) measures the cost of borrowing expressed as a yearly rate. In the United States, the APR is calculated as a periodic rate times the number of payment periods per year and, as a result, some writers use APR as a general synonym for the stated annual interest rate. Nevertheless, APR is a term with legal connotations; its calculation follows regulatory standards that vary internationally. Therefore, "stated annual interest rate" is the preferred general term for an annual interest rate that does not account for compounding within the year.

The periodic interest rate is the stated annual interest rate divided by m, where m is the number of compounding periods in one year. Using our previous example, we can solve for EAR as follows: $(1.04)^2 - 1 = 8.16$ percent.

The concept of EAR extends to continuous compounding. Suppose we have a rate of 8 percent compounded continuously. We can find the EAR in the same way as above by finding the appropriate future value factor. In this case, a \$1 investment would grow to $\$1e^{0.08(1.0)} = \$1.0833$. The interest earned for one year represents an effective annual rate of 8.33 percent and is larger than the 8.16 percent EAR with semiannual compounding because interest is compounded more frequently. With continuous compounding, we can solve for the effective annual rate as follows:

$$\text{EAR} = e^{r_s} - 1 \tag{6}$$

We can reverse the formulas for EAR with discrete and continuous compounding to find a periodic rate that corresponds to a particular effective annual rate. Suppose we want to find the appropriate periodic rate for a given effective annual rate of 8.16 percent with semiannual compounding. We can use Equation 5 to find the periodic rate:

$$0.0816 = (1 + \text{Periodic rate})^2 - 1$$
$$1.0816 = (1 + \text{Periodic rate})^2$$
$$(1.0816)^{1/2} - 1 = \text{Periodic rate}$$
$$(1.04) - 1 = \text{Periodic rate}$$
$$4\% = \text{Periodic rate}$$

To calculate the continuously compounded rate (the stated annual interest rate with continuous compounding) corresponding to an effective annual rate of 8.33 percent, we find the interest rate that satisfies Equation 6:

$$0.0833 = e^{r_s} - 1$$
$$1.0833 = e^{r_s}$$

To solve this equation, we take the natural logarithm of both sides. (Recall that the natural log of e^{r_s} is $\ln e^{r_s} = r_s$.) Therefore, $\ln 1.0833 = r_s$, resulting in $r_s = 8$ percent. We see that a stated annual rate of 8 percent with continuous compounding is equivalent to an EAR of 8.33 percent.

4. THE FUTURE VALUE OF A SERIES OF CASH FLOWS

In this section, we consider series of cash flows, both even and uneven. We begin with a list of terms commonly used when valuing cash flows that are distributed over many time periods.

- An **annuity** is a finite set of level sequential cash flows.
- An **ordinary annuity** has a first cash flow that occurs one period from now (indexed at $t = 1$).

- An **annuity due** has a first cash flow that occurs immediately (indexed at $t = 0$).
- A **perpetuity** is a perpetual annuity, or a set of level never-ending sequential cash flows, with the first cash flow occurring one period from now.

4.1. Equal Cash Flows—Ordinary Annuity

Consider an ordinary annuity paying 5 percent annually. Suppose we have five separate deposits of $1,000 occurring at equally spaced intervals of one year, with the first payment occurring at $t = 1$. Our goal is to find the future value of this ordinary annuity after the last deposit at $t = 5$. The increment in the time counter is one year, so the last payment occurs five years from now. As the time line in Figure 3 shows, we find the future value of each $1,000 deposit as of $t = 5$ with Equation 2, $FV_N = PV(1 + r)^N$. The arrows in Figure 3 extend from the payment date to $t = 5$. For instance, the first $1,000 deposit made at $t = 1$ will compound over four periods. Using Equation 2, we find that the future value of the first deposit at $t = 5$ is $1,000(1.05)^4 = \$1,215.51$. We calculate the future value of all other payments in a similar fashion. (Note that we are finding the future value at $t = 5$, so the last payment does not earn any interest.) With all values now at $t = 5$, we can add the future values to arrive at the future value of the annuity. This amount is $5,525.63.

We can arrive at a general annuity formula if we define the annuity amount as A, the number of time periods as N, and the interest rate per period as r. We can then define the future value as

$$FV_N = A[(1 + r)^{N-1} + (1 + r)^{N-2} + (1 + r)^{N-3} + \ldots + (1 + r)^1 + (1 + r)^0]$$

which simplifies to

$$FV_N = A\left[\frac{(1 + r)^N - 1}{r}\right] \qquad (7)$$

The term in brackets is the future value annuity factor. This factor gives the future value of an ordinary annuity of $1 per period. Multiplying the future value annuity factor by the annuity amount gives the future value of an ordinary annuity. For the ordinary annuity in Figure 3, we find the future value annuity factor from Equation 7 as

$$\left[\frac{(1.05)^5 - 1}{0.05}\right] = 5.525631$$

FIGURE 3   The Future Value of a Five-Year Ordinary Annuity

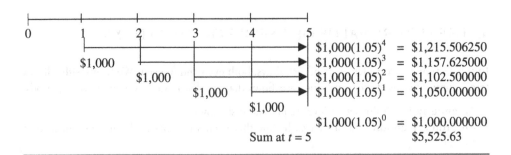

$$
\begin{array}{ll}
\$1,000(1.05)^4 & = \$1,215.506250 \\
\$1,000(1.05)^3 & = \$1,157.625000 \\
\$1,000(1.05)^2 & = \$1,102.500000 \\
\$1,000(1.05)^1 & = \$1,050.000000 \\
\\
\$1,000(1.05)^0 & = \$1,000.000000 \\
\text{Sum at } t = 5 & \quad\ \ \$5,525.63
\end{array}
$$

With an annuity amount $A = \$1,000$, the future value of the annuity is $\$1,000(5.525631) = \$5,525.63$, an amount that agrees with our earlier work.

The next example illustrates how to find the future value of an ordinary annuity using the formula in Equation 7.

EXAMPLE 7   The Future Value of an Annuity

Suppose your company's defined contribution retirement plan allows you to invest up to €20,000 per year. You plan to invest €20,000 per year in a stock index fund for the next 30 years. Historically, this fund has earned 9 percent per year on average. Assuming that you actually earn 9 percent a year, how much money will you have available for retirement after making the last payment?

Solution: Use Equation 7 to find the future amount:

$$A = €20,000$$
$$r = 9\% = 0.09$$
$$N = 30$$
$$\text{FV annuity factor} = \frac{(1+r)^N - 1}{r} = \frac{(1.09)^{30} - 1}{0.09} = 136.307539$$
$$\text{FV}_N = €20,000(136.307539)$$
$$= €2,726,150.77$$

Assuming the fund continues to earn an average of 9 percent per year, you will have €2,726,150.77 available at retirement.

4.2. Unequal Cash Flows

In many cases, cash flow streams are unequal, precluding the simple use of the future value annuity factor. For instance, an individual investor might have a savings plan that involves unequal cash payments depending on the month of the year or lower savings during a planned vacation. One can always find the future value of a series of unequal cash flows by compounding the cash flows one at a time. Suppose you have the five cash flows described in Table 2, indexed relative to the present ($t = 0$).

All of the payments shown in Table 2 are different. Therefore, the most direct approach to finding the future value at $t = 5$ is to compute the future value of each payment as of $t = 5$ and then sum the individual future values. The total future value at Year 5 equals $\$19,190.76$, as shown in the third column. Later in this chapter, you will learn shortcuts to take when the cash flows are close to even; these shortcuts will allow you to combine annuity and single-period calculations.

TABLE 2   A Series of Unequal Cash Flows and Their Future Values at 5 Percent

Time	Cash Flow ($)	Future Value at Year 5
$t = 1$	1,000	$\$1,000(1.05)^4 = \$1,215.51$
$t = 2$	2,000	$\$2,000(1.05)^3 = \$2,315.25$
$t = 3$	4,000	$\$4,000(1.05)^2 = \$4,410.00$
$t = 4$	5,000	$\$5,000(1.05)^1 = \$5,250.00$
$t = 5$	6,000	$\$6,000(1.05)^0 = \$6,000.00$
		Sum = $\$19,190.76$

5. THE PRESENT VALUE OF A SINGLE CASH FLOW

5.1. Finding the Present Value of a Single Cash Flow

Just as the future value factor links today's present value with tomorrow's future value, the present value factor allows us to discount future value to present value. For example, with a 5 percent interest rate generating a future payoff of $105 in one year, what current amount invested at 5 percent for one year will grow to $105? The answer is $100; therefore, $100 is the present value of $105 to be received in one year at a discount rate of 5 percent.

Given a future cash flow that is to be received in N periods and an interest rate per period of r, we can use the formula for future value to solve directly for the present value as follows:

$$FV_N = PV(1 + r)^N$$

$$PV = FV_N \left[\frac{1}{(1 + r)^N} \right]$$

$$PV = FV_N (1 + r)^{-N}$$

(8)

We see from Equation 8 that the present value factor, $(1 + r)^{-N}$, is the reciprocal of the future value factor, $(1 + r)^N$.

EXAMPLE 8   The Present Value of a Lump Sum

An insurance company has issued a Guaranteed Investment Contract (GIC) that promises to pay $100,000 in six years with an 8 percent return rate. What amount of money must the insurer invest today at 8 percent for six years to make the promised payment?

Solution: We can use Equation 8 to find the present value using the following data:

$$FV_N = \$100,000$$

$$r = 8\% = 0.08$$

$$N = 6$$

$$PV = FV_N(1 + r)^{-N}$$

$$= \$100,000\left[\frac{1}{(1.08)^6}\right]$$

$$= \$100,000(0.6301696)$$

$$= \$63,016.96$$

FIGURE 4   The Present Value of a Lump Sum to Be Received at Time $t = 6$

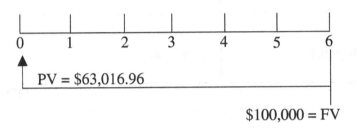

We can say that $63,016.96 today, with an interest rate of 8 percent, is equivalent to $100,000 to be received in six years. Discounting the $100,000 makes a future $100,000 equivalent to $63,016.96 when allowance is made for the time value of money. As the time line in Figure 4 shows, the $100,000 has been discounted six full periods.

EXAMPLE 9   The Projected Present Value of a More Distant Future Lump Sum

Suppose you own a liquid financial asset that will pay you $100,000 in 10 years from today. Your daughter plans to attend college four years from today, and you want to know what the asset's present value will be at that time. Given an 8 percent discount rate, what will the asset be worth four years from today?

Solution: The value of the asset is the present value of the asset's promised payment. At $t = 4$, the cash payment will be received six years later. With this information, you can solve for the value four years from today using Equation 8:

$$FV_N = \$100{,}000$$
$$r = 8\% = 0.08$$
$$N = 6$$
$$PV = FV_N(1 + r)^{-N}$$
$$= \$100{,}000\frac{1}{(1.08)^6}$$
$$= \$100{,}000(0.6301696)$$
$$= \$63{,}016.96$$

FIGURE 5   The Relationship between Present Value and Future Value

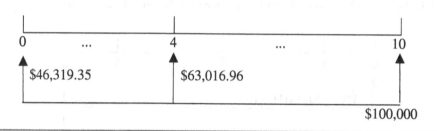

The time line in Figure 5 shows the future payment of \$100,000 that is to be received at $t = 10$. The time line also shows the values at $t = 4$ and at $t = 0$. Relative to the payment at $t = 10$, the amount at $t = 4$ is a projected present value, while the amount at $t = 0$ is the present value (as of today).

Present value problems require an evaluation of the present value factor, $(1 + r)^{-N}$. Present values relate to the discount rate and the number of periods in the following ways:

- For a given discount rate, the farther in the future the amount to be received, the smaller that amount's present value.
- Holding time constant, the larger the discount rate, the smaller the present value of a future amount.

5.2. The Frequency of Compounding

Recall that interest may be paid semiannually, quarterly, monthly, or even daily. To handle interest payments made more than once a year, we can modify the present value formula (Equation 8) as follows. Recall that r_s is the quoted interest rate and equals the periodic interest rate multiplied by the number of compounding periods in each year. In general, with more than one compounding period in a year, we can express the formula for present value as

$$PV = FV_N \left(1 + \frac{r_s}{m}\right)^{-mN}$$ (9)

where
   m = number of compounding periods per year
   r_s = quoted annual interest rate
   N = number of years

The formula in Equation 9 is quite similar to that in Equation 8. As we have already noted, present value and future value factors are reciprocals. Changing the frequency of compounding does not alter this result. The only difference is the use of the periodic interest rate and the corresponding number of compounding periods.

The following example illustrates Equation 9.

EXAMPLE 10   The Present Value of a Lump Sum with Monthly Compounding

The manager of a Canadian pension fund knows that the fund must make a lump-sum payment of C\$5 million 10 years from now. She wants to invest an amount today in a GIC so that it will grow to the required amount. The current interest rate on GICs is 6 percent a year, compounded monthly. How much should she invest today in the GIC?

Solution: Use Equation 9 to find the required present value:

$$FV_N = C\$5,000,000$$
$$r_s = 6\% = 0.06$$
$$m = 12$$
$$r_s/m = 0.06/12 = 0.005$$
$$N = 10$$
$$mN = 12(10) = 120$$
$$PV = FV_N \left(1 + \frac{r_s}{m}\right)^{-mN}$$
$$= C\$5,000,000(1.005)^{-120}$$
$$= C\$5,000,000(0.549633)$$
$$= C\$2,748,163.67$$

In applying Equation 9, we use the periodic rate (in this case, the monthly rate) and the appropriate number of periods with monthly compounding (in this case, 10 years of monthly compounding, or 120 periods).

---

6. THE PRESENT VALUE OF A SERIES OF CASH FLOWS

Many applications in investment management involve assets that offer a series of cash flows over time. The cash flows may be highly uneven, relatively even, or equal. They may occur over relatively short periods of time, longer periods of time, or even stretch on indefinitely. In this section, we discuss how to find the present value of a series of cash flows.

6.1. The Present Value of a Series of Equal Cash Flows

We begin with an ordinary annuity. Recall that an ordinary annuity has equal annuity payments, with the first payment starting one period into the future. In total, the annuity makes N payments, with the first payment at $t = 1$ and the last at $t = N$. We can express the present value of an ordinary annuity as the sum of the present values of each individual annuity payment, as follows:

$$PV = \frac{A}{(1+r)} + \frac{A}{(1+r)^2} + \frac{A}{(1+r)^3} + \ldots + \frac{A}{(1+r)^{N-1}} + \frac{A}{(1+r)^N} \qquad (10)$$

where
A = the annuity amount
r = the interest rate per period corresponding to the frequency of annuity payments (for example, annual, quarterly, or monthly)
N = the number of annuity payments

Because the annuity payment (A) is a constant in this equation, it can be factored out as a common term. Thus the sum of the interest factors has a shortcut expression:

$$PV = A \left[\frac{1 - \frac{1}{(1+r)^N}}{r} \right] \qquad (11)$$

In much the same way that we computed the future value of an ordinary annuity, we find the present value by multiplying the annuity amount by a present value annuity factor (the term in brackets in Equation 11).

EXAMPLE 11   The Present Value of an Ordinary Annuity

Suppose you are considering purchasing a financial asset that promises to pay €1,000 per year for five years, with the first payment one year from now. The required rate of return is 12 percent per year. How much should you pay for this asset?

Solution: To find the value of the financial asset, use the formula for the present value of an ordinary annuity given in Equation 11 with the following data:

$$A = €1,000$$
$$r = 12\% = 0.12$$
$$N = 5$$

$$PV = A\left[\frac{1-\frac{1}{(1+r)^N}}{r}\right]$$

$$= €1{,}000\left[\frac{1-\frac{1}{(1.12)^5}}{0.12}\right]$$

$$= €1{,}000(3.604776)$$
$$= €3{,}604.78$$

The series of cash flows of €1,000 per year for five years is currently worth €3,604.78 when discounted at 12 percent.

FIGURE 6   An Annuity Due of $100 per Period

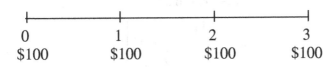

Keeping track of the actual calendar time brings us to a specific type of annuity with level payments: the annuity due. An annuity due has its first payment occurring today ($t = 0$). In total, the annuity due will make N payments. Figure 6 presents the time line for an annuity due that makes four payments of $100.

As Figure 6 shows, we can view the four-period annuity due as the sum of two parts: a $100 lump sum today and an ordinary annuity of $100 per period for three periods. At a 12 percent discount rate, the four $100 cash flows in this annuity due example will be worth $340.18.[7]

Expressing the value of the future series of cash flows in today's dollars gives us a convenient way of comparing annuities. The next example illustrates this approach.

EXAMPLE 12   An Annuity Due as the Present Value of an Immediate Cash Flow Plus an Ordinary Annuity

You are retiring today and must choose to take your retirement benefits either as a lump sum or as an annuity. Your company's benefits officer presents you with two

---

[7]There is an alternative way to calculate the present value of an annuity due. Compared to an ordinary annuity, the payments in an annuity due are each discounted one less period. Therefore, we can modify Equation 11 to handle annuities due by multiplying the right-hand side of the equation by $(1 + r)$:

$$PV(\text{Annuity due}) = A\{[1 - (1 + r)^{-N}]/r\}(1 + r)$$

alternatives: an immediate lump sum of $2 million or an annuity with 20 payments of $200,000 a year with the first payment starting today. The interest rate at your bank is 7 percent per year compounded annually. Which option has the greater present value? (Ignore any tax differences between the two options.)

Solution: To compare the two options, find the present value of each at time $t = 0$ and choose the one with the larger value. The first option's present value is $2 million, already expressed in today's dollars. The second option is an annuity due. Because the first payment occurs at $t = 0$, you can separate the annuity benefits into two pieces: an immediate $200,000 to be paid today ($t = 0$) and an ordinary annuity of $200,000 per year for 19 years. To value this option, you need to find the present value of the ordinary annuity using Equation 11 and then add $200,000 to it.

$$A = \$200,000$$
$$N = 19$$
$$r = 7\% = 0.07$$

$$PV = A \left[\frac{1 - \dfrac{1}{(1+r)^N}}{r} \right]$$

$$= \$200,000 \left[\frac{1 - \dfrac{1}{(1.07)^{19}}}{0.07} \right]$$

$$= \$200,000(10.335595)$$
$$= \$2,067,119.05$$

The 19 payments of $200,000 have a present value of $2,067,119.05. Adding the initial payment of $200,000 to $2,067,119.05, we find that the total value of the annuity option is $2,267,119.05. The present value of the annuity is greater than the lump sum alternative of $2 million.

We now look at another example reiterating the equivalence of present and future values.

EXAMPLE 13   The Projected Present Value of an Ordinary Annuity

A German pension fund manager anticipates that benefits of €1 million per year must be paid to retirees. Retirements will not occur until 10 years from now at time $t = 10$. Once benefits begin to be paid, they will extend until $t = 39$ for a total of 30 payments. What is the present value of the pension liability if the appropriate annual discount rate for plan liabilities is 5 percent compounded annually?

Solution: This problem involves an annuity with the first payment at $t = 10$. From the perspective of $t = 9$, we have an ordinary annuity with 30 payments. We can compute the present value of this annuity with Equation 11 and then look at it on a time line.

$$A = €1,000,000$$
$$r = 5\% = 0.05$$
$$N = 30$$

$$PV = A \left[\frac{1 - \frac{1}{(1+r)^N}}{r} \right]$$

$$= €1,000,000 \left[\frac{1 - \frac{1}{(1.05)^{30}}}{0.05} \right]$$

$$= €1,000,000(15.372451)$$
$$= €15,372,451.03$$

On the time line, we have shown the pension payments of €1 million extending from $t = 10$ to $t = 39$. The bracket and arrow indicate the process of finding the present value of the annuity, discounted back to $t = 9$. The present value of the pension benefits as of $t = 9$ is €15,372,451.03. The problem is to find the present value today (at $t = 0$).

Now we can rely on the equivalence of present value and future value. As Figure 7 shows, we can view the amount at $t = 9$ as a future value from the vantage point of $t = 0$. We compute the present value of the amount at $t = 9$ as follows:

$$FV_N = €15,372,451.03 \text{ (the present value at } t = 9\text{)}$$
$$N = 9$$
$$r = 5\% = 0.05$$
$$PV = FV_N(1 + r)^{-N}$$
$$= €15,372,451.03(1.05)^{-9}$$
$$= €15,372,451.03(0.644609)$$
$$= €9,909,219.00$$

The present value of the pension liability is €9,909,219.00.

FIGURE 7   The Present Value of an Ordinary Annuity with First Payment at Time $t = 10$ (in Millions)

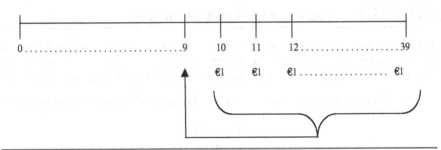

Example 13 illustrates three procedures emphasized in this chapter:

1. finding the present or future value of any cash flow series;
2. recognizing the equivalence of present value and appropriately discounted future value; and
3. keeping track of the actual calendar time in a problem involving the time value of money.

6.2. The Present Value of an Infinite Series of Equal Cash Flows—Perpetuity

Consider the case of an ordinary annuity that extends indefinitely. Such an ordinary annuity is called a perpetuity (a perpetual annuity). To derive a formula for the present value of a perpetuity, we can modify Equation 10 to account for an infinite series of cash flows:

$$PV = A \sum_{t=1}^{\infty} \left[\frac{1}{(1 + r)^t} \right] \tag{12}$$

As long as interest rates are positive, the sum of present value factors converges and

$$PV = \frac{A}{r} \tag{13}$$

To see this, look back at Equation 11, the expression for the present value of an ordinary annuity. As N (the number of periods in the annuity) goes to infinity, the term $1/(1 + r)^N$ approaches 0 and Equation 11 simplifies to Equation 13. This equation will reappear when we value dividends from stocks because stocks have no predefined life span. (A stock paying constant dividends is similar to a perpetuity.) With the first payment a year from now, a perpetuity of $10 per year with a 20 percent required rate of return has a present value of $10/0.2 = $50.

Equation 13 is valid only for a perpetuity with level payments. In our development above, the first payment occurred at $t = 1$; therefore, we compute the present value as of $t = 0$.

Other assets also come close to satisfying the assumptions of a perpetuity. Certain government bonds and preferred stocks are typical examples of financial assets that make level payments for an indefinite period of time.

EXAMPLE 14   The Present Value of a Perpetuity

The British government once issued a type of security called a consol bond, which promised to pay a level cash flow indefinitely. If a consol bond paid £100 per year in perpetuity, what would it be worth today if the required rate of return were 5 percent?

Solution: To answer this question, we can use Equation 13 with the following data:

$$A = £100$$
$$r = 5\% = 0.05$$
$$PV = A/r$$

$$= \text{£}100/0.05$$
$$= \text{£}2,000$$

The bond would be worth £2,000.

6.3. Present Values Indexed at Times Other than $t = 0$

In practice with investments, analysts frequently need to find present values indexed at times other than $t = 0$. Subscripting the present value and evaluating a perpetuity beginning with $100 payments in Year 2, we find $PV_1 = \$100/0.05 = \$2,000$ at a 5 percent discount rate. Further, we can calculate today's PV as $PV_0 = \$2,000/1.05 = \$1,904.76$.

Consider a similar situation in which cash flows of $6 per year begin at the end of the 4th year and continue at the end of each year thereafter, with the last cash flow at the end of the 10th year. From the perspective of the end of the third year, we are facing a typical seven-year ordinary annuity. We can find the present value of the annuity from the perspective of the end of the third year and then discount that present value back to the present. At an interest rate of 5 percent, the cash flows of $6 per year starting at the end of the fourth year will be worth $34.72 at the end of the third year ($t = 3$) and $29.99 today ($t = 0$).

The next example illustrates the important concept that an annuity or perpetuity beginning sometime in the future can be expressed in present value terms one period prior to the first payment. That present value can then be discounted back to today's present value.

EXAMPLE 15   The Present Value of a Projected Perpetuity

Consider a level perpetuity of £100 per year with its first payment beginning at $t = 5$. What is its present value today (at $t = 0$), given a 5 percent discount rate?

Solution: First, we find the present value of the perpetuity at $t = 4$ and then discount that amount back to $t = 0$. (Recall that a perpetuity or an ordinary annuity has its first payment one period away, explaining the $t = 4$ index for our present value calculation.)

i. Find the present value of the perpetuity at $t = 4$:

$$A = \text{£}100$$
$$r = 5\% = 0.05$$
$$PV = A/r$$
$$= \text{£}100/0.05$$
$$= \text{£}2,000$$

ii. Find the present value of the future amount at $t = 4$. From the perspective of $t = 0$, the present value of £2,000 can be considered a future value. Now we need to find the present value of a lump sum:

$$FV_N = £2,000 \text{ (the present value at } t = 4)$$
$$r = 5\% = 0.05$$
$$N = 4$$
$$PV = FV_N(1 + r)^{-N}$$
$$= £2,000(1.05)^{-4}$$
$$= £2,000(0.822702)$$
$$= £1,645.40$$

Today's present value of the perpetuity is £1,645.40.

As discussed earlier, an annuity is a series of payments of a fixed amount for a specified number of periods. Suppose we own a perpetuity. At the same time, we issue a perpetuity obligating us to make payments; these payments are the same size as those of the perpetuity we own. However, the first payment of the perpetuity we issue is at $t = 5$; payments then continue on forever. The payments on this second perpetuity exactly offset the payments received from the perpetuity we own at $t = 5$ and all subsequent dates. We are left with level nonzero net cash flows at $t = 1, 2, 3,$ and 4. This outcome exactly fits the definition of an annuity with four payments. Thus we can construct an annuity as the difference between two perpetuities with equal, level payments but differing starting dates. The next example illustrates this result.

EXAMPLE 16   The Present Value of an Ordinary Annuity as the Present Value of a Current Minus Projected Perpetuity

Given a 5 percent discount rate, find the present value of a four-year ordinary annuity of £100 per year starting in Year 1 as the difference between the following two level perpetuities:

Perpetuity 1   £100 per year starting in Year 1 (first payment at $t = 1$)
Perpetuity 2   £100 per year starting in Year 5 (first payment at $t = 5$)

Solution: If we subtract Perpetuity 2 from Perpetuity 1, we are left with an ordinary annuity of £100 per period for four years (payments at $t = 1, 2, 3, 4$). Subtracting the present value of Perpetuity 2 from that of Perpetuity 1, we arrive at the present value of the four-year ordinary annuity:

$$PV_0(\text{Perpetuity 1}) = £100/0.05 = £2,000$$
$$PV_4(\text{Perpetuity 2}) = £100/0.05 = £2,000$$
$$PV_0(\text{Perpetuity 2}) = £2,000/(1.05)^4 = £1,645.40$$
$$PV_0(\text{Annuity}) = PV_0(\text{Perpetuity 1}) - PV_0(\text{Perpetuity 2})$$
$$= £2,000 - £1,645.40$$
$$= £354.60$$

The four-year ordinary annuity's present value is equal to £2,000 − £1,645.40 = £354.60.

Solution to 2: In this case, we can speak of a positive compound rate of decrease or a negative compound growth rate. Using Equation 14, we find

$$g = \sqrt[5]{₩727.5/₩796.4} - 1$$
$$= \sqrt[5]{0.913486} - 1$$
$$= 0.982065 - 1$$
$$= -0.017935 \text{ or about } -1.8\%$$

In contrast to the positive sales growth, the rate of growth in net profit was approximately −1.8 percent during the 2012–2017 period.

EXAMPLE 18   Calculating a Growth Rate (2)

Toyota Motor Corporation, one of the largest automakers in the world, had consolidated vehicle sales of 8.96 million units in 2018 (fiscal year ending 31 March 2018). This is substantially more than consolidated vehicle sales of 7.35 million units six years earlier in 2012. What was the growth rate in number of vehicles sold by Toyota from 2012 to 2018?

Solution: Using Equation 14, we find

$$g = \sqrt[6]{8.96/7.35} - 1$$
$$= \sqrt[6]{1.219048} - 1$$
$$= 1.033563 - 1$$
$$= 0.033563 \text{ or about } 3.4\%$$

The rate of growth in vehicles sold was approximately 3.4 percent during the 2012–2018 period. Note that we can also refer to 3.4 percent as the compound annual growth rate because it is the single number that compounds the number of vehicles sold in 2012 forward to the number of vehicles sold in 2018. Table 4 lists the number of vehicles sold by Toyota from 2012 to 2018.

Table 4 also shows 1 plus the one-year growth rate in number of vehicles sold. We can compute the 1 plus six-year cumulative growth in number of vehicles sold from 2012 to 2018 as the product of quantities (1 + one-year growth rate). We arrive at the same result as when we divide the ending number of vehicles sold, 8.96 million, by the beginning number of vehicles sold, 7.35 million:

$$\frac{8.96}{7.35} = \left(\frac{8.87}{7.35}\right)\left(\frac{9.12}{8.87}\right)\left(\frac{8.97}{9.12}\right)\left(\frac{8.68}{8.97}\right)\left(\frac{8.97}{8.68}\right)\left(\frac{8.96}{8.97}\right)$$

$$= (1 + g_1)(1 + g_2)(1 + g_3)(1 + g_4)(1 + g_5)(1 + g_6)$$

$$1.219048 = (1.206803)(1.028185)(0.983553)(0.967670)(1.033410)(0.998885)$$

TABLE 4   Number of Vehicles Sold, 2012–2018

Year	Number of Vehicles Sold (Millions)	$(1 + g)_t$	t
2012	7.35		0
2013	8.87	8.87/7.35 = 1.206803	1
2014	9.12	9.12/8.87 = 1.028185	2
2015	8.97	8.97/9.12 = 0.983553	3
2016	8.68	8.68/8.97 = 0.967670	4
2017	8.97	8.97/8.68 = 1.033410	5
2018	8.96	8.96/8.97 = 0.998885	6

Source: www.toyota.com.

The right-hand side of the equation is the product of 1 plus the one-year growth rate in number of vehicles sold for each year. Recall that, using Equation 14, we took the sixth root of 8.96/7.35 = 1.219048. In effect, we were solving for the single value of g which, when compounded over six periods, gives the correct product of 1 plus the one-year growth rates.[8]

In conclusion, we do not need to compute intermediate growth rates as in Table 4 to solve for a compound growth rate g. Sometimes, however, the intermediate growth rates are interesting or informative. For example, most of the 21.9 percent increase in vehicles sold by Toyota from 2012 to 2018 occurred in 2013 as sales increased by 20.7 percent from 2012 to 2013. Elsewhere in Toyota Motor's disclosures, the company noted that all regions except Europe showed a substantial increase in sales in 2013. We can also analyze the variability in growth rates when we conduct an analysis as in Table 4. Sales continued to increase in 2014 but then declined in 2015 and 2016. Sales then increased but the sales in 2017 and 2018 are about the same as in 2015.

The compound growth rate is an excellent summary measure of growth over multiple time periods. In our Toyota Motors example, the compound growth rate of 3.4 percent is the single growth rate that, when added to 1, compounded over six years, and multiplied by the 2012 number of vehicles sold, yields the 2018 number of vehicles sold.

7.2. Solving for the Number of Periods

In this section, we demonstrate how to solve for the number of periods given present value, future value, and interest or growth rates.

---

[8]The compound growth rate that we calculate here is an example of a geometric mean, specifically the geometric mean of the growth rates. We define the geometric mean in Chapter 2, which is on statistical concepts.

EXAMPLE 19   The Number of Annual Compounding Periods Needed for an Investment to Reach a Specific Value

You are interested in determining how long it will take an investment of €10,000,000 to double in value. The current interest rate is 7 percent compounded annually. How many years will it take €10,000,000 to double to €20,000,000?

Solution: Use Equation 2, $FV_N = PV(1 + r)^N$, to solve for the number of periods, N, as follows:

$$(1 + r)^N = FV_N/PV = 2$$
$$N \ln(1 + r) = \ln(2)$$
$$N = \ln(2)/\ln(1 + r)$$
$$= \ln(2)/\ln(1.07) = 10.24$$

With an interest rate of 7 percent, it will take approximately 10 years for the initial €10,000,000 investment to grow to €20,000,000. Solving for N in the expression $(1.07)^N = 2.0$ requires taking the natural logarithm of both sides and using the rule that $\ln(x^N) = N \ln(x)$. Generally, we find that $N = [\ln(FV/PV)]/\ln(1 + r)$. Here, $N = \ln(€20,000,000/€10,000,000)/\ln(1.07) = \ln(2)/\ln(1.07) = 10.24$.[9]

7.3. Solving for the Size of Annuity Payments

In this section, we discuss how to solve for annuity payments. Mortgages, auto loans, and retirement savings plans are classic examples of applications of annuity formulas.

EXAMPLE 20   Calculating the Size of Payments on a Fixed-Rate Mortgage

You are planning to purchase a $120,000 house by making a down payment of $20,000 and borrowing the remainder with a 30-year fixed-rate mortgage with monthly payments. The first payment is due at $t = 1$. Current mortgage interest rates are quoted at 8 percent with monthly compounding. What will your monthly mortgage payments be?

---

[9]To quickly approximate the number of periods, practitioners sometimes use an ad hoc rule called the **Rule of 72**: Divide 72 by the stated interest rate to get the approximate number of years it would take to double an investment at the interest rate. Here, the approximation gives $72/7 = 10.3$ years. The Rule of 72 is loosely based on the observation that it takes 12 years to double an amount at a 6 percent interest rate, giving $6 \times 12 = 72$. At a 3 percent rate, one would guess it would take twice as many years, $3 \times 24 = 72$.

Solution: The bank will determine the mortgage payments such that at the stated periodic interest rate, the present value of the payments will be equal to the amount borrowed (in this case, $100,000). With this fact in mind, we can use Equation 11,

$PV = A \left[\frac{1 - \frac{1}{(1+r)^N}}{r} \right]$, to solve for the annuity amount, A, as the present value divided by

the present value annuity factor:

$$PV = \$100,000$$

$$r_s = 8\% = 0.08$$

$$m = 12$$

$$r_s/m = 0.08/12 = 0.006667$$

$$N = 30$$

$$mN = 12 \times 30 = 360$$

$$\text{Present value annuity factor} = \frac{1 - \frac{1}{[1 + (r_s/m)]^{mN}}}{r_s/m} = \frac{1 - \frac{1}{(1.006667)^{360}}}{0.006667}$$

$$= 136.283494$$

$$A = PV/\text{Present value annuity factor}$$

$$= \$100,000/136.283494$$

$$= \$733.76$$

The amount borrowed, $100,000, is equivalent to 360 monthly payments of $733.76 with a stated interest rate of 8 percent. The mortgage problem is a relatively straightforward application of finding a level annuity payment.

Next, we turn to a retirement-planning problem. This problem illustrates the complexity of the situation in which an individual wants to retire with a specified retirement income. Over the course of a life cycle, the individual may be able to save only a small amount during the early years but then may have the financial resources to save more during later years. Savings plans often involve uneven cash flows, a topic we will examine in the last part of this chapter. When dealing with uneven cash flows, we take maximum advantage of the principle that dollar amounts indexed at the same point in time are additive—the **cash flow additivity principle**.

EXAMPLE 21   The Projected Annuity Amount Needed to Fund a Future-Annuity Inflow

Jill Grant is 22 years old (at $t = 0$) and is planning for her retirement at age 63 (at $t = 41$). She plans to save $2,000 per year for the next 15 years ($t = 1$ to $t = 15$). She wants to have retirement income of $100,000 per year for 20 years, with the first retirement payment starting at $t = 41$. How much must Grant save each year from $t = 16$ to $t = 40$

FIGURE 8   Solving for Missing Annuity Payments (in Thousands)

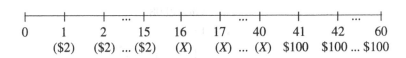

in order to achieve her retirement goal? Assume she plans to invest in a diversified stock-and-bond mutual fund that will earn 8 percent per year on average.

Solution: To help solve this problem, we set up the information on a time line. As Figure 8 shows, Grant will save $2,000 (an outflow) each year for Years 1 to 15. Starting in Year 41, Grant will start to draw retirement income of $100,000 per year for 20 years. In the time line, the annual savings is recorded in parentheses ($2) to show that it is an outflow. The problem is to find the savings, recorded as *X*, from Year 16 to Year 40.

Solving this problem involves satisfying the following relationship: The present value of savings (outflows) equals the present value of retirement income (inflows). We could bring all the dollar amounts to $t = 40$ or to $t = 15$ and solve for *X*.

Let us evaluate all dollar amounts at $t = 15$ (we encourage the reader to repeat the problem by bringing all cash flows to $t = 40$). As of $t = 15$, the first payment of *X* will be one period away (at $t = 16$). Thus we can value the stream of *X*s using the formula for the present value of an ordinary annuity.

This problem involves three series of level cash flows. The basic idea is that the present value of the retirement income must equal the present value of Grant's savings. Our strategy requires the following steps:

1. Find the future value of the savings of $2,000 per year and index it at $t = 15$. This value tells us how much Grant will have saved.
2. Find the present value of the retirement income at $t = 15$. This value tells us how much Grant needs to meet her retirement goals (as of $t = 15$). Two substeps are necessary. First, calculate the present value of the annuity of $100,000 per year at $t = 40$. Use the formula for the present value of an annuity. (Note that the present value is indexed at $t = 40$ because the first payment is at $t = 41$.) Next, discount the present value back to $t = 15$ (a total of 25 periods).
3. Now compute the difference between the amount Grant has saved (Step 1) and the amount she needs to meet her retirement goals (Step 2). Her savings from $t = 16$ to $t = 40$ must have a present value equal to the difference between the future value of her savings and the present value of her retirement income.

Our goal is to determine the amount Grant should save in each of the 25 years from $t = 16$ to $t = 40$. We start by bringing the $2,000 savings to $t = 15$, as follows:

$$A = \$2,000$$

$$r = 8\% = 0.08$$

$$N = 15$$

$$FV = A\left[\frac{(1+r)^N - 1}{r}\right]$$

$$= \$2,000\left[\frac{(1.08)^{15} - 1}{0.08}\right]$$

$$= \$2,000(27.152114)$$

$$= \$54,304.23$$

At $t = 15$, Grant's initial savings will have grown to \$54,304.23.

Now we need to know the value of Grant's retirement income at $t = 15$. As stated earlier, computing the retirement present value requires two substeps. First, find the present value at $t = 40$ with the formula in Equation 11; second, discount this present value back to $t = 15$. Now we can find the retirement income present value at $t = 40$:

$$A = \$100,000$$

$$r = 8\% = 0.08$$

$$N = 20$$

$$PV = A\left[\frac{1 - \dfrac{1}{(1+r)^N}}{r}\right]$$

$$= \$100,000\left[\frac{1 - \dfrac{1}{(1.08)^{20}}}{0.08}\right]$$

$$= \$100,000(9.818147)$$

$$= \$981,814.74$$

The present value amount is as of $t = 40$, so we must now discount it back as a lump sum to $t = 15$:

$$FV_N = \$981,814.74$$

$$N = 25$$

$$r = 8\% = 0.08$$

$$PV = FV_N(1+r)^{-N}$$

$$= \$981,814.74(1.08)^{-25}$$

$$= \$981,814.74(0.146018)$$

$$= \$143,362.53$$

Now recall that Grant will have saved $54,304.23 by $t = 15$. Therefore, in present value terms, the annuity from $t = 16$ to $t = 40$ must equal the difference between the amount already saved ($54,304.23) and the amount required for retirement ($143,362.53). This amount is equal to $143,362.53 - $54,304.23 = $89,058.30. Therefore, we must now find the annuity payment, A, from $t = 16$ to $t = 40$ that has a present value of $89,058.30. We find the annuity payment as follows:

$$PV = \$89,058.30$$

$$r = 8\% = 0.08$$

$$N = 25$$

$$\text{Present value annuity factor} = \left[\frac{1 - \dfrac{1}{(1+r)^N}}{r} \right]$$

$$= \left[\frac{1 - \dfrac{1}{(1.08)^{25}}}{0.08} \right]$$

$$= 10.674776$$

$$A = PV/\text{Present value annuity factor}$$

$$= \$89,058.30/10.674776$$

$$= \$8,342.87$$

Grant will need to increase her savings to $8,342.87 per year from $t = 16$ to $t = 40$ to meet her retirement goal of having a fund equal to $981,814.74 after making her last payment at $t = 40$.

7.4. Review of Present and Future Value Equivalence

As we have demonstrated, finding present and future values involves moving amounts of money to different points on a time line. These operations are possible because present value and future value are equivalent measures separated in time. Table 5 illustrates this equivalence; it lists the timing of five cash flows, their present values at $t = 0$, and their future values at $t = 5$.

To interpret Table 5, start with the third column, which shows the present values. Note that each $1,000 cash payment is discounted back the appropriate number of periods to find the present value at $t = 0$. The present value of $4,329.48 is exactly equivalent to the series of cash flows. This information illustrates an important point: A lump sum can actually generate an annuity. If we place a lump sum in an account that earns the stated interest rate for all periods, we can generate an annuity that is equivalent to the lump sum. Amortized loans, such as mortgages and car loans, are examples of this principle.

TABLE 5   The Equivalence of Present and Future Values

Time	Cash Flow ($)	Present Value at $t = 0$	Future Value at $t = 5$
1	1,000	$\$1{,}000(1.05)^{-1} = \$952.38$	$\$1{,}000(1.05)^{4} = \$1{,}215.51$
2	1,000	$\$1{,}000(1.05)^{-2} = \$907.03$	$\$1{,}000(1.05)^{3} = \$1{,}157.63$
3	1,000	$\$1{,}000(1.05)^{-3} = \$863.84$	$\$1{,}000(1.05)^{2} = \$1{,}102.50$
4	1,000	$\$1{,}000(1.05)^{-4} = \$822.70$	$\$1{,}000(1.05)^{1} = \$1{,}050.00$
5	1,000	$\$1{,}000(1.05)^{-5} = \$783.53$	$\$1{,}000(1.05)^{0} = \$1{,}000.00$
		Sum: $4,329.48	Sum: $5,525.64

To see how a lump sum can fund an annuity, assume that we place $4,329.48 in the bank today at 5 percent interest. We can calculate the size of the annuity payments by using Equation 11. Solving for A, we find

$$A = \frac{PV}{\dfrac{1 - [1/(1 + r)^{N}]}{r}}$$

$$= \frac{\$4{,}329.48}{\dfrac{1 - [1/(1.05)^{5}]}{0.05}}$$

$$= \$1{,}000$$

Table 6 shows how the initial investment of $4,329.48 can actually generate five $1,000 withdrawals over the next five years.

To interpret Table 6, start with an initial present value of $4,329.48 at $t = 0$. From $t = 0$ to $t = 1$, the initial investment earns 5 percent interest, generating a future value of $4,329.48(1.05) = $4,545.95. We then withdraw $1,000 from our account, leaving $4,545.95 - $1,000 = $3,545.95 (the figure reported in the last column for time period 1). In the next period, we earn one year's worth of interest and then make a $1,000 withdrawal. After the fourth withdrawal, we have $952.38, which earns 5 percent. This amount then grows to $1,000 during the year, just enough for us to make the last withdrawal. Thus the

TABLE 6   How an Initial Present Value Funds an Annuity

Time Period	Amount Available at the Beginning of the Time Period ($)	Ending Amount before Withdrawal	Withdrawal ($)	Amount Available after Withdrawal ($)
1	4,329.48	$\$4{,}329.48(1.05) = \$4{,}545.95$	1,000	3,545.95
2	3,545.95	$\$3{,}545.95(1.05) = \$3{,}723.25$	1,000	2,723.25
3	2,723.25	$\$2{,}723.25(1.05) = \$2{,}859.41$	1,000	1,859.41
4	1,859.41	$\$1{,}859.41(1.05) = \$1{,}952.38$	1,000	952.38
5	952.38	$\$952.38(1.05) = \$1{,}000$	1,000	0

initial present value, when invested at 5 percent for five years, generates the $1,000 five-year ordinary annuity. The present value of the initial investment is exactly equivalent to the annuity.

Now we can look at how future value relates to annuities. In Table 5, we reported that the future value of the annuity was $5,525.64. We arrived at this figure by compounding the first $1,000 payment forward four periods, the second $1,000 forward three periods, and so on. We then added the five future amounts at $t = 5$. The annuity is equivalent to $5,525.64 at $t = 5$ and $4,329.48 at $t = 0$. These two dollar measures are thus equivalent. We can verify the equivalence by finding the present value of $5,525.64, which is $5,525.64 × $(1.05)^{-5} = $4,329.48$. We found this result above when we showed that a lump sum can generate an annuity.

To summarize what we have learned so far: A lump sum can be seen as equivalent to an annuity, and an annuity can be seen as equivalent to its future value. Thus present values, future values, and a series of cash flows can all be considered equivalent as long as they are indexed at the same point in time.

7.5. The Cash Flow Additivity Principle

The cash flow additivity principle—the idea that amounts of money indexed at the same point in time are additive—is one of the most important concepts in time value of money mathematics. We have already mentioned and used this principle; this section provides a reference example for it.

Consider the two series of cash flows shown on the time line in Figure 9. The series are denoted A and B. If we assume that the annual interest rate is 2 percent, we can find the future value of each series of cash flows as follows. Series A's future value is $100(1.02) + $100 = 202. Series B's future value is $200(1.02) + $200 = 404. The future value of (A + B) is $202 + $404 = $606 by the method we have used up to this point. The alternative way to find the future value is to add the cash flows of each series, A and B (call it A + B), and then find the future value of the combined cash flow, as shown in Figure 9.

FIGURE 9   The Additivity of Two Series of Cash Flows

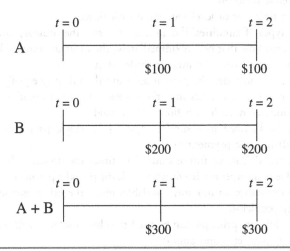

The third time line in Figure 9 shows the combined series of cash flows. Series A has a cash flow of $100 at $t = 1$, and Series B has a cash flow of $200 at $t = 1$. The combined series thus has a cash flow of $300 at $t = 1$. We can similarly calculate the cash flow of the combined series at $t = 2$. The future value of the combined series (A + B) is $300(1.02) + $300 = $606, the same result we found when we added the future values of each series.

The additivity and equivalence principles also appear in another common situation. Suppose cash flows are $4 at the end of the first year and $24 (actually separate payments of $4 and $20) at the end of the second year. Rather than finding present values of the first year's $4 and the second year's $24, we can treat this situation as a $4 annuity for two years and a second-year $20 lump sum. If the discount rate were 6 percent, the $4 annuity would have a present value of $7.33 and the $20 lump sum a present value of $17.80, for a total of $25.13.

8. SUMMARY

In this chapter, we have explored a foundation topic in investment mathematics, the time value of money. We have developed and reviewed the following concepts for use in financial applications:

- The interest rate, r, is the required rate of return; r is also called the discount rate or opportunity cost.
- An interest rate can be viewed as the sum of the real risk-free interest rate and a set of premiums that compensate lenders for risk: an inflation premium, a default risk premium, a liquidity premium, and a maturity premium.
- The future value, FV, is the present value, PV, times the future value factor, $(1 + r)^N$.
- The interest rate, r, makes current and future currency amounts equivalent based on their time value.
- The stated annual interest rate is a quoted interest rate that does not account for compounding within the year.
- The periodic rate is the quoted interest rate per period; it equals the stated annual interest rate divided by the number of compounding periods per year.
- The effective annual rate is the amount by which a unit of currency will grow in a year with interest on interest included.
- An annuity is a finite set of level sequential cash flows.
- There are two types of annuities, the annuity due and the ordinary annuity. The annuity due has a first cash flow that occurs immediately; the ordinary annuity has a first cash flow that occurs one period from the present (indexed at $t = 1$).
- On a time line, we can index the present as 0 and then display equally spaced hash marks to represent a number of periods into the future. This representation allows us to index how many periods away each cash flow will be paid.
- Annuities may be handled in a similar approach as single payments if we use annuity factors rather than single-payment factors.
- The present value, PV, is the future value, FV, times the present value factor, $(1 + r)^{-N}$.
- The present value of a perpetuity is A/r, where A is the periodic payment to be received forever.
- It is possible to calculate an unknown variable, given the other relevant variables in time value of money problems.
- The cash flow additivity principle can be used to solve problems with uneven cash flows by combining single payments and annuities.

PRACTICE PROBLEMS

1. The table below gives current information on the interest rates for two two-year and two eight-year maturity investments. The table also gives the maturity, liquidity, and default risk characteristics of a new investment possibility (Investment 3). All investments promise only a single payment (a payment at maturity). Assume that premiums relating to inflation, liquidity, and default risk are constant across all time horizons.

Investment	Maturity (in Years)	Liquidity	Default Risk	Interest Rate (%)
1	2	High	Low	2.0
2	2	Low	Low	2.5
3	7	Low	Low	r_3
4	8	High	Low	4.0
5	8	Low	High	6.5

Based on the information in the above table, address the following:
   A. Explain the difference between the interest rates on Investment 1 and Investment 2.
   B. Estimate the default risk premium.
   C. Calculate upper and lower limits for the interest rate on Investment 3, r_3.

2. A couple plans to set aside $20,000 per year in a conservative portfolio projected to earn 7 percent a year. If they make their first savings contribution one year from now, how much will they have at the end of 20 years?

3. Two years from now, a client will receive the first of three annual payments of $20,000 from a small business project. If she can earn 9 percent annually on her investments and plans to retire in six years, how much will the three business project payments be worth at the time of her retirement?

4. To cover the first year's total college tuition payments for his two children, a father will make a $75,000 payment five years from now. How much will he need to invest today to meet his first tuition goal if the investment earns 6 percent annually?

5. A client can choose between receiving 10 annual $100,000 retirement payments, starting one year from today, or receiving a lump sum today. Knowing that he can invest at a rate of 5 percent annually, he has decided to take the lump sum. What lump sum today will be equivalent to the future annual payments?

6. You are considering investing in two different instruments. The first instrument will pay nothing for three years, but then it will pay $20,000 per year for four years. The second instrument will pay $20,000 for three years and $30,000 in the fourth year. All payments are made at year-end. If your required rate of return on these investments is 8 percent annually, what should you be willing to pay for:
   A. The first instrument?
   B. The second instrument (use the formula for a four-year annuity)?

7. Suppose you plan to send your daughter to college in three years. You expect her to earn two-thirds of her tuition payment in scholarship money, so you estimate that your payments will be $10,000 a year for four years. To estimate whether you have set aside enough money, you ignore possible inflation in tuition payments and assume that you can earn 8 percent annually on your investments. How much should you set aside now to cover these payments?

8. A client plans to send a child to college for four years starting 18 years from now. Having set aside money for tuition, she decides to plan for room and board also. She estimates these costs at $20,000 per year, payable at the beginning of each year, by the time her child goes to college. If she starts next year and makes 17 payments into a savings account paying 5 percent annually, what annual payments must she make?

9. A couple plans to pay their child's college tuition for 4 years starting 18 years from now. The current annual cost of college is C$7,000, and they expect this cost to rise at an annual rate of 5 percent. In their planning, they assume that they can earn 6 percent annually. How much must they put aside each year, starting next year, if they plan to make 17 equal payments?

10. The nominal risk-free rate is *best* described as the sum of the real risk-free rate and a premium for:
    A. maturity.
    B. liquidity.
    C. expected inflation.

11. Which of the following risk premiums is most relevant in explaining the difference in yields between 30-year bonds issued by the US Treasury and 30-year bonds issued by a small private issuer?
    A. Inflation
    B. Maturity
    C. Liquidity

12. A bank quotes a stated annual interest rate of 4.00%. If that rate is equal to an effective annual rate of 4.08%, then the bank is compounding interest:
    A. daily.
    B. quarterly.
    C. semiannually.

13. The value in six years of $75,000 invested today at a stated annual interest rate of 7% compounded quarterly is *closest* to:
    A. $112,555.
    B. $113,330.
    C. $113,733.

14. A client requires £100,000 one year from now. If the stated annual rate is 2.50% compounded weekly, the deposit needed today is *closest* to:
    A. £97,500.
    B. £97,532.
    C. £97,561.

15. For a lump sum investment of ¥250,000 invested at a stated annual rate of 3% compounded daily, the number of months needed to grow the sum to ¥1,000,000 is *closest* to:
    A. 555.
    B. 563.
    C. 576.

16. Given a €1,000,000 investment for four years with a stated annual rate of 3% compounded continuously, the difference in its interest earnings compared with the same investment compounded daily is *closest* to:
    A. €1.
    B. €6.
    C. €455.

17. An investment pays €300 annually for five years, with the first payment occurring today. The present value (PV) of the investment discounted at a 4% annual rate is *closest* to:
    A. €1,336.
    B. €1,389.
    C. €1,625.

18. A perpetual preferred stock makes its first quarterly dividend payment of $2.00 in five quarters. If the required annual rate of return is 6% compounded quarterly, the stock's present value is *closest* to:
    A. $31.
    B. $126.
    C. $133.

19. A saver deposits the following amounts in an account paying a stated annual rate of 4%, compounded semiannually:

Year	End-of-Year Deposits ($)
1	4,000
2	8,000
3	7,000
4	10,000

At the end of Year 4, the value of the account is *closest* to:
    A. $30,432
    B. $30,447
    C. $31,677

20. An investment of €500,000 today that grows to €800,000 after six years has a stated annual interest rate *closest* to:
    A. 7.5% compounded continuously.
    B. 7.7% compounded daily.
    C. 8.0% compounded semiannually.

21. A sweepstakes winner may select either a perpetuity of £2,000 a month beginning with the first payment in one month or an immediate lump sum payment of £350,000. If the annual discount rate is 6% compounded monthly, the present value of the perpetuity is:
   A. less than the lump sum.
   B. equal to the lump sum.
   C. greater than the lump sum.

22. At a 5% interest rate per year compounded annually, the present value (PV) of a 10-year ordinary annuity with annual payments of $2,000 is $15,443.47. The PV of a 10-year annuity due with the same interest rate and payments is *closest* to:
   A. $14,708.
   B. $16,216.
   C. $17,443.

23. Grandparents are funding a newborn's future university tuition costs, estimated at $50,000/year for four years, with the first payment due as a lump sum in 18 years. Assuming a 6% effective annual rate, the required deposit today is *closest* to:
   A. $60,699.
   B. $64,341.
   C. $68,201.

24. The present value (PV) of an investment with the following year-end cash flows (CF) and a 12% required annual rate of return is *closest* to:

Year	Cash Flow (€)
1	100,000
2	150,000
5	−10,000

   A. €201,747.
   B. €203,191.
   C. €227,573.

25. A sports car, purchased for £200,000, is financed for five years at an annual rate of 6% compounded monthly. If the first payment is due in one month, the monthly payment is *closest* to:
   A. £3,847.
   B. £3,867.
   C. £3,957.

26. Given a stated annual interest rate of 6% compounded quarterly, the level amount that, deposited quarterly, will grow to £25,000 at the end of 10 years is *closest* to:
   A. £461.
   B. £474.
   C. £836.

27. Given the following time line and a discount rate of 4% a year compounded annually, the present value (PV), as of the end of Year 5 (PV_5), of the cash flow received at the end of Year 20 is *closest* to:

  A. $22,819.
  B. $27,763.
  C. $28,873.

28. A client invests €20,000 in a four-year certificate of deposit (CD) that annually pays interest of 3.5%. The annual CD interest payments are automatically reinvested in a separate savings account at a stated annual interest rate of 2% compounded monthly. At maturity, the value of the combined asset is *closest* to:

  A. €21,670.
  B. €22,890.
  C. €22,950.

CHAPTER 2

ORGANIZING, VISUALIZING, AND DESCRIBING DATA

Pamela Peterson Drake, PhD, CFA

Jian Wu, PhD

LEARNING OUTCOMES

The candidate should be able to:

- Identify and compare data types;
- Describe how data are organized for quantitative analysis;
- Interpret frequency and related distributions;
- Interpret a contingency table;
- Describe ways that data may be visualized and evaluate uses of specific visualizations;
- Describe how to select among visualization types;
- Calculate and interpret measures of central tendency;
- Select among alternative definitions of mean to address an investment problem;
- Calculate quantiles and interpret related visualizations;
- Calculate and interpret measures of dispersion;
- Calculate and interpret target downside deviation;
- Interpret skewness;
- Interpret kurtosis;
- Interpret correlation between two variables.

1. INTRODUCTION

Data have always been a key input for securities analysis and investment management, but the acceleration in the availability and the quantity of data has also been driving the rapid evolution of the investment industry. With the rise of big data and machine learning techniques, investment practitioners are embracing an era featuring large volume, high

Quantitative Methods for Investment Analysis, Second Edition, by Pamela Peterson Drake, PhD, CFA, Jian Wu, PhD. Copyright © 2020 by CFA Institute.

velocity, and a wide variety of data—allowing them to explore and exploit this abundance of information for their investment strategies.

While this data-rich environment offers potentially tremendous opportunities for investors, turning data into useful information is not so straightforward. Organizing, cleaning, and analyzing data are crucial to the development of successful investment strategies; otherwise, we end up with "garbage in and garbage out" and failed investments. It is often said that 80% of an analyst's time is spent on finding, organizing, cleaning, and analyzing data, while just 20% of her/his time is taken up by model development. So, the importance of having a properly organized, cleansed, and well-analyzed dataset cannot be over-emphasized. With this essential requirement met, an appropriately executed data analysis can detect important relationships within data, uncover underlying structures, identify outliers, and extract potentially valuable insights. Utilizing both visual tools and quantitative methods, like the ones covered in this chapter, is the first step in summarizing and understanding data that will be crucial inputs to an investment strategy.

This chapter provides a foundation for understanding important concepts that are an indispensable part of the analytical tool kit needed by investment practitioners, from junior analysts to senior portfolio managers. These basic concepts pave the way for more sophisticated tools that will be developed as the quantitative methods topic unfolds and that are integral to gaining competencies in the investment management techniques and asset classes that are presented later in the CFA curriculum.

Section 2 covers core data types, including continuous and discrete numerical data, nominal and ordinal categorical data, and structured versus unstructured data. Organizing data into arrays and data tables and summarizing data in frequency distributions and contingency tables are discussed in Section 3. Section 4 introduces the important topic of data visualization using a range of charts and graphics to summarize, explore, and better understand data. Section 5 covers the key measures of central tendency, including several variants of mean that are especially useful in investments. Quantiles and their investment applications are the focus of Section 6. Key measures of dispersion are discussed in Section 7. The shape of data distributions—specifically, skewness and kurtosis—are covered in Sections 8 and 9, respectively. Section 10 provides a graphical introduction to covariance and correlation between two variables. The chapter concludes with a Summary.

2. DATA TYPES

Data can be defined as a collection of numbers, characters, words, and text—as well as images, audio, and video—in a raw or organized format to represent facts or information. To choose the appropriate statistical methods for summarizing and analyzing data and to select suitable charts for visualizing data, we need to distinguish among different data types. We will discuss data types under three different perspectives of classifications: numerical versus categorical data; cross-sectional versus time-series versus panel data; and structured versus unstructured data.

2.1. Numerical versus Categorical Data

From a statistical perspective, data can be classified into two basic groups: numerical data and categorical data.

2.1.1. Numerical Data

Numerical data are values that represent measured or counted quantities as a number and are also called **quantitative data**. Numerical (quantitative) data can be split into two types: continuous data and discrete data.

Continuous data are data that can be measured and can take on any numerical value in a specified range of values. For example, the future value of a lump-sum investment measures the amount of money to be received after a certain period of time bearing an interest rate. The future value could take on a range of values depending on the time period and interest rate. Another common example of continuous data is the price returns of a stock that measures price change over a given period in percentage terms.

Discrete data are numerical values that result from a counting process. So, practically speaking, the data are limited to a finite number of values. For example, the frequency of discrete compounding, m, counts the number of times that interest is accrued and paid out in a given year. The frequency could be monthly ($m = 12$), quarterly ($m = 4$), semi-yearly ($m = 2$), or yearly ($m = 1$).

2.1.2. Categorical Data

Categorical data (also called **qualitative data**) are values that describe a quality or characteristic of a group of observations and therefore can be used as labels to divide a dataset into groups to summarize and visualize. Usually they can take only a limited number of values that are mutually exclusive. Examples of categorical data for classifying companies include bankrupt versus not bankrupt and dividends increased versus no dividend action.

Nominal data are categorical values that are not amenable to being organized in a logical order. An example of nominal data is the classification of publicly listed stocks into 11 sectors, as shown in Exhibit 1, that are defined by the Global Industry Classification Standard (GICS). GICS, developed by Morgan Stanley Capital International (MSCI) and Standard & Poor's (S&P), is a four-tiered, hierarchical industry classification system consisting of

EXHIBIT 1   Equity Sector Classification by GICS

Sector (Text Label)	Code (Numerical Label)
Energy	10
Materials	15
Industrials	20
Consumer Discretionary	25
Consumer Staples	30
Health Care	35
Financials	40
Information Technology	45
Communication Services	50
Utilities	55
Real Estate	60

Source: S&P Global Market Intelligence.

11 sectors, 24 industry groups, 69 industries, and 158 sub-industries. Each sector is defined by a unique text label, as shown in the column named "Sector."

Text labels are a common format to represent nominal data, but nominal data can also be coded with numerical labels. As shown below, the column named "Code" contains a corresponding GICS code of each sector as a numerical value. However, the nominal data in numerical format do not indicate ranking, and any arithmetic operations on nominal data are not meaningful. In this example, the energy sector with the code 10 does not represent a lower or higher rank than the real estate sector with the code 60. Often, financial models, such as regression models, require input data to be numerical; so, nominal data in the input dataset must be coded numerically before applying an algorithm (that is, a process for problem solving) for performing the analysis. This would be mainly to identify the category (here, sector) in the model.

Ordinal data are categorical values that can be logically ordered or ranked. For example, the Morningstar and Standard & Poor's star ratings for investment funds are ordinal data in which one star represents a group of funds judged to have had relatively the worst performance, with two, three, four, and five stars representing groups with increasingly better performance or quality as evaluated by those firms.

Ordinal data may also involve numbers to identify categories. For example, in ranking growth-oriented investment funds based on their five-year cumulative returns, we might assign the number 1 to the top performing 10% of funds, the number 2 to next best performing 10% of funds, and so on; the number 10 represents the bottom performing 10% of funds. Despite the fact that categories represented by ordinal data can be ranked higher or lower compared to each other, they do not necessarily establish a numerical difference between each category. Importantly, such investment fund ranking tells us nothing about the difference in performance between funds ranked 1 and 2 compared with the difference in performance between funds ranked 3 and 4 or 9 and 10.

Having discussed different data types from a statistical perspective, it is important to note that at first glance, identifying data types may seem straightforward. In some situations, where categorical data are coded in numerical format, they should be distinguished from numerical data. A sound rule of thumb: Meaningful arithmetic operations can be performed on numerical data but not on categorical data.

EXAMPLE 1   Identifying Data Types (I)

Identify the data type for each of the following kinds of investment-related information:

1. *Number of coupon payments for a corporate bond.* As background, a corporate bond is a contractual obligation between an issuing corporation (i.e., borrower) and bondholders (i.e., lenders) in which the issuer agrees to pay interest—in the form of fixed coupon payments—on specified dates, typically semi-annually, over the life of the bond (i.e., to its maturity date) and to repay principal (i.e., the amount borrowed) at maturity.
2. *Cash dividends per share paid by a public company.* Note that cash dividends are a distribution paid to shareholders based on the number of shares owned.
3. *Credit ratings for corporate bond issues.* As background, credit ratings gauge the bond issuer's ability to meet the promised payments on the bond. Bond rating agencies

typically assign bond issues to discrete categories that are in descending order of credit quality (i.e., increasing probability of non-payment or default).

4. *Hedge fund classification types.* Note that hedge funds are investment vehicles that are relatively unconstrained in their use of debt, derivatives, and long and short investment strategies. Hedge fund classification types group hedge funds by the kind of investment strategy they pursue.

Solution to 1: Number of coupon payments are discrete data. For example, a newly-issued 5-year corporate bond paying interest semi-annually (quarterly) will make 10 (20) coupon payments during its life. In this case, coupon payments are limited to a finite number of values; so, they are discrete.

Solution to 2: Cash dividends per share are continuous data since they can take on any non-negative values.

Solution to 3: Credit ratings are ordinal data. A rating places a bond issue in a category, and the categories are ordered with respect to the expected probability of default. But arithmetic operations cannot be done on credit ratings, and the difference in the expected probability of default between categories of highly rated bonds, for example, is not necessarily equal to that between categories of lowly rated bonds.

Solution to 4: Hedge fund classification types are nominal data. Each type groups together hedge funds with similar investment strategies. In contrast to credit ratings for bonds, however, hedge fund classification schemes do not involve a ranking. Thus, such classification schemes are not ordinal data.

2.2. Cross-Sectional versus Time-Series versus Panel Data

Another data classification standard is based on how data are collected, and it categorizes data into three types: cross-sectional, time series, and panel.

Prior to the description of the data types, we need to explain two data-related terminologies: variable and observation. A **variable** is a characteristic or quantity that can be measured, counted, or categorized and is subject to change. A variable can also be called a field, an attribute, or a feature. For example, stock price, market capitalization, dividend and dividend yield, earnings per share (EPS), and price-to-earnings ratio (P/E) are basic data variables for the financial analysis of a public company. An **observation** is the value of a specific variable collected at a point in time or over a specified period of time. For example, last year DEF, Inc. recorded EPS of $7.50. This value represented a 15% annual increase.

Cross-sectional data are a list of the observations of a specific variable from multiple observational units at a given point in time. The observational units can be individuals, groups, companies, trading markets, regions, etc. For example, January inflation rates (i.e., the variable) for each of the euro-area countries (i.e., the observational units) in the European Union for a given year constitute cross-sectional data.

Time-series data are a sequence of observations for a single observational unit of a specific variable collected over time and at discrete and typically equally spaced intervals of time, such as daily, weekly, monthly, annually, or quarterly. For example, the daily closing prices (i.e., the variable) of a particular stock recorded for a given month constitute time-series data.

EXHIBIT 2   Earnings per Share in Euros of Three Eurozone Companies in a Given Year

Time Period	Company A	Company B	Company C
Q1	13.53	0.84	−0.34
Q2	4.36	0.96	0.08
Q3	13.16	0.79	−2.72
Q4	12.95	0.19	0.09

Panel data are a mix of time-series and cross-sectional data that are frequently used in financial analysis and modeling. Panel data consist of observations through time on one or more variables for multiple observational units. The observations in panel data are usually organized in a matrix format called a data table. Exhibit 2 is an example of panel data showing quarterly earnings per share (i.e., the variable) for three companies (i.e., the observational units) in a given year by quarter. Each column is a time series of data that represents the quarterly EPS observations from Q1 to Q4 of a specific company, and each row is cross-sectional data that represent the EPS of all three companies of a particular quarter.

2.3. Structured versus Unstructured Data

Categorizing data into structured and unstructured types is based on whether or not the data are in a highly organized form.

Structured data are highly organized in a pre-defined manner, usually with repeating patterns. The typical forms of structured data are one-dimensional arrays, such as a time series of a single variable, or two-dimensional data tables, where each column represents a variable or an observation unit and each row contains a set of values for the same columns. Structured data are relatively easy to enter, store, query, and analyze without much manual processing. Typical examples of structured company financial data are:

- Market data: data issued by stock exchanges, such as intra-day and daily closing stock prices and trading volumes.
- Fundamental data: data contained in financial statements, such as earnings per share, price to earnings ratio, dividend yield, and return on equity.
- Analytical data: data derived from analytics, such as cash flow projections or forecasted earnings growth.

Unstructured data, in contrast, are data that do not follow any conventionally organized forms. Some common types of unstructured data are text—such as financial news, posts in social media, and company filings with regulators—and also audio/video, such as managements' earnings calls and presentations to analysts.

Unstructured data are a relatively new classification driven by the rise of alternative data (i.e., data generated from unconventional sources, like electronic devices, social media, sensor networks, and satellites, but also by companies in the normal course of business) and its growing adoption in the financial industry. Unstructured data are typically alternative data as they are usually collected from unconventional sources. By indicating the source from which the data are generated, such data can be classified into three groups:

- Produced by individuals (i.e., via social media posts, web searches, etc.);

- Generated by business processes (i.e., via credit card transactions, corporate regulatory filings, etc.); and
- Generated by sensors (i.e., via satellite imagery, foot traffic by mobile devices, etc.).

Unstructured data may offer new market insights not normally contained in data from traditional sources and may provide potential sources of returns for investment processes. Unlike structured data, however, utilizing unstructured data in investment analysis is challenging. Typically, financial models are able to take only structured data as inputs; therefore, unstructured data must first be transformed into structured data that models can process.

Exhibit 3 shows an excerpt from Form 10-Q (Quarterly Report) filed by Company XYZ with the US Securities and Exchange Commission (SEC) for the fiscal quarter ended 31 March 20XX. The form is an unstructured mix of text and tables, so it cannot be directly used by computers as input to financial models. The SEC has utilized eXtensible Business Reporting Language (XBRL) to structure such data. The data extracted from the XBRL submission can be organized into five tab-delimited TXT format files that contain information about the submission, including taxonomy tags (i.e., financial statement items), dates, units of measure (uom), values (i.e., for the tag items), and more—making it readable by computer. Exhibit 4 shows an excerpt from one of the now structured data tables downloaded from the SEC's EDGAR (Electronic Data Gathering, Analysis, and Retrieval) database.

EXHIBIT 3   Excerpt from 10-Q of Company XYZ for Fiscal Quarter Ended 31 March 20XX

Company XYZ
Form 10-Q
Fiscal Quarter Ended 31 March 20XX
Table of Contents

Part I		Page
Item 1	Financial Statements	1
Item 2	Management's Discussion and Analysis of Financial Condition and Results of Operations	21
Item 3	Quantitative and Qualitative Disclosures About Market Risk	32
Item 4	Controls and Procedures	32
Part II		
Item 1	Legal Proceedings	33
Item 1A	Risk Factors	33
Item 2	Unregistered Sales of Equity Securities and Use of Proceeds	43
Item 3	Defaults Upon Senior Securities	43
Item 4	Mine Safety Disclosures	43
Item 5	Other Information	43
Item 6	Exhibits	44

Condensed Consolidated Statements of Operations (Unaudited)
(in millions, except number of shares, which are reflected in thousands and per share amounts)

	31 March 20XX
Net sales:	
Products	$46,565
Services	11,450
Total net sales	58,015
Cost of sales:	
Products	32,047
Services	4,147
Total cost of sales	36,194
Gross margin	21,821
Operating expenses:	
Research and development	3,948
Selling, general and administrative	4,458
Total operating expenses	8,406
Operating income	13,415
Other income/(expense), net	378
Income before provision for income taxes	13,793
Provision for income taxes	2,232
Net income	$11,561

Source: EDGAR.

EXHIBIT 4   Structured Data Extracted from Form 10-Q of Company XYZ for Fiscal Quarter Ended 31 March 20XX

adsh	tag	ddate	uom	value
0000320193-19-000066	RevenueFromContract WithCustomerExcluding AssessedTax	20XX0331	USD	$58,015,000,000
0000320193-19-000066	GrossProfit	20XX0331	USD	$21,821,000,000
0000320193-19-000066	OperatingExpenses	20XX0331	USD	$8,406,000,000
0000320193-19-000066	OperatingIncomeLoss	20XX0331	USD	$13,415,000,000
0000320193-19-000066	NetIncomeLoss	20XX0331	USD	$11,561,000,000

Source: EDGAR.

EXAMPLE 2   Identifying Data Types (II)

1. Which of the following is *most likely* to be structured data?
   A. Social media posts where consumers are commenting on what they think of a company's new product.
   B. Daily closing prices during the past month for all companies listed on Japan's Nikkei 225 stock index.
   C. Audio and video of a CFO explaining her company's latest earnings announcement to securities analysts.

2. Which of the following statements describing panel data is *most accurate*?
   A. It is a sequence of observations for a single observational unit of a specific variable collected over time at discrete and equally spaced intervals.
   B. It is a list of observations of a specific variable from multiple observational units at a given point in time.
   C. It is a mix of time-series and cross-sectional data that are frequently used in financial analysis and modeling.

3. Which of the following data series is *least likely* to be sortable by values?
   A. Daily trading volumes for stocks listed on the Shanghai Stock Exchange.
   B. EPS for a given year for technology companies included in the S&P 500 Index.
   C. Dates of first default on bond payments for a group of bankrupt European manufacturing companies.

4. Which of the following best describes a time series?
   A. Daily stock prices of the XYZ stock over a 60-month period.
   B. Returns on four-star rated Morningstar investment funds at the end of the most recent month.
   C. Stock prices for all stocks in the FTSE100 on 31 December of the most recent calendar year.

Solution to 1: B is correct as daily closing prices constitute structured data. A is incorrect as social media posts are unstructured data. C is incorrect as audio and video are unstructured data.

Solution to 2: C is correct as it most accurately describes panel data. A is incorrect as it describes time-series data. B is incorrect as it describes cross-sectional data.

Solution to 3: C is correct as dates are ordinal data that can be sorted by chronological order but not by value. A and B are incorrect as both daily trading volumes and earnings per share (EPS) are numerical data, so they can be sorted by values.

Solution to 4: A is correct since a time series is a sequence of observations of a specific variable (XYZ stock price) collected over time (60 months) and at discrete intervals of time (daily). B and C are both incorrect as they are cross-sectional data.

3. DATA SUMMARIZATION

Given the wide variety of possible formats of **raw data**, which are data available in their original form as collected, such data typically cannot be used by humans or computers to directly extract information and insights. Organizing data into a one-dimensional array or a two-dimensional array is typically the first step in data analytics and modeling. In this section, we will illustrate the construction of these typical data organization formats. We will also introduce two useful tools that can efficiently summarize one-variable and two-variable data: frequency distributions and contingency tables, respectively. Both of them can give us a quick snapshot of the data and allow us to find patterns in the data and associations between variables.

3.1. Organizing Data for Quantitative Analysis

Quantitative analysis and modeling typically require input data to be in a clean and formatted form, so raw data are usually not suitable for use directly by analysts. Depending upon the number of variables, raw data can be organized into two typical formats for quantitative analysis: one-dimensional arrays and two-dimensional rectangular arrays.

A **one-dimensional array** is the simplest format for representing a collection of data of the same data type, so it is suitable for representing a single variable. Exhibit 5 is an example of a one-dimensional array that shows the closing price for the first 10 trading days for ABC Inc. stock after the company went public. Closing prices are time-series data collected at daily intervals, so it is natural to organize them into a time-ordered sequence. The time-series format also facilitates future data updates to the existing dataset. In this case, closing prices for future trading sessions can be easily added to the end of the array with no alteration of previously formatted data.

More importantly, in contrast to compiling the data randomly in an unorganized manner, organizing such data by its time-series nature preserves valuable information beyond the basic **descriptive statistics** that summarize central tendency and spread variation in the data's distribution. For example, by simply plotting the data against time, we can learn whether the data demonstrate any increasing or decreasing trends over time or whether the time series repeats certain patterns in a systematic way over time.

A **two-dimensional rectangular array** (also called a **data table**) is one of the most popular forms for organizing data for processing by computers or for presenting data visually for consumption by humans. Similar to the structure in an Excel spreadsheet, a data table is comprised of columns and rows to hold multiple variables and multiple observations, respectively. When a data table is used to organize the data of one single observational unit (i.e., a single company), each column represents a different variable (feature or attribute) of that observational unit, and each row holds an observation for the different variables; successive rows represent the observations for successive time periods. In other words, observations of each variable are a time-series sequence that is sorted in either ascending or descending time order. Consequently, observations of different variables must be sorted and aligned to the same time scale. **Example 3** shows how to organize a raw dataset for a company collected online into a machine-readable data table.

EXHIBIT 5   One-Dimensional Array: Daily
Closing Price of ABC Inc. Stock

Observation by Day	Stock Price ($)
1	57.21
2	58.26
3	58.64
4	56.19
5	54.78
6	54.26
7	56.88
8	54.74
9	52.42
10	50.14

EXAMPLE 3   Organizing a Company's Raw Data into a Data Table

Suppose you are conducting a valuation analysis of ABC Inc., which has been listed on the stock exchange for two years. The metrics to be used in your valuation include revenue, earnings per share (EPS), and dividends paid per share (DPS). You have retrieved the last two years of ABC's quarterly data from the exchange's website, which is shown in Exhibit 6. The data available online are pre-organized into a tabular format, where each column represents a fiscal year and each row represents a particular quarter with values of the three measures clustered together.

Use the data to construct a two-dimensional rectangular array (i.e., data table) with the columns representing the metrics for valuation and the observations arranged in a time-series sequence.

Solution: To construct a two-dimensional rectangular array, we first need to determine the data table structure. The columns have been specified to represent the three valuation metrics (i.e., variables): revenue, EPS and DPS. The rows should be the observations for each variable in a time ordered sequence. In this example, the data for the valuation measures will be organized in the same quarterly intervals as the raw data retrieved online, starting from Q1 Year 1 to Q4 Year 2. Then, the observations from the original table can be placed accordingly into the data table by variable name and by filing quarter. Exhibit 7 shows the raw data reorganized in the two-dimensional rectangular array (by date and associated valuation metric), which can now be used in financial analysis and is readable by a computer.

It is worth pointing out that in case of missing values while organizing data, how to handle them depends largely on why the data are missing. In this example, dividends (DPS) in the first five quarters are missing because ABC Inc. did not authorize (and pay) any dividends. So, filling the dividend column with zeros is appropriate. If revenue, EPS, and DPS of a given quarter are missing due to particular data source

EXHIBIT 6   Metrics of ABC Inc. Retrieved Online

Fiscal Quarter	Year 1 (Fiscal Year)	Year 2 (Fiscal Year)
March		
Revenue	$3,784(M)	$4,097(M)
EPS	1.37	−0.34
DPS	N/A	N/A
June		
Revenue	$4,236(M)	$5,905(M)
EPS	1.78	3.89
DPS	N/A	0.25
September		
Revenue	$4,187(M)	$4,997(M)
EPS	−3.38	−2.88
DPS	N/A	0.25
December		
Revenue	$3,889(M)	$4,389(M)
EPS	−8.66	−3.98
DPS	N/A	0.25

EXHIBIT 7   Data Table for ABC Inc.

	Revenue ($ Million)	EPS ($)	DPS ($)
Q1 Year 1	3,784	1.37	0
Q2 Year 1	4,236	1.78	0
Q3 Year 1	4,187	−3.38	0
Q4 Year 1	3,889	−8.66	0
Q1 Year 2	4,097	−0.34	0
Q2 Year 2	5,905	3.89	0.25
Q3 Year 2	4,997	−2.88	0.25
Q4 Year 2	4,389	−3.98	0.25

issues, however, these missing values cannot be simply replaced with zeros; this action would result in incorrect interpretation. Instead, the missing values might be replaced with the latest available data or with interpolated values, depending on how the data will be consumed or modeled.

3.2. Summarizing Data Using Frequency Distributions

We now discuss various tabular formats for describing data based on the count of observations. These tables are a necessary step toward building a true visualization of a dataset. Later, we shall see how bar charts, tree-maps, and heat maps, among other graphic tools, are used to visualize important properties of a dataset.

A **frequency distribution** (also called a one-way table) is a tabular display of data constructed either by counting the observations of a variable by distinct values or groups or by tallying the values of a numerical variable into a set of numerically ordered bins. It is an important tool for initially summarizing data by groups or bins for easier interpretation.

Constructing a frequency distribution of a categorical variable is relatively straightforward and can be stated in the following two basic steps:

1. Count the number of observations for each unique value of the variable.
2. Construct a table listing each unique value and the corresponding counts, and then sort the records by number of counts in descending or ascending order to facilitate the display.

Exhibit 8 shows a frequency distribution of a portfolio's stock holdings by sectors (the variables), which are defined by GICS. The portfolio contains a total of 479 stocks that have been individually classified into 11 GICS sectors (first column). The stocks are counted by sector and are summarized in the second column, absolute frequency. The **absolute frequency**, or simply the raw frequency, is the actual number of observations counted for each unique value of the variable (i.e., each sector). Often it is desirable to express the frequencies in terms of percentages, so we also show the **relative frequency** (in the third column), which is calculated as the absolute frequency of each unique value of the variable divided by the total number of observations. The relative frequency provides a normalized measure of the distribution of the data, allowing comparisons between datasets with different numbers of total observations.

EXHIBIT 8   Frequency Distribution for a Portfolio by Sector

Sector (Variable)	Absolute Frequency	Relative Frequency
Industrials	73	15.2%
Information Technology	69	14.4%
Financials	67	14.0%
Consumer Discretionary	62	12.9%
Health Care	54	11.3%
Consumer Staples	33	6.9%
Real Estate	30	6.3%
Energy	29	6.1%
Utilities	26	5.4%
Materials	26	5.4%
Communication Services	10	2.1%
Total	**479**	**100.0%**

A frequency distribution table provides a snapshot of the data, and it facilitates finding patterns. Examining the distribution of absolute frequency in Exhibit 8, we see that the largest number of stocks (73), accounting for 15.2% of the stocks in the portfolio, are held in companies in the industrials sector. The sector with the least number of stocks (10) is communication services, which represents just 2.1% of the stocks in the portfolio.

It is also easy to see that the top four sectors (i.e., industrials, information technology, financials, and consumer discretionary) have very similar relative frequencies, between 15.2% and 12.9%. Similar relative frequencies, between 6.9% and 5.4%, are also seen among several other sectors. Note that the absolute frequencies add up to the total number of stocks in the portfolio (479), and the sum of the relative frequencies should be equal to 100%.

Frequency distributions also help in the analysis of large amounts of numerical data. The procedure for summarizing numerical data is a bit more involved than that for summarizing categorical data because it requires creating non-overlapping bins (also called **intervals** or buckets) and then counting the observations falling into each bin. One procedure for constructing a frequency distribution for numerical data can be stated as follows:

1. Sort the data in ascending order.
2. Calculate the range of the data, defined as Range = Maximum value − Minimum value.
3. Decide on the number of bins (*k*) in the frequency distribution.
4. Determine bin width as Range/*k*.
5. Determine the first bin by adding the bin width to the minimum value. Then, determine the remaining bins by successively adding the bin width to the prior bin's end point and stopping after reaching a bin that includes the maximum value.
6. Determine the number of observations falling into each bin by counting the number of observations whose values are equal to or exceed the bin minimum value yet are less than the bin's maximum value. The exception is in the last bin, where the maximum value is equal to the last bin's maximum, and therefore, the observation with the maximum value is included in this bin's count.
7. Construct a table of the bins listed from smallest to largest that shows the number of observations falling into each bin.

In Step 4, when rounding the bin width, round up (rather than down) to ensure that the final bin includes the maximum value of the data.

These seven steps are basic guidelines for constructing frequency distributions. In practice, however, we may want to refine the above basic procedure. For example, we may want the bins to begin and end with whole numbers for ease of interpretation. Another practical refinement that promotes interpretation is to start the first bin at the nearest whole number below the minimum value.

As this procedure implies, a frequency distribution groups data into a set of bins, where each bin is defined by a unique set of values (i.e., beginning and ending points). Each observation falls into only one bin, and the total number of bins covers all the values represented in the data. The frequency distribution is the list of the bins together with the corresponding measures of frequency.

To illustrate the basic procedure, suppose we have 12 observations sorted in ascending order (*Step 1*):

−4.57, −4.04, −1.64, 0.28, 1.34, 2.35, 2.38, 4.28, 4.42, 4.68, 7.16, and 11.43.

The minimum observation is −4.57, and the maximum observation is +11.43. So, the range is +11.43 − (−4.57) = 16 (*Step 2*).

EXHIBIT 9   Determining Endpoints of the Bins

−4.57	+	4.0	=	−0.57
−0.57	+	4.0	=	3.43
3.43	+	4.0	=	7.43
7.40	+	4.0	=	11.43

If we set $k = 4$ (*Step 3*), then the bin width is $16/4 = 4$ (*Step 4*).

Exhibit 9 shows the repeated addition of the bin width of 4 to determine the endpoint for each of the bins (*Step 5*).

Thus, the bins are [−4.57 to −0.57), [−0.57 to 3.43), [3.43 to 7.43), and [7.43 to 11.43], where the notation [−4.57 to −0.57) indicates −4.57 ≤ observation < −0.57. The parentheses indicate that the endpoints are not included in the bins, and the square brackets indicate that the beginning points and the last endpoint are included in the bin. Exhibit 10 summarizes Steps 5 through 7.

Note that the bins do not overlap, so each observation can be placed uniquely into one bin, and the last bin includes the maximum value.

We turn to these issues in discussing the construction of frequency distributions for daily returns of the fictitious Euro-Asia-Africa (EAA) Equity Index. The dataset of daily returns of the EAA Equity Index spans a five-year period and consists of 1,258 observations with a minimum value of −4.1% and a maximum value of 5.0%. Thus, the range of the data is 5% − (−4.1%) = 9.1%, approximately. (The mean daily return—mean as a measure of central tendency will be discussed shortly—is 0.04%.)

The decision on the number of bins (k) into which we should group the observations often involves inspecting the data and exercising judgment. How much detail should we include? If we use too few bins, we will summarize too much and may lose pertinent characteristics. Conversely, if we use too many bins, we may not summarize enough and may introduce unnecessary noise.

We can establish an appropriate value for k by evaluating the usefulness of the resulting bin width. A large number of empty bins may indicate that we are attempting to over-organize the data to present too much detail. Starting with a relatively small bin width, we can see whether or not the bins are mostly empty and whether or not the value of k associated with that bin width is too large. If the bins are mostly empty, implying that k is too large, we can consider increasingly larger bins (i.e., smaller values of k) until we have a frequency distribution that effectively summarizes the distribution.

EXHIBIT 10   Frequency Distribution

Bin				Absolute Frequency
A	−4.57	≤ observation <	−0.57	3
B	−0.57	≤ observation <	3.43	4
C	3.43	≤ observation <	7.43	4
D	7.43	≤ observation ≤	11.43	1

Suppose that for ease of interpretation we want to use a bin width stated in whole rather than fractional percentages. In the case of the daily EAA Equity Index returns, a 1 percent bin width would be associated with $9.1/1 = 9.1$ bins, which can be rounded up to $k = 10$ bins. That number of bins will cover a range of $1\% \times 10 = 10\%$. By constructing the frequency distribution in this manner, we will also have bins that end and begin at a value of 0 percent, thereby allowing us to count the negative and positive returns in the data. Without too much work, we have found an effective way to summarize the data.

Exhibit 11 shows the frequency distribution for the daily returns of the EAA Equity Index using return bins of 1 percent, where the first bin includes returns from −5.0 percent to −4.0 percent (exclusive, meaning < −4 percent) and the last bin includes daily returns from 4.0 percent to 5.0 percent (inclusive, meaning ≤5 percent). Note that to facilitate interpretation, the first bin starts at the nearest whole number below the minimum value (so, at −5.0 percent).

Exhibit 11 includes two other useful ways to present the data (which can be computed in a straightforward manner once we have established the absolute and relative frequency distributions): the cumulative absolute frequency and the cumulative relative frequency. The **cumulative absolute frequency** cumulates (meaning, adds up) the absolute frequencies as we move from the first bin to the last bin. Similarly, the **cumulative relative frequency** is a sequence of partial sums of the relative frequencies. For the last bin, the cumulative absolute frequency will equal the number observations in the dataset (1,258), and the cumulative relative frequency will equal 100 percent.

As Exhibit 11 shows, the absolute frequencies vary widely, ranging from 1 to 555. The bin encompassing returns between 0 percent and 1 percent has the most observations (555), and the corresponding relative frequency tells us these observations account for 44.12 percent of the total number of observations. The frequency distribution gives us a sense of not only where most of the observations lie but also whether the distribution is evenly spread. It is easy to see that the vast majority of observations (37.36 percent + 44.12 percent = 81.48 percent) lie in the middle two bins spanning −1 percent to 1 percent. We can also see that not many observations are greater than 3 percent or less than −4 percent. Moreover, as there are bins

EXHIBIT 11   Frequency Distribution for Daily Returns of EAA Equity Index

Return Bin (%)	Absolute Frequency	Relative Frequency (%)	Cumulative Absolute Frequency	Cumulative Relative Frequency (%)
−5.0 to −4.0	1	0.08	1	0.08
−4.0 to −3.0	7	0.56	8	0.64
−3.0 to −2.0	23	1.83	31	2.46
−2.0 to −1.0	77	6.12	108	8.59
−1.0 to 0.0	470	37.36	578	45.95
0.0 to 1.0	555	44.12	1,133	90.06
1.0 to 2.0	110	8.74	1,243	98.81
2.0 to 3.0	13	1.03	1,256	99.84
3.0 to 4.0	1	0.08	1,257	99.92
4.0 to 5.0	1	0.08	1,258	100.00

with 0 percent as ending or beginning points, we are able to count positive and negative returns in the data. Looking at the cumulative relative frequency in the last column, we see that the bin of -1 percent to 0 percent shows a cumulative relative frequency of 45.95 percent. This indicates that 45.95 percent of the observations lie below the daily return of 0 percent and that 54.05 percent of the observations are positive daily returns.

It is worth noting that other than being summarized in tables, frequency distributions also can be effectively represented in visuals, which will be discussed shortly in the section on data visualization.

EXAMPLE 4 Constructing a Frequency Distribution of Country Index Returns

Suppose we have the annual equity index returns of a given year for 18 different countries, as shown in Exhibit 12, and we are asked to summarize the data.

Construct a frequency distribution table from these data and state some key findings from the summarized data.

Solution: The first step in constructing a frequency distribution table is to sort the return data in ascending order:
The second step is to calculate the range of the data, which is 9.9% − 5.5% = 4.4%.

EXHIBIT 12   Annual Equity Index Returns for 18 Countries

Market	Index Return (%)
Country A	7.7
Country B	8.5
Country C	9.1
Country D	5.5
Country E	7.1
Country F	9.9
Country G	6.2
Country H	6.8
Country I	7.5
Country J	8.9
Country K	7.4
Country L	8.6
Country M	9.6
Country N	7.7
Country O	6.8
Country P	6.1
Country Q	8.8
Country R	7.9

Market	Index Return (%)
Country D	5.5
Country P	6.1
Country G	6.2
Country H	6.8
Country O	6.8
Country E	7.1
Country K	7.4
Country I	7.5
Country A	7.7
Country N	7.7
Country R	7.9
Country B	8.5
Country L	8.6
Country Q	8.8
Country J	8.9
Country C	9.1
Country M	9.6
Country F	9.9

The third step is to decide on the number of bins. Here, we will use $k = 5$.
The fourth step is to determine the bin width. Here, it is $4.4\%/5 = 0.88\%$, which we will round up to 1.0%.
The fifth step is to determine the bins, which are as follows:

    5.0% + 1.0% = 6.0%
    6.0% + 1.0% = 7.0%
    7.0% + 1.0% = 8.0%
    8.0% + 1.0% = 9.0%
    9.0% + 1.0% = 10.0%

For ease of interpretation, the first bin is set to begin with the nearest whole number (5.0 percent) below the minimum value (5.5 percent) of the data series.
The sixth step requires counting the return observations falling into each bin, and the seventh (last) step is use these results to construct the final frequency distribution table. Exhibit 13 presents the frequency distribution table, which summarizes the data in Exhibit 12 into five bins spanning 5 to 10 percent. Note that with 18 countries, the relative frequency for one observation is calculated as $1/18 = 5.56$ percent.

As Exhibit 13 shows, there is substantial variation in these equity index returns. One-third of the observations fall in the 7.0 to 8.0% bin, making it the bin with the most observations. Both the 6.0 to 7.0% bin and the 8.0 to 9.0% bin hold four

EXHIBIT 13   Frequency Distribution of Equity Index Returns

Return Bin (%)	Absolute Frequency	Relative Frequency (%)	Cumulative Absolute Frequency	Cumulative Relative Frequency (%)
5.0 to 6.0	1	5.56	1	5.56
6.0 to 7.0	4	22.22	5	27.78
7.0 to 8.0	6	33.33	11	61.11
8.0 to 9.0	4	22.22	15	83.33
9.0 to 10.0	3	16.67	18	100.00

observations each, accounting for 22.22 percent of the total number of the observations, respectively. The two remaining bins have fewer observations, one or three observations, respectively.

3.3. Summarizing Data Using a Contingency Table

We have shown that the frequency distribution table is a powerful tool to summarize data for one variable. How can we summarize data for two variables simultaneously? A contingency table provides a solution to this question.

A **contingency table** is a tabular format that displays the frequency distributions of two or more categorical variables simultaneously and is used for finding patterns between the variables. A contingency table for two categorical variables is also known as a two-way table. Contingency tables are constructed by listing all the levels (i.e., categories) of one variable as rows and all the levels of the other variable as columns in the table. A contingency table having R levels of one variable in rows and C levels of the other variable in columns is referred to as an $R \times C$ table. Note that each variable in a contingency table must have a finite number of levels, which can be either ordered (ordinal data) or unordered (nominal data). Importantly, the data displayed in the cells of the contingency table can be either a frequency (count) or a relative frequency (percentage) based on either overall total, row totals, or column totals.

Exhibit 14 presents a 5 × 3 contingency table that summarizes the number of stocks (i.e., frequency) in a particular portfolio of 1,000 stocks by two variables, sector and company market capitalization. Sector has five levels, with each one being a GICS-defined sector. Market capitalization (commonly referred to as market cap) is defined for a company as the number of shares outstanding times the price per share. The stocks in this portfolio are categorized by three levels of market capitalization: large cap, more than $10 billion; mid cap, $10 billion to $2 billion; and small cap, less than $2 billion.

The entries in the cells of the contingency table show the number of stocks of each sector with a given level of market cap. For example, there are 275 small-cap health care stocks, making it the portfolio's largest subgroup in terms of frequency. These data are also called **joint frequencies** because you are joining one variable from the row (i.e., sector) and the other variable from the column (i.e., market cap) to count observations. The joint frequencies are then added across rows and across columns, and these corresponding sums

EXHIBIT 14   Portfolio Frequencies by Sector and Market Capitalization

| Sector Variable (5 Levels) | Market Capitalization Variable (3 Levels) | | | |
	Small	Mid	Large	Total
Communication Services	55	35	20	110
Consumer Staples	50	30	30	110
Energy	175	95	20	290
Health Care	275	105	55	435
Utilities	20	25	10	55
Total	575	290	135	1,000

are called **marginal frequencies**. For example, the marginal frequency of health care stocks in the portfolio is the sum of the joint frequencies across all three levels of market cap, so 435 (= 275 + 105 + 55). Similarly, adding the joint frequencies of small-cap stocks across all five sectors gives the marginal frequency of small-cap stocks of 575 (= 55 + 50 + 175 + 275 + 20).

Clearly, health care stocks and small-cap stocks have the largest marginal frequencies among sector and market cap, respectively, in this portfolio. Note the marginal frequencies represent the frequency distribution for each variable. Finally, the marginal frequencies for each variable must sum to the total number of stocks (overall total) in the portfolio—here, 1,000 (shown in the lower right cell).

Similar to the one-way frequency distribution table, we can express frequency in percentage terms as relative frequency by using one of three options. We can divide the joint frequencies by: a) the total count; b) the marginal frequency on a row; or c) the marginal frequency on a column.

Exhibit 15 shows the contingency table using relative frequencies based on total count. It is readily apparent that small-cap health care and energy stocks comprise the largest portions of the total portfolio, at 27.5 percent (= 275/1,000) and 17.5 percent (= 175/1,000),

EXHIBIT 15   Relative Frequencies as Percentage of Total

| Sector Variable (5 Levels) | Market Capitalization Variable (3 Levels) | | | |
	Small	Mid	Large	Total
Communication Services	5.5%	3.5%	2.0%	11.0%
Consumer Staples	5.0%	3.0%	3.0%	11.0%
Energy	17.5%	9.5%	2.0%	29.0%
Health Care	27.5%	10.5%	5.5%	43.5%
Utilities	2.0%	2.5%	1.0%	5.5%
Total	57.5%	29.0%	13.5%	100%

EXHIBIT 16   Relative Frequencies: Sector as Percentage of Market Cap

| Sector Variable (5 Levels) | Market Capitalization Variable (3 Levels) | | | Total |
	Small	Mid	Large	
Communication Services	9.6%	12.1%	14.8%	11.0%
Consumer Staples	8.7%	10.3%	22.2%	11.0%
Energy	30.4%	32.8%	14.8%	29.0%
Health Care	47.8%	36.2%	40.7%	43.5%
Utilities	3.5%	8.6%	7.4%	5.5%
Total	100.0%	100.0%	100.0%	**100.0%**

respectively, followed by mid-cap health care and energy stocks, at 10.5 percent and 9.5 percent, respectively. Together, these two sectors make up nearly three-quarters of the portfolio (43.5% + 29.0% = 72.5%).

Exhibit 16 shows relative frequencies based on marginal frequencies of market cap (i.e., columns). From this perspective, it is clear that the health care and energy sectors dominate the other sectors at each level of market capitalization: 78.3 percent (= 275/575 + 175/575), 69.0 percent (= 105/290 + 95/290), and 55.6 percent (= 55/135 + 20/135), for small, mid, and large caps, respectively. Note that there may be a small rounding error difference between these results and the numbers shown in Exhibit 15.

In conclusion, the findings from these contingency tables using frequencies and relative frequencies indicate that in terms of the number of stocks, the portfolio can be generally described as a small- to mid-cap–oriented health care and energy sector portfolio that also includes stocks of several other defensive sectors.

As an analytical tool, contingency tables can be used in different applications. One application is for evaluating the performance of a classification model (in this case, the contingency table is called a **confusion matrix**). Suppose we have a model for classifying companies into two groups: those that default on their bond payments and those that do not default. The confusion matrix for displaying the model's results will be a 2 × 2 table showing the frequency of actual defaults versus the model's predicted frequency of defaults. Exhibit 17 shows such a confusion matrix for a sample of 2,000 non-investment-grade bonds. Using company characteristics and other inputs, the model correctly predicts 300 cases of bond defaults and 1,650 cases of no defaults.

EXHIBIT 17   Confusion Matrix for Bond Default Prediction Model

| Predicted | Actual Default | | Total |
Default	Yes	No	
Yes	300	40	**340**
No	10	1,650	**1,660**
Total	**310**	**1,690**	**2,000**

We can also observe that this classification model incorrectly predicts default in 40 cases where no default actually occurred and also incorrectly predicts no default in 10 cases where default actually did occur. Later in the text you will learn how to construct a confusion matrix, how to calculate related model performance metrics, and how to use them to evaluate and tune a classification model.

Another application of contingency tables is to investigate potential association between two categorical variables. For example, revisiting Exhibit 14, one may ask whether the distribution of stocks by sectors is independent of the levels of market capitalization? Given the dominance of small-cap and mid-cap health care and energy stocks, the answer is likely, no.

One way to test for a potential association between categorical variables is to perform a **chi-square test of independence**. Essentially, the procedure involves using the marginal frequencies in the contingency table to construct a table with expected values of the observations. The actual values and expected values are used to derive the chi-square test statistic. This test statistic is then compared to a value from the chi-square distribution for a given level of significance. If the test statistic is greater than the chi-square distribution value, then there is evidence to reject the claim of independence, implying a significant association exists between the categorical variables. The following example describes how a contingency table is used to set up this test of independence.

EXAMPLE 5   Contingency Tables and Association between Two Categorical Variables

Suppose we randomly pick 315 investment funds and classify them two ways: by fund style, either a growth fund or a value fund; and by risk level, either low risk or high risk. Growth funds primarily invest in stocks whose earnings are expected to grow at a faster rate than earnings for the broad stock market. Value funds primarily invest in stocks that appear to be undervalued relative to their fundamental values. Risk here refers to volatility in the return of a given investment fund, so low (high) volatility implies low (high) risk. The data are summarized in a 2 × 2 contingency table shown in Exhibit 18.

1. Calculate the number of growth funds and number of value funds out of the total funds.
2. Calculate the number of low-risk and high-risk funds out of the total funds.
3. Describe how the contingency table is used to set up a test for independence between fund style and risk level.

Solution to 1: The task is to calculate the marginal frequencies by fund style, which is done by adding joint frequencies across the rows. Therefore, the marginal frequency for growth is $73 + 26 = 99$, and the marginal frequency for value is $183 + 33 = 216$.

EXHIBIT 18   Contingency Table by Investment Fund Style and Risk Level

	Low Risk	High Risk
Growth	73	26
Value	183	33

Solution to 2: The task is to calculate the marginal frequencies by fund risk, which is done by adding joint frequencies down the columns. Therefore, the marginal frequency for low risk is $73 + 183 = 256$, and the marginal frequency for high risk is $26 + 33 = 59$.

Solution to 3: Based on the procedure mentioned for conducting a chi-square test of independence, we would perform the following three steps.

    Step 1: Add the marginal frequencies and overall total to the contingency table. We have also included the relative frequency table for observed values.

EXHIBIT 19A   Observed Marginal Frequencies and Relative Frequencies

	Observed Values				Observed Values		
	Low Risk	**High Risk**			**Low Risk**	**High Risk**	
Growth	73	26	**99**	Growth	74%	26%	**100%**
Value	183	33	**216**	Value	85%	15%	**100%**
	256	**59**	**315**				

    Step 2: Use the marginal frequencies in the contingency table to construct a table with expected values of the observations. To determine expected values for each cell, multiply the respective row total by the respective column total, then divide by the overall total. So, for $cell_{i,j}$ (in *ith* row and *jth* column):

$$\text{Expected Value}_{i,j} = (\text{Total Row } i \times \text{Total Column } j)/\text{Overall Total} \qquad (1)$$

For example,

      Expected value for Growth/Low Risk is: $(99 \times 256)/315 = 80.46$; and

      Expected value for Value/High Risk is: $(216 \times 59)/315 = 40.46$.

    The table of expected values (and accompanying relative frequency table) are:

EXHIBIT 19B   Expected Marginal Frequencies and Relative Frequencies

	Observed Values				Observed Values		
	Low Risk	**High Risk**			**Low Risk**	**High Risk**	
Growth	80.457	18.543	**99**	Growth	81%	19%	**100%**
Value	175.543	40.457	**216**	Value	81%	19%	**100%**
	256	**59**	**315**				

    Step 3: Use the actual values and the expected values of observation counts to derive the chi-square test statistic, which is then compared to a value from the chi-square distribution for a given level of significance. If the test statistic is greater than the chi-square distribution value, then there is evidence of a significant association between the categorical variables.

4. DATA VISUALIZATION

Visualization is the presentation of data in a pictorial or graphical format for the purpose of increasing understanding and for gaining insights into the data. As has been said, "a picture is worth a thousand words." In this section, we discuss a variety of charts that are useful for understanding distributions, making comparisons, and exploring potential relationships among data. Specifically, we will cover visualizing frequency distributions of numerical and categorical data by using plots that represent multi-dimensional data for discovering relationships and by interpreting visuals that display unstructured data.

4.1. Histogram and Frequency Polygon

A **histogram** is a chart that presents the distribution of numerical data by using the height of a bar or column to represent the absolute frequency of each bin or interval in the distribution.

To construct a histogram from a continuous variable, we first need to split the data into bins and summarize the data into a frequency distribution table, such as the one we constructed in Exhibit 11. In a histogram, the y-axis generally represents the absolute frequency or the relative frequency in percentage terms, while the x-axis usually represents the bins of the variable. Using the frequency distribution table in Exhibit 11, we plot the histogram of daily returns of the EAA Equity Index, as shown in Exhibit 20. The bars are of equal width, representing the bin width of 1 percent for each return interval. The bars are usually drawn with no spaces in between, but small gaps can also be added between adjacent bars to increase readability, as in this exhibit. In this case, the height of each bar represents the absolute frequency for each return bin. A quick glance can tell us that the return bin 0 to 1 percent (exclusive) has the highest frequency, with more than 500 observations (555, to be exact), and it is represented by the tallest bar in the histogram.

An advantage of the histogram is that it can effectively present a large amount of numerical data that has been grouped into a frequency distribution and can allow a quick inspection of the shape, center, and spread of the distribution to better understand it. For example, in Exhibit 20, despite the histogram of daily EAA Equity Index returns appearing bell-shaped and roughly symmetrical, most bars to the right side of the origin (i.e., zero) are taller than those on the left side, indicating that more observations lie in the bins in positive territory. Remember that in the earlier discussion of this return distribution, it was noted that 54.1 percent of the observations are positive daily returns.

As mentioned, histograms can also be created with relative frequencies—the choice of using absolute versus relative frequency depends on the question being answered. An absolute frequency histogram best answers the question of how many items are in each bin, while a relative frequency histogram gives the proportion or percentage of the total observations in each bin.

Another graphical tool for displaying frequency distributions is the frequency polygon. To construct a **frequency polygon**, we plot the midpoint of each return bin on the x-axis and the absolute frequency for that bin on the y-axis. We then connect neighboring points with a straight line. Exhibit 20 shows the frequency polygon that overlays the histogram. In the graph, for example, the return interval 1 to 2 percent (exclusive) has a frequency of 110, so we plot the return-interval midpoint of 0.5 percent (which is 1.50 percent on the x-axis) and a frequency of 110 (on the y-axis). Importantly, the frequency polygon can quickly convey a visual understanding of the distribution since it displays frequency as an area under the curve.

EXHIBIT 20   Histogram Overlaid with Frequency Polygon for Daily Returns of EAA Equity Index

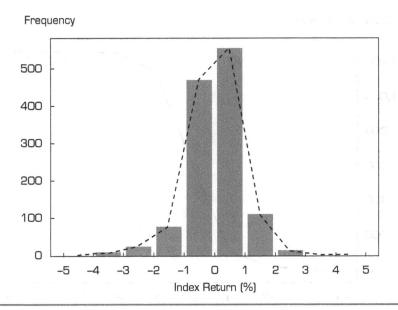

Another form for visualizing frequency distributions is the **cumulative frequency distribution chart**. Such a chart can plot either the cumulative absolute frequency or the cumulative relative frequency on the *y*-axis against the upper limit of the interval. The cumulative frequency distribution chart allows us to see the number or the percentage of the observations that lie below a certain value. To construct the cumulative frequency distribution, we graph the returns in the fourth (i.e., Cumulative Absolute Frequency) or fifth (i.e., Cumulative Relative Frequency) column of Exhibit 11 against the upper limit of each return interval.

Exhibit 21 presents the graph of the cumulative absolute frequency distribution for the daily returns on the EAA Equity Index. Notice that the cumulative distribution tends to flatten out when returns are extremely negative or extremely positive because the frequencies in these bins are quite small. The steep slope in the middle of Exhibit 21 reflects the fact that most of the observations—[(470 + 555)/1,258], or 81.5 percent—lie in the neighborhood of −1.0 to 1.0 percent.

4.2. Bar Chart

As we have demonstrated, the histogram is an efficient graphical tool to present the frequency distribution of numerical data. The frequency distribution of categorical data can be plotted in a similar type of graph called a **bar chart**. In a bar chart, each bar represents a distinct category, with the bar's height proportional to the frequency of the corresponding category.

Similar to plotting a histogram, the construction of a bar chart with one categorical variable first requires a frequency distribution table summarized from the variable. Note that the bars can be plotted vertically or horizontally. In a vertical bar chart, the *y*-axis still represents the absolute frequency or the relative frequency. Different from the histogram,

EXHIBIT 21   Cumulative Absolute Frequency Distribution of Daily Returns of EAA Equity Index

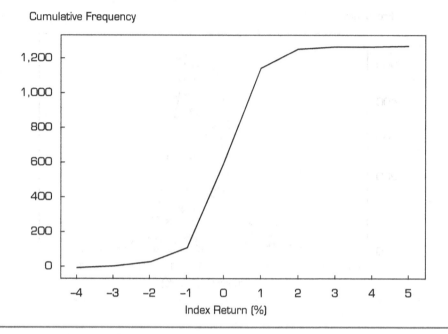

however, is that the x-axis in a bar chart represents the mutually exclusive categories to be *compared* rather than bins that group numerical data.

For example, using the marginal frequencies for the five GICS sectors shown in the last column in Exhibit 14, we plot a horizontal bar chart in Exhibit 22 to show the frequency of stocks by sector in the portfolio. The bars are of equal width to represent each sector, and sufficient space should be between adjacent bars to separate them from each other. Because this is a horizontal bar chart—in this case, the x-axis shows the absolute frequency and the y-axis represents the sectors—the length of each bar represents the absolute frequency of each sector. Since sectors are nominal data with no logical ordering, the bars representing sectors may be arranged in any order. However, in the particular case where the categories in a bar chart are ordered by frequency in descending order and the chart includes a line displaying cumulative relative frequency, then it is called a Pareto Chart. The chart is often used to highlight dominant categories or the most important groups.

Bar charts provide a snapshot to show the comparison between categories of data. As shown in Exhibit 22, the sector in which the portfolio holds most stocks is the health care sector, with 435 stocks, followed by the energy sector, with 290 stocks. The sector in which the portfolio has the least number of stocks is utilities, with 55 stocks. To compare categories more accurately, in some cases we may add the frequency count to the right end of each bar (or the top end of each bar in the case of a vertical bar chart).

The bar chart shown in Exhibit 22 can present the frequency distribution of only one categorical variable. In the case of two categorical variables, we need an enhanced version of the bar chart, called a **grouped bar chart** (also known as a **clustered bar chart**), to show joint frequencies. Using the joint frequencies by sector and by level of market capitalization given

EXHIBIT 22   Frequency by Sector for Stocks in a Portfolio

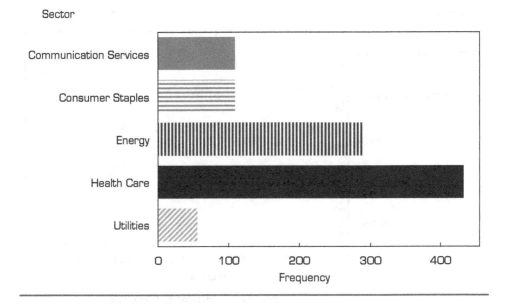

in Exhibit 14, for example, we show how a grouped bar chart is constructed in Exhibit 23. While the *y*-axis still represents the same categorical variable (the distinct GICS sectors as in Exhibit 22), in Exhibit 23 three bars are clustered side-by-side within the same sector to represent the three respective levels of market capitalization. The bars within each cluster should be colored or patterned differently to distinguish between them, but the color or pattern schemes for the sub-groups must be identical across the sector clusters, as shown by the legend at the upper right of Exhibit 23. Additionally, the bars in each sector cluster must always be placed in the same order throughout the chart. It is easy to see that the small-cap heath care stocks are the sub-group with the highest frequency (275), and we can also see that small-cap stocks are the largest sub-group within each sector—except for utilities, where mid cap is the largest.

An alternative form for presenting the joint frequency distribution of two categorical variables is a **stacked bar chart**. In the vertical version of a stacked bar chart, the bars representing the sub-groups are placed on top of each other to form a single bar. Each subsection of the bar is shown in a different color or pattern to represent the contribution of each sub-group, and the overall height of the stacked bar represents the marginal frequency for the category. Exhibit 23 can be replotted in a stacked bar chart, as shown in Exhibit 24.

We have shown that the frequency distribution of categorical data can be clearly and efficiently presented by using a bar chart. However, it is worth noting that applications of bar charts may be extended to more general cases when categorical data are associated with numerical data. For example, suppose we want to show a company's quarterly profits over the past one year. In this case, we can plot a vertical bar chart where each bar represents one of the four quarters in a time order and its height indicates the value of profits for that quarter.

EXHIBIT 23   Frequency by Sector and Level of Market Capitalization for Stocks in a Portfolio

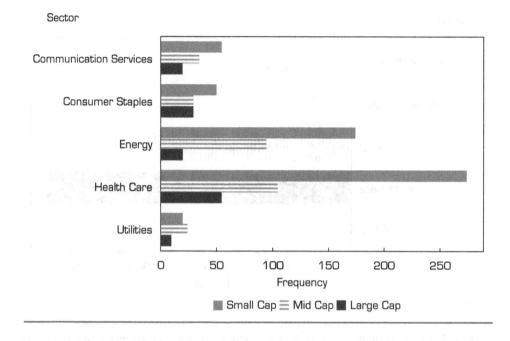

EXHIBIT 24   Frequency by Sector and Level of Market Capitalization in a Stacked Bar Chart

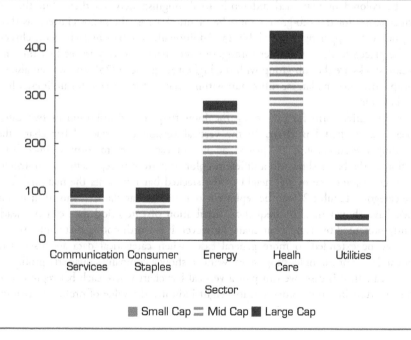

EXHIBIT 25   Tree-Map for Frequency Distribution by Sector in a Portfolio

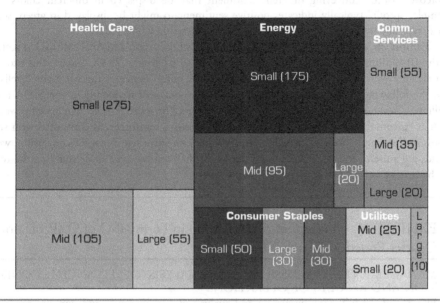

4.3. Tree-Map

In addition to bar charts and grouped bar charts, another graphical tool for displaying categorical data is a **tree-map**. It consists of a set of shaded rectangles to represent distinct groups, and the area of each rectangle is proportional to the value of the corresponding group. For example, referring back to the marginal frequencies by GICS sector in Exhibit 14, we plot a tree-map in Exhibit 25 to represent the frequency distribution by sector for stocks in the portfolio. The tree-map clearly shows that health care is the sector with the largest number of stocks in the portfolio, which is represented by the rectangle with the largest area.

Note that this example also depicts one more categorical variable (i.e., level of market capitalization). The tree-map can represent data with additional dimensions by displaying a set of nested rectangles. To show the joint frequencies of sub-groups by sector and level of market capitalization, as given in Exhibit 14, we can split each existing rectangle for sector into three sub-rectangles to represent small-cap, mid-cap, and large-cap stocks, respectively. In this case, the area of each nested rectangle would be proportional to the number of stocks in each market capitalization sub-group. The exhibit clearly shows that small-cap health care is the sub-group with the largest number of stocks. It is worth noting a caveat for using tree-maps: Tree-maps become difficult to read if the hierarchy involves more than three levels.

4.4. Word Cloud

So far, we have shown how to visualize the frequency distribution of numerical data or categorical data. However, can we find a chart to depict the frequency of unstructured data—particularly, textual data? A **word cloud** (also known as **tag cloud**) is a visual device for representing textual data. A word cloud consists of words extracted from a source of textual data, with the size of each distinct word being proportional to the frequency with which it appears in the given text. Note that common words (e.g., "a," "it," "the") are generally stripped out to focus on key words that convey the most meaningful information. This format allows us to quickly perceive the most frequent terms among the given text to provide information about the nature of the text, including topic and whether or not the text conveys positive or negative news. Moreover, words conveying different sentiment may be displayed in different colors. For example, "profit" typically indicates positive sentiment so might be displayed in green, while "loss" typically indicates negative sentiment and may be shown in red.

Exhibit 26 is an excerpt from the Management's Discussion and Analysis (MDA) section of the 10-Q filing for QXR Inc. for the quarter ended 31 March 20XX. Taking this text, we can create a word cloud, as shown in Exhibit 27. A quick glance at the word cloud tells us that the following words stand out (i.e., they were used most frequently in the MDA text): "billion," "revenue," "year," "income," "growth," and "financial." Note that specific words, such as "income" and "growth," typically convey positive sentiment, as contrasted with such words as "loss" and "decline," which typically convey negative sentiment. In conclusion, word clouds are a useful tool for visualizing textual data that can facilitate understanding the topic of the text as well as the sentiment it may convey.

EXHIBIT 26   Excerpt of MDA Section in Form 10-Q of QXR Inc. for Quarter Ended 31 March 20XX

MANAGEMENT'S DISCUSSION AND ANALYSIS OF FINANCIAL CONDITION AND RESULTS OF OPERATIONS
Please read the following discussion and analysis of our financial condition and results of operations together with our consolidated financial statements and related notes included under Part I, Item 1 of this Quarterly Report on Form 10-Q.

EXECUTIVE OVERVIEW OF RESULTS

Below are our key financial results for the three months ended March 31, 20XX (consolidated unless otherwise noted):

- Revenues of $36.3 billion and revenue growth of 17 percent year over year, constant currency revenue growth of 19 percent year over year.
- Major segment revenues of $36.2 billion with revenue growth of 17 percent year over year and other segments' revenues of $170 million with revenue growth of 13 percent year over year.
- Revenues from the United States, EMEA, APAC, and Other Americas were $16.5 billion, $11.8 billion, $6.1 billion, and $1.9 billion, respectively.
- Cost of revenues was $16.0 billion, consisting of TAC of $6.9 billion and other cost of revenues of $9.2 billion. Our TAC as a percentage of advertising revenues were 22 percent.
- Operating expenses (excluding cost of revenues) were $13.7 billion, including the EC AFS fine of $1.7 billion.
- Income from operations was $6.6 billion.
- Other income (expense), net, was $1.5 billion.
- Effective tax rate was 18 percent
- Net income was $6.7 billion with diluted net income per share of $9.50.
- Operating cash flow was $12.0 billion.
- Capital expenditures were $4.6 billion.

EXHIBIT 27   Word Cloud Visualizing Excerpted Text in MDA Section in Form 10-Q of QXR Inc.

4.5. Line Chart

A **line chart** is a type of graph used to visualize ordered observations. Often a line chart is used to display the change of data series over time. Note that the frequency polygon in Exhibit 20 and the cumulative frequency distribution chart in Exhibit 21 are also line charts but used particularly in those instances for representing data frequency distributions.

Constructing a line chart is relatively straightforward: We first plot all the data points against horizontal and vertical axes and then connect the points by straight line segments. For example, to show the 10-day daily closing prices of ABC Inc. stock presented in Exhibit 5, we first construct a chart with the x-axis representing time (in days) and the y-axis representing stock price (in dollars). Next, plot each closing price as points against both axes, and then use straight line segments to join the points together, as shown in Exhibit 28.

An important benefit of a line chart is that it facilitates showing changes in the data and underlying trends in a clear and concise way. This helps to understand the current data and also helps with forecasting the data series. In Exhibit 28, for example, it is easy to spot the price changes over the first 10 trading days since ABC's initial public offering (IPO). We see that the stock price peaked on Day 3 and then traded lower. Following a partial recovery on Day 7, it declined steeply to around $50 on Day 10. In contrast, although the

EXHIBIT 28   Daily Closing Prices of ABC Inc.'s Stock and Its Sector Index

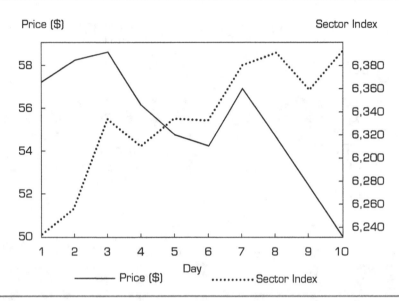

one-dimensional data array table in Exhibit 5 displays the same values as the line chart, the data table by itself does not provide a quick snapshot of changes in the data or facilitate understanding underlying trends. This is why line charts are helpful for visualization, particularly in cases of large amounts of data (i.e., hundreds, or even thousands, of data points).

A line chart is also capable of accommodating more than one set of data points, which is especially helpful for making comparisons. We can add a line to represent each group of data (e.g., a competitor's stock price or a sector index), and each line would have a distinct color or line pattern identified in a legend. For example, Exhibit 28 also includes a plot of ABC's sector index (i.e., the sector index for which ABC stock is a member, like health care or energy) over the same period. The sector index is displayed with its own distinct color or line pattern to facilitate comparison. Note also that because the sector index has a different range (approximately 6,230 to 6,390) than ABC's stock ($50 to $59 per share), we need a secondary y-axis to correctly display the sector index, which is on the right-hand side of the exhibit.

This comparison can help us understand whether ABC's stock price movement over the period is due to potential mispricing of its share issuance or instead due to industry-specific factors that also affect its competitors' stock prices. The comparison shows that over the period, the sector index moved in a nearly opposite trend versus ABC's stock price movement. This indicates that the steep decline in ABC's stock price is less likely attributable to sector-specific factors and more likely due to potential over-pricing of its IPO or to other company-specific factors.

When an observational unit (here, ABC Inc.) has more than two features (or variables) of interest, it would be useful to show the multi-dimensional data all in one chart to gain insights from a more holistic view. How can we add an additional dimension to a two-dimensional line chart? We can replace the data points with varying-sized bubbles to

EXHIBIT 29   Quarterly Revenue and EPS of ABC Incorporated

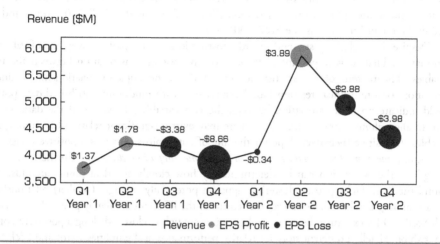

represent a third dimension of the data. Moreover, these bubbles may even be patterned, shaded or color coded to present additional information. This version of a line chart is called a **bubble line chart**.

Exhibit 7, for example, presented three types of quarterly data for ABC Inc. for use in a valuation analysis. We would like to plot two of them, revenue and earnings per share (EPS), over the two-year period. As shown in Exhibit 29, with the x-axis representing time (i.e., quarters) and the y-axis representing revenue in millions of dollars, we can plot the revenue data points against both axes to form a typical line chart. Next, each marker representing a revenue data point is replaced by a circular bubble with its size proportional to the magnitude of the EPS in the corresponding quarter. Moreover, the bubbles are shaded in a binary scheme with lightly shaded representing profits and dark shading representing losses. In this way, the bubble line chart reflects the changes for both revenue and EPS simultaneously, and it also shows whether the EPS represents a profit or a loss.

As depicted, ABC's earning were quite volatile during its initial two years as a public company. Earnings started off as a profit of $1.37/share but finished the first year with a big loss of −$8.66/share, during which time revenue experienced only small fluctuations. Furthermore, while revenues and earnings both subsequently recovered sharply—peaking in Q2 of Year 2—revenues then declined, and the company returned to significant losses (−3.98/share) by the end of Year 2.

4.6. Scatter Plot

A **scatter plot** is a type of graph for visualizing the joint variation in two numerical variables. It is a useful tool for displaying and understanding potential relationships between the variables.

A scatter plot is constructed with the x-axis representing one variable and the y-axis representing the other variable. It uses dots to indicate the values of the two variables for a particular point in time, which are plotted against the corresponding axes. Suppose an analyst is investigating potential relationships between sector index returns and returns for the broad market, such as the S&P 500 Index. Specifically, he or she is interested in the relative performance of two sectors, information technology (IT) and utilities, compared to the market index over a specific five-year period. The analyst has obtained the sector and market index returns for each month over the five years under investigation and plotted the data points in the scatter plots, shown in Exhibit 30 for IT versus the S&P 500 returns and in Exhibit 31 for utilities versus the S&P 500 returns.

Despite their relatively straightforward construction, scatter plots convey lots of valuable information. First, it is important to inspect for any potential association between the two variables. The pattern of the scatter plot may indicate no apparent relationship, a linear association, or a non-linear relationship. A scatter plot with randomly distributed data points would indicate no clear association between the two variables. However, if the data points seem to align along a straight line, then there may exist a significant relationship among the variables. A positive (negative) slope for the line of data points indicates a positive (negative) association, *meaning the variables move in the same (opposite) direction*. Furthermore, the strength of the association can be determined by how closely the data points are clustered around the line. Tight (loose) clustering signals a potentially stronger (weaker) relationship.

Examining Exhibit 30, we can see the returns of the IT sector are highly positively associated with S&P 500 Index returns because the data points are tightly clustered along a positively sloped line. Exhibit 31 tells a different story for relative performance of the utilities sector and S&P 500 index returns: The data points appear to be distributed in no discernable pattern, indicating no clear relationship among these variables. Second, observing the data points located toward the ends of each axis, which represent the maximum or minimum values, provides a quick sense of the data range. Third, assuming that a relationship among the variables is apparent, inspecting the scatter plot can help to spot extreme values (i.e., outliers). For example, an outlier data point is readily detected in Exhibit 30, as indicated by the arrow. As you will learn later in the CFA Program curriculum, finding these extreme values and handling them with appropriate measures is an important part of the financial modeling process.

EXHIBIT 30   Scatter Plot of Information Technology Sector Index Return vs. S&P 500 Index Return

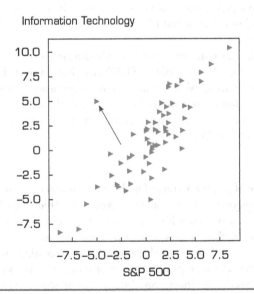

EXHIBIT 31   Scatter Plot of Utilities Sector Index Return vs. S&P 500 Index Return

Information Technology

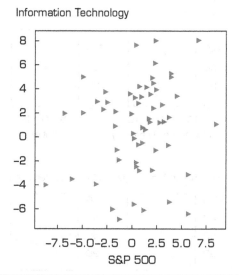

Scatter plots are a powerful tool for finding patterns between two variables, for assessing data range, and for spotting extreme values. In practice, however, there are situations where we need to inspect for pairwise associations among many variables—for example, when conducting feature selection from dozens of variables to build a predictive model.

A **scatter plot matrix** is a useful tool for organizing scatter plots between pairs of variables, making it easy to inspect all pairwise relationships in one combined visual. For example, suppose the analyst would like to extend his or her investigation by adding another sector index. He or she can use a scatter plot matrix, as shown in Exhibit 32, which now incorporates four variables, including index returns for the S&P 500 and for three sectors: IT, utilities, and financials.

The scatter plot matrix contains each combination of bivariate scatter plot (i.e., S&P 500 vs. each sector, IT vs. utilities, IT vs. financials, and financials vs. utilities) as well as univariate frequency distribution histograms for each variable plotted along the diagonal. In this way, the scatter plot matrix provides a concise visual summary of each variable and of potential relationships among them. Importantly, the construction of the scatter plot matrix is typically a built-in function in most major statistical software packages, so it is relatively easy to implement. It is worth pointing out that the upper triangle of the matrix is the mirror image of the lower triangle, so the compact form of the scatter plot matrix that uses only the lower triangle is also appropriate.

With the addition of the financial sector, the bottom panel of Exhibit 32 reveals the following additional information, which can support sector allocation in the portfolio construction process:

• Strong positive relationship between returns of financial and S&P 500;
• Positive relationship between returns of financial and IT; and
• No clear relationship between returns of financial and utilities.

EXHIBIT 32   Pairwise Scatter Plot Matrix

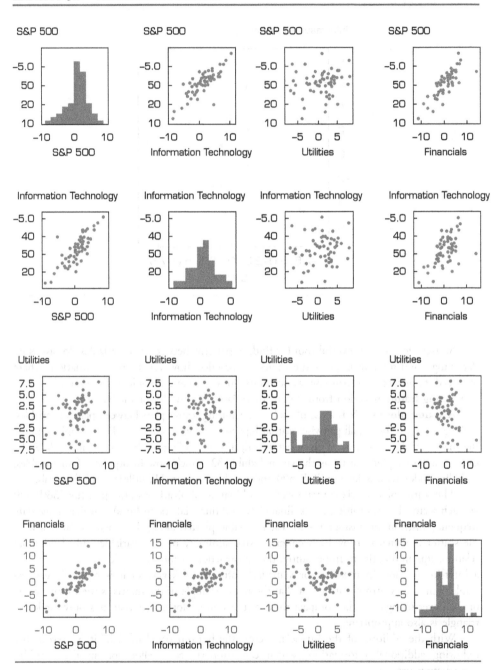

It is important to note that despite their usefulness, scatter plots and scatter plot matrixes should not be considered as substitutes for robust statistical tests; rather, they should be used alongside such tests for best results.

EXHIBIT 33   Frequencies by Sector and Market Capitalization in Heat Map

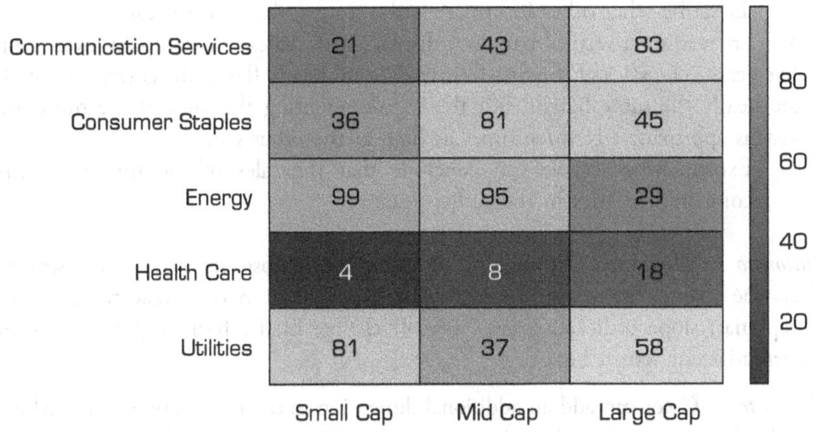

4.7. Heat Map

A **heat map** is a type of graphic that organizes and summarizes data in a tabular format and represents them using a color spectrum. For example, given a portfolio, we can create a contingency table that summarizes the joint frequencies of the stock holdings by sector and by level of market capitalization, as in Exhibit 33.

Cells in the chart are shaded or color-coded to differentiate high values from low values by using the shading (color) scheme defined in the shading (color) spectrum on the right side of the chart. As shown by the heat map, this portfolio has the largest exposure (in terms of number of stocks) to small- and mid-cap energy stocks. It has substantial exposures to large-cap communications services, mid-cap consumer staples, and small-cap utilities; however, exposure to the health care sector is limited. In sum, the heat map reveals this portfolio to be relatively well-diversified among sectors and market-cap levels. Besides their use in displaying frequency distributions, heat maps are commonly used for visualizing the degree of correlation among different variables.

EXAMPLE 6   Evaluating Data Visuals

1. You have a cumulative absolute frequency distribution graph (similar to the one in Exhibit 21) of daily returns over a five-year period for an index of Asian equity markets.
    Interpret the meaning of the slope of such a graph.
2. You are creating a word cloud for a visual representation of text on a company's quarterly earnings announcements over the past three years. The word cloud uses font size to indicate word frequency. This particular company has experienced both quarterly profits and losses during the period under investigation.
    Describe how the word cloud might be used to convey information besides word frequency.
3. You are examining a scatter plot of monthly stock returns, similar to the one in Exhibit 30, for two technology companies: one is a hardware manufacturer, and the

other is a software developer. The scatter plot shows a strong positive association among their returns.

Describe what other information the scatter plot can provide.

4. You are reading a vertical bar chart displaying the sales of a company over the past five years. The sales of the first four years seem nearly flat as the corresponding bars are nearly the same height, but the bar representing the sales of the most recent year is approximately three times as high as the other bars.

Explain whether we can conclude that the sales of the fifth year tripled compared to sales in the earlier years.

Solution to 1: The slope of the graph of a cumulative absolute frequency distribution reflects the change in the number of observations between two adjacent return bins. A steep (flat) slope indicates a large (small) change in the frequency of observations between adjacent return bins.

Solution to 2: Color can add an additional dimension to the information conveyed in the word cloud. For example, red can be used for "losses" and other words conveying negative sentiment, and green can be used for "profit" and other words indicative of positive sentiment.

Solution to 3: Besides the sign and degree of association of the stocks' returns, the scatter plot can provide a visual representation of whether the association is linear or non-linear, the maximum and minimum values for the return observations, and an indication of which observations may have extreme values (i.e., are potential outliers).

Solution to 4: Typically, the heights of bars in a vertical bar chart are proportional to the values that they represent. However, if the graph is using a truncated y-axis (i.e., one that does not start at zero), then values are not accurately represented by the height of bars. Therefore, we need to examine the y-axis of the bar chart before concluding that sales in the fifth year were triple the sales of the prior years.

4.8. Guide to Selecting among Visualization Types

We have introduced and discussed a variety of different visualization types that are regularly used in investment practice. When it comes to selecting a chart for visualizing data, the intended purpose is the key consideration: Is it for exploring and/or presenting distributions or relationships, or is it for making comparisons? Given your intended purpose, the best selection is typically the simplest visual that conveys the message or achieves the specific goal. Exhibit 34 presents a flow chart for facilitating selection among the visualization types we have discussed. Finally, note that some visualization types, such as bar chart and heat map, may be suitable for several different purposes.

Data visualization is a powerful tool to show data and gain insights into data. However, we need to be cautious that a graph could be misleading if data are mispresented or the graph is poorly constructed. There are numerous different ways that may lead to a misleading graph. We list four typical pitfalls here that analysts should avoid.

First, an improper chart type is selected to present data, which would hinder the accurate interpretation of data. For example, to investigate the correlation between two data series, we

EXHIBIT 34   Flow Chart of Selecting Visualization Types

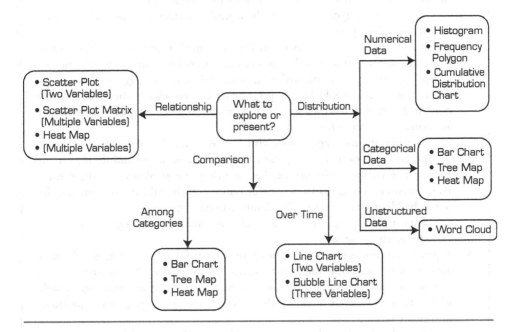

can construct a scatter plot to visualize the joint variation between two variables. In contrast, plotting the two data series separately in a line chart would make it rather difficult to examine the relationship.

Second, data are selectively plotted in favor of the conclusion an analyst intends to draw. For example, data presented for an overly short time period may appear to show a trend that is actually noise—that is, variation within the data's normal range if examining the data over a longer time period. So, presenting data for too short a time window may mistakenly point to a non-existing trend.

Third, data are improperly plotted in a truncated graph that has a *y*-axis that does not start at zero. In some situations, the truncated graph can create the false impression of significant differences when there is actually only a small difference. For example, suppose a vertical bar chart is used to compare annual revenues of two companies, one with $9 billion and the other with $10 billion. If the *y*-axis starts at $8 billion, then the bar heights would inaccurately imply that the latter company's revenue is twice the former company's revenue.

Last, but not least, is the improper scaling of axes. For example, given a line chart, setting a higher than necessary maximum on the *y*-axis tends to compress the graph into an area close to the *x*-axis. This causes the graph to appear to be less steep and less volatile than if it was properly plotted. In sum, analysts need to avoid these misuses of visualization when charting data and must ensure the ethical use of data visuals.

EXAMPLE 7   Selecting Visualization Types

1. A portfolio manager plans to buy several stocks traded on a small emerging market exchange but is concerned whether the market can provide sufficient liquidity to

support her purchase order size. As the first step, she wants to analyze the daily trading volumes of one of these stocks over the past five years.

Explain which type of chart can best provide a quick view of trading volume for the given period.

2. An analyst is building a model to predict stock market downturns. According to the academic literature and his practitioner knowledge and expertise, he has selected 10 variables as potential predictors. Before continuing to construct the model, the analyst would like to get a sense of how closely these variables are associated with the broad stock market index and whether any pair of variables are associated with each other.

Describe the most appropriate visual to select for this purpose.

3. Central Bank members meet regularly to assess the economy and decide on any interest rate changes. Minutes of their meetings are published on the Central Bank's website. A quantitative researcher wants to analyze the meeting minutes for use in building a model to predict future economic growth.

Explain which type of chart is most appropriate for creating an overview of the meeting minutes.

4. A private investor wants to add a stock to her portfolio, so she asks her financial adviser to compare the three-year financial performances (by quarter) of two companies. One company experienced consistent revenue and earnings growth, while the other experienced volatile revenue and earnings growth, including quarterly losses.

Describe the chart the adviser should use to best show these performance differences.

Solution to 1: The five-year history of daily trading volumes contains a large amount of numerical data. Therefore, a histogram is the best chart for grouping these data into frequency distribution bins and for showing a quick snapshot of the shape, center, and spread of the data's distribution.

Solution to 2: To inspect for a potential relationship between two variables, a scatter plot is a good choice. But with 10 variables, plotting individual scatter plots is not an efficient approach. Instead, utilizing a scatter plot matrix would give the analyst a good overview in one comprehensive visual of all the pairwise associations between the variables.

Solution to 3: Since the meeting minutes consist of textual data, a word cloud would be the most suitable tool to visualize the textual data and facilitate the researcher's understanding of the topic of the text as well as the sentiment, positive or negative, it may convey.

Solution to 4: The best chart for making this comparison would be a bubble line chart using two different color lines to represent the quarterly revenues for each company. The bubble sizes would then indicate the magnitude of each company's quarterly earnings, with green bubbles signifying profits and red bubbles indicating losses.

5. MEASURES OF CENTRAL TENDENCY

So far, we have discussed methods we can use to organize and present data so that they are more understandable. The frequency distribution of an asset return series, for example, reveals much about the nature of the risks that investors may encounter in a particular asset. Although frequency distributions, histograms, and contingency tables provide a convenient way to summarize a series of observations, these methods are just a first step toward describing the data. In this section, we discuss the use of quantitative measures that explain characteristics of data. Our focus is on measures of central tendency and other measures of location. A **measure of central tendency** specifies where the data are centered. Measures of central tendency are probably more widely used than any other statistical measure because they can be computed and applied relatively easily. **Measures of location** include not only measures of central tendency but other measures that illustrate the location or distribution of data.

In the following subsections, we explain the common measures of central tendency—the arithmetic mean, the median, the mode, the weighted mean, the geometric mean, and the harmonic mean. We also explain other useful measures of location, including quartiles, quintiles, deciles, and percentiles.

A **statistic** is a summary measure of a set of observations, and descriptive statistics summarize the central tendency and spread variation in the distribution of data. If the statistic summarizes the set of all possible observations of a **population,** we refer to the statistic as a parameter. If the statistic summarizes a set of observations that is a subset of the population, we refer to the statistic as a **sample statistic,** often leav8ing off the word "sample" and simply referring to it as a statistic. While measures of central tendency and location can be calculated for populations and **samples,** our focus is on sample measures (i.e., sample statistics) as it is rare that an investment manager would be dealing with an entire population of data.

5.1. The Arithmetic Mean

Analysts and portfolio managers often want one number that describes a representative possible outcome of an investment decision. The arithmetic mean is one of the most frequently used measures of the center of data.

Definition of Arithmetic Mean. The **arithmetic mean** is the sum of the values of the observations divided by the number of observations.

5.1.1. The Sample Mean
The sample mean is the arithmetic mean or arithmetic average computed for a sample. As you will see, we use the terms "mean" and "average" interchangeably. Often, we cannot observe every member of a population; instead, we observe a subset or sample of the population.

Sample Mean Formula. The **sample mean** or average, $\overline{X}$ (read "X-bar"), is the arithmetic mean value of a sample:

$$\overline{X} = \frac{\sum_{i=1}^{n} X_i}{n} \tag{2}$$

where n is the number of observations in the sample.

Equation 2 tells us to sum the values of the observations (X_i) and divide the sum by the number of observations. For example, if a sample of market capitalizations for six publicly traded Australian companies contains the values (in AUD billions) 35, 30, 22, 18, 15, and 12, the sample mean market cap is $132/6 =$ A\$22 billion. As previously noted, the sample mean is a statistic (that is, a descriptive measure of a sample).

Means can be computed for individual units or over time. For instance, the sample might be the return on equity (ROE) in a given year for a sample of 25 companies in the FTSE Eurotop 100, an index of Europe's 100 largest companies. In this case, we calculate the mean ROE in that year as an average across 25 individual units. When we examine the characteristics of some units at a specific point in time (such as ROE for the FTSE Eurotop 100), we are examining cross-sectional data; the mean of these observations is the cross-sectional mean. If the sample consists of the historical monthly returns on the FTSE Eurotop 100 for the past five years, however, then we have time-series data; the mean of these observations is the time-series mean. We will examine specialized statistical methods related to the behavior of time series in the chapter on time-series analysis (Chapter 9).

Except in cases of large datasets with many observations, we should not expect any of the actual observations to equal the mean; sample means provide only a summary of the data being analyzed. Also, although in some cases the number of values below the mean is quite close to the number of values above the mean, this need not be the case. As an analyst, you will often need to find a few numbers that describe the characteristics of the distribution, and we will consider more later. The mean is generally the statistic that you use as a measure of the typical outcome for a distribution. You can then use the mean to compare the performance of two different markets. For example, you might be interested in comparing the stock market performance of investments in Asia Pacific with investments in Europe. You can use the mean returns in these markets to compare investment results.

EXAMPLE 8   Calculating a Cross-Sectional Mean

Suppose we want to examine the performance of a sample of selected stock indexes from 11 different countries. The 52-week percentage change is reported in Exhibit 35 for Year 1, Year 2, and Year 3 for the sample of indexes.

EXHIBIT 35   Annual Returns for Years 1 to 3 for Selected Countries' Stock Indexes

Index	52-Week Return (%)		
	Year 1	Year 2	Year 3
Country A	−15.6	−5.4	6.1
Country B	7.8	6.3	−1.5
Country C	5.3	1.2	3.5
Country D	−2.4	−3.1	6.2
Country E	−4.0	−3.0	3.0
Country F	5.4	5.2	−1.0
Country G	12.7	6.7	−1.2
Country H	3.5	4.3	3.4

Index	52-Week Return (%)		
	Year 1	Year 2	Year 3
Country I	6.2	7.8	3.2
Country J	8.1	4.1	-0.9
Country K	11.5	3.4	1.2

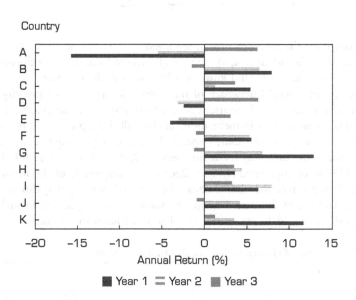

Using the data provided, calculate the sample mean return for the 11 indexes for each year.

Solution: For Year 3, the calculation applies Equation 2 to the returns for Year 3: (6.1 − 1.5 + 3.5 + 6.2 + 3.0 − 1.0 − 1.2 + 3.4 + 3.2 − 0.9 + 1.2)/11 = 22.0/11 = 2.0%. Using a similar calculation, the sample mean is 3.5% for Year 1 and 2.5% for Year 2.

5.1.2. Properties of the Arithmetic Mean
The arithmetic mean can be likened to the center of gravity of an object. Exhibit 36 expresses this analogy graphically by plotting nine hypothetical observations on a bar. The nine observations are 2, 4, 4, 6, 10, 10, 12, 12, and 12; the arithmetic mean is 72/9 = 8. The observations are plotted on the bar with various heights based on their frequency (that is, 2 is one

unit high, 4 is two units high, and so on). When the bar is placed on a fulcrum, it balances only when the fulcrum is located at the point on the scale that corresponds to the arithmetic mean.

As analysts, we often use the mean return as a measure of the typical outcome for an asset. As in **Example 8**, however, some outcomes are above the mean and some are below it. We can calculate the distance between the mean and each outcome, which is the deviation. Mathematically, it is always true that the sum of the deviations around the mean equals 0. We can see this by using the definition of the arithmetic mean shown in Equation 2, multiplying both sides of the equation by n: $n\overline{X} = \sum_{i=1}^{n} X_i$. The sum of the deviations from the mean is calculated as follows:

$$\sum_{i=1}^{n}(X_i - \overline{X}) = \sum_{i=1}^{n}X_i - \sum_{i=1}^{n}\overline{X} = \sum_{i=1}^{n}X_i - n\,\overline{X} = 0.$$

Deviations from the arithmetic mean are important information because they indicate risk. The concept of deviations around the mean forms the foundation for the more complex concepts of variance, skewness, and kurtosis, which we will discuss later.

A property and potential drawback of the arithmetic mean is its sensitivity to extreme values, or outliers. Because all observations are used to compute the mean and are given equal weight (i.e., importance), the arithmetic mean can be pulled sharply upward or downward by extremely large or small observations, respectively. For example, suppose we compute the arithmetic mean of the following seven numbers: 1, 2, 3, 4, 5, 6, and 1,000. The mean is $1,021/7 = 145.86$, or approximately 146. Because the magnitude of the mean, 146, is so much larger than most of the observations (the first six), we might question how well it represents the location of the data. Perhaps the most common approach in such cases is to report the median, or middle value, in place of or in addition to the mean.

EXHIBIT 36   Center of Gravity Analogy for the Arithmetic Mean

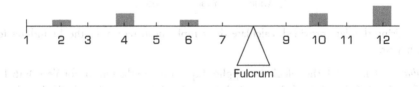

5.1.3. Outliers
In practice, although an extreme value or outlier in a financial dataset may just represent a rare value in the population, it may also reflect an error in recording the value of an observation or an observation generated from a different population from that producing the other observations in the sample. In the latter two cases, in particular, the arithmetic mean could be misleading. So, what do we do? The first step is to examine the data, either by inspecting the sample observations if the sample is not too large or by using visualization approaches. Once we are comfortable that we have identified and eliminated errors (that is, we have cleaned the data), we can then address what to do with extreme values in the sample. When dealing with a sample that has extreme values, there may be a possibility of transforming the variable (e.g., a log transformation) or of selecting another variable that

achieves the same purpose. However, if alternative model specifications or variable transformations are not possible, then here are three options for dealing with extreme values:

Option 1. Do nothing; use the data without any adjustment.
Option 2. Delete all the outliers.
Option 3. Replace the outliers with another value.

The first option is appropriate if the values are legitimate, correct observations, and it is important to reflect the whole of the sample distribution. Outliers may contain meaningful information, so excluding or altering these values may reduce valuable information. Further, because identifying a data point as extreme leaves it up to the judgment of the analyst, leaving in all observations eliminates that need to judge a value as extreme.

The second option excludes the extreme observations. One measure of central tendency in this case is the **trimmed mean**, which is computed by excluding a stated small percentage of the lowest and highest values and then computing an arithmetic mean of the remaining values. For example, a 5 percent trimmed mean discards the lowest 2.5 percent and the highest 2.5 percent of values and computes the mean of the remaining 95 of values. A trimmed mean is used in sports competitions when judges' lowest and highest scores are discarded in computing a contestant's score.

The third option involves substituting values for the extreme values. A measure of central tendency in this case is the **winsorized mean**. It is calculated by assigning a stated percentage of the lowest values equal to one specified low value and a stated percentage of the highest values equal to one specified high value, and then it computes a mean from the restated data. For example, a 95 percent winsorized mean sets the bottom 2.5 percent of values equal to the value at or below which 2.5 percent of all the values lie (as will be seen shortly, this is called the "2.5th percentile" value) and the top 2.5 percent of values equal to the value at or below which 97.5 percent of all the values lie (the "97.5th percentile" value).

In **Exhibit 37**, we show the differences among these options for handling outliers using daily returns for the fictitious Euro-Asia-Africa (EAA) Equity Index in Exhibit 11.

EXHIBIT 37   Handling Outliers: Daily Returns to an Index

Consider the fictitious EAA Equity Index. Using daily returns on the EAA Equity Index for the period of five years, consisting of 1,258 trading days, we can see the effect of trimming and winsorizing the data:

The trimmed mean eliminates the lowest 2.5 percent of returns, which in this sample is any daily return less than −1.934 percent, and it eliminates the highest 2.5 percent, which in this sample is any daily return greater than 1.671 percent. The result of this trimming is that the mean is calculated using 1,194 observations instead of the original sample's 1,258 observations.

The winsorized mean substitutes −1.934 percent for any return below −1.934 and substitutes 1.671 percent for any return above 1.671. The result in this case is that the trimmed and winsorized means are above the arithmetic mean.

	Arithmetic Mean (%)	Trimmed Mean [Trimmed 5%] (%)	Winsorized Mean [95%] (%)
Mean	0.035	0.048	0.038
Number of Observations	1,258	1,194	1,258

5.2. The Median

A second important measure of central tendency is the median.

Definition of Median. The **median** is the value of the middle item of a set of items that has been sorted into ascending or descending order. In an odd-numbered sample of n items, the median is the value of the item that occupies the $(n + 1)/2$ position. In an even-numbered sample, we define the median as the mean of the values of items occupying the $n/2$ and $(n + 2)/2$ positions (the two middle items).

Suppose we have a return on assets (in %) for each of three companies: 0.0, 2.0, and 2.1. With an odd number of observations ($n = 3$), the median occupies the $(n + 1)/2 = 4/2 = $ 2nd position. The median is 2.0 percent. The value of 2.0 percent is the middlemost observation: One lies above it, and one lies below it. Whether we use the calculation for an even- or odd-numbered sample, an equal number of observations lie above and below the median. A distribution has only one median.

A potential advantage of the median is that, unlike the mean, extreme values do not affect it. For example, if a sample consists of the observations of 1, 2, 3, 4, 5, 6 and 1,000, the median is 4. The median is not influenced by the extremely large outcome of 1,000. In other words, the median is affected less by outliers than the mean and therefore is useful in describing data that follow a distribution that is not symmetric, such as revenues.

The median, however, does not use all the information about the size of the observations; it focuses only on the relative position of the ranked observations. Calculating the median may also be more complex. To do so, we need to order the observations from smallest to largest, determine whether the sample size is even or odd, and then on that basis, apply one of two calculations. Mathematicians express this disadvantage by saying that the median is less mathematically tractable than the mean.

We use the data from Exhibit 35 to demonstrate finding the median, reproduced in Exhibit 38 in ascending order of the return for Year 3, with the ranked position from

EXHIBIT 38   Returns on Selected Country Stock Indexes for Year 3 in Ascending Order

Index	Year 3 Return (%)		Position
Country B	−1.5		1
Country G	−1.2		2
Country F	−1.0		3
Country J	−0.9		4
Country K	1.2		5
Country E	3.0	←	6
Country I	3.2		7
Country H	3.4		8
Country C	3.5		9
Country A	6.1		10
Country D	6.2		11

1 (lowest) to 11 (highest) indicated. Because this sample has 11 observations, the median is the value in the sorted array that occupies the $(11 + 1)/2 = 6$th position. Country E's index occupies the sixth position and is the median. The arithmetic mean for Year 3 for this sample of indexes is 2.0 percent, whereas the median is 3.0.

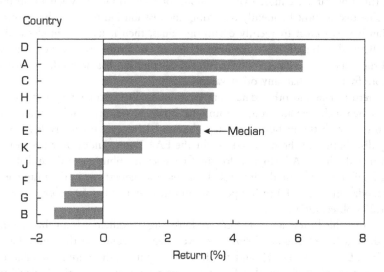

If a sample has an even number of observations, the median is the mean of the two values in the middle. For example, if our sample in Exhibit 38 had 12 indexes instead of 11, the median would be the mean of the values in the sorted array that occupy the sixth and the seventh positions.

EXHIBIT 39   Histogram of Daily Returns on the EAA Equity Index

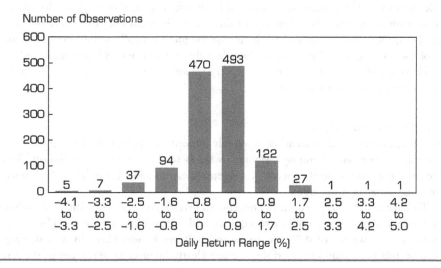

5.3. The Mode

The third important measure of central tendency is the mode.

Definition of Mode. The **mode** is the most frequently occurring value in a distribution.

A distribution can have more than one mode, or even no mode. When a distribution has a single value that is most frequently occurring, the distribution is said to be **unimodal**. If a distribution has two most frequently occurring values, then it has two modes and is called **bimodal**. If the distribution has three most frequently occurring values, then it is **trimodal**. When all the values in a dataset are different, the distribution has no mode because no value occurs more frequently than any other value.

Stock return data and other data from continuous distributions may not have a modal outcome. When such data are grouped into bins, however, we often find an interval (possibly more than one) with the highest frequency: the **modal interval** (or intervals). Consider the frequency distribution of the daily returns for the EAA Equity Index over five years that we looked at in Exhibit 11. A histogram for the frequency distribution of these daily returns is shown in Exhibit 39. The modal interval always has the highest bar in the histogram; in this case, the modal interval is 0.0 to 0.9 percent, and this interval has 493 observations out of a total of 1,258 observations.

Notice that this histogram in Exhibit 39 looks slightly different from the one in Exhibit 11, since this one has 11 bins and follows the seven-step procedure exactly. Thus, the bin width is 0.828 [=(5.00 − −4.11)/11], and the first bin begins at the minimum value of −4.11 percent. It was noted previously that for ease of interpretation, in practice bin width is often rounded up to the nearest whole number; the first bin can start at the nearest whole number below the minimum value. These refinements and the use of 10 bins were incorporated into the histogram in Exhibit 11, which has a modal interval of 0.0 to 1.0 percent.

The mode is the only measure of central tendency that can be used with nominal data. For example, when we categorize investment funds into different styles and assign a number to each style, the mode of these categorized data is the most frequent investment fund style.

5.4. Other Concepts of Mean

Earlier we explained the arithmetic mean, which is a fundamental concept for describing the central tendency of data. An advantage of the arithmetic mean over two other measures of central tendency, the median and mode, is that the mean uses all the information about the size of the observations. The mean is also relatively easy to work with mathematically.

However, other concepts of mean are very important in investments. In the following sections, we discuss such concepts.

5.4.1. The Weighted Mean

The concept of weighted mean arises repeatedly in portfolio analysis. In the arithmetic mean, all sample observations are equally weighted by the factor $1/n$. In working with portfolios, we often need the more general concept of weighted mean to allow for different (i.e., unequal) weights on different observations.

To illustrate the weighted mean concept, an investment manager with $100 million to invest might allocate $70 million to equities and $30 million to bonds. The portfolio, therefore, has a weight of 0.70 on stocks and 0.30 on bonds. How do we calculate the return on this portfolio? The portfolio's return clearly involves an averaging of the returns on the stock and bond investments. The mean that we compute, however, must reflect the fact that stocks have a 70% weight in the portfolio and bonds have a 30% weight. The way to reflect this weighting is to multiply the return on the stock investment by 0.70 and the return on the bond investment by 0.30, then sum the two results. This sum is an example of a weighted mean. It would be incorrect to take an arithmetic mean of the return on the stock and bond investments, equally weighting the returns on the two asset classes.

Weighted Mean Formula. The **weighted mean** $\overline{X}_w$ (read "X-bar sub-w"), for a set of observations $X_1, X_2, \ldots, X_n$ with corresponding weights of $w_1, w_2, \ldots, w_n$, is computed as:

$$\overline{X}_w = \sum_{i=1}^{n} w_i X_i, \tag{3}$$

In the context of portfolios, a positive weight represents an asset held long and a negative weight represents an asset held short.

The formula for the weighted mean can be compared to the formula for the arithmetic mean. For a set of observations $X_1, X_2, \ldots, X_n$, let the weights $w_1, w_2, \ldots, w_n$ all equal $1/n$. Under this assumption, the formula for the weighted mean is $(1/n)\sum_{i=1}^{n} X_i$. This is the formula for the arithmetic mean. Therefore, the arithmetic mean is a special case of the weighted mean in which all the weights are equal.

EXAMPLE 9   Calculating a Weighted Mean

Using the country index data shown in Exhibit 35, consider a portfolio that consists of three funds that track three countries' indexes: County C, Country G, and Country K. The portfolio weights and index returns are as follows:

Using the information provided, calculate the returns on the portfolio for each year.

Index Tracked by Fund	Allocation (%)	Annual Return (%)		
		Year 1	Year 2	Year 3
Country C	25%	5.3	1.2	3.5
Country G	45%	12.7	6.7	-1.2
Country K	30%	11.5	3.4	1.2

Solution: Converting the percentage asset allocation to decimal form, we find the mean return as the weighted average of the funds' returns. We have:

Mean portfolio return for Year 1	$= 0.25\,(5.3) + 0.45\,(12.7) + 0.30\,(11.5)$
	$= 10.50\%$
Mean portfolio return for Year 2	$= 0.25\,(1.2) + 0.45\,(6.7) + 0.30\,(3.4)$
	$= 4.34\%$
Mean portfolio return for Year 3	$= 0.25\,(3.5) + 0.45\,(-1.2) + 0.30\,(1.2)$
	$= 0.70\%$

This example illustrates the general principle that a portfolio return is a weighted sum. Specifically, a portfolio's return is the weighted average of the returns on the assets in the portfolio; the weight applied to each asset's return is the fraction of the portfolio invested in that asset.

Market indexes are computed as weighted averages. For market-capitalization weighted indexes, such as the CAC-40 in France, the TOPIX in Japan, or the S&P 500 in the United States, each included stock receives a weight corresponding to its market value divided by the total market value of all stocks in the index.

Our illustrations of weighted mean use past data, but they might just as well use forward-looking data. When we take a weighted average of forward-looking data, the weighted mean is the expected value. Suppose we make one forecast for the year-end level of the S&P 500 assuming economic expansion and another forecast for the year-end level of the S&P 500 assuming economic contraction. If we multiply the first forecast by the probability of expansion and the second forecast by the probability of contraction and then add these weighted forecasts, we are calculating the expected value of the S&P 500 at year-end. If we take a weighted average of possible future returns on the S&P 500, where the weights are the probabilities, we are computing the S&P 500's expected return. The probabilities must sum to 1, satisfying the condition on the weights in the expression for weighted mean, Equation 3.

5.4.2. The Geometric Mean

The geometric mean is most frequently used to average rates of change over time or to compute the growth rate of a variable. In investments, we frequently use the geometric mean to either average a time series of rates of return on an asset or a portfolio or to compute the growth rate of a financial variable, such as earnings or sales. The geometric mean is defined by the following formula.

Geometric Mean Formula. The **geometric mean**, $\overline{X}_G$, of a set of observations $X_1, X_2, \ldots, X_n$ is:

$$\overline{X}_G = \sqrt[n]{X_1 X_2 X_3 \ldots X_n}. \text{ with } X_i \geq 0 \text{ for } i = 1, 2, \ldots, n. \tag{4}$$

Equation 4 has a solution, and the geometric mean exists only if the product under the square root sign is non-negative. Therefore, we must impose the restriction that all the observations X_i are greater than or equal to zero. We can solve for the geometric mean directly with any calculator that has an exponentiation key (on most calculators, y^x). We can also solve for the geometric mean using natural logarithms. Equation 4 can also be stated as

$$ln\overline{X}_G = \tfrac{1}{n}ln(X_1X_2X_3...X_n),$$

or, because the logarithm of a product of terms is equal to the sum of the logarithms of each of the terms, as

$$ln\overline{X}_G = \frac{\sum_{i=1}^{n} lnX_i}{n}.$$

When we have computed $ln\overline{X}_G$, then $\overline{X}_G = e^{ln\overline{X}_G}$ (on most calculators, the key for this step is e^x).

Risky assets can have negative returns up to -100 percent (if their price falls to zero), so we must take some care in defining the relevant variables to average in computing a geometric mean. We cannot just use the product of the returns for the sample and then take the nth root because the returns for any period could be negative. We must recast the returns to make them positive. We do this by adding 1.0 to the returns expressed as decimals, where R_t represents the return in period t. The term $(1 + R_t)$ represents the year-ending value relative to an initial unit of investment at the beginning of the year. As long as we use $(1 + R_t)$, the observations will never be negative because the biggest negative return is -100%. The result is the geometric mean of $1 + R_t$; by then subtracting 1.0 from this result, we obtain the geometric mean of the individual returns R_t.

An equation that summarizes the calculation of the geometric mean return, R_G, is a slightly modified version of Equation 4 in which X_i represents "1 + return in decimal form." Because geometric mean returns use time series, we use a subscript t indexing time as well. We calculate one plus the geometric mean return as:

$$1 + R_G = \sqrt[T]{(1 + R_1)(1 + R_2)...(1 + R_T)}.$$

We can represent this more compactly as:

$$1 + R_G = \left[\prod_{t=1}^{T}(1 + R_t)\right]^{\frac{1}{T}},$$

where the capital Greek letter 'pi,' Π, denotes the arithmetical operation of multiplication of the T terms. Once we subtract one, this becomes the formula for the geometric mean return.

For example, the returns on Country B's index are given in Exhibit 35 as 7.8, 6.3, and -1.5 percent. Putting the returns into decimal form and adding 1.0 produces 1.078, 1.063, and 0.985. Using Equation 4, we have $\sqrt[3]{(1.078)(1.063)(0.985)} = \sqrt[3]{1.128725} = 1.041189$. This number is 1 plus the geometric mean rate of return. Subtracting 1.0 from this result, we have $1.041189 - 1.0 = 0.041189$, or approximately 4.12 percent. This is lower than the arithmetic mean for County B's index of 4.2 percent.

Geometric Mean Return Formula. Given a time series of holding period returns R_t, $t = 1, 2,$ ..., T, the geometric mean return over the time period spanned by the returns R_1 through R_T is:

$$R_G = \left[\prod_{t=1}^{T} (1 + R_t) \right]^{\frac{1}{T}} - 1. \qquad\qquad (5)$$

We can use Equation 5 to solve for the geometric mean return for any return data series. Geometric mean returns are also referred to as compound returns. If the returns being averaged in Equation 5 have a monthly frequency, for example, we may call the geometric mean monthly return the compound monthly return. The next example illustrates the computation of the geometric mean while contrasting the geometric and arithmetic means.

EXAMPLE 10   Geometric and Arithmetic Mean Returns

Using the data in Exhibit 35, calculate the arithmetic mean and the geometric mean returns over the three years for each of the three stock indexes: those of Country D, Country E, and Country F.

Solution: The arithmetic mean returns calculations are:

	Annual Return (%)			Sum $\sum_{i=1}^{3} R_i$	Arithmetic Mean
	Year 1	year 2	year 3		
Country D	-2.4	-3.1	6.2	0.7	0.233
Country E	-4.0	-3.0	3.0	-4.0	-1.333
Country F	5.4	5.2	-1.0	9.6	3.200

Geometric mean returns calculations are:

	1 + Return in Decimal Form $(1 + R_t)$			Product $\prod_{t}^{T}(1 + R_t)$	3rd root $[\prod_{t}^{3}(1 + R_t)]^{\frac{1}{3}}$	Geometric mean return (%)
	Year 1	Year 2	Year 3			
Country D	0.976	0.969	1.062	1.00438	1.00146	0.146
Country E	0.960	0.970	1.030	0.95914	0.98619	-1.381
Country F	1.054	1.052	0.990	1.09772	1.03157	3.157

In **Example 10**, the geometric mean return is less than the arithmetic mean return for each country's index returns. In fact, the geometric mean is always less than or equal to the arithmetic mean. The only time that the two means will be equal is when there is no variability in the observations—that is, when all the observations in the series are the same.

In general, the difference between the arithmetic and geometric means increases with the variability within the sample; the more disperse the observations, the greater the difference between the arithmetic and geometric means. Casual inspection of the returns in Exhibit 35 and the associated graph of means suggests a greater variability for Country A's index relative to the other indexes, and this is confirmed with the greater deviation of the geometric mean return (-5.38 percent) from the arithmetic mean return (-4.97 percent), as we show in Exhibit 40. How should the analyst interpret these results?

The geometric mean return represents the growth rate or compound rate of return on an investment. One unit of currency invested in a fund tracking the Country B index at the beginning of Year 1 would have grown to $(1.078)(1.063)(0.985) = 1.128725$ units of currency, which is equal to 1 plus the geometric mean return compounded over three periods: $[1 + 0.041189]^3 = 1.128725$, confirming that the geometric mean is the compound rate of return. With its focus on the profitability of an investment over a multi-period horizon, the geometric mean is of key interest to investors. The arithmetic mean return, focusing on average single-period performance, is also of interest. Both arithmetic and geometric means have a role to play in investment management, and both are often reported for return series.

For reporting historical returns, the geometric mean has considerable appeal because it is the rate of growth or return we would have to earn each year to match the actual, cumulative investment performance. Suppose we purchased a stock for €100 and two years later it was worth €100, with an intervening year at €200. The geometric mean of 0 percent is clearly the compound rate of growth during the two years, which we can confirm by compounding the returns: $[(1 + 1.00)(1 - 0.50)]^{1/2} - 1 = 0$ percent. Specifically, the ending amount is the beginning amount times $(1 + R_G)^2$. The geometric mean is an excellent measure of past performance.

EXHIBIT 40   Arithmetic and Geometric Mean Returns for Country Stock Indexes: Years 1 to 3

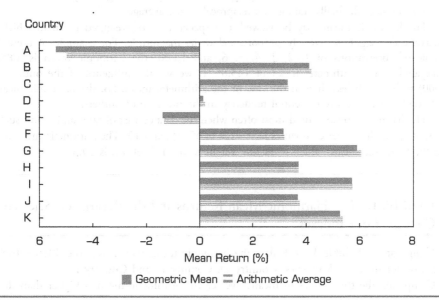

The arithmetic mean, which is [100% + −50%]/2 = 25% in the above example, can distort our assessment of historical performance. As we noted previously, the arithmetic mean is always greater than or equal to the geometric mean. If we want to estimate the average return over a one-period horizon, we should use the arithmetic mean because the arithmetic mean is the average of one-period returns. If we want to estimate the average returns over more than one period, however, we should use the geometric mean of returns because the geometric mean captures how the total returns are linked over time. In a forward-looking context, a financial analyst calculating expected risk premiums may find that the weighted mean is appropriate, with the probabilities of the possible outcomes used as the weights.

Dispersion in cash flows or returns causes the arithmetic mean to be larger than the geometric mean. The more dispersion in the sample of returns, the more divergence exists between the arithmetic and geometric means. If there is zero variance in a sample of observations, the geometric and arithmetic return are equal.

5.4.3. The Harmonic Mean

The arithmetic mean, the weighted mean, and the geometric mean are the most frequently used concepts of mean in investments. A fourth concept, the **harmonic mean**, $\overline{X}_H$, is another measure of central tendency. The harmonic mean is appropriate in cases in which the variable is a rate or a ratio. The terminology "harmonic" arises from its use of a type of series involving reciprocals known as a harmonic series.

Harmonic Mean Formula. The harmonic mean of a set of observations X_1, X_2, ..., X_n is:

$$\overline{X}_H = \frac{n}{\sum_{i=1}^{n}(1/X_i)} \text{ with } X_i > 0 \text{ for } i = 1, 2, ..., n. \qquad (6)$$

The harmonic mean is the value obtained by summing the reciprocals of the observations— terms of the form $1/X_i$—then averaging that sum by dividing it by the number of observations n, and, finally, taking the reciprocal of the average.

The harmonic mean may be viewed as a special type of weighted mean in which an observation's weight is inversely proportional to its magnitude. For example, if there is a sample of observations of 1, 2, 3, 4, 5, 6, and 1,000, the harmonic mean is 2.8560. Compared to the arithmetic mean of 145.8571, we see the influence of the outlier (the 1,000) to be much less than in the case of the arithmetic mean. So, the harmonic mean is quite useful as a measure of central tendency in the presence of outliers.

The harmonic mean is used most often when the data consist of rates and ratios, such as P/Es. Suppose three peer companies have P/Es of 45, 15, and 15. The arithmetic mean is 25, but the harmonic mean, which gives less weight to the P/E of 45, is 19.3.

EXAMPLE 11   Harmonic Mean Returns and the Returns on Selected Country Stock Indexes

Using data in Exhibit 35, calculate the harmonic mean return over the 2016–2018 period for three stock indexes: Country D, Country E, and Country F. Comparing the three types of means, we see the arithmetic mean is higher than the

Calculating the Harmonic Mean for the Indexes

Index	Inverse of 1 + Return, or $\frac{1}{(1+X_i)}$ where X_i is the return in decimal form			$\sum_i^n 1/X_i$	$\dfrac{n}{\sum_i^n 1/X_i}$	Harmonic Mean (%)
	Year 1	Year 2	Year 3			
Country D	1.02459	1.03199	0.94162	2.99820	1.00060	0.05999
Country E	1.04167	1.03093	0.97087	3.04347	0.98572	−1.42825
Country F	0.94877	0.95057	1.01010	2.90944	1.03113	3.11270

geometric mean return, and the geometric mean return is higher than the harmonic mean return. We can see the differences in these means in the following graph:

Harmonic, Geometric, and Arithmetic Means of Selected Country Indexes

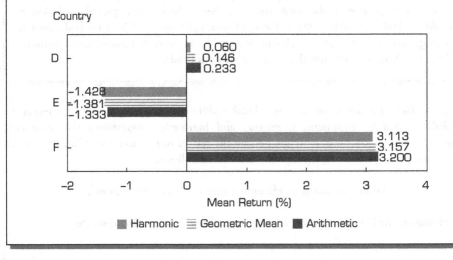

The harmonic mean is a relatively specialized concept of the mean that is appropriate for averaging ratios ("amount per unit") when the ratios are repeatedly applied to a fixed quantity to yield a variable number of units. The concept is best explained through an illustration. A well-known application arises in the investment strategy known as **cost averaging**, which involves the periodic investment of a fixed amount of money. In this application, the ratios we are averaging are prices per share at different purchase dates, and we are applying those prices to a constant amount of money to yield a variable number of shares. An illustration of the harmonic mean to cost averaging is provided in **Example 12**.

EXAMPLE 12   Cost Averaging and the Harmonic Mean

Suppose an investor purchases €1,000 of a security each month for $n = 2$ months. The share prices are €10 and €15 at the two purchase dates. What is the average price paid for the security?

Purchase in the first month = €1,000/€10 = 100 shares
Purchase in the second month = €1,000/€15 = 66.67 shares

The purchases are 166.67 shares in total, and the price paid per share is €2,000/166.67 = €12.

The average price paid is in fact the harmonic mean of the asset's prices at the purchase dates. Using Equation 6, the harmonic mean price is 2/[(1/10) + (1/15)] = €12. The value €12 is less than the arithmetic mean purchase price (€10 + €15)/2 = €12.5.

However, we could find the correct value of €12 using the weighted mean formula, where the weights on the purchase prices equal the shares purchased at a given price as a proportion of the total shares purchased. In our example, the calculation would be (100/166.67)€10.00 + (66.67/166.67)€15.00 = €12. If we had invested varying amounts of money at each date, we could not use the harmonic mean formula. We could, however, still use the weighted mean formula.

Since they use the same data but involve different progressions in their respective calculations (that is, arithmetic, geometric, and harmonic progressions) the arithmetic, geometric, and harmonic means are mathematically related to one another. While we will not go into the proof of this relationship, the basic result follows:

$$\text{Arithmetic mean} \times \text{Harmonic mean} = \text{Geometric mean}^2.$$

However, the key question is: Which mean to use in what circumstances?

EXAMPLE 13   Calculating the Arithmetic, Geometric, and Harmonic Means for P/Es

Each year in December, a securities analyst selects her 10 favorite stocks for the next year. Exhibit 41 gives the P/E, the ratio of share price to projected earnings per share (EPS), for her top-10 stock picks for the next year.
    For these 10 stocks,

1. Calculate the arithmetic mean P/E.
2. Calculate the geometric mean P/E.
3. Calculate the harmonic mean P/E.

EXHIBIT 41   Analyst's 10 Favorite Stocks
for Next Year

Stock	P/E
Stock 1	22.29
Stock 2	15.54
Stock 3	9.38
Stock 4	15.12
Stock 5	10.72
Stock 6	14.57
Stock 7	7.20
Stock 8	7.97
Stock 9	10.34

Stock	P/E	Natural Log of the P/E $ln(X_i)$	Inverse of the P/E $1/X_i$
Stock 1	22.29	3.1041	0.0449
Stock 2	15.54	2.7434	0.0644
Stock 3	9.38	2.2386	0.1066
Stock 4	15.12	2.7160	0.0661
Stock 5	10.72	2.3721	0.0933
Stock 6	14.57	2.6790	0.0686
Stock 7	7.20	1.9741	0.1389
Stock 8	7.97	2.0757	0.1255
Stock 9	10.34	2.3360	0.0967
Stock 10	8.35	2.1223	0.1198
Sum	121.48	24.3613	0.9247

Solution:

1. The arithmetic mean is 121.48/10 = 12.1480.
2. The geometric mean is $e^{24.3613/10}$ = 11.4287.
3. The harmonic mean is 10/0.9247 = 10.8142.

EXHIBIT 42   Deciding Which Central Tendency Measure to Use

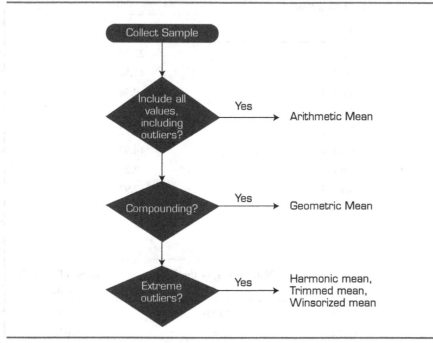

A mathematical fact concerning the harmonic, geometric, and arithmetic means is that unless all the observations in a dataset have the same value, the harmonic mean is less than the geometric mean, which, in turn, is less than the arithmetic mean. The choice of which mean to use depends on many factors, as we describe in Exhibit 42:

- Are there outliers that we want to include?
- Is the distribution symmetric?
- Is there compounding?
- Are there extreme outliers?

6. OTHER MEASURES OF LOCATION: QUANTILES

Having discussed measures of central tendency, we now examine an approach to describing the location of data that involves identifying values at or below which specified proportions of the data lie. For example, establishing that 25, 50, and 75 percent of the annual returns on a portfolio are at or below the values −0.05, 0.16, and 0.25, respectively, provides concise information about the distribution of portfolio returns. Statisticians use the word **quantile** (or **fractile**) as the most general term for a value at or below which a stated fraction of the data lies. In the following section, we describe the most commonly used quantiles—quartiles, quintiles, deciles, and percentiles—and their application in investments.

6.1. Quartiles, Quintiles, Deciles, and Percentiles

We know that the median divides a distribution of data in half. We can define other dividing lines that split the distribution into smaller sizes. **Quartiles** divide the distribution into quarters, **quintiles** into fifths, **deciles** into tenths, and **percentiles** into hundredths. Given a set of observations, the yth percentile is the value at or below which $y\%$ of observations lie. Percentiles are used frequently, and the other measures can be defined with respect to them. For example, the first quartile (Q_1) divides a distribution such that 25% of the observations lie at or below it; therefore, the first quartile is also the 25th percentile. The second quartile (Q_2) represents the 50th percentile, and the third quartile (Q_3) represents the 75th percentile (i.e., 75% of the observations lie at or below it). The **interquartile range** (IQR) is the difference between the third quartile and the first quartile, or IQR $= Q_3 - Q_1$.

When dealing with actual data, we often find that we need to approximate the value of a percentile. For example, if we are interested in the value of the 75th percentile, we may find that no observation divides the sample such that exactly 75% of the observations lie at or below that value. The following procedure, however, can help us determine or estimate a percentile. The procedure involves first locating the position of the percentile within the set of observations and then determining (or estimating) the value associated with that position.

Let P_y be the value at or below which $y\%$ of the distribution lies, or the yth percentile. (For example, P_{18} is the point at or below which 18% of the observations lie; this implies that $100 - 18 = 82\%$ of the observations are greater than P_{18}.) The formula for the position (or location) of a percentile in an array with n entries sorted in ascending order is:

$$L_y = (n+1)\tfrac{y}{100,} \qquad\qquad (7)$$

where y is the percentage point at which we are dividing the distribution, and L_y is the location (L) of the percentile (P_y) in the array sorted in ascending order. The value of L_y may or may not be a whole number. In general, as the sample size increases, the percentile location calculation becomes more accurate; in small samples it may be quite approximate.

To summarize:

- When the location, L_y, is a whole number, the location corresponds to an actual observation. For example, if we are determining the third quartile (Q_3) in a sample of size $n = 11$, then L_y would be $L_{75} = (11 + 1)(75/100) = 9$, and the third quartile would be $P_{75} = X_9$, where X_i is defined as the value of the observation in the ith $(i = L_{75}$, so 9th), position of the data sorted in ascending order.
- When L_y is not a whole number or integer, L_y lies between the two closest integer numbers (one above and one below), and we use **linear interpolation** between those two places to determine P_y. Interpolation means estimating an unknown value on the basis of two known values that surround it (i.e., lie above and below it); the term "linear" refers to a straight-line estimate.

Example 14 illustrates the calculation of various quantiles for the daily return on the EAA Equity Index.

EXAMPLE 14   Percentiles, Quintiles, and Quartiles for the EAA Equity Index

Using the daily returns on the fictitious EAA Equity Index over five years and ranking them by return, from lowest to highest daily return, we show the return bins from 1 (the lowest 5 percent) to 20 (the highest 5 percent) as follows:

Note that because of the continuous nature of returns, it is not likely for a return to fall on the boundary for any bin other than the minimum (Bin = 1) and maximum (Bin = 20).

1. Identify the 10th and 90th percentiles.
2. Identify the first, second, and third quintiles.
3. Identify the first and third quartiles.
4. Identify the median.
5. Calculate the interquartile range.

EXHIBIT 43   EAA Equity Index Daily Returns Grouped by Size of Return

| Bin | Cumulative Percentage of Sample Trading Days (%) | Daily Return (%) Between* | | Number of Observations |
		Lower Bound	Upper Bound	
1	5	−4.108	−1.416	63
2	10	−1.416	−0.876	63
3	15	−0.876	−0.629	63
4	20	−0.629	−0.432	63
5	25	−0.432	−0.293	63
6	30	−0.293	−0.193	63
7	35	−0.193	−0.124	62
8	40	−0.124	−0.070	63
9	45	−0.070	−0.007	63
10	50	−0.007	0.044	63
11	55	0.044	0.108	63
12	60	0.108	0.173	63
13	65	0.173	0.247	63
14	70	0.247	0.343	62
15	75	0.343	0.460	63
16	80	0.460	0.575	63
17	85	0.575	0.738	63
18	90	0.738	0.991	63
19	95	0.991	1.304	63
20	100	1.304	5.001	63

Solution to 1: The 10th and 90th percentiles correspond to the bins or ranked returns that include 10 percent and 90 percent of the daily returns, respectively. The 10th percentile corresponds to the return of −0.876 percent (and includes returns of that much and lower), and the 90th percentile corresponds to the return of 0.991 percent (and lower).

Solution to 2: The first quintile corresponds to the lowest 20 percent of the ranked data, or −0.432 percent (and lower).

The second quintile corresponds to the lowest 40 percent of the ranked data, or −0.070 percent (and lower).

The third quintile corresponds to the lowest 60 percent of the ranked data, or 0.173 percent (and lower).

Solution to 3: The first quartile corresponds to the lowest 25 percent of the ranked data, or −0.293 percent (and lower).

The third quartile corresponds to the lowest 75 percent of the ranked data, or 0.460 percent (and lower).

Solution to 4: The median is the return for which 50 percent of the data lies on either side, which is 0.044 percent, the highest daily return in the 10th bin out of 20.

Solution to 5: The interquartile range is the difference between the third and first quartiles, 0.460 percent and −0.293 percent, or 0.753 percent.

One way to visualize the dispersion of data across quartiles is to use a diagram, such as a box and whisker chart. A **box and whisker plot** consists of a "box" with "whiskers" connected to the box, as shown in Exhibit 44. The "box" represents the lower bound of the second quartile and the upper bound of the third quartile, with the median or arithmetic average noted as a measure of central tendency of the entire distribution. The whiskers are the lines that run from the box and are bounded by the "fences," which represent the lowest and highest values of the distribution.

There are several variations for box and whisker displays. For example, for ease in detecting potential outliers, the fences of the whiskers may be a function of the interquartile range instead of the highest and lowest values like that in Exhibit 44.

EXHIBIT 44   Box and Whisker Plot

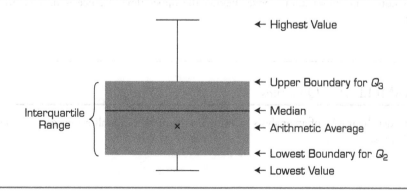

EXHIBIT 45   Box and Whisker Chart for EAA Equity Index Daily Returns

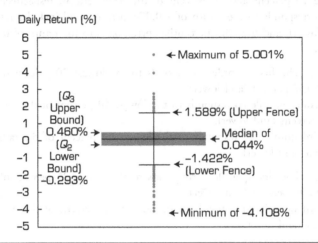

In Exhibit 44, visually, the interquartile range is the height of the box and the fences are set at extremes. But another form of box and whisker plot typically uses 1.5 times the interquartile range for the fences. Thus, the upper fence is 1.5 times the interquartile range added to the upper bound of Q_3, and the lower fence is 1.5 times the interquartile range subtracted from the lower bound of Q_2. Observations beyond the fences (i.e., outliers) may also be displayed.

We can see the role of outliers in such a box and whisker plot using the EAA Equity Index daily returns, as shown in Exhibit 45. Referring back to Exhibit 43 (**Example 13**), we know:

- The maximum and minimum values of the distribution are 5.001 and −4.108, respectively, while the median (50th percentile) value is 0.044.
- The interquartile range is 0.753 [= 0.460 − (−0.293)], and when multiplied by 1.5 and added to the Q_3 upper bound of 0.460 gives an upper fence of 1.589 [= (1.5 × 0.753) + 0.460].
- The lower fence is determined in a similar manner, using the Q_2 lower bound, to be −1.422 [= −(1.5 × 0.753) + (−0.293)].

As noted, any observation above (below) the upper (lower) fence is deemed to be an outlier.

EXAMPLE 15   Quantiles

Consider the results of an analysis focusing on the market capitalizations of a sample of 100 firms:

Bin	Cumulative Percentage of Sample (%)	Market Capitalization (in billions of €)		Number of Observations
		Lower Bound	Upper Bound	
1	5	0.28	15.45	5
2	10	15.45	21.22	5
3	15	21.22	29.37	5
4	20	29.37	32.57	5
5	25	32.57	34.72	5
6	30	34.72	37.58	5
7	35	37.58	39.90	5
8	40	39.90	41.57	5
9	45	41.57	44.86	5
10	50	44.86	46.88	5
11	55	46.88	49.40	5
12	60	49.40	51.27	5
13	65	51.27	53.58	5
14	70	53.58	56.66	5
15	75	56.66	58.34	5
16	80	58.34	63.10	5
17	85	63.10	67.06	5
18	90	67.06	73.00	5
19	95	73.00	81.62	5
20	100	81.62	96.85	5

Using this information, answer the following five questions.

1. The tenth percentile corresponds to observations in bins:
   A. 2.
   B. 1 and 2.
   C. 19 and 20.

2. The second quintile corresponds to observations in bins:
   A. 8.
   B. 5, 6, 7, and 8.
   C. 6, 7, 8, 9, and 10.

3. The fourth quartile corresponds to observations in bins:
   A. 17.
   B. 17, 18, 19, and 20.
   C. 16, 17, 18, 19, and 20.

4. The median is *closest* to:
   A. 44.86.

   B. 46.88.
   C. 49.40.

5. The interquartile range is *closest* to:
   A. 20.76.
   B. 23.62.
   C. 25.52.

Solution to 1: B is correct because the tenth percentile corresponds to the lowest 10 percent of the observations in the sample, which are in bins 1 and 2.

Solution to 2: B is correct because the second quintile corresponds to the second 20 percent of observations. The first 20% consists of bins 1 through 4. The second 20 percent of observations consists of bins 5 through 8.

Solution to 3: C is correct because a quartile consists of 25 percent of the data, and the last 25 percent of the 20 bins are 16 through 20.

Solution to 4: B is correct because this is the center of the 20 bins. The market capitalization of 46.88 is the highest value of the 10th bin and the lowest value of the 11th bin.

Solution to 5: B is correct because the interquartile range is the difference between the lowest value in the second quartile and the highest value in the third quartile. The lowest value of the second quartile is 34.72, and the highest value of the third quartile is 58.34. Therefore, the interquartile range is $58.34 - 34.72 = 23.62$.

6.2. Quantiles in Investment Practice

In this section, we briefly discuss the use of quantiles in investments. Quantiles are used in portfolio performance evaluation as well as in investment strategy development and research.

   Investment analysts use quantiles every day to rank performance—for example, the performance of portfolios. The performance of investment managers is often characterized in terms of the percentile or quartile in which they fall relative to the performance of their peer group of managers. The Morningstar investment fund star rankings, for example, associate the number of stars with percentiles of performance relative to similar-style investment funds.

   Another key use of quantiles is in investment research. For example, analysts often refer to the set of companies with returns falling below the 10th percentile cutoff point as the bottom return decile. Dividing data into quantiles based on some characteristic allows analysts to evaluate the impact of that characteristic on a quantity of interest. For instance, empirical finance studies commonly rank companies based on the market value of their equity and then sort them into deciles. The first decile contains the portfolio of those companies with the smallest market values, and the tenth decile contains those companies with the largest market values. Ranking companies by decile allows analysts to compare the performance of small companies with large ones.

7. MEASURES OF DISPERSION

Few would disagree with the importance of expected return or mean return in investments: The mean return tells us where returns, and investment results, are centered. To more completely understand an investment, however, we also need to know how returns are dispersed around the mean. **Dispersion** is the variability around the central tendency. If mean return addresses reward, then dispersion addresses risk.

In this section, we examine the most common measures of dispersion: range, mean absolute deviation, variance, and standard deviation. These are all measures of **absolute dispersion**. Absolute dispersion is the amount of variability present without comparison to any reference point or benchmark.

These measures are used throughout investment practice. The variance or standard deviation of return is often used as a measure of risk pioneered by Nobel laureate Harry Markowitz. Other measures of dispersion, mean absolute deviation and range, are also useful in analyzing data.

7.1. The Range

We encountered range earlier when we discussed the construction of frequency distributions. It is the simplest of all the measures of dispersion.

Definition of Range. The **range** is the difference between the maximum and minimum values in a dataset:

$$\text{Range} = \text{Maximum value} - \text{Minimum value}. \qquad (8)$$

As an illustration of range, consider Exhibit 35, our example of annual returns for countries' stock indexes. The range of returns for Year 1 is the difference between the returns of Country G's index and Country A's index, or $12.7 - (-15.6) = 28.3$ percent. The range of returns for Year 3 is the difference between the returns for the County D index and the Country B index, or $6.2 - (-1.5) = 7.7$ percent.

An alternative definition of range specifically reports the maximum and minimum values. This alternative definition provides more information than does the range as defined in Equation 8. In other words, in the above-mentioned case for Year 1, the range is reported as "from 12.7 percent to −15.6 percent."

One advantage of the range is ease of computation. A disadvantage is that the range uses only two pieces of information from the distribution. It cannot tell us how the data are distributed (that is, the shape of the distribution). Because the range is the difference between the maximum and minimum returns, it can reflect extremely large or small outcomes that may not be representative of the distribution.

7.2. The Mean Absolute Deviation

Measures of dispersion can be computed using all the observations in the distribution rather than just the highest and lowest. But how should we measure dispersion? Our previous discussion on properties of the arithmetic mean introduced the notion of distance or deviation from the mean $(X_i - \overline{X})$ as a fundamental piece of information used in statistics.

We could compute measures of dispersion as the arithmetic average of the deviations around the mean, but we would encounter a problem: The deviations around the mean always sum to 0. If we computed the mean of the deviations, the result would also equal 0. Therefore, we need to find a way to address the problem of negative deviations canceling out positive deviations.

One solution is to examine the absolute deviations around the mean as in the **mean absolute deviation**. This is also known as the average absolute deviation.

Mean Absolute Deviation Formula. The mean absolute deviation (MAD) for a sample is:

$$MAD = \frac{\sum_{i=1}^{n} |X_i - \overline{X}|}{n}, \tag{9}$$

where $\overline{X}$ is the sample mean, n is the number of observations in the sample, and the $|\ |$ indicate the absolute value of what is contained within these bars.

In calculating MAD, we ignore the signs of the deviations around the mean. For example, if $X_i = -11.0$ and $\overline{X} = 4.5$, the absolute value of the difference is $|-11.0 - 4.5| = |-15.5| = 15.5$. The mean absolute deviation uses all of the observations in the sample and is thus superior to the range as a measure of dispersion. One technical drawback of MAD is that it is difficult to manipulate mathematically compared with the next measure we will introduce, sample variance. **Example 16** illustrates the use of the range and the mean absolute deviation in evaluating risk.

EXAMPLE 16   Mean Absolute Deviation for Selected Countries' Stock Index Returns

---

Using the country stock index returns in Exhibit 35, calculate the mean absolute deviation of the index returns for each year. Note the sample mean returns ($\overline{X}$) are 3.5 percent, 2.5 percent, and 2.0 percent for Years 1, 2, and 3, respectively.

	Absolute Value of Deviation from the Mean $|X_i - \overline{X}|$		
	Year 1	Year 2	Year 3
Country A	19.1	7.9	4.1
Country B	4.3	3.8	3.5
Country C	1.8	1.3	1.5
Country D	5.9	5.6	4.2
Country E	7.5	5.5	1.0
Country F	1.9	2.7	3.0
Country G	9.2	4.2	3.2
Country H	0.0	1.8	1.4
Country I	2.7	5.3	1.2
Country J	4.6	1.6	2.9

	Absolute Value of Deviation from the Mean $\lvert X_i - \overline{X} \rvert$		
	Year 1	Year 2	Year 3
Country K	8.0	0.9	0.8
Sum	65.0	40.6	26.8
MAD	5.91	3.69	2.44

Solution: For Year 3, for example, the sum of the absolute deviations from the arithmetic mean ($\overline{X} = 2.0$) is 26.8. We divide this by 11, with the resulting MAD of 2.44.

7.3. Sample Variance and Sample Standard Deviation

The mean absolute deviation addressed the issue that the sum of deviations from the mean equals zero by taking the absolute value of the deviations. A second approach to the treatment of deviations is to square them. The variance and standard deviation, which are based on squared deviations, are the two most widely used measures of dispersion. **Variance** is defined as the average of the squared deviations around the mean. **Standard deviation** is the positive square root of the variance. The following discussion addresses the calculation and use of variance and standard deviation.

7.3.1. Sample Variance
In investments, we often do not know the mean of a population of interest, usually because we cannot practically identify or take measurements from each member of the population. We then estimate the population mean using the mean from a sample drawn from the population, and we calculate a sample variance or standard deviation.
Sample Variance Formula. The **sample variance**, s^2, is:

$$s^2 = \frac{\sum_{i=1}^{n}(X_i - \overline{X})^2}{n - 1}, \tag{10}$$

where $\overline{X}$ is the sample mean and n is the number of observations in the sample.

Given knowledge of the sample mean, we can use Equation 10 to calculate the sum of the squared differences from the mean, taking account of all n items in the sample, and then to find the mean squared difference by dividing the sum by $n - 1$. Whether a difference from the mean is positive or negative, squaring that difference results in a positive number. Thus, variance takes care of the problem of negative deviations from the mean canceling out positive deviations by the operation of squaring those deviations.

For the sample variance, by dividing by the sample size minus 1 (or $n - 1$) rather than n, we improve the statistical properties of the sample variance. In statistical terms, the sample variance defined in Equation 10 is an unbiased estimator of the population variance (a concept covered later in the curriculum on sampling). The quantity $n - 1$ is also known as the number of degrees of freedom in estimating the population variance. To estimate the population variance with s^2, we must first calculate the sample mean, which itself is an estimated parameter. Therefore, once we have computed the sample mean, there are only $n - 1$ independent pieces of information from the sample; that is, if you know the sample mean and $n - 1$ of the observations, you could calculate the missing sample observation.

7.3.2. Sample Standard Deviation

Because the variance is measured in squared units, we need a way to return to the original units. We can solve this problem by using standard deviation, the square root of the variance. Standard deviation is more easily interpreted than the variance because standard deviation is expressed in the same unit of measurement as the observations. By taking the square root, we return the values to the original unit of measurement. Suppose we have a sample with values in euros. Interpreting the standard deviation in euros is easier than interpreting the variance in squared euros.

Sample Standard Deviation Formula. The **sample standard deviation**, s, is:

$$s = \sqrt{\frac{\sum_{i=1}^{n}(X_i - \overline{X})^2}{n - 1}}, \tag{11}$$

where $\overline{X}$ is the sample mean and n is the number of observations in the sample.

To calculate the sample standard deviation, we first compute the sample variance. We then take the square root of the sample variance. The steps for computing the sample variance and the standard deviation are provided in Exhibit 46.

We illustrate the process of calculating the sample variance and standard deviation in **Example 17** using the returns of the selected country stock indexes presented in Exhibit 35.

EXHIBIT 46   Steps to Calculate Sample Standard Deviation and Variance

Step	Description	Notation
1	Calculate the sample mean.	$\overline{X}$
2	Calculate the deviations from the sample mean.	$(X_i - \overline{X})$
3	Calculate each observation's squared deviation from the sample mean.	$(X_i - \overline{X})^2$
4	Sum the squared deviations from the mean.	$\sum_{i=1}^{n}(X_i - \overline{X})^2$
5	Divide the sum of squared deviations from the mean by $n - 1$. This is the variance (s^2).	$\frac{\sum_{i=1}^{n}(X_i - \overline{X})^2}{n-1}$
6	Take the square root of the sum of the squared deviations divided by $n - 1$. This is the standard deviation (s).	$\sqrt{\frac{\sum_{i=1}^{n}(X_i - \overline{X})^2}{n-1}}$

EXAMPLE 17   Calculating Sample Variance and Standard Deviation for Returns on Selected Country Stock Indexes

Using the sample information on country stock indexes in Exhibit 35, calculate the sample variance and standard deviation of the sample of index returns for Year 3.

Index	Sample Observation	Deviation from the Sample Mean	Squared Deviation
Country A	6.1	4.1	16.810
Country B	−1.5	−3.5	12.250
Country C	3.5	1.5	2.250
Country D	6.2	4.2	17.640
Country E	3.0	1.0	1.000
Country F	−1.0	−3.0	9.000
Country G	−1.2	−3.2	10.240
Country H	3.4	1.4	1.960
Country I	3.2	1.2	1.440
Country J	−0.9	−2.9	8.410
Country K	1.2	−0.8	0.640
Sum	**22.0**	**0.0**	**81.640**

Solution: Sample variance = 81.640/10 = 8.164
Sample standard deviation = $\sqrt{8.164}$ = 2.857

In addition to looking at the cross-sectional standard deviation as we did in **Example 17**, we could also calculate the standard deviation of a given country's returns across time (that is, the three years). Consider Country F, which has an arithmetic mean return of 3.2 percent. The sample standard deviation is calculated as:

$$\sqrt{\frac{(0.054 - 0.032)^2 + (0.052 - 0.032)^2 + (-0.01 - 0.032)^2}{2}}$$

$$= \sqrt{\frac{0.000484 + 0.000400 + 0.001764}{2}}$$

$$= \sqrt{0.001324}$$

$$= 3.6387\%.$$

Because the standard deviation is a measure of dispersion about the arithmetic mean, we usually present the arithmetic mean and standard deviation together when summarizing data. When we are dealing with data that represent a time series of percentage changes, presenting the geometric mean—representing the compound rate of growth—is also very helpful.

7.3.3. Dispersion and the Relationship between the Arithmetic and the Geometric Means

We can use the sample standard deviation to help us understand the gap between the arithmetic mean and the geometric mean. The relation between the arithmetic mean $(\overline{X})$ and geometric mean $(\overline{X}_G)$ is:

$$\overline{X}_G \approx \overline{X} - \frac{s^2}{2}.$$

In other words, the larger the variance of the sample, the wider the difference between the geometric mean and the arithmetic mean.

Using the data for Country F from **Example 8**, the geometric mean return is 3.1566 percent, the arithmetic mean return is 3.2 percent, and the factor $s^2/2$ is 0.001324/2 = 0.0662 percent:

$$3.1566\% \approx 3.2\% - 0.0662\%$$

$$3.1566\% \approx 3.1338\%.$$

This relation informs us that the more disperse or volatile the returns, the larger the gap between the geometric mean return and the arithmetic mean return.

7.4. Target Downside Deviation

An asset's variance or standard deviation of returns is often interpreted as a measure of the asset's risk. Variance and standard deviation of returns take account of returns above and below the mean, or upside and downside risks, respectively. However, investors are typically concerned only with **downside risk**—for example, returns below the mean or below some specified minimum target return. As a result, analysts have developed measures of downside risk.

In practice, we may be concerned with values of return (or another variable) below some level other than the mean. For example, if our return objective is 6.0 percent annually (our minimum acceptable return), then we may be concerned particularly with returns below 6.0 percent a year. The 6.0 percent is the target. The target downside deviation, also referred to as the **target semideviation**, is a measure of dispersion of the observations (here, returns) below the target. To calculate a sample target semideviation, we first specify the target. After identifying observations below the target, we find the sum of the squared negative deviations from the target, divide that sum by the total number of observations in the sample minus 1, and, finally, take the square root.

Sample Target Semideviation Formula. The target semideviation, s_{Target}, is:

$$s_{Target} = \sqrt{\sum_{\text{for all} X_i \leq B}^{n} \frac{(X_i - B)^2}{n-1}}, \tag{12}$$

where B is the target and n is the total number of sample observations. We illustrate this in **Example 18**.

EXAMPLE 18   Calculating Target Downside Deviation

Suppose the monthly returns on a portfolio are as shown:

1. Calculate the target downside deviation when the target return is 3 percent.
2. If the target return were 4 percent, would your answer be different from that for question 1? Without using calculations, explain how would it be different?

Monthly Portfolio Returns

Month	Return (%)
January	5
February	3
March	-1
April	-4
May	4
June	2
July	0
August	4
September	3
October	0
November	6
December	5

Month	Observation	Deviation from the 3% Target	Deviations below the Target	Squared Deviations below the Target
January	5	2	—	—
February	3	0	—	—
March	-1	-4	-4	16
April	-4	-7	-7	49
May	4	1	—	—
June	2	-1	-1	1
July	0	-3	-3	9
August	4	1	—	—
September	3	0	—	—
October	0	-3	-3	9
November	6	3	—	—
December	5	2	—	—
Sum				84

Solution to 1: **Target semideviation** $= \sqrt{\frac{84}{11}} = 2.7634\%$

Solution to 2: If the target return is higher, then the existing deviations would be larger and there would be several more values in the deviations and squared deviations below the target; so, the target semideviation would be larger.

How does the target downside deviation relate to the sample standard deviation? We illustrate the differences between the target downside deviation and the standard deviation in **Example 19**, using the data in **Example 18**.

EXAMPLE 19   Comparing the Target Downside Deviation with the Standard Deviation

1. Given the data in **Example 18**, calculate the sample standard deviation.
2. Given the data in **Example 18**, calculate the target downside deviation if the target is 2 percent.
3. Compare the standard deviation, the target downside deviation if the target is 2 percent, and the target downside deviation if the target is 3 percent.

Solution to 1: The sample standard deviation is $\sqrt{\frac{96.2500}{11}} = 2.958\%$.

Solution to 2: The target semideviation with 2% target $= \sqrt{\frac{53}{11}} = 2.195\%$.
Solution to 3: The standard deviation is based on the deviation from the mean, which is 2.25 percent. The standard deviation includes all deviations from the mean, not just those below it. This results in a sample standard deviation of 2.958 percent.

Month	Observation	Deviation from the Mean	Squared Deviation
January	5	2.75	7.5625
February	3	0.75	0.5625
March	-1	-3.25	10.5625
April	-4	-6.25	39.0625
May	4	1.75	3.0625
June	2	-0.25	0.0625
July	0	-2.25	5.0625
August	4	1.75	3.0625
September	3	0.75	0.5625
October	0	-2.25	5.0625
November	6	3.75	14.0625
December	5	2.75	7.5625
Sum	27		**96.2500**

Month	Observation	Deviation from the 2% Target	Deviations below the Target	Squared Deviations below the Target
January	5	3	—	—
February	3	1	—	—
March	-1	-3	-3	9
April	-4	-6	-6	36
May	4	2	—	—
June	2	0	—	—
July	0	-2	-2	4
August	4	2	—	—
September	3	1	—	—
October	0	-2	-2	4
November	6	4	—	—
December	5	3	—	—

Considering just the four observations below the 2 percent target, the target semideviation is 2.195 percent. It is less than the sample standard deviation since target semideviation captures only the downside risk (i.e., deviations below the target). Considering target semideviation with a 3 percent target, there are now five observations below 3 percent, so the target semideviation is higher, at 2.763 percent.

7.5. Coefficient of Variation

We noted earlier that the standard deviation is more easily interpreted than variance because standard deviation uses the same units of measurement as the observations. We may sometimes find it difficult to interpret what standard deviation means in terms of the relative degree of variability of different sets of data, however, either because the datasets have markedly different means or because the datasets have different units of measurement. In this section, we explain a measure of relative dispersion, the coefficient of variation that can be useful in such situations. **Relative dispersion** is the amount of dispersion relative to a reference value or benchmark.

The coefficient of variation is helpful in such situations as that just described (i.e., datasets with markedly different means or different units of measurement).

Coefficient of Variation Formula. The **coefficient of variation**, CV, is the ratio of the standard deviation of a set of observations to their mean value:

$$CV = s/\overline{X}, \tag{13}$$

where s is the sample standard deviation and $\overline{X}$ is the sample mean.

When the observations are returns, for example, the coefficient of variation measures the amount of risk (standard deviation) per unit of reward (mean return). An issue that may arise, especially when dealing with returns, is that if $\overline{X}$ is negative, the statistic is meaningless.

The CV may be stated as a multiple (e.g., 2 times) or as a percentage (e.g., 200 percent). Expressing the magnitude of variation among observations relative to their average size, the coefficient of variation permits direct comparisons of dispersion across different datasets. Reflecting the correction for scale, the coefficient of variation is a scale-free measure (that is, it has no units of measurement).

We illustrate the usefulness of coefficient of variation for comparing datasets with markedly different standard deviations using two hypothetical samples of companies in **Example 20**.

EXAMPLE 20   Coefficient of Variation of Returns on Assets

Suppose an analyst collects the return on assets (in percentage terms) for ten companies for each of two industries:

These data can be represented graphically as the following:

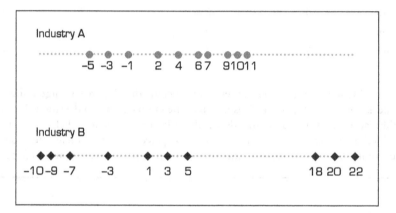

1. Calculate the average return on assets (ROA) for each industry.
2. Calculate the standard deviation of ROA for each industry.
3. Calculate the coefficient of variation of ROA for each industry.

Company	Industry A	Industry B
1	-5	-10
2	-3	-9
3	-1	-7
4	2	-3
5	4	1
6	6	3
7	7	5
8	9	18
9	10	20
10	11	22

Solution to 1: The arithmetic mean for both industries is the sum divided by 10, or 40/10 = 4%.

Solution to 2: The standard deviation using Equation 11 for Industry A is 5.60, and for Industry B the standard deviation is 12.12.

Solution to 3:

The coefficient of variation for Industry A = 5.60/4 = 1.40.
The coefficient of variation for Industry B = 12.12/4 = 3.03.

Though the two industries have the same arithmetic mean ROA, the dispersion is different—with Industry B's returns on assets being much more disperse than those of Industry A. The coefficients of variation for these two industries reflects this, with Industry B having a larger coefficient of variation. The interpretation is that the risk per unit of mean return is more than two times (2.16 = 3.03/1.40) greater for Industry B compared to Industry A.

8. THE SHAPE OF THE DISTRIBUTIONS: SKEWNESS

Mean and variance may not adequately describe an investment's distribution of returns. In calculations of variance, for example, the deviations around the mean are squared, so we do not know whether large deviations are likely to be positive or negative. We need to go beyond measures of central tendency and dispersion to reveal other important characteristics of the distribution. One important characteristic of interest to analysts is the degree of symmetry in return distributions.

If a return distribution is symmetrical about its mean, each side of the distribution is a mirror image of the other. Thus, equal loss and gain intervals exhibit the same frequencies. If the mean is zero, for example, then losses from −5 percent to −3 percent occur with about the same frequency as gains from 3 percent to 5 percent.

One of the most important distributions is the normal distribution, depicted in Exhibit 47. This symmetrical, bell-shaped distribution plays a central role in the mean–variance model of portfolio selection; it is also used extensively in financial risk management. The normal distribution has the following characteristics:

- Its mean, median, and mode are equal.
- It is completely described by two parameters—its mean and variance (or standard deviation).

But with any distribution other than a normal distribution, more information than the mean and variance is needed to characterize its shape.

A distribution that is not symmetrical is **skewed**. A return distribution with positive skew has frequent small losses and a few extreme gains. A return distribution with negative skew has frequent small gains and a few extreme losses. Exhibit 48 shows continuous positively and negatively skewed distributions. The continuous positively skewed distribution shown has a long tail on its right side; the continuous negatively skewed distribution shown has a long tail on its left side.

EXHIBIT 47   The Normal Distribution

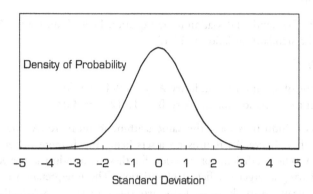

For a continuous positively skewed unimodal distribution, the mode is less than the median, which is less than the mean. For the continuous negatively skewed unimodal distribution, the mean is less than the median, which is less than the mode. For a given expected return and standard deviation, investors should be attracted by a positive skew because the mean return lies above the median. Relative to the mean return, positive skew amounts to limited, though frequent, downside returns compared with somewhat unlimited, but less frequent, upside returns.

Skewness is the name given to a statistical measure of skew. (The word "skewness" is also sometimes used interchangeably for "skew.") Like variance, skewness is computed using each observation's deviation from its mean. **Skewness** (sometimes referred to as relative skewness) is computed as the average cubed deviation from the mean standardized by dividing by the standard deviation cubed to make the measure free of scale. A symmetric distribution has skewness of 0, a positively skewed distribution has positive skewness, and a negatively skewed distribution has negative skewness, as given by this measure.

We can illustrate the principle behind the measure by focusing on the numerator. Cubing, unlike squaring, preserves the sign of the deviations from the mean. If a distribution is positively skewed with a mean greater than its median, then more than half of the deviations from the mean are negative and less than half are positive. However, for the sum of the cubed deviations to be positive, the losses must be small and likely and the gains less likely but more extreme. Therefore, if skewness is positive, the average magnitude of positive deviations is larger than the average magnitude of negative deviations.

The approximation for computing **sample skewness** when n is large (100 or more) is:

$$\text{Skewness} \approx \left(\tfrac{1}{n}\right) \frac{\sum_{i=1}^{n} (X_i - \overline{X})^3}{s^3}.$$

EXHIBIT 48   Properties of Skewed Distributions

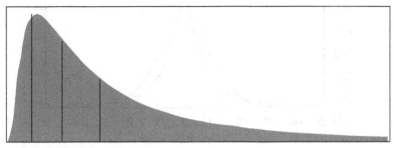

A. Positively Skewed

Density of Probability

Mode Median Mean

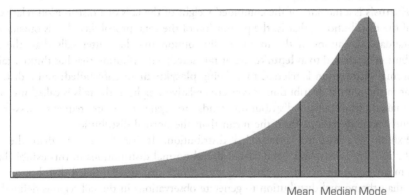

B. Negatively Skewed

Density of Probability

Mean Median Mode

A simple example illustrates that a symmetrical distribution has a skewness measure equal to 0. Suppose we have the following data: 1, 2, 3, 4, 5, 6, 7, 8, and 9. The mean outcome is 5, and the deviations are −4, −3, −2, −1, 0, 1, 2, 3, and 4. Cubing the deviations yields −64, −27, −8, −1, 0, 1, 8, 27, and 64, with a sum of 0. The numerator of skewness (and so skewness itself) is thus equal to 0, supporting our claim.

As you will learn as the CFA Program curriculum unfolds, different investment strategies may tend to introduce different types and amounts of skewness into returns.

9. THE SHAPE OF THE DISTRIBUTIONS: KURTOSIS

In the previous section, we discussed how to determine whether a return distribution deviates from a normal distribution because of skewness. Another way in which a return distribution might differ from a normal distribution is its relative tendency to generate large deviations

EXHIBIT 49   Fat-Tailed Distribution Compared to the Normal Distribution

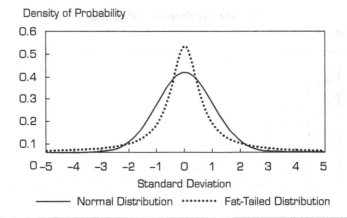

from the mean. Most investors would perceive a greater chance of extremely large deviations from the mean as increasing risk.

Kurtosis is a measure of the combined weight of the tails of a distribution relative to the rest of the distribution—that is, the proportion of the total probability that is outside of, say, 2.5 standard deviations of the mean. A distribution that has fatter tails than the normal distribution is referred to as **leptokurtic** or **fat-tailed**; a distribution that has thinner tails than the normal distribution is referred to as being **platykurtic** or **thin-tailed**; and a distribution similar to the normal distribution as concerns relative weight in the tails is called **mesokurtic**. A fat-tailed (thin-tailed) distribution tends to generate more-frequent (less-frequent) extremely large deviations from the mean than the normal distribution.

Exhibit 49 illustrates a fat-tailed distribution. It has fatter tails than the normal distribution. By construction, the fat-tailed and normal distributions in this exhibit have the same mean, standard deviation, and skewness. Note that this fat-tailed distribution is more likely than the normal distribution to generate observations in the tail regions defined by the intersection of graphs near a standard deviation of about ±2.5. This fat-tailed distribution is also more likely to generate observations that are near the mean, defined here as the region ±1 standard deviation around the mean. In compensation, to have probabilities sum to 1, this distribution generates fewer observations in the regions between the central region and the two tail regions.

The calculation for kurtosis involves finding the average of deviations from the mean raised to the fourth power and then standardizing that average by dividing by the standard deviation raised to the fourth power. A normal distribution has kurtosis of 3.0, so a fat-tailed distribution has a kurtosis of above 3 and a thin-tailed distribution of below 3.0.

Excess kurtosis is the kurtosis relative to the normal distribution. For a large sample size ($n = 100$ or more), **sample excess kurtosis** (K_E) is approximately as follows:

$$K_E \approx \left[\left(\frac{1}{n}\right) \frac{\sum_{i=1}^{n} (X_i - \overline{X})^4}{s^4} \right] - 3.$$

As with skewness, this measure is free of scale. Many statistical packages report estimates of sample **excess kurtosis**, labeling this as simply "kurtosis."

Excess kurtosis thus characterizes kurtosis relative to the normal distribution. A normal distribution has excess kurtosis equal to 0. A fat-tailed distribution has excess kurtosis greater than 0, and a thin-tailed distribution has excess kurtosis less than 0. A return distribution with positive excess kurtosis—a fat-tailed return distribution—has more frequent extremely large deviations from the mean than a normal distribution.

Summarizing:

If kurtosis is ...	then excess kurtosis is ...	Therefore, the distribution is ...	And we refer to the distribution as being ...
above 3.0	above 0.	fatter-tailed than the normal distribution.	fat-tailed (leptokurtic).
equal to 3.0	equal to 0.	similar in tails to the normal distribution.	mesokurtic.
less than 3.0	less than 0.	thinner-tailed than the normal distribution.	thin-tailed (platykurtic).

Most equity return series have been found to be fat-tailed. If a return distribution is fat-tailed and we use statistical models that do not account for the distribution, then we will underestimate the likelihood of very bad or very good outcomes. Using the data on the daily returns of the fictitious EAA Equity Index, we see the skewness and kurtosis of these returns in **Exhibit 50**.

EXHIBIT 50   Skewness and Kurtosis of EAA Equity Index Daily Returns

We can see this graphically, comparing the distribution of the daily returns with a normal distribution with the same mean and standard deviation:

	Daily Return (%)
Arithmetic mean	0.0347
Standard deviation	0.8341

	Measure of Symmetry
Skewness	–0.4260
Excess kurtosis	3.7962

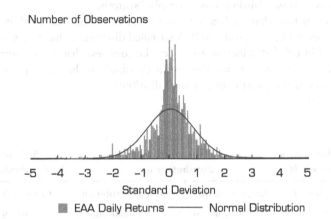

Using both the statistics and the graph, we see the following:

- The distribution is negatively skewed, as indicated by the negative calculated skewness of −0.4260 and the influence of observations below the mean of 0.0347%.
- The highest frequency of returns occurs within the −0.5 to 0.0 standard deviations from the mean (i.e., negatively skewed).
- The distribution is fat-tailed, as indicated by the positive excess kurtosis of 3.7962. We can see fat tails, a concentration of returns around the mean, and fewer observations in the regions between the central region and the two-tail regions.

EXAMPLE 21   Interpreting Skewness and Kurtosis

Consider the daily trading volume for a stock for one year, as shown in the graph below. In addition to the count of observations within each bin or interval, the number of observations anticipated based on a normal distribution (given the sample arithmetic average and standard deviation) is provided in the chart as well. The average trading volume per day for this stock in this year is 8.6 million shares, and the standard deviation is 4.9 million shares.

Histogram of Daily Trading Volume for a Stock for One Year

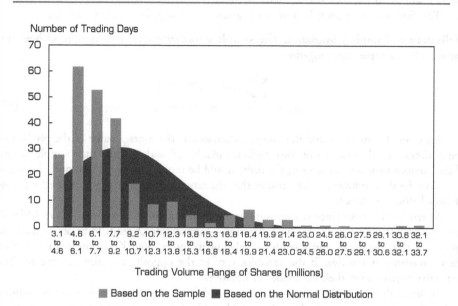

Number of Trading Days

Trading Volume Range of Shares (millions)

■ Based on the Sample   ■ Based on the Normal Distribution

1. Describe whether or not this distribution is skewed. If so, what could account for this situation?
2. Describe whether or not this distribution displays kurtosis. How would you make this determination?

Solution to 1: The distribution appears to be skewed to the right, or positively skewed. This is likely due to: (1) no possible negative trading volume on a given trading day, so the distribution is truncated at zero; and (2) greater-than-typical trading occurring relatively infrequently, such as when there are company-specific announcements.

The actual skewness for this distribution is 2.1090, which supports this interpretation.

Solution to 2: The distribution appears to have excess kurtosis, with a right-side fat tail and with maximum shares traded in the 4.6 to 6.1 million range, exceeding what is expected if the distribution was normally distributed. There are also fewer observations than expected between the central region and the tail.

The actual excess kurtosis for this distribution is 5.2151, which supports this interpretation.

10. CORRELATION BETWEEN TWO VARIABLES

Now that we have some understanding of sample variance and standard deviation, we can more formally consider the concept of correlation between two random variables that we previously explored visually in the scatter plots in Section 4. **Correlation** is a measure of the linear relationship between two random variables.

The first step is to consider how two variables vary together, their covariance.

Definition of Sample Covariance. The **sample covariance** (s_{XY}) is a measure of how two variables in a sample move together:

$$s_{XY} = \frac{\sum_{i=1}^{n}(X_i - \overline{X})(Y_i - \overline{Y})}{n-1}. \tag{14}$$

Equation 14 indicates that the sample covariance is the average value of the product of the deviations of observations on two random variables (X_i and Y_i) from their sample means. If the random variables are returns, the units would be returns squared. Also, note the use of $n-1$ in the denominator, which ensures that the sample covariance is an unbiased estimate of population covariance.

Stated simply, covariance is a measure of the joint variability of two random variables. If the random variables vary in the same direction—for example, X tends to be above its mean when Y is above its mean, and X tends to be below its mean when Y is below its mean—then their covariance is positive. If the variables vary in the opposite direction relative to their respective means, then their covariance is negative.

By itself, the size of the covariance measure is difficult to interpret as it is not normalized and so depends on the magnitude of the variables. This brings us to the normalized version of covariance, which is the correlation coefficient.

Definition of Sample Correlation Coefficient. The **sample correlation coefficient** is a standardized measure of how two variables in a sample move together. The sample correlation coefficient (r_{XY}) is the ratio of the sample covariance to the product of the two variables' standard deviations:

$$r_{XY} = \frac{s_{XY}}{s_X s_Y}. \tag{15}$$

Importantly, the correlation coefficient expresses the strength of the linear relationship between the two random variables.

10.1. Properties of Correlation

We now discuss the correlation coefficient, or simply correlation, and its properties in more detail, as follows:

1. Correlation ranges from -1 and $+1$ for two random variables, X and Y:

$$-1 \leq r_{XY} \leq +1.$$

2. A correlation of 0 (uncorrelated variables) indicates an absence of any linear (that is, straight-line) relationship between the variables.
3. A positive correlation close to $+1$ indicates a strong positive linear relationship. A correlation of 1 indicates a perfect linear relationship.
4. A negative correlation close to -1 indicates a strong negative (that is, inverse) linear relationship. A correlation of -1 indicates a perfect inverse linear relationship.

   We will make use of scatter plots, similar to those used previously in our discussion of data visualization, to illustrate correlation. In contrast to the correlation coefficient, which expresses the relationship between two data series using a single number, a scatter plot depicts the relationship graphically. Therefore, scatter plots are a very useful tool for the sensible interpretation of a correlation coefficient.

   Exhibit 51 shows examples of scatter plots. Panel A shows the scatter plot of two variables with a correlation of +1. Note that all the points on the scatter plot in Panel A lie on a straight line with a positive slope. Whenever variable X increases by one unit, variable Y increases by two units. Because all of the points in the graph lie on a straight line, an increase of one unit in X is associated with exactly a two-unit increase in Y, regardless of the level of X. Even if the slope of the line were different (but positive), the correlation between the two variables would still be +1 as long as all the points lie on that straight line. Panel B shows a scatter plot for two variables with a correlation coefficient of −1. Once again, the plotted observations all fall on a straight line. In this graph, however, the line has a negative slope. As X increases by one unit, Y decreases by two units, regardless of the initial value of X.

EXHIBIT 51   Scatter Plots Showing Various Degrees of Correlation

A. Variables with a Correlation of +1

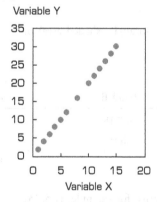

B. Variables with a Correlation of −1

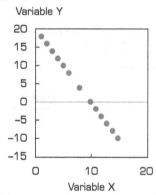

C. Variables with a Correlation of 0

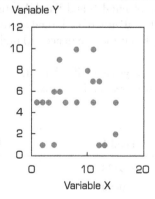

D. Variables with a Strong Nonlinear Association

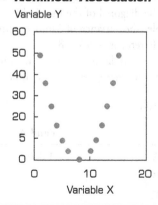

Panel C shows a scatter plot of two variables with a correlation of 0; they have no linear relation. This graph shows that the value of variable X tells us nothing about the value of variable Y. Panel D shows a scatter plot of two variables that have a non-linear relationship. Because the correlation coefficient is a measure of the linear association between two variables, it would not be appropriate to use the correlation coefficient in this case.

Example 22 is meant to reinforce your understanding of how to interpret covariance and correlation.

EXAMPLE 22   Interpreting the Correlation Coefficient

Consider the statistics for the returns over twelve months for three funds, A, B, and C, shown in Exhibit 52.

EXHIBIT 52

	Fund A	Fund B	Fund C
Arithmetic average	2.9333	3.2250	2.6250
Standard deviation	2.4945	2.4091	3.6668

The covariances are represented in the upper-triangle (shaded area) of the matrix shown in Exhibit 53.

EXHIBIT 53

	Fund A	Fund B	Fund C
Fund A	6.2224	5.7318	-3.6682
Fund B		5.8039	-2.3125
Fund C			13.4457

The covariance of Fund A and Fund B returns, for example, is 5.7318.

Why show just the upper-triangle of this matrix? Because the covariance of Fund A and Fund B returns is the same as the covariance of Fund B and Fund A returns.

The diagonal of the matrix in Exhibit 53 is the variance of each fund's return. For example, the variance of Fund A returns is 6.2224, but the covariance of Fund A and Fund B returns is 5.7138.

The correlations among the funds' returns are given in Exhibit 54, where the correlations are reported in the upper-triangle (shaded area) of the matrix. Note that the

EXHIBIT 54

	Fund A	Fund B	Fund C
Fund A	1.0000	0.9538	-0.4010
Fund B		1.0000	-0.2618
Fund C			1.0000

correlation of a fund's returns with itself is $+1$, so the diagonal in the correlation matrix consists of 1.000.

1. Interpret the correlation between Fund A's returns and Fund B's returns.
2. Interpret the correlation between Fund A's returns and Fund C's returns.
3. Describe the relationship of the covariance of these returns and the correlation of returns.

Solutions

1. The correlation of Fund A and Fund B returns is 0.9538, which is positive and close to 1.0. This means that when returns of Fund A tend to be above their mean, Fund B's returns also tend to be above their mean. Graphically, we would observe a positive, but not perfect, linear relationship between the returns for the two funds.
2. The correlation of Fund A's returns and Fund C's returns is -0.4010, which indicates that when Fund A's returns are above their mean, Fund B's returns tend to be below their mean. This implies a negative slope when graphing the returns of these two funds, but it would not be a perfect inverse relationship.
3. There are two negative correlations: Fund A returns with Fund C returns, and Fund B returns with Fund C returns. What determines the sign of the correlation is the sign of the covariance, which in each of these cases is negative. When the covariance between fund returns is positive, such as between Fund A and Fund B returns, the correlation is positive. This follows from the fact that the correlation coefficient is the ratio of the covariance of the two funds' returns to the product of their standard deviations.

10.2. Limitations of Correlation Analysis

Exhibit 51 illustrates that correlation measures the linear association between two variables, but it may not always be reliable. Two variables can have a strong *nonlinear* relation and still have a very low correlation. For example, the relation $Y = (X - 4)^2$ is a nonlinear relation contrasted to the linear relation $Y = 2X - 4$. The nonlinear relation between variables X and Y is shown in Panel D. Below a level of 4 for X, Y increases with decreasing values of X. When X is 4 or greater, however, Y increases whenever X increases. Even though these two variables are perfectly associated, there is no linear association between them (hence, no meaningful correlation).

Correlation may also be an unreliable measure when outliers are present in one or both of the variables. As we have seen, outliers are small numbers of observations at either extreme (small or large) of a sample. The correlation may be quite sensitive to outliers. In such a situation, we should consider whether it makes sense to exclude those outlier observations and whether they are noise or news. As a general rule, we must determine whether a computed sample correlation changes greatly by removing outliers. We must also use judgment to determine whether those outliers contain information about the two variables' relationship (and should thus be included in the correlation analysis) or contain no information (and should thus be excluded). If they are to be excluded from the correlation analysis, as we have seen previously, outlier observations can be handled by trimming or winsorizing the dataset.

Importantly, keep in mind that correlation does not imply causation. Even if two variables are highly correlated, one does not necessarily cause the other in the sense that certain values of one variable bring about the occurrence of certain values of the other.

Moreover, with visualizations too, including scatter plots, we must be on guard against unconsciously making judgments about causal relationships that may or may not be supported by the data.

The term **spurious correlation** has been used to refer to: 1) correlation between two variables that reflects chance relationships in a particular dataset; 2) correlation induced by a calculation that mixes each of two variables with a third variable; and 3) correlation between two variables arising not from a direct relation between them but from their relation to a third variable.

As an example of the chance relationship, consider the monthly US retail sales of beer, wine, and liquor and the atmospheric carbon dioxide levels from 2000–2018. The correlation is 0.824, indicating that there is a positive relation between the two. However, there is no reason to suspect that the levels of atmospheric carbon dioxide are related to the retail sales of beer, wine, and liquor.

As an example of the second kind of spurious correlation, two variables that are uncorrelated may be correlated if divided by a third variable. For example, consider a cross-sectional sample of companies' dividends and total assets. While there may be a low correlation between these two variables, dividing each by market capitalization may increase the correlation.

As an example of the third kind of spurious correlation, height may be positively correlated with the extent of a person's vocabulary, but the underlying relationships are between age and height and between age and vocabulary.

Investment professionals must be cautious in basing investment strategies on high correlations. Spurious correlations may suggest investment strategies that appear profitable but actually would not be, if implemented.

A further issue is that correlation does not tell the whole story about the data. Consider Anscombe's Quartet, discussed in **Exhibit 55**, where very dissimilar graphs can be developed with variables that have the same mean, same standard deviation, and same correlation.

EXHIBIT 55   Anscombe's Quartet

Francis Anscombe, a British statistician, developed datasets that illustrate why just looking at summary statistics (that is, mean, standard deviation, and correlation) does not fully describe the data. He created four datasets (designated I, II, III, and IV), each with two variables, X and Y, such that:

- The Xs in each dataset have the same mean and standard deviation, 9.00 and 3.32, respectively.
- The Ys in each dataset have the same mean and standard deviation, 7.50 and 2.03, respectively.
- The Xs and Ys in each dataset have the same correlation of 0.82.

While the X variable has the same values for I, II, and III in the quartet of datasets, the Y variables are quite different, creating different relationships. The four datasets are:

I. An approximate linear relationship between X and Y.
II. A curvilinear relationship between X and Y.
III. A linear relationship except for one outlier.
IV. A constant X with the exception of one outlier.

Observation	I		II		III		IV	
	X	Y	X	Y	X	Y	X	Y
1	10	8.04	10	9.14	10	7.46	8	6.6
2	8	6.95	8	8.14	8	6.77	8	5.8
3	13	7.58	13	8.74	13	12.74	8	7.7
4	9	8.81	9	8.77	9	7.11	8	8.8
5	11	8.33	11	9.26	11	7.81	8	8.5
6	14	9.96	14	8.1	14	8.84	8	7
7	6	7.24	6	6.13	6	6.08	8	5.3
8	4	4.26	4	3.1	4	5.39	19	13
9	12	10.8	12	9.13	12	8.15	8	5.6
10	7	4.82	7	7.26	7	6.42	8	7.9
11	5	5.68	5	4.74	5	5.73	8	6.9
N	11	11	11	11	11	11	11	11
Mean	9.00	7.50	9.00	7.50	9.00	7.50	9.00	7.50
Standard deviation	3.32	2.03	3.32	2.03	3.32	2.03	3.32	2.03
Correlation	0.82		0.82		0.82		0.82	

Depicting the quartet visually,

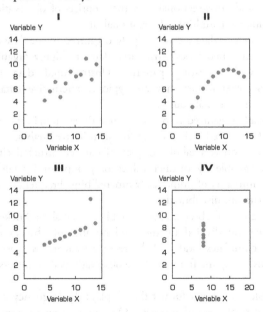

The bottom line? Knowing the means and standard deviations of the two variables, as well as the correlation between them, does not tell the entire story.

Source: Francis John Anscombe, "Graphs in Statistical Analysis," *The American Statistician* 27 (February 1973): 17–21.

11. SUMMARY

In this chapter, we have presented tools and techniques for organizing, visualizing, and describing data that permit us to convert raw data into useful information for investment analysis.

- Data can be defined as a collection of numbers, characters, words, and text—as well as images, audio, and video—in a raw or organized format to represent facts or information.
- From a statistical perspective, data can be classified as numerical data and categorical data. Numerical data (also called quantitative data) are values that represent measured or counted quantities as a number. Categorical data (also called qualitative data) are values that describe a quality or characteristic of a group of observations and usually take only a limited number of values that are mutually exclusive.
- Numerical data can be further split into two types: continuous data and discrete data. Continuous data can be measured and can take on any numerical value in a specified range of values. Discrete data are numerical values that result from a counting process and therefore are limited to a finite number of values.
- Categorical data can be further classified into two types: nominal data and ordinal data. Nominal data are categorical values that are not amenable to being organized in a logical order, while ordinal data are categorical values that can be logically ordered or ranked.
- Based on how they are collected, data can be categorized into three types: cross-sectional, time series, and panel. Time-series data are a sequence of observations for a single observational unit on a specific variable collected over time and at discrete and typically equally spaced intervals of time. Cross-sectional data are a list of the observations of a specific variable from multiple observational units at a given point in time. Panel data are a mix of time-series and cross-sectional data that consists of observations through time on one or more variables for multiple observational units.
- Based on whether or not data are in a highly organized form, they can be classified into structured and unstructured types. Structured data are highly organized in a pre-defined manner, usually with repeating patterns. Unstructured data do not follow any conventionally organized forms; they are typically alternative data as they are usually collected from unconventional sources.
- Raw data are typically organized into either a one-dimensional array or a two-dimensional rectangular array (also called a data table) for quantitative analysis.
- A frequency distribution is a tabular display of data constructed either by counting the observations of a variable by distinct values or groups or by tallying the values of a numerical variable into a set of numerically ordered bins. Frequency distributions permit us to evaluate how data are distributed.
- The relative frequency of observations in a bin (interval or bucket) is the number of observations in the bin divided by the total number of observations. The cumulative relative frequency cumulates (adds up) the relative frequencies as we move from the first bin to the last, thus giving the fraction of the observations that are less than the upper limit of each bin.
- A contingency table is a tabular format that displays the frequency distributions of two or more categorical variables simultaneously. One application of contingency tables is for evaluating the performance of a classification model (using a confusion matrix). Another application of contingency tables is to investigate a potential association between two categorical variables by performing a chi-square test of independence.

- Visualization is the presentation of data in a pictorial or graphical format for the purpose of increasing understanding and for gaining insights into the data.
- A histogram is a bar chart of data that have been grouped into a frequency distribution. A frequency polygon is a graph of frequency distributions obtained by drawing straight lines joining successive midpoints of bars representing the class frequencies.
- A bar chart is used to plot the frequency distribution of categorical data, with each bar representing a distinct category and the bar's height (or length) proportional to the frequency of the corresponding category. Grouped bar charts or stacked bar charts can present the frequency distribution of multiple categorical variables simultaneously.
- A tree-map is a graphical tool to display categorical data. It consists of a set of colored rectangles to represent distinct groups, and the area of each rectangle is proportional to the value of the corresponding group. Additional dimensions of categorical data can be displayed by nested rectangles.
- A word cloud is a visual device for representing textual data, with the size of each distinct word being proportional to the frequency with which it appears in the given text.
- A line chart is a type of graph used to visualize ordered observations and often to display the change of data series over time. A bubble line chart is a special type of line chart that uses varying-sized bubbles as data points to represent an additional dimension of data.
- A scatter plot is a type of graph for visualizing the joint variation in two numerical variables. It is constructed by drawing dots to indicate the values of the two variables plotted against the corresponding axes. A scatter plot matrix organizes scatter plots between pairs of variables into a matrix format to inspect all pairwise relationships between more than two variables in one combined visual.
- A heat map is a type of graphic that organizes and summarizes data in a tabular format and represents it using a color spectrum. It is often used in displaying frequency distributions or visualizing the degree of correlation among different variables.
- The key consideration when selecting among chart types is the intended purpose of visualizing data (i.e., whether it is for exploring/presenting distributions or relationships or for making comparisons).
- A population is defined as all members of a specified group. A sample is a subset of a population.
- A parameter is any descriptive measure of a population. A sample statistic (statistic, for short) is a quantity computed from or used to describe a sample.
- Sample statistics—such as measures of central tendency, measures of dispersion, skewness, and kurtosis—help with investment analysis, particularly in making probabilistic statements about returns.
- Measures of central tendency specify where data are centered and include the mean, median, and mode (i.e., the most frequently occurring value).
- The arithmetic mean is the sum of the observations divided by the number of observations. It is the most frequently used measure of central tendency.
- The median is the value of the middle item (or the mean of the values of the two middle items) when the items in a set are sorted into ascending or descending order. The median is not influenced by extreme values and is most useful in the case of skewed distributions.
- The mode is the most frequently observed value and is the only measure of central tendency that can be used with nominal data. A distribution may be unimodal (one mode), bimodal (two modes), trimodal (three modes), or have even more modes.

- A portfolio's return is a weighted mean return computed from the returns on the individual assets, where the weight applied to each asset's return is the fraction of the portfolio invested in that asset.
- The geometric mean, $\overline{X}_G$, of a set of observations $X_1, X_2, ..., X_n$, is $\overline{X}_G = \sqrt[n]{X_1 X_2 X_3 ... X_n}$, with $X_i \geq 0$ for $i = 1, 2, ..., n$. The geometric mean is especially important in reporting compound growth rates for time-series data. The geometric mean will always be less than an arithmetic mean whenever there is variance in the observations.
- The harmonic mean, $\overline{X}_H$, is a type of weighted mean in which an observation's weight is inversely proportional to its magnitude.
- Quantiles—such as the median, quartiles, quintiles, deciles, and percentiles—are location parameters that divide a distribution into halves, quarters, fifths, tenths, and hundredths, respectively.
- A box and whiskers plot illustrates the interquartile range (the "box") as well as a range outside of the box that is based on the interquartile range, indicated by the "whiskers."
- Dispersion measures—such as the range, mean absolute deviation (MAD), variance, standard deviation, target downside deviation, and coefficient of variation—describe the variability of outcomes around the arithmetic mean.
- The range is the difference between the maximum value and the minimum value of the dataset. The range has only a limited usefulness because it uses information from only two observations.
- The MAD for a sample is the average of the absolute deviations of observations from the

  mean, $\dfrac{\sum_{i=1}^{n} |X_i - \overline{X}|}{n}$, where $\overline{X}$ is the sample mean and n is the number of observations in the sample.
- The variance is the average of the squared deviations around the mean, and the standard deviation is the positive square root of variance. In computing sample variance (s^2) and sample standard deviation (s), the average squared deviation is computed using a divisor equal to the sample size minus 1.
- The target downside deviation, or target semideviation, is a measure of the risk of being below a given target. It is calculated as the square root of the average squared deviations from the target, but it includes only those observations below the target (B), or

$$\sqrt{\sum_{\text{for all } X_i \leq B}^{n} \frac{(X_i - B)^2}{n - 1}}.$$

- The coefficient of variation, CV, is the ratio of the standard deviation of a set of observations to their mean value. By expressing the magnitude of variation among observations relative to their average size, the CV permits direct comparisons of dispersion across different datasets. Reflecting the correction for scale, the CV is a scale-free measure (i.e., it has no units of measurement).
- Skew or skewness describes the degree to which a distribution is asymmetric about its mean. A return distribution with positive skewness has frequent small losses and a few extreme gains compared to a normal distribution. A return distribution with negative skewness has frequent small gains and a few extreme losses compared to a normal distribution. Zero skewness indicates a symmetric distribution of returns.
- Kurtosis measures the combined weight of the tails of a distribution relative to the rest of the distribution. A distribution with fatter tails than the normal distribution is referred to

as fat-tailed (leptokurtic); a distribution with thinner tails than the normal distribution is referred to as thin-tailed (platykurtic). Excess kurtosis is kurtosis minus 3, since 3 is the value of kurtosis for all normal distributions.

- The correlation coefficient is a statistic that measures the association between two variables. It is the ratio of covariance to the product of the two variables' standard deviations. A positive correlation coefficient indicates that the two variables tend to move together, whereas a negative coefficient indicates that the two variables tend to move in opposite directions. Correlation does not imply causation, simply association. Issues that arise in evaluating correlation include the presence of outliers and spurious correlation.

PRACTICE PROBLEMS

1. Published ratings on stocks ranging from 1 (strong sell) to 5 (strong buy) are examples of which measurement scale?
   A. Ordinal
   B. Continuous
   C. Nominal

2. Data values that are categorical and not amenable to being organized in a logical order are *most likely* to be characterized as:
   A. ordinal data.
   B. discrete data.
   C. nominal data.

3. Which of the following data types would be classified as being categorical?
   A. Discrete
   B. Nominal
   C. Continuous

4. A fixed-income analyst uses a proprietary model to estimate bankruptcy probabilities for a group of firms. The model generates probabilities that can take any value between 0 and 1. The resulting set of estimated probabilities would *most likely* be characterized as:
   A. ordinal data.
   B. discrete data.
   C. continuous data.

5. An analyst uses a software program to analyze unstructured data—specifically, management's earnings call transcript for one of the companies in her research coverage. The program scans the words in each sentence of the transcript and then classifies the sentences as having negative, neutral, or positive sentiment. The resulting set of sentiment data would *most likely* be characterized as:
   A. ordinal data.
   B. discrete data.
   C. nominal data.

Use the following information to answer Questions 6 and 7.

An equity analyst gathers total returns for three country equity indexes over the past four years. The data are presented below.

Time Period	Index A	Index B	Index C
Year t–3	15.56%	11.84%	–4.34%
Year t–2	–4.12%	–6.96%	9.32%
Year t–1	11.19%	10.29%	–12.72%
Year t	8.98%	6.32%	21.44%

6. Each individual column of data in the table can be *best* characterized as:
   A. panel data.
   B. time-series data.
   C. cross-sectional data.

7. Each individual row of data in the table can be *best* characterized as:
   A. panel data.
   B. time-series data.
   C. cross-sectional data.

8. A two-dimensional rectangular array would be most suitable for organizing a collection of raw:
   A. panel data.
   B. time-series data.
   C. cross-sectional data.

9. In a frequency distribution, the absolute frequency measure:
   A. represents the percentages of each unique value of the variable.
   B. represents the actual number of observations counted for each unique value of the variable.
   C. allows for comparisons between datasets with different numbers of total observations.

10. An investment fund has the return frequency distribution shown in the following exhibit.

Return Interval (%)	Absolute Frequency
–10.0 to –7.0	3
–7.0 to –4.0	7
–4.0 to –1.0	10
–1.0 to +2.0	12
+2.0 to +5.0	23
+5.0 to +8.0	5

Which of the following statements is correct?
A.   The relative frequency of the bin "–1.0 to +2.0" is 20%.
B.   The relative frequency of the bin "+2.0 to +5.0" is 23%.
C.   The cumulative relative frequency of the bin "+5.0 to +8.0" is 91.7%.

11.   An analyst is using the data in the following exhibit to prepare a statistical report.

Portfolio's Deviations from Benchmark Return for a 12-Year Period (%)

Year 1	2.48	Year 7	–9.19
Year 2	–2.59	Year 8	–5.11
Year 3	9.47	Year 9	1.33
Year 4	–0.55	Year 10	6.84
Year 5	–1.69	Year 11	3.04
Year 6	–0.89	Year 12	4.72

The cumulative relative frequency for the bin –1.71% ≤ x < 2.03% is *closest* to:
A.   0.250.
B.   0.333.
C.   0.583.

Use the following information to answer Questions 12 and 13.

A fixed-income portfolio manager creates a contingency table of the number of bonds held in her portfolio by sector and bond rating. The contingency table is presented here:

	Bond Rating		
Sector	**A**	**AA**	**AAA**
Communication Services	25	32	27
Consumer Staples	30	25	25
Energy	100	85	30
Health Care	200	100	63
Utilities	22	28	14

12.   The marginal frequency of energy sector bonds is *closest* to:
A.   27.
B.   85.
C.   215.

13.   The relative frequency of AA rated energy bonds, based on the total count, is *closest* to:
A.   10.5%.
B.   31.5%.
C.   39.5%.

The following information relates to Questions 14–15

The following histogram shows a distribution of the S&P 500 Index annual returns for a 50-year period:>

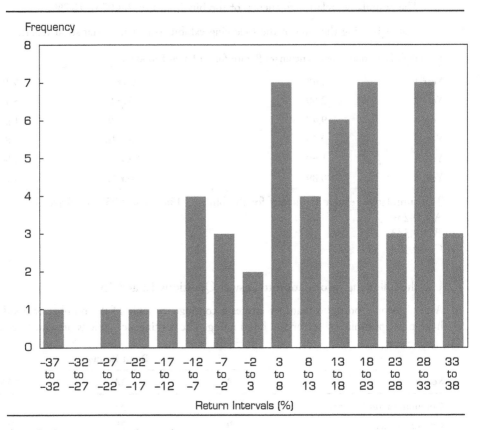

14. The bin containing the median return is:
    A. 3% to 8%.
    B. 8% to 13%.
    C. 13% to 18%.

15. Based on the previous histogram, the distribution is *best* described as being:
    A. unimodal.
    B. bimodal.
    C. trimodal.

16. The following is a frequency polygon of monthly exchange rate changes in the US dollar/Japanese yen spot exchange rate for a four-year period. A positive change represents yen appreciation (the yen buys more dollars), and a negative change represents yen depreciation (the yen buys fewer dollars).

Monthly Changes in the US Dollar/Japanese Yen Spot Exchange Rate

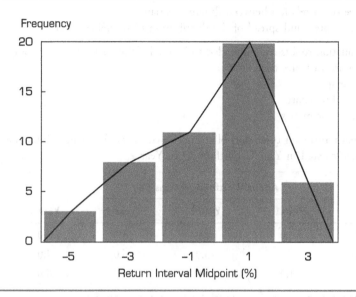

Based on the chart, yen appreciation:
A.   occurred more than 50% of the time.
B.   was less frequent than yen depreciation.
C.   in the 0.0 to 2.0 interval occurred 20% of the time.

17.   A bar chart that orders categories by frequency in descending order and includes a line
      displaying cumulative relative frequency is referred to as a:
      A.   Pareto Chart.
      B.   grouped bar chart.
      C.   frequency polygon.

18.   Which visualization tool works *best* to represent unstructured, textual data?
      A.   Tree-Map
      B.   Scatter plot
      C.   Word cloud

19.   A tree-map is best suited to illustrate:
      A.   underlying trends over time.
      B.   joint variations in two variables.
      C.   value differences of categorical groups.

20.   A line chart with two variables—for example, revenues and earnings per share—is best
      suited for visualizing:
      A.   the joint variation in the variables.
      B.   underlying trends in the variables over time.
      C.   the degree of correlation between the variables.

21. A heat map is best suited for visualizing the:
    A. frequency of textual data.
    B. degree of correlation between different variables.
    C. shape, center, and spread of the distribution of numerical data.

22. Which valuation tool is recommended to be used if the goal is to make comparisons of three or more variables over time?
    A. Heat map
    B. Bubble line chart
    C. Scatter plot matrix

23. The annual returns for three portfolios are shown in the following exhibit. Portfolios P and R were created in Year 1, Portfolio Q in Year 2.

	Annual Portfolio Returns (%)				
	Year 1	Year 2	Year 3	Year 4	Year 5
Portfolio P	−3.0	4.0	5.0	3.0	7.0
Portfolio Q		−3.0	6.0	4.0	8.0
Portfolio R	1.0	−1.0	4.0	4.0	3.0

The median annual return from portfolio creation to Year 5 for:
A. Portfolio P is 4.5%.
B. Portfolio Q is 4.0%.
C. Portfolio R is higher than its arithmetic mean annual return.

24. At the beginning of Year X, an investor allocated his retirement savings in the asset classes shown in the following exhibit and earned a return for Year X as also shown.

Asset Class	Asset Allocation (%)	Asset Class Return for Year X (%)
Large-cap US equities	20.0	8.0
Small-cap US equities	40.0	12.0
Emerging market equities	25.0	−3.0
High-yield bonds	15.0	4.0

The portfolio return for Year X is *closest to*:
A. 5.1%.
B. 5.3%.
C. 6.3%.

25. The following exhibit shows the annual returns for Fund Y.

	Fund Y (%)
Year 1	19.5
Year 2	−1.9
Year 3	19.7
Year 4	35.0
Year 5	5.7

The geometric mean return for Fund Y is *closest* to:
A. 14.9%.
B. 15.6%.
C. 19.5%.

26. A portfolio manager invests €5,000 annually in a security for four years at the prices shown in the following exhibit.

	Purchase Price of Security (€ per unit)
Year 1	62.00
Year 2	76.00
Year 3	84.00
Year 4	90.00

The average price is *best* represented as the:
A. harmonic mean of €76.48.
B. geometric mean of €77.26.
C. arithmetic average of €78.00.

The following information relates to Questions 27–28.

The following exhibit shows the annual MSCI World Index total returns for a 10-year period.

Year 1	15.25%	Year 6	30.79%
Year 2	10.02%	Year 7	12.34%
Year 3	20.65%	Year 8	-5.02%
Year 4	9.57%	Year 9	16.54%
Year 5	-40.33%	Year 10	27.37%

27. The fourth quintile return for the MSCI World Index is *closest* to:
A. 20.65%.
B. 26.03%.
C. 27.37%.

28. For Year 6–Year 10, the mean absolute deviation of the MSCI World Index total returns is *closest* to:
A. 10.20%.
B. 12.74%.
C. 16.40%.

29. Annual returns and summary statistics for three funds are listed in the following exhibit:

	Annual Returns (%)		
Year	Fund ABC	Fund XYZ	Fund PQR
Year 1	−20.0	−33.0	−14.0
Year 2	23.0	−12.0	−18.0
Year 3	−14.0	−12.0	6.0
Year 4	5.0	−8.0	−2.0
Year 5	−14.0	11.0	3.0
Mean	−4.0	−10.8	−5.0
Standard deviation	17.8	15.6	10.5

The fund with the highest absolute dispersion is:
A. Fund PQR if the measure of dispersion is the range.
B. Fund XYZ if the measure of dispersion is the variance.
C. Fund ABC if the measure of dispersion is the mean absolute deviation.

30. The mean monthly return and the standard deviation for three industry sectors are shown in the following exhibit.

Sector	Mean Monthly Return (%)	Standard Deviation of Return (%)
Utilities (UTIL)	2.10	1.23
Materials (MATR)	1.25	1.35
Industrials (INDU)	3.01	1.52

Based on the coefficient of variation, the riskiest sector is:
A. utilities.
B. materials.
C. industrials.

31. The average return for Portfolio A over the past twelve months is 3%, with a standard deviation of 4%. The average return for Portfolio B over this same period is also 3%, but with a standard deviation of 6%. The geometric mean return of Portfolio A is 2.85%. The geometric mean return of Portfolio B is:
A. less than 2.85%.
B. equal to 2.85%.
C. greater than 2.85%.

32. An analyst calculated the excess kurtosis of a stock's returns as −0.75. From this information, we conclude that the distribution of returns is:
A. normally distributed.
B. thin-tailed compared to the normal distribution.
C. fat-tailed compared to the normal distribution.

33. When analyzing investment returns, which of the following statements is correct?
   A. The geometric mean will exceed the arithmetic mean for a series with non-zero variance.
   B. The geometric mean measures an investment's compound rate of growth over multiple periods.
   C. The arithmetic mean measures an investment's terminal value over multiple periods.

The following information relates to Questions 34–38

A fund had the following experience over the past 10 years:

Year	Return
1	4.5%
2	6.0%
3	1.5%
4	–2.0%
5	0.0%
6	4.5%
7	3.5%
8	2.5%
9	5.5%
10	4.0%

34. The arithmetic mean return over the 10 years is *closest* to:
   A. 2.97%.
   B. 3.00%.
   C. 3.33%.

35. The geometric mean return over the 10 years is *closest* to:
   A. 2.94%.
   B. 2.97%.
   C. 3.00%.

36. The harmonic mean return over the 10 years is *closest* to:
   A. 2.94%.
   B. 2.97%.
   C. 3.00%.

37. The standard deviation of the 10 years of returns is *closest* to:
   A. 2.40%.
   B. 2.53%.
   C. 7.58%.

38. The target semideviation of the returns over the 10 years if the target is 2% is *closest* to:
   A. 1.42%.
   B. 1.50%.
   C. 2.01%.

39. A correlation of 0.34 between two variables, X and Y, is *best* described as:
   A. changes in X causing changes in Y.
   B. a positive association between X and Y.
   C. a curvilinear relationship between X and Y.

40. Which of the following is a potential problem with interpreting a correlation coefficient?
   A. Outliers
   B. Spurious correlation
   C. Both outliers and spurious correlation

The following relates to Questions 41 and 42

An analyst is evaluating the tendency of returns on the portfolio of stocks she manages to move along with bond and real estate indexes. She gathered monthly data on returns and the indexes:

	Returns (%)		
	Portfolio Returns	Bond Index Returns	Real Estate Index Returns
Arithmetic average	5.5	3.2	7.8
Standard deviation	8.2	3.4	10.3

	Portfolio Returns and Bond Index Returns	Portfolio Returns and Real Estate Index Returns
Covariance	18.9	–55.9

41. Without calculating the correlation coefficient, the correlation of the portfolio returns and the bond index returns is:
   A. negative.
   B. zero.
   C. positive.

42. Without calculating the correlation coefficient, the correlation of the portfolio returns and the real estate index returns is:
   A. negative.
   B. zero.
   C. positive.

43. Consider two variables, A and B. If variable A has a mean of –0.56, variable B has a mean of 0.23, and the covariance between the two variables is positive, the correlation between these two variables is:
   A. negative.
   B. zero.
   C. positive.

The following information relates to Questions 44–45.

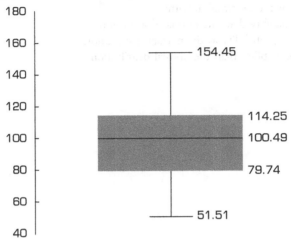

44. The median is *closest* to:
    A. 34.51.
    B. 100.49.
    C. 102.98.

45. The interquartile range is *closest* to:
    A. 13.76.
    B. 25.74.
    C. 34.51.

The following information relates to Questions 46–48

An analyst examined a cross-section of annual returns for 252 stocks and calculated the following statistics:

Arithmetic Average	9.986%
Geometric Mean	9.909%
Variance	0.001723
Skewness	0.704
Excess Kurtosis	0.503

46. The coefficient of variation is closest to:
    A. 0.02.
    B. 0.42.
    C. 2.41.

47. This distribution is best described as:
    A. negatively skewed.
    B. having no skewness.
    C. positively skewed.

48. Compared to the normal distribution, this sample's distribution is best described as having tails of the distribution with:
   A. less probability than the normal distribution.
   B. the same probability as the normal distribution.
   C. more probability than the normal distribution.

CHAPTER 3

PROBABILITY CONCEPTS

Richard A. DeFusco, PhD, CFA
Dennis W. McLeavey, DBA, CFA
Jerald E. Pinto, PhD, CFA
David E. Runkle, PhD, CFA

LEARNING OUTCOMES

The candidate should be able to:

- define a random variable, an outcome, an event, mutually exclusive events, and exhaustive events;
- state the two defining properties of probability and distinguish among empirical, subjective, and a priori probabilities;
- state the probability of an event in terms of odds for and against the event;
- distinguish between unconditional and conditional probabilities;
- explain the multiplication, addition, and total probability rules;
- calculate and interpret 1) the joint probability of two events, 2) the probability that at least one of two events will occur, given the probability of each and the joint probability of the two events, and 3) a joint probability of any number of independent events;
- distinguish between dependent and independent events;
- calculate and interpret an unconditional probability using the total probability rule;
- explain the use of conditional expectation in investment applications;
- explain the use of a tree diagram to represent an investment problem;
- calculate and interpret covariance and correlation;
- calculate and interpret the expected value, variance, and standard deviation of a random variable and of returns on a portfolio;
- calculate and interpret covariance given a joint probability function;
- calculate and interpret an updated probability using Bayes' formula;
- identify the most appropriate method to solve a particular counting problem and solve counting problems using factorial, combination, and permutation concepts.

Quantitative Methods for Investment Analysis, Second Edition, by Richard A. DeFusco, PhD, CFA, Dennis W. McLeavey, DBA, CFA, Jerald E. Pinto, PhD, CFA, David E. Runkle, PhD, CFA. Copyright © 2019 by CFA Institute.

1. INTRODUCTION

All investment decisions are made in an environment of risk. The tools that allow us to make decisions with consistency and logic in this setting come under the heading of probability. This chapter presents the essential probability tools needed to frame and address many real-world problems involving risk. We illustrate how these tools apply to such issues as predicting investment manager performance, forecasting financial variables, and pricing bonds so that they fairly compensate bondholders for default risk. Our focus is practical. We explore in detail the concepts that are most important to investment research and practice. One such concept is independence, as it relates to the predictability of returns and financial variables. Another is expectation, as analysts continually look to the future in their analyses and decisions. Analysts and investors must also cope with variability. We present variance, or dispersion around expectation, as a risk concept important in investments. The reader will acquire specific skills in using portfolio expected return and variance.

The basic tools of probability, including expected value and variance, are set out in Section 2 of this chapter. Section 3 introduces covariance and correlation (measures of relatedness between random quantities) and the principles for calculating portfolio expected return and variance. Two topics end the chapter: Bayes' formula and outcome counting. Bayes' formula is a procedure for updating beliefs based on new information. In several areas, including a widely used option-pricing model, the calculation of probabilities involves defining and counting outcomes. The chapter ends with a discussion of principles and shortcuts for counting.

2. PROBABILITY, EXPECTED VALUE, AND VARIANCE

The probability concepts and tools necessary for most of an analyst's work are relatively few and simple but require thought to apply. This section presents the essentials for working with probability, expectation, and variance, drawing on examples from equity and fixed income analysis.

An investor's concerns center on returns. The return on a risky asset is an example of a **random variable**, a quantity whose **outcomes** (possible values) are uncertain. For example, a portfolio may have a return objective of 10 percent a year. The portfolio manager's focus at the moment may be on the likelihood of earning a return that is less than 10 percent over the next year. Ten percent is a particular value or outcome of the random variable "portfolio return." Although we may be concerned about a single outcome, frequently our interest may be in a set of outcomes: The concept of "event" covers both.

- **Definition of Event.** An **event** is a specified set of outcomes.

We may specify an event to be a single outcome—for example, *the portfolio earns a return of 10 percent*. (We use italics to highlight statements that define events.) We can capture the portfolio manager's concerns by defining the event as *the portfolio earns a return below 10 percent*. This second event, referring as it does to all possible returns greater than or equal to −100 percent (the worst possible return) but less than 10 percent, contains an infinite number of outcomes. To save words, it is common to use a capital letter in italics to represent a defined event. We could define A = *the portfolio earns a return of 10 percent* and B = *the portfolio earns a return below 10 percent*.

To return to the portfolio manager's concern, how likely is it that the portfolio will earn a return below 10 percent?

The answer to this question is a **probability**: a number between 0 and 1 that measures the chance that a stated event will occur. If the probability is 0.40 that the portfolio earns a return below 10 percent, there is a 40 percent chance of that event happening. If an event is impossible, it has a probability of 0. If an event is certain to happen, it has a probability of 1. If an event is impossible or a sure thing, it is not random at all. So, 0 and 1 bracket all the possible values of a probability.

Probability has two properties, which together constitute its definition.

- **Definition of Probability.** The two defining properties of a probability are as follows:
    1. The probability of any event E is a number between 0 and 1: $0 \le P(E) \le 1$.
    2. The sum of the probabilities of any set of mutually exclusive and **exhaustive** events equals 1.

P followed by parentheses stands for "the probability of (the event in parentheses)," as in $P(E)$ for "the probability of event E." We can also think of P as a rule or function that assigns numerical values to events consistent with Properties 1 and 2.

In the above definition, the term mutually exclusive means that only one event can occur at a time; **exhaustive** means that the events cover all possible outcomes. The events $A = the$ *portfolio earns a return of 10 percent* and $B = the$ *portfolio earns a return below 10 percent* are mutually exclusive because A and B cannot both occur at the same time. For example, a return of 8.1 percent means that B has occurred and A has not occurred. Although events A and B are mutually exclusive, they are not exhaustive because they do not cover outcomes such as a return of 11 percent. Suppose we define a third event: $C = the$ *portfolio earns a return above 10 percent.* Clearly, A, B, and C are mutually exclusive and exhaustive events. Each of $P(A)$, $P(B)$, and $P(C)$ is a number between 0 and 1, and $P(A) + P(B) + P(C) = 1$.

The most basic kind of mutually exclusive and exhaustive events is the set of all the distinct possible outcomes of the random variable. If we know both that set and the assignment of probabilities to those outcomes—the probability distribution of the random variable—we have a complete description of the random variable, and we can assign a probability to any event that we might describe.[1] The probability of any event is the sum of the probabilities of the distinct outcomes included in the definition of the event. Suppose the event of interest is $D = the$ *portfolio earns a return above the risk-free rate,* and we know the probability distribution of portfolio returns. Assume the risk-free rate is 4 percent. To calculate $P(D)$, the probability of D, we would sum the probabilities of the outcomes that satisfy the definition of the event; that is, we would sum the probabilities of portfolio returns greater than 4 percent.

Earlier, to illustrate a concept, we assumed a probability of 0.40 for a portfolio earning less than 10 percent, without justifying the particular assumption. We also talked about using a probability distribution of outcomes to calculate the probability of events, without explaining how a probability distribution might be estimated. Making actual financial decisions using inaccurate probabilities might have grave consequences. How, in practice, do we estimate probabilities? This topic is a field of study in itself, but there are three broad approaches to estimating probabilities. In investments, we often estimate the probability of an event as a relative frequency of occurrence based on historical data. This method produces an **empirical**

---

[1]In the chapter on common probability distributions (Chapter 4), we describe some of the probability distributions most frequently used in investment applications.

probability. For example, **Thanatawee (2013)** reports that of his sample of 1,927 yearly observations for nonfinancial SET (Stock Exchange of Thailand) firms during the years 2002 to 2010, 1,382 were dividend paying firms and 545 were non dividend paying firms. The empirical probability of a Thai firm paying a dividend is thus 1,382/1,927 = 0.72, approximately. We will point out empirical probabilities in several places as they appear in this chapter.

Relationships must be stable through time for empirical probabilities to be accurate. We cannot calculate an empirical probability of an event not in the historical record or a reliable empirical probability for a very rare event. There are cases, then, in which we may adjust an empirical probability to account for perceptions of changing relationships. In other cases, we have no empirical probability to use at all. We may also make a personal assessment of probability without reference to any particular data. Each of these three types of probability is a **subjective probability**, one drawing on personal or subjective judgment. Subjective probabilities are of great importance in investments. Investors, in making buy and sell decisions that determine asset prices, often draw on subjective probabilities. Subjective probabilities appear in various places in this chapter, notably in our discussion of Bayes' formula.

In a more narrow range of well-defined problems, we can sometimes deduce probabilities by reasoning about the problem. The resulting probability is an **a priori probability**, one based on logical analysis rather than on observation or personal judgment. We will use this type of probability in **Example 6**. The counting methods we discuss later are particularly important in calculating an a priori probability. Because a priori and empirical probabilities generally do not vary from person to person, they are often grouped as **objective probabilities**.

In business and elsewhere, we often encounter probabilities stated in terms of odds—for instance, "the odds for E" or the "odds against E." For example, as of August 2018, analysts' fiscal year 2019 EPS forecasts for JetBlue Airways ranged from \$1.50 to \$2.20. Suppose one analyst asserts that the odds for the company beating the highest estimate, \$2.20, are 1 to 7. Suppose a second analyst argues that the odds against that happening are 15 to 1. What do those statements imply about the probability of the company's EPS beating the highest estimate? We interpret probabilities stated in terms of odds as follows:

- **Probability Stated as Odds.** Given a probability $P(E)$,
  1. Odds for $E = P(E)/[1 - P(E)]$. The odds for E are the probability of E divided by 1 minus the probability of E. Given odds for E of "a to b," the implied probability of E is $a/(a + b)$.

In the example, the statement that the odds for *the company's EPS for FY2019 beating \$2.20* are 1 to 7 means that the speaker believes the probability of the event is $1/(1 + 7) = 1/8 = 0.125$.

  2. Odds against $E = [1 - P(E)]/P(E)$, the reciprocal of odds for E. Given odds against E of "a to b," the implied probability of E is $b/(a + b)$.

The statement that the odds against *the company's EPS for FY2019 beating \$2.20* are 15 to 1 is consistent with a belief that the probability of the event is $1/(1 + 15) = 1/16 = 0.0625$.

To further explain odds for an event, if $P(E) = 1/8$, the odds for E are $(1/8)/(7/8) = (1/8)(8/7) = 1/7$, or "1 to 7." For each occurrence of E, we expect seven cases of nonoccurrence; out of eight cases in total, therefore, we expect E to happen once, and the probability of E is 1/8. In wagering, it is common to speak in terms of the odds against something, as in Statement 2. For odds of "15 to 1" against E (an implied probability of E of 1/16), a \$1 wager on E, if successful, returns \$15 in profits plus the \$1 staked in the wager. We can calculate the bet's anticipated profit as follows:

Win: Probability = 1/16; Profit =$15

Loss: Probability = 15/16; Profit =–$1

Anticipated profit = (1/16)($15) + (15/16)(–$1) = $0

Weighting each of the wager's two outcomes by the respective probability of the outcome, if the odds (probabilities) are accurate, the anticipated profit of the bet is $0.

EXAMPLE 1   Profiting from Inconsistent Probabilities

You are examining the common stock of two companies in the same industry in which an important antitrust decision will be announced next week. The first company, SmithCo Corporation, will benefit from a governmental decision that there is no antitrust obstacle related to a merger in which it is involved. You believe that SmithCo's share price reflects a 0.85 probability of such a decision. A second company, Selbert Corporation, will equally benefit from a "go ahead" ruling. Surprisingly, you believe Selbert stock reflects only a 0.50 probability of a favorable decision. Assuming your analysis is correct, what investment strategy would profit from this pricing discrepancy?

  Consider the logical possibilities. One is that the probability of 0.50 reflected in Selbert's share price is accurate. In that case, Selbert is fairly valued but SmithCo is overvalued, as its current share price overestimates the probability of a "go ahead" decision. The second possibility is that the probability of 0.85 is accurate. In that case, SmithCo shares are fairly valued, but Selbert shares, which build in a lower probability of a favorable decision, are undervalued. You diagram the situation as shown in Table 1.

  The 0.50 probability column shows that Selbert shares are a better value than SmithCo shares. Selbert shares are also a better value if a 0.85 probability is accurate. Thus SmithCo shares are overvalued relative to Selbert shares.

  Your investment actions depend on your confidence in your analysis and on any investment constraints you face (such as constraints on selling stock short).[2] A conservative strategy would be to buy Selbert shares and reduce or eliminate any current position in SmithCo. The most aggressive strategy is to short SmithCo stock (relatively overvalued) and simultaneously buy the stock of Selbert (relatively undervalued). This strategy is known as **pairs arbitrage trade**: a trade in two closely related stocks involving the short sale of one and the purchase of the other.

TABLE 1   Worksheet for Investment Problem

	True Probability of a "Go Ahead" Decision	
	0.50	**0.85**
SmithCo	Shares Overvalued	Shares Fairly Valued
Selbert	Shares Fairly Valued	Shares Undervalued

---

[2] *Selling short* or *shorting stock* means selling borrowed shares in the hope of repurchasing them later at a lower price.

The prices of SmithCo and Selbert shares reflect probabilities that are not **consistent**. According to one of the most important probability results for investments, the **Dutch Book Theorem**,[3] inconsistent probabilities create profit opportunities. In our example, investors, by their buy and sell decisions to exploit the inconsistent probabilities, should eliminate the profit opportunity and inconsistency.

To understand the meaning of a probability in investment contexts, we need to distinguish between two types of probability: unconditional and conditional. Both unconditional and conditional probabilities satisfy the definition of probability stated earlier, but they are calculated or estimated differently and have different interpretations. They provide answers to different questions.

The probability in answer to the straightforward question "What is the probability of this event A?" is an **unconditional probability**, denoted $P(A)$. Unconditional probability is also frequently referred to as **marginal probability**.[4]

Suppose the question is "What is the probability that *the stock earns a return above the risk-free rate* (event A)?" The answer is an unconditional probability that can be viewed as the ratio of two quantities. The numerator is the sum of the probabilities of stock returns above the risk-free rate. Suppose that sum is 0.70. The denominator is 1, the sum of the probabilities of all possible returns. The answer to the question is $P(A) = 0.70$.

Contrast the question "What is the probability of A?" with the question "What is the probability of A, given that B has occurred?" The probability in answer to this last question is a **conditional probability**, denoted $P(A \mid B)$ (read: "the probability of A given B").

Suppose we want to know the probability that *the stock earns a return above the risk-free rate* (event A), given that *the stock earns a positive return* (event B). With the words "given that," we are restricting returns to those larger than 0 percent—a new element in contrast to the question that brought forth an unconditional probability. The conditional probability is calculated as the ratio of two quantities. The numerator is the sum of the probabilities of stock returns above the risk-free rate; in this particular case, the numerator is the same as it was in the unconditional case, which we gave as 0.70. The denominator, however, changes from 1 to the sum of the probabilities for all outcomes (returns) above 0 percent. Suppose that number is 0.80, a larger number than 0.70 because returns between 0 and the risk-free rate have some positive probability of occurring. Then $P(A \mid B) = 0.70/0.80 = 0.875$. If we observe that the stock earns a positive return, the probability of a return above the risk-free rate is greater than the unconditional probability, which is the probability of the event given no other information. The result is intuitive.[5] To review, an unconditional

---

[3] The theorem's name comes from the terminology of wagering. Suppose someone places a $100 bet on X at odds of 10 to 1 against X, and later he is able to place a $600 bet against X at odds of 1 to 1 against X. Whatever the outcome of X, that person makes a riskless profit (equal to $400 if X occurs or $500 if X does not occur) because the implied probabilities are inconsistent. **Ramsey (1931)** presented the problem of inconsistent probabilities. See also **Lo (1999)**.

[4] In analyses of probabilities presented in tables, unconditional probabilities usually appear at the ends or *margins* of the table, hence the term *marginal probability*. Because of possible confusion with the way *marginal* is used in economics (roughly meaning *incremental*), we use the term *unconditional probability* throughout this discussion.

[5] In this example, the conditional probability is greater than the unconditional probability. The conditional probability of an event may, however, be greater than, equal to, or less than the unconditional probability, depending on the facts. For instance, the probability that *the stock earns a return above the risk-free rate* given that *the stock earns a negative return* is 0.

probability is the probability of an event without any restriction; it might even be thought of as a stand-alone probability. A conditional probability, in contrast, is a probability of an event given that another event has occurred.

In discussing approaches to calculating probability, we gave one empirical estimate of the probability that a change in dividends is a dividend decrease. That probability was an unconditional probability. Given additional information on company characteristics, could an investor refine that estimate? Investors continually seek an information edge that will help improve their forecasts. In mathematical terms, they are attempting to frame their view of the future using probabilities conditioned on relevant information or events. Investors do not ignore useful information; they adjust their probabilities to reflect it. Thus, the concepts of conditional probability (which we analyze in more detail below), as well as related concepts discussed further on, are extremely important in investment analysis and financial markets.

To state an exact definition of conditional probability, we first need to introduce the concept of joint probability. Suppose we ask the question "What is the probability of both A and B happening?" The answer to this question is a **joint probability**, denoted $P(AB)$ (read: "the probability of A and B"). If we think of the probability of A and the probability of B as sets built of the outcomes of one or more random variables, the joint probability of A and B is the sum of the probabilities of the outcomes they have in common. For example, consider two events: *the stock earns a return above the risk-free rate* (A) and *the stock earns a positive return* (B). The outcomes of A are contained within (a subset of) the outcomes of B, so $P(AB)$ equals $P(A)$. We can now state a formal definition of conditional probability that provides a formula for calculating it.

- **Definition of Conditional Probability.** The conditional probability of A given that B has occurred is equal to the joint probability of A and B divided by the probability of B (assumed not to equal 0).

$$P(A \mid B) = P(AB)/P(B), \; P(B) \neq 0 \tag{1}$$

Sometimes we know the conditional probability $P(A \mid B)$ and we want to know the joint probability $P(AB)$. We can obtain the joint probability from the following **multiplication rule for probabilities**, which is Equation 1 rearranged.

- **Multiplication Rule for Probability.** The joint probability of A and B can be expressed as

$$P(AB) = P(A \mid B)P(B) \tag{2}$$

EXAMPLE 2 Conditional Probabilities and Predictability of Mutual Fund Performance (1)

Vidal-Garcia (2013) examined whether historical performance predicts future performance for a sample of mutual funds that included 1,050 actively managed equity funds in six European countries over a 13-year period. Funds were classified into nine investment styles based on combinations of investment focus (growth, blend, and

TABLE 2   Persistence of Returns for Large Value Funds in France over a 13-Year Period

	Year 2 Winner	Year 2 Loser
Year 1 Winner	65.5%	34.5%
Year 1 Loser	15.5%	84.5%

Source: Vidal-Garcia (2013), Table 4.

value) and funds' market capitalization (small, mid, and large cap). One approach Vidal-Garcia used involved calculating each fund's annual benchmark-adjusted return by subtracting a benchmark return from the annual return of the fund. MSCI (Morgan Stanley Capital International) style indexes were used as benchmarks. For each style of fund in each country, funds were classified as winners or losers for each of two consecutive years. The top 50 percent of funds by benchmark-adjusted return for a given year were labeled winners; the bottom 50 percent were labeled losers. An excerpt from the results of the study for 135 French funds classified as large value funds is given in Table 2. It shows the percentage of those funds that were winners in two consecutive years, winner in one year and then loser in the next year, losers then winners, and losers in both years. The winner–winner entry, for example, shows that 65.5 percent of the first-year winner funds were also winners in the second year. Note that the four entries in the table can be viewed as conditional probabilities.

Based on the data in Table 2, answer the following questions:

1. State the four events needed to define the four conditional probabilities.
2. State the four entries of the table as conditional probabilities using the form P(*this event* | *that event*) = number.
3. Are the conditional probabilities in Part 2 empirical, a priori, or subjective probabilities?
4. Using information in the table, calculate the probability of the event a *fund is a loser in both Year 1 and Year 2.* (Note that because 50 percent of funds are categorized as losers in each year, the unconditional probability that a fund is labeled a loser in either year is 0.5.)

Solution to 1: The four events needed to define the conditional probabilities are as follows:

    Fund is a Year 1 winner
    Fund is a Year 1 loser
    Fund is a Year 2 loser
    Fund is a Year 2 winner

Solution to 2: From Row 1:

    P(*fund is a Year 2 winner* | *fund is a Year 1 winner*) = 0.655
    P(*fund is a Year 2 loser* | *fund is a Year 1 winner*) = 0.345

From Row 2:

> *P(fund is a Year 2 winner | fund is a Year 1 loser)* = 0.155
> *P(fund is a Year 2 loser | fund is a Year 1 loser)* = 0.845

Solution to 3: These probabilities are calculated from data, so they are empirical probabilities.

Solution to 4: The estimated probability is 0.423. Let A represent the event that a *fund is a Year 2 loser*, and let B represent the event that *the fund is a Year 1 loser*. Therefore, the event AB is the event that a *fund is a loser in both Year 1 and Year 2*. From Table 2, $P(A \mid B) = 0.845$ and $P(B) = 0.50$. Thus, using Equation 2, we find that

$$P(AB) = P(A \mid B)P(B) = 0.845(0.50) = 0.4225$$

or a probability of approximately 0.423.

Equation 2 states that the joint probability of A and B equals the probability of A given B times the probability of B. Because $P(AB) = P(BA)$, the expression $P(AB) = P(BA) = P(B \mid A)$ $P(A)$ is equivalent to Equation 2.

When we have two events, A and B, that we are interested in, we often want to know the probability that either A or B occurs. Here the word "or" is inclusive, meaning that either A or B occurs or that both A and B occur. Put another way, the probability of A or B is the probability that at least one of the two events occurs. Such probabilities are calculated using the **addition rule for probabilities**.

- **Addition Rule for Probabilities.** Given events A and B, the probability that A or B occurs, or both occur, is equal to the probability that A occurs, plus the probability that B occurs, minus the probability that both A and B occur.

$$P(A \text{ or } B) = P(A) + P(B) - P(AB) \tag{3}$$

If we think of the individual probabilities of A and B as sets built of outcomes of one or more random variables, the first step in calculating the probability of A or B is to sum the probabilities of the outcomes in A to obtain $P(A)$. If A and B share any outcomes, then if we now added $P(B)$ to $P(A)$, we would count twice the probabilities of those shared outcomes. So we add to $P(A)$ the quantity $[P(B) - P(AB)]$, which is the probability of outcomes in B net of the probability of any outcomes already counted when we computed $P(A)$. Figure 1 illustrates this process; we avoid double-counting the outcomes in the intersection of A and B by subtracting $P(AB)$. As an example of the calculation, if $P(A) = 0.50$, $P(B) = 0.40$, and $P(AB) = 0.20$, then $P(A \text{ or } B) = 0.50 + 0.40 - 0.20 = 0.70$. Only if the two events A and B were mutually exclusive, so that $P(AB) = 0$, would it be correct to state that $P(A \text{ or } B) = P(A) + P(B)$.

FIGURE 1   Addition Rule for Probabilities

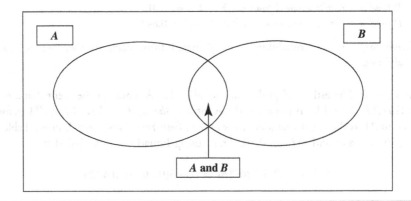

The next example shows how much useful information can be obtained using the few probability rules presented to this point.

EXAMPLE 3   Probability of a Limit Order Executing

You have two buy limit orders outstanding on the same stock. A limit order to buy stock at a stated price is an order to buy at that price or lower. A number of vendors, including an internet service that you use, supply the estimated probability that a limit order will be filled within a stated time horizon, given the current stock price and the price limit. One buy order (Order 1) was placed at a price limit of $10. The probability that it will execute within one hour is 0.35. The second buy order (Order 2) was placed at a price limit of $9.75; it has a 0.25 probability of executing within the same one-hour time frame.

1. What is the probability that either Order 1 or Order 2 will execute?
2. What is the probability that Order 2 executes, given that Order 1 executes?

Solution to 1: The probability is 0.35. The two probabilities that are given are $P(Order\ 1\ executes) = 0.35$ and $P(Order\ 2\ executes) = 0.25$. Note that if Order 2 executes, it is certain that Order 1 also executes because the price must pass through $10 to reach $9.75. Thus,

$$P(Order\ 1\ executes \mid Order\ 2\ executes) = 1$$

and

$$P(Order\ 1\ executes\ \text{and}\ Order\ 2\ executes) = P(Order\ 1\ executes \mid Order\ 2\ executes)P(Order\ 2\ executes) = 1(0.25) = 0.25$$

To answer the question, we use the addition rule for probabilities:

$$P(Order\ 1\ executes\ \text{or}\ Order\ 2\ executes) = P(Order\ 1\ executes) \\ + P(Order\ 2\ executes) - P(Order\ 1\ executes\ \text{and}\ Order\ 2\ executes) \\ = 0.35 + 0.25 - 0.25 = 0.35$$

Note that the outcomes for which Order 2 executes are a subset of the outcomes for which Order 1 executes. After you count the probability that Order 1 executes, you have counted the probability of the outcomes for which Order 2 also executes. Therefore, the answer to the question is the probability that Order 1 executes, 0.35.

Solution to 2: If the first order executes, the probability that the second order executes is 0.714. In the solution to Part 1, you found that P(*Order 1 executes* and *Order 2 executes*) = P(*Order 1 executes* | *Order 2 executes*)P(*Order 2 executes*) = 1(0.25) = 0.25. An equivalent way to state this joint probability is useful here:

$$P(\textit{Order 1 executes} \text{ and } \textit{Order 2 executes}) = 0.25$$
$$= P(\textit{Order 2 executes} \mid \textit{Order 1 executes})P(\textit{Order 1 executes})$$

Because P(*Order 1 executes*) = 0.35 was a given, you have one equation with one unknown:

$$0.25 = P(\textit{Order 2 executes} \mid \textit{Order 1 executes})(0.35)$$

You conclude that P(*Order 2 executes* | *Order 1 executes*) = 0.25/0.35 = 5/7, or about 0.714. You can also use Equation 1 to obtain this answer.

Of great interest to investment analysts are the concepts of independence and dependence. These concepts bear on such basic investment questions as which financial variables are useful for investment analysis, whether asset returns can be predicted, and whether superior investment managers can be selected based on their past records.

Two events are independent if the occurrence of one event does not affect the probability of occurrence of the other event.

- **Definition of Independent Events.** Two events A and B are **independent** if and only if $P(A \mid B) = P(A)$ or, equivalently, $P(B \mid A) = P(B)$.

When two events are not independent, they are **dependent**: The probability of occurrence of one is related to the occurrence of the other. If we are trying to forecast one event, information about a dependent event may be useful, but information about an independent event will not be useful. For example, if two events are mutually exclusive, then knowledge that one event has occurred gives us information that the other (mutually exclusive) event cannot occur.

When two events are independent, the multiplication rule for probabilities, Equation 2, simplifies because $P(A \mid B)$ in that equation then equals $P(A)$.

- **Multiplication Rule for Independent Events.** When two events are independent, the joint probability of A and B equals the product of the individual probabilities of A and B.

$$P(AB) = P(A)P(B) \qquad\qquad (4)$$

Therefore, if we are interested in two independent events with probabilities of 0.75 and 0.50, respectively, the probability that both will occur is $0.375 = 0.75(0.50)$. The multiplication rule for independent events generalizes to more than two events; for example, if A, B, and C are independent events, then $P(ABC) = P(A)P(B)P(C)$.

EXAMPLE 4   BankCorp's Earnings per Share (1)

As part of your work as a banking industry analyst, you build models for forecasting earnings per share of the banks you cover. Today you are studying BankCorp. The historical record shows that in 55 percent of recent quarters BankCorp's EPS has increased sequentially, and in 45 percent of quarters EPS has decreased or remained unchanged sequentially.[6] At this point in your analysis, you are assuming that changes in sequential EPS are independent.

Earnings per share for 2Q:Year 1 (that is, EPS for the second quarter of Year 1) were larger than EPS for 1Q:Year 1.

1. What is the probability that 3Q:Year 1 EPS will be larger than 2Q:Year 1 EPS (a positive change in sequential EPS)?
2. What is the probability that EPS decreases or remains unchanged in the next two quarters?

Solution to 1: Under the assumption of independence, the probability that 3Q:Year 1 EPS will be larger than 2Q:Year 1 EPS is the unconditional probability of positive change, 0.55. The fact that 2Q:Year 1 EPS was larger than 1Q:Year 1 EPS is not useful information, as the next change in EPS is independent of the prior change.

Solution to 2: The probability is $0.2025 = 0.45(0.45)$.

The following example illustrates how difficult it is to satisfy a set of independent criteria even when each criterion by itself is not necessarily stringent.

EXAMPLE 5   Screening Stocks for Investment

You have developed a stock screen—a set of criteria for selecting stocks. Your investment universe (the set of securities from which you make your choices) is the Russell 1000 Index, an index of 1,000 large-capitalization US equities. Your criteria capture different aspects of the selection problem; you believe that the criteria are independent of each other, to a close approximation.

Criterion	Fraction of Russell 1000 Stocks Meeting Criterion
First valuation criterion	0.50
Second valuation criterion	0.50
Analyst coverage criterion	0.25
Profitability criterion for company	0.55
Financial strength criterion for company	0.67

---

[6] *Sequential* comparisons of quarterly EPS are with the immediate prior quarter. A sequential comparison stands in contrast to a comparison with the same quarter one year ago (another frequent type of comparison).

How many stocks do you expect to pass your screen?

Only 23 stocks out of 1,000 pass through your screen. If you define five events— *the stock passes the first valuation criterion, the stock passes the second valuation criterion, the stock passes the analyst coverage criterion, the company passes the profitability criterion, the company passes the financial strength criterion* (say events *A, B, C, D,* and *E,* respectively)—then the probability that a stock will pass all five criteria, under independence, is

$$P(ABCDE) = P(A)P(B)P(C)P(D)P(E) = (0.50)(0.50)(0.25)(0.55)(0.67)$$
$$= 0.023031$$

Although only one of the five criteria is even moderately strict (the strictest lets 25 percent of stocks through), the probability that a stock can pass all five is only 0.023031, or about 2 percent. The size of the list of candidate investments is 0.023031 (1,000) = 23.031, or 23 stocks.

An area of intense interest to investment managers and their clients is whether records of past performance are useful in identifying repeat winners and losers. The following example shows how this issue relates to the concept of independence.

EXAMPLE 6   Conditional Probabilities and Predictability of Mutual Fund Performance (2)

The purpose of the **Vidal-Garcia (2013)** study, introduced in **Example 2**, was to address the question of repeat European mutual fund winners and losers. If the status of a fund as a winner or a loser in one year is independent of whether it is a winner in the next year, the practical value of performance ranking is questionable. Using the four events defined in **Example 2** as building blocks, we can define the following events to address the issue of predictability of mutual fund performance:

Fund is a Year 1 winner and *fund is a Year 2 winner*
Fund is a Year 1 winner and *fund is a Year 2 loser*
Fund is a Year 1 loser and *fund is a Year 2 winner*
Fund is a Year 1 loser and *fund is a Year 2 loser*

In Part 4 of **Example 2**, you calculated that

P(fund is a Year 2 loser and *fund is a Year 1 loser)* = 0.423

If the ranking in one year is independent of the ranking in the next year, what will you expect *P(fund is a Year 2 loser* and *fund is a Year 1 loser)* to be? Interpret the empirical probability 0.423.

By the multiplication rule for independent events, *P(fund is a Year 2 loser* and *fund is a Year 1 loser)* = *P(fund is a Year 2 loser)P(fund is a Year 1 loser)*. Because 50 percent of funds are categorized as losers in each year, the unconditional probability that a fund is labeled a loser in either year is 0.50. Thus $P(fund\ is\ a\ Year\ 2\ loser)P(fund\ is\ a\ Year\ 1\ loser) = 0.50(0.50) = 0.25$. If the status of a fund as a loser in one year is independent of whether it is a loser in the prior year, we conclude that $P(fund\ is\ a\ Year\ 2\ loser$ and $fund\ is\ a\ Year\ 1\ loser) = 0.25$. This probability is a priori because it is obtained from reasoning about the problem. You could also reason that the four events described above define categories and that if funds are randomly assigned to the four categories, there is a 1/4 probability of *fund is a Year 1 loser* and *fund is a Year 2 loser*. If the classifications in Year 1 and Year 2 were dependent, then the assignment of funds to categories would not be random. The empirical probability of 0.423 is above 0.25. Is this apparent predictability the result of chance? A test conducted by Vidal-Garcia indicated a less than 1 percent chance of observing the tabled data if the Year 1 and Year 2 rankings were independent.

In investments, the question of whether one event (or characteristic) provides information about another event (or characteristic) arises in both time-series settings (through time) and cross-sectional settings (among units at a given point in time). **Examples 4** and **6** examined independence in a time-series setting. **Example 5** illustrated independence in a cross-sectional setting. Independence/dependence relationships are often also explored in both settings using regression analysis, a technique we discuss in a later chapter.

In many practical problems, we logically analyze a problem as follows: We formulate scenarios that we think affect the likelihood of an event that interests us. We then estimate the probability of the event, given the scenario. When the scenarios (conditioning events) are mutually exclusive and exhaustive, no possible outcomes are left out. We can then analyze the event using the **total probability rule**. This rule explains the unconditional probability of the event in terms of probabilities conditional on the scenarios.

The total probability rule is stated below for two cases. Equation 5 gives the simplest case, in which we have two scenarios. One new notation is introduced: If we have an event or scenario S, the event not-S, called the **complement** of S, is written S^C.[7] Note that $P(S) + P(S^C) = 1$, as either S or not-S must occur. Equation 6 states the rule for the general case of n mutually exclusive and exhaustive events or scenarios.

- **The Total Probability Rule.**

$$P(A) = P(AS) + P(AS^C)$$
$$= P(A|S)P(S) + P(A|S^C)P(S^C) \tag{5}$$

$$P(A) = P(AS_1) + P(AS_2) + ... + P(AS_n)$$
$$= P(A|S_1)P(S_1) + P(A|S_2)P(S_2) + ... + P(A|S_n)P(S_n) \tag{6}$$

where $S_1, S_2, ..., S_n$ are mutually exclusive and exhaustive scenarios or events.

---

[7]For readers familiar with mathematical treatments of probability, S, a notation usually reserved for a concept called the sample space, is being appropriated to stand for *scenario.*

Equation 6 states the following: The probability of any event [$P(A)$] can be expressed as a weighted average of the probabilities of the event, given scenarios [terms such $P(A \mid S_1)$]; the weights applied to these conditional probabilities are the respective probabilities of the scenarios [terms such as $P(S_1)$ multiplying $P(A \mid S_1)$], and the scenarios must be mutually exclusive and exhaustive. Among other applications, this rule is needed to understand Bayes' formula, which we discuss later in the chapter.

In the next example, we use the total probability rule to develop a consistent set of views about BankCorp's earnings per share.

EXAMPLE 7   BankCorp's Earnings per Share (2)

You are continuing your investigation into whether you can predict the direction of changes in BankCorp's quarterly EPS. You define four events:

Event	Probability
A = *Change in sequential EPS is positive next quarter*	0.55
A^C = *Change in sequential EPS is 0 or negative next quarter*	0.45
S = *Change in sequential EPS is positive in the prior quarter*	0.55
S^C = *Change in sequential EPS is 0 or negative in the prior quarter*	0.45

On inspecting the data, you observe some persistence in EPS changes: Increases tend to be followed by increases, and decreases by decreases. The first probability estimate you develop is *P(change in sequential EPS is positive next quarter | change in sequential EPS is 0 or negative in the prior quarter)* = $P(A \mid S^C)$ = 0.40. The most recent quarter's EPS (2Q:Year 1) is announced, and the change is a positive sequential change (the event S). You are interested in forecasting EPS for 3Q:Year 1.

1. Write this statement in probability notation: "the probability that the change in sequential EPS is positive next quarter, given that the change in sequential EPS is positive the prior quarter."
2. Calculate the probability in Part 1. (Calculate the probability that is consistent with your other probabilities or beliefs.)

Solution to 1: In probability notation, this statement is written $P(A \mid S)$.

Solution to 2: The probability is 0.673 that the change in sequential EPS is positive for 3Q:Year 1, given the positive change in sequential EPS for 2Q:Year 1, as shown below.

According to Equation 5, $P(A) = P(A \mid S)P(S) + P(A \mid S^C)P(S^C)$. The values of the probabilities needed to calculate $P(A \mid S)$ are already known: $P(A) = 0.55$, $P(S) = 0.55$, $P(S^C) = 0.45$, and $P(A \mid S^C) = 0.40$. Substituting into Equation 5,

$$0.55 = P(A \mid S)(0.55) + 0.40(0.45)$$

Solving for the unknown, $P(A \mid S) = [0.55 - 0.40(0.45)]/0.55 = 0.672727$, or 0.673.

You conclude that *P(change in sequential EPS is positive next quarter | change in sequential EPS is positive the prior quarter)* = 0.673. Any other probability is not consistent with your other estimated probabilities. Reflecting the persistence in EPS changes, this conditional probability of a positive EPS change, 0.673, is greater than the unconditional probability of an EPS increase, 0.55.

In the chapter on statistical concepts and market returns, we discussed the concept of a weighted average or weighted mean. The example highlighted in that chapter was that portfolio return is a weighted average of the returns on the individual assets in the portfolio, where the weight applied to each asset's return is the fraction of the portfolio invested in that asset. The total probability rule, which is a rule for stating an unconditional probability in terms of conditional probabilities, is also a weighted average. In that formula, probabilities of scenarios are used as weights. Part of the definition of weighted average is that the weights sum to 1. The probabilities of mutually exclusive and exhaustive events do sum to 1 (this is part of the definition of probability). The next weighted average we discuss, the expected value of a random variable, also uses probabilities as weights.

The expected value of a random variable is an essential quantitative concept in investments. Investors continually make use of expected values—in estimating the rewards of alternative investments, in forecasting EPS and other corporate financial variables and ratios, and in assessing any other factor that may affect their financial position. The expected value of a random variable is defined as follows:

- **Definition of Expected Value.** The **expected value** of a random variable is the probability-weighted average of the possible outcomes of the random variable. For a random variable X, the expected value of X is denoted $E(X)$.

Expected value (for example, expected stock return) looks either to the future, as a forecast, or to the "true" value of the mean (the population mean, discussed in the chapter on statistical concepts and market returns). We should distinguish expected value from the concepts of historical or sample mean. The sample mean also summarizes in a single number a central value. However, the sample mean presents a central value for a particular set of observations as an equally weighted average of those observations. To summarize, the contrast is forecast versus historical, or population versus sample.

EXAMPLE 8   BankCorp's Earnings per Share (3)

You continue with your analysis of BankCorp's EPS. In Table 3, you have recorded a probability distribution for BankCorp's EPS for the current fiscal year.

TABLE 3   Probability Distribution for BankCorp's EPS

Probability	EPS ($)
0.15	2.60
0.45	2.45
0.24	2.20
0.16	2.00
1.00	

What is the expected value of BankCorp's EPS for the current fiscal year?

Following the definition of expected value, list each outcome, weight it by its probability, and sum the terms.

$$E(EPS) = 0.15(\$2.60) + 0.45(\$2.45) + 0.24(\$2.20) + 0.16(\$2.00)$$
$$= \$2.3405$$

The expected value of EPS is \$2.34.

An equation that summarizes your calculation in **Example 8** is

$$E(X) = P(X_1)X_1 + P(X_2)X_2 + \ldots + P(X_n)X_n = \sum_{i=1}^{n} P(X_i)X_i \qquad (7)$$

where X_i is one of n possible outcomes of the random variable X.[8]

The expected value is our forecast. Because we are discussing random quantities, we cannot count on an individual forecast being realized (although we hope that, on average, forecasts will be accurate). It is important, as a result, to measure the risk we face. Variance and standard deviation measure the dispersion of outcomes around the expected value or forecast.

- **Definition of Variance.** The **variance** of a random variable is the expected value (the probability-weighted average) of squared deviations from the random variable's expected value:

$$\sigma^2(X) = E\{[X - E(X)]^2\} \qquad (8)$$

The two notations for variance are $\sigma^2(X)$ and $\text{Var}(X)$.

Variance is a number greater than or equal to 0 because it is the sum of squared terms. If variance is 0, there is no dispersion or risk. The outcome is certain, and the quantity X is not random at all. Variance greater than 0 indicates dispersion of outcomes. Increasing variance indicates increasing dispersion, all else equal. Variance of X is a quantity in the squared units of X. For example, if the random variable is return in percent, variance of return is in units of percent squared. Standard deviation is easier to interpret than variance, as it is in the same units as the random variable. If the random variable is return in percent, standard deviation of return is also in units of percent. In the following example, when the variance of returns is stated as a percent or amount of money, to conserve space the chapter may suppress showing the unit squared. Note that when the variance of returns is stated as a decimal, the complication of dealing with units of "percent squared" does not arise.

- **Definition of Standard Deviation. Standard deviation** is the positive square root of variance.

---

[8]For simplicity, we model all random variables in this chapter as discrete random variables, which have a countable set of outcomes. For continuous random variables, which are discussed along with discrete random variables in the chapter on common probability distributions, the operation corresponding to summation is integration.

The best way to become familiar with these concepts is to work examples.

EXAMPLE 9   BankCorp's Earnings per Share (4)

In **Example 8**, you calculated the expected value of BankCorp's EPS as $2.34, which is your forecast. Now you want to measure the dispersion around your forecast. Table 4 shows your view of the probability distribution of EPS for the current fiscal year.

What are the variance and standard deviation of BankCorp's EPS for the current fiscal year?

The order of calculation is always expected value, then variance, then standard deviation. Expected value has already been calculated. Following the definition of variance above, calculate the deviation of each outcome from the mean or expected value, square each deviation, weight (multiply) each squared deviation by its probability of occurrence, and then sum these terms.

$$\sigma^2(\text{EPS}) = P(\$2.60)[\$2.60 - E(\text{EPS})]^2 + P(\$2.45)[\$2.45 - E(\text{EPS})]^2$$
$$+ P(\$2.20)[\$2.20 - E(\text{EPS})]^2 + P(\$2.00)[\$2.00 - E(\text{EPS})]^2$$
$$= 0.15(2.60 - 2.34)^2 + 0.45(2.45 - 2.34)^2$$
$$+ 0.24(2.20 - 2.34)^2 + 0.16(2.00 - 2.34)^2$$
$$= 0.01014 + 0.005445 + 0.004704 + 0.018496 = 0.038785$$

Standard deviation is the positive square root of 0.038785:

$$\sigma(\text{EPS}) = 0.038785^{1/2} = 0.196939, \text{ or approximately } 0.20.$$

TABLE 4   Probability Distribution for BankCorp's EPS

Probability	EPS ($)
0.15	2.60
0.45	2.45
0.24	2.20
0.16	2.00
1.00	

An equation that summarizes your calculation of variance in **Example 9** is

$$\sigma^2(X) = P(X_1)[X_1 - E(X)]^2 + P(X_2)[X_2 - E(X)]^2$$
$$+ \dots + P(X_n)[X_n - E(X)]^2 = \sum_{i=1}^{n} P(X_i)[X_i - E(X)]^2 \tag{9}$$

where X_i is one of n possible outcomes of the random variable X.

In investments, we make use of any relevant information available in making our forecasts. When we refine our expectations or forecasts, we are typically making adjustments based on new information or events; in these cases we are using **conditional expected values**. The expected value of a random variable X given an event or scenario S is denoted $E(X \mid S)$. Suppose the random variable X can take on any one of n distinct outcomes $X_1, X_2, ..., X_n$ (these outcomes form a set of mutually exclusive and exhaustive events). The expected value of X conditional on S is the first outcome, X_1, times the probability of the first outcome given S, $P(X_1 \mid S)$, plus the second outcome, X_2, times the probability of the second outcome given S, $P(X_2 \mid S)$, and so forth.

$$E(X \mid S) = P(X_1 \mid S)X_1 + P(X_2 \mid S)X_2 + ... + P(X_n \mid S)X_n \tag{10}$$

We will illustrate this equation shortly.

Parallel to the total probability rule for stating unconditional probabilities in terms of conditional probabilities, there is a principle for stating (unconditional) expected values in terms of conditional expected values. This principle is the **total probability rule for expected value**.

- **The Total Probability Rule for Expected Value.**

$$E(X) = E(X \mid S)P(S) + E(X \mid S^C)P(S^C) \tag{11}$$

$$E(X) = E(X \mid S_1)P(S_1) + E(X \mid S_2)P(S_2) + ... + E(X \mid S_n)P(S_n) \tag{12}$$

where $S_1, S_2, ..., S_n$ are mutually exclusive and exhaustive scenarios or events.

The general case, Equation 12, states that the expected value of X equals the expected value of X given Scenario 1, $E(X \mid S_1)$, times the probability of Scenario 1, $P(S_1)$, plus the expected value of X given Scenario 2, $E(X \mid S_2)$, times the probability of Scenario 2, $P(S_2)$, and so forth.

To use this principle, we formulate mutually exclusive and exhaustive scenarios that are useful for understanding the outcomes of the random variable. This approach was employed in developing the probability distribution of BankCorp's EPS in **Examples 8** and **9**, as we now discuss.

The earnings of BankCorp are interest rate sensitive, benefiting from a declining interest rate environment. Suppose there is a 0.60 probability that BankCorp will operate in a *declining interest rate environment* in the current fiscal year and a 0.40 probability that it will operate in a *stable interest rate environment* (assessing the chance of an increasing interest rate environment as negligible). If a *declining interest rate environment* occurs, the probability that EPS will be $2.60 is estimated at 0.25, and the probability that EPS will be $2.45 is estimated at 0.75. Note that 0.60, the probability of *declining interest rate environment*, times 0.25, the probability of $2.60 EPS given a *declining interest rate environment*, equals 0.15, the (unconditional) probability of $2.60 given in the table in **Examples 8** and **9**. The probabilities are consistent. Also, 0.60(0.75) = 0.45, the probability of $2.45 EPS given in Tables 3 and 4. The **tree diagram** in Figure 2 shows the rest of the analysis.

FIGURE 2   BankCorp's Forecasted EPS

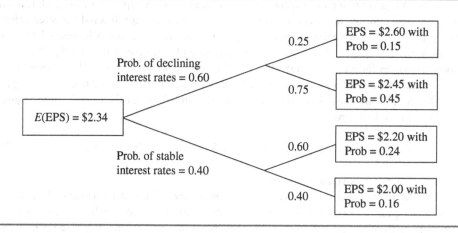

A declining interest rate environment points us to the **node** of the tree that branches off into outcomes of $2.60 and $2.45. We can find expected EPS given a declining interest rate environment as follows, using Equation 10:

$$E(\text{EPS} \mid \text{declining interest rate environment}) = 0.25(\$2.60) + 0.75(\$2.45)$$
$$= \$2.4875$$

If interest rates are stable,

$$E(\text{EPS} \mid \text{stable interest rate environment}) = 0.60(\$2.20) + 0.40(\$2.00)$$
$$= \$2.12$$

Once we have the new piece of information that interest rates are stable, for example, we revise our original expectation of EPS from $2.34 downward to $2.12. Now using the total probability rule for expected value,

$$E(\text{EPS}) = E(\text{EPS} \mid \text{declining interest rate environment})$$
$$P(\text{declining interest rate environment})$$
$$+ E(\text{EPS} \mid \text{stable interest rate environment})$$
$$P(\text{stable interest rate environment})$$

So $E(\text{EPS}) = \$2.4875(0.60) + \$2.12(0.40) = \$2.3405$ or about $2.34.

This amount is identical to the estimate of the expected value of EPS calculated directly from the probability distribution in **Example 8**. Just as our probabilities must be consistent, so must our expected values, unconditional and conditional; otherwise our investment actions may create profit opportunities for other investors at our expense.

To review, we first developed the factors or scenarios that influence the outcome of the event of interest. After assigning probabilities to these scenarios, we formed expectations conditioned on the different scenarios. Then we worked backward to formulate an expected value as of today. In the problem just worked, EPS was the event of interest, and the interest rate environment was the factor influencing EPS.

We can also calculate the variance of EPS given each scenario:

$$\sigma^2(\text{EPS} \mid declining\ interest\ rate\ environment)$$
$$= P(\$2.60 \mid declining\ interest\ rate\ environment)$$
$$\times [\$2.60 - E(\text{EPS} \mid declining\ interest\ rate\ environment)]^2$$
$$+ P(\$2.45 \mid declining\ interest\ rate\ environment)$$
$$\times [\$2.45 - E(\text{EPS} \mid declining\ interest\ rate\ environment)]^2$$
$$= 0.25(\$2.60 - \$2.4875)^2 + 0.75(\$2.45 - \$2.4875)^2$$
$$= 0.004219$$

$$\sigma^2(\text{EPS} \mid stable\ interest\ rate\ environment)$$
$$= P(\$2.20 \mid stable\ interest\ rate\ environment)$$
$$\times [\$2.20 - E(\text{EPS} \mid stable\ interest\ rate\ environment)]^2$$
$$+ P(\$2.00 \mid stable\ interest\ rate\ environment)$$
$$\times [\$2.00 - E(\text{EPS} \mid stable\ interest\ rate\ environment)]^2$$
$$= 0.60(\$2.20 - \$2.12)^2 + 0.40(\$2.00 - \$2.12)^2 = 0.0096$$

These are **conditional variances**, the variance of EPS given a *declining interest rate environment* and the variance of EPS given a *stable interest rate environment*. The relationship between unconditional variance and conditional variance is a relatively advanced topic.[9] The main points are 1) that variance, like expected value, has a conditional counterpart to the unconditional concept and 2) that we can use conditional variance to assess risk given a particular scenario.

EXAMPLE 10   BankCorp's Earnings per Share (5)

Continuing with BankCorp, you focus now on BankCorp's cost structure. One model you are researching for BankCorp's operating costs is

$$\widehat{Y} = a + bX$$

---

[9]The unconditional variance of EPS is the sum of two terms: 1) the expected value (probability-weighted average) of the conditional variances (parallel to the total probability rules) and 2) the variance of conditional expected values of EPS. The second term arises because the variability in conditional expected value is a source of risk. Term 1 is $\sigma^2(\text{EPS}) = P(declining\ interest\ rate\ environment)\ \sigma^2(\text{EPS} \mid declining\ interest\ rate\ environment) + P(stable\ interest\ rate\ environment)\ \sigma^2(\text{EPS} \mid stable\ interest\ rate\ environment) = 0.60$ (0.004219) + 0.40(0.0096) = 0.006371. Term 2 is $\sigma^2[E(\text{EPS} \mid interest\ rate\ environment)] = 0.60$ ($\$2.4875 - \$2.34)^2 + 0.40(\$2.12 - \$2.34)^2 = 0.032414$. Summing the two terms, unconditional variance equals 0.006371 + 0.032414 = 0.038785.

FIGURE 3   BankCorp's Forecasted Operating Costs

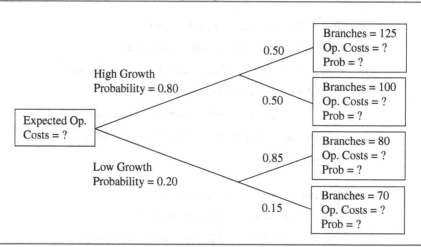

where $\hat{Y}$ is a forecast of operating costs in millions of dollars and X is the number of branch offices. $\hat{Y}$ represents the expected value of Y given X, or $E(Y \mid X)$. ($\hat{Y}$ is a notation used in regression analysis, which we discuss in a later chapter.) You interpret the intercept a as fixed costs and b as variable costs. You estimate the equation as

$$\hat{Y} = 12.5 + 0.65X$$

BankCorp currently has 66 branch offices, and the equation estimates that $12.5 + 0.65(66) = \$55.4$ million. You have two scenarios for growth, pictured in the tree diagram in Figure 3.

1. Compute the forecasted operating costs given the different levels of operating costs, using $\hat{Y} = 12.5 + 0.65X$. State the probability of each level of the number of branch offices. These are the answers to the questions in the terminal boxes of the tree diagram.
2. Compute the expected value of operating costs under the high growth scenario. Also calculate the expected value of operating costs under the low growth scenario.
3. Answer the question in the initial box of the tree: What are BankCorp's expected operating costs?

Solution to 1: Using $\hat{Y} = 12.5 + 0.65X$, from top to bottom, we have

Operating Costs	Probability
$\hat{Y} = 12.5 + 0.65(125) = \$93.75$ million	$0.80(0.50) = 0.40$
$\hat{Y} = 12.5 + 0.65(100) = \$77.50$ million	$0.80(0.50) = 0.40$
$\hat{Y} = 12.5 + 0.65(80) = \$64.50$ million	$0.20(0.85) = 0.17$
$\hat{Y} = 12.5 + 0.65(70) = \$58.00$ million	$0.20(0.15) = 0.03$
	Sum $= 1.00$

Solution to 2: Dollar amounts are in millions.

$$E(\text{operating costs}|high\ growth) = 0.50(\$93.75) + 0.50(\$77.50)$$
$$= \$85.625$$

$$E(\text{operating costs}|low\ growth) = 0.85(\$64.50) + 0.15(\$58.00)$$
$$= \$63.525$$

Solution to 3: Dollar amounts are in millions.

$$E(\text{operating costs}) = E(\text{operating costs} \mid high\ growth)P(high\ growth)$$
$$+ E(\text{operating costs} \mid low\ growth)P(low\ growth)$$
$$= \$85.625(0.80) + \$63.525(0.20) = \$81.205$$

BankCorp's expected operating costs are \$81.205 million.

We will see conditional probabilities again when we discuss Bayes' formula. This section has introduced a few problems that can be addressed using probability concepts. The following problem draws on these concepts, as well as on analytical skills.

EXAMPLE 11   The Default Risk Premium for a One-Period Debt Instrument

As the co-manager of a short-term bond portfolio, you are reviewing the pricing of a speculative-grade, one-year-maturity, zero-coupon bond. For this type of bond, the return is the difference between the amount paid and the principal value received at maturity. Your goal is to estimate an appropriate default risk premium for this bond. You define the default risk premium as the extra return above the risk-free return that will compensate investors for default risk. If R is the promised return (yield-to-maturity) on the debt instrument and R_F is the risk-free rate, the default risk premium is $R - R_F$. You assess the probability that the bond defaults as $P(\text{the bond defaults}) = 0.06$. Looking at current money market yields, you find that one-year US Treasury bills (T-bills) are offering a return of 2 percent, an estimate of R_F. As a first step, you make the simplifying assumption that bondholders will recover nothing in the event of a default. What is the minimum default risk premium you should require for this instrument?

The challenge in this type of problem is to find a starting point. In many problems, including this one, an effective first step is to divide up the possible outcomes into mutually exclusive and exhaustive events in an economically logical way. Here, from the viewpoint of a bondholder, the two events that affect returns are *the bond defaults* and *the bond does not default*. These two events cover all outcomes. How do these events affect a bondholder's returns? A second step is to compute the value of the bond for the two events. We have no specifics on bond **face value**, but we can compute value per $1 or one unit of currency invested.

	The Bond Defaults	*The Bond Does Not Default*
Bond value	$0	$(1 + R)$

The third step is to find the expected value of the bond (per $1 invested).

$$E(\text{bond}) = \$0 \times P(\textit{the bond defaults}) + \$(1 + R)[1 - P(\textit{the bond defaults})]$$

So $E(\text{bond}) = \$(1 + R)[1 - P(\textit{the bond defaults})]$. The expected value of the T-bill per $1 invested is $(1 + R_F)$. In fact, this value is certain because the T-bill is risk free. The next step requires economic reasoning. You want the default premium to be large enough so that you expect to at least break even compared with investing in the T-bill. This outcome will occur if the expected value of the bond equals the expected value of the T-bill per $1 invested.

$$\text{Expected Value of Bond} = \text{Expected Value of T-Bill}$$
$$\$(1 + R)[1 - P(\textit{the bond defaults})] = (1 + R_F)$$

Solving for the promised return on the bond, you find $R = \{(1 + R_F)/[1 - P(\textit{the bond defaults})]\} - 1$. Substituting the values in the statement of the problem, $R = [1.02/(1 - 0.06)] - 1 = 1.08511 - 1 = 0.08511$ or about 8.51 percent, and default risk premium is $R - R_F = 8.51\% - 2\% = 6.51\%$.

You require a default risk premium of at least 651 basis points. You can state the matter as follows: If the bond is priced to yield 8.51 percent, you will earn a 651 basis-point spread and receive the bond principal with 94 percent probability. If the bond defaults, however, you will lose everything. With a premium of 651 basis points, you expect to just break even relative to an investment in T-bills. Because an investment in the zero-coupon bond has variability, if you are risk averse you will demand that the premium be larger than 651 basis points.

This analysis is a starting point. Bondholders usually recover part of their investment after a default. A next step would be to incorporate a recovery rate.

In this section, we have treated random variables such as EPS as stand-alone quantities. We have not explored how descriptors such as expected value and variance of EPS may be functions of other random variables. Portfolio return is one random variable that is clearly a function of other random variables, the random returns on the individual securities in the portfolio. To analyze a portfolio's expected return and variance of return, we must understand these quantities are a function of characteristics of the individual securities' returns. Looking at the dispersion or variance of portfolio return, we see that the way individual security returns move together or covary is important. To understand the significance of these movements, we need to explore some new concepts, covariance and correlation. The next section, which deals with portfolio expected return and variance of return, introduces these concepts.

3. PORTFOLIO EXPECTED RETURN AND VARIANCE OF RETURN

Modern portfolio theory makes frequent use of the idea that investment opportunities can be evaluated using expected return as a measure of reward and variance of return as a measure of risk. The calculation and interpretation of portfolio expected return and variance of return are fundamental skills. In this section, we will develop an understanding of portfolio expected return and variance of return.[10] Portfolio return is determined by the returns on the individual holdings. As a result, the calculation of portfolio variance, as a function of the individual asset returns, is more complex than the variance calculations illustrated in the previous section.

We work with an example of a portfolio that is 50 percent invested in an S&P 500 Index fund, 25 percent invested in a US long-term corporate bond fund, and 25 percent invested in a fund indexed to the MSCI EAFE Index (representing equity markets in Europe, Australasia, and the Far East). Table 5 shows these weights.

We first address the calculation of the expected return on the portfolio. In the previous section, we defined the expected value of a random variable as the probability-weighted average of the possible outcomes. Portfolio return, we know, is a weighted average of the returns on the securities in the portfolio. Similarly, the expected return on a portfolio is a weighted average of the expected returns on the securities in the portfolio, using exactly the same weights. When we have estimated the expected returns on the individual securities, we immediately have portfolio expected return. This convenient fact follows from the properties of expected value.

- **Properties of Expected Value.** Let w_i be any constant and R_i be a random variable.
    1. The expected value of a constant times a random variable equals the constant times the expected value of the random variable.

$$E(w_i R_i) = w_i E(R_i)$$

    2. The expected value of a weighted sum of random variables equals the weighted sum of the expected values, using the same weights.

$$E(w_1 R_1 + w_2 R_2 + \dots + w_n R_n) = w_1 E(R_1) + w_2 E(R_2) + \dots + w_n E(R_n) \qquad (13)$$

Suppose we have a random variable with a given expected value. If we multiply each outcome by 2, for example, the random variable's expected value is multiplied by 2 as well. That is the

TABLE 5   Portfolio Weights

Asset Class	Weights
S&P 500	0.50
US long-term corporate bonds	0.25
MSCI EAFE	0.25

---

[10]Although we outline a number of basic concepts in this section, we do not present mean–variance analysis per se. For a presentation of mean–variance analysis, see the treatments in standard investment textbooks such as Bodie, Kane, and Marcus (2017), Elton, Gruber, Brown, and Goetzmann (2013), and Reilly and Brown (2018).

meaning of Part 1. The second statement is the rule that directly leads to the expression for portfolio expected return. A portfolio with n securities is defined by its portfolio weights, w_1, $w_2, \ldots, w_n$, which sum to 1. So portfolio return, R_p, is $R_p = w_1 R_1 + w_2 R_2 + \ldots + w_n R_n$. We can state the following principle:

- **Calculation of Portfolio Expected Return.** Given a portfolio with n securities, the expected return on the portfolio is a weighted average of the expected returns on the component securities:

$$E(R_p) = E(w_1 R_1 + w_2 R_2 + \ldots + w_n R_n)$$
$$= w_1 E(R_1) + w_2 E(R_2) + \ldots + w_n E(R_n)$$

Suppose we have estimated expected returns on the assets in the portfolio, as given in Table 6. We calculate the expected return on the portfolio as 11.75 percent:

$$E(R_p) = w_1 E(R_1) + w_2 E(R_2) + w_3 E(R_3)$$
$$= 0.50(13\%) + 0.25(6\%) + 0.25(15\%) = 11.75\%$$

In the previous section, we studied variance as a measure of dispersion of outcomes around the expected value. Here we are interested in portfolio variance of return as a measure of investment risk. Letting R_p stand for the return on the portfolio, portfolio variance is $\sigma^2(R_p) = E\{[R_p - E(R_p)]^2\}$ according to Equation 8. How do we implement this definition? In the chapter on statistical concepts and market returns, we learned how to calculate a historical or sample variance based on a sample of returns. Now we are considering variance in a forward-looking sense. We will use information about the individual assets in the portfolio to obtain portfolio variance of return. To avoid clutter in notation, we write ER_p for $E(R_p)$. We need the concept of covariance.

- **Definition of Covariance.** Given two random variables R_i and R_j, the covariance between R_i and R_j is

$$\text{Cov}(R_i, R_j) = E[(R_i - ER_i)(R_j - ER_j)] \qquad (14)$$

Alternative notations are $\sigma(R_i, R_j)$ and σ_{ij}.

Equation 14 states that the covariance between two random variables is the probability-weighted average of the cross-products of each random variable's deviation from its own expected value. The above measure is the population covariance and it is forward-looking. Sometimes analysts look at historical covariance for guidance on developing expectations for the future. For this purpose, the sample covariance, which is computed using a sample of

TABLE 6   Weights and Expected Returns

Asset Class	Weight	Expected Return (%)
S&P 500	0.50	13
US long-term corporate bonds	0.25	6
MSCI EAFE	0.25	15

historical data about the two variables, is appropriate. The sample covariance between two random variables R_i and R_j, based on a sample of past data of size n is

$$\text{Cov}(R_i,R_j) = \sum_{i=1}^{n}(R_{i,t} - \overline{R}_i)(R_{j,t} - \overline{R}_j)/(n - 1) \qquad (15)$$

The sample covariance is the average value of the product of the deviations of observations on two random variables from their sample means.[11] If the random variables are returns, the units of both forward-looking covariance and historical variance would be returns squared. In this chapter, we will consider covariance in a forward-looking sense, unless mentioned otherwise.

We will return to discuss covariance after we establish the need for the concept. Working from the definition of variance, we find

$$\sigma^2(R_p) = E[(R_p - ER_p)^2]$$

$$= E\{[w_1 R_1 + w_2 R_2 + w_3 R_3 - E(w_1 R_1 + w_2 R_2 + w_3 R_3)]^2\}$$

$$= E\{[w_1 R_1 + w_2 R_2 + w_3 R_3 - w_1 ER_1 - w_2 ER_2 - w_3 ER_3]^2\}$$

(using Equation 13)

$$= E\{[w_1(R_1 - ER_1) + w_2(R_2 - ER_2) + w_3(R_3 - ER_3)]^2\}$$

(rearranging)

$$= E\{[w_1(R_1 - ER_1) + w_2(R_2 - ER_2) + w_3(R_3 - ER_3)]$$
$$\times [w_1(R_1 - ER_1) + w_2(R_2 - ER_2) + w_3(R_3 - ER_3)]\}$$

(what squaring means)

$$= E[w_1 w_1(R_1 - ER_1)(R_1 - ER_1) + w_1 w_2(R_1 - ER_1)(R_2 - ER_2)$$
$$+ w_1 w_3(R_1 - ER_1)(R_3 - ER_3) + w_2 w_1(R_2 - ER_2)(R_1 - ER_1)$$
$$+ w_2 w_2(R_2 - ER_2)(R_2 - ER_2) + w_2 w_3(R_2 - ER_2)(R_3 - ER_3)$$
$$+ w_3 w_1(R_3 - ER_3)(R_1 - ER_1) + w_3 w_2(R_3 - ER_3)(R_2 - ER_2)$$
$$+ w_3 w_3(R_3 - ER_3)(R_3 - ER_3)]$$

(doing the multiplication)

$$= w_1^2 E[(R_1 - ER_1)^2] + w_1 w_2 E[(R_1 - ER_1)(R_2 - ER_2)]$$
$$+ w_1 w_3 E[(R_1 - ER_1)(R_3 - ER_3)] + w_2 w_1 E[(R_2 - ER_2)(R_1 - ER_1)]$$
$$+ w_2^2 E[(R_2 - ER_2)^2] + w_2 w_3 E[(R_2 - ER_2)(R_3 - ER_3)]$$
$$+ w_3 w_1 E[(R_3 - ER_3)(R_1 - ER_1)] + w_3 w_2 E[(R_3 - ER_3)(R_2 - ER_2)]$$
$$+ w_3^2 E[(R_3 - ER_3)^2]$$

(recalling that the w_i terms are constants)

$$= w_1^2 \sigma^2(R_1) + w_1 w_2 \text{Cov}(R_1,R_2) + w_1 w_3 \text{Cov}(R_1,R_3)$$
$$+ w_1 w_2 \text{Cov}(R_1,R_2) + w_2^2 \sigma^2(R_2) + w_2 w_3 \text{Cov}(R_2,R_3)$$
$$+ w_1 w_3 \text{Cov}(R_1,R_3) + w_2 w_3 \text{Cov}(R_2,R_3) + w_3^2 \sigma^2(R_3) \qquad (16)$$

---

[11]The use of $n - 1$ in the denominator is a technical point; it ensures that the sample covariance is an unbiased estimate of population covariance.

The last step follows from the definitions of variance and covariance.[12] For the italicized covariance terms in Equation 16, we used the fact that the order of variables in covariance does not matter: $Cov(R_2,R_1) = Cov(R_1,R_2)$, for example. As we will show, the diagonal variance terms $\sigma^2(R_1)$, $\sigma^2(R_2)$, and $\sigma^2(R_3)$ can be expressed as $Cov(R_1,R_1)$, $Cov(R_2,R_2)$, and $Cov(R_3,R_3)$, respectively. Using this fact, the most compact way to state Equation 16 is

$$\sigma^2(R_p) = \sum_{i=1}^{3} \sum_{j=1}^{3} w_i w_j Cov(R_i,R_j).$$ The double summation signs say: "Set $i = 1$ and let j run from 1 to 3; then set $i = 2$ and let j run from 1 to 3; next set $i = 3$ and let j run from 1 to 3; finally, add the nine terms." This expression generalizes for a portfolio of any size n to

$$\sigma^2(R_p) = \sum_{i=1}^{n} \sum_{j=1}^{n} w_i w_j Cov(R_i,R_j) \tag{17}$$

We see from Equation 16 that individual variances of return constitute part, but not all, of portfolio variance. The three variances are actually outnumbered by the six covariance terms off the diagonal. For three assets, the ratio is 1 to 2, or 50 percent. If there are 20 assets, there are 20 variance terms and $20(20) - 20 = 380$ off-diagonal covariance terms. The ratio of variance terms to off-diagonal covariance terms is less than 6 to 100, or 6 percent. A first observation, then, is that as the number of holdings increases, covariance[13] becomes increasingly important, all else equal.

What exactly is the effect of covariance on portfolio variance? The covariance terms capture how the co-movements of returns affect portfolio variance. For example, consider two stocks: One tends to have high returns (relative to its expected return) when the other has low returns (relative to its expected return). The returns on one stock tend to offset the returns on the other stock, lowering the variability or variance of returns on the portfolio. Like variance, the units of covariance are hard to interpret, and we will introduce a more intuitive concept shortly. Meanwhile, from the definition of covariance, we can establish two essential observations about covariance.

1. We can interpret the sign of covariance as follows:
    Covariance of returns is negative if, when the return on one asset is above its expected value, the return on the other asset tends to be below its expected value (an average inverse relationship between returns).
    Covariance of returns is 0 if returns on the assets are unrelated.
    Covariance of returns is positive when the returns on both assets tend to be on the same side (above or below) their expected values at the same time (an average positive relationship between returns).
2. The covariance of a random variable with itself (*own covariance*) is its own variance:
    $Cov(R,R) = E\{[R - E(R)][R - E(R)]\} = E\{[R - E(R)]^2\} = \sigma^2(R)$.

---

[12]Useful facts about variance and covariance include: 1) The variance of a constant *times* a random variable equals the constant squared times the variance of the random variable, or $\sigma^2(wR) = w^2\sigma^2(R)$; 2) The variance of a constant *plus* a random variable equals the variance of the random variable, or $\sigma^2(w + R) = \sigma^2(R)$ because a constant has zero variance; 3) The covariance between a constant and a random variable is zero.

[13]When the meaning of covariance as "off-diagonal covariance" is obvious, as it is here, we omit the qualifying words. Covariance is usually used in this sense.

TABLE 7   Inputs to Portfolio Expected Return and Variance

A. Inputs to Portfolio Expected Return

Asset	A	B	C
	$E(R_A)$	$E(R_B)$	$E(R_C)$

B. Covariance Matrix: The Inputs to Portfolio Variance of Return

Asset	A	B	C
A	**$Cov(R_A,R_A)$**	$Cov(R_A,R_B)$	$Cov(R_A,R_C)$
B	$Cov(R_B,R_A)$	**$Cov(R_B,R_B)$**	$Cov(R_B,R_C)$
C	$Cov(R_C,R_A)$	$Cov(R_C,R_B)$	**$Cov(R_C,R_C)$**

A complete list of the covariances constitutes all the statistical data needed to compute portfolio variance of return. Covariances are often presented in a square format called a **covariance matrix**. Table 7 summarizes the inputs for portfolio expected return and variance of return.

With three assets, the covariance matrix has $3^2 = 3 \times 3 = 9$ entries, but it is customary to treat the diagonal terms, the variances, separately from the off-diagonal terms. These diagonal terms are bolded in Table 7. This distinction is natural, as security variance is a single-variable concept. So there are $9 - 3 = 6$ covariances, excluding variances. But $Cov(R_B,R_A) = Cov(R_A, R_B)$, $Cov(R_C,R_A) = Cov(R_A,R_C)$, and $Cov(R_C,R_B) = Cov(R_B,R_C)$. The covariance matrix below the diagonal is the mirror image of the covariance matrix above the diagonal. As a result, there are only $6/2 = 3$ distinct covariance terms to estimate. In general, for n securities, there are $n(n - 1)/2$ distinct covariances to estimate and n variances to estimate.

Suppose we have the covariance matrix shown in Table 8. We will be working in returns stated as percents and the table entries are in units of percent squared $(\%^2)$. The terms $38\%^2$ and $400\%^2$ are 0.0038 and 0.0400, respectively, stated as decimals; correctly working in percents and decimals leads to identical answers.

Taking Equation 16 and grouping variance terms together produces the following:

$$
\begin{aligned}
\sigma^2(R_p) &= w_1^2\sigma^2(R_1) + w_2^2\sigma^2(R_2) + w_3^2\sigma^2(R_3) + 2w_1w_2Cov(R_1,R_2) \\
&\quad + 2w_1w_3Cov(R_1,R_3) + 2w_2w_3Cov(R_2,R_3) \\
&= (0.50)^2(400) + (0.25)^2(81) + (0.25)^2(441) \\
&\quad + 2(0.50)(0.25)(45) + 2(0.50)(0.25)(189) \\
&\quad + 2(0.25)(0.25)(38) \\
&= 100 + 5.0625 + 27.5625 + 11.25 + 47.25 + 4.75 = 195.875
\end{aligned}
\tag{18}
$$

TABLE 8   Covariance Matrix

	S&P 500	US Long-Term Corporate Bonds	MSCI EAFE
S&P 500	400	45	189
US long-term corporate bonds	45	81	38
MSCI EAFE	189	38	441

The variance is 195.875. Standard deviation of return is $195.875^{1/2} = 14$ percent. To summarize, the portfolio has an expected annual return of 11.75 percent and a standard deviation of return of 14 percent.

Let us look at the first three terms in the calculation above. Their sum, $100 + 5.0625 + 27.5625 = 132.625$, is the contribution of the individual variances to portfolio variance. If the returns on the three assets were independent, covariances would be 0 and the standard deviation of portfolio return would be $132.625^{1/2} = 11.52$ percent as compared to 14 percent before. The portfolio would have less risk. Suppose the covariance terms were negative. Then a negative number would be added to 132.625, so portfolio variance and risk would be even smaller. At the same time, we have not changed expected return. For the same expected portfolio return, the portfolio has less risk. This risk reduction is a diversification benefit, meaning a risk-reduction benefit from holding a portfolio of assets. The diversification benefit increases with decreasing covariance. This observation is a key insight of modern portfolio theory. It is even more intuitively stated when we can use the concept of correlation. Then we can say that as long as security returns are not perfectly positively correlated, diversification benefits are possible. Furthermore, the smaller the correlation between security returns, the greater the cost of not diversifying (in terms of risk-reduction benefits forgone), all else equal.

- **Definition of Correlation.** The correlation between two random variables, R_i and R_j, is defined as $\rho(R_i,R_j) = \text{Cov}(R_i,R_j)/[\sigma(R_i)\sigma(R_j)]$. Alternative notations are $\text{Corr}(R_i,R_j)$ and ρ_{ij}.

The above definition of correlation is forward-looking because it involves dividing the forward-looking covariance by the product of forward-looking standard deviations. We can similarly compute an historical or sample correlation by dividing historical or sample covariance between two variables by the product of sample standard deviations of the two variables.

Frequently, covariance is substituted out using the relationship $\text{Cov}(R_i,R_j) = \rho(R_i,R_j)\sigma(R_i)\sigma(R_j)$. Like covariance, the correlation coefficient is a measure of linear association. However, the division indicated in the definition of correlation makes correlation a pure number (one without a unit of measurement) and places bounds on its largest and smallest possible values, which are $+1$ and -1, respectively. If two variables have a strong positive linear relation, then their correlation will be close to $+1$. If two variables have a strong negative linear relation, then their correlation will be close to -1. If two variables have a weak linear relation, then their correlation will be close to 0. Using the above definition, we can state a correlation matrix from data in the covariance matrix alone. Table 9 shows the correlation matrix.

TABLE 9   Correlation Matrix of Returns

	S&P 500	US Long-Term Corporate Bonds	MSCI EAFE
S&P 500	1.00	0.25	0.45
US long-term corporate bonds	0.25	1.00	0.20
MSCI EAFE	0.45	0.20	1.00

For example, the covariance between long-term bonds and MSCI EAFE is 38, from Table 8. The standard deviation of long-term bond returns is $81^{1/2} = 9$ percent, that of MSCI EAFE returns is $441^{1/2} = 21$ percent, from diagonal terms in Table 8. The correlation ρ(Return on long-term bonds, Return on EAFE) is $38/[(9\%)(21\%)] = 0.201$, rounded to 0.20. The correlation of the S&P 500 with itself equals 1: The calculation is its own covariance divided by its standard deviation squared.

EXAMPLE 12   Portfolio Expected Return and Variance of Return

You have a portfolio of two mutual funds, A and B, 75 percent invested in A, as shown in Table 10.

TABLE 10   Mutual Fund Expected Returns, Return Variances, and Covariances

Fund	A	B
	$E(R_A) = 20\%$	$E(R_B) = 12\%$
Covariance Matrix		
Fund	A	B
A	625	120
B	120	196

1. Calculate the expected return of the portfolio.
2. Calculate the correlation matrix for this problem. Carry out the answer to two decimal places.
3. Compute portfolio standard deviation of return.

Solution to 1: $E(R_p) = w_A E(R_A) + (1 - w_A)E(R_B) = 0.75(20\%) + 0.25(12\%) = 18\%$. Portfolio weights must sum to 1: $w_B = 1 - w_A$.

Solution to 2: $\sigma(R_A) = 625^{1/2} = 25$ percent $\sigma(R_B) = 196^{1/2} = 14$ percent. There is one distinct covariance and thus one distinct correlation: $\rho(R_A,R_B) = \text{Cov}(R_A,R_B)/[\sigma(R_A)\sigma(R_B)] = 120/[25(14)] = 0.342857$, or 0.34 Table 11 shows the correlation matrix.

Diagonal terms are always equal to 1 in a correlation matrix.

TABLE 11   Correlation Matrix

	A	B
A	1.00	0.34
B	0.34	1.00

Solution to 3:

$$\sigma^2(R_p) = w_A^2 \sigma^2(R_A) + w_B^2 \sigma^2(R_B) + 2w_A w_B \text{Cov}(R_A, R_B)$$
$$= (0.75)^2(625) + (0.25)^2(196) + 2(0.75)(0.25)(120)$$
$$= 351.5625 + 12.25 + 45 = 408.8125$$
$$\sigma(R_p) = 408.8125^{1/2} = 20.22 \text{ percent}$$

How do we estimate return covariance and correlation? Frequently, we make forecasts on the basis of historical covariance or use other methods based on historical return data, such as a market model regression.[14] We can also calculate covariance using the **joint probability function** of the random variables, if that can be estimated. The joint probability function of two random variables X and Y, denoted $P(X, Y)$, gives the probability of joint occurrences of values of X and Y. For example, $P(3, 2)$, is the probability that X equals 3 and Y equals 2.

Suppose that the joint probability function of the returns on BankCorp stock (R_A) and the returns on NewBank stock (R_B) has the simple structure given in Table 12.

The expected return on BankCorp stock is $0.20(25\%) + 0.50(12\%) + 0.30(10\%) = 14\%$. The expected return on NewBank stock is $0.20(20\%) + 0.50(16\%) + 0.30(10\%) = 15\%$. The joint probability function above might reflect an analysis based on whether banking industry conditions are good, average, or poor. Table 13 presents the calculation of covariance.

TABLE 12   Joint Probability Function of BankCorp and NewBank Returns (Entries Are Joint Probabilities)

	$R_B = 20\%$	$R_B = 16\%$	$R_B = 10\%$
$R_A = 25\%$	0.20	0	0
$R_A = 12\%$	0	0.50	0
$R_A = 10\%$	0	0	0.30

TABLE 13   Covariance Calculations

Banking Industry Condition	Deviations BankCorp	Deviations NewBank	Product of Deviations	Probability of Condition	Probability-Weighted Product
Good	25−14	20−15	55	0.20	11
Average	12−14	16−15	−2	0.50	−1
Poor	10−14	10−15	20	0.30	6
					$\text{Cov}(R_A, R_B) = 16$

Note: Expected return for BankCorp is 14% and for NewBank, 15%.

---

[14]See any of the textbooks mentioned in Footnote 10.

The first and second columns of numbers show, respectively, the deviations of BankCorp and NewBank returns from their mean or expected value. The next column shows the product of the deviations. For example, for good industry conditions, $(25 - 14)(20 - 15) = 11(5) = 55$. Then 55 is multiplied or weighted by 0.20, the probability that banking industry conditions are good: $55(0.20) = 11$. The calculations for average and poor banking conditions follow the same pattern. Summing up these probability-weighted products, we find that $\text{Cov}(R_A,R_B) = 16$.

A formula for computing the covariance between random variables R_A and R_B is

$$\text{Cov}(R_A,R_B) = \sum_i \sum_j P(R_{A,i}, R_{B,j})(R_{A,i} - ER_A)(R_{B,j} - ER_B) \qquad (19)$$

The formula tells us to sum all possible deviation cross-products weighted by the appropriate joint probability. In the example we just worked, as Table 12 shows, only three joint probabilities are nonzero. Therefore, in computing the covariance of returns in this case, we need to consider only three cross-products:

$$\begin{aligned}
\text{Cov}(R_A,R_B) &= P(25,20)[(25 - 14)(20 - 15)] + P(12,16)[(12 - 14)(16 - 15)] \\
&\quad + P(10,10)[(10 - 14)(10 - 15)] \\
&= 0.20(11)(5) + 0.50(-2)(1) + 0.30(-4)(-5) \\
&= 11 - 1 + 6 = 16
\end{aligned}$$

One theme of this chapter has been independence. Two random variables are independent when every possible pair of events—one event corresponding to a value of X and another event corresponding to a value of Y—are independent events. When two random variables are independent, their joint probability function simplifies.

- **Definition of Independence for Random Variables.** Two random variables X and Y are independent if and only if $P(X,Y) = P(X)P(Y)$.

For example, given independence, $P(3,2) = P(3)P(2)$. We multiply the individual probabilities to get the joint probabilities. *Independence* is a stronger property than *uncorrelatedness* because correlation addresses only linear relationships. The following condition holds for independent random variables and, therefore, also holds for uncorrelated random variables.

- **Multiplication Rule for Expected Value of the Product of Uncorrelated Random Variables.** The expected value of the product of uncorrelated random variables is the product of their expected values.

$$E(XY) = E(X)E(Y) \text{ if } X \text{ and } Y \text{ are uncorrelated.}$$

Many financial variables, such as revenue (price times quantity), are the product of random quantities. When applicable, the above rule simplifies calculating expected value of a product of random variables.[15]

---

[15]Otherwise, the calculation depends on conditional expected value; the calculation can be expressed as $E(XY) = E(X)\,E(Y|X)$.

4. TOPICS IN PROBABILITY

In the remainder of the chapter we discuss two topics that can be important in solving investment problems. We start with Bayes' formula: what probability theory has to say about learning from experience. Then we move to a discussion of shortcuts and principles for counting.

4.1. Bayes' Formula

When we make decisions involving investments, we often start with viewpoints based on our experience and knowledge. These viewpoints may be changed or confirmed by new knowledge and observations. Bayes' formula is a rational method for adjusting our viewpoints as we confront new information.[16] Bayes' formula and related concepts have been applied in many business and investment decision-making contexts, including the evaluation of mutual fund performance.[17]

Bayes' formula makes use of Equation 6, the total probability rule. To review, that rule expressed the probability of an event as a weighted average of the probabilities of the event, given a set of scenarios. Bayes' formula works in reverse; more precisely, it reverses the "given that" information. Bayes' formula uses the occurrence of the event to infer the probability of the scenario generating it. For that reason, Bayes' formula is sometimes called an inverse probability. In many applications, including the one illustrating its use in this section, an individual is updating his beliefs concerning the causes that may have produced a new observation.

- **Bayes' Formula.** Given a set of prior probabilities for an event of interest, if you receive new information, the rule for updating your probability of the event is

Updated probability of event given the new information

$$= \frac{\text{Probability of the new information given event}}{\text{Unconditional probability of the new information}} \times \text{Prior probability of event}$$

In probability notation, this formula can be written concisely as:

$$P(\text{Event} \mid \text{Information}) = \frac{P(\text{Information} \mid \text{Event})}{P(\text{Information})} P(\text{Event})$$

To illustrate Bayes' formula, we work through an investment example that can be adapted to any actual problem. Suppose you are an investor in the stock of DriveMed, Inc. Positive earnings surprises relative to consensus EPS estimates often result in positive stock returns, and negative surprises often have the opposite effect. DriveMed is preparing to release last quarter's EPS result, and you are interested in which of these three events happened: *last quarter's EPS exceeded the consensus EPS estimate,* or *last quarter's EPS exactly met the consensus EPS estimate,* or *last quarter's EPS fell short of the consensus EPS estimate.* This list of the alternatives is mutually exclusive and exhaustive.

---

[16]Named after the Reverend Thomas Bayes (1702–61).
[17]See Huij and Verbeek (2007).

On the basis of your own research, you write down the following **prior probabilities** (or priors, for short) concerning these three events:

- *P(EPS exceeded consensus)* = 0.45
- *P(EPS met consensus)* = 0.30
- *P(EPS fell short of consensus)* = 0.25

These probabilities are "prior" in the sense that they reflect only what you know now, before the arrival of any new information.

The next day, DriveMed announces that it is expanding factory capacity in Singapore and Ireland to meet increased sales demand. You assess this new information. The decision to expand capacity relates not only to current demand but probably also to the prior quarter's sales demand. You know that sales demand is positively related to EPS. So now it appears more likely that last quarter's EPS will exceed the consensus.

The question you have is, "In light of the new information, what is the updated probability that the prior quarter's EPS exceeded the consensus estimate?"

Bayes' formula provides a rational method for accomplishing this updating. We can abbreviate the new information as *DriveMed expands*. The first step in applying Bayes' formula is to calculate the probability of the new information (here: *DriveMed expands*), given a list of events or scenarios that may have generated it. The list of events should cover all possibilities, as it does here. Formulating these conditional probabilities is the key step in the updating process. Suppose your view is

$$P(DriveMed\ expands\ |\ EPS\ exceeded\ consensus) = 0.75$$

$$P(DriveMed\ expands\ |\ EPS\ met\ consensus) = 0.20$$

$$P(DriveMed\ expands\ |\ EPS\ fell\ short\ of\ consensus) = 0.05$$

Conditional probabilities of an observation (here: *DriveMed expands*) are sometimes referred to as **likelihoods**. Again, likelihoods are required for updating the probability.

Next, you combine these conditional probabilities or likelihoods with your prior probabilities to get the unconditional probability for DriveMed expanding, *P(DriveMed expands)*, as follows:

$$
\begin{aligned}
P(&DriveMed\ expands) \\
&= P(DriveMed\ expands\ |\ EPS\ exceeded\ consensus) \\
&\quad \times P(EPS\ exceeded\ consensus) \\
&\quad + P(DriveMed\ expands\ |\ EPS\ met\ consensus) \\
&\quad \times P(EPS\ met\ consensus) \\
&\quad + P(DriveMed\ expands\ |\ EPS\ fell\ short\ of\ consensus) \\
&\quad \times P(EPS\ fell\ short\ of\ consensus) \\
&= 0.75(0.45) + 0.20(0.30) + 0.05(0.25) = 0.41,\ or\ 41\%
\end{aligned}
$$

This is Equation 6, the total probability rule, in action. Now you can answer your question by applying Bayes' formula:

$P(EPS\ exceeded\ consensus\ |\ DriveMed\ expands)$

$$= \frac{P(DriveMed\ expands\ |\ EPS\ exceeded\ consensus)}{P(DriveMed\ expands)} P(EPS\ exceeded\ consensus)$$

$$= (0.75/0.41)(0.45) = 1.829268(0.45) = 0.823171$$

Prior to DriveMed's announcement, you thought the probability that DriveMed would beat consensus expectations was 45 percent. On the basis of your interpretation of the announcement, you update that probability to 82.3 percent. This updated probability is called your **posterior probability** because it reflects or comes after the new information.

The Bayes' calculation takes the prior probability, which was 45 percent, and multiplies it by a ratio—the first term on the right-hand side of the equal sign. The denominator of the ratio is the probability that DriveMed expands, as you view it without considering (conditioning on) anything else. Therefore, this probability is unconditional. The numerator is the probability that DriveMed expands, if last quarter's EPS actually exceeded the consensus estimate. This last probability is larger than unconditional probability in the denominator, so the ratio (1.83 roughly) is greater than 1. As a result, your updated or posterior probability is larger than your prior probability. Thus, the ratio reflects the impact of the new information on your prior beliefs.

EXAMPLE 13   Inferring whether DriveMed's EPS Met Consensus EPS

You are still an investor in DriveMed stock. To review the givens, your prior probabilities are $P(EPS\ exceeded\ consensus) = 0.45$, $P(EPS\ met\ consensus) = 0.30$, and $P(EPS\ fell\ short\ of\ consensus) = 0.25$. You also have the following conditional probabilities:

$$P(DriveMed\ expands\ |\ EPS\ exceeded\ consensus) = 0.75$$
$$P(DriveMed\ expands\ |\ EPS\ met\ consensus) = 0.20$$
$$P(DriveMed\ expands\ |\ EPS\ fell\ short\ of\ consensus) = 0.05$$

Recall that you updated your probability that last quarter's EPS exceeded the consensus estimate from 45 percent to 82.3 percent after DriveMed announced it would expand. Now you want to update your other priors.

1. Update your prior probability that DriveMed's EPS met consensus.
2. Update your prior probability that DriveMed's EPS fell short of consensus.
3. Show that the three updated probabilities sum to 1. (Carry each probability to four decimal places.)
4. Suppose, because of lack of prior beliefs about whether DriveMed would meet consensus, you updated on the basis of prior probabilities that all three possibilities were equally likely: $P(EPS\ exceeded\ consensus) = P(EPS\ met\ consensus) = P(EPS\ fell\ short\ of\ consensus) = 1/3$. What is your estimate of the probability $P(EPS\ exceeded\ consensus\ |\ DriveMed\ expands)$?

Solution to 1: The probability is $P(EPS\ met\ consensus\ |\ DriveMed\ expands) =$

$$\frac{P(DriveMed\ expands\ |\ EPS\ met\ consensus)}{P(DriveMed\ expands)} P(EPS\ met\ consensus)$$

The probability $P(DriveMed\ expands)$ is found by taking each of the three conditional probabilities in the statement of the problem, such as $P(DriveMed\ expands\ |\ EPS\ exceeded\ consensus)$; multiplying each one by the prior probability of the conditioning event, such as $P(EPS\ exceeded\ consensus)$; then adding the three products. The calculation is unchanged from the problem in the text above: $P(DriveMed\ expands) = 0.75(0.45) + 0.20(0.30) + 0.05(0.25) = 0.41$, or 41 percent. The other probabilities needed, $P(DriveMed\ expands\ |\ EPS\ met\ consensus) = 0.20$ and $P(EPS\ met\ consensus) = 0.30$, are givens. So

> $P(EPS\ met\ consensus\ |\ DriveMed\ expands)$
> $= [P(DriveMed\ expands\ |\ EPS\ met\ consensus)/P(DriveMed\ expands)]$
> $P(EPS\ met\ consensus)$
> $= (0.20/0.41)(0.30) = 0.487805(0.30) = 0.146341$

After taking account of the announcement on expansion, your updated probability that last quarter's EPS for DriveMed just met consensus is 14.6 percent compared with your prior probability of 30 percent.

Solution to 2: $P(DriveMed\ expands)$ was already calculated as 41 percent. Recall that $P(DriveMed\ expands\ |\ EPS\ fell\ short\ of\ consensus) = 0.05$ and $P(EPS\ fell\ short\ of\ consensus) = 0.25$ are givens.

> $P(EPS\ fell\ short\ of\ consensus\ |\ DriveMed\ expands)$
> $= [P(DriveMed\ expands\ |\ EPS\ fell\ short\ of\ consensus)/$
> $P(DriveMed\ expands)]P(EPS\ fell\ short\ of\ consensus)$
> $= (0.05/0.41)(0.25) = 0.121951(0.25) = 0.030488$

As a result of the announcement, you have revised your probability that DriveMed's EPS fell short of consensus from 25 percent (your prior probability) to 3 percent.

Solution to 3: The sum of the three updated probabilities is

> $P(EPS\ exceeded\ consensus\ |\ DriveMed\ expands) + P(EPS\ met\ consensus\ |$
> $DriveMed\ expands) + P(EPS\ fell\ short\ of\ consensus\ |\ DriveMed\ expands)$
> $= 0.8232 + 0.1463 + 0.0305 = 1.0000$

The three events (*EPS exceeded consensus, EPS met consensus, EPS fell short of consensus*) are mutually exclusive and exhaustive: One of these events or statements must be true, so the conditional probabilities must sum to 1. Whether we are talking about conditional or unconditional probabilities, whenever we have a complete set of the distinct possible events or outcomes, the probabilities must sum to 1. This calculation serves as a check on your work.

Solution to 4: Using the probabilities given in the question,

$$P(DriveMed\ expands)$$
$$= P(DriveMed\ expands\mid EPS\ exceeded\ consensus)$$
$$P(EPS\ exceeded\ consensus) + P(DriveMed\ expands\mid$$
$$EPS\ met\ consensus)P(EPS\ met\ consensus) + P(DriveMed\ expands\mid$$
$$EPS\ fell\ short\ of\ consensus)P(EPS\ fell\ short\ of\ consensus)$$
$$= 0.75(1/3) + 0.20(1/3) + 0.05(1/3) = 1/3$$

Not surprisingly, the probability of DriveMed expanding is 1/3 because the decision maker has no prior beliefs or views regarding how well EPS performed relative to the consensus estimate. Now we can use Bayes' formula to find $P(EPS\ exceeded\ consensus\mid DriveMed\ expands) = [P(DriveMed\ expands\mid EPS\ exceeded\ consensus)/P(DriveMed\ expands)]\ P(EPS\ exceeded\ consensus) = [(0.75/(1/3)](1/3) = 0.75$ or 75 percent. This probability is identical to your estimate of $P(DriveMed\ expands\mid EPS\ exceeded\ consensus)$.

When the prior probabilities are equal, the probability of information given an event equals the probability of the event given the information. When a decision-maker has equal prior probabilities (called **diffuse priors**), the probability of an event is determined by the information.

4.2. Principles of Counting

The first step in addressing a question often involves determining the different logical possibilities. We may also want to know the number of ways that each of these possibilities can happen. In the back of our mind is often a question about probability. How likely is it that I will observe this particular possibility? Records of success and failure are an example. When we evaluate a market timer's record, one well-known evaluation method uses counting methods presented in this section.[18] An important investment model, the binomial option pricing model, incorporates the combination formula that we will cover shortly. We can also use the methods in this section to calculate what we called a priori probabilities in Section 2. When we can assume that the possible outcomes of a random variable are equally likely, the probability of an event equals the number of possible outcomes favorable for the event divided by the total number of outcomes.

In counting, enumeration (counting the outcomes one by one) is of course the most basic resource. What we discuss in this section are shortcuts and principles. Without these shortcuts and principles, counting the total number of outcomes can be very difficult and prone to error. The first and basic principle of counting is the multiplication rule.

---

[18]Henriksson and Merton (1981).

- **Multiplication Rule of Counting.** If one task can be done in n_1 ways, and a second task, given the first, can be done in n_2 ways, and a third task, given the first two tasks, can be done in n_3 ways, and so on for k tasks, then the number of ways the k tasks can be done is $(n_1)(n_2)(n_3) \ldots (n_k)$.

Suppose we have three steps in an investment decision process. The first step can be done in two ways, the second in four ways, and the third in three ways. Following the multiplication rule, there are $(2)(4)(3) = 24$ ways in which we can carry out the three steps.

Another illustration is the assignment of members of a group to an equal number of positions. For example, suppose you want to assign three security analysts to cover three different industries. In how many ways can the assignments be made? The first analyst may be assigned in three different ways. Then two industries remain. The second analyst can be assigned in two different ways. Then one industry remains. The third and last analyst can be assigned in only one way. The total number of different assignments equals $(3)(2)(1) = 6$. The compact notation for the multiplication we have just performed is 3! (read: 3 factorial). If we had n analysts, the number of ways we could assign them to n tasks would be

$$n! = n(n-1)(n-2)(n-3)\ldots1$$

or **n factorial**. (By convention, $0! = 1$.) To review, in this application we repeatedly carry out an operation (here, job assignment) until we use up all members of a group (here, three analysts). With n members in the group, the multiplication formula reduces to n factorial.[19]

The next type of counting problem can be called labeling problems.[20] We want to give each object in a group a label, to place it in a category. The following example illustrates this type of problem.

A mutual fund guide ranked 18 bond mutual funds by total returns for the last year. The guide also assigned each fund one of five risk labels: *high risk* (four funds), *above-average risk* (four funds), *average risk* (three funds), *below-average risk* (four funds), and *low risk* (three funds); as $4 + 4 + 3 + 4 + 3 = 18$, all the funds are accounted for. How many different ways can we take 18 mutual funds and label 4 of them high risk, 4 above-average risk, 3 average risk, 4 below-average risk, and 3 low risk, so that each fund is labeled?

The answer is close to 13 billion. We can label any of 18 funds *high risk* (the first slot), then any of 17 remaining funds, then any of 16 remaining funds, then any of 15 remaining funds (now we have 4 funds in the *high risk* group); then we can label any of 14 remaining funds *above-average risk*, then any of 13 remaining funds, and so forth. There are 18! possible sequences. However, order of assignment within a category does not matter. For example, whether a fund occupies the first or third slot of the four funds labeled *high risk*, the fund has the same label (*high risk*). Thus there are 4! ways to assign a given group of four funds to the four *high risk* slots. Making the same argument for the other categories, in total there are $(4!)(4!)(3!)(4!)(3!)$ equivalent sequences. To eliminate such redundancies from the 18! total, we divide 18! by $(4!)(4!)(3!)(4!)(3!)$. We have $18!/[(4!)(4!)(3!)(4!)(3!)] = 18!/[(24)(24)(6)(24)(6)] = 12,864,852,000$. This procedure generalizes as follows.

---

[19]The shortest explanation of n factorial is that it is the number of ways to order n objects in a row. In all the problems to which we apply this counting method, we must use up all the members of a group (sampling without replacement).

[20]This discussion follows Kemeny, Schleifer, Snell, and Thompson (1972) in terminology and approach.

- **Multinomial Formula (General Formula for Labeling Problems).** The number of ways that n objects can be labeled with k different labels, with n_1 of the first type, n_2 of the second type, and so on, with $n_1 + n_2 + \ldots + n_k = n$, is given by

$$\frac{n!}{n_1! \ n_2! \ldots n_k!}$$

The multinomial formula with two different labels ($k = 2$) is especially important. This special case is called the combination formula. A **combination** is a listing in which the order of the listed items does not matter. We state the combination formula in a traditional way, but no new concepts are involved. Using the notation in the formula below, the number of objects with the first label is $r = n_1$ and the number with the second label is $n - r = n_2$ (there are just two categories, so $n_1 + n_2 = n$). Here is the formula:

- **Combination Formula (Binomial Formula).** The number of ways that we can choose r objects from a total of n objects, when the order in which the r objects are listed does not matter, is

$$_nC_r = \binom{n}{r} = \frac{n!}{(n-r)! \ r!}$$

Here $_nC_r$ and $\binom{n}{r}$ are shorthand notations for $n!/(n-r)!r!$ (read: n choose r, or n combination r).

    If we label the r objects as *belongs to the group* and the remaining objects as *does not belong to the group*, whatever the group of interest, the combination formula tells us how many ways we can select a group of size r. We can illustrate this formula with the binomial option pricing model. This model describes the movement of the underlying asset as a series of moves, price up (U) or price down (D). For example, two sequences of five moves containing three up moves, such as UUUDD and UDUUD, result in the same final stock price. At least for an option with a payoff dependent on final stock price, the number but not the order of up moves in a sequence matters. How many sequences of five moves *belong to the group with three up moves?* The answer is 10, calculated using the combination formula ("5 choose 3"):

$$_5C_3 = 5!/[(5 - 3)!3!]$$
$$= [(5)(4)(3)(2)(1)]/[(2)(1)(3)(2)(1)] = 120/12 = 10 \text{ ways}$$

A useful fact can be illustrated as follows: $_5C_3 = 5!/(2!3!)$ equals $_5C_2 = 5!/(3!2!)$, as $3 + 2 = 5$; $_5C_4 = 5!/(1!4!)$ equals $_5C_1 = 5!/(4!1!)$, as $4 + 1 = 5$. This symmetrical relationship can save work when we need to calculate many possible combinations.

    Suppose jurors want to select three companies out of a group of five to receive the first-, second-, and third-place awards for the best annual report. In how many ways can the jurors make the three awards? Order does matter if we want to distinguish among the three awards (the rank within the group of three); clearly the question makes order important. On the other hand, if the question were "In how many ways can the jurors choose three winners, without regard to place of finish?" we would use the combination formula.

To address the first question above, we need to count ordered listings such as *first place, New Company; second place, Fir Company; third place, Well Company*. An ordered listing is known as a **permutation**, and the formula that counts the number of permutations is known as the permutation formula.[21]

- **Permutation Formula.** The number of ways that we can choose *r* objects from a total of *n* objects, when the order in which the *r* objects are listed does matter, is

$$_nP_r = \frac{n!}{(n-r)!}$$

So the jurors have $_5P_3$ = 5!/(5 − 3)! = [(5)(4)(3)(2)(1)]/[(2)(1)] = 120/2 = 60 ways in which they can make their awards. To see why this formula works, note that [(5)(4)(3)(2)(1)]/[(2)(1)] reduces to (5)(4)(3), after cancellation of terms. This calculation counts the number of ways to fill three slots choosing from a group of five people, according to the multiplication rule of counting. This number is naturally larger than it would be if order did not matter (compare 60 to the value of 10 for "5 choose 3" that we calculated above). For example, *first place, Well Company; second place, Fir Company; third place, New Company* contains the same three companies as *first place, New Company; second place, Fir Company; third place, Well Company*. If we were concerned only with award winners (without regard to place of finish), the two listings would count as one combination. But when we are concerned with the order of finish, the listings count as two permutations.

Answering the following questions may help you apply the counting methods we have presented in this section.

1. Does the task that I want to measure have a finite number of possible outcomes? If the answer is yes, you may be able to use a tool in this section, and you can go to the second question. If the answer is no, the number of outcomes is infinite, and the tools in this section do not apply.
2. Do I want to assign every member of a group of size *n* to one of *n* slots (or tasks)? If the answer is yes, use *n* factorial. If the answer is no, go to the third question.
3. Do I want to count the number of ways to apply one of three or more labels to each member of a group? If the answer is yes, use the multinomial formula. If the answer is no, go to the fourth question.
4. Do I want to count the number of ways that I can choose *r* objects from a total of *n*, when the order in which I list the *r* objects does not matter (can I give the *r* objects a label)? If the answer to these questions is yes, the combination formula applies. If the answer is no, go to the fifth question.
5. Do I want to count the number of ways I can choose *r* objects from a total of *n*, when the order in which I list the *r* objects is important? If the answer is yes, the permutation formula applies. If the answer is no, go to question 6.
6. Can the multiplication rule of counting be used? If it cannot, you may have to count the possibilities one by one, or use more advanced techniques than those presented here.[22]

---

[21]A more formal definition states that a permutation is an ordered subset of *n* distinct objects.
[22]Feller (1957) contains a very full treatment of counting problems and solution methods.

5. SUMMARY

In this chapter, we have discussed the essential concepts and tools of probability. We have applied probability, expected value, and variance to a range of investment problems.

- A random variable is a quantity whose outcome is uncertain.
- Probability is a number between 0 and 1 that describes the chance that a stated event will occur.
- An event is a specified set of outcomes of a random variable.
- Mutually exclusive events can occur only one at a time. Exhaustive events cover or contain all possible outcomes.
- The two defining properties of a probability are, first, that $0 \leq P(E) \leq 1$ (where $P(E)$ denotes the probability of an event E), and second, that the sum of the probabilities of any set of mutually exclusive and exhaustive events equals 1.
- A probability estimated from data as a relative frequency of occurrence is an empirical probability. A probability drawing on personal or subjective judgment is a subjective probability. A probability obtained based on logical analysis is an a priori probability.
- A probability of an event E, $P(E)$, can be stated as odds for $E = P(E)/[1 - P(E)]$ or odds against $E = [1 - P(E)]/P(E)$.
- Probabilities that are inconsistent create profit opportunities, according to the Dutch Book Theorem.
- A probability of an event *not* conditioned on another event is an unconditional probability. The unconditional probability of an event A is denoted $P(A)$. Unconditional probabilities are also called marginal probabilities.
- A probability of an event given (conditioned on) another event is a conditional probability. The probability of an event A given an event B is denoted $P(A \mid B)$.
- The probability of both A and B occurring is the joint probability of A and B, denoted $P(AB)$.
- $P(A \mid B) = P(AB)/P(B)$, $P(B) \neq 0$.
- The multiplication rule for probabilities is $P(AB) = P(A \mid B)P(B)$.
- The probability that A or B occurs, or both occur, is denoted by $P(A \text{ or } B)$.
- The addition rule for probabilities is $P(A \text{ or } B) = P(A) + P(B) - P(AB)$.
- When events are independent, the occurrence of one event does not affect the probability of occurrence of the other event. Otherwise, the events are dependent.
- The multiplication rule for independent events states that if A and B are independent events, $P(AB) = P(A)P(B)$. The rule generalizes in similar fashion to more than two events.
- According to the total probability rule, if S_1, S_2, ..., S_n are mutually exclusive and exhaustive scenarios or events, then $P(A) = P(A \mid S_1)P(S_1) + P(A \mid S_2)P(S_2) + ... + P(A \mid S_n)P(S_n)$.
- The expected value of a random variable is a probability-weighted average of the possible outcomes of the random variable. For a random variable X, the expected value of X is denoted $E(X)$.
- The total probability rule for expected value states that $E(X) = E(X \mid S_1)P(S_1) + E(X \mid S_2)P(S_2) + ... + E(X \mid S_n)P(S_n)$, where S_1, S_2, ..., S_n are mutually exclusive and exhaustive scenarios or events.
- The variance of a random variable is the expected value (the probability-weighted average) of squared deviations from the random variable's expected value $E(X)$: $\sigma^2(X) = E\{[X - E(X)]^2\}$, where $\sigma^2(X)$ stands for the variance of X.
- Variance is a measure of dispersion about the mean. Increasing variance indicates increasing dispersion. Variance is measured in squared units of the original variable.

- Standard deviation is the positive square root of variance. Standard deviation measures dispersion (as does variance), but it is measured in the same units as the variable.
- Covariance is a measure of the co-movement between random variables.
- The covariance between two random variables R_i and R_j in a forward-looking sense is the expected value of the cross-product of the deviations of the two random variables from their respective means: $\text{Cov}(R_i, R_j) = E\{[R_i - E(R_i)][R_j - E(R_j)]\}$. The covariance of a random variable with itself is its own variance.
- The historical or sample covariance between two random variables R_i and R_j based on a sample of past data of size n is the average value of the product of the deviations of observations on two random variables from their sample means:

$$\text{Cov}(R_i, R_j) = \sum_{i=1}^{n}(R_{i,t} - \overline{R}_i)(R_{j,t} - \overline{R}_j)/(n-1)$$

- Correlation is a number between -1 and $+1$ that measures the co-movement (linear association) between two random variables: $\rho(R_i, R_j) = \text{Cov}(R_i, R_j)/[\sigma(R_i)\ \sigma(R_j)]$.
- If two variables have a very strong linear relation, then the absolute value of their correlation will be close to 1. If two variables have a weak linear relation, then the absolute value of their correlation will be close to 0.
- If the correlation coefficient is positive, the two variables are directly related; if the correlation coefficient is negative, the two variables are inversely related.
- To calculate the variance of return on a portfolio of n assets, the inputs needed are the n expected returns on the individual assets, n variances of return on the individual assets, and $n(n-1)/2$ distinct covariances.
- Portfolio variance of return is $\sigma^2(R_p) = \sum_{i=1}^{n}\sum_{j=1}^{n}w_iw_j\text{Cov}(R_i, R_j)$.
- The calculation of covariance in a forward-looking sense requires the specification of a joint probability function, which gives the probability of joint occurrences of values of the two random variables.
- When two random variables are independent, the joint probability function is the product of the individual probability functions of the random variables.
- Bayes' formula is a method for updating probabilities based on new information.
- Bayes' formula is expressed as follows: Updated probability of event given the new information = [(Probability of the new information given event)/(Unconditional probability of the new information)] × Prior probability of event.
- The multiplication rule of counting says, for example, that if the first step in a process can be done in 10 ways, the second step, given the first, can be done in 5 ways, and the third step, given the first two, can be done in 7 ways, then the steps can be carried out in $(10)(5)(7) = 350$ ways.
- The number of ways to assign every member of a group of size n to n slots is $n! = n\ (n-1) (n-2)(n-3)\ \dots\ 1$. (By convention, $0! = 1$.)
- The number of ways that n objects can be labeled with k different labels, with n_1 of the first type, n_2 of the second type, and so on, with $n_1 + n_2 + \dots + n_k = n$, is given by $n!/(n_1!n_2!\ \dots\ n_k!)$. This expression is the multinomial formula.
- A special case of the multinomial formula is the combination formula. The number of ways to choose r objects from a total of n objects, when the order in which the r objects are listed does not matter, is

$$_nC_r = \binom{n}{r} = \frac{n!}{(n-r)!r!}$$

- The number of ways to choose r objects from a total of n objects, when the order in which the r objects are listed does matter, is

$$_nP_r = \frac{n!}{(n-r)!}$$

This expression is the permutation formula.

REFERENCES

Bodie, Zvi, Alex Kane, and Alan J. Marcus. 2017. *Essentials of Investments*, 11th edition. New York: McGraw-Hill Irwin.

Elton, Edwin J., Martin J. Gruber, Stephen J. Brown, and William N. Goetzmann. 2013. *Modern Portfolio Theory and Investment Analysis*, 9th edition. Hoboken, NJ: Wiley.

Feller, William. 1957. *An Introduction to Probability Theory and Its Applications, Vol. I*, 2nd edition. New York: Wiley.

Henriksson, Roy D. and Robert C. Merton. 1981. "On Market Timing and Investment Performance, II. Statistical Procedures for Evaluating Forecasting Skills." *Journal of Business*, vol. 54, no. 4:513–533. 10.1086/296144

Huij, Joop and Marno Verbeek. 2007. "Cross-sectional learning and short-run persistence in mutual fund performance." *Journal of Banking & Finance*, vol. 31:973–997. 10.1016/j.jbankfin.2006.08.002

Kemeny, John G., Arthur Schleifer, Jr., J. Laurie Snell, and Gerald L. Thompson. 1972. *Finite Mathematics with Business Applications*, 2nd edition. Englewood Cliffs, NJ: Prentice-Hall.

Lo, Andrew W. 1999. "The Three P's of Total Risk Management." *Financial Analysts Journal*, vol. 55, no. 1:13–26. 10.2469/faj.v55.n1.2238

Ramsey, Frank P. 1931. "Truth and Probability." In *The Foundations of Mathematics and Other Logical Essays*, edited by R.B. Braithwaite. London: Routledge and Keegan Paul.

Reilly, Frank K. and Keith C. Brown. 2018. *Investment Analysis and Portfolio Management*, 11th edition. Mason, OH: Cengage South-Western.

Thanatawee, Yordying. 2013. "Ownership Structure with Dividend Policy: Evidence from Thailand." *International Journal of Economics and Finance*, vol. 5, no. 1:121–132.

Vidal-Garcia, Javier. 2013. "The Persistence of European Mutual Fund Performance." *Research in International Business and Finance*, vol. 28:45–67. 10.1016/j.ribaf.2012.09.004

PRACTICE PROBLEMS

1. Suppose that 5 percent of the stocks meeting your stock-selection criteria are in the telecommunications (telecom) industry. Also, dividend-paying telecom stocks are 1 percent of the total number of stocks meeting your selection criteria. What is the probability that a stock is dividend paying, given that it is a telecom stock that has met your stock selection criteria?

2. You are using the following three criteria to screen potential acquisition targets from a list of 500 companies:

Criterion	Fraction of the 500 Companies Meeting the Criterion
Product lines compatible	0.20
Company will increase combined sales growth rate	0.45
Balance sheet impact manageable	0.78

    If the criteria are independent, how many companies will pass the screen?

3. You apply both valuation criteria and financial strength criteria in choosing stocks. The probability that a randomly selected stock (from your investment universe) meets your valuation criteria is 0.25. Given that a stock meets your valuation criteria, the probability that the stock meets your financial strength criteria is 0.40. What is the probability that a stock meets both your valuation and financial strength criteria?

4. Suppose the prospects for recovering principal for a defaulted bond issue depend on which of two economic scenarios prevails. Scenario 1 has probability 0.75 and will result in recovery of $0.90 per $1 principal value with probability 0.45, or in recovery of $0.80 per $1 principal value with probability 0.55. Scenario 2 has probability 0.25 and will result in recovery of $0.50 per $1 principal value with probability 0.85, or in recovery of $0.40 per $1 principal value with probability 0.15.

    A. Compute the probability of each of the four possible recovery amounts: $0.90, $0.80, $0.50, and $0.40.
    B. Compute the expected recovery, given the first scenario.
    C. Compute the expected recovery, given the second scenario.
    D. Compute the expected recovery.
    E. Graph the information in a tree diagram.

5. You have developed a set of criteria for evaluating distressed credits. Companies that do not receive a passing score are classed as likely to go bankrupt within 12 months. You gathered the following information when validating the criteria:
    - Forty percent of the companies to which the test is administered will go bankrupt within 12 months: P(*nonsurvivor*) = 0.40.
    - Fifty-five percent of the companies to which the test is administered pass it: P(*pass test*) = 0.55.
    - The probability that a company will pass the test given that it will subsequently survive 12 months, is 0.85: P(*pass test | survivor*) = 0.85.

    A. What is P(*pass test | nonsurvivor*)?
    B. Using Bayes' formula, calculate the probability that a company is a survivor, given that it passes the test; that is, calculate P(survivor | pass test).
    C. What is the probability that a company is a *nonsurvivor*, given that it fails the test?
    D. Is the test effective?

6. In probability theory, exhaustive events are *best* described as events:
    A. with a probability of zero.
    B. that are mutually exclusive.
    C. that include all potential outcomes.

7. Which probability estimate *most likely* varies greatly between people?
   A. An *a priori* probability
   B. An empirical probability
   C. A subjective probability

8. If the probability that Zolaf Company sales exceed last year's sales is 0.167, the odds for exceeding sales are *closest* to:
   A. 1 to 5.
   B. 1 to 6.
   C. 5 to 1.

9. The probability of an event given that another event has occurred is a:
   A. joint probability.
   B. marginal probability.
   C. conditional probability.

10. After estimating the probability that an investment manager will exceed his benchmark return in each of the next two quarters, an analyst wants to forecast the probability that the investment manager will exceed his benchmark return over the two-quarter period in total. Assuming that each quarter's performance is independent of the other, which probability rule should the analyst select?
    A. Addition rule
    B. Multiplication rule
    C. Total probability rule

11. Which of the following is a property of two dependent events?
    A. The two events must occur simultaneously.
    B. The probability of one event influences the probability of the other event.
    C. The probability of the two events occurring is the product of each event's probability.

12. Which of the following *best* describes how an analyst would estimate the expected value of a firm under the scenarios of bankruptcy and survivorship? The analyst would use:
    A. the addition rule.
    B. conditional expected values.
    C. the total probability rule for expected value.

13. An analyst developed two scenarios with respect to the recovery of $100,000 principal from defaulted loans:

Scenario	Probability of Scenario (%)	Amount Recovered ($)	Probability of Amount (%)
1	40	50,000	60
		30,000	40
2	60	80,000	90
		60,000	10

The amount of the expected recovery is *closest* to:
A. $36,400.
B. $63,600.
C. $81,600.

14. US and Spanish bonds have return standard deviations of 0.64 and 0.56, respectively. If the correlation between the two bonds is 0.24, the covariance of returns is *closest* to:
    A. 0.086.
    B. 0.670.
    C. 0.781.

15. The covariance of returns is positive when the returns on two assets tend to:
    A. have the same expected values.
    B. be above their expected value at different times.
    C. be on the same side of their expected value at the same time.

16. Which of the following correlation coefficients indicates the weakest linear relationship between two variables?
    A. −0.67
    B. −0.24
    C. 0.33

17. An analyst develops the following covariance matrix of returns:

	Hedge Fund	Market Index
Hedge Fund	256	110
Market Index	110	81

The correlation of returns between the hedge fund and the market index is *closest* to:
    A. 0.005.
    B. 0.073.
    C. 0.764.

18. All else being equal, as the correlation between two assets approaches +1.0, the diversification benefits:
    A. decrease.
    B. stay the same.
    C. increase.

19. Given a portfolio of five stocks, how many unique covariance terms, excluding variances, are required to calculate the portfolio return variance?
    A. 10
    B. 20
    C. 25

20. The probability distribution for a company's sales is:

Probability	Sales ($ millions)
0.05	70
0.70	40
0.25	25

The standard deviation of sales is *closest* to:
A. $9.81 million.
B. $12.20 million.
C. $32.40 million.

21. Which of the following statements is *most* accurate? If the covariance of returns between two assets is 0.0023, then:
A. the assets' risk is near zero.
B. the asset returns are unrelated.
C. the asset returns have a positive relationship.

22. An analyst produces the following joint probability function for a foreign index (FI) and a domestic index (DI).

	$R_{DI} = 30\%$	$R_{DI} = 25\%$	$R_{DI} = 15\%$
$R_{FI} = 25\%$	0.25		
$R_{FI} = 15\%$		0.50	
$R_{FI} = 10\%$			0.25

The covariance of returns on the foreign index and the returns on the domestic index is *closest* to:
A. 26.39.
B. 26.56.
C. 28.12.

23. A manager will select 20 bonds out of his universe of 100 bonds to construct a portfolio. Which formula provides the number of possible portfolios?
A. Permutation formula
B. Multinomial formula
C. Combination formula

24. A firm will select two of four vice presidents to be added to the investment committee. How many different groups of two are possible?
A. 6
B. 12
C. 24

25. From an approved list of 25 funds, a portfolio manager wants to rank 4 mutual funds from most recommended to least recommended. Which formula is *most* appropriate to calculate the number of possible ways the funds could be ranked?
A. Permutation formula
B. Multinomial formula
C. Combination formula

CHAPTER 4

COMMON PROBABILITY DISTRIBUTIONS

Richard A. DeFusco, PhD, CFA
Dennis W. McLeavey, DBA, CFA
Jerald E. Pinto, PhD, CFA
David E. Runkle, PhD, CFA

LEARNING OUTCOMES

The candidate should be able to:

- define a probability distribution and distinguish between discrete and continuous random variables and their probability functions;
- describe the set of possible outcomes of a specified discrete random variable;
- interpret a cumulative distribution function;
- calculate and interpret probabilities for a random variable, given its cumulative distribution function;
- define a discrete uniform random variable, a Bernoulli random variable, and a binomial random variable;
- calculate and interpret probabilities given the discrete uniform and the binomial distribution functions;
- construct a binomial tree to describe stock price movement;
- define the continuous uniform distribution and calculate and interpret probabilities, given a continuous uniform distribution;
- explain the key properties of the normal distribution;
- distinguish between a univariate and a multivariate distribution and explain the role of correlation in the multivariate normal distribution;
- determine the probability that a normally distributed random variable lies inside a given interval;

Quantitative Methods for Investment Analysis, Second Edition, by Richard A. DeFusco, PhD, CFA, Dennis W. McLeavey, DBA, CFA, Jerald E. Pinto, PhD, CFA, David E. Runkle, PhD, CFA. Copyright © 2019 by CFA Institute.

- define the standard normal distribution, explain how to standardize a random variable, and calculate and interpret probabilities using the standard normal distribution;
- define shortfall risk, calculate the safety-first ratio, and select an optimal portfolio using Roy's safety-first criterion;
- explain the relationship between normal and lognormal distributions and why the lognormal distribution is used to model asset prices;
- distinguish between discretely and continuously compounded rates of return and calculate and interpret a continuously compounded rate of return, given a specific holding period return;
- describe Monte Carlo simulation.

1. INTRODUCTION TO COMMON PROBABILITY DISTRIBUTIONS

In nearly all investment decisions we work with random variables. The return on a stock and its earnings per share are familiar examples of random variables. To make probability statements about a random variable, we need to understand its probability distribution. A **probability distribution** specifies the probabilities of the possible outcomes of a random variable.

In this chapter, we present important facts about four probability distributions and their investment uses. These four distributions—the uniform, binomial, normal, and lognormal—are used extensively in investment analysis. They are used in such basic valuation models as the Black–Scholes–Merton option pricing model, the binomial option pricing model, and the capital asset pricing model. With the working knowledge of probability distributions provided in this chapter, you will also be better prepared to study and use other quantitative methods such as hypothesis testing, regression analysis, and time-series analysis.

After discussing probability distributions, we end the chapter with a brief introduction to Monte Carlo simulation, a computer-based tool for obtaining information on complex problems. For example, an investment analyst may want to experiment with an investment idea without actually implementing it. Or she may need to price a complex option for which no simple pricing formula exists. In these cases and many others, Monte Carlo simulation is an important resource. To conduct a Monte Carlo simulation, the analyst must identify risk factors associated with the problem and specify probability distributions for them. Hence, Monte Carlo simulation is a tool that requires an understanding of probability distributions.

Before we discuss specific probability distributions, we define basic concepts and terms. We then illustrate the operation of these concepts through the simplest distribution, the uniform distribution. That done, we address probability distributions that have more applications in investment work but also greater complexity.

2. DISCRETE RANDOM VARIABLES

A **random variable** is a quantity whose future outcomes are uncertain. The two basic types of random variables are discrete random variables and continuous random variables. A **discrete random variable** can take on at most a countable number of possible values. For example, a discrete random variable X can take on a limited number of outcomes x_1, x_2, ..., x_n (n possible outcomes), or a discrete random variable Y can take on an unlimited number of outcomes $y_1, y_2, \dots$ (without end).[1] Because we can count all the possible outcomes of X and Y (even if we go on forever in the case of Y), both X and Y satisfy the definition of a discrete random variable. By contrast, we cannot count the outcomes of a **continuous random variable**. We cannot describe the possible outcomes of a continuous random variable Z with a list $z_1, z_2, \dots$ because the outcome $(z_1 + z_2)/2$, not in the list, would always be possible. Rate of return is an example of a continuous random variable.

In working with a random variable, we need to understand its possible outcomes. For example, a majority of the stocks traded on the New Zealand Stock Exchange are quoted in ticks of NZ\$0.01. Quoted stock price is thus a discrete random variable with possible values NZ\$0, NZ\$0.01, NZ\$0.02, ... But we can also model stock price as a continuous random variable (as a lognormal random variable, to look ahead). In many applications, we have a choice between using a discrete or a continuous distribution. We are usually guided by which distribution is most efficient for the task we face. This opportunity for choice is not surprising, as many discrete distributions can be approximated with a continuous distribution, and vice versa. In most practical cases, a probability distribution is only a mathematical idealization, or approximate model, of the relative frequencies of a random variable's possible outcomes.

EXAMPLE 1 The Distribution of Bond Price

You are researching a probability model for bond price, and you begin by thinking about the characteristics of bonds that affect price. What are the lowest and the highest possible values for bond price? Why? What are some other characteristics of bonds that may affect the distribution of bond price?

The lowest possible value of bond price is 0, when the bond is worthless. Identifying the highest possible value for bond price is more challenging. The promised payments on a coupon bond are the coupons (interest payments) plus the face amount (principal). The price of a bond is the present discounted value of these promised payments. Because investors require a return on their investments, 0 percent is the lower limit on the discount rate that investors would use to discount a bond's promised payments. At a discount rate of 0 percent, the price of a bond is the sum of the face value and the remaining coupons without any discounting. The discount rate thus places the upper limit on bond price. Suppose, for example, that face value is \$1,000 and two \$40 coupons remain; the interval \$0 to \$1,080 captures all possible values of the bond's price. This upper limit decreases through time as the number of remaining payments decreases.

Other characteristics of a bond also affect its price distribution. Pull to par value is one such characteristic: As the maturity date approaches, the standard deviation of bond price tends to grow smaller as bond price converges to par value. Embedded options also affect bond price. For example, with bonds that are currently callable, the issuer may retire the bonds at a prespecified premium above par; this option of the issuer cuts off part of the bond's upside. Modeling bond price distribution is a challenging problem.

---

[1] We follow the convention that an uppercase letter represents a random variable and a lowercase letter represents an outcome or specific value of the random variable. Thus X refers to the random variable, and x refers to an outcome of X. We subscript outcomes, as in x_1 and x_2, when we need to distinguish among different outcomes in a list of outcomes of a random variable.

Every random variable is associated with a probability distribution that describes the variable completely. We can view a probability distribution in two ways. The basic view is the **probability function**, which specifies the probability that the random variable takes on a specific value: $P(X = x)$ is the probability that a random variable X takes on the value x. (Note that capital X represents the random variable and lowercase x represents a specific value that the random variable may take.) For a discrete random variable, the shorthand notation for the probability function is $p(x) = P(X = x)$. For continuous random variables, the probability function is denoted $f(x)$ and called the **probability density function** (PDF), or just the density.[2]

A probability function has two key properties (which we state, without loss of generality, using the notation for a discrete random variable):

- $0 \leq p(x) \leq 1$, because probability is a number between 0 and 1.
- The sum of the probabilities $p(x)$ over all values of X equals 1. If we add up the probabilities of all the distinct possible outcomes of a random variable, that sum must equal 1.

We are often interested in finding the probability of a range of outcomes rather than a specific outcome. In these cases, we take the second view of a probability distribution, the cumulative distribution function (CDF). The **cumulative distribution function**, or distribution function for short, gives the probability that a random variable X is less than or equal to a particular value x, $P(X \leq x)$. For both discrete and continuous random variables, the shorthand notation is $F(x) = P(X \leq x)$. How does the cumulative distribution function relate to the probability function? The word "cumulative" tells the story. To find $F(x)$, we sum up, or cumulate, values of the probability function for all outcomes less than or equal to x. The function of the CDF is parallel to that of cumulative relative frequency, which we discussed in the chapter on statistical concepts and market returns.

Next, we illustrate these concepts with examples and show how we use discrete and continuous distributions. We start with the simplest distribution, the discrete uniform.

2.1. The Discrete Uniform Distribution

The simplest of all probability distributions is the discrete uniform distribution. Suppose that the possible outcomes are the integers (whole numbers) 1 to 8, inclusive, and the probability that the random variable takes on any of these possible values is the same for all outcomes (that is, it is uniform). With eight outcomes, $p(x) = 1/8$, or 0.125, for all values of X ($X = 1$, 2, 3, 4, 5, 6, 7, 8); the statement just made is a complete description of this discrete uniform random variable. The distribution has a finite number of specified outcomes, and each outcome is equally likely. Table 1 summarizes the two views of this random variable, the probability function and the cumulative distribution function.

We can use Table 1 to find three probabilities: $P(X \leq 7)$, $P(4 \leq X \leq 6)$, and $P(4 < X \leq 6)$. The following examples illustrate how to use the CDF to find the probability that a random variable will fall in any interval (for any random variable, not only the uniform).

- The probability that X is less than or equal to 7, $P(X \leq 7)$, is the next-to-last entry in the third column, 0.875 or 87.5 percent.

---

[2]The technical term for the probability function of a discrete random variable, probability mass function (PMF), is used less frequently.

TABLE 1 Probability Function and Cumulative Distribution Function for a Discrete Uniform Random Variable

X = x	Probability Function $p(x) = P(X = x)$	Cumulative Distribution Function $F(x) = P(X \le x)$
1	0.125	0.125
2	0.125	0.250
3	0.125	0.375
4	0.125	0.500
5	0.125	0.625
6	0.125	0.750
7	0.125	0.875
8	0.125	1.000

- To find $P(4 \le X \le 6)$, we need to find the sum of three probabilities: $p(4)$, $p(5)$, and $p(6)$. We can find this sum in two ways. We can add $p(4)$, $p(5)$, and $p(6)$ from the second column. Or we can calculate the probability as the difference between two values of the cumulative distribution function:

$$F(6) = P(X \le 6) = p(6) + p(5) + p(4) + p(3) + p(2) + p(1)$$
$$F(3) = P(X \le 3) = p(3) + p(2) + p(1)$$

so

$$P(4 \le X \le 6) = F(6) - F(3) = p(6) + p(5) + p(4) = 3/8$$

So we calculate the second probability as $F(6) - F(3) = 3/8$.
- The third probability, $P(4 < X \le 6)$, the probability that X is less than or equal to 6 but greater than 4, is $p(5) + p(6)$. We compute it as follows, using the CDF:

$$P(4 < X \le 6) = P(X \le 6) - P(X \le 4) = F(6) - F(4) = p(6) + p(5) = 2/8$$

So we calculate the third probability as $F(6) - F(4) = 2/8$.

Suppose we want to check that the discrete uniform probability function satisfies the general properties of a probability function given earlier. The first property is $0 \le p(x) \le 1$. We see that $p(x) = 1/8$ for all x in the first column of the table. (Note that $p(x)$ equals 0 for numbers x such as –14 or 12.215 that are not in that column.) The first property is satisfied. The second property is that the probabilities sum to 1. The entries in the second column of Table 1 do sum to 1.

The CDF has two other characteristic properties:

- The CDF lies between 0 and 1 for any x: $0 \le F(x) \le 1$.
- As we increase x, the CDF either increases or remains constant.

Check these statements by looking at the third column in Table 1.

We now have some experience working with probability functions and CDFs for discrete random variables. Later in this chapter, we will discuss Monte Carlo simulation, a methodology driven by random numbers. As we will see, the uniform distribution has an important technical use: It is the basis for generating random numbers, which in turn produce random observations for all other probability distributions.[3]

2.2. The Binomial Distribution

In many investment contexts, we view a result as either a success or a failure, or as binary (twofold) in some other way. When we make probability statements about a record of successes and failures, or about anything with binary outcomes, we often use the binomial distribution. What is a good model for how a stock price moves through time? Different models are appropriate for different uses. Cox, Ross, and Rubinstein (1979) developed an option pricing model based on binary moves, price up or price down, for the asset underlying the option. Their binomial option pricing model was the first of a class of related option pricing models that have played an important role in the development of the derivatives industry. That fact alone would be sufficient reason for studying the binomial distribution, but the binomial distribution has uses in decision making as well.

The building block of the binomial distribution is the **Bernoulli random variable**, named after the Swiss probabilist Jakob Bernoulli (1654–1704). Suppose we have a trial (an event that may repeat) that produces one of two outcomes. Such a trial is a **Bernoulli trial**. If we let Y equal 1 when the outcome is success and Y equal 0 when the outcome is failure, then the probability function of the Bernoulli random variable Y is

$$p(1) = P(Y = 1) = p$$
$$p(0) = P(Y = 0) = 1 - p$$

where p is the probability that the trial is a success. Our next example is the very first step on the road to understanding the binomial option pricing model.

EXAMPLE 2   One-Period Stock Price Movement as a Bernoulli Random Variable

---

Suppose we describe stock price movement in the following way. Stock price today is S. Next period stock price can move up or down. The probability of an up move is p, and the probability of a down move is $1 - p$. Thus, stock price is a Bernoulli random variable with probability of success (an up move) equal to p. When the stock moves up, ending price is uS, with u equal to 1 plus the rate of return if the stock moves up.

---

[3]See Hillier (2014). Random numbers initially generated by computers are usually random positive integer numbers that are converted to approximate continuous uniform random numbers between 0 and 1. Then the continuous uniform random numbers are used to produce random observations on other distributions, such as the normal, using various techniques. We will discuss random observation generation further in the section on Monte Carlo simulation.

For example, if the stock earns 0.01 or 1 percent on an up move, $u = 1.01$. When the stock moves down, ending price is dS, with d equal to 1 plus the rate of return if the stock moves down. For example, if the stock earns –0.01 or –1 percent on a down move, $d = 0.99$. Figure 1 shows a diagram of this model of stock price dynamics.

FIGURE 1   One-Period Stock Price as a Bernoulli Random Variable

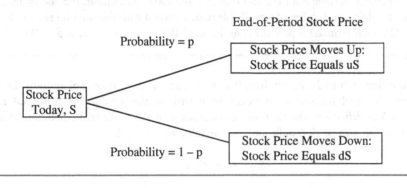

We will continue with the above example later. In the model of stock price movement in Example 2, success and failure at a given trial relate to up moves and down moves, respectively. In the following example, success is a profitable trade and failure is an unprofitable one.

EXAMPLE 3   A Trading Desk Evaluates Block Brokers (1)

You work in equities trading at an institutional money manager that regularly trades with several block brokers. Blocks are orders to sell or buy that are too large for the liquidity ordinarily available in dealer networks or stock exchanges. Your firm has known interests in certain kinds of stock. Block brokers call your trading desk when they want to sell blocks of stocks that they think your firm may be interested in buying. You know that these transactions have definite risks. For example, if the broker's client (the seller of the shares) has unfavorable information on the stock, or if the total amount he is selling through all channels is not truthfully communicated to you, you may see an immediate loss on the trade. From time to time, your firm audits the performance of block brokers. Your firm calculates the post-trade, market-risk-adjusted dollar returns on stocks purchased from block brokers. On that basis, you classify each trade as unprofitable or profitable. You have summarized the performance of the brokers in a spreadsheet, excerpted in Table 2 for November of last year. (The broker names are coded BB001 and BB002.)

TABLE 2   Block Trading Gains and Losses

	Profitable Trades	Losing Trades
BB001	3	9
BB002	5	3

View each trade as a Bernoulli trial. Calculate the percentage of profitable trades with the two block brokers for last November. These are estimates of p, the underlying probability of a successful (profitable) trade with each broker.

Your firm has logged $3 + 9 = 12$ trades (the row total) with block broker BB001. Because 3 of the 12 trades were profitable, the percentage of profitable trades was 3/12 or 25 percent. With broker BB002, the percentage of profitable trades was 5/8 or 62.5 percent. A trade is a Bernoulli trial, and the above calculations provide estimates of the underlying probability of a profitable trade (success) with the two brokers. For broker BB001, your estimate is $\hat{p} = 0.25$; for broker BB002, your estimate is $\hat{p} = 0.625$.[4]

In n Bernoulli trials, we can have 0 to n successes. If the outcome of an individual trial is random, the total number of successes in n trials is also random. A **binomial random variable** X is defined as the number of successes in n Bernoulli trials. A binomial random variable is the sum of Bernoulli random variables Y_i, $i = 1, 2, ..., n$:

$$X = Y_1 + Y_2 + ... + Y_n$$

where Y_i is the outcome on the ith trial (1 if a success, 0 if a failure). We know that a Bernoulli random variable is defined by the parameter p. The number of trials, n, is the second parameter of a binomial random variable. The binomial distribution makes these assumptions:

- The probability, p, of success is constant for all trials.
- The trials are independent.

The second assumption has great simplifying force. If individual trials were correlated, calculating the probability of a given number of successes in n trials would be much more complicated.

Under the above two assumptions, a binomial random variable is completely described by two parameters, n and p. We write

$$X \sim B(n,p)$$

which we read as "X has a binomial distribution with parameters n and p." You can see that a Bernoulli random variable is a binomial random variable with $n = 1$: $Y \sim B(1, p)$.

Now we can find the general expression for the probability that a binomial random variable shows x successes in n trials. We can think in terms of a model of stock price dynamics that can be generalized to allow any possible stock price movements if the periods are made extremely small. Each period is a Bernoulli trial: With probability p, the stock price moves up; with probability $1 - p$, the price moves down. A success is an up move, and x is the number of up moves or successes in n periods (trials). With each period's moves independent and p constant, the number of up moves in n periods is a binomial random variable. We now develop an expression for $P(X = x)$, the probability function for a binomial random variable.

---

[4]The "hat" over p indicates that it is an estimate of p, the underlying probability of a profitable trade with the broker.

Any sequence of n periods that shows exactly x up moves must show $n - x$ down moves. We have many different ways to order the up moves and down moves to get a total of x up moves, but given independent trials, any sequence with x up moves must occur with probability $p^x(1 - p)^{n-x}$. Now we need to multiply this probability by the number of different ways we can get a sequence with x up moves. Using a basic result in counting from the chapter on probability concepts, there are

$$\frac{n!}{(n-x)!x!}$$

different sequences in n trials that result in x up moves (or successes) and $n - x$ down moves (or failures). Recall from the chapter on probability concepts (Chapter 3) that n factorial ($n!$) is defined as $n(n - 1)(n - 2) \ldots 1$ (and $0! = 1$ by convention). For example, $5! = (5)(4)(3)(2)(1) = 120$. The combination formula $n!/[(n - x)!x!]$ is denoted by

$$\binom{n}{x}$$

(read "n combination x" or "n choose x"). For example, over three periods, exactly three different sequences have two up moves: UUD, UDU, and DUU. We confirm this by

$$\binom{3}{2} = \frac{3!}{(3-2)!2!} = \frac{(3)(2)(1)}{(1)(2)(1)} = 3$$

If, hypothetically, each sequence with two up moves had a probability of 0.15, then the total probability of two up moves in three periods would be $3 \times 0.15 = 0.45$. This example should persuade you that for X distributed $B(n, p)$, the probability of x successes in n trials is given by

$$p(x) = P(X = x) = \binom{n}{x}p^x(1-p)^{n-x} = \frac{n!}{(n-x)!x!}p^x(1-p)^{n-x} \tag{1}$$

Some distributions are always symmetric, such as the normal, and others are always asymmetric or skewed, such as the lognormal. The binomial distribution is symmetric when the probability of success on a trial is 0.50, but it is asymmetric or skewed otherwise.

We illustrate Equation 1 (the probability function) and the CDF through the symmetrical case. Consider a random variable distributed $B(n = 5, p = 0.50)$. Table 3 contains a complete description of this random variable. The fourth column of Table 3 is Column 2, n combination x, times Column 3, $p^x(1 - p)^{n-x}$; Column 4 gives the probability for each value of the number of up moves from the first column. The fifth column, cumulating the entries in the fourth column, is the cumulative distribution function.

What would happen if we kept $n = 5$ but sharply lowered the probability of success on a trial to 10 percent? "Probability for Each Way" for $X = 0$ (no up moves) would then be about 59 percent: $0.10^0(1 - 0.10)^5 = 0.59049$. Because zero successes could still happen one way (Column 2), $p(0) = 59$ percent. You may want to check that given $p = 0.10$, $P(X \le 2) = 99.14$ percent: The probability of two or fewer up moves would be more than 99 percent. The random variable's probability would be massed on 0, 1, and 2 up moves, and the

TABLE 3   Binomial Probabilities, $p = 0.50$ and $n = 5$

Number of Up Moves, x (1)	Number of Possible Ways to Reach x Up Moves (2)	Probability for Each Way (3)	Probability for x, $p(x)$ (4) = (2) × (3)	$F(x) = P(X \leq x)$ (5)
0	1	$0.50^0(1 - 0.50)^5 = 0.03125$	0.03125	0.03125
1	5	$0.50^1(1 - 0.50)^4 = 0.03125$	0.15625	0.18750
2	10	$0.50^2(1 - 0.50)^3 = 0.03125$	0.31250	0.50000
3	10	$0.50^3(1 - 0.50)^2 = 0.03125$	0.31250	0.81250
4	5	$0.50^4(1 - 0.50)^1 = 0.03125$	0.15625	0.96875
5	1	$0.50^5(1 - 0.50)^0 = 0.03125$	0.03125	1.00000

probability of larger outcomes would be minute. The outcomes of 3 and larger would be the long right tail, and the distribution would be right skewed. On the other hand, if we set $p = 0.90$, we would have the mirror image of the distribution with $p = 0.10$. The distribution would be left skewed.

With an understanding of the binomial probability function in hand, we can continue with our example of block brokers.

EXAMPLE 4   A Trading Desk Evaluates Block Brokers (2)

You now want to evaluate the performance of the block brokers in Example 3. You begin with two questions:

1. If you are paying a fair price on average in your trades with a broker, what should be the probability of a profitable trade?
2. Did each broker meet or miss that expectation on probability?

You also realize that the brokers' performance has to be evaluated in light of the sample's size, and for that you need to use the binomial probability function (Equation 1). You thus address the following (referring to the data in Example 3):

3. Under the assumption that the prices of trades were fair,
    A. calculate the probability of three or fewer profitable trades with broker BB001.
    B. calculate the probability of five or more profitable trades with broker BB002.

Solution to 1 and 2: If the price you trade at is fair, 50 percent of the trades you do with a broker should be profitable.[5] The rate of profitable trades with broker BB001 was 25 percent. Therefore, broker BB001 missed your performance expectation. Broker BB002, at 62.5 percent profitable trades, exceeded your expectation.

---

[5] Of course, you need to adjust for the direction of the overall market after the trade (any broker's record will be helped by a bull market) and perhaps make other risk adjustments. Assume that these adjustments have been made.

Solution to 3:

A.   For broker BB001, the number of trades (the trials) was $n = 12$, and 3 were profitable. You are asked to calculate the probability of three or fewer profitable trades, $F(3) = p(3) + p(2) + p(1) + p(0)$.

Suppose the underlying probability of a profitable trade with BB001 is $p = 0.50$. With $n = 12$ and $p = 0.50$, according to Equation 1 the probability of three profitable trades is

$$p(3) = \binom{n}{x} p^x (1-p)^{n-x} = \binom{12}{3}(0.50^3)(0.50^9)$$

$$= \frac{12!}{(12-3)!3!}0.50^{12} = 220(0.000244) = 0.053711$$

The probability of exactly 3 profitable trades out of 12 is 5.4 percent if broker BB001 were giving you fair prices. Now you need to calculate the other probabilities:

$$p(2) = [12!/(12-2)!2!](0.50^2)(0.50^{10}) = 66(0.000244) = 0.016113$$

$$p(1) = [12!/(12-1)!1!](0.50^1)(0.50^{11}) = 12(0.000244) = 0.00293$$

$$p(0) = [12!/(12-0)!0!](0.50^0)(0.50^{12}) = 1(0.000244) = 0.000244$$

Adding all the probabilities, $F(3) = 0.053711 + 0.016113 + 0.00293 + 0.000244 = 0.072998$ or 7.3 percent. The probability of doing 3 or fewer profitable trades out of 12 would be 7.3 percent if your trading desk were getting fair prices from broker BB001.

B.   For broker BB002, you are assessing the probability that the underlying probability of a profitable trade with this broker was 50 percent, despite the good results. The question was framed as the probability of doing five or more profitable trades if the underlying probability is 50 percent: $1 - F(4) = p(5) + p(6) + p(7) + p(8)$. You could calculate $F(4)$ and subtract it from 1, but you can also calculate $p(5) + p(6) + p(7) + p(8)$ directly.

You begin by calculating the probability that exactly 5 out of 8 trades would be profitable if BB002 were giving you fair prices:

$$p(5) = \binom{8}{5}(0.50^5)(0.50^3)$$

$$= 56(0.003906) = 0.21875$$

The probability is about 21.9 percent. The other probabilities are

$$p(6) = 28(0.003906) = 0.109375$$

$$p(7) = 8(0.003906) = 0.03125$$

$$p(8) = 1(0.003906) = 0.003906$$

So $p(5) + p(6) + p(7) + p(8) = 0.21875 + 0.109375 + 0.03125 + 0.003906 = 0.363281$ or 36.3 percent.[6] A 36.3 percent probability is substantial; the underlying probability of executing a fair trade with BB002 might well have been 0.50 despite your success with BB002 in November of last year. If one of the trades with BB002 had been reclassified from profitable to unprofitable, exactly half the trades would have been profitable. In summary, your trading desk is getting at least fair prices from BB002; you will probably want to accumulate additional evidence before concluding that you are trading at better-than-fair prices.

The magnitude of the profits and losses in these trades is another important consideration. If all profitable trades had small profits but all unprofitable trades had large losses, for example, you might lose money on your trades even if the majority of them were profitable.

In the next example, the binomial distribution helps in evaluating the performance of an investment manager.

EXAMPLE 5   Meeting a Tracking Objective

You work for a pension fund sponsor. You have assigned a new money manager to manage a $500 million portfolio indexed on the MSCI EAFE (Europe, Australasia, and Far East) Index, which is designed to measure developed-market equity performance excluding the United States and Canada. After research, you believe it is reasonable to expect that the manager will keep portfolio return within a band of 75 basis points (bps) of the benchmark's return, on a quarterly basis.[7] To quantify this expectation further, you will be satisfied if portfolio return is within the 75 bps band 90 percent of the time. The manager meets the objective in six out of eight quarters. Of course, six out of eight quarters is a 75 percent success rate. But how does the manager's record precisely relate to your expectation of a 90 percent success rate and the sample size, 8 observations? To answer this question, you must find the probability that, given an assumed true or underlying success rate of 90 percent, performance could be as bad as or worse than that delivered. Calculate the probability (by hand or with a spreadsheet).

Specifically, you want to find the probability that portfolio return is within the 75 bps band in six or fewer quarters out of the eight in the sample. With $n = 8$ and $p = 0.90$, this probability is $F(6) = p(6) + p(5) + p(4) + p(3) + p(2) + p(1) + p(0)$. Start with

$$p(6) = (8!/6!2!)(0.90^6)(0.10^2) = 28(0.005314) = 0.148803$$

and work through the other probabilities:

$$p(5) = (8!/5!3!)(0.90^5)(0.10^3) = 56(0.00059) = 0.033067$$
$$p(4) = (8!/4!4!)(0.90^4)(0.10^4) = 70(0.000066) = 0.004593$$
$$p(3) = (8!/3!5!)(0.90^3)(0.10^5) = 56(0.000007) = 0.000408$$
$$p(2) = (8!/2!6!)(0.90^2)(0.10^6) = 28(0.000001) = 0.000023$$
$$p(1) = (8!/1!7!)(0.90^1)(0.10^7) = 8(0.00000009) = 0.00000072$$
$$p(0) = (8!/0!8!)(0.90^0)(0.10^8) = 1(0.00000001) = 0.00000001$$

Summing all these probabilities, you conclude that $F(6) = 0.148803 + 0.033067 + 0.004593 + 0.000408 + 0.000023 + 0.00000072 + 0.00000001 = 0.186895$ or 18.7 percent. There is a moderate 18.7 percent probability that the manager would show the record he did (or a worse record) if he had the skill to meet your expectations 90 percent of the time.

You can use other evaluation concepts such as tracking error or tracking risk, defined as the standard deviation of return differences between a portfolio and its benchmark, to assess the manager's performance. The calculation above would be only one input into any conclusions that you reach concerning the manager's performance. But to answer problems involving success rates, you need to be skilled in using the binomial distribution.

Two descriptors of a distribution that are often used in investments are the mean and the variance (or the standard deviation, the positive square root of variance).[8] Table 4 gives the expressions for the mean and variance of binomial random variables. Because a single Bernoulli random variable, $Y \sim B(1, p)$, takes on the value 1 with probability p and the value 0 with probability $1 - p$, its mean or weighted-average outcome is p. Its variance is $p(1 - p)$.[9] A general binomial random variable, $B(n, p)$, is the sum of n Bernoulli random variables, and so the mean of a $B(n, p)$ random variable is np. Given that a $B(1, p)$ variable has variance $p(1 - p)$, the variance of a $B(n, p)$ random variable is n times that value, or $np(1 - p)$, assuming that all the trials (Bernoulli random variables) are independent. We can

TABLE 4   Mean and Variance of Binomial Random Variables

	Mean	Variance
Bernoulli, $B(1, p)$	p	$p(1 - p)$
Binomial, $B(n, p)$	np	$np(1 - p)$

[8]The mean (or arithmetic mean) is the sum of all values in a distribution or dataset, divided by the number of values summed. The variance is a measure of dispersion about the mean. See the chapter on statistical concepts and market returns for further details on these concepts (Chapter 3).
[9]We can show that $p(1 - p)$ is the variance of a Bernoulli random variable as follows, noting that a Bernoulli random variable can take on only one of two values, 1 or 0: $\sigma^2(Y) = E[(Y - EY)^2] = E[(Y - p)^2] = (1 - p)^2 p + (0 - p)^2(1 - p) = (1 - p)[(1 - p)p + p^2] = p(1 - p)$.

illustrate the calculation for two binomial random variables with differing probabilities as follows:

Random Variable	Mean	Variance
$B(n = 5, p = 0.50)$	$2.50 = 5(0.50)$	$1.25 = 5(0.50)(0.50)$
$B(n = 5, p = 0.10)$	$0.50 = 5(0.10)$	$0.45 = 5(0.10)(0.90)$

For a $B(n = 5, p = 0.50)$ random variable, the expected number of successes is 2.5 with a standard deviation of $1.118 = (1.25)^{1/2}$; for a $B(n = 5, p = 0.10)$ random variable, the expected number of successes is 0.50 with a standard deviation of $0.67 = (0.45)^{1/2}$.

EXAMPLE 6   The Expected Number of Defaults in a Bond Portfolio

Suppose as a bond analyst you are asked to estimate the number of bond issues expected to default over the next year in an unmanaged high-yield bond portfolio with 25 US issues from distinct issuers. The credit ratings of the bonds in the portfolio are tightly clustered around Moody's B2/Standard & Poor's B, meaning that the bonds are speculative with respect to the capacity to pay interest and repay principal. The estimated annual default rate for B2/B rated bonds is 10.7 percent.

1. Over the next year, what is the expected number of defaults in the portfolio, assuming a **binomial model** for defaults?
2. Estimate the standard deviation of the number of defaults over the coming year.
3. Critique the use of the binomial probability model in this context.

Solution to 1: For each bond, we can define a Bernoulli random variable equal to 1 if the bond defaults during the year and zero otherwise. With 25 bonds, the expected number of defaults over the year is $np = 25(0.107) = 2.675$ or approximately 3.

Solution to 2: The variance is $np(1 - p) = 25(0.107)(0.893) = 2.388775$. The standard deviation is $(2.388775)^{1/2} = 1.55$. Thus, a two standard deviation confidence interval about the expected number of defaults would run from approximately 0 to approximately 6, for example.

Solution to 3: An assumption of the binomial model is that the trials are independent. In this context, a trial relates to whether an individual bond issue will default over the next year. Because the issuing companies probably share exposure to common economic factors, the trials may not be independent. Nevertheless, for a quick estimate of the expected number of defaults, the binomial model may be adequate.

Earlier, we looked at a simple one-period model for stock price movement. Now we extend the model to describe stock price movement on three consecutive days. Each day is an independent trial. The stock moves up with constant probability p (the **up transition probability**); if it moves up, u is 1 plus the rate of return for an up move. The stock moves down with constant probability $1 - p$ (the **down transition probability**); if it moves down, d is 1 plus the rate of return for a down move. We graph stock price movement in Figure 2, where we now associate each of the $n = 3$ stock price moves with time indexed by t. The shape of the graph suggests why it is a called a **binomial tree**. Each boxed value from which successive moves or outcomes branch in the tree is called a **node**; in this example, a node is potential value for the stock price at a specified time.

We see from the tree that the stock price at $t = 3$ has four possible values: *uuuS*, *uudS*, *uddS*, and *dddS*. The probability that the stock price equals *any* one of these four values is given by the binomial distribution. For example, three sequences of moves result in a final stock price of *uudS*: These are *uud*, *udu*, and *duu*. These sequences have two up moves out of three moves in total; the combination formula confirms that the number of ways to get two up moves (successes) in three periods (trials) is $3!/(3 - 2)!2! = 3$. Next note that each of these sequences, *uud*, *udu*, and *duu*, has probability $p^2(1 - p)$. So $P(S_3 = uudS) = 3p^2(1 - p)$, where S_3 indicates the stock's price after three moves.

The binomial random variable in this application is the number of up moves. Final stock price distribution is a function of the initial stock price, the *number* of up moves, and the *size* of the up moves and down moves. We cannot say that stock price itself is a binomial random variable; rather, it is a function of a binomial random variable, as well as of u and d, and initial price. This richness is actually one key to why this way of modeling stock price is useful: It allows us to choose values of these parameters to approximate various distributions for stock price (using a large number of time periods).[10] One distribution that can be approximated is the lognormal, an important continuous distribution model for stock price that we will discuss later. The flexibility extends further. In the tree shown above, the transition probabilities are the same at each node: p for an up move and $1 - p$ for a down move. That standard formula describes a process in which stock return volatility is constant through time. Option experts, however, sometimes model changing volatility through time using a binomial tree in which the probabilities for up and down moves differ at different nodes.

The binomial tree also supplies the possibility of testing a condition or contingency at any node. This flexibility is useful in investment applications such as option pricing. Consider an American call option on a dividend-paying stock. (Recall that an American option can be

FIGURE 2   A Binomial Model of Stock Price Movement

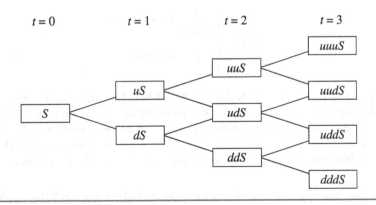

---

[10]For example, we can split 20 days into 100 subperiods, taking care to use compatible values for u and d.

exercised at any time before expiration, at any node on the tree.) Just before an ex-dividend date, it may be optimal to exercise an American call option on stock to buy the stock and receive the dividend.[11] If we model stock price with a binomial tree, we can test, at each node, whether exercising the option is optimal. Also, if we know the value of the call at the four terminal nodes at $t = 3$ and we have a model for discounting values by one period, we can step backward one period to $t = 2$ to find the call's value at the three nodes there. Continuing back recursively, we can find the call's value today. This type of recursive operation is easily programmed on a computer. As a result, binomial trees can value options even more complex than American calls on stock.[12]

3. CONTINUOUS RANDOM VARIABLES

In the previous section, we considered discrete random variables (i.e., random variables whose set of possible outcomes is countable). In contrast, the possible outcomes of continuous random variables are never countable. If 1.250 is one possible value of a continuous random variable, for example, we cannot name the next higher or lower possible value. Technically, the range of possible outcomes of a continuous random variable is the real line (all real numbers between $-\infty$ and $+\infty$) or some subset of the real line.

In this section, we focus on the two most important continuous distributions in investment work, the normal and lognormal. As we did with discrete distributions, we introduce the topic through the uniform distribution.

3.1. Continuous Uniform Distribution

The continuous uniform distribution is the simplest continuous probability distribution. The uniform distribution has two main uses. As the basis of techniques for generating random numbers, the uniform distribution plays a role in Monte Carlo simulation. As the probability distribution that describes equally likely outcomes, the uniform distribution is an appropriate probability model to represent a particular kind of uncertainty in beliefs in which all outcomes appear equally likely.

The PDF for a uniform random variable is

$$f(x) = \begin{cases} \dfrac{1}{b-a} & \text{for } a < x < b \\ 0 & \text{otherwise} \end{cases}$$

For example, with $a = 0$ and $b = 8$, $f(x) = 1/8$ or 0.125. We graph this density in Figure 3. The graph of the density function plots as a horizontal line with a value of 0.125.

What is the probability that a uniform random variable with limits $a = 0$ and $b = 8$ is less than or equal to 3, or $F(3) = P(X \le 3)$? When we were working with the discrete uniform random variable with possible outcomes 1, 2, ..., 8, we summed individual

FIGURE 3   Continuous Uniform Distribution

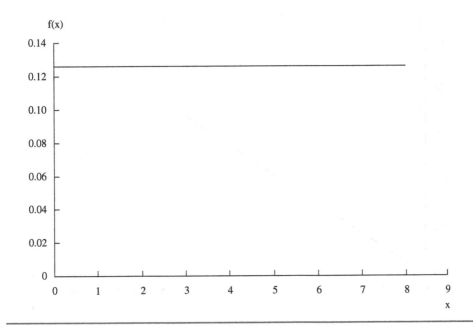

probabilities: $p(1) + p(2) + p(3) = 0.375$. In contrast, the probability that a continuous uniform random variable, or any continuous random variable, assumes any given fixed value is 0. To illustrate this point, consider the narrow interval 2.510 to 2.511. Because that interval holds an infinity of possible values, the sum of the probabilities of values in that interval alone would be infinite if each individual value in it had a positive probability. To find the probability $F(3)$, we find the area under the curve graphing the PDF, between 0 to 3 on the x axis. In calculus, this operation is called integrating the probability function $f(x)$ from 0 to 3. This area under the curve is a rectangle with base $3 - 0 = 3$ and height $1/8$. The area of this rectangle equals base times height: $3(1/8) = 3/8$ or 0.375. So $F(3) = 3/8$ or 0.375.

The interval from 0 to 3 is three-eighths of the total length between the limits of 0 and 8, and $F(3)$ is three-eighths of the total probability of 1. The middle line of the expression for the CDF captures this relationship.

$$F(x) = \begin{cases} 0 \text{ for } x \le a \\ \dfrac{x - a}{b - a} \text{ for } a < x < b \\ 1 \text{ for } x \ge b \end{cases}$$

For our problem, $F(x) = 0$ for $x \le 0$, $F(x) = x/8$ for $0 < x < 8$, and $F(x) = 1$ for $x \ge 8$. We graph this CDF in Figure 4.

The mathematical operation that corresponds to finding the area under the curve of a PDF $f(x)$ from a to b is the integral of $f(x)$ from a to b:

$$P(a \le X \le b) = \int_a^b f(x)\,dx \qquad\qquad (2)$$

FIGURE 4   Continuous Uniform Cumulative Distribution

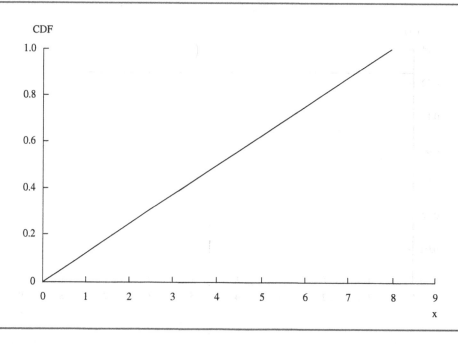

where $\int dx$ is the symbol for summing $\int$ over small changes dx, and the limits of integration (a and b) can be any real numbers or $-\infty$ and $+\infty$. All probabilities of continuous random variables can be computed using Equation 2. For the uniform distribution example considered above, $F(7)$ is Equation 2 with lower limit $a = 0$ and upper limit $b = 7$. The integral corresponding to the CDF of a uniform distribution reduces to the three-line expression given previously. To evaluate Equation 2 for nearly all other continuous distributions, including the normal and lognormal, we rely on spreadsheet functions, computer programs, or tables of values to calculate probabilities. Those tools use various numerical methods to evaluate the integral in Equation 2.

Recall that the probability of a continuous random variable equaling any fixed point is 0. This fact has an important consequence for working with the cumulative distribution function of a continuous random variable: For any continuous random variable X, $P(a \leq X \leq b) = P(a < X \leq b) = P(a \leq X < b) = P(a < X < b)$, because the probabilities at the endpoints a and b are 0. For discrete random variables, these relations of equality are not true, because probability accumulates at points.

EXAMPLE 7   Probability That a Lending Facility Covenant Is Breached

You are evaluating the bonds of a below-investment-grade borrower at a low point in its business cycle. You have many factors to consider, including the terms of the company's bank lending facilities. The contract creating a bank lending facility such as an unsecured line of credit typically has clauses known as covenants. These covenants place restrictions on what the borrower can do. The company will be in breach of a covenant in the lending facility if the interest coverage ratio, EBITDA/interest, calculated on EBITDA over the four trailing quarters, falls below 2.0. EBITDA is earnings before interest, taxes, depreciation, and amortization. Compliance with the covenants will be checked at the end of the current quarter. If the covenant is breached, the bank can demand immediate repayment of all borrowings on the facility. That action would probably trigger a liquidity crisis for the company. With a high degree of confidence, you forecast interest charges of $25 million. Your estimate of EBITDA runs from $40 million on the low end to $60 million on the high end.

Address two questions (treating projected interest charges as a constant):

1. If the outcomes for EBITDA are equally likely, what is the probability that EBITDA/interest will fall below 2.0, breaching the covenant?
2. Estimate the mean and standard deviation of EBITDA/interest. For a continuous uniform random variable, the mean is given by $\mu = (a + b)/2$ and the variance is given by $\sigma^2 = (b - a)^2/12$.

Solution to 1: EBITDA/interest is a continuous uniform random variable because all outcomes are equally likely. The ratio can take on values between 1.6 = ($40 million)/ ($25 million) on the low end and 2.4 = ($60 million/$25 million) on the high end. The range of possible values is 2.4 - 1.6 = 0.8. What fraction of the possible values falls below 2.0, the level that triggers default? The distance between 2.0 and 1.6 is 0.40; the value 0.40 is one-half the total length of 0.8, or 0.4/0.8 = 0.50. So, the probability that the covenant will be breached is 50 percent.

Solution to 2: In Solution 1, we found that the lower limit of EBITDA/interest is 1.6. This lower limit is *a*. We found that the upper limit is 2.4. This upper limit is *b*. Using the formula given above,

$$\mu = (a + b)/2 = (1.6 + 2.4)/2 = 2.0$$

The variance of the interest coverage ratio is

$$\sigma^2 = (b - a)^2/12 = (2.4 - 1.6)^2/12 = 0.053333$$

The standard deviation is the positive square root of the variance, $0.230940 = (0.053333)^{1/2}$. The standard deviation is not particularly useful as a risk measure for a uniform distribution, however. The probability that lies within various standard deviation bands around the mean is sensitive to different specifications of the upper and lower limits (although Chebyshev's inequality is always satisfied).[13] Here, a one standard deviation interval around the mean of 2.0 runs from 1.769 to 2.231 and captures 0.462/0.80 = 0.5775 or 57.8 percent of the probability. A two standard deviation interval runs from 1.538 to 2.462, which extends past both the lower and upper limits of the random variable.

---

[13]Chebyshev's inequality is discussed in the chapter, "Organizing, Visualizing, and Describing Data," on statistical concepts and market returns.

3.2. The Normal Distribution

The normal distribution may be the most extensively used probability distribution in quantitative work. It plays key roles in modern portfolio theory and in several risk management technologies. Because it has so many uses, the normal distribution must be thoroughly understood by investment professionals.

The role of the normal distribution in statistical inference and regression analysis is vastly extended by a crucial result known as the central limit theorem. The central limit theorem states that the sum (and mean) of a large number of independent random variables is approximately normally distributed.[14]

The French mathematician Abraham de Moivre (1667–1754) introduced the normal distribution in 1733 in developing a version of the central limit theorem. As Figure 5 shows, the normal distribution is symmetrical and bell-shaped. The range of possible outcomes of the normal distribution is the entire real line: all real numbers lying between $-\infty$ and $+\infty$. The tails of the bell curve extend without limit to the left and to the right.

The defining characteristics of a normal distribution are as follows:

- The normal distribution is completely described by two parameters—its mean, μ, and variance, σ^2. We indicate this as $X \sim N(\mu, \sigma^2)$ (read "X follows a normal distribution with mean μ and variance σ^2"). We can also define a normal distribution in terms of the mean and the standard deviation, σ (this is often convenient because σ is measured in the same units as X and μ). As a consequence, we can answer any probability question about a normal random variable if we know its mean and variance (or standard deviation).

FIGURE 5   Two Normal Distributions

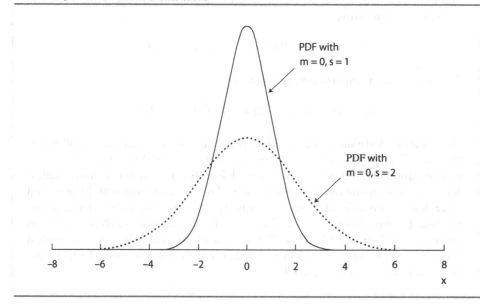

- The normal distribution has a skewness of 0 (it is symmetric). The normal distribution has a kurtosis of 3; its excess kurtosis (kurtosis − 3.0) equals 0.[15] As a consequence of symmetry, the mean, median, and the mode are all equal for a normal random variable.
- A linear combination of two or more normal random variables is also normally distributed.

These bullet points concern a single variable or univariate normal distribution: the distribution of one normal random variable. A **univariate distribution** describes a single random variable. A **multivariate distribution** specifies the probabilities for a group of related random variables. You will encounter the **multivariate normal distribution** in investment work and chapter and should know the following about it.

When we have a group of assets, we can model the distribution of returns on each asset individually, or the distribution of returns on the assets as a group. "As a group" means that we take account of all the statistical interrelationships among the return series. One model that has often been used for security returns is the multivariate normal distribution. A multivariate normal distribution for the returns on n stocks is completely defined by three lists of parameters:

1. The list of the mean returns on the individual securities (n means in total);
2. The list of the securities' variances of return (n variances in total); and
3. The list of all the distinct pairwise return correlations: $n(n - 1)/2$ distinct correlations in total.[16]

The need to specify correlations is a distinguishing feature of the multivariate normal distribution in contrast to the univariate normal distribution.

The statement "assume returns are normally distributed" is sometimes used to mean a joint normal distribution. For a portfolio of 30 securities, for example, portfolio return is a weighted average of the returns on the 30 securities. A weighted average is a linear combination. Thus, portfolio return is normally distributed if the individual security returns are (joint) normally distributed. To review, in order to specify the normal distribution for portfolio return, we need the means, variances, and the distinct pairwise correlations of the component securities.

With these concepts in mind, we can return to the normal distribution for one random variable. The curves graphed in Figure 5 are the normal density function:

$$f(x) = \frac{1}{\sigma\sqrt{2\pi}} \exp\left(\frac{-(x - \mu)^2}{2\sigma^2}\right) \text{ for } -\infty < x < +\infty \tag{3}$$

The two densities graphed in Figure 5 correspond to a mean of $\mu = 0$ and standard deviations of $\sigma = 1$ and $\sigma = 2$. The normal density with $\mu = 0$ and $\sigma = 1$ is called the **standard normal distribution** (or **unit normal distribution**). Plotting two normal

---

[15]If we have a sample of size n from a normal distribution, we may want to know the possible variation in sample skewness and kurtosis. For a normal random variable, the standard deviation of sample skewness is $6/n$ and the standard deviation of sample kurtosis is $24/n$.

[16]For example, a distribution with two stocks (a bivariate normal distribution) has two means, two variances, and one correlation: $2(2 - 1)/2$. A distribution with 30 stocks has 30 means, 30 variances, and 435 distinct correlations: $30(30 - 1)/2$. The return correlation of Dow Chemical with American Express stock is the same as the correlation of American Express with Dow Chemical stock, so these are counted as one distinct correlation.

distributions with the same mean and different standard deviations helps us appreciate why standard deviation is a good measure of dispersion for the normal distribution: Observations are much more concentrated around the mean for the normal distribution with $\sigma = 1$ than for the normal distribution with $\sigma = 2$.

Although not literally accurate, the normal distribution can be considered an approximate model for returns. Nearly all the probability of a normal random variable is contained within three standard deviations of the mean. For realistic values of mean return and return standard deviation for many assets, the normal probability of outcomes below −100 percent is very small. Whether the approximation is useful in a given application is an empirical question. For example, the normal distribution is a closer fit for quarterly and yearly holding period returns on a diversified equity portfolio than it is for daily or weekly returns.[17] A persistent departure from normality in most equity return series is kurtosis greater than 3, the fat-tails problem. So when we approximate equity return distributions with the normal distribution, we should be aware that the normal distribution tends to underestimate the probability of extreme returns.[18] Option returns are skewed. Because the normal is a symmetrical distribution, we should be cautious in using the normal distribution to model the returns on portfolios containing significant positions in options.

The normal distribution, however, is less suitable as a model for asset prices than as a model for returns. A normal random variable has no lower limit. This characteristic has several implications for investment applications. An asset price can drop only to 0, at which point the asset becomes worthless. As a result, practitioners generally do not use the normal distribution to model the distribution of asset prices. Also note that moving from any level of asset price to 0 translates into a return of −100 percent. Because the normal distribution extends below 0 without limit, it cannot be literally accurate as a model for asset returns.

Having established that the normal distribution is the appropriate model for a variable of interest, we can use it to make the following probability statements:

- Approximately 50 percent of all observations fall in the interval $\mu \pm (2/3)\sigma$.
- Approximately 68 percent of all observations fall in the interval $\mu \pm \sigma$.
- Approximately 95 percent of all observations fall in the interval $\mu \pm 2\sigma$.
- Approximately 99 percent of all observations fall in the interval $\mu \pm 3\sigma$.

One, two, and three standard deviation intervals are illustrated in Figure 6. The intervals indicated are easy to remember but are only approximate for the stated probabilities. More-precise intervals are $\mu \pm 1.96\sigma$ for 95 percent of the observations and $\mu \pm 2.58\sigma$ for 99 percent of the observations.

In general, we do not observe the population mean or the population standard deviation of a distribution, so we need to estimate them.[19] We estimate the population mean, μ, using the sample mean, $\overline{X}$ (sometimes denoted as $\hat{\mu}$) and estimate the population standard deviation, σ, using the sample standard deviation, s (sometimes denoted as $\hat{\sigma}$).

---

[17]See Fama (1976) and Campbell, Lo, and MacKinlay (1997).

[18]Fat tails can be modeled by a mixture of normal random variables or by a Student's t-distribution with a relatively small number of degrees of freedom. See Kon (1984) and Campbell, Lo, and MacKinlay (1997). We discuss the Student's t-distribution in the chapter on sampling and estimation (Chapter 5).

[19]A population is all members of a specified group, and the population mean is the arithmetic mean computed for the population. A sample is a subset of a population, and the sample mean is the arithmetic mean computed for the sample. For more information on these concepts, see the chapter "Organizing, Visualizing, and Describing Data," on statistical concepts and market returns.

FIGURE 6   Units of Standard Deviation

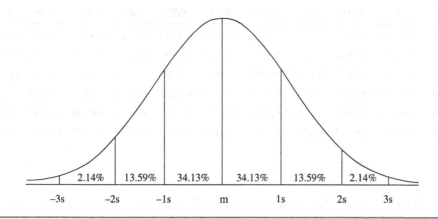

| 2.14% | 13.59% | 34.13% | 34.13% | 13.59% | 2.14% |

−3s		−2s		−1s	m	1s	2s	3s

There are as many different normal distributions as there are choices for mean (μ) and variance (σ^2). We can answer all of the above questions in terms of any normal distribution. Spreadsheets, for example, have functions for the normal CDF for any specification of mean and variance. For the sake of efficiency, however, we would like to refer all probability statements to a single normal distribution. The standard normal distribution (the normal distribution with $\mu = 0$ and $\sigma = 1$) fills that role.

There are two steps in **standardizing** a random variable X: Subtract the mean of X from X, then divide that result by the standard deviation of X. If we have a list of observations on a normal random variable, X, we subtract the mean from each observation to get a list of deviations from the mean, then divide each deviation by the standard deviation. The result is the standard normal random variable, Z. (Z is the conventional symbol for a standard normal random variable.) If we have $X \sim N(\mu,\sigma^2)$ (read "X follows the normal distribution with parameters μ and σ^2"), we standardize it using the formula

$$Z = (X - \mu)/\sigma \tag{4}$$

Suppose we have a normal random variable, X, with $\mu = 5$ and $\sigma = 1.5$. We standardize X with $Z = (X - 5)/1.5$. For example, a value $X = 9.5$ corresponds to a standardized value of 3, calculated as $Z = (9.5 - 5)/1.5 = 3$. The probability that we will observe a value as small as or smaller than 9.5 for $X \sim N(5,1.5)$ is exactly the same as the probability that we will observe a value as small as or smaller than 3 for $Z \sim N(0,1)$. We can answer all probability questions about X using standardized values and probability tables for Z. We generally do not know the population mean and standard deviation, so we often use the sample mean $\overline{X}$ for μ and the sample standard deviation s for σ.

Standard normal probabilities can also be computed with spreadsheets, statistical and econometric software, and programming languages. Tables of the cumulative distribution function for the standard normal random variable are in the back of this book. Table 5 shows an excerpt from those tables. $N(x)$ is a conventional notation for the CDF of a standard normal variable.[20]

---

[20]Another often-seen notation for the CDF of a standard normal variable is $\Phi(x)$.

TABLE 5 $P(Z \leq x) = N(x)$ for $x \geq 0$ or $P(Z \leq z) = N(z)$ for $z \geq 0$

x or z	0	0.01	0.02	0.03	0.04	0.05	0.06	0.07	0.08	0.09
0.00	0.5000	0.5040	0.5080	0.5120	0.5160	0.5199	0.5239	0.5279	0.5319	0.5359
0.10	0.5398	0.5438	0.5478	0.5517	0.5557	0.5596	0.5636	0.5675	0.5714	0.5753
0.20	0.5793	0.5832	0.5871	0.5910	0.5948	0.5987	0.6026	0.6064	0.6103	0.6141
0.30	0.6179	0.6217	0.6255	0.6293	0.6331	0.6368	0.6406	0.6443	0.6480	0.6517
0.40	0.6554	0.6591	0.6628	0.6664	0.6700	0.6736	0.6772	0.6808	0.6844	0.6879
0.50	0.6915	0.6950	0.6985	0.7019	0.7054	0.7088	0.7123	0.7157	0.7190	0.7224

To find the probability that a standard normal variable is less than or equal to 0.24, for example, locate the row that contains 0.20, look at the 0.04 column, and find the entry 0.5948. Thus, $P(Z \leq 0.24) = 0.5948$ or 59.48 percent.

The following are some of the most frequently referenced values in the standard normal table:

- The 90th percentile point is 1.282: $P(Z \leq 1.282) = N(1.282) = 0.90$ or 90 percent, and 10 percent of values remain in the right tail.
- The 95th percentile point is 1.65: $P(Z \leq 1.65) = N(1.65) = 0.95$ or 95 percent, and 5 percent of values remain in the right tail. Note the difference between the use of a percentile point when dealing with one tail rather than two tails. Earlier, we used 1.65 standard deviations for the 90 percent confidence interval, where 5 percent of values lie outside that interval on each of the two sides. Here we use 1.65 because we are concerned with the 5 percent of values that lie only on one side, the right tail.
- The 99th percentile point is 2.327: $P(Z \leq 2.327) = N(2.327) = 0.99$ or 99 percent, and 1 percent of values remain in the right tail.

The tables that we give for the normal CDF include probabilities for $x \leq 0$. Many sources, however, give tables only for $x \geq 0$. How would one use such tables to find a normal probability? Because of the symmetry of the normal distribution, we can find all probabilities using tables of the CDF of the standard normal random variable, $P(Z \leq x) = N(x)$, for $x \geq 0$. The relations below are helpful for using tables for $x \geq 0$, as well as in other uses:

- For a non-negative number x, use $N(x)$ from the table. Note that for the probability to the right of x, we have $P(Z \geq x) = 1.0 - N(x)$.
- For a negative number $-x$, $N(-x) = 1.0 - N(x)$: Find $N(x)$ and subtract it from 1. All the area under the normal curve to the left of x is $N(x)$. The balance, $1.0 - N(x)$, is the area and probability to the right of x. By the symmetry of the normal distribution around its mean, the area and the probability to the right of x are equal to the area and the probability to the left of $-x$, $N(-x)$.
- For the probability to the right of $-x$, $P(Z \geq -x) = N(x)$.

EXAMPLE 8   Probabilities for a Common Stock Portfolio

Assume the portfolio mean return is 12 percent and the standard deviation of return estimate is 22 percent per year.

You want to calculate the following probabilities, assuming that a normal distribution describes returns. (You can use the excerpt from the table of normal probabilities to answer these questions.)

1. What is the probability that portfolio return will exceed 20 percent?
2. What is the probability that portfolio return will be between 12 percent and 20 percent? In other words, what is $P(12\% \leq \text{Portfolio return} \leq 20\%)$?
3. You can buy a one-year T-bill that yields 5.5 percent. This yield is effectively a one-year risk-free interest rate. What is the probability that your portfolio's return will be equal to or less than the risk-free rate?

If X is portfolio return, standardized portfolio return is $Z = (X - \bar{X})/s = (X - 12\%)/22\%$. We use this expression throughout the solutions.

Solution to 1: For $X = 20\%$, $Z = (20\% - 12\%)/22\% = 0.363636$. You want to find P $(Z > 0.363636)$. First note that $P(Z > x) = P(Z \geq x)$ because the normal is a continuous distribution. Recall that $P(Z \geq x) = 1.0 - P(Z \leq x)$ or $1 - N(x)$. Rounding 0.363636 to 0.36, according to the table, $N(0.36) = 0.6406$. Thus, $1 - 0.6406 = 0.3594$. The probability that portfolio return will exceed 20 percent is about 36 percent if your normality assumption is accurate.

Solution to 2: $P(12\% \leq \text{Portfolio return} \leq 20\%) = N(Z \text{ corresponding to } 20\%) - N(Z$ corresponding to 12%). For the first term, $Z = (20\% - 12\%)/22\% = 0.36$ approximately, and $N(0.36) = 0.6406$ (as in Solution 1). To get the second term immediately, note that 12 percent is the mean, and for the normal distribution 50 percent of the probability lies on either side of the mean. Therefore, $N(Z \text{ corresponding to } 12\%)$ must equal 50 percent. So $P(12\% \leq \text{Portfolio return} \leq 20\%) = 0.6406 - 0.50 = 0.1406$ or approximately 14 percent.

Solution to 3: If X is portfolio return, then we want to find $P(\text{Portfolio return} \leq 5.5\%)$. This question is more challenging than Parts 1 or 2, but when you have studied the solution below you will have a useful pattern for calculating other shortfall probabilities.

There are three steps, which involve standardizing the portfolio return: First, subtract the portfolio mean return from each side of the inequality: $P(\text{Portfolio return} - 12\% \leq 5.5\% - 12\%)$. Second, divide each side of the inequality by the standard deviation of portfolio return: $P[(\text{Portfolio return} - 12\%)/22\% \leq (5.5\% - 12\%)/22\%] = P(Z \leq -0.295455) = N(-0.295455)$. Third, recognize that on the left-hand side we have a standard normal variable, denoted by Z. As we pointed out above, $N(-x) = 1 - N(x)$. Rounding -0.29545 to -0.30 for use with the excerpted table, we have $N(-0.30) = 1 - N$ $(0.30) = 1 - 0.6179 = 0.3821$, roughly 38 percent. The probability that your portfolio will underperform the one-year risk-free rate is about 38 percent.

We can get the answer above quickly by subtracting the mean portfolio return from 5.5 percent, dividing by the standard deviation of portfolio return, and evaluating the result (-0.295455) with the standard normal CDF.

3.3. Applications of the Normal Distribution

Modern portfolio theory (MPT) makes wide use of the idea that the value of investment opportunities can be meaningfully measured in terms of mean return and variance of return. In economic theory, **mean–variance analysis** holds exactly when investors are risk averse; when they choose investments so as to maximize expected utility, or satisfaction; and when either 1) returns are normally distributed, or 2) investors have quadratic utility functions.[21] Mean–variance analysis can still be useful, however—that is, it can hold approximately— when either assumption 1 or 2 is violated. Because practitioners prefer to work with observables such as returns, the proposition that returns are at least approximately normally distributed has played a key role in much of MPT.

Mean–variance analysis generally considers risk symmetrically in the sense that standard deviation captures variability both above and below the mean. An alternative approach evaluates only downside risk. We discuss one such approach, safety-first rules, as it provides an excellent illustration of the application of normal distribution theory to practical investment problems. **Safety-first rules** focus on **shortfall risk**, the risk that portfolio value will fall below some minimum acceptable level over some time horizon. The risk that the assets in a defined benefit plan will fall below plan liabilities is an example of a shortfall risk.

Suppose an investor views any return below a level of R_L as unacceptable. Roy's safety-first criterion states that the optimal portfolio minimizes the probability that portfolio return, R_P, falls below the threshold level, R_L.[22] In symbols, the investor's objective is to choose a portfolio that minimizes $P(R_P < R_L)$. When portfolio returns are normally distributed, we can calculate $P(R_P < R_L)$ using the number of standard deviations that R_L lies below the expected portfolio return, $E(R_P)$. The portfolio for which $E(R_P) - R_L$ is largest relative to standard deviation minimizes $P(R_P < R_L)$. Therefore, if returns are normally distributed, the safety-first optimal portfolio *maximizes* the safety-first ratio (SFRatio):

$$\text{SFRatio} = [E(R_P) - R_L]/\sigma_P$$

The quantity $E(R_P) - R_L$ is the distance from the mean return to the shortfall level. Dividing this distance by σ_P gives the distance in units of standard deviation. There are two steps in choosing among portfolios using Roy's criterion (assuming normality):[23]

1. Calculate each portfolio's SFRatio.
2. Choose the portfolio with the highest SFRatio.

For a portfolio with a given safety-first ratio, the probability that its return will be less than R_L is $N(-\text{SFRatio})$, and the safety-first optimal portfolio has the lowest such probability. For example, suppose an investor's threshold return, R_L, is 2 percent. He is presented with two portfolios. Portfolio 1 has an expected return of 12 percent with a standard deviation of 15 percent. Portfolio 2 has an expected return of 14 percent with a standard deviation of 16 percent. The SFRatios are $0.667 = (12 - 2)/15$ and $0.75 = (14 - 2)/16$ for Portfolios 1

[21]Utility functions are mathematical representations of attitudes toward risk and return.
[22]A.D. Roy (1952) introduced this criterion.
[23]If there is an asset offering a risk-free return over the time horizon being considered, and if R_L is less than or equal to that risk-free rate, then it is optimal to be fully invested in the risk-free asset. Holding the risk-free asset in this case eliminates the chance that the threshold return is not met.

and 2, respectively. For the superior Portfolio 2, the probability that portfolio return will be less than 2 percent is $N(-0.75) = 1 - N(0.75) = 1 - 0.7734 = 0.227$ or about 23 percent, assuming that portfolio returns are normally distributed.

You may have noticed the similarity of SFRatio to the Sharpe ratio. If we substitute the risk-free rate, R_F, for the critical level R_L, the SFRatio becomes the Sharpe ratio. The safety-first approach provides a new perspective on the Sharpe ratio: When we evaluate portfolios using the Sharpe ratio, the portfolio with the highest Sharpe ratio is the one that minimizes the probability that portfolio return will be less than the risk-free rate (given a normality assumption).

EXAMPLE 9   The Safety-First Optimal Portfolio for a Client

You are researching asset allocations for a client in Canada with a C$800,000 portfolio. Although her investment objective is long-term growth, at the end of a year she may want to liquidate C$30,000 of the portfolio to fund educational expenses. If that need arises, she would like to be able to take out the C$30,000 without invading the initial capital of C$800,000. Table 6 shows three alternative allocations.

Address these questions (assume normality for Parts 2 and 3):

1. Given the client's desire not to invade the C$800,000 principal, what is the shortfall level, R_L? Use this shortfall level to answer Part 2.
2. According to the safety-first criterion, which of the three allocations is the best?
3. What is the probability that the return on the safety-first optimal portfolio will be less than the shortfall level?

Solution to 1: Because C$30,000/C$800,000 is 3.75 percent, for any return less than 3.75 percent the client will need to invade principal if she takes out C$30,000. So $R_L = 3.75$ percent.

Solution to 2: To decide which of the three allocations is safety-first optimal, select the alternative with the highest ratio $[E(R_P) - R_L]/\sigma_P$:

$$\text{Allocation A: } 0.787037 = (25 - 3.75)/27$$
$$\text{Allocation B: } 0.90625 = (11 - 3.75)/8$$
$$\text{Allocation C: } 0.5125 = (14 - 3.75)/20$$

Allocation B, with the largest ratio (0.90625), is the best alternative according to the safety-first criterion.

Solution to 3: To answer this question, note that $P(R_B < 3.75) = N(-0.90625)$. We can round 0.90625 to 0.91 for use with tables of the standard normal CDF. First, we

TABLE 6   Mean and Standard Deviation for Three Allocations (in Percent)

	A	B	C
Expected annual return	25	11	14
Standard deviation of return	27	8	20

calculate $N(-0.91) = 1 - N(0.91) = 1 - 0.8186 = 0.1814$ or about 18.1 percent. Using a spreadsheet function for the standard normal CDF on -0.90625 without rounding, we get 18.24 percent or about 18.2 percent. The safety-first optimal portfolio has a roughly 18 percent chance of not meeting a 3.75 percent return threshold.

Several points are worth noting. First, if the inputs were even slightly different, we could get a different ranking. For example, if the mean return on B were 10 rather than 11 percent, A would be superior to B. Second, if meeting the 3.75 percent return threshold were a necessity rather than a wish, C\$830,000 in one year could be modeled as a liability. Fixed income strategies such as cash flow matching could be used to offset or immunize the C\$830,000 quasi-liability.

Roy's safety-first rule was the earliest approach to addressing shortfall risk. The standard mean-variance portfolio selection process can also accommodate a shortfall risk constraint.[24]

In many investment contexts besides Roy's safety-first criterion, we use the normal distribution to estimate a probability. For example, Kolb, Gay, and Hunter (1985) developed an expression based on the standard normal distribution for the probability that a futures trader will exhaust his liquidity because of losses in a futures contract. Another arena in which the normal distribution plays an important role is financial risk management. Financial institutions such as investment banks, security dealers, and commercial banks have formal systems to measure and control financial risk at various levels, from trading positions to the overall risk for the firm.[25] Two mainstays in managing financial risk are Value at Risk (VaR) and stress testing/scenario analysis. **Stress testing/scenario analysis**, a complement to VaR, refers to a set of techniques for estimating losses in extremely unfavorable combinations of events or scenarios. **Value at Risk** (VaR) is a money measure of the minimum value of losses expected over a specified time period (for example, a day, a quarter, or a year) at a given level of probability (often 0.05 or 0.01). Suppose we specify a one-day time horizon and a level of probability of 0.05, which would be called a 95 percent one-day VaR.[26] If this VaR equaled €5 million for a portfolio, there would be a 0.05 probability that the portfolio would lose €5 million or more in a single day (assuming our assumptions were correct). One of the basic approaches to estimating VaR, the variance-covariance or analytical method, assumes that returns follow a normal distribution. For more information on VaR, see Chance and Brooks (2016).

3.4. The Lognormal Distribution

Closely related to the normal distribution, the lognormal distribution is widely used for modeling the probability distribution of share and other asset prices. For example, the lognormal appears in the Black–Scholes–Merton option pricing model.

---

[24]See Leibowitz and Henriksson (1989), for example.

[25]**Financial risk** is risk relating to asset prices and other financial variables. The contrast is to other, nonfinancial risks (for example, relating to operations and technology), which require different tools to manage.

[26]In 95 percent one-day VaR, the 95 percent refers to the confidence in the value of VaR and is equal to $1 - 0.05$; this is a traditional way to state VaR.

FIGURE 7   Two Lognormal Distributions

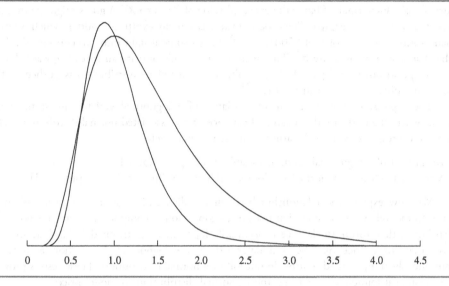

The Black–Scholes–Merton model assumes that the price of the asset underlying the option is lognormally distributed.

A random variable Y follows a lognormal distribution if its natural logarithm, ln Y, is normally distributed. The reverse is also true: If the natural logarithm of random variable Y, ln Y, is normally distributed, then Y follows a lognormal distribution. If you think of the term lognormal as "the log is normal," you will have no trouble remembering this relationship.

The two most noteworthy observations about the lognormal distribution are that it is bounded below by 0 and it is skewed to the right (it has a long right tail). Note these two properties in the graphs of the PDFs of two lognormal distributions in Figure 7. Asset prices are bounded from below by 0. In practice, the lognormal distribution has been found to be a usefully accurate description of the distribution of prices for many financial assets. On the other hand, the normal distribution is often a good approximation for returns. For this reason, both distributions are very important for finance professionals.

Like the normal distribution, the lognormal distribution is completely described by two parameters. Unlike the other distributions we have considered, a lognormal distribution is defined in terms of the parameters of a *different* distribution. The two parameters of a lognormal distribution are the mean and standard deviation (or variance) of its associated normal distribution: the mean and variance of ln Y, given that Y is lognormal. Remember, we must keep track of two sets of means and standard deviations (or variances): the mean and standard deviation (or variance) of the associated normal distribution (these are the parameters), and the mean and standard deviation (or variance) of the lognormal variable itself.

The expressions for the mean and variance of the lognormal variable itself are challenging. Suppose a normal random variable X has expected value μ and variance σ^2. Define $Y = \exp(X)$. Remember that the operation indicated by $\exp(X)$ or e^X is the opposite operation from taking logs.[27] Because ln $Y = \ln [\exp(X)] = X$ is normal (we assume X is normal), Y is lognormal. What is the expected value of $Y = \exp(X)$? A guess might be that the expected value of Y is $\exp(\mu)$. The expected value is actually $\exp(\mu + 0.50\sigma^2)$, which is larger than $\exp(\mu)$ by a factor of $\exp(0.50\sigma^2) > 1$.[28] To get some insight into this concept, think of what happens if we increase σ^2. The distribution spreads out; it can spread upward, but it cannot spread downward past 0. As a result, the center of its distribution is pushed to the right—the distribution's mean increases.[29]

The expressions for the mean and variance of a lognormal variable are summarized below, where μ and σ^2 are the mean and variance of the associated normal distribution (refer to these expressions as needed, rather than memorizing them):

- Mean (μ_L) of a lognormal random variable = $\exp(\mu + 0.50\sigma^2)$
- Variance (σ_L^2) of a lognormal random variable = $\exp(2\mu + \sigma^2) \times [\exp(\sigma^2) - 1]$

We now explore the relationship between the distribution of stock return and stock price. In the following we show that if a stock's continuously compounded return is normally distributed, then future stock price is necessarily lognormally distributed.[30] Furthermore, we show that stock price may be well described by the lognormal distribution even when continuously compounded returns do not follow a normal distribution. These results provide the theoretical foundation for using the lognormal distribution to model prices.

To outline the presentation that follows, we first show that the stock price at some future time T, S_T, equals the current stock price, S_0, multiplied by e raised to power $r_{0,T}$, the continuously compounded return from 0 to T; this relationship is expressed as $S_T = S_0\exp(r_{0,T})$. We then show that we can write $r_{0,T}$ as the sum of shorter-term continuously compounded returns and that if these shorter-period returns are normally distributed, then $r_{0,T}$ is normally distributed (given certain assumptions) or approximately normally distributed (not making those assumptions). As S_T is proportional to the log of a normal random variable, S_T is lognormal.

To supply a framework for our discussion, suppose we have a series of equally spaced observations on stock price: $S_0, S_1, S_2, ..., S_T$. Current stock price, S_0, is a known quantity and so is nonrandom. The future prices (such as S_1), however, are random variables. The **price relative**, S_1/S_0, is an ending price, S_1, over a beginning price, S_0; it is equal to 1 plus the holding period return on the stock from $t = 0$ to $t = 1$:

$$S_1/S_0 = 1 + R_{0,1}$$

For example, if $S_0 = \$30$ and $S_1 = \$34.50$, then $S_1/S_0 = \$34.50/\$30 = 1.15$. Therefore, $R_{0,1} = 0.15$ or 15 percent. In general, price relatives have the form

$$S_{t+1}/S_t = 1 + R_{t,t+1}$$

---

[27]The quantity $e \approx 2.7182818$.
[28]Note that $\exp(0.50\sigma^2) > 1$ because $\sigma^2 > 0$.
[29]Luenberger (1998) is the source of this explanation.
[30]Continuous compounding treats time as essentially continuous or unbroken, in contrast to discrete compounding, which treats time as advancing in discrete finite intervals. Continuously compounded returns are the model for returns in so-called **continuous time** finance models such as the Black–Scholes–Merton option pricing model. See the chapter on the time value of money (Chapter 1) for more information on compounding.

where $R_{t,t+1}$ is the rate of return from t to $t + 1$.

An important concept is the continuously compounded return associated with a holding period return such as $R_{0,1}$. The **continuously compounded return** associated with a holding period is the natural logarithm of 1 plus that holding period return, or equivalently, the natural logarithm of the ending price over the beginning price (the price relative).[31] For example, if we observe a one-week holding period return of 0.04, the equivalent continuously compounded return, called the one-week continuously compounded return, is $\ln(1.04) = 0.039221$; €1.00 invested for one week at 0.039221 continuously compounded gives €1.04, equivalent to a 4 percent one-week holding period return. The continuously compounded return from t to $t + 1$ is

$$r_{t,t+1} = \ln(S_{t+1}/S_t) = \ln(1 + R_{t,t+1}) \tag{5}$$

For our example, $r_{0,1} = \ln(S_1/S_0) = \ln(1 + R_{0,1}) = \ln(\$34.50/\$30) = \ln(1.15) = 0.139762$. Thus, 13.98 percent is the continuously compounded return from $t = 0$ to $t = 1$. The continuously compounded return is smaller than the associated holding period return. If our investment horizon extends from $t = 0$ to $t = T$, then the continuously compounded return to T is

$$r_{0,T} = \ln(S_T/S_0)$$

Applying the function exp to both sides of the equation, we have $\exp(r_{0,T}) = \exp[\ln(S_T/S_0)] = S_T/S_0$, so

$$S_T = S_0\exp(r_{0,T})$$

We can also express S_T/S_0 as the product of price relatives:

$$S_T/S_0 = (S_T/S_{T-1})(S_{T-1}/S_{T-2})...(S_1/S_0)$$

Taking logs of both sides of this equation, we find that continuously compounded return to time T is the sum of the one-period continuously compounded returns:

$$r_{0,T} = r_{T-1,T} + r_{T-2,T-1} + ...r_{0,1} \tag{6}$$

Using holding period returns to find the ending value of a $1 investment involves the multiplication of quantities (1 + holding period return). Using continuously compounded returns involves addition.

A key assumption in many investment applications is that returns are **independently and identically distributed (IID)**. Independence captures the proposition that investors cannot predict future returns using past returns (i.e., weak-form market efficiency). Identical distribution captures the assumption of stationarity.[32]

Assume that the one-period continuously compounded returns (such as $r_{0,1}$) are IID random variables with mean μ and variance σ^2 (but making no normality or other distributional assumption). Then

---

[31]In this chapter we use lowercase r to refer specifically to continuously compounded returns.
[32]Stationarity implies that the mean and variance of return do not change from period to period.

$$E(r_{0,T}) = E(r_{T-1,T}) + E(r_{T-2,T-1}) + \ldots + E(r_{0,1}) = \mu T \qquad (7)$$

(we add up μ for a total of T times) and

$$\sigma^2(r_{0,T}) = \sigma^2 T \qquad (8)$$

(as a consequence of the independence assumption). The variance of the T holding period continuously compounded return is T multiplied by the variance of the one-period continuously compounded return; also, $\sigma(r_{0,T}) = \sigma\sqrt{T}$. If the one-period continuously compounded returns on the right-hand side of Equation 6 are normally distributed, then the T holding period continuously compounded return, $r_{0,T}$, is also normally distributed with mean μT and variance $\sigma^2 T$. This relationship is so because a linear combination of normal random variables is also normal. But even if the one-period continuously compounded returns are not normal, their sum, $r_{0,T}$, is approximately normal according to a result in statistics known as the central limit theorem.[33] Now compare $S_T = S_0\exp(r_{0,T})$ to $Y = \exp(X)$, where X is normal and Y is lognormal (as we discussed above). Clearly, we can model future stock price S_T as a lognormal random variable because $r_{0,T}$ should be at least approximately normal. This assumption of normally distributed returns is the basis in theory for the lognormal distribution as a model for the distribution of prices of shares and other assets.

Continuously compounded returns play a role in many option pricing models, as mentioned earlier. An estimate of volatility is crucial for using option pricing models such as the Black–Scholes–Merton model. **Volatility** measures the standard deviation of the continuously compounded returns on the underlying asset.[34] In practice, we very often estimate volatility using a historical series of continuously compounded daily returns. We gather a set of daily holding period returns and then use Equation 5 to convert them into continuously compounded daily returns. We then compute the standard deviation of the continuously compounded daily returns and annualize that number using Equation 8.[35] (By convention, volatility is stated as an annualized measure.)[36] Example 10 illustrates the estimation of volatility for the shares of Astra International.

---

[33]We mentioned the central limit theorem earlier in our discussion of the normal distribution. To give a somewhat fuller statement of it, according to the central limit theorem the sum (as well as the mean) of a set of independent, identically distributed random variables with finite variances is normally distributed, whatever distribution the random variables follow. We discuss the central limit theorem in the chapter on sampling (Chapter 5).

[34]Volatility is also called the instantaneous standard deviation, and as such is denoted σ. The underlying asset, or simply the underlying, is the asset underlying the option. For more information on these concepts, see Chance and Brooks (2016).

[35]To compute the standard deviation of a set or sample of n returns, we sum the squared deviation of each return from the mean return and then divide that sum by $n - 1$. The result is the sample variance. Taking the square root of the sample variance gives the sample standard deviation. To review the calculation of standard deviation, see the chapter "Organizing, Visualizing, and Describing Data," on statistical concepts and market returns.

[36]Annualizing is often done on the basis of 250 days in a year, the approximate number of days markets are open for trading. The 250-day number may lead to a better estimate of volatility than the 365-day number. Thus if daily volatility were 0.01, we would state volatility (on an annual basis) as $0.01\sqrt{250} = 0.1581$.

EXAMPLE 10   Volatility as Used in Option Pricing Models

Suppose you are researching Astra International (Indonesia Stock Exchange: ASII) and are interested in Astra's price action in a week in which international economic news had significantly affected the Indonesian stock market. You decide to use volatility as a measure of the variability of Astra shares during that week. Table 7 shows closing prices during that week.

Use the data in Table 7 to do the following:

1. Estimate the volatility of Astra shares. (Annualize volatility based on 250 days in a year.)
2. Identify the probability distribution for Astra share prices if continuously compounded daily returns follow the normal distribution.

Solution to 1: First, use Equation 5 to calculate the continuously compounded daily returns; then find their standard deviation in the usual way. (In the calculation of sample variance to get sample standard deviation, use a divisor of 1 less than the sample size.)

$\ln(7,000/6,950) = 0.007168$
$\ln(6,850/7,000) = -0.021661$
$\ln(6,600/6,850) = -0.037179$
$\ln(6,350/6,600) = -0.038615$

 Sum $= -0.090287$
 Mean $= -0.022572$
 Variance $= 0.000452$
 Standard Deviation $= 0.021261$

The standard deviation of continuously compounded daily returns is 0.021261. Equation 8 states that $\hat{\sigma}(r_{0,T}) = \hat{\sigma}\sqrt{T}$. In this example, $\hat{\sigma}$ is the sample standard deviation of one-period continuously compounded returns. Thus, $\hat{\sigma}$ refers to 0.021261. We want to annualize, so the horizon T corresponds to one year. As $\hat{\sigma}$ is in days, we set T equal to the number of trading days in a year (250).

We find that annualized volatility for Astra stock that week was 33.6 percent, calculated as $0.021261\sqrt{250} = 0.336165$.

Note that the sample mean, −0.022572, is a possible estimate of the mean, μ, of the continuously compounded one-period or daily returns. The sample mean can be

TABLE 7   Astra International Daily Closing Prices

Day	Closing Price (IDR)
Monday	6,950
Tuesday	7,000
Wednesday	6,850
Thursday	6,600
Friday	6,350

translated into an estimate of the expected continuously compounded annual return using Equation 7: $\hat{\mu}T = -0.022572(250)$ (using 250 to be consistent with the calculation of volatility). But four observations are far too few to estimate expected returns. The variability in the daily returns overwhelms any information about expected return in a series this short.

Solution to 2: Astra share prices should follow the lognormal distribution if the continuously compounded daily returns on Astra shares follow the normal distribution.

We have shown that the distribution of stock price is lognormal, given certain assumptions. What are the mean and variance of S_T if S_T follows the lognormal distribution? Earlier in this section, we gave bullet-point expressions for the mean and variance of a lognormal random variable. In the bullet-point expressions, the $\hat{\mu}$ and $\hat{\sigma}^2$ would refer, in the context of this discussion, to the mean and variance of the T horizon (not the one-period) continuously compounded returns (assumed to follow a normal distribution), compatible with the horizon of S_T.[37] Related to the use of mean and variance (or standard deviation), earlier in this chapter we used those quantities to construct intervals in which we expect to find a certain percentage of the observations of a normally distributed random variable. Those intervals were symmetric about the mean. Can we state similar, symmetric intervals for a lognormal random variable? Unfortunately, we cannot. Because the lognormal distribution is not symmetric, such intervals are more complicated than for the normal distribution, and we will not discuss this specialist topic here.[38]

Finally, we have presented the relation between the mean and variance of continuously compounded returns associated with different time horizons (see Equations 7 and 8), but how are the means and variances of holding period returns and continuously compounded returns related? As analysts, we typically think in terms of holding period returns rather than continuously compounded returns, and we may desire to convert means and standard deviations of holding period returns to means and standard deviations of continuously compounded returns for an option application, for example. To effect such conversions (and those in the other direction, from a continuous compounding to a holding period basis), we can use the expressions in Ferguson (1993).

4. INTRODUCTION TO MONTE CARLO SIMULATION

With an understanding of probability distributions, we are now prepared to learn about a computer-based technique in which probability distributions play an integral role. The technique is called Monte Carlo simulation. **Monte Carlo simulation** in finance involves the use of computer software to represent the operation of a complex financial system. A characteristic feature of Monte Carlo simulation is the generation of a large number of random samples from a specified probability distribution or distributions to represent the role of risk in the system.

Monte Carlo simulation has several quite distinct uses. One use is in planning, where Monte Carlo simulation allows us to experiment with a proposed policy before actually

---

[37]The expression for the mean is $E(S_T) = S_0 \exp[E(r_{0,T}) + 0.5\sigma^2(r_{0,T})]$, for example.

[38]See **Hull (2017)** for a discussion of lognormal confidence intervals.

implementing it. For example, investment performance can be evaluated with reference to a benchmark or a liability. Defined benefit pension plans often invest assets with reference to plan liabilities. Pension liabilities are a complex random process. In a Monte Carlo asset-liability financial planning study, the functioning of pension assets and liabilities is simulated over time, given assumptions about how assets are invested, the work force, and other variables. A key specification in this and all Monte Carlo simulations is the probability distributions of the various sources of risk (including interest rates and security market returns, in this case). The implications of different investment policy decisions on the plan's funded status can be assessed through simulated time. The experiment can be repeated for another set of assumptions.

Monte Carlo simulation is also widely used to develop estimates of VaR. In this application, we simulate the portfolio's profit and loss performance for a specified time horizon. Repeated trials within the simulation (each trial involving a draw of random observations from a probability distribution) produce a frequency distribution for changes in portfolio value. The point that defines the cutoff for the least favorable 5 percent of simulated changes is an estimate of 95 percent VaR, for example.

In an extremely important use, Monte Carlo simulation is a tool for valuing complex securities, particularly some **European-style options**, options that are exercisable only at maturity, for which no analytic pricing formula is available. For other securities, such as mortgage-backed securities with complex embedded options, Monte Carlo simulation is also an important modeling resource.

Researchers use Monte Carlo simulation to test their models and tools. How critical is a particular assumption to the performance of a model? Because we control the assumptions when we do a simulation, we can run the model through a Monte Carlo simulation to examine a model's sensitivity to a change in our assumptions.

To understand the technique of Monte Carlo simulation, let us present the process as a series of steps—these can be viewed as providing an overview rather than a detailed recipe for implementing a Monte Carlo simulation in its many varied applications. To illustrate the steps, we take the case of using Monte Carlo simulation to value a type of option for which no analytic pricing formula is available, an Asian call option on a stock. An **Asian call option** is a European-style option with a value at maturity equal to the difference between the stock price at maturity and the average stock price during the life of the option, or $0, whichever is greater. For instance, if the final stock price is $34 with an average value of $31 over the life of the option, the value of the option at maturity is $3 (the greater of $34 − $31 = $3 and $0). Steps 1 through 3 of the process describe specifying the simulation; Steps 4 through 7 describe running the simulation.

1. Specify the quantities of interest in terms of underlying variables. Here the quantity of interest is the option value, and the underlying variable is the stock price. Then, specify the starting value(s) of the underlying variable(s).
   To illustrate the steps, we are using the case of valuing an Asian call option on stock. We use C_{iT} to represent the value of the option at maturity T. The subscript i in C_{iT} indicates that C_{iT} is a value resulting from the ith **simulation trial**, each simulation trial involving a drawing of random values (an iteration of Step 4).
2. Specify a time grid. Take the horizon in terms of calendar time and split it into a number of subperiods, say K in total. Calendar time divided by the number of subperiods, K, is the time increment, Δt.

3. Specify distributional assumptions for the risk factors that drive the underlying variables. For example, stock price is the underlying variable for the Asian call, so we need a model for stock price movement. Say we choose the following model for changes in stock price, where Z_k stands for the standard normal random variable:

$$\Delta(\text{Stock price}) = (\mu \times \text{Prior stock price} \times \Delta t) + (\sigma \times \text{Prior stock price} \times Z_k)$$

The term, Z_k is a risk factor in the simulation. Through our choice of μ and σ, we control the distribution of stock price. Although this example has one risk factor, a given simulation may have multiple risk factors.

4. Using a computer program or spreadsheet function, draw K random values of each risk factor. In our example, the spreadsheet function would produce a draw of K values of the standard normal variable Z_k: $Z_1, Z_2, Z_3, \dots, Z_K$.

5. Calculate the underlying variables using the random observations generated in Step 4. Using the above model of stock price dynamics, the result is K observations on changes in stock price. An additional calculation is needed to convert those changes into K stock prices (using initial stock price, which is given). Another calculation produces the average stock price during the life of the option (the sum of K stock prices divided by K).

6. Compute the quantities of interest. In our example, the first calculation is the value of an Asian call at maturity, C_{iT}. A second calculation discounts this terminal value back to the present to get the call value as of today, C_{i0}. We have completed one simulation trial. (The subscript i in C_{i0} stands for the ith simulation trial, as it does in C_{iT}.) In a Monte Carlo simulation, a running tabulation is kept of statistics relating to the distribution of the quantities of interest, including their mean value and standard deviation, over the simulation trials to that point.

7. Iteratively go back to Step 4 until a specified number of trials, I, is completed. Finally, produce statistics for the simulation. The key value for our example is the mean value of C_{i0} for the total number of simulation trials. This mean value is the Monte Carlo estimate of the value of the Asian call.

In Step 4 of our example, a computer function produced a set of random observations on a standard normal random variable. Recall that for a uniform distribution, all possible numbers are equally likely. The term **random number generator** refers to an algorithm that produces uniformly distributed random numbers between 0 and 1. In the context of computer simulations, the term **random number** refers to an observation drawn from a uniform distribution. For other distributions, the term "random observation" is used in this context.

It is a remarkable fact that random observations from any distribution can be produced using the uniform random variable with endpoints 0 and 1. To see why this is so, consider the inverse transformation method of producing random observations. Suppose we are interested in obtaining random observations for a random variable, X, with cumulative distribution function $F(x)$. Recall that $F(x)$ evaluated at x is a number between 0 and 1. Suppose a random outcome of this random variable is 3.21 and that $F(3.21) = 0.25$ or 25 percent. Define an inverse of F, call it F^{-1}, that can do the following: Substitute the probability 0.25 into F^{-1} and it returns the random outcome 3.21. In other words, $F^{-1}(0.25) = 3.21$. To generate random observations on X, the steps are 1) generate a uniform random number, r, between 0 and 1 using the random number generator and 2) evaluate $F^{-1}(r)$ to obtain a random observation on X. Random observation generation is a field of study in itself, and we have briefly discussed the inverse transformation method here just to illustrate a point. As a generalist you do not need to address the technical details of converting random numbers into random observations, but you do need to know that random observations from any distribution can be generated using a uniform random variable.

In Examples 11 and 12, we give an application of Monte Carlo simulation to a question of great interest to investment practice: the potential gains from market timing.

EXAMPLE 11   Valuing a Lookback Option Using Monte Carlo Simulation

A standard lookback call option on stock has a value at maturity equal to (Value of the stock at maturity – Minimum value of stock during the life of the option prior to maturity) or $0, whichever is greater. If the minimum value reached prior to maturity was $20.11 and the value of the stock at maturity is $23, for example, the call is worth $23 – $20.11 = $2.89.

Briefly discuss how you might use Monte Carlo simulation in valuing a lookback call option.

Solution: In the text, we described how we could use Monte Carlo simulation to value an Asian option, a complex European-style option. Just as we can calculate the average value of the stock over a simulation trial to value an Asian option, we can also calculate the minimum value of the stock over a simulation trial. Then, for a given simulation trial, we can calculate the terminal value of the call, given the minimum value of the stock for the simulation trial. We can then discount back this terminal value to the present to get the value of the call today ($t = 0$). The average of these $t = 0$ values over all simulation trials is the Monte Carlo simulated value of the lookback call option.

Monte Carlo simulation is a complement to analytical methods. It provides only statistical estimates, not exact results. Analytical methods, where available, provide more insight into cause-and-effect relationships. For example, the Black–Scholes–Merton option pricing model for the value of a European call option is an analytical method, expressed as a formula. It is a much more efficient method for valuing such a call than is Monte Carlo simulation. As an analytical expression, the Black–Scholes–Merton model permits the analyst to quickly gauge the sensitivity of call value to changes in current stock price and the other variables that determine call value. In contrast, Monte Carlo simulations do not directly provide such precise insights. However, only some types of options can be priced with analytical expressions. As financial product innovations proceed, the field of applications for Monte Carlo simulation continues to grow.

5. SUMMARY

In this chapter, we have presented the most frequently used probability distributions in investment analysis and the Monte Carlo simulation.

- A probability distribution specifies the probabilities of the possible outcomes of a random variable.
- The two basic types of random variables are discrete random variables and continuous random variables. Discrete random variables take on at most a countable number of possible

outcomes that we can list as $x_1, x_2, \ldots$ In contrast, we cannot describe the possible outcomes of a continuous random variable Z with a list $z_1, z_2, \ldots$ because the outcome $(z_1 + z_2)/2$, not in the list, would always be possible.

- The probability function specifies the probability that the random variable will take on a specific value. The probability function is denoted $p(x)$ for a discrete random variable and $f(x)$ for a continuous random variable. For any probability function $p(x)$, $0 \le p(x) \le 1$, and the sum of $p(x)$ over all values of X equals 1.
- The cumulative distribution function, denoted $F(x)$ for both continuous and discrete random variables, gives the probability that the random variable is less than or equal to x.
- The discrete uniform and the continuous uniform distributions are the distributions of equally likely outcomes.
- The binomial random variable is defined as the number of successes in n Bernoulli trials, where the probability of success, p, is constant for all trials and the trials are independent. A Bernoulli trial is an experiment with two outcomes, which can represent success or failure, an up move or a down move, or another binary (two-fold) outcome.
- A binomial random variable has an expected value or mean equal to np and variance equal to $np(1-p)$.
- A binomial tree is the graphical representation of a model of asset price dynamics in which, at each period, the asset moves up with probability p or down with probability $(1-p)$. The binomial tree is a flexible method for modeling asset price movement and is widely used in pricing options.
- The normal distribution is a continuous symmetric probability distribution that is completely described by two parameters: its mean, μ, and its variance, σ^2.
- A univariate distribution specifies the probabilities for a single random variable. A multivariate distribution specifies the probabilities for a group of related random variables.
- To specify the normal distribution for a portfolio when its component securities are normally distributed, we need the means, standard deviations, and all the distinct pairwise correlations of the securities. When we have those statistics, we have also specified a multivariate normal distribution for the securities.
- For a normal random variable, approximately 68 percent of all possible outcomes are within a one standard deviation interval about the mean, approximately 95 percent are within a two standard deviation interval about the mean, and approximately 99 percent are within a three standard deviation interval about the mean.
- A normal random variable, X, is standardized using the expression $Z = (X - \mu)/\sigma$, where μ and σ are the mean and standard deviation of X. Generally, we use the sample mean $\bar{X}$ as an estimate of μ and the sample standard deviation s as an estimate of σ in this expression.
- The standard normal random variable, denoted Z, has a mean equal to 0 and variance equal to 1. All questions about any normal random variable can be answered by referring to the cumulative distribution function of a standard normal random variable, denoted $N(x)$ or $N(z)$.
- Shortfall risk is the risk that portfolio value will fall below some minimum acceptable level over some time horizon.
- Roy's safety-first criterion, addressing shortfall risk, asserts that the optimal portfolio is the one that minimizes the probability that portfolio return falls below a threshold level. According to Roy's safety-first criterion, if returns are normally distributed, the safety-first optimal portfolio P is the one that maximizes the quantity $[E(R_P) - R_L]/\sigma_P$, where R_L is the minimum acceptable level of return.

- A random variable follows a lognormal distribution if the natural logarithm of the random variable is normally distributed. The lognormal distribution is defined in terms of the mean and variance of its associated normal distribution. The lognormal distribution is bounded below by 0 and skewed to the right (it has a long right tail).
- The lognormal distribution is frequently used to model the probability distribution of asset prices because it is bounded below by zero.
- Continuous compounding views time as essentially continuous or unbroken; discrete compounding views time as advancing in discrete finite intervals.
- The continuously compounded return associated with a holding period is the natural log of 1 plus the holding period return, or equivalently, the natural log of ending price over beginning price.
- If continuously compounded returns are normally distributed, asset prices are lognormally distributed. This relationship is used to move back and forth between the distributions for return and price. Because of the central limit theorem, continuously compounded returns need not be normally distributed for asset prices to be reasonably well described by a lognormal distribution.
- Monte Carlo simulation involves the use of a computer to represent the operation of a complex financial system. A characteristic feature of Monte Carlo simulation is the generation of a large number of random samples from specified probability distribution(s) to represent the operation of risk in the system. Monte Carlo simulation is used in planning, in financial risk management, and in valuing complex securities. Monte Carlo simulation is a complement to analytical methods but provides only statistical estimates, not exact results.

REFERENCES

Campbell, John, Andrew Lo, and A. Craig MacKinlay. 1997. *The Econometrics of Financial Markets.* Princeton, NJ: Princeton University Press.

Chance, Don M. and Robert Brooks. 2016. *An Introduction to Derivatives and Risk Management,* 10th ed. Mason, OH: South-Western.

Cox, Jonathan, Stephen Ross, and Mark Rubinstein. 1979. "Options Pricing: A Simplified Approach." *Journal of Financial Economics,* vol. 7:229–263. 10.1016/0304-405X(79)90015-1

Fama, Eugene. 1976. *Foundations of Finance.* New York: Basic Books.

Ferguson, Robert. 1993. "Some Formulas for Evaluating Two Popular Option Strategies." *Financial Analysts Journal,* vol. 49, no. 5:71–76. 10.2469/faj.v49.n5.71

Hillier, Frederick S. 2014. *Introduction to Operations Research,* 10th edition. New York: McGraw-Hill.

Hull, John. 2017. *Options, Futures, and Other Derivatives,* 10th edition. Upper Saddle River, NJ: Pearson.

Kolb, Robert W., Gerald D. Gay, and William C. Hunter. 1985. "Liquidity Requirements for Financial Futures Investments." *Financial Analysts Journal,* vol. 41, no. 3:60–68. 10.2469/faj.v41.n3.60

Kon, Stanley J. 1984. "Models of Stock Returns—A Comparison." *Journal of Finance,* vol. 39:147–165.

Leibowitz, Martin and Roy Henriksson. 1989. "Portfolio Optimization with Shortfall Constraints: A Confidence-Limit Approach to Managing Downside Risk." *Financial Analysts Journal,* vol. 45, no. 2:34–41. 10.2469/faj.v45.n2.34

Luenberger, David G. 1998. *Investment Science.* New York: Oxford University Press.

Roy, A.D. 1952. "Safety-First and the Holding of Assets." *Econometrica,* vol. 20:431–439. 10.2307/1907413

PRACTICE PROBLEMS

1. A European put option on stock conveys the right to sell the stock at a prespecified price, called the exercise price, at the maturity date of the option. The value of this put at maturity is (exercise price − stock price) or $0, whichever is greater. Suppose the exercise price is $100 and the underlying stock trades in ticks of $0.01. At any time before maturity, the terminal value of the put is a random variable.
   A. Describe the distinct possible outcomes for terminal put value. (Think of the put's maximum and minimum values and its minimum price increments.)
   B. Is terminal put value, at a time before maturity, a discrete or continuous random variable?
   C. Letting Y stand for terminal put value, express in standard notation the probability that terminal put value is less than or equal to $24. No calculations or formulas are necessary.

2. Define the term "binomial random variable." Describe the types of problems for which the binomial distribution is used.

3. The value of the cumulative distribution function $F(x)$, where x is a particular outcome, for a discrete uniform distribution:
   A. sums to 1.
   B. lies between 0 and 1.
   C. decreases as x increases.

4. For a binomial random variable with five trials, and a probability of success on each trial of 0.50, the distribution will be:
   A. skewed.
   B. uniform.
   C. symmetric.

5. In a discrete uniform distribution with 20 potential outcomes of integers 1 to 20, the probability that X is greater than or equal to 3 but less than 6, $P(3 \le X < 6)$, is:
   A. 0.10.
   B. 0.15.
   C. 0.20.

6. Over the last 10 years, a company's annual earnings increased year over year seven times and decreased year over year three times. You decide to model the number of earnings increases for the next decade as a binomial random variable.
   A. What is your estimate of the probability of success, defined as an increase in annual earnings?
   For Parts B, C, and D of this problem, assume the estimated probability is the actual probability for the next decade.
   B. What is the probability that earnings will increase in exactly 5 of the next 10 years?
   C. Calculate the expected number of yearly earnings increases during the next 10 years.
   D. Calculate the variance and standard deviation of the number of yearly earnings increases during the next 10 years.

E.   The expression for the probability function of a binomial random variable depends on two major assumptions. In the context of this problem, what must you assume about annual earnings increases to apply the binomial distribution in Part B? What reservations might you have about the validity of these assumptions?

7.   A portfolio manager annually outperforms her benchmark 60 percent of the time. Assuming independent annual trials, what is the probability that she will outperform her benchmark four or more times over the next five years?
   A.   0.26
   B.   0.34
   C.   0.48

8.   You are examining the record of an investment newsletter writer who claims a 70 percent success rate in making investment recommendations that are profitable over a one-year time horizon. You have the one-year record of the newsletter's seven most recent recommendations. Four of those recommendations were profitable. If all the recommendations are independent and the newsletter writer's skill is as claimed, what is the probability of observing four or fewer profitable recommendations out of seven in total?

9.   You are forecasting sales for a company in the fourth quarter of its fiscal year. Your low-end estimate of sales is €14 million, and your high-end estimate is €15 million. You decide to treat all outcomes for sales between these two values as equally likely, using a continuous uniform distribution.
   A.   What is the expected value of sales for the fourth quarter?
   B.   What is the probability that fourth-quarter sales will be less than or equal to €14,125,000?

10. State the approximate probability that a normal random variable will fall within the following intervals:
   A.   Mean plus or minus one standard deviation.
   B.   Mean plus or minus two standard deviations.
   C.   Mean plus or minus three standard deviations.

11. Find the area under the normal curve up to $z = 0.36$; that is, find $P(Z \leq 0.36)$. Interpret this value.

12. If the probability that a portfolio outperforms its benchmark in any quarter is 0.75, the probability that the portfolio outperforms its benchmark in three or fewer quarters over the course of a year is *closest* to:
   A.   0.26
   B.   0.42
   C.   0.68

13. In futures markets, profits or losses on contracts are settled at the end of each trading day. This procedure is called marking to market or daily resettlement. By preventing a trader's losses from accumulating over many days, marking to market reduces the risk that traders will default on their obligations. A futures markets trader needs a liquidity pool to meet the daily mark to market. If liquidity is exhausted, the trader may be forced to unwind his position at an unfavorable time.
   Suppose you are using financial futures contracts to hedge a risk in your portfolio. You have a liquidity pool (cash and cash equivalents) of λ dollars per contract and a time

horizon of T trading days. For a given size liquidity pool, λ, Kolb, Gay, and Hunter (1985) developed an expression for the probability stating that you will exhaust your liquidity pool within a T-day horizon as a result of the daily mark to market. Kolb et al. assumed that the expected change in futures price is 0 and that futures price changes are normally distributed. With σ representing the standard deviation of daily futures price changes, the standard deviation of price changes over a time horizon to day T is $\sigma\sqrt{T}$, given continuous compounding. With that background, the Kolb et al. expression is

$$\text{Probability of exhausting liquidity pool} = 2[1 - N(x)]$$

where $x = \lambda/(\sigma\sqrt{T})$. Here x is a standardized value of λ. $N(x)$ is the standard normal cumulative distribution function. For some intuition about $1 - N(x)$ in the expression, note that the liquidity pool is exhausted if losses exceed the size of the liquidity pool at any time up to and including T; the probability of that event happening can be shown to be proportional to an area in the right tail of a standard normal distribution, $1 - N(x)$. Using the Kolb et al. expression, answer the following questions:

A. Your hedging horizon is five days, and your liquidity pool is \$2,000 per contract. You estimate that the standard deviation of daily price changes for the contract is \$450. What is the probability that you will exhaust your liquidity pool in the five-day period?

B. Suppose your hedging horizon is 20 days, but all the other facts given in Part A remain the same. What is the probability that you will exhaust your liquidity pool in the 20-day period?

14. Which of the following is characteristic of the normal distribution?
    A. Asymmetry
    B. Kurtosis of 3
    C. Definitive limits or boundaries

15. Which of the following assets *most likely* requires the use of a multivariate distribution for modeling returns?
    A. A call option on a bond
    B. A portfolio of technology stocks
    C. A stock in a market index

16. The total number of parameters that fully characterizes a multivariate normal distribution for the returns on two stocks is:
    A. 3.
    B. 4.
    C. 5.

17. A client has a portfolio of common stocks and fixed-income instruments with a current value of £1,350,000. She intends to liquidate £50,000 from the portfolio at the end of the year to purchase a partnership share in a business. Furthermore, the client would like to be able to withdraw the £50,000 without reducing the initial capital of £1,350,000. The following table shows four alternative asset allocations.

Mean and Standard Deviation for Four Allocations (in Percent)

	A	B	C	D
Expected annual return	16	12	10	9
Standard deviation of return	24	17	12	11

Address the following questions (assume normality for Parts B and C):

A. Given the client's desire not to invade the £1,350,000 principal, what is the shortfall level, R_L? Use this shortfall level to answer Part B.

B. According to the safety-first criterion, which of the allocations is the best?

C. What is the probability that the return on the safety-first optimal portfolio will be less than the shortfall level, R_L?

Please refer to Exhibit 1 for Questions 18 and 19.

EXHIBIT 1.   Z-Table Values, $P(Z \leq z) = N(z)$ for $z \geq 0$

Z	0.00	0.01	0.02	0.03	0.04	0.05	0.06	0.07	0.08	0.09
0.00	0.5000	0.5040	0.5080	0.5120	0.5160	0.5199	0.5239	0.5279	0.5319	0.5359
0.1	0.5398	0.5438	0.5478	0.5517	0.5557	0.5596	0.5636	0.5675	0.5714	0.5753
0.2	0.5793	0.5832	0.5871	0.5910	0.5948	0.5987	0.6026	0.6064	0.6103	0.6141
0.3	0.6179	0.6217	0.6255	0.6293	0.6331	0.6368	0.6406	0.6443	0.6480	0.6517
0.4	0.6554	0.6591	0.6628	0.6664	0.6700	0.6736	0.6772	0.6808	0.6844	0.6879
0.5	0.6915	0.6950	0.6985	0.7019	0.7054	0.7088	0.7123	0.7157	0.7190	0.7224

18. A portfolio has an expected mean return of 8 percent and standard deviation of 14 percent. The probability that its return falls between 8 and 11 percent is *closest* to:

A. 8.3%

B. 14.8%.

C. 58.3%.

19. A portfolio has an expected return of 7% with a standard deviation of 13%. For an investor with a minimum annual return target of 4%, the probability that the portfolio return will fail to meet the target is *closest* to:

A. 33%.

B. 41%.

C. 59%.

20.

A. Define Monte Carlo simulation and explain its use in finance.

B. Compared with analytical methods, what are the strengths and weaknesses of Monte Carlo simulation for use in valuing securities?

21. Which of the following is a continuous random variable?

A. The value of a futures contract quoted in increments of $0.05

B. The total number of heads recorded in 1 million tosses of a coin

C. The rate of return on a diversified portfolio of stocks over a three-month period

22. X is a discrete random variable with possible outcomes $X = \{1,2,3,4\}$. Three functions $f(x)$, $g(x)$, and $h(x)$ are proposed to describe the probabilities of the outcomes in X.

	Probability Function		
$X = x$	$f(x) = P(X = x)$	$g(x) = P(X = x)$	$h(x) = P(X = x)$
1	−0.25	0.20	0.20
2	0.25	0.25	0.25
3	0.50	0.50	0.30
4	0.25	0.05	0.35

The conditions for a probability function are satisfied by:
A. $f(x)$.
B. $g(x)$.
C. $h(x)$.

23. The cumulative distribution function for a discrete random variable is shown in the following table.

	Cumulative Distribution Function
$X = x$	$F(x) = P(X \leq x)$
1	0.15
2	0.25
3	0.50
4	0.60
5	0.95
6	1.00

The probability that X will take on a value of either 2 or 4 is *closest* to:
A. 0.20.
B. 0.35.
C. 0.85.

24. Which of the following events can be represented as a Bernoulli trial?
A. The flip of a coin
B. The closing price of a stock
C. The picking of a random integer between 1 and 10

25. The weekly closing prices of Mordice Corporation shares are as follows:

Date	Closing Price (€)
1 August	112
8 August	160
15 August	120

The continuously compounded return of Mordice Corporation shares for the period August 1 to August 15 is *closest to*:
A. 6.90%
B. 7.14%
C. 8.95%

26. A stock is priced at $100.00 and follows a one-period binomial process with an up move that equals 1.05 and a down move that equals 0.97. If 1 million Bernoulli trials are conducted, and the average terminal stock price is $102.00, the probability of an up move (*p*) is *closest* to:
A. 0.375.
B. 0.500.
C. 0.625.

27. A call option on a stock index is valued using a three-step binomial tree with an up move that equals 1.05 and a down move that equals 0.95. The current level of the index is $190, and the option exercise price is $200. If the option value is positive when the stock price exceeds the exercise price at expiration and $0 otherwise, the number of terminal nodes with a positive payoff is:
A. one.
B. two.
C. three.

28. A random number between zero and one is generated according to a continuous uniform distribution. What is the probability that the first number generated will have a value of exactly 0.30?
A. 0%
B. 30%
C. 70%

29. A Monte Carlo simulation can be used to:
A. directly provide precise valuations of call options.
B. simulate a process from historical records of returns.
C. test the sensitivity of a model to changes in assumptions.

30. A limitation of Monte Carlo simulation is:
A. its failure to do "what if" analysis.
B. that it requires historical records of returns.
C. its inability to independently specify cause-and-effect relationships.

31. Which parameter equals zero in a normal distribution?
A. Kurtosis
B. Skewness
C. Standard deviation

32. An analyst develops the following capital market projections.

	Stocks	Bonds
Mean Return	10%	2%
Standard Deviation	15%	5%

Assuming the returns of the asset classes are described by normal distributions, which of the following statements is correct?
A. Bonds have a higher probability of a negative return than stocks.
B. On average, 99 percent of stock returns will fall within two standard deviations of the mean.
C. The probability of a bond return less than or equal to 3 percent is determined using a Z-score of 0.25.

33. A client holding a £2,000,000 portfolio wants to withdraw £90,000 in one year without invading the principal. According to Roy's safety-first criterion, which of the following portfolio allocations is optimal?

	Allocation A	Allocation B	Allocation C
Expected annual return	6.5%	7.5%	8.5%
Standard deviation of returns	8.35%	10.21%	14.34%

A. Allocation A
B. Allocation B
C. Allocation C

34. In contrast to normal distributions, lognormal distributions:
A. are skewed to the left.
B. have outcomes that cannot be negative.
C. are more suitable for describing asset returns than asset prices.

35. The lognormal distribution is a more accurate model for the distribution of stock prices than the normal distribution because stock prices are:
A. symmetrical.
B. unbounded.
C. non-negative.

36. The price of a stock at $t = 0$ is $208.25 and at $t = 1$ is $186.75. The continuously compounded rate of return for the stock from $t = 0$ to $t = 1$ is closest to:
A. −10.90%.
B. −10.32%.
C. 11.51%.

CHAPTER 5

SAMPLING AND ESTIMATION

Richard A. DeFusco, PhD, CFA
Dennis W. McLeavey, DBA, CFA
Jerald E. Pinto, PhD, CFA
David E. Runkle, PhD, CFA

LEARNING OUTCOMES

The candidate should be able to:

- define simple random sampling and a sampling distribution;
- explain sampling error;
- distinguish between simple random and stratified random sampling;
- distinguish between time-series and cross-sectional data;
- explain the central limit theorem and its importance;
- calculate and interpret the standard error of the sample mean;
- identify and describe desirable properties of an estimator;
- distinguish between a point estimate and a confidence interval estimate of a population parameter;
- describe properties of Student's *t*-distribution and calculate and interpret its degrees of freedom;
- calculate and interpret a confidence interval for a population mean, given a normal distribution with 1) a known population variance, 2) an unknown population variance, or 3) an unknown population variance and a large sample size;
- describe the issues regarding selection of the appropriate sample size, data-mining bias, sample selection bias, survivorship bias, look-ahead bias, and time-period bias.

Quantitative Methods for Investment Analysis, Second Edition, by Richard A. DeFusco, PhD, CFA, Dennis W. McLeavey, DBA, CFA, Jerald E. Pinto, PhD, CFA, and David E. Runkle, PhD, CFA. Copyright © 2019 by CFA Institute.

1. INTRODUCTION

Each day, we observe the high, low, and close of stock market indexes from around the world. Indexes such as the S&P 500 Index and the Nikkei-Dow Jones Average are samples of stocks. Although the S&P 500 and the Nikkei do not represent the populations of US or Japanese stocks, we view them as valid indicators of the whole population's behavior. As analysts, we are accustomed to using this sample information to assess how various markets from around the world are performing. Any statistics that we compute with sample information, however, are only estimates of the underlying population parameters. A sample, then, is a subset of the population—a subset studied to infer conclusions about the population itself.

This chapter explores how we sample and use sample information to estimate population parameters. In the next section, we discuss **sampling**—the process of obtaining a sample. In investments, we continually make use of the mean as a measure of central tendency of random variables, such as return and earnings per share. Even when the probability distribution of the random variable is unknown, we can make probability statements about the population mean using the central limit theorem. In Section 3, we discuss and illustrate this key result. Following that discussion, we turn to statistical estimation. Estimation seeks precise answers to the question "What is this parameter's value?"

The central limit theorem and estimation are the core of the body of methods presented in this chapter. In investments, we apply these and other statistical techniques to financial data; we often interpret the results for the purpose of deciding what works and what does not work in investments. We end this chapter with a discussion of the interpretation of statistical results based on financial data and the possible pitfalls in this process.

2. SAMPLING

In this section, we present the various methods for obtaining information on a population (all members of a specified group) through samples (part of the population). The information on a population that we try to obtain usually concerns the value of a **parameter**, a quantity computed from or used to describe a population of data. When we use a sample to estimate a parameter, we make use of sample statistics (statistics, for short). A statistic is a quantity computed from or used to describe a sample of data.

We take samples for one of two reasons. In some cases, we cannot possibly examine every member of the population. In other cases, examining every member of the population would not be economically efficient. Thus, savings of time and money are two primary factors that cause an analyst to use sampling to answer a question about a population. In this section, we discuss two methods of random sampling: simple random sampling and stratified random sampling. We then define and illustrate the two types of data an analyst uses: cross-sectional data and time-series data.

2.1. Simple Random Sampling

Suppose a telecommunications equipment analyst wants to know how much major customers will spend on average for equipment during the coming year. One strategy is to survey the population of telecom equipment customers and inquire what their purchasing plans are. In statistical terms, the characteristics of the population of customers' planned expenditures would then usually be expressed by descriptive measures such as the mean and variance. Surveying all companies, however, would be very costly in terms of time and money.

Alternatively, the analyst can collect a representative sample of companies and survey them about upcoming telecom equipment expenditures. In this case, the analyst will compute the sample mean expenditure, $\bar{X}$, a statistic. This strategy has a substantial advantage over polling the whole population because it can be accomplished more quickly and at lower cost.

Sampling, however, introduces error. The error arises because not all the companies in the population are surveyed. The analyst who decides to sample is trading time and money for sampling error.

When an analyst chooses to sample, he must formulate a sampling plan. A **sampling plan** is the set of rules used to select a sample. The basic type of sample from which we can draw statistically sound conclusions about a population is the **simple random sample** (random sample, for short).

- **Definition of Simple Random Sample.** A simple random sample is a subset of a larger population created in such a way that each element of the population has an equal probability of being selected to the subset.

The procedure of drawing a sample to satisfy the definition of a simple random sample is called **simple random sampling**. How is simple random sampling carried out? We need a method that ensures randomness—the lack of any pattern—in the selection of the sample. For a finite (limited) population, the most common method for obtaining a random sample involves the use of random numbers (numbers with assured properties of randomness). First, we number the members of the population in sequence. For example, if the population contains 500 members, we number them in sequence with three digits, starting with 001 and ending with 500. Suppose we want a simple random sample of size 50. In that case, using a computer random-number generator or a table of random numbers, we generate a series of three-digit random numbers. We then match these random numbers with the number codes of the population members until we have selected a sample of size 50.

Sometimes we cannot code (or even identify) all the members of a population. We often use **systematic sampling** in such cases. With systematic sampling, we select every kth member until we have a sample of the desired size. The sample that results from this procedure should be approximately random. Real sampling situations may require that we take an approximately random sample.

Suppose the telecommunications equipment analyst polls a random sample of telecom equipment customers to determine the average equipment expenditure. The sample mean will provide the analyst with an estimate of the population mean expenditure. Any difference between the sample mean and the population mean is called **sampling error**.

- **Definition of Sampling Error.** Sampling error is the difference between the observed value of a statistic and the quantity it is intended to estimate.

A random sample reflects the properties of the population in an unbiased way, and sample statistics, such as the sample mean, computed on the basis of a random sample are valid estimates of the underlying population parameters.

A sample statistic is a random variable. In other words, not only do the original data from the population have a distribution but so does the sample statistic.

This distribution is the statistic's **sampling distribution**.

- **Definition of Sampling Distribution of a Statistic.** The sampling distribution of a statistic is the distribution of all the distinct possible values that the statistic can assume when computed from samples of the same size randomly drawn from the same population.

In the case of the sample mean, for example, we refer to the "sampling distribution of the sample mean" or the distribution of the sample mean. We will have more to say about sampling distributions later in this chapter. Next, however, we look at another sampling method that is useful in investment analysis.

2.2. Stratified Random Sampling

The simple random sampling method just discussed may not be the best approach in all situations. One frequently used alternative is stratified random sampling.

- **Definition of Stratified Random Sampling.** In stratified random sampling, the population is divided into subpopulations (strata) based on one or more classification criteria. Simple random samples are then drawn from each stratum in sizes proportional to the relative size of each stratum in the population. These samples are then pooled to form a stratified random sample.

In contrast to simple random sampling, stratified random sampling guarantees that population subdivisions of interest are represented in the sample. Another advantage is that estimates of parameters produced from stratified sampling have greater precision—that is, smaller variance or dispersion—than estimates obtained from simple random sampling.

Bond indexing is one area in which stratified sampling is frequently applied. **Indexing** is an investment strategy in which an investor constructs a portfolio to mirror the performance of a specified index. In pure bond indexing, also called the full-replication approach, the investor attempts to fully replicate an index by owning all the bonds in the index in proportion to their market value weights. Many bond indexes consist of thousands of issues, however, so pure bond indexing is difficult to implement. In addition, transaction costs would be high because many bonds do not have liquid markets. Although a simple random sample could be a solution to the cost problem, the sample would probably not match the index's major risk factors—interest rate sensitivity, for example. Because the major risk factors of fixed-income portfolios are well known and quantifiable, stratified sampling offers a more effective approach. In this approach, we divide the population of index bonds into groups of similar duration (interest rate sensitivity), cash flow distribution, sector, credit quality, and call exposure. We refer to each group as a stratum or cell (a term frequently used in this context). Then, we choose a sample from each stratum proportional to the relative market weighting of the stratum in the index to be replicated.

EXAMPLE 1   Bond Indexes and Stratified Sampling

Suppose you are the manager of a mutual fund indexed to the Bloomberg Barclays US Government/Credit Index. You are exploring several approaches to indexing, including a stratified sampling approach. You first distinguish among agency bonds, US Treasury bonds, and investment grade corporate bonds. For each of these three groups, you define 10 maturity intervals—1 to 2 years, 2 to 3 years, 3 to 4 years, 4 to 6 years, 6 to 8 years, 8 to 10 years, 10 to 12 years, 12 to 15 years, 15 to 20 years, and 20 to 30 years —and also separate the bonds with coupons (annual interest rates) of 6 percent or less from the bonds with coupons of more than 6 percent.

1. How many cells or strata does this sampling plan entail?
2. If you use this sampling plan, what is the minimum number of issues the indexed portfolio can have?
3. Suppose that in selecting among the securities that qualify for selection within each cell, you apply a criterion concerning the liquidity of the security's market. Is the sample obtained random? Explain your answer.

Solution to 1: We have 3 issuer classifications, 10 maturity classifications, and 2 coupon classifications. So, in total, this plan entails $3(10)(2) = 60$ different strata or cells. (This answer is an application of the multiplication rule of counting discussed in Chapter 3, which is on probability concepts.)

Solution to 2: You cannot have fewer than one issue for each cell, so the portfolio must include at least 60 issues.

Solution to 3: If you apply any additional criteria to the selection of securities for the cells, not every security that might be included has an equal probability of being selected. As a result, the sampling is not random. In practice, indexing using stratified sampling usually does not strictly involve random sampling because the selection of bond issues within cells is subject to various additional criteria. Because the purpose of sampling in this application is not to make an inference about a population parameter but rather to index a portfolio, lack of randomness is not in itself a problem in this application of stratified sampling.

In the next section, we discuss the kinds of data used by financial analysts in sampling and practical issues that arise in selecting samples.

2.3. Time-Series and Cross-Sectional Data

Investment analysts commonly work with both time-series and cross-sectional data. A time series is a sequence of returns collected at discrete and equally spaced intervals of time (such as a historical series of monthly stock returns). Cross-sectional data are data on some characteristic of individuals, groups, geographical regions, or companies at a single point in time. The book value per share at the end of a given year for all New York Stock Exchange-listed companies is an example of cross-sectional data.

Economic or financial theory offers no basis for determining whether a long or short time period should be selected to collect a sample. As analysts, we might have to look for subtle clues. For example, combining data from a period of fixed exchange rates with data from a period of floating exchange rates would be inappropriate. The variance of exchange rates when exchange rates were fixed would certainly be less than when rates were allowed to float. As a consequence, we would not be sampling from a population described by a single set of parameters.[1] Tight versus loose **monetary policy** also influences the distribution of returns to stocks; thus, combining data from tight-money and loose-money periods would be inappropriate. **Example 2** illustrates the problems that can arise when sampling from more than one distribution.

---

[1] When the mean or variance of a time series is not constant through time, the time series is not stationary.

EXAMPLE 2   Calculating Sharpe Ratios: One or Two Years of Quarterly Data

Analysts often use the Sharpe ratio to evaluate the performance of a managed portfolio. The **Sharpe ratio** is the average return in excess of the risk-free rate divided by the standard deviation of returns. This ratio measures the excess return earned per unit of standard deviation of return.

To compute the Sharpe ratio, suppose that an analyst collects eight quarterly excess returns (i.e., total return in excess of the risk-free rate). During the first year, the investment manager of the portfolio followed a low-risk strategy, and during the second year, the manager followed a high-risk strategy. For each of these years, the analyst also tracks the quarterly excess returns of some benchmark against which the manager will be evaluated. For each of the two years, the Sharpe ratio for the benchmark is 0.21. Table 1 gives the calculation of the Sharpe ratio of the portfolio.

For the first year, during which the manager followed a low-risk strategy, the average quarterly return in excess of the risk-free rate was 1 percent with a standard deviation of 4.62 percent. The Sharpe ratio is thus $1/4.62 = 0.22$. The second year's results mirror the first year except for the higher average return and volatility. The Sharpe ratio for the second year is $4/18.48 = 0.22$. The Sharpe ratio for the benchmark is 0.21 during the first and second years. Because larger Sharpe ratios are better than smaller ones (providing more return per unit of risk), the manager appears to have outperformed the benchmark.

Now, suppose the analyst believes a larger sample to be superior to a small one. She thus decides to pool the two years together and calculate a Sharpe ratio based on eight quarterly observations. The average quarterly excess return for the two years is the average of each year's average excess return. For the two-year period, the average excess return is $(1 + 4)/2 = 2.5$ percent per quarter. The standard deviation for all eight quarters measured from the sample mean of 2.5 percent is 12.57 percent. The portfolio's Sharpe ratio for the two-year period is now $2.5/12.57 = 0.199$; the Sharpe ratio for the benchmark remains 0.21. Thus, when returns for the two-year period are pooled, the manager appears to have provided less return per unit of risk than the benchmark and less when compared with the separate yearly results.

The problem with using eight quarters of return data is that the analyst has violated the assumption that the sampled returns come from the same population. As a

TABLE 1   Calculation of Sharpe Ratios: Low-Risk and High-Risk Strategies

Quarter/Measure	Year 1 Excess Returns	Year 2 Excess Returns
Quarter 1	-3%	-12%
Quarter 2	5	20
Quarter 3	-3	-12
Quarter 4	5	20
Quarterly average	1%	4%
Quarterly standard deviation	4.62%	18.48%
Sharpe ratio = 0.22 = 1/4.62 = 4/18.48		

result of the change in the manager's investment strategy, returns in Year 2 followed a different distribution than returns in Year 1. Clearly, during Year 1, returns were generated by an underlying population with lower mean and variance than the population of the second year. Combining the results for the first and second years yielded a sample that was representative of no population. Because the larger sample did not satisfy model assumptions, any conclusions the analyst reached based on the larger sample are incorrect. For this example, she was better off using a smaller sample than a larger sample because the smaller sample represented a more homogeneous distribution of returns.

The second basic type of data is cross-sectional data.[2] With cross-sectional data, the observations in the sample represent a characteristic of individuals, groups, geographical regions, or companies at a single point in time. The telecommunications analyst discussed previously is essentially collecting a cross-section of planned capital expenditures for the coming year.

Whenever we sample cross-sectionally, certain assumptions must be met if we wish to summarize the data in a meaningful way. Again, a useful approach is to think of the observation of interest as a random variable that comes from some underlying population with a given mean and variance. As we collect our sample and begin to summarize the data, we must be sure that all the data do, in fact, come from the same underlying population. For example, an analyst might be interested in how efficiently companies use their inventory assets. Some companies, however, turn over their inventory more quickly than others because of differences in their operating environments (e.g., grocery stores turn over inventory more quickly than automobile manufacturers, in general). So the distribution of inventory turnover rates may not be characterized by a single distribution with a given mean and variance. Therefore, summarizing inventory turnover across all companies might be inappropriate. If random variables are generated by different underlying distributions, the sample statistics computed from combined samples are not related to one underlying population parameter. The size of the sampling error in such cases is unknown.

In instances such as these, analysts often summarize company-level data by industry. Attempting to summarize by industry partially addresses the problem of differing underlying distributions, but large corporations are likely to be in more than one industrial sector, so analysts should be sure they understand how companies are assigned to the industry groups.

Whether we deal with time-series data or cross-sectional data, we must be sure to have a random sample that is representative of the population we wish to study. With the objective of inferring information from representative samples, we now turn to the next part of this chapter, which focuses on the central limit theorem as well as point and interval estimates of the population mean.

---

[2] The reader may also encounter two types of datasets that have both time-series and cross-sectional aspects. **Panel data** consist of observations through time on a single characteristic of multiple observational units. For example, the annual inflation rate of the Eurozone countries over a five-year period would represent panel data. **Longitudinal data** consist of observations on characteristic(s) of the same observational unit through time. Observations on a set of financial ratios for a single company over a 10-year period would be an example of longitudinal data. Both panel and longitudinal data may be represented by arrays (matrixes) in which successive rows represent the observations for successive time periods.

3. DISTRIBUTION OF THE SAMPLE MEAN

Earlier in this chapter, we presented a telecommunications equipment analyst who decided to sample in order to estimate mean planned capital expenditures by his customers. Supposing that the sample is representative of the underlying population, how can the analyst assess the sampling error in estimating the population mean? Viewed as a formula that takes a function of the random outcomes of a random variable, the sample mean is itself a random variable with a probability distribution. That probability distribution is called the statistic's sampling distribution.[3] To estimate how closely the sample mean can be expected to match the underlying population mean, the analyst needs to understand the sampling distribution of the mean. Fortunately, we have a result, the central limit theorem, that helps us understand the sampling distribution of the mean for many of the estimation problems we face.

3.1. The Central Limit Theorem

One of the most practically useful theorems in probability theory, the central limit theorem has important implications for how we construct confidence intervals and test hypotheses. Formally, it is stated as follows:

- **The Central Limit Theorem.** Given a population described by any probability distribution having mean μ and finite variance σ^2, the sampling distribution of the sample mean $\bar{X}$ computed from samples of size n from this population will be approximately normal with mean μ (the population mean) and variance σ^2/n (the population variance divided by n) when the sample size n is large.

The central limit theorem allows us to make quite precise probability statements about the population mean by using the sample mean, *whatever the distribution of the population* (so long as it has finite variance), because the sample mean follows an approximate normal distribution for large-size samples. The obvious question is, "When is a sample's size large enough that we can assume the sample mean is normally distributed?" In general, when sample size n is greater than or equal to 30, we can assume that the sample mean is approximately normally distributed.[4]

The central limit theorem states that the variance of the distribution of the sample mean is σ^2/n. The positive square root of variance is standard deviation. The standard deviation of a sample statistic is known as the standard error of the statistic. The standard error of the sample mean is an important quantity in applying the central limit theorem in practice.

- **Definition of the Standard Error of the Sample Mean.** For sample mean $\bar{X}$ calculated from a sample generated by a population with standard deviation σ, the standard error of the sample mean is given by one of two expressions:

---

[3] Sometimes confusion arises because "sample mean" is also used in another sense. When we calculate the sample mean for a particular sample, we obtain a definite number, say 8. If we state that "the sample mean is 8" we are using "sample mean" in the sense of a particular outcome of sample mean as a random variable. The number 8 is of course a constant and does not have a probability distribution. In this discussion, we are not referring to "sample mean" in the sense of a constant number related to a particular sample.

[4] When the underlying population is very nonnormal, a sample size well in excess of 30 may be required for the normal distribution to be a good description of the sampling distribution of the mean.

$$\sigma \bar{X} = \frac{\sigma}{\sqrt{n}} \tag{1}$$

when we know σ, the population standard deviation, or by

$$s \bar{X} = \frac{s}{\sqrt{n}} \tag{2}$$

when we do not know the population standard deviation and need to use the sample standard deviation, s, to estimate it.[5]

In practice, we almost always need to use Equation 2. The estimate of s is given by the square root of the sample variance, s^2, calculated as follows:

$$s^2 = \frac{\sum_{i=1}^{n}(X_i - \bar{X})^2}{n-1} \tag{3}$$

We will soon see how we can use the sample mean and its standard error to make probability statements about the population mean by using the technique of confidence intervals. First, however, we provide an illustration of the central limit theorem's force.

EXAMPLE 3   The Central Limit Theorem

It is remarkable that the sample mean for large sample sizes will be distributed normally regardless of the distribution of the underlying population. To illustrate the central limit theorem in action, we specify in this example a distinctly nonnormal distribution and use it to generate a large number of random samples of size 100. We then calculate the sample mean for each sample. The frequency distribution of the calculated sample means is an approximation of the sampling distribution of the sample mean for that sample size. Does that sampling distribution look like a normal distribution?

We return to the telecommunications analyst studying the capital expenditure plans of telecom businesses. Suppose that capital expenditures for communications equipment form a continuous uniform random variable with a **lower bound** equal to $0 and an upper bound equal to $100—for short, call this a uniform (0, 100) random variable.

---

[5] We need to note a technical point: When we take a sample of size n from a finite population of size N, we apply a shrinkage factor to the estimate of the standard error of the sample mean that is called the finite population correction factor (FPC). The FPC is equal to $[(N-n)/(N-1)]^{1/2}$. Thus, if $N = 100$ and $n = 20$, $[(100-20)/(100-1)]^{1/2} = 0.898933$. If we have estimated a standard error of, say, 20, according to Equation 1 or Equation 2, the new estimate is $20(0.898933) = 17.978663$. The FPC applies only when we sample from a finite population without replacement; most practitioners also do not apply the FPC if sample size n is very small relative to N (say, less than 5 percent of N). For more information on the finite population correction factor, see **Daniel and Terrell (1995)**.

TABLE 2   Frequency Distribution: 200 Random Samples of a
Uniform (0,100) Random Variable

Range of Sample Means ($ Million)	Absolute Frequency
$42.5 \leq \bar{X} < 44$	1
$44 \leq \bar{X} < 45.5$	6
$45.5 \leq \bar{X} < 47$	22
$47 \leq \bar{X} < 48.5$	39
$48.5 \leq \bar{X} < 50$	41
$50 \leq \bar{X} < 51.5$	39
$51.5 \leq \bar{X} < 53$	23
$53 \leq \bar{X} < 54.5$	12
$54.5 \leq \bar{X} < 56$	12
$56 \leq \bar{X} < 57.5$	5

Note: $\bar{X}$ is the mean capital expenditure for each sample.

The probability function of this continuous uniform random variable has a rather simple shape that is anything but normal. It is a horizontal line with a vertical intercept equal to 1/100. Unlike a normal random variable, for which outcomes close to the mean are most likely, all possible outcomes are equally likely for a uniform random variable.

To illustrate the power of the central limit theorem, we conduct a Monte Carlo simulation to study the capital expenditure plans of telecom businesses.[6] In this simulation, we collect 200 random samples of the capital expenditures of 100 companies (200 random draws, each consisting of the capital expenditures of 100 companies with $n = 100$). In each simulation trial, 100 values for capital expenditure are generated from the uniform (0, 100) distribution. For each random sample, we then compute the sample mean. We conduct 200 simulation trials in total. Because we have specified the distribution generating the samples, we know that the population mean capital expenditure is equal to ($0 + $100 million)/2 = $50 million; the population variance of capital expenditures is equal to $(100 - 0)^2/12 = 833.33$; thus, the standard deviation is $28.87 million and the standard error is $28.87/\sqrt{100} = 2.887$ under the central limit theorem.[7]

The results of this Monte Carlo experiment are tabulated in Table 2 in the form of a frequency distribution. This distribution is the estimated sampling distribution of the sample mean.

The frequency distribution can be described as bell-shaped and centered close to the population mean of 50. The most frequent, or modal, range, with 41 observations, is 48.5 to 50. The overall average of the sample means is $49.92, with a standard error

---

[6] Monte Carlo simulation involves the use of a computer to represent the operation of a system subject to risk. An integral part of Monte Carlo simulation is the generation of a large number of random samples from a specified probability distribution or distributions.

[7] If a is the lower limit of a uniform random variable and b is the upper limit, then the random variable's mean is given by $(a + b)/2$ and its variance is given by $(b - a)^2/12$. The chapter on common probability distributions (Chapter 4) fully describes continuous uniform random variables.

equal to $2.80. The calculated standard error is close to the value of 2.887 given by the central limit theorem. The discrepancy between calculated and expected values of the mean and standard deviation under the central limit theorem is a result of random chance (sampling error).

In summary, although the distribution of the underlying population is very nonnormal, the simulation has shown that a normal distribution well describes the estimated sampling distribution of the sample mean, with mean and standard error consistent with the values predicted by the central limit theorem.

To summarize, according to the central limit theorem, when we sample from any distribution, the distribution of the sample mean will have the following properties as long as our sample size is large:

- The distribution of the sample mean $\bar{X}$ will be approximately normal.
- The mean of the distribution of $\bar{X}$ will be equal to the mean of the population from which the samples are drawn.
- The variance of the distribution of $\bar{X}$ will be equal to the variance of the population divided by the sample size.

We next discuss the concepts and tools related to estimating the population parameters, with a special focus on the population mean. We focus on the population mean because analysts are more likely to meet interval estimates for the population mean than any other type of interval estimate.

4. POINT AND INTERVAL ESTIMATES OF THE POPULATION MEAN

Statistical inference traditionally consists of two branches, hypothesis testing and estimation. Hypothesis testing addresses the question "Is the value of this parameter (say, a population mean) equal to some specific value (0, for example)?" In this process, we have a hypothesis concerning the value of a parameter, and we seek to determine whether the evidence from a sample supports or does not support that hypothesis. We discuss hypothesis testing in detail in the chapter on hypothesis testing (Chapter 6).

The second branch of statistical inference, and the focus of this chapter, is estimation. Estimation seeks an answer to the question "What is this parameter's (for example, the population mean's) value?" In estimating, unlike in hypothesis testing, we do not start with a hypothesis about a parameter's value and seek to test it. Rather, we try to make the best use of the information in a sample to form one of several types of estimates of the parameter's value. With estimation, we are interested in arriving at a rule for best calculating a single number to estimate the unknown population parameter (a point estimate). Together with calculating a point estimate, we may also be interested in calculating a range of values that brackets the unknown population parameter with some specified level of probability (a confidence interval). In Section 4.1 we discuss point estimates of parameters and then, in Section 4.2, the formulation of confidence intervals for the population mean.

4.1. Point Estimators

An important concept introduced in this chapter is that sample statistics viewed as formulas involving random outcomes are random variables. The formulas that we use to compute the sample mean and all the other sample statistics are examples of estimation formulas or **estimators**. The particular value that we calculate from sample observations using an estimator is called an **estimate**. An estimator has a sampling distribution; an estimate is a fixed number pertaining to a given sample and thus has no sampling distribution. To take the example of the mean, the calculated value of the sample mean in a given sample, used as an estimate of the population mean, is called a **point estimate** of the population mean. As **Example 3** illustrated, the formula for the sample mean can and will yield different results in repeated samples as different samples are drawn from the population.

In many applications, we have a choice among a number of possible estimators for estimating a given parameter. How do we make our choice? We often select estimators because they have one or more desirable statistical properties. Following is a brief description of three desirable properties of estimators: unbiasedness (lack of bias), efficiency, and consistency.[8]

- **Definition of Unbiasedness.** An unbiased estimator is one whose expected value (the mean of its sampling distribution) equals the parameter it is intended to estimate.

For example, the expected value of the sample mean, $\bar{X}$, equals μ, the population mean, so we say that the sample mean is an unbiased estimator (of the population mean). The sample variance, s^2, which is calculated using a divisor of $n - 1$ (Equation 3), is an unbiased estimator of the population variance, σ^2. If we were to calculate the sample variance using a divisor of n, the estimator would be biased: Its expected value would be smaller than the population variance. We would say that sample variance calculated with a divisor of n is a biased estimator of the population variance.

Whenever one unbiased estimator of a parameter can be found, we can usually find a large number of other unbiased estimators. How do we choose among alternative unbiased estimators? The criterion of efficiency provides a way to select from among unbiased estimators of a parameter.

- **Definition of Efficiency.** An unbiased estimator is efficient if no other unbiased estimator of the same parameter has a sampling distribution with smaller variance.

To explain the definition, in repeated samples we expect the estimates from an efficient estimator to be more tightly grouped around the mean than estimates from other unbiased estimators. Efficiency is an important property of an estimator.[9] Sample mean $\bar{X}$ is an efficient estimator of the population mean; sample variance s^2 is an efficient estimator of σ^2.

Recall that a statistic's sampling distribution is defined for a given sample size. Different sample sizes define different sampling distributions. For example, the variance of sampling distribution of the sample mean is smaller for larger sample sizes. Unbiasedness and efficiency are properties of an estimator's sampling distribution that hold for any size sample. An unbiased estimator is unbiased equally in a sample of size 10 and in a sample of size 1,000. In some problems, however, we cannot find estimators that have such desirable properties as

---

[8] See Daniel and Terrell (1995) or Greene (2018) for a thorough treatment of the properties of estimators.

[9] An efficient estimator is sometimes referred to as the best unbiased estimator.

unbiasedness in small samples.[10] In this case, statisticians may justify the choice of an estimator based on the properties of the estimator's sampling distribution in extremely large samples, the estimator's so-called asymptotic properties. Among such properties, the most important is consistency.

• **Definition of Consistency.** A consistent estimator is one for which the probability of estimates close to the value of the population parameter increases as sample size increases.

Somewhat more technically, we can define a consistent estimator as an estimator whose sampling distribution becomes concentrated on the value of the parameter it is intended to estimate as the sample size approaches infinity. The sample mean, in addition to being an efficient estimator, is also a consistent estimator of the population mean: As sample size n goes to infinity, its standard error, $\sigma/\sqrt{n}$, goes to 0 and its sampling distribution becomes concentrated right over the value of population mean, μ. To summarize, we can think of a consistent estimator as one that tends to produce more and more accurate estimates of the population parameter as we increase the sample's size. If an estimator is consistent, we may attempt to increase the accuracy of estimates of a population parameter by calculating estimates using a larger sample. For an inconsistent estimator, however, increasing sample size does not help to increase the probability of accurate estimates.

4.2. Confidence Intervals for the Population Mean

When we need a single number as an estimate of a population parameter, we make use of a point estimate. However, because of sampling error, the point estimate is not likely to equal the population parameter in any given sample. Often, a more useful approach than finding a point estimate is to find a range of values that we expect to bracket the parameter with a specified level of probability—an interval estimate of the parameter. A confidence interval fulfills this role.

• **Definition of Confidence Interval.** A confidence interval is a range for which one can assert with a given probability $1 - \alpha$, called the **degree of confidence**, that it will contain the parameter it is intended to estimate. This interval is often referred to as the $100(1 - \alpha)\%$ confidence interval for the parameter.

The endpoints of a confidence interval are referred to as the lower and upper confidence limits. In this chapter, we are concerned only with two-sided confidence intervals— confidence intervals for which we calculate both lower and upper limits.[11]

Confidence intervals are frequently given either a probabilistic interpretation or a practical interpretation. In the probabilistic interpretation, we interpret a 95 percent confidence interval for the population mean as follows. In repeated sampling, 95 percent of such confidence intervals will, in the long run, include or bracket the population mean. For example, suppose we sample from the population 1,000 times, and based on each sample, we

---

[10] Such problems frequently arise in regression and time-series analyses.

[11] It is also possible to define two types of one-sided confidence intervals for a population parameter. A lower one-sided confidence interval establishes a lower limit only. Associated with such an interval is an assertion that with a specified degree of confidence the population parameter equals or exceeds the lower limit. An upper one-sided confidence interval establishes an upper limit only; the related assertion is that the population parameter is less than or equal to that upper limit, with a specified degree of confidence. Investment researchers rarely present one-sided confidence intervals, however.

construct a 95 percent confidence interval using the calculated sample mean. Because of random chance, these confidence intervals will vary from each other, but we expect 95 percent, or 950, of these intervals to include the unknown value of the population mean. In practice, we generally do not carry out such repeated sampling. Therefore, in the practical interpretation, we assert that we are 95 percent confident that a single 95 percent confidence interval contains the population mean. We are justified in making this statement because we know that 95 percent of all possible confidence intervals constructed in the same manner will contain the population mean. The confidence intervals that we discuss in this chapter have structures similar to the following basic structure:

- **Construction of Confidence Intervals.** A $100(1 - \alpha)\%$ confidence interval for a parameter has the following structure:

$$\text{Point estimate} \pm \text{Reliability factor} \times \text{Standard error}$$

where

Point estimate = a point estimate of the parameter (a value of a sample statistic)
Reliability factor = a number based on the assumed distribution of the point estimate and the degree of confidence $(1 - \alpha)$ for the confidence interval
Standard error = the standard error of the sample statistic providing the point estimate[12]

The most basic confidence interval for the population mean arises when we are sampling from a normal distribution with known variance. The reliability factor in this case is based on the standard normal distribution, which has a mean of 0 and a variance of 1. A standard normal random variable is conventionally denoted by Z. The notation z_α denotes the point of the standard normal distribution such that α of the probability remains in the right tail. For example, 0.05 or 5 percent of the possible values of a standard normal random variable are larger than $z_{0.05} = 1.65$.

Suppose we want to construct a 95 percent confidence interval for the population mean and, for this purpose, we have taken a sample of size 100 from a normally distributed population with known variance of $\sigma^2 = 400$ (so, $\sigma = 20$). We calculate a sample mean of $\bar{X} = 25$. Our point estimate of the population mean is, therefore, 25. If we move 1.96 standard deviations above the mean of a normal distribution, 0.025 or 2.5 percent of the probability remains in the right tail; by symmetry of the normal distribution, if we move 1.96 standard deviations below the mean, 0.025 or 2.5 percent of the probability remains in the left tail. In total, 0.05 or 5 percent of the probability is in the two tails and 0.95 or 95 percent lies in between. So, $z_{0.025} = 1.96$ is the reliability factor for this 95 percent confidence interval. Note the relationship $100(1 - \alpha)\%$ for the confidence interval and the $z_{\alpha/2}$ for the reliability factor. The standard error of the sample mean, given by Equation 1, is $\sigma_{\bar{X}} = 20/\sqrt{100} = 2$. The confidence interval, therefore, has a lower limit of $\bar{X} - 1.96\sigma_{\bar{X}} = 25 - 1.96(2) = 25 - 3.92 = 21.08$. The upper limit of the confidence interval is $\bar{X} + 1.96\sigma_{\bar{X}} = 25 + 1.96(2) = 25 + 3.92 = 28.92$. The 95 percent confidence interval for the population mean spans 21.08 to 28.92.

- **Confidence Intervals for the Population Mean (Normally Distributed Population with Known Variance).** A $100(1 - \alpha)\%$ confidence interval for population mean μ when we are sampling from a normal distribution with known variance σ^2 is given by

---

[12] The quantity (reliability factor) × (standard error) is sometimes called the precision of the estimator; larger values of the product imply lower precision in estimating the population parameter.

$$\bar{X} \pm z_{\alpha/2}\frac{\sigma}{\sqrt{n}} \tag{4}$$

The reliability factors for the most frequently used confidence intervals are as follows.

- **Reliability Factors for Confidence Intervals Based on the Standard Normal Distribution.** We use the following reliability factors when we construct confidence intervals based on the standard normal distribution:[13]
  - 90 percent confidence intervals: Use $z_{0.05} = 1.65$
  - 95 percent confidence intervals: Use $z_{0.025} = 1.96$
  - 99 percent confidence intervals: Use $z_{0.005} = 2.58$

These reliability factors highlight an important fact about all confidence intervals. As we increase the degree of confidence, the confidence interval becomes wider and gives us less precise information about the quantity we want to estimate. "The surer we want to be, the less we have to be sure of."[14]

In practice, the assumption that the sampling distribution of the sample mean is at least approximately normal is frequently reasonable, either because the underlying distribution is approximately normal or because we have a large sample and the central limit theorem applies. However, rarely do we know the population variance in practice. When the population variance is unknown but the sample mean is at least approximately normally distributed, we have two acceptable ways to calculate the confidence interval for the population mean. We will soon discuss the more conservative approach, which is based on Student's t-distribution (the t-distribution, for short).[15] In investment literature, it is the most frequently used approach in both estimation and hypothesis tests concerning the mean when the population variance is not known, whether sample size is small or large.

A second approach to confidence intervals for the population mean, based on the standard normal distribution, is the z-alternative. It can be used only when sample size is large. (In general, a sample size of 30 or larger may be considered large.) In contrast to the confidence interval given in Equation 4, this confidence interval uses the sample standard deviation, s, in computing the standard error of the sample mean (Equation 2).

- **Confidence Intervals for the Population Mean—The z-Alternative (Large Sample, Population Variance Unknown).** A $100(1 - \alpha)\%$ confidence interval for population mean μ when sampling from any distribution with unknown variance and when sample size is large is given by

$$\bar{X} \pm z_{\alpha/2}\frac{s}{\sqrt{n}} \tag{5}$$

Because this type of confidence interval appears quite often, we illustrate its calculation in **Example 4**.

---

[13] Most practitioners use values for $z_{0.05}$ and $z_{0.005}$ that are carried to two decimal places. For reference, more exact values for $z_{0.05}$ and $z_{0.005}$ are 1.645 and 2.575, respectively. For a quick calculation of a 95 percent confidence interval, $z_{0.025}$ is sometimes rounded from 1.96 to 2.

[14] **Freund and Williams (1977)**, p. 266.

[15] The distribution of the statistic t is called Student's t-distribution after the pen name "Student" used by W. S. Gosset, who published his work in 1908.

EXAMPLE 4   Confidence Interval for the Population Mean of Sharpe Ratios—z-Statistic

---

Suppose an investment analyst takes a random sample of US equity mutual funds and calculates the average Sharpe ratio. The sample size is 100, and the average Sharpe ratio is 0.45. The sample has a standard deviation of 0.30. Calculate and interpret the 90 percent confidence interval for the population mean of all US equity mutual funds by using a reliability factor based on the standard normal distribution.

The reliability factor for a 90 percent confidence interval, as given earlier, is $z_{0.05} = 1.65$. The confidence interval will be

$$\bar{X} \pm z_{0.05} \frac{s}{\sqrt{n}} = 0.45 \pm 1.65 \frac{0.30}{\sqrt{100}} = 0.45 \pm 1.65(0.03) = 0.45 \pm 0.0495$$

The confidence interval spans 0.4005 to 0.4995, or 0.40 to 0.50, carrying two decimal places. The analyst can say with 90 percent confidence that the interval includes the population mean.

In this example, the analyst makes no specific assumption about the probability distribution describing the population. Rather, the analyst relies on the central limit theorem to produce an approximate normal distribution for the sample mean.

As **Example 4** shows, even if we are unsure of the underlying population distribution, we can still construct confidence intervals for the population mean as long as the sample size is large because we can apply the central limit theorem.

We now turn to the conservative alternative, using the t-distribution, for constructing confidence intervals for the population mean when the population variance is not known. For confidence intervals based on samples from normally distributed populations with unknown variance, the theoretically correct reliability factor is based on the t-distribution. Using a reliability factor based on the t-distribution is essential for a small sample size. Using a t reliability factor is appropriate when the population variance is unknown, even when we have a large sample and could use the central limit theorem to justify using a z reliability factor. In this large sample case, the t-distribution provides more-conservative (wider) confidence intervals.

The t-distribution is a symmetrical probability distribution defined by a single parameter known as **degrees of freedom (DF)**. Each value for the number of degrees of freedom defines one distribution in this family of distributions. We will shortly compare t-distributions with the standard normal distribution, but first we need to understand the concept of degrees of freedom. We can do so by examining the calculation of the sample variance.

Equation 3 gives the unbiased estimator of the sample variance that we use. The term in the denominator, $n - 1$, which is the sample size minus 1, is the number of degrees of freedom in estimating the population variance when using Equation 3. We also use $n - 1$ as the number of degrees of freedom for determining reliability factors based on the t-distribution. The term degrees of freedom is used because in a random sample, we assume that observations are selected independently of each other. The numerator of the sample variance, however, uses the sample mean. How does the use of the sample mean affect the number of observations collected independently for the sample variance formula? With a

FIGURE 1   Student's *t*-Distribution versus the Standard Normal Distribution

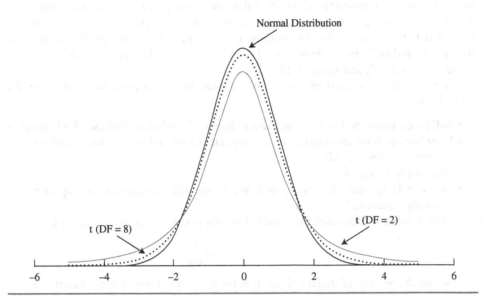

sample of size 10 and a mean of 10 percent, for example, we can freely select only 9 observations. Regardless of the 9 observations selected, we can always find the value for the 10th observation that gives a mean equal to 10 percent. From the standpoint of the sample variance formula, then, there are 9 degrees of freedom. Given that we must first compute the sample mean from the total of *n* independent observations, only *n* – 1 observations can be chosen independently for the calculation of the sample variance. The concept of degrees of freedom comes up frequently in statistics, and you will see it often in later chapters.

Suppose we sample from a normal distribution. The ratio $z = (\bar{X} - \mu)/(\sigma/\sqrt{n})$ is distributed normally with a mean of 0 and standard deviation of 1; however, the ratio $t = (\bar{X} - \mu)/(s/\sqrt{n})$ follows the *t*-distribution with a mean of 0 and *n* – 1 degrees of freedom. The ratio represented by *t* is not normal because *t* is the ratio of two random variables, the sample mean and the sample standard deviation. The definition of the standard normal random variable involves only one random variable, the sample mean. As degrees of freedom increase, however, the *t*-distribution approaches the standard normal distribution. Figure 1 shows the standard normal distribution and two *t*-distributions, one with DF = 2 and one with DF = 8.

Of the three distributions shown in Figure 1, the standard normal distribution has tails that approach zero faster than the tails of the two *t*-distributions. The *t*-distribution is also symmetrically distributed around its mean value of zero, just like the normal distribution. As the degrees of freedom increase, the *t*-distribution approaches the standard normal. The *t*-distribution with DF = 8 is closer to the standard normal than the *t*-distribution with DF = 2.

Beyond plus and minus four standard deviations from the mean, the area under the standard normal distribution appears to approach 0; both *t*-distributions continue to show some area under each curve beyond four standard deviations, however. The *t*-distributions have fatter tails, but the tails of the *t*-distribution with DF = 8 more closely resemble the normal distribution's tails. As the degrees of freedom increase, the tails of the *t*-distribution become less fat.

Frequently referred to values for the t-distribution are presented in tables at the end of the book. For each degree of freedom, five values are given: $t_{0.10}$, $t_{0.05}$, $t_{0.025}$, $t_{0.01}$, and $t_{0.005}$. The values for $t_{0.10}$, $t_{0.05}$, $t_{0.025}$, $t_{0.01}$, and $t_{0.005}$ are such that, respectively, 0.10, 0.05, 0.025, 0.01, and 0.005 of the probability remains in the right tail, for the specified number of degrees of freedom.[16] For example, for DF = 30, $t_{0.10} = 1.310$, $t_{0.05} = 1.697$, $t_{0.025} = 2.042$, $t_{0.01} = 2.457$, and $t_{0.005} = 2.750$.

We now give the form of confidence intervals for the population mean using the t-distribution.

- **Confidence Intervals for the Population Mean (Population Variance Unknown)— t-Distribution.** If we are sampling from a population with unknown variance and either of the conditions below holds:
  - the sample is large, or
  - the sample is small, but the population is normally distributed, or approximately normally distributed,

  then a $100(1 - \alpha)\%$ confidence interval for the population mean μ is given by

$$\bar{X} \pm t_{\alpha/2}\frac{s}{\sqrt{n}} \tag{6}$$

  where the number of degrees of freedom for $t_{\alpha/2}$ is $n - 1$ and n is the sample size.

Example 5 reprises the data of **Example 4** but uses the t-statistic rather than the z-statistic to calculate a confidence interval for the population mean of Sharpe ratios.

EXAMPLE 5 Confidence Interval for the Population Mean of Sharpe Ratios—t-Statistic

As in **Example 4**, an investment analyst seeks to calculate a 90 percent confidence interval for the population mean Sharpe ratio of US equity mutual funds based on a random sample of 100 US equity mutual funds. The sample mean Sharpe ratio is 0.45, and the sample standard deviation of the Sharpe ratios is 0.30. Now recognizing that the population variance of the distribution of Sharpe ratios is unknown, the analyst decides to calculate the confidence interval using the theoretically correct t-statistic.

Because the sample size is 100, DF = 99. In the tables in the back of the book, the closest value is DF = 100. Using DF = 100 and reading down the 0.05 column, we find that $t_{0.05} = 1.66$. This reliability factor is slightly larger than the reliability factor $z_{0.05} = 1.65$ that was used in **Example 4**. The confidence interval will be

$$\bar{X} \pm t_{0.05}\frac{s}{\sqrt{n}} = 0.45 \pm 1.66\frac{0.30}{\sqrt{100}} = 0.45 \pm 1.66(0.03) = 0.45 \pm 0.0498$$

The confidence interval spans 0.4002 to 0.4998, or 0.40 to 0.50, carrying two decimal places. To two decimal places, the confidence interval is unchanged from the one computed in **Example 4**.

---

[16] The values $t_{0.10}$, $t_{0.05}$, $t_{0.025}$, $t_{0.01}$, and $t_{0.005}$ are also referred to as one-sided critical values of t at the 0.10, 0.05, 0.025, 0.01, and 0.005 significance levels, for the specified number of degrees of freedom.

Table 3 summarizes the various reliability factors that we have used.

TABLE 3   Basis of Computing Reliability Factors

Sampling from:	Statistic for Small Sample Size	Statistic for Large Sample Size
Normal distribution with known variance	z	z
Normal distribution with unknown variance	t	t^*
Nonnormal distribution with known variance	not available	z
Nonnormal distribution with unknown variance	not available	t^*

*Use of z also acceptable.

4.3. Selection of Sample Size

What choices affect the width of a confidence interval? To this point we have discussed two factors that affect width: the choice of statistic (t or z) and the choice of degree of confidence (affecting which specific value of t or z we use). These two choices determine the reliability factor. (Recall that a confidence interval has the structure Point estimate $\pm$ Reliability factor $\times$ Standard error.)

The choice of sample size also affects the width of a confidence interval. All else equal, a larger sample size decreases the width of a confidence interval. Recall the expression for the standard error of the sample mean:

$$\text{Standard error of the sample mean} = \frac{\text{Sample standard deviation}}{\sqrt{\text{Sample size}}}$$

We see that the standard error varies inversely with the square root of sample size. As we increase sample size, the standard error decreases and consequently the width of the confidence interval also decreases. The larger the sample size, the greater precision with which we can estimate the population parameter.[17] All else equal, larger samples are good, in that sense. In practice, however, two considerations may operate against increasing sample size. First, as we saw in **Example 2** concerning the Sharpe ratio, increasing the size of a sample may result in sampling from more than one population. Second, increasing sample size may involve additional expenses that outweigh the value of additional precision. Thus three issues that the analyst should weigh in selecting sample size are the need for precision, the risk of sampling from more than one population, and the expenses of different sample sizes.

---

[17] A formula exists for determining the sample size needed to obtain a desired width for a confidence interval. Define E = Reliability factor $\times$ Standard error. The smaller E is, the smaller the width of the confidence interval, because $2E$ is the confidence interval's width. The sample size to obtain a desired value of E at a given degree of confidence $(1 - \alpha)$ is $n = [(t_{\alpha/2}s)/E]^2$.

EXAMPLE 6 A Money Manager Estimates Net Client Inflows

A money manager wants to obtain a 95 percent confidence interval for fund inflows and outflows over the next six months for his existing clients. He begins by calling a random sample of 10 clients and inquiring about their planned additions to and withdrawals from the fund. The manager then computes the change in cash flow for each client sampled as a percentage change in total funds placed with the manager. A positive percentage change indicates a net cash inflow to the client's account, and a negative percentage change indicates a net cash outflow from the client's account. The manager weights each response by the relative size of the account within the sample and then computes a weighted average.

As a result of this process, the money manager computes a weighted average of 5.5 percent. Thus, a point estimate is that the total amount of funds under management will increase by 5.5 percent in the next six months. The standard deviation of the observations in the sample is 10 percent. A histogram of past data looks fairly close to normal, so the manager assumes the population is normal.

1. Calculate a 95 percent confidence interval for the population mean and interpret your findings.

The manager decides to see what the confidence interval would look like if he had used a sample size of 20 or 30 and found the same mean (5.5 percent) and standard deviation (10 percent).

2. Using the sample mean of 5.5 percent and standard deviation of 10 percent, compute the confidence interval for sample sizes of 20 and 30. For the sample size of 30, use Equation 6.
3. Interpret your results from Parts 1 and 2.

Solution to 1: Because the population variance is unknown and the sample size is small, the manager must use the t-statistic in Equation 6 to calculate the confidence interval. Based on the sample size of 10, DF $= n - 1 = 10 - 1 = 9$. For a 95 percent confidence interval, he needs to use the value of $t_{0.025}$ for DF $= 9$. According to the tables in Appendix B at the end of this volume, this value is 2.262. Therefore, a 95 percent confidence interval for the population mean is

$$\bar{X} \pm t_{0.025} \frac{s}{\sqrt{n}} = 5.5\% \pm 2.262 \frac{10\%}{\sqrt{10}}$$
$$= 5.5\% \pm 2.262(3.162)$$
$$= 5.5\% \pm 7.15\%$$

The confidence interval for the population mean spans −1.65 percent to +12.65 percent.[18] The manager can be confident at the 95 percent level that this range includes the population mean.

Solution to 2: Table 4 gives the calculations for the three sample sizes.

---

[18] We assumed in this example that sample size is sufficiently small compared with the size of the client base that we can disregard the finite population correction factor (mentioned in Footnote 6).

TABLE 4   The 95 Percent Confidence Interval for Three Sample Sizes

Distribution	95% Confidence Interval	Lower Bound	Upper Bound	Relative Size
$t(n = 10)$	5.5% $\pm$ 2.262(3.162)	−1.65%	12.65%	100.0%
$t(n = 20)$	5.5% $\pm$ 2.093(2.236)	0.82	10.18	65.5
$t(n = 30)$	5.5% $\pm$ 2.045(1.826)	1.77	9.23	52.2

Solution to 3: The width of the confidence interval decreases as we increase the sample size. This decrease is a function of the standard error becoming smaller as n increases. The reliability factor also becomes smaller as the number of degrees of freedom increases. The last column of Table 4 shows the relative size of the width of confidence intervals based on $n = 10$ to be 100 percent. Using a sample size of 20 reduces the confidence interval's width to 65.5 percent of the interval width for a sample size of 10. Using a sample size of 30 cuts the width of the interval almost in half. Comparing these choices, the money manager would obtain the most precise results using a sample of 30.

Having covered many of the fundamental concepts of sampling and estimation, we are in a good position to focus on sampling issues of special concern to analysts. The quality of inferences depends on the quality of the data as well as on the quality of the sampling plan used. Financial data pose special problems, and sampling plans frequently reflect one or more biases. The next section of this chapter discusses these issues.

5. MORE ON SAMPLING

We have already seen that the selection of sample period length may raise the issue of sampling from more than one population. There are, in fact, a range of challenges to valid sampling that arise in working with financial data. In this section we discuss four such sampling-related issues: data-mining bias, sample selection bias, look-ahead bias, and time-period bias. All of these issues are important for point and interval estimation and hypothesis testing. As we will see, if the sample is biased in any way, then point and interval estimates and any other conclusions that we draw from the sample will be in error.

5.1. Data-Mining Bias

Data mining relates to overuse of the same or related data in ways that we shall describe shortly. Data-mining bias refers to the errors that arise from such misuse of data. Investment strategies that reflect data-mining biases are often not successful in the future. Nevertheless, both investment practitioners and researchers have frequently engaged in data mining. Analysts thus need to understand and guard against this problem.

Data-mining is the practice of determining a model by extensive searching through a dataset for statistically significant patterns (that is, repeatedly "drilling" in the same data until finding something that appears to work).[19] In exercises involving statistical significance we set a significance level, which is the probability of rejecting the hypothesis we are testing when the hypothesis is in fact correct.[20] Because rejecting a true hypothesis is undesirable, the investigator often sets the significance level at a relatively small number such as 0.05 or 5 percent.[21] Suppose we test the hypothesis that a variable does not predict stock returns, and we test in turn 100 different variables. Let us also suppose that in truth none of the 100 variables has the ability to predict stock returns. Using a 5 percent significance level in our tests, we would still expect that 5 out of 100 variables would appear to be significant predictors of stock returns because of random chance alone. We have mined the data to find some apparently significant variables. In essence, we have explored the same data again and again until we found some after-the-fact pattern or patterns in the dataset. This is the sense in which data mining involves overuse of data. If we were to just report the significant variables, without also reporting the total number of variables that we tested that were unsuccessful as predictors, we would be presenting a very misleading picture of our findings. Our results would appear to be far more significant than they actually were, because a series of tests such as the one just described invalidates the conventional interpretation of a given significance level (such as 5 percent), according to the theory of inference.

How can we investigate the presence of data-mining bias? With most financial data, the most ready means is to conduct out-of-sample tests of the proposed variable or strategy. An **out-of-sample test** uses a sample that does not overlap the time period(s) of the sample(s) on which a variable, strategy, or model, was developed. If a variable or investment strategy is the result of data mining, it should generally not be significant in out-of-sample tests. A variable or investment strategy that is statistically and economically significant in out-of-sample tests, and that has a plausible economic basis, may be the basis for a valid investment strategy. Caution is still warranted, however. The most crucial out-of-sample test is future investment success. If the strategy becomes known to other investors, prices may adjust so that the strategy, however well tested, does not work in the future. To summarize, the analyst should be aware that many apparently profitable investment strategies may reflect data-mining bias and thus be cautious about the future applicability of published investment research results.

Untangling the extent of data mining can be complex. To assess the significance of an investment strategy, we need to know how many unsuccessful strategies were tried not only by the current investigator but also by *previous* investigators using the same or related datasets. Much research, in practice, closely builds on what other investigators have done, and so reflects intergenerational data mining, to use the terminology of **McQueen and Thorley (1999)**. **Intergenerational data mining** involves using information developed by previous

---

[19] Some researchers use the term *data snooping* instead of data mining.

[20] To convey an understanding of data mining, it is very helpful to introduce some basic concepts related to hypothesis testing. The chapter on hypothesis testing (Chapter 6) contains further discussion of significance levels and tests of significance.

[21] In terms of our previous discussion of confidence intervals, significance at the 5 percent level corresponds to a hypothesized value for a population statistic falling outside a 95 percent confidence interval based on an appropriate sample statistic (e.g., the sample mean, when the hypothesis concerns the population mean).

researchers using a dataset to guide current research using the same or a related dataset.[22] Analysts have accumulated many observations about the peculiarities of many financial datasets, and other analysts may develop models or investment strategies that will tend to be supported within a dataset based on their familiarity with the prior experience of other analysts. As a consequence, the importance of those new results may be overstated. Research has suggested that the magnitude of this type of data-mining bias may be considerable.[23]

With the background of the above definitions and explanations, we can understand **McQueen and Thorley's (1999)** cogent exploration of data mining in the context of the popular Motley Fool "Foolish Four" investment strategy. The Foolish Four strategy, first presented in 1996, was a version of the Dow Dividend Strategy that was tuned by its developers to exhibit an even higher arithmetic mean return than the Dow Dividend Strategy over 1973 to 1993.[24] From 1973 to 1993, the Foolish Four portfolio had an average annual return of 25 percent, and the claim was made in print that the strategy should have similar returns in the future. As McQueen and Thorley discussed, however, the Foolish Four strategy was very much subject to data-mining bias, including bias from intergenerational data mining, as the strategy's developers exploited observations about the dataset made by earlier workers. McQueen and Thorley highlighted the data-mining issues by taking the Foolish Four portfolio one step further. They mined the data to create a "Fractured Four" portfolio that earned nearly 35 percent over 1973 to 1996, beating the Foolish Four strategy by almost 8 percentage points. Observing that all of the Foolish Four stocks did well in even years but not odd years and that the second-to-lowest-priced high-yielding stock was relatively the best-performing stock in odd years, the strategy of the Fractured Four portfolio was to hold the Foolish Four stocks with equal weights in even years and hold only the second-to-lowest-priced stock in odd years. How likely is it that a performance difference between even and odd years reflected underlying economic forces, rather than a chance pattern of the data over the particular time period? Probably, very unlikely. Unless an investment strategy reflected underlying economic forces, we would not expect it to have any value in a forward-looking sense. Because the Foolish Four strategy also partook of data mining, the same issues applied to it. McQueen and Thorley found that in an out-of-sample test over the 1949–72 period, the Foolish Four strategy had about the same mean return as buying and holding the DJIA, but with higher risk. If the higher taxes and transaction costs of the Foolish Four strategy were accounted for, the comparison would have been even more unfavorable.

McQueen and Thorley presented two signs that can warn analysts about the potential existence of data mining:

---

[22] The term "intergenerational" comes from viewing each round of researchers as a generation. Campbell, Lo, and MacKinlay (1997) have called intergenerational data mining "data snooping." The latter phrase, however, is commonly used as a synonym of data mining; thus McQueen and Thorley's terminology is less ambiguous. The term "intragenerational data mining" is available when we want to highlight that the reference is to an investigator's new or independent data mining.

[23] For example, Lo and MacKinlay (1990) concluded that the magnitude of this type of bias on tests of the capital asset pricing model was considerable.

[24] The Dow Dividend Strategy, also known as Dogs of the Dow Strategy, consists of holding an equally weighted portfolio of the 10 highest-yielding DJIA stocks as of the beginning of a year. At the time of McQueen and Thorley's research, the Foolish Four strategy was as follows: At the beginning of each year, the Foolish Four portfolio purchases a 4-stock portfolio from the 5 lowest-priced stocks of the 10 highest-yielding DJIA stocks. The lowest-priced stock of the five is excluded, and 40 percent is invested in the second-to-lowest-priced stock, with 20 percent weights in the remaining three.

- *Too much digging/too little confidence.* The testing of many variables by the researcher is the "too much digging" warning sign of a data-mining problem. Unfortunately, many researchers do not disclose the number of variables examined in developing a model. Although the number of variables examined may not be reported, we should look closely for verbal hints that the researcher searched over many variables. The use of terms such as "we noticed (or noted) that" or "someone noticed (or noted) that," with respect to a pattern in a dataset, should raise suspicions that the researchers were trying out variables based on their own or others' observations of the data.
- *No story/no future.* The absence of an explicit economic rationale for a variable or trading strategy is the "no story" warning sign of a data-mining problem. Without a plausible economic rationale or story for why a variable should work, the variable is unlikely to have predictive power. In a demonstration exercise using an extensive search of variables in an international financial database, **Leinweber (1997)** found that butter production in a particular country remote from the United States explained 75 percent of the variation in US stock returns as represented by the S&P 500. Such a pattern, with no plausible economic rationale, is highly likely to be a random pattern particular to a specific time period.[25] What if we do have a plausible economic explanation for a significant variable? McQueen and Thorley caution that a plausible economic rationale is a necessary but not a sufficient condition for a trading strategy to have value. As we mentioned earlier, if the strategy is publicized, market prices may adjust to reflect the new information as traders seek to exploit it; as a result, the strategy may no longer work.

5.2. Sample Selection Bias

When researchers look into questions of interest to analysts or portfolio managers, they may exclude certain stocks, bonds, portfolios, or time periods from the analysis for various reasons— perhaps because of data availability. When data availability leads to certain assets being excluded from the analysis, we call the resulting problem **sample selection bias**. For example, you might sample from a database that tracks only companies currently in existence. Many mutual fund databases, for instance, provide historical information about only those funds that currently exist. Databases that report historical balance sheet and income statement information suffer from the same sort of bias as the mutual fund databases: Funds or companies that are no longer in business do not appear there. So, a study that uses these types of databases suffers from a type of sample selection bias known as **survivorship bias**.

Dimson, Marsh, and Staunton (2002) raised the issue of survivorship bias in international indexes:

> An issue that has achieved prominence is the impact of market survival on estimated long-run returns. Markets can experience not only disappointing performance but also total loss of value through confiscation, hyperinflation, nationalization, and market failure. By measuring the performance of markets that survive over long intervals, we draw inferences that are conditioned on survival. Yet, as pointed out by **Brown, Goetzmann, and Ross (1995)** and **Goetzmann and Jorion (1999)**, one cannot determine in advance which markets will survive and which will perish. (p. 41)

---

[25] In the finance literature, such a random but irrelevant-to-the-future pattern is sometimes called an artifact of the dataset.

Survivorship bias sometimes appears when we use both stock price and accounting data. For example, many studies in finance have used the ratio of a company's market price to book equity per share (i.e., the price-to-book ratio, P/B) and found that P/B is inversely related to a company's returns (see Fama and French 1992, 1993). P/B is also used to create many popular value and growth indexes. If the database that we use to collect accounting data excludes failing companies, however, a survivorship bias might result. **Kothari, Shanken, and Sloan (1995)** investigated just this question and argued that failing stocks would be expected to have low returns and low P/Bs. If we exclude failing stocks, then those stocks with low P/Bs that are included will have returns that are higher on average than if all stocks with low P/Bs were included. Kothari, Shanken, and Sloan suggested that this bias is responsible for the previous findings of an inverse relationship between average return and P/B.[26] The only advice we can offer at this point is to be aware of any biases potentially inherent in a sample. Clearly, sample selection biases can cloud the results of any study.

A sample can also be biased because of the removal (or delisting) of a company's stock from an exchange.[27] For example, the Center for Research in Security Prices at the University of Chicago is a major provider of return data used in academic research. When a delisting occurs, CRSP attempts to collect returns for the delisted company, but many times, it cannot do so because of the difficulty involved; CRSP must simply list delisted company returns as missing. A study in the *Journal of Finance* by **Shumway and Warther (1999)** documented the bias caused by delisting for CRSP NASDAQ return data. The authors showed that delistings associated with poor company performance (e.g., bankruptcy) are missed more often than delistings associated with good or neutral company performance (e.g., merger or moving to another exchange). In addition, delistings occur more frequently for small companies.

Sample selection bias occurs even in markets where the quality and consistency of the data are quite high. Newer asset classes such as hedge funds may present even greater problems of sample selection bias. Hedge funds are a heterogeneous group of investment vehicles typically organized so as to be free from regulatory oversight. In general, hedge funds are not required to publicly disclose performance (in contrast to, say, mutual funds). Hedge funds themselves decide whether they want to be included in one of the various databases of hedge fund performance. Hedge funds with poor track records clearly may not wish to make their records public, creating a problem of self-selection bias in hedge fund databases. Further, as pointed out by **Fung and Hsieh (2002)**, because only hedge funds with good records will volunteer to enter a database, in general, overall past hedge fund industry performance will tend to appear better than it really is. Furthermore, many hedge fund databases drop funds that go out of business, creating survivorship bias in the database. Even if the database does not drop defunct hedge funds, in the attempt to eliminate survivorship bias, the problem remains of hedge funds that stop reporting performance because of poor results.[28]

5.3. Look-Ahead Bias

A test design is subject to **look-ahead bias** if it uses information that was not available on the test date. For example, tests of trading rules that use stock market returns and accounting

---

[26] See Fama and French (1996, p. 80) for discussion of data snooping and survivorship bias in their tests.
[27] Delistings occur for a variety of reasons: merger, bankruptcy, liquidation, or migration to another exchange.
[28] See Fung and Hsieh (2002) and ter Horst and Verbeek (2007) for more details on the problems of interpreting hedge fund performance. Note that an offsetting type of bias may occur if successful funds stop reporting performance because they no longer want new cash inflows.

balance sheet data must account for look-ahead bias. In such tests, a company's book value per share is commonly used to construct the P/B variable. Although the market price of a stock is available for all market participants at the same point in time, fiscal year-end book equity per share might not become publicly available until sometime in the following quarter.

5.4. Time-Period Bias

A test design is subject to **time-period bias** if it is based on a time period that may make the results time-period specific. A short time series is likely to give period specific results that may not reflect a longer period. A long time series may give a more accurate picture of true investment performance; its disadvantage lies in the potential for a structural change occurring during the time frame that would result in two different return distributions. In this situation, the distribution that would reflect conditions before the change differs from the distribution that would describe conditions after the change.

EXAMPLE 7   Biases in Investment Research

An analyst is reviewing the empirical evidence on historical US equity returns. She finds that value stocks (i.e., those with low P/Bs) outperformed growth stocks (i.e., those with high P/Bs) in some recent time periods. After reviewing the US market, the analyst wonders whether value stocks might be attractive in the United Kingdom. She investigates the performance of value and growth stocks in the UK market for a 14-year period. To conduct this research, the analyst does the following:

- obtains the current composition of the Financial Times Stock Exchange (FTSE) All Share Index, which is a market-capitalization–weighted index;
- eliminates the few companies that do not have December fiscal year-ends;
- uses year-end book values and market prices to rank the remaining universe of companies by P/Bs at the end of the year;
- based on these rankings, divides the universe into 10 portfolios, each of which contains an equal number of stocks;
- calculates the equal-weighted return of each portfolio and the return for the FTSE All Share Index for the 12 months following the date each ranking was made; and
- subtracts the FTSE returns from each portfolio's returns to derive excess returns for each portfolio.

Describe and discuss each of the following biases introduced by the analyst's research design:

- survivorship bias;
- look-ahead bias; and
- time-period bias.

Survivorship Bias
A test design is subject to survivorship bias if it fails to account for companies that have gone bankrupt, merged, or otherwise departed the database. In this example, the analyst used the current list of FTSE stocks rather than the actual list of stocks that existed at

the start of each year. To the extent that the computation of returns excluded companies removed from the index, the performance of the portfolios with the lowest P/B is subject to survivorship bias and may be overstated. At some time during the testing period, those companies not currently in existence were eliminated from testing. They would probably have had low prices (and low P/Bs) and poor returns.

Look-Ahead Bias

A test design is subject to look-ahead bias if it uses information unavailable on the test date. In this example, the analyst conducted the test under the assumption that the necessary accounting information was available at the end of the fiscal year. For example, the analyst assumed that book value per share for a given fiscal year was available on 31 December of that year. Because this information is not released until several months after the close of a fiscal year, the test may have contained look-ahead bias. This bias would make a strategy based on the information appear successful, but it assumes perfect forecasting ability.

Time-Period Bias

A test design is subject to time-period bias if it is based on a time period that may make the results time-period specific. Although the test covered a period extending more than 10 years, that period may be too short for testing an anomaly. Ideally, an analyst should test market anomalies over several business cycles to ensure that results are not period specific. This bias can favor a proposed strategy if the time period chosen was favorable to the strategy.

6. SUMMARY

In this chapter, we have presented basic concepts and results in sampling and estimation. We have also emphasized the challenges faced by analysts in appropriately using and interpreting financial data. As analysts, we should always use a critical eye when evaluating the results from any study. The quality of the sample is of the utmost importance: If the sample is biased, the conclusions drawn from the sample will be in error.

- To draw valid inferences from a sample, the sample should be random.
- In simple random sampling, each observation has an equal chance of being selected. In stratified random sampling, the population is divided into subpopulations, called strata or cells, based on one or more classification criteria; simple random samples are then drawn from each stratum.
- Stratified random sampling ensures that population subdivisions of interest are represented in the sample. Stratified random sampling also produces more-precise parameter estimates than simple random sampling.
- Time-series data are a collection of observations at equally spaced intervals of time. Cross-sectional data are observations that represent individuals, groups, geographical regions, or companies at a single point in time.
- The central limit theorem states that for large sample sizes, for any underlying distribution for a random variable, the sampling distribution of the sample mean for that variable will

be approximately normal, with mean equal to the population mean for that random variable and variance equal to the population variance of the variable divided by sample size.

- Based on the central limit theorem, when the sample size is large, we can compute confidence intervals for the population mean based on the normal distribution regardless of the distribution of the underlying population. In general, a sample size of 30 or larger can be considered large.

- An estimator is a formula for estimating a parameter. An estimate is a particular value that we calculate from a sample by using an estimator.

- Because an estimator or statistic is a random variable, it is described by some probability distribution. We refer to the distribution of an estimator as its sampling distribution. The standard deviation of the sampling distribution of the sample mean is called the standard error of the sample mean.

- The desirable properties of an estimator are *unbiasedness* (the expected value of the estimator equals the population parameter), *efficiency* (the estimator has the smallest variance), and *consistency* (the probability of accurate estimates increases as sample size increases).

- The two types of estimates of a parameter are point estimates and interval estimates. A point estimate is a single number that we use to estimate a parameter. An interval estimate is a range of values that brackets the population parameter with some probability.

- A confidence interval is an interval for which we can assert with a given probability $1 - \alpha$, called the degree of confidence, that it will contain the parameter it is intended to estimate. This measure is often referred to as the $100(1 - \alpha)\%$ confidence interval for the parameter.

- A $100(1 - \alpha)\%$ confidence interval for a parameter has the following structure: Point estimate $\pm$ Reliability factor $\times$ Standard error, where the reliability factor is a number based on the assumed distribution of the point estimate and the degree of confidence $(1 - \alpha)$ for the confidence interval and where standard error is the standard error of the sample statistic providing the point estimate.

- A $100(1 - \alpha)\%$ confidence interval for population mean μ when sampling from a normal distribution with known variance σ^2 is given by $\bar{X} \pm z_{\alpha/2}\frac{\sigma}{\sqrt{n}}$, where $z_{\alpha/2}$ is the point of the standard normal distribution such that $\alpha/2$ remains in the right tail.

- Student's *t*-distribution is a family of symmetrical distributions defined by a single parameter, degrees of freedom.

- A random sample of size n is said to have $n - 1$ degrees of freedom for estimating the population variance, in the sense that there are only $n - 1$ independent deviations from the mean on which to base the estimate.

- The degrees of freedom number for use with the *t*-distribution is also $n - 1$.

- The *t*-distribution has fatter tails than the standard normal distribution but converges to the standard normal distribution as degrees of freedom go to infinity.

- A $100(1 - \alpha)\%$ confidence interval for the population mean μ when sampling from a normal distribution with unknown variance (a *t*-distribution confidence interval) is given by $\bar{X} \pm t_{\alpha/2}(s/\sqrt{n})$, where $t_{\alpha/2}$ is the point of the *t*-distribution such that $\alpha/2$ remains in the right tail and s is the sample standard deviation. This confidence interval can also be used, because of the central limit theorem, when dealing with a large sample from a population with unknown variance that may not be normal.

- We may use the confidence interval $\bar{X} \pm z_{\alpha/2}(s/\sqrt{n})$ as an alternative to the *t*-distribution confidence interval for the population mean when using a large sample from a population with unknown variance. The confidence interval based on the *z*-statistic is less conservative (narrower) than the corresponding confidence interval based on a *t*-distribution.

- Three issues in the selection of sample size are the need for precision, the risk of sampling from more than one population, and the expenses of different sample sizes.
- Sample data in investments can have a variety of problems. *Survivorship bias* occurs if companies are excluded from the analysis because they have gone out of business or because of reasons related to poor performance. *Data-mining bias* comes from finding models by repeatedly searching through databases for patterns. *Look-ahead bias* exists if the model uses data not available to market participants at the time the market participants act in the model. Finally, time-period bias is present if the time period used makes the results time-period specific or if the time period used includes a point of structural change.

REFERENCES

Brown, Stephen, William Goetzmann, and Stephen Ross. 1995. "Survival." *Journal of Finance*, vol. 50:853–873. 10.1111/j.1540-6261.1995.tb04039.x.

Campbell, John, Andrew Lo, and A. Craig MacKinlay. 1997. *The Econometrics of Financial Markets*. Princeton, NJ: Princeton University Press.

Daniel, Wayne W. and James C. Terrell. 1995. *Business Statistics for Management & Economics*, 7th edition. Boston: Houghton-Mifflin.

Dimson, Elroy, Paul Marsh, and Mike Staunton. 2002. *Triumphs of the Optimists: 101 Years of Global Investment Returns*. Princeton, NJ: Princeton University Press.

Fama, Eugene F. and Kenneth R. French. 1996. "Multifactor Explanations of Asset Pricing Anomalies." *Journal of Finance*, vol. 51, no. 1:55–84. 10.1111/j.1540-6261.1996.tb05202.x.

Freund, John E and Frank J. Williams. 1977. *Elementary Business Statistics*, 3rd edition. Englewood Cliffs, NJ: Prentice-Hall.

Fung, William and David Hsieh. 2002. "Hedge-Fund Benchmarks: Information Content and Biases." *Financial Analysts Journal*, vol. 58, no. 1:22–34. 10.2469/faj.v58.n1.2507.

Goetzmann, William and Philippe Jorion. 1999. "Re-Emerging Markets." *Journal of Financial and Quantitative Analysis*, vol. 34, no. 1:1–32. 10.2307/2676244.

Greene, William H. 2018. *Econometric Analysis*, 8th edition. Upper Saddle River, NJ: Prentice-Hall.

Kothari, S.P., Jay Shanken, and Richard G. Sloan. 1995. "Another Look at the Cross-Section of Expected Stock Returns." *Journal of Finance*, vol. 50, no. 1:185–224. 10.1111/j.1540-6261.1995.tb05171.x.

Leinweber, David. 1997. *Stupid Data Mining Tricks: Over-Fitting the S&P 500*. Monograph. Pasadena, CA: First Quadrant.

Lo, Andrew W. and A. Craig MacKinlay. 1990. "Data Snooping Biases in Tests of Financial Asset Pricing Models." *Review of Financial Studies*, vol. 3:175–208. 10.1093/rfs/3.2.175.

McQueen, Grant and Steven Thorley. 1999. "Mining Fools Gold." *Financial Analysts Journal*, vol. 55, no. 2:61–72. 10.2469/faj.v55.n2.2261.

Shumway, Tyler and Vincent A. Warther. 1999. "The Delisting Bias in CRSP's Nasdaq Data and Its Implications for the Size Effect." *Journal of Finance*, vol. 54, no. 6:2361–2379. 10.1111/0022-1082.00192.

ter Horst, Jenke and Marno Verbeek. 2007. "Fund Liquidation, Self-selection, and Look-ahead Bias in the Hedge Fund Industry." *Review of Finance*, vol. 11:605–632. 10.1093/rof/rfm012.

PRACTICE PROBLEMS

1. Peter Biggs wants to know how growth managers performed last year. Biggs assumes that the population cross-sectional standard deviation of growth manager returns is 6 percent and that the returns are independent across managers.
   A. How large a random sample does Biggs need if he wants the standard deviation of the sample means to be 1 percent?
   B. How large a random sample does Biggs need if he wants the standard deviation of the sample means to be 0.25 percent?

2. Petra Munzi wants to know how value managers performed last year. Munzi estimates that the population cross-sectional standard deviation of value manager returns is 4 percent and assumes that the returns are independent across managers.
   A. Munzi wants to build a 95 percent confidence interval for the mean return. How large a random sample does Munzi need if she wants the 95 percent confidence interval to have a total width of 1 percent?
   B. Munzi expects a cost of about $10 to collect each observation. If she has a $1,000 budget, will she be able to construct the confidence interval she wants?

3. Assume that the equity risk premium is normally distributed with a population mean of 6 percent and a population standard deviation of 18 percent. Over the last four years, equity returns (relative to the risk-free rate) have averaged –2.0 percent. You have a large client who is very upset and claims that results this poor should *never* occur. Evaluate your client's concerns.
   A. Construct a 95 percent confidence interval around the population mean for a sample of four-year returns.
   B. What is the probability of a –2.0 percent or lower average return over a four-year period?

4. Compare the standard normal distribution and Student's *t*-distribution.

5. Find the reliability factors based on the *t*-distribution for the following confidence intervals for the population mean (DF = degrees of freedom, n = sample size):
   A. A 99 percent confidence interval, DF = 20.
   B. A 90 percent confidence interval, DF = 20.
   C. A 95 percent confidence interval, n = 25.
   D. A 95 percent confidence interval, n = 16.

6. Assume that monthly returns are normally distributed with a mean of 1 percent and a sample standard deviation of 4 percent. The population standard deviation is unknown. Construct a 95 percent confidence interval for the sample mean of monthly returns if the sample size is 24.

7. Ten analysts have given the following fiscal year earnings forecasts for a stock:

Forecast (X_i)	Number of Analysts (n_i)
1.40	1
1.43	1
1.44	3
1.45	2
1.47	1
1.48	1
1.50	1

Because the sample is a small fraction of the number of analysts who follow this stock, assume that we can ignore the finite population correction factor. Assume that the analyst forecasts are normally distributed.

A. What are the mean forecast and standard deviation of forecasts?

B. Provide a 95 percent confidence interval for the population mean of the forecasts.

8. Thirteen analysts have given the following fiscal-year earnings forecasts for a stock:

Forecast (X_i)	Number of Analysts (n_i)
0.70	2
0.72	4
0.74	1
0.75	3
0.76	1
0.77	1
0.82	1

Because the sample is a small fraction of the number of analysts who follow this stock, assume that we can ignore the finite population correction factor.

A. What are the mean forecast and standard deviation of forecasts?

B. What aspect of the data makes us uncomfortable about using t-tables to construct confidence intervals for the population mean forecast?

9. Explain the differences between constructing a confidence interval when sampling from a normal population with a known population variance and sampling from a normal population with an unknown variance.

10. An exchange rate has a given expected future value and standard deviation.
    A. Assuming that the exchange rate is normally distributed, what are the probabilities that the exchange rate will be at least 2 or 3 standard deviations away from its mean?
    B. Assume that you do not know the distribution of exchange rates. Use Chebyshev's inequality (that at least $1 - 1/k^2$ proportion of the observations will be within k standard deviations of the mean for any positive integer k greater than 1) to calculate the maximum probabilities that the exchange rate will be at least 2 or 3 standard deviations away from its mean.

11. Although he knows security returns are not independent, a colleague makes the claim that because of the central limit theorem, if we diversify across a large number of investments, the portfolio standard deviation will eventually approach zero as n becomes large. Is he correct?

12. Why is the central limit theorem important?

13. What is wrong with the following statement of the central limit theorem?

Central Limit Theorem. "If the random variables X_1, X_2, X_3, ..., X_n are a random sample of size n from any distribution with finite mean μ and variance σ^2, then the distribution of $\bar{X}$ will be approximately normal, with a standard deviation of $\sigma/\sqrt{n}$."

14. Suppose we take a random sample of 30 companies in an industry with 200 companies. We calculate the sample mean of the ratio of cash flow to total debt for the prior year. We find that this ratio is 23 percent. Subsequently, we learn that the population cash flow to total debt ratio (taking account of all 200 companies) is 26 percent. What is the explanation for the discrepancy between the sample mean of 23 percent and the population mean of 26 percent?
    A. Sampling error.
    B. Bias.
    C. A lack of consistency.

15. Alcorn Mutual Funds is placing large advertisements in several financial publications. The advertisements prominently display the returns of 5 of Alcorn's 30 funds for the past 1-, 3-, 5-, and 10-year periods. The results are indeed impressive, with all of the funds beating the major market indexes and a few beating them by a large margin. Is the Alcorn family of funds superior to its competitors?

16. Julius Spence has tested several predictive models in order to identify undervalued stocks. Spence used about 30 company-specific variables and 10 market-related variables to predict returns for about 5,000 North American and European stocks. He found that a final model using eight variables applied to telecommunications and computer stocks yields spectacular results. Spence wants you to use the model to select investments. Should you? What steps would you take to evaluate the model?

17. The *best* approach for creating a stratified random sample of a population involves:
    A. drawing an equal number of simple random samples from each subpopulation.
    B. selecting every *k*th member of the population until the desired sample size is reached.
    C. drawing simple random samples from each subpopulation in sizes proportional to the relative size of each subpopulation.

18. A population has a non-normal distribution with mean E and variance σ^2. The sampling distribution of the sample mean computed from samples of large size from that population will have:
    A. the same distribution as the population distribution.
    B. its mean approximately equal to the population mean.
    C. its variance approximately equal to the population variance.

19. A sample mean is computed from a population with a variance of 2.45. The sample size is 40. The standard error of the sample mean is *closest* to:
    A. 0.039.
    B. 0.247.
    C. 0.387.

20. An estimator with an expected value equal to the parameter that it is intended to estimate is described as:
    A. efficient.
    B. unbiased.
    C. consistent.

21. If an estimator is consistent, an increase in sample size will increase the:
    A. accuracy of estimates.
    B. efficiency of the estimator.
    C. unbiasedness of the estimator.

22. For a two-sided confidence interval, an increase in the degree of confidence will result in:
    A. a wider confidence interval.
    B. a narrower confidence interval.
    C. no change in the width of the confidence interval.

23. As the *t*-distribution's degrees of freedom decrease, the *t*-distribution *most likely*:
    A. exhibits tails that become fatter.
    B. approaches a standard normal distribution.
    C. becomes asymmetrically distributed around its mean value.

24. For a sample size of 17, with a mean of 116.23 and a variance of 245.55, the width of a 90 percent confidence interval using the appropriate *t*-distribution is *closest to*:
    A. 13.23.
    B. 13.27.
    C. 13.68.

25. For a sample size of 65 with a mean of 31 taken from a normally distributed population with a variance of 529, a 99 percent confidence interval for the population mean will have a lower limit *closest* to:
   A. 23.64.
   B. 25.41.
   C. 30.09.

26. An increase in sample size is *most likely* to result in a:
   A. wider confidence interval.
   B. decrease in the standard error of the sample mean.
   C. lower likelihood of sampling from more than one population.

27. A report on long-term stock returns focused exclusively on all currently publicly traded firms in an industry is *most likely* susceptible to:
   A. look-ahead bias.
   B. survivorship bias.
   C. intergenerational data mining.

28. Which sampling bias is *most likely* investigated with an out-of-sample test?
   A. Look-ahead bias
   B. Data-mining bias
   C. Sample selection bias

29. Which of the following characteristics of an investment study *most likely* indicates time-period bias?
   A. The study is based on a short time-series.
   B. Information not available on the test date is used.
   C. A structural change occurred prior to the start of the study's time series.

CHAPTER 6

HYPOTHESIS TESTING

Richard A. DeFusco, PhD, CFA
Dennis W. McLeavey, DBA, CFA
Jerald E. Pinto, PhD, CFA
David E. Runkle, PhD, CFA

LEARNING OUTCOMES

The candidate should be able to:

- define a hypothesis, describe the steps of hypothesis testing, and describe and interpret the choice of the null and alternative hypotheses;
- distinguish between one-tailed and two-tailed tests of hypotheses;
- explain a test statistic, Type I and Type II errors, a significance level, and how significance levels are used in hypothesis testing;
- explain a decision rule, the power of a test, and the relation between confidence intervals and hypothesis tests;
- distinguish between a statistical result and an economically meaningful result;
- explain and interpret the *p*-value as it relates to hypothesis testing;
- identify the appropriate test statistic and interpret the results for a hypothesis test concerning the population mean of both large and small samples when the population is normally or approximately normally distributed and the variance is 1) known or 2) unknown;
- identify the appropriate test statistic and interpret the results for a hypothesis test concerning the equality of the population means of two at least approximately normally distributed populations, based on independent random samples with 1) equal or 2) unequal assumed variances;
- identify the appropriate test statistic and interpret the results for a hypothesis test concerning the mean difference of two normally distributed populations;
- identify the appropriate test statistic and interpret the results for a hypothesis test concerning 1) the variance of a normally distributed population, and 2) the equality of the

Quantitative Methods for Investment Analysis, Second Edition, by Richard A. DeFusco, PhD, CFA, Dennis W. McLeavey, DBA, CFA, Jerald E. Pinto, PhD, CFA, David E. Runkle, PhD, CFA. Copyright © 2019 by CFA Institute

variances of two normally distributed populations based on two independent random samples;
- formulate a test of the hypothesis that the population correlation coefficient equals zero and determine whether the hypothesis is rejected at a given level of significance;
- distinguish between parametric and nonparametric tests and describe situations in which the use of nonparametric tests may be appropriate.

1. INTRODUCTION

Analysts often confront competing ideas about how financial markets work. Some of these ideas develop through personal research or experience with markets; others come from interactions with colleagues; and many others appear in the professional literature on finance and investments. In general, how can an analyst decide whether statements about the financial world are probably true or probably false?

When we can reduce an idea or assertion to a definite statement about the value of a quantity, such as an underlying or population mean, the idea becomes a statistically testable statement or hypothesis. The analyst may want to explore questions such as the following:

- Is the underlying mean return on this mutual fund different from the underlying mean return on its benchmark?
- Did the volatility of returns on this stock change after the stock was added to a stock market index?
- Are a security's bid-ask spreads related to the number of dealers making a market in the security?
- Do data from a national bond market support a prediction of an economic theory about the term structure of interest rates (the relationship between yield and maturity)?

To address these questions, we use the concepts and tools of hypothesis testing. Hypothesis testing is part of statistical inference, the process of making judgments about a larger group (a population) on the basis of a smaller group actually observed (a sample). The concepts and tools of hypothesis testing provide an objective means to gauge whether the available evidence supports the hypothesis. After a statistical test of a hypothesis we should have a clearer idea of the probability that a hypothesis is true or not, although our conclusion always stops short of certainty. Hypothesis testing has been a powerful tool in the advancement of investment knowledge and science. As Robert L. Kahn of the Institute for Social Research (Ann Arbor, Michigan) has written, "The mill of science grinds only when hypothesis and data are in continuous and abrasive contact."

The main emphases of this chapter are the framework of hypothesis testing and tests concerning mean, variance, and correlation, three quantities frequently used in investments. We give an overview of the procedure of hypothesis testing in the next section. We then address testing hypotheses about the mean and hypotheses about the differences between means. In the fourth section of this chapter, we address testing hypotheses about a single variance, the differences between variances, and a correlation coefficient. We end the chapter with an overview of some other important issues and techniques in statistical inference.

2. HYPOTHESIS TESTING

Hypothesis testing, as we have mentioned, is part of the branch of statistics known as statistical inference. Traditionally, the field of statistical inference has two subdivisions: **estimation** and **hypothesis testing**. Estimation addresses the question "What is this parameter's (e.g., the population mean's) value?" The answer is in the form of a confidence interval built around a point estimate. Take the case of the mean: We build a confidence interval for the population mean around the sample mean as a point estimate. For the sake of specificity, suppose the sample mean is 50 and a 95 percent confidence interval for the population mean is 50 ± 10 (the confidence interval runs from 40 to 60). If this confidence interval has been properly constructed, there is a 95 percent probability that the interval from 40 to 60 contains the population mean's value.[1] The second branch of statistical inference, hypothesis testing, has a somewhat different focus. A hypothesis testing question is "Is the value of the parameter (say, the population mean) 45 (or some other specific value)?" The assertion "the population mean is 45" is a hypothesis. A **hypothesis** is defined as a statement about one or more populations.

This section focuses on the concepts of hypothesis testing. The process of hypothesis testing is part of a rigorous approach to acquiring knowledge known as the scientific method. The scientific method starts with observation and the formulation of a theory to organize and explain observations. We judge the correctness of the theory by its ability to make accurate predictions —for example, to predict the results of new observations.[2] If the predictions are correct, we continue to maintain the theory as a possibly correct explanation of our observations. When risk plays a role in the outcomes of observations, as in finance, we can only try to make unbiased, probability-based judgments about whether the new data support the predictions. Statistical hypothesis testing fills that key role of testing hypotheses when chance plays a role. In an analyst's day-to-day work, he may address questions to which he might give answers of varying quality. When an analyst correctly formulates the question into a testable hypothesis and carries out and reports on a hypothesis test, he has provided an element of support to his answer consistent with the standards of the scientific method. Of course, the analyst's logic, economic reasoning, information sources, and perhaps other factors also play a role in our assessment of the answer's quality.[3]

We organize this introduction to hypothesis testing around the following list of seven steps.

- **Steps in Hypothesis Testing.** The steps in testing a hypothesis are as follows:[4]
  1. Stating the hypotheses.
  2. Identifying the appropriate test statistic and its probability distribution.
  3. Specifying the significance level.
  4. Stating the decision rule.

---

[1] We discussed the construction and interpretation of confidence intervals in the chapter on sampling and estimation (Chapter 5).

[2] To be testable, a theory must be capable of making predictions that can be shown to be wrong.

[3] See Freeley and Steinberg (2013) for a discussion of critical thinking applied to reasoned decision making.

[4] This list is based on one in Daniel and Terrell (1995).

5. Collecting the data and calculating the test statistic.
6. Making the statistical decision.
7. Making the economic or investment decision.

We will explain each of these steps using as illustration a hypothesis test concerning the sign of the risk premium on US stocks. The steps above constitute a traditional approach to hypothesis testing. We will end the section with a frequently used alternative to those steps, the p-value approach.

The first step in hypothesis testing is stating the hypotheses. We always state two hypotheses: the null hypothesis (or null), designated H_0, and the alternative hypothesis, designated H_a.

- **Definition of Null Hypothesis.** The null hypothesis is the hypothesis to be tested. For example, we could hypothesize that the population mean risk premium for US equities is less than or equal to zero.

The null hypothesis is a proposition that is considered true unless the sample we use to conduct the hypothesis test gives convincing evidence that the null hypothesis is false. When such evidence is present, we are led to the alternative hypothesis.

- **Definition of Alternative Hypothesis.** The alternative hypothesis is the hypothesis accepted when the null hypothesis is rejected. Our alternative hypothesis is that the population mean risk premium for US equities is greater than zero.

Suppose our question concerns the value of a population parameter, θ, in relation to one possible value of the parameter, θ_0 (these are read, respectively, "theta" and "theta sub zero").[5] Examples of a population parameter include the population mean, μ, and the population variance, σ^2. We can formulate three different sets of hypotheses, which we label according to the assertion made by the alternative hypothesis.

- **Formulations of Hypotheses.** In the following discussion we formulate the null and alternative hypotheses in three different ways:
  1. H_0: $\theta = \theta_0$ versus H_a: $\theta \neq \theta_0$ (a "not equal to" alternative hypothesis)
  2. H_0: $\theta \leq \theta_0$ versus H_a: $\theta > \theta_0$ (a "greater than" alternative hypothesis)
  3. H_0: $\theta \geq \theta_0$ versus H_a: $\theta < \theta_0$ (a "less than" alternative hypothesis)

In our US example, $\theta = \mu_{RP}$ and represents the population mean risk premium on US equities. Also, $\theta_0 = 0$ and we are using the second of the above three formulations.

The first formulation is a **two-sided hypothesis test** (or **two-tailed hypothesis test**): We reject the null in favor of the alternative if the evidence indicates that the population parameter is either smaller or larger than θ_0. In contrast, Formulations 2 and 3 are each a **one-sided hypothesis test** (or **one-tailed hypothesis test**). For Formulations 2 and 3, we reject the null only if the evidence indicates that the population parameter is respectively greater than or less than θ_0. The alternative hypothesis has one side.

Notice that in each case above, we state the null and alternative hypotheses such that they account for all possible values of the parameter. With Formulation 1, for example, the parameter is either equal to the hypothesized value θ_0 (under the null hypothesis) or not equal

[5]Greek letters, such as σ, are reserved for population parameters; Roman letters in italics, such as s, are used for sample statistics.

to the hypothesized value θ_0 (under the alternative hypothesis). Those two statements logically exhaust all possible values of the parameter.

Despite the different ways to formulate hypotheses, we always conduct a test of the null hypothesis at the point of equality, $\theta = \theta_0$. Whether the null is H_0: $\theta = \theta_0$, H_0: $\theta \leq \theta_0$, or H_0: $\theta \geq \theta_0$, we actually test $\theta = \theta_0$. The reasoning is straightforward. Suppose the hypothesized value of the parameter is 5. Consider H_0: $\theta \leq 5$, with a "greater than" alternative hypothesis, H_a: $\theta > 5$. If we have enough evidence to reject H_0: $\theta = 5$ in favor of H_a: $\theta > 5$, we definitely also have enough evidence to reject the hypothesis that the parameter, θ, is some smaller value, such as 4.5 or 4. To review, the calculation to test the null hypothesis is the same for all three formulations. What is different for the three formulations, we will see shortly, is how the calculation is evaluated to decide whether or not to reject the null.

How do we choose the null and alternative hypotheses? Probably most common are "not equal to" alternative hypotheses. We reject the null because the evidence indicates that the parameter is either larger or smaller than θ_0. Sometimes, however, we may have a "suspected" or "hoped for" condition for which we want to find supportive evidence.[6] In that case, we can formulate the alternative hypothesis as the statement that this condition is true; the null hypothesis that we test is the statement that this condition is not true. If the evidence supports rejecting the null and accepting the alternative, we have statistically confirmed what we thought was true. For example, economic theory suggests that investors require a positive risk premium on stocks (the **risk premium** is defined as the expected return on stocks minus the risk-free rate). Following the principle of stating the alternative as the "hoped for" condition, we formulate the following hypotheses:

H_0: The population mean risk premium on US stocks is less than or equal to 0.

H_a: The population mean risk premium on US stocks is positive.

Note that "greater than" and "less than" alternative hypotheses reflect the beliefs of the researcher more strongly than a "not equal to" alternative hypothesis. To emphasize an attitude of neutrality, the researcher may sometimes select a "not equal to" alternative hypothesis when a one-sided alternative hypothesis is also reasonable.

The second step in hypothesis testing is identifying the appropriate test statistic and its probability distribution.

- **Definition of Test Statistic.** A test statistic is a quantity, calculated based on a sample, whose value is the basis for deciding whether or not to reject the null hypothesis.

The focal point of our statistical decision is the value of the test statistic. Frequently, the test statistic has the form[7]

$$\text{Test statistic} = \frac{\text{Sample statistic} - \text{Value of the population parameter under } H_0}{\text{Standard error of the sample statistic}} \qquad (1)$$

---

[6]Part of this discussion of the selection of hypotheses follows Bowerman, O'Connell, and Murphree (2016).

[7]In some cases, the test statistic may have a different form. For example, as we discuss in Section 4.3, the form of the test statistic for correlation coefficient is different.

For our risk premium example, the population parameter of interest is the population mean risk premium, μ_{RP}. We label the hypothesized value of the population mean under H_0 as μ_0. Restating the hypotheses using symbols, we test H_0: $\mu_{RP} \leq \mu_0$ versus H_a: $\mu_{RP} > \mu_0$. However, because under the null we are testing $\mu_0 = 0$, we write H_0: $\mu_{RP} \leq 0$ versus H_a: $\mu_{RP} > 0$.

The sample mean provides an estimate of the population mean. Therefore, we can use the sample mean risk premium calculated from historical data, $\overline{X}_{RP}$, as the sample statistic in Equation 1. The standard deviation of the sample statistic, known as the standard error of the statistic, is the denominator in Equation 1. For this example, the sample statistic is a sample mean. For a sample mean, $\overline{X}$, calculated from a sample generated by a population with standard deviation σ, the standard error is given by one of two expressions:

$$\sigma_{\overline{X}} = \frac{\sigma}{\sqrt{n}} \tag{2}$$

when we know σ (the population standard deviation), or

$$s_{\overline{X}} = \frac{s}{\sqrt{n}} \tag{3}$$

when we do not know the population standard deviation and need to use the sample standard deviation s to estimate it. For this example, because we do not know the population standard deviation of the process generating the return, we use Equation 3. The test statistic is thus

$$\frac{\overline{X}_{RP} - \mu_0}{s_{\overline{X}}} = \frac{\overline{X}_{RP} - 0}{s/\sqrt{n}}$$

In making the substitution of 0 for μ_0, we use the fact already highlighted that we test any null hypothesis at the point of equality, as well as the fact that $\mu_0 = 0$ here.

We have identified a test statistic to test the null hypothesis. What probability distribution does it follow? We will encounter four distributions for test statistics in this chapter:

1. the t-distribution (for a t-test);
2. the standard normal or z-distribution (for a z-test);
3. the chi-square (χ^2) distribution (for a chi-square test); and
4. the F-distribution (for an F-test).

We will discuss the details later, but assume we can conduct a z-test based on the central limit theorem because our US sample has many observations.[8] To summarize, the test statistic for the hypothesis test concerning the mean risk premium is $\overline{X}_{RP}/s_{\overline{X}}$. We can conduct a z-test because we can plausibly assume that the test statistic follows a standard normal distribution.

---

[8] The central limit theorem says that the sampling distribution of the sample mean will be approximately normal with mean μ and variance σ^2/n when the sample size is large. The sample we will use for this example has 118 observations.

EXHIBIT 1   Type I and Type II Errors in Hypothesis Testing

Decision	True Situation	
	H_0 True	H_0 False
Do not reject H_0	Correct Decision	Type II Error
Reject H_0 (accept H_a)	Type I Error	Correct Decision

The third step in hypothesis testing is specifying the significance level. When the test statistic has been calculated, two actions are possible: 1) We reject the null hypothesis or 2) we do not reject the null hypothesis. The action we take is based on comparing the calculated test statistic to a specified possible value or values. The comparison values we choose are based on the level of significance selected. The level of significance reflects how much sample evidence we require to reject the null. Analogous to its counterpart in a court of law, the required standard of proof can change according to the nature of the hypotheses and the seriousness of the consequences of making a mistake. There are four possible outcomes when we test a null hypothesis:

1. We reject a false null hypothesis. This is a correct decision.
2. We reject a true null hypothesis. This is called a **Type I error**.
3. We do not reject a false null hypothesis. This is called a **Type II error**.
4. We do not reject a true null hypothesis. This is a correct decision.

We illustrate these outcomes in Exhibit 1.

When we make a decision in a hypothesis test, we run the risk of making either a Type I or a Type II error. These are mutually exclusive errors: If we mistakenly reject the null, we can only be making a Type I error; if we mistakenly fail to reject the null, we can only be making a Type II error.

The probability of a Type I error in testing a hypothesis is denoted by the Greek letter alpha, α. This probability is also known as the **level of significance** of the test. For example, a level of significance of 0.05 for a test means that there is a 5 percent probability of rejecting a true null hypothesis. The probability of a Type II error is denoted by the Greek letter beta, β.

Controlling the probabilities of the two types of errors involves a trade-off. All else equal, if we decrease the probability of a Type I error by specifying a smaller significance level (say 0.01 rather than 0.05), we increase the probability of making a Type II error because we will reject the null less frequently, including when it is false. The only way to reduce the probabilities of both types of errors simultaneously is to increase the sample size, n.

Quantifying the trade-off between the two types of error in practice is usually impossible because the probability of a Type II error is itself hard to quantify. Consider H_0: $\theta \leq 5$ versus H_a: $\theta > 5$. Because every true value of θ greater than 5 makes the null hypothesis false, each value of θ greater than 5 has a different β (Type II error probability). In contrast, it is sufficient to state a Type I error probability for $\theta = 5$, the point at which we conduct the test of the null hypothesis. Thus, in general, we specify only α, the probability of a Type I error, when we conduct a hypothesis test. Whereas the significance level of a test is the probability of incorrectly rejecting the null, the **power of a test** is the probability of *correctly* rejecting the null—that is, the probability of rejecting the null when it is false.[9] When more than one test statistic is available to conduct a hypothesis test, we should prefer the most powerful, all else equal.[10]

To summarize, the standard approach to hypothesis testing involves specifying a level of significance (probability of Type I error) only. It is most appropriate to specify this significance level prior to calculating the test statistic. If we specify it after calculating the test statistic, we may be influenced by the result of the calculation, which detracts from the objectivity of the test.

We can use three conventional significance levels to conduct hypothesis tests: 0.10, 0.05, and 0.01. Qualitatively, if we can reject a null hypothesis at the 0.10 level of significance, we have *some evidence* that the null hypothesis is false. If we can reject a null hypothesis at the 0.05 level, we have *strong evidence* that the null hypothesis is false. And if we can reject a null hypothesis at the 0.01 level, we have *very strong evidence* that the null hypothesis is false. For the risk premium example, we will specify a 0.05 significance level.

The fourth step in hypothesis testing is stating the decision rule. The general principle is simply stated. When we test the null hypothesis, if we find that the calculated value of the test statistic is more extreme than a given value or values determined by the specified level of significance, α, we reject the null hypothesis. We say the result is **statistically significant**. Otherwise, we do not reject the null hypothesis and we say the result is not statistically significant. The value or values with which we compare the calculated test statistic to make our decision are the rejection points (critical values) for the test.[11]

- **Definition of a Rejection Point (Critical Value) for the Test Statistic.** A rejection point (critical value) for a test statistic is a value with which the computed test statistic is compared to decide whether to reject or not reject the null hypothesis.

For a one-tailed test, we indicate a rejection point using the symbol for the test statistic with a subscript indicating the specified probability of a Type I error, ; for example, z_α. For a two-tailed test, we indicate $z_{\alpha/2}$. To illustrate the use of rejection points, suppose we are using a z-test and have chosen a 0.05 level of significance.

- For a test of H_0: $\theta = \theta_0$ versus H_a: $\theta \neq \theta_0$, two rejection points exist, one negative and one positive. For a two-sided test at the 0.05 level, the total probability of a Type I error must sum to 0.05. Thus, $0.05/2 = 0.025$ of the probability should be in each tail of the distribution of the test statistic under the null. Consequently, the two rejection points are $z_{0.025} = 1.96$ and $-z_{0.025} = -1.96$. Let z represent the calculated value of the test statistic. We reject the null if we find that $z < -1.96$ or $z > 1.96$. We do not reject if $-1.96 \leq z \leq 1.96$.
- For a test of H_0: $\theta \leq \theta_0$ versus H_a: $\theta > \theta_0$ at the 0.05 level of significance, the rejection point is $z_{0.05} = 1.645$. We reject the null hypothesis if $z > 1.645$. The value of the standard normal distribution such that 5 percent of the outcomes lie to the right is $z_{0.05} = 1.645$.
- For a test of H_0: $\theta \geq \theta_0$ versus H_a: $\theta < \theta_0$, the rejection point is $-z_{0.05} = -1.645$. We reject the null hypothesis if $z < -1.645$.

Exhibit 2 illustrates a test H_0: $\mu = \mu_0$ versus H_a: $\mu \neq \mu_0$ at the 0.05 significance level using a z-test. The "acceptance region" is the traditional name for the set of values of the test

---

[9]The power of a test is, in fact, 1 minus the probability of a Type II error.

[10]We do not always have information on the relative power of the test for competing test statistics, however.

[11]"Rejection point" is a descriptive synonym for the more traditional term "critical value."

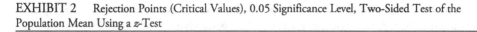

EXHIBIT 2   Rejection Points (Critical Values), 0.05 Significance Level, Two-Sided Test of the
Population Mean Using a z-Test

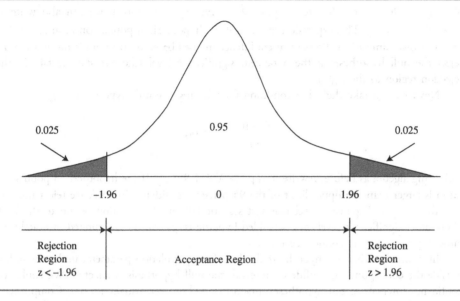

0.025   0.95   0.025

        −1.96   0   1.96

    Rejection   Rejection
    Region   Acceptance Region   Region
    z < −1.96   z > 1.96

statistic for which we do not reject the null hypothesis. (The traditional name, however, is
inaccurate. We should avoid using phrases such as "accept the null hypothesis" because such a
statement implies a greater degree of conviction about the null than is warranted when we fail
to reject it.)[12] On either side of the acceptance region is a rejection region (or critical region).
If the null hypothesis that $\mu = \mu_0$ is true, the test statistic has a 2.5 percent chance of falling
in the left rejection region and a 2.5 percent chance of falling in the right rejection region.
Any calculated value of the test statistic that falls in either of these two regions causes us to
reject the null hypothesis at the 0.05 significance level. The rejection points of 1.96 and
−1.96 are seen to be the dividing lines between the acceptance and rejection regions.

Exhibit 2 affords a good opportunity to highlight the relationship between confidence
intervals and hypothesis tests. A 95 percent confidence interval for the population mean, μ,
based on sample mean, $\overline{X}$, is given by $\overline{X} - 1.96\ s_{\overline{X}}$ to $\overline{X} + 1.96\ s_{\overline{X}}$, where $s_{\overline{X}}$ is the
standard error of the sample mean (Equation 3).[13]

Now consider one of the conditions for rejecting the null hypothesis:

$$\frac{\overline{X} - \mu_0}{s_{\overline{X}}} > 1.96$$

_____

[12]The analogy in some courts of law (for example, in the United States) is that if a jury does not return a
verdict of guilty (the alternative hypothesis), it is most accurate to say that the jury has failed to reject the
null hypothesis, namely, that the defendant is innocent.
[13]Just as with the hypothesis test, we can use this confidence interval, based on the standard normal
distribution, when we have large samples. An alternative hypothesis test and confidence interval uses the t-
distribution, which requires concepts that we introduce in the next section.

Here, μ_0 is the hypothesized value of the population mean. The condition states that rejection is warranted if the test statistic exceeds 1.96. Multiplying both sides by $s_{\overline{X}}$, we have $\overline{X} - \mu_0 > 1.96 \; s_{\overline{X}}$, or after rearranging, $\overline{X} - 1.96 \; s_{\overline{X}} > \mu_0$, which we can also write as $\mu_0 < \overline{X} - 1.96 \; s_{\overline{X}}$. This expression says that if the hypothesized population mean, μ_0, is less than the lower limit of the 95 percent confidence interval based on the sample mean, we must reject the null hypothesis at the 5 percent significance level (the test statistic falls in the rejection region to the right).

Now, we can take the other condition for rejecting the null hypothesis:

$$\frac{\overline{X} - \mu_0}{s_{\overline{X}}} < -1.96$$

and, using algebra as before, rewrite it as $\mu_0 > \overline{X} + 1.96 \; s_{\overline{X}}$. If the hypothesized population mean is larger than the upper limit of the 95 percent confidence interval, we reject the null hypothesis at the 5 percent level (the test statistic falls in the rejection region to the left). Thus, an α significance level in a two-sided hypothesis test can be interpreted in exactly the same way as a $(1 - \alpha)$ confidence interval.

In summary, when the hypothesized value of the population parameter under the null is outside the corresponding confidence interval, the null hypothesis is rejected. We could use confidence intervals to test hypotheses; practitioners, however, usually do not. Computing a test statistic (one number, versus two numbers for the usual confidence interval) is more efficient. Also, analysts encounter actual cases of one-sided confidence intervals only rarely. Furthermore, only when we compute a test statistic can we obtain a p-value, a useful quantity relating to the significance of our results (we will discuss p-values shortly).

To return to our risk premium test, we stated hypotheses $H_0: \mu_{RP} \leq 0$ versus $H_a: \mu_{RP} > 0$. We identified the test statistic as $\overline{X}_{RP}/s_{\overline{X}}$ and stated that it follows a standard normal distribution. We are, therefore, conducting a one-sided z-test. We specified a 0.05 significance level. For this one-sided z-test, the rejection point at the 0.05 level of significance is 1.645. We will reject the null if the calculated z-statistic is larger than 1.645. Exhibit 3 illustrates this test.

The fifth step in hypothesis testing is collecting the data and calculating the test statistic. The quality of our conclusions depends not only on the appropriateness of the statistical model but also on the quality of the data we use in conducting the test. We first need to check for measurement errors in the recorded data. Some other issues to be aware of include sample selection bias and time-period bias. Sample selection bias refers to bias introduced by systematically excluding some members of the population according to a particular attribute. One type of sample selection bias is survivorship bias. For example, if we define our sample as US bond mutual funds currently operating and we collect returns for just these funds, we will systematically exclude funds that have not survived to the present date. Nonsurviving funds are likely to have underperformed surviving funds, on average; as a result the performance reflected in the sample may be biased upward. Time-period bias refers to the possibility that when we use a time-series sample, our statistical conclusion may be sensitive to the starting and ending dates of the sample.[14]

To continue with the risk premium hypothesis, we focus on US equities. According to Dimson, Marsh, and Staunton (2018) for the period 1900 to 2017 inclusive (118 annual observations), the arithmetic mean equity risk premium for US stocks relative to bill returns,

---

[14]These issues are discussed further in the chapter on sampling (Chapter 5).

EXHIBIT 3   Rejection Point (Critical Value), 0.05 Significance Level, One-Sided Test of the Population Mean Using a z-Test

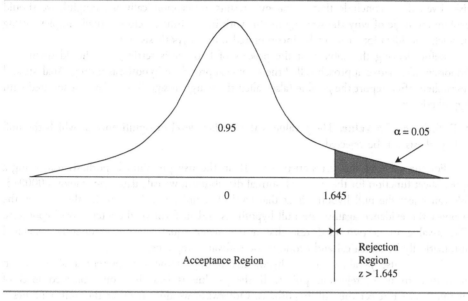

0.95

$\alpha = 0.05$

0   1.645

Acceptance Region

Rejection Region
$z > 1.645$

$\overline{X}_{RP}$, was 7.5 percent per year. The sample standard deviation of the annual risk premiums was 19.5 percent. Using Equation 3, the standard error of the sample mean is $s_{\overline{X}} = s/\sqrt{n} = 19.5\%/\sqrt{118} = 1.795\%$. The test statistic is $z = \overline{X}_{RP}/s_{\overline{X}} = 7.5\%/1.795\% = 4.18$.

The sixth step in hypothesis testing is making the statistical decision. For our example, because the test statistic $z = 4.18$ is larger than the rejection point of 1.645, we reject the null hypothesis in favor of the alternative hypothesis that the risk premium on US stocks is positive. The first six steps are the statistical steps. The final decision concerns our use of the statistical decision.

The seventh and final step in hypothesis testing is making the economic or investment decision. The economic or investment decision takes into consideration not only the statistical decision but also all pertinent economic issues. In the sixth step, we found strong statistical evidence that the US risk premium is positive. The magnitude of the estimated risk premium, 7.5 percent a year, is economically very meaningful as well. Based on these considerations, an investor might decide to commit funds to US equities. A range of nonstatistical considerations, such as the investor's tolerance for risk and financial position, might also enter the decision-making process.

The preceding discussion raises an issue that often arises in this decision-making step. We frequently find that slight differences between a variable and its hypothesized value are statistically significant but not economically meaningful. For example, we may be testing an investment strategy and reject a null hypothesis that the mean return to the strategy is zero based on a large sample. Equation 1 shows that the smaller the standard error of the sample statistic (the divisor in the formula), the larger the value of the test statistic and the greater the chance the null will be rejected, all else equal. The standard error decreases as the sample size, n, increases, so that for very large samples, we can reject the null for small departures from it.

We may find that although a strategy provides a statistically significant positive mean return, the results are not economically significant when we account for transaction costs, taxes, and risk. Even if we conclude that a strategy's results are economically meaningful, we should explore the logic of why the strategy might work in the future before actually implementing it. Such considerations cannot be incorporated into a hypothesis test.

Before leaving the subject of the process of hypothesis testing, we should discuss an important alternative approach called the p-value approach to hypothesis testing. Analysts and researchers often report the p-value (also called the marginal significance level) associated with hypothesis tests.

- **Definition of p-Value.** The p-value is the smallest level of significance at which the null hypothesis can be rejected.

For the value of the test statistic of 4.18 in the risk premium hypothesis test, using a spreadsheet function for the standard normal distribution, we calculate a p-value of 0.000015. We can reject the null hypothesis at that level of significance. The smaller the p-value, the stronger the evidence against the null hypothesis and in favor of the alternative hypothesis. The p-value for a two-sided test that a parameter equals zero is frequently generated automatically by statistical and econometric software programs.[15]

We can use p-values in the hypothesis testing framework presented above as an alternative to using rejection points. If the p-value is less than our specified level of significance, we reject the null hypothesis. Otherwise, we do not reject the null hypothesis. Using the p-value in this fashion, we reach the same conclusion as we do using rejection points. For example, because 0.000015 is less than 0.05, we would reject the null hypothesis in the risk premium test. The p-value, however, provides more precise information on the strength of the evidence than does the rejection points approach. The p-value of 0.000015 indicates that the null is rejected at a far smaller level of significance than 0.05.

If one researcher examines a question using a 0.05 significance level and another researcher uses a 0.01 significance level, the reader may have trouble comparing the findings. This concern has given rise to an approach to presenting the results of hypothesis tests that features p-values and omits specification of the significance level (Step 3). The interpretation of the statistical results is left to the consumer of the research. This has sometimes been called the p-value approach to hypothesis testing.[16]

---

[15] We can use spreadsheets to calculate p-values as well. In Microsoft Excel, for example, we may use the worksheet functions TDIST, NORMSDIST, CHIDIST, and FDIST to calculate p-values for t-tests, z-tests, chi-square tests, and F-tests, respectively.

[16] Davidson and MacKinnon (1993) argued the merits of this approach: "The P value approach does not necessarily force us to make a decision about the null hypothesis. If we obtain a P value of, say, 0.000001, we will almost certainly want to reject the null. But if we obtain a P value of, say, 0.04, or even 0.004, we are not *obliged* to reject it. We may simply file the result away as information that casts some doubt on the null hypothesis, but that is not, by itself, conclusive. We believe that this somewhat agnostic attitude toward test statistics, in which they are merely regarded as pieces of information that we may or may not want to act upon, is usually the most sensible one to take." (p. 80)

3. HYPOTHESIS TESTS CONCERNING THE MEAN

Hypothesis tests concerning the mean are among the most common in practice. In this section we discuss such tests for several distinct types of problems. In one type (discussed in Section 3.1), we test whether the population mean of a single population is equal to (or greater or less than) some hypothesized value. Then, in Sections 3.2 and 3.3, we address inference on means based on two samples. Is an observed difference between two sample means due to chance or different underlying (population) means? When we have two random samples that are independent of each other—no relationship exists between the measurements in one sample and the measurements in the other—the techniques of Section 3.2 apply. When the samples are dependent, the methods of Section 3.3 are appropriate.[17]

3.1. Tests Concerning a Single Mean

An analyst who wants to test a hypothesis concerning the value of an underlying or population mean will conduct a *t*-test in the great majority of cases. A **t-test** is a hypothesis test using a statistic (*t*-statistic) that follows a *t*-distribution. The *t*-distribution is a probability distribution defined by a single parameter known as degrees of freedom (DF). Each value of degrees of freedom defines one distribution in this family of distributions. The *t*-distribution is closely related to the standard normal distribution. Like the standard normal distribution, a *t*-distribution is symmetrical with a mean of zero. However, the *t*-distribution is more spread out: It has a standard deviation greater than 1 (compared to 1 for the standard normal)[18] and more probability for outcomes distant from the mean (it has fatter tails than the standard normal distribution). As the number of degrees of freedom increases with sample size, the spread decreases and the *t*-distribution approaches the standard normal distribution as a limit.

Why is the *t*-distribution the focus for the hypothesis tests of this section? In practice, investment analysts need to estimate the population standard deviation by calculating a sample standard deviation. That is, the population variance (or standard deviation) is unknown. For hypothesis tests concerning the population mean of a normally distributed population with unknown variance, the theoretically correct test statistic is the *t*-statistic. What if a normal distribution does not describe the population? The *t*-test is **robust** to moderate departures from normality, except for outliers and strong skewness.[19] When we have large samples, departures of the underlying distribution from the normal are of increasingly less concern. The sample mean is approximately normally distributed in large samples according to the central limit theorem, whatever the distribution describing the population. In general, a sample size of 30 or more usually can be treated as a large sample and a sample size of 29 or less is treated as a small sample.[20]

---

[17]When we want to test whether the population means of more than two populations are equal, we use analysis of variance (ANOVA). We introduce ANOVA in its most common application, regression analysis, in the chapter on linear regression (Chapter 7).

[18]The formula for the variance of a *t*-distribution is $DF/(DF - 2)$.

[19]See Moore, McCabe, and Craig (2016). A statistic is robust if the required probability calculations are insensitive to violations of the assumptions.

[20]Although this generalization is useful, we caution that the sample size needed to obtain an approximately normal sampling distribution for the sample mean depends on how non-normal the original population is. For some populations, "large" may be a sample size well in excess of 30.

- **Test Statistic for Hypothesis Tests of the Population Mean (Practical Case—Population Variance Unknown).** If the population sampled has unknown variance and either of the conditions below holds:
  1. the sample is large, or
  2. the sample is small but the population sampled is normally distributed, or approximately normally distributed, then the test statistic for hypothesis tests concerning a single population mean, μ, is

$$t_{n-1} = \frac{\overline{X} - \mu_0}{s/\sqrt{n}} \tag{4}$$

where

t_{n-1} = t-statistic with $n-1$ degrees of freedom (n is the sample size)
$\overline{X}$ = the sample mean
μ_0 = the hypothesized value of the population mean
s = the sample standard deviation

The denominator of the t-statistic is an estimate of the sample mean standard error, $s_{\overline{X}} = s/\sqrt{n}$.[21]

In Example 1, because the sample size is small, the test is called a small sample test concerning the population mean.

EXAMPLE 1 Risk and Return Characteristics of an Equity Mutual Fund (1)

You are analyzing Sendar Equity Fund, a midcap growth fund that has been in existence for 24 months. During this period, it has achieved a mean monthly return of 1.50 percent with a sample standard deviation of monthly returns of 3.60 percent. Given its level of systematic (market) risk and according to a pricing model, this mutual fund was expected to have earned a 1.10 percent mean monthly return during that time period. Assuming returns are normally distributed, are the actual results consistent with an underlying or population mean monthly return of 1.10 percent?

1. Formulate null and alternative hypotheses consistent with the description of the research goal.
2. Identify the test statistic for conducting a test of the hypotheses in Part 1.

---

[21] A technical note, for reference, is required. When the sample comes from a finite population, estimates of the standard error of the mean, whether from Equation 2 or Equation 3, overestimate the true standard error. To address this, the computed standard error is multiplied by a shrinkage factor called the finite population correction factor (fpc), equal to $\sqrt{(N-n)/(N-1)}$, where N is the population size and n is the sample size. When the sample size is small relative to the population size (less than 5 percent of the population size), the fpc is usually ignored. The overestimation problem arises only in the usual situation of sampling without replacement (after an item is selected, it cannot be picked again) as opposed to sampling with replacement.

3. Identify the rejection point or points for the hypothesis tested in Part 1 at the 0.10 level of significance.
4. Determine whether the null hypothesis is rejected or not rejected at the 0.10 level of significance. (Use the tables in the back of this book.)

Solution to 1: We have a "not equal to" alternative hypothesis, where μ is the underlying mean return on Sendar Equity Fund—H_0: $\mu = 1.10$ versus H_a: $\mu \neq 1.10$.

Solution to 2: Because the population variance is not known, we use a *t*-test with $24 - 1 = 23$ degrees of freedom.

Solution to 3: Because this is a two-tailed test, we have the rejection point $t_{\alpha/2,n-1} = t_{0.05,23}$. In the table for the *t*-distribution, we look across the row for 23 degrees of freedom to the 0.05 column, to find 1.714. The two rejection points for this two-sided test are -1.714 and 1.714. We will reject the null if we find that $t < -1.714$ or $t > 1.714$.

Solution to 4:

$$t_{23} = \frac{1.50 - 1.10}{3.60/\sqrt{24}} = \frac{0.40}{0.734847} = 0.544331 \text{ or } 0.544$$

Because 0.544 does not satisfy either $t > 1.714$ or $t < -1.714$, we do not reject the null hypothesis.

The confidence interval approach provides another perspective on this hypothesis test. The theoretically correct $100(1 - \alpha)\%$ confidence interval for the population mean of a normal distribution with unknown variance, based on a sample of size n, is

$$\overline{X} - t_{\alpha/2}s_{\overline{X}} \quad \text{to} \quad \overline{X} + t_{\alpha/2}s_{\overline{X}}$$

where $t_{\alpha/2}$ is the value of t such that $\alpha/2$ of the probability remains in the right tail and where $-t_{\alpha/2}$ is the value of t such that $\alpha/2$ of the probability remains in the left tail, for $n - 1$ degrees of freedom. Here, the 90 percent confidence interval runs from $1.5 - (1.714)(0.734847) = 0.240$ to $1.5 + (1.714)(0.734847) = 2.760$, compactly [0.240, 2.760]. The hypothesized value of mean return, 1.10, falls within this confidence interval, and we see from this perspective also that the null hypothesis is not rejected. At a 10 percent level of significance, we conclude that a population mean monthly return of 1.10 percent is consistent with the 24-month observed data series. Note that 10 percent is a relatively high probability of rejecting the hypothesis of a 1.10 percent population mean monthly return when it is true.

EXAMPLE 2 A Slowdown in Payments of Receivables

FashionDesigns, a supplier of casual clothing to retail chains, is concerned about a possible slowdown in payments from its customers. The controller's office measures the rate of payment by the average number of days in receivables.[22] FashionDesigns has generally maintained an average of 45 days in receivables. Because it would be too costly to analyze all of the company's receivables frequently, the controller's office uses sampling to track customers' payment rates. A random sample of 50 accounts shows a mean number of days in receivables of 49 with a standard deviation of 8 days.

1. Formulate null and alternative hypotheses consistent with determining whether the evidence supports the suspected condition that customer payments have slowed.
2. Identify the test statistic for conducting a test of the hypotheses in Part 1.
3. Identify the rejection point or points for the hypothesis tested in Part 1 at the 0.05 and 0.01 levels of significance.
4. Determine whether the null hypothesis is rejected or not rejected at the 0.05 and 0.01 levels of significance.

Solution to 1: The suspected condition is that the number of days in receivables has increased relative to the historical rate of 45 days, which suggests a "greater than" alternative hypothesis. With μ as the population mean number of days in receivables, the hypotheses are $H_0: \mu \leq 45$ versus $H_a: \mu > 45$.

Solution to 2: Because the population variance is not known, we use a *t*-test with $50 - 1 = 49$ degrees of freedom.

Solution to 3: The rejection point is found across the row for degrees of freedom of 49. To find the one-tailed rejection point for a 0.05 significance level, we use the 0.05 column: The value is 1.677. To find the one-tailed rejection point for a 0.01 level of significance, we use the 0.01 column: The value is 2.405. To summarize, at a 0.05 significance level, we reject the null if we find that $t > 1.677$; at a 0.01 significance level, we reject the null if we find that $t > 2.405$.

Solution to 4:

$$t_{49} = \frac{49 - 45}{8/\sqrt{50}} = \frac{4}{1.131371} = 3.536$$

Because $3.536 > 1.677$, the null hypothesis is rejected at the 0.05 level. Because $3.536 > 2.405$, the null hypothesis is also rejected at the 0.01 level. We can say with a high level of confidence that FashionDesigns has experienced a slowdown in customer payments. The level of significance, 0.01, is a relatively low probability of rejecting the hypothesized mean of 45 days or less. Rejection gives us confidence that the mean has increased above 45 days.

---

[22]This measure represents the average length of time that the business must wait after making a sale before receiving payment. The calculation is (Accounts receivable)/(Average sales per day).

We stated above that when population variance is not known, we use a *t*-test for tests concerning a single population mean. Given at least approximate normality, the *t*-test is always called for when we deal with small samples and do not know the population variance. For large samples, the central limit theorem states that the sample mean is approximately normally distributed, whatever the distribution of the population. So the *t*-test is still appropriate, but an alternative test may be more useful when sample size is large.

For large samples, practitioners sometimes use a *z*-test in place of a *t*-test for tests concerning a mean.[23] The justification for using the *z*-test in this context is twofold. First, in large samples, the sample mean should follow the normal distribution at least approximately, as we have already stated, fulfilling the normality assumption of the *z*-test. Second, the difference between the rejection points for the *t*-test and *z*-test becomes quite small when sample size is large. For a two-sided test at the 0.05 level of significance, the rejection points for a *z*-test are 1.96 and –1.96. For a *t*-test, the rejection points are 2.045 and –2.045 for DF = 29 (about a 4 percent difference between the *z* and *t* rejection points) and 2.009 and –2.009 for DF = 50 (about a 2.5 percent difference between the *z* and *t* rejection points). Because the *t*-test is readily available as statistical program output and theoretically correct for unknown population variance, we present it as the test of choice.

In a very limited number of cases, we may know the population variance; in such cases, the *z*-test is theoretically correct.[24]

- **The *z*-Test Alternative.**
  1. If the population sampled is normally distributed with known variance σ^2, then the test statistic for a hypothesis test concerning a single population mean, μ, is

$$z = \frac{\overline{X} - \mu_0}{\sigma/\sqrt{n}} \tag{5}$$

  2. If the population sampled has unknown variance and the sample is large, in place of a *t*-test, an alternative test statistic (relying on the central limit theorem) is

$$z = \frac{\overline{X} - \mu_0}{s/\sqrt{n}} \tag{6}$$

In the above equations,

   σ = the known population standard deviation
   s = the sample standard deviation
   μ_0 = the hypothesized value of the population mean

When we use a *z*-test, we most frequently refer to a rejection point in the list below.

---

[23] These practitioners choose between *t*-tests and *z*-tests based on sample size. For small samples ($n < 30$), they use a *t*-test, and for large samples, a *z*-test.

[24] For example, in Monte Carlo simulation, we prespecify the probability distributions for the risk factors. If we use a normal distribution, we know the true values of mean and variance. Monte Carlo simulation involves the use of a computer to represent the operation of a system subject to risk; we discuss Monte Carlo simulation in the chapter on common probability distributions (Chapter 4).

- **Rejection Points for a z-Test.**
  A. Significance level of $\alpha = 0.10$.
     1. H_0: $\theta = \theta_0$ versus H_a: $\theta \neq \theta_0$. The rejection points are $z_{0.05} = 1.645$ and $-z_{0.05} = -1.645$.
        Reject the null hypothesis if $z > 1.645$ or if $z < -1.645$.
     2. H_0: $\theta \leq \theta_0$ versus H_a: $\theta > \theta_0$. The rejection point is $z_{0.10} = 1.28$.
        Reject the null hypothesis if $z > 1.28$.
     3. H_0: $\theta \geq \theta_0$ versus H_a: $\theta < \theta_0$. The rejection point is $-z_{0.10} = -1.28$.
        Reject the null hypothesis if $z < -1.28$.
  B. Significance level of $\alpha = 0.05$.
     1. H_0: $\theta = \theta_0$ versus H_a: $\theta \neq \theta_0$. The rejection points are $z_{0.025} = 1.96$ and $-z_{0.025} = -1.96$.
        Reject the null hypothesis if $z > 1.96$ or if $z < -1.96$.
     2. H_0: $\theta \leq \theta_0$ versus H_a: $\theta > \theta_0$. The rejection point is $z_{0.05} = 1.645$.
        Reject the null hypothesis if $z > 1.645$.
     3. H_0: $\theta \geq \theta_0$ versus H_a: $\theta < \theta_0$. The rejection point is $-z_{0.05} = -1.645$.
        Reject the null hypothesis if $z < -1.645$.
  C. Significance level of $\alpha = 0.01$.
     1. H_0: $\theta = \theta_0$ versus H_a: $\theta \neq \theta_0$. The rejection points are $z_{0.005} = 2.575$ and $-z_{0.005} = -2.575$.
        Reject the null hypothesis if $z > 2.575$ or if $z < -2.575$.
     2. H_0: $\theta \leq \theta_0$ versus H_a: $\theta > \theta_0$. The rejection point is $z_{0.01} = 2.33$.
        Reject the null hypothesis if $z > 2.33$.
     3. H_0: $\theta \geq \theta_0$ versus H_a: $\theta < \theta_0$. The rejection point is $-z_{0.01} = -2.33$.
        Reject the null hypothesis if $z < -2.33$.

Next, we present a historical example of conducting a hypothesis test on the potential impact of negative internal control disclosure by a company on its stock price.

EXAMPLE 3   The Effect of Control Deficiency Disclosures under the Sarbanes–Oxley Act on Share Prices

The Sarbanes–Oxley Act came into effect in 2002 and introduced major changes to the regulation of corporate governance and financial practice in the United States. One of the requirements of this Act is for firms to periodically assess and report certain types of internal control deficiencies to the audit committee, external auditors, and to the Securities and Exchange Commission (SEC). When a company makes an internal control weakness disclosure, does it convey information that affects the market value of the firm's stock?

Gupta and Nayar (2007) addressed this question by studying a number of voluntary disclosures made in the very early days of Sarbanes–Oxley implementation. Their final sample for this study consisted of 90 firms that had made control deficiency disclosures to the SEC from March 2003 to July 2004. This 90-firm sample was termed the "full sample." These firms were further examined to see if there were any other contemporaneous announcements, such as earnings announcements, associated with the control deficiency disclosures. Of the 90 firms, 45 did not have any such confounding announcements, and the sample of these firms was termed the "clean sample."

The announcement day of the internal control weakness was designated $t = 0$. If these announcements provide *new* information useful for equity valuation, the information should cause a change in stock prices and returns once it is available. Only one component of stock returns is of interest: the return in excess of that predicted given a stock's market risk or beta, called the abnormal return. Significant negative (positive) abnormal returns indicate that investors perceive unfavorable (favorable) corporate news in the internal control weakness announcement. Although Gupta and Nayar examined abnormal returns for various time horizons or event windows, we report a selection of their findings for the window [0, +1], which includes a two-day period of the day of and the day after the announcement. The researchers chose to use z-tests for statistical significance.

Full sample (90 firms). The null hypothesis that the average abnormal stock return during [0, +1] was 0 would be true if stock investors did not find either positive or negative information in the announcement.

    Mean abnormal return $= -3.07$ percent.

    z-statistic for abnormal return $= -5.938$.

Clean sample (45 firms). The null hypothesis that the average abnormal stock return during [0, +1] was 0 would be true if stock investors did not find either positive or negative information in the announcement.

    Mean abnormal return $= -1.87$ percent.

    z-statistic for abnormal return $= -3.359$.

1. With respect to both of the cases, suppose that the null hypothesis reflects the belief that investors do not, on average, perceive either positive or negative information in control deficiency disclosures. State one set of hypotheses (a null hypothesis and an alternative hypothesis) that covers both cases.
2. Determine whether the null hypothesis formulated in Part 1 is rejected or not rejected at the 0.05 and 0.01 levels of significance for the *full sample* case. Interpret the results.
3. Determine whether the null hypothesis formulated in Part 1 is rejected or not rejected at the 0.05 and 0.01 levels of significance for the *clean sample* case. Interpret the results.

Solution to 1: A set of hypotheses consistent with no information in control deficiency disclosures relevant to stock investors is

H_0: The population mean abnormal return during [0, +1] equals 0.

H_a: The population mean abnormal return during [0, +1] does not equal 0.

Solution to 2: From the information on rejection points for *z*-tests, we know that we reject the null hypothesis at the 0.05 significance level if $z > 1.96$ or if $z < -1.96$, and at the 0.01 significance level if $z > 2.575$ or if $z < -2.575$. The *z*-statistic reported by the researchers is −5.938, which is significant at the 0.05 and 0.01 levels. The null is rejected. The control deficiency disclosures appear to contain valuation-relevant information.

Because it is possible that significant results could be due to outliers, the researchers also reported the number of cases of positive and negative abnormal returns. The ratio of cases of positive to negative abnormal returns was 32:58, which tends to support the conclusion from the *z*-test of statistically significant negative abnormal returns.

Solution to 3: The *z*-statistic reported by the researchers for the clean sample is −3.359, which is significant at the 0.05 and 0.01 levels. Although both the mean abnormal return and the *z*-statistic are smaller in magnitude for the clean sample than for the full sample, the results continue to be statistically significant.

The ratio of cases of positive to negative abnormal returns was 16:29, which tends to support the conclusion from the *z*-test of statistically significant negative abnormal returns.

Nearly all practical situations involve an unknown population variance. Exhibit 4 summarizes our discussion for tests concerning the population mean when the population variance is unknown.

3.2. Tests Concerning Differences between Means

We often want to know whether a mean value—for example, a mean return—differs between two groups. Is an observed difference due to chance or to different underlying values for the mean? We have two samples, one for each group. When it is reasonable to believe that the samples are from populations at least approximately normally distributed and that the samples are also independent of each other, the techniques of this section apply. We discuss two *t*-tests for a test concerning differences between the means of two populations. In one case, the population variances, although unknown, can be assumed to be equal. Then, we efficiently combine the observations from both samples to obtain a pooled estimate of the common but unknown population variance. A pooled estimate is an estimate drawn from the combination of two different samples. In the second case, we do not assume that the unknown population variances are equal, and an approximate *t*-test is then available. Letting μ_1 and μ_2 stand, respectively, for the population means of the first and second populations, we most often

EXHIBIT 4   Test Concerning the Population Mean (Population Variance Unknown)

	Large Sample ($n \geq 30$)	Small Sample ($n < 30$)
Population normal	*t*-Test (*z*-Test alternative)	*t*-Test
Population non-normal	*t*-Test (*z*-Test alternative)	Not Available

want to test whether the population means, although unknown, are equal or whether one is larger than the other. Thus we usually formulate the following hypotheses:

1   H_0: $\mu_1 - \mu_2 = 0$ versus H_a: $\mu_1 - \mu_2 \neq 0$ (the alternative is that $\mu_1 \neq \mu_2$)
2   H_0: $\mu_1 - \mu_2 \leq 0$ versus H_a: $\mu_1 - \mu_2 > 0$ (the alternative is that $\mu_1 > \mu_2$)
3   H_0: $\mu_1 - \mu_2 \geq 0$ versus H_a: $\mu_1 - \mu_2 < 0$ (the alternative is that $\mu_1 < \mu_2$)

We can, however, formulate other hypotheses, such as H_0: $\mu_1 - \mu_2 = 2$ versus H_a: $\mu_1 - \mu_2 \neq 2$. The procedure is the same.

The definition of the *t*-test follows.

- **Test Statistic for a Test of the Difference between Two Population Means (Normally Distributed Populations, Population Variances Unknown but Assumed Equal).** When we can assume that the two populations are normally distributed and that the unknown population variances are equal, a *t*-test based on independent random samples is given by

$$t = \frac{(\overline{X}_1 - \overline{X}_2) - (\mu_1 - \mu_2)}{\left(\frac{s_p^2}{n_1} + \frac{s_p^2}{n_2}\right)^{1/2}} \tag{7}$$

where $s_p^2 = \frac{(n_1-1)s_1^2+(n_2-1)s_2^2}{n_1+n_2-2}$ is a pooled estimator of the common variance. The number of degrees of freedom is $n_1 + n_2 - 2$.

EXAMPLE 4   Mean Returns on the S&P BSE SENSEX: A Test of Equality across Two Time Periods

The S&P BSE SENSEX is an index designed to measure the performance of the Indian stock market. The realized mean monthly return on this index in years 2012–2014 appears to have been substantially different than the mean return in years 2015–2017. Was the difference statistically significant? The data, shown in Exhibit 5, indicate that the difference in standard deviations during these two periods is small. Therefore, assuming equal population variances for returns in the two periods is not unreasonable.

1.   Formulate null and alternative hypotheses consistent with a two-sided hypothesis test.
2.   Identify the test statistic for conducting a test of the hypotheses in Part 1.

EXHIBIT 5   S&P BSE SENSEX Monthly Return and Standard Deviation for Two Time Periods

Time Period	Number of Months (n)	Mean Monthly Return (%)	Standard Deviation
2012 through 2014	36	1.694	4.115
2015 through 2017	36	0.665	3.779

Source of data returns: https://www.asiaindex.co.in/indices/equity/sp-bse-sensex accessed 18 August 2018.

3. Identify the rejection point or points for the hypothesis tested in Part 1 at the 0.10, 0.05, and 0.01 levels of significance.
4. Determine whether the null hypothesis is rejected or not rejected at the 0.10, 0.05, and 0.01 levels of significance.

Solution to 1: Letting μ_1 represent the population mean return for the 2012 through 2014 and μ_2 represent the population mean return for the 2015 through 2017, we formulate the following hypotheses:

$$H_0: \mu_1 - \mu_2 = 0 \text{ versus } H_a: \mu_1 - \mu_2 \neq 0$$

Solution to 2: Because the two samples are drawn from two different time periods, they are independent samples. The population variances are not known but can be assumed to be equal. Given all these considerations, the *t*-test given in Equation 7 has $36 + 36 - 2 = 70$ degrees of freedom.

Solution to 3: In the tables (Appendix B), for a two-sided test, the rejection points are ± 1.667, ± 1.994, and ± 2.648 for, respectively, the 0.10, 0.05, and 0.01 levels for DF = 70. To summarize, at the 0.10 level, we will reject the null if $t < -1.667$ or $t > 1.667$; at the 0.05 level, we will reject the null if $t < -1.994$ or $t > 1.994$; and at the 0.01 level, we will reject the null if $t < -2.648$ or $t > 2.648$.

Solution to 4: In calculating the test statistic, the first step is to calculate the pooled estimate of variance:

$$s_p^2 = \frac{(n_1 - 1)s_1^2 + (n_2 - 1)s_2^2}{n_1 + n_2 - 2}$$

$$= \frac{(36 - 1)(4.115)^2 + (36 - 1)(3.779)^2}{36 + 36 - 2}$$

$$= \frac{1{,}092.4923}{70}$$

$$= 15.6070$$

$$t = \frac{(\overline{X}_1 - \overline{X}_2) - (\mu_1 - \mu_2)}{\left(\dfrac{s_p^2}{n_1} + \dfrac{s_p^2}{n_2}\right)^{1/2}}$$

$$= \frac{(1.694 - 0.665) - 0}{\left(\dfrac{15.6070}{36} + \dfrac{15.6070}{36}\right)^{1/2}}$$

$$= \frac{1.029}{0.9312}$$

$$= 1.11$$

The calculated *t* statistic of 1.11 is not significant at the 0.10 level, so it is also not significant at the 0.05 and 0.01 levels. Therefore, we do not reject the null hypothesis at any of the three levels.

In many cases of practical interest, we cannot assume that population variances are equal. The following test statistic is often used in the investment literature in such cases:

- **Test Statistic for a Test of the Difference between Two Population Means (Normally Distributed Populations, Unequal and Unknown Population Variances).** When we can assume that the two populations are normally distributed but do not know the population variances and cannot assume that they are equal, an approximate *t*-test based on independent random samples is given by

$$t = \frac{(\overline{X}_1 - \overline{X}_2) - (\mu_1 - \mu_2)}{\left(\frac{s_1^2}{n_1} + \frac{s_2^2}{n_2}\right)^{1/2}} \tag{8}$$

where we use tables of the *t*-distribution using modified degrees of freedom computed with the formula

$$DF = \frac{\left(\frac{s_1^2}{n_1} + \frac{s_2^2}{n_2}\right)^2}{\frac{(s_1^2/n_1)^2}{n_1} + \frac{(s_2^2/n_2)^2}{n_2}} \tag{9}$$

A practical tip is to compute the *t*-statistic before computing the degrees of freedom. Whether or not the *t*-statistic is significant will sometimes be obvious.

EXAMPLE 5   Recovery Rates on Defaulted Bonds: A Hypothesis Test

How are the required yields on risky corporate bonds determined? Two key factors are the expected probability of default and the expected amount that will be recovered in the event of default, or the recovery rate. Jankowitsch, Nagler, and Subrahmanyam (2014) examine the recovery rates of defaulted bonds in the US corporate bond market based on an extensive set of traded prices and volumes around various types of default events. For their study period, 2002 to 2012, Jankowitsch et al. confirm that the type of default event (e.g., distressed exchanges and formal bankruptcy filings), the seniority of the bond, and the industry of the firm are important in explaining the recovery rate. In one of their analyses, they focus on non-financial firms, and find that electricity firms recover more in default than firms in the retail industry. We want to test if the difference in recovery rates between those two types of firms is statistically significant. With μ_1 denoting the population mean recovery rate for the bonds of electricity firms and μ_2 denoting the population mean recovery rate for the bonds of retail firms, the hypotheses are H_0: $\mu_1 - \mu_2 = 0$ versus H_a: $\mu_1 - \mu_2 \neq 0$.

Exhibit 6 excerpts from their findings.

We assume that the populations (recovery rates) are normally distributed and that the samples are independent. Based on the data in the table, address the following:

1. Discuss whether we should choose a test based on Equation 8 or Equation 7.
2. Calculate the test statistic to test the null hypothesis given above.
3. What is the value of the test's modified degrees of freedom?
4. Determine whether to reject the null hypothesis at the 0.10 level.

EXHIBIT 6   Recovery Rates by Industry of Firm

Electricity			Retail		
Number of Observations	Average Price[a]	Standard Deviation	Number of Observations	Average Price[a]	Standard Deviation
39	$48.03	$22.67	33	$33.40	$34.19

[a] This is the average traded price over the default day and the following 30 days after default; the average price provides an indication of the amount of money that can be recovered.

Source: Jankowitsch, Nagler, and Subrahmanyam (2013), Table 2.

Solution to 1: The sample standard deviation for the recovery rate on the bonds of electricity firms ($22.67) appears much smaller than the sample standard deviation of the bonds for retail firms ($34.19). Therefore, we should not assume equal variances, and accordingly, we should employ the approximate t-test given in Equation 8.

Solution to 2: The test statistic is

$$t = \frac{(\overline{X}_1 - \overline{X}_2)}{\left(\frac{s_1^2}{n_1} + \frac{s_2^2}{n_2}\right)^{1/2}}$$

where

$\overline{X}_1$ = sample mean recovery rate for electricity firms = 48.03
$\overline{X}_2$ = sample mean recovery rate for retail firms = 33.40
s_1^2 = sample variance for electricity firms = 22.67^2 = 513.9289
s_2^2 = sample variance for retail firms = 34.19^2 = 1,168.9561
n_1 = sample size of the electricity firms sample = 39
n_2 = sample size of the retail firms sample = 33

Thus, $t = (48.03 - 33.40)/[(513.9289/39) + (1,168.9561/33)]^{1/2} = 14.63/(13.177664 + 35.422912)^{1/2} = 14.63/6.971411 = 2.099$. The calculated t-statistic is thus 2.099.

Solution to 3:

$$DF = \frac{\left(\frac{s_1^2}{n_1} + \frac{s_2^2}{n_2}\right)^2}{\frac{(s_1^2/n_1)^2}{n_1} + \frac{(s_2^2/n_2)^2}{n_2}} = \frac{\left(\frac{513.9289}{39} + \frac{1,168.9561}{33}\right)^2}{\frac{(513.9289/39)^2}{39} + \frac{(1,168.9561/33)^2}{33}}$$

$$= \frac{2362.016009}{42.476304} = 55.61 \text{ or } 56 \text{ degrees of freedom}$$

Solution to 4: The closest entry to DF = 56 in the tables for the t-distribution is DF = 60. For $\alpha = 0.10$, we find $t_{\alpha/2} = 1.671$. Thus, we reject the null if $t < -1.671$ or

$t > 1.671$. Based on the computed value of 2.099, we reject the null hypothesis at the 0.10 level. Some evidence exists that recovery rates differ between electricity and retail industries. Why? Studies on recovery rates suggest that the higher recovery rates of electricity firms may be explained by their higher levels of tangible assets.

3.3. Tests Concerning Mean Differences

In the previous section, we presented two *t*-tests for discerning differences between population means. The tests were based on two samples. An assumption for those tests' validity was that the samples were independent—i.e., unrelated to each other. When we want to conduct tests on two means based on samples that we believe are dependent, the methods of this section apply.

The *t*-test in this section is based on data arranged in **paired observations**, and the test itself is sometimes called a **paired comparisons test**. Paired observations are observations that are dependent because they have something in common. A paired comparisons test is a statistical test for differences in dependent items. For example, we may be concerned with the dividend policy of companies before and after a change in the tax law affecting the taxation of dividends. We then have pairs of "before" and "after" observations for the same companies. We may test a hypothesis about the mean of the differences (mean differences) that we observe across companies. In other cases, the paired observations are not on the same units. For example, we may be testing whether the mean returns earned by two investment strategies were equal over a study period. The observations here are dependent in the sense that there is one observation for each strategy in each month, and both observations depend on underlying market risk factors. Because the returns to both strategies are likely to be related to some common risk factors, such as the market return, the samples are dependent. By calculating a standard error based on differences, the *t*-test presented below takes account of correlation between the observations.

Letting A represent "after" and B "before," suppose we have observations for the random variables X_A and X_B and that the samples are dependent. We arrange the observations in pairs. Let d_i denote the difference between two paired observations. We can use the notation $d_i = x_{Ai} - x_{Bi}$, where x_{Ai} and x_{Bi} are the *i*th pair of observations, $i = 1, 2, ..., n$ on the two variables. Let μ_d stand for the population mean difference. We can formulate the following hypotheses, where μ_{d0} is a hypothesized value for the population mean difference:

1. $H_0: \mu_d = \mu_{d0}$ versus $H_a: \mu_d \neq \mu_{d0}$
2. $H_0: \mu_d \leq \mu_{d0}$ versus $H_a: \mu_d > \mu_{d0}$
3. $H_0: \mu_d \geq \mu_{d0}$ versus $H_a: \mu_d < \mu_{d0}$

In practice, the most commonly used value for μ_{d0} is 0.

As usual, we are concerned with the case of normally distributed populations with unknown population variances, and we will formulate a *t*-test. To calculate the *t*-statistic, we first need to find the sample mean difference:

$$\bar{d} = \frac{1}{n}\sum_{i=1}^{n} d_i \tag{10}$$

where n is the number of pairs of observations. The sample variance, denoted by s_d^2, is

$$s_d^2 = \frac{\sum_{i=1}^{n}(d_i - \overline{d})^2}{n-1} \tag{11}$$

Taking the square root of this quantity, we have the sample standard deviation, s_d, which then allows us to calculate the standard error of the mean difference as follows:[25]

$$s_{\overline{d}} = \frac{s_d}{\sqrt{n}} \tag{12}$$

- **Test Statistic for a Test of Mean Differences (Normally Distributed Populations, Unknown Population Variances).** When we have data consisting of paired observations from samples generated by normally distributed populations with unknown variances, a t-test is based on

$$t = \frac{\overline{d} - \mu_{d0}}{s_{\overline{d}}} \tag{13}$$

with $n - 1$ degrees of freedom, where n is the number of paired observations, $\overline{d}$ is the sample mean difference (as given by Equation 10), and $s_{\overline{d}}$ is the standard error of $\overline{d}$ (as given by Equation 12).

Exhibit 7 reports the quarterly returns for a six-year period for two managed portfolios specializing in precious metals. The two portfolios were closely similar in risk (as measured by standard deviation of return and other measures) and had nearly identical expense ratios. A major investment services company rated Portfolio B more highly than Portfolio A. In investigating the portfolios' relative performance, suppose we want to test the hypothesis that the mean quarterly return on Portfolio A equaled the mean quarterly return on Portfolio B during the six-year period. Because the two portfolios shared essentially the same set of risk factors, their returns were not independent, so a paired comparisons test is appropriate. Let μ_d stand for the population mean value of difference between the returns on the two portfolios during this period. We test $H_0: \mu_d = 0$ versus $H_a: \mu_d \neq 0$ at a 0.05 significance level.

The sample mean difference, $\overline{d}$, between Portfolio A and Portfolio B is –0.65 percent per quarter. The standard error of the sample mean difference is $s\overline{d} = 6.71/\sqrt{24} = 1.369673$. The calculated test statistic is $t = (-0.65 - 0)/1.369673 = -0.475$ with $n - 1 = 24 - 1 = 23$ degrees of freedom. At the 0.05 significance level, we reject the null if $t > 2.069$ or if $t < -2.069$. Because –0.475 is not less than –2.069, we fail to reject the null. At the 0.10 significance level, we reject the null if $t > 1.714$ or if $t < -1.714$. Thus, the difference in mean quarterly returns is not significant at any conventional significance level.

The following example illustrates the application of this test to evaluate two competing investment strategies.

---

[25]We can also use the following equivalent expression, which makes use of the correlation between the two variables: $s\overline{d} = \sqrt{s_A^2 + s_B^2 - 2r(X_A,X_B)s_A s_B}/\sqrt{n}$ where s_A^2 is the sample variance of X_A, s_B^2 is the sample variance of X_B, and $r(X_A, X_B)$ is the sample correlation between X_A and X_B.

EXHIBIT 7   Quarterly Returns on Two Managed Portfolios

Quarter	Portfolio A (%)	Portfolio B (%)	Difference (Portfolio A – Portfolio B)
4Q:Year 6	11.40	14.64	–3.24
3Q:Year 6	–2.17	0.44	–2.61
2Q:Year 6	10.72	19.51	–8.79
1Q:Year 6	38.91	50.40	–11.49
4Q:Year 5	4.36	1.01	3.35
3Q:Year 5	5.13	10.18	–5.05
2Q:Year 5	26.36	17.77	8.59
1Q:Year 5	–5.53	4.76	–10.29
4Q:Year 4	5.27	–5.36	10.63
3Q:Year 4	–7.82	–1.54	–6.28
2Q:Year 4	2.34	0.19	2.15
1Q:Year 4	–14.38	–12.07	–2.31
4Q:Year 3	–9.80	–9.98	0.18
3Q:Year 3	19.03	26.18	–7.15
2Q:Year 3	4.11	–2.39	6.50
1Q:Year 3	–4.12	–2.51	–1.61
4Q:Year 2	–0.53	–11.32	10.79
3Q:Year 2	5.06	0.46	4.60
2Q:Year 2	–14.01	–11.56	–2.45
1Q:Year 2	12.50	3.52	8.98
4Q:Year 1	–29.05	–22.45	–6.60
3Q:Year 1	3.60	0.10	3.50
2Q:Year 1	–7.97	–8.96	0.99
1Q:Year 1	–8.62	–0.66	–7.96
Mean	1.87	2.52	–0.65

Sample standard deviation of differences = 6.71

EXAMPLE 6   A Comparison of Two Portfolios

You are investigating whether the performance of a portfolio of stocks from the entire world differs from the performance of a portfolio of only US stocks. For the worldwide portfolio, you choose to focus on Vanguard Total World Stock Index ETF. This ETF seeks to track the performance of the FTSE Global All Cap Index, which is a market-capitalization-weighted index designed to measure the market performance of stock of companies from both developed and emerging markets. For the US portfolio, you choose to focus on SPDR S&P 500, an ETF that seeks to track the performance of the

EXHIBIT 8   Monthly Return Summary for Vanguard Total World Stock Index ETF and
SPDR S&P 500 ETF: August 2013 to July 2018 ($n = 60$)

Strategy	Mean Return	Standard Deviation
Worldwide	0.79%	2.93%
US	1.06	2.81
Difference	−0.27	1.00[a]

[a] Sample standard deviation of differences.
Source of data returns: finance.yahoo.com accessed 18 August 2018.

S&P 500 Index. You analyze the monthly returns on both ETFs from August 2013 to
July 2018 and prepare the following summary table.
From Exhibit 8 we have $\bar{d} = -0.27\%$ and $s_d = 1.00\%$.

1. Formulate null and alternative hypotheses consistent with a two-sided test that the
    mean difference between the worldwide and only US strategies equals 0.
2. Identify the test statistic for conducting a test of the hypotheses in Part 1.
3. Identify the rejection point or points for the hypothesis tested in Part 1 at the 0.01
    level of significance.
4. Determine whether the null hypothesis is rejected or not rejected at the 0.01 level
    of significance. (Use the tables in the back of this volume.)
5. Discuss the choice of a paired comparisons test.

Solution to 1: With μ_d as the underlying mean difference between the worldwide and
US strategies, we have H_0: $\mu_d = 0$ versus H_a: $\mu_d \neq 0$.

Solution to 2: Because the population variance is unknown, the test statistic is a *t*-test
with $60 - 1 = 59$ degrees of freedom.

Solution to 3: In the table for the *t*-distribution, the closest entry to DF = 59 is
DF = 60. We look across the row for 60 degrees of freedom to the 0.005 column, to
find 2.66. We will reject the null if we find that $t > 2.66$ or $t < -2.66$.

Solution to 4:

$$t_{59} = \frac{-0.27}{1.00/\sqrt{60}} = \frac{-0.27}{0.129099} = -2.09$$

Because −2.09 > −2.66, we cannot reject the null hypothesis. Accordingly, we conclude
that the difference in mean returns for the two strategies is not statistically significant.

Solution to 5: Several US stocks that are part of the S&P 500 index are also included in
the Vanguard Total World Stock Index ETF. The profile of the World ETF indicates
that nine of the top ten holdings in the ETF are US stocks. As a result, they are not
independent samples; in general, the correlation of returns on the Vanguard Total
World Stock Index ETF and SPDR S&P 500 ETF should be positive. Because the
samples are dependent, a paired comparisons test was appropriate.

4. HYPOTHESIS TESTS CONCERNING VARIANCE AND CORRELATION

Because variance and standard deviation are widely used quantitative measures of risk in investments, analysts should be familiar with hypothesis tests concerning variance. The correlation between two variables is also widely used in investments. For example, investment managers often need to understand the correlations among returns on different assets. Therefore, analysts should also be familiar with hypothesis tests concerning correlation. The tests of variance and correlation discussed in this section make regular appearances in investment literature. Next, we examine two types of tests concerning variance: tests concerning the value of a single population variance and tests concerning the differences between two population variances. We then examine how to test the significance of a correlation coefficient.

4.1. Tests Concerning a Single Variance

In this section, we discuss testing hypotheses about the value of the variance, σ^2, of a single population. We use σ_0^2 to denote the hypothesized value of σ^2. We can formulate hypotheses as follows:

1. $H_0:\sigma^2 = \sigma_0^2$ versus $H_a:\sigma^2 \neq \sigma_0^2$ (a "not equal to" alternative hypothesis)
2. $H_0:\sigma^2 \leq \sigma_0^2$ versus $H_a:\sigma^2 > \sigma_0^2$ (a "greater than" alternative hypothesis)
3. $H_0:\sigma^2 \geq \sigma_0^2$ versus $H_a:\sigma^2 < \sigma_0^2$ (a "less than" alternative hypothesis)

In tests concerning the variance of a single normally distributed population, we make use of a chi-square test statistic, denoted χ^2. The chi-square distribution, unlike the normal and t-distributions, is asymmetrical. Like the t-distribution, the chi-square distribution is a family of distributions. A different distribution exists for each possible value of degrees of freedom, $n - 1$ (n is sample size). Unlike the t-distribution, the chi-square distribution is bounded below by 0; χ^2 does not take on negative values.

- **Test Statistic for Tests Concerning the Value of a Population Variance (Normal Population).** If we have n independent observations from a normally distributed population, the appropriate test statistic is

$$\chi^2 = \frac{(n-1)s^2}{\sigma_0^2} \qquad (14)$$

with $n - 1$ degrees of freedom. In the numerator of the expression is the sample variance, calculated as

$$s^2 = \frac{\sum_{i=1}^{n}(X_i - \overline{X})^2}{n-1} \qquad (15)$$

In contrast to the t-test, for example, the chi-square test is sensitive to violations of its assumptions. If the sample is not actually random or if it does not come from a normally distributed population, inferences based on a chi-square test are likely to be faulty.

If we choose a level of significance, α, the rejection points for the three kinds of hypotheses are as follows:

- **Rejection Points for Hypothesis Tests on the Population Variance.**
  1. "Not equal to" H_a: Reject the null hypothesis if the test statistic is greater than the upper $\alpha/2$ point (denoted $\chi^2_{\alpha/2}$) or less than the lower $\alpha/2$ point (denoted $\chi^2_{1-\alpha/2}$) of the chi-square distribution with DF $= n - 1$.[26]
  2. "Greater than" H_a: Reject the null hypothesis if the test statistic is greater than the upper α point of the chi-square distribution with DF $= n - 1$.
  3. "Less than" H_a: Reject the null hypothesis if the test statistic is less than the lower α point of the chi-square distribution with DF $= n - 1$.

EXAMPLE 7   Risk and Return Characteristics of an Equity Mutual Fund (2)

You continue with your analysis of Sendar Equity Fund, a midcap growth fund that has been in existence for only 24 months. Recall that during this period, Sendar Equity achieved a sample standard deviation of monthly returns of 3.60 percent. You now want to test a claim that the specific investment approach followed by Sendar result in a standard deviation of monthly returns of less than 4 percent.

1. Formulate null and alternative hypotheses consistent with the verbal description of the research goal.
2. Identify the test statistic for conducting a test of the hypotheses in Part 1.
3. Identify the rejection point or points for the hypothesis tested in Part 1 at the 0.05 level of significance.
4. Determine whether the null hypothesis is rejected or not rejected at the 0.05 level of significance. (Use the tables in the back of this volume.)

Solution to 1: We have a "less than" alternative hypothesis, where σ is the underlying standard deviation of return on Sendar Equity Fund. Being careful to square standard deviation to obtain a test in terms of variance, the hypotheses are $H_0: \sigma^2 \geq 16.0$ versus $H_a: \sigma^2 < 16.0$.

Solution to 2: The test statistic is χ^2 with $24 - 1 = 23$ degrees of freedom.

Solution to 3: The lower 0.05 rejection point is found on the line for DF $= 23$, under the 0.95 column (95 percent probability in the right tail, to give 0.95 probability of getting a test statistic this large or larger). The rejection point is 13.091. We will reject the null if we find that χ^2 is less than 13.091.

---

[26]Just as with other hypothesis tests, the chi-square test can be given a confidence interval interpretation. Unlike confidence intervals based on z- or t-statistics, however, chi-square confidence intervals for variance are asymmetric. A two-sided confidence interval for population variance, based on a sample of size n, has a lower limit $L = (n-1)s^2/\chi^2_{\alpha/2}$ and an upper limit $U = (n-1)s^2/\chi^2_{1-\alpha/2}$. Under the null hypothesis, the hypothesized value of the population variance should fall within these two limits.

Solution to 4:

$$\chi^2 = \frac{(n-1)s^2}{\sigma_0^2} = \frac{23 \times 3.60^2}{4^2} = \frac{298.08}{16} = 18.63$$

Because 18.63 (the calculated value of the test statistic) is not less than 13.091, we do not reject the null hypothesis. We cannot conclude that Sendar's investment disciplines result in a standard deviation of monthly returns of less than 4 percent.

4.2. Tests Concerning the Equality (Inequality) of Two Variances

Suppose we have a hypothesis about the relative values of the variances of two normally distributed populations with means μ_1 and μ_2 and variances σ_1^2 and σ_2^2. We can formulate all hypotheses as one of the choices below:

1. $H_0: \sigma_1^2 = \sigma_2^2$ versus $H_a: \sigma_1^2 \neq \sigma_2^2$
2. $H_0: \sigma_1^2 \leq \sigma_2^2$ versus $H_a: \sigma_1^2 > \sigma_2^2$
3. $H_0: \sigma_1^2 \geq \sigma_2^2$ versus $H_a: \sigma_1^2 < \sigma_2^2$

Note that at the point of equality, the null hypothesis $\sigma_1^2 = \sigma_2^2$ implies that the ratio of population variances equals 1: $\sigma_1^2/\sigma_2^2 = 1$. Given independent random samples from these populations, tests related to these hypotheses are based on an *F*-test, which is the ratio of sample variances. Suppose we use n_1 observations in calculating the sample variance s_1^2 and n_2 observations in calculating the sample variance s_2^2. Tests concerning the difference between the variances of two populations make use of the *F*-distribution. Like the chi-square distribution, the *F*-distribution is a family of asymmetrical distributions bounded from below by 0. Each *F*-distribution is defined by two values of degrees of freedom, called the numerator and denominator degrees of freedom.[27] The *F*-test, like the chi-square test, is not robust to violations of its assumptions.

- **Test Statistic for Tests Concerning Differences between the Variances of Two Populations (Normally Distributed Populations).** Suppose we have two samples, the first with n_1 observations and sample variance s_1^2, the second with n_2 observations and sample variance s_2^2. The samples are random, independent of each other, and generated by normally distributed populations. A test concerning differences between the variances of the two populations is based on the ratio of sample variances

$$F = \frac{s_1^2}{s_2^2} \tag{16}$$

---

[27]The relationship between the chi-square and *F*-distributions is as follows: If χ_1^2 is one chi-square random variable with *m* degrees of freedom and χ_2^2 is another chi-square random variable with *n* degrees of freedom, then $F = (\chi_1^2/m)/(\chi_2^2/n)$ follows an *F*-distribution with *m* numerator and *n* denominator degrees of freedom.

with $DF_1 = n_1 - 1$ numerator degrees of freedom and $DF_2 = n_2 - 1$ denominator degrees of freedom. Note that DF_1 and DF_2 are the divisors used in calculating s_1^2 and s_2^2, respectively.

A convention, or usual practice, is to use the larger of the two ratios s_1^2/s_2^2 or s_2^2/s_1^2 as the actual test statistic. When we follow this convention, the value of the test statistic is always greater than or equal to 1; tables of critical values of F then need include only values greater than or equal to 1. Under this convention, the rejection point for any formulation of hypotheses is a single value in the right-hand side of the relevant F-distribution. Note that the labeling of populations as "1" or "2" is arbitrary in any case.

- **Rejection Points for Hypothesis Tests on the Relative Values of Two Population Variances.** Follow the convention of using the larger of the two ratios s_1^2/s_2^2 and s_2^2/s_1^2 and consider two cases:
  1. A "not equal to" alternative hypothesis: Reject the null hypothesis at the α significance level if the test statistic is greater than the upper $\alpha/2$ point of the F-distribution with the specified numerator and denominator degrees of freedom.
  2. A "greater than" or "less than" alternative hypothesis: Reject the null hypothesis at the α significance level if the test statistic is greater than the upper α point of the F-distribution with the specified number of numerator and denominator degrees of freedom.

Thus, if we conduct a two-sided test at the $\alpha = 0.01$ level of significance, we need to find the rejection point in F-tables at the $\alpha/2 = 0.01/2 = 0.005$ significance level for a one-sided test (Case 1). But a one-sided test at 0.01 uses rejection points in F-tables for $\alpha = 0.01$ (Case 2). As an example, suppose we are conducting a two-sided test at the 0.05 significance level. We calculate a value of F of 2.77 with 12 numerator and 19 denominator degrees of freedom. Using the F-tables for $0.05/2 = 0.025$ in the back of the volume, we find that the rejection point is 2.72. Because the value 2.77 is greater than 2.72, we reject the null hypothesis at the 0.05 significance level.

If the convention stated above is not followed and we are given a calculated value of F less than 1, can we still use F-tables? The answer is yes; using a reciprocal property of F-statistics, we can calculate the needed value. The easiest way to present this property is to show a calculation. Suppose our chosen level of significance is 0.05 for a two-tailed test and we have a value of F of 0.11, with 7 numerator degrees of freedom and 9 denominator degrees of freedom. We take the reciprocal, $1/0.11 = 9.09$. Then we look up this value in the F-tables for 0.025 (because it is a two-tailed test) with degrees of freedom reversed: F for 9 numerator and 7 denominator degrees of freedom. In other words, $F_{9,7} = 1/F_{7,9}$ and 9.09 exceeds the critical value of 4.82, so $F_{7,9} = 0.11$ is significant at the 0.05 level.

EXAMPLE 8   Volatility and the Global Financial Crisis of the Late 2000s

You are investigating whether the population variance of returns on the KOSPI Index of the South Korean stock market changed subsequent to the global financial crisis that peaked in 2008. For this investigation, you are considering 1999 to 2006 as the pre-crisis period and 2010 to 2017 as the post-crisis period. You gather the data in Exhibit 9 for 418 weeks of returns during 1999 to 2006 and 418 weeks of returns during 2010 to 2017. You have specified a 0.01 level of significance.

EXHIBIT 9   KOSPI Index Returns and Variance before and after the Global Financial Crisis of the Late 2000s

	n	Mean Weekly Return (%)	Variance of Returns
Before crisis: 1999 to 2006	418	0.307	18.203
After crisis: 2010 to 2017	418	0.114	3.919

Source of data for returns: finance.yahoo.com accessed 19 August 2018.

1. Formulate null and alternative hypotheses consistent with the verbal description of the research goal.
2. Identify the test statistic for conducting a test of the hypotheses in Part 1.
3. Determine whether or not to reject the null hypothesis at the 0.01 level of significance. (Use the F-tables in the back of this volume.)

Solution to 1: We have a "not equal to" alternative hypothesis:

$$H_0: \sigma^2_{Before} = \sigma^2_{After} \quad \text{versus} \quad H_a: \sigma^2_{Before} \neq \sigma^2_{After}$$

Solution to 2: To test a null hypothesis of the equality of two variances, we use $F = s_1^2/s_2^2$ with $418 - 1 = 417$ numerator and denominator degrees of freedom.

Solution to 3: The "before" sample variance is larger, so following a convention for calculating F-statistics, the "before" sample variance goes in the numerator: $F = 18.203/3.919 = 4.645$. Because this is a two-tailed test, we use F-tables for the 0.005 level (= 0.01/2) to give a 0.01 significance level. In the tables in the back of the volume, the closest value to 417 degrees of freedom is 120 degrees of freedom. At the 0.01 level, the rejection point is 1.61. Because 4.645 is greater than the critical value 1.61, we reject the null hypothesis that the population variance of returns is the same in the pre- and post-global financial crisis periods.[28] It seems that the South Korean market was more volatile before the financial crisis.

EXAMPLE 9   The Volatility of Derivatives Expiration Days

Since 2001, the financial markets in the United States have seen the quadruple occurrence of stock option, index option, index futures, and single stock futures expirations on the same day during four months of the year. Such days are known as "quadruple witching days." You are interested in investigating whether quadruple witching days exhibit greater volatility than normal days. Exhibit 10 presents the daily

---

[28]The critical value decreases as the degrees of freedom increase. Therefore, the critical value for 417 degrees of freedom is even smaller than 1.61, and we can reject the null hypothesis.

EXHIBIT 10   Standard Deviation of Return: Normal Trading Days
and Derivatives Expiration Days

Type of Day	n	Standard Deviation (%)
Normal trading	138	0.821
Options/futures expiration	16	1.217

standard deviation of return for normal days and options/futures expiration days during
a four-year period. The tabled data refer to options and futures on the 30 stocks that
constitute the Dow Jones Industrial Average.

1. Formulate null and alternative hypotheses consistent with the belief that quadruple
    witching days display above-normal volatility.
2. Identify the test statistic for conducting a test of the hypotheses in Part 1.
3. Determine whether to reject the null hypothesis at the 0.05 level of significance.
    (Use the F-tables in the back of this volume.)

Solution to 1: We have a "greater than" alternative hypothesis:

$$H_0: \sigma^2_{\text{Expirations}} \leq \sigma^2_{\text{Normal}} \quad \text{versus} \quad H_a: \sigma^2_{\text{Expirations}} > \sigma^2_{\text{Normal}}$$

Solution to 2: Let σ^2_1 represent the variance of quadruple witching days, and σ^2_2
represent the variance of normal days, following the convention for the selection of the
numerator and the denominator stated earlier. To test the null hypothesis, we use
$F = s^2_1/s^2_2$ with $16 - 1 = 15$ numerator and $138 - 1 = 137$ denominator degrees of
freedom.

Solution to 3: $F = (1.217)^2/(0.821)^2 = 1.481/0.674 = 2.20$. Because this is a one-
tailed test at the 0.05 significance level, we use F-tables for the 0.05 level directly. In
the tables in the back of the volume, the closest value to 137 degrees of freedom is 120
degrees of freedom. At the 0.05 level, the rejection point is 1.75. Because 2.20 is
greater than 1.75, we reject the null hypothesis. It appears that quadruple witching days
have above-normal volatility.

4.3. Tests Concerning Correlation

In many contexts in investments, we want to assess the strength of the linear relationship
between two variables—the correlation between them. A common approach is to use the
correlation coefficient. A significance test of a correlation coefficient allows us to assess
whether the relationship between two random variables is the result of chance. If we decide
that the relationship does not result from chance, we are inclined to use this information in
predictions because a good prediction of one variable will help us predict the other variable.

   If the correlation coefficient between two variables is zero, we would conclude that there is
no linear relation between the two variables. We use a test of significance to assess whether the

correlation is different from zero. After we estimate a correlation coefficient, we need to ask whether the estimated correlation is significantly different from 0. Before we can answer this question, we must know some details about the distribution of the underlying variables themselves. For purposes of simplicity, assume that both of the variables are normally distributed.[29]

We propose two hypotheses: the null hypothesis, H_0, that the correlation in the population is 0 ($\rho = 0$); and the alternative hypothesis, H_a, that the correlation in the population is different from 0 ($\rho \neq 0$). The alternative hypothesis is a test that the correlation is not equal to 0; therefore, a two-tailed test is appropriate. As long as the two variables are distributed normally, we can test to determine whether the null hypothesis should be rejected using the sample correlation, r. The formula for the t-test is

$$t = \frac{r\sqrt{n-2}}{\sqrt{1-r^2}} \tag{17}$$

This test statistic has a t-distribution with $n - 2$ degrees of freedom if the null hypothesis is true. One practical observation concerning Equation 17 is that the magnitude of r needed to reject the null hypothesis H_0: $\rho = 0$ decreases as sample size n increases, for two reasons. First, as n increases, the number of degrees of freedom increases and the absolute value of the critical value t_c decreases. Second, the absolute value of the numerator increases with larger n, resulting in larger-magnitude t-values. For example, with sample size $n = 12$, $r = 0.58$ results in a t-statistic of 2.252 that is just significant at the 0.05 level ($t_c = 2.228$). With a sample size $n = 32$, a smaller sample correlation $r = 0.35$ yields a t-statistic of 2.046 that is just significant at the 0.05 level ($t_c = 2.042$); the $r = 0.35$ would not be significant with a sample size of 12 even at the 0.10 significance level. Another way to make this point is that sampling from the same population, a false null hypothesis H_0: $\rho = 0$ is more likely to be rejected as we increase sample size, all else equal, because a higher number of observations increases the numerator of the test statistic.

EXAMPLE 10   Testing the Yen–Canadian Dollar Return Correlation

The sample correlation between the GBP monthly returns to Japanese yen and Canadian dollar is 0.5132 for the period from January 2011 through December 2017 (*Source of exchange rate data*: http://fx.sauder.ubc.ca/).

Can we reject a null hypothesis that the underlying or population correlation equals 0 at the 0.05 level of significance?

Solution: With 84 months from January 2011 through December 2017, we use the following statistic to test the null hypothesis, H_0, that the true correlation in the

---

[29]Actually, we must assume that each observation (x, y) on the two variables (X, Y) is a random observation from a bivariate normal distribution. Informally, in a bivariate or two-variable normal distribution, each individual variable is normally distributed and their joint relationship is completely described by the correlation, ρ, between them. For more details, see, for example, Daniel and Terrell (1995) and Greene (2018).

population is 0, against the alternative hypothesis, H_a, that the correlation in the population is different from 0:

$$t = \frac{0.5132\sqrt{84-2}}{\sqrt{1-0.5132^2}} = 5.4146$$

In the tables at the back of this volume, at the 0.05 significance level, the critical level for this test statistic is 1.99 ($n = 84$, degrees of freedom $= 82$). When the test statistic is either larger than 1.99 or smaller than -1.99, we can reject the hypothesis that the correlation in the population is 0. The test statistic is 5.4146, so we can reject the null hypothesis.

5. OTHER ISSUES: NONPARAMETRIC INFERENCE

The hypothesis-testing procedures we have discussed to this point have two characteristics in common. First, they are concerned with parameters, and second, their validity depends on a definite set of assumptions. Mean and variance, for example, are two parameters, or defining quantities, of a normal distribution. The tests also make specific assumptions—in particular, assumptions about the distribution of the population producing the sample. Any test or procedure with either of the above two characteristics is a **parametric test** or procedure. In some cases, however, we are concerned about quantities other than parameters of distributions. In other cases, we may believe that the assumptions of parametric tests do not hold for the particular data we have. In such cases, a nonparametric test or procedure can be useful. A **nonparametric test** is a test that is not concerned with a parameter, or a test that makes minimal assumptions about the population from which the sample comes.[30]

We primarily use nonparametric procedures in three situations: when the data we use do not meet distributional assumptions, when the data are given in ranks, or when the hypothesis we are addressing does not concern a parameter.

The first situation occurs when the data available for analysis suggest that the distributional assumptions of the parametric test are not satisfied. For example, we may want to test a hypothesis concerning the mean of a population but believe that neither a t-test nor a z-test is appropriate because the sample is small and may come from a markedly non-normally distributed population. In that case, we may use a nonparametric test. The nonparametric test will frequently involve the conversion of observations (or a function of observations) into ranks according to magnitude, and sometimes it will involve working with only "greater than" or "less than" relationships (using the signs $+$ and $-$ to denote those relationships). Characteristically, one must refer to specialized statistical tables to determine the rejection points of the test statistic, at least for small samples.[31] Such tests, then, typically interpret the

---

[30]Some writers make a distinction between "nonparametric" and "distribution-free" tests. They refer to procedures that do not concern the parameters of a distribution as nonparametric and to procedures that make minimal assumptions about the underlying distribution as distribution free. We follow a commonly accepted, inclusive usage of the term nonparametric.

[31]For large samples, there is often a transformation of the test statistic that permits the use of tables for the standard normal or t-distribution.

EXHIBIT 11   Nonparametric Alternatives to Parametric Tests Concerning Means

	Parametric	**Nonparametric**
Tests concerning a single mean	*t*-test	Wilcoxon signed-rank test
	z-test	
Tests concerning differences between means	*t*-test Approximate *t*-test	Mann–Whitney U test
Tests concerning mean differences (paired comparisons tests)	*t*-test	Wilcoxon signed-rank test Sign test

null hypothesis as a thesis about ranks or signs. In Exhibit 11, we give examples of nonparametric alternatives to the parametric tests concerning means we have discussed in this chapter.[32] The reader should consult a comprehensive business statistics textbook for an introduction to such tests, and a specialist textbook for details.[33]

We pointed out that when we use nonparametric tests, we often convert the original data into ranks. In some cases, the original data are already ranked. In those cases, we also use nonparametric tests because parametric tests generally require a stronger measurement scale than ranks. For example, if our data were the rankings of investment managers, hypotheses concerning those rankings would be tested using nonparametric procedures. Ranked data also appear in many other finance contexts. For example, Heaney, Koga, Oliver, and Tran (1999) studied the relationship between the size of Japanese companies (as measured by revenue) and their use of derivatives. The companies studied used derivatives to hedge one or more of five types of risk exposure: interest rate risk, foreign exchange risk, commodity price risk, marketable security price risk, and credit risk. The researchers gave a "perceived scope of risk exposure" score to each company that was equal to the number of types of risk exposure that the company reported hedging. Although revenue is measured on a strong scale (a ratio scale), scope of risk exposure is measured on only an ordinal scale.[34] The researchers thus employed nonparametric statistics to explore the relationship between derivatives usage and size.

A third situation in which we use nonparametric procedures occurs when our question does not concern a parameter. For example, if the question concerns whether a sample is random or not, we use the appropriate nonparametric test (a so-called "runs test"). Another type of question nonparametrics can address is whether a sample came from a population following a particular probability distribution (using the Kolmogorov–Smirnov test, for example).

We end this chapter by describing in some detail a nonparametric statistic that has often been used in investment research, the Spearman rank correlation.

---

[32]In some cases, there are several nonparametric alternatives to a parametric test.

[33]See, for example, Hettmansperger and McKean (2010) or Siegel and Castellan (1988).

[34]We discussed scales of measurement in the chapter "Organizing, Visualizing, and Describing Data."

5.1. Nonparametric Tests Concerning Correlation: The Spearman Rank Correlation Coefficient

Earlier in this chapter, we examined the t-test of the hypothesis that two variables are uncorrelated, based on the correlation coefficient. As we pointed out there, this test relies on fairly stringent assumptions. When we believe that the population under consideration meaningfully departs from those assumptions, we can employ a test based on the **Spearman rank correlation coefficient**, r_S. The Spearman rank correlation coefficient is essentially equivalent to the usual correlation coefficient calculated on the *ranks* of the two variables (say X and Y) within their respective samples. Thus it is a number between -1 and $+1$, where -1 ($+1$) denotes a perfect inverse (positive) straight-line relationship between the variables and 0 represents the absence of any straight-line relationship (no correlation). The calculation of r_S requires the following steps:

1. Rank the observations on X from largest to smallest. Assign the number 1 to the observation with the largest value, the number 2 to the observation with second-largest value, and so on. In case of ties, we assign to each tied observation the average of the ranks that they jointly occupy. For example, if the third- and fourth-largest values are tied, we assign both observations the rank of 3.5 (the average of 3 and 4). Perform the same procedure for the observations on Y.
2. Calculate the difference, d_i, between the ranks of each pair of observations on X and Y.
3. Then, with n the sample size, the Spearman rank correlation is given by[35]

$$r_s = 1 - \frac{6\sum_{i=1}^{n} d_i^2}{n(n^2 - 1)} \qquad (18)$$

Suppose an investor wants to invest in a diversified emerging markets mutual fund. He has narrowed the field to 10 such funds, which are rated as 5-star funds by Morningstar. In examining the funds, a question arises as to whether the funds' most recent reported Sharpe ratios and expense ratios as of mid-2018 are related. Because the assumptions of the t-test on the correlation coefficient may not be met, it is appropriate to conduct a test on the rank correlation coefficient.[36] Exhibit 12 presents the calculation of r_S. The first two rows contain the original data. The row of X ranks converts the Sharpe ratios to ranks; the row of Y ranks converts the expense ratios to ranks. We want to test $H_0: \rho = 0$ versus $H_a: \rho \neq 0$, where ρ is defined in this context as the population correlation of X and Y after ranking. For small samples, the rejection points for the test based on r_S must be looked up in Exhibit 13. For large samples (say $n > 30$), we can conduct a t-test using

---

[35]Calculating the usual correlation coefficient on the ranks would yield approximately the same result as Equation 18.

[36]The expense ratio (the ratio of a fund's operating expenses to average net assets) is bounded both from below (by zero) and from above. The Sharpe ratio is also observed within a limited range, in practice. Thus, neither variable can be normally distributed, and hence jointly they cannot follow a bivariate normal distribution. In short, the assumptions of a t-test are not met.

EXHIBIT 12 The Spearman Rank Correlation: An Example

	Mutual Fund									
	1	2	3	4	5	6	7	8	9	10
Sharpe Ratio (X)	0.65	0.80	0.68	0.72	0.64	0.54	0.71	0.76	0.62	0.64
Expense Ratio (Y)	1.04	1.05	1.79	1.26	1.33	1.64	1.01	3.20	6.81	1.07
X Rank	5.5	1	5.5	3	7.5	10	4	2	9	7.5
Y Rank	9	8	3	6	5	4	10	2	1	7
d_i	−3.5	−7	2.5	−3	2.5	6	−6	0	8	0.5
d_i^2	12.25	49	6.25	9	6.25	36	36	0	64	0.25

$$r_s = 1 - \frac{6 \sum d_i^2}{10(100-1)} = 1 - \frac{6(219)}{10(100-1)} = -0.3273$$

Source of Sharpe and Expense Ratios: http://markets.on.nytimes.com/research/screener/mutual_funds/mutual_funds .asp, accessed 19 August 2018.

$$t = \frac{(n-2)^{1/2} r_s}{(1 - r_s^2)^{1/2}} \tag{19}$$

based on $n - 2$ degrees of freedom.

In the example at hand, a two-tailed test with a 0.05 significance level, Exhibit 13 gives the upper-tail rejection point for $n = 10$ as 0.6364 (we use the 0.025 column for a two-tailed test at a 0.05 significance level). Accordingly, we reject the null hypothesis if r_S is less than −0.6364 or greater than 0.6364. With r_S equal to −0.3273, we do not reject the null hypothesis.

In the mutual fund example, we converted observations on two variables into ranks. If one or both of the original variables were in the form of ranks, we would need to use r_S to investigate correlation.

5.2. Nonparametric Inference: Summary

Nonparametric statistical procedures extend the reach of inference because they make few assumptions, can be used on ranked data, and may address questions unrelated to parameters. Quite frequently, nonparametric tests are reported alongside parametric tests. The reader can then assess how sensitive the statistical conclusion is to the assumptions underlying the parametric test. However, if the assumptions of the parametric test are met, the parametric test (where available) is generally preferred to the nonparametric test because the parametric test usually permits us to draw sharper conclusions.[37] For complete coverage of all the nonparametric procedures that may be encountered in the finance and investment literature, it is best to consult a specialist textbook.[38]

---

[37] To use a concept introduced in an earlier section, the parametric test is often more powerful.

[38] See, for example, Hettmansperger and McKean (2010) or Siegel and Castellan (1988).

EXHIBIT 13   Spearman Rank Correlation Distribution Approximate Upper-Tail Rejection Points

Sample Size: n	$\alpha = 0.05$	$\alpha = 0.025$	$\alpha = 0.01$
5	0.8000	0.9000	0.9000
6	0.7714	0.8286	0.8857
7	0.6786	0.7450	0.8571
8	0.6190	0.7143	0.8095
9	0.5833	0.6833	0.7667
10	0.5515	0.6364	0.7333
11	0.5273	0.6091	0.7000
12	0.4965	0.5804	0.6713
13	0.4780	0.5549	0.6429
14	0.4593	0.5341	0.6220
15	0.4429	0.5179	0.6000
16	0.4265	0.5000	0.5824
17	0.4118	0.4853	0.5637
18	0.3994	0.4716	0.5480
19	0.3895	0.4579	0.5333
20	0.3789	0.4451	0.5203
21	0.3688	0.4351	0.5078
22	0.3597	0.4241	0.4963
23	0.3518	0.4150	0.4852
24	0.3435	0.4061	0.4748
25	0.3362	0.3977	0.4654
26	0.3299	0.3894	0.4564
27	0.3236	0.3822	0.4481
28	0.3175	0.3749	0.4401
29	0.3113	0.3685	0.4320
30	0.3059	0.3620	0.4251

Note: The corresponding lower tail critical value is obtained by changing the sign of the upper-tail critical value.

6. SUMMARY

In this chapter, we have presented the concepts and methods of statistical inference and hypothesis testing.

- A hypothesis is a statement about one or more populations.
- The steps in testing a hypothesis are as follows:
  1. Stating the hypotheses.
  2. Identifying the appropriate test statistic and its probability distribution.

3. Specifying the significance level.
4. Stating the decision rule.
5. Collecting the data and calculating the test statistic.
6. Making the statistical decision.
7. Making the economic or investment decision.

- We state two hypotheses: The null hypothesis is the hypothesis to be tested; the alternative hypothesis is the hypothesis accepted when the null hypothesis is rejected.
- There are three ways to formulate hypotheses:
  1. $H_0: \theta = \theta_0$ versus $H_a: \theta \neq \theta_0$
  2. $H_0: \theta \leq \theta_0$ versus $H_a: \theta > \theta_0$
  3. $H_0: \theta \geq \theta_0$ versus $H_a: \theta < \theta_0$
  where θ_0 is a hypothesized value of the population parameter and θ is the true value of the population parameter. In the above, Formulation 1 is a two-sided test and Formulations 2 and 3 are one-sided tests.
- When we have a "suspected" or "hoped for" condition for which we want to find supportive evidence, we frequently set up that condition as the alternative hypothesis and use a one-sided test. To emphasize a neutral attitude, however, the researcher may select a "not equal to" alternative hypothesis and conduct a two-sided test.
- A test statistic is a quantity, calculated on the basis of a sample, whose value is the basis for deciding whether to reject or not reject the null hypothesis. To decide whether to reject, or not to reject, the null hypothesis, we compare the computed value of the test statistic to a critical value (rejection point) for the same test statistic.
- In reaching a statistical decision, we can make two possible errors: We may reject a true null hypothesis (a Type I error), or we may fail to reject a false null hypothesis (a Type II error).
- The level of significance of a test is the probability of a Type I error that we accept in conducting a hypothesis test. The probability of a Type I error is denoted by the Greek letter alpha, α. The standard approach to hypothesis testing involves specifying a level of significance (probability of Type I error) only.
- The power of a test is the probability of correctly rejecting the null (rejecting the null when it is false).
- A decision rule consists of determining the rejection points (critical values) with which to compare the test statistic to decide whether to reject or not to reject the null hypothesis. When we reject the null hypothesis, the result is said to be statistically significant.
- The $(1 - \alpha)$ confidence interval represents the range of values of the test statistic for which the null hypothesis will not be rejected at an α significance level.
- The statistical decision consists of rejecting or not rejecting the null hypothesis. The economic decision takes into consideration all economic issues pertinent to the decision.
- The p-value is the smallest level of significance at which the null hypothesis can be rejected. The smaller the p-value, the stronger the evidence against the null hypothesis and in favor of the alternative hypothesis. The p-value approach to hypothesis testing does not involve setting a significance level; rather it involves computing a p-value for the test statistic and allowing the consumer of the research to interpret its significance.
- For hypothesis tests concerning the population mean of a normally distributed population with unknown (known) variance, the theoretically correct test statistic is the t-statistic (z-statistic). In the unknown variance case, given large samples (generally, samples of 30 or

more observations), the z-statistic may be used in place of the t-statistic because of the force of the central limit theorem.

- The t-distribution is a symmetrical distribution defined by a single parameter: degrees of freedom. Compared to the standard normal distribution, the t-distribution has fatter tails.

- When we want to test whether the observed difference between two means is statistically significant, we must first decide whether the samples are independent or dependent (related). If the samples are independent, we conduct tests concerning differences between means. If the samples are dependent, we conduct tests of mean differences (paired comparisons tests).

- When we conduct a test of the difference between two population means from normally distributed populations with unknown variances, if we can assume the variances are equal, we use a t-test based on pooling the observations of the two samples to estimate the common (but unknown) variance. This test is based on an assumption of independent samples.

- When we conduct a test of the difference between two population means from normally distributed populations with unknown variances, if we cannot assume that the variances are equal, we use an approximate t-test using modified degrees of freedom given by a formula. This test is based on an assumption of independent samples.

- In tests concerning two means based on two samples that are not independent, we often can arrange the data in paired observations and conduct a test of mean differences (a paired comparisons test). When the samples are from normally distributed populations with unknown variances, the appropriate test statistic is a t-statistic. The denominator of the t-statistic, the standard error of the mean differences, takes account of correlation between the samples.

- In tests concerning the variance of a single, normally distributed population, the test statistic is chi-square (χ^2) with $n - 1$ degrees of freedom, where n is sample size.

- For tests concerning differences between the variances of two normally distributed populations based on two random, independent samples, the appropriate test statistic is based on an F-test (the ratio of the sample variances).

- The F-statistic is defined by the numerator and denominator degrees of freedom. The numerator degrees of freedom (number of observations in the sample minus 1) is the divisor used in calculating the sample variance in the numerator. The denominator degrees of freedom (number of observations in the sample minus 1) is the divisor used in calculating the sample variance in the denominator. In forming an F-test, a convention is to use the larger of the two ratios, s_1^2/s_2^2 or s_2^2/s_1^2, as the actual test statistic.

- In tests concerning correlation, we use a t-statistic to test whether a population correlation coefficient is significantly different from 0. If we have n observations for two variables, this test statistic has a t-distribution with $n - 2$ degrees of freedom.

- A parametric test is a hypothesis test concerning a parameter or a hypothesis test based on specific distributional assumptions. In contrast, a nonparametric test either is not concerned with a parameter or makes minimal assumptions about the population from which the sample comes.

- A nonparametric test is primarily used in three situations: when data do not meet distributional assumptions, when data are given in ranks, or when the hypothesis we are addressing does not concern a parameter.

- The Spearman rank correlation coefficient is calculated on the ranks of two variables within their respective samples.

REFERENCES

Bowerman, Bruce L., Richard T. O'Connell, Richard T., and Emily S. Murphree, Emily S. 2016. *Business Statistics in Practice*, 8th edition. New York: McGraw-Hill/Irwin.

Daniel, Wayne W. and James C. Terrell, James C. 1995. *Business Statistics for Management & Economics*, 7th edition. Boston: Houghton-Mifflin.

Davidson, Russell and James G. MacKinnon, James G. 1993. *Estimation and Inference in Econometrics*. New York: Oxford University Press.

Dimson, Elroy, Paul Marsh, Paul, and Mike Staunton, Mike. 2018. "Credit Suisse Global Investment Returns Yearbook 2018 (Summary Edition)." Credit Suisse Research Institute.

Freeley, Austin J. and David L. Steinberg, David L. 2013. *Argumentation and Debate: Critical Thinking for Reasoned Decision Making*, 13th edition. Boston, MA: Wadsworth Cengage Learning.

Gupta, Parveen P. and Nandkumar Nayar, Nandkumar. 2007. "Information Content of Control Deficiency Disclosures under the Sarbanes-Oxley Act: An Empirical Investigation." *International Journal of Disclosure and Governance*, vol. 4:3–23. 10.1057/palgrave.jdg.2050047.

Heaney, Richard, Chitoshi Koga, Chitoshi, Barry Oliver, Barry, and Alfred Tran, Alfred. 1999. "The Size Effect and Derivative Usage in Japan." Working paper: The Australian National University.

Hettmansperger, Thomas P. and Joseph W. McKean, Joseph W. 2010. *Robust Nonparametric Statistical Methods*, 2nd edition. Boca Raton, FL: CRC Press.

Jankowitsch, Rainer, Florian Nagler, Florian, and Marti G. Subrahmanyam, Marti G. 2014. "The Determinants of Recovery Rates in the US Corporate Bond Market." *Journal of Financial Economics*, vol. 114, no. 1:155–177.

Moore, David S., George P. McCabe, George P., and Bruce Craig, Bruce. 2016. *Introduction to the Practice of Statistics*, 9th edition. New York: W.H. Freeman.

Siegel, Sidney and N. John Castellan, N. John. 1988. *Nonparametric Statistics for the Behavioral Sciences*, 2nd edition. New York: McGraw-Hill.

PRACTICE PROBLEMS

1. Which of the following statements about hypothesis testing is correct?
   A. The null hypothesis is the condition a researcher hopes to support.
   B. The alternative hypothesis is the proposition considered true without conclusive evidence to the contrary.
   C. The alternative hypothesis exhausts all potential parameter values not accounted for by the null hypothesis.

2. Identify the appropriate test statistic or statistics for conducting the following hypothesis tests. (Clearly identify the test statistic and, if applicable, the number of degrees of freedom. For example, "We conduct the test using an x-statistic with y degrees of freedom.")
   A. H_0: $\mu = 0$ versus H_a: $\mu \neq 0$, where μ is the mean of a normally distributed population with unknown variance. The test is based on a sample of 15 observations.
   B. H_0: $\mu = 0$ versus H_a: $\mu \neq 0$, where μ is the mean of a normally distributed population with unknown variance. The test is based on a sample of 40 observations.
   C. H_0: $\mu \leq 0$ versus H_a: $\mu > 0$, where μ is the mean of a normally distributed population with known variance σ^2. The sample size is 45.

    D. H_0: $\sigma^2 = 200$ versus H_a: $\sigma^2 \neq 200$, where σ^2 is the variance of a normally distributed population. The sample size is 50.

    E. $H_0 : \sigma_1^2 = \sigma_2^2$ versus $H_a : \sigma_1^2 \neq \sigma_2^2$, where σ_1^2 is the variance of one normally distributed population and σ_2^2 is the variance of a second normally distributed population. The test is based on two independent random samples.

    F. H_0: (Population mean 1) − (Population mean 2) = 0 versus H_a: (Population mean 1) − (Population mean 2) $\neq$ 0, where the samples are drawn from normally distributed populations with unknown variances. The observations in the two samples are correlated.

    G. H_0: (Population mean 1) − (Population mean 2) = 0 versus H_a: (Population mean 1) − (Population mean 2) $\neq$ 0, where the samples are drawn from normally distributed populations with unknown but assumed equal variances. The observations in the two samples (of size 25 and 30, respectively) are independent.

3. For each of the following hypothesis tests concerning the population mean, μ, state the rejection point condition or conditions for the test statistic (e.g., $t > 1.25$); n denotes sample size.

    A. H_0: $\mu = 10$ versus H_a: $\mu \neq 10$, using a t-test with $n = 26$ and $\alpha = 0.05$

    B. H_0: $\mu = 10$ versus H_a: $\mu \neq 10$, using a t-test with $n = 40$ and $\alpha = 0.01$

    C. H_0: $\mu \leq 10$ versus H_a: $\mu > 10$, using a t-test with $n = 40$ and $\alpha = 0.01$

    D. H_0: $\mu \leq 10$ versus H_a: $\mu > 10$, using a t-test with $n = 21$ and $\alpha = 0.05$

    E. H_0: $\mu \geq 10$ versus H_a: $\mu < 10$, using a t-test with $n = 19$ and $\alpha = 0.10$

    F. H_0: $\mu \geq 10$ versus H_a: $\mu < 10$, using a t-test with $n = 50$ and $\alpha = 0.05$

4. For each of the following hypothesis tests concerning the population mean, μ, state the rejection point condition or conditions for the test statistic (e.g., $z > 1.25$); n denotes sample size.

    A. H_0: $\mu = 10$ versus H_a: $\mu \neq 10$, using a z-test with $n = 50$ and $\alpha = 0.01$

    B. H_0: $\mu = 10$ versus H_a: $\mu \neq 10$, using a z-test with $n = 50$ and $\alpha = 0.05$

    C. H_0: $\mu = 10$ versus H_a: $\mu \neq 10$, using a z-test with $n = 50$ and $\alpha = 0.10$

    D. H_0: $\mu \leq 10$ versus H_a: $\mu > 10$, using a z-test with $n = 50$ and $\alpha = 0.05$

5. Willco is a manufacturer in a mature cyclical industry. During the most recent industry cycle, its net income averaged $30 million per year with a standard deviation of $10 million ($n = 6$ observations). Management claims that Willco's performance during the most recent cycle results from new approaches and that we can dismiss profitability expectations based on its average or normalized earnings of $24 million per year in prior cycles.

    A. With μ as the population value of mean annual net income, formulate null and alternative hypotheses consistent with testing Willco management's claim.

    B. Assuming that Willco's net income is at least approximately normally distributed, identify the appropriate test statistic.

    C. Identify the rejection point or points at the 0.05 level of significance for the hypothesis tested in Part A.

    D. Determine whether or not to reject the null hypothesis at the 0.05 significance level.

The following information relates to Questions 6–7

Performance in Forecasting Quarterly Earnings per Share

	Number of Forecasts	Mean Forecast Error (Predicted – Actual)	Standard Deviations of Forecast Errors
Analyst A	101	0.05	0.10
Analyst B	121	0.02	0.09

6. Investment analysts often use earnings per share (EPS) forecasts. One test of forecasting quality is the zero-mean test, which states that optimal forecasts should have a mean forecasting error of 0. (Forecasting error = Predicted value of variable – Actual value of variable.)

   You have collected data (shown in the table above) for two analysts who cover two different industries: Analyst A covers the telecom industry; Analyst B covers automotive parts and suppliers.

   A. With μ as the population mean forecasting error, formulate null and alternative hypotheses for a zero-mean test of forecasting quality.

   B. For Analyst A, using both a t-test and a z-test, determine whether to reject the null at the 0.05 and 0.01 levels of significance.

   C. For Analyst B, using both a t-test and a z-test, determine whether to reject the null at the 0.05 and 0.01 levels of significance.

7. Reviewing the EPS forecasting performance data for Analysts A and B, you want to investigate whether the larger average forecast errors of Analyst A are due to chance or to a higher underlying mean value for Analyst A. Assume that the forecast errors of both analysts are normally distributed and that the samples are independent.

   A. Formulate null and alternative hypotheses consistent with determining whether the population mean value of Analyst A's forecast errors (μ_1) are larger than Analyst B's (μ_2).

   B. Identify the test statistic for conducting a test of the null hypothesis formulated in Part A.

   C. Identify the rejection point or points for the hypothesis tested in Part A, at the 0.05 level of significance.

   D. Determine whether or not to reject the null hypothesis at the 0.05 level of significance.

8. The table below gives data on the monthly returns on the S&P 500 and small-cap stocks for a forty-year period and provides statistics relating to their mean differences. Furthermore, the entire sample period is split into two subperiods of 20 years each and the returns data for these subperiods is also given in the table.

Measure	S&P 500 Return (%)	Small-Cap Stock Return (%)	Differences (S&P 500– Small-Cap Stock)
Entire sample period, 480 months			
Mean	1.0542	1.3117	–0.258
Standard deviation	4.2185	5.9570	3.752
First subperiod, 240 months			
Mean	0.6345	1.2741	–0.640
Standard deviation	4.0807	6.5829	4.096
Second subperiod, 240 months			
Mean	1.4739	1.3492	0.125
Standard deviation	4.3197	5.2709	3.339

Let μ_d stand for the population mean value of difference between S&P 500 returns and small-cap stock returns. Use a significance level of 0.05 and suppose that mean differences are approximately normally distributed.

A. Formulate null and alternative hypotheses consistent with testing whether any difference exists between the mean returns on the S&P 500 and small-cap stocks.

B. Determine whether or not to reject the null hypothesis at the 0.05 significance level for the entire sample period.

C. Determine whether or not to reject the null hypothesis at the 0.05 significance level for the first subperiod.

D. Determine whether or not to reject the null hypothesis at the 0.05 significance level for the second subperiod.

9. During a 10-year period, the standard deviation of annual returns on a portfolio you are analyzing was 15 percent a year. You want to see whether this record is sufficient evidence to support the conclusion that the portfolio's underlying variance of return was less than 400, the return variance of the portfolio's benchmark.

A. Formulate null and alternative hypotheses consistent with the verbal description of your objective.

B. Identify the test statistic for conducting a test of the hypotheses in Part A.

C. Identify the rejection point or points at the 0.05 significance level for the hypothesis tested in Part A.

D. Determine whether the null hypothesis is rejected or not rejected at the 0.05 level of significance.

10. You are investigating whether the population variance of returns on the S&P 500/ BARRA Growth Index changed subsequent to the October 1987 market crash. You gather the following data for 120 months of returns before October 1987 and for 120 months of returns after October 1987. You have specified a 0.05 level of significance.

Time Period	n	Mean Monthly Return (%)	Variance of Returns
Before October 1987	120	1.416	22.367
After October 1987	120	1.436	15.795

A. Formulate null and alternative hypotheses consistent with the verbal description of the research goal.

B. Identify the test statistic for conducting a test of the hypotheses in Part A.

C. Determine whether or not to reject the null hypothesis at the 0.05 level of significance. (Use the *F*-tables in the back of this volume.)

11. The following table shows the sample correlations between the monthly returns for four different mutual funds and the S&P 500. The correlations are based on 36 monthly observations. The funds are as follows:

Fund 1   Large-cap fund
Fund 2   Mid-cap fund
Fund 3   Large-cap value fund
Fund 4   Emerging markets fund
S&P 500   US domestic stock index

	Fund 1	Fund 2	Fund 3	Fund 4	S&P 500
Fund 1	1				
Fund 2	0.9231	1			
Fund 3	0.4771	0.4156	1		
Fund 4	0.7111	0.7238	0.3102	1	
S&P 500	0.8277	0.8223	0.5791	0.7515	1

Test the null hypothesis that each of these correlations, individually, is equal to zero against the alternative hypothesis that it is not equal to zero. Use a 5 percent significance level.

12. In the step "stating a decision rule" in testing a hypothesis, which of the following elements must be specified?

A. Critical value

B. Power of a test

C. Value of a test statistic

13. Which of the following statements is correct with respect to the null hypothesis?

A. It is considered to be true unless the sample provides evidence showing it is false.

B. It can be stated as "not equal to" provided the alternative hypothesis is stated as "equal to."

C. In a two-tailed test, it is rejected when evidence supports equality between the hypothesized value and population parameter.

14. An analyst is examining a large sample with an unknown population variance. To test the hypothesis that the historical average return on an index is less than or equal to 6%, which of the following is the *most* appropriate test?
    A. One-tailed z-test
    B. Two-tailed z-test
    C. One-tailed F-test

15. A hypothesis test for a normally-distributed population at a 0.05 significance level implies a:
    A. 95% probability of rejecting a true null hypothesis.
    B. 95% probability of a Type I error for a two-tailed test.
    C. 5% critical value rejection region in a tail of the distribution for a one-tailed test.

16. Which of the following statements regarding a one-tailed hypothesis test is correct?
    A. The rejection region increases in size as the level of significance becomes smaller.
    B. A one-tailed test more strongly reflects the beliefs of the researcher than a two-tailed test.
    C. The absolute value of the rejection point is larger than that of a two-tailed test at the same level of significance.

17. The value of a test statistic is *best* described as the basis for deciding whether to:
    A. reject the null hypothesis.
    B. accept the null hypothesis.
    C. reject the alternative hypothesis.

18. Which of the following is a Type I error?
    A. Rejecting a true null hypothesis
    B. Rejecting a false null hypothesis
    C. Failing to reject a false null hypothesis

19. A Type II error is *best* described as:
    A. rejecting a true null hypothesis.
    B. failing to reject a false null hypothesis.
    C. failing to reject a false alternative hypothesis.

20. The level of significance of a hypothesis test is *best* used to:
    A. calculate the test statistic.
    B. define the test's rejection points.
    C. specify the probability of a Type II error.

21. You are interested in whether excess risk-adjusted return (alpha) is correlated with mutual fund expense ratios for US large-cap growth funds. The following table presents the sample.

Mutual Fund	1	2	3	4	5	6	7	8	9
Alpha (X)	−0.52	−0.13	−0.60	−1.01	−0.26	−0.89	−0.42	−0.23	−0.60
Expense Ratio (Y)	1.34	0.92	1.02	1.45	1.35	0.50	1.00	1.50	1.45

   A. Formulate null and alternative hypotheses consistent with the verbal description of the research goal.

B. Identify the test statistic for conducting a test of the hypotheses in Part A.

C. Justify your selection in Part B.

D Determine whether or not to reject the null hypothesis at the 0.05 level of significance.

22. All else equal, is specifying a smaller significance level in a hypothesis test likely to increase the probability of a:

	Type I error?	Type II error?
A.	No	No
B.	No	Yes
C.	Yes	No

23. The probability of correctly rejecting the null hypothesis is the:
   A. *p*-value.
   B. power of a test.
   C. level of significance.

24. The power of a hypothesis test is:
   A. equivalent to the level of significance.
   B. the probability of not making a Type II error.
   C. unchanged by increasing a small sample size.

25. When making a decision in investments involving a statistically significant result, the:
   A. economic result should be presumed meaningful.
   B. statistical result should take priority over economic considerations.
   C. economic logic for the future relevance of the result should be further explored.

26. An analyst tests the profitability of a trading strategy with the null hypothesis being that the average abnormal return before trading costs equals zero. The calculated *t*-statistic is 2.802, with critical values of $\pm$ 2.756 at significance level $\alpha = 0.01$. After considering trading costs, the strategy's return is near zero. The results are *most likely*:
   A. statistically but not economically significant.
   B. economically but not statistically significant.
   C. neither statistically nor economically significant.

27. Which of the following statements is correct with respect to the *p*-value?
   A. It is a less precise measure of test evidence than rejection points.
   B. It is the largest level of significance at which the null hypothesis is rejected.
   C. It can be compared directly with the level of significance in reaching test conclusions.

28. Which of the following represents a correct statement about the *p*-value?
   A. The *p*-value offers less precise information than does the rejection points approach.
   B. A larger *p*-value provides stronger evidence in support of the alternative hypothesis.
   C. A *p*-value less than the specified level of significance leads to rejection of the null hypothesis.

29. Which of the following statements on p-value is correct?
    A. The p-value is the smallest level of significance at which H_0 can be rejected.
    B. The p-value indicates the probability of making a Type II error.
    C. The lower the p-value, the weaker the evidence for rejecting the H_0.

30. The following table shows the significance level (α) and the p-value for three hypothesis tests.

	α	p-value
Test 1	0.05	0.10
Test 2	0.10	0.08
Test 3	0.10	0.05

The evidence for rejecting H_0 is strongest for:
    A. Test 1.
    B. Test 2.
    C. Test 3.

31. Which of the following tests of a hypothesis concerning the population mean is *most* appropriate?
    A. A z-test if the population variance is unknown and the sample is small
    B. A z-test if the population is normally distributed with a known variance
    C. A t-test if the population is non-normally distributed with unknown variance and a small sample

32. For a small sample with unknown variance, which of the following tests of a hypothesis concerning the population mean is most appropriate?
    A. A t-test if the population is normally distributed
    B. A t-test if the population is non-normally distributed
    C. A z-test regardless of the normality of the population distribution

33. For a small sample from a normally distributed population with unknown variance, the *most* appropriate test statistic for the mean is the:
    A. z-statistic.
    B. t-statistic.
    C. χ^2 statistic.

34. An investment consultant conducts two independent random samples of 5-year performance data for US and European absolute return hedge funds. Noting a 50-basis point-return advantage for US managers, the consultant decides to test whether the two means are statistically different from one another at a 0.05 level of significance. The two populations are assumed to be normally distributed with unknown but equal variances. Results of the hypothesis test are contained in the tables below.

	Sample Size	Mean Return %	Standard Deviation
US Managers	50	4.7	5.4
European Managers	50	4.2	4.8

Null and Alternative Hypotheses	$H_0: \mu_{US} - \mu_E = 0; H_a: \mu_{US} - \mu_E \neq 0$
Test Statistic	0.4893
Critical Value Rejection Points	± 1.984

μ_{US} is the mean return for US funds and μ_E is the mean return for European funds. The results of the hypothesis test indicate that the:
A.   null hypothesis is not rejected.
B.   alternative hypothesis is statistically confirmed.
C.   difference in mean returns is statistically different from zero.

35.   A pooled estimator is used when testing a hypothesis concerning the:
A.   equality of the variances of two normally distributed populations.
B.   difference between the means of two at least approximately normally distributed populations with unknown but assumed equal variances.
C.   difference between the means of two at least approximately normally distributed populations with unknown and assumed unequal variances.

36.   When evaluating mean differences between two dependent samples, the *most* appropriate test is a:
A.   chi-square test.
B.   paired comparisons test.
C.   *z*-test.

37.   A fund manager reported a 2% mean quarterly return over the past ten years for its entire base of 250 client accounts that all follow the same investment strategy. A consultant employing the manager for 45 client accounts notes that their mean quarterly returns were 0.25% less over the same period. The consultant tests the hypothesis that the return disparity between the returns of his clients and the reported returns of the fund manager's 250 client accounts are significantly different from zero. Assuming normally distributed populations with unknown population variances, the *most* appropriate test statistic is:
A.   a paired comparisons *t*-test.
B.   a *t*-test of the difference between the two population means.
C.   an approximate *t*-test of mean differences between the two populations.

38.   A chi-square test is *most* appropriate for tests concerning:
A.   a single variance.
B.   differences between two population means with variances assumed to be equal.
C.   differences between two population means with variances assumed to not be equal.

39. Which of the following should be used to test the difference between the variances of two normally distributed populations?
    A. t-test
    B. F-test
    C. Paired comparisons test

40. Jill Batten is analyzing how the returns on the stock of Stellar Energy Corp. are related with the previous month's percent change in the US Consumer Price Index for Energy (CPIENG). Based on 248 observations, she has computed the sample correlation between the Stellar and CPIENG variables to be –0.1452. She also wants to determine whether the sample correlation is statistically significant. The critical value for the test statistic at the 0.05 level of significance is approximately 1.96. Batten should conclude that the statistical relationship between Stellar and CPIENG is:
    A. significant, because the calculated test statistic has a lower absolute value than the critical value for the test statistic.
    B. significant, because the calculated test statistic has a higher absolute value than the critical value for the test statistic.
    C. not significant, because the calculated test statistic has a higher absolute value than the critical value for the test statistic.

41. In which of the following situations would a non-parametric test of a hypothesis *most likely* be used?
    A. The sample data are ranked according to magnitude.
    B. The sample data come from a normally distributed population.
    C. The test validity depends on many assumptions about the nature of the population.

42. An analyst is examining the monthly returns for two funds over one year. Both funds' returns are non-normally distributed. To test whether the mean return of one fund is greater than the mean return of the other fund, the analyst can use:
    A. a parametric test only.
    B. a nonparametric test only.
    C. both parametric and nonparametric tests.

CHAPTER 7

INTRODUCTION TO LINEAR REGRESSION

Richard A. DeFusco, PhD, CFA
Dennis W. McLeavey, DBA, CFA
Jerald E. Pinto, PhD, CFA
David E. Runkle, PhD, CFA

LEARNING OUTCOMES

The candidate should be able to:

- distinguish between the dependent and independent variables in a linear regression;
- explain the assumptions underlying linear regression and interpret regression coefficients;
- calculate and interpret the standard error of estimate, the coefficient of determination, and a confidence interval for a regression coefficient;
- formulate a null and alternative hypothesis about a population value of a regression coefficient and determine the appropriate test statistic and whether the null hypothesis is rejected at a given level of significance;
- calculate the predicted value for the dependent variable, given an estimated regression model and a value for the independent variable;
- calculate and interpret a confidence interval for the predicted value of the dependent variable; and
- describe the use of analysis of variance (ANOVA) in regression analysis, interpret ANOVA results, and calculate and interpret the *F*-statistic.

Quantitative Methods for Investment Analysis, Second Edition, by Richard A. DeFusco, PhD, CFA, Dennis W. McLeavey, DBA, CFA, Jerald E. Pinto, PhD, CFA, and David E. Runkle, PhD, CFA. Copyright © 2019 by CFA Institute.

1. INTRODUCTION

Financial analysts often need to examine whether a variable is able to explain another variable. For example, she or he might want to know whether the spread between a company's return on invested capital and its cost of capital helps to explain the company's value in the marketplace. Regression analysis is a tool for examining this issue. We introduce basic concepts in regression analysis, a powerful technique for examining the ability of one or more variables (independent variables) to explain or predict another variable (the dependent variable).

We first describe linear regression with one independent variable. We then explain the assumptions of the linear regression model, the standard error of estimate, and the coefficient of determination. We then address testing hypotheses concerning the population values of the intercept and slope coefficient of a regression model. The next section describes the uses of **analysis of variance (ANOVA)** in a regression. The subsequent section explains prediction intervals.

2. LINEAR REGRESSION

Linear regression with one independent variable, sometimes called simple linear regression, models the relationship between two variables as a straight line. When the linear relationship between the two variables is significant, linear regression provides a simple model for forecasting the value of one variable, known as the **dependent variable**, given the value of the second variable, known as the **independent variable**. The following sections explain linear regression in more detail.

2.1. Linear Regression with One Independent Variable

As a financial analyst, you will often want to understand the relationship between financial or economic variables or to predict the value of one variable using information about the value of another variable. For example, you may want to know the impact of changes in the 10-year Treasury bond yield on the earnings yield of the S&P 500 Index (the earnings yield is the reciprocal of the price-to-earnings ratio). If the relationship between those two variables is linear, you can use linear regression to summarize it.

Linear regression allows us to use one variable to make predictions about another, test hypotheses about the relation between two variables, and quantify the strength of the relationship between the two variables. We first focus on linear regression with a single independent variable. In subsequent coverage of the regression topic, we will examine regression with more than one independent variable.

Regression analysis begins with the dependent variable (denoted Y), the variable that you are seeking to explain. The independent variable (denoted X) is the variable you are using to explain changes in the dependent variable. For example, you might try to explain small-stock returns (the dependent variable) based on returns to the S&P 500 (the independent variable). Or you might try to explain inflation (the dependent variable) as a function of growth in a country's money supply (the independent variable).

Linear regression assumes a linear relationship between the dependent and the independent variables. The following regression equation describes that relation:

$$Y_i = b_0 + b_1 X_i + \varepsilon_i, \; i = 1, \ldots, n. \tag{1}$$

This equation states that the dependent variable, Y, is equal to the intercept, b_0, plus a slope coefficient, b_1, times the independent variable, X, plus an **error term**, ε. The error term represents the portion of the dependent variable that cannot be explained by the independent variable. We refer to the intercept b_0 and the slope coefficient b_1 as the **regression coefficients**.

Regression analysis uses two principal types of data: cross sectional and time series. Cross-sectional data involve many observations of X and Y for the same time period. Those observations could come from different companies, asset classes, investment funds, people, countries, or other entities, depending on the regression model. For example, a cross-sectional model might use data from many companies to test whether predicted earnings-per-share growth explains differences in price-to-earnings ratios (P/Es) during a specific time period. The word *explain* is frequently used in describing regression relationships. One estimate of a company's P/E that does not depend on any other variable is the average P/E. If a regression of a P/E on an independent variable tends to give more accurate estimates of P/E than just assuming that the company's P/E equals the average P/E, we say that the independent variable helps *explain* P/Es because using that independent variable improves our estimates. Finally, note that if we use cross-sectional observations in a regression, we usually denote the observations as $i = 1, 2, \ldots, n$.

Time-series data use many observations from different time periods for the same company, asset class, investment fund, person, country, or other entity, depending on the regression model. For example, a time-series model might use monthly data from many years to test whether US inflation rates determine US short-term interest rates. If we use time-series data in a regression, we usually denote the observations as $t = 1, 2, \ldots, T$. Note that in the sections that follow we primarily use the notation $i = 1, 2, \ldots, n$ even for time series.

Exactly how does linear regression estimate b_0 and b_1? Linear regression, also known as linear least squares, computes a line that best fits the observations; it chooses values for the intercept, b_0, and slope, b_1, that minimize the sum of the squared vertical distances between the observations and the regression line. Linear regression chooses the **estimated parameters** or **fitted parameters** $\hat{b}_0$ and $\hat{b}_1$ (hats over the symbols for coefficients indicate estimated values) in Equation 1 to minimize

$$\sum_{i=1}^{n} (Y_i - \hat{b}_0 - \hat{b}_1 X_i)^2. \tag{2}$$

In this expression, the term $(Y_i - \hat{b}_0 - \hat{b}_1 X_i)^2$ means the squared difference between the dependent variable and the predicted value of the dependent variable. Using this method to estimate the values of $\hat{b}_0$ and $\hat{b}_1$, we can fit a line through the observations of X and Y that best explains the value that Y takes for any particular value of X.

Note that we never observe the population parameter values b_0 and b_1 in a regression model. Instead, we observe only $\hat{b}_0$ and $\hat{b}_1$, which are estimates of the population parameter values. Thus, predictions must be based on the parameters' estimated values, and testing is based on estimated values in relation to the hypothesized population values.

Suppose that we want to estimate the regression relation between the annual rate of inflation (the dependent variable) and the annual rate of money supply growth (the independent variable) for six industrialized countries. Exhibit 1 shows the average annual growth rate

EXHIBIT 1   Annual Money Supply Growth Rate and Inflation Rate by Country, 1980–2018

Country	Money Supply Growth Rate (%)	Inflation Rate (%)
Australia	10.31	3.93
Japan	3.95	0.30
South Korea	16.10	4.61
Switzerland	5.34	1.58
United Kingdom	11.56	3.89
United States	6.18	2.63
Average	8.91	2.63

Source: The World Bank.

in the money supply and the average annual inflation rate from 1980 to 2018 for the six countries ($n = 6$).

Exhibit 2 gives a visual example of how linear regression works. The figure shows a scatter plot constructed by using the data for each country in Exhibit 1 to mark a point on a graph and the linear regression that results from estimating the following equation: Long-term rate of inflation $= b_0 + b_1$ (Long-term rate of money supply growth) $+ \varepsilon$.

The vertical distance from each of the six data points to the fitted regression line is the regression residual, which is the difference between the actual value of the dependent variable and the predicted value of the dependent variable made by the regression equation. Linear regression chooses the estimated coefficients $\hat{b}_0$ and $\hat{b}_1$ in Equation 1 such that the sum of the squared vertical distances is minimized. The estimated regression equation is

EXHIBIT 2   Fitted Regression Line Explaining the Inflation Rate Using Growth in the Money Supply by Country, 1980–2018

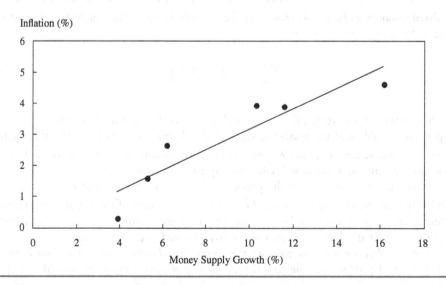

Source: The World Bank.

Long-term inflation $= -0.0011 + 0.3290$ (Long-term money supply growth). Note that we have entered the monthly rates as decimals. Also, we used rounded numbers in the formulas discussed later to estimate the regression equation.

According to this regression equation, if the long-term money supply growth is 0 for any country, the long-term rate of inflation in that country is predicted to be -0.11 percent. For every 1 percentage point (pp) increase in the long-term rate of money supply growth for a country (say, from 3 to 4 percent), the long-term inflation rate is predicted to increase by 0.329 pps. In a regression such as this one, which contains one independent variable, the slope coefficient equals $cov(Y, X)/var(X)$. Exhibit 3 shows how to compute the slope coefficient from the data in Exhibit 1. The individual observations of countries' average annual money supply growth from 1980–2018 are denoted X_i, and individual observations of countries' annual average inflation rate from 1980–2018 are denoted Y_i. The next two columns show the calculations for the inputs to the slope coefficient: the sample covariance and the sample variance of X. The last column is included because we need the sample standard deviation of Y to compute the coefficient of determination, the subject of a later section.

EXHIBIT 3   Sample Covariance and Sample Variances: Annual Money Supply Growth Rate and Inflation Rate by Country, 1980–2018

Country	Money Supply Growth Rate X_i	Inflation Rate Y_i	Cross-Product $(X_i-\overline{X})(Y_i-\overline{Y})$	Squared Deviations $(X_i-\overline{X})^2$	Squared Deviations $(Y_i-\overline{Y})^2$
Australia	0.1031	0.0393	0.000155	0.000196	0.000123
Japan	0.0395	0.0030	0.001250	0.002460	0.000635
South Korea	0.1610	0.0461	0.001287	0.005170	0.000320
Switzerland	0.0534	0.0158	0.000443	0.001274	0.000154
United Kingdom	0.1156	0.0389	0.000284	0.000702	0.000114
United States	0.0618	0.0263	0.000052	0.000745	0.000004
Sum	0.5344	0.1694	0.003471	0.010547	0.001350
Average	0.0891	0.0282			
Covariance			0.000694		
Variance				0.002109	0.000270
Standard deviation				0.045924	0.016432

Notes:

1. Divide the cross-product sum by $n - 1$ (with $n = 6$) to obtain the covariance of X and Y.

2. Divide the squared deviations' sums by $n - 1$ (with $n = 6$) to obtain the variances of X and Y.

3. We have not used full precision in the table's calculations. Had we used full precision in all calculations, some of the table's entries would be slightly different but would not materially affect our conclusions.

Source: The World Bank.

$$\text{cov}(Y, X) = 0.000694.$$

$$\text{var}(X) = 0.002109.$$

$$\text{cov}(Y, X)/\text{var}(X) = 0.000694/0.002109.$$

$$\hat{b}_1 = 0.329.$$

In a linear regression, the fitted regression line passes through the point corresponding to the means of the dependent and the independent variables. As shown in Exhibit 4 (excerpted from Exhibit 3), from 1980 to 2018, the mean long-term growth rate of the money supply for these six countries was 8.91 percent, whereas the mean long-term inflation rate was 2.82 percent.

Because the point (8.91, 2.82) lies on the regression line $\hat{b}_0 = \overline{Y} - \hat{b}_1\overline{X}$, we can solve for the intercept using this point as follows:

$$\hat{b}_0 = 0.0282 - 0.329(0.0891) = -0.0011.$$

We are showing how to solve the linear regression equation step by step to make the source of the numbers clear. Typically, an analyst will use the data analysis function on a spreadsheet or a statistical package to perform linear regression analysis. Later, we will discuss how to use regression residuals to quantify the uncertainty in a regression model.

3. ASSUMPTIONS OF THE LINEAR REGRESSION MODEL

We have discussed how to interpret the coefficients in a linear regression model. Now we turn to the statistical assumptions underlying this model. Suppose that we have n observations of both the dependent variable, Y, and the independent variable, X, and we want to estimate Equation 1:

$$Y_i = b_0 + b_1X_i + \varepsilon_i, i = 1, \ldots, n.$$

To be able to draw valid conclusions from a linear regression model with a single independent variable, we need to make the following six assumptions, known as the classic normal linear regression model assumptions:

1. The relationship between the dependent variable, Y, and the independent variable, X, is linear in the parameters b_0 and b_1. This requirement means that b_0 and b_1 are raised to the first power only and that neither b_0 nor b_1 is multiplied or divided by another regression parameter (as in b_0/b_1, for example). The requirement does not exclude X from being raised to a power other than 1.
2. The independent variable, X, is not random.
3. The expected value of the error term is 0: $E(\varepsilon) = 0$.

EXHIBIT 4   Excerpt from Exhibit 3

	Money Supply Growth Rate	Inflation Rate
Average	8.91%	2.82%

4. The variance of the error term is the same for all observations: $E(\varepsilon_i^2) = \sigma_\varepsilon^2$, $i = 1, \ldots, n$.
5. The error term, ε, is uncorrelated across observations. Consequently, $E(\varepsilon_i\varepsilon_j) = 0$ for all i not equal to j.[1]
6. The error term, ε, is normally distributed.

Now we can take a closer look at each of these assumptions.

Assumption 1 is critical for a valid linear regression. If the relationship between the independent and dependent variables is nonlinear in the parameters, then estimating that relation with a linear regression model will produce invalid results. For example, $Y_i = b_0 e^{b_1 X_i} + \varepsilon_i$ is nonlinear in b_1, so we could not apply the linear regression model to it.

Even if the dependent variable is nonlinear, linear regression can be used as long as the regression is linear in the parameters. So, for example, linear regression can be used to estimate the equation $Y_i = b_0 + b_1 X_i^2 + \varepsilon_i$.

Assumptions 2 and 3 ensure that linear regression produces the correct estimates of b_0 and b_1. Although we assume that the independent variable in the regression model is not random, that assumption is clearly often not true (for an explanation of why we may still rely on the results of regression models in such circumstances, see Greene 2018).

Assumptions 4, 5, and 6 let us use the linear regression model to determine the distribution of the estimated parameters $\hat{b}_0$ and $\hat{b}_1$ and thus test whether those coefficients have a particular value.

- Assumption 4, that the variance of the error term is the same for all observations, is also known as the homoskedasticity assumption. We will discuss how to test for and correct violations of this assumption at a later stage of our coverage of the regression topic.
- Assumption 5, that the errors are uncorrelated across observations, is also necessary for correctly estimating the variances of the estimated parameters $\hat{b}_0$ and $\hat{b}_1$. We will discuss violations of this assumption at a later stage of our coverage.
- Assumption 6, that the error term is normally distributed, allows us to easily test a particular hypothesis about a linear regression model. For large sample sizes, we may be able to drop the assumption of normality by appealing to the central limit theorem (see Greene 2018). Asymptotic theory shows that in many cases, the test statistics produced by standard regression programs are valid even if the error term is not normally distributed.

EXAMPLE 1 Evaluating Economic Forecasts

If economic forecasts were completely accurate, every prediction of a change in an economic variable in a quarter would exactly match the actual change that occurs in that quarter. Even though forecasts may be inaccurate, we hope that they are at least unbiased—that is, that the expected value of the forecast error is zero. An unbiased forecast can be expressed as $E(\text{Actual change} - \text{Predicted change}) = 0$. In fact, most evaluations of forecast accuracy test whether forecasts are unbiased (see, for example, Keane and Runkle 1990).

In the euro area, the Survey of Professional Forecasters (SPF), conducted by the European Central bank (ECB), gathers professional forecasters' predictions about

---

[1] $\text{var}(\varepsilon_i) = E[\varepsilon_i - E(\varepsilon_i)]^2 = E(\varepsilon_i - 0)^2 = E(\varepsilon_i)^2$; $\text{cov}(\varepsilon_i, \varepsilon_j) = E\{[\varepsilon_i - E(\varepsilon_i)][\varepsilon_j - E(\varepsilon_j)]\} = E[(\varepsilon_i - 0)(\varepsilon_j - 0)] = E(\varepsilon_i\varepsilon_j) = 0$.

many economic variables. Since 1999, the SPF has gathered predictions on the euro area inflation rate using the change in the Harmonised Index of Consumer Prices (HICP) for the prices of consumer goods and services acquired by households to measure inflation. Exhibit 5 shows a scatter plot of the mean forecast made in the first quarter of a year for the percentage change in the HICP during that year and the actual percentage change in the HICP, from 1999 through 2018, along with the fitted regression line for the following equation: Actual percentage change $= b_0 + b_1$(Predicted percentage change) $+ \varepsilon$. If the forecasts are unbiased, the intercept, b_0, should be 0 and the slope, b_1, should be 1. We should also find E(Actual change $-$ Predicted change) $= 0$. If forecasts are actually unbiased, as long as $b_0 = 0$ and $b_1 = 1$, the error term, Actual change $- b_0 - b_1$(Predicted change), will have an expected value of 0, as required by Assumption 3 of the linear regression model. With unbiased forecasts, any other values of b_0 and b_1 would yield an error term with an expected value different from 0.

EXHIBIT 5   Actual Change in Euro Area HICP vs. Predicted Change

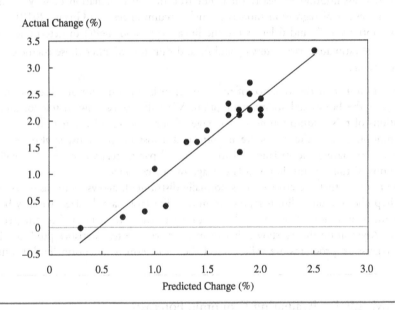

Source: European Central Bank.

If $b_0 = 0$ and $b_1 = 1$, our best guess of actual change in HICP would be 0 if professional forecasters' predictions of change in HICP were 0. For every 1 pp increase in the prediction of change by the professional forecasters, the regression model would predict a 1 pp increase in actual change.

The fitted regression line in Exhibit 5 comes from the following equation: Actual change $= -0.7558 + 1.5922$(Predicted change). It seems that the estimated values of b_0 and b_1 are not particularly close to the values of b_0 and b_1 that are consistent with unbiased forecasts: 0 and 1, respectively. Later we will discuss how to test the hypotheses that $b_0 = 0$ and $b_1 = 1$.

4. THE STANDARD ERROR OF ESTIMATE

The linear regression model sometimes describes the relationship between two variables quite well, but sometimes it does not. We must be able to distinguish between these two cases to use regression analysis effectively. Therefore, in this section and the next, we discuss statistics that measure how well a given linear regression model captures the relationship between the dependent and independent variables.

Exhibit 5, for example, shows what appears to be a strong relation between predicted inflation and actual inflation. If we knew professional forecasters' predictions for inflation in a particular quarter, we would be reasonably certain that we could use this regression model to forecast actual inflation relatively accurately.

In other cases, however, the relation between the dependent and independent variables is not strong. Exhibit 6 shows a scatter plot of the monthly returns of the S&P 500 Index and the monthly inflation rate in the United States from January 1990 through June 2018, along with the fitted regression line for the equation: Returns to S&P 500 = b_0 + b_1(Rate of inflation) + ε. In this figure, the actual observations are generally much farther from the fitted regression line than in Exhibit 5. Using the estimated regression equation to predict monthly stock returns assuming a particular level of inflation might result in an inaccurate forecast.

As noted, the regression relation in Exhibit 6 appears less precise than that in Exhibit 5. The standard error of estimate (sometimes called the standard error of the regression) measures this uncertainty. This statistic is very much like the standard deviation for a single variable, except that it measures the standard deviation of $\hat{\varepsilon}_i$, the residual term in the regression.

The formula for the standard error of estimate (SEE) for a linear regression model with one independent variable is

$$\text{SEE} = \left(\frac{\sum_{i=1}^{n} (Y_i - \hat{b}_0 - \hat{b}_1 X_i)^2}{n-2} \right)^{1/2} = \left(\frac{\sum_{i=1}^{n} (\hat{\varepsilon}_i)^2}{n-2} \right)^{1/2}. \tag{3}$$

In the numerator of this equation, we are computing the difference between the dependent variable's actual value for each observation and its predicted value $(\hat{b}_0 + \hat{b}_1 X_i)$ for each observation. The difference between the actual and predicted values of the dependent variable is the regression residual, $\hat{\varepsilon}_i$, which is often referred to as the error term.

Equation 3 looks very much like the formula for computing a standard deviation, except that $n - 2$ appears in the denominator instead of $n - 1$. We use $n - 2$ because the sample includes n observations and the linear regression model estimates two parameters $(\hat{b}_0$ and $\hat{b}_1)$; the difference between the number of observations and the number of parameters is $n - 2$. This difference is also called the degrees of freedom; it is the denominator needed to ensure that the estimated standard error of estimate is unbiased.

EXHIBIT 6   Fitted Regression Line Explaining Stock Returns by Inflation during 1990–2019

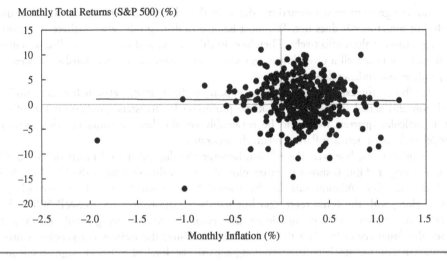

Sources: Bureau of Labor Statistics and finance.yahoo.com as of 23 November 2019.

EXAMPLE 2   Computing the Standard Error of Estimate

Recall that the estimated regression equation for the inflation and money supply growth data shown in Exhibit 2 was $Y_i = -0.0011 + 0.3290X_i$. Exhibit 7 uses this estimated equation to compute the data needed for the standard error of estimate.

EXHIBIT 7   Computing the Standard Error of Estimate

Country	Money Supply Growth Rate X_i	Inflation Rate Y_i	Predicted Inflation Rate $\widehat{Y}_i$	Regression Residual $Y_i - \widehat{Y}_i$	Squared Residual $(Y_i - \widehat{Y}_i)^2$
Australia	0.1031	0.0393	0.0328	0.0065	0.000042
Japan	0.0395	0.0030	0.0119	−0.0089	0.000079
South Korea	0.1610	0.0461	0.0519	−0.0058	0.000034
Switzerland	0.0534	0.0158	0.0165	−0.0007	0.000000
United Kingdom	0.1156	0.0389	0.0369	0.0020	0.000004
United States	0.0618	0.0263	0.0192	0.0071	0.000050
Sum					0.000209

Source: The World Bank.

The first and second columns of data in Exhibit 7 show the long-term money supply growth rates, X_i, and long-term inflation rates, Y_i, for the six countries. The third column of data shows the predicted value of the dependent variable from the fitted regression equation for each observation. For the United States, for example, the predicted value of long-term inflation is $-0.0011 + 0.3291(0.0618) = 0.0192$, or 1.92 percent. The next-to-last column contains the regression residual, which is the difference between the actual value of the dependent variable, Y_i, and the predicted value of the dependent variable, $(\hat{Y}_i = \hat{b}_0 + \hat{b}_1 X_i)$. So, for the United States, the residual is $0.0263 - 0.0192 = 0.0071$, or 0.71 percent. The last column contains the squared regression residual. The sum of the squared residuals is 0.000050. By applying the formula for the standard error of estimate, we obtain

$$\left(\frac{0.000050}{6-2} \right)^{\frac{1}{2}} = 0.003536.$$

Thus, the standard error of estimate is about 0.35 percent.

Later, we will combine this estimate with estimates of the uncertainty about the parameters in this regression to determine confidence intervals for predicting inflation rates from money supply growth. We will see that smaller standard errors result in more accurate predictions.

5. THE COEFFICIENT OF DETERMINATION

Although the standard error of estimate gives some indication of how certain we can be about a particular prediction of Y using the regression equation, it still does not tell us how well the independent variable explains variation in the dependent variable. The coefficient of determination does exactly this: It measures the fraction of the total variation in the dependent variable that is explained by the independent variable.

We can compute the coefficient of determination in two ways. The simpler method, which can be used in a linear regression with one independent variable, is to square the correlation coefficient between the dependent and independent variables. The historical or sample correlation between two variables can be computed by dividing the sample covariance between those two variables by the product of sample standard deviations of the two variables. For example, the correlation coefficient between the long-term rate of money growth and the long-term rate of inflation between 1980 and 2018 for six industrialized countries is computed using data reported in Exhibit 3 as $0.000694/(0.045924 \times 0.016432) = 0.9197$. Thus, the coefficient of determination in the regression shown in Exhibit 1 is $(0.9197)^2 = 0.8458$. So, in this regression, the long-term rate of money supply growth explains approximately 84.6 percent of the variation in the long-term rate of inflation across the countries between 1980 and 2018. (Relatedly, note that the square root of the coefficient of determination in a linear regression with one independent variable, after attaching the sign of the estimated slope coefficient, gives the correlation coefficient between the dependent and independent variables.)

The problem with this method is that it cannot be used when we have more than one independent variable. Therefore, we need an alternative method of computing the coefficient of determination for multiple independent variables. We now present the logic behind that alternative.

If we did not know the regression relationship, our best guess for the value of any particular observation of the dependent variable would simply be $\overline{Y}$, the mean of the dependent variable. One measure of accuracy in predicting Y_i based on $\overline{Y}$ is the sample variance of Y_i, $\sum_{i=1}^{n}\frac{(Y_i-\overline{Y})^2}{n-1}$. An alternative to using $\overline{Y}$ to predict a particular observation Y_i is using the regression relationship to make that prediction. In that case, our predicted value would be $\hat{Y}_i = \hat{b}_0 + \hat{b}_1 X_i$. If the regression relationship works well, the error in predicting Y_i using $\hat{Y}_i$ should be much smaller than the error in predicting Y_i using $\overline{Y}$. If we call $\sum_{i=1}^{n}(Y_i-\overline{Y})^2$ the total variation of Y and $\sum_{i=1}^{n}(Y_i-\hat{Y}_i)^2$ the unexplained variation from the regression, then we can measure the explained variation from the regression using the following equation:

$$\text{Total variation} = \text{Unexplained variation} + \text{Explained variation.} \qquad (4)$$

The coefficient of determination is the fraction of the total variation that is explained by the regression. This gives us the relationship

$$R^2 = \frac{\text{Explained variation}}{\text{Total variation}} = \frac{\text{Total variation} - \text{Unexplained variation}}{\text{Total variation}}$$

$$= 1 - \frac{\text{Unexplained variation}}{\text{Total variation}}. \qquad (5)$$

Note that total variation equals explained variation plus unexplained variation, as shown in Equation 4. Most regression programs report the coefficient of determination as R^2. In addition, regression programs also report multiple R, which is the correlation between the actual values and the forecast values of Y. The coefficient of determination is the square of multiple R.

EXAMPLE 3   Inflation Rate and Growth in the Money Supply

Using the data in Exhibit 7, we can see that the unexplained variation from the regression, which is the sum of the squared residuals, equals 0.000230. Exhibit 8 shows the computation of total variation in the dependent variable, the long-term rate of inflation.

EXHIBIT 8   Computing Total Variation

Country	Money Supply Growth Rate X_i	Inflation Rate Y_i	Deviation from Mean $Y_i - \overline{Y}$	Squared Deviation $(Y_i - \overline{Y})^2$
Australia	0.1031	0.0393	0.0111	0.000123
Japan	0.0395	0.0030	−0.0252	0.000635

Country	Money Supply Growth Rate X_i	Inflation Rate Y_i	Deviation from Mean $Y_i - \bar{Y}$	Squared Deviation $(Y_i - \bar{Y})^2$
South Korea	0.1610	0.0461	0.0179	0.000320
Switzerland	0.0534	0.0158	−0.0124	0.000154
United Kingdom	0.1156	0.0389	0.0107	0.000114
United States	0.0618	0.0263	−0.0019	0.000004
	Average:	0.0282	Sum:	0.001350

Source: International Monetary Fund.

The average inflation rate for this period is 2.82 percent. The next-to-last column shows the amount by which each country's long-term inflation rate deviates from that average; the last column shows the square of that deviation. The sum of those squared deviations is the total variation in Y for the sample (0.001350), shown in Exhibit 8. Compute the coefficient of determination for the regression.

Solution: The coefficient of determination for the regression is

$$\frac{\text{Total variation} - \text{Unexplained variation}}{\text{Total variation}} = \frac{0.001350 - 0.000209}{0.001350} = 0.8452.$$

Note that this method gives the same result that we obtained earlier, the slight difference being explained by rounding. We will use this method again in the subsequent coverage of the regression topic; when we have more than one independent variable, this method is the only way to compute the coefficient of determination.

6. HYPOTHESIS TESTING

In this section, we address testing hypotheses concerning the population values of the intercept or slope coefficient of a regression model. This topic is critical in practice. For example, we may want to check a stock's valuation using the capital asset pricing model; we hypothesize that the stock has a market-average beta or level of systematic risk. Or we may want to test the hypothesis that economists' forecasts of the inflation rate are unbiased (not overestimates or underestimates, on average). In each case, does the evidence support the hypothesis? Such questions as these can be addressed with hypothesis tests within a regression model. Such tests are often t-tests of the value of the intercept or slope coefficients. To understand the concepts involved in this test, it is useful to first review a simple, equivalent approach based on confidence intervals.

We can perform a hypothesis test using the confidence interval approach if we know three things: (1) the estimated parameter value, $\hat{b}_0$ or $\hat{b}_1$, (2) the hypothesized value of the parameter, b_0 or b_1, and (3) a confidence interval around the estimated parameter. A confidence interval is an interval of values that we believe includes the true parameter value, b_1, with a given degree of confidence. To compute a confidence interval, we must select the significance level for the test and know the standard error of the estimated coefficient.

Suppose we regress a stock's returns on a stock market index's returns and find that the slope coefficient $(\hat{b}_1)$ is 1.5, with a standard error $(s_{\hat{b}_1})$ of 0.200. Assume we used 62 monthly observations in our regression analysis. The hypothesized value of the parameter (b_1) is 1.0, the market average slope coefficient. The estimated and population slope coefficients are often called beta, because the population coefficient is often represented by the lowercase Greek letter beta (β) rather than the b_1 that we use in our coverage. Our null hypothesis is that $b_1 = 1.0$ and $\hat{b}_1$ is the estimate for b_1. We will use a 95 percent confidence interval for our test, or we could say that the test has a significance level of 0.05.

Our confidence interval will span the range $\hat{b}_1 - t_c s_{\hat{b}_1}$ to $\hat{b}_1 + t_c s_{\hat{b}_1}$, or

$$\hat{b}_1 \pm t_c s_{\hat{b}_1}, \qquad (6)$$

where t_c is the critical t-value (note that we use the t-distribution for this test because we are using a sample estimate of the standard error, s_b, rather than its true population value). The critical value for the test depends on the number of degrees of freedom for the t-distribution under the null hypothesis. The number of degrees of freedom equals the number of observations minus the number of parameters estimated. In a regression with one independent variable, there are two estimated parameters, the intercept term and the coefficient on the independent variable. For 62 observations and two parameters estimated in this example, we have 60 degrees of freedom $(62 - 2)$. For 60 degrees of freedom, the table of critical values in the back of the book shows that the critical t-value at the 0.05 significance level is 2.00. Substituting the values from our example into Equation 6 gives us the interval

$$\hat{b}_1 \pm t_c s_{\hat{b}_1} = 1.5 \pm 2.00(0.200)$$
$$= 1.5 \pm 0.400$$
$$= 1.10 \text{ to } 1.90.$$

A 95 percent confidence interval is the interval, based on the sample value, that we would expect to include the population value with a 95 percent degree of confidence. Because we are testing the null hypothesis that $b_1 = 1.0$ and because our confidence interval does not include 1.0, we can reject the null hypothesis.

In practice, the most common way to test a hypothesis using a regression model is with a t-test of significance. To test the hypothesis, we can compute the statistic

$$t = \frac{\hat{b}_1 - b_1}{s_{\hat{b}_1}}. \qquad (7)$$

This test statistic has a t-distribution with $n - 2$ degrees of freedom because two parameters were estimated in the regression. We compare the absolute value of the t-statistic with t_c. If the absolute value of t is greater than t_c, then we can reject the null hypothesis. Substituting the values from the previous example into this relationship gives the t-statistic associated with the test that the stock's beta equals 1.0 $(b_1 = 1.0)$.

$$t = \frac{\hat{b}_1 - b_1}{s_{\hat{b}_1}}$$

$$= (1.5 - 1.0)/0.200$$

$$= 2.50.$$

Because $t > t_c$, we reject the null hypothesis that $b_1 = 1.0$.

The t-statistic in the previous example is 2.50, and at the 0.05 significance level, $t_c = 2.00$; thus, we reject the null hypothesis because $t > t_c$. This statement is equivalent to saying that we are 95 percent confident that the interval for the slope coefficient does not contain the value 1.0. If we were performing this test at the 0.01 level, however, t_c would be 2.66 and we would not reject the hypothesis because t would not be greater than t_c at this significance level. A 99 percent confidence interval for the slope coefficient does contain the value 1.0.

The choice of significance level is always a matter of judgment. When we use higher levels of confidence, the t_c increases. This choice leads to wider confidence intervals and to a decreased likelihood of rejecting the null hypothesis. Analysts often choose the 0.05 level of significance, which indicates a 5 percent chance of rejecting the null hypothesis when, in fact, it is true (a Type I error). Of course, decreasing the level of significance from 0.05 to 0.01 decreases the probability of Type I error, but it increases the probability of Type II error—failing to reject the null hypothesis when, in fact, it is false.

Often, financial analysts do not simply report whether their tests reject a particular hypothesis about a regression parameter. Instead, they report the p-value or probability value for a particular hypothesis. The p-value is the smallest level of significance at which the null hypothesis can be rejected. It allows the reader to interpret the results rather than be told that a certain hypothesis has been rejected or accepted. In most regression software packages, the p-values printed for regression coefficients apply to a test of null hypothesis that the true parameter is equal to 0 against the alternative that the parameter is not equal to 0, given the estimated coefficient and the standard error for that coefficient. For example, if the p-value is 0.005, we can reject the hypothesis that the true parameter is equal to 0 at the 0.5% significance level (99.5 percent confidence).

The standard error of the estimated coefficient is an important input for a hypothesis test concerning the regression coefficient (and for a confidence interval for the estimated coefficient). Stronger regression results lead to smaller standard errors of an estimated parameter and result in tighter confidence intervals. If the standard error $(s_{\hat{b}_1})$ in the previous example were 0.100 instead of 0.200, the confidence interval range would be half as large and the t-statistic twice as large. With a standard error this small, we would reject the null hypothesis even at the 0.01 significance level because we would have $t = (1.5 - 1)/0.1 = 5.00$ and $t_c = 2.66$.

With this background, we can turn to hypothesis tests using actual regression results. The next three examples illustrate hypothesis tests in a variety of typical investment contexts.

EXAMPLE 4   Estimating Beta for Bayer AG

Bayer AG is a chemicals conglomerate focused on crop science and health care. The company's stock trades on the Xetra Börse Frankfurt in Germany. Suppose you are an investor in Bayer's stock and want an estimate of its beta. As in the text example, you hypothesize that Bayer has an average level of market risk and that its required return in excess of the risk-free rate is the same as the market's required excess return. One regression that summarizes these statements is

$$(R - R_F) = \alpha + \beta(R_M - R_F) + \varepsilon, \tag{8}$$

where R_F is the periodic risk-free rate of return (known at the beginning of the period), R_M is the periodic return on the market, R is the periodic return to the stock of the company, and β measures the sensitivity of the required excess return to the excess return to the market. Estimating this equation with linear regression provides an estimate of β, $\hat{\beta}$, which tells us the size of the required return premium for the security, given expectations about market returns.[2]

Suppose we want to test the null hypothesis, H_0, that $\beta = 1$ for Bayer stock to see whether the stock has the same required return premium as the market as a whole. We need data on returns to Bayer stock, a risk-free interest rate, and the returns to the market index. For this example, we use data from October 2014 through October 2019 ($n = 60$). The return to Bayer stock is R. The monthly return to 10-year German government bonds is R_F. The return to the DAX Index is R_M. This index is the primary broad measure of the German equity market. We are estimating two parameters, so the number of degrees of freedom is $n - 2 = 60 - 2 = 58$. Exhibit 9 shows the results from the regression $(R - R_F) = \alpha + \beta(R_M - R_F) + \varepsilon$.

EXHIBIT 9   Estimating Beta for Bayer AG

Regression Statistics

Multiple R	0.7552		
R^2	0.5703		
Standard error of estimate	0.0547		
Observations	60		
	Coefficients	**Standard Error**	**t-Statistic**
Alpha	−0.00962	0.0073	−1.3161
Beta	1.1275	0.1285	8.7747

Sources: finance.yahoo.com.
Note: The *t*-statistics for a coefficient automatically reported by statistical software programs assume that the null hypothesis states that the coefficient is equal to 0.

1. Test the null hypothesis, H_0, that β for Bayer equals 1 ($\beta = 1$) against the alternative hypothesis that β does not equal 1 ($\beta \neq 1$) using the confidence interval approach.
2. Test the above null hypothesis using a *t*-test.

---

[2]Beta (β) is typically estimated using 60 months of historical data, but the data-sample length sometimes varies. Although monthly data are typically used, some financial analysts estimate β using daily data. The expected excess return for Bayer stock above the risk-free rate $(R - R_F)$ is $\beta(R_M - R_F)$, given a particular excess return to the market above the risk-free rate $(R_M - R_F)$. This result holds because we regress $(R - R_F)$ against $(R_M - R_F)$. For example, if a stock's beta is 1.5, its expected excess return is 1.5 times that of the market portfolio.

3. How much of Bayer stock's excess return variation can be attributed to company-specific risk?

Solution to 1: The estimated $\hat{\beta}$ from the regression is 1.1275. The estimated standard error for that coefficient in the regression, $s_{\hat{\beta}}$, is 0.1285. The regression equation has 58 degrees of freedom $(60 - 2)$, so the critical value for the test statistic is approximately $t_c = 2.00$ at the 0.05 significance level. Therefore, the 95 percent confidence interval for the data for any hypothesized value of β is shown by the range

$$\hat{\beta} \pm t_c s_{\hat{\beta}} = 1.1275 \pm 2.00(0.1285)$$

$$= 0.8705 \text{ to } 1.3845.$$

In this case, the hypothesized parameter value is $\beta = 1$, and the value 1 falls inside this confidence interval, so we cannot reject the hypothesis at the 0.05 significance level. This means that we cannot reject the hypothesis that Bayer stock has the same systematic risk as the market as a whole.

Solution to 2: The t-statistic for the test of whether the slope is equal to the average of the stocks in the market is computed using the following equation:

$$t = \frac{\hat{\beta} - \beta}{s_{\hat{\beta}}} = \frac{1.1275 - 1.0}{0.1285} = 0.9922.$$

The absolute value of this t-statistic is less than the critical t-value of 2.00. Therefore, neither approach allows us to reject the null hypothesis. Note that the t-statistic associated with $\hat{\beta}$ in the regression results in Table 5 is 8.7745. Given the significance level we are using, we cannot reject the null hypothesis that $\beta = 1$, but we can reject the hypothesis that $\beta = 0$.

Solution to 3: The R^2 in this regression is 0.5703. This result suggests that about 57 percent of the total variation in the excess return to Bayer stock (the return to Bayer above the risk-free rate) can be explained by excess return to the market portfolio. The remaining 43 percent of Bayer stock's excess return variation is the nonsystematic component, which can be attributed to company-specific risk.

In the next example, we show a regression hypothesis test with a one-sided alternative.

EXAMPLE 5   Explaining Company Value Based on Returns to Invested Capital

Some financial analysts have argued that one good way to measure a company's ability to create wealth is to compare the company's return on invested capital (ROIC) with its weighted-average cost of capital (WACC). If a company has an ROIC greater than its cost of capital, the company is creating wealth; if its ROIC is less than its cost of capital, it is destroying wealth (Sonkin and Johnson 2017).

Enterprise value (EV) is a market-price-based measure of company value defined as the market value of equity and debt minus the value of cash and investments. Invested capital (IC) is an accounting measure of company value defined as the sum of the book values of equity and debt. Higher ratios of EV to IC should reflect greater success at wealth creation in general. Mauboussin (1996) argued that the spread between ROIC and WACC helps explain the ratio of EV to IC. Using data on companies in the food-processing industry, we can test the relationship between EV/IC and (the ROIC–WACC spread) using the regression model given in Equation 9.

$$EV_i/IC_i = b_0 + b_1(ROIC_i - WACC_i) + \varepsilon_i, \tag{9}$$

where the subscript i is an index to identify the company. Our null hypothesis is H_0: $b_1 \leq 0$, and we specify a significance level of 0.05. If we reject the null hypothesis, we have evidence of a statistically significant relationship between EV/IC and (the ROIC–WACC spread). Equation 9 is estimated using data from nine food-processing companies. The results of this regression are displayed in Exhibit 10 and Exhibit 11.

EXHIBIT 10   Explaining Enterprise Value/Invested Capital by the ROIC–WACC Spread

Regression Statistics

Multiple R	0.9469		
R^2	0.8966		
Standard error of estimate	0.7422		
Observations	9		
	Coefficients	**Standard Error**	**t-Statistic**
Intercept	1.3478	0.3511	3.8391
Spread	30.0169	3.8519	7.7928

Note: The data relate to 2001.

Source: Nelson, Moskow, Lee, and Valentine (2003).

We reject the null hypothesis based on the t-statistic of 7.7928 on the estimated slope coefficient. There is a statistically significant positive relationship between the return spread (ROIC–WACC spread) and the ratio of EV to IC in our sample of companies. Exhibit 11 illustrates the strong positive relationship. The R^2 of 0.8966 indicates that the return spread explains about 90 percent of the variation in the ratio of EV to IC among the food-processing companies in the sample in 2001. The coefficient on the return spread of 30.0169 implies that the predicted increase in EV/IC is $0.01(30.0169) = 0.3002$, or about 30 percent, for a 1 pp increase in the return spread for our sample of companies.

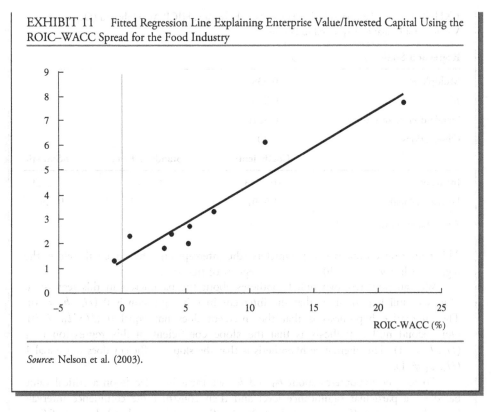

EXHIBIT 11   Fitted Regression Line Explaining Enterprise Value/Invested Capital Using the ROIC–WACC Spread for the Food Industry

Source: Nelson et al. (2003).

In the final example of this section, the null hypothesis for a *t*-test of the slope coefficient is that the value of slope equals 1, in contrast to the null hypothesis that it equals 0 as in prior examples.

EXAMPLE 6   Testing Whether Inflation Forecasts Are Unbiased

Example 1 introduced the concept of testing for bias in forecasts. That example showed that if a forecast is unbiased, its expected error is 0. We can examine whether a time series of forecasts for a particular economic variable is unbiased by comparing the forecast at each date with the actual value of the economic variable announced after the forecast. If the forecasts are unbiased, then, by definition, the average realized forecast error should be close to 0. In that case, the value of b_0 (the intercept) should be 0 and the value of b_1 (the slope) should be 1, as discussed in **Example 1**.

Refer once again to Exhibit 5, which shows the mean forecast made by professional economic forecasters in the first quarter of a year for the percentage change in euro area HICP during that year and the actual percentage change from 1999 through 2018 ($n = 20$). To test whether the forecasts are unbiased, we must estimate the regression shown in **Example 1**. We report the results of this regression in Exhibit 12. The equation to be estimated is

$$\text{Actual percentage change in HICP}_t = b_0 + b_1(\text{Predicted change}_t) + \varepsilon_t.$$

EXHIBIT 12   Testing Whether Forecasts of Euro Area HICP Are Unbiased (Dependent Variable: CPI Change Expressed in Percent)

Regression Statistics

Multiple R	0.9382		
R^2	0.8802		
Standard error of estimate	0.3216		
Observations	20		
	Coefficients	**Standard Error**	**t-Statistic**
Intercept	−0.7558	0.2274	−3.3236
Forecast (slope)	1.5902	0.1383	11.4998

Source: European Central Bank.

This regression estimates two parameters (the intercept and the slope); therefore, the regression has $n - 2 = 20 - 2 = 18$ degrees of freedom.

We can now test two null hypotheses about the parameters in this regression. Our first null hypothesis is that the intercept in this regression is 0 (H_0: $b_0 = 0$). The alternative hypothesis is that the intercept does not equal 0 (H_a: $b_0 \neq 0$). Our second null hypothesis is that the slope coefficient in this regression is 1 (H_0: $b_1 = 1$). The alternative hypothesis is that the slope coefficient does not equal 1 (H_a: $b_1 \neq 1$).

To test the hypotheses about b_0 and b_1, we must first decide on a critical value based on a particular significance level and then construct the confidence intervals for each parameter. If we choose the 0.05 significance level, with 18 degrees of freedom, the critical value, t_c, is approximately 2.1. The estimated value of the parameter $\hat{b}_0$ is −0.7558, and the estimated value of the standard error for $\hat{b}_0(s_{\hat{b}_0})$ is 0.2274. Let B_0 stand for any particular hypothesized value. Therefore, under the null hypothesis that $b_0 = B_0$, a 95% confidence interval for b_0 is $\hat{b}_0 \pm t_c s_{\hat{b}_0}$:

$$-0.7558 \pm 2.1(0.2274)$$

$$= -1.2333 \text{ to } -0.2783.$$

In this case, B_0 is 0. The value of 0 falls outside this confidence interval, so we can reject the first null hypothesis that $b_0 = 0$. We will explain how to interpret this result shortly.

Our second null hypothesis is based on the same sample as our first null hypothesis. Therefore, the critical value for testing that hypothesis is the same as the critical value for testing the first hypothesis ($t_c = 2.1$). The estimated value of the parameter $\hat{b}_1$ is 1.5902, and the estimated value of the standard error for $\hat{b}_1$, $s_{\hat{b}_1}$, is 0.1383. Therefore, the 95% confidence interval for any particular hypothesized value of b_1 can be constructed as follows:

$$\hat{b}_1 \pm t_c s_{\hat{b}_1}$$

$$= 1.5902 \pm 2.1(0.1383)$$

$$= 1.2998 \text{ to } 1.8806.$$

In this case, our hypothesized value of b_1 is 1. The value 1 falls outside this confidence interval, so we can reject the null hypothesis that $b_1 = 1$ at the 0.05 significance level. Because we did reject at least one of the two null hypotheses (in this example, we have rejected both the null hypotheses, $b_0 = 0$ and $b_1 = 1$) about the parameters in this model, we can reject the hypothesis that the forecasts of HICP change were unbiased. Note that jointly testing the hypothesis $b_0 = 0$ and $b_1 = 1$ would require us to take into account the covariance of $\hat{b}_0$ and $\hat{b}_1$. For information on testing joint hypotheses of this type, see Greene (2018).

A>s an analyst, you often will need forecasts of economic variables to help you make recommendations about asset allocation, expected returns, and other investment decisions. The hypothesis tests just conducted suggest that you can reject the hypothesis that the HICP predictions in the Survey of Professional Forecasters are unbiased. If you need an unbiased forecast of future percentage change in HICP for your asset-allocation decision, you might not want to use these forecasts. You may also want to do some further exploration. For example, a study of forecasts in the European Central Bank Survey of Professional Forecasters by Genre, Kenny, Meyler, and Timmermann (2013) found that the inflation forecasts were worse when the financial crisis period is included. Therefore, you may want to re-estimate the regression equation after excluding the financial crisis period and retest the null hypotheses that $b_0 = 0$ and $b_1 = 1$. Similarly, you may want to look for evidence of any outliers, small numbers of observations at either extreme (small or large) of a sample, in a scatter plot of realized and forecasted inflation, and redo the previous analysis after excluding these outliers.

7. ANALYSIS OF VARIANCE IN A REGRESSION WITH ONE INDEPENDENT VARIABLE

Analysis of variance (ANOVA) is a statistical procedure for dividing the total variability of a variable into components that can be attributed to different sources. In regression analysis, we use ANOVA to determine the usefulness of the independent variable or variables in explaining variation in the dependent variable. An important statistical test conducted in analysis of variance is the *F*-test. The *F*-statistic tests whether all the slope coefficients in a linear regression are equal to 0. In a regression with one independent variable, this is a test of the null hypothesis H_0: $b_1 = 0$ against the alternative hypothesis H_a: $b_1 \neq 0$.

To correctly determine the test statistic for the null hypothesis that the slope coefficient equals 0, we need to know the following:

- the total number of observations (n);
- the total number of parameters to be estimated (in a regression with one independent variable, this number is 2: the intercept and the slope coefficient);
- the sum of squared errors or residuals, $\sum_{i=1}^{n}(Y_i - \hat{Y}_i)^2$, abbreviated SSE (this value is also known as the residual sum of squares); and

- the regression sum of squares, $\sum_{i=1}^{n}(\hat{Y}_i - \overline{Y})^2$, abbreviated RSS (this value is the amount of total variation in Y that is explained in the regression equation; total variation (TSS) is the sum of SSE and RSS).

The F-test for determining whether the slope coefficient equals 0 is based on an F-statistic, constructed using these four values. The F-statistic measures how well the regression equation explains the variation in the dependent variable. The F-statistic is the ratio of the average regression sum of squares to the average sum of the squared errors. The average regression sum of squares is computed by dividing the regression sum of squares by the number of slope parameters estimated (in this case, 1). The average sum of squared errors is computed by dividing the sum of squared errors by the number of observations, n, minus the total number of parameters estimated (in this case, 2: the intercept and the slope). These two divisors are the degrees of freedom for an F-test. If there are n observations, the F-test for the null hypothesis that the slope coefficient is equal to 0 is here denoted $F_{(\# \text{ slope parameters}),(n- \# \text{ parameters})} = F_{1,n-2}$, and the test has 1 and $n - 2$ degrees of freedom.

Suppose, for example, that the independent variable in a regression model explains none of the variation in the dependent variable. Then the predicted value for the regression model, $\hat{Y}_i$, is the average value of the dependent variable $\overline{Y}$. In this case, the regression sum of squares $\sum_{i=1}^{n}(\hat{Y}_i - \overline{Y})^2$ is 0. Therefore, the F-statistic is 0. If the independent variable explains little of the variation in the dependent variable, the value of the F-statistic will be very small.

The formula for the F-statistic in a regression with one independent variable is

$$F = \frac{\text{RSS}/1}{\text{SSE}/(n-2)} = \frac{\text{Mean regression sum of squares}}{\text{Mean squared error}}. \tag{10}$$

If the regression model does a good job of explaining variation in the dependent variable, then this ratio should be high. The explained regression sum of squares per estimated parameter will be high relative to the unexplained variation for each degree of freedom. Critical values for this F-statistic are given in Appendix D at the end of this volume.

Even though the F-statistic is commonly computed by regression software packages, analysts typically do not use ANOVA and F-tests in regressions with just one independent variable. Why not? In such regressions, the F-statistic is the square of the t-statistic for the slope coefficient. Therefore, the F-test duplicates the t-test for the significance of the slope coefficient. This relation is not true for regressions with two or more slope coefficients. Nevertheless, the one-slope-coefficient case gives a foundation for understanding the multiple-slope-coefficient cases.

Often, mutual fund performance is evaluated based on whether the fund has positive alpha—significantly positive excess risk-adjusted returns. One commonly used method of risk adjustment is based on the capital asset pricing model. Consider the regression

$$(R_i - R_F) = \alpha_i + \beta_i(R_M - R_F) + \varepsilon_i, \tag{11}$$

where R_F is the periodic risk-free rate of return (known at the beginning of the period), R_M is the periodic return on the market, R_i is the periodic return to Mutual Fund i, and β_i is the fund's beta. A fund has zero risk-adjusted excess return if $\alpha_i = 0$. If $\alpha_i = 0$, then $(R_i - R_F) = \beta_i(R_M - R_F) + \varepsilon_i$, and taking expectations, $E(R_i) = R_F + \beta_i(R_M - R_F)$, implying that β_i

completely explains the fund's mean excess returns. If, for example, $\alpha_i > 0$, the fund is earning higher returns than expected given its beta.

In summary, to test whether a fund has a positive alpha, we must test the null hypothesis that the fund has no risk-adjusted excess returns (H_0: $\alpha = 0$) against the alternative hypothesis of non-zero risk-adjusted returns (H_a: $\alpha \neq 0$). Note that the Greek letter alpha, α, is traditionally used to represent the intercept in Equation 11 and should not be confused with another traditional usage of α to represent a significance level.

EXAMPLE 7   Performance Evaluation: The Dreyfus Appreciation Fund

Exhibit 13 presents results evaluating the excess return to the Dreyfus Appreciation Fund from January 2014 through December 2018. Note that the estimated beta in this regression, $\hat{\beta}_i$, is 0.9119. The Dreyfus Appreciation Fund was estimated to be less risky than the market as a whole.

EXHIBIT 13   Performance Evaluation of Dreyfus Appreciation Fund, January 2014 to December 2018

Regression Statistics

Multiple R	0.9082
R^2	0.8248
Standard error of estimate	0.0303
Observations	60

ANOVA	Degrees of Freedom (df)	Sum of Squares (SS)	Mean Sum of Squares (MSS)	F
Regression	1	0.2507	0.2507	272.97
Residual	58	0.0533	0.000918	
Total	59	0.3039		

	Coefficients	Standard Error	t-Statistic
Alpha	−0.0076	0.0046	−1.6683
Beta	0.9119	0.0552	16.5218

Sources: finance.yahoo.com as of 21 October 2019; the Federal Reserve.

1. Test whether the fund had a significant excess return beyond the return associated with the market risk of the fund.
2. Based on the *t*-test, discuss whether the beta of the fund is likely to be zero.
3. Use Equation 10 to compute the *F*-statistic. Based on the *F*-test, determine whether the beta of the fund is likely to be zero.

Solution to 1: The estimated alpha ($\hat{\alpha}$) in this regression is negative (−0.0076). The absolute value of the coefficient is about 1.7 times the size of the standard error for that coefficient (0.0046), so the t-statistic for the coefficient is -1.6683. Therefore, we cannot reject the null hypothesis ($\alpha = 0$) that the fund did not have a significant excess return beyond the return associated with the market risk of the fund. The negative alpha is therefore non-significant.

Solution to 2: Because the t-statistic for the slope coefficient in this regression is 16.52, the p-value for that coefficient is less than 0.0001 and is approximately zero. Therefore, the probability that the true value of this coefficient is 0 is microscopic.

Solution to 3: The ANOVA portion of Exhibit 13 provides the data we need to compute the F-statistic. In this case,

- the total number of observations (n) is 60;
- the total number of parameters to be estimated is 2 (intercept and slope);
- the sum of squared errors or residuals, SSE, is 0.0533; and
- the regression sum of squares, RSS, is 0.2507.

Therefore, the F-statistic to test whether the slope coefficient is equal to 0 is

$$\frac{0.2507/1}{0.0533/(60-2)} = 272.81.$$

The ANOVA output would show that the p-value for this F-statistic is less than 0.0001 and is exactly the same as the p-value for the t-statistic for the slope coefficient. Therefore, the F-test tells us nothing more than we already knew from the t-test. Note also that the F-statistic (272.81) is the square of the t-statistic (16.5218). (The slight difference is due to rounding.)

8. PREDICTION INTERVALS

Financial analysts often want to use regression results to make predictions about a dependent variable. For example, we might ask, "How fast will the sales of XYZ Corporation grow this year if real GDP grows by 4 percent?" But we are not merely interested in making these forecasts; we also want to know how certain we should be about the forecasts' results. For example, if we predicted that sales for XYZ Corporation would grow by 6 percent this year, our prediction would mean more if we were 95 percent confident that sales growth would fall in the interval from 5 to 7 percent, rather than only 25 percent confident that this outcome would occur. Therefore, we need to understand how to compute confidence intervals around regression forecasts.

We must take into account two sources of uncertainty when using the regression model $Y_i = b_0 + b_1 X_i + \varepsilon_i$, $i = 1, \ldots, n$, and the estimated parameters $\hat{b}_0$ and $\hat{b}_1$ to make a prediction. First, the error term itself contains uncertainty. The standard deviation of the error term, σ_ε, can be estimated from the standard error of estimate for the regression equation. A second source of uncertainty in making predictions about Y, however, comes from uncertainty in the estimated parameters $\hat{b}_0$ and $\hat{b}_1$.

If we knew the true values of the regression parameters, b_0 and b_1, then the variance of our prediction of Y, given any particular predicted (or assumed) value of X, would simply be s^2, the squared standard error of estimate. The variance would be s^2 because the prediction, $\hat{Y}$, would come from the equations $\hat{Y} = b_0 + b_1 X$ and $(Y - \hat{Y}) = \varepsilon$.

Because we must estimate the regression parameters $\hat{b}_0$ and $\hat{b}_1$, however, our prediction of Y, $\hat{Y}$, given any particular predicted value of X, is actually $\hat{Y} = \hat{b}_0 + \hat{b}_1 X$. The estimated variance of the prediction error, s_f^2, of Y, given X, is

$$s_f^2 = s^2 \left[1 + \frac{1}{n} + \frac{(X - \overline{X})^2}{(n-1)s_x^2} \right].$$

This estimated variance depends on

- the squared standard error of estimate, s^2;
- the number of observations, n;
- the value of the independent variable, X, used to predict the dependent variable;
- the estimated mean, $\overline{X}$; and
- variance, s_x^2, of the independent variable.

Once we have this estimate of the variance of the prediction error, determining a prediction interval around the prediction is very similar to estimating a confidence interval around an estimated parameter, as shown earlier. We need to take the following four steps to determine the prediction interval for the prediction:

1. Make the prediction.
2. Compute the variance of the prediction error using Equation 12.
3. Choose a significance level, α, for the forecast. For example, the 0.05 level, given the degrees of freedom in the regression, determines the critical value for the forecast interval, t_c.
4. Compute the $(1 - \alpha)$ percent prediction interval for the prediction—namely, $\hat{Y} \pm t_c s_f$.

EXAMPLE 8   Predicting the Ratio of Enterprise Value to Invested Capital

We continue with the example of explaining the ratio of enterprise value to invested capital among food-processing companies by the spread between the return to invested capital and the weighted-average cost of capital (ROIC–WACC). In **Example 5**, we estimated the regression given in Exhibit 10.

EXHIBIT 10   Explaining Enterprise Value/Invested Capital by the ROIC–WACC Spread (repeated)

Regression Statistics

Multiple R	0.9469		
R^2	0.8966		
Standard error of estimate	0.7422		
Observations	9		
	Coefficients	**Standard Error**	**t-Statistic**
Intercept	1.3478	0.3511	3.8391
Spread	30.0169	3.8519	7.7928

Source: Nelson et al. (2003).

You are interested in predicting the ratio of enterprise value to invested capital for a company if the return spread between ROIC and WACC is 10 pps. What is the 95 percent prediction interval for the ratio of enterprise value to invested capital for that company?

Using the data provided in Exhibit 10, take the following steps:

1. Make the prediction: Expected EV/IC $= 1.3478 + 30.0169(0.10) = 4.3495$. This regression suggests that if the return spread between ROIC and WACC (X_i) is 10%, the predicted EV/IC will be 4.3495.
2. Compute the variance of the prediction error. To compute the variance of the forecast error, we must know
    - the standard error of the estimate of the equation, $s = 0.7422$ (as shown in Exhibit 10);
    - the mean return spread, $\overline{X} = 0.0647$ (this computation is not shown in the table); and
    - the variance of the mean return spread in the sample, $s_x^2 = 0.004641$ (this computation is not shown in the table).

Using these data, you can compute the variance of the forecast error (s_f^2) for predicting EV/IC for a company with a 10 percent spread between ROIC and WACC:

$$s_f^2 = 0.7422^2 \left[1 + \frac{1}{9} + \frac{(0.10 - 0.0647)^2}{(9-1)0.004641} \right]$$

$$= 0.630556.$$

In this example, the variance of the forecast error is 0.630556, and the standard deviation of the forecast error is $s_f = (0.630556)^{1/2} = 0.7941$.

3. Determine the critical value of the *t*-statistic. Given a 95 percent confidence interval and $9 - 2 = 7$ degrees of freedom, the critical value of the *t*-statistic, t_c, is 2.365 using the tables in the back of this volume.

4. Compute the prediction interval. The 95 percent confidence interval for EV/IC extends from $4.3495 - 2.365(0.7941)$ to $4.3495 + 2.365(0.7941)$, or 2.4715 to 6.2275.

In summary, if the spread between the ROIC and the WACC is 10 percent, the 95 percent prediction interval for EV/IC will extend from 2.4715 to 6.2275. The small sample size is reflected in the relatively large prediction interval.

Finally, if the regression assumptions are violated, hypothesis tests and predictions based on linear regression will not be valid. Although there are tests for violations of regression assumptions, often uncertainty exists as to whether an assumption has been violated. This limitation will be discussed in detail in our further coverage of the regression topic.

9. SUMMARY

- The dependent variable in a linear regression is the variable that the regression model tries to explain. The independent variables are the variables that a regression model uses to explain the dependent variable.
- If there is one independent variable in a linear regression and there are n observations of the dependent and independent variables, the regression model is $Y_i = b_0 + b_1 X_i + \varepsilon_i$, $i = 1, \ldots, n$, where Y_i is the dependent variable, X_i is the independent variable, and ε_i is the error term. In this model, the coefficient b_0 is the intercept. The intercept is the predicted value of the dependent variable when the independent variable has a value of zero. In this model, the coefficient b_1 is the slope of the regression line. If the value of the independent variable increases by one unit, then the model predicts that the value of the dependent variable will increase by b_1 units.
- The assumptions of the classic normal linear regression model are the following:
  - A linear relation exists between the dependent variable and the independent variable.
  - The independent variable is not random.
  - The expected value of the error term is 0.
  - The variance of the error term is the same for all observations (homoskedasticity).
  - The error term is uncorrelated across observations.
  - The error term is normally distributed.
- The estimated parameters in a linear regression model minimize the sum of the squared regression residuals.
- The standard error of estimate measures how well the regression model fits the data. If the SEE is small, the model fits well.
- The coefficient of determination measures the fraction of the total variation in the dependent variable that is explained by the independent variable. In a linear regression with one independent variable, the simplest way to compute the coefficient of determination is to square the correlation of the dependent and independent variables.
- To calculate a confidence interval for an estimated regression coefficient, we must know the standard error of the estimated coefficient and the critical value for the t-distribution at the chosen level of significance, t_c.
- To test whether the population value of a regression coefficient, b_1, is equal to a particular hypothesized value, B_1, we must know the estimated coefficient, $\hat{b}_1$, the standard error of

the estimated coefficient, $s_{\hat{b}_1}$, and the critical value for the t-distribution at the chosen level of significance, t_c. The test statistic for this hypothesis is $(\hat{b}_1 - B_1)/s_{\hat{b}_1}$. If the absolute value of this statistic is greater than t_c, then we reject the null hypothesis that $b_1 = B_1$.

- In the regression model $Y_i = b_0 + b_1 X_i + \varepsilon_i$, if we know the estimated parameters, $\hat{b}_0$ and $\hat{b}_1$, for any value of the independent variable, X, then the predicted value of the dependent variable Y is $\hat{Y} = \hat{b}_0 + \hat{b}_1 X$.

- The prediction interval for a regression equation for a particular predicted value of the dependent variable is $\hat{Y} \pm t_c s_f$, where s_f is the square root of the estimated variance of the prediction error and t_c is the critical level for the t-statistic at the chosen significance level. This computation specifies a $(1 - \alpha)$ percent confidence interval. For example, if $\alpha = 0.05$, then this computation yields a 95% confidence interval.

REFERENCES

Genre, Veronique, Geoff Kenny, Aidan Meyler, and Allan Timmermann. 2013. "Combining Expert Forecasts: Can Anything Beat the Simple Average?" *International Journal of Forecasting* 29 (1): 108–21. doi:10.1016/j.ijforecast.2012.06.004.

Greene, William H. 2018. *Economic Analysis*. 8th ed. Upper Saddle River, NJ: Prentice-Hall.

Keane, Michael P., and David E. Runkle. 1990. "Testing the Rationality of Price Forecasts: New Evidence from Panel Data." *American Economic Review* 80 (4): 714–35.

Nelson, David C., Robert B. Moskow, Tiffany Lee, and Gregg Valentine. 2003. *Food Investor's Handbook*. New York: Credit Suisse First Boston.

Sonkin, Paul D., and Paul Johnson. 2017. *Pitch the Perfect Investment*. New York: Wiley.

PRACTICE PROBLEMS

1. Julie Moon is an energy analyst examining electricity, oil, and natural gas consumption in different regions over different seasons. She ran a regression explaining the variation in energy consumption as a function of temperature. The total variation of the dependent variable was 140.58, the explained variation was 60.16, and the unexplained variation was 80.42. She had 60 monthly observations.
   A. Compute the coefficient of determination.
   B. What was the sample correlation between energy consumption and temperature?
   C. Compute the standard error of the estimate of Moon's regression model.
   D. Compute the sample standard deviation of monthly energy consumption.

2. You are examining the results of a regression estimation that attempts to explain the unit sales growth of a business you are researching. The analysis of variance output for the regression is given in the table below. The regression was based on five observations ($n = 5$).

ANOVA	df	SS	MSS	F	Significance F
Regression	1	88.0	88.0	36.667	0.00904
Residual	3	7.2	2.4		
Total	4	95.2			

    A. How many independent variables are in the regression to which the ANOVA refers?

    B. Define Total SS.

    C. Calculate the sample variance of the dependent variable using information in the above table.

    D. Define regression SS and explain how its value of 88 is obtained in terms of other quantities reported in the above table.

    E. What hypothesis does the *F*-statistic test?

    F. Explain how the value of the *F*-statistic of 36.667 is obtained in terms of other quantities reported in the above table.

    G. Is the *F*-test significant at the 5 percent significance level?

3. An economist collected the monthly returns for KDL's portfolio and a diversified stock index. The data collected are shown below:

Month	Portfolio Return (%)	Index Return (%)
1	1.11	−0.59
2	72.10	64.90
3	5.12	4.81
4	1.01	1.68
5	−1.72	−4.97
6	4.06	−2.06

The economist calculated the correlation between the two returns and found it to be 0.996. The regression results with the KDL return as the dependent variable and the index return as the independent variable are given as follows:

Regression Statistics

Multiple R	0.996
R^2	0.992
Standard error	2.861
Observations	6

ANOVA	DF	SS	MSS	F	Significance F
Regression	1	4,101.62	4,101.62	500.79	0
Residual	4	32.76	8.19		
Total	5	4,134.38			

	Coefficients	Standard Error	t-Statistic	p-Value
Intercept	2.252	1.274	1.768	0.1518
Slope	1.069	0.0477	22.379	0

When reviewing the results, Andrea Fusilier suspected that they were unreliable. She found that the returns for Month 2 should have been 7.21 percent and 6.49 percent, instead of the large values shown in the first table. Correcting these values resulted in a revised correlation of 0.824 and the revised regression results shown as follows:

Regression Statistics

Multiple R	0.824				
R^2	0.678				
Standard error	2.062				
Observations	6				

ANOVA	DF	SS	MSS	F	Significance F
Regression	1	35.89	35.89	35.89	0.044
Residual	4	17.01	4.25		
Total	5	52.91			

	Coefficients	Standard Error	t-Statistic	p-Value
Intercept	2.242	0.863	2.597	0.060
Slope	0.623	0.214	2.905	0.044

Explain how the bad data affected the results.

The following information relates to Questions 4–9

Kenneth McCoin, CFA, is a fairly tough interviewer. Last year, he handed each job applicant a sheet of paper with the information in the following table, and he then asked several questions about regression analysis. Some of McCoin's questions, along with a sample of the answers he received to each, are given below. McCoin told the applicants that the independent variable is the ratio of net income to sales for restaurants with a market cap of more than $100 million and the dependent variable is the ratio of cash flow from operations to sales for those restaurants. Which of the choices provided is the best answer to each of McCoin's questions?

Regression Statistics

Multiple R	0.8623
R^2	0.7436
Standard error	0.0213
Observations	24

ANOVA	df	SS	MSS	F	Significance F
Regression	1	0.029	0.029000	63.81	0
Residual	22	0.010	0.000455		
Total	23	0.040			

	Coefficients	Standard Error	t-Statistic	p-Value
Intercept	0.077	0.007	11.328	0
Slope	0.826	0.103	7.988	0

4. What is the value of the coefficient of determination?
   A. 0.8261
   B. 0.7436
   C. 0.8623

	Standard Error of the Estimate	R^2
A	Decrease	Decrease
B	Decrease	Increase
C	Increase	Decrease

5. Suppose that you deleted several of the observations that had small residual values. If you re-estimated the regression equation using this reduced sample, what would likely happen to the standard error of the estimate and the R^2?

6. What is the correlation between X and Y?
   A. −0.7436
   B. 0.7436
   C. 0.8623

7. Where did the *F*-value in the ANOVA table come from?
   A. You look up the *F*-value in a table. The *F* depends on the numerator and denominator degrees of freedom.
   B. Divide the "mean square" for the regression by the "mean square" of the residuals.
   C. The *F*-value is equal to the reciprocal of the *t*-value for the slope coefficient.

8. If the ratio of net income to sales for a restaurant is 5 percent, what is the predicted ratio of cash flow from operations to sales?
   A. $0.007 + 0.103(5.0) = 0.524$.
   B. $0.077 − 0.826(5.0) = −4.054$.
   C. $0.077 + 0.826(5.0) = 4.207$.

9. Is the relationship between the ratio of cash flow to operations and the ratio of net income to sales significant at the 5 percent level?
   A. No, because the R^2 is greater than 0.05.
   B. No, because the p-values of the intercept and slope are less than 0.05.
   C. Yes, because the p-values for F and t for the slope coefficient are less than 0.05.

The following information relates to Questions 10–14

Howard Golub, CFA, is preparing to write a research report on Stellar Energy Corp. common stock. One of the world's largest companies, Stellar is in the business of refining and marketing oil. As part of his analysis, Golub wants to evaluate the sensitivity of the stock's returns to various economic factors. For example, a client recently asked Golub whether the price of Stellar Energy Corp. stock has tended to rise following increases in retail energy prices. Golub believes the association between the two variables is negative, but he does not know the strength of the association.

Golub directs his assistant, Jill Batten, to study the relationships between Stellar monthly common stock returns versus the previous month's percentage change in the US Consumer Price Index for Energy (CPIENG) and Stellar monthly common stock returns versus the previous month's percentage change in the US Producer Price Index for Crude Energy Materials (PPICEM). Golub wants Batten to run both a correlation and a linear regression analysis. In response, Batten compiles the summary statistics shown in Exhibit 1 for the 248 months between January 1980 and August 2000. All of the data are in decimal form, where 0.01 indicates a 1% return. Batten also runs a regression analysis using Stellar monthly returns as the dependent variable and the monthly change in CPIENG as the independent variable. Exhibit 2 displays the results of this regression model.

EXHIBIT 1   Descriptive Statistics

		Lagged Monthly Change	
	Monthly Return Stellar Common Stock	CPIENG	PPICEM
Mean	0.0123	0.0023	0.0042
Standard deviation	0.0717	0.0160	0.0534
Covariance, Stellar vs. CPIENG	−0.00017		
Covariance, Stellar vs. PPICEM	−0.00048		
Covariance, CPIENG vs. PPICEM	0.00044		
Correlation, Stellar vs. CPIENG	−0.1452		

EXHIBIT 2   Regression Analysis with CPIENG

Regression Statistics

Multiple R	0.1452
R^2	0.0211
Standard error of the estimate	0.0710
Observations	248

	Coefficients	Standard Error	t-Statistic
Intercept	0.0138	0.0046	3.0275
Slope coefficient	−0.6486	0.2818	−2.3014

	Data Type	Expected Value of Error Term
A	Time series	0
B	Time series	ε_i
C	Cross sectional	0

10. Did Batten's regression analyze cross-sectional or time-series data, and what was the expected value of the error term from that regression?

11. Based on the regression, which used data in decimal form, if the CPIENG *decreases* by 1.0 percent, what is the expected return on Stellar common stock during the next period?
    A. 0.0073 (0.73%)
    B. 0.0138 (1.38%)
    C. 0.0203 (2.03%)

12. Based on Batten's regression model, the coefficient of determination indicates that:
    A. Stellar's returns explain 2.11% of the variability in CPIENG.
    B. Stellar's returns explain 14.52% of the variability in CPIENG.
    C. changes in CPIENG explain 2.11% of the variability in Stellar's returns.

13. For Batten's regression model, the standard error of the estimate shows that the standard deviation of:
    A. the residuals from the regression is 0.0710.
    B. values estimated from the regression is 0.0710.
    C. Stellar's observed common stock returns is 0.0710.

14. For the analysis run by Batten, which of the following is an *incorrect* conclusion from the regression output?
    A. The estimated intercept coefficient from Batten's regression is statistically significant at the 0.05 level.
    B. In the month after the CPIENG declines, Stellar's common stock is expected to exhibit a positive return.
    C. Viewed in combination, the slope and intercept coefficients from Batten's regression are not statistically significant at the 0.05 level.

The following information relates to Questions 15–24

Anh Liu is an analyst researching whether a company's debt burden affects investors' decision to short the company's stock. She calculates the short interest ratio (the ratio of short interest to average daily share volume, expressed in days) for 50 companies as of the end of 2016 and compares this ratio with the companies' debt ratio (the ratio of total liabilities to total assets, expressed in decimal form).

Liu provides a number of statistics in Exhibit 1. She also estimates a simple regression to investigate the effect of the debt ratio on a company's short interest ratio. The results of this simple regression, including the analysis of variance (ANOVA), are shown in Exhibit 2.

In addition to estimating a regression equation, Liu graphs the 50 observations using a scatter plot, with the short interest ratio on the vertical axis and the debt ratio on the horizontal axis.

EXHIBIT 1   Summary Statistics

Statistic	Debt Ratio X_i	Short Interest Ratio Y_i
Sum	19.8550	192.3000
Average	0.3971	3.8460
Sum of squared deviations from the mean	$\sum_{i=1}^{n}(X_i - \bar{X})^2 = 2.2225.$	$\sum_{i=1}^{n}(Y_i - \bar{Y})^2 = 412.2042.$
Sum of cross-products of deviations from the mean	$\sum_{i=1}^{n}(X_i - \bar{X})(Y_i - \bar{Y}) = -9.2430.$	

EXHIBIT 2   Regression of the Short Interest Ratio on the Debt Ratio

ANOVA	Degrees of Freedom (df)	Sum of Squares (SS)	Mean Square (MS)
Regression	1	38.4404	38.4404
Residual	48	373.7638	7.7867
Total	49	412.2042	

Regression Statistics

Multiple R	0.3054		
R^2	0.0933		
Standard error of estimate	2.7905		
Observations	50		
	Coefficients	Standard Error	t-Statistic
Intercept	5.4975	0.8416	6.5322
Debt ratio	−4.1589	1.8718	−2.2219

Liu is considering three interpretations of these results for her report on the relationship between debt ratios and short interest ratios:

Interpretation 1: Companies' higher debt ratios cause lower short interest ratios.
Interpretation 2: Companies' higher short interest ratios cause higher debt ratios.
Interpretation 3: Companies with higher debt ratios tend to have lower short interest ratios.

She is especially interested in using her estimation results to predict the short interest ratio for MQD Corporation, which has a debt ratio of 0.40.

15. Based on Exhibits 1 and 2, if Liu were to graph the 50 observations, the scatter plot summarizing this relation would be *best* described as:
    A. horizontal.
    B. upward sloping.
    C. downward sloping.

16. Based on Exhibit 1, the sample covariance is *closest to*:
    A. −9.2430.
    B. −0.1886.
    C. 8.4123.

17. Based on Exhibits 1 and 2, the correlation between the debt ratio and the short interest ratio is *closest to*:
    A. −0.3054.
    B. 0.0933.
    C. 0.3054.

18. Which of the interpretations *best* describes Liu's findings for her report?
    A. Interpretation 1
    B. Interpretation 2
    C. Interpretation 3

19. The dependent variable in Liu's regression analysis is the:
    A. intercept.
    B. debt ratio.
    C. short interest ratio.

20. Based on Exhibit 2, the degrees of freedom for the *t*-test of the slope coefficient in this regression are:
    A. 48.
    B. 49.
    C. 50.

21. The upper bound for the 95 percent confidence interval for the coefficient on the debt ratio in the regression is *closest* to:
    A. −1.0199.
    B. −0.3947.
    C. 1.4528.

22. Which of the following should Liu conclude from these results shown in Exhibit 2?
    A. The average short interest ratio is 5.4975.
    B. The estimated slope coefficient is statistically significant at the 0.05 level.
    C. The debt ratio explains 30.54 percent of the variation in the short interest ratio.

23. Based on Exhibit 2, the short interest ratio expected for MQD Corporation is *closest* to:
    A. 3.8339.
    B. 5.4975.
    C. 6.2462.

24 Based on Liu's regression results in Exhibit 2, the *F*-statistic for testing whether the slope coefficient is equal to zero is *closest* to:
    A   -2.2219.
    B   3.5036.
    C   4.9367.

The following information relates to Questions 25–30

Elena Vasileva recently joined EnergyInvest as a junior portfolio analyst. Vasileva's supervisor asks her to evaluate a potential investment opportunity in Amtex, a multinational oil and gas corporation based in the United States. Vasileva's supervisor suggests using regression analysis to examine the relation between Amtex shares and returns on crude oil.

Vasileva notes the following assumptions of regression analysis:

Assumption 1   The error term is uncorrelated across observations.
Assumption 2   The variance of the error term is the same for all observations.
Assumption 3   The expected value of the error term is equal to the mean value of the dependent variable.

Vasileva runs a regression of Amtex share returns on crude oil returns using the monthly data she collected. Selected data used in the regression are presented in Exhibit 1, and selected regression output is presented in Exhibit 2.

Vasileva expects the crude oil return next month, Month 37, to be −0.01. She computes the variance of the prediction error to be 0.0022.

EXHIBIT 1   Selected Data for Crude Oil Returns and Amtex Share Returns

	Oil Return (X_i)	Amtex Return (Y_i)	Cross-Product $(X_i - \bar{X})(Y_i - \bar{Y})$	Predicted Amtex Return $(\hat{Y})$	Regression Residual $(Y_i - \hat{Y})$	Squared Residual $(Y_i - \hat{Y})^2$
Month 1	−0.032000	0.033145	−0.000388	0.002011	−0.031134	0.000969
⋮	⋮	⋮	⋮	⋮	⋮	⋮
Month 36	0.028636	0.062334	0.002663	0.016282	−0.046053	0.002121
Sum			0.085598			0.071475
Average	−0.018056	0.005293				

EXHIBIT 2   Selected Regression Output, Dependent Variable: Amtex Share Return

	Coefficient	Standard Error
Intercept	0.0095	0.0078
Oil return	0.2354	0.0760

Note: The critical t-value for a two-sided t-test at the 1% significance level (df = 34) is 2.728.

25. Which of Vasileva's assumptions regarding regression analysis is *incorrect?*
    A. Assumption 1
    B. Assumption 2
    C. Assumption 3

26. Based on Exhibit 1, the standard error of the estimate is *closest* to:
    A. 0.044558.
    B. 0.045850.
    C. 0.050176.

27. Based on Exhibit 2, Vasileva should reject the null hypothesis that:
    A. the slope is less than or equal to 0.15.
    B. the intercept is less than or equal to 0.
    C. crude oil returns do not explain Amtex share returns.

28. Based on Exhibit 2, Vasileva should compute the:
    A. 99% confidence interval for the slope coefficient to be 0.1594 to 0.3114.
    B. 95% confidence interval for the intercept to be −0.0037 to 0.0227.
    C. 95% confidence interval for the slope coefficient to be 0.0810 to 0.3898.

29. Based on Exhibit 2 and Vasileva's prediction of the crude oil return for Month 37, the estimate of Amtex share return for Month 37 is *closest* to:
    A. −0.0024.
    B. 0.0071.
    C. 0.0119.

30. Using information from Exhibit 2, Vasileva should compute the 95% prediction interval for Amtex share return for Month 37 to be:
    A. −0.0882 to 0.1025.
    B. −0.0835 to 0.1072.
    C. 0.0027 to 0.0116.

The following information relates to Question 31–33

Doug Abitbol is a portfolio manager for Polyi Investments, a hedge fund that trades in the United States. Abitbol manages the hedge fund with the help of Robert Olabudo, a junior portfolio manager.

Abitbol looks at economists' inflation forecasts and would like to examine the relationship between the US Consumer Price Index (US CPI) consensus forecast and actual US CPI using regression analysis. Olabudo estimates regression coefficients to test whether the consensus forecast is unbiased. Regression results are presented in Exhibit 1. Additionally,

EXHIBIT 1   Regression Output: Estimating US CPI

Regression Statistics			
Multiple R	0.9929		
R^2	0.9859		
Standard error of estimate	0.0009		
Observations	60		
	Coefficients	**Standard Error**	**t-Statistic**
Intercept	0.0001	0.0002	0.5351
US CPI consensus forecast	0.9830	0.0155	63.6239

Notes:
1. The absolute value of the critical value for the *t*-statistic is 2.0 at the 5% level of significance.
2. The standard deviation of the US CPI consensus forecast is $s_x = 0.7539$.
3. The mean of the US CPI consensus forecast is $\bar{X} = 1.3350$.

Olabudo calculates the 95 percent prediction interval of the actual CPI using a US CPI consensus forecast of 2.8.

To conclude their meeting, Abitbol and Olabudo discuss the limitations of regression analysis. Olabudo notes the following limitations of regression analysis:

Limitation 1: Public knowledge of regression relationships may negate their future usefulness.
Limitation 2: Hypothesis tests and predictions based on linear regression will not be valid if regression assumptions are violated.

31. Based on Exhibit 1, Olabudo should:
    A. conclude that the inflation predictions are unbiased.
    B. reject the null hypothesis that the slope coefficient equals 1.
    C. reject the null hypothesis that the intercept coefficient equals 0.

32. Based on Exhibit 1, Olabudo should calculate a prediction interval for the actual US CPI *closest* to:
    A. 2.7506 to 2.7544.
    B. 2.7521 to 2.7529.
    C. 2.7981 to 2.8019.

33. Which of Olabudo's noted limitations of regression analysis is correct?
    A. Only Limitation 1
    B. Only Limitation 2
    C. Both Limitation 1 and Limitation 2

CHAPTER 8

MULTIPLE REGRESSION

Richard A. DeFusco, PhD, CFA
Dennis W. McLeavey, DBA, CFA
Jerald E. Pinto, PhD, CFA
David E. Runkle, PhD, CFA

LEARNING OUTCOMES

The candidate should be able to:

- formulate a multiple regression equation to describe the relation between a dependent variable and several independent variables, and determine the statistical significance of each independent variable;
- interpret estimated regression coefficients and their *p*-values;
- formulate a null and an alternative hypothesis about the population value of a regression coefficient, calculate the value of the test statistic, and determine whether to reject the null hypothesis at a given level of significance;
- interpret the results of hypothesis tests of regression coefficients;
- calculate and interpret a predicted value for the dependent variable, given an estimated regression model and assumed values for the independent variables;
- explain the assumptions of a multiple regression model;
- calculate and interpret the *F*-statistic, and describe how it is used in regression analysis;
- distinguish between and interpret the R^2 and adjusted R^2 in multiple regression;
- evaluate how well a regression model explains the dependent variable by analyzing the output of the regression equation and an ANOVA table;
- formulate and interpret a multiple regression, including qualitative independent variables;
- explain the types of heteroskedasticity and how heteroskedasticity and serial correlation affect statistical inference;
- describe multicollinearity, and explain its causes and effects in regression analysis;

Quantitative Methods for Investment Analysis, Second Edition, by Richard A. DeFusco, PhD, CFA, Dennis W. McLeavey, DBA, CFA, Jerald E. Pinto, PhD, CFA, and David E. Runkle, PhD, CFA. Copyright © 2019 by CFA Institute.

- describe how model misspecification affects the results of a regression analysis, and describe how to avoid common forms of misspecification;
- interpret an estimated logistic regression;
- evaluate and interpret a multiple regression model and its results.

1. INTRODUCTION

As financial analysts, we often need to use more sophisticated statistical methods than correlation analysis or regression involving a single independent variable. For example, a mutual fund analyst might want to know whether returns to a technology mutual fund behaved more like the returns to a growth stock index or like the returns to a value stock index. An investor might be interested in the factors that determine whether analysts cover a stock. Or analysts researching individual companies may want to understand what factors (such as macroeconomic variables) drive the demand for the company's products or services. We can answer these questions using linear regression with more than one independent variable—multiple linear regression.

We first introduce and illustrate the basic concepts and models of multiple regression analysis. These models rest on assumptions that are sometimes violated in practice. We then discuss three commonly occurring violations of regression assumptions. We address practical concerns, such as how to diagnose an assumption violation and what remedial steps to take when a model assumption has been violated. The subsequent section outlines some guidelines for building good regression models and discusses ways that analysts sometimes go wrong in this endeavor. We then discuss a class of models whose dependent variable is qualitative in nature. Specifically, we discuss logistic regression that plays an important role in machine learning for Big Data analysis.

2. MULTIPLE LINEAR REGRESSION

As investment analysts, we often hypothesize that more than one variable explains the behavior of a variable in which we are interested. The variable we seek to explain is called the dependent variable. The variables that we believe explain the dependent variable are called the independent variables. They may also be termed explanatory variables, predictor variables, or simply regressors. A tool that permits us to examine the relationship (if any) between the two types of variables is multiple linear regression. **Multiple linear regression** allows us to determine the effect of more than one independent variable on a particular dependent variable.

A **multiple linear regression model** has the general form

$$Y_i = b_0 + b_1 X_{1i} + b_2 X_{2i} + \ldots + b_k X_{ki} + \varepsilon_i, \quad i = 1, 2, \ldots n, \tag{1}$$

where
  Y_i = the ith observation of the dependent variable Y
  X_{ji} = the ith observation of the independent variable X_j, $j = 1, 2, \ldots, k$
  b_0 = the intercept of the equation
  $b_1, \ldots, b_k$ = the slope coefficients for each of the independent variables
  ε_i = the error term
  n = the number of observations

A slope coefficient, b_j, measures how much the dependent variable, Y, changes when the independent variable, X_j, changes by one unit, holding all other independent variables constant. For example, if $b_1 = 1$ and all the other independent variables remain constant, then we predict that if X_1 increases by one unit, Y will also increase by one unit. If $b_1 = -1$ and all the other independent variables are held constant, then we predict that if X_1 increases by one unit, Y will decrease by one unit. Multiple linear regression estimates b_0, ..., b_k. In this chapter, we will refer to both the intercept, b_0, and the slope coefficients, b_1, ..., b_k, as **regression coefficients**. As we proceed with our discussion, keep in mind that a regression equation has k slope coefficients and $k + 1$ regression coefficients.

Although Equation 1 may seem to apply only to cross-sectional data because the notation for the observations is the same ($i = 1$, ..., n), all these results apply to time-series data as well. For example, if we analyze data from many time periods for one company, we would typically use the notation Y_t, X_{1t}, X_{2t}, ..., X_{kt}, in which the first subscript denotes the variable and the second denotes the tth time period.

In practice, we use software to estimate a multiple regression model. **Exhibit 1** presents an application of multiple regression analysis in investment practice. In the course of discussing a hypothesis test, **Exhibit 1** presents typical regression output and its interpretation.

EXHIBIT 1   Explaining the Bid–Ask Spread

As the manager of the trading desk at an investment management firm, you have noticed that the average bid–ask spreads of different NASDAQ-listed stocks can vary widely. When the ratio of a stock's bid–ask spread to its price is higher than for another stock, your firm's costs of trading in that stock tend to be higher. You have formulated the hypothesis that NASDAQ stocks' percentage bid–ask spreads are related to the number of market makers and the company's stock market capitalization. You have decided to investigate your hypothesis using multiple regression analysis.

You specify a regression model in which the dependent variable measures the percentage bid–ask spread, and the independent variables measure the number of market makers and the company's stock market capitalization. The regression is estimated using data from December 31, 2013, for 2,587 NASDAQ-listed stocks. Based on earlier published research exploring bid–ask spreads, you express the dependent and independent variables as natural logarithms, a so-called **log-log regression model**. A log-log regression model may be appropriate when one believes that proportional changes in the dependent variable bear a constant relationship to proportional changes in the independent variable(s), as we illustrate next. You formulate the multiple regression:

$$Y_i = b_0 + b_1 X_{1i} + b_2 X_{2i} + \varepsilon_i, \qquad (2)$$

where

   Y_i = the natural logarithm of (Bid–ask spread/Stock price) for stock i
   X_{1i} = the natural logarithm of the number of NASDAQ market makers for stock i
   X_{2i} = the natural logarithm of the market capitalization (measured in millions of US$) of company i

In a log-log regression, such as Equation 2, the slope coefficients are interpreted as elasticities assumed to be constant. For example, a value of $b_2 = -0.75$ would mean that for a 1% increase in the market capitalization, we expect Bid–ask spread/Stock price to decrease by 0.75%, holding all other independent variables constant [note that $\Delta (\ln X) \approx \Delta X/X$, where Δ represents "change in" and $\Delta X/X$ is a proportional change in X].

Reasoning that greater competition tends to lower costs, you suspect that the greater the number of market makers, the smaller the percentage bid–ask spread. Therefore, you formulate a first null hypothesis (H_0) and alternative hypothesis (H_a):

$$H_0: b_1 \geq 0$$

$$H_a: b_1 < 0$$

The null hypothesis is the hypothesis that the "suspected" condition is not true. If the evidence supports rejecting the null hypothesis and accepting the alternative hypothesis, you have statistically confirmed your suspicion. An alternative valid formulation is a two-sided test, $H_0: b_1 = 0$ versus $H_a: b_1 \neq 0$, which reflects the beliefs of the researcher less strongly.

You also believe that the stocks of companies with higher market capitalization may have more-liquid markets, tending to lower percentage bid–ask spreads. Therefore, you formulate a second null hypothesis and alternative hypothesis:

$$H_0: b_2 \geq 0$$

$$H_a: b_2 < 0$$

For both tests, we use a t-test, rather than a z-test, because we do not know the population variance of b_1 and b_2. Suppose that you choose a 0.01 significance level for both tests.

Results from Regressing ln(Bid–Ask Spread/Price) on ln(Number of Market Makers) and ln(Market Capitalization)

	Coefficient	Standard Error	t-Statistic
Intercept	1.5949	0.2275	7.0105
ln(Number of NASDAQ market makers)	−1.5186	0.0808	−18.7946
ln(Company's market capitalization)	−0.3790	0.0151	−25.0993

ANOVA	DF	SS	MSS	F	Significance F
Regression	2	3,728.1334	1,864.0667	2,216.75	0.00
Residual	2,584	2,172.8870	0.8409		
Total	2,586	5,901.0204			
Residual standard error			0.9170		
Multiple R^2			0.6318		
Observations			2,587		

Note: "DF" = degrees of freedom.
Source: Center for Research in Security Prices, University of Chicago.

The table shows the results of estimating this linear regression. If the regression result is not significant, we may follow the useful principle of not proceeding to interpret the individual regression coefficients. Thus, the analyst might look first at the **analysis of variance (ANOVA)** section, which addresses the regression's overall significance.

- The ANOVA section reports quantities related to the overall explanatory power and significance of the regression. SS stands for sum of squares, and MSS stands for mean sum of squares (SS divided by DF). The F-test reports the overall significance of the regression. For example, an entry of 0.01 for the significance of F means that the regression is significant at the 0.01 level. In our illustration the regression is even more significant because the significance of F is 0 at two decimal places.

Having ascertained that the overall regression is highly significant, an analyst might turn to the first listed column in the first section of the regression output.

- The Coefficient column gives the estimates of the intercept, b_0, and the slope coefficients, b_1 and b_2. The estimated intercept is positive, but both estimated slope coefficients are negative. Are these estimated regression coefficients significantly different from zero? The Standard Error column gives the standard error (the standard deviation) of the estimated regression coefficients. The test statistic for hypotheses concerning the population value of a regression coefficient has the form (Estimated regression coefficient − Hypothesized population value of the regression coefficient)/(Standard error of the regression coefficient). This is a t-test. Under the null hypothesis, the hypothesized population value of the regression coefficient is 0. Thus (Estimated regression coefficient)/(Standard error of the regression coefficient) is the t-statistic given in the third column. For example, the t-statistic for the intercept is $1.5949/0.2275 = 7.0105$. To evaluate the significance of the t-statistic, we need to determine a quantity called degrees of freedom (DF). When calculating the degrees of freedom lost in the regression, we add 1 to the number of independent variables to account for the intercept term. The calculation is: Degrees of freedom = Number of observations − (Number of independent variables + 1) = $n - (k + 1)$.
- The final section of the regression results table presents two measures of how well the estimated regression fits or explains the data. The first is the standard deviation of the regression residual, the residual standard error. This standard deviation is called the standard error of estimate (SEE). The second measure quantifies the degree of linear association between the dependent variable and all the independent variables jointly. This measure is known as multiple R^2 or simply R^2 (the square of the correlation between predicted and actual values of the dependent variable). Multiple R^2 is also known as the multiple coefficient of determination, or simply the coefficient of determination. A value of 0 for R^2 indicates no linear association; a value of 1 indicates perfect linear association. The final item in **Exhibit 1** is the number of observations in the sample (2,587).

Having reviewed the meaning of typical regression output, we can return to complete the hypothesis tests. The estimated regression supports the hypothesis that the greater the number of market makers, the smaller the percentage bid–ask spread: We reject H_0: $b_1 \geq 0$ in favor of H_a: $b_1 < 0$. The results also support the belief that the stocks of companies with higher market capitalization have lower percentage bid–ask spreads: We reject H_0: $b_2 \geq 0$ in favor of H_a: $b_2 < 0$.

To see that the null hypothesis is rejected for both tests, we can use t-test tables. For both tests, DF = 2,587 − 3 = 2,584. The tables do not give critical values for degrees of freedom that large. The critical value for a one-tailed test with DF = 200 at the 0.01 significance level is 2.345; for a larger number of degrees of freedom, the critical value would be even smaller in magnitude. Therefore, in our one-sided tests, we reject the null hypothesis in favor of the alternative hypothesis if

$$t = \frac{\hat{b}_j - b_j}{s_{\hat{b}_j}} = \frac{\hat{b}_j - 0}{s_{\hat{b}_j}} < -2.345,$$

where

$\hat{b}_j$ = the regression estimate of b_j, $j = 1, 2$
b_j = the hypothesized value[1] of the coefficient (0)
$s_{\hat{b}_j}$ = the estimated standard error of $\hat{b}_j$

The t-values of −18.7946 and −25.0993 for the estimates of b_1 and b_2, respectively, are both less than −2.345.

Before proceeding further, we should address the interpretation of a prediction stated in natural logarithm terms. We can convert a natural logarithm to the original units by taking the antilogarithm. To illustrate this conversion, suppose that a particular stock has 20 NASDAQ market makers and a market capitalization of $100 million. The natural logarithm of the number of NASDAQ market makers is equal to ln 20 = 2.9957, and the natural logarithm of the company's market cap (in millions) is equal to ln 100 = 4.6052. With these values, the regression model predicts that the natural log of the ratio of the bid–ask spread to the stock price will be 1.5949 + (−1.5186 × 2.9957) + (−0.3790 × 4.6052) = −4.6997. We take the antilogarithm of −4.6997 by raising e to that power: $e^{-4.6997} = 0.0091$. The predicted bid–ask spread will be 0.91 percent of the stock price. The operation illustrated (taking the antilogarithm) recovers the value of a variable in the original units as $e^{\ln X} = X$. Later we state the assumptions of the multiple regression model; before using an estimated regression to make predictions in actual practice, we should assure ourselves that those assumptions are satisfied.

In Exhibit 1, we presented output common to most regression software programs. Many software programs also report p-values for the regression coefficients (the entry 0.00 for the significance of F was a p-value for the F-test). For each regression coefficient, the p-value would be the smallest level of significance at which we can reject a null hypothesis that the population value of the coefficient is 0, in a two-sided test. The lower the p-value, the stronger the evidence against that null hypothesis. A p-value quickly allows us to determine if an independent variable is significant at a conventional significance level, such as 0.05, or at any other standard we believe is appropriate.

---

[1]To economize on notation in stating test statistics, in this context we use b_j to represent the hypothesized value of the parameter (elsewhere we use it to represent the unknown population parameter).

Having estimated Equation 1, we can write

$$\hat{Y}_i = \hat{b}_0 + \hat{b}_1 X_{1i} + \hat{b}_2 X_{2i}$$
$$= 1.5949 - 1.5186 X_{1i} - 0.3790 X_{2i}$$

where $\hat{Y}_i$ stands for the predicted value of Y_i, and $\hat{b}_0$, $\hat{b}_1$, and $\hat{b}_2$ stand for the estimated values of b_0, b_1, and b_2, respectively. How should we interpret the estimated slope coefficients -1.5186 and -0.3790?

Interpreting the slope coefficients in a multiple linear regression model is different than doing so in the one-independent-variable regressions explored in earlier coverage of the topic of simple regression. Suppose we have a one-independent-variable regression that we estimate as $\hat{Y}_i = 0.50 + 0.75 X_{1i}$. The interpretation of the slope estimate 0.75 is that for every 1-unit increase in X_1, we expect Y to increase by 0.75 units. If we were to add, however, a second independent variable to the equation, we would generally find that the estimated coefficient on X_1 is *not* 0.75 unless the second independent variable were uncorrelated with X_1. In other words, the slope coefficient of a dependent variable may depend upon other independent variables.

The slope coefficients in a multiple regression are known as **partial regression coefficients** or **partial slope coefficients** and need to be interpreted with care (the terminology comes from the fact that they correspond to the partial derivatives of Y with respect to the independent variables).

Suppose the coefficient on X_1 in a regression with the second independent variable was 0.60. Can we say that for every 1-unit increase in X_1, we expect Y to increase by 0.60 units? Not without qualification. For every 1-unit increase in X_1, we still expect Y to increase by 0.75 units when X_2 is not held constant. We would interpret 0.60 as the expected increase in Y for a 1-unit increase X_1 *holding the second independent variable constant.*

To explain what the shorthand reference "holding the second independent constant" refers to, if we were to regress X_1 on X_2, the residuals from that regression would represent the part of X_1 that is uncorrelated with X_2. We could then regress Y on those residuals in a one-independent-variable regression. We would find that the slope coefficient on the residuals would be 0.60; by construction, 0.60 would represent the expected effect on Y of a 1-unit increase in X_1 after removing the part of X_1 that is correlated with X_2. Consistent with this explanation, we can view 0.60 as the expected net effect on Y of a 1-unit increase in X_1, after accounting for any effects of the other independent variables on the expected value of Y. To reiterate, a partial regression coefficient measures the expected change in the dependent variable for a 1-unit increase in an independent variable, holding all the other independent variables constant.

To apply this process to the regression in Exhibit 1, we see that the estimated coefficient on the natural logarithm of market capitalization is -0.3790. Therefore, the model predicts that an increase of 1 in the natural logarithm of the company's market capitalization is associated with a -0.3790 change in the natural logarithm of the ratio of the bid–ask spread to the stock price, holding the natural logarithm of the number of market makers constant. We need to be careful not to expect that the natural logarithm of the ratio of the bid–ask spread to the stock price would differ by -0.3790 if we compared two stocks for which the natural logarithm of the company's market capitalization differed by 1, because in all likelihood the number of market makers for the two stocks would differ as well, which would affect the dependent variable. The value -0.3790 is the expected net effect of difference in log market capitalizations, net of the effect of the log number of market makers on the expected value of the dependent variable.

2.1. Assumptions of the Multiple Linear Regression Model

Before we can conduct correct statistical inference on a multiple linear regression model (a model with more than one independent variable estimated using ordinary least squares, OLS, an estimation method based on the criterion of minimizing the sum of the squared residuals of a regression), we need to know the assumptions underlying that model. Suppose we have n observations on the dependent variable, Y, and the independent variables, X_1, X_2, ..., X_k, and we want to estimate the equation $Y_i = b_0 + b_1X_{1i} + b_2X_{2i} + ... + b_kX_{ki} + \varepsilon_i$.

In order to make a valid inference from a multiple linear regression model, we need to make the following six assumptions, which as a group define the classical normal multiple linear regression model:

1. The relationship between the dependent variable, Y, and the independent variables, X_1, X_2, ..., X_k, is linear as described in Equation 1.
2. The independent variables $(X_1, X_2, ..., X_k)$ are not random, which means that they are fixed and known; no exact linear relation exists between two or more of the independent variables or combinations of independent variables.
3. The expected value of the error term, conditioned on the independent variables, is 0: $E(\varepsilon \mid X_1, X_2, ..., X_k) = 0$.
4. The variance of the error term is the same for all observations:[2] $E(\varepsilon_i^2) = \sigma_\varepsilon^2$.
5. The error term is uncorrelated across observations: $E(\varepsilon_i\varepsilon_j) = 0, j \neq i$.
6. The error term is normally distributed.

Note that these assumptions are almost exactly the same as those for the single-variable linear regression model. Assumption 2 is modified such that no exact linear relation exists between two or more independent variables or combinations of independent variables. If this part of Assumption 2 is violated, then we cannot compute linear regression estimates. Also, even if no exact linear relationship exists between two or more independent variables, or combinations of independent variables, linear regression may encounter problems if two or more of the independent variables or combinations thereof are highly correlated. Such a high correlation is known as multicollinearity, which we will discuss later. We will also discuss the consequences of conducting regression analysis premised on Assumptions 4 and 5 being met when, in fact, they are violated.

EXHIBIT 2   Factors Explaining the Valuations of Multinational Corporations

Kyaw, Manley, and Shetty (2011) examined which factors affect the valuation of a multinational corporation (MNC). Specifically, they wanted to know whether political risk, transparency, and geographic diversification affected the valuations of MNCs. They used data for 450 US MNCs from 1998 to 2003. The valuations of these corporations were measured using Tobin's q, a commonly used measure of corporate valuation that is calculated as the ratio of the sum of the market value of a corporation's equity and the book value of long-term debt to the sum of the book values of equity and long-term debt. The authors regressed Tobin's q of MNCs on variables representing political risk, transparency, and geographic diversification. The authors

---

[2]$\text{Var}(\varepsilon) = E(\varepsilon^2)$ and $\text{Cov}(\varepsilon_i\varepsilon_j) = E(\varepsilon_i\varepsilon_j)$ because $E(\varepsilon) = 0$.

also included some additional variables that may affect company valuation, including size, leverage, and beta. They used the equation

$$\text{Tobin's } q_{i,t} = b_0 + b_1(\text{Size}_{i,t}) + b_2(\text{Leverage}_{i,t}) + b_3(\text{Beta}_{i,t}) + b_4(\text{Political risk}_{i,t})$$
$$+ b_5(\text{Transparency}_{i,t}) + b_6(\text{Geographic diversification}_{i,t}) + \varepsilon_{i,t},$$

where

> Tobin's $q_{i,t}$ = the Tobin's q for MNC i in year t, with Tobin's q computed as (Market value of equity + Book value of long-term debt)/(Book value of equity + Book value of long-term debt)
>
> Size$_{i,t}$ = the natural log of the total sales of MNC i in the year t in millions of US$
>
> Leverage$_{i,t}$ = the ratio of total debt to total assets of MNC i in year t
>
> Beta$_{i,t}$ = the beta of the stock of MNC i in year t
>
> Political risk$_{i,t}$ = the at-risk-proportion of international operations of MNC i in year t, calculated as [1 − (number of safe countries/total number of foreign countries in which the firm has operations)], using national risk coding from *Euromoney*
>
> Transparency$_{i,t}$ = the "transparency %" (representing the level of disclosure) of MNC i in year t, using survey data from *S&P Transparency & Disclosure*
>
> Geographic diversification$_{i,t}$ = foreign sales of MNC i in year t expressed as a percentage of its total sales in that year

The following table shows the results of their analysis.

Results from Regressing Tobin's q on Factors Affecting the Value of Multinational Corporations

	Coefficient	Standard Error	t-Statistic
Intercept	19.829	4.798	4.133
Size	−0.712	0.228	−3.123
Leverage	−3.897	0.987	−3.948
Beta	−1.032	0.261	−3.954
Political risk	−2.079	0.763	−2.725
Transparency	−0.129	0.050	−2.580
Geographic diversification	0.021	0.010	2.100

Notes: This study combines time series observations with cross-sectional observations; such data are commonly referred to as panel data. In such a setting, the standard errors need to be corrected for bias by using a clustered standard error approach as in Petersen (2009). The standard errors reported in this exhibit are clustered standard errors.
Size is the natural log of total sales. A log transformation (either natural log or log base 10) is commonly used for independent variables that can take a wide range of values; company size and fund size are two such variables. One reason to use the log transformation is to improve the statistical properties of the residuals. If the authors had not taken the log of sales and instead used sales as the independent variable, the regression model probably would not have explained Tobin's q as well.
Source: Kyaw, Manley, and Shetty (2011).

Suppose that we use the regression results to test the null hypothesis that the size of a multinational corporation has no effect on its value. Our null hypothesis is that the coefficient on the size variable equals 0 (H_0: $b_1 = 0$), and our alternative hypothesis is that the coefficient does not equal 0 (H_a: $b_1 \neq 0$). The t-statistic for testing that hypothesis is

$$t = \frac{\hat{b}_1 - b_1}{s_{\hat{b}_1}} = \frac{-0.712 - 0}{0.228} = -3.12.$$

With 450 observations and 7 coefficients, the t-statistic has $450 - 7 = 443$ degrees of freedom. At the 0.05 significance level, the critical value for t is about 1.97. The absolute value of computed t-statistic on the size coefficient is 3.12, which suggests strongly that we can reject the null hypothesis that size is unrelated to MNC value. In fact, the critical value for t is about 2.6 at the 0.01 significance level.

Because $Size_{i,t}$ is the natural (base e or 2.72) log of sales, an increase of 1 in $Size_{i,t}$ is the same as a 2.72-fold increase in sales. Thus, the estimated coefficient of approximately -0.7 for $Size_{i,t}$ implies that every 2.72-fold increase in sales of the MNC (an increase of 1 in $Size_{i,t}$) is associated with an expected decrease of 0.7 in Tobin's $q_{i,t}$ of the MNC, *holding constant the other five independent variables in the regression.*

Now suppose we want to test the null hypothesis that geographic diversification is not related to Tobin's q. We want to test whether the coefficient on geographic diversification equals 0 (H_0: $b_6 = 0$) against the alternative hypothesis that the coefficient on geographic diversification does not equal 0 (H_a: $b_6 \neq 0$). The t-statistic to test this hypothesis is

$$t = \frac{\hat{b}_6 - b_6}{s_{\hat{b}_6}} = \frac{0.021 - 0}{0.010} = 2.10.$$

The critical value of the t-test is 1.97 at the 0.05 significance level. Therefore, at the 0.05 significance level, we can reject the null hypothesis that geographic diversification has no effect on MNC valuation. We can interpret the coefficient on geographic diversification of 0.021 as implying that an increase of 1 in the percentage of MNC's sales that are foreign sales is associated with an expected 0.021 increase in Tobin's q for the MNC, holding all other independent variables constant.

EXHIBIT 3   Explaining Returns to the Fidelity Select Technology Portfolio

Suppose you are considering an investment in the Fidelity Select Technology Portfolio (FSPTX), a US mutual fund specializing in technology stocks. You want to know whether the fund behaves more like a large-cap growth fund or a large-cap value fund. You decide to estimate the regression

$$Y_t = b_0 + b_1 X_{1t} + b_2 X_{2t} + \varepsilon_t,$$

where
  Y_t = the monthly return to the FSPTX
  X_{1t} = the monthly return to the S&P 500 Growth Index
  X_{2t} = the monthly return to the S&P 500 Value Index

The S&P 500 Growth and S&P 500 Value indexes represent predominantly large-cap growth and value stocks, respectively.

The regression results show the results of this linear regression using monthly data from August 2014 through August 2019. The estimated intercept in the regression is 0.0011. Thus, if both the return to the S&P 500 Growth Index and the return to the S&P 500 Value Index equal 0 in a specific month, the regression model predicts that the return to the FSPTX will be 0.11 percent. The coefficient on the large-cap growth index is 1.5850, and the coefficient on the large-cap value index return is −0.3902. Therefore, if in a given month the return to the S&P 500 Growth Index was 1 percent and the return to the S&P 500 Value Index was −2%, the model predicts that the return to the FSPTX would be 0.0011 + 1.5850(0.01) − 0.3902(−0.02) = 2.48%.

Results from Regressing the FSPTX Returns on the S&P 500 Growth and S&P 500 Value Indexes

	Coefficient	Standard Error	t-Statistic
Intercept	0.0011	0.0025	0.4405
S&P 500 Growth Index	1.5850	0.1334	11.88
S&P 500 Value Index	−0.3902	0.1332	−2.93

ANOVA	DF	SS	MSS	F	Significance F
Regression	2	0.1198	0.0599	178.01	3.07E-25
Residual	57	0.0192	0.0003		
Total	59	0.1389			
Residual standard error		0.0183			
Multiple R^2		0.862			
Observations		60			

Source: finance.yahoo.com.

We may want to know whether the coefficient on the returns to the S&P 500 Value Index is statistically significant. Our null hypothesis states that the coefficient equals 0 (H_0: $b_2 = 0$); our alternative hypothesis states that the coefficient does not equal 0 (H_a: $b_2 \neq 0$).

Our test of the null hypothesis uses a t-test constructed as follows:

$$ t = \frac{\hat{b}_2 - b_2}{s_{\hat{b}_2}} = \frac{-0.3902 - 0}{0.1332} 2.93 $$

where

$\hat{b}_2$ = the regression estimate of b_2
b_2 = the hypothesized value of the coefficient (0)
$s_{\hat{b}_2}$ = the estimated standard error of $\hat{b}_2$

This regression has 60 observations and three coefficients (two independent variables and the intercept); therefore, the t-test has $60 - 3 = 57$ degrees of freedom. At the 0.05 significance level, the critical value for the test statistic is about 2.00. The absolute value of the test statistic is 2.93. Because the test statistic's absolute value is more than the critical value (2.93 > 2.00), we reject the null hypothesis that $b_2 = 0$. (Note that the t-tests reported in the regression results table, as well as the other regression tables, are tests of the null hypothesis that the population value of a regression coefficient equals 0.)

Similar analysis shows that at the 0.05 significance level, we cannot reject the null hypothesis that the intercept equals 0 (H_0: $b_0 = 0$) in favor of the alternative hypothesis that the intercept does not equal 0 (H_a: $b_0 \neq 0$). The results also show that the t-statistic for testing that hypothesis is 0.4405, a result smaller in absolute value than the critical value of 2.00. However, at the 0.05 significance level we *can* reject the null hypothesis that the coefficient on the S&P 500 Growth Index equals 0 (H_0: $b_1 = 0$) in favor of the alternative hypothesis that the coefficient does not equal 0 (H_a: $b_1 \neq 0$). The t-statistic for testing that hypothesis is 11.88, a result far above the critical value of 2.00. Thus, multiple regression analysis suggests that returns to the FSPTX are very closely associated with the returns to the S&P 500 Growth Index, but they are negatively related to S&P 500 Value Index. This regression is related to return-based style analysis, one of the most frequent applications of regression analysis in the investment profession. For more information, see Sharpe (1988), who pioneered this field, and Buetow, Johnson, and Runkle (2000).

2.2. Predicting the Dependent Variable in a Multiple Regression Model

Financial analysts often want to predict the value of the dependent variable in a multiple regression based on assumed values of the independent variables. We have previously discussed how to make such a prediction in the case of only one independent variable. The process for making that prediction with multiple linear regression is very similar.

To predict the value of a dependent variable using a multiple linear regression model, we follow these three steps:

1. Obtain estimates $\hat{b}_0$, $\hat{b}_1$, $\hat{b}_2$, ..., $\hat{b}_k$ of the regression parameters b_0, b_1, b_2, ..., b_k.
2. Determine the assumed values of the independent variables, $\hat{X}_{1i}$, $\hat{X}_{2i}$, ..., $\hat{X}_{ki}$.

3. Compute the predicted value of the dependent variable, $\hat{Y}_i$, using the equation

$$\hat{Y}_i = \hat{b}_0 + \hat{b}_1 \hat{X}_{1i} + \hat{b}_2 \hat{X}_{2i} + \dots + \hat{b}_k \hat{X}_{ki} \tag{3}$$

Two practical points concerning using an estimated regression to predict the dependent variable are in order. First, we should be confident that the assumptions of the regression model are met. Second, we should be cautious about predictions based on values of the independent variables that are outside the range of the data on which the model was estimated; such predictions are often unreliable.

EXAMPLE 1   Predicting a Multinational Corporation's Tobin's q

In Exhibit 2, we explained the Tobin's q for US multinational corporations (MNC) based on the natural log of sales, leverage, beta, political risk, transparency, and geographic diversification. To review the regression equation:

$$\text{Tobin's } q_{i,t} = b_0 + b_1(\text{Size}_{i,t}) + b_2(\text{Leverage}_{i,t}) + b_3(\text{Beta}_{i,t}) + b_4(\text{Political risk}_{i,t})$$
$$+ b_5(\text{Transparency}_{i,t}) + b_6(\text{Geographic diversification}_{i,t}) + \varepsilon_i.$$

Now we can use the results of the regression (excerpted here) to predict the Tobin's q for a US MNC.

Regression results

	Coefficient
Intercept	19.829
Size	−0.712
Leverage	−3.897
Beta	−1.032
Political risk	−2.079
Transparency	−0.129
Geographic diversification	0.021

Suppose that a particular MNC has the following data for a given year:
- Total sales of $7,600 million. The natural log of total sales in millions of US$ equals ln(7,600) = 8.94.
- Leverage (Total debt/Total assets) of 0.45.
- Beta of 1.30.
- Political risk of 0.47, implying that the ratio of the number of safe countries to the total number of foreign countries in which the MNC has operations is 0.53.
- Transparency score of 65, indicating 65 percent "yes" answers to survey questions related to the corporation's transparency.
- Geographic diversification of 30, indicating that 30 percent of the corporation's sales are in foreign countries.

What is the predicted Tobin's q for the above MNC?

Solution: The predicted Tobin's q for the MNC, based on the regression, is:

$$19.829 + (-0.712 \times 8.94) + (-3.897 \times 0.45) + (-1.032 \times 1.30) + (-2.079 \times 0.47) + (-0.129 \times 65) + (0.021 \times 30) = 1.64.$$

When predicting the dependent variable using a linear regression model, we encounter two types of uncertainty: uncertainty in the regression model itself, as reflected in the standard error of estimate, and uncertainty about the estimates of the regression model's parameters. In earlier coverage of the regression topic, we presented procedures for constructing a prediction interval for linear regression with one independent variable. For multiple regression, however, computing a prediction interval to properly incorporate both types of uncertainty requires matrix algebra, which is outside the scope of our discussion (see Greene 2018 for more information).

2.3. Testing Whether All Population Regression Coefficients Equal Zero

Earlier, we illustrated how to conduct hypothesis tests on regression coefficients individually. What if we now want to test the significance of the regression as a whole? As a group, do the independent variables help explain the dependent variable? To address this question, we test the null hypothesis that all the slope coefficients in a regression are simultaneously equal to 0. In this section, we further discuss ANOVA with regard to a regression's explanatory power and the inputs for an F-test of the above null hypothesis.

If none of the independent variables in a regression model helps explain the dependent variable, the slope coefficients should all equal 0. In a multiple regression, however, we cannot test the null hypothesis that *all* slope coefficients equal 0 based on t-tests that *each individual* slope coefficient equals 0, because the individual tests do not account for the effects of interactions among the independent variables. For example, a classic symptom of multicollinearity is that we can reject the hypothesis that all the slope coefficients equal 0 even though none of the t-statistics for the individual estimated slope coefficients is significant. Conversely, we can construct unusual examples in which the estimated slope coefficients are significantly different from 0 although jointly they are not.

To test the null hypothesis that all the slope coefficients in the multiple regression model are jointly equal to 0 ($H_0\text{: } b_1 = b_2 = ... = b_k = 0$) against the alternative hypothesis that at least one slope coefficient is not equal to 0, we must use an F-test. The F-test is viewed as a test of the regression's overall significance.

To correctly calculate the test statistic for the null hypothesis, we need four inputs:

- Total number of observations, n.
- Total number of regression coefficients to be estimated, $k + 1$, where k is the number of slope coefficients.
- Sum of squared errors or residuals, $\sum_{i=1}^{n} (Y_i - \hat{Y}_i)^2 = \sum_{i=1}^{n} \hat{\varepsilon}_i^2$, abbreviated SSE, also known as the residual sum of squares, the unexplained variation. In a table of regression output, this is the number under the "SS" column in the row "Residual."
- Regression sum of squares, $\sum_{i=1}^{n} (\hat{Y}_i - \overline{Y})^2$, abbreviated RSS. This amount is the variation in Y from its mean that the regression equation explains (explained variation).

Excerpt from Exhibit 1:

ANOVA	DF	SS	MSS	F	Significance F
Regression	2	3,728.1334	1,864.0667	2,216.7505	0.00
Residual	2,584	2,172.8870	0.8409		
Total	2,586	5,901.0204			

In a table of regression output, this is the number under the "SS" column in the row "Regression."

The F-test for determining whether the slope coefficients equal 0 is based on an F-statistic calculated using the four values listed above. The F-statistic measures how well the regression equation explains the variation in the dependent variable; it is the ratio of the mean regression sum of squares to the mean squared error.

We compute the mean regression sum of squares by dividing the regression sum of squares by the number of slope coefficients estimated, k. We compute the mean squared error by dividing the sum of squared errors by the number of observations, n, minus $(k + 1)$. The two divisors in these computations are the degrees of freedom for calculating an F-statistic. For n observations and k slope coefficients, the F-test for the null hypothesis that the slope coefficients are all equal to 0 is denoted $F_{k,n-(k+1)}$. The subscript indicates that the test should have k degrees of freedom in the numerator (numerator degrees of freedom) and $n - (k + 1)$ degrees of freedom in the denominator (denominator degrees of freedom).

The formula for the F-statistic is

$$F = \frac{RSS/k}{SSE/[n - (k + 1)]} = \frac{\text{Mean regression sum of squares}}{\text{Mean squared error}} = \frac{MSR}{MSE}, \quad (4)$$

where MSR is the mean regression sum of squares and MSE is the mean squared error. In our regression output tables, MSR and MSE are the first and second quantities under the MSS (mean sum of squares) column in the ANOVA section of the output. If the regression model does a good job of explaining variation in the dependent variable, then the ratio MSR/MSE will be large.

What does this F-test tell us when the independent variables in a regression model explain none of the variation in the dependent variable? In this case, each predicted value in the regression model, $\hat{Y}_i$, has the average value of the dependent variable, $\overline{Y}$, and the regression sum of squares, $\sum_{i=1}^{n}(\hat{Y}_i - \overline{Y})^2$ is 0. Therefore, the F-statistic for testing the null hypothesis (that all the slope coefficients are equal to 0) has a value of 0 when the independent variables do not explain the dependent variable at all.

To specify the details of making the statistical decision when we have calculated F, we reject the null hypothesis at the α significance level if the calculated value of F is greater than the upper α critical value of the F distribution with the specified numerator and denominator degrees of freedom. Note that we use a one-tailed F-test (because MSR necessarily increases relative to MSE as the explanatory power of the regression increases.)

We can illustrate the test using Exhibit 1, in which we investigated whether the natural log of the number of NASDAQ market makers and the natural log of the stock's market capitalization explained the natural log of the bid–ask spread divided by price. Assume that we set the significance level for this test to $\alpha = 0.05$ (i.e., a 5 percent probability that we will mistakenly reject the null hypothesis if it is true). Excerpt from Exhibit 1 presents the results of variance computations for this regression.

This model has two slope coefficients ($k = 2$), so two degrees of freedom are in the numerator of this F-test. With 2,587 observations in the sample, the number of degrees of freedom in the denominator of the F-test is $n - (k + 1) = 2,587 - 3 = 2,584$. The sum of the squared errors is 2,172.8870. The regression sum of squares is 3,728.1334. Therefore, the F-test for the null hypothesis that the two slope coefficients in this model equal 0 is

$$\frac{3,728.1334/2}{2,172.8870/2,584} = 2,216.7505.$$

This test statistic is distributed as an $F_{2,2,584}$ random variable under the null hypothesis that the slope coefficients are equal to 0. In Exhibit 1 for the 0.05 significance level, we look at the second column, which shows F-distributions with two degrees of freedom in the numerator. Near the bottom of the column, we find that the critical value of the F-test needed to reject the null hypothesis is between 3.00 and 3.07. (We see a range of values because the denominator has more than 120 degrees of freedom but less than an infinite number of degrees of freedom.) The actual value of the F-test statistic at 2,216.75 is much greater, so we reject the null hypothesis that coefficients of both independent variables equal 0. In fact, regression results in Exhibit 1 under "Significance F," reports a p-value of 0. This p-value means that the smallest level of significance at which the null hypothesis can be rejected is practically 0. The large value for this F-statistic implies a very small probability of incorrectly rejecting the null hypothesis (a mistake known as a Type I error).

2.4. Adjusted R^2

In our coverage of simple regression, we presented the coefficient of determination, R^2, as a measure of the goodness of fit of an estimated regression to the data. In a multiple linear regression, however, R^2 is less appropriate as a measure of whether a regression model fits the data well (goodness of fit). Recall that R^2 is defined as

$$\frac{\text{Total variation} - \text{Unexplained variation}}{\text{Total variation}}.$$

The numerator equals the regression sum of squares, RSS. Thus, R^2 states RSS as a fraction of the total sum of squares, $\sum_{i=1}^{n}(Y_i - \overline{Y})^2$. If we add regression variables to the model, the amount of unexplained variation will decrease; RSS will increase if the new independent variable explains any of the unexplained variation in the model. Such a reduction occurs when the new independent variable is even slightly correlated with the dependent variable and is not a linear combination of other independent variables in the regression (note that we say that variable y is a linear combination of variables x and z, or even more variables, if $y = ax + bz$ for some constants a and b). Consequently, we can increase R^2 simply by including many additional independent variables that explain even a slight amount of the previously unexplained variation, even if the amount they explain is not statistically significant.

Some financial analysts use an alternative measure of goodness of fit called **adjusted R^2**, or $\overline{R}^2$. This measure of fit does not automatically increase when another variable is added to a regression; it is adjusted for degrees of freedom. Adjusted R^2 is typically part of the multiple regression output produced by statistical software packages.

The relation between R^2 and $\overline{R}^2$ is

$$\overline{R}^2 = 1 - \left(\frac{n-1}{n-k-1}\right)(1 - R^2),$$

where n is the number of observations and k is the number of independent variables (the number of slope coefficients). Note that if $k \geq 1$, then R^2 is strictly greater than adjusted R^2. When a new independent variable is added, $\overline{R}^2$ can decrease if adding that variable results in only a small increase in R^2. In fact, $\overline{R}^2$ can be negative, although R^2 is always nonnegative. When $\overline{R}^2$ is negative, we can effectively consider its value to be 0. If we use $\overline{R}^2$ to compare regression models, it is important that the dependent variable be defined the same way in both models and that the sample sizes used to estimate the models are the same. For example, it makes a difference for the value of $\overline{R}^2$ if the dependent variable is GDP (gross domestic product) or ln(GDP), even if the independent variables are identical. Furthermore, we should be aware that a high $\overline{R}^2$ does not necessarily indicate that the regression is well specified in the sense of including the correct set of variables. One reason for caution is that a high $\overline{R}^2$ may reflect peculiarities of the dataset used to estimate the regression. To evaluate a regression model, we need to take many other factors into account, as we discuss later in the section on model specification.

3. USING DUMMY VARIABLES IN REGRESSIONS

Financial analysts often need to use qualitative variables as independent variables in a regression. One such type of variable that we will focus on is called a **dummy variable**. It takes on a value of 1 if a particular condition is true and 0 if that condition is false. We will see that one purpose of using dummy variables is to distinguish between "groups" or "categories" of data.

3.1. Defining a Dummy Variable

A dummy variable may arise in several ways in datasets:

i. It may reflect an inherent property of the data (e.g., belonging to an industry or a region). For example, a company belongs to health care industry (dummy variable = 1) or it does not (dummy variable = 0). The data on such variables are collected directly along with the rest of the independent variables for each observation.

ii. It may be an identified characteristic of the data. We may introduce such a binary variable by a condition that is either true or false. For example, the date may be before 2008 (prior to the onset of financial crisis, dummy variable = 0) or after 2008 (after the onset of the financial crisis, dummy variable = 1).

iii. Alternatively, it may be constructed from some characteristic of the data. The dummy variable would reflect a condition that is either true or false. Examples would include satisfying a condition, such as particular company size (dummy = 1 if revenues exceed 1bn, otherwise it equals 0).

We need to exercise care when choosing the number of dummy variables in a regression. If we want to distinguish among n categories, we need $n - 1$ dummy variables. So, if we use dummy variables to denote companies belonging to one of 11 industries, we would use 10 dummies. We still apply the analysis to 11 categories, but the one to which we do not assign a dummy will be referred to as the "base" or "control" group. If, for example, we wish to analyze a dataset with three mutual fund types, we need two dummies. The reason for the need to use $n - 1$ dummy variables is that we must not violate assumption 2 that no exact linear relationship must exist between two or more of the independent variables. If we were to make the mistake of including dummy variables for all n categories rather than $n - 1$, the regression procedure would fail due to the complete violation of assumption 2.

3.2. Visualizing and Interpreting Dummy Variables

One of the most common types of dummy variables are so-called intercept dummies. Consider a regression model for the dependent variable Y that involves one continuous independent variable (X) and one dummy variable (D).

$$Y = b_0 + d_0 D + b_1 X + \varepsilon. \qquad (5)$$

This single regression model can be shown to estimate two lines of best fit corresponding to the value of the dummy variable:

- If $D = 0$, then the equation becomes $Y = b_0 + b_1 X + \varepsilon$.
- If $D = 1$, then the equation becomes $Y = (b_0 + d_0) + b_1 X + \varepsilon$.

Exhibit 4 shows a graphical illustration. This scenario can be interpreted as an intercept shift shown by the d_0 distance. The shift can be positive or negative (it is positive in the illustration). The line where the dummy takes the value of zero ($D = 0$) relates to the base category; the other line where the dummy variable takes the value of 1 ($D = 1$) relates to the category to which we apply the dummy variable.

EXHIBIT 4   Intercept Dummy

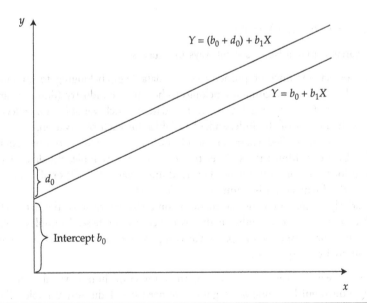

A different scenario would reflect dummies that allow for slope differences. We will refer to those as slope dummies. They can be explained using a simple model with one continuous variable (x) and one dummy variable (D).

$$Y = b_0 + b_1 X + d_1 (D \times X) + \varepsilon. \tag{6}$$

The presence of such slope dummy can be interpreted as a change in the slope between the categories captured by the dummy variable:

$$\text{If } D = 0, \text{ then } Y = b_0 + b_1 X + \varepsilon.$$
$$\text{If } D = 1, \text{ then } Y = b_0 + (b_1 + d_1) X + \varepsilon.$$

As before, the case of $D = 0$ is the base or control group. The dummy variable allows for slopes to differ between the two categories. For the base category, the relationship between x and y is shown by the less steep line $Y = b_0 + b_1 X$. For the other category, the relationship between Y and X is shown by the steeper sloping line $Y = b_0 + (b_1 + d_1)X$. This difference between slopes may be positive or negative depending on the scenario.

It is also possible to use dummies in both slope and intercept. To do so we combine the two previous models. We let the dummy variable "interact" with the continuous independent variable x.

$$Y = b_0 + d_0 D + b_1 X + d_1 (D \times X) + \varepsilon. \tag{7}$$

EXHIBIT 5   Slope Dummy Variables

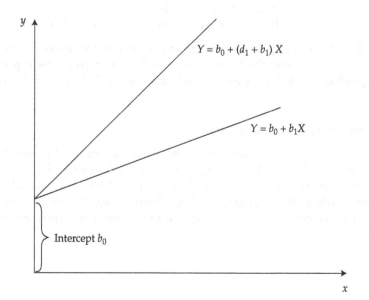

EXHIBIT 6   Slope and Intercept Dummies

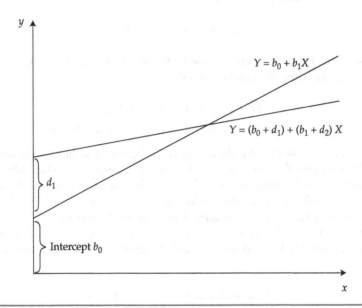

$Y = b_0 + b_1 X$

$Y = (b_0 + d_1) + (b_1 + d_2) X$

d_1

Intercept b_0

Note: The graph shows a scenario where $d_1 > 0$ and $d_2 < 0$.

These scenarios are based on only two data categories. We may, however, have more categories with more dummies and more independent variables. The graphs would simply show more lines of best fit, one relating to each category.

$$\text{If } D = 0, \text{ then } Y = b_0 + b_1 X + \varepsilon.$$
$$\text{If } D = 1, \text{ then } Y = (b_0 + d_0) + (b_1 + d_1)X + \varepsilon.$$

This allows for both a change in intercept and a change in slope across the two groups. In this more complex treatment, the difference between the two categories now depends on both an intercept effect (d_0) and a slope effect ($d_1 X$) that vary with the size of the independent variable.

3.3. Testing for Statistical Significance

One of the purposes of using dummy variables is to distinguish between "groups" or "categories" of data. To test whether a regression function is different for one group versus another is straightforward with dummy variables with the help of t-tests. Individual t-tests on the dummy variable coefficients indicate if that difference is significantly different from zero. Exhibit 7 illustrates the use of dummy variables in a regression using a cross-section of mutual fund data.

EXHIBIT 7 Analysis of Mutual Funds in Different Categories

William James is a fund analyst at an investment consultancy firm. He has been tasked with analyzing how mutual fund characteristics affect fund returns measured as the average returns over the past 5 years. He uses a large database of US mutual funds that include a number of style classes. The dependent variable is the average annual return over the last 5 years. The independent variables that the analyst chose to focus on are fund expense ratio, the natural logarithm of fund size and fund age, and two dummy variables to denote fund style (style being Value, Blend, or Growth).

As there are three possible style categories, he uses $n - 1 = 2$ dummy variables. The dummy variable BLEND has a value of 1 if the observation (the mutual fund) is "Blend" and a value of 0 if it is not. The GROWTH dummy has a value of 1 if the fund is labelled as "Growth"; otherwise, it equals zero. The base or "control" category, for which we do not use a specific dummy, is the "Value" category. In this regression, for simplicity we are only allowing for an effect on the intercept of the regression, not the slopes of the independent variables.

He estimates the following cross-sectional regression model:

$$\text{Fund returns} = b_0 + d_1\text{BLEND} + d_2\text{GROWTH}$$
$$+ b_1\text{Expense ratio} + b_2\text{Portfolio cash}$$
$$+ b_3\text{Fund age} + b_4\text{Log of assets} + e.$$

Mutual Funds Regression Output

Regression Statistics	
R^2	0.1230
Adjusted R^2	0.1228
Standard Error	4.224
Observations	23,025

ANOVA	DF	SS	MS	F	Significance F
Regression	6	57,636.46	9,606	538	0
Residual	23,018	410,816.9	17.85		
Total	23,024	468,453.3			

	Coefficients	Standard Error	t-Statistic	P-value
Intercept	−2.909	0.299	−9.7376	2.30177E-22
Annual_expense_ratio_	−0.586	0.0495	−11.824	3.623E-32
Portfolio_cash	−0.032	0.0029	−11.168	6.93514E-29
Fund age	0.074	0.0033	22.605	6.3821E-112
Log of assets	0.267	0.0141	18.924	2.92142E-79
Blend dummy	0.661	0.0678	9.749	2.0673E-22
Growth dummy	2.498	0.0748	33.394	8.2581E-239

The regression output, shown next, suggests that while the R^2 is relatively low at 0.12, the slope coefficients are statistically significant. The results suggest that fund returns are negatively impacted by the level of expenses and cash holdings (coefficients of −0.58 and −0.03, respectively), which we would intuitively expect. The results also indicate that older funds perform better, with a positive age coefficient of 0.074.

The estimated coefficients for the dummy variables show the estimated difference between the returns on different types of funds. At 0.66 and 2.50, the coefficients of the dummy variables suggest that Blend funds deliver average returns that exceed those in the Value category by 0.66 percent per year, while Growth funds deliver 2.50 percent over and above the base, "Value," category. The intercept coefficient, also statistically significant, suggests that average annual negative return of 2.91 percent is unexplained by the independent variables in the model.

We can also use the F-test to analyze the null hypothesis that jointly the independent variables (including the dummies) all equal 0. Regression results shows the value of the F-statistic at 538, which we compare to the critical value. Appendix D (the F-distribution table) shows the critical values for this F-test. If we choose a significance level of 0.01 and look in column 6 (because the numerator has 6 degrees of freedom), we see that the critical value is 2.96 when the denominator has 120 degrees of freedom. The denominator actually has 23,024 degrees of freedom, so the critical value of the F-statistic is smaller than 2.96 (for DF = 120) but larger than 2.8 (for an infinite number of degrees of freedom). The value of the F-test statistic is 538, so we can reject the null hypothesis that the coefficients jointly are equal to 0.

James decides to extend his study of mutual funds by introducing slope dummies. The initial results indicated a relationship between returns and fund age, although the magnitude was small at 0.07 percent for each year of age. He wonders whether this relationship between performance and age differs between different fund types. For example, does the age factor affect Growth or Blend funds more than it affects Value funds? In other words, is the improvement in performance with fund age different for the different types of funds?

To explore this hypothesis—that the impact of Fund age is different across types of funds—he introduces two additional independent variables, one that is a multiple of "Fund age × Blend dummy" and the second "Fund age × Growth dummy." He estimates the following model:

Fund Returns (avg over 5 years)
$= b_0 + b_1$ Expense ratio $+ b_2$ Portfolio cash $+ b_3$ Fund age $+ b_4$ Log of assets
$+ d_1$ (Blend dummy) $+ d_2$ (Growth dummy) $+$ "Fund age × Blend dummy"
$+$ "Fund age × Growth dummy" $+ \varepsilon$.

When the Blend dummy is equal to 1, the interaction term takes on the value of "Fund age." For observations when the Growth dummy is equal to 1, the second interaction term takes on the value of "Fund age." The regression results are as follows:

The regression results feature the original intercept and slope coefficient variables plus the new slope coefficients of the interaction dummies. The values and statistical significance of the intercept and slope coefficient show little change. But the revised model provides more information about the Fund age variable. For our default base or control group—Value funds—we observe the Fund age slope coefficient of 0.065, suggesting that those funds see extra return with the passage of time (i.e., fund age).

Regression Statistics					
R^2	0.123				
Adjusted R^2	0.123				
Standard Error	4.224				
Observations	23,025				

ANOVA	DF	SS	MS	F	Significance F
Regression	8	57,760.46	7,220	404.6	0
Residual	23,016	410,692.9	17.84		
Total	23,024	468,453.3			

	Coefficients	Standard Error	t-Statistic	P-value
Intercept	−2.81	0.306	−9.183	4.54531E-20
Annual_expense_ratio	−0.587	0.0496	−11.839	3.0289E-32
Portfolio_cash	−0.032	0.0029	−11.211	4.28797E-29
Fund age	0.065	0.0059	11.012	3.91371E-28
Log of assets	0.267	0.0141	18.906	4.05994E-79
Blend dummy	0.603	0.1088	5.546	2.95478E-08
Growth dummy	2.262	0.1204	18.779	4.27618E-78
Age × Blend	0.0049	0.0077	0.627	0.530817435
Age × Growth	0.0201	0.0081	2.478	0.01323

In this model, we also have the interaction dummies, of which "Fund age × Growth" has a statistically significant coefficient. For Growth funds, the extra annual return with each additional year of age is the sum of the "Age" and "Fund age × Growth" coefficients (i.e., 0.065 percent plus 0.02 percent). So, the overall "slope" coefficient for the performance of Growth (with respect to Age) is the sum of the two coefficients. One can interpret the overall output as suggesting that Growth funds deliver returns that exceed those of Value funds by 2.26 percent (the Growth Intercept) plus 0.085 percent for each year of age. Another way to interpret this result is to imagine a two-dimensional space similar to the one in Exhibit 6. The coefficient of the "Fund age × Growth" variable would give the extra slope implied by growth over and above the slope coefficient of the "Fund age" variable.

4. VIOLATIONS OF REGRESSION ASSUMPTIONS

Earlier we presented the assumptions of the multiple linear regression model. Inference based on an estimated regression model rests on those assumptions being satisfied. In applying regression analysis to financial data, analysts need to be able to diagnose violations of regression assumptions, understand the consequences of violations, and know the remedial steps to take. In the following sections, we discuss three regression violations: **heteroskedasticity**, serial correlation, and multicollinearity.

4.1. Heteroskedasticity

So far, we have made an important assumption that the variance of error in a regression is constant across observations. In statistical terms, we assumed that the errors were homoskedastic. Errors in financial data, however, are often **heteroskedastic**: The variance of the errors differs across observations. In this section, we discuss how heteroskedasticity affects statistical analysis, how to test for heteroskedasticity, and how to correct for it.

We can see the difference between homoskedastic and heteroskedastic errors by comparing two graphs. Exhibit 8 shows the values of the dependent and independent variables and a fitted regression line for a model with homoskedastic errors. There is no systematic relationship between the value of the independent variable and the regression residuals (the vertical distance between a plotted point and the fitted regression line). Exhibit 9 shows the values of the dependent and independent variables and a fitted regression line for a model with heteroskedastic errors. Here, a systematic relationship is visually apparent: On average, the regression residuals grow much larger as the size of the independent variable increases.

4.1.1. The Consequences of Heteroskedasticity

What are the consequences when the assumption of constant error variance is violated? Although heteroskedasticity does not affect the consistency (Greene 2018) of the regression parameter estimators, it can lead to mistakes in inference. Informally, an estimator of a

EXHIBIT 8   Regression with Homoskedasticity

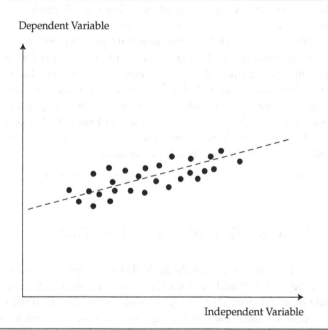

EXHIBIT 9   Regression with Heteroskedasticity

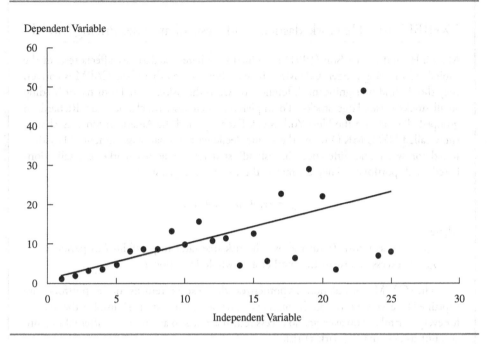

regression parameter is consistent if the probability that estimates of a regression parameter differ from the true value of the parameter decreases as the number of observations used in the regression increases. When errors are heteroskedastic, the F-test for the overall significance of the regression is unreliable. This unreliability occurs because the mean squared error is a biased estimator of the true population variance given heteroskedasticity. Furthermore, t-tests for the significance of individual regression coefficients are unreliable because heteroskedasticity introduces bias into estimators of the standard error of regression coefficients. If a regression shows significant heteroskedasticity, the standard errors and test statistics computed by regression programs will be incorrect unless they are adjusted for heteroskedasticity.

In regressions with financial data, the most likely results of heteroskedasticity are that the estimated standard errors will be underestimated and the t-statistics inflated. When we ignore heteroskedasticity, we tend to find significant relationships where none actually exist. Sometimes, however, failure to adjust for heteroskedasticity results in standard errors that are too large (and t-statistics that are too small). The consequences in practice may be serious if we are using regression analysis in the development of investment strategies. As Exhibit 10 shows, the issue impinges even on our understanding of financial models.

EXHIBIT 10   Heteroskedasticity and Tests of an Asset Pricing Model

MacKinlay and Richardson (1991) examined how heteroskedasticity affects tests of the capital asset pricing model (CAPM). These authors argued that if the CAPM is correct, they should find no significant differences between the risk-adjusted returns for holding small stocks versus large stocks. To implement their test, MacKinlay and Richardson grouped all stocks on the New York Stock Exchange and the American Stock Exchange (now called NYSE MKT) by market-value decile with annual reassignment. They then tested for systematic differences in risk-adjusted returns across market-capitalization-based stock portfolios. They estimated the following regression:

$$r_{i,t} = \alpha_i + \beta_i r_{m,t} + \varepsilon_{i,t}$$

where

$r_{i,t}$ = excess return (return above the risk-free rate) to portfolio i in period t
$r_{m,t}$ = excess return to the market as a whole in period t

The CAPM formulation hypothesizes that excess returns on a portfolio are explained by excess returns on the market as a whole. That hypothesis implies that $\alpha_i = 0$ for every portfolio i; on average, no excess return accrues to any portfolio after taking into account its systematic (market) risk.

Using data from January 1926 to December 1988 and a market index based on equal-weighted returns, MacKinlay and Richardson failed to reject the CAPM at the 0.05 level when they assumed that the errors in the regression model are normally distributed and homoskedastic. They found, however, that they could reject the CAPM when they corrected their test statistics to account for heteroskedasticity. They rejected the hypothesis that there are no size-based, risk-adjusted excess returns in historical data.

We have stated that effects of heteroskedasticity on statistical inference can be severe. To be more precise about this concept, we should distinguish between two broad kinds of heteroskedasticity: unconditional and conditional.

Unconditional heteroskedasticity occurs when heteroskedasticity of the error variance is not correlated with the independent variables in the multiple regression. Although this form of heteroskedasticity violates Assumption 4 of the linear regression model, it creates no major problems for statistical inference.

The type of heteroskedasticity that causes the most problems for statistical inference is **conditional heteroskedasticity**—heteroskedasticity in the error variance that is correlated with (conditional on) the values of the independent variables in the regression. Fortunately, many statistical software packages easily test and correct for conditional heteroskedasticity.

4.1.2. Testing for Heteroskedasticity

Because of conditional heteroskedasticity's consequences on inference, the analyst must be able to diagnose its presence. The Breusch–Pagan test is widely used in finance research because of its generality.

Breusch and Pagan (1979) suggested the following test for conditional heteroskedasticity: Regress the squared residuals from the estimated regression equation on the independent variables in the regression. If no conditional heteroskedasticity exists, the independent variables will not explain much of the variation in the squared residuals. If conditional heteroskedasticity is present in the original regression, however, the independent variables will explain a significant portion of the variation in the squared residuals. The independent variables can explain the variation because each observation's squared residual will be correlated with the independent variables if the independent variables affect the variance of the errors.

Breusch and Pagan showed that under the null hypothesis of no conditional heteroskedasticity, nR^2 (from the regression of the squared residuals on the independent variables from the original regression) will be a χ^2 random variable with the number of degrees of freedom equal to the number of independent variables in the regression (for more on the Breusch–Pagan test, see Greene 2018). Therefore, the null hypothesis states that the regression's squared error term is uncorrelated with the independent variables. The alternative hypothesis states that the squared error term is correlated with the independent variables. Exhibit 11 illustrates the Breusch–Pagan test for conditional heteroskedasticity.

EXHIBIT 11   Testing for Conditional Heteroskedasticity in the Relation between Interest Rates and Expected Inflation

Suppose an analyst wants to know how closely nominal interest rates are related to expected inflation to determine how to allocate assets in a fixed-income portfolio. The analyst wants to test the Fisher effect, the hypothesis suggested by Irving Fisher that nominal interest rates increase by 1 percentage point for every 1 percentage point increase in expected inflation. The Fisher effect assumes the following relation between nominal interest rates, real interest rates, and expected inflation:

$$i = r + \pi^e,$$

where
  i = the nominal rate
  r = the real interest rate (assumed constant)
  π^e = the expected rate of inflation

To test the Fisher effect using time-series data, we could specify the following regression model for the nominal interest rate:

$$i_t = b_0 + b_1\pi_t^e + \varepsilon_t. \tag{8}$$

Noting that the Fisher effect predicts that the coefficient on the inflation variable is 1, we can state the null and alternative hypotheses as

$$H_0: b_1 = 1 \text{ and}$$

$$H_a: b_1 \neq 1.$$

We might also specify a 0.05 significance level for the test. Before we estimate Equation 8 we must decide how to measure expected inflation (π_t^e) and the nominal interest rate (i_t).

The Survey of Professional Forecasters (SPF) has compiled data on the quarterly inflation expectations of professional forecasters using annualized median SPF prediction of current-quarter growth in the GDP deflator. We use those data as our measure of expected inflation. We use three-month US Treasury bill returns as our measure of the (risk-free) nominal interest rate. We use quarterly data from the fourth quarter of 1968 to the fourth quarter of 2013 to estimate Equation 8 The regression results are shown next.

To make the statistical decision on whether the data support the Fisher effect, we calculate the following t-statistic, which we then compare to its critical value:

$$t = \frac{\hat{b}_1 - b_1}{s_{\hat{b}_1}} = \frac{1.1744 - 1}{0.0761} = 2.29.$$

With a 0.05 significance level and $181 - 2 = 179$ degrees of freedom, the critical t-value is about 1.97. If we have conducted a valid test, we can reject at the 0.05 significance level the hypothesis that the true coefficient in this regression is 1 and that the Fisher effect holds. The t-test assumes that the errors are homoskedastic. Before we accept the validity of the t-test, therefore, we should test whether the errors are conditionally heteroskedastic. If those errors prove to be conditionally heteroskedastic, then the test is invalid.

We can perform the **Breusch–Pagan test** for conditional heteroskedasticity on the squared residuals from the Fisher effect regression. The test regresses the squared residuals on the predicted inflation rate. The R^2 in the squared residuals regression (not shown here) is 0.0666. The test statistic from this regression, nR^2, is $181 \times 0.0666 = 12.0546$. Under the null hypothesis of no conditional heteroskedasticity, this test statistic is a χ^2 random variable with one degree of freedom (because there is only one independent variable).

We should be concerned about heteroskedasticity only for large values of the test statistic. Therefore, we should use a one-tailed test to determine whether we can reject the null hypothesis. The critical value of the test statistic for a variable from a χ^2

Results from Regressing T-Bill Returns on Predicted Inflation

	Coefficient	Standard Error	t-Statistic
Intercept	0.0116	0.0033	3.5152
Inflation prediction	1.1744	0.0761	15.4323
Residual standard error	0.0233		
Multiple R^2	0.5708		
Observations	181		
Durbin–Watson statistic	0.2980		

Note: The Durbin–Watson statistic will be explained in the section on serial correlation.
Source: Federal Reserve Bank of Philadelphia, US Department of Commerce.

distribution with one degree of freedom at the 0.05 significance level is 3.84. The test statistic from the Breusch–Pagan test is 12.0546, so we can reject the hypothesis of no conditional heteroskedasticity at the 0.05 level. In fact, we can even reject the hypothesis of no conditional heteroskedasticity at the 0.01 significance level, because the critical value of the test statistic in the case is 6.63. As a result, we conclude that the error term in the Fisher effect regression is conditionally heteroskedastic. The standard errors computed in the original regression are not correct, because they do not account for heteroskedasticity. Therefore, we cannot accept the *t*-test as valid.

In Exhibit 11, we concluded that a *t*-test that we might use to test the Fisher effect was not valid. Does that mean that we cannot use a regression model to investigate the Fisher effect? Fortunately, no. A methodology is available to adjust regression coefficients' standard error to correct for heteroskedasticity. Using an adjusted standard error for $\hat{b}_1$, we can reconduct the *t*-test. As we shall see in the next section, using this valid *t*-test we will not reject the null hypothesis in Exhibit 11. That is, our statistical conclusion will change after we correct for heteroskedasticity.

4.1.3. Correcting for Heteroskedasticity

Financial analysts need to know how to correct for heteroskedasticity, because such a correction may reverse the conclusions about a particular hypothesis test—and thus affect a particular investment decision. In Exhibit 10, for instance, MacKinlay and Richardson reversed their investment conclusions after correcting their model's significance tests for heteroskedasticity.

We can use two different methods to correct for the effects of conditional heteroskedasticity in linear regression models. The first method, computing **robust standard errors**, corrects the standard errors of the linear regression model's estimated coefficients to account for the conditional heteroskedasticity. The second method, **generalized least squares**, modifies the original equation to eliminate the heteroskedasticity. The new, modified regression equation is then estimated under the assumption that heteroskedasticity is no longer a problem. The technical details behind these two methods of correcting for conditional heteroskedasticity are outside the scope of this discussion. Many statistical software packages can easily compute robust standard errors, however, and we recommend using them. Note that robust standard errors are also known as **heteroskedasticity-consistent standard errors** or **White-corrected standard errors**.

Returning to the subject of Exhibit 11 concerning the Fisher effect, recall that we concluded that the error variance was heteroskedastic. If we correct the regression coefficients' standard errors for conditional heteroskedasticity, we get the results shown in Exhibit 12. In comparing the standard errors with those in Exhibit 11, we see that the standard error for the intercept changes very little but the standard error for the coefficient on predicted inflation (the slope coefficient) increases by about 22 percent (from 0.0761 to 0.0931). Note also that the regression coefficients are the same in both tables because the results correct only the standard errors in Exhibit 11.

We can now conduct a valid *t*-test of the null hypothesis that the slope coefficient has a true value of 1 by using the robust standard error for $\hat{b}_1$. We find that $t = (1.1744 - 1)/0.0931 = 1.8733$. This number is smaller than the critical value of 1.97 needed to reject the

EXHIBIT 12   Results from Regressing T-Bill Returns on Predicted Inflation (Standard Errors Corrected for Conditional Heteroskedasticity)

	Coefficients	Standard Error	t-Statistic
Intercept	0.0116	0.0034	3.4118
Inflation prediction	1.1744	0.0931	12.6144
Residual standard error	0.0233		
Multiple R^2	0.5708		
Observations	181		

Source: Federal Reserve Bank of Philadelphia, US Department of Commerce.

null hypothesis that the slope equals 1 (remember, this is a two-tailed test). So, we can no longer reject the null hypothesis that the slope equals 1 because of the greater uncertainty (standard error) around the coefficient estimate. Thus, in this example, correcting for the statistically significant conditional heteroskedasticity had an effect on the result of the hypothesis test about the slope of the predicted inflation coefficient. Exhibit 10 concerning tests of the CAPM is a similar case. In other cases, however, our statistical decision might not change based on using robust standard errors in the t-test.

4.2. Serial Correlation

A more common—and potentially more serious—problem than violation of the homoskedasticity assumption is the violation of the assumption that regression errors are uncorrelated across observations. Trying to explain a particular financial relation over a number of periods is risky because errors in financial regression models are often correlated through time.

When regression errors are correlated across observations, we say that they are **serially correlated** (or autocorrelated). Serial correlation most typically arises in time-series regressions. In this section, we discuss three aspects of serial correlation: its effect on statistical inference, tests for it, and methods to correct for it.

4.2.1. The Consequences of Serial Correlation

As with heteroskedasticity, the principal problem caused by serial correlation in a linear regression is an incorrect estimate of the regression coefficient standard errors computed by statistical software packages. As long as none of the independent variables is a lagged value of the dependent variable (a value of the dependent variable from a previous period), then the estimated parameters themselves will be consistent and need not be adjusted for the effects of serial correlation. If, however, one of the independent variables is a lagged value of the dependent variable—for example, if the T-bill return from the previous month was an independent variable in the Fisher effect regression—then serial correlation in the error term will cause all the parameter estimates from linear regression to be inconsistent and they will not be valid estimates of the true parameters (we will address this later).

In none of the regressions examined so far is an independent variable a lagged value of the dependent variable. Thus, in these regressions any effect of serial correlation appears in the regression coefficient standard errors. We will examine here the positive serial correlation case because that case is so common. **Positive serial correlation** is serial correlation in which a positive error for one observation increases the chance of a positive error for another observation. Positive serial correlation also means that a negative error for one observation increases the chance of a negative error for another observation. In contrast, with **negative serial correlation**, a positive error for one observation increases the chance of a negative error for another observation, and a negative error for one observation increases the chance of a positive error for another. In examining positive serial correlation, we make the common assumption that serial correlation takes the form of **first-order serial correlation**, or serial correlation between adjacent observations. In a time-series context, that assumption means the sign of the error term tends to persist from one period to the next.

Although positive serial correlation does not affect the consistency of the estimated regression coefficients, it does affect our ability to conduct valid statistical tests. First, the *F*-statistic to test for overall significance of the regression may be inflated because the mean squared error (MSE) will tend to underestimate the population error variance. Second, positive serial correlation typically causes the ordinary least squares (OLS) standard errors for the regression coefficients to underestimate the true standard errors. Consequently, if positive serial correlation is present in the regression, standard linear regression analysis will typically lead us to compute artificially small standard errors for the regression coefficient. These small standard errors will cause the estimated *t*-statistics to be inflated, suggesting significance where perhaps there is none. The inflated *t*-statistics may, in turn, lead us to incorrectly reject null hypotheses about population values of the parameters of the regression model more often than we would if the standard errors were correctly estimated. This Type I error could lead to improper investment recommendations.

4.2.2. Testing for Serial Correlation

We can choose from a variety of tests for serial correlation in a regression model (see Greene 2018), but the most common is based on a statistic developed by Durbin and Watson (1951); in fact, many statistical software packages compute the Durbin–Watson statistic automatically. The equation for the Durbin–Watson test statistic is

$$\text{DW} = \frac{\sum_{t=2}^{T} (\hat{\varepsilon}_t - \hat{\varepsilon}_{t-1})^2}{\sum_{t=1}^{T} \hat{\varepsilon}_t^2}, \tag{9}$$

where $\hat{\varepsilon}_t$ is the regression residual for period t. We can rewrite this equation as

$$\frac{\frac{1}{T-1}\sum_{t=2}^{T} (\hat{\varepsilon}_t^2 - 2\hat{\varepsilon}_t\hat{\varepsilon}_{t-1} + \hat{\varepsilon}_{t-1}^2)}{\frac{1}{T-1}\sum_{t=1}^{T} \hat{\varepsilon}_t^2} \approx \frac{\text{Var}(\hat{\varepsilon}_t) - 2\,\text{Cov}(\hat{\varepsilon}_t,\hat{\varepsilon}_{t-1}) + \text{Var}(\hat{\varepsilon}_{t-1})}{\text{Var}(\hat{\varepsilon}_t)}.$$

If the variance of the error is constant through time, then we expect $\text{Var}(\hat{\varepsilon}_t) = \hat{\sigma}_\varepsilon^2$ for all t, where we use $\hat{\sigma}_\varepsilon^2$ to represent the estimate of the constant error variance. If the errors are also not serially correlated, then we expect $\text{Cov}(\hat{\varepsilon}_t, \hat{\varepsilon}_{t-1}) = 0$. In that case, the Durbin–Watson statistic is approximately equal to

$$\frac{\hat{\sigma}_\varepsilon^2 - 0 + \hat{\sigma}_\varepsilon^2}{\hat{\sigma}_\varepsilon^2} = 2.$$

This equation tells us that if the errors are homoskedastic and not serially correlated, then the Durbin–Watson statistic will be close to 2. Therefore, we can test the null hypothesis that the errors are not serially correlated by testing whether the Durbin–Watson statistic differs significantly from 2.

If the sample is very large, the Durbin–Watson statistic will be approximately equal to $2(1 - r)$, where r is the sample correlation between the regression residuals from one period and those from the previous period. This approximation is useful because it shows the value of the Durbin–Watson statistic for differing levels of serial correlation. The Durbin–Watson statistic can take on values ranging from 0 (in the case of serial correlation of $+1$) to 4 (in the case of serial correlation of -1):

- If the regression has no serial correlation, then the regression residuals will be uncorrelated through time and the value of the Durbin–Watson statistic will be equal to $2(1 - 0) = 2$.
- If the regression residuals are positively serially correlated, then the Durbin–Watson statistic will be less than 2. For example, if the serial correlation of the errors is 1, then the value of the Durbin–Watson statistic will be 0.
- If the regression residuals are negatively serially correlated, then the Durbin–Watson statistic will be greater than 2. For example, if the serial correlation of the errors is -1, then the value of the Durbin–Watson statistic will be 4.

Returning to Exhibit 11, which explored the Fisher effect, the Durbin–Watson statistic for the OLS regression is 0.2980. This result means that the regression residuals are positively serially correlated:

$$DW = 0.2980$$
$$\approx 2(1-r)$$
$$r \approx 1-DW/2$$
$$= 1-0.2980/2$$
$$= 0.8510.$$

This outcome raises the concern that OLS standard errors may be incorrect because of positive serial correlation. Does the observed Durbin–Watson statistic (0.2980) provide enough evidence to warrant rejecting the null hypothesis of no positive serial correlation?

We should reject the null hypothesis of no serial correlation if the Durbin–Watson statistic is below a critical value, d^*. Unfortunately, Durbin and Watson also showed that for a given sample we cannot know the true critical value, d^*. Instead, we can determine only that d^* lies either between two values, d_u (an upper value) and d_l (a lower value), or outside those values. Exhibit 13 depicts the upper and lower values of d^* as they relate to the results of the Durbin–Watson statistic.

From Exhibit 13 we learn the following:

- When the Durbin–Watson (DW) statistic is less than d_l, we reject the null hypothesis of no positive serial correlation.
- When the DW statistic falls between d_l and d_u, the test results are inconclusive.
- When the DW statistic is greater than d_u, we fail to reject the null hypothesis of no positive serial correlation (sometimes serial correlation in a regression model is negative rather than positive). For a null hypothesis of no serial correlation, the null hypothesis is rejected if

EXHIBIT 13   Value of the Durbin–Watson Statistic

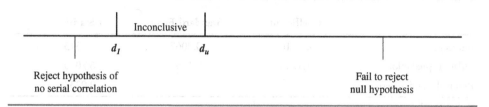

DW < d_1, indicating significant positive serial correlation) or if DW > 4 − d_1, indicating significant negative serial correlation).

Returning to Exhibit 11, the Fisher effect regression has one independent variable and 181 observations. The Durbin–Watson statistic is 0.2980. We can reject the null hypothesis of no correlation in favor of the alternative hypothesis of positive serial correlation at the 0.05 level because the Durbin–Watson statistic is far below d_l for $k = 1$ and $n = 100$ (1.65). The level of d_l would be even higher for a sample of 181 observations. This finding of significant positive serial correlation suggests that the OLS standard errors in this regression probably significantly underestimate the true standard errors.

4.2.3. Correcting for Serial Correlation

We have two alternative remedial steps when a regression has significant serial correlation. First, we can adjust the coefficient standard errors for the linear regression parameter estimates to account for the serial correlation. Second, we can modify the regression equation itself to eliminate the serial correlation. We recommend using the first method for dealing with serial correlation; the second method may result in inconsistent parameter estimates unless implemented with extreme care.

Two of the most prevalent methods for adjusting standard errors were developed by Hansen (1982) and Newey and West (1987). These methods are standard features in many statistical software packages and the correction is known by various names, including serial-correlation consistent standard errors, serial correlation and heteroskedasticity adjusted standard errors, and robust standard errors. An additional advantage of these methods is that they simultaneously correct for conditional heteroskedasticity.

Exhibit 14 shows the results of correcting the standard errors from Exhibit 11 for serial correlation and heteroskedasticity using the Newey–West method. Note that the coefficients for both the intercept and the slope are the same as in the original regression. The robust standard errors are now much larger, however—more than twice the OLS standard errors in Exhibit 11. Because of the severe serial correlation in the regression error, OLS greatly underestimates the uncertainty about the estimated parameters in the regression.

Note also that the serial correlation has not been eliminated, but the standard error has been corrected to account for the serial correlation.

Now suppose we want to test our original null hypothesis (the Fisher effect) that the coefficient on the predicted inflation term equals 1 (H_0: $b_1 = 1$) against the alternative that the coefficient on the inflation term is not equal to 1 (H_a: $b_1 \neq 1$). With the corrected standard errors, the value of the test statistic for this null hypothesis is

EXHIBIT 14   Results from Regressing T-Bill Returns on Predicted Inflation (Standard Errors Corrected for Conditional Heteroskedasticity and Serial Correlation)

	Coefficient	Standard Error	t-Statistic
Intercept	0.0116	0.0067	1.7313
Inflation prediction	1.1744	0.1751	6.7070
Residual standard error			0.0233
Multiple R^2	0.5708		
Observations	181		

Source: Federal Reserve Bank of Philadelphia, US Department of Commerce.

$$\frac{\hat{b}_1 - b_1}{s_{\hat{b}_1}} = \frac{1.1744 - 1}{0.1751} = 0.996.$$

The critical values for both the 0.05 and 0.01 significance level are much larger than 0.996 (the *t*-test statistic), so we cannot reject the null hypothesis. This conclusion is the same as that reached in Exhibit 10, where the correction was only for heteroskedasticity.

This shows that for some hypotheses, serial correlation and conditional heteroskedasticity could have a big effect on whether we accept or reject those hypotheses. In addition, serial correlation can also affect forecast accuracy.

4.3. Multicollinearity

The second assumption of the multiple linear regression model is that no exact linear relationship exists between two or more of the independent variables. When one of the independent variables is an exact linear combination of other independent variables, it becomes mechanically impossible to estimate the regression. Suppose we tried to explain a company's credit ratings with a regression that included net sales, cost of goods sold, and gross profit as independent variables. Because Gross profit = Net sales − Cost of goods sold, by definition there is an exact linear relationship between these variables. This type of blunder is relatively obvious (and easy to avoid). The problem just described, known as perfect collinearity, is much less of a practical concern than multicollinearity. **Multicollinearity** occurs when two or more independent variables (or combinations of independent variables) are highly (but not perfectly) correlated with each other. With multicollinearity we can estimate the regression, but the interpretation of the regression output becomes problematic. Multicollinearity is a serious practical concern because approximate linear relationships among financial variables are common.

4.3.1. The Consequences of Multicollinearity

Although the presence of multicollinearity does not affect the consistency of the OLS estimates of the regression coefficients, the estimates become extremely imprecise and unreliable. Furthermore, it becomes practically impossible to distinguish the individual impacts of the independent variables on the dependent variable. These consequences are reflected in inflated OLS standard errors for the regression coefficients. With inflated standard errors, t-tests on the coefficients have little power (ability to reject the null hypothesis).

4.3.2. Detecting Multicollinearity

In contrast to the cases of heteroskedasticity and serial correlation, we shall not provide a formal statistical test for multicollinearity. In practice, multicollinearity is often a matter of degree rather than of absence or presence.

The analyst should be aware that using the magnitude of pairwise correlations among the independent variables to assess multicollinearity, as has occasionally been suggested, is generally inadequate. Although very high pairwise correlations among independent variables can indicate multicollinearity, it is not necessary for such pairwise correlations to be high for there to be a problem of multicollinearity. Stated another way, high pairwise correlations among the independent variables are not a necessary condition for multicollinearity, and low pairwise correlations do not mean that multicollinearity is not a problem. Even if pairs of independent variables have low correlation, there may be linear combinations of the independent variables that are very highly correlated, creating a multicollinearity problem. The only case in which correlation between independent variables may be a reasonable indicator of multicollinearity occurs in a regression with exactly two independent variables.

The classic symptom of multicollinearity is a high R^2 (and significant F-statistic), even though the t-statistics on the estimated slope coefficients are not significant. The insignificant t-statistics reflect inflated standard errors. Although the coefficients might be estimated with great imprecision, as reflected in low t-statistics, the independent variables *as a group* may do a good job of explaining the dependent variable. A high R^2 would reflect this effectiveness. Exhibit 15 illustrates this diagnostic.

EXHIBIT 15   Multicollinearity in Explaining Returns to the Fidelity Select Technology Portfolio

In Exhibit 3 we regressed returns to the Fidelity Select Technology Portfolio (FSPTX) on returns to the S&P 500 Growth Index and the S&P 500 Value Index using data from August 2014 through August 2019. The regression results are reproduced next. The t-statistic of 11.88 on the growth index return is greater than 2, indicating that the coefficient on the growth index differs significantly from 0 at standard significance levels. The t-statistic on the value index return is −2.93 and is therefore also statistically significant. This result suggests that the returns to the FSPTX are linked to the returns to the growth index and negatively associated with the returns to the value index. Note that the coefficient on the growth index, however, is 1.585. This result implies that returns on the FSPTX are more volatile than are returns on the growth index.

Note also that this regression explains a significant amount of the variation in the returns to the FSPTX. Specifically, the R^2 from this regression is 0.8627. Thus, approximately 86% of the variation in the returns to the FSPTX is explained by returns to the S&P 500 Growth and S&P 500 Value Indexes.

Now suppose we run another linear regression that adds returns to the S&P 500 itself to the returns to the S&P 500 Growth and S&P 500 Value Indexes. The S&P 500 includes the component stocks of these two style indexes, so we are introducing a severe multicollinearity problem.

Results from Regressing the FSPTX Returns on the S&P 500 Growth and Value Indexes

	Coefficient	Standard Error	t-Statistic
Intercept	0.0011	0.0025	0.4406
S&P 500 Growth Index	1.5850	0.1334	11.8843
S&P 500 Value Index	−0.3902	0.1332	−2.93

ANOVA	DF	SS	MSS	F	Significance F
Regression	2	0.1198	0.0599	178	0.000
Residual	57	0.0192	0.0003		
Total	59	0.1390			

Residual standard error	0.0183
Multiple R^2	0.862
Observations	60

Results from Regressing the FSPTX Returns on Returns to the S&P 500 Growth and S&P 500 Value Indexes and the S&P 500 Index

	Coefficient	Standard Error	t-Statistic
Intercept	0.0008	0.0025	0.4047
S&P 500 Growth Index	−0.1873	4.1890	−0.0447
S&P 500 Value Index	−1.8717	3.7387	−0.5274
S&P 500 Index	3.3522	7.9194	−0.4233

ANOVA	DF	SS	MSS	F	Significance F
Regression	3	0.1198	0.0399	117.02	4.26E-24
Residual	56	0.0191	0.0003		
Total	59	0.1389			

Residual standard error	0.0185
Multiple R^2	0.8624
Observations	60

Source: finance.yahoo.com.

The regression results are shown next. Note that the R^2 in this regression has changed almost imperceptibly from the R^2 in the previous regression (increasing from 0.8620 to 0.8624), but now the standard errors of the coefficients of the independent variables are much larger. Adding the return to the S&P 500 to the previous regression does not explain any more of the variance in the returns to the FSPTX than the previous regression did, but now none of the coefficients is statistically significant. This is the classic case of multicollinearity.

EXHIBIT 16   Problems in Linear Regression and Their Solutions

Problem	Effect	Solution
Heteroskedasticity	Incorrect standard errors	Use robust standard errors (corrected for conditional heteroskedasticity)
Serial correlation	Incorrect standard errors (additional problems if a lagged value of the dependent variable is used as an independent variable)	Use robust standard errors (corrected for serial correlation)
Multicollinearity	High R^2 and low *t*-statistics	Remove one or more independent variables; often no solution based in theory

Multicollinearity may be a problem even when we do not observe the classic symptom of insignificant *t*-statistics but a highly significant *F*-test. Advanced textbooks provide further tools to help diagnose multicollinearity (Greene 2018).

4.3.3. Correcting for Multicollinearity

The most direct solution to multicollinearity is excluding one or more of the regression variables. In the previous example, we can see that the S&P 500 total returns should not be included if both the S&P 500 Growth and S&P 500 Value Indexes are included because the returns to the entire S&P 500 Index are a weighted average of the return to growth stocks and value stocks. In many cases, however, no easy solution is available to the problem of multicollinearity, and you will need to experiment with including or excluding different independent variables to determine the source of multicollinearity.

4.4. Heteroskedasticity, Serial Correlation, Multicollinearity: Summarizing the Issues

We have discussed some of the problems that heteroskedasticity, serial correlation, and multicollinearity may cause in interpreting regression results. These violations of regression assumptions, we have noted, all lead to problems in making valid inferences. The analyst should check that model assumptions are fulfilled before interpreting statistical tests.

Exhibit 16 gives a summary of these problems, the effect they have on the linear regression results (an analyst can see these effects using regression software), and the solutions to these problems.

5. MODEL SPECIFICATION AND ERRORS IN SPECIFICATION

Until now, we have assumed that whatever regression model we estimate is correctly specified. **Model specification** refers to the set of variables included in the regression and the regression equation's functional form. In the following, we first give some broad guidelines for correctly specifying a regression. Then, we turn to three types of model misspecification: misspecified functional form, regressors that are correlated with the error term, and additional time-series misspecification. Each of these types of misspecification invalidates statistical inference using OLS; most of these misspecifications will cause the estimated regression coefficients to be inconsistent.

5.1. Principles of Model Specification

In discussing the principles of model specification, we need to acknowledge that there are competing philosophies about how to approach model specification. Furthermore, our purpose for using regression analysis may affect the specification we choose. The following principles have fairly broad application, however.

- *The model should be grounded in cogent economic reasoning.* We should be able to supply the economic reasoning behind the choice of variables, and the reasoning should make sense. When this condition is fulfilled, we increase the chance that the model will have predictive value with new data. This approach contrasts to the variable-selection process known as **data mining**. With data mining, the investigator essentially develops a model that maximally exploits the characteristics of a specific dataset. Data mining is used in the different sense of discovering patterns in large datasets.
- *The functional form chosen for the variables in the regression should be appropriate given the nature of the variables.* As one illustration, consider studying mutual fund **market timing** based on fund and market returns alone. One might reason that for a successful timer, a plot of mutual fund returns against market returns would show curvature because a successful timer would tend to increase (decrease) beta when market returns were high (low). The model specification should reflect the expected nonlinear relationship. In other cases, we may transform the data such that a regression assumption is better satisfied.
- *The model should be parsimonious.* In this context, parsimonious means accomplishing a lot with a little. We should expect each variable included in a regression to play an essential role.
- *The model should be examined for violations of regression assumptions before being accepted.* We have already discussed detecting the presence of heteroskedasticity, serial correlation, and multicollinearity. As a result of such diagnostics, we may conclude that we need to revise the set of included variables and/or their functional form.
- *The model should be tested and be found useful out of sample before being accepted.* The term "out of sample" refers to observations outside the dataset on which the model was estimated. A plausible model may not perform well out of sample because economic relationships have changed since the sample period. That possibility is itself useful to know. A second explanation, however, may be that relationships have not changed but that the model explains only a specific dataset.

Having given some broad guidance on model specification, we turn to a discussion of specific model specification errors. Understanding these errors will help an analyst develop better models and be a more informed consumer of investment research.

5.2. Misspecified Functional Form

Whenever we estimate a regression, we must assume that the regression has the correct functional form. This assumption can fail in several ways:

- Omitted variable(s). One or more important variables could be omitted from regression.
- Inappropriate variable scaling. One or more of the regression variables may need to be transformed (for example, by taking the natural logarithm of the variable) before estimating the regression.

- Inappropriate data pooling. The regression model pools data from different samples that should not be pooled.

First, consider the effects of omitting an important independent variable from a regression (omitted variable bias). If the true regression model was

$$Y_i = b_0 + b_1 X_{1i} + b_2 X_{2i} + \varepsilon_i, \tag{10}$$

but we estimate the model

$$Y_i = a_0 + a_1 X_{1i} + \varepsilon_i,$$

then our regression model would be misspecified (note the different notation when X_{2i} is omitted, because the intercept term and slope coefficient on X_{1i} will generally not be the same as when X_{2i} is included). What is wrong with the model?

If the omitted variable (X_2) is correlated with the remaining variable (X_1), then the error term in the model will be correlated with (X_1) and the estimated values of the regression coefficients a_0 and a_1 would be biased and inconsistent. In addition, the estimates of the standard errors of those coefficients will also be inconsistent. So, we can use neither the coefficient estimates nor the estimated standard errors to make statistical tests.

EXHIBIT 17   Omitted Variable Bias and the Bid–Ask Spread

In this example, we extend our examination of the bid–ask spread to show the effect of omitting an important variable from a regression. In Example 1, we showed that the natural logarithm of the ratio [(Bid–ask spread)/Price] was significantly related to both the natural logarithm of the number of market makers and the natural logarithm of the market capitalization of the company. We repeat the regression results from Exhibit 1 next.

Results from Regressing ln(Bid–Ask Spread/Price) on ln(Number of Market Makers) and ln (Market Capitalization) (repeated)

	Coefficients	Standard Error	t-Statistic
Intercept	1.5949	0.2275	7.0105
ln(Number of NASDAQ market makers)	−1.5186	0.0808	−18.7946
ln(Company's market capitalization)	−0.3790	0.0151	−25.0993

ANOVA	DF	SS	MSS	F	Significance F
Regression	2	3,728.1334	1,864.0667	2,216.7505	0.00
Residual	2,584	2,172.8870	0.8409		
Total	2,586	5,901.0204			

Residual standard error	0.9170
Multiple R^2	0.6318
Observations	2,587

Source: Center for Research in Security Prices, University of Chicago.

Results from Regressing ln(Bid–Ask Spread/Price) on ln(Number of Market Makers)

		Coefficients	Standard Error	t-Statistic
Intercept		5.0707	0.2009	25.2399
ln(Number of NASDAQ market makers)		−3.1027	0.0561	−55.3066
ANOVA	**DF**	**SS**	**MSS**	**F**	**Significance F**
Regression	1	3,200.3918	3,200.3918	3,063.3655	0.00
Residual	2,585	2,700.6287	1.0447		
Total	2,586	5,901.0204			
Residual standard error		1.0221			
Multiple R^2		0.5423			
Observations		2,587			

Source: Center for Research in Security Prices, University of Chicago.

If we did not include the natural log of market capitalization as an independent variable in the regression and regressed the natural logarithm of the ratio [(Bid–ask spread)/Price] only on the natural logarithm of the number of market makers for the stock, the results would be as shown next.

Note that the coefficient on ln(Number of NASDAQ market makers) changed from −1.5186 in the original (correctly specified) regression to −3.1027 in the misspecified regression. Also, the intercept changed from 1.5949 in the correctly specified regression to 5.0707 in the misspecified regression. These results illustrate that omitting an independent variable that should be in the regression can cause the remaining regression coefficients to be inconsistent.

A second common cause of misspecification in regression models is the use of the wrong form of the data in a regression when a transformed version of the data is appropriate. For example, sometimes analysts fail to account for curvature or nonlinearity in the relationship between the dependent variable and one or more of the independent variables, instead specifying a linear relation among variables. When we are specifying a regression model, we should consider whether economic theory suggests a nonlinear relation. We can often confirm the nonlinearity by plotting the data, as we will illustrate in Example 2. If the relationship between the variables becomes linear when one or more of the variables is represented as a proportional change in the variable, we may be able to correct the misspecification by taking the natural logarithm of the variable(s) we want to represent as a proportional change. Other times, analysts use unscaled data in regressions when scaled data (such as dividing net income or cash flow by sales) are more appropriate. In Exhibit 1, we scaled the bid–ask spread by stock price because what a given bid–ask spread means in terms of transactions costs for a given size investment depends on the price of the stock. If we had not scaled the bid–ask spread, the regression would have been misspecified.

EXAMPLE 2 Nonlinearity and the Bid–Ask Spread

In Exhibit 1, we showed that the natural logarithm of the ratio [(Bid–ask spread)/Price] was significantly related to both the natural logarithm of the number of market makers and the natural logarithm of the company's market capitalization. But why did we take the natural logarithm of each of the variables in the regression? We began a discussion of this question in Exhibit 1, which we continue now.

What does theory suggest about the nature of the relationship between the ratio (Bid–ask spread)/Price, or the percentage bid–ask spread, and its determinants (the independent variables)? Stoll (1978) builds a theoretical model of the determinants of percentage bid–ask spread in a dealer market. In his model, the determinants enter multiplicatively in a particular fashion. In terms of the independent variables introduced in Exhibit 1, the functional form assumed is

$$[(\text{Bid–ask spread})/\text{Price}]_i = c(\text{Number of market makers})_i^{b_1}$$
$$\times (\text{Market capitalization})_i^{b_2},$$

where c is a constant. The relationship of the percentage bid–ask spread with the number of market makers and market capitalization is not linear in the original variables (the form of the model is analogous to the Cobb–Douglas production function in economics). If we take the natural log of both sides of this model, however, we have a log-log regression that is linear in the transformed variables:

$$Y_i = b_0 + b_1 X_{1i} + b_2 X_{2i} + \varepsilon_i,$$

where

Y_i = the natural logarithm of the ratio (Bid–ask spread)/Price for stock i
b_0 = a constant that equals $\ln(c)$
X_{1i} = the natural logarithm of the number of market makers for stock i
X_{2i} = the natural logarithm of the market capitalization of company i
ε_i = the error term (note: added to the model)

As mentioned in Exhibit 1, a slope coefficient in the log-log model is interpreted as an elasticity—precisely, the partial elasticity of the dependent variable with respect to the independent variable (partial means holding the other independent variables constant).

We can plot the data to assess whether the variables are linearly related after the logarithmic transformation. For example, in Exhibit 18 we show a scatterplot of the natural logarithm of the number of market makers for a stock (on the x-axis) and the natural logarithm of (Bid–ask spread)/Price (on the y-axis) as well as a regression line showing the linear relation between the two transformed variables. The relation between the two transformed variables is clearly linear.

If we do not take log of the ratio (Bid–ask spread)/Price, the plot is not linear. Exhibit 19 shows a plot of the natural logarithm of the number of market makers for a stock (on the x-axis) and the ratio (Bid–ask spread)/Price expressed as a percentage (on the y-axis) as well as a regression line that attempts to show a linear relation between the two variables. We see that the relation between the two variables is very nonlinear.

EXHIBIT 18   Linear Regression When Two Variables Have a Linear Relation

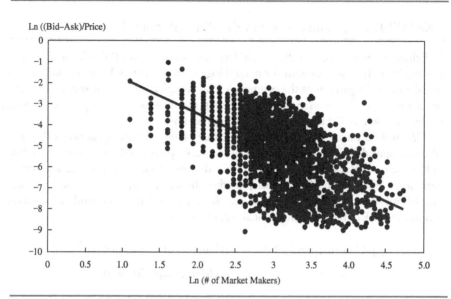

EXHIBIT 19   Linear Regression When Two Variables Have a Nonlinear Relation

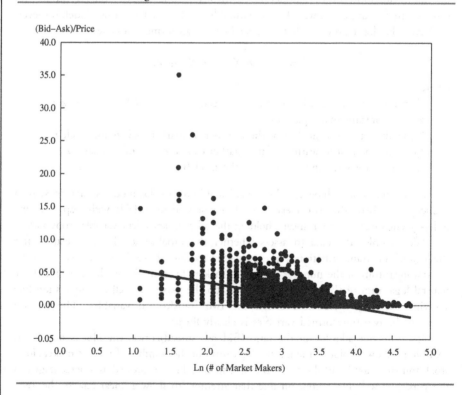

EXHIBIT 20   Results from Regressing Bid–Ask Spread/Price on ln(Number of Market Makers) and ln(Market Cap)

	Coefficients	Standard Error	t-Statistic
Intercept	0.0674	0.0035	19.2571
ln(Number of NASDAQ market makers)	−0.0142	0.0012	−11.8333
ln(Company's market cap)	−0.0016	0.0002	−8.0000

ANOVA	DF	SS	MSS	F	Significance F
Regression	2	0.1539	0.0770	392.3338	0.00
Residual	2,584	0.5068	0.0002		
Total	2,586	0.6607			

Residual standard error	0.0140
Multiple R^2	0.2329
Observations	2,587

Source: Center for Research in Security Prices, University of Chicago.

Note that the relation between (Bid–ask spread)/Price and ln(Market cap) is also nonlinear, while the relation between ln(Bid–ask spread)/Price and ln(Market cap) is linear; we omit these scatterplots to save space. Consequently, we should not estimate a regression with (Bid–ask spread)/Price as the dependent variable. Consideration of the need to ensure that predicted bid–ask spreads are positive would also lead us to not use (Bid–ask spread)/Price as the dependent variable. If we use the non-transformed ratio (Bid–ask spread)/Price as the dependent variable, the estimated model could predict negative values of the bid–ask spread. This result would be nonsensical; in reality, no bid–ask spread is negative (it is hard to motivate traders to simultaneously buy high and sell low), so a model that predicts negative bid–ask spreads is certainly misspecified. In our data sample, the bid–ask spread for each of the 2,587 companies is positive. We illustrate the problem of negative values of the predicted bid–ask spreads now.

Exhibit 20 shows the results of a regression with (Bid–ask spread)/ Price as the dependent variable and the natural logarithm of the number of market makers and the natural logarithm of the company's market capitalization as the independent variables.

1. Suppose that for a particular NASDAQ-listed stock, the number of market makers is 50 and the market capitalization is $6 billion. What is the predicted ratio of bid–ask spread to price for this stock based on the model just shown?

Solution to 1: The natural log of the number of market makers equals ln 50 = 3.9120, and the natural log of the stock's market capitalization (in millions) is ln 6,000 = 8.6995. In this case, the predicted ratio of bid–ask spread to price is 0.0674 + (−0.0142 × 3.9120) + (−0.0016 × 8.6995) = −0.0021. Therefore, the model predicts that the ratio of bid–ask spread to stock price is −0.0021 or −0.21% of the stock price.

2. Does the predicted bid–ask spread for this stock make sense? If not, how could this problem be avoided?

Solution to 2: The predicted bid–ask spread is negative, which does not make economic sense. This problem could be avoided by using log of (Bid–ask spread)/Price as the dependent variable. Whether the natural log of the percentage bid–ask spread, Y, is positive or negative, the percentage bid–ask spread found as e^Y is positive because a positive number raised to any power is positive. The constant e is positive ($e \approx 2.7183$).

Often, analysts must decide whether to scale variables before they compare data across companies. For example, in financial statement analysis, analysts often compare companies using **common size statements**. In a common size income statement, all the line items in a company's income statement are divided by the company's revenues. Common size statements make comparability across companies much easier. An analyst can use common size statements to quickly compare trends in gross margins (or other income statement variables) for a group of companies.

Issues of comparability also appear for analysts who want to use regression analysis to compare the performance of a group of companies. Exhibit 21 illustrates this issue.

EXHIBIT 21   Scaling and the Relation between Cash Flow from Operations and Free Cash Flow

Suppose we go back to the year 2001 and want to explain free cash flow to the firm as a function of cash flow from operations in 2001 for 11 family clothing stores in the United States with market capitalizations of more than $100 million as of the end of 2001.

To investigate this issue, the analyst might use free cash flow as the dependent variable and cash flow from operations as the independent variable in single-independent-variable linear regression. Next, we show the results of that regression. Note that the t-statistic for the slope coefficient for cash flow from operations is quite high (6.5288), the significance level for the F-statistic for the regression is very low (0.0001), and the R^2 is quite high. We might be tempted to believe that this regression is a success and that for a family clothing store, if cash flow from operations increased by $1.00, we could confidently predict that free cash flow to the firm would increase by $0.3579.

But is this specification correct? The regression does not account for size differences among the companies in the sample.

We can account for size differences by using common size cash flow results across companies. We scale the variables by dividing cash flow from operations and free cash flow to the firm by the company's sales before using regression analysis. We will use (Free cash flow to the firm/Sales) as the dependent variable and (Cash flow from operations/Sales) as the independent variable. The results are shown next. Note that the t-statistic for the slope coefficient on (Cash flow from operations/Sales) is 1.6262, so it is not significant at the 0.05 level. Note also that the significance level of the F-statistic is 0.1383, so we cannot reject at the 0.05 level the hypothesis that the regression does not explain variation in (Free cash flow/Sales) among family clothing stores. Finally, note that the R^2 in this regression is much lower than that of the previous regression.

Results from Regressing the Free Cash Flow on Cash Flow from Operations for Family Clothing Stores

	Coefficients	Standard Error	*t*-Statistic
Intercept	0.7295	27.7302	0.0263
Cash flow from operations	0.3579	0.0548	6.5288

ANOVA	DF	SS	MSS	F	Significance F
Regression	1	245,093.7836	245,093.7836	42.6247	0.0001
Residual	9	51,750.3139	5,750.0349		
Total	10	296,844.0975			

Residual standard error	75.8290
Multiple R^2	0.8257
Observations	11

Results from Regressing the Free Cash Flow/Sales on Cash Flow from Operations/Sales for Family Clothing Stores

	Coefficient	Standard Error	*t*-Statistic
Intercept	−0.0121	0.0221	−0.5497
Cash flow from operations/Sales	0.4749	0.2920	1.6262

ANOVA	DF	SS	MSS	F	Significance F
Regression	1	0.0030	0.0030	2.6447	0.1383
Residual	9	0.0102	0.0011		
Total	10	0.0131			

Residual standard error	0.0336
Multiple R^2	0.2271
Observations	11

Which regression makes more sense? Usually, the scaled regression makes more sense. We want to know what happens to free cash flow (as a fraction of sales) if a change occurs in cash flow from operations (as a fraction of sales). Without scaling, the results of the regression can be based solely on scale differences across companies rather than on the companies' underlying economics.

A third common form of misspecification in regression models is pooling data from different samples that should not be pooled. This type of misspecification can best be illustrated graphically. Exhibit 22 shows two clusters of data on variables X and Y with a fitted

EXHIBIT 22   Plot of Two Series with Changing Means

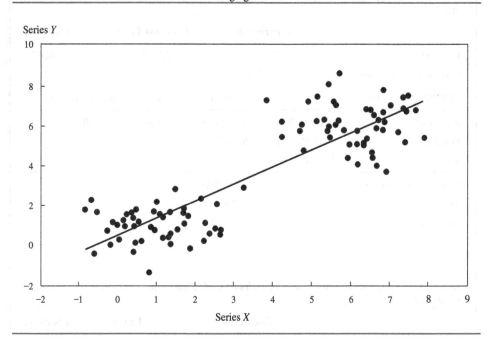

regression line. The data could represent the relationship between two financial variables at two different time periods, for example.

In each cluster of data on X and Y, the correlation between the two variables is virtually 0. Because the means of both X and Y are different for the two clusters of data in the combined sample, X and Y are highly correlated. The correlation is spurious (misleading), however, because it reflects differences in the relationship between X and Y during two different time periods.

5.3. Time-Series Misspecification (Independent Variables Correlated with Errors)

In the previous section, we discussed the misspecification that arises when a relevant independent variable is omitted from a regression. In this section, we discuss problems that arise from the kinds of variables included in the regression, particularly in a time-series context. In models that use time-series data to explain the relations among different variables, it is particularly easy to violate Regression Assumption 3: that the error term has mean 0, conditioned on the independent variables. If this assumption is violated, the estimated regression coefficients will be biased and inconsistent.

Three common problems that create this type of time-series misspecification are:

- including lagged dependent variables as independent variables in regressions with serially correlated errors;

- including a function of a dependent variable as an independent variable, sometimes as a result of the incorrect dating of variables; and
- independent variables that are measured with error.

The next examples demonstrate these problems.

Suppose that an analyst includes the first lagged value of the dependent variable in a multiple regression that, as a result, has significant serial correlation in the errors. For example, the analyst might use the regression equation

$$Y_t = b_0 + b_1 X_{1t} + b_2 Y_{t-1} + \varepsilon_t. \tag{11}$$

Because we assume that the error term is serially correlated, by definition the error term is correlated with the dependent variable. Consequently, the lagged dependent variable, Y_{t-1}, will be correlated with the error term, violating the assumption that the independent variables are uncorrelated with the error term. As a result, the estimates of the regression coefficients will be biased and inconsistent.

EXHIBIT 23 Fisher Effect with a Lagged Dependent Variable

In our discussion of serial correlation, we concluded from a test using the Durbin–Watson test that the error term in the Fisher effect equation (Equation 8) showed positive (first-order) serial correlation, using three-month T-bill returns as the dependent variable and inflation expectations of professional forecasters as the independent variable. Observations on the dependent and independent variables were quarterly. We now modify that regression by including the previous quarter's three-month T-bill returns as an additional independent variable.

At first glance, these regression results look very interesting: The coefficient on the lagged T-bill return appears to be highly significant. But on closer consideration, we must ignore these regression results because the regression is fundamentally misspecified. As long as the error term is serially correlated, including lagged T-bill returns as an independent variable in the regression will cause all the coefficient estimates to be biased and inconsistent. Therefore, this regression is not usable for either testing a hypothesis or for forecasting.

Results from Regressing T-Bill Returns on Predicted Inflation and Lagged T-Bill Returns

	Coefficient	Standard Error	*t*-Statistic
Intercept	−0.0005	0.0014	−0.3571
Inflation prediction	0.1843	0.0455	4.0505
Lagged T-bill return	0.8796	0.0295	29.8169
Residual standard error	0.0095		
Multiple R^2	0.9285		
Observations	181		

Source: Federal Reserve Bank of Philadelphia, US Department of Commerce.

A second common time-series misspecification in investment analysis is to forecast the past. What does that mean? If we forecast the future (say we predict at time t the value of variable Y in period $t + 1$), we must base our predictions on information we knew at time t. We could use a regression to make that forecast using the equation

$$Y_{t+1} = b_0 + b_1 X_{1t} + \varepsilon_{t+1}. \tag{12}$$

In this equation, we predict the value of Y in time $t + 1$ using the value of X in time t. The error term, ε_{t+1}, is unknown at time t and thus should be uncorrelated with X_{1t}.

Unfortunately, analysts sometimes use regressions that try to forecast the value of a dependent variable at time $t + 1$ based on independent variable(s) that are functions of the value of the dependent variable at time $t + 1$. In such a model, the independent variable(s) would be correlated with the error term, so the equation would be misspecified. As an example, an analyst may try to explain the cross-sectional returns for a group of companies during a particular year using the market-to-book ratio and the market capitalization for those companies at the end of the year. ("Market-to-book ratio" is the ratio of price per share divided by book value per share.) If the analyst believes that such a regression predicts whether companies with high market-to-book ratios or high market capitalizations will have high returns, the analyst is mistaken. This is because for any given period, the higher the return during the period, the higher the market capitalization and the market-to-book period will be at the end of the period. In this case, if all the cross-sectional data come from period $t + 1$, a high value of the dependent variable (returns) actually causes a high value of the independent variables (market capitalization and the market-to-book ratio) rather than the other way around. In this type of misspecification, the regression model effectively includes the dependent variable on both the right-and left-hand sides of the regression equation.

The third common time-series misspecification arises when an independent variable is measured with error. Suppose a financial theory tells us that a particular variable X_t, such as expected inflation, should be included in the regression model. But we cannot directly observe X_t; instead, we can observe actual inflation, $Z_t = X_t + u_t$, where we assume u_t is an error term that is uncorrelated with X_t. Even in this best of circumstances, using Z_t in the regression instead of X_t will cause the regression coefficient estimates to be biased and inconsistent. To see why, assume we want to estimate the regression

$$Y_t = b_0 + b_1 X_t + \varepsilon_t,$$

but we substitute Z_t for X_t. Then we would estimate

$$Y_t = b_0 + b_1 Z_t + (-b_1 u_t + \varepsilon_t).$$

But $Z_t = X_t + u_t$, Z_t is correlated with the error term $(-b_1 u_t + \varepsilon_t)$. Therefore, our estimated model violates the assumption that the error term is uncorrelated with the independent variable. Consequently, the estimated regression coefficients will be biased and inconsistent.

EXHIBIT 24   The Fisher Effect with Measurement Error

Recall from Exhibit 11 on the Fisher effect that based on our initial analysis in which we did not correct for heteroskedasticity and serial correlation, we rejected the hypothesis that three-month T-bill returns moved one-for-one with expected inflation.

What if we used actual inflation instead of expected inflation as the independent variable? Note first that

$$\pi = \pi^e + v,$$

where

$$\pi = \text{actual rate of inflation}$$
$$\pi^e = \text{expected rate of inflation}$$
$$v = \text{the difference between actual and expected inflation}$$

Because actual inflation measures expected inflation with error, the estimators of the regression coefficients using T-bill yields as the dependent variable and actual inflation as the independent variable will not be consistent. (Note that a consistent estimator is one for which the probability of estimates close to the value of the population parameter increases as sample size increases.)

The following regression output shows the results of using actual inflation as the independent variable. The estimates in this exhibit are quite different from those

Results from Regressing T-Bill Returns on Predicted Inflation (repeated)

	Coefficient	Standard Error	*t*-Statistic
Intercept	0.0116	0.0033	3.5152
Inflation prediction	1.1744	0.0761	15.4323
Residual standard error	0.0223		
Multiple R^2	0.5708		
Observations	181		
Durbin–Watson statistic	0.2980		

Results from Regressing T-Bill Returns on Actual Inflation

	Coefficient	Standard Error	*t*-Statistic
Intercept	0.0227	0.0034	6.6765
Actual inflation	0.8946	0.0761	11.7556
Residual standard error	0.0267		
Multiple R^2	0.4356		
Observations	181		

Source: Federal Reserve Bank of Philadelphia, US Department of Commerce.

presented in the previous exhibit. Note that the slope coefficient on actual inflation is much lower than the slope coefficient on predicted inflation in the previous regression. This result is an illustration of a general proposition: In a single-independent-variable regression, if we select a version of that independent variable that is measured with error, the estimated slope coefficient on that variable will be biased toward 0. Note that this proposition does not generalize to regressions with more than one independent variable. Of course, we ignore serially-correlated errors in this example, but because the regression coefficients are inconsistent (due to measurement error), testing or correcting for serial correlation is not worthwhile.

5.4. Other Types of Time-Series Misspecification

By far the most frequent source of misspecification in linear regressions that use time series from two or more different variables is nonstationarity. Very roughly, **nonstationarity** means that a variable's properties, such as mean and variance, are not constant through time. We will postpone our discussion about stationarity to the later coverage on time-series analysis, but we can list some examples in which we need to use stationarity tests before we use regression statistical inference.

• Relations among time series with trends (for example, the relation between consumption and GDP).
• Relations among time series that may be **random walks** (time series for which the best predictor of next period's value is this period's value). Exchange rates are often random walks.

The time-series examples in our discussion were carefully chosen such that nonstationarity was unlikely to be an issue for any of them. But nonstationarity can be a very severe problem for analyzing the relations among two or more time series in practice. Analysts must understand these issues before they apply linear regression to analyzing the relations among time series. Otherwise, they may rely on invalid statistical inference.

6. MODELS WITH QUALITATIVE DEPENDENT VARIABLES

In this section, we explain what qualitative dependent variables are, how the regression models that feature such variables work, and how the regression results can be interpreted.

6.1. Models with Qualitative Dependent Variables

Qualitative dependent variables (also called **categorical dependent variables**) are outcome variables that describe data that fit into categories. For example, to predict whether or not a company will go bankrupt, we need to use a qualitative dependent variable (bankrupt or not) as the dependent variable and use data on the company's financial performance (e.g., return on equity, debt-to-equity ratio, or debt rating) as independent variables. The qualitative dependent variable in this example here is a binary variable. This is one of many potential scenarios in which financial analysts need to be able to explain the outcomes of a qualitative dependent variable that describes data that belong to two categories. It is also possible to carry out analysis where the dependent variable can fall into more than two categories. For example, Moody's Bank Financial Strength Rating is a qualitative variable that indicates the Moody's rating or category—A, B, C, D, or E—of a bank.

In contrast to a linear regression, the dependent variable here is not continuous in nature but is discrete and in the simple scenario has two categories. Unfortunately, for estimating such a model, linear regression is not the best statistical method to use. If we use the qualitative dependent variable $Y = \{$bankrupt $(= 1)$ or not bankrupt $(= 0)\}$ as the dependent variable in a regression with financial variables as the independent variables, then we are estimating a linear probability model:

$$l_i = b_0 + b_1 X_{1i} + b_2 X_{2i} + b_3 X_{3i} + \varepsilon_i. \tag{13}$$

Unfortunately, the predicted value of the dependent variable could be much greater than 1 or much lower than 0 depending on the estimated coefficients b_i and the value of observed X_is. Of course, these results would be invalid. The probability of bankruptcy (or of anything, for that matter) cannot be greater than 1.0 or less than 0. Another issue with the use of linear regression is that it assumes the relationship between the probability of bankruptcy and each financial variable to be linear throughout the range of the financial variable. However, we may not expect that. For example, we may expect that the probability of bankruptcy and debt-to-equity ratio are not linearly related for very low or high levels of debt-to-equity ratio.

To address these issues associated with linear regression, we should apply a nonlinear transformation to the probability of bankruptcy and relate the transformed probabilities linearly to the independent variables. There are many possible transformations, which are closely related except when the probability is quite low or high.

The most commonly used transformation is the logistic transformation. Denote by "p" the probability that a company goes bankrupt, or more generally, a condition is fulfilled or an event happens. The logistic transformation is $\ln\left(\frac{p}{1-p}\right)$. The ratio $\frac{p}{1-p}$ is a ratio of probabilities—the probability that the event of interest happens (p) divided by the probability that it does not happen $(1 - p)$. This ratio is called the odds of an event happening. For example, if the probability of a company going bankrupt is 0.75, then $\frac{p}{1-p}$ is $0.75/(1 - 0.75) = 0.75/0.25 = 3$. So, the odds of bankruptcy is 3, which indicates that the probability of bankruptcy is three times as large as the probability of the company not going bankrupt. The natural logarithm of the odds of an event happening is called log odds or logit.

The logistic transformation tends to linearize the relationship between the dependent and independent variables. Instead of a linear regression to estimate the probability of bankruptcy, we should use **logistic regression (logit model)** or **discriminant analysis** for this kind of estimation.

Logistic regression models are used to estimate the probability of a discrete outcome given the values of the independent variables used to explain that outcome. Logistic regression is widely used in machine learning where the objective is classification. Logistic regression involves using the logistic transformation of the event probability as the dependent variable:

$$\ln\left(\frac{p}{1-p}\right) = b_0 + b_1 X_1 + b_2 X_2 + b_3 X_3 + \varepsilon. \tag{14}$$

EXHIBIT 25   Linear Probability Models versus Logit Models

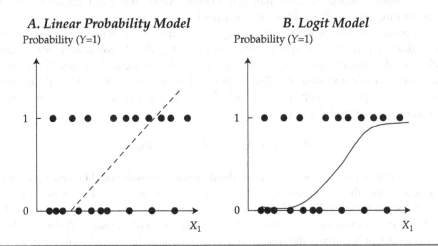

A. Linear Probability Model
Probability (Y=1)

B. Logit Model
Probability (Y=1)

The event probability can be derived from Equation 14 as:

$$p = \frac{1}{1 + \exp[-(b_0 + b_1 X_1 + b_2 X_2 + b_3 X_3)]}. \tag{15}$$

This nonlinear function takes on the sigmoidal shape shown in Exhibit 25. The shape is approximately linear except when probability estimates are close to zero or one. One can see in the exhibit that the nonlinear transformation constrains probability estimates to be between 0 and 1. We can also see that mathematically. As $(b_0 + b_1 X_1 + b_2 X_2 + b_3 X_3)$ approaches positive infinity, p approaches 1; and as $(b_0 + b_1 X_1 + b_2 X_2 + b_3 X_3)$ approaches negative infinity, p approaches 0. Logistic regression assumes a logistic distribution for the error term; this distribution is similar in shape to the normal distribution but has heavier tails.

For a binary p, $\ln\left(\frac{p}{1-p}\right)$ is undefined for both $p = 0$ and $p = 1$. In such a case, logistic regression coefficients are estimated by maximum likelihood method rather than by least squares. The maximum likelihood method estimates logistic regression coefficients that make it most likely that the choices in the sample would have occurred by maximizing the likelihood function for the data. We need to assume the probability distribution of p to construct the likelihood function. Because p is binary, the Bernoulli distribution is chosen as its probability distribution. Maximum likelihood method is an iterative method in which the goal is to maximize log likelihood. Each iteration results in a higher log likelihood, and the iterating process stops when the difference in the log likelihood of two successive iterations is quite small.

Because the logit model has the logistic transformation of event probability as the dependent variable, the interpretation of regression coefficients is not as simple or intuitive as an ordinary linear regression. In a linear regression, the slope coefficient of an independent variable is the change in the dependent variable per unit change in the independent variable, holding all other independent variables constant. In the logit model, the slope coefficient is the change in the "log odds" that the event happens per unit change in the independent variable, holding all other independent variables constant. The exponent of the slope coefficient is the "odds ratio," which is the ratio of odds that the event happens with a unit increase in the independent variable to the odds that the event happens without the increase in the independent variable. The test of the hypothesis that a logit regression coefficient is significantly different from zero is similar to the test in an ordinary linear regression.

We can evaluate the overall performance of a logit regression by examining the likelihood ratio chi-square test statistic. Most statistical analysis packages report this statistic along with the *p*-value or the probability of obtaining this statistic if there is no collective effect of the independent variables on the probability of the event. The *p*-value helps us evaluate the overall statistical significance of the model.

There is no equivalent measure in logistic regression of the R^2 statistic of an ordinary linear regression since logistic regression cannot be fitted using a least square approach. However, researchers have proposed different measures for logistic regression to capture the explained variation. These measures are called pseudo-R^2 and must be interpreted with caution. The pseudo-R^2 in logistic regression may be used to compare different specifications of the same model but is not appropriate for comparing models based on different datasets.

Qualitative dependent variable models can be useful not only for portfolio management but also for business management. For example, we might want to predict whether a client is likely to continue investing in a company or to withdraw assets from the company. We might also want to explain how particular demographic characteristics might affect the probability that a potential investor will sign on as a new client or evaluate the effectiveness of a particular direct-mail advertising campaign based on the demographic characteristics of the target audience. These issues can be analyzed with a logit model. Logistic regression also plays an important role in Big Data analysis—for example, in binary classification problems in machine learning and in neural networks, a topic explained at a later stage.

EXHIBIT 26   Explaining Financing Choice

Grundy and Verwijmeren (2019) investigate what investment characteristics determine the financing choice of a company. We can employ a logit model to address the question. The sample consists of 680 investments financed with debt or equity by US firms between 1995 and 2017 for which the information on investments' characteristics could be obtained. Because the dependent variable in the regression analysis is a binary variable, a logit model is used.

The variables in the logit model are as follows:

Dependent variable:

EQUITY = a binary variable that takes on a value of 1 if equity is used to finance an investment and 0 if debt is used

Independent variables:

TANGIBLE & NON-UNIQUE = a binary variable that takes on a value of 1 if the investment is in a tangible asset and the asset is redeployable

R&D = a binary variable that takes on a value of 1 if the investment has R&D-like characteristics

LN(INVESTMENT LIFE) = natural log of the expected life span of the investment in years

TIME UNTIL PAYOFFS = an ordered categorical variable to capture the time until positive payoffs from the investment begin

INVESTMENT LIFE UNCERTAINTY = a binary variable that takes on a value of 1 if the investment has a relatively uncertain lifespan

VOLATILITY = a binary variable that takes on a value of 1 if the investment is relatively more risky

NEED FOR MONITORING = an ordered categorical variable based on an assessment of the need for monitoring of the investment. Takes one of three values: low, medium, or high.

The authors of the study are examining whether the choice of financing type, either equity or debt, is related to characteristics of the investment being financed. One hypothesis is that equity is more likely to be used when the investment being undertaken has more uncertainty associated with its payoffs. Correspondingly, debt financing is more likely to be used for investments in tangible or investments with a greater need for monitoring. Neither of these hypotheses provides a clear prediction regarding the relationship between investment life and the financing method used. The following table shows an excerpt from the results of the logit estimation: Model 1 of Table II of Grundy and Verwijmeren (2019).

As the results in the table indicate, the absolute value of z-statistics for TANGIBLE & NON-UNIQUE, R&D, TIME UNTIL PAYOFFS, VOLATILITY, and NEED FOR MONITORING is equal to or higher than the critical value at the 0.05 level for the z-statistic (1.96). For each of these variables at the 0.05 level of significance, we can reject the null hypothesis that the coefficient equals 0 in favor of the alternative hypothesis that the coefficient is not equal to 0. The statistically significant coefficients suggest that investments with R&D-like characteristics, more time until positive payoffs begin, and more volatility are likely to be equity-financed; investments in tangible and non-unique assets and investments with greater need for monitoring are more likely to be debt-financed. Thus, both of the original hypotheses are confirmed with respect to the factors that determine the choice of financing by a firm.

Explaining Financing Choice Using a Logit Model

DEPENDENT VARIABLE EQUITY INDEPENDENT VARIABLES	Coefficient	Standard Error	z-Statistic
TANGIBLE & NON-UNIQUE	−1.18	0.29	−4.07
R&D	0.90	0.46	1.96
LN(INVESTMENT LIFE)	−0.39	0.26	−1.50
TIME UNTIL PAYOFFS	1.49	0.31	4.81
INVESTMENT LIFE UNCERTAINTY	0.13	0.39	0.33
VOLATILITY	1.29	0.35	3.69
NEED FOR MONITORING	−0.98	0.31	−3.16
Pseudo-R^2		0.28	

Notes: The research paper does not include the z-statistics. However, we can compute them as the ratio of coefficient and standard error.

Neither of the two remaining independent variables is statistically significant at the 0.05 level in this logit analysis. The absolute values of z-statistics on these two variables are 1.50 or less, so neither one reaches the critical value of 1.96 needed to reject the null hypothesis (that the associated coefficient is significantly different from 0). This result shows that once we take into account the factors included in the analysis, the other factors—life of the investment and uncertainty of investment life—have no power to explain the financing choice.

The estimated regression coefficient for an independent variable is the change in "log odds" that the investment is financed by equity per unit change in that independent variable, holding all other independent variables constant. Consider an investment that does not have R&D-like characteristics. So, R&D takes a value of 0. Suppose that for this investment, after we input the values of R&D and all the other independent variables in the estimated logit model, we get −0.6577. So, the log odds for this investment, that is not R&D-like, being financed by equity equal −0.6577.

The estimated regression coefficient of 0.90 for R&D implies that if this investment had R&D-like characteristics while other characteristics were held constant, the log odds for this investment being financed by equity would increase to −0.6577 + 0.90 = 0.2423. Therefore, the odds of this investment with R&D-like characteristics being financed by equity would be exp(0.2423) = 1.2742. In other words, the probability of equity financing is about 1.27 times as large as the probability of debt financing: $\frac{p}{1-p}$ = 1.2742, where p is the probability of the investment being financed by equity. Solving this equation for p results in 0.5603 or 56.03 percent. We could have also computed this using Equation 8:

$$p = \frac{1}{1 + \exp[-(0.2423)]} = 0.5603.$$

The exponent of estimated regression coefficient of 0.90 for R&D = exp(0.90) = 2.4596 (or 1.2742/0,5180). This "odds ratio" is the ratio of odds that the investment is equity financed if it has R&D-like characteristics to the odds that the investment is equity financed if it does not have R&D-like characteristics.

EXAMPLE 3   Explaining CEO Awards

Use the following information to answer Questions 1–8.

CEOs receive substantial attention in the media. Various publications, such as *Bloomberg Businessweek* and *Forbes,* confer prestigious business awards to a small number of CEOs. Studies, such as those by Malmendier and Tate (2009), find that after receiving an award, the performance of the CEO, as measured by the firm's stock return and return on assets, declines. They also find that award-winning CEOs spend more time on activities outside their companies and underperform relative to non-winning CEOs. Kim Dalton is a financial analyst interested in determining which CEOs are likely to win an award. Her sample consists of observations of company characteristics for each month in which an award is given to CEOs of companies in the

S&P 1500 index for a 10-year period in the 2000s. Dalton employs a logistic regression for her analysis.

The dependent variable in the logistic regression is the logistic transformation of AWARD, a binary variable that takes on a value of 1 for a CEO winning an award in the award month and 0 for non-winning CEOs. The independent variables include BOOK-TO-MARKET (the ratio of the company's book equity and market capitalization); LNSIZE (the natural log of the market value of the company's equity); RETURN-1TO3, RETURN-4TO6, RETURN-7TO12 (total return during months 1–3, 4–6, and 7–12 prior to the award month, respectively); LNTENURE (the natural log of the CEO's tenure with a firm in number of years); and FEMALE (a dummy variable that takes on a value of 1 if the CEO is a female).

In this attempt to explain CEO award winning, Dalton is examining whether CEOs of companies with a low book-to-market ratio, larger companies (as captured by their market values), and companies with higher returns in recent months are more likely to win an award. Dalton is also examining if female CEOs and older CEOs are more likely to receive an award. The following table shows the results of the logit estimation.

1. Which of the following is the reason for Kim Dalton choosing a logit regression for her analysis?
   A. AWARD is a binary variable.
   B. FEMALE is a binary variable.
   C. Two binary variables are in the model.

2. CEOs of which of the following companies are most likely to win an award?
   A. Large companies with a high book-to-market ratio that have achieved high stock returns in months 7–12 before the award month.
   B. Large companies with a low book-to-market ratio that have achieved high stock returns in months 4–6 before the award month.
   C. Large companies with a low book-to-market ratio that have achieved high stock returns in months 7–12 before the award month.

Explaining CEO Award Winning Using a Logit Model

	Coefficient	Standard Error	z-Statistic	p-Value
Intercept	−2.5169	2.2675	−1.11	0.267
BOOK-TO-MARKET	−0.0618	0.0243	−2.54	0.011
LNSIZE	1.3515	0.5201	2.60	0.009
RETURN-1TO3	0.3684	0.5731	0.64	0.520
RETURN-4TO6	0.1734	0.5939	0.29	0.770
RETURN-7TO12	0.9345	0.2250	4.15	0.000
LNTENURE	1.2367	0.5345	2.31	0.021
FEMALE	0.8100	0.3632	2.23	0.026
Likelihood ratio chi-square		323.16		
Prob > chi-square		0.000		
Pseudo R^2		0.226		

3. Which of the following types of CEOs are most likely to win an award?
   A. Females with a long tenure with the company.
   B. Females with a short tenure with the company.
   C. Males with a long tenure with the company.

4. Consider a company for which the log odds of its CEO winning an award based on the estimated regression model work out to -2.3085. The CEO of the company is a male. What would be the log odds of the CEO winning an award if the CEO was a female, while all the other variables are held constant?
   A. -4.0154
   B. -3.1185
   C. -1.4985

5. What are the odds of the male CEO mentioned in the previous question winning an award?
   A. 0.0807
   B. 0.0994
   C. 0.2235

6. Assuming the odds of the male CEO winning an award are 0.0994, what is the probability of the male CEO winning an award?
   A. 9.04%
   B. 9.94%
   C. 18.27%

7. What is the ratio of odds that a female CEO wins an award to the odds that a male CEO wins an award?
   A. 0.0807
   B. 0.4449
   C. 2.2479

8. In estimating the logit regression model, Dalton has used returns expressed in fractions. For example, a return of 10% is entered as 0.10. Therefore, one unit is 1 or 100%. Consider the company with a male CEO discussed earlier. For this company, the total return during months 7 to 12 prior to the award month was 11%. We know that the log odds of its CEO winning an award based on the estimated regression model work out to -2.3085. What would be the log odds of its CEO winning an award if the total return during months 7 to 12 prior to the award month was 12%?
   A. -1.3740
   B. -2.2991
   C. -2.3178

Solution to 1: A is correct. AWARD being a binary dependent variable requires that we use a nonlinear estimation model, such as logit.

B is incorrect because FEMALE is an independent variable. Having a binary independent variable does not make ordinary linear regression inappropriate for estimating the model.

C is incorrect. The total number of binary variables in the model is not relevant to the choice of the estimation procedure. What matters in the context of this question is whether the dependent variable is binary or not.

Solution to 2: C is correct. LNSIZE and RETURN-7TO12 have a significantly positive relationship, while BOOK-TO-MARKET has a significantly negative relationship with log odds of a CEO winning an award.

A is incorrect because the book-to-market ratio has a significantly negative relationship with log odds of a CEO winning an award.

B is incorrect because RETURN-4TO6 has a z-statistic of only 0.29 and is not statistically significant at the 10% level of significance.

Solution to 3: A is correct. The binary variable FEMALE is positive and statistically significant, indicating that female CEOs are more likely to win an award than male CEOs. LNTENURE is also positive and statistically significant, indicating that CEOs with a longer tenure with the company are more likely to win an award. Therefore, female CEOs with longer tenure are most likely to win an award.

Solution to 4: C is correct. The binary variable FEMALE has a slope coefficient of 0.8100. Therefore, the log odds for a female CEO instead of a male CEO, while other variables are held constant, will be $-2.3085 + 0.8100 = -1.4985$.

Solution to 5: B is correct. The log odds of the CEO winning an award are -2.3085. This means that the odds of the CEO winning an award are $\exp(-2.3085) = 0.0994$.

Solution to 6: A is correct. Given that the odds (of the CEO winning an award) are 0.0994, we know that $p/(1 - p) = 0.0994$, where p is the probability of the CEO winning an award. Solving this equation for p results in 0.0904 or 9.04%. We could have also computed this using Equation 15: $p = 1/(1 + \exp[-(2.3085)]) = 0.0904$.

Solution to 7: C is correct. The binary variable FEMALE has a slope coefficient of 0.8100. Therefore, the odds ratio for a female CEO winning an award to a male CEO winning an award is $\exp(0.8100) = 2.2479$. In other words, the odds of a female CEO winning an award are about 2.25 times the odds of a male CEO winning an award.

Solution to 8: B is correct. The variable RETURN-7TO12 has a slope coefficient of 0.9345. Therefore, for every 1 unit or 100% increase in this variable, log odds increase by 0.9345. In the previous question, the variable increases by 0.01 unit or 1%. Accordingly, log odds would increase by $0.01 \times 0.9345 = 0.009345$. So, the log odds would be the $-2.3085 + 0.009345 = -2.2991$.

7. SUMMARY

We have presented the multiple linear regression model and discussed violations of regression assumptions, model specification and misspecification, and models with qualitative variables.

- The general form of a multiple linear regression model is $Y_i = b_0 + b_1X_{1i} + b_2X_{2i} + \ldots + b_kX_{ki} + \varepsilon_i$.
- We conduct hypothesis tests concerning the population values of regression coefficients using t-tests of the form

$$t = \frac{\hat{b}_j - b_j}{s_{\hat{b}_j}}.$$

- The lower the p-value reported for a test, the more significant the result.
- The assumptions of classical normal multiple linear regression model are as follows:
  1. A linear relation exists between the dependent variable and the independent variables.
  2. The independent variables are not random. Also, no exact linear relation exists between two or more of the independent variables.
  3. The expected value of the error term, conditioned on the independent variables, is 0.
  4. The variance of the error term is the same for all observations.
  5. The error term is uncorrelated across observations.
  6. The error term is normally distributed.

- To make a prediction using a multiple linear regression model, we take the following three steps:
  1. Obtain estimates of the regression coefficients.
  2. Determine the assumed values of the independent variables.
  3. Compute the predicted value of the dependent variable.

- When predicting the dependent variable using a linear regression model, we encounter two types of uncertainty: uncertainty in the regression model itself, as reflected in the standard error of estimate, and uncertainty about the estimates of the regression coefficients.
- The F-test is reported in an ANOVA table. The F-statistic is used to test whether at least one of the slope coefficients on the independent variables is significantly different from 0.

$$F = \frac{RSS/k}{SSE/[n - (k + 1)]} = \frac{\text{Mean regression sum of squares}}{\text{Mean squared error}}.$$

Under the null hypothesis that all the slope coefficients are jointly equal to 0, this test statistic has a distribution of $F_{k, n-(k+1)}$, where the regression has n observations and k independent variables. The F-test measures the overall significance of the regression.

- R^2 is nondecreasing in the number of independent variables, so it is less reliable as a measure of goodness of fit in a regression with more than one independent variable than in a one-independent-variable regression.
  Analysts often choose to use adjusted R^2 because it does not necessarily increase when one adds an independent variable.
- Dummy variables in a regression model can help analysts determine whether a particular qualitative independent variable explains the model's dependent variable. A dummy variable takes on the value of 0 or 1. If we need to distinguish among n categories, the regression should include $n - 1$ dummy variables.
- When using intercept dummies, the intercept of the regression measures the average value of the dependent variable of the omitted category, and the coefficient on each dummy

Quantitative Investment Analysis

variable measures the average incremental effect of that dummy variable on the dependent variable.

- When using slope dummies, the coefficient on each dummy measures the average incremental effect on the slope coefficient of the independent variable.
- If a regression shows significant conditional heteroskedasticity, the standard errors and test statistics computed by regression programs will be incorrect unless they are adjusted for heteroskedasticity.
- One simple test for conditional heteroskedasticity is the Breusch–Pagan test. Breusch and Pagan showed that, under the null hypothesis of no conditional heteroskedasticity, nR^2 (from the regression of the squared residuals on the independent variables from the original regression) will be a χ^2 random variable with the number of degrees of freedom equal to the number of independent variables in the regression.
- The principal effect of serial correlation in a linear regression is that the standard errors and test statistics computed by regression programs will be incorrect unless adjusted for serial correlation. Positive serial correlation typically inflates the t-statistics of estimated regression coefficients as well as the F-statistic for the overall significance of the regression.
- The most commonly used test for serial correlation is based on the Durbin–Watson statistic. If the Durbin–Watson statistic differs sufficiently from 2, then the regression errors have significant serial correlation.
- Multicollinearity occurs when two or more independent variables (or combinations of independent variables) are highly (but not perfectly) correlated with each other. With multicollinearity, the regression coefficients may not be individually statistically significant even when the overall regression is significant, as judged by the F-statistic.
- Model specification refers to the set of variables included in the regression and the regression equation's functional form. The following principles can guide model specification:
  - The model should be grounded in cogent economic reasoning.
  - The functional form chosen for the variables in the regression should be appropriate given the nature of the variables.
  - The model should be parsimonious.
  - The model should be examined for violations of regression assumptions before being accepted.
  - The model should be tested and found useful out of sample before being accepted.
- If a regression is misspecified, then statistical inference using OLS is invalid and the estimated regression coefficients may be inconsistent.
- Assuming that a model has the correct functional form when in fact it does not is one example of misspecification. This assumption may be violated in several ways:
  - One or more important variables could be omitted from the regression.
  - One or more of the regression variables may need to be transformed before estimating the regression.
  - The regression model pools data from different samples that should not be pooled.
- Another type of misspecification occurs when independent variables are correlated with the error term. This is a violation of Regression Assumption 3, that the error term has a mean of 0, and causes the estimated regression coefficients to be biased and inconsistent. Three common problems that create this type of time-series misspecification are:

- including lagged dependent variables as independent variables in regressions with serially correlated errors;
- including a function of the dependent variable as an independent variable, sometimes as a result of the incorrect dating of variables; and
- independent variables that are measured with error.

- Logit models estimate the probability of a discrete outcome (the value of a qualitative dependent variable, such as whether a company enters bankruptcy) given the values of the independent variables used to explain that outcome. The logit model, which is based on the logistic distribution, estimates the probability that $Y = 1$ (a condition is fulfilled) given the values of the independent variables.

REFERENCES

Altman, Edward I. 1968. "Financial Ratios, Discriminant Analysis and the Prediction of Corporate Bankruptcy." *Journal of Finance*, vol. 23: 589–609. 10.1111/j.1540-6261.1968.tb00843.x.

Altman, E. I., R. Halderman, and P. Narayanan. 1977. "Zeta Analysis: A New Model to Identify Bankruptcy Risk of Corporations." *Journal of Banking & Finance*, vol. 1: 29–54. 10.1016/0378-4266 (77)90017-6.

Bhabra, Harjeet S. and Jiayin Huang. 2013. "An Empirical Investigation of Mergers and Acquisitions by Chinese Listed Companies, 1997–2007." *Journal of Multinational Financial Management*, vol. 23: 186–207. 10.1016/j.mulfin.2013.03.002.

Breusch, T. and A. Pagan. 1979. "A Simple Test for Heteroscedasticity and Random Coefficient Variation." *Econometrica*, vol. 47: 1287–1294. 10.2307/1911963.

Buetow, Gerald W., Jr., Robert R. Johnson, and David E. Runkle. 2000. "The Inconsistency of Return-Based Style Analysis." *Journal of Portfolio Management*, vol. 26, no. 3: 61–77. 10.3905/ jpm.2000.319722.

Durbin, J. and G.S. Watson. 1951. "Testing for Serial Correlation in Least Squares Regression, II." *Biometrika*, vol. 38: 159–178. 10.1093/biomet/38.1-2.159.

Greene, William H. 2018. *Economic Analysis*, 8th edition. New York: Pearson Education.

Grundy, Bruce D. and Patrick Verwijmeren. 2019. "The External Financing of Investment" (3 April). https://papers.ssrn.com/sol3/papers.cfm?abstract_id=2986127.

Gujarati, Damodar N., Dawn C. Porter, and Sangeetha Gunasekar. 2011. *Basic Econometrics*, 5th edition. New York: McGraw-Hill Irwin.

Hansen, Lars Peter. 1982. "Large Sample Properties of Generalized Method of Moments Estimators." *Econometrica*, vol. 50, no. 4: 1029–1054. 10.2307/1912775.

Keane, Michael P. and David E. Runkle. 1998. "Are Financial Analysts' Forecasts of Corporate Profits Rational?" *Journal of Political Economy*, vol. 106, no. 4: 768–805. 10.1086/250029.

Kyaw, NyoNyo A., John Manley, and Anand Shetty. 2011. "Factors in Multinational Valuations: Transparency, Political Risk, and Diversification." *Journal of Multinational Financial Management*, vol. 21: 55–67.

MacKinlay, A. Craig and Matthew P. Richardson. 1991. "Using Generalized Methods of Moments to Test Mean–Variance Efficiency." *Journal of Finance*, vol. 46, no. 2: 511–527. 10.1111/ j.1540-6261.1991.tb02672.x.

Malmendier, Ulrike and Geoffrey Tate. 2009. "Superstar CEOs." *Quarterly Journal of Economics* 124 (4): 1593–638. 10.1162/qjec.2009.124.4.1593.

Mankiw, N. Gregory. 2015. *Macroeconomics*, 9th edition. New York: Worth Publishers.

Mitchell, T. 1997. *Machine Learning*. McGraw-Hill.

Newey, Whitney K. and Kenneth D. West. 1987. "A Simple, Positive Semi-definite, Heteroskedasticity and Autocorrelation Consistent Covariance Matrix." *Econometrica*, vol. 55, no. 3: 703–708. 10.2307/1913610.

Petersen, Mitchell A. 2009. "Estimating Standard Errors in Finance Panel Data Sets: Comparing Approaches." *Review of Financial Studies*, vol. 22, no. 1: 435–480. 10.1093/rfs/hhn053.

Samuel, A. July 1959. "Some Studies in Machine Learning Using the Game of Checkers." *IBM Journal of Research and Development* 3 (3): 210–29. 10.1147/rd.33.0210.

Sharpe, William F. 1988. "Determining a Fund's Effective Asset Mix." *Investment Management Review*, November/December:59–69.

Siegel, Jeremy J. 2014. *Stocks for the Long Run*, 5th edition. New York: McGraw-Hill.

Stoll, Hans R. 1978. "The Pricing of Security Dealer Services: An Empirical Study of Nasdaq Stocks." *Journal of Finance*, vol. 33, no. 4: 1153–1172. 10.1111/j.1540-6261.1978.tb02054.x.

Theobald, O. 2017. *Machine Learning for Absolute Beginners*. Independently published.

Tibshirani, R. 1996. "Regression Shrinkage and Selection via the Lasso." *Journal of the Royal Statistical Society. Series B. Methodological* 58 (1): 267–88. 10.1111/j.2517-6161.1996.tb02080.x.

Wang, W., Y. Huang, Y. Wang, and L. Wang. 2014. "Generalized Autoencoder: A Neural Network Framework for Dimensionality Reduction." *2014 IEEE Conference on Computer Vision and Pattern Recognition Workshops*: 490–497.

PRACTICE PROBLEMS

1. With many US companies operating globally, the effect of the US dollar's strength on a US company's returns has become an important investment issue. You would like to determine whether changes in the US dollar's value and overall US equity market returns affect an asset's returns. You decide to use the S&P 500 Index to represent the US equity market.

   A. Write a multiple regression equation to test whether changes in the value of the dollar and equity market returns affect an asset's returns. Use the notations below.

   R_{it} = return on the asset in period t

   R_{Mt} = return on the S&P 500 in period t

   ΔX_t = change in period t in the log of a trade-weighted index of the foreign exchange value of US dollar against the currencies of a broad group of major US trading partners.

   B. You estimate the regression for Archer Daniels Midland Company (NYSE: ADM). You regress its monthly returns for the period January 1990 to December 2002 on S&P 500 Index returns and changes in the log of the trade-weighted exchange value of the US dollar. The table below shows the coefficient estimates and their standard errors.

   Coefficient Estimates from Regressing ADM's Returns: Monthly Data, January 1990–December 2002

	Coefficient	Standard Error
Intercept	0.0045	0.0062
R_{Mt}	0.5373	0.1332
ΔX_t	−0.5768	0.5121
$n = 156$		

Determine whether S&P 500 returns affect ADM's returns. Then determine whether changes in the value of the US dollar affect ADM's returns. Use a 0.05 significance level to make your decisions.

C. Based on the estimated coefficient on R_{Mt}, is it correct to say that "for a 1 percentage point increase in the return on the S&P 500 in period t, we expect a 0.5373 percentage point increase in the return on ADM"?

2. One of the most important questions in financial economics is what factors determine the cross-sectional variation in an asset's returns. Some have argued that book-to-market ratio and size (market value of equity) play an important role.

A. Write a multiple regression equation to test whether book-to-market ratio and size explain the cross-section of asset returns. Use the notations below.

$$(B/M)_i = \text{book-to-market ratio for asset } i$$
$$R_i = \text{return on asset } i \text{ in a particular month}$$
$$\text{Size}_i = \text{natural log of the market value of equity for asset } i$$

B. The table below shows the results of the linear regression for a cross-section of 66 companies. The size and book-to-market data for each company are for December 2001. The return data for each company are for January 2002.

Results from Regressing Returns on the Book-to-Market Ratio and Size

	Coefficient	Standard Error
Intercept	0.0825	0.1644
(B/M)$_i$	−0.0541	0.0588
Size$_i$	−0.0164	0.0350
$n = 66$		

Source: FactSet.

Determine whether the book-to-market ratio and size are each useful for explaining the cross-section of asset returns. Use a 0.05 significance level to make your decision.

3. There is substantial cross-sectional variation in the number of financial analysts who follow a company. Suppose you hypothesize that a company's size (market cap) and financial risk (debt-to-equity ratios) influence the number of financial analysts who follow a company. You formulate the following regression model:

$$(\text{Analyst following})_i = b_0 + b_1 \text{Size}_i + b_2 (D/E)_i + \varepsilon_i$$

where

> (Analyst following)$_i$ = the natural log of $(1 + n)$, where n_i is the number of analysts following company i
>
> Size$_i$ = the natural log of the market capitalization of company i in millions of dollars

(D/E)$_i$ = the debt-to-equity ratio for company i

In the definition of Analyst following, 1 is added to the number of analysts following a company because some companies are not followed by any analysts, and the natural log of 0 is indeterminate. The following table gives the coefficient estimates of the above regression model for a randomly selected sample of 500 companies. The data are for the year 2002.

Coefficient Estimates from Regressing Analyst Following on Size and Debt-to-Equity Ratio

	Coefficient	Standard Error	t-Statistic
Intercept	−0.2845	0.1080	−2.6343
Size$_i$	0.3199	0.0152	21.0461
(D/E)$_i$	−0.1895	0.0620	−3.0565
$n = 500$			

Source: First Call/Thomson Financial, Compustat.

A. Consider two companies, both of which have a debt-to-equity ratio of 0.75. The first company has a market capitalization of $100 million, and the second company has a market capitalization of $1 billion. Based on the above estimates, how many more analysts will follow the second company than the first company?

B. Suppose the p-value reported for the estimated coefficient on (D/E)$_i$ is 0.00236. State the interpretation of 0.00236.

4. In early 2001, US equity marketplaces started trading all listed shares in minimal increments (ticks) of $0.01 (decimalization). After decimalization, bid–ask spreads of stocks traded on the NASDAQ tended to decline. In response, spreads of NASDAQ stocks cross-listed on the Toronto Stock Exchange (TSE) tended to decline as well. Researchers Oppenheimer and Sabherwal (2003) hypothesized that the percentage decline in TSE spreads of cross-listed stocks was related to company size, the predecimalization ratio of spreads on NASDAQ to those on the TSE, and the percentage decline in NASDAQ spreads. The following table gives the regression coefficient estimates from estimating that relationship for a sample of 74 companies. Company size is measured by the natural logarithm of the book value of company's assets in thousands of Canadian dollars.

Coefficient Estimates from Regressing Percentage Decline in TSE Spreads on Company Size, Predecimalization Ratio of NASDAQ to TSE Spreads, and Percentage Decline in NASDAQ Spreads

	Coefficient	t-Statistic
Intercept	−0.45	−1.86
Size$_i$	0.05	2.56
(Ratio of spreads)$_i$	−0.06	−3.77
(Decline in NASDAQ spreads)$_i$	0.29	2.42
$n = 74$		

Source: Oppenheimer and Sabherwal (2003).

The average company in the sample has a book value of assets of C\$900 million and a predecimalization ratio of spreads equal to 1.3. Based on the above model, what is the predicted decline in spread on the TSE for a company with these average characteristics, given a 1 percentage point decline in NASDAQ spreads?

5. The neglected-company effect claims that companies that are followed by fewer analysts will earn higher returns on average than companies that are followed by many analysts. To test the neglected-company effect, you have collected data on 66 companies and the number of analysts providing earnings estimates for each company. You decide to also include size as an independent variable, measuring size as the log of the market value of the company's equity, to try to distinguish any small-company effect from a neglected-company effect. The small-company effect asserts that small-company stocks may earn average higher risk-adjusted returns than large-company stocks.

   The table below shows the results from estimating the model $R_i = b_0 + b_1\text{Size}_i + b_2(\text{Number of analysts})_i + \varepsilon_i$ for a cross-section of 66 companies. The size and number of analysts for each company are for December 2001. The return data are for January 2002.

Results from Regressing Returns on Size and Number of Analysts

	Coefficient	Standard Error	t-Statistic
Intercept	0.0388	0.1556	0.2495
Size$_i$	−0.0153	0.0348	−0.4388
(Number of analysts)$_i$	0.0014	0.0015	0.8995

ANOVA	DF	SS	MSS
Regression	2	0.0094	0.0047
Residual	63	0.6739	0.0107
Total	65	0.6833	

Residual standard error	0.1034
R-squared	0.0138
Observations	66

Source: First Call/Thomson Financial, FactSet.

A. What test would you conduct to see whether the two independent variables are *jointly* statistically related to returns (H_0: $b_1 = b_2 = 0$)?

B. What information do you need to conduct the appropriate test?

C. Determine whether the two variables jointly are statistically related to returns at the 0.05 significance level.

D. Explain the meaning of adjusted R^2 and state whether adjusted R^2 for the regression would be smaller than, equal to, or larger than 0.0138.

6. Some developing nations are hesitant to open their equity markets to foreign investment because they fear that rapid inflows and outflows of foreign funds will increase volatility. In July 1993, India implemented substantial equity market reforms, one of which allowed foreign institutional investors into the Indian equity markets. You want to test whether the volatility of returns of stocks traded on the Bombay Stock Exchange (BSE) increased after July 1993, when foreign institutional investors were first allowed to invest in India. You have collected monthly return data for the BSE from February 1990 to December 1997. Your dependent variable is a measure of return volatility of stocks traded on the BSE; your independent variable is a dummy variable that is coded 1 if foreign investment was allowed during the month and 0 otherwise.

You believe that market return volatility actually *decreases* with the opening up of equity markets. The table below shows the results from your regression.

Results from Dummy Regression for Foreign Investment in India with a Volatility Measure as the Dependent Variable

	Coefficient	Standard Error	t-Statistic
Intercept	0.0133	0.0020	6.5351
Dummy	−0.0075	0.0027	−2.7604
n = 95			

Source: FactSet.

A. State null and alternative hypotheses for the slope coefficient of the dummy variable that are consistent with testing your stated belief about the effect of opening the equity markets on stock return volatility.

B. Determine whether you can reject the null hypothesis at the 0.05 significance level (in a one-sided test of significance).

C. According to the estimated regression equation, what is the level of return volatility before and after the market-opening event?

7. Both researchers and the popular press have discussed the question as to which of the two leading US political parties, Republicans or Democrats, is better for the stock market.

A. Write a regression equation to test whether overall market returns, as measured by the annual returns on the S&P 500 Index, tend to be higher when the Republicans or the Democrats control the White House. Use the notations below.

$$R_{Mt} = \text{return on the S\&P 500 in period } t$$

$$\text{Party}_t = \text{the political party controlling the White House (1 for a Republican president; 0 for a Democratic president) in period } t$$

B.   The table below shows the results of the linear regression from Part A using annual
data for the S&P 500 and a dummy variable for the party that controlled the
White House. The data are from 1926 to 2002.

Results from Regressing S&P 500 Returns on a Dummy Variable for the Party That Controlled
the White House, 1926–2002

	Coefficient	Standard Error	t-Statistic		
Intercept	0.1494	0.0323	4.6270		
Party$_t$	−0.0570	0.0466	−1.2242		
ANOVA	DF	SS	MSS	F	Significance F
Regression	1	0.0625	0.0625	1.4987	0.2247
Residual	75	3.1287	0.0417		
Total	76	3.1912			
Residual standard error		0.2042			
R-squared		0.0196			
Observations		77			

Source: FactSet.

Based on the coefficient and standard error estimates, verify to two decimal places the
t-statistic for the coefficient on the dummy variable reported in the table.
C.   Determine at the 0.05 significance level whether overall US equity market returns
tend to differ depending on the political party controlling the White House.

8.   Problem 3 addressed the cross-sectional variation in the number of financial analysts
who follow a company. In that problem, company size and debt-to-equity ratios were
the independent variables. You receive a suggestion that membership in the S&P 500
Index should be added to the model as a third independent variable; the hypothesis is
that there is greater demand for analyst coverage for stocks included in the S&P 500
because of the widespread use of the S&P 500 as a benchmark.
A.   Write a multiple regression equation to test whether analyst following is
systematically higher for companies included in the S&P 500 Index. Also include
company size and debt-to-equity ratio in this equation. Use the notations below.
(Analyst following)$_i$ = natural log of (1 + Number of analysts following company i)
Size$_i$ = natural log of the market capitalization of company i in
millions of dollars
(D/E)$_i$ = debt-to-equity ratio for company i
S&P$_i$ = inclusion of company i in the S&P 500 Index (1 if included,
0 if not included)
In the above specification for analyst following, 1 is added to the number of
analysts following a company because some companies are not followed by any
analyst, and the natural log of 0 is indeterminate.
B.   State the appropriate null hypothesis and alternative hypothesis in a two-sided test
of significance of the dummy variable.

C. The following table gives estimates of the coefficients of the above regression model
    for a randomly selected sample of 500 companies. The data are for the year 2002.
    Determine whether you can reject the null hypothesis at the 0.05 significance level
    (in a two-sided test of significance).

Coefficient Estimates from Regressing Analyst Following on Size, Debt-to-Equity Ratio, and S&P 500 Membership, 2002

	Coefficient	Standard Error	t-Statistic
Intercept	−0.0075	0.1218	−0.0616
Size$_i$	0.2648	0.0191	13.8639
(D/E)$_i$	−0.1829	0.0608	−3.0082
S&P$_i$	0.4218	0.0919	4.5898
n = 500			

Source: First Call/Thomson Financial, Compustat.

D. Consider a company with a debt-to-equity ratio of 2/3 and a market capitalization
    of $10 billion. According to the estimated regression equation, how many analysts
    would follow this company if it were not included in the S&P 500 Index, and how
    many would follow if it were included in the index?
E. In Problem 3, using the sample, we estimated the coefficient on the size variable as
    0.3199, versus 0.2648 in the above regression. Discuss whether there is an
    inconsistency in these results.

9. You believe there is a relationship between book-to-market ratios and subsequent
   returns. The output from a cross-sectional regression and a graph of the actual and
   predicted relationship between the book-to-market ratio and return are shown below.

Results from Regressing Returns on the Book-to-Market Ratio

	Coefficient	Standard Error	t-Statistic
Intercept	12.0130	3.5464	3.3874
$\left(\frac{Book\ value}{Market\ value}\right)_i$	−9.2209	8.4454	−1.0918

ANOVA	DF	SS	MSS	F	Significance F
Regression	1	154.9866	154.9866	1.1921	0.2831
Residual	32	4162.1895	130.0684		
Total	33	4317.1761			

Residual standard error	11.4048
R-squared	0.0359
Observations	34

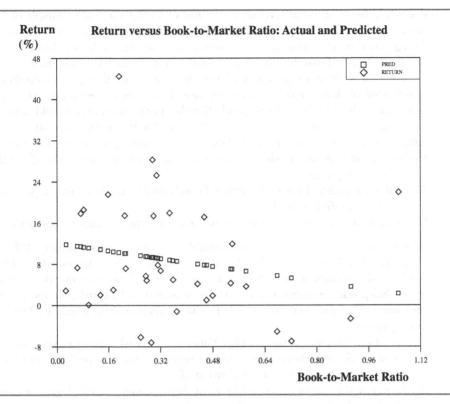

Return versus Book-to-Market Ratio: Actual and Predicted

A. You are concerned with model specification problems and regression assumption violations. Focusing on assumption violations, discuss symptoms of conditional heteroskedasticity based on the graph of the actual and predicted relationship.

B. Describe in detail how you could formally test for conditional heteroskedasticity in this regression.

C. Describe a recommended method for correcting for conditional heteroskedasticity.

10. You are examining the effects of the January 2001 NYSE implementation of the trading of shares in minimal increments (ticks) of $0.01 (decimalization). In particular, you are analyzing a sample of 52 Canadian companies cross-listed on both the NYSE and the Toronto Stock Exchange (TSE). You find that the bid–ask spreads of these shares decline on both exchanges after the NYSE decimalization. You run a linear regression analyzing the decline in spreads on the TSE, and find that the decline on the TSE is related to company size, predecimalization ratio of NYSE to TSE spreads, and decline in the NYSE spreads. The relationships are statistically significant. You want to be sure, however, that the results are not influenced by conditional heteroskedasticity. Therefore, you regress the squared residuals of the regression model on the three independent variables. The R^2 for this regression is 14.1 percent. Perform a statistical test to determine if conditional heteroskedasticity is present.

11. You are analyzing if institutional investors such as mutual funds and pension funds prefer to hold shares of companies with less volatile returns. You have the percentage of

shares held by institutional investors at the end of 1998 for a random sample of 750 companies. For these companies, you compute the standard deviation of daily returns during that year. Then you regress the institutional holdings on the standard deviation of returns. You find that the regression is significant at the 0.01 level and the F-statistic is 12.98. The R^2 for this regression is 1.7 percent. As expected, the regression coefficient of the standard deviation of returns is negative. Its t-statistic is -3.60, which is also significant at the 0.01 level. Before concluding that institutions prefer to hold shares of less volatile stocks, however, you want to be sure that the regression results are not influenced by conditional heteroskedasticity. Therefore, you regress the squared residuals of the regression model on the standard deviation of returns. The R^2 for this regression is 0.6 percent.

A. Perform a statistical test to determine if conditional heteroskedasticity is present at the 0.05 significance level.

B. In view of your answer to Part A, what remedial action, if any, is appropriate?

12. In estimating a regression based on monthly observations from January 1987 to December 2002 inclusive, you find that the coefficient on the independent variable is positive and significant at the 0.05 level. You are concerned, however, that the t-statistic on the independent variable may be inflated because of serial correlation between the error terms. Therefore, you examine the Durbin–Watson statistic, which is 1.8953 for this regression.

A. Based on the value of the Durbin–Watson statistic, what can you say about the serial correlation between the regression residuals? Are they positively correlated, negatively correlated, or not correlated at all?

B. Compute the sample correlation between the regression residuals from one period and those from the previous period.

C. Perform a statistical test to determine if serial correlation is present. Assume that the critical values for 192 observations when there is a single independent variable are about 0.09 above the critical values for 100 observations.

13. The book-to-market ratio and the size of a company's equity are two factors that have been asserted to be useful in explaining the cross-sectional variation in subsequent returns. Based on this assertion, you want to estimate the following regression model:

$$R_i = b_0 + b_1 \left(\frac{\text{Book}}{\text{Market}} \right)_i + b_2 \text{Size}_i + \varepsilon_i$$

where
R_i = Return of company i's shares (in the following period)
$\left(\frac{\text{Book}}{\text{Market}} \right)_i$ = company i's book-to-market ratio
Size_i = Market value of company i's equity
A colleague suggests that this regression specification may be erroneous, because he believes that the book-to-market ratio may be strongly related to (correlated with) company size.

A. To what problem is your colleague referring, and what are its consequences for regression analysis?

Regression of Return on Book-to-Market and Size

	Coefficient	Standard Error	*t*-Statistic
Intercept	14.1062	4.220	3.3427
$\left(\frac{\text{Book}}{\text{Market}}\right)_i$	−12.1413	9.0406	−1.3430
Size$_i$	−0.00005502	0.00005977	−0.92047
R-squared	0.06156		
Observations	34		

Correlation Matrix

	Book-to-Market Ratio	Size
Book-to-Market Ratio	1.0000	
Size	−0.3509	1.0000

B. With respect to multicollinearity, critique the choice of variables in the regression model above.

C. State the classic symptom of multicollinearity and comment on that basis whether multicollinearity appears to be present, given the additional fact that the *F*-test for the above regression is not significant.

14. You are analyzing the variables that explain the returns on the stock of the Boeing Company. Because overall market returns are likely to explain a part of the returns on Boeing, you decide to include the returns on a value-weighted index of all the companies listed on the NYSE, AMEX, and NASDAQ as an independent variable. Further, because Boeing is a large company, you also decide to include the returns on the S&P 500 Index, which is a value-weighted index of the larger market-capitalization companies. Finally, you decide to include the changes in the US dollar's value. To conduct your test, you have collected the following data for the period 1990–2002.

R_t = monthly return on the stock of Boeing in month t

R_{ALLt} = monthly return on a value-weighted index of all the companies listed on the NYSE, AMEX, and NASDAQ in month t

R_{SPt} = monthly return on the S&P 500 Index in month t

ΔX_t = change in month t in the log of a trade-weighted index of the foreign exchange value of the US dollar against the currencies of a broad group of major US trading partners

The following table shows the output from regressing the monthly return on Boeing stock on the three independent variables.

Regression of Boeing Returns on Three Explanatory Variables: Monthly Data, January 1990–
December 2002

	Coefficient	Standard Error	t-Statistic
Intercept	0.0026	0.0066	0.3939
R_{ALLt}	−0.1337	0.6219	−0.2150
R_{SPt}	0.8875	0.6357	1.3961
ΔX_t	0.2005	0.5399	0.3714

ANOVA	DF	SS	MSS
Regression	3	0.1720	0.0573
Residual	152	0.8947	0.0059
Total	155	1.0667	

Residual standard error	0.0767
R-squared	0.1610
Observations	156

Source: FactSet, Federal Reserve Bank of Philadelphia.

From the t-statistics, we see that none of the explanatory variables is statistically
significant at the 5 percent level or better. You wish to test, however, if the three
variables *jointly* are statistically related to the returns on Boeing.

A. Your null hypothesis is that all three population slope coefficients equal 0—that the
three variables *jointly* are statistically not related to the returns on Boeing. Conduct
the appropriate test of that hypothesis.

B. Examining the regression results, state the regression assumption that may be
violated in this example. Explain your answer.

C. State a possible way to remedy the violation of the regression assumption identified
in Part B.

15. You are analyzing the cross-sectional variation in the number of financial analysts that
follow a company (also the subject of Problems 3 and 8). You believe that there is less
analyst following for companies with a greater debt-to-equity ratio and greater analyst
following for companies included in the S&P 500 Index. Consistent with these beliefs,
you estimate the following regression model.

$$(\text{Analysts following})_i = b_0 + b_1(\text{D/E})_i + b_2(\text{S\&P})_i + \varepsilon_i$$

where

$(\text{Analysts following})_i$ = natural log of (1 + Number of analysts following company i)
$(\text{D/E})_i$ = debt-to-equity ratio for company i
$\text{S\&P}_i$ = inclusion of company i in the S&P 500 Index (1 if included; 0 if
not included)

In the preceding specification, 1 is added to the number of analysts following a company
because some companies are not followed by any analysts, and the natural log of 0 is
indeterminate. The following table gives the coefficient estimates of the above regression
model for a randomly selected sample of 500 companies. The data are for the year 2002.

Coefficient Estimates from Regressing Analyst Following on Debt-to-Equity Ratio and S&P 500 Membership, 2002

	Coefficient	Standard Error	t-Statistic
Intercept	1.5367	0.0582	26.4038
$(D/E)_i$	−0.1043	0.0712	−1.4649
$S\&P_i$	1.2222	0.0841	14.5327
$n = 500$			

Source: First Call/Thomson Financial, Compustat.

You discuss your results with a colleague. She suggests that this regression specification may be erroneous, because analyst following is likely to be also related to the size of the company.

A. What is this problem called, and what are its consequences for regression analysis?

B. To investigate the issue raised by your colleague, you decide to collect data on company size also. You then estimate the model after including an additional variable, Size i, which is the natural log of the market capitalization of company i in millions of dollars. The following table gives the new coefficient estimates.

Coefficient Estimates from Regressing Analyst Following on Size, Debt-to-Equity Ratio, and S&P 500 Membership, 2002

	Coefficient	Standard Error	t-Statistic
Intercept	−0.0075	0.1218	−0.0616
$Size_i$	0.2648	0.0191	13.8639
$(D/E)_i$	−0.1829	0.0608	−3.0082
$S\&P_i$	0.4218	0.0919	4.5898
$n = 500$			

Source: First Call/Thomson Financial, Compustat.

What do you conclude about the existence of the problem mentioned by your colleague in the original regression model you had estimated?

16. You have noticed that hundreds of non-US companies are listed not only on a stock exchange in their home market but also on one of the exchanges in the United States. You have also noticed that hundreds of non-US companies are listed only in their home market and not in the United States. You are trying to predict whether or not a non-US company will choose to list on a US exchange. One of the factors that you think will affect whether or not a company lists in the United States is its size relative to the size of other companies in its home market.

A. What kind of a dependent variable do you need to use in the model?

B. What kind of a model should be used?

The following information relates to Questions 17–22

Gary Hansen is a securities analyst for a mutual fund specializing in small-capitalization growth stocks. The fund regularly invests in initial public offerings (IPOs). If the fund subscribes to an offer, it is allocated shares at the offer price. Hansen notes that IPOs frequently are underpriced, and the price rises when open market trading begins. The initial return for an IPO is calculated as the change in price on the first day of trading divided by the offer price. Hansen is developing a regression model to predict the initial return for IPOs. Based on past research, he selects the following independent variables to predict IPO initial returns:

Underwriter rank	=	1–10, where 10 is highest rank
Pre-offer price adjustment[a]	=	(Offer price − Initial filing price)/Initial filing price
Offer size ($ millions)	=	Shares sold × Offer price
Fraction retained[a]	=	Fraction of total company shares retained by insiders

[a]Expressed as a decimal

Hansen collects a sample of 1,725 recent IPOs for his regression model. Regression results appear in Exhibit 1, and ANOVA results appear in Exhibit 2.

Hansen wants to use the regression results to predict the initial return for an upcoming IPO. The upcoming IPO has the following characteristics:

- Underwriter rank = 6
- Pre-offer price adjustment = 0.04
- Offer size = $40 million
- Fraction retained = 0.70

EXHIBIT 1 Hansen's Regression Results Dependent Variable: IPO Initial Return (Expressed in Decimal Form, i.e., 1% = 0.01)

Variable	Coefficient (b_j)	Standard Error	t-Statistic
Intercept	0.0477	0.0019	25.11
Underwriter rank	0.0150	0.0049	3.06
Pre-offer price adjustment	0.4350	0.0202	21.53
Offer size	−0.0009	0.0011	−0.82
Fraction retained	0.0500	0.0260	1.92

EXHIBIT 2 Selected ANOVA Results for Hansen's Regression

	Degrees of Freedom (DF)	Sum of Squares (SS)
Regression	4	51.433
Residual	1,720	91.436
Total	1,724	142.869
Multiple R-squared = 0.36		

Because he notes that the pre-offer price adjustment appears to have an important effect on initial return, Hansen wants to construct a 95 percent confidence interval for the coefficient on this variable. He also believes that for each 1 percent increase in pre-offer price adjustment, the initial return will increase by less than 0.5 percent, holding other variables constant. Hansen wishes to test this hypothesis at the 0.05 level of significance.

Before applying his model, Hansen asks a colleague, Phil Chang, to review its specification and results. After examining the model, Chang concludes that the model suffers from two problems: 1) conditional heteroskedasticity, and 2) omitted variable bias. Chang makes the following statements:

Statement 1.   "Conditional heteroskedasticity will result in consistent coefficient estimates, but both the *t*-statistics and *F*-statistic will be biased, resulting in false inferences."

Statement 2.   "If an omitted variable is correlated with variables already included in the model, coefficient estimates will be biased and inconsistent and standard errors will also be inconsistent."

Selected values for the *t*-distribution and *F*-distribution appear in Exhibits 3 and 4, respectively.

EXHIBIT 3   Selected Values for the *t*-Distribution (DF = ∞)

Area in Right Tail	*t*-Value
0.050	1.645
0.025	1.960
0.010	2.326
0.005	2.576

EXHIBIT 4   Selected Values for the *F*-Distribution ($\alpha = 0.01$) (DF1/DF2: Numerator/Denominator Degrees of Freedom)

		DF1	
		4	∞
DF2	4	16.00	13.50
	∞	3.32	1.00

17. Based on Hansen's regression, the predicted initial return for the upcoming IPO is *closest* to:
    A.   0.0943.
    B.   0.1064.
    C.   0.1541.

18. The 95 percent confidence interval for the regression coefficient for the pre-offer price adjustment is *closest* to:
    A.   0.156 to 0.714.
    B.   0.395 to 0.475.
    C.   0.402 to 0.468.

	Null Hypothesis	Conclusion about b_j (0.05 Level of Significance)
A	H_0: $b_j = 0.5$	Reject H_0
B	H_0: $b_j \geq 0.5$	Fail to reject H_0
C	H_0: $b_j \geq 0.5$	Reject H_0

19. The *most* appropriate null hypothesis and the *most* appropriate conclusion regarding Hansen's belief about the magnitude of the initial return relative to that of the pre-offer price adjustment (reflected by the coefficient b_j) are:

20. The *most* appropriate interpretation of the multiple R-squared for Hansen's model is that:
    A. unexplained variation in the dependent variable is 36 percent of total variation.
    B. correlation between predicted and actual values of the dependent variable is 0.36.
    C. correlation between predicted and actual values of the dependent variable is 0.60.

21. Is Chang's Statement 1 correct?
    A. Yes.
    B. No, because the model's F-statistic will not be biased.
    C. No, because the model's t-statistics will not be biased.

22. Is Chang's Statement 2 correct?
    A. Yes.
    B. No, because the model's coefficient estimates will be unbiased.
    C. No, because the model's coefficient estimates will be consistent.

The following information relates to Questions 23–28

Adele Chiesa is a money manager for the Bianco Fund. She is interested in recent findings showing that certain business condition variables predict excess US stock market returns (one-month market return minus one-month T-bill return). She is also familiar with evidence showing how US stock market returns differ by the political party affiliation of the US president. Chiesa estimates a multiple regression model to predict monthly excess stock market returns accounting for business conditions and the political party affiliation of the US president:

Excess stock market return$_t$ = a_0 + a_1Default spread$_{t-1}$ + a_2Term spread$_{t-1}$ + a_3Pres party dummy$_{t-1}$ + e_t

Default spread is equal to the yield on Baa bonds minus the yield on Aaa bonds. Term spread is equal to the yield on a 10-year constant-maturity US Treasury index minus the yield on a 1-year constant-maturity US Treasury index. Pres party dummy is equal to 1 if the US president is a member of the Democratic Party and 0 if a member of the Republican Party.

Chiesa collects 432 months of data (all data are in percent form, i.e., 0.01 = 1 percent). The regression is estimated with 431 observations because the independent variables are lagged one month. The regression output is in Exhibit 1. Exhibits 2 through 5 contain critical values for selected test statistics.

EXHIBIT 1   Multiple Regression Output (the Dependent Variable Is the One-Month Market Return in Excess of the One-Month T-Bill Return)

	Coefficient	t-Statistic	p-Value
Intercept	−4.60	−4.36	<0.01
Default spread$_{t-1}$	3.04	4.52	<0.01
Term spread$_{t-1}$	0.84	3.41	<0.01
Pres party dummy$_{t-1}$	3.17	4.97	<0.01
Number of observations		431	
Test statistic from Breusch–Pagan (BP) test		7.35	
R^2		0.053	
Adjusted R^2		0.046	
Durbin–Watson (DW)		1.65	
Sum of squared errors (SSE)		19,048	
Regression sum of squares (SSR)		1,071	

An intern working for Chiesa has a number of questions about the results in Exhibit 1:

Question 1.   How do you test to determine whether the overall regression model is significant?

Question 2.   Does the estimated model conform to standard regression assumptions? For instance, is the error term serially correlated, or is there conditional heteroskedasticity?

Question 3.   How do you interpret the coefficient for the Pres party dummy variable?

Question 4.   Default spread appears to be quite important. Is there some way to assess the precision of its estimated coefficient? What is the economic interpretation of this variable?

After responding to her intern's questions, Chiesa concludes with the following statement: "Predictions from Exhibit 1 are subject to parameter estimate uncertainty, but not regression model uncertainty."

EXHIBIT 2   Critical Values for the Durbin–Watson Statistic ($\alpha = 0.05$)

N	K = 3	
	d_l	d_u
420	1.825	1.854
430	1.827	1.855
440	1.829	1.857

EXHIBIT 3　Table of the Student's t-Distribution (One-Tailed Probabilities for DF $= \infty$)

P	t
0.10	1.282
0.05	1.645
0.025	1.960
0.01	2.326

EXHIBIT 4　Values of χ^2

	Probability in Right Tail			
DF	0.975	0.95	0.05	0.025
1	0.0001	0.0039	3.841	5.024
2	0.0506	0.1026	5.991	7.378
3	0.2158	0.3518	7.815	9.348
4	0.4840	0.7110	9.488	11.14

EXHIBIT 5　Table of the F-Distribution (Critical Values for Right-Hand Tail Area Equal to 0.05) Numerator: DF1 and Denominator: DF2

	DF1				
DF2	1	2	3	4	427
1	161	200	216	225	254
2	18.51	19.00	19.16	19.25	19.49
3	10.13	9.55	9.28	9.12	8.53
4	7.71	6.94	6.59	6.39	5.64
427	3.86	3.02	2.63	2.39	1.17

23. Regarding the intern's Question 1, is the regression model as a whole significant at the 0.05 level?
    A. No, because the calculated F-statistic is less than the critical value for F.
    B. Yes, because the calculated F-statistic is greater than the critical value for F.
    C. Yes, because the calculated χ^2 statistic is greater than the critical value for χ^2.

24. Which of the following is Chiesa's *best* response to Question 2 regarding serial correlation in the error term? At a 0.05 level of significance, the test for serial correlation indicates that there is:
    A. no serial correlation in the error term.
    B. positive serial correlation in the error term.
    C. negative serial correlation in the error term.

25. Regarding Question 3, the Pres party dummy variable in the model indicates that the mean monthly value for the excess stock market return is:
    A. 1.43 percent larger during Democratic presidencies than Republican presidencies.
    B. 3.17 percent larger during Democratic presidencies than Republican presidencies.
    C. 3.17 percent larger during Republican presidencies than Democratic presidencies.

26. In response to Question 4, the 95 percent confidence interval for the regression coefficient for the default spread is *closest* to:
    A. 0.13 to 5.95.
    B. 1.72 to 4.36.
    C. 1.93 to 4.15.

27. With respect to the default spread, the estimated model indicates that when business conditions are:
    A. strong, expected excess returns will be higher.
    B. weak, expected excess returns will be lower.
    C. weak, expected excess returns will be higher.

28. Is Chiesa's concluding statement correct regarding parameter estimate uncertainty and regression model uncertainty?
    A. Yes.
    B. No, predictions are not subject to parameter estimate uncertainty.
    C. No, predictions are subject to regression model uncertainty and parameter estimate uncertainty.

The following information relates to Questions 29–36

Doris Honoré is a securities analyst with a large wealth management firm. She and her colleague Bill Smith are addressing three research topics: how investment fund characteristics affect fund total returns, whether a fund rating system helps predict fund returns, and whether stock and bond market returns explain the returns of a portfolio of utility shares run by the firm.

To explore the first topic, Honoré decides to study US mutual funds using a sample of 555 large-cap US equity funds. The sample includes funds in style classes of value, growth, and blend (i.e., combining value and growth characteristics). The dependent variable is the average annualized rate of return (in percent) over the past five years. The independent variables are fund expense ratio, portfolio turnover, the natural logarithm of fund size, fund age, and three dummy variables. The multiple manager dummy variable has a value of 1 if the fund has multiple managers (and a value of 0 if it has a single manager). The fund style is indicated by a growth dummy (value of 1 for growth funds and 0 otherwise) and a blend dummy (value of 1 for blend funds and 0 otherwise). If the growth and blend dummies are both zero, the fund is a value fund. The regression output is given in Exhibit 1.

EXHIBIT 1   Multiple Regression Output for Large-Cap Mutual Fund Sample

	Coefficient	Standard Error	t-Statistic
Intercept	10.9375	1.3578	8.0551
Expense ratio (%)	−1.4839	0.2282	−6.5039
Portfolio turnover (%)	0.0017	0.0016	1.0777
ln (fund size in $)	0.1467	0.0612	2.3976
Manager tenure (years)	−0.0098	0.0102	−0.9580
Multiple manager dummy	0.0628	0.1533	0.4100
Fund age (years)	−0.0123	0.0047	−2.6279
Growth dummy	2.4368	0.1886	12.9185
Blend dummy	0.5757	0.1881	3.0611

ANOVA	DF	SS	MSS
Regression	8	714.169	89.2712
Residual	546	1583.113	2.8995
Total	554	2297.282	

Multiple R	0.5576
R^2	0.3109
Adjusted R^2	0.3008
Standard error (%)	1.7028
Observations	555

Based on the results shown in Exhibit 1, Honoré wants to test the hypothesis that all of the regression coefficients are equal to zero. For the 555 fund sample, she also wants to compare the performance of growth funds with the value funds.

Honoré is concerned about the possible presence of multicollinearity in the regression. She states that adding a new independent variable that is highly correlated with one or more independent variables already in the regression model, has three potential consequences:

1. The R^2 is expected to decline.
2. The regression coefficient estimates can become imprecise and unreliable.
3. The standard errors for some or all of the regression coefficients will become inflated.

Another concern for the regression model (in Exhibit 1) is conditional heteroskedasticity. Honoré is concerned that the presence of heteroskedasticity can cause both the F-test for the overall significance of the regression and the t-tests for significance of individual regression coefficients to be unreliable. She runs a regression of the squared residuals from the model in Exhibit 1 on the eight independent variables, and finds the R^2 is 0.0669.

As a second research project, Honoré wants to test whether including Morningstar's rating system, which assigns a one- through five-star rating to a fund, as an independent variable will improve the predictive power of the regression model. To do this, she needs to examine whether values of the independent variables in a given period predict fund return in the next period. Smith suggests three different methods of adding the Morningstar ratings to the model:

- Method 1: Add an independent variable that has a value equal to the number of stars in the rating of each fund.
- Method 2: Add five dummy variables, one for each rating.
- Method 3: Add dummy variables for four of the five ratings.

As a third research project, Honoré wants to establish whether bond market returns (proxied by returns of long-term US Treasuries) and stock market returns (proxied by returns of the S&P 500 Index) explain the returns of a portfolio of utility stocks being recommended to clients. Exhibit 2 presents the results of a regression of 10 years of monthly percentage total returns for the utility portfolio on monthly total returns for US Treasuries and the S&P 500.

EXHIBIT 2   Regression Analysis of Utility Portfolio Returns

	Coefficient	Standard Error	t-Statistic	p-Value
Intercept	−0.0851	0.2829	−0.3008	0.7641
US Treasury	0.4194	0.0848	4.9474	<0.0001
S&P 500	0.6198	0.0666	9.3126	<0.0001

ANOVA	DF	SS	MSS	F	Significance F
Regression	2	827.48	413.74	46.28	<0.0001
Residual	117	1045.93	8.94		
Total	119	1873.41			

Multiple R	0.6646
R^2	0.4417
Adjusted R^2	0.4322
Standard error (%)	2.99
Observations	120

For the time-series model in Exhibit 2, Honoré says that positive serial correlation would not require that the estimated coefficients be adjusted, but that the standard errors of the regression coefficients would be underestimated. This issue would cause the t-statistics of the regression coefficients to be inflated. Honoré tests the null hypothesis that the there is no serial correlation in the regression residuals and finds that the Durbin–Watson statistic is equal to 1.81. The critical values at the 0.05 significance level for the Durbin–Watson statistic are $d_l = 1.63$ and $d_u = 1.72$.

Smith asks whether Honoré should have estimated the models in Exhibit 1 and Exhibit 2 using a probit or logit model instead of using a traditional regression analysis.

29. Considering Exhibit 1, the F-statistic is closest to:
    A.   3.22.
    B.   8.06.
    C.   30.79.

30. Based on Exhibit 1, the difference between the predicted annualized returns of a growth
fund and an otherwise similar value fund is *closest* to:
A. 1.86%.
B. 2.44%.
C. 3.01%.

31. Honoré describes three potential consequences of multicollinearity. Are all three
consequences correct?
A. Yes
B. No, 1 is incorrect
C. No, 2 is incorrect

32. Which of the three methods suggested by Smith would *best* capture the ability of the
Morningstar rating system to predict mutual fund performance?
A. Method 1
B. Method 2
C. Method 3

33. Honoré is concerned about the consequences of heteroskedasticity. Is she correct
regarding the effect of heteroskedasticity on the reliability of the *F*-test and *t*-tests?
A. Yes
B. No, she is incorrect with regard to the *F*-test
C. No, she is incorrect with regard to the *t*-tests

34. Is Honoré's description of the effects of positive serial correlation (in Exhibit 2) correct
regarding the estimated coefficients and the standard errors?
A. Yes
B. No, she is incorrect about only the estimated coefficients
C. No, she is incorrect about only the standard errors of the regression coefficients

35. Based on her estimated Durbin–Watson statistic, Honoré should:
A. fail to reject the null hypothesis.
B. reject the null hypothesis because there is significant positive serial correlation.
C. reject the null hypothesis because there is significant negative serial correlation.

36. Should Honoré have estimated the models in Exhibit 1 and Exhibit 2 using probit or
logit models instead of traditional regression analysis?
A. Both should be estimated with probit or logit models.
B. Neither should be estimated with probit or logit models.
C. Only the analysis in Exhibit 1 should be done with probit or logit models.

The following information relates to Questions 37–45

Brad Varden, a junior analyst at an actively managed mutual fund, is responsible for research
on a subset of the 500 large-cap equities the fund follows. Recently, the fund has been paying
close attention to management turnover and to publicly available environmental, social, and
governance (ESG) ratings. Varden is given the task of investigating whether any significant
relationship exists between a company's profitability and either of these two characteristics.
Colleen Quinni, a senior analyst at the fund, suggests that as an initial step in his

investigation, Varden should perform a multiple regression analysis on the variables and report back to her.

Varden knows that Quinni is an expert at quantitative research, and she once told Varden that after you get an idea, you should formulate a hypothesis, test the hypothesis, and analyze the results. Varden expects to find that ESG rating is negatively related to ROE and CEO tenure is positively related to ROE. He considers a relationship meaningful when it is statistically significant at the 0.05 level. To begin, Varden collects values for ROE, CEO tenure, and ESG rating for a sample of 40 companies from the large-cap security universe. He performs a multiple regression with ROE (in percent) as the dependent variable and ESG rating and CEO tenure (in years) as the independent variables: $Y_i = b_0 + b_1 X_{1i} + b_2 X_{2i} + \varepsilon_i$.

Exhibit 1 shows the regression results.

EXHIBIT 1   Regression Statistics

$\widehat{Y}_i = 9.442 + 0.069X_{1i} + 0.681X_{2i}$

	Coefficient	Standard Error	t-Statistic	p-Value
Intercept	9.442	3.343	2.824	0.008
b_1 (ESG variable)	0.069	0.058	1.201	0.238
b_2 (Tenure variable)	0.681	0.295	2.308	0.027

ANOVA	DF	SS	MSS	F	Significance F
Regression	2	240.410	120.205	4.161	0.023
Residual	37	1069.000	28.892		
Total	39	1309.410			

Multiple R	0.428
R^2	0.183
Adjusted R^2	0.139
Standard error (%)	5.375
Observations	40

DF Associates is one of the companies Varden follows. He wants to predict its ROE using his regression model. DF Associates' corporate ESG rating is 55, and the company's CEO has been in that position for 10.5 years.

Varden also wants to check on the relationship between these variables and the dividend growth rate (divgr), so he completes the correlation matrix shown in Exhibit 2.

EXHIBIT 2   Correlation Matrix

	ROE	ESG	Tenure	Divgr
ROE	1.0			
ESG	0.446	1.0		
Tenure	0.369	0.091	1.0	
Divgr	0.117	0.046	0.028	1.0

Investigating further, Varden determines that dividend growth is not a linear combination of CEO tenure and ESG rating. He is unclear about how additional independent variables would affect the significance of the regression, so he asks Quinni, "Given this correlation matrix, will both R^2 and adjusted R^2 automatically increase if I add dividend growth as a third independent variable?"

The discussion continues, and Quinni asks two questions.

1. What does your F-statistic of 4.161 tell you about the regression?
2. In interpreting the overall significance of your regression model, which statistic do you believe is most relevant: R^2, adjusted R^2, or the F-statistic?

Varden answers both questions correctly and says he wants to check two more ideas. He believes the following:

1. ROE is less correlated with the dividend growth rate in firms whose CEO has been in office more than 15 years, and
2. CEO tenure is a normally distributed random variable.

Later, Varden includes the dividend growth rate as a third independent variable and runs the regression on the fund's entire group of 500 large-cap equities. He finds that the adjusted R^2 is much higher than the results in Exhibit 1. He reports this to Quinni and says, "Adding the dividend growth rate gives a model with a higher adjusted R^2. The three-variable model is clearly better." Quinni cautions, "I don't think you can conclude that yet."

37. Based on Exhibit 1 and given Varden's expectations, which is the *best* null hypothesis and conclusion regarding CEO tenure?
    A. $b_2 \leq 0$; reject the null hypothesis
    B. $b_2 = 0$; cannot reject the null hypothesis
    C. $b_2 \geq 0$; reject the null hypothesis

38. At a significance level of 1%, which of the following is the *best* interpretation of the regression coefficients with regard to explaining ROE?
    A. ESG is significant, but tenure is not.
    B. Tenure is significant, but ESG is not.
    C. Neither ESG nor tenure is significant.

39. Based on Exhibit 1, which independent variables in Varden's model are significant at the 0.05 level?
    A. ESG only
    B. Tenure only
    C. Neither ESG nor tenure

40. Based on Exhibit 1, the predicted ROE for DF Associates is *closest* to:
    A. 10.957%.
    B. 16.593%.
    C. 20.388%.

41. Based on Exhibit 2, Quinni's *best* answer to Varden's question about the effect of adding a third independent variable is:
    A. no for R^2 and no for adjusted R^2.
    B. yes for R^2 and no for adjusted R^2.
    C. yes for R^2 and yes for adjusted R^2.

42. Based on Exhibit 1, Varden's *best* answer to Quinni's question about the *F*-statistic is:
    A. both independent variables are significant at the 0.05 level.
    B. neither independent variable is significant at the 0.05 level.
    C. at least one independent variable is significant at the 0.05 level.

43. Varden's *best* answer to Quinni's question about overall significance is:
    A. R^2.
    B. adjusted R^2.
    C. the *F*-statistic.

44. If Varden's beliefs about ROE and CEO tenure are true, which of the following would violate the assumptions of multiple regression analysis?
    A. The assumption about CEO tenure distribution only
    B. The assumption about the ROE/dividend growth correlation only
    C. The assumptions about both the ROE/dividend growth correlation and CEO tenure distribution

45. The *best* rationale for Quinni's caution about the three-variable model is that the:
    A. dependent variable is defined differently.
    B. sample sizes are different in the two models.
    C. dividend growth rate is positively correlated with the other independent variables.

CHAPTER 9

TIME-SERIES ANALYSIS

Richard A. DeFusco, PhD, CFA

Dennis W. McLeavey, DBA, CFA

Jerald E. Pinto, PhD, CFA

David E. Runkle, PhD, CFA

LEARNING OUTCOMES

The candidate should be able to:

- calculate and evaluate the predicted trend value for a time series, modeled as either a linear trend or a log-linear trend, given the estimated trend coefficients;
- describe factors that determine whether a linear or a log-linear trend should be used with a particular time series and evaluate limitations of trend models;
- explain the requirement for a time series to be covariance stationary and describe the significance of a series that is not stationary;
- describe the structure of an autoregressive (AR) model of order p and calculate one- and two-period-ahead forecasts given the estimated coefficients;
- explain how autocorrelations of the residuals can be used to test whether the autoregressive model fits the time series;
- explain mean reversion and calculate a mean-reverting level;
- contrast in-sample and out-of-sample forecasts and compare the forecasting accuracy of different time-series models based on the root mean squared error criterion;
- explain the instability of coefficients of time-series models;
- describe characteristics of random walk processes and contrast them to covariance stationary processes;
- describe implications of unit roots for time-series analysis, explain when unit roots are likely to occur and how to test for them, and demonstrate how a time series with a unit root can be transformed so it can be analyzed with an AR model;
- describe the steps of the unit root test for nonstationarity and explain the relation of the test to autoregressive time-series models;

Quantitative Methods for Investment Analysis, Second Edition, by Richard A. DeFusco, PhD, CFA, Dennis W. McLeavey, DBA, CFA, Jerald E. Pinto, PhD, CFA, and David E. Runkle, PhD, CFA. Copyright © 2015 by CFA Institute.

- explain how to test and correct for seasonality in a time-series model and calculate and interpret a forecasted value using an AR model with a seasonal lag;
- explain autoregressive conditional heteroskedasticity (ARCH) and describe how ARCH models can be applied to predict the variance of a time series;
- explain how time-series variables should be analyzed for nonstationarity and/or cointegration before use in a linear regression; and
- determine an appropriate time-series model to analyze a given investment problem and justify that choice.

1. INTRODUCTION TO TIME-SERIES ANALYSIS

As financial analysts, we often use time-series data to make investment decisions. A **time series** is a set of observations on a variable's outcomes in different time periods: the quarterly sales for a particular company during the past five years, for example, or the daily returns on a traded security. In this chapter, we explore the two chief uses of time-series models: to explain the past and to predict the future of a time series. We also discuss how to estimate time-series models, and we examine how a model describing a particular time series can change over time. The following two examples illustrate the kinds of questions we might want to ask about time series.

Suppose it is the beginning of 2020 and we are managing a US-based investment portfolio that includes Swiss stocks. Because the value of this portfolio would decrease if the Swiss franc depreciates with respect to the dollar, and vice versa, holding all else constant, we are considering whether to hedge the portfolio's exposure to changes in the value of the franc.

EXHIBIT 1   Swiss Franc/US Dollar Exchange Rate, Monthly Average of Daily Data

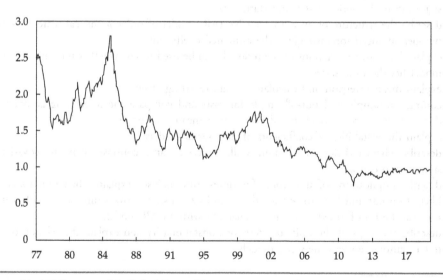

Source: Board of Governors of the Federal Reserve System.

To help us in making this decision, we decide to model the time series of the franc/dollar exchange rate. Exhibit 1 shows monthly data on the franc/dollar exchange rate. The data are monthly averages of daily exchange rates. Has the exchange rate been more stable since 1987 than it was in previous years? Has the exchange rate shown a long-term trend? How can we best use past exchange rates to predict future exchange rates?

As another example, suppose it is the beginning of 2020. We cover retail stores for a sell-side firm and want to predict retail sales for the coming year. Exhibit 2 shows monthly data on US retail sales. The data are not seasonally adjusted, hence the spikes around the holiday season at the turn of each year. Because the reported sales in the stores' financial statements are not seasonally adjusted, we model seasonally unadjusted retail sales. How can we model the trend in retail sales? How can we adjust for the extreme seasonality reflected in the peaks and troughs occurring at regular intervals? How can we best use past retail sales to predict future retail sales?

Some fundamental questions arise in time-series analysis: How do we model trends? How do we predict the future value of a time series based on its past values? How do we model seasonality? How do we choose among time-series models? And how do we model changes in the variance of time series over time? We address each of these issues in this chapter.

We first describe typical challenges in applying the linear regression model to time-series data. We present linear and log-linear trend models, which describe, respectively, the value and the natural log of the value of a time series as a linear function of time. We then present autoregressive time-series models—which explain the current value of a time series in terms of one or more lagged values of the series. Such models are among the most commonly used in investments, and the section addresses many related concepts and issues. We then turn our attention to random walks. Because such time series are not covariance stationary, they cannot be modeled using autoregressive models unless they can be transformed into stationary series. We therefore explore appropriate transformations and tests of stationarity. The subsequent sections address moving-average time-series models and discuss the problem of

EXHIBIT 2   Monthly US Retail Sales

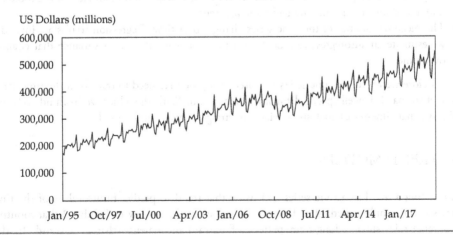

Source: US Department of Commerce, Census Bureau.

seasonality in time series and how to address it. We also cover autoregressive moving-average models, a more complex alternative to autoregressive models. The last two topics are modeling changing variance of the error term in a time series and the consequences of regression of one time series on another when one or both time series may not be covariance stationary.

2. CHALLENGES OF WORKING WITH TIME SERIES

Throughout the chapter, our objective will be to apply linear regression to a given time series. Unfortunately, in working with time series, we often find that the assumptions of the linear regression model are not satisfied. To apply time-series analysis, we need to assure ourselves that the linear regression model assumptions are met. When those assumptions are not satisfied, in many cases we can transform the time series or specify the regression model differently, so that the assumptions of the linear regression model are met.

We can illustrate assumption difficulties in the context of a common time-series model, an autoregressive model. Informally, an autoregressive model is one in which the independent variable is a lagged (that is, past) value of the dependent variable, such as the model $x_t = b_0 + b_1 x_{t-1} + \varepsilon_t$ (we could also write the equation as $y_t = b_0 + b_1 y_{t-1} + \varepsilon_t$). Specific problems that we often encounter in dealing with time series include the following:

- The residual errors are correlated instead of being uncorrelated. In the calculated regression, the difference between x_t and $b_0 + b_1 x_{t-1}$ is called the residual error (ε_t). The linear regression assumes that this error term is not correlated across observations. The violation of that assumption is frequently more critical in terms of its consequences in the case of time-series models involving past values of the time series as independent variables than for other models (such as cross-sectional models) in which the dependent and independent variables are distinct. As we discussed in the chapter on multiple regression (Chapter 8), in a regression in which the dependent and independent variables are distinct, serial correlation of the errors in this model does not affect the consistency of our estimates of intercept or slope coefficients. By contrast, in an autoregressive time-series regression, such as $x_t = b_0 + b_1 x_{t-1} + \varepsilon_t$, serial correlation in the error term causes estimates of the intercept (b_0) and slope coefficient (b_1) to be inconsistent.
- The mean or variance of the time series changes over time. Regression results are invalid if we estimate an autoregressive model for a time series with mean or variance that changes over time.

Before we try to use time series for forecasting, we may need to transform the time-series model so that it is well specified for linear regression. With this objective in mind, you will observe that time-series analysis is relatively straightforward and logical.

3. TREND MODELS

Estimating a trend in a time series and using that trend to predict future values of the time series is the simplest method of forecasting. For example, we saw in Exhibit 2 that monthly US retail sales show a long-term pattern of upward movement—that is, a **trend**. In this section, we examine two types of trends—linear trends and log-linear trends—and discuss how to choose between them.

3.1. Linear Trend Models

The simplest type of trend is a **linear trend**, one in which the dependent variable changes at a constant rate with time. If a time series, y_t, has a linear trend, then we can model the series using the following regression equation:

$$y_t = b_0 + b_1 t + \varepsilon_t, \ t = 1, 2, \ldots, T, \tag{1}$$

where

y_t = the value of the time series at time t (value of the dependent variable)
b_0 = the y-intercept term
b_1 = the slope coefficient
t = time, the independent or explanatory variable
ε_t = a random error term

In Equation 1, the trend line, $b_0 + b_1 t$, predicts the value of the time series at time t (where t takes on a value of 1 in the first period of the sample and increases by 1 in each subsequent period). Because the coefficient b_1 is the slope of the trend line, we refer to b_1 as the trend coefficient. We can estimate the two coefficients, b_0 and b_1, using ordinary least squares, denoting the estimated coefficients as $\widehat{b}_0$ and $\widehat{b}_1$. Recall that ordinary least squares is an estimation method based on the criterion of minimizing the sum of a regression's squared residuals.

Now we demonstrate how to use these estimates to predict the value of the time series in a particular period. Recall that t takes on a value of 1 in Period 1. Therefore, the predicted or fitted value of y_t in Period 1 is $\widehat{y}_1 = \widehat{b}_0 + \widehat{b}_1(1)$. Similarly, in a subsequent period—say, the sixth period—the fitted value is $\widehat{y}_6 = \widehat{b}_0 + \widehat{b}_1(6)$. Now suppose that we want to predict the value of the time series for a period outside the sample—say, period $T + 1$. The predicted value of y_t for period $T + 1$ is $\widehat{y}_{T+1} = \widehat{b}_0 + \widehat{b}_1(T + 1)$. For example, if $\widehat{b}_0$ is 5.1 and $\widehat{b}_1$ is 2, then at $t = 5$ the predicted value of y_5 is 15.1 and at $t = 6$ the predicted value of y_6 is 17.1. Note that each consecutive observation in this time series increases by $\widehat{b}_1 = 2$, irrespective of the level of the series in the previous period.

EXAMPLE 1   The Trend in the US Consumer Price Index

It is January 2020. As a fixed-income analyst in the trust department of a bank, Lisette Miller is concerned about the future level of inflation and how it might affect portfolio value. Therefore, she wants to predict future inflation rates. For this purpose, she first needs to estimate the linear trend in inflation. To do so, she uses the monthly US Consumer Price Index (CPI) inflation data, expressed as an annual percentage rate, (1% is represented as 1.0) shown in Exhibit 3. The data include 228 months from January 1995 through June 2019, and the model to be estimated is $y_t = b_0 + b_1 t + \varepsilon_t, \ t = 1, 2, \ldots, 294$. The table in Exhibit 4 shows the results of estimating this equation. With 294 observations and two parameters, this model has 292 degrees of freedom. At the 0.05 significance level, the critical value for a t-statistic is 1.97. The intercept $(\widehat{b}_0 = 2.7845)$ is statistically significant because the value of the t-statistic for the coefficient is well above the critical value. The trend coefficient is negative

EXHIBIT 3   Monthly CPI Inflation, Not Seasonally Adjusted

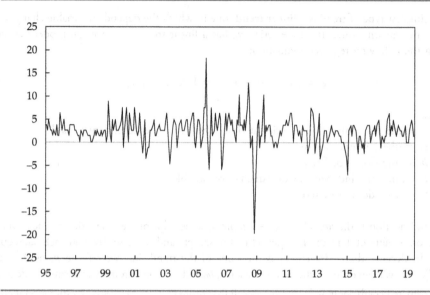

Source: Bureau of Labor Statistics.

$(\widehat{b}_1 = -0.0037)$, suggesting a slightly declining trend in inflation during the sample time period. However, the trend is not statistically significant because the absolute value of the *t*-statistic for the coefficient is below the critical value. The estimated regression equation can be written as

$$y_t = 2.7845 - 0.0037t$$

EXHIBIT 4   Estimating a Linear Trend in Inflation: Monthly Observations, January 1995– June 2019

Regression Statistics

R^2	0.0099		
Standard error	3.1912		
Observations	294		
Durbin–Watson	1.2145		
	Coefficient	**Standard Error**	**t-Statistic**
Intercept	2.7845	0.3732	7.4611
t (Trend)	−0.0037	0.0022	−1.68

Source: US Bureau of Labor Statistics.

Because the trend line slope is estimated to be –0.0037, Miller concludes that the linear trend model's best estimate is that the annualized rate of inflation declined at a rate of about 37 bps per month during the sample time period. The decline is not statistically significantly different from zero.

In January 1995, the first month of the sample, the predicted value of inflation is $\hat{y}_1 = 2.7845 - 0.0037(1) = 2.7808\%$. In June 2019, the 294th, or last, month of the sample, the predicted value of inflation is $\hat{y}_{228} = 2.7845 - 0.0037(294) = 1.697\%$. Note, though, that these predicted values are for in-sample periods. A comparison of these values with the actual values indicates how well Miller's model fits the data; however, a main purpose of the estimated model is to predict the level of inflation for out-of-sample periods. For example, for June 2020 (12 months after the end of the sample), $t = 294 + 12 = 306$, and the predicted level of inflation is $\hat{y}_{306} = 2.7845 - 0.0037(306) = 1.6523\%$.

Exhibit 5 shows the inflation data along with the fitted trend. Consistent with the negative but small and statistically insignificant trend coefficient, the fitted trend line is slightly downward sloping. Note that inflation does not appear to be above or below the trend line for a long period of time. No persistent differences exist between the trend and actual inflation. The residuals (actual minus trend values) appear to be unpredictable and uncorrelated in time. Therefore, using a linear trend line to model inflation rates from 1995 through 2019 does not appear to violate the assumptions of the linear regression model. Note also that the R^2 in this model is quite low, indicating great uncertainty in the inflation forecasts from this model. In fact, the estimated model explains only 0.99% of the variation in monthly inflation. Although linear trend models have their uses, they are often inappropriate for economic data. Most economic

EXHIBIT 5   Monthly CPI Inflation with Trend

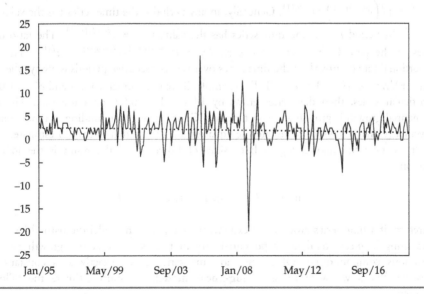

Source: US Bureau of Labor Statistics.

time series reflect trends with changing slopes and/or intercepts over time. The linear trend model identifies the slope and intercept that provides the best linear fit for all past data. The model's deviation from the actual data can be greatest near the end of a data series, which can compromise forecasting accuracy. Later in this chapter, we will examine whether we can build a better model of inflation than a model that uses only a trend line.

3.2. Log-Linear Trend Models

Sometimes a linear trend does not correctly model the growth of a time series. In those cases, we often find that fitting a linear trend to a time series leads to persistent rather than uncorrelated errors. If the residuals from a linear trend model are persistent, then we need to employ an alternative model satisfying the conditions of linear regression. For financial time series, an important alternative to a linear trend is a log-linear trend. Log-linear trends work well in fitting time series that have exponential growth.

Exponential growth means constant growth at a particular rate. For example, annual growth at a constant rate of 5% is exponential growth. How does exponential growth work? Suppose we describe a time series by the following equation:

$$y_t = e^{b_0 + b_1 t}, t = 1, 2, ..., T. \tag{2}$$

Exponential growth is growth at a constant rate $(e^{b_1} - 1)$ with continuous compounding. For instance, consider values of the time series in two consecutive periods. In Period 1, the time series has the value $y_1 = e^{b_0 + b_1(1)}$, and in Period 2, it has the value $y_2 = e^{b_0 + b_1(2)}$. The resulting ratio of the values of the time series in the first two periods is $y_2/y_1 = \left(e^{b_0 + b_1(2)} \right) / \left(e^{b_0 + b_1(1)} \right) = e^{b_1(1)}$. Generally, in any period t, the time series has the value $y_t = e^{b_0 + b_1(t)}$. In period $t + 1$, the time series has the value $y_{t+1} = e^{b_0 + b_1(t+1)}$. The ratio of the values in the periods $(t + 1)$ and t is $y_{t+1}/y_t = e^{b_0 + b_1(t+1)} / e^{b_0 + b_1(t)} = e^{b_1(1)}$. Thus, the proportional rate of growth in the time series over two consecutive periods is always the same: $(y_{t+1} - y_t)/y_t = y_{t+1}/y_t - 1 = e^{b_1} - 1$. For example, if we use annual periods and $e^{b_1} = 1.04$ for a particular series, then that series grows by $1.04 - 1 = 0.04$, or 4% a year. Therefore, exponential growth is growth at a constant rate. Continuous compounding is a mathematical convenience that allows us to restate the equation in a form that is easy to estimate.

If we take the natural log of both sides of Equation 2, the result is the following equation:

$$\ln y_t = b_0 + b_1 t, t = 1, 2, \ldots, T$$

Therefore, if a time series grows at an exponential rate, we can model the natural log of that series using a linear trend (an exponential growth rate is a compound growth rate with continuous compounding). Of course, no time series grows exactly at a constant rate. Consequently, if we want to use a **log-linear model**, we must estimate the following equation:

$$\ln y_t = b_0 + b_1 t + \varepsilon_t, t = 1, 2, \ldots, T. \tag{3}$$

Note that this equation is linear in the coefficients b_0 and b_1. In contrast to a linear trend model, in which the predicted trend value of y_t is $\widehat{b_0} + \widehat{b_1} t$, the predicted trend value of y_t in a log-linear trend model is $e^{\widehat{b_0} + \widehat{b_1} t}$ because $e^{\ln y_t} = y_t$.

Examining Equation 3, we see that a log-linear model predicts that $\ln y_t$ will increase by b_1 from one time period to the next. The model predicts a constant growth rate in y_t of $e^{b_1} - 1$. For example, if $b_1 = 0.05$, then the predicted growth rate of y_t in each period is $e^{0.05} - 1 = 0.051271$, or 5.13%. In contrast, the linear trend model (Equation 1) predicts that y_t grows by a constant amount from one period to the next.

Example 2 illustrates the problem of nonrandom residuals in a linear trend model, and Example 3 shows a log-linear regression fit to the same data.

EXAMPLE 2   A Linear Trend Regression for Quarterly Sales at Starbucks

In September 2019, technology analyst Ray Benedict wants to use Equation 1 to fit the data on quarterly sales for Starbucks Corporation shown in Exhibit 6. Starbucks' fiscal year ends in June. Benedict uses 74 observations on Starbucks' sales from the second quarter of fiscal year 2001 (starting in April 2001) to the third quarter of fiscal year 2019 (ending in June 2019) to estimate the linear trend regression model $y_t = b_0 + b_1 t + \varepsilon_t, t = 1, 2, \ldots, 74$. Exhibit 7 shows the results of estimating this equation.

EXHIBIT 6   Starbucks Quarterly Sales by Fiscal Year

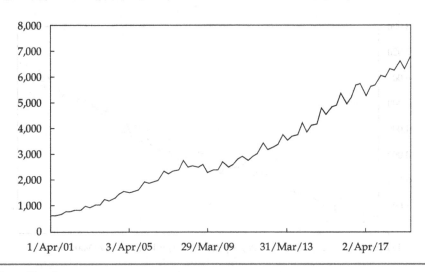

Source: Bloomberg.

EXHIBIT 7   Estimating a Linear Trend in Starbucks Sales

Regression Statistics

R^2	0.9603
Standard error	353.36
Observations	74
Durbin–Watson	0.40

	Coefficient	Standard Error	*t*-Statistic
Intercept	137.4213	82.99	1.6559
t (Trend)	80.2060	1.9231	41.7066

Source: Bloomberg.

At first glance, the results shown in Exhibit 7 seem quite reasonable: The trend coefficient is highly statistically significant. When Benedict plots the data on Starbucks' sales and the trend line, however, he sees a different picture. As Exhibit 8 shows, before 2008 the trend line is persistently below sales. Subsequently, until 2015, the trend line is persistently above sales and then varies somewhat thereafter.

Recall a key assumption underlying the regression model: that the regression errors are not correlated across observations. If a trend is persistently above or below the value of the time series, however, the residuals (the difference between the time series and the trend) are serially correlated. Exhibit 9 shows the residuals (the

EXHIBIT 8   Starbucks Quarterly Sales with Trend

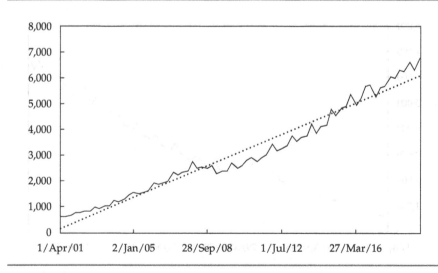

Source: Bloomberg.

EXHIBIT 9   Residual from Predicting Starbucks Sales with a Trend

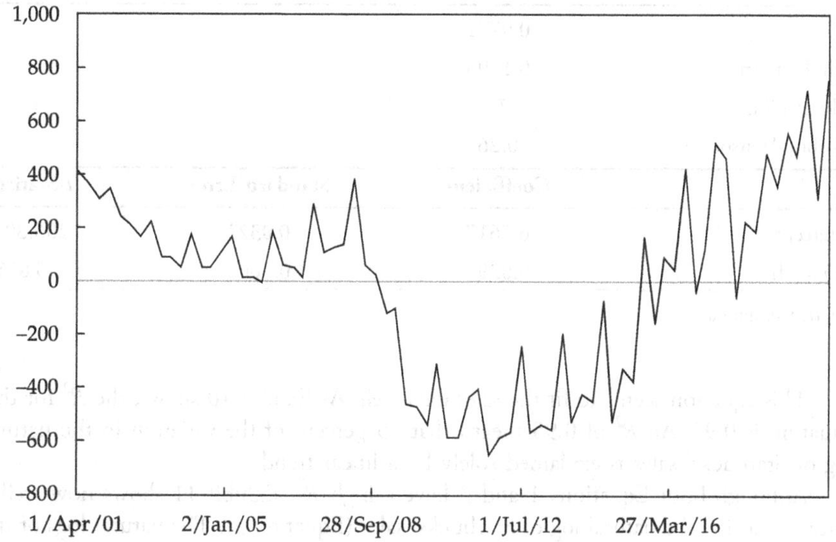

Source: Bloomberg.

difference between sales and the trend) from estimating a linear trend model with the raw sales data. The figure shows that the residuals are persistent: They are consistently negative from 2008 to 2015 and consistently positive from 2001 to 2008 and from 2017 to 2019.

Because of this persistent serial correlation in the errors of the trend model, using a linear trend to fit sales at Starbucks would be inappropriate, even though the R^2 of the equation is high (0.96). The assumption of uncorrelated residual errors has been violated. Because the dependent and independent variables are not distinct, as in cross-sectional regressions, this assumption violation is serious and causes us to search for a better model.

EXAMPLE 3   A Log-Linear Regression for Quarterly Sales at Starbucks

Having rejected a linear trend model in **Example 2**, technology analyst Benedict now tries a different model for the quarterly sales for Starbucks Corporation from the second quarter of 2001 to the third quarter of 2019. The curvature in the data plot shown in Exhibit 6 provides a hint that an exponential curve may fit the data. Consequently, he estimates the following linear equation:

$$\ln y_t = b_0 + b_1 t + \varepsilon_t,\ t = 1, 2, \ldots, 74$$

EXHIBIT 10   Estimating a Linear Trend in Lognormal Starbucks Sales

Regression Statistics

R^2	0.9771
Standard error	0.1393
Observations	74
Durbin–Watson	0.26

	Coefficient	Standard Error	t-Statistic
Intercept	6.7617	0.0327	206.80
t (Trend)	0.0295	0.0008	36.875

Source: Compustat.

This equation seems to fit the sales data well. As Exhibit 10 shows, the R^2 for this equation is 0.95. An R^2 of 0.95 means that 95 percent of the variation in the natural log of Starbucks' sales is explained solely by a linear trend.

Although both Equations 1 and 3 have a high R^2, Exhibit 11 shows how well a linear trend fits the natural log of Starbucks' sales (Equation 3). The natural logs of the sales data lie very close to the linear trend during the sample period, and log sales are not substantially above or below the trend for long periods of time. Thus, a log-linear trend model seems better suited for modeling Starbucks' sales than a linear trend model is.

1. Benedict wants to use the results of estimating Equation 3 to predict Starbucks' sales in the future. What is the predicted value of Starbucks' sales for the fourth quarter of 2019?

EXHIBIT 11   Natural Log of Starbucks Quarterly Sales

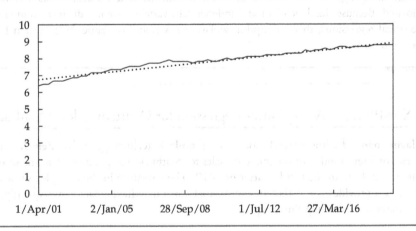

Source: Compustat.

Solution to 1: The estimated value $\hat{b}_0$ is 6.7617, and the estimated value $\hat{b}_1$ is 0.0295. Therefore, for fourth quarter of 2019 ($t = 75$), the estimated model predicts that ln $\hat{y}_{75} = 6.7617 + 0.0295(75) = 8.9742$ and that sales will be $\hat{y} = e^{\ln \hat{y}_{75}} = e^{8.9742} =$ \$7,896.7 million. Note that a $\hat{b}_1$ of 0.0295 implies that the exponential growth rate per quarter in Starbucks' sales will be 2.99475% ($e^{0.0464} - 1 = 0.0299475$).

2. How much different is the previous forecast from the prediction of the linear trend model?

Solution to 2: Exhibit 7 showed that for the linear trend model, the estimated value of $\hat{b}_0$ is 137.4213 and the estimated value of $\hat{b}_1$ is 80.2060. Thus, if we predict Starbucks' sales for the fourth quarter of 2019 ($t = 75$) using the linear trend model, the forecast is $\hat{y}_{75} = 137.4213 + 80.2060(75) = \$6,152.87$ million. This forecast is far below the prediction made by the log-linear regression model. Later we will examine whether we can build a better model of Starbucks' quarterly sales than a model that uses only a log-linear trend.

3.3. Trend Models and Testing for Correlated Errors

Both the linear trend model and the log-linear trend model are single-variable regression models. If they are to be correctly specified, the regression model assumptions must be satisfied. In particular, the regression error for one period must be uncorrelated with the regression error for all other periods. In **Example 2** in the previous section, we could infer an obvious violation of that assumption from a visual inspection of a plot of residuals (Exhibit 9). The log-linear trend model of **Example 3** appeared to fit the data much better, but we still need to confirm that the uncorrelated errors assumption is satisfied. To address that question formally, we must carry out a Durbin–Watson test on the residuals.

Logical Ordering of Time-Series Observations

In contrast to cross-sectional observations, time-series observations have a logical ordering. They must be processed in chronological order of the time periods involved. For example, we should not make a prediction of the inflation rate using a CPI series in which the order of the observations had been scrambled, because time patterns such as growth in the independent variables can negatively affect the statistical properties of the estimated regression coefficients.

In the chapter on regression analysis, we showed how to test whether regression errors are serially correlated using the Durbin–Watson statistic. For example, if the trend models shown in **Examples 1** and **3** really capture the time-series behavior of inflation and the log of Starbucks' sales, then the Durbin–Watson statistic for both of those models should not differ significantly from 2.0. Otherwise, the errors in the model are either positively or negatively serially correlated, and that correlation can be used to build a better forecasting model for those time series.

In **Example 1**, estimating a linear trend in the monthly CPI inflation yielded a Durbin–Watson statistic of 1.09. Is this result significantly different from 2.0? To find out, we need to test the null hypothesis of no positive serial correlation. For a sample with 228 observations and one independent variable, the critical value, d_l, for the Durbin–Watson test statistic at the 0.05 significance level is above 1.77. Because the value of the Durbin–Watson statistic (1.09) is below this critical value, we can reject the hypothesis of no positive serial correlation in the errors. (Remember that significantly small values of the Durbin–Watson statistic indicate positive serial correlation; significantly large values point to negative serial correlation; here the Durbin–Watson statistic of 1.09 indicates positive serial correlation.) We can conclude that a regression equation that uses a linear trend to model inflation has positive serial correlation in the errors. We will need a different kind of regression model because this one violates the least squares assumption of no serial correlation in the errors.

In **Example 3**, estimating a linear trend with the natural logarithm of sales for the Starbucks example yielded a Durbin–Watson statistic of 0.12. Suppose we wish to test the null hypothesis of no positive serial correlation. The critical value, d_l, is above 1.60 at the 0.05 significance level. The value of the Durbin–Watson statistic (0.12) is below this critical value, so we can reject the null hypothesis of no positive serial correlation in the errors. We can conclude that a regression equation that uses a trend to model the log of Starbucks' quarterly sales has positive serial correlation in the errors. So, for this series as well, we need to build a different kind of model.

Overall, we conclude that the trend models sometimes have the limitation that errors are serially correlated. Existence of serial correlation suggests that we can build better forecasting models for such time series than trend models.

4. AUTOREGRESSIVE (AR) TIME-SERIES MODELS

A key feature of the log-linear model's depiction of time series, and a key feature of time series in general, is that current-period values are related to previous-period values. For example, Starbucks' sales for the current period are related to its sales in the previous period. An **autoregressive model (AR)**, a time series regressed on its own past values, represents this relationship effectively. When we use this model, we can drop the normal notation of y as the dependent variable and x as the independent variable because we no longer have that distinction to make. Here we simply use x_t. For example, Equation 4 shows a first-order autoregression, AR(1), for the variable x_t:

$$x_t = b_0 + b_1 x_{t-1} + \varepsilon_t. \tag{4}$$

Thus, in an AR(1) model, we use only the most recent past value of x_t to predict the current value of x_t. In general, a pth-order autoregression, AR(p), for the variable x_t is shown by

$$x_t = b_0 + b_1 x_{t-1} + b_2 x_{t-2} + \ldots + b_p x_{t-p} + \varepsilon_t. \tag{5}$$

In this equation, p past values of x_t are used to predict the current value of x_t. In the next section, we discuss a key assumption of time-series models that include lagged values of the dependent variable as independent variables.

4.1. Covariance-Stationary Series

Note that the independent variable (x_{t-1}) in Equation 4 is a random variable. This fact may seem like a mathematical subtlety, but it is not. If we use ordinary least squares to estimate Equation 4 when we have a randomly distributed independent variable that is a lagged value of the dependent variable, our statistical inference may be invalid. To make a valid statistical inference, we must make a key assumption in time-series analysis: We must assume that the time series we are modeling is **covariance stationary**.[1]

What does it mean for a time series to be covariance stationary? The basic idea is that a time series is covariance stationary if its properties, such as mean and variance, do not change over time. A covariance stationary series must satisfy three principal requirements. First, the expected value of the time series must be constant and finite in all periods: $E(y_t) = \mu$ and $|\mu| < \infty$, $t = 1, 2, \ldots, T$ (for this first requirement, we use the absolute value to rule out the case in which the mean is negative without limit—i.e., minus infinity). Second, the variance of the time series must be constant and finite in all periods. Third, the covariance of the time series with itself for a fixed number of periods in the past or future must be constant and finite in all periods. The second and third requirements can be summarized as follows:

$$\text{cov}(y_t, y_{t-s}) = \lambda_s; \ |\lambda_s| < \infty; \ t = 1, 2, \ldots, T; \ s = 0, \pm 1, \pm 2, \ldots, \pm T$$

where λ signifies a constant. (Note that when s in this equation equals 0, this equation imposes the condition that the variance of the time series is finite, because the covariance of a random variable with itself is its variance: $\text{cov}(y_t, y_t) = \text{var}(y_t)$.) What happens if a time series is not covariance stationary but we model it using Equation 4? The estimation results will have no economic meaning. For a non-covariance-stationary time series, estimating the regression in Equation 4 will yield spurious results. In particular, the estimate of b_1 will be biased, and any hypothesis tests will be invalid.

How can we tell if a time series is covariance stationary? We can often answer this question by looking at a plot of the time series. If the plot shows roughly the same mean and variance over time without any significant seasonality, then we may want to assume that the time series is covariance stationary.

Some of the time series we looked at in the exhibits appear to be covariance stationary. For example, the inflation data shown in Exhibit 3 appear to have roughly the same mean and variance over the sample period. Many of the time series one encounters in business and investments, however, are not covariance stationary. For example, many time series appear to grow (or decline) steadily over time and thus have a mean that is nonconstant, which implies that they are nonstationary. As an example, the time series of quarterly sales in Exhibit 8 clearly shows the mean increasing as time passes. Thus, Starbucks' quarterly sales are not covariance stationary (in general, any time series accurately described with a linear or

---

[1]"Weakly stationary" is a synonym for covariance stationary. Note that the terms "stationary" and "stationarity" are often used to mean "covariance stationary" or "covariance stationarity," respectively. You may also encounter the more restrictive concept of "strictly" stationary, which has little practical application. For details, see Diebold (2008).

log-linear trend model is not covariance stationary, although a transformation of the original series might be covariance stationary). Macroeconomic time series such as those relating to income and consumption are often strongly trending as well. A time series with seasonality (regular patterns of movement with the year) also has a nonconstant mean, as do other types of time series that we discuss later (in particular, random walks are not covariance stationary).

Exhibit 2 showed that monthly retail sales (not seasonally adjusted) are also not covariance stationary. Sales in December are always much higher than sales in other months (these are the regular large peaks), and sales in January are always much lower (these are the regular large drops after the December peaks). On average, sales also increase over time, so the mean of sales is not constant.

Later we will show that we can often transform a nonstationary time series into a stationary time series. But whether a stationary time series is original or transformed, a warning is necessary: Stationarity in the past does not guarantee stationarity in the future. There is always the possibility that a well-specified model will fail when the state of the world changes and yields a different underlying model that generates the time series.

4.2. Detecting Serially Correlated Errors in an Autoregressive Model

We can estimate an autoregressive model using ordinary least squares if the time series is covariance stationary and the errors are uncorrelated. Unfortunately, our previous test for serial correlation, the Durbin–Watson statistic, is invalid when the independent variables include past values of the dependent variable. Therefore, for most time-series models, we cannot use the Durbin–Watson statistic. Fortunately, we can use other tests to determine whether the errors in a time-series model are serially correlated. One such test reveals whether the autocorrelations of the error term are significantly different from 0. This test is a t-test involving a residual autocorrelation and the standard error of the residual autocorrelation. As background for the test, we next discuss autocorrelation in general before moving to residual autocorrelation.

The **autocorrelations** of a time series are the correlations of that series with its own past values. The order of the correlation is given by k, where k represents the number of periods lagged. When $k = 1$, the autocorrelation shows the correlation of the variable in one period with its occurrence in the previous period. For example, the **kth-order autocorrelation** (ρ_k) is

$$\rho_k = \frac{\text{cov}(x_t, x_{t-k})}{\sigma_x^2} = \frac{E[(x_t - \mu)(x_{t-k} - \mu)]}{\sigma_x^2}$$

where E stands for the expected value. Note that we have the relationship $\text{cov}(x_t, x_{t-k}) \leq \sigma_x^2$, with equality holding when $k = 0$. This means that the absolute value of ρ_k is less than or equal to 1.

Of course, we can never directly observe the autocorrelations, ρ_k. Instead, we must estimate them. Thus, we replace the expected value of x_t, μ, with its estimated value, $\bar{x}$, to compute the estimated autocorrelations. The kth-order estimated autocorrelation of the time series x_t, which we denote $\hat{\rho}_k$, is

$$\hat{\rho}_k = \frac{\sum_{t=k+1}^{T} [(x_t - \bar{x})(x_{t-k} - \bar{x})]}{\sum_{t=1}^{T} (x_t - \bar{x})^2}$$

Analogous to the definition of autocorrelations for a time series, we can define the autocorrelations of the error term for a time-series model as[2]

$$\begin{aligned} \rho_{\varepsilon,k} &= \frac{\text{cov}(\varepsilon_t, \varepsilon_{t-k})}{\sigma_\varepsilon^2} \\ &= \frac{E[(\varepsilon_t - 0)(\varepsilon_{t-k} - 0)]}{\sigma_\varepsilon^2} \\ &= \frac{E(\varepsilon_t \varepsilon_{t-k})}{\sigma_\varepsilon^2} \end{aligned}$$

We assume that the expected value of the error term in a time-series model is 0.[3]

We can determine whether we are using the correct time-series model by testing whether the autocorrelations of the error term (**error autocorrelations**) differ significantly from 0. If they do, the model is not specified correctly. We estimate the error autocorrelation using the sample autocorrelations of the residuals (**residual autocorrelations**) and their sample variance.

A test of the null hypothesis that an error autocorrelation at a specified lag equals 0 is based on the residual autocorrelation for that lag and the standard error of the residual correlation, which is equal to $1/\sqrt{T}$, where T is the number of observations in the time series (Diebold 2008). Thus, if we have 100 observations in a time series, the standard error for each of the estimated autocorrelations is 0.1. We can compute the t-test of the null hypothesis that the error correlation at a particular lag equals 0 by dividing the residual autocorrelation at that lag by its standard error $(1/\sqrt{T})$.

How can we use information about the error autocorrelations to determine whether an autoregressive time-series model is correctly specified? We can use a simple three-step method. First, estimate a particular autoregressive model—say, an AR(1) model. Second, compute the autocorrelations of the residuals from the model.[4] Third, test to see whether the residual autocorrelations differ significantly from 0. If significance tests show that the residual autocorrelations differ significantly from 0, the model is not correctly specified; we may need to modify it in ways that we will discuss shortly.[5] We now present an example to demonstrate how this three-step method works.

---

[2]Whenever we refer to autocorrelation without qualification, we mean autocorrelation of the time series itself rather than autocorrelation of the error term or residuals.

[3]This assumption is similar to the one made in earlier coverage of regression analysis about the expected value of the error term.

[4]We can compute these residual autocorrelations easily with most statistical software packages. In Microsoft Excel, for example, to compute the first-order residual autocorrelation, we compute the correlation of the residuals from Observations 1 through $T - 1$ with the residuals from Observations 2 through T.

[5]Often, econometricians use additional tests for the significance of residual autocorrelations. For example, the Box–Pierce Q-statistic is frequently used to test the joint hypothesis that all autocorrelations of the residuals are equal to 0. For further discussion, see Diebold (2008).

EXAMPLE 4   Predicting Gross Margins for Intel Corporation

Analyst Melissa Jones decides to use a time-series model to predict Intel Corporation's gross margin [(Sales − Cost of goods sold)/Sales] using quarterly data from the first quarter of 1999 through the second quarter of 2019. She does not know the best model for gross margin but believes that the current-period value will be related to the previous-period value. She decides to start out with a first-order autoregressive model, AR(1): Gross margin$_t$ = b_0 + b_1(Gross margin$_{t-1}$) + ε_t. Her observations on the dependent variable are 1Q 2003 through 2Q 2019. Exhibit 12 shows the results of estimating this AR(1) model, along with the autocorrelations of the residuals from that model.

The first thing to note about Exhibit 12 is that both the intercept ($\hat{b}_0$ = 0.1513) and the coefficient on the first lag ($\hat{b}_1$ = 0.7462) of the gross margin are highly significant in the regression equation. The first lag of a time series is the value of the time series in the previous period. The t-statistic for the intercept is about 3.2, whereas the t-statistic for the first lag of the gross margin is more than 9. With 65 observations and two parameters, this model has 63 degrees of freedom. At the 0.05 significance level, the critical value for a t-statistic is about 2.0. Therefore, Jones must reject the null hypotheses that the intercept is equal to 0 (b_0 = 0) and the coefficient on the first lag is equal to 0 (b_1 = 0) in favor of the alternative hypothesis that the coefficients, individually, are not equal to 0. But are these statistics valid? Although the Durbin–Watson statistic is presented in Exhibit 12, it cannot be used to test serial correlation

EXHIBIT 12   Autoregression: AR(1) Model Gross Margin of Intel Quarterly Observations, January 2003–June 2019

Regression Statistics

R^2	0.5746
Standard error	0.03002
Observations	65
Durbin–Watson	1.743

	Coefficient	Standard Error	t-Statistic
Intercept	0.1513	0.0480	3.15
Gross margin$_{t-1}$	0.7462	0.0809	9.2236

Autocorrelations of the Residual

Lag	Autocorrelation	Standard Error	t-Statistic
1	0.1308	0.1240	1.0545
2	−0.2086	0.1240	−1.6818
3	0.0382	0.1240	0.3080
4	0.0608	0.1240	0.4903

Source: Bloomberg.

when the independent variables include past values of the dependent variable. The correct approach is to test whether the residuals from this model are serially correlated.

At the bottom of Exhibit 12, the first four autocorrelations of the residual are displayed along with the standard error and the *t*-statistic for each of those autocorrelations.[6] The sample has 65 observations, so the standard error for each of the autocorrelations is $1/\sqrt{65} = 0.1240$. Exhibit 12 shows that none of the first four autocorrelations has a *t*-statistic larger than 1.6818 in absolute value. Therefore, Jones can conclude that none of these autocorrelations differs significantly from 0. Consequently, she can assume that the residuals are not serially correlated and that the model is correctly specified, and she can validly use ordinary least squares to estimate the parameters and the parameters' standard errors in the autoregressive model (for other tests for serial correlation of residuals, see Diebold 2008).

Now that Jones has concluded that this model is correctly specified, how can she use it to predict Intel's gross margin in the next period? The estimated equation is Gross margin$_t$ = 0.1513 + 0.7462(Gross margin$_{t-1}$) + ε_t. The expected value of the error term is 0 in any period. Therefore, this model predicts that gross margin in period $t + 1$ will be Gross margin$_{t+1}$ = 0.1513 + 0.7462(Gross margin$_t$). For example, if gross margin is 55% in this quarter (0.55), the model predicts that in the next quarter gross margin will increase to 0.1513 + 0.7462(0.55) = 0.5617, or 56.17 percent. However, if gross margin is currently 65% (0.65), the model predicts that in the next quarter, gross margin will fall to 0.1513 + 0.7462(0.65) = 0.6363, or 63.63 percent. As we show in the following section, the model predicts that gross margin will increase if it is below a certain level (59.61 percent) and decrease if it is above that level.

4.3. Mean Reversion

We say that a time series shows **mean reversion** if it tends to fall when its level is above its mean and rise when its level is below its mean. Much like the temperature in a room controlled by a thermostat, a mean-reverting time series tends to return to its long-term mean. How can we determine the value that the time series tends toward? If a time series is currently at its mean-reverting level, then the model predicts that the value of the time series will be the same in the next period. At its mean-reverting level, we have the relationship $x_{t+1} = x_t$. For an AR(1) model ($x_{t+1} = b_0 + b_1 x_t$), the equality $x_{t+1} = x_t$ implies the level $x_t = b_0 + b_1 x_t$ or that the mean-reverting level, x_t, is given by

$$x_t = \frac{b_0}{1 - b_1}$$

So the AR(1) model predicts that the time series will stay the same if its current value is $b_0/(1 - b_1)$, increase if its current value is below $b_0/(1 - b_1)$, and decrease if its current value is above $b_0/(1 - b_1)$.

---

[6]For seasonally unadjusted data, analysts often compute the same number of autocorrelations as there are observations in a year (for example, four for quarterly data). The number of autocorrelations computed also often depends on sample size, as discussed in Diebold (2008).

In the case of gross margins for Intel, the mean-reverting level for the model shown in Exhibit 12 is $0.1513/(1 - 0.7462) = 0.5961$. If the current gross margin is above 0.5961, the model predicts that the gross margin will fall in the next period. If the current gross margin is below 0.5961, the model predicts that the gross margin will rise in the next period. As we will discuss later, all covariance-stationary time series have a finite mean-reverting level.

4.4. Multiperiod Forecasts and the Chain Rule of Forecasting

Often, financial analysts want to make forecasts for more than one period. For example, we might want to use a quarterly sales model to predict sales for a company for each of the next four quarters. To use a time-series model to make forecasts for more than one period, we must examine how to make multiperiod forecasts using an AR(1) model. The one-period-ahead forecast of x_t from an AR(1) model is as follows:

$$\widehat{x}_{t+1} = \widehat{b}_0 + \widehat{b}_1 x_t \qquad (6)$$

If we want to forecast x_{t+2} using an AR(1) model, our forecast will be based on

$$\widehat{x}_{t+2} = \widehat{b}_0 + \widehat{b}_1 x_{t+1} \qquad (7)$$

Unfortunately, we do not know x_{t+1} in period t, so we cannot use Equation 7 directly to make a two-period-ahead forecast. We can, however, use our forecast of x_{t+1} and the AR(1) model to make a prediction of x_{t+2}. The **chain rule of forecasting** is a process in which the next period's value, predicted by the forecasting equation, is substituted into the equation to give a predicted value two periods ahead. Using the chain rule of forecasting, we can substitute the predicted value of x_{t+1} into Equation 7 to get $\widehat{x}_{t+2} = \widehat{b}_0 + \widehat{b}_1 \widehat{x}_{t+1}$. We already know $\widehat{x}_{t+1}$ from our one-period-ahead forecast in Equation 6. Now we have a simple way of predicting x_{t+2}.

Multiperiod forecasts are more uncertain than single-period forecasts because each forecast period has uncertainty. For example, in forecasting x_{t+2}, we first have the uncertainty associated with forecasting x_{t+1} using x_t, and then we have the uncertainty associated with forecasting x_{t+2} using the forecast of x_{t+1}. In general, the more periods a forecast has, the more uncertain it is. Note that if a forecasting model is well specified, the prediction errors from the model will not be serially correlated. If the prediction errors for each period are not serially correlated, then the variance of a multiperiod forecast will be higher than the variance of a single-period forecast.

EXAMPLE 5   Multiperiod Prediction of Intel's Gross Margin

Suppose that at the beginning of 2020, we want to predict Intel's gross margin in two periods using the model shown in Exhibit 12. Assume that Intel's gross margin in the current period is 63 percent. The one-period-ahead forecast of Intel's gross margin from this model is $0.6214 = 0.1513 + 0.7462(0.63)$. By substituting the one-period-ahead forecast, 0.6214, back into the regression equation, we can derive the following two-period-ahead forecast: $0.6150 = 0.1513 + 0.7462(0.6214)$. Therefore, if the current gross margin for Intel is 63 percent, the model predicts that Intel's gross margin in two quarters will be 61.50 percent.

EXAMPLE 6   Modeling US CPI Inflation

Analyst Lisette Miller has been directed to build a time-series model for monthly US inflation. Inflation and expectations about inflation, of course, have a significant effect on bond returns. For a 24-year period beginning January 1995 and ending December 2018, she selects as data the annualized monthly percentage change in the CPI. Which model should Miller use?

The process of model selection parallels that of Example 4 relating to Intel's gross margins. The first model Miller estimates is an AR(1) model, using the previous month's inflation rate as the independent variable: $\text{Inflation}_t = b_0 + b_1(\text{Inflation}_{t-1}) + \varepsilon_t$, $t = 1, 2, \ldots, 359$. To estimate this model, she uses monthly CPI inflation data from January 1995 to December 2018 ($t = 1$ denotes February 1995). Exhibit 13 shows the results of estimating this model.

As Exhibit 13 shows, both the intercept ($\widehat{b}_0 = 1.3346$) and the coefficient on the first lagged value of inflation ($\widehat{b}_1 = 0.3984$) are highly statistically significant, with large t-statistics. With 287 observations and two parameters, this model has 285 degrees of freedom. The critical value for a t-statistic at the 0.05 significance level is about 1.97. Therefore, Miller can reject the individual null hypotheses that the intercept is equal to 0 ($b_0 = 0$) and the coefficient on the first lag is equal to 0 ($b_1 = 0$) in favor of the alternative hypothesis that the coefficients, individually, are not equal to 0.

Are these statistics valid? Miller will know when she tests whether the residuals from this model are serially correlated. With 287 observations in this sample, the

EXHIBIT 13   Monthly CPI Inflation at an Annual Rate: AR(1) Model—Monthly Observations, February 1995–December 2018

Regression Statistics

R^2	0.1586
Standard error	2.9687
Observations	287
Durbin–Watson	1.8442

	Coefficient	Standard Error	t-Statistic
Intercept	1.3346	0.2134	6.2540
Inflation$_{t-1}$	0.3984	0.0544	7.3235

Autocorrelations of the Residual

Lag	Autocorrelation	Standard Error	t-Statistic
1	0.0777	0.0590	1.3175
2	−0.1653	0.0590	−2.8013
3	−0.1024	0.0590	−1.7362
4	−0.0845	0.0590	1.4324

Source: US Bureau of Labor Statistics.

EXHIBIT 14   Monthly CPI Inflation at an Annual Rate: AR(2) Model—Monthly Observations, March 1995–December 2018

Regression Statistics

R^2	0.1907		
Standard error	2.9208		
Observations	286		
Durbin–Watson	1.9934		
	Coefficient	**Standard Error**	**t-Statistic**
Intercept	1.5996	0.2245	7.1252
Inflation$_{t-1}$	0.4759	0.0583	8.1636
Inflation$_{t-2}$	-0.1964	0.0583	-3.368

Autocorrelations of the Residual

Lag	Autocorrelation	Standard Error	t-Statistic
1	0.0032	0.0591	0.0536
2	0.0042	0.0591	0.0707
3	-0.0338	0.0591	-0.5696
4	0.0155	0.0591	1.7692

Source: US Bureau of Labor Statistics.

standard error for each of the estimated autocorrelations is $1/\sqrt{287} = 0.0590$. The critical value for the t-statistic is 1.97. Because the second estimated autocorrelation has t-statistic larger than 1.97 in absolute value, Miller concludes that the autocorrelations are significantly different from 0. This model is thus misspecified because the residuals are serially correlated.

    If the residuals in an autoregressive model are serially correlated, Miller can eliminate the correlation by estimating an autoregressive model with more lags of the dependent variable as explanatory variables. Exhibit 14 shows the result of estimating a second time-series model, an AR(2) model using the same data as in the analysis shown in Exhibit 13. With 286 observations and three parameters, this model has 283 degrees of freedom. Because the degrees of freedom are almost the same as those for the estimates shown in Exhibit 13, the critical value of the t-statistic at the 0.05 significance level also is almost the same (1.97). If she estimates the equation with two lags— Inflation$_t$ = b_0 + b_1(Inflation$_{t-1}$) + b_2(Inflation$_{t-2}$) + ε_t—Miller finds that all three of the coefficients in the regression model (an intercept and the coefficients on two lags of the dependent variable) differ significantly from 0. The bottom portion of Exhibit 14 shows that none of the first four autocorrelations of the residual has a t-statistic greater in absolute value than the critical value of 1.97. Therefore, Miller fails to reject the hypothesis that the individual autocorrelations of the residual equal 0. She concludes that this model is correctly specified because she finds no evidence of serial correlation in the residuals.

1. The analyst selected an AR(2) model because the residuals from the AR(1) model were serially correlated. Suppose that in a given month, inflation had been 4% at an annual rate in the previous month and 3% in the month before that. What would be the difference in the analyst forecast of inflation for that month if she had used an AR(1) model instead of the AR(2) model?

Solution to 1: The AR(1) model shown in Exhibit 13 predicted that inflation in the next month would be 1.3346 + 0.3984(4) = 2.93 percent, approximately, whereas the AR(2) model shown in Exhibit 14 predicts that inflation in the next month will be 1.5996 + 0.4759(4) – 0.1964(3) = 2.91 percent approximately. If the analyst had used the incorrect AR(1) model, she would have predicted inflation to be 2 bps higher (2.93 percent versus 2.91 percent) than when using the AR(2) model. Although in this case the difference in the predicted inflation is actually very small, this kind of scenario illustrates that using an incorrect forecast could adversely affect the quality of her company's investment choices.

4.5. Comparing Forecast Model Performance

One way to compare the forecast performance of two models is to compare the variance of the forecast errors that the two models make. The model with the smaller forecast error variance will be the more accurate model, and it will also have the smaller standard error of the time-series regression. (This standard error usually is reported directly in the output for the time-series regression.)

In comparing forecast accuracy among models, we must distinguish between in-sample forecast errors and out-of-sample forecast errors. **In-sample forecast errors** are the residuals from a fitted time-series model. For example, when we estimated a linear trend with raw inflation data from January 1995 to December 2018, the in-sample forecast errors were the residuals from January 1995 to December 2018. If we use this model to predict inflation outside this period, the differences between actual and predicted inflation are **out-of-sample forecast errors**.

EXAMPLE 7   In-Sample Forecast Comparisons of US CPI Inflation

In **Example 6**, the analyst compared an AR(1) forecasting model of monthly US inflation with an AR(2) model of monthly US inflation and decided that the AR(2) model was preferable. Exhibit 13 showed that the standard error from the AR(1) model of inflation is 2.9687, and Exhibit 14 showed that the standard error from the AR(2) model is 2.9208. Therefore, the AR(2) model had a lower in-sample forecast error variance than the AR(1) model had, which is consistent with our belief that the AR(2) model was preferable. Its standard error is 2.9208/2.9687 = 98.39 percent of the forecast error of the AR(1) model.

Often, we want to compare the forecasting accuracy of different models after the sample period for which they were estimated. We wish to compare the out-of-sample forecast accuracy of the models. Out-of-sample forecast accuracy is important because the future is always out of sample. Although professional forecasters distinguish between out-of-sample and in-sample forecasting performance, many articles that analysts read contain only in-sample forecast evaluations. Analysts should be aware that out-of-sample performance is critical for evaluating a forecasting model's real-world contribution.

Typically, we compare the out-of-sample forecasting performance of forecasting models by comparing their **root mean squared error (RMSE)**, which is the square root of the average squared error. The model with the smallest RMSE is judged the most accurate. The following example illustrates the computation and use of RMSE in comparing forecasting models.

EXAMPLE 8   Out-of-Sample Forecast Comparisons of US CPI Inflation

Suppose we want to compare the forecasting accuracy of the AR(1) and AR(2) models of US inflation estimated over 1995 to 2018, using data on US inflation from January 2019 to September 2019.

For each month from January 2019 to September 2019, the first column of numbers in Exhibit 15 shows the actual annualized inflation rate during the month. The second and third columns show the rate of inflation in the previous two months.

EXHIBIT 15   Out-of-Sample Forecast Error Comparisons: January 2019–September 2019 US CPI Inflation (Annualized)

Date	Infl(t)	Infl(t–1)	Infl(t–2)	AR(1) Error	Squared Error	AR(2) Error	Squared Error
2019							
January	0.0000	0.0000	0.0000	0.1335	0.0178	–1.6000	2.5599
February	2.4266	0.0000	0.0000	–2.2931	5.2585	0.8266	0.6833
March	4.9070	2.4266	0.0000	–3.8068	14.4916	2.1522	4.6320
April	3.6600	4.9070	2.4266	–1.5716	2.4699	0.2014	0.0406
May	1.2066	3.6600	4.9070	0.3850	0.1482	–1.1714	1.3722
June	1.2066	1.2066	3.6600	–0.5924	0.3510	–0.2488	0.0619
July	3.6600	1.2066	1.2066	–3.0458	9.2770	1.7228	2.9680
August	1.2066	3.6600	1.2066	0.3850	0.1482	–1.8982	3.6030
September	0.0000	1.2066	3.6600	0.6142	0.3772	–1.4554	2.1181
				Average	3.6155	Average	2.0043
				RMSE	1.9014	RMSE	1.4157

Note: Any apparent discrepancies between error and squared error results are due to rounding.
Source: US Bureau of Labor Statistics.

The fourth column shows the out-of-sample errors (Actual – Forecast) from the AR(1) model shown in Exhibit 13. The fifth column shows the squared errors from the AR(1) model. The sixth column shows the out-of-sample errors from the AR(2) model shown in Exhibit 14. The final column shows the squared errors from the AR(2) model. The bottom of the table displays the average squared error and the RMSE. According to these measures, the AR(2) model was slightly more accurate than the AR(1) model in its out-of-sample forecasts of inflation from January 2019 to September 2019. The RMSE from the AR(2) model was only $1.4157/1.9014 = 74.46$ percent as large as the RMSE from the AR(1) model. Therefore, the AR(2) model was more accurate both in sample and out of sample. Of course, this was a small sample to use in evaluating out-of-sample forecasting performance. Sometimes, an analyst may have conflicting information about whether to choose an AR(1) or an AR(2) model. We must also consider regression coefficient stability. We will continue the comparison between these two models in the following section.

4.6. Instability of Regression Coefficients

One of the important issues an analyst faces in modeling a time series is the sample period to use. The estimates of regression coefficients of the time-series model can change substantially across different sample periods used for estimating the model. Often, the regression coefficient estimates of a time-series model estimated using an earlier sample period can be quite different from those of a model estimated using a later sample period. Similarly, the estimates can be different between models estimated using relatively shorter and longer sample periods. Further, the choice of model for a particular time series can also depend on the sample period. For example, an AR(1) model may be appropriate for the sales of a company in one particular sample period, but an AR(2) model may be necessary for an earlier or later sample period (or for a longer or shorter sample period). Thus, the choice of a sample period is an important decision in modeling a financial time series.

Unfortunately, there is usually no clear-cut basis in economic or financial theory for determining whether to use data from a longer or shorter sample period to estimate a time-series model. We can get some guidance, however, if we remember that our models are valid only for covariance-stationary time series. For example, we should not combine data from a period when exchange rates were fixed with data from a period when exchange rates were floating. The exchange rates in these two periods would not likely have the same variance because exchange rates are usually much more volatile under a floating-rate regime than when rates are fixed. Similarly, many US analysts consider it inappropriate to model US inflation or interest-rate behavior since the 1960s as a part of one sample period, because the Federal Reserve had distinct policy regimes during this period. A simple way to determine appropriate samples for time-series estimation is to look at graphs of the data to see whether the time series looks stationary before estimation begins. If we know that a government policy changed on a specific date, we might also test whether the time-series relation was the same before and after that date.

In the following example, we illustrate how the choice of a longer versus a shorter period can affect the decision of whether to use, for example, a first- or second-order time-series model. We then show how the choice of the time-series model (and the associated regression coefficients) affects our forecast. Finally, we discuss which sample period, and accordingly which model and corresponding forecast, is appropriate for the time series analyzed in the example.

EXAMPLE 9 Instability in Time-Series Models of US Inflation

In **Example 6**, the analyst Lisette Miller concluded that US CPI inflation should be modeled as an AR(2) time series. A colleague examined her results and questioned estimating one time-series model for inflation in the United States since 1984, given that the Federal Reserve responded aggressively to the financial crisis that emerged in 2007. He argues that the inflation time series from 1995 to 2018 has two **regimes** or underlying models generating the time series: one running from 1995 through 2007 and another starting in 2008. Therefore, the colleague suggests that Miller estimate a new time-series model for US inflation starting in 2008. Because of his suggestion, Miller first estimates an AR(1) model for inflation using data for a sample period from 2008 to 2018. Exhibit 16 shows her AR(1) estimates.

The bottom part of Exhibit 16 shows that the first four autocorrelations of the residuals from the AR(1) model are quite small. None of these autocorrelations has a t-statistic larger than 1.99, the critical value for significance. Consequently, Miller cannot reject the null hypothesis that the residuals are serially uncorrelated. The AR(1) model is correctly specified for the sample period from 2008 to 2018, so there is no need to estimate the AR(2) model. This conclusion is very different from that reached in Example 6 using data from 1995 to 2018. In that example, Miller initially rejected the AR(1) model because

EXHIBIT 16   Autoregression: AR(1) Model Monthly CPI Inflation at an Annual Rate, January 2008–December 2018

Regression Statistics

R^2	0.2536
Standard error	3.0742
Observations	132
Durbin–Watson	1.8164

	Coefficient	Standard Error	t-Statistic
Intercept	0.8431	0.2969	2.8397
Inflation$_{t-1}$	0.5036	0.0758	6.6438

Autocorrelations of the Residual

Lag	Autocorrelation	Standard Error	t-Statistic
1	0.0999	0.087	1.1479
2	−0.1045	0.087	−1.2015
3	−0.1568	0.087	−1.8051
4	0.0500	0.087	0.5750

Source: US Bureau of Labor Statistics.

EXHIBIT 17   Monthly CPI Inflation

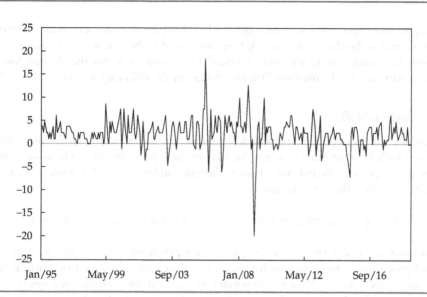

Source: US Bureau of Labor Statistics.

its residuals exhibited serial correlation. When she used a larger sample, an AR(2) model initially appeared to fit the data much better than did an AR(1) model.

How deeply does our choice of sample period affect our forecast of future inflation? Suppose that in a given month, inflation was 4 percent at an annual rate, and the month before that it was 3 percent. The AR(1) model shown in Exhibit 16 predicts that inflation in the next month will be 0.8431 + 0.5036(4) ≈ 2.86 percent. Therefore, the forecast of the next month's inflation using the 2008 to 2018 sample is 2.86 percent. Remember from the analysis following **Example 6** that the AR(2) model for the 1995 to 2018 sample predicts inflation of 2.91 percent in the next month. Thus, using the correctly specified model for the shorter sample produces an inflation forecast 0.05 pps below the forecast made from the correctly specified model for the longer sample period. Such a difference might substantially affect a particular investment decision.

Which model is correct? Exhibit 17 suggests an answer. Monthly US inflation was so much more volatile during the middle part of the study period than in the earlier or later years that inflation is probably not a covariance-stationary time series from 1995 to 2018. Therefore, we can reasonably believe that the data have more than one regime and Miller should estimate a separate model for inflation from 2009 to 2018, as shown previously. In fact, the standard deviation of annualized monthly inflation rates is just 2.86 percent for 1995–2007 but 3.54 percent for 2008–2018, largely because of volatility during the 2008 crisis. As the example shows, experience (such as knowledge of government policy changes) and judgment play a vital role in determining how to model a time series. Simply relying on autocorrelations of the residuals from a time-series model cannot tell us the correct sample period for our analysis.

5. RANDOM WALKS AND UNIT ROOTS

So far, we have examined those time series in which the time series has a tendency to revert to its mean level as the change in a variable from one period to the next follows a mean-reverting pattern. In contrast, there are many financial time series in which the changes follow a random pattern. We discuss these "random walks" in the following section.

5.1. Random Walks

A random walk is one of the most widely studied time-series models for financial data. A **random walk** is a time series in which the value of the series in one period is the value of the series in the previous period plus an unpredictable random error. A random walk can be described by the following equation:

$$x_t = x_{t-1} + \varepsilon_t, \mathrm{E}(\varepsilon_t) = 0, \mathrm{E}(\varepsilon_t^2) = \sigma^2, \mathrm{cov}(\varepsilon_t, \varepsilon_s) = \mathrm{E}(\varepsilon_t \varepsilon_s) = 0 \text{ if } t \neq s. \qquad (8)$$

Equation 8 means that the time series x_t is in every period equal to its value in the previous period plus an error term, ε_t, that has constant variance and is uncorrelated with the error term in previous periods. Note two important points. First, this equation is a special case of an AR(1) model with $b_0 = 0$ and $b_1 = 1.$[7] Second, the expected value of ε_t is zero. Therefore, the best forecast of x_t that can be made in period $t - 1$ is x_{t-1}. In fact, in this model, x_{t-1} is the best forecast of x in every period after $t - 1$.

Random walks are quite common in financial time series. For example, many studies have tested whether and found that currency exchange rates follow a random walk. Consistent with the second point made in the previous paragraph, some studies have found that sophisticated exchange rate forecasting models cannot outperform forecasts made using the random walk model and that the best forecast of the future exchange rate is the current exchange rate.

Unfortunately, we cannot use the regression methods we have discussed so far to estimate an AR(1) model on a time series that is actually a random walk. To see why this is so, we must determine why a random walk has no finite mean-reverting level or finite variance. Recall that if x_t is at its mean-reverting level, then $x_t = b_0 + b_1 x_t$, or $x_t = b_0/(1 - b_1)$. In a random walk, however, $b_0 = 0$ and $b_1 = 1$, so $b_0/(1 - b_1) = 0/0$. Therefore, a random walk has an undefined mean-reverting level.

What is the variance of a random walk? Suppose that in Period 1, the value of x_1 is 0. Then we know that $x_2 = 0 + \varepsilon_2$. Therefore, the variance of $x_2 = \mathrm{var}(\varepsilon_2) = \sigma^2$. Now $x_3 = x_2 + \varepsilon_3 = \varepsilon_2 + \varepsilon_3$. Because the error term in each period is assumed to be uncorrelated with the error terms in all other periods, the variance of $x_3 = \mathrm{var}(\varepsilon_2) + \mathrm{var}(\varepsilon_3) = 2\sigma^2$. By a similar argument, we can show that for any period t, the variance of $x_t = (t - 1)\sigma^2$. But this means that as t grows large, the variance of x_t grows without an upper bound: It approaches infinity. This lack of upper bound, in turn, means that a random walk is not a covariance-stationary time series, because a covariance-stationary time series must have a finite variance.

---

[7]Equation 8 with a nonzero intercept added (as in Equation 9, given later) is sometimes referred to as a random walk with drift.

What is the practical implication of these issues? *We cannot use standard regression analysis on a time series that is a random walk.* We can, however, attempt to convert the data to a covariance-stationary time series if we suspect that the time series is a random walk. In statistical terms, we can difference it.

We difference a time series by creating a new time series—say, y_t—that in each period is equal to the difference between x_t and x_{t-1}. This transformation is called **first-differencing** because it subtracts the value of the time series in the first prior period from the current value of the time series. Sometimes the first difference of x_t is written as $\Delta x_t = x_t - x_{t-1}$. Note that the first difference of the random walk in Equation 8 yields

$$y_t = x_t - x_{t-1} = \varepsilon_t, \mathrm{E}(\varepsilon_t) = 0, \mathrm{E}(\varepsilon_t^2) = \sigma^2, \mathrm{cov}(\varepsilon_t, \varepsilon_s) = \mathrm{E}(\varepsilon_t \varepsilon_s) = 0 \text{ for t} \neq \text{s}$$

The expected value of ε_t is 0. Therefore, the best forecast of y_t that can be made in period $t - 1$ is 0. This implies that the best forecast is that there will be no change in the value of the current time series, x_{t-1}.

The first-differenced variable, y_t, is covariance stationary. How is this so? First, note that this model ($y_t = \varepsilon_t$) is an AR(1) model with $b_0 = 0$ and $b_1 = 0$. We can compute the mean-reverting level of the first-differenced model as $b_0/(1 - b_1) = 0/1 = 0$. Therefore, a first-differenced random walk has a mean-reverting level of 0. Note also that the variance of y_t in each period is $\mathrm{var}(\varepsilon_t) = \sigma^2$. Because the variance and the mean of y_t are constant and finite in each period, y_t is a covariance-stationary time series and we can model it using linear regression. Of course, modeling the first-differenced series with an AR(1) model does not help us predict the future, because $b_0 = 0$ and $b_1 = 0$. We simply conclude that the original time series is, in fact, a random walk.

Had we tried to estimate an AR(1) model for a time series that was a random walk, our statistical conclusions would have been incorrect because AR models cannot be used to estimate random walks or any time series that is not covariance stationary. The following example illustrates this issue with exchange rates.

EXAMPLE 10   The Yen/US Dollar Exchange Rate

Financial analysts often assume that exchange rates are random walks. Consider an AR(1) model for the Japanese yen/US dollar exchange rate (JPY/USD). Exhibit 18 shows the results of estimating the model using month-end observations from October 1980 through August 2019.

The results in Exhibit 18 suggest that the yen/US dollar exchange rate is a random walk because the estimated intercept does not appear to be significantly different from 0 and the estimated coefficient on the first lag of the exchange rate is very close to 1. Can we use the *t*-statistics in Exhibit 18 to test whether the exchange rate is a random walk? Unfortunately, no, because the standard errors in an AR model are invalid if the model is estimated using a data series that is a random walk (remember, a random walk is not covariance stationary). If the exchange rate is, in fact, a random walk, we might come to an incorrect conclusion based on faulty statistical tests and then invest incorrectly. We can use a test presented in the next section to test whether the time series is a random walk.

EXHIBIT 18   Yen/US Dollar Exchange Rate: AR(1) Model Month-End Observations, October 1980–August 2019

Regression Statistics

R^2	0.9897
Standard error	4.5999
Observations	467
Durbin–Watson	1.9391

	Coefficient	Standard Error	t-Statistic
Intercept	0.8409	0.6503	1.2931
JPY/USD$_{t-1}$	0.9919	0.0047	211.0426

Autocorrelations of the Residual

Lag	Autocorrelation	Standard Error	t-Statistic
1	0.0302	0.0465	0.6495
2	0.0741	0.0465	1.5935
3	0.0427	0.0465	0.9183
4	−0.0034	0.0465	0.0731

Source: US Federal Reserve Board of Governors.

Suppose the exchange rate is a random walk, as we now suspect. If so, the first-differenced series, $y_t = x_t - x_{t-1}$, will be covariance stationary. We present the results from estimating $y_t = b_0 + b_1 y_{t-1} + \varepsilon_t$ in Exhibit 19. If the exchange rate is a random walk, then $b_0 = 0$, $b_1 = 0$, and the error term will not be serially correlated.

In Exhibit 19, neither the intercept nor the coefficient on the first lag of the first-differenced exchange rate differs significantly from 0, and no residual autocorrelations differ significantly from 0. These findings are consistent with the yen/US dollar exchange rate being a random walk.

We have concluded that the differenced regression is the model to choose. Now we can see that we would have been seriously misled if we had based our model choice on an R^2 comparison. In Exhibit 18, the R^2 is 0.9897, whereas in Exhibit 19, the R^2 is 0.0008. How can this be, if we just concluded that the model in Exhibit 19 is the one that we should use? In Exhibit 18, the R^2 measures how well the exchange rate in one period predicts the exchange rate in the next period. If the exchange rate is a random walk, its current value will be an extremely good predictor of its value in the next period, and thus the R^2 will be extremely high. At the same time, if the exchange rate is a random walk, then changes in the exchange rate should be completely unpredictable. Exhibit 19 estimates whether changes in the exchange rate from one month to the next can be predicted by changes in the exchange rate over the previous month. If they cannot be predicted, the R^2 in Exhibit 19 should be very low. In fact, it is low (0.0008). This comparison provides a good example of the general rule that we cannot necessarily choose which model is correct solely by comparing the R^2 from the two models.

EXHIBIT 19 First-Differenced Yen/US Dollar Exchange Rate: AR(1) Model Month-End Observations, November 1980–August 2019

Regression Statistics

R^2	0.0008
Standard error	4.6177
Observations	466
Durbin–Watson	2.0075

	Coefficient	Standard Error	t-Statistic
Intercept	−0.2185	0.2142	−1.0200
JPY/USD$_{t-1}$ − JPY/USD$_{t-2}$	0.0287	0.0464	0.6185

Autocorrelations of the Residual

Lag	Autocorrelation	Standard Error	t-Statistic
1	−0.0023	0.0463	−0.0501
2	0.0724	0.0463	1.5643
3	0.0387	0.0463	0.8361
4	−0.0062	0.0463	−0.1329

Source: US Federal Reserve Board of Governors.

The exchange rate is a random walk, and changes in a random walk are by definition unpredictable. Therefore, we cannot profit from an investment strategy that predicts changes in the exchange rate.

To this point, we have discussed only simple random walks—that is, random walks without drift. In a random walk without drift, the best predictor of the time series in the next period is its current value. A random walk with drift, however, should increase or decrease by a constant amount in each period. The equation describing a random walk with drift is a special case of the AR(1) model:

$$
\begin{aligned}
x_t &= b_0 + b_1 x_{t-1} + \varepsilon_t, \\
b_1 &= 1, b_0 \neq 0, \text{ or} \\
x_t &= b_0 + x_{t-1} + \varepsilon_t, \text{E}(\varepsilon_t) = 0.
\end{aligned}
\tag{9}
$$

A random walk with drift has $b_0 \neq 0$, compared to a simple random walk, which has $b_0 = 0$.

We have already seen that $b_1 = 1$ implies an undefined mean-reversion level and thus nonstationarity. Consequently, we cannot use an AR model to analyze a time series that is a random walk with drift until we transform the time series by taking first differences. If we first-difference Equation 9, the result is $y_t = x_t - x_{t-1}$, $y_t = b_0 + \varepsilon_t$, $b_0 \neq 0$.

5.2. The Unit Root Test of Nonstationarity

In this section, we discuss how to use random walk concepts to determine whether a time series is covariance stationary. This approach focuses on the slope coefficient in the random-walk-with-drift case of an AR(1) model in contrast with the traditional autocorrelation approach, which we discuss first.

The examination of the autocorrelations of a time series at various lags is a well-known prescription for inferring whether or not a time series is stationary. Typically, for a stationary time series, either autocorrelations at all lags are statistically indistinguishable from zero or the autocorrelations drop off rapidly to zero as the number of lags becomes large. Conversely, the autocorrelations of a nonstationary time series do not exhibit those characteristics. However, this approach is less definite than a currently more popular test for nonstationarity known as the Dickey–Fuller test for a unit root.

We can explain what is known as the unit root problem in the context of an AR(1) model. If a time series comes from an AR(1) model, then to be covariance stationary, the absolute value of the lag coefficient, b_1, must be less than 1.0. We could not rely on the statistical results of an AR(1) model if the absolute value of the lag coefficient were greater than or equal to 1.0 because the time series would not be covariance stationary. If the lag coefficient is equal to 1.0, the time series has a **unit root**: It is a random walk and is not covariance stationary (note that when b_1 is greater than 1 in absolute value, we say that there is an "explosive root"). By definition, all random walks, with or without a drift term, have unit roots.

How do we test for unit roots in a time series? If we believed that a time series, x_t, was a random walk with drift, it would be tempting to estimate the parameters of the AR(1) model $x_t = b_0 + b_1 x_{t-1} + \varepsilon_t$ using linear regression and conduct a t-test of the hypothesis that $b_1 = 1$. Unfortunately, if $b_1 = 1$, then x_t is not covariance stationary and the t-value of the estimated coefficient, $\hat{b}_1$, does not actually follow the t-distribution; consequently, a t-test would be invalid.

Dickey and Fuller (1979) developed a regression-based unit root test based on a transformed version of the AR(1) model $x_t = b_0 + b_1 x_{t-1} + \varepsilon_t$. Subtracting x_{t-1} from both sides of the AR(1) model produces

$$x_t - x_{t-1} = b_0 + (b_1 - 1)x_{t-1} + \varepsilon_t,$$

or

$$x_t - x_{t-1} = b_0 + g_1 x_{t-1} + \varepsilon_t, \quad E(\varepsilon_t) = 0, \tag{10}$$

where $g_1 = (b_1 - 1)$. If $b_1 = 1$, then $g_1 = 0$ and thus a test of $g_1 = 0$ is a test of $b_1 = 1$. If there is a unit root in the AR(1) model, then g_1 will be 0 in a regression where the dependent variable is the first difference of the time series and the independent variable is the first lag of the time series. The null hypothesis of the Dickey–Fuller test is H_0: $g_1 = 0$—that is, that the time series has a unit root and is nonstationary—and the alternative hypothesis is H_a: $g_1 < 0$, that the time series does not have a unit root and is stationary.

To conduct the test, one calculates a t-statistic in the conventional manner for $\hat{g}_1$ but instead of using conventional critical values for a t-test, one uses a revised set of values computed by Dickey and Fuller; the revised critical values are larger in absolute value than the conventional critical values. A number of software packages incorporate Dickey–Fuller tests.

EXAMPLE 11   (Historical Example)

AstraZeneca's Quarterly Sales (1)

In January 2012, equity analyst Aron Berglin is building a time-series model for the quarterly sales of AstraZeneca, a British/Swedish biopharmaceutical company head-quartered in London. He is using AstraZeneca's quarterly sales in US dollars for January 2000 to December 2011 and any lagged sales data that he may need prior to 2000 to build this model. He finds that a log-linear trend model seems better suited for modeling AstraZeneca's sales than does a linear trend model. However, the Durbin–Watson statistic from the log-linear regression is just 0.7064, which causes him to reject the hypothesis that the errors in the regression are serially uncorrelated. He concludes that he cannot model the log of AstraZeneca's quarterly sales using only a time trend line. He decides to model the log of AstraZeneca's quarterly sales using an AR(1) model. He uses ln Sales$_t$ = b_0 + b_1(ln Sales$_{t-1}$) + ε_t.

Before he estimates this regression, the analyst should use the Dickey–Fuller test to determine whether there is a unit root in the log of AstraZeneca's quarterly sales. If he uses the sample of quarterly data on AstraZeneca's sales from the first quarter of 2000 through the fourth quarter of 2011, takes the natural log of each observation, and computes the Dickey–Fuller t-test statistic, the value of that statistic might cause him to fail to reject the null hypothesis that there is a unit root in the log of AstraZeneca's quarterly sales.

If a time series appears to have a unit root, how should we model it? One method that is often successful is to model the first-differenced series as an autoregressive time series. The following example demonstrates this method.

EXAMPLE 12   AstraZeneca's Quarterly Sales (2)

The plot of the log of AstraZeneca's quarterly sales is shown in Exhibit 20. By looking at the plot, Berglin is convinced that the log of quarterly sales is not covariance stationary (that it has a unit root).

So he creates a new series, y_t, that is the first difference of the log of AstraZeneca's quarterly sales. Exhibit 21 shows that series.

Berglin compares Exhibit 21 to Exhibit 20 and notices that first-differencing the log of AstraZeneca's quarterly sales eliminates the strong upward trend that was present in the log of AstraZeneca's sales. Because the first-differenced series has no strong trend, Berglin is better off assuming that the differenced series is covariance stationary rather than assuming that AstraZeneca's sales or the log of AstraZeneca's sales is a covariance-stationary time series.

Now suppose Berglin decides to model the new series using an AR(1) model. Berglin uses ln(Sales$_t$) – ln(Sales$_{t-1}$) = b_0 + b_1[ln(Sales$_{t-1}$) – ln(Sales$_{t-2}$)] + ε_t. Exhibit 22 shows the results of that regression.

The lower part of Exhibit 22 suggests that the first four autocorrelations of residuals in this model are not statistically significant. With 48 observations and two

EXHIBIT 20   Log of AstraZeneca's Quarterly Sales

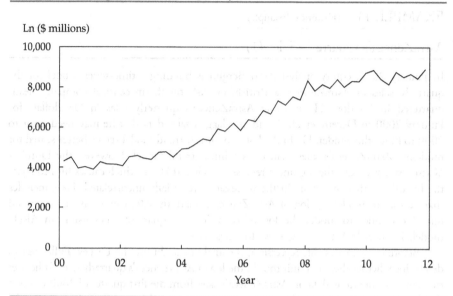

Source: Compustat.

EXHIBIT 21   Log Difference, AstraZeneca's Quarterly Sales

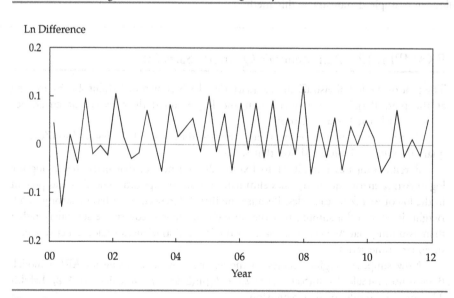

Source: Compustat.

EXHIBIT 22   Log Differenced Sales: AR(1) Model of AstraZeneca Quarterly Observations, January 2000–December 2011

Regression Statistics

R^2	0.3005
Standard error	0.0475
Observations	48
Durbin–Watson	1.6874

	Coefficient	Standard Error	t-Statistic
Intercept	0.0222	0.0071	3.1268
ln Sales$_{t-1}$ – ln Sales$_{t-2}$	-0.5493	0.1236	-4.4442

Autocorrelations of the Residual

Lag	Autocorrelation	Standard Error	t-Statistic
1	0.2809	0.1443	1.9466
2	-0.0466	0.1443	-0.3229
3	0.0081	0.1443	0.0561
4	0.2647	0.1443	1.8344

Source: Compustat.

parameters, this model has 46 degrees of freedom. The critical value for a *t*-statistic in this model is above 2.0 at the 0.05 significance level. None of the *t*-statistics for these autocorrelations has an absolute value larger than 2.0. Therefore, we fail to reject the null hypotheses that each of these autocorrelations is equal to 0 and conclude instead that no significant autocorrelation is present in the residuals.

This result suggests that the model is well specified and that we could use the estimates. Both the intercept $(\hat{b}_0 = 0.0222)$ and the coefficient $(\hat{b}_1 = -0.5493)$ on the first lag of the new first-differenced series are statistically significant.

1. Explain how to interpret the estimated coefficients in the model.

Solution to 1: The value of the intercept (0.0222) implies that if sales have not changed in the current quarter $(y_t = \ln Sales_t - \ln Sales_{t-1} = 0)$, sales will grow by 2.22 percent next quarter.[8] If sales have changed during this quarter, however, the model predicts that sales will grow by 2.22 percent minus 0.5493 times the sales growth in this quarter.

2. AstraZeneca's sales in the third and fourth quarters of 2011 were $8,405 million and $8,872 million, respectively. If we use the previous model soon after the end of the fourth quarter of 2011, what will be the predicted value of AstraZeneca's sales for the first quarter of 2012?

---

[8]Note that 2.22 percent is the exponential growth rate, not [(Current quarter sales/Previous quarter sales) – 1]. The difference between these two methods of computing growth is usually small.

Solution to 2: Let us say that t is the fourth quarter of 2011, so $t - 1$ is the third quarter of 2011 and $t + 1$ is the first quarter of 2012. Then we would have to compute $\hat{y}_{t+1} = 0.0222 - 0.5493y_t$. To compute $\hat{y}_{t+1}$, we need to know $y_t = \ln \text{Sales}_t - \ln \text{Sales}_{t-1}$. In the third quarter of 2011, AstraZeneca's sales were \$8,405 million, so $\ln \text{Sales}_{t-1} = \ln 8{,}405 = 9.0366$. In the fourth quarter of 2011, AstraZeneca's sales were \$8,872 million, so $\ln \text{Sales}_t = \ln 8{,}872 = 9.0907$. Thus $y_t = 9.0907 - 9.0366 = 0.0541$. Therefore, $\hat{y}_{t+1} = 0.0222 - 0.5493(0.0541) = -0.0075$. If $\hat{y}_{t+1} = -0.0075$, then $-0.0075 = \ln \text{Sales}_{t+1} - \ln \text{Sales}_t = \ln(\text{Sales}_{t+1}/\text{Sales}_t)$. If we exponentiate both sides of this equation, the result is

$$e^{-0.0075} = \left(\frac{\text{Sales}_{t+1}}{\text{Sales}_t}\right)$$

$$\text{Sales}_{t+1} = \text{Sales}_t e^{-0.0075}$$

$$= \$8{,}872 \text{ million} \times 0.9925$$

$$= \$8{,}805 \text{ million}$$

Thus, based on fourth quarter sales for 2011, this model would have predicted that AstraZeneca's sales in the first quarter of 2012 would be \$8,805 million. This sales forecast might have affected our decision to buy AstraZeneca's stock at the time.

6. MOVING-AVERAGE TIME-SERIES MODELS

So far, many of the forecasting models we have used have been autoregressive models. Because most financial time series have the qualities of an autoregressive process, autoregressive time-series models are probably the most frequently used time-series models in financial forecasting. Some financial time series, however, seem to more closely follow another kind of time-series model, called a moving-average model. For example, as we will show, returns on the S&P BSE 100 Index can be better modeled as a moving-average process than as an autoregressive process.

In this section, we present the fundamentals of moving-average models so that you can ask the right questions when considering their use. We first discuss how to smooth past values with a moving average and then how to forecast a time series using a moving-average model. Even though both methods include the words "moving average" in the name, they are very different.

6.1. Smoothing Past Values with an n-Period Moving Average

Suppose you are analyzing the long-term trend in the past sales of a company. In order to focus on the trend, you may find it useful to remove short-term fluctuations or noise by smoothing out the time series of sales. One technique to smooth out period-to-period fluctuations in the value of a time series is an **n-period moving average**. An n-period moving average of the current and past $n - 1$ values of a time series, x_t, is calculated as

$$\frac{x_t + x_{t-1} + \cdots + x_{t-(n-1)}}{n}. \tag{11}$$

The following example demonstrates how to compute a moving average of AstraZeneca's quarterly sales.

EXAMPLE 13   AstraZeneca's Quarterly Sales (3)

Suppose we want to compute the four-quarter moving average of AstraZeneca's sales as of the beginning of the first quarter of 2012. AstraZeneca's sales in the previous four quarters were as follows: 1Q 2011, \$8,490 million; 2Q 2011, \$8,601 million; 3Q 2011, \$8,405 million; and 4Q 2011, \$8,872 million. The four-quarter moving average of sales as of the beginning of the first quarter of 2012 is thus (8,490 + 8,601 + 8,405 + 8,872)/4 = \$8,592 million.

We often plot the moving average of a series with large fluctuations to help discern any patterns in the data. Exhibit 23 shows monthly retail sales for the United States from December 1995 to June 2019, along with a 12-month moving average of the data (data from January 1995 are used to compute the 12-month moving average).

EXHIBIT 23   Monthly US Real Retail Sales and 12-Month Moving Average of Retail Sales

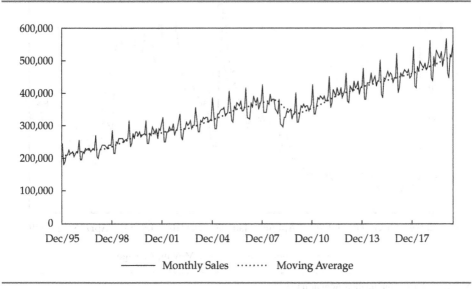

— Monthly Sales   ········ Moving Average

Source: Bloomberg.

As Exhibit 23 shows, each year has a very strong peak in retail sales (December) followed by a sharp drop in sales (January). Because of the extreme seasonality in the data, a 12-month moving average can help us focus on the long-term movements in retail sales instead of seasonal fluctuations. Note that the moving average does not have the sharp seasonal fluctuations of the original retail sales data. Rather, the moving average of retail sales grows steadily—for example, from 1995 through the second half of 2008—and then declines for about a year and grows steadily thereafter. We can see that trend more easily by looking at a 12-month moving average than by looking at the time series itself.

Exhibit 24 shows monthly Europe Brent Crude Oil spot prices along with a 12-month moving average of oil prices. Although these data do not have the same sharp regular seasonality displayed in the retail sales data in Exhibit 23, the moving average smooths out the monthly fluctuations in oil prices to show the longer-term movements.

Exhibit 24 also shows one weakness with a moving average: It always lags large movements in the actual data. For example, when oil prices rose quickly in late 2007 and the first half of 2008, the moving average rose only gradually. When oil prices fell sharply toward the end of 2008, the moving average also lagged. Consequently, a simple moving average of the recent past, though often useful in smoothing out a time series, may not be the best predictor of the future. A main reason for this is that a simple moving average gives equal weight to all the periods in the moving average. In order to forecast the future values of a time series, it is often better to use a more sophisticated moving-average time-series model. We discuss such models in the following section.

EXHIBIT 24   Monthly Europe Brent Crude Oil Price and 12-Month Moving Average of Prices

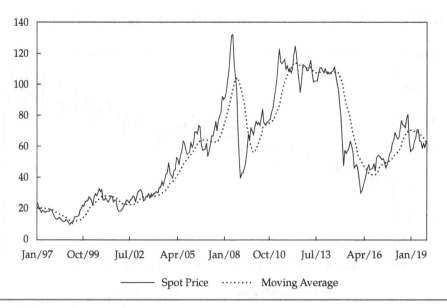

Source: US Energy Information Administration.

6.2. Moving-Average Time-Series Models for Forecasting

Suppose that a time series, x_t, is consistent with the following model:

$$x_t = \varepsilon_t + \theta\varepsilon_{t-1}, \mathrm{E}(\varepsilon_t) = 0, \mathrm{E}(\varepsilon_t^2) = \sigma^2,$$
$$\mathrm{cov}(\varepsilon_t,\varepsilon_s) = \mathrm{E}(\varepsilon_t\varepsilon_s) = 0 \text{ for t} \neq \text{s} \tag{12}$$

This equation is called a moving-average model of order 1, or simply an MA(1) model. Theta (θ) is the parameter of the MA(1) model.[9]

Equation 12 is a moving-average model because in each period, x_t is a moving average of ε_t and ε_{t-1}, two uncorrelated random variables that each have an expected value of zero. Unlike the simple moving-average model of Equation 11, this moving-average model places different weights on the two terms in the moving average (1 on ε_t, and θ on ε_{t-1}).

We can see if a time series fits an MA(1) model by looking at its autocorrelations to determine whether x_t is correlated only with its preceding and following values. First, we examine the variance of x_t in Equation 12 and its first two autocorrelations. Because the expected value of x_t is 0 in all periods and ε_t is uncorrelated with its own past values, the first autocorrelation is not equal to 0, but the second and higher autocorrelations are equal to 0. Further analysis shows that all autocorrelations except for the first will be equal to 0 in an MA(1) model. Thus for an MA(1) process, any value x_t is correlated with x_{t-1} and x_{t+1} but with no other time-series values; we could say that an MA(1) model has a memory of one period.

Of course, an MA(1) model is not the most complex moving-average model. A qth-order moving-average model, denoted MA(q) and with varying weights on lagged terms, can be written as

$$x_t = \varepsilon_t + \theta_1\varepsilon_{t-1} + \cdots + \theta_q\varepsilon_{t-q}, \mathrm{E}(\varepsilon_t) = 0, \mathrm{E}(\varepsilon_t^2) = \sigma^2,$$
$$\mathrm{cov}(\varepsilon_t,\varepsilon_s) = \mathrm{E}(\varepsilon_t\varepsilon_s) = 0 \text{ for t} \neq \text{s} \tag{13}$$

How can we tell whether an MA(q) model fits a time series? We examine the autocorrelations. For an MA(q) model, the first q autocorrelations will be significantly different from 0, and all autocorrelations beyond that will be equal to 0; an MA(q) model has a memory of q periods. This result is critical for choosing the right value of q for an MA model. We discussed this result previously for the specific case of $q = 1$ that all autocorrelations except for the first will be equal to 0 in an MA(1) model.

How can we distinguish an autoregressive time series from a moving-average time series? Once again, we do so by examining the autocorrelations of the time series itself. The autocorrelations of most autoregressive time series start large and decline gradually, whereas the autocorrelations of an MA(q) time series suddenly drop to 0 after the first q autocorrelations. We are unlikely to know in advance whether a time series is autoregressive or moving average. Therefore, the autocorrelations give us our best clue about how to model the time series. Most time series, however, are best modeled with an autoregressive model.

---

[9]Note that a moving-average time-series model is very different from a simple moving average, as discussed in Section 6.1. The simple moving average is based on observed values of a time series. In a moving-average time-series model, we never directly observe ε_t or any other ε_{t-j}, but we can infer how a particular moving-average model will imply a particular pattern of serial correlation for a time series, as we will discuss.

EXAMPLE 14   (Historical Example)
A Time-Series Model for Monthly Returns on the S&P BSE 100 Index

The S&P BSE 100 Index is designed to reflect the performance of India's top 100 large-cap companies listed on the BSE Ltd. (formerly Bombay Stock Exchange). Are monthly returns on the S&P BSE 100 Index autocorrelated? If so, we may be able to devise an investment strategy to exploit the autocorrelation. What is an appropriate time-series model for S&P BSE 100 monthly returns?

Exhibit 25 shows the first six autocorrelations of returns to the S&P BSE 100 using monthly data from January 2000 through December 2013. Note that all of the autocorrelations are quite small. Do they reach significance? With 168 observations, the critical value for a t-statistic in this model is about 1.98 at the 0.05 significance level. None of the autocorrelations has a t-statistic larger in absolute value than the critical value of 1.98. Consequently, we fail to reject the null hypothesis that those autocorrelations, individually, do not differ significantly from 0.

If returns on the S&P BSE 100 were an MA(q) time series, then the first q autocorrelations would differ significantly from 0. None of the autocorrelations is statistically significant, however, so returns to the S&P BSE 100 appear to come from an MA(0) time series. An MA(0) time series in which we allow the mean to be nonzero takes the following form:[10]

EXHIBIT 25   Annualized Monthly Returns to the S&P BSE 100, January 2000–December 2013

Autocorrelations

Lag	Autocorrelation	Standard Error	t-Statistic
1	0.1103	0.0772	1.4288
2	−0.0045	0.0772	−0.0583
3	0.0327	0.0772	0.4236
4	0.0370	0.0772	0.4793
5	−0.0218	0.0772	−0.2824
6	0.0191	0.0772	0.2474
Observations	168		

Source: BSE Ltd.

---

[10]On the basis of investment theory and evidence, we expect that the mean monthly return on the S&P BSE 100 is positive ($\mu > 0$). We can also generalize Equation 13 for an MA(q) time series by adding a constant term, μ. Including a constant term in a moving-average model does not change the expressions for the variance and autocovariances of the time series. A number of early studies of weak-form market efficiency used Equation 14 as the model for stock returns. See Garbade (1982).

$$x_t = \mu + \varepsilon_t, \; E(\varepsilon_t) = 0, \; E(\varepsilon_t^2) = \sigma^2,$$
$$\text{cov}(\varepsilon_t, \varepsilon_s) = E(\varepsilon_t \varepsilon_s) = 0 \text{ for } t \neq s \qquad (14)$$

which means that the time series is not predictable. This result should not be surprising, because most research suggests that short-term returns to stock indexes are difficult to predict.

We can see from this example how examining the autocorrelations allowed us to choose between the AR and MA models. If returns to the S&P BSE 100 had come from an AR(1) time series, the first autocorrelation would have differed significantly from 0 and the autocorrelations would have declined gradually. Not even the first autocorrelation is significantly different from 0, however. Therefore, we can be sure that returns to the S&P BSE 100 do not come from an AR(1) model—or from any higher-order AR model, for that matter. This finding is consistent with our conclusion that the S&P BSE 100 series is MA(0).

7. SEASONALITY IN TIME-SERIES MODELS

As we analyze the results of the time-series models in this chapter, we encounter complications. One common complication is significant **seasonality**, a case in which the series shows regular patterns of movement within the year. At first glance, seasonality might appear to rule out using autoregressive time-series models. After all, autocorrelations will differ by season. This problem can often be solved, however, by using seasonal lags in an autoregressive model.

A seasonal lag is usually the value of the time series one year before the current period, included as an extra term in an autoregressive model. Suppose, for example, that we model a particular quarterly time series using an AR(1) model, $x_t = b_0 + b_1 x_{t-1} + \varepsilon_t$. If the time series had significant seasonality, this model would not be correctly specified. The seasonality would be easy to detect because the seasonal autocorrelation (in the case of quarterly data, the fourth autocorrelation) of the error term would differ significantly from 0. Suppose this quarterly model has significant seasonality. In this case, we might include a seasonal lag in the autoregressive model and estimate

$$x_t = b_0 + b_1 x_{t-1} + b_2 x_{t-4} + \varepsilon_t \qquad (15)$$

to test whether including the seasonal lag would eliminate statistically significant autocorrelation in the error term.

In **Examples 15** and **16**, we illustrate how to test and adjust for seasonality in a time-series model. We also illustrate how to compute a forecast using an autoregressive model with a seasonal lag.

EXAMPLE 15   Seasonality in Sales at Starbucks

Earlier, we concluded that we could not model the log of Starbucks' quarterly sales using only a time-trend line (as shown in **Example 3**) because the Durbin–Watson statistic from the regression provided evidence of positive serial correlation in the error term. Based on methods presented in this chapter, we might next investigate using the first difference of log sales to remove an exponential trend from the data to obtain a covariance-stationary time series.

Using quarterly data from the last quarter of 2001 to the second quarter of 2019, we estimate the following AR(1) model using ordinary least squares: $(\ln \text{Sales}_t - \ln \text{Sales}_{t-1}) = b_0 + b_1(\ln \text{Sales}_{t-1} - \ln \text{Sales}_{t-2}) + \varepsilon_t$. Exhibit 26 shows the results of the regression.

The first thing to note in Exhibit 26 is the strong seasonal autocorrelation of the residuals. The bottom portion of the table shows that the fourth autocorrelation has a value of 0.7630 and a t-statistic of 6. With 72 observations and two parameters, this model has 70 degrees of freedom.[11] The critical value for a t-statistic is about 1.99 at the 0.05 significance level. Given this value of the t-statistic, we must reject the null hypothesis that the fourth autocorrelation is equal to 0 because the t-statistic is larger than the critical value of 1.99.

In this model, the fourth autocorrelation is the seasonal autocorrelation because this AR(1) model is estimated with quarterly data. Exhibit 26 shows the strong and statistically significant seasonal autocorrelation that occurs when a time series with strong seasonality is modeled without taking the seasonality into account. Therefore, the AR(1) model is misspecified, and we should not use it for forecasting.

EXHIBIT 26   Log Differenced Sales: AR(1) Model—Starbucks, Quarterly Observations, 2001–2019

Regression Statistics

R^2	0.2044
Standard error	0.0611
Observations	72
Durbin–Watson	1.9904

	Coefficient	Standard Error	t-Statistic
Intercept	0.0469	0.0080	5.8625
$\ln \text{Sales}_{t-1} - \ln \text{Sales}_{t-2}$	−0.4533	0.1069	−4.2404

Autocorrelations of the Residual

Lag	Autocorrelation	Standard Error	t-Statistic
1	0.0051	0.1179	−0.0433
2	−0.1676	0.1179	−1.4218
3	−0.0130	0.1179	−0.1099
4	0.7630	0.1179	6.4720

Source: Bloomberg.

---

[11]In this example, we restrict the start of the sample period to the beginning of 2001, and we do not use prior observations for the lags. Accordingly, the number of observations decreases with an increase in the number of lags. In Exhibit 26, the first observation is for the third quarter of 2001 because we use up to two lags. In Exhibit 27, the first observation is for the second quarter of 2002 because we use up to five lags.

EXHIBIT 27   Log Differenced Sales: AR(1) Model with Seasonal Lag—Starbucks, Quarterly Observations, 2005–2019

Regression Statistics

R^2	0.7032
Standard error	0.0373
Observations	69
Durbin–Watson	2.0392

	Coefficient	Standard Error	*t*-Statistic
Intercept	0.0107	0.0059	1.8136
ln Sales$_{t-1}$ – ln Sales$_{t-2}$	–0.1540	0.0729	–2.1125
ln Sales$_{t-4}$ – ln Sales$_{t-5}$	0.7549	0.0720	10.4847

Autocorrelations of the Residual

Lag	Autocorrelation	Standard Error	*t*-Statistic
1	0.0135	0.1204	0.1121
2	–0.0171	0.1204	–0.1420
3	0.1589	0.1204	1.3198
4	–0.1498	0.1204	–1.2442

Source: Compustat.

Suppose we decide to use an autoregressive model with a seasonal lag because of the seasonal autocorrelation. We are modeling quarterly data, so we estimate Equation 15: $(\ln \text{Sales}_t - \ln \text{Sales}_{t-1}) = b_0 + b_1(\ln \text{Sales}_{t-1} - \ln \text{Sales}_{t-2}) + b_2(\ln \text{Sales}_{t-4} - \ln \text{Sales}_{t-5}) + \varepsilon_t$. Adding the seasonal difference ln Sales$_{t-4}$ – ln Sales$_{t-5}$ is an attempt to remove a consistent quarterly pattern in the data and could also eliminate a seasonal nonstationarity if one existed. The estimates of this equation appear in Exhibit 27.

Note the autocorrelations of the residual shown at the bottom of Exhibit 27. None of the *t*-statistics on the first four autocorrelations is now significant. Because the overall regression is highly significant (an *F*-test, not shown in the exhibit, is significant at the 0.01 level), we can take an AR(1) model with a seasonal lag as a reasonable working model for Starbucks sales. (A model having only a seasonal lag term was investigated and not found to improve on this model.)

How can we interpret the coefficients in this model? To predict the current quarter's sales growth at Starbucks, we need to know two things: sales growth in the previous quarter and sales growth four quarters ago. If sales remained constant in each of those two quarters, the model in Exhibit 27 would predict that sales will grow by 0.0107 (1.07%) in the current quarter. If sales grew by 1 percent last quarter and by 2% four quarters ago, then the model would predict that sales growth this quarter will be 0.0107 – 0.0154(0.01) + 0.7549(0.02) = 0.0256, or 2.56 percent. Note that all of these growth rates are exponential growth rates. Notice also that the R^2 in the model with the seasonal lag (0.7032 in Exhibit 27) was more than three times higher than the R^2 in the model without the seasonal lag (0.2044 in Exhibit 26). Again, the seasonal lag model does a much better job of explaining the data.

EXAMPLE 16   (Historical Example)
Retail Sales Growth

We want to predict the growth in monthly retail sales of Canadian furniture and home furnishing stores so that we can decide whether to recommend the shares of these stores. We decide to use non-seasonally adjusted data on retail sales. To begin with, we estimate an AR(1) model with observations on the annualized monthly growth in retail sales from January 1995 to December 2012. We estimate the following equation: Sales growth$_t = b_0 + b_1$(Sales growth$_{t-1}$) $+ \varepsilon_t$. Exhibit 28 shows the results from this model.

The autocorrelations of the residuals from this model, shown at the bottom of Exhibit 28, indicate that seasonality is extremely significant in this model. With 216

EXHIBIT 28   Monthly Retail Sales Growth of Canadian Furniture and Home Furnishing Stores: AR(1) Model, January 1995–December 2012

Regression Statistics			
R^2	0.0509		
Standard error	1.8198		
Observations	216		
Durbin–Watson	2.0956		
	Coefficient	Standard Error	t-Statistic
Intercept	1.0518	0.1365	7.7055
Sales growth$_{t-1}$	-0.2252	0.0665	-3.3865
Autocorrelations of the Residual			
Lag	Autocorrelation	Standard Error	t-Statistic
1	-0.0109	0.0680	-0.1603
2	-0.1949	0.0680	-2.8662
3	0.1173	0.0680	1.7250
4	-0.0756	0.0680	-1.1118
5	-0.1270	0.0680	-1.8676
6	-0.1384	0.0680	-2.0353
7	-0.1374	0.0680	-2.0206
8	-0.0325	0.0680	-0.4779
9	0.1207	0.0680	1.7750
10	-0.2197	0.0680	-3.2309
11	-0.0342	0.0680	-0.5029
12	0.7620	0.0680	11.2059

Source: Statistics Canada (Government of Canada).

observations and two parameters, this model has 214 degrees of freedom. At the 0.05 significance level, the critical value for a *t*-statistic is about 1.97. The 12th-lag autocorrelation (the seasonal autocorrelation, because we are using monthly data) has a value of 0.7620 and a *t*-statistic of 11.21. The *t*-statistic on this autocorrelation is larger than the critical value (1.97), implying that we can reject the null hypothesis that the 12th autocorrelation is 0. Note also that many of the other *t*-statistics for autocorrelations shown in the table differ significantly from 0. Consequently, the model shown in Exhibit 28 is misspecified, so we cannot rely on it to forecast sales growth.

Suppose we add the seasonal lag of sales growth (the 12th lag) to the AR(1) model to estimate the equation Sales growth$_t$ = b_0 + b_1(Sales growth$_{t-1}$) + b_2(Sales growth$_{t-12}$) + ε_t. In this example, although we state that the sample period begins in

EXHIBIT 29   Monthly Retail Sales Growth of Canadian Furniture and Home Furnishing Stores: AR(1) Model with Seasonal Lag, January 1995–December 2012

Regression Statistics

R^2	0.6724
Standard error	1.0717
Observations	216
Durbin–Watson	2.1784

	Coefficient	Standard Error	*t*-Statistic
Intercept	0.2371	0.0900	2.6344
Sales growth$_{t-1}$	−0.0792	0.0398	−1.9899
Sales growth$_{t-12}$	0.7798	0.0388	20.0979

Autocorrelations of the Residual

Lag	Autocorrelation	Standard Error	*t*-Statistic
1	−0.0770	0.0680	−1.1324
2	−0.0374	0.0680	−0.5500
3	0.0292	0.0680	0.4294
4	−0.0358	0.0680	−0.5265
5	−0.0399	0.0680	−0.5868
6	0.0227	0.0680	0.3338
7	−0.0967	0.0680	−1.4221
8	0.1241	0.0680	1.8250
9	0.0499	0.0680	0.7338
10	−0.0631	0.0680	−0.9279
11	0.0231	0.0680	0.3397
12	−0.1168	0.0680	−1.7176

Source: Statistics Canada (Government of Canada).

1995, we use prior observations for the lags. This results in the same number of observations irrespective of the number of lags. Exhibit 29 presents the results of estimating this equation. The estimated value of the seasonal autocorrelation (the 12th autocorrelation) has fallen to –0.1168. None of the first 12 autocorrelations has a t-statistic with an absolute value greater than the critical value of 1.97 at the 0.05 significance level. We can conclude that there is no significant serial correlation in the residuals from this model. Because we can reasonably believe that the model is correctly specified, we can use it to predict retail sales growth. Note that the R^2 in Exhibit 29 is 0.6724, much larger than the R^2 in Exhibit 28 (computed by the model without the seasonal lag).

How can we interpret the coefficients in the model? To predict growth in retail sales in this month, we need to know last month's retail sales growth and retail sales growth 12 months ago. If retail sales remained constant both last month and 12 months ago, the model in Exhibit 29 would predict that retail sales will grow at an annual rate of about 23.7 percent this month. If retail sales grew at an annual rate of 10 percent last month and at an annual rate of 5% 12 months ago, the model in Exhibit 29 would predict that retail sales will grow in the current month at an annual rate of 0.2371 – 0.0792(0.10) + 0.7798(0.05) = 0.2682, or 26.8 percent.

8. AUTOREGRESSIVE MOVING-AVERAGE MODELS

So far, we have presented autoregressive and moving-average models as alternatives for modeling a time series. The time series we have considered in examples have usually been explained quite well with a simple autoregressive model (with or without seasonal lags).[12] Some statisticians, however, have advocated using a more general model, the autoregressive moving-average (ARMA) model. The advocates of ARMA models argue that these models may fit the data better and provide better forecasts than do plain autoregressive (AR) models. However, as we discuss later in this section, there are severe limitations to estimating and using these models. Because you may encounter ARMA models, we next provide a brief overview.

An ARMA model combines both autoregressive lags of the dependent variable and moving-average errors. The equation for such a model with p autoregressive terms and q moving-average terms, denoted ARMA(p, q), is

$$x_t = b_0 + b_1 x_{t-1} + \cdots + b_p x_{t-p} + \varepsilon_t + \theta_1 \varepsilon_{t-1} + \cdots + \theta_q \varepsilon_{t-q},$$
$$E(\varepsilon_t) = 0, E(\varepsilon_t^2) = \sigma^2, \text{cov}(\varepsilon_t, \varepsilon_s) = E(\varepsilon_t \varepsilon_s) = 0 \text{ for } t \neq s$$
(16)

where $b_1, b_2, \ldots, b_p$ are the autoregressive parameters and $\theta_1, \theta_2, \ldots, \theta_q$ are the moving-average parameters.

Estimating and using ARMA models has several limitations. First, the parameters in ARMA models can be very unstable. In particular, slight changes in the data sample or the initial guesses for the values of the ARMA parameters can result in very different final

---

[12]For the returns on the S&P BSE 100 (see **Example 14**), we chose a moving-average model over an autoregressive model.

estimates of the ARMA parameters. Second, choosing the right ARMA model is more of an art than a science. The criteria for deciding on p and q for a particular time series are far from perfect. Moreover, even after a model is selected, that model may not forecast well.

To reiterate, ARMA models can be very unstable, depending on the data sample used and the particular ARMA model estimated. Therefore, you should be skeptical of claims that a particular ARMA model provides much better forecasts of a time series than any other ARMA model. In fact, in most cases, you can use an AR model to produce forecasts that are just as accurate as those from ARMA models without nearly as much complexity. Even some of the strongest advocates of ARMA models admit that these models should not be used with fewer than 80 observations, and they do not recommend using ARMA models for predicting quarterly sales or gross margins for a company using even 15 years of quarterly data.

9. AUTOREGRESSIVE CONDITIONAL HETEROSKEDASTICITY MODELS

Up to now, we have ignored any issues of heteroskedasticity in time-series models and have assumed homoskedasticity. **Heteroskedasticity** is the dependence of the error term variance on the independent variable; **homoskedasticity** is the independence of the error term variance from the independent variable. We have assumed that the error term's variance is constant and does not depend on the value of the time series itself or on the size of previous errors. At times, however, this assumption is violated and the variance of the error term is not constant. In such a situation, the standard errors of the regression coefficients in AR, MA, or ARMA models will be incorrect, and our hypothesis tests would be invalid. Consequently, we can make poor investment decisions based on those tests.

For example, suppose you are building an autoregressive model of a company's sales. If heteroskedasticity is present, then the standard errors of the regression coefficients of your model will be incorrect. It is likely that because of heteroskedasticity, one or more of the lagged sales terms may appear statistically significant when in fact they are not. Therefore, if you use this model for your decision making, you may make some suboptimal decisions.

In work responsible in part for his shared 2003 Nobel Prize in Economics, Robert F. Engle in 1982 first suggested a way of testing whether the variance of the error in a particular time-series model in one period depends on the variance of the error in previous periods. He called this type of heteroskedasticity "autoregressive conditional heteroskedasticity" (ARCH).

As an example, consider the ARCH(1) model

$$\varepsilon_t \sim N(0, a_0 + a_1 \varepsilon_{t-1}^2) \tag{17}$$

where the distribution of ε_t, conditional on its value in the previous period, ε_{t-1}, is normal, with mean 0 and variance $a_0 + a_1 \varepsilon_{t-1}^2$. If $a_1 = 0$, the variance of the error in every period is just a_0. The variance is constant over time and does not depend on past errors. Now suppose that $a_1 > 0$. Then the variance of the error in one period depends on how large the squared error was in the previous period. If a large error occurs in one period, the variance of the error in the next period will be even larger.

Engle showed that we can test whether a time series is ARCH(1) by regressing the squared residuals from a previously estimated time-series model (AR, MA, or ARMA) on a constant and one lag of the squared residuals. We can estimate the linear regression equation

$$\widehat{\varepsilon}_t^2 = a_0 + a_1 \widehat{\varepsilon}_{t-1}^2 + u_t \tag{18}$$

where u_t is an error term. If the estimate of a_1 is statistically significantly different from zero, we conclude that the time series is ARCH(1). If a time-series model has ARCH(1) errors, then the variance of the errors in period $t + 1$ can be predicted in period t using the formula $\widehat{\sigma}_{t+1}^2 = \widehat{a}_0 + \widehat{a}_1 \widehat{\varepsilon}_t^2$.

EXAMPLE 17   Testing for ARCH(1) in Monthly Inflation

Analyst Lisette Miller wants to test whether monthly data on CPI inflation contain autoregressive conditional heteroskedasticity. She could estimate Equation 18 using the residuals from the time-series model. Based on the analyses in **Examples 6** through **9**, she has concluded that if she modeled monthly CPI inflation from 1995 to 2018, there would not be much difference in the performance of AR(1) and AR(2) models in forecasting inflation. The AR(1) model is clearly better for the period 2008–2018. She decides to further explore the AR(1) model for the entire period 1995 to 2018. Exhibit 30 shows the results of testing whether the errors in that model are ARCH(1). Because the test involves the first lag of residuals of the estimated time-series model, the number of observations in the test is one less than that in the model.

The t-statistic for the coefficient on the previous period's squared residuals is greater than 4.8. Therefore, Miller easily rejects the null hypothesis that the variance of the error does not depend on the variance of previous errors. Consequently, the test statistics she computed in Exhibit 30 are not valid, and she should not use them in deciding her investment strategy.

It is possible Miller's conclusion—that the AR(1) model for monthly inflation has ARCH in the errors—may have been due to the sample period used (1995–2018). In

---

EXHIBIT 30   Test for ARCH(1) in an AR(1) Model: Residuals from Monthly CPI Inflation at an Annual Rate, March 1995–December 2018

Regression Statistics

R^2	0.0759		
Standard error	23.7841		
Observations	286		
Durbin–Watson	2.0569		

	Coefficient	Standard Error	t-Statistic
Intercept	6.3626	1.4928	4.2622
$\widehat{\varepsilon}_{t-1}^2$	0.2754	0.0570	4.8316

Source: US Bureau of Labor Statistics.

EXHIBIT 31   Test for ARCH(1) in an AR(1) Model: Monthly CPI Inflation at an Annual Rate, February 2008–December 2018

Regression Statistics

R^2	0.1113		
Standard error	24.64		
Observations	131		
Durbin–Watson	2.0385		
	Coefficient	**Standard Error**	**t-Statistic**
Intercept	6.2082	2.2873	2.7142
$\widehat{\varepsilon}^2_{t-1}$	0.3336	0.0830	4.0229

Source: US Bureau of Labor Statistics.

Example 9, she used a shorter sample period, 2008–2018, and concluded that monthly CPI inflation follows an AR(1) process. (These results were shown in Exhibit 16.) Exhibit 30 shows that errors for a time-series model of inflation for the entire sample (1995–2018) have ARCH errors. Do the errors estimated with a shorter sample period (2008–2018) also display ARCH? For the shorter sample period, Miller estimated an AR(1) model using monthly inflation data. Now she tests to see whether the errors display ARCH. Exhibit 31 shows the results.

In this sample, the coefficient on the previous period's squared residual has a t-statistic of 4.0229. Consequently, Miller rejects the null hypothesis that the errors in this regression have no autoregressive conditional heteroskedasticity. The error variance appears to be heteroskedastic, and Miller cannot rely on the t-statistics.

Suppose a model contains ARCH(1) errors. What are the consequences of that fact? First, if ARCH exists, the standard errors for the regression parameters will not be correct. We will need to use generalized least squares[13] or other methods that correct for heteroskedasticity to correctly estimate the standard error of the parameters in the time-series model. Second, if ARCH exists and we have it modeled—for example, as ARCH(1)—we can predict the variance of the errors. Suppose, for instance, that we want to predict the variance of the error in inflation using the estimated parameters from Exhibit 30: $\widehat{\sigma}^2_t = 6.3626 + 0.2754\widehat{\varepsilon}^2_{t-1}$. If the error in one period were 0 percent, the predicted variance of the error in the next period would be $6.3626 + 0.2754(0) = 6.3626$. If the error in one period were 1 percent, the predicted variance of the error in the next period would be $6.3626 + 0.2754(1^2) = 6.6380$.

---

[13]See Greene (2018).

Engle and other researchers have suggested many generalizations of the ARCH(1) model, including ARCH(p) and generalized autoregressive conditional heteroskedasticity (GARCH) models. In an ARCH(p) model, the variance of the error term in the current period depends linearly on the squared errors from the previous p periods: $\sigma_t^2 = a_0 + a_1\varepsilon_{t-1}^2 + \cdots + a_p\varepsilon_{t-p}^2$. GARCH models are similar to ARMA models of the error variance in a time series. Just like ARMA models, GARCH models can be finicky and unstable: Their results can depend greatly on the sample period and the initial guesses of the parameters in the GARCH model. Financial analysts who use GARCH models should be well aware of how delicate these models can be, and they should examine whether GARCH estimates are robust to changes in the sample and the initial guesses about the parameters.[14]

10. REGRESSIONS WITH MORE THAN ONE TIME SERIES

Up to now, we have discussed time-series models only for one time series. Although in the chapter on correlation and regression and on multiple regression we used linear regression to analyze the relationship among different time series, in those chapters we completely ignored unit roots. A time series that contains a unit root is not covariance stationary. If any time series in a linear regression contains a unit root, ordinary least squares estimates of regression test statistics may be invalid.

To determine whether we can use linear regression to model more than one time series, let us start with a single independent variable; that is, there are two time series, one corresponding to the dependent variable and one corresponding to the independent variable. We will then extend our discussion to multiple independent variables.

We first use a unit root test, such as the Dickey–Fuller test, for each of the two time series to determine whether either of them has a unit root.[15] There are several possible scenarios related to the outcome of these tests. One possible scenario is that we find that neither of the time series has a unit root. Then we can safely use linear regression to test the relations between the two time series. Otherwise, we may have to use additional tests, as we discuss later in this section.

EXAMPLE 18   Unit Roots and the Fisher Effect

Researchers at an asset management firm examined the Fisher effect by estimating the regression relation between expected inflation and US Treasury bill (T-bill) returns. They used 181 quarterly observations on expected inflation rates and T-bill returns from the sample period extending from the fourth quarter of 1968 through the fourth quarter of 2013. They used linear regression to analyze the relationship between the two time series. The results of this regression would be valid if both time series are covariance stationary; that is, neither of the two time series has a unit root. So, if they compute the Dickey–Fuller t-test statistic of the hypothesis of a unit root separately for

---

[14]For more on ARCH, GARCH, and other models of time-series variance, see **Hamilton (1994)**.

[15]For theoretical details of unit root tests, see Greene (2018) or **Tsay (2010)**. Unit root tests are available in some econometric software packages, such as EViews.

each time series and find that they can reject the null hypothesis that the T-bill return series has a unit root and the null hypothesis that the expected inflation time series has a unit root, then they can use linear regression to analyze the relation between the two series. In that case, the results of their analysis of the Fisher effect would be valid.

A second possible scenario is that we reject the hypothesis of a unit root for the independent variable but fail to reject the hypothesis of a unit root for the dependent variable. In this case, the error term in the regression would not be covariance stationary. Therefore, one or more of the following linear regression assumptions would be violated: (1) that the expected value of the error term is 0, (2) that the variance of the error term is constant for all observations, and (3) that the error term is uncorrelated across observations. Consequently, the estimated regression coefficients and standard errors would be inconsistent. The regression coefficients might appear significant, but those results would be spurious.[16] Thus we should not use linear regression to analyze the relation between the two time series in this scenario.

A third possible scenario is the reverse of the second scenario: We reject the hypothesis of a unit root for the dependent variable but fail to reject the hypothesis of a unit root for the independent variable. In this case also, like the second scenario, the error term in the regression would not be covariance stationary, and we cannot use linear regression to analyze the relation between the two time series.

EXAMPLE 19   (Historical Example)
Unit Roots and Predictability of Stock Market Returns
by Price-to-Earnings Ratio

Johann de Vries is analyzing the performance of the South African stock market. He examines whether the percentage change in the Johannesburg Stock Exchange (JSE) All Share Index can be predicted by the price-to-earnings ratio (P/E) for the index. Using monthly data from January 1994 to December 2013, he runs a regression using $(P_t - P_{t-1})/P_{t-1}$ as the dependent variable and P_{t-1}/E_{t-2} as the independent variable, where P_t is the value of the JSE index at time t and E_t is the earnings on the index. De Vries finds that the regression coefficient is negative and statistically significant and the value of the R^2 for the regression is quite high. What additional analysis should he perform before accepting the regression as valid?

De Vries needs to perform unit root tests for each of the two time series. If one of the two time series has a unit root, implying that it is not stationary, the results of the linear regression are not meaningful and cannot be used to conclude that stock market returns are predictable by P/E.[17]

---

[16]The problem of spurious regression for nonstationary time series was first discussed by Granger and Newbold (1974).

[17]Barr and Kantor (1999) contains evidence that the P/E time series is nonstationary.

The next possibility is that both time series have a unit root. In this case, we need to establish whether the two time series are **cointegrated** before we can rely on regression analysis.[18] Two time series are cointegrated if a long-term financial or economic relationship exists between them such that they do not diverge from each other without bound in the long run. For example, two time series are cointegrated if they share a common trend.

In the fourth scenario, both time series have a unit root but are not cointegrated. In this scenario, as in the second and third scenarios, the error term in the linear regression will not be covariance stationary, some regression assumptions will be violated, the regression coefficients and standard errors will not be consistent, and we cannot use them for hypothesis tests. Consequently, linear regression of one variable on the other would be meaningless.

Finally, the fifth possible scenario is that both time series have a unit root but they are cointegrated. In this case, the error term in the linear regression of one time series on the other will be covariance stationary. Accordingly, the regression coefficients and standard errors will be consistent, and we can use them for hypothesis tests. However, we should be very cautious in interpreting the results of a regression with cointegrated variables. The cointegrated regression estimates the long-term relation between the two series but may not be the best model of the short-term relation between the two series. Short-term models of cointegrated series (error correction models) are discussed in **Engle and Granger (1987)** and **Tsay (2010)**, but these are specialist topics.

Now let us look at how we can test for cointegration between two time series that each have a unit root, as in the fourth and fifth scenarios.[19] Engle and Granger suggested the following test. If y_t and x_t are both time series with a unit root, we should do the following:

1.   Estimate the regression $y_t = b_0 + b_1 x_t + \varepsilon_t$.
2.   Test whether the error term from the regression in Step 1 has a unit root using a Dickey–Fuller test. Because the residuals are based on the estimated coefficients of the regression, we cannot use the standard critical values for the Dickey–Fuller test. Instead, we must use the critical values computed by Engle and Granger, which take into account the effect of uncertainty about the regression parameters on the distribution of the Dickey–Fuller test.
3.   If the (Engle–Granger) Dickey–Fuller test fails to reject the null hypothesis that the error term has a unit root, then we conclude that the error term in the regression is not covariance stationary. Therefore, the two time series are not cointegrated. In this case, any regression relation between the two series is spurious.
4.   If the (Engle–Granger) Dickey–Fuller test rejects the null hypothesis that the error term has a unit root, then we may assume that the error term in the regression is covariance stationary and that the two time series are cointegrated. The parameters and standard errors from linear regression will be consistent and will let us test hypotheses about the long-term relation between the two series.

---

[18]Engle and Granger (1987) first discussed cointegration.

[19]Consider a time series, x_t, that has a unit root. For many such financial and economic time series, the first difference of the series, $x_t - x_{t-1}$, is stationary. We say that such a series, whose first difference is stationary, has a *single* unit root. However, for some time series, even the first difference may not be stationary and further differencing may be needed to achieve stationarity. Such a time series is said to have *multiple* unit roots. In this section, we consider only the case in which each nonstationary series has a single unit root (which is quite common).

EXAMPLE 20   Testing for Cointegration between Intel Sales and Nominal GDP

Suppose we want to test whether the natural log of Intel's sales and the natural log of GDP are cointegrated (that is, whether there is a long-term relation between GDP and Intel sales). We want to test this hypothesis using quarterly data from the first quarter of 1995 through the fourth quarter of 2019. Here are the steps:

1. Test whether the two series each have a unit root. If we cannot reject the null hypothesis of a unit root for both series, implying that both series are nonstationary, we must then test whether the two series are cointegrated.

2. Having established that each series has a unit root, we estimate the regression ln Intel sales$_t$ = b_0 + b_1(ln GDP$_t$) + ε_t, then conduct the (Engle–Granger) Dickey–Fuller test of the hypothesis that there is a unit root in the error term of this regression using the residuals from the estimated regression. If we reject the null hypothesis of a unit root in the error term of the regression, we reject the null hypothesis of no cointegration. That is, the two series would be cointegrated. If the two series are cointegrated, we can use linear regression to estimate the long-term relation between the natural log of Intel sales and the natural log of GDP.

We have so far discussed models with a single independent variable. We now extend the discussion to a model with two or more independent variables, so that there are three or more time series. The simplest possibility is that none of the time series in the model has a unit root. Then, we can safely use multiple regression to test the relation among the time series.

EXAMPLE 21   Unit Roots and Returns to the Fidelity Select Technology Fund

---

In earlier coverage of multiple regression, we used a multiple linear regression model to examine whether returns to either the S&P 500 Growth Index or the S&P 500 Value Index explain returns to the Fidelity Select Technology Portfolio using monthly observations between October 2015 and August 2019. Of course, if any of the three time series has a unit root, then the results of our regression analysis may be invalid. Therefore, we could use a Dickey–Fuller test to determine whether any of these series has a unit root.

If we reject the hypothesis of unit roots for all three series, we can use linear regression to analyze the relation among the series. In that case, the results of our analysis of the factors affecting returns to the Fidelity Select Technology Portfolio would be valid.

If at least one time series (the dependent variable or one of the independent variables) has a unit root while at least one time series (the dependent variable or one of the independent variables) does not, the error term in the regression cannot be covariance stationary. Consequently, we should not use multiple linear regression to analyze the relation among the time series in this scenario.

Another possibility is that each time series, including the dependent variable and each of the independent variables, has a unit root. If this is the case, we need to establish whether the time series are cointegrated. To test for cointegration, the procedure is similar to that for a model with a single independent variable. First, estimate the regression $y_t = b_0 + b_1 x_{1t} + b_2 x_{2t} + \ldots + b_k x_{kt} + \varepsilon_t$. Then conduct the (Engle–Granger) Dickey–Fuller test of the hypothesis that there is a unit root in the errors of this regression using the residuals from the estimated regression.

If we cannot reject the null hypothesis of a unit root in the error term of the regression, we cannot reject the null hypothesis of no cointegration. In this scenario, the error term in the multiple regression will not be covariance stationary, so we cannot use multiple regression to analyze the relationship among the time series.

If we can reject the null hypothesis of a unit root in the error term of the regression, we can reject the null hypothesis of no cointegration. However, modeling three or more time series that are cointegrated may be difficult. For example, an analyst may want to predict a retirement services company's sales based on the country's GDP and the total population over age 65. Although the company's sales, GDP, and the population over 65 may each have a unit root and be cointegrated, modeling the cointegration of the three series may be difficult, and doing so is beyond the scope of this volume. Analysts who have not mastered all these complex issues should avoid forecasting models with multiple time series that have unit roots; the regression coefficients may be inconsistent and may produce incorrect forecasts.

11. OTHER ISSUES IN TIME SERIES

Time-series analysis is an extensive topic and includes many highly complex issues. Our objective in this chapter has been to present those issues in time series that are the most important for financial analysts and can also be handled with relative ease. In this section, we briefly discuss some of the issues that we have not covered but could be useful for analysts.

In this chapter, we have shown how to use time-series models to make forecasts. We have also introduced the RMSE as a criterion for comparing forecasting models. However, we have not discussed measuring the uncertainty associated with forecasts made using time-series models. The uncertainty of these forecasts can be very large, and should be taken into account when making investment decisions. Fortunately, the same techniques apply to evaluating the uncertainty of time-series forecasts as apply to evaluating the uncertainty about forecasts from linear regression models. To accurately evaluate forecast uncertainty, we need to consider both the uncertainty about the error term and the uncertainty about the estimated parameters in the time-series model. Evaluating this uncertainty is fairly complicated when using regressions with more than one independent variable.

In this chapter, we used the US CPI inflation series to illustrate some of the practical challenges analysts face in using time-series models. We used information on US Federal Reserve policy to explore the consequences of splitting the inflation series in two. In financial time-series work, we may suspect that a time series has more than one regime but lack the information to attempt to sort the data into different regimes. If you face such a problem, you may want to investigate other methods, especially switching regression models, to identify multiple regimes using only the time series itself.

If you are interested in these and other advanced time-series topics, you can learn more from Diebold (2008) and Tsay (2010).

12. SUGGESTED STEPS IN TIME-SERIES FORECASTING

The following is a step-by-step guide to building a model to predict a time series.

1. Understand the investment problem you have, and make an initial choice of model. One alternative is a regression model that predicts the future behavior of a variable based on hypothesized causal relationships with other variables. Another is a time-series model that attempts to predict the future behavior of a variable based on the past behavior of the same variable.

2. If you have decided to use a time-series model, compile the time series and plot it to see whether it looks covariance stationary. The plot might show important deviations from covariance stationarity, including the following:
    *   a linear trend,
    *   an exponential trend,
    *   seasonality, or
    *   a significant shift in the time series during the sample period (for example, a change in mean or variance).

3. If you find no significant seasonality or shift in the time series, then perhaps either a linear trend or an exponential trend will be sufficient to model the time series. In that case, take the following steps:
    *   Determine whether a linear or exponential trend seems most reasonable (usually by plotting the series).
    *   Estimate the trend.
    *   Compute the residuals.
    *   Use the Durbin–Watson statistic to determine whether the residuals have significant serial correlation. If you find no significant serial correlation in the residuals, then the trend model is sufficient to capture the dynamics of the time series and you can use that model for forecasting.

4. If you find significant serial correlation in the residuals from the trend model, use a more complex model, such as an autoregressive model. First, however, reexamine whether the time series is covariance stationary. The following is a list of violations of stationarity, along with potential methods to adjust the time series to make it covariance stationary:
    *   If the time series has a linear trend, first-difference the time series.
    *   If the time series has an exponential trend, take the natural log of the time series and then first-difference it.
    *   If the time series shifts significantly during the sample period, estimate different time-series models before and after the shift.
    *   If the time series has significant seasonality, include seasonal lags (discussed in Step 7).

5. After you have successfully transformed a raw time series into a covariance-stationary time series, you can usually model the transformed series with a short autoregression.[20] To decide which autoregressive model to use, take the following steps:
   - Estimate an AR(1) model.
   - Test to see whether the residuals from this model have significant serial correlation.
   - If you find no significant serial correlation in the residuals, you can use the AR(1) model to forecast.

6. If you find significant serial correlation in the residuals, use an AR(2) model and test for significant serial correlation of the residuals of the AR(2) model.
   - If you find no significant serial correlation, use the AR(2) model.
   - If you find significant serial correlation of the residuals, keep increasing the order of the AR model until the residual serial correlation is no longer significant.

7. Your next move is to check for seasonality. You can use one of two approaches:
   - Graph the data and check for regular seasonal patterns.
   - Examine the data to see whether the seasonal autocorrelations of the residuals from an AR model are significant (for example, the fourth autocorrelation for quarterly data) and whether the autocorrelations before and after the seasonal autocorrelations are significant. To correct for seasonality, add seasonal lags to your AR model. For example, if you are using quarterly data, you might add the fourth lag of a time series as an additional variable in an AR(1) or an AR(2) model.

8. Next, test whether the residuals have autoregressive conditional heteroskedasticity. To test for ARCH(1), for example, do the following:
   - Regress the squared residual from your time-series model on a lagged value of the squared residual.
   - Test whether the coefficient on the squared lagged residual differs significantly from 0.
   - If the coefficient on the squared lagged residual does not differ significantly from 0, the residuals do not display ARCH and you can rely on the standard errors from your time-series estimates.
   - If the coefficient on the squared lagged residual does differ significantly from 0, use generalized least squares or other methods to correct for ARCH.

9. Finally, you may also want to perform tests of the model's out-of-sample forecasting performance to see how the model's out-of-sample performance compares to its in-sample performance.

   Using these steps in sequence, you can be reasonably sure that your model is correctly specified.

---

[20]Most financial time series can be modeled using an autoregressive process. For a few time series, a moving-average model may fit better. To see whether this is the case, examine the first five or six autocorrelations of the time series. If the autocorrelations suddenly drop to 0 after the first q autocorrelations, a moving-average model (of order q) is appropriate. If the autocorrelations start large and decline gradually, an autoregressive model is appropriate.

SUMMARY

- The predicted trend value of a time series in period t is $\widehat{b}_0 + \widehat{b}_1 t$ in a linear trend model; the predicted trend value of a time series in a log-linear trend model is $e^{\widehat{b}_0 + \widehat{b}_1 t}$.
- Time series that tend to grow by a constant amount from period to period should be modeled by linear trend models, whereas time series that tend to grow at a constant rate should be modeled by log-linear trend models.
- Trend models often do not completely capture the behavior of a time series, as indicated by serial correlation of the error term. If the Durbin–Watson statistic from a trend model differs significantly from 2, indicating serial correlation, we need to build a different kind of model.
- An autoregressive model of order p, denoted AR(p), uses p lags of a time series to predict its current value: $x_t = b_0 + b_1 x_{t-1} + b_2 x_{t-2} + \ldots + b_p x_{t-p} + \varepsilon_t$.
- A time series is covariance stationary if the following three conditions are satisfied: First, the expected value of the time series must be constant and finite in all periods. Second, the variance of the time series must be constant and finite in all periods. Third, the covariance of the time series with itself for a fixed number of periods in the past or future must be constant and finite in all periods. Inspection of a nonstationary time-series plot may reveal an upward or downward trend (nonconstant mean) and/or nonconstant variance. The use of linear regression to estimate an autoregressive time-series model is not valid unless the time series is covariance stationary.
- For a specific autoregressive model to be a good fit to the data, the autocorrelations of the error term should be 0 at all lags.
- A time series is mean reverting if it tends to fall when its level is above its long-run mean and rise when its level is below its long-run mean. If a time series is covariance stationary, then it will be mean reverting.
- The one-period-ahead forecast of a variable x_t from an AR(1) model made in period t for period $t + 1$ is $\widehat{x}_{t+1} = \widehat{b}_0 + \widehat{b}_1 x_t$. This forecast can be used to create the two-period-ahead forecast from the model made in period t, $\widehat{x}_{t+2} = \widehat{b}_0 + \widehat{b}_1 x_{t+1}$. Similar results hold for AR (p) models.
- In-sample forecasts are the in-sample predicted values from the estimated time-series model. Out-of-sample forecasts are the forecasts made from the estimated time-series model for a time period different from the one for which the model was estimated. Out-of-sample forecasts are usually more valuable in evaluating the forecasting performance of a time-series model than are in-sample forecasts. The root mean squared error (RMSE), defined as the square root of the average squared forecast error, is a criterion for comparing the forecast accuracy of different time-series models; a smaller RMSE implies greater forecast accuracy.
- Just as in regression models, the coefficients in time-series models are often unstable across different sample periods. In selecting a sample period for estimating a time-series model, we should seek to assure ourselves that the time series was stationary in the sample period.
- A random walk is a time series in which the value of the series in one period is the value of the series in the previous period plus an unpredictable random error. If the time series is a random walk, it is not covariance stationary. A random walk with drift is a random walk with a nonzero intercept term. All random walks have unit roots. If a time series has a unit root, then it will not be covariance stationary.

- If a time series has a unit root, we can sometimes transform the time series into one that is covariance stationary by first-differencing the time series; we may then be able to estimate an autoregressive model for the first-differenced series.
- An n-period moving average of the current and past $(n-1)$ values of a time series, x_t, is calculated as $[x_t + x_{t-1} + \ldots + x_{t-(n-1)}]/n$.
- A moving-average model of order q, denoted MA(q), uses q lags of a random error term to predict its current value.
- The order q of a moving-average model can be determined using the fact that if a time series is a moving-average time series of order q, its first q autocorrelations are nonzero while autocorrelations beyond the first q are zero.
- The autocorrelations of most autoregressive time series start large and decline gradually, whereas the autocorrelations of an MA(q) time series suddenly drop to 0 after the first q autocorrelations. This helps in distinguishing between autoregressive and moving-average time series.
- If the error term of a time-series model shows significant serial correlation at seasonal lags, the time series has significant seasonality. This seasonality can often be modeled by including a seasonal lag in the model, such as adding a term lagged four quarters to an AR(1) model on quarterly observations.
- The forecast made in time t for time $t+1$ using a quarterly AR(1) model with a seasonal lag would be $x_{t+1} = \hat{b}_0 + \hat{b}_1 x_t + \hat{b}_2 x_{t-3}$.
- ARMA models have several limitations: The parameters in ARMA models can be very unstable; determining the AR and MA order of the model can be difficult; and even with their additional complexity, ARMA models may not forecast well.
- The variance of the error in a time-series model sometimes depends on the variance of previous errors, representing autoregressive conditional heteroskedasticity (ARCH). Analysts can test for first-order ARCH in a time-series model by regressing the squared residual on the squared residual from the previous period. If the coefficient on the squared residual is statistically significant, the time-series model has ARCH(1) errors.
- If a time-series model has ARCH(1) errors, then the variance of the errors in period $t+1$ can be predicted in period t using the formula $\hat{\sigma}^2_{t+1} = \hat{a}_0 + \hat{a}_1 \hat{\varepsilon}^2_t$.
- If linear regression is used to model the relationship between two time series, a test should be performed to determine whether either time series has a unit root:
  . If neither of the time series has a unit root, then we can safely use linear regression.
  . If one of the two time series has a unit root, then we should not use linear regression.
  . If both time series have a unit root and the time series are cointegrated, we may safely use linear regression; however, if they are not cointegrated, we should not use linear regression. The (Engle–Granger) Dickey–Fuller test can be used to determine whether time series are cointegrated.

REFERENCES

Barr, G. D. I. and B. S. Kantor. 1999. "Price–Earnings Ratios on the Johannesburg Stock Exchange—Are They a Good Value?" *SA Journal of Accounting Research* 13 (1): 1–23.

Dickey, David A. and Wayne A. Fuller. 1979. "Distribution of the Estimators for Autoregressive Time Series with a Unit Root." *Journal of the American Statistical Association* 74 (366): 427–31. 10.2307/2286348.

Diebold, Francis X. 2008. *Elements of Forecasting*, 4th ed. Cincinnati: South-Western.

Engle, Robert F. and Clive W. J. Granger. 1987. "Co-Integration and Error Correction: Representation, Estimation, and Testing." *Econometrica* 55 (2): 251–76. 10.2307/1913236.

Garbade, Kenneth. 1982. *Securities Markets*. New York: McGraw-Hill.

Granger, Clive W. J. and Paul Newbold. 1974. "Spurious Regressions in Econometrics." *Journal of Econometrics* 2 (2): 111–20. 10.1016/0304-4076(74)90034-7.

Greene, William H., *Econometric Analysis, New York*. 2018. NY: Pearson.

Hamilton, James D. 1994. *Time Series Analysis*. Princeton, NJ: Princeton University Press.

Tsay, Ruey S. 2010. *Analysis of Financial Time Series*, 3rd ed. New York: Wiley.

PRACTICE PROBLEMS

Note: In the problems and solutions for this chapter, we use the hat ($\hat{}$) to indicate an estimate if we are trying to differentiate between an estimated and an actual value. However, we suppress the hat when we are clearly showing regression output.

1. The civilian unemployment rate (UER) is an important component of many economic models. Exhibit 1 gives regression statistics from estimating a linear trend model of the unemployment rate: $UER_t = b_0 + b_1 t + \varepsilon_t$.

EXHIBIT 1   Estimating a Linear Trend in the Civilian Unemployment Rate: Monthly Observations, January 2013–August 2019

Regression Statistics			
R^2	0.9316		
Standard error	0.3227		
Observations	80		
Durbin–Watson	0.1878		
	Coefficient	**Standard Error**	*t*-**Statistic**
Intercept	7.2237	0.0728	99.1704
Trend	–0.0510	0.0016	–32.6136

   A. Using the regression output in the previous table, what is the model's prediction of the unemployment rate for July 2013?

   B. How should we interpret the Durbin–Watson (DW) statistic for this regression? What does the value of the DW statistic say about the validity of a *t*-test on the coefficient estimates?

2. Exhibit 2 compares the predicted civilian unemployment rate (PRED) with the actual civilian unemployment rate (UER) from January 2013 to August 2019. The predicted results come from estimating the linear time trend model $UER_t = b_0 + b_1 t + \varepsilon_t$. What can we conclude about the appropriateness of this model?

EXHIBIT 2   Predicted and Actual Civilian Unemployment Rates

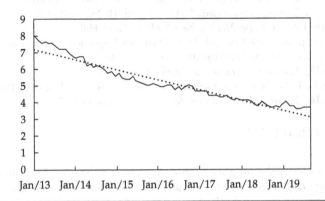

Jan/13 Jan/14 Jan/15 Jan/16 Jan/17 Jan/18 Jan/19

3. You have been assigned to analyze automobile manufacturers, and as a first step in your analysis, you decide to model monthly sales of lightweight vehicles to determine sales growth in that part of the industry. Exhibit 3 gives lightweight vehicle monthly sales (annualized) from January 1992 to December 2000.

EXHIBIT 3   Lightweight Vehicle Sales

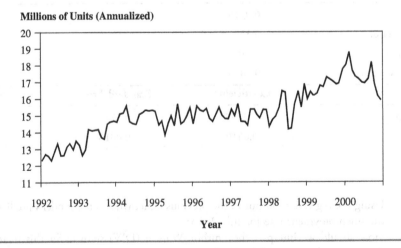

Millions of Units (Annualized)

Year

Monthly sales in the lightweight vehicle sector, $Sales_t$, have been increasing over time, but you suspect that the growth rate of monthly sales is relatively constant. Write the simplest time-series model for $Sales_t$ that is consistent with your perception.

4. Exhibit 4 shows a plot of the first differences in the civilian unemployment rate (UER) between January 2013 and August 2019, $\Delta UER_t = UER_t - UER_{t-1}$.

EXHIBIT 4   Change in Civilian Unemployment Rate

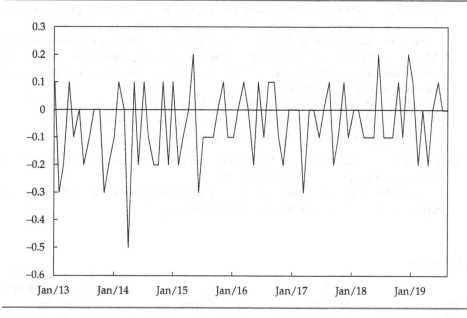

A. Has differencing the data made the new series, ΔUER_t, covariance stationary? Explain your answer.

B. Given the graph of the change in the unemployment rate shown in the figure, describe the steps we should take to determine the appropriate autoregressive time-series model specification for the series ΔUER_t.

5. Exhibit 5 gives the regression output of an AR(1) model on first differences in the unemployment rate. Describe how to interpret the DW statistic for this regression.

EXHIBIT 5   Estimating an AR(1) Model of Changes in the Civilian Unemployment Rate: Monthly Observations, February 2013–August 2019

Regression Statistics

R^2	0.0546
Standard error	0.1309
Observations	79
Durbin–Watson	2.0756

	Coefficient	Standard Error	*t*-Statistic
Intercept	−0.0668	0.0158	−4.2278
ΔUER_{t-1}	−0.2320	0.1100	−2.191

6. Assume that changes in the civilian unemployment rate are covariance stationary and that an AR(1) model is a good description for the time series of changes in the

unemployment rate. Specifically, we have $\Delta UER_t = -0.0668 - 0.2320\Delta UER_{t-1}$ (using the coefficient estimates given in the previous problem). Given this equation, what is the mean-reverting level to which changes in the unemployment rate converge?

7. Suppose the following model describes changes in the civilian unemployment rate: $\Delta UER_t = -0.0668 - 0.2320\Delta UER_{t-1}$. The current change (first difference) in the unemployment rate is 0.0300. Assume that the mean-reverting level for changes in the unemployment rate is -0.0542.

   A. What is the best prediction of the next change?

   B. What is the prediction of the change following the next change?

   C. Explain your answer to Part B in terms of equilibrium.

8. Exhibit 6 gives the actual sales, log of sales, and changes in the log of sales of Cisco Systems for the period 1Q 2019 to 4Q 2019.

   Forecast the first- and second-quarter sales of Cisco Systems for 2020 using the regression $\Delta \ln(Sales_t) = 0.0068 + 0.2633\Delta \ln(Sales_{t-1})$.

EXHIBIT 6

Date	Actual Sales ($ Millions)	Log of Sales	Changes in Log of Sales $\Delta \ln(Sales_t)$
1Q 2019	13,072	9.4782	0.0176
2Q 2019	12,446	9.4292	-0.0491
3Q 2019	12,958	9.4695	0.403
4Q 2019	13,428	9.5051	0.0356
1Q 2020			
2Q 2020			

9. Exhibit 7 gives the actual change in the log of sales of Cisco Systems from 1Q 2019 to 4Q 2019, along with the forecasts from the regression model $\Delta \ln(Sales_t) = 0.0068 + 0.2633\Delta \ln(Sales_{t-1})$ estimated using data from 1Q 2001 to 4Q 2018. (Note that the observations after the fourth quarter of 2018 are out of sample.)

EXHIBIT 7

Date	Actual Value of Changes in the Log of Sales $\Delta \ln(Sales_t)$	Forecast Value of Changes in the Log of Sales $\Delta \ln(Sales_t)$
1Q 2019	0.0176	0.0147
2Q 2019	-0.0491	0.0107
3Q 2019	0.4030	0.0096
4Q 2019	0.0356	0.0093

    A. Calculate the RMSE for the out-of-sample forecast errors.

    B. Compare the forecasting performance of the model given with that of another model having an out-of-sample RMSE of 2 percent.

10. A. The AR(1) model for the civilian unemployment rate, $\Delta UER_t = -0.0405 - 0.4674\Delta UER_{t-1}$, was developed with five years of data. What would be the drawback to using the AR(1) model to predict changes in the civilian unemployment rate 12 months or more ahead, as compared with 1 month ahead?

    B. For purposes of estimating a predictive equation, what would be the drawback to using 30 years of civilian unemployment data rather than only 5 years?

11. Exhibit 8 shows monthly observations on the natural log of lightweight vehicle sales, ln (Sales$_t$), for January 1992 to December 2000.

EXHIBIT 8   Lightweight Vehicle Sales

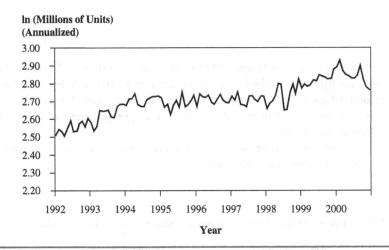

    A. Using the figure, comment on whether the specification $\ln(Sales_t) = b_0 + b_1[\ln(Sales_{t-1})] + \varepsilon_t$ is appropriate.

    B. State an appropriate transformation of the time series.

12. Exhibit 9 shows a plot of first differences in the log of monthly lightweight vehicle sales over the same period as in Problem 11. Has differencing the data made the resulting series, $\Delta\ln(Sales_t) = \ln(Sales_t) - \ln(Sales_{t-1})$, covariance stationary?

EXHIBIT 9   Change in Natural Log of Lightweight Vehicle Sales

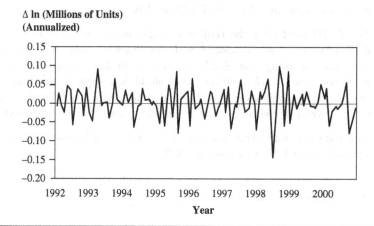

13. Using monthly data from January 1992 to December 2000, we estimate the following equation for lightweight vehicle sales: $\Delta\ln(Sales_t) = 2.7108 + 0.3987\Delta\ln(Sales_{t-1}) + \varepsilon_t$. Exhibit 10 gives sample autocorrelations of the errors from this model.
   A. Use the information in the table to assess the appropriateness of the specification given by the equation.
   B. If the residuals from the AR(1) model above violate a regression assumption, how would you modify the AR(1) specification?

EXHIBIT 10   Different Order Autocorrelations of Differences in the Logs of Vehicle Sales

Lag	Autocorrelation	Standard Error	t-Statistic
1	0.9358	0.0962	9.7247
2	0.8565	0.0962	8.9005
3	0.8083	0.0962	8.4001
4	0.7723	0.0962	8.0257
5	0.7476	0.0962	7.7696
6	0.7326	0.0962	7.6137
7	0.6941	0.0962	7.2138
8	0.6353	0.0962	6.6025
9	0.5867	0.0962	6.0968
10	0.5378	0.0962	5.5892
11	0.4745	0.0962	4.9315
12	0.4217	0.0962	4.3827

14. Exhibit 11 shows the quarterly sales of Cisco Systems from 3Q 2001 to 2Q 2019.

EXHIBIT 11   Quarterly Sales at Cisco

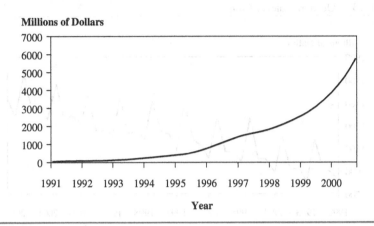

Exhibit 12 gives the regression statistics from estimating the model $\Delta \ln(\text{Sales}_t) = b_0 + b_1 \Delta \ln(\text{Sales}_{t-1}) + \varepsilon_t$.

EXHIBIT 12   Change in the Natural Log of Sales for Cisco Quarterly Observations, 3Q 1991–4Q 2000

Regression Statistics

R^2	0.2899		
Standard error	0.0408		
Observations	38		
Durbin–Watson	1.5707		

	Coefficient	Standard Error	*t*-Statistic
Intercept	0.0661	0.0175	3.7840
$\Delta \ln(\text{Sales}_{t-1})$	0.4698	0.1225	3.8339

A. Describe the salient features of the quarterly sales series.

B. Describe the procedures we should use to determine whether the AR(1) specification is correct.

C. Assuming the model is correctly specified, what is the long-run change in the log of sales toward which the series will tend to converge?

15. Exhibit 13 shows the quarterly sales of Avon Products from 1Q 1992 to 2Q 2002. Describe the salient features of the data shown.

EXHIBIT 13   Quarterly Sales at Avon

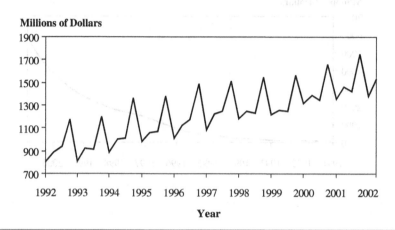

16. Exhibit 14 shows the autocorrelations of the residuals from an AR(1) model fit to the changes in the gross profit margin (GPM) of the Home Depot, Inc.

EXHIBIT 14   Autocorrelations of the Residuals from Estimating the Regression $\Delta GPM_t = 0.0006 - 0.3330\Delta GPM_{t-1} + \varepsilon_t$, 1Q 1992–4Q 2001 (40 Observations)

Lag	Autocorrelation
1	−0.1106
2	−0.5981
3	−0.1525
4	0.8496
5	−0.1099

Exhibit 15 shows the output from a regression on changes in the GPM for Home Depot, where we have changed the specification of the AR regression.

EXHIBIT 15   Change in Gross Profit Margin for Home Depot, 1Q 1992–4Q 2001

Regression Statistics

R^2	0.9155		
Standard error	0.0057		
Observations	40		
Durbin–Watson	2.6464		

	Coefficient	Standard Error	t-Statistic
Intercept	−0.0001	0.0009	−0.0610
ΔGPM_{t-1}	−0.0608	0.0687	−0.8850
ΔGPM_{t-4}	0.8720	0.0678	12.8683

A. Identify the change that was made to the regression model.
B. Discuss the rationale for changing the regression specification.

17. Suppose we decide to use an autoregressive model with a seasonal lag because of the seasonal autocorrelation in the previous problem. We are modeling quarterly data, so we estimate Equation 15: $(\ln Sales_t - \ln Sales_{t-1}) = b_0 + b_1(\ln Sales_{t-1} - \ln Sales_{t-2}) + b_2(\ln Sales_{t-4} - \ln Sales_{t-5}) + \varepsilon_t$. Exhibit 16 shows the regression statistics from this equation.

EXHIBIT 16   Log Differenced Sales: AR(1) Model with Seasonal Lag Johnson & Johnson Quarterly Observations, January 1985–December 2001

Regression Statistics

R^2	0.4220		
Standard error	0.0318		
Observations	68		
Durbin–Watson	1.8784		

	Coefficient	Standard Error	t-Statistic
Intercept	0.0121	0.0053	2.3055
Lag 1	−0.0839	0.0958	−0.8757
Lag 4	0.6292	0.0958	6.5693

Autocorrelations of the Residual

Lag	Autocorrelation	Standard Error	t-Statistic
1	0.0572	0.1213	0.4720
2	−0.0700	0.1213	−0.5771
3	0.0065	0.1213	−0.0532
4	−0.0368	0.1213	−0.3033

  A. Using the information in Exhibit 16, determine whether the model is correctly
     specified.
  B. If sales grew by 1 percent last quarter and by 2 percent four quarters ago, use the
     model to predict the sales growth for this quarter.

18. Describe how to test for autoregressive conditional heteroskedasticity (ARCH) in the
    residuals from the AR(1) regression on first differences in the civilian unemployment
    rate, $\Delta UER_t = b_0 + b_1 \Delta UER_{t-1} + \varepsilon_t$.

19. Suppose we want to predict the annualized return of the five-year T-bill using the
    annualized return of the three-month T-bill with monthly observations from January
    1993 to December 2002. Our analysis produces the data shown in Exhibit 17.
    Can we rely on the regression model in Exhibit 17 to produce meaningful predictions?
    Specify what problem might be a concern with this regression.

EXHIBIT 17   Regression with Three-Month T-Bill as the Independent Variable and the Five-Year
T-Bill as the Dependent Variable: Monthly Observations, January 1993–December 2002

Regression Statistics

R^2	0.5829		
Standard error	0.6598		
Observations	120		
Durbin–Watson	0.1130		
	Coefficient	**Standard Error**	**t-Statistic**
Intercept	3.0530	0.2060	14.8181
Three-month	0.5722	0.0446	12.8408

The following information relates to Questions 20–26

Angela Martinez, an energy sector analyst at an investment bank, is concerned about the future level of oil prices and how it might affect portfolio values. She is considering whether to recommend a hedge for the bank portfolio's exposure to changes in oil prices. Martinez examines West Texas Intermediate (WTI) monthly crude oil price data, expressed in US dollars per barrel, for the 181-month period from August 2000 through August 2015. The end-of-month WTI oil price was $51.16 in July 2015 and $42.86 in August 2015 (Month 181).

After reviewing the time-series data, Martinez determines that the mean and variance of the time series of oil prices are not constant over time. She then runs the following four regressions using the WTI time-series data.

- Linear trend model: Oil price$_t$ = b_0 + $b_1 t$ + e_t.
- Log-linear trend model: ln Oil price$_t$ = b_0 + $b_1 t$ + e_t.
- AR(1) model: Oil price$_t$ = b_0 + b_1Oil price$_{t-1}$ + e_t.
- AR(2) model: Oil price$_t$= b_0 + b_1Oil price$_{t-1}$ + b_2Oil price$_{t-2}$ + e_t.

Exhibit 1 presents selected data from all four regressions, and Exhibit 2 presents selected autocorrelation data from the AR(1) models.

EXHIBIT 1   Crude Oil Price per Barrel, August 2000–August 2015

	Regression Statistics (t-statistics for coefficients are reported in parentheses)			
	Linear	Log-Linear	AR(1)	AR(2)
R^2	0.5703	0.6255	0.9583	0.9656
Standard error	18.6327	0.3034	5.7977	5.2799
Observations	181	181	180	179
Durbin–Watson	0.10	0.08	1.16	2.08
RMSE			2.0787	2.0530
Coefficients:				
Intercept	28.3278	3.3929	1.5948	2.0017
	(10.1846)	(74.9091)	(1.4610)	(1.9957)
t (Trend)	0.4086	0.0075		
	(15.4148)	(17.2898)		
Oil price$_{t-1}$			0.9767	1.3946
			(63.9535)	(20.2999)
Oil price$_{t-2}$				−0.4249
				(−6.2064)

EXHIBIT 2   Autocorrelations of the Residual from AR(1) Model

Lag	Autocorrelation	t-Statistic
1	0.4157	5.5768
2	0.2388	3.2045
3	0.0336	0.4512
4	−0.0426	−0.5712

Note: At the 5 percent significance level, the critical value for a *t*-statistic is 1.97.

In Exhibit 1, at the 5 percent significance level, the lower critical value for the Durbin–Watson test statistic is 1.75 for both the linear and log-linear regressions.

After reviewing the data and regression results, Martinez draws the following conclusions.

Conclusion 1.   The time series for WTI oil prices is covariance stationary.

Conclusion 2.   Out-of-sample forecasting using the AR(1) model appears to be more accurate than that of the AR(2) model.

20. Based on Exhibit 1, the predicted WTI oil price for October 2015 using the linear trend model is *closest* to:
   A. $29.15.
   B. $74.77.
   C. $103.10.

21. Based on Exhibit 1, the predicted WTI oil price for September 2015 using the log-linear trend model is *closest* to:
   A. $29.75.
   B. $29.98.
   C. $116.50.

22. Based on the regression output in Exhibit 1, there is evidence of positive serial correlation in the errors in:
   A. the linear trend model but not the log-linear trend model.
   B. both the linear trend model and the log-linear trend model.
   C. neither the linear trend model nor the log-linear trend model.

23. Martinez's Conclusion 1 is:
   A. correct.
   B. incorrect because the mean and variance of WTI oil prices are not constant over time.
   C. incorrect because the Durbin–Watson statistic of the AR(2) model is greater than 1.75.

24. Based on Exhibit 1, the forecasted oil price in September 2015 based on the AR(2) model is *closest* to:
   A. $38.03.
   B. $40.04.
   C. $61.77.

25. Based on the data for the AR(1) model in Exhibits 1 and 2, Martinez can conclude that the:
    A. residuals are not serially correlated.
    B. autocorrelations do not differ significantly from zero.
    C. standard error for each of the autocorrelations is 0.0745.

26. Based on the mean-reverting level implied by the AR(1) model regression output in Exhibit 1, the forecasted oil price for September 2015 is *most likely* to be:
    A. less than $42.86.
    B. equal to $42.86.
    C. greater than $42.86.

The following information relates to Question 27–35

Max Busse is an analyst in the research department of a large hedge fund. He was recently asked to develop a model to predict the future exchange rate between two currencies. Busse gathers monthly exchange rate data from the most recent 10-year period and runs a regression based on the following AR(1) model specification:

Regression 1: $x_t = b_0 + b_1 x_{t-1} + \varepsilon_t$, where x_t is the exchange rate at time t.

Based on his analysis of the time series and the regression results, Busse reaches the following conclusions:

Conclusion 1.   The variance of x_t increases over time.
Conclusion 2.   The mean-reverting level is undefined.
Conclusion 3. b_0 does not appear to be significantly different from 0.

Busse decides to do additional analysis by first-differencing the data and running a new regression.

Regression 2: $y_t = b_0 + b_1 y_{t-1} + \varepsilon_t$, where $y_t = x_t - x_{t-1}$.

Exhibit 1 shows the regression results.

EXHIBIT 1   First-Differenced Exchange Rate AR(1) Model: Month-End Observations, Last 10 Years

Regression Statistics

R^2	0.0017
Standard error	7.3336
Observations	118
Durbin–Watson	1.9937

	Coefficient	Standard Error	t-Statistic
Intercept	-0.8803	0.6792	-1.2960
$x_{t-1} - x_{t-2}$	0.0412	0.0915	0.4504

Autocorrelations of the Residual

Lag	Autocorrelation	Standard Error	t-Statistic
1	0.0028	0.0921	0.0300
2	0.0205	0.0921	0.2223
3	0.0707	0.0921	0.7684
4	0.0485	0.0921	0.5271

Note: The critical *t*-statistic at the 5 percent significance level is 1.98.

Busse decides that he will need to test the data for nonstationarity using a Dickey–Fuller test. To do so, he knows he must model a transformed version of Regression 1.

Busse's next assignment is to develop a model to predict future quarterly sales for PoweredUP, Inc., a major electronics retailer. He begins by running the following regression:

Regression 3: $\ln \text{Sales}_t - \ln \text{Sales}_{t-1} = b_0 + b_1(\ln \text{Sales}_{t-1} - \ln \text{Sales}_{t-2}) + \varepsilon_t$.

Exhibit 2 presents the results of this regression.

EXHIBIT 2   Log Differenced Sales AR(1) Model: PoweredUP, Inc., Last 10 Years of Quarterly Sales

Regression Statistics

R^2	0.2011
Standard error	0.0651
Observations	38
Durbin–Watson	1.9677

	Coefficient	Standard Error	*t*-Statistic
Intercept	0.0408	0.0112	3.6406
ln Sales$_{t-1}$ – ln Sales$_{t-2}$	−0.4311	0.1432	−3.0099

Autocorrelations of the Residual

Lag	Autocorrelation	Standard Error	*t*-Statistic
1	0.0146	0.1622	0.0903
2	−0.1317	0.1622	−0.8119
3	−0.1123	0.1622	−0.6922
4	0.6994	0.1622	4.3111

Note: The critical *t*-statistic at the 5 percent significance level is 2.02.

Because the regression output from Exhibit 2 raises some concerns, Busse runs a different regression. These regression results, along with quarterly sales data for the past five quarters, are presented in Exhibits 3 and 4, respectively.

EXHIBIT 3   Log Differenced Sales AR(1) Model with Seasonal Lag: PoweredUP, Inc., Last 10 Years of Quarterly Sales

Regression Statistics

R^2	0.6788
Standard error	0.0424
Observations	35
Durbin–Watson	1.8799

	Coefficient	Standard Error	t-Statistic
Intercept	0.0092	0.0087	1.0582
ln $Sales_{t-1}$ – ln $Sales_{t-2}$	−0.1279	0.1137	−1.1252
ln $Sales_{t-4}$ – ln $Sales_{t-5}$	0.7239	0.1093	6.6209

Autocorrelations of the Residual

Lag	Autocorrelation	Standard Error	t-Statistic
1	0.0574	0.1690	0.3396
2	0.0440	0.1690	0.2604
3	0.1923	0.1690	1.1379
4	−0.1054	0.1690	−0.6237

Note: The critical t-statistic at the 5 percent significance level is 2.03.

EXHIBIT 4   Most Recent Quarterly Sales Data (in billions)

Dec 2015 ($Sales_{t-1}$)	$3.868
Sep 2015 ($Sales_{t-2}$)	$3.780
June 2015 ($Sales_{t-3}$)	$3.692
Mar 2015 ($Sales_{t-4}$)	$3.836
Dec 2014 ($Sales_{t-5}$)	$3.418

After completing his work on PoweredUP, Busse is asked to analyze the relationship of oil prices and the stock prices of three transportation companies. His firm wants to know whether the stock prices can be predicted by the price of oil. Exhibit 5 shows selected information from the results of his analysis.

EXHIBIT 5   Analysis Summary of Stock Prices for Three Transportation Stocks and the Price of Oil

	Unit Root?	Linear or Exponential Trend?	Serial Correlation of Residuals in Trend Model?	ARCH(1)?	Comments
Company 1	Yes	Exponential	Yes	Yes	Not cointegrated with oil price
Company 2	Yes	Linear	Yes	No	Cointegrated with oil price
Company 3	No	Exponential	Yes	No	Not cointegrated with oil price
Oil Price	Yes				

To assess the relationship between oil prices and stock prices, Busse runs three regressions using the time series of each company's stock prices as the dependent variable and the time series of oil prices as the independent variable.

27. Which of Busse's conclusions regarding the exchange rate time series is consistent with both the properties of a covariance-stationary time series and the properties of a random walk?
    A. Conclusion 1
    B. Conclusion 2
    C. Conclusion 3

28. Based on the regression output in Exhibit 1, the first-differenced series used to run Regression 2 is consistent with:
    A. a random walk.
    B. covariance stationarity.
    C. a random walk with drift.

29. Based on the regression results in Exhibit 1, the *original* time series of exchange rates:
    A. has a unit root.
    B. exhibits stationarity.
    C. can be modeled using linear regression.

30. In order to perform the nonstationarity test, Busse should transform the Regression 1 equation by:
    A. adding the second lag to the equation.
    B. changing the regression's independent variable.
    C. subtracting the independent variable from both sides of the equation.

31. Based on the regression output in Exhibit 2, what should lead Busse to conclude that the Regression 3 equation is not correctly specified?
    A. The Durbin–Watson statistic
    B. The *t*-statistic for the slope coefficient
    C. The *t*-statistics for the autocorrelations of the residual

32. Based on the regression output in Exhibit 3 and sales data in Exhibit 4, the forecasted value of quarterly sales for March 2016 for PoweredUP is *closest* to:
    A. $4.193 billion.
    B. $4.205 billion.
    C. $4.231 billion.

33. Based on Exhibit 5, Busse should conclude that the variance of the error terms for Company 1:
    A. is constant.
    B. can be predicted.
    C. is homoskedastic.

34. Based on Exhibit 5, for which company would the regression of stock prices on oil prices be expected to yield valid coefficients that could be used to estimate the long-term relationship between stock price and oil price?
    A. Company 1
    B. Company 2
    C. Company 3

35. Based on Exhibit 5, which single time-series model would *most likely* be appropriate for Busse to use in predicting the future stock price of Company 3?
    A. Log-linear trend model
    B. First-differenced AR(2) model
    C. First-differenced log AR(1) model

CHAPTER 10

MACHINE LEARNING

Kathleen DeRose, CFA
Matthew Dixon, PhD, FRM
Christophe Le Lannou

LEARNING OUTCOMES

The candidate should be able to:

- distinguish between supervised machine learning, unsupervised machine learning, and deep learning;
- describe overfitting and identify methods of addressing it;
- describe supervised machine learning algorithms—including penalized regression, support vector machine, k-nearest neighbor, classification and regression tree, ensemble learning, and random forest—and determine the problems for which they are best suited;
- describe unsupervised machine learning algorithms—including principal components analysis, k-means clustering, and hierarchical clustering—and determine the problems for which they are best suited;
- describe neural networks, deep learning nets, and reinforcement learning.

1. INTRODUCTION

Investment firms are increasingly using technology at every step of the investment management value chain—from improving their understanding of clients to uncovering new sources of alpha and executing trades more efficiently. Machine learning techniques, a central part of that technology, are the subject of this chapter. These techniques first appeared in finance in the 1990s and have since flourished with the explosion of data and cheap computing power.

This chapter provides a high-level view of machine learning (ML). It covers a selection of key ML algorithms and their investment applications. Investment practitioners should be equipped with a basic understanding of the types of investment problems that machine learning can address, an idea of how the algorithms work, and the vocabulary to interact

Quantitative Methods for Investment Analysis, Second Edition, by Kathleen DeRose, CFA, Matthew Dixon, PhD, FRM, Christophe Le Lannou. Copyright © 2020 by CFA Institute.

with machine learning and data science experts. While investment practitioners need not master the details and mathematics of machine learning, as domain experts in investments they can play an important role in the implementation of these techniques by being able to source appropriate model inputs, interpret model outputs, and translate outputs into appropriate investment actions.

Section 2 gives an overview of machine learning in investment management. Section 3 defines machine learning and the types of problems that can be addressed by supervised and unsupervised learning. Section 4 describes evaluating machine learning algorithm performance. Key supervised machine learning algorithms are covered in Section 5, and Section 6 describes key unsupervised machine learning algorithms. Neural networks, deep learning nets, and reinforcement learning are covered in Section 7. Section 8 provides a decision flowchart for selecting the appropriate ML algorithm. The chapter concludes with a summary.

2. MACHINE LEARNING AND INVESTMENT MANAGEMENT

The growing volume and exploding diversity of data, as well as the perceived increasing economic value of insights extracted from these data, have inspired rapid growth in data science. This newly emerging field combines mathematics, computer science, and business analytics. It also strikes out in a new direction that relies on learning—from basic learning functions that map relationships between variables to advanced neural networks that mimic physical processes that absorb, order, and adapt to information.

Machine learning has theoretical and practical implications for investment management. For example, machine learning could potentially reshape accepted wisdom about asset risk premiums and reconfigure investment management business processes. Large datasets and learning models are already affecting investment management practices—from client profiling to asset allocation, stock selection, portfolio construction and risk management, and trading.

Machine learning applications are at each step of the asset and wealth management value chain. Chatbots answer basic retirement savings questions, learning from their interactions with investors. Machine learning methods can be used to generate alpha signals used in security selection by creating a non-linear forecast for a single time series, by deriving a forecast from a suite of predefined factors, or even by choosing input signals from existing or newly found data. For example, researchers using textual analysis have found that year-over-year changes in annual (10-K) and quarterly (10-Q) filings, particularly negative changes in the management discussion and risk sections, can strongly predict equity returns.

Machine learning methods can help calculate target portfolio weights that incorporate client restrictions and then dynamically weight them to maximize a Sharpe ratio. Another use of machine learning methods is better estimation of the variance–covariance matrix via principal components analysis, which reduces the number of variables needed to explain the variation in the data. Research suggests that machine learning solutions outperform mean–variance optimization in portfolio construction. Machine learning techniques are already creating better order flow management tools with non-linear trading algorithms that reduce the costs of implementing portfolio decisions. These developments have caused an evolution in the automation of tools, processes, and businesses (such as robo-advising).

3. WHAT IS MACHINE LEARNING?

We now discuss some fundamental concepts of machine learning, including a definition and an overview of key types of machine learning, such as supervised and unsupervised ML.

3.1. Defining Machine Learning

Statistical approaches and machine learning techniques both analyze observations to reveal some underlying process; however, they diverge in their assumptions, terminology, and techniques. Statistical approaches rely on foundational assumptions and explicit models of structure, such as observed samples that are assumed to be drawn from a specified underlying probability distribution. These a priori restrictive assumptions can fail in reality.

In contrast, machine learning seeks to extract knowledge from large amounts of data with fewer such restrictions. The goal of machine learning algorithms is to automate decision-making processes by generalizing (i.e., learning) from known examples to determine an underlying structure in the data. The emphasis is on the ability of the algorithm to generate structure or predictions from data without any human help. An elementary way to think of ML algorithms is to "find the pattern, apply the pattern."

Machine learning techniques are better able than statistical approaches (such as linear regression) to handle problems with many variables (high dimensionality) or with a high degree of non-linearity. ML algorithms are particularly good at detecting change, even in highly non-linear systems, because they can detect the preconditions of a model's break or anticipate the probability of a regime switch.

Machine learning is broadly divided into three distinct classes of techniques: supervised learning, unsupervised learning, and deep learning/reinforcement learning.

3.2. Supervised Learning

Supervised learning involves ML algorithms that infer patterns between a set of inputs (the Xs) and the desired output (Y). The inferred pattern is then used to map a given input set into a predicted output. Supervised learning requires a **labeled dataset**, one that contains matched sets of observed inputs and the associated output. Applying the ML algorithm to this dataset to infer the pattern between the inputs and output is called training the algorithm. Once the algorithm has been trained, the inferred pattern can be used to predict output values based on new inputs (i.e., ones not in the training dataset).

Multiple regression is an example of supervised learning. A regression model takes matched data (Xs, Y) and uses it to estimate parameters that characterize the relationship between Y and the Xs. The estimated parameters can then be used to predict Y on a new, different set of Xs. The difference between the predicted and actual Y is used to evaluate how well the regression model predicts out-of-sample (i.e., using new data).

The terminology used with ML algorithms differs from that used in regression. Exhibit 1 provides a visual of the supervised learning model training process and a translation between regression and ML terminologies.

In supervised machine learning, the dependent variable (Y) is the **target** and the independent variables (Xs) are known as **features**. The labeled data (training dataset) is used to train the supervised ML algorithm to infer a pattern-based prediction rule. The fit of

EXHIBIT 1   Overview of Supervised Learning

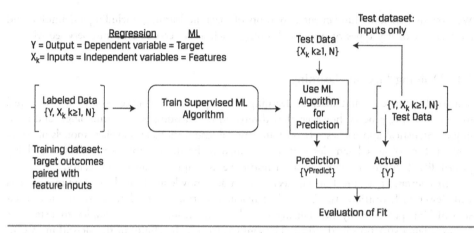

the ML model is evaluated using labeled test data in which the predicted targets ($Y^{Predict}$) are compared to the actual targets (Y^{Actual}).

An example of supervised learning is the case in which ML algorithms are used to predict whether credit card transactions are fraudulent or legitimate. In the credit card example, the target is a binary variable with a value of 1 for "fraudulent" or 0 for "non-fraudulent." The features are the transaction characteristics. The chosen ML algorithm uses these data elements to train a model to predict the likelihood of fraud more accurately in new transactions. The ML program "learns from experience" if the percentage of correctly predicted credit card transactions increases as the amount of input from a growing credit card database increases. One possible ML algorithm to use would be to fit a logistic regression model to the data to provide an estimate of the probability a transaction is fraudulent.

Supervised learning can be divided into two categories of problems—regression and classification—with the distinction between them being determined by the nature of the target (Y) variable. If the target variable is continuous, then the task is one of regression (even if the ML technique used is not "regression"; note this nuance of ML terminology). If the target variable is categorical or ordinal (i.e., a ranked category), then it is a classification problem. Regression and classification use different ML techniques.

Regression focuses on making predictions of continuous target variables. Most readers are already familiar with multiple linear regression (e.g., ordinary least squares) models, but other supervised learning techniques exist, including non-linear models. These non-linear models are useful for problems involving large datasets with large numbers of features, many of which may be correlated. Some examples of problems belonging to the regression category are using historical stock market returns to forecast stock price performance or using historical corporate financial ratios to forecast the probability of bond default.

Classification focuses on sorting observations into distinct categories. In a regression problem, when the dependent variable (target) is categorical, the model relating the outcome to the independent variables (features) is called a "classifier." You should already be familiar with logistic regression as a type of classifier. Many classification models are binary classifiers, as in the case of fraud detection for credit card transactions. Multi-category classification is not uncommon, as in the case of classifying firms into multiple credit rating categories. In assigning ratings, the outcome variable is ordinal, meaning the categories have a distinct order or ranking (e.g., from low to high creditworthiness). Ordinal variables are intermediate between categorical variables and continuous variables on a scale of measurement.

3.3. Unsupervised Learning

Unsupervised learning is machine learning that does not make use of labeled data. More formally, in unsupervised learning, we have inputs (Xs) that are used for analysis without any target (Y) being supplied. In unsupervised learning, because the ML algorithm is not given labeled training data, the algorithm seeks to discover structure within the data themselves. As such, unsupervised learning is useful for exploring new datasets because it can provide human experts with insights into a dataset too big or too complex to visualize.

Two important types of problems that are well suited to unsupervised machine learning are reducing the dimension of data and sorting data into clusters, known as dimension reduction and clustering, respectively.

Dimension reduction focuses on reducing the number of features while retaining variation across observations to preserve the information contained in that variation. Dimension reduction may have several purposes. It may be applied to data with a large number of features to produce a lower dimensional representation (i.e., with fewer features) that can fit, for example, on a computer screen. Dimension reduction is also used in many quantitative investment and risk management applications where it is critical to identify the most predictive factors underlying asset price movements.

Clustering focuses on sorting observations into groups (clusters) such that observations in the same cluster are more similar to each other than they are to observations in other clusters. Groups are formed based on a set of criteria that may or may not be pre-specified (such as the number of groups). Clustering has been used by asset managers to sort companies into groupings driven by data (e.g., based on their financial statement data or corporate characteristics) rather than conventional groupings (e.g., based on sectors or countries).

3.4. Deep Learning and Reinforcement Learning

More broadly in the field of artificial intelligence, additional categories of machine learning algorithms are distinguished. In **deep learning**, sophisticated algorithms address complex tasks, such as image classification, face recognition, speech recognition, and natural language processing. Deep learning is based on **neural networks** (NNs), also called artificial neural networks (ANNs)—highly flexible ML algorithms that have been successfully applied to a variety of supervised and unsupervised tasks characterized by large datasets, non-linearities, and interactions among features. In **reinforcement learning**, a computer learns from interacting with itself or data generated by the same algorithm. Deep learning and reinforcement learning principles have been combined to create efficient algorithms for solving a range of highly complex problems in robotics, health care, and finance.

3.5. Summary of ML Algorithms and How to Choose among Them

Exhibit 2 is a guide to the various machine learning algorithms organized by algorithm type (supervised or unsupervised) and by type of variables (continuous, categorical, or both). We will not cover linear or logistic regression since they are covered elsewhere in chapters on quantitative methods (Chapters 7–9). The extensions of linear regression, such as penalized regression and least absolute shrinkage and selection operator (LASSO), as well as the other ML algorithms shown in Exhibit 2, will be covered in this chapter.

EXHIBIT 2   Guide to ML Algorithms

	ML Algorithm Type	
Variables	**Supervised** (Target Variable)	**Unsupervised** (No Target Variable)
Continuous	**Regression**	**Dimension Reduction**
	• Linear; Penalized Regression/LASSO	• Principal Components Analysis (PCA)
	• Logistic	**Clustering**
	• Classification and Regression Tree (CART)	• K-Means
	• Random Forest	• Hierarchical
Categorical	**Classification**	**Dimension Reduction**
	• Logistic	• Principal Components Analysis (PCA)
	• Support Vector Machine (SVM)	**Clustering**
	• K-Nearest Neighbor (KNN)	• K-Means
	• Classification and Regression Tree (CART)	• Hierarchical
Continuous or Categorical	Neural Networks	Neural Networks
	Deep Learning	Deep Learning
	Reinforcement Learning	Reinforcement Learning

EXAMPLE 1   Machine Learning Overview

1. Which of the following *best* describes machine learning? Machine learning:
   A. is a type of computer algorithm used just for linear regression.
   B. is a set of algorithmic approaches aimed at generating structure or predictions from data without human intervention by finding a pattern and then applying the pattern.
   C. is a set of computer-driven approaches adapted to extracting information from linear, labeled datasets.

2. Which of the following statements is *most* accurate? When attempting to discover groupings of data without any target (*Y*) variable:
   A. an unsupervised ML algorithm is used.
   B. an ML algorithm that is given labeled training data is used.
   C. a supervised ML algorithm is used.

3. Which of the following statements concerning supervised learning *best* distinguishes it from unsupervised learning? Supervised learning involves:
   A. training on labeled data to infer a pattern-based prediction rule.
   B. training on unlabeled data to infer a pattern-based prediction rule.
   C. learning from unlabeled data by discovering underlying structure in the data themselves.

4. Which of the following *best* describes dimension reduction? Dimension reduction:
   A. focuses on classifying observations in a dataset into known groups using labeled training data.
   B. focuses on clustering observations in a dataset into unknown groups using unlabeled data.
   C. focuses on reducing the number of features in a dataset while retaining variation across observations to preserve the information in that variation.

Solution to 1: B is correct. A is incorrect because machine learning algorithms are typically not used for linear regression. C is incorrect because machine learning is not limited to extracting information from linear, labeled datasets.

Solution to 2: A is correct. B is incorrect because the term "labeled training data" means the target (*Y*) is provided. C is incorrect because a supervised ML algorithm is meant to predict a target (*Y*) variable.

Solution to 3: A is correct. B is incorrect because supervised learning uses labeled training data. C is incorrect because it describes unsupervised learning.

Solution to 4: C is correct. A is incorrect because it describes classification, not dimension reduction. B is incorrect because it describes clustering, not dimension reduction.

4. OVERVIEW OF EVALUATING ML ALGORITHM PERFORMANCE

Machine learning algorithms promise several advantages relative to a structured statistical approach in exploring and analyzing the structure of very large datasets. ML algorithms have the ability to uncover complex interactions between feature variables and the target variable, and they can process massive amounts of data quickly. Moreover, many ML algorithms can easily capture non-linear relationships and may be able to recognize and predict structural changes between features and the target. These advantages mainly derive from the non-parametric and non-linear models that allow more flexibility when inferring relationships.

The flexibility of ML algorithms comes with a price, however. ML algorithms can produce overly complex models with results that are difficult to interpret, may be sensitive to noise or particulars of the data, and may fit the training data too well. An ML algorithm that fits the training data too well will typically not predict well using new data. This problem is known as **overfitting**, and it means that the fitted algorithm does not **generalize** well to new data. A model that generalizes well is a model that retains its explanatory power when predicting using out-of-sample (i.e., new) data. An overfit model has incorporated the noise or random fluctuations in the training data into its learned relationship. The problem is that these aspects often do not apply to new data the algorithm receives and so will negatively impact the model's ability to generalize, therefore reducing its overall predictive value. The evaluation of any ML algorithm thus focuses on its prediction error on new data rather than on its goodness of fit on the data with which the algorithm was fitted (i.e., trained).

Generalization is an objective in model building, so the problem of overfitting is a challenge to attaining that objective. These two concepts are the focus of the discussion below.

4.1. Generalization and Overfitting

To properly describe generalization and overfitting of an ML model, it is important to note the partitioning of the dataset to which the model will be applied. The dataset is typically divided into three non-overlapping samples: (1) **training sample** used to train the model, (2) **validation sample** for validating and tuning the model, and (3) **test sample** for testing the model's ability to predict well on new data. The training and validation samples are often referred to as being "in-sample," and the test sample is commonly referred to as being "out-of-sample." We will return shortly to the topic of partitioning the dataset.

To be valid and useful, any supervised machine learning model must generalize well beyond the training data. The model should retain its explanatory power when tested out-of-sample. As mentioned, one common reason for failure to generalize is overfitting. Think of overfitting as tailoring a custom suit that fits only one person. Continuing the analogy, underfitting is similar to making a baggy suit that fits no one, whereas robust fitting, the desired result, is similar to fashioning a universal suit that fits all people of similar dimensions.

The concepts of underfitting, overfitting, and good (or robust) fitting are illustrated in Exhibit 3. Underfitting means the model does not capture the relationships in the data. The left graph shows four errors in this underfit model (three misclassified circles and one misclassified triangle). Overfitting means training a model to such a degree of specificity to the training data that the model begins to incorporate noise coming from quirks or spurious correlations; it mistakes randomness for patterns and relationships. The algorithm may have memorized the data, rather than learned from it, so it has perfect hindsight but no foresight. The main contributors to overfitting are thus high noise levels in the data and too much complexity in the model. The middle graph shows no errors in this overfit model. **Complexity** refers to the number of features, terms, or branches in the model and to whether the model is linear or non-linear (non-linear is more complex). As models become more complex, overfitting risk increases. A good fit/robust model fits the training (in-sample) data well and generalizes well to out-of-sample data, both within acceptable degrees of error. The right graph shows that the good fitting model has only one error, the misclassified circle.

4.2. Errors and Overfitting

To capture these effects and calibrate degree of fit, data scientists compare error rates in- and out-of-sample as a function of both the data and the algorithm. Total in-sample errors (E_{in})

EXHIBIT 3   Underfitting, Overfitting, and Good Fitting

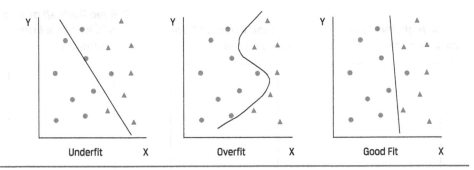

are generated by the predictions of the fitted relationship relative to actual target outcomes on the training sample. Total out-of-sample errors (E_{out}) are from either the validation or test samples. Low or no in-sample error but large out-of-sample error are indicative of poor generalization. Data scientists decompose the total out-of-sample error into three sources:

1. **Bias error**, or the degree to which a model fits the training data. Algorithms with erroneous assumptions produce high bias with poor approximation, causing underfitting and high in-sample error.
2. **Variance error**, or how much the model's results change in response to new data from validation and test samples. Unstable models pick up noise and produce high variance, causing overfitting and high out-of-sample error.
3. **Base error** due to randomness in the data.

A **learning curve** plots the accuracy rate (= 1 – error rate) in the validation or test samples (i.e., out-of-sample) against the amount of data in the training sample, so it is useful for describing under- and overfitting as a function of bias and variance errors. If the model is robust, out-of-sample accuracy increases as the training sample size increases. This implies that error rates experienced in the validation or test samples (E_{out}) and in the training sample (E_{in}) converge toward each other and toward a desired error rate (or, alternatively, the base error). In an underfitted model with high bias error, shown in the left panel of Exhibit 4, high error rates cause convergence below the desired accuracy rate. Adding more training samples will not improve the model to the desired performance level. In an overfitted model with high variance error, shown in the middle panel of Exhibit 4, the validation sample and training sample error rates fail to converge. In building models, data scientists try to simultaneously minimize both bias and variance errors while selecting an algorithm with good predictive or classifying power, as seen in the right panel of Exhibit 4.

Out-of-sample error rates are also a function of model complexity. As complexity increases in the training set, error rates (E_{in}) fall and bias error shrinks. As complexity increases in the test set, however, error rates (E_{out}) rise and variance error rises. Typically, linear functions are more susceptible to bias error and underfitting, while non-linear functions are more prone to variance error and overfitting. Therefore, an optimal point of model complexity exists where the bias and variance error curves intersect and in- and out-of-sample error rates are minimized. A **fitting curve**, which shows in- and out-of-sample error rates

EXHIBIT 4   Learning Curves: Accuracy in Validation and Training Samples

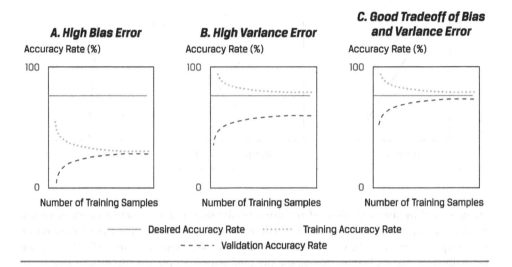

(E_{in} and E_{out}) on the *y*-axis plotted against model complexity on the *x*-axis, is presented in Exhibit 5 and illustrates this trade-off.

Finding the optimal point (managing overfitting risk)—the point just before the total error rate starts to rise (due to increasing variance error)—is a core part of the machine learning process and the key to successful generalization. Data scientists express the trade-off between overfitting and generalization as a trade-off between *cost* (the difference between in- and out-of-sample error rates) and *complexity*. They use the trade-off between cost and complexity to calibrate and visualize under- and overfitting and to optimize their models.

EXHIBIT 5   Fitting Curve Shows Trade-Off between Bias and Variance Errors and Model Complexity

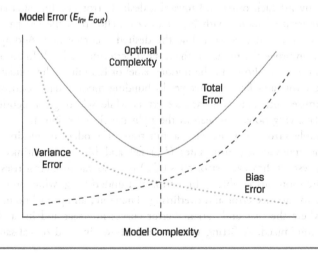

4.3. Preventing Overfitting in Supervised Machine Learning

We have seen that overfitting impairs generalization, but overfitting potential is endemic to the supervised machine learning process due to the presence of noise. So, how do data scientists combat this risk? Two common methods are used to reduce overfitting: (1) preventing the algorithm from getting too complex during selection and training, which requires estimating an overfitting penalty, and (2) proper data sampling achieved by using **cross-validation**, a technique for estimating out-of-sample error directly by determining the error in validation samples.

The first strategy comes from Occam's razor, the problem-solving principle that the simplest solution tends to be the correct one. In supervised machine learning, it means limiting the number of features and penalizing algorithms that are too complex or too flexible by constraining them to include only parameters that reduce out-of-sample error.

The second strategy comes from the principle of avoiding sampling bias. But sampling bias can creep into machine learning in many ways. The challenge is having a large enough dataset to make both training and testing possible on representative samples. An unrepresentative sample or reducing the training sample size too much could obscure its true patterns, thereby increasing bias. In supervised machine learning, the technique for reducing sampling bias is through careful partitioning of the dataset into three groups: (1) training sample, the set of labeled training data where the target variable (Y) is known;(2) validation sample, the set of data used for making structural choices on the degree of model complexity, comparing various solutions, and tuning the selected model, thereby validating the model; and (3) test sample, the set of data held aside for testing to confirm the model's predictive or classifying power. The goal, of course, is to deploy the tested model on fresh data from the same domain.

To mitigate the problem of such **holdout samples** (i.e., data samples not used to train the model) reducing the training set size too much, modelers use special cross-validation techniques. One such technique is **k-fold cross-validation**, in which the data (excluding test sample and fresh data) are shuffled randomly and then are divided into k equal sub-samples, with $k - 1$ samples used as training samples and one sample, the kth, used as a validation sample. Note that k is typically set at 5 or 10. This process is then repeated k times, which helps minimize both bias and variance by insuring that each data point is used in the training set $k - 1$ times and in the validation set once. The average of the k validation errors (mean E_{val}) is then taken as a reasonable estimate of the model's out-of-sample error (E_{out}). A limitation of k-fold cross-validation is that it cannot be used with time-series data, where only the most recent data can reasonably be used for model validation.

In sum, mitigating overfitting risk by avoiding excessive out-of-sample error is critical to creating a supervised machine learning model that generalizes well to fresh datasets drawn from the same distribution. The main techniques used to mitigate overfitting risk in model construction are complexity reduction (or regularization) and cross-validation.

EXAMPLE 2   Evaluating ML Algorithm Performance

Shreya Anand is a portfolio manager based in the Mumbai headquarters office of an investment firm, where she runs a high-dividend-yield fund for wealthy clients. Anand has some knowledge of data science from her university studies. She is interested in classifying companies in the NIFTY 200 Index—an index of large- and mid-cap companies listed on the National Stock Exchange of India—into two categories: dividend increase and no dividend increase. She assembles data for training, validating, and testing an ML-based model that consists of 1,000 observations of NIFTY 200 companies, each consisting of 25 features (fundamental and technical) and the labeled target (dividend increase or no dividend increase).

After training her model, Anand discovers that while it is good at correctly classifying using the training sample, it does not perform well on new data. In consulting her colleagues about this issue, Anand hears conflicting explanations about what constitutes good generalization in an ML model:

Statement 1.   The model retains its explanatory power when predicting using new data (i.e., out-of-sample).

Statement 2.   The model shows low explanatory power after training using in-sample data (i.e., training data).

Statement 3.   The model loses its explanatory power when predicting using new data (i.e., out-of-sample).

1. Which statement made to Anand is *most* accurate?
    A. Statement 1
    B. Statement 2
    C. Statement 3

2. Anand's model is *most likely* being impaired by which of the following?
    A. Underfitting and bias error
    B. Overfitting and variance error
    C. Overfitting and bias error

3. By implementing which one of the following actions can Anand address the problem?
    A. Estimate and incorporate into the model a penalty that decreases in size with the number of included features.
    B. Use the k-fold cross-validation technique to estimate the model's out-of-sample error, and then adjust the model accordingly.
    C. Use an unsupervised learning model.

Solution to 1: A, Statement 1, is correct. B, Statement 2, is incorrect because it describes a poorly fitting model with high bias. C, Statement 3, is incorrect because it describes an overfitted model with poor generalization.

Solution to 2: B is correct. Anand's model is good at correctly classifying using the training sample, but it does not perform well using new data. The model is overfitted, so it has high variance error.

Solution to 3: B is correct. A is incorrect because the penalty should increase in size with the number of included features. C is incorrect because Anand is using labeled data for classification, and unsupervised learning models do not use labeled data.

5. SUPERVISED MACHINE LEARNING ALGORITHMS

Supervised machine learning models are trained using labeled data, and depending on the nature of the target (*Y*) variable, they can be divided into two types: regression for a continuous target variable and classification for a categorical or ordinal target variable. As shown in Exhibit 2 under regression, we will now cover penalized regression and LASSO. Then, as shown under classification, we will introduce support vector machine (SVM), *k*-nearest neighbor (KNN), and classification and regression tree (CART) algorithms. Note that CART, as its name implies, can be used for both classification and regression problems.

In the following discussion, assume we have a number of observations of a target variable, *Y*, and *n* real valued features, $X_1, \ldots, X_n$, that we may use to establish a relationship (regression or classification) between **X** (a vector of the X_i) and *Y* for each observation in our dataset.

5.1. Penalized Regression

Penalized regression is a computationally efficient technique used in prediction problems. In practice, penalized regression has been useful for reducing a large number of features to a manageable set and for making good predictions in a variety of large datasets, especially where features are correlated (i.e., when classical linear regression breaks down).

In a large dataset context, we may have many features that potentially could be used to explain *Y*. When a model is fit to training data, the model may so closely reflect the characteristics of the specific training data that the model does not perform well on new data. Features may be included that reflect noise or randomness in the training dataset that will not be present in new or future data used for making predictions. That is the problem of overfitting, and penalized regression can be described as a technique to avoid overfitting. In prediction, out-of-sample performance is key, so relatively parsimonious models (that is, models in which each variable plays an essential role) tend to work well because they are less subject to overfitting.

Let us suppose that we standardize our data so the features have a mean of 0 and a variance of 1. Standardization of features will allow us to compare the magnitudes of regression coefficients for the feature variables. In ordinary linear regression (i.e., ordinary least squares, or OLS), the regression coefficients $\widehat{b}_0 \widehat{b}_1, ..., \widehat{b}_K$ are chosen to *minimize* the sum of the squared residuals (i.e., the sum of the squared difference between the actual values, Y_i, and the predicted values, $\widehat{Y}_i$), or

$$\sum_{i=1}^{n} (Y_i - \widehat{Y}_i)^2.$$

Penalized regression includes a constraint such that the regression coefficients are chosen to minimize the sum of squared residuals *plus* a penalty term that increases in size with the number of included features. So, in a penalized regression, a feature must make a sufficient contribution to model fit to offset the penalty from including it. Therefore, only the more important features for explaining *Y* will remain in the penalized regression model.

In one popular type of penalized regression, **LASSO**, or least absolute shrinkage and selection operator, the penalty term has the following form, with $\lambda > 0$:

$$\text{Penalty term} = \lambda \sum_{k=1}^{K} |\hat{b}_k|$$

In addition to minimizing the sum of the squared residuals, LASSO involves minimizing the sum of the absolute values of the regression coefficients (see the following expression). The greater the number of included features (i.e., variables with non-zero coefficients), the larger the penalty term. Therefore, penalized regression ensures that a feature is included only if the sum of squared residuals declines by more than the penalty term increases. All types of penalized regression involve a trade-off of this type. Also, since LASSO eliminates the least important features from the model, it automatically performs a type of feature selection.

$$\sum_{i=1}^{n} (Y_i - \hat{Y}_i)^2 + \lambda \sum_{k=1}^{K} |\hat{b}_K|$$

Lambda (λ) is a **hyperparameter**—a parameter whose value must be set by the researcher before learning begins—of the regression model and will determine the balance between fitting the model versus keeping the model parsimonious. In practice, a hyperparameter is set by reviewing model performance repeatedly at different settings on the validation set, and hence the test set is also essential to avoid overfitting of hyperparameters to the validation data.

Note that in the case where $\lambda = 0$, the LASSO penalized regression is equivalent to an OLS regression. When using LASSO or other penalized regression techniques, the penalty term is added only during the model building process (i.e., when fitting the model to the training data). Once the model has been built, the penalty term is no longer needed, and the model is then evaluated by the sum of the squared residuals generated using the test dataset.

With today's availability of fast computation algorithms, investment analysts are increasingly using LASSO and other regularization techniques to remove less pertinent features and build parsimonious models. **Regularization** describes methods that reduce statistical variability in high-dimensional data estimation problems—in this case, reducing regression coefficient estimates toward zero and thereby avoiding complex models and the risk of overfitting. LASSO has been used, for example, for forecasting default probabilities in industrial sectors where scores of potential features, many collinear, have been reduced to fewer than 10 variables, which is important given the relatively small number (about 100) of observations of default.

Regularization methods can also be applied to non-linear models. A long-term challenge of the asset management industry in applying mean–variance optimization has been the estimation of stable covariance matrixes and asset weights for large portfolios. Asset returns typically exhibit strong multi-collinearity, making the estimation of the covariance matrix highly sensitive to noise and outliers, so the resulting optimized asset weights are highly unstable. Regularization methods have been used to address this problem. The relatively parsimonious models produced by applying penalized regression methods, such as LASSO, tend to work well because they are less subject to overfitting.

EXHIBIT 6   Scatterplots and Linear Separation of Labeled Data

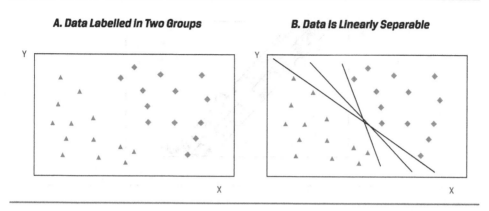

A. Data Labelled In Two Groups   **B. Data Is Linearly Separable**

5.2. Support Vector Machine

Support vector machine (SVM) is one of the most popular algorithms in machine learning. It is a powerful supervised algorithm used for classification, regression, and outlier detection. Despite its complicated-sounding name, the notion is relatively straightforward and best explained with a few pictures. The left panel in Exhibit 6 presents a simple dataset with two features (x and y coordinates) labeled in two groups (triangles and crosses). These binary labeled data are noticeably separated into two distinct regions, which could represent stocks with positive and negative returns in a given year. These two regions can be easily separated by an infinite number of straight lines; three of them are shown in the right panel of Exhibit 6. The data are thus linearly separable, and any of the straight lines shown would be called a **linear classifier**—a binary classifier that makes its classification decision based on a linear combination of the features of each data point.

With two dimensions or features (x and y), linear classifiers can be represented as straight lines. Observations with n features can be represented in an n-dimension space, and the dataset would be linearly separable if the observations can be separated into two distinct regions by a linear space boundary. The general term for such a space boundary is an n-dimensional hyperplane, which with $n = 1$ is called a line and with $n = 2$ is called a plane.

Support vector machine is a linear classifier that determines the hyperplane that optimally separates the observations into two sets of data points. The intuitive idea behind the SVM algorithm is maximizing the probability of making a correct prediction (here, that an observation is a triangle or a cross) by determining the boundary that is the furthest away from all the observations. In Exhibit 7, SVM separates the data by the maximum margin, where the margin is the shaded strip that divides the observations into two groups. The straight line in the middle of the shaded strip is the discriminant boundary, or boundary, for short. We can see that the SVM algorithm produces the widest shaded strip (i.e., the one with the maximum margin on either side of the boundary). The margin is determined by the observations closest to the boundary (the circled points) in each set, and these observations are called support vectors. Adding more training data away from the support vectors will not affect the boundary. In our training datasets, however, adding data points which are close to the hyperplane may move the margin by changing the set of support vectors.

EXHIBIT 7   Linear Support Vector Machine Classifier

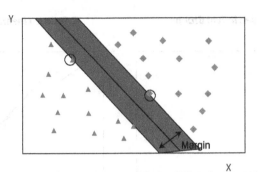

In Exhibit 7, SVM is classifying all observations perfectly. Most real-world datasets, however, are not linearly separable. Some observations may fall on the wrong side of the boundary and be misclassified by the SVM algorithm. The SVM algorithm handles this problem by an adaptation called **soft margin classification**, which adds a penalty to the objective function for observations in the training set that are misclassified. In essence, the SVM algorithm will choose a discriminant boundary that optimizes the trade-off between a wider margin and a lower total error penalty.

As an alternative to soft margin classification, a non-linear SVM algorithm can be run by introducing more advanced, non-linear separation boundaries. These algorithms may reduce the number of misclassified instances in the training datasets but are more complex and, so, are prone to overfitting.

SVM has many applications in investment management. It is particularly suited for small to medium-size but complex high-dimensional datasets, such as corporate financial statements or bankruptcy databases. Investors seek to predict company failures for identifying stocks to avoid or to short sell, and SVM can generate a binary classification (e.g., bankruptcy likely versus bankruptcy unlikely) using many fundamental and technical feature variables. SVM can effectively capture the characteristics of such data with many features while being resilient to outliers and correlated features. SVM can also be used to classify text from documents (e.g., news articles, company announcements, and company annual reports) into useful categories for investors (e.g., positive sentiment and negative sentiment).

5.3. *K*-Nearest Neighbor

K-nearest neighbor (KNN) is a supervised learning technique used most often for classification and sometimes for regression. The idea is to classify a new observation by finding similarities (i.e., nearness) between this new observation and the existing data. Going back to the scatterplot in Exhibit 6, let us assume we have a new observation: The diamond in Exhibit 8 needs to be classified as belonging to either the cross or the triangle category. If $k = 1$, the diamond will be classified into the same category as its nearest neighbor (i.e., the triangle in the left panel). The right panel in Exhibit 8 presents the case where $k = 5$, so the algorithm will look at the diamond's five nearest neighbors, which are three triangles and two crosses. The decision rule is to choose the classification with the largest number of nearest neighbors

EXHIBIT 8   *K*-Nearest Neighbor Algorithm

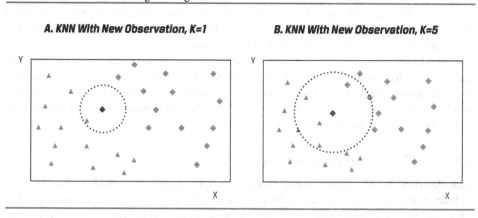

out of the five being considered. So, the diamond is again classified as belonging to the tri-angle category.

Let us suppose we have a database of corporate bonds classified by credit rating that also contains detailed information on the characteristics of these bonds. Such features would include those of the issuing company (e.g., asset size, industry, leverage ratios, cash flow ratios) and of the bond issue itself (e.g., tenor, fixed/floating coupon, embedded options). Now, assume a new bond is about to be issued with no credit rating. By nature, corporate bonds with similar issuer and issue characteristics should be given a similar credit rating. So, by using KNN, we can predict the implied credit rating of the new bond based on the similarities of its characteristics to those of the bonds in our database.

KNN is a straightforward, intuitive model that is still very powerful because it is non-parametric; the model makes no assumptions about the distribution of the data. Moreover, it can be used directly for multi-class classification. A critical challenge of KNN, however, is defining what it means to be similar (or near). Besides the selection of features, an impor-tant decision relates to the distance metric used to model similarity because an inappropriate measure will generate poorly performing models. The choice of a correct distance measure may be even more subjective for ordinal or categorical data. For example, if an analyst is looking at the similarities in market performance of various equities, he or she may consider using the correlation between the stocks' historical returns as an appropriate measure of similarity.

Knowledge of the data and understanding of the business objectives of the analysis are critical aspects in the process of defining similarity. KNN results can be sensitive to inclusion of irrelevant or correlated features, so it may be necessary to select features manually. By doing so, the analyst removes less valuable information to keep the most relevant and perti-nent information. If done correctly, this process should generate a more representative dis-tance measure. KNN algorithms tend to work better with a small number of features.

Finally, the number *k*, the hyperparameter of the model, must be chosen with the understanding that different values of *k* can lead to different conclusions. For predicting the credit rating of an unrated bond, for example, should *k* be the 3, 15, or 50 bonds most similar to the unrated bond? If *k* is an even number, there may be ties and no clear classifi-cation. Choosing a value for *k* that is too small would result in a high error rate and sensitivity to local outliers, but choosing a value for k that is too large would dilute the concept of nearest neighbors by averaging too many outcomes. In practice, several different techniques can be used to determine an optimal value for k, taking into account the number of categories and their partitioning of the feature space.

The KNN algorithm has many applications in the investment industry, including bankruptcy prediction, stock price prediction, corporate bond credit rating assignment, and customized equity and bond index creation. For example, KNN is useful for determining bonds that are similar and those that are dissimilar, which is critical information for creating a custom, diversified bond index.

5.4. Classification and Regression Tree

Classification and regression tree (CART) is another common supervised machine learning technique that can be applied to predict either a categorical target variable, producing a classification tree, or a continuous target variable, producing a regression tree. CART is commonly applied to binary classification or regression.

CART will be discussed in the context of a simplified model for classifying companies by whether they are likely to increase their dividends to shareholders. Such a classification requires a binary tree: a combination of an initial root node, decision nodes, and terminal nodes. The root node and each decision node represent a single feature (f) and a cutoff value (c) for that feature. As shown in Panel A of Exhibit 9, we start at the initial root node for a new data point. In this case, the initial root node represents the feature investment opportunities growth (IOG), designated as X1, with a cutoff value of 10%. From the initial root node, the data are partitioned at decision nodes into smaller and smaller subgroups until terminal nodes that contain the predicted labels are formed. In this case, the predicted labels are either dividend increase (the cross) or no dividend increase (the dash).

Also shown in Panel A of Exhibit 9, if the value of feature IOG (X1) is greater than 10 percent (Yes), then we proceed to the decision node for free cash flow growth (FCFG), designated as X2, which has a cutoff value of 20 percent. Now, if the value of FCFG is not greater than 20 percent (No), then CART will predict that that data point belongs to the no dividend increase (dash) category, which represents a terminal node. Conversely, if the value of X2 is greater than 20 percent (Yes), then CART will predict that that data point belongs to the dividend increase (cross) category, which represents another terminal node.

It is important to note that the same feature can appear several times in a tree in combination with other features. Moreover, some features may be relevant only if other conditions have been met. For example, going back to the initial root node, if IOG is not greater than 10 percent (X1 ≤ 10 percent) and FCFG is greater than 10 percent, then IOG appears again as another decision node, but this time it is lower down in the tree and has a cutoff value of 5 percent.

We now turn to how the CART algorithm selects features and cutoff values for them. Initially, the classification model is trained from the labeled data, which in this hypothetical case are 10 instances of companies having a dividend increase (the crosses) and 10 instances of companies with no dividend increase (the dashes). As shown in Panel B of Exhibit 9, at the initial root node and at each decision node, the feature space (i.e., the plane defined by X1 and X2) is split into two rectangles for values above and below the cutoff value for the particular feature represented at that node. This can be seen by noting the distinct patterns of the lines that emanate from the decision nodes in Panel A. These same distinct patterns are used for partitioning the feature space in Panel B.

EXHIBIT 9   Classification and Regression Tree—Decision Tree and Partitioning of the Feature Space

A. Decision Tree

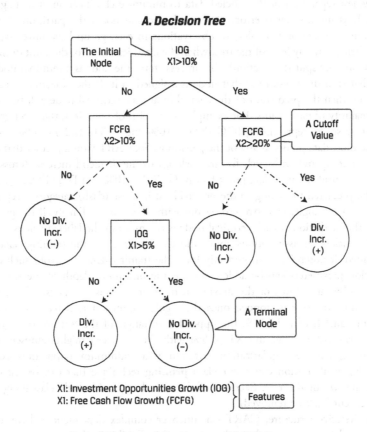

X1: Investment Opportunities Growth (IOG)
X1: Free Cash Flow Growth (FCFG)   } Features

B. Partitioning of the Feature (X1, X2) Space

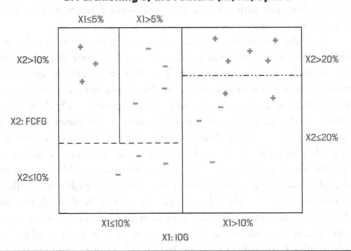

The CART algorithm chooses the feature and the cutoff value at each node that generates the widest separation of the labeled data to minimize classification error (e.g., by a criterion, such as mean-squared error). After each decision node, the partition of the feature space becomes smaller and smaller, so observations in each group have lower within-group error than before. At any level of the tree, when the classification error does not diminish much more from another split (bifurcation), the process stops, the node is a terminal node, and the category that is in the majority at that node is assigned to it. If the objective of the model is classification, then the prediction of the algorithm at each terminal node will be the category with the majority of data points. For example, in Panel B of Exhibit 9, the top right rectangle of the feature space, representing IOG (X1) > 10% and FCFG (X2)> 20%, contains five crosses, the most data points of any of the partitions. So, CART would predict that a new data point (i.e., a company) with such features belongs to the dividend increase (cross) category. However, if instead the new data point had IOG (X1) > 10% and FCFG (X2) $\leq$ 20%, then it would be predicted to belong to the no dividend increase (dash) category—represented by the lower right rectangle, with two crosses but with three dashes. Finally, if the goal is regression, then the prediction at each terminal node is the mean of the labeled values.

CART makes no assumptions about the characteristics of the training data, so if left unconstrained, it potentially can perfectly learn the training data. To avoid such overfitting, regularization parameters can be added, such as the maximum depth of the tree, the minimum population at a node, or the maximum number of decision nodes. The iterative process of building the tree is stopped once the regularization criterion has been reached. For example, in Panel B of Exhibit 9, the upper left rectangle of the feature space (determined by X1 $\leq$ 10%, X2 > 10%, and X1 $\leq$ 5% with three crosses) might represent a terminal node resulting from a regularization criterion with minimum population equal to 3. Alternatively, regularization can occur via a **pruning** technique that can be used afterward to reduce the size of the tree. Sections of the tree that provide little classifying power are pruned (i.e., cut back or removed).

By its iterative structure, CART can uncover complex dependencies between features that other models cannot reveal. As demonstrated in Exhibit 9, the same feature can appear several times in combination with other features and some features may be relevant only if other conditions have been met.

As shown in Exhibit 10, high profitability is a critical feature for predicting whether a stock is an attractive investment or a value trap (i.e., an investment that, although apparently priced cheaply, is likely to be unprofitable). This feature is relevant only if the stock is cheap: For example, in this hypothetical case, if P/E is less than 15, leverage is high (debt to total capital > 50%) and sales are expanding (sales growth > 15%). Said another way, high profitability is irrelevant in this context if the stock is not cheap *and* if leverage is not high *and* if sales are not expanding. Multiple linear regression typically fails in such situations where the relationship between the features and the outcome is non-linear.

CART models are popular supervised machine learning models because the tree provides a visual explanation for the prediction. This contrasts favorably with other algorithms that are often considered to be "black boxes" because it may be difficult to understand the reasoning behind their outcomes and thus to place trust in them. CART is a powerful tool to build expert systems for decision-making processes. It can induce robust rules despite noisy data and complex relationships between high numbers of features. Typical applications of CART in investment management include, among others, enhancing detection of fraud

EXHIBIT 10   Stylized Decision Tree—Attractive Investment or Value Trap?

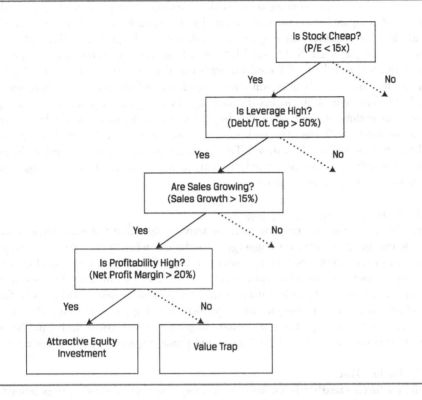

in financial statements, generating consistent decision processes in equity and fixed-income selection, and simplifying communication of investment strategies to clients.

5.5. Ensemble Learning and Random Forest

Instead of basing predictions on the results of a single model as in the previous discussion, why not use the predictions of a group—or an ensemble—of models? Each single model will have a certain error rate and will make noisy predictions. But by taking the average result of many predictions from many models, we can expect to achieve a reduction in noise as the average result converges toward a more accurate prediction. This technique of combining the predictions from a collection of models is called **ensemble learning**, and the combination of multiple learning algorithms is known as the **ensemble method**. Ensemble learning typically produces more accurate and more stable predictions than the best single model. In fact, in many prestigious machine learning competitions, an ensemble method is often the winning solution.

Ensemble learning can be divided into two main categories: (1) aggregation of heterogeneous learners (i.e., different types of algorithms combined with a voting classifier) or (2) aggregation of homogeneous learners (i.e., a combination of the same algorithm using different training data that are based, for example, on a bootstrap aggregating, or bagging, technique, as discussed later).

5.5.1. Voting Classifiers

Suppose you have been working on a machine learning project for some time and have trained and compared the results of several algorithms, such as SVM, KNN, and CART. A **majority-vote classifier** will assign to a new data point the predicted label with the most votes. For example, if the SVM and KNN models are both predicting the category "stock outperformance" and the CART model is predicting the category "stock underperformance," then the majority-vote classifier will choose stock outperformance." The more individual models you have trained, the higher the accuracy of the aggregated prediction up to a point. There is an optimal number of models beyond which performance would be expected to deteriorate from overfitting. The trick is to look for diversity in the choice of algorithms, modeling techniques, and hypotheses. The (extreme) assumption here is that if the predictions of the individual models are independent, then we can use the law of large numbers to achieve a more accurate prediction.

5.5.2. Bootstrap Aggregating (Bagging)

Alternatively, one can use the same machine learning algorithm but with different training data. **Bootstrap aggregating** (or **bagging**) is a technique whereby the original training dataset is used to generate n new training datasets or bags of data. Each new bag of data is generated by random sampling with replacement from the initial training set. The algorithm can now be trained on n independent datasets that will generate n new models. Then, for each new observation, we can aggregate the n predictions using a majority-vote classifier for a classification or an average for a regression. Bagging is a very useful technique because it helps to improve the stability of predictions and protects against overfitting the model.

5.5.3. Random Forest

A **random forest classifier** is a collection of a large number of decision trees trained via a bagging method. For example, a CART algorithm would be trained using each of the n independent datasets (from the bagging process) to generate the multitude of different decision trees that make up the random forest classifier.

To derive even more individual predictions, added diversity can be generated in the trees by randomly reducing the number of features available during training. So, if each observation has n features, one can randomly select a subset of m features (where $m < n$) that will then be considered by the CART algorithm for splitting the dataset at each of the decision nodes. The number of subset features (m), the number of trees to use, the minimum size (population) of each node (or leaf), and the maximum depth of each tree are all hyperparameters that can be tuned to improve overall model prediction accuracy. For any new observation, we let all the classifier trees (i.e., the random forest) undertake classification by majority vote—implementing a machine learning version of the wisdom of crowds. The process involved in random forest construction tends to reduce variance and protect against overfitting on the training data. It also reduces the ratio of noise to signal because errors cancel out across the collection of slightly different classification trees. However, an important drawback of random forest is that it lacks the ease of interpretability of individual trees; as a result, it is considered a relatively black box type of algorithm.

Exhibit 11 presents three scatterplots of actual and predicted defaults by small and medium-sized businesses with respect to two features, X and Y—for example, firm profitability and leverage, respectively. The left plot shows the actual cases of default in light shade and no default in dark shade, while the middle and right plots present the predicted defaults

EXHIBIT 11   Credit Defaults of Small- and Medium-Sized Borrowers

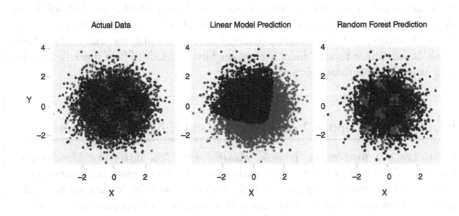

Source: Bacham and Zhao (2017).

and no defaults (also in light and dark shades, respectively). It is clear from the middle plot, which is based on a traditional linear regression model, that the model fails to predict the complex non-linear relationship between the features. Conversely, the right plot, which presents the prediction results of a random forest model, shows that this model performs very well in matching the actual distribution of the data.

Ensemble Learning with Random Forest

In making use of voting across classifier trees, random forest is an example of ensemble learning: Incorporating the output of a collection of models produces classifications that have better signal-to-noise ratios than the individual classifiers. A good example is a credit card fraud detection problem that comes from an open source dataset on Kaggle.[1] Here, the data contained several anonymized features that might be used to explain which transactions were fraudulent. The difficulty in the analysis arises from the fact that the rate of fraudulent transactions is very low; in a sample of 284,807 transactions, only 492 were fraudulent (0.17 percent). This is akin to finding a needle in a haystack. Applying a random forest classification algorithm with an oversampling technique—which involves increasing the proportional representation of fraudulent data in the training set—does extremely well. Despite the lopsided sample, it delivers **precision** (the ratio of correctly predicted fraudulent cases to all predicted fraudulent cases) of 89 percent and **recall** (the ratio of correctly predicted fraudulent cases to all actual fraudulent cases) of 82 percent.

---

[1]See www.kaggle.com/mlg-ulb/creditcardfraud (accessed 1 October 2018).

Despite its relative simplicity, random forest is a powerful algorithm with many invest-ment applications. These include, for example, use in factor-based investment strategies for asset allocation and investment selection or use in predicting whether an IPO will be suc-cessful (e.g., percent oversubscribed, first trading day close/IPO price) given the attributes of the IPO offering and the corporate issuer. Later, in a mini-case study, Deep Neural Network–Based Equity Factor Model, we present further details of how supervised machine learning is used for fundamental factor modeling.

EXAMPLE 3   Support Vector Machine and *K*-Nearest Neighbor

Rachel Lee is a fixed-income portfolio manager with Zeta Investment Management Company. Zeta manages an investment-grade bond portfolio for small, conservative insti-tutions and a non-investment-grade (i.e., high-yield) bond portfolio for yield-seeking, high-net-worth individuals. Both portfolios can hold unrated bonds if the characteristics of the unrated bonds closely match those of the respective portfolio's average holding.

Lee is discussing an upcoming straight, 10-year fixed-coupon bond issue with senior credit analyst Marc Watson. Watson comments that although the bond's issuer, Biotron Corporation, has not had this issue rated, his analysis of the company's prof-itability, cash flow, leverage, and coverage ratios places the issue near the borderline between low investment-grade (Baa3/BBB–) and high non-investment-grade (Ba1/BB+) bonds.

Lee decides to use machine learning methods to confirm the implied credit rating of Biotron Corporation.

1. State the type of problem being addressed by Lee.
2. State two ML algorithms that Lee could use to explore the implied credit rating of Biotron Corporation, and then describe how each algorithm could be applied.

Lee decides to apply the two identified ML algorithms. Both algorithms clearly support a high non-investment-grade rating. Watson states that because both ML algorithms agree on the rating, he has confidence in relying on the rating.

3. State one argument in support of Watson's viewpoint.

Solution to 1: Lee is addressing a supervised learning classification problem because she must determine whether Biotron's upcoming bond issue would be classified as investment grade or non-investment grade.

Solution to 2: One suitable ML algorithm is SVM. The SVM algorithm is a linear classifier that aims to find the optimal hyperplane—the one that separates observations into two distinct sets by the maximum margin. So, SVM is well suited to binary clas-sification problems, such as the one facing Lee (investment grade versus non-invest-ment grade). In this case, Lee could train the SVM algorithm on data—characteristics (features) and rating (target)—of low investment-grade (Baa3/BBB–) and high non-investment-grade (Ba1/BB+) bonds. Lee would then note on which side of the margin the new data point (Biotron's new bonds) lies.

The KNN algorithm is also well suited for classification problems because it clas-sifies a new observation by finding similarities (or nearness) between the new observation and the existing data. Training the algorithm with data as for SVM, the decision rule for classifying Biotron's new bonds is which classification is in the majority among its *k*-nearest neighbors. Note that *k* (a hyperparameter) must be pre-specified by Lee.

Solution to 3: If the ML algorithms disagreed on the classification, the classification would be more likely to be sensitive to the algorithm's approach to classifying data. Because the classification of Biotron's new issue appears robust to the choice of ML algorithm (i.e., both algorithms agree on the rating), the resulting classification will more likely be correct.

EXAMPLE 4 CART and Ensemble Learning

Laurie Kim is a portfolio manager at Hilux LLC, a high-yield bond investment firm. The economy has been in recession for several months, and high-yield bond prices have declined precipitously as credit spreads have widened in response to the weak macroeconomic environment. Kim, however, believes this is a good time to buy because she expects to profit as credit spreads narrow and high-yield bond prices rise in anticipation of economic recovery.

   Based on her analysis, Kim believes that corporate high-yield bonds in the credit quality range of B/B2 to CCC/Caa2 are the most attractive. However, she must carefully select which bonds to buy and which bonds to avoid because of the elevated default risk caused by the currently weak economy.

   To help with her bond selection, Kim turns to Hilux's data analytics team. Kim has supplied them with historical data consisting of 19 fundamental and 5 technical factors for several thousand high-yield bond issuers and issues labeled to indicate default or no default. Kim requests that the team develop an ML-based model using all the factors provided that will make accurate classifications in two categories: default and no default. Exploratory data analysis suggests considerable non-linearities among the feature set.

1. State the type of problem being addressed by Kim.
2. Describe the dimensionality of the model that Kim requests her analytics team to develop.
3. Evaluate whether a CART model is appropriate for addressing her problem.
4. Describe how a CART model operates at each node of the tree.
5. Describe how the team might avoid overfitting and improve the predictive power of a CART model.
6. Describe how ensemble learning might be used by the team to develop even better predictions for Kim's selection of corporate high-yield bonds.

Solution to 1: Kim is addressing a classification problem because she must determine whether bonds that she is considering purchasing in the credit quality range of B/B2 to CCC/Caa2 will default or not default.

Solution to 2: With 19 fundamental and 5 technical factors (i.e., the features), the dimensionality of the model is 24.

Solution to 3: The CART model is an algorithm for addressing classification problems. Its ability to handle complex, non-linear relationships makes it a good choice to address the modeling problem at hand. An important advantage of CART is that its results are relatively straightforward to visualize and interpret, which should help Kim explain her recommendations based on the model to Hilux's investment committee and the firm's clients.

Solution to 4: At each node in the decision tree, the algorithm will choose the feature and the cutoff value for the selected feature that generates the widest separation of the labeled data to minimize classification error.

Solution to 5: The team can avoid overfitting and improve the predictive power of the CART model by adding regularization parameters. For example, the team could specify the maximum depth of the tree, the minimum population at a node, or the maximum number of decision nodes. The iterative process of building nodes will be stopped once the regularization criterion has been reached. Alternatively, a pruning technique can be used afterward to remove parts of the CART model that provide little power to correctly classify instances into default or no default categories.

Solution to 6: The analytics team might use ensemble learning to combine the predictions from a collection of models, where the average result of many predictions leads to a reduction in noise and thus more accurate predictions. Ensemble learning can be achieved by an aggregation of either heterogeneous learners—different types of algorithms combined with a voting classifier—or homogeneous learners—a combination of the same algorithm but using different training data based on the bootstrap aggregating (i.e., bagging) technique. The team may also consider developing a random forest classifier (i.e., a collection of many decision trees) trained via a bagging method.

CASE STUDY: CLASSIFICATION OF WINNING AND LOSING FUNDS

The following case study was developed and written by Matthew Dixon, PhD, FRM.

A research analyst for a fund of funds has been tasked with identifying a set of attractive exchange-traded funds (ETFs) and mutual funds (MFs) in which to invest. She decides to use machine learning to identify the best (i.e., winners) and worst (i.e., losers) performing funds and the features which are most important in such an identification. Her aim is to train a model to correctly classify the winners and losers and then to use it to predict future outperformers. She is unsure of which type of machine learning classification model (i.e., classifier) would work best, so she reports and cross-compares her findings using several different well-known machine learning algorithms.

The goal of this case is to demonstrate the application of machine learning classification to fund selection. Therefore, the analyst will use the following classifiers to identify the best and worst performing funds:

- classification and regression tree (CART),
- support vector machine (SVM),
- *k*-nearest neighbors (KNN), and
- random forests.

Data Description

In the following experiments, the performance of each fund is learned by the machine learning algorithms based on fund type and size, asset class composition, fundamentals (i.e., valuation multiples), and sector composition characteristics. To form a cross-sectional classifier, the sector composition and fund size reported on 15 February 2019 are assumed to be representative of the latest month over which the fund return is reported. **Exhibit 12** presents a description of the dataset.

EXHIBIT 12   Dataset Description
Dataset: MF and ETF Data

There are two separate datasets, one for MFs and one for ETFs, consisting of fund type, size, asset class composition, fundamental financial ratios, sector weights, and monthly total return labeled to indicate the fund as being a winner, a loser, or neither. Number of observations: 6,085 MFs and 1,594 ETFs.
    Features: Up to 21, as shown below:
General (six features):
1. cat_investment*: Fund type, either "blend," "growth," or "value"
2. net_assets: Total net assets in US dollars
3. cat_size: Investment category size, either "small," "medium," or "large" market capitalization stocks
4. portfolio_cash**: The ratio of cash to total assets in the fund
5. portfolio_stocks: The ratio of stocks to total assets in the fund
6. portfolio_bonds: The ratio of bonds to total assets in the fund

Fundamentals (four features):
1. price_earnings: The ratio of price per share to earnings per share
2. price_book: The ratio of price per share to book value per share
3. price_sales: The ratio of price per share to sales per share
4. price_cashflow: The ratio of price per share to cash flow per share

Sector weights (for 11 sectors) provided as percentages:
1. basic_materials
2. consumer_cyclical
3. financial_services
4. real_estate
5. consumer_defensive
6. healthcare
7. utilities
8. communication_services
9. energy

10. industrials
11. technology

Labels:

Winning and losing ETFs or MFs are determined based on whether their returns are
one standard deviation or more above or below the distribution of one-month fund
returns across all ETFs or across all MFs, respectively. More precisely, the labels are:
1, if fund_return_1 month ≥ mean(fund_return_1 month) + one std.dev(fund_
return_1 month), indicating a winning fund;
–1, if fund_return_1 month ≤ mean(fund_return_1 month) – one std.dev(fund_re-
turn_1 month), indicating a losing fund; and
0, otherwise.

*Feature appears in the ETF dataset only.
**Feature appears in the MF dataset only.
Data sources: Kaggle, Yahoo Finance on 15 February 2019.

Methodology

The classification model is trained to determine whether a fund's performance is one standard deviation or more above the mean return (Label 1), within one standard deviation of
the mean return (Label 0), or one standard deviation or more below the mean return
(Label -1), where the mean return and standard deviation are either for all ETFs or all
MFs, depending on the particular fund's type (ETF or MF). Performance is based on the
one-month return of each fund as of 15 February 2019.

This procedure results in most of the funds being labeled as "0" (or average). After
removing missing values in the dataset, there are 1,594 and 6,085 observations in the ETF
and MF datasets, respectively. The data table is a 7,679 × 22 matrix, with 7,679 rows for
each fund observation (1,594 for ETFs and 6,085 for MFs) and 22 columns for the 21 features plus the return label, and all data are recorded as of 15 February 2019.

The aim of the experiment is to identify not only winning and losing funds but also the
features which are useful for distinguishing winners from losers. An important caveat, however, is that no claim is made that such features are causal.

A separate multi-classifier, with three classes, is run for each dataset. Four types of
machine learning algorithms are used to build each classifier: (i) CART, (ii) SVM, (iii)
KNN, and (iv) random forest. Random forest is an example of an ensemble method (based
on bagging), whereas the other three algorithms do not use bagging.

A typical experimental design would involve using 70 percent of the data for training
and holding 15 percent for tuning model hyperparameters and the remaining 15 percent
of the data for testing. For simplicity, we shall not tune the hyperparameters but simply
use the default settings without attempting to fine tune each one for best performance. So,
in this case, we do not withhold 15 percent of the data for validation but instead train the
classifier on a random split of 70 percent of the dataset, with the remaining 30 percent of
the dataset used for testing. Crucially, for fairness of evaluation, each algorithm is trained
and tested on identical data: The same 70 percent of observations are used for training each

algorithm, and the same 30 percent are used for testing each one. The most important hyperparameters and settings for the algorithms are shown in **Exhibit 13**.

EXHIBIT 13   Parameter Settings for the Four Machine Learning Classifiers

---

1. CART: maximum tree depth: 5 levels
2. SVM: cost parameter: 1.0
3. KNN: number of nearest neighbors: 4
4. Random forest: number of trees: 100; maximum tree depth: 20 levels

---

The choices of hyperparameter values for the four machine learning classifiers are supported by theory, academic research, practice, and experimentation to yield a satisfactory bias–variance trade-off. For SVM, the cost parameter is a penalty on the margin of the decision boundary. A large cost parameter forces the SVM to use a thin margin, whereas a smaller cost parameter widens the margin. For random forests, recall that this is an ensemble method which uses multiple decision trees to classify, typically by majority vote. Importantly, no claim is made that these choices of hyperparameters are universally optimal for any dataset.

Results

The results of each classifier are evaluated separately on the test portion of the ETF and MF datasets. The evaluation metrics used are based on Type I and Type II classification errors, where a Type I error is a false positive (FP) and a Type II error is a false negative (FN). Correct classifications are true positive (TP) and true negative (TN).

- The first evaluation metric is **accuracy**, the percentage of correctly predicted classes out of total predictions. So, high accuracy implies low Type I and Type II errors.
- **F1 score**, the second evaluation metric, is the weighted average of precision and recall. Precision is the ratio of correctly predicted positive classes to all predicted positive classes, and recall is the ratio of correctly predicted positive classes to all actual positive classes.

F1 score is a more appropriate evaluation metric to use than accuracy when there is unequal class distribution (i.e., class imbalance) in the dataset, as is the case here. As mentioned, most of the funds in the ETF and MF datasets are designated as indicating average performers.

Exhibit 14 shows the comparative performance results for each algorithm applied to the ETF dataset. These results show the random forest model is the most accurate (0.812), but once class imbalance is accounted for using F1 score (0.770), random forest is about as good as CART. Generally, ensemble methods, such as random forest, are expected to be at least as good as their single-model counterparts because ensemble forecasts generalize better out-of-sample. Importantly, while the relative accuracies and F1 scores across the different methods provide a basis for comparison, they do not speak to the absolute performance. In this regard, values approaching 1 suggest an excellent model, whereas values of approximately

1/3 would indicate the model is useless: 1/3 is premised on three (+1, 0, -1) equally distributed labels. However, because the distribution of classes is often not balanced, this ratio typically requires some adjustment.

EXHIBIT 14   Comparison of Accuracy and F1 Score for Each Classifier Applied to the ETF Dataset

	CART	SVM	KNN	Random Forest
Accuracy	0.770	0.774	0.724	0.812
F1 score	0.769	0.693	0.683	0.770

Exhibit 15 shows that the random forest model outperforms all the other classifiers
under both metrics when applied to the MF dataset. Overall, the accuracy and F1 score
for the SVM and KNN methods are similar for each dataset, and these algorithms are dominated by CART and random forest, especially in the larger MF dataset. The difference in
performance between the two datasets for all the algorithms is to be expected, since the
MF dataset is approximately four times larger than the ETF dataset and a larger sample set
generally leads to better model performance. Moreover, the precise explanation of why random forest and CART outperform SVM and KNN is beyond the scope of this case. Suffice
it to say that random forests are well known to be more robust to noise than most other
classifiers.

EXHIBIT 15   Comparison of Accuracy and F1 Score for Each Classifier Applied to the Mutual
Fund Dataset

	CART	SVM	KNN	Random Forest
Accuracy	0.959	0.859	0.856	0.969
F1 score	0.959	0.847	0.855	0.969

Exhibit 16 presents results on the relative importance of the features in the random forest model for both the ETF (Panel A) and MF (Panel B) datasets. Relative importance is
determined by **information gain**, which quantifies the amount of information that the feature holds about the response. Information gain can be regarded as a form of non-linear correlation between Y and X. Note the horizontal scale of Panel B (MF dataset) is more than
twice as large as that of Panel A (ETF dataset), and the bar colors represent the feature rankings, not the features themselves.

The prices-to-sales (price_sales) and prices-to-earnings (price_earnings) ratios are
observed to be important indicators of performance, at about 0.08–0.09 and 0.06–0.07,
respectively, in the random forest models for each dataset. The ratio of stocks to total assets
(portfolio_stocks), at 0.06, is another key feature. Moreover, the industrials, health care, and
communication services sector weightings are relatively important in the ETF dataset, while
the real estate, consumer defensive, and energy sector weightings are key features in the MF
dataset for differentiating between winning and losing funds.

Another important observation is that the category of the fund size (cat_size) is by far
the most important feature in the model's performance for the MF dataset (≈ 0.20), whereas
it is of much less importance for model performance using the ETF dataset (≈ 0.04).
Conversely, net assets is a relatively important feature for model performance using the

EXHIBIT 16   Relative Importance of Features in the Random Forest Model

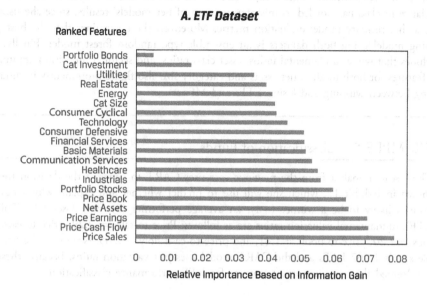

A. ETF Dataset

Ranked Features

Relative Importance Based on Information Gain

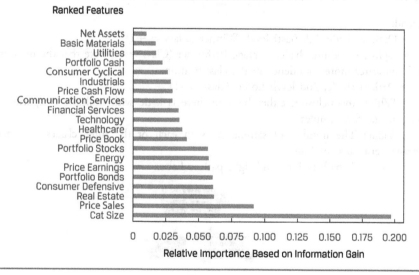

B. Mutual Fund Dataset

Ranked Features

Relative Importance Based on Information Gain

ETF dataset (0.065), while it is the least important feature when the random forest model is applied to the MF dataset (0.01).

Conclusion

The research analyst has trained and tested machine learning–based models that she can use to identify potential winning and losing ETFs and MFs. Her classification models use input features based on fund type and size, asset class composition, fundamentals, and sector composition characteristics. She is more confident in her assessment of MFs than of ETFs, owing to the substantially larger sample size of the former. She is also confident that any imbalance in class has not led to misinterpretation of her models' results, since she uses F1 score as her primary model evaluation metric. Moreover, she determines that the best performing model using both datasets is an ensemble-type random forest model. Finally, she concludes that while fundamental ratios, asset class ratios, and sector composition are important features for both models, net assets and category size also figure prominently in discriminating between winning and losing ETFs and MFs.

EXAMPLE 5   Classification of Funds

The research analyst from the previous case uses CART to generate the decision tree shown in Exhibit 17, which she will use to predict whether and explain why a new ETF is likely to be a winner (+1), an average performer (0), or a loser (-1). This ETF's fundamental valuation ratios are as follows: Price-to-sales = 2.29, price-to-earnings = 7.20, price-to-book = 1.41, and price-to-cash flow = 2.65. Note that the sample size is 1,067 ETFs and the CART model uses just valuation ratios, because these are deemed the most important features for ETF performance classification.

EXHIBIT 17   CART-Based Decision Tree for EFT Performance Classification

Legend:
- Darkest shade, 5th (last) level: Winner (Class = +1)
- Light to medium shade: Average Performer (Class = 0); note that the medium shade indicates more confidence in the classification.
- Darkest shade, 2nd level: Loser (Class = -1)
- White: Inconclusive, either because there is a tie with multiple categories or there are too few samples
- Value: The number of sample cases in each of the three classes: Winner, Average Performer, or Loser
- Path: Left path is True and right path is False.

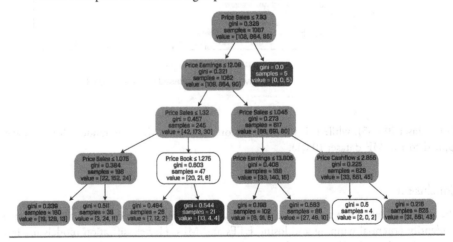

1. Explain the CART model's prediction for performance of the new ETF: winner, loser, or average performer.

2. Calculate the probability that the fund will be in the class predicted by the CART model.

3. Explain why the analyst should be cautious in basing the ETF's predicted performance solely on the CART-generated decision tree.

Solution to 1: Based on its valuation ratios (P/S = 2.29; P/E = 7.20; P/B = 1.41), the new ETF is predicted to be a winner because the decision path leads to the dark shaded, 5th level ("winner") terminal node. The split criteria and decisions are as follows:

Initial node: P/S ≤ 7.93 and EFT P/S = 2.29, so True.
2nd-level node: P/E ≤ 12.08 and EFT P/E = 7.20, so True.
3rd-level node: P/S ≤ 1.32 and EFT P/S = 2.29, so False.
4th-level node: P/B ≤ 1.275 and EFT P/B = 1.41, so False.
5th-level (terminal) node: darkest shaded terminal node indicates "winner."

Solution to 2: The output from the CART model in the darkest shaded, 5th level (winner) terminal node is [13, 4, 4], which indicates it includes 13 funds of Class +1 (winners), 4 funds of Class 0 (average performers), and 4 funds of Class –1 (losers). Thus, the probability predicted by the CART model that this ETF will be in the "winner" class is 13/21, or 62 percent. There are also equal probabilities of it being an average performer (19 percent) or a loser (19 percent).

Solution to 3: There are several reasons why the analyst should be cautious in basing the ETF's predicted performance solely on the CART-generated decision tree. First, this CART model had a maximum depth of just five levels. Truncating at five levels facilitates visualization, but a more realistic decision path is likely to be nuanced and so would require greater depth. Second, only some of the important variables (from Exhibit 16) were used in generating this tree, again for simplicity of visualization. A CART model using additional features, including fund asset class ratios, sector composition, and, especially, net assets would be expected to generate a more accurate (using F1 score) model. Finally, the number of funds reaching the darkest shaded, 5th level ("winner") terminal node (21) is small compared to the total sample size (1,067), so there may be too few clear winners (13) under this decision path from which to draw a statistically significant conclusion. Besides increasing the maximum tree depth and adding more features, another approach the analyst might take in this case for achieving a more accurate model is random forest; being an ensemble classifier, a random forest model would generalize out-of-sample better than any single CART model.

6. UNSUPERVISED MACHINE LEARNING ALGORITHMS

Unsupervised learning is machine learning that does not use labeled data (i.e., no target variable); thus, the algorithms are tasked with finding patterns within the data themselves. The two main types of unsupervised ML algorithms shown in Exhibit 2 are dimension reduction, using principal components analysis, and clustering, which includes *k*-means and hierarchical clustering. These will now be described in turn.

6.1. Principal Components Analysis

Dimension reduction is an important type of unsupervised learning that is used widely in practice. When many features are in a dataset, representing the data visually or fitting models to the data may become extremely complex and "noisy" in the sense of reflecting random influences specific to a dataset. In such cases, dimension reduction may be necessary. Dimension reduction aims to represent a dataset with many typically correlated features by a smaller set of features that still does well in describing the data.

A long-established statistical method for dimension reduction is **principal components analysis (PCA)**. PCA is used to summarize or transform highly correlated features of data into a few main, uncorrelated composite variables. A **composite variable** is a variable that combines two or more variables that are statistically strongly related to each other. Informally, PCA involves transforming the covariance matrix of the features and involves two key concepts: eigenvectors and eigenvalues. In the context of PCA, **eigenvectors** define new, mutually uncorrelated composite variables that are linear combinations of the original features. As a vector, an eigenvector also represents a direction. Associated with each eigenvector is an eigenvalue. An **eigenvalue** gives the proportion of total variance in the initial data that is explained by each eigenvector. The PCA algorithm orders the eigenvectors from highest to lowest according to their eigenvalues—that is, in terms of their usefulness in explaining the total variance in the initial data (this will be shown shortly using a scree plot). PCA selects as the first principal component the eigenvector that explains the largest proportion of variation in the dataset (the eigenvector with the largest eigenvalue). The second principal component explains the next-largest proportion of variation remaining after the first principal component; this process continues for the third, fourth, and subsequent principal components. Because the principal components are linear combinations of the initial feature set, only a few principal components are typically required to explain most of the total variance in the initial feature covariance matrix.

Exhibit 18 shows a hypothetical dataset with three features, so it is plotted in three dimensions along the *x*-, *y*-, and *z*-axes. Each data point has a measurement (*x*, *y*, *z*), and the data should be standardized so that the mean of each series (*x*'s, *y*'s, and *z*'s) is 0 and the standard deviation is 1. Assume PCA has been applied, revealing the first two principal components, PC1 and PC2. With respect to PC1, a perpendicular line dropped from each data point to PC1 shows the vertical distance between the data point and PC1, representing **projection error**. Moreover, the distance between each data point in the direction that is parallel to PC1 represents the spread or variation of the data along PC1. The PCA algorithm operates in such a way that it finds PC1 by selecting the line for which the sum of the projection errors for all data points is minimized and for which the sum of the spread between all the data is maximized. As a consequence of these selection criteria, PC1 is the unique vector that accounts for the largest proportion of the variance in the initial data. The next-largest portion of the remaining variance is best explained by PC2, which is at right angles to PC1 and thus is uncorrelated with PC1. The data points can now be represented by the first two principal components. This

EXHIBIT 18   First and Second Principal Components of a Hypothetical Three-Dimensional Dataset

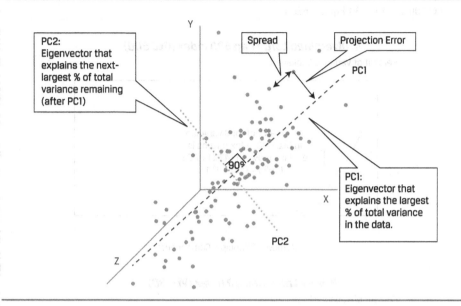

example demonstrates the effectiveness of the PCA algorithm in summarizing the variability of the data and the resulting dimension reduction.

It is important to know how many principal components to retain because there is a trade-off between a lower-dimensional, more manageable view of a complex dataset when a few are selected and some loss of information. **Scree plots**, which show the proportion of total variance in the data explained by each principal component, can be helpful in this regard (see the accompanying sidebar). In practice, the smallest number of principal components that should be retained is that which the scree plot shows as explaining a desired proportion of total variance in the initial dataset (often 85 percent to 95 percent).

Scree Plots for the Principal Components of Returns to the Hypothetical DLC 500 and VLC 30 Equity Indexes

In this illustration, researchers use scree plots and decide that three principal components are sufficient for explaining the returns to the hypothetical Diversified Large Cap (DLC) 500 and Very Large Cap (VLC) 30 equity indexes over the last 10-year period. The DLC 500 can be thought of as a diversified index of large-cap companies covering all economic sectors, while the VLC 30 is a more concentrated index of the 30 largest publicly traded companies. The dataset consists of index prices and more than 2,000 fundamental and technical features. Multi-collinearity among the features is a typical problem because that many features or combinations of features tend to have overlaps. To mitigate the problem, PCA can be used to capture the information and variance in the data. The following scree plots show that of the 20 principal components generated, the first 3 together explain about 90 percent and 86 percent of the variance in the

Scree Plots of Percent of Total Variance Explained by Each Principal Component for Hypothetical
DLC 500 and VLC 30 Equity Indexes

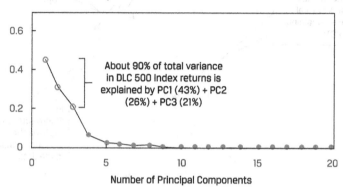

A. Diversified Large Cap 500 Index (DLC 500)

Percent of Variance Explained

About 90% of total variance
in DLC 500 Index returns is
explained by PC1 (43%) + PC2
(26%) + PC3 (21%)

Number of Principal Components

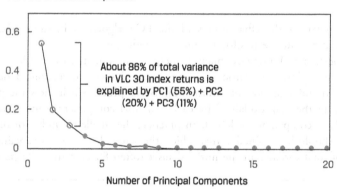

B. Very Large Cap 30 Index (VLC 30)

Percent of Variance Explained

About 86% of total variance
in VLC 30 Index returns is
explained by PC1 (55%) + PC2
(20%) + PC3 (11%)

Number of Principal Components

value of the DLC 500 and VLC 30 indexes, respectively. The scree plots indicate that for
each of these indexes, the incremental contribution to explaining the variance structure of
the data is quite small after about the fifth principal component. Therefore, these less useful principal components can be ignored without much loss of information.

The main drawback of PCA is that since the principal components are combinations of
the dataset's initial features, they typically cannot be easily labeled or directly interpreted by

the analyst. Compared to modeling data with variables that represent well-defined concepts, the end user of PCA may perceive PCA as something of a black box.

Reducing the number of features to the most relevant predictors is very useful, even when working with datasets having as few as 10 or so features. Notably, dimension reduction facilitates visually representing the data in two or three dimensions. It is typically performed as part of exploratory data analysis, before training another supervised or unsupervised learning model. Machine learning models are quicker to train, tend to reduce overfitting (by avoiding the curse of dimensionality), and are easier to interpret if provided with lower-dimensional datasets.

6.2. Clustering

Clustering is another type of unsupervised machine learning, which is used to organize data points into similar groups called clusters. A **cluster** contains a subset of observations from the dataset such that all the observations within the same cluster are deemed "similar." The aim is to find a good clustering of the data—meaning that the observations inside each cluster are similar or close to each other (a property known as cohesion) and the observations in two different clusters are as far away from one another or are as dissimilar as possible (a property known as separation). Exhibit 19 depicts this intra-cluster cohesion and inter-cluster separation.

Clustering algorithms are particularly useful in the many investment problems and applications in which the concept of similarity is important. Applied to grouping companies, for example, clustering may uncover important similarities and differences among companies that are not captured by standard classifications of companies by industry and sector. In portfolio management, clustering methods have been used for improving portfolio diversification.

In practice, expert human judgment has a role in using clustering algorithms. In the first place, one must establish what it means to be similar. Each company can be considered an observation with multiple features, including such financial statement items as total revenue and profit to shareholders, a wide array of financial ratios, or any other potential model inputs. Based on these features, a measure of similarity, or distance, between two observations (i.e., companies) can be defined. The smaller the distance, the more similar the observations; the larger the distance, the more dissimilar the observations.

A commonly used definition of distance is the Euclidian distance, the straight-line distance between two points. A closely related distance useful in portfolio diversification is correlation, which is the average Euclidian distance between a set of standardized points. Roughly a dozen different distance measures are used regularly in ML. In practice, the

EXHIBIT 19   Evaluating Clustering—Intra-Cluster Cohesion and Inter-Cluster Separation

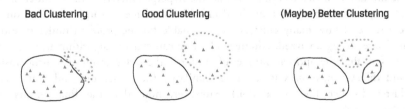

Bad Clustering   Good Clustering   (Maybe) Better Clustering

choice of the distance measures depends on the nature of the data (numerical or not) and the business problem being investigated. Once the relevant distance measure is defined, similar observations can be grouped together. We now introduce two of the more popular clustering approaches: k-means and hierarchical clustering.

6.2.1. K-Means Clustering

K-means is an algorithm that repeatedly partitions observations into a fixed number, k, of non-overlapping clusters. The number of clusters, k, is a model hyperparameter. Each cluster is characterized by its **centroid** (i.e., center), and each observation is assigned by the algorithm to the cluster with the centroid to which that observation is closest. Notably, once the clusters are formed, there is no defined relationship between them.

The k-means algorithm follows an iterative process. It is illustrated in Exhibit 20 for k = 3 and a set of observations on a variable that can be described by two features. In Exhibit 20, the horizontal and vertical axes represent, respectively, the first and second features. For example, an investment analyst may want to group a set of firms into three groups according to two numerical measures of management quality. The algorithm groups the observations in the following steps:

1. K-means starts by determining the position of the k (here, 3) initial random centroids.
2. The algorithm then analyzes the features for each observation. Based on the distance measure that is used, k-means assigns each observation to its closest centroid, which defines a cluster.
3. Using the observations within each cluster, k-means then calculates the new (k) centroids for each cluster, where the centroid is the average value of their assigned observations.
4. K-means then reassigns the observations to the new centroids, redefining the clusters in terms of included and excluded observations.
5. The process of recalculating the new (k) centroids for each cluster is reiterated.
6. K-means then reassigns the observations to the revised centroids, again redefining the clusters in terms of observations that are included and excluded.

The k-means algorithm will continue to iterate until no observation is reassigned to a new cluster (i.e., no need to recalculate new centroids). The algorithm has then converged and reveals the final k clusters with their member observations. The k-means algorithm has minimized intra-cluster distance (thereby maximizing cohesion) and has maximized inter-cluster distance (thereby maximizing separation) under the constraint that $k = 3$.

The k-means algorithm is fast and works well on very large datasets, those with hundreds of millions of observations. However, the final assignment of observations to clusters can depend on the initial location of the centroids. To address this problem, the algorithm can be run several times using different sets of initial centroids, and then one can choose the clustering that is most useful given the business purpose.

One limitation of this technique is that the hyperparameter, k, the number of clusters in which to partition the data, must be decided before k-means can be run. So, one needs to have a sense of how many clusters are reasonable for the problem under investigation and the dataset being analyzed. Alternatively, one can run the algorithm using a range of values for k to find the optimal number of clusters—the k that minimizes intra-cluster distance and thereby maximizes intra-cluster similarity (i.e., cohesion) and that maximizes inter-cluster distance (i.e., separation). However, note that the final results can be

EXHIBIT 20   Example of 3-Means Algorithm

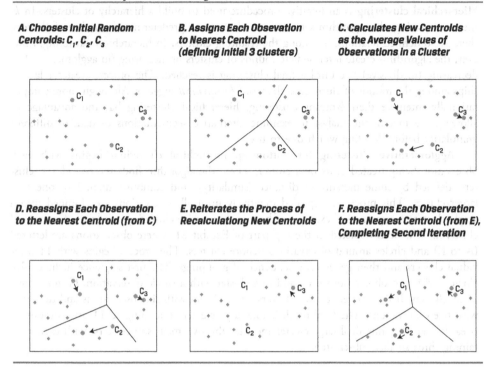

A. Chooses Initial Random Centroids: C_1, C_2, C_3

B. Assigns Each Obsevation to Nearest Centroid (defining initial 3 clusters)

C. Calculates New Centroids as the Average Values of Observations in a Cluster

D. Reassigns Each Observation to the Nearest Centroid (from C)

E. Reiterates the Process of Recalculationg New Centroids

F. Reassigns Each Observation to the Nearest Centroid (from E), Completing Second Iteration

subjective and dependent on the context of the problem and the particular training set. In practice, it is common to make the final choice of k based on face validity, such that the clusters feel sensible and are interpretable. This decision is greatly assisted by using summary information about the centroids and ranges of values and naming example items in each cluster.

For example, consider the Russell 3000 Index, which tracks the 3,000 highest market capitalization stocks in the United States. These 3,000 stocks can be grouped in 10, 50, or even more clusters based on their financial characteristics (e.g., total assets, total revenue, profitability, leverage) and operating characteristics (e.g., employee headcount, R&D intensity). Because companies in the same standard industry classification can have very different financial and operating characteristics, using k-means to derive different clusters can provide insights and understanding into the nature of peer groups. As mentioned, the exact choice of the k, the number of clusters, will depend on the level of precision or segmentation desired. In a similar vein, clustering can be used to classify collective investment vehicles or hedge funds as an alternative to standard classifications. Clustering analysis can also help visualize the data and facilitate detecting trends or outliers.

In sum, the k-means algorithm is among the most used algorithms in investment practice, particularly in data exploration for discovering patterns in high-dimensional data or as a method for deriving alternatives to existing static industry classifications.

6.2.2. Hierarchical Clustering: Agglomerative and Divisive

Hierarchical clustering is an iterative procedure used to build a hierarchy of clusters. In *k*-means clustering, the algorithm segments the data into a predetermined number of clusters; there is no defined relationship among the resulting clusters. In hierarchical clustering, however, the algorithms create intermediate rounds of clusters of increasing (in agglomerative) or decreasing (in divisive) size until a final clustering is reached. The process creates relationships among the rounds of clusters, as the word *hierarchical* suggests. Although more computationally intensive than *k*-means clustering, hierarchical clustering has the advantage of allowing the investment analyst to examine alternative segmentations of data of different granularity before deciding which one to use.

Agglomerative clustering (or bottom-up hierarchical clustering) begins with each observation being treated as its own cluster. Then, the algorithm finds the two closest clusters, defined by some measure of distance (similarity), and combines them into one new larger cluster. This process is repeated iteratively until all observations are clumped into a single cluster. A hypothetical example of how agglomerative clustering develops a hierarchical clustering scheme is depicted in the top part of Exhibit 21, where observations are lettered (A to K) and circles around observations denote clusters. The process begins with 11 individual clusters and then generates a sequence of groupings. The first sequence includes five clusters with two observations each and one cluster with a single observation, G, for a total of six clusters. It then generates two clusters—one cluster with six observations and the other with five observations. The final result is one large cluster containing all 11 observations. It is easily seen that this final large cluster includes the two main sub-clusters, with each containing three smaller sub-clusters.

EXHIBIT 21   Agglomerative and Divisive Hierarchical Clustering

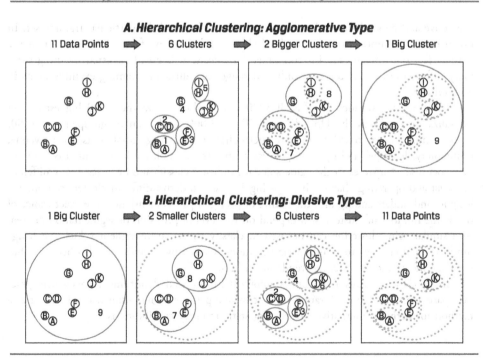

By contrast, **divisive clustering** (or top-down hierarchical clustering) starts with all the observations belonging to a single cluster. The observations are then divided into two clusters based on some measure of distance (similarity). The algorithm then progressively partitions the intermediate clusters into smaller clusters until each cluster contains only one observation. Divisive clustering is depicted in the bottom part of Exhibit 21, which begins with all 11 observations in one large cluster. Next, the algorithm generates two smaller clusters, one with six observations and the other with five observations, and then six clusters, with two observations each except for observation G, which is its own cluster. Finally, 11 clusters are generated, with each cluster containing only one observation.

Although this is not a typical outcome (because the two methods generally use different algorithms), in this hypothetical illustration, the agglomerative and divisive clustering methods produced the same result: two main sub-clusters each having three smaller sub-clusters. The analyst could decide between using a six- or a two-cluster representation of the data. The agglomerative method is the approach typically used with large datasets because of the algorithm's fast computing speed. The agglomerative clustering algorithm makes clustering decisions based on local patterns without initially accounting for the global structure of the data. As such, the agglomerative method is well suited for identifying small clusters. However, because the divisive method starts with a holistic representation of the data, the divisive clustering algorithm is designed to account for the global structure of the data and thus is better suited for identifying large clusters.

To decide on the closest clusters for combining in the agglomerative process or for dividing in the divisive process, an explicit definition for the distance between two clusters is required. Some commonly used definitions for the distance between two clusters involve finding the minimum, the maximum, or the average of the straight-line distances between all the pairs of observations in each cluster.

6.2.3. Dendrograms

A type of tree diagram for visualizing a hierarchical cluster analysis is known as a **dendrogram**, which highlights the hierarchical relationships among the clusters. Exhibit 22 shows a dendrogram representation for the clustering shown in Exhibit 21. First, a few technical points on dendrograms bear mentioning—although they may not all be apparent in Exhibit 22. The x-axis shows the clusters, and the y-axis indicates some distance measure. Clusters are represented by a horizontal line, the arch, which connects two vertical lines, called dendrites, where the height of each arch represents the distance between the two clusters being considered. Shorter dendrites represent a shorter distance (and greater similarity) between clusters. The horizontal dashed lines cutting across the dendrites show the number of clusters into which the data are split at each stage.

The agglomerative algorithm starts at the bottom of the dendrite, where each observation is its own cluster (A to K). Agglomerative clustering then generates the six larger clusters (1 to 6). For example, Clusters A and B combine to form Cluster 1, and Observation G remains its own cluster, now Cluster 4. Moving up the dendrogram, two larger clusters are formed, where, for example, Cluster 7 includes Clusters 1 to 3. Finally, at the top of the dendrogram is the single large cluster (9). The dendrogram readily shows how this largest cluster is composed of the two main sub-clusters (7 and 8), each having three smaller sub-clusters (1 to 3 and 4 to 6, respectively). The dendrogram also facilitates visualization of divisive clustering by starting at the top of the largest cluster and then working downward until the bottom is reached, where all 11 single-observation clusters are shown.

EXHIBIT 22   Dendrogram of Agglomerative Hierarchical Clustering

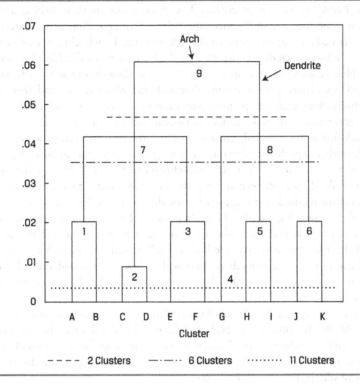

Clustering has many applications in investment management. For example, portfolio diversification can be approached as a clustering problem with the aim of optimally diversifying risks by investing in assets from multiple different clusters. Because the clusters have maximum inter-cluster separation, diversifying among them helps ensure that the portfolio reflects a wide diversity of characteristics with well-diversified risk. In contrast, information that investments are concentrated in a cluster indicates a high probability of concentrated risk. Finally, it is important to note that while the results of clustering algorithms are often difficult to evaluate (because the resulting clusters themselves are not explicitly defined), they are still very useful in practice for uncovering important underlying structure (namely, similarities among observations) in complex datasets.

EXAMPLE 6   Investment Uses of Clustering Algorithms

István Perényi is a portfolio manager of the Europe Diversified Equity Fund ("the Fund") within the Diversified Investment Management Company (DIMCO) fund family. The Fund is benchmarked to the STOXX Europe 600 Index, which spans 17 countries, 19 industry sectors, and three market capitalization groupings (large-, mid-, and small-cap).

Examining the Fund's most recent performance, Perényi is concerned that the Fund's holdings, although approximately aligned with the STOXX Europe 600

Index's country weights, may have unrecognized risk biases and concentrations. Perényi asks Elsa Lund, DIMCO's chief risk officer, to investigate the Fund's diversification. Lund asks her analysts for ideas on how Perényi's request can be addressed and receives three suggestions:

Suggestion 1.   Estimate the country, industry, and market cap exposures of each Fund holding, aggregate them, and compare the aggregate exposures to the benchmark's exposures. Then, examine mismatches for evidence of unexpected biases or concentrations.

Suggestion 2.   Identify inherent groupings among fund holdings based on a broad set of eight numerical (operating and financial) measures related to the holdings' characteristics. Then, examine the groupings for evidence of unexpected biases or concentrations.

Suggestion 3.   Regress the return of the Fund on a set of country equity market indexes and sector indexes based on the Fund's benchmark. Then, examine the regression coefficients for evidence of unexpected biases or concentrations.

Lund has several questions for analyst Greg Kane about using one or more clustering machine learning algorithms in relation to addressing Perényi's request.

Lund asks whether any information needs to be specified for the ML clustering algorithms no matter which one is used. Kane replies that only the distance measure that the algorithm will use and the hyperparameter, k, for k-means clustering need to be specified.

Lund further asks whether there would be an advantage to using k-means clustering as opposed to hierarchical clustering. Kane replies that in his opinion, hierarchical clustering is the more appropriate algorithm.

1. Which analyst suggestion is *most likely* to be implemented using machine learning?
    A. Suggestion 1
    B. Suggestion 2
    C. Suggestion 3

2. Kane's reply to Lund's first question about specification of ML clustering models is:
    A. correct.
    B. not correct, because other hyperparameters must also be specified.
    C. not correct, because the feature set for describing the measure used to group holdings must also be specified.

3. The best justification for Kane's preference for hierarchical clustering in his reply to Lund's second question is that Kane is *most likely* giving consideration to:
    A. the speed of the algorithms.
    B. the dimensionality of the dataset.
    C. the need to specify the hyperparameter, k, in using a k-means algorithm.

Solution to 1: B is correct. A machine learning clustering algorithm could be used to implement Suggestion 2. A and C are incorrect because Suggestions 1 and 3, respectively, can be addressed easily using traditional regression analysis.

Solution to 2: C is correct. Beyond specifying a distance measure and the *k* for *k*-means, whichever clustering algorithm is selected, the feature set used to group holdings by similarities must also be specified. Operating and financial characteristics of the companies represented in the Fund's portfolio are examples of such features.

Solution to 3: C is correct. The value of the hyperparameter, *k*, the number of distinct groups into which the STOXX Europe 600 Index can be segmented, is not known and needs to be specified in advance by the analyst. Using a hierarchical algorithm, the sorting of observations into clusters will occur without any prior input on the analyst's part.

CASE STUDY: CLUSTERING STOCKS BASED ON CO-MOVEMENT SIMILARITY

The following case study was developed and written by Matthew Dixon, PhD, FRM.

An endowment fund's Investment Committee is seeking three "buy" recommendations for the fund's large-cap equity portfolio. An analyst working for the Investment Committee is given a subset of eight stocks from the S&P 500 Index and asked to determine the co-movement similarity (i.e., correlation) of their returns. Specifically, for diversification purposes, the Investment Committee wants the correlation of returns between the recommended stocks to be low, so the analyst decides to use clustering to identify the most similar stocks and then choose one stock from each cluster. Although this case study focuses mainly on hierarchical agglomerative clustering, the analyst's results using other clustering algorithms (i.e., divisive clustering and *k*-means) are also briefly discussed. **Exhibit 23** provides a description of the data used by the analyst.

EXHIBIT 23   Dataset of Eight Stocks from the S&P 500 Index

Description: Daily adjusted closing prices of eight S&P 500 member stocks
Trading Dates: 30 May 2017 to 24 May 2019
Number of Observations: 501
Stocks (Ticker Symbols): AAPL, F, FB, GM, GS, GOOG, JPM, and UBS

The following steps are taken by the analyst to perform the hierarchical agglomerative cluster analysis:

1. Collect panel data on adjusted closing prices for the stocks under investigation.
2. Calculate the daily log returns for each stock, where each time series of stock returns is an *n*-vector ($n = 500$).
3. Run the agglomerative hierarchical clustering algorithm.

a. The algorithm calculates the pairwise distance (i.e., Euclidean distance) between vectors of any two stocks' returns. Each pairwise distance is an element of a distance matrix (i.e., dissimilarity matrix) with zero diagonals.

b. The algorithm starts with each stock as its own cluster, finds the pair of clusters which are closest to each other, and then redefines them as a new cluster.

c. The algorithm finds the distances from this new cluster to the remaining return clusters. Using a process called average (centroid) linkage, it determines the distances from the center of the new cluster to the centers of the remaining clusters. Note that there are several other linkage methods, but whichever method is selected, the algorithm proceeds in the same fashion: It combines the pair of clusters which are closest, redefines them as a new cluster, and recalculates the distances to the remaining clusters.

4. Repeat Step 3c until the data are aggregated into a single large cluster.

5. Plot the resulting dendrogram to visualize the hierarchical clusters and draw the highest horizontal line intersecting three (i.e., the desired number of clusters, since the Investment Committee wants three "buy" recommendations) vertical lines (or dendrites) to determine the appropriate cluster configuration.

Exhibit 24 shows for illustrative purposes a subset of the panel data on daily returns, calculated from the adjusted closing prices of the eight stocks collected in Step 1. The clustering is performed on the daily returns.

The results of the remaining steps are described using the distance matrix shown in Exhibit 25.

The distance matrix reveals the closest pair of stocks is JPM and GS, with a distance of 0.215. Therefore, this pair becomes the first combined cluster as shown in the dendrogram in Exhibit 26. Note that the vertical distance connecting the various clusters represents the Euclidean distance between clusters, so the arch between this pair has a height of 0.215. Now that JPM and GS are paired in a cluster (i.e., GS_JPM), we treat the mean of their two return vectors as a new point.

From the distance matrix, the average distance of UBS to the new cluster (i.e., GS_JPM) is the sum of the distance between UBS and JPM, 0.243, and the distance between UBS and GS, 0.281, divided by two, which is 0.262 (= (0.243 + 0.281)/2). Since this distance is smaller than the distance between any of the other unpaired stock clusters, UBS is merged with this cluster to create a new cluster (i.e., GS_JPM_UBS). The height of the arch in the dendrogram for this new cluster is 0.262, which is now observed

EXHIBIT 24   Subset of Stock Returns, Calculated from Adjusted Closing Prices, for Clustering

Date	JPM	UBS	GS	FB	AAPL	GOOG	GM	F
2017-05-31	−0.021	−0.007	−0.033	−0.006	−0.006	−0.011	0.012	0.004
2017-06-01	0.011	0.013	0.018	0.000	0.003	0.002	0.015	0.026
2017-06-02	−0.005	−0.002	−0.008	0.014	0.015	0.009	0.001	−0.005
2017-06-05	0.002	−0.007	0.003	0.000	−0.010	0.008	0.000	−0.009
2017-06-06	0.002	0.002	0.003	−0.005	0.003	−0.007	−0.001	−0.012

EXHIBIT 25   Distance Matrix for Hierarchical Agglomerative Clustering

	JPM	UBS	GS	FB	AAPL	GOOG	GM	F
JPM	0.000	0.243	0.215	0.456	0.364	0.332	0.358	0.348
UBS	0.243	0.000	0.281	0.460	0.380	0.338	0.384	0.385
GS	0.215	0.281	0.000	0.471	0.375	0.345	0.383	0.393
FB	0.456	0.460	0.471	0.000	0.437	0.357	0.491	0.480
AAPL	0.364	0.380	0.375	0.437	0.000	0.307	0.445	0.456
GOOG	0.332	0.338	0.345	0.357	0.307	0.000	0.405	0.422
GM	0.358	0.384	0.383	0.491	0.445	0.405	0.000	0.334
F	0.348	0.385	0.393	0.480	0.456	0.422	0.334	0.000

to contain three banking sector stocks. Although not shown in the dendrogram, the cluster is identified by the return vector averaged over the three stocks.

The next closest pair of points, whether stock to stock or stock to cluster, is AAPL and GOOG, with a distance of 0.307, so the algorithm merges these two points into a second cluster (i.e., AAPL_GOOG), with an arch height of 0.307. Next, GM and F are paired into a third cluster (i.e., F_GM), with an arch height of 0.334. Finally, the first two clusters are merged to form a five-stock cluster (i.e., GS_JPM_UBS_AAPL_GOOG), with an arch height of 0.356. Note that this value is determined by taking the average distance between the three banks and AAPL and GOOG: 0.356 = (0.364 + 0.380 + 0.375 + 0.332 + 0.338 + 0.345)/6. The result is three separate clusters: the five-stock cluster, F_GM, and FB by itself. Also, note the horizontal dashed line that cuts the dendrogram into three distinct clusters, with FB as its own cluster.

This agglomerative hierarchical clustering analysis reveals some interesting preliminary results—largely grouping the stocks by their sectors but also uncovering some anomalies.

EXHIBIT 26   Dendrogram for Hierarchical Agglomerative Clustering

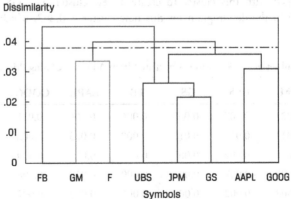

In particular, FB is found to behave quite differently, in terms of return co-movement similarity, from the other technology stocks (AAPL and GOOG). Also, AAPL and GOOG are found to behave more like the bank stocks and less like the auto stocks (F and GM), which appear in their own cluster.

In contrast to agglomerative clustering, the divisive clustering algorithm starts with all stocks assigned to one large cluster and then splits the cluster into sub-clusters recursively, until each stock occupies its own cluster. Determining how to split the first cluster requires searching over all combinations of possible splits, so it is too numerically intensive to cover the details here. However, results of the first two splits for divisive clustering, into three clusters, are shown in **Exhibit 27**. Results for *k*-means, with *k* = 3, and agglomerative clustering are also presented.

EXHIBIT 27   Comparison of Results of Different Clustering Algorithms

	Agglomerative	*K*-means	Divisive
AAPL	3	2	2
F	2	1	1
FB	1	2	3
GM	2	1	1
GOOG	3	2	2
GS	3	3	1
JPM	3	3	1
UBS	3	3	1

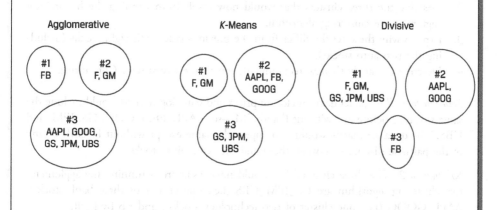

Whereas the assignment of the cluster number (1, 2, 3), shown in the upper panel, can be taken as arbitrary across each algorithm, the useful information is in the grouping of like stocks. As seen in the stylized clusters in the lower panel, all three clustering algorithms agree that bank stocks belong in the same cluster. Both hierarchical agglomerative and k-means algorithms also agree that auto stocks belong in their own separate cluster. K-means clusters the stocks precisely by industry sector, whereas hierarchical agglomerative and divisive clustering identify FB as an outlier and place it in its own cluster. In general, the most agreement is expected between the two hierarchical clustering algorithms, although their results are not guaranteed to match, even when using the same linkage process. K-means starts with three clusters ($k = 3$) and iteratively swaps points in and out of these clusters using a partitioning mechanism different from that of hierarchical clustering. Thus, k-means results are typically not expected to match those of hierarchical clustering.

In conclusion, based on the analyses of the co-movement similarity of returns among the eight stocks using the agglomerative clustering algorithm and the Investment Committee's requirement that the correlation of returns between the recommended stocks should be low, the analyst's recommendation should be as follows:

- buy FB,
- buy the most attractive of the two auto stocks (F or GM), and
- buy the most attractive of the three bank stocks (GS, JPM, or UBS).

EXAMPLE 7 Hierarchical Agglomerative Clustering

Assume the analyst is given the same set of stocks as previously excluding F and GM (i.e., no auto stocks)—so now, six stocks. Using the information from this mini-case study, answer the following questions:

1. Describe how the inputs to the hierarchical agglomerative clustering algorithm would differ from those in the mini-case study.
2. Describe the three clusters that would now result from running the hierarchical agglomerative clustering algorithm.
3. Explain why these results differ from the previous case, with eight stocks (including the two auto stocks).
4. Describe the analyst's new recommendation to the Investment Committee.

Solution to 1: The panel data on closing prices and daily log returns would include the same stocks as before but without F and GM—so, AAPL, FB, GOOG, GS, JPM, and UBS. The distance matrix would also appear the same except without F, GM, or any of the pairwise distances between them and the remaining stocks.

Solution to 2: The three clusters that would now result from running the agglomerative clustering algorithm are GS_JPM_UBS (i.e., one cluster of three bank stocks), AAPL_GOOG (i.e., one cluster of two technology stocks), and FB by itself.

Solution to 3: The agglomerative clustering algorithm now combines GS and JPM and then UBS, as before, to form a bank cluster. Next, and as previously, the algorithm combines AAPL and GOOG into a cluster. However, without the auto stocks, there is no need to combine AAPL_GOOG with the bank cluster. There are now three distinct clusters, since (as before) the algorithm treats FB as its own cluster, given the high degree of return co-movement dissimilarity between FB and the other clusters (i.e., AAPL_GOOG, and GS_JPM_UBS).

Solution to 4: The analyst's new recommendation to the Investment Committee would be to buy FB, buy the cheapest of AAPL or GOOG, and buy the most attractive of the three bank stocks (GS, JPM, or UBS).

7. NEURAL NETWORKS, DEEP LEARNING NETS, AND REINFORCEMENT LEARNING

The artificial intelligence revolution has been driven in large part by advances in neural networks, deep learning algorithms, and reinforcement learning. These sophisticated algorithms can address highly complex machine learning tasks, such as image classification, face recognition, speech recognition, and natural language processing. These complicated tasks are characterized by non-linearities and interactions between large numbers of feature inputs. We now provide an overview of these algorithms and their investment applications.

7.1. Neural Networks

Neural networks (also called artificial neural networks, or ANNs) are a highly flexible type of ML algorithm that have been successfully applied to a variety of tasks characterized by non-linearities and complex interactions among features. Neural networks are commonly used for classification and regression in supervised learning but are also important in reinforcement learning, which does not require human-labeled training data.

Exhibit 28 shows the connection between multiple regression and neural networks. Panel A represents a hypothetical regression for data using four inputs, the features x_1 to x_4, and one output—the predicted value of the target variable y. Panel B shows a schematic representation of a basic neural network, which consists of nodes (circles) connected by links (arrows connecting nodes). Neural networks have three types of layers: an input layer (here with a node for each of the four features); hidden layers, where learning occurs in training and inputs are processed on trained nets; and an output layer (here consisting of a single node for the target variable y), which passes information outside the network.

Besides the network structure, another important difference between multiple regression and neural networks is that the nodes in the neural network's hidden layer transform the inputs in a non-linear fashion into new values that are then combined into the target value. For example, consider the popular rectified linear unit (ReLU) function, $f(x) = \max(0, x)$, which takes on a value of zero if there is a negative input and takes on the value of the input if it is positive. In this case, y will be equal to β_1 times z_1, where z_1 is the maximum of $(x_1 + x_2 + x_3)$ or 0, plus β_2 times z_2, the maximum of $(x_2 + x_4)$ or 0, plus β_3 times z_3, the maximum of $(x_2 + x_3 + x_4)$ or 0, plus an error term.

EXHIBIT 28   Regression and Neural Networks (Regression with Transformed Features)

A. Conceptual Illustration of Regression

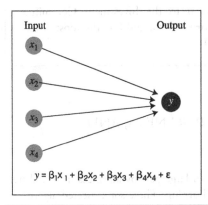

B. Conceptual Illustration of Hypothetical Neural Network

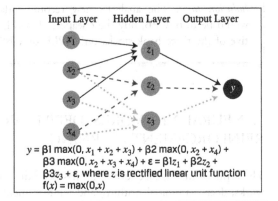

Note that for neural networks, the feature inputs would be scaled (i.e., standardized) to account for differences in the units of the data. For example, if the inputs were positive numbers, each could be scaled by its maximum value so that their values lie between 0 and 1.

Exhibit 29 shows a more complex neural network, with an input layer consisting of four nodes (i.e., four features), one hidden layer consisting of five hidden nodes, and an output node. These three numbers—4, 5, and 1—for the neural network are hyperparameters that determine the structure of the neural network.

EXHIBIT 29   A More Complex Neural Network with One Hidden Layer

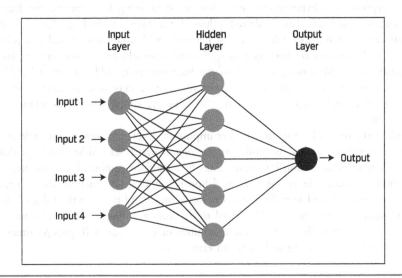

Now consider any of the nodes to the right of the input layer. These nodes are sometimes called "neurons" because they process information received. Take the topmost hidden node. Four links connect to that node from the inputs, so the node gets four values transmitted by the links. Each link has a weight meant to represent its importance (initially these weights may be assigned randomly). Each node has, conceptually, two functional parts: a summation operator and an activation function. Once the node receives the four input values, the **summation operator** multiplies each value by its respective weight and then sums the weighted values to form the total net input. The total net input is then passed to the **activation function**, which transforms this input into the final output of the node. Informally, the activation function operates like a light dimmer switch that decreases or increases the strength of the input. The activation function, which is chosen by the modeler (i.e., a hyperparameter), is characteristically non-linear, such as an S-shaped (sigmoidal) function (with output range of 0 to 1) or the rectified linear unit function shown in Panel B of Exhibit 28. Non-linearity implies that the rate of change of output differs at different levels of input.

This activation function is shown in Exhibit 30, where in the left graph a negative total net input is transformed via the S-shaped function into an output close to 0. This low output implies the node does not trigger, so there is nothing to pass to the next node. Conversely, in the right graph a positive total net input is transformed into an output close to 1, so the node does trigger. The output of the activation function is then transmitted to the next set of nodes if there is a second hidden layer or, as in this case, to the output layer node as the predicted value. The process of transmission just described (think of forward pointing arrows in Exhibit 29) is referred to as **forward propagation**.

Starting with an initialized set of random network weights (i.e., the weights assigned to each of the links), training a neural network in a supervised learning context is an iterative process in which predictions are compared to actual values of labeled data and evaluated

EXHIBIT 30   Activation Function as "Light Dimmer Switch" at Each Node in a Neural Network

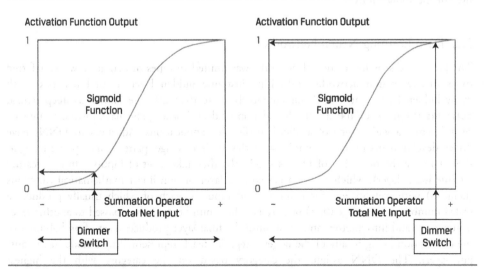

by a specified performance measure (e.g., mean squared error). Then, the network weights are adjusted to reduce total error of the network. (If the process of adjustment works backward through the layers of the network, this process is called **backward propagation**.) Learning takes place through this process of adjustment to the network weights with the aim of reducing total error. Without proliferating notation relating to nodes, the gist of the updating can be expressed informally as

> New weight = (Old weight) − (Learning rate)
>   × (Partial derivative of the total error with respect to the old weight),

where partial derivative is a gradient or rate of change of the total error with respect to the change in the old weight and **learning rate** is a hyperparameter that affects the magnitude of adjustments. When learning is completed, all the network weights have assigned values; these are the parameters of the network.

The structure of a network in which all the features are interconnected with non-linear activation functions allows neural networks to uncover and approximate complex non-linear relationships among features. Broadly speaking, when more nodes and more hidden layers are specified, a neural network's ability to handle complexity tends to increase (but so does the risk of overfitting).

Asset pricing is a noisy, stochastic process with potentially unstable relationships that challenge modeling processes, so researchers are asking if machine learning can improve our understanding of how markets work. Research comparing statistical and machine learning methods' abilities to explain and predict equity prices so far indicates that simple neural networks produce models of equity returns at the individual stock and portfolio level that are superior to models built using traditional statistical methods due to their ability to capture dynamic and interacting variables. This suggests that ML-based models, such as neural networks, may simply be better able to cope with the non-linear relationships inherent in security prices. However, the trade-offs in using neural networks are their lack of interpretability (i.e., black box nature) and the large amounts of data and high computation intensity needed to train such models; thus, neural networks may not be a good choice in many investment applications.

7.2. Deep Learning Neural Networks

The previous discussion of neural networks was limited to types of neural networks referred to as shallow neural networks—exhibiting just one hidden layer. Neural networks with many hidden layers—at least 2 but potentially more than 20—are known as **deep neural networks** (DNNs). DNNs are the foundation of deep learning and have proven to be successful across a wide range of artificial intelligence applications. Advances in DNNs have driven developments in many complex activities, such as image, pattern, and speech recognition. To state the operation of DNNs succinctly, they take a set of inputs x from a feature set (the input layer), which are then passed to a layer of non-linear mathematical functions (neurons) with weights w_{ij} (for neuron i and input j), each of which usually produces a scaled number in the range (0, 1) or (−1, 1). These numbers are then passed to another layer of functions and into another and so on until the final layer produces a set of probabilities of the observation being in any of the target categories (each represented by a node in the output layer). The DNN assigns the category based on the category with the highest probability. The DNN is trained on large datasets; during training, the weights, w_i, are determined to minimize a specified loss function.

In practice, while the number of nodes in the input and the output layers are typically determined by the characteristics of the features and predicted output, many model hyperparameters still must be decided, particularly the number of hidden layers, the number of nodes per hidden layer, and their connectivity and activation architecture. The objective is to choose them to achieve the best out-of-sample performance, but it is still a challenge with no simple solution. As such, a good starting point is a reasonable guess for hyperparameters based on experience and literature. The researcher can then observe the result and adjust the hyperparameters incrementally until the model performance goal is reached. In practice, DNNs require substantial time to train, and systematically varying the hyperparameters may not be feasible. So, for many problems with relatively small datasets, one can start with just two or three hidden layers and a few hundred nodes before tuning the parameters until a model with acceptable predictive power is achieved.

DNNs have been shown to be useful in general for pattern recognition problems (e.g., character and image recognition), credit card fraud detection, vision and control problems in autonomous cars, natural language processing (such as machine translation), and other applications. DNNs have become hugely successful because of a confluence of three developments: (1) the availability of large quantities of machine-readable data to train models, (2) advances in analytical methods for fitting these models, and (3) fast computers, especially new chips in the graphics processing unit (GPU) class, tailored for the type of calculations done on DNNs.

Several financial firms are experimenting with DNNs for trading as well as automating their internal processes. Culkin and Das (2017) described how they trained DNNs to price options, mimicking the Black–Scholes–Merton model. Their research used the same six input parameters for the model as input layer features—spot price, strike, time to maturity, dividend yield, risk-free interest rate, and volatility—with four hidden layers of 100 neurons each and one output layer. The predicted option prices out-of-sample were very close to the actual option prices: A regression of predicted option prices on actual prices had an R^2 of 99.8 percent.

7.3. Reinforcement Learning

Reinforcement learning (RL) made headlines in 2017 when DeepMind's AlphaGo program beat the reigning world champion at the ancient game of Go. The RL framework involves an agent that is designed to perform actions that will maximize its rewards over time, taking into consideration the constraints of its environment. In the case of AlphaGo, a virtual gamer (the agent) uses his or her console commands (the actions) with the information on the screen (the environment) to maximize his or her score (the reward). Unlike supervised learning, reinforcement learning has neither direct labeled data for each observation nor instantaneous feedback. With RL, the algorithm needs to observe its environment, learn by testing new actions (some of which may not be immediately optimal), and reuse its previous experiences. The learning subsequently occurs through millions of trials and errors. Academics and practitioners are applying RL in a similar way in investment strategies where the agent could be a virtual trader who follows certain trading rules (the actions) in a specific market (the environment) to maximize its profits (its reward). The success of RL in dealing with the complexities of financial markets is still an open question.

EXAMPLE 8   Deep Neural Networks

Glen Mitsui is the chief investment officer for a large Australian state's Public Employees' Pension Fund (PEPF), which currently has assets under management (AUM) of A\$20 billion. The fund manages one-quarter of its assets internally, with A\$5 billion mostly in domestic government and corporate fixed-income instruments and domestic equities. The remaining three-quarters of AUM, or A\$15 billion, is managed by nearly 100 mostly active external asset managers and is invested in a wide range of asset classes, including foreign fixed income and equities, domestic and foreign hedge funds, REITs, commodities, and derivatives.

PEPF has a small staff of four investment professionals tasked with selecting and monitoring these external managers to whom it pays more than A\$400 million in fees annually. Performance (compared to appropriate benchmarks) of many of PEPF's external managers has been lagging over the past several years. After studying the situation, Mitsui concludes that style drift may be an important factor in explaining such underperformance, for which PEPF is not happy to pay. Mitsui believes that machine learning may help and consults with Frank Monroe, professor of data analysis at Epsilon University.

Monroe suggests using a deep neural network model that collects and analyzes the real-time trading data of PEPF's external managers and compares them to well-known investment styles (e.g., high dividend, minimum volatility, momentum, growth, value) to detect potential style drift. Mitsui arranges for Monroe to meet with PEPF's investment committee (IC) to discuss the matter. As a junior data analyst working with Monroe, you must help him satisfy the following requests from the IC:

1. Define a deep neural network.
2. Evaluate Monroe's opinion on the applicability of deep neural networks to Mitsui's problem.
3. Describe the functions of the three groups of layers of a deep neural network.

Solution to 1: A deep neural network is a neural network (NN) with many hidden layers (at least 2 but often more than 20). NNs and DNNs have been successfully applied to a wide variety of complex tasks characterized by non-linearities and interactions among features, particularly pattern recognition problems.

Solution to 2: Mitsui wants to detect patterns of potential style drift in the daily trading of nearly 100 external asset managers in many markets. This task will involve the processing of huge amounts of complicated data. Monroe is correct that a DNN is well suited to PEPF's needs.

Solution to 3: The input layer, the hidden layers, and the output layer constitute the three groups of layers of DNNs. The input layer receives the inputs (i.e., features) and has as many nodes as there are dimensions of the feature set. The hidden layers consist of nodes, each comprising a summation operator and an activation function that are connected by links. These hidden layers are, in effect, where the model is learned. The final layer, the output layer, produces a set of probabilities of an observation being in any of the target style categories (each represented by a node in the output layer). For example, if there are three target style categories, then three nodes in the output layer are activated to produce outputs that sum to one. So, output (Style Category I, 0.7; Style Category II, 0.2; Style Category III, 0.1) would indicate that the model assigns the greatest probability to an observation being in Style Category I and the least probability to Style Category III. The DNN assigns the observation to the style category with the highest probability.

CASE STUDY: DEEP NEURAL NETWORK–BASED EQUITY FACTOR MODEL

The following case study was developed and written by Matthew Dixon, PhD, FRM.

An investment manager wants to select stocks based on their predicted performance using a fundamental equity factor model. She seeks to capture superior performance from stocks with the largest excess return using a non-linear factor model and so chooses a deep neural network to predict the stock returns. The goal of this mini-case study is to demonstrate the application of deep neural networks to fundamental equity factor modeling. We shall focus on using feed-forward (i.e., forward propagation) network regression in place of ordinary least squares linear regression. Since neural networks are prone to over-fitting, we shall use LASSO penalization, the same penalty score–based approach used previously with regression, to mitigate this issue.

Introduction

Cross-sectional fundamental factor models are used extensively by investment managers to capture the effects of company-specific factors on individual securities. A fixed universe of N assets is first chosen, together with a set of K fundamental factors. Each asset's sensitivity (i.e., exposure or loading) to a fundamental factor is represented by beta, B, and the factors are represented by factor returns (f_t). There are two standard approaches to estimating a factor model: (i) adopt time-series regression (TSR) to recover loadings if factors are known or (ii) use cross-sectional regression (CSR) to recover factor returns from known loadings. We shall follow the CSR approach; the factor exposures are used to predict a stock's return (r_t) by estimating the factor returns using multivariate linear regression (where ϵ_t is the model error at time t):

$$r_t = Bf_t + \epsilon_t.$$

However, this CSR model is too simplistic to capture non-linear relationships between stock returns and fundamental factors. So, instead we use a deep neural network to learn the non-linear relationships between the betas (B) and asset returns (r_t) at each time t. The goal of deep learning is to find the network weights which minimize the out-of-sample mean squared error (MSE) between the predicted stock returns, $\hat{r}$, and the observed stock returns, r. We shall see that simply increasing the number of neurons in the network will increase predictive performance using the in-sample data but to the detriment of out-of-sample performance; this phenomenon is the bias–variance trade-off. To mitigate this effect, we add a LASSO penalty term to the loss function to automatically shrink the number of non-zero weights in the network. In doing so, we shall see that this leads to better out-of-sample predictive performance.

Note that each weight corresponds to a link between a node in the previous and current layer. Reducing the number of weights generally means that the number of connections—not the number of nodes—is reduced. The exception is when all weights from the neurons in the previous layer are set to zero—in which case the number of nodes in the current layer would be reduced. In the special case when the previous layer is the input layer, the number of features is also reduced.

We shall illustrate the data preparation and the neural network fitting using six fundamental equity factors. This choice of number and type of fundamental factor is arbitrary, and an investment manager may use many more factors in her or his model, often representing industry sectors and sub-sectors using dummy variables.

Data Description

A description of the stock price and fundamental equity factor data used for training and evaluating the neural network is shown in **Exhibit 31**.

EXHIBIT 31   Dataset of S&P 500 Stocks and Fundamental Factors

Description:

A subset of S&P 500 Index stocks, historical monthly adjusted closing prices, and corresponding monthly fundamental factor loadings.
Time period: June 2010 to November 2018
Number of periods: 101
Number of stocks (N): 218 stocks
Number of features (K): 6
Features: Fundamental equity factors:
1. Current enterprise value (i.e., market values of equity + preferred stock + debt − cash − short-term investments)
2. Current enterprise value to trailing 12-month EBITDA
3. Price-to-sales ratio
4. Price-to-earnings ratio
5. Price-to-book ratio
6. Log of stock's market capitalization (i.e., share price × number of shares outstanding)

Output: Monthly return for each stock over the following month.

EXHIBIT 32   Extract of Six Factor Loadings and Return for Three Selected Stocks

TICKER	CURR_EV ($ Mil.)	CURR_EV_TO_ T12M_EBITDA (X)	PX_TO_ SALES (X)	PX_TO_ EARN (X)	PX_TO_ BOOK (X)	LOG_CAP ($ Mil.)	RETURN (%)
SWK	10,775.676	30.328	1.138	16.985	1.346	9.082970	-0.132996
STZ	7,433.553	15.653	1.052	10.324	1.480	8.142253	-0.133333
SRE	19,587.124	10.497	1.286	10.597	1.223	9.314892	-0.109589

We define the universe as the top 250 stocks from the S&P 500, ranked by market capitalization as of June 2010. All stock prices and factor loadings are sourced from Bloomberg.
An illustrative extract of the data is given in Exhibit 32. Note that after removing stocks
with missing factor loadings, we are left with 218 stocks.

Experimental Design

The method used to train the deep neural network is time-series cross-validation (i.e., walk-
forward optimization), as depicted in Exhibit 33. At each time period, the investment manager fits a new model; each factor (f_1 to f_6) is a feature in the network, and the loadings of
the factors for each stock is a feature vector observation (i.e., the set of observations for each
stock for each period), leading to $N = 218$ observations of pairs of feature vectors and output (monthly return, r_t) in the training set per period. The network is initially trained at
period t, and then it is tested over the next period, $t + 1$, which also has $N = 218$ observations of pairs of feature vectors and output. In the next iteration, the $t + 1$ data become the

EXHIBIT 33   Time-Series Cross-Validation on Asset Returns (Walk-Forward Optimization)—The
First Three Iterations

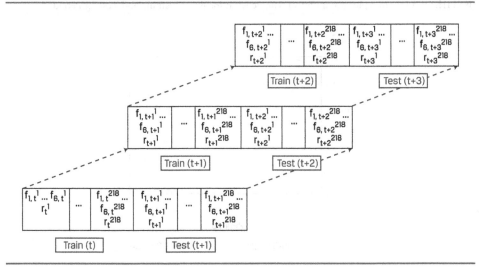

new training set and the revised model is tested on the $t + 2$ data. The walk-forward optimization of the neural network continues until the last iteration: model training with $t + 99$ data (from Period 100) and testing with $t + 100$ data (from the last period, 101).

    We use a feed-forward neural network with six input nodes (i.e., neurons), two hidden layers, and one output neuron. There are 50 neurons in each hidden layer to intentionally over-specify the number of parameters needed in the model, meaning bias (variance) is substantially lower (higher) than optimal. LASSO penalization is then used to automatically shrink the parameter set. Additionally, it is important for the number of nodes in each hidden layer not to exceed the number of observations in the training set (50 nodes per layer versus 218 observations). The model training in period t involves finding the optimal bias-versus-variance trade-off. Once fitted, we record the in-sample MSE and the out-of-sample MSE in addition to the optimal regularization parameter. This procedure is then repeated sequentially over the horizon of 100 remaining periods, tuning the hyperparameters at each stage using cross-validation. The end result of this procedure is a fitted model, trained monthly on the current cross-sectional data and for which hyperparameters have been tuned at each step.

Results

Exhibit 34 presents the results from model evaluation; it compares the in-sample and out-of-sample MSEs of the deep neural network over all 101 months. Note that the out-of-sample error (dotted line) is typically significantly larger than the in-sample error (solid line). However, as the time periods pass and the model is repeatedly trained and tested, the difference between the out-of-sample and in-sample MSEs narrows dramatically.

    Exhibit 35 shows the effect of LASSO regularization on the in-sample MSE (lower panel, B) and the out-of-sample MSE (upper panel, A) for the first iteration of the time-series cross-validation (training with data from period t and testing with data from period $t + 1$). The degree of LASSO regularization needed is found by cross-validation using 50 neurons in each hidden layer. Increasing the LASSO regularization, which reduces the number

EXHIBIT 34   In-Sample and Out-of-Sample MSE for Each Training and Testing Period

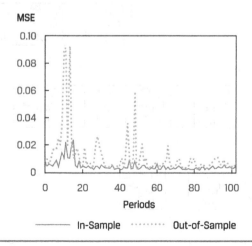

EXHIBIT 35   LASSO Regularization for Optimizing Bias–Variance Trade-Off (First Iteration)

A.

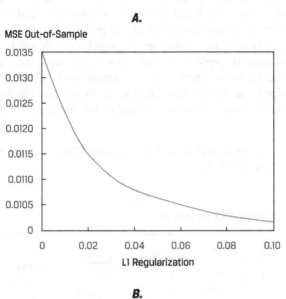

MSE Out-of-Sample

B.

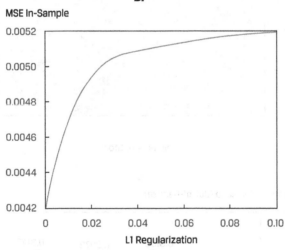

MSE In-Sample

of non-zero weights in the model, introduces more bias and hence increases the in-sample error. Conversely, increasing the LASSO regularization reduces the model's variance and thereby reduces the out-of-sample error. Overall, the amount of LASSO regularization needed is significant, at 0.10; typically the regularization hyperparameter is between 0.001 and 1.0. Also, the out-of-sample and in-sample MSEs have not yet converged. There is still a substantial gap, of roughly 0.0051 (= 0.01025 – 0.0052), and the slope of the curves in each plot suggests the optimal value of the regularization hyperparameter is significantly more than 0.10. Note that the value of the regularization hyperparameter is not interpretable and does not correspond to the number of weights eliminated. Suffice it to say, the larger the value of the regularization hyperparameter, the more the loss is being penalized.

It is important to recognize that although the out-of-sample MSE of this deep learning neural network is key to characterizing its predictive performance, it does not necessarily follow that a stock selection strategy based on the neural network will be successful. This is because the neural network predicts the next month's expected (i.e., mean) asset returns and not the full distribution of returns. Hence a simple stock selection strategy—measured by information ratios (recall the information ratio, or IR, is alpha divided by nonsystematic risk, so it measures the abnormal return per unit of risk for a well-diversified portfolio) of

EXHIBIT 36   Information Ratios from Back-Testing a Stock Selection Strategy Using Top Performers from the Neural Network

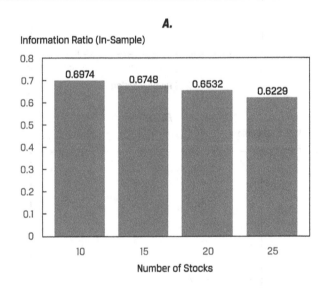

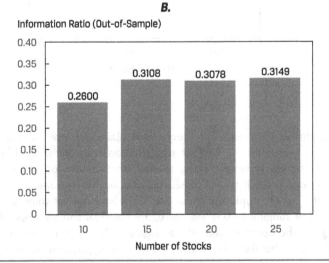

the portfolio returns—that selects stocks ranked by predicted returns will not necessarily lead to positive information ratios.

Exhibit 36 presents the information ratios found by back-testing a simple stock selection strategy that picks the top performing stocks determined by the neural network's forecasted returns realized in month $t +1$ using features observed in month t. Note these IRs do not account for transaction costs, interest rates, or any other fees. The upper panel (A) shows the best-case scenario; the neural network in-sample prediction is used to select the n (where n is 10, 15, 20, or 25) top performing stocks. The IRs are shown for each of the different-sized portfolios; they range from 0.697 to 0.623. Note that as a rule of thumb, IRs in the range of 0.40–0.60 are considered quite good. The lower panel (B) shows the IRs from back-test results for the same strategy applied to the out-of-sample data. The out-of-sample IRs range from 0.260 to 0.315 and so are substantially smaller than in-sample IRs.

Importantly, the out-of-sample performance provides the most realistic assessment of the likely future investment performance from applying this deep learning neural network to stock selection. It is a baseline for further model refinements, including adding more fundamental and macroeconomic factors. With such refinements, it can be expected that the out-of-sample IRs should improve substantially.

EXAMPLE 9   Deep Learning–Based Fundamental Factor Model

A research analyst, Jane Hinton, has been tasked with further developing the deep learning–based fundamental factor model. She decides to refine the model by adding four more fundamental factors (such as debt leverage and R&D intensity) given by firm characteristics and by including dummy variables for 11 industrial sectors. Moreover, she additionally expands the universe of stocks to 420 from 218 by using a supplementary data source.

1. Describe how Jane would modify the inputs of the neural network architecture for this new dataset.
2. Describe the size of the new training and test datasets.
3. Describe any additional changes to the architecture and hyperparameters of the neural network that Jane would likely need to make to ensure good performance of the network.
4. Explain how Jane should evaluate whether the new model leads to improved portfolio performance.

Solution to 1: Jane adds four more fundamental factors and 11 dummy variables, to represent each industrial sector, for a total of 21 (= 4 + 11 + 6) features. Therefore, the refined neural network will have 21 input neurons. The output layer will remain the same. Note that concerns of collinearity of the features through the dummy variables or high correlation, which are problematic for linear regression, are not an issue for a deep learning–based model.

Solution to 2: There are now data on 420 stocks, for each of the 101 time periods, consisting of factor loadings for the 21 features and the monthly return for each stock.

Per the time-series cross-validation method, the test dataset in the current iteration will become the training dataset in the next iteration.

Solution to 3: Jane should find the new optimal LASSO regularization hyperparameter using time-series cross-validation. Alternatively, she may find the optimal bias–variance trade-off by first increasing the number of neurons in the hidden layers and then performing the cross-validation.

Solution to 4: Once Jane has found the optimal LASSO hyperparameter and network architecture, she will use the model to forecast the out-of-sample monthly asset returns (i.e., the model forecasts from factor loadings which are not in the training set). She will then rank and select the top predicted performers and finally measure the realized monthly portfolio return. She will then repeat the experiment by moving forward one month in the dataset and repeating the out-of-sample forecast of the asset returns, until she has generated forecasts for all time periods. Finally, Jane will calculate the information ratios from the mean and standard deviation of the monthly portfolio excess returns.

EXAMPLE 10 Summing Up the Major Types of Machine Learning

1. As used in supervised machine learning, classification problems involve the following *except*:
   A. binary target variables.
   B. continuous target variables.
   C. categorical target variables.

2. Which of the following *best* describes penalized regression? Penalized regression:
   A. is unrelated to multiple linear regression.
   B. involves a penalty term that is added to the predicted target variable.
   C. is a category of general linear models used when the number of features and overfitting are concerns.

3. CART is *best* described as:
   A. an unsupervised ML algorithm.
   B. a clustering algorithm based on decision trees.
   C. a supervised ML algorithm that accounts for non-linear relationships among the features.

4. A neural network is *best* described as a technique for machine learning that is:
   A. exactly modeled on the human nervous system.
   B. based on layers of nodes connected by links when the relationships among the features are usually non-linear.
   C. based on a tree structure of nodes when the relationships among the features are linear.

5. Hierarchical clustering is *best* described as a technique in which:
   A. the grouping of observations is unsupervised.

    B. features are grouped into a pre-specified number, *k*, of clusters.

    C. observations are classified according to predetermined labels.

6. Dimension reduction techniques are *best* described as a means to reduce a set of features to a manageable size:

    A. without regard for the variation in the data.

    B. while increasing the variation in the data.

    C. while retaining as much of the variation in the data as possible.

Solution to 1: B is correct. A and C are incorrect because when the target variable is binary or categorical (not continuous), the problem is a classification problem.

Solution to 2: C is correct. A is incorrect because penalized regression is related to multiple linear regression. B is incorrect because penalized regression involves adding a penalty term to the sum of the squared regression residuals.

Solution to 3: C is correct. A is incorrect because CART is a supervised ML algorithm. B is incorrect because CART is a classification and regression algorithm, not a clustering algorithm.

Solution to 4: B is correct. A is incorrect because neural networks are not exactly modeled on the human nervous system. C is incorrect because neural networks are not based on a tree structure of nodes when the relationships among the features are linear.

Solution to 5: A is correct. B is incorrect because it refers to *k*-means clustering. C is incorrect because it refers to classification, which involves supervised learning.

Solution to 6: C is correct because dimension reduction techniques, such as PCA, are aimed at reducing the feature set to a manageable size while retaining as much of the variation in the data as possible.

8. CHOOSING AN APPROPRIATE ML ALGORITHM

Exhibit 37 presents a simplified decision flowchart for choosing among the machine learning algorithms which have been discussed. The dark-shaded ovals contain the supervised ML algorithms, the light-shaded ovals contain the unsupervised ML algorithms, and the key questions to consider are shown in the unshaded rounded rectangles.

    First, start by asking, are the data complex, having many features that are highly correlated? If yes, then dimension reduction using principal components analysis is appropriate.

    Next, is the problem one of classification or numerical prediction? If numerical prediction, then depending on whether the data have non-linear characteristics, the choice of ML algorithms is from a set of regression algorithms—either penalized regression/LASSO for linear data or CART, random forest, or neural networks for non-linear data.

    If the problem is one of classification, then depending on whether the data are labeled, the choice is either from a set of classification algorithms using labeled data or from a set of clustering algorithms using unlabeled data.

EXHIBIT 37   Stylized Decision Flowchart for Choosing ML Algorithms

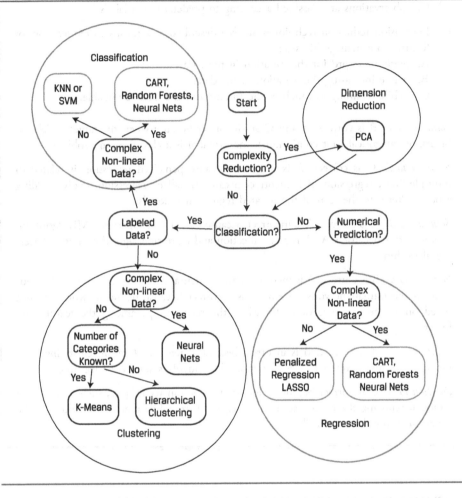

If the data are labeled, then depending on whether the data have non-linear character-istics, the choice of classification algorithm would be *K*-nearest neighbor and support vector machine for linear data or CART, random forest, or neural networks (or deep neural net-works) for non-linear data.

Finally, if the data are unlabeled, the choice of clustering algorithm depends on whether the data have non-linear characteristics. The choice of clustering algorithm would be neural networks (or deep neural networks) for non-linear data or for linear data, *K*-means with a known number of categories and hierarchical clustering with an unknown number of categories.

9. SUMMARY

Machine learning methods are gaining usage at many stages in the investment management value chain. Among the major points made are the following:

- Machine learning aims at extracting knowledge from large amounts of data by learning from known examples to determine an underlying structure in the data. The emphasis is on generating structure or predictions without human intervention. An elementary way to think of ML algorithms is to "find the pattern, apply the pattern."
- Supervised learning depends on having labeled training data as well as matched sets of observed inputs (X's, or features) and the associated output (Y, or target). Supervised learning can be divided into two categories: regression and classification. If the target variable to be predicted is continuous, then the task is one of regression. If the target variable is categorical or ordinal (e.g., determining a firm's rating), then it is a classification problem.
- With unsupervised learning, algorithms are trained with no labeled data, so they must infer relations between features, summarize them, or present underlying structure in their distributions that has not been explicitly provided. Two important types of problems well suited to unsupervised ML are dimension reduction and clustering.
- In deep learning, sophisticated algorithms address complex tasks (e.g., image classification, natural language processing). Deep learning is based on neural networks, highly flexible ML algorithms for solving a variety of supervised and unsupervised tasks characterized by large datasets, non-linearities, and interactions among features. In reinforcement learning, a computer learns from interacting with itself or data generated by the same algorithm.
- Generalization describes the degree to which an ML model retains its explanatory power when predicting out-of-sample. Overfitting, a primary reason for lack of generalization, is the tendency of ML algorithms to tailor models to the training data at the expense of generalization to new data points.
- Bias error is the degree to which a model fits the training data. Variance error describes how much a model's results change in response to new data from validation and test samples. Base error is due to randomness in the data. Out-of-sample error equals bias error plus variance error plus base error.
- K-fold cross-validation is a technique for mitigating the holdout sample problem (excessive reduction of the training set size). The data (excluding test sample and fresh data) are shuffled randomly and then divided into k equal sub-samples, with $k - 1$ samples used as training samples and one sample, the kth, used as a validation sample.
- Regularization describes methods that reduce statistical variability in high-dimensional data estimation or prediction problems via reducing model complexity.
- LASSO (least absolute shrinkage and selection operator) is a popular type of penalized regression where the penalty term involves summing the absolute values of the regression coefficients. The greater the number of included features, the larger the penalty. So, a feature must make a sufficient contribution to model fit to offset the penalty from including it.
- Support vector machine (SVM) is a classifier that aims to seek the optimal hyperplane— the one that separates the two sets of data points by the maximum margin (and thus is typically used for classification).
- K-nearest neighbor (KNN) is a supervised learning technique most often used for classification. The idea is to classify a new observation by finding similarities ("nearness") between it and its k-nearest neighbors in the existing dataset.

- Classification and regression tree (CART) can be applied to predict either a categorical target variable, producing a classification tree, or a continuous target variable, producing a regression tree.
- A binary CART is a combination of an initial root node, decision nodes, and terminal nodes. The root node and each decision node represent a single feature (f) and a cutoff value (c) for that feature. The CART algorithm iteratively partitions the data into subgroups until terminal nodes are formed that contain the predicted label.
- Ensemble learning is a technique of combining the predictions from a collection of models. It typically produces more accurate and more stable predictions than any single model.
- A random forest classifier is a collection of many different decision trees generated by a bagging method or by randomly reducing the number of features available during training.
- Principal components analysis (PCA) is an unsupervised ML algorithm that reduces highly correlated features into fewer uncorrelated composite variables by transforming the feature covariance matrix. PCA produces eigenvectors that define the principal components (i.e., the new uncorrelated composite variables) and eigenvalues, which give the proportion of total variance in the initial data that is explained by each eigenvector and its associated principal component.
- K-means is an unsupervised ML algorithm that partitions observations into a fixed number (k) of non-overlapping clusters. Each cluster is characterized by its centroid, and each observation belongs to the cluster with the centroid to which that observation is closest.
- Hierarchical clustering is an unsupervised iterative algorithm that is used to build a hierarchy of clusters. Two main strategies are used to define the intermediary clusters (i.e., those clusters between the initial dataset and the final set of clustered data).
- Agglomerative (bottom-up) hierarchical clustering begins with each observation being its own cluster. Then, the algorithm finds the two closest clusters, defined by some measure of distance, and combines them into a new, larger cluster. This process is repeated until all observations are clumped into a single cluster.
- Divisive (top-down) hierarchical clustering starts with all observations belonging to a single cluster. The observations are then divided into two clusters based on some measure of distance. The algorithm then progressively partitions the intermediate clusters into smaller clusters until each cluster contains only one observation.
- Neural networks consist of nodes connected by links. They have three types of layers: an input layer, hidden layers, and an output layer. Learning takes place in the hidden layer nodes, each of which consists of a summation operator and an activation function. Neural networks have been successfully applied to a variety of investment tasks characterized by non-linearities and complex interactions among variables.
- Neural networks with many hidden layers (at least 2 but often more than 20) are known as deep neural networks (DNNs) and are the backbone of the artificial intelligence revolution.
- Reinforcement learning (RL) involves an agent that should perform actions that will maximize its rewards over time, taking into consideration the constraints of its environment.

REFERENCES

Bacham, Dinesh and Janet Zhao. 2017. "Machine Learning: Challenges, Lessons, and Opportunities in Credit Risk Modeling." *Moody's Analytics Risk Perspectives* 9: 28–35.

Culkin, Robert and Sanjiv R. Das. 2017. "Machine Learning in Finance: The Case of Deep Learning for Option Pricing." *Journal of Investment Management* 15 (4): 92–100.

PRACTICE PROBLEMS

The following information relates to Questions 1–10

Alef Associates manages a long-only fund specializing in global small-cap equities. Since its founding a decade ago, Alef maintains a portfolio of 100 stocks (out of an eligible universe of about 10,000 stocks). Some of these holdings are the result of screening the universe for attractive stocks based on several ratios that use readily available market and accounting data; others are the result of investment ideas generated by Alef's professional staff of five securities analysts and two portfolio managers.

Although Alef's investment performance has been good, its chief investment officer, Paul Moresanu, is contemplating a change in the investment process aimed at achieving even better returns. After attending multiple workshops and being approached by data vendors, Moresanu feels that data science should play a role in the way Alef selects its investments. He has also noticed that much of Alef's past outperformance is due to stocks that became takeover targets. After some research and reflection, Moresanu writes the following email to the Alef's CEO.

Subject: Investment Process Reorganization

I have been thinking about modernizing the way we select stock investments. Given that our past success has put Alef Associates in an excellent financial position, now seems to be a good time to invest in our future. What I propose is that we continue managing a portfolio of 100 global small-cap stocks but restructure our process to benefit from machine learning (ML). Importantly, the new process will still allow a role for human insight, for example, in providing domain knowledge. In addition, I think we should make a special effort to identify companies that are likely to be acquired. Specifically, I suggest following the four steps which would be repeated every quarter.

Step 1. We apply ML techniques to a model including fundamental and technical variables (features) to predict next quarter's return for each of the 100 stocks currently in our portfolio. Then, the 20 stocks with the lowest estimated return are identified for replacement.

Step 2. We utilize ML techniques to divide our investable universe of about 10,000 stocks into 20 different groups, based on a wide variety of the most relevant financial and non-financial characteristics. The idea is to prevent unintended portfolio concentration by selecting stocks from each of these distinct groups.

Step 3.   For each of the 20 different groups, we use labeled data to train a model that will predict the five stocks (in any given group) that are most likely to become acquisition targets in the next one year.

Step 4.   Our five experienced securities analysts are each assigned four of the groups, and then each analyst selects their one best stock pick from each of their assigned groups. These 20 "high-conviction" stocks will be added to our portfolio (in replacement of the 20 relatively underperforming stocks to be sold in Step 1).

A couple of additional comments related to the above:

Comment 1.   The ML algorithms will require large amounts of data. We would first need to explore using free or inexpensive historical datasets and then evaluate their usefulness for the ML-based stock selection processes before deciding on using data that requires subscription.

Comment 2.   As time passes, we expect to find additional ways to apply ML techniques to refine Alef's investment processes.

What do you think?
Paul Moresanu

1.   The machine learning techniques appropriate for executing Step 1 are *most* likely to be based on:
     A.   regression
     B.   classification
     C.   clustering

2.   Assuming regularization is utilized in the machine learning technique used for executing Step 1, which of the following ML models would be *least* appropriate:
     A.   Regression tree with pruning.
     B.   LASSO with lambda (λ) equal to 0.
     C.   LASSO with lambda (λ) between 0.5 and 1.

3.   Which of the following machine learning techniques is *most* appropriate for executing Step 2:
     A.   K-Means Clustering
     B.   Principal Components Analysis (PCA)
     C.   Classification and Regression Trees (CART)

4.   The hyperparameter in the ML model to be used for accomplishing Step 2 is?
     A.   100, the number of small-cap stocks in Alef's portfolio.
     B.   10,000, the eligible universe of small-cap stocks in which Alef can potentially invest.
     C.   20, the number of different groups (i.e. clusters) into which the eligible universe of small-cap stocks will be divided.

5.   The target variable for the labelled training data to be used in Step 3 is *most* likely which one of the following?
     A.   A continuous target variable.
     B.   A categorical target variable.
     C.   An ordinal target variable.

6. Comparing two ML models that could be used to accomplish Step 3, which statement(s) *best* describe(s) the advantages of using Classification and Regression Trees (CART) instead of K-Nearest Neighbor (KNN)?

    Statement I.   For CART there is no requirement to specify an initial hyperparameter (like K).

    Statement II.   For CART there is no requirement to specify a similarity (or distance) measure.

    Statement III. For CART the output provides a visual explanation for the prediction.

    A. Statement I only.
    B. Statement III only.
    C. Statements I, II and III.

7. Assuming a Classification and Regression Tree (CART) model is used to accomplish Step 3, which of the following is *most* likely to result in model overfitting?
    A. Using the k–fold cross-validation method
    B. Including an overfitting penalty (i.e., regularization term).
    C. Using a fitting curve to select a model with low bias error and high variance error.

8. Assuming a Classification and Regression Tree (CART) model is initially used to accomplish Step 3, as a further step which of the following techniques is most likely to result in more accurate predictions?
    A. Discarding CART and using the predictions of a Support Vector Machine (SVM) model instead.
    B. Discarding CART and using the predictions of a K-Nearest Neighbor (KNN) model instead.
    C. Combining the predictions of the CART model with the predictions of other models – such as logistic regression, SVM, and KNN – via ensemble learning.

9. Regarding Comment #2, Moresanu has been thinking about the applications of neural networks (NNs) and deep learning (DL) to investment management. Which statement(s) *best* describe(s) the tasks for which NNs and DL are well-suited?

    Statement I.   NNs and DL are well-suited for image and speech recognition, and natural language processing.

    Statement II.   NNs and DL are well-suited for developing single variable ordinary least squares regression models.

    Statement III. NNs and DL are well-suited for modelling non-linearities and complex interactions among many features.

    A. Statement II only.
    B. Statements I and III.
    C. Statements I, II and III.

10. Regarding neural networks (NNs) that Alef might potentially implement, which of the following statements is *least* accurate?
    A. NNs must have at least 10 hidden layers to be considered deep learning nets.
    B. The activation function in a node operates like a light dimmer switch since it decreases or increases the strength of the total net input.
    C. The summation operator receives input values, multiplies each by a weight, sums up the weighted values into the total net input, and passes it to the activation function.

CHAPTER 11

BIG DATA PROJECTS

Sreekanth Mallikarjun, PhD
Ahmed Abbasi, PhD

LEARNING OUTCOMES

The candidate should be able to:

- state and explain steps in a data analysis project;
- describe objectives, steps, and examples of preparing and wrangling data;
- describe objectives, methods, and examples of data exploration;
- describe objectives, steps, and techniques in model training;
- describe preparing, wrangling, and exploring text-based data for financial forecasting;
- describe methods for extracting, selecting and engineering features from textual data;
- evaluate the fit of a machine learning algorithm.

1. INTRODUCTION

Big data (also referred to as alternative data) encompasses data generated by financial markets (e.g., stock and bond prices), businesses (e.g., company financials, production volumes), governments (e.g., economic and trade data), individuals (e.g., credit card purchases, social media posts), sensors (e.g., satellite imagery, traffic patterns), and the Internet of Things, or IoT, (i.e., the network of interrelated digital devices that can transfer data among themselves without human interaction). A veritable explosion in big data has occurred over the past decade or so, especially in unstructured data generated from social media (e.g., posts, tweets, blogs), email and text communications, web traffic, online news sites, electronic images, and other electronic information sources. The prospects are for exponential growth in big data to continue.

Investment managers are increasingly using big data in their investment processes as they strive to discover signals embedded in such data that can provide them with an information edge. They seek to augment structured data with a plethora of unstructured data

Quantitative Methods for Investment Analysis, Second Edition, by Sreekanth Mallikarjun, PhD, and Ahmed Abbasi, PhD. Copyright © 2019 by CFA Institute.

to develop improved forecasts of trends in asset prices, detect anomalies, etc. A typical example involves a fund manager using financial text data from 10-K reports for forecasting stock sentiment (i.e., positive or negative), which can then be used as an input to a more comprehensive forecasting model that includes corporate financial data.

Unlike structured data (numbers and values) that can be readily organized into data tables to be read and analyzed by computers, unstructured data typically require specific methods of preparation and refinement before being usable by machines (i.e., computers) and useful to investment professionals. Given the volume, variety, and velocity of available big data, it is important for portfolio managers and investment analysts to have a basic understanding of how unstructured data can be transformed into structured data suitable as inputs to machine learning (ML) methods (in fact, for any type of modeling methods) that can potentially improve their financial forecasts.

This chapter describes the steps in using big data, both structured and unstructured, in financial forecasting. The concepts and methods are then demonstrated in a case study of an actual big data project. The project uses text-based data derived from financial documents to train an ML model to classify text into positive or negative sentiment classes for the respective stocks and then to predict sentiment.

Section 2 of the chapter covers a description of the key characteristics of big data. Section 3 provides an overview of the steps in executing a financial forecasting project using big data. We then describe in Sections 4–6 key aspects of data preparation and wrangling, data exploration, and model training using structured data and unstructured (textual) data. In Section 7, we bring these pieces together by covering the execution of an actual big data project. A summary in Section 8 concludes the chapter.

2. BIG DATA IN INVESTMENT MANAGEMENT

Big data differs from traditional data sources based on the presence of a set of characteristics commonly referred to as the 3Vs: volume, variety, and velocity.

Volume refers to the quantity of data. The US Library of Congress, which is tasked with archiving both digital and physical information artifacts in the United States, has collected hundreds of terabytes of data (one terabyte equals 1,024 gigabytes, which are equal to 1,048,576 megabytes). Several years ago, one of the authors managed an archival project for the Library of Congress in which many terabytes of online content were collected—a copious amount of data at the time. However, in most US industry sectors today, the average company collects more data than the Library of Congress! In big data conversations, terabytes have been replaced with petabytes and exabytes (one exabyte equals 1,024 petabytes, which are equal to 1,048,576 terabytes). The classic grains of sand analogy puts these volumes into perspective: If a megabyte is a tablespoon of sand, then a petabyte is a 1.6-kilometer-long beach and an exabyte is a beach extending about 1,600 kilometers.

Variety pertains to the array of available data sources. Organizations are now dealing with structured, semi-structured, and unstructured data from within and outside the enterprise. Variety includes traditional transactional data; user-generated text, images, and videos; social media; sensor-based data; web and mobile clickstreams; and spatial-temporal data. Effectively leveraging the variety of available data presents both opportunities and challenges, including such legal and ethical issues as data privacy.

Velocity is the speed at which data are created. Many large organizations collect several petabytes of data every hour. With respect to unstructured data, more than one billion new tweets (i.e., a message of 280 characters or less posted on the social media website Twitter) are generated every three days; five billion search queries occur daily. Such information has important implications for real-time predictive analytics in various financial applications. Analyzing such data in motion poses challenges since relevant patterns and insights might be moving targets relative to situations of data at rest.

When using big data for inference or prediction, there is a "fourth V": *Veracity relates to the credibility and reliability of different data sources.* Determining the credibility and reliability of data sources is an important part of any empirical investigation. The issue of veracity becomes critically important for big data, however, because of the varied sources of these large datasets. Big data amplifies the age-old challenge of disentangling quality from quantity. Social media, including blogs, forums, and social networking sites, are plagued with spam; by some estimates, as much as 10 to 15 percent of such content is completely fake. Similarly, according to our research, web spam accounts for more than 20 percent of all content on the worldwide web. Clickstreams from website and mobile traffic are equally susceptible to noise. Furthermore, deriving deep semantic knowledge from text remains challenging in certain instances despite significant advances in natural language processing (NLP).

These Vs have numerous implications for financial technology (commonly referred to as fintech) pertaining to investment management. Machine learning assessments of creditworthiness, which have traditionally relied on structured financial metrics, are being enhanced by incorporating text derived from financial statements, news articles, and call transcripts. Customers in the financial industry are being segmented based not only on their transactional data but also on their views and preferences expressed on social media (to the degree permissible under applicable privacy agreements). Big data also affords opportunities for enhanced fraud detection and risk management.

3. STEPS IN EXECUTING A DATA ANALYSIS PROJECT: FINANCIAL FORECASTING WITH BIG DATA

In the era of big data, firms treat data like they do important assets. However, effective big data analytics are critical to allow appropriate data monetization. Let us take financial forecasting as an application area. Numerous forecasting tasks in this domain can benefit from predictive analytics models built using machine learning methods. One common example is predicting whether stock prices (for an individual stock or a portfolio) will go up or down in value at some specific point in the future. Traditionally, financial forecasting relied on various financial and accounting numbers, ratios, and metrics coupled with statistical or mathematical models. More recently, machine learning models have been commonly utilized. However, with the proliferation of textual big data (e.g., online news articles, internet financial forums, social networking platforms), such unstructured data have been shown to offer insights faster (as they are real-time) and have enhanced predictive power.

Textual big data provides several valuable types of information, including topics and sentiment. Topics are what people are talking about (e.g., a firm, an industry, a particular event). Sentiment is how people feel about what they are discussing. For instance, they might express positive, negative, or neutral views (i.e., sentiments) toward a topic of discussion. One study conducted in the United States found that positive sentiment on Twitter could predict the trend for the Dow Jones Industrial Average up to three days later with nearly 87 percent accuracy.

Deriving such insights requires supplementing traditional data with textual big data. As depicted in Exhibit 1, the inclusion of big data has immediate implications for building the machine learning model as well as downstream implications for financial forecasting and analysis. We begin with the top half of Exhibit 1, which shows the traditional (i.e., with structured data) *ML Model Building Steps:*

1. *Conceptualization of the modeling task.* This crucial first step entails determining what the output of the model should be (e.g., whether the price of a stock will go up/down one week from now), how this model will be used and by whom, and how it will be embedded in existing or new business processes.
2. *Data collection.* The data traditionally used for financial forecasting tasks are mostly numeric data derived from internal and external sources. Such data are typically already in a structured tabular format, with columns of features, rows of instances, and each cell representing a particular value.
3. *Data preparation and wrangling.* This step involves cleansing and preprocessing of the raw data. Cleansing may entail resolving missing values, out-of-range values, and the like. Preprocessing may involve extracting, aggregating, filtering, and selecting relevant data columns.
4. *Data exploration.* This step encompasses exploratory data analysis, feature selection, and feature engineering.
5. *Model training.* This step involves selecting the appropriate ML method (or methods), evaluating performance of the trained model, and tuning the model accordingly.

Note that these steps are iterative because model building is an iterative process. The insights gained from one iteration may inform the next iteration, beginning with reconceptualization. In contrast with structured data sources, textual big data originating in online news articles, social media, internal/external documents (such as public financial statements), and other openly available data sources are unstructured.

The *Text ML Model Building Steps* used for the unstructured data sources of big data are shown in the bottom half of Exhibit 1. They differ from those used for traditional data sources and are typically intended to create output information that is structured. The differences in steps between the text model and traditional model account for the characteristics of big data: volume, velocity, variety, and veracity. In this chapter, we mostly focus on the variety and veracity dimensions of big data as they manifest themselves in text. The major differences in the *Text ML Model Building Steps* are in the first four steps:

1. *Text problem formulation.* Analysts begin by determining how to formulate the text classification problem, identifying the exact inputs and outputs for the model. Perhaps we are interested in computing sentiment scores (structured output) from text (unstructured input). Analysts must also decide how the text ML model's classification output will be utilized.
2. *Data (text) curation.* This step involves gathering relevant external text data via web services or **web spidering (scraping or crawling) programs** that extract raw content from a source, typically web pages. Annotation of the text data with high-quality, reliable target (dependent) variable labels might also be necessary for supervised learning and performance evaluation purposes. For instance, experts might need to label whether a given expert assessment of a stock is bearish or bullish.

EXHIBIT 1   Model Building for Financial Forecasting Using Big Data: Structured (Traditional) vs. Unstructured (Text)

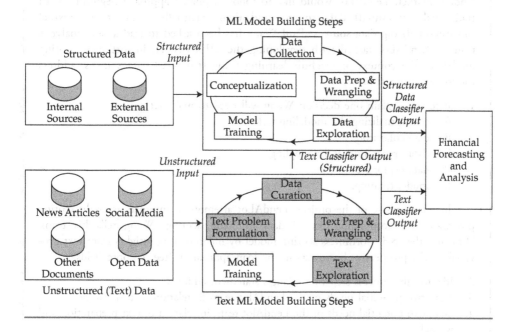

3. *Text preparation and wrangling.* This step involves critical cleansing and preprocessing tasks necessary to convert streams of unstructured data into a format that is usable by traditional modeling methods designed for structured inputs.
4. *Text exploration.* This step encompasses text visualization through techniques, such as word clouds, and text feature selection and engineering.

The resulting output (e.g., sentiment prediction scores) can either be combined with other structured variables or used directly for forecasting and/or analysis.

Next, we describe two key steps from the *ML Model Building Steps* depicted in Exhibit 1 that typically differ for structured data versus textual big data: data/text preparation and wrangling and data/text exploration. We then discuss model training. Finally, we focus on applying these steps to a case study related to classifying and predicting stock sentiment from financial texts.

EXAMPLE 1   Steps in ML Model Building

LendALot Corporation is a B2C (business-to-consumer) lender that has traditionally outsourced potential customers' creditworthiness scoring to a third-party firm. Given the recent advances in machine learning (ML)-based fintech that goes beyond traditional repayment history and ability-to-repay assessments derived from structured data, LendALot would like to develop in-house, ML-based credit scoring capabilities to enhance borrower risk assessment and differentiate itself in the B2C lending market. LendALot would like to follow a phased approach beginning with traditional (structured) data sources and then eventually incorporating textual (unstructured) big data sources. Paul Wang has been asked to lead a new analytics team at LendALot tasked with developing the ML-based creditworthiness scoring model. In the context of machine learning using structured data sources, address the following questions.

1. State and explain one decision Wang will need to make related to:
    A. conceptualizing the modeling task.
    B. data collection.
    C. data preparation and wrangling.
    D. data exploration.
    E. model training.

In a later phase of the project, LendALot attempts to improve its credit scoring processes by incorporating textual data in credit scoring. Wang tells his team, "Enhance the creditworthiness scoring model by incorporating insights from text provided by the prospective borrowers in the loan application free response fields."

2. Identify the process step that Wang's statement addresses.
3. State two potential needs of the LendAlot team in relation to text curation.
4. State two potential needs of the LendAlot team in relation to text preparation and wrangling.

Solution to 1:

A. In the conceptualization step, Wang will need to decide how the output of the ML model will be specified (e.g., a binary classification of creditworthiness), how the model will be used and by whom, and how it will be embedded in LendALot's business processes.
B. In the data collection phase, Wang must decide on what data—internal, external, or both—to use for credit scoring.
C. In the data preparation and wrangling step, Wang will need to decide on data cleansing and preprocessing needs. Cleansing may entail resolving missing values, extreme values, etc. Preprocessing may involve extracting, aggregating, filtering, and selecting relevant data columns.
D. In the data exploration phase, Wang will need to decide which exploratory data analysis methods are appropriate, which features to use in building a credit scoring model, and which features may need to be engineered.
E. In the model training step, Wang must decide which ML algorithm(s) to use. Assuming labeled training data are available, the choice will be among supervised learning algorithms. Decisions will need to be made on how model fit is measured and how the model is validated and tuned.

Solution to 2: Wang's statement relates to the initial step of text problem formulation.

Solution to 3: Related to text curation, the team will be using internal data (from loan applications). They will need to ensure that the text comment fields on the loan applications have been correctly implemented and enabled. If these fields are not required, they need to ensure there is a sufficient response rate to analyze.

Solution to 4: Related to text preparation and wrangling, the team will need to carry out the critical tasks of text cleansing and text preprocessing. These two tasks are necessary to convert an unstructured stream of data into structured values for use by traditional modeling methods.

4. DATA PREPARATION AND WRANGLING

Data preparation and wrangling involve cleansing and organizing raw data into a consolidated format. The resulting dataset is suitable to use for further analyses and training a machine learning (ML) model. This is a critical stage, the foundation, in big data projects. Most of the project time is spent on this step, and the quality of the data affects the training of the selected ML model. Domain knowledge—that is, the involvement of specialists in the particular field in which the data are obtained and used—is beneficial and often necessary to successfully execute this step. Data preparation is preceded by data collection, so we discuss the data collection process first.

Before the data collection process even begins, it is important to state the problem, define objectives, identify useful data points, and conceptualize the model. Conceptualization is like a blueprint on a drawing board, a modifiable plan that is necessary to initiate the model building process. A project overview is established by determining the ML model type— supervised or unsupervised—and data sources/collection plans with respect to the needs of the project.

Data collection involves searching for and downloading the raw data from one or multiple sources. Data can be stored in different formats, sources, and locations. As databases are the most common primary sources, building necessary queries with the help of database administrators is critical. Database schemas are built with certain assumptions and exceptions, and it is safest to clarify the database architecture with an administrator or database architect before downloading the necessary data. Data also exist in the form of spreadsheets, comma-separated values (csv) files, text files, and other formats. Care must be taken before using such data, and documentation (often referred to as "Readme" files) must be referred to, if available. **Readme files** are text files provided with the raw data that contain information related to a data file. They are useful for understanding the data and how they can be interpreted correctly.

Alternatively, third-party data vendors can be sources of clean data. External data usually can be accessed through an **application programming interface (API)**—a set of well-defined methods of communication between various software components—or the vendors can deliver the required data in the form of csv files or other formats (as previously mentioned). Using external data can save time and resources that would otherwise go into data preparation and wrangling; however, vendor contracts come with a price. Depending on the big data project constraints, a decision must be made regarding the use of internal or external data based on the trade-offs between time, financial costs, and accuracy. For projects using internal user data, external data might not be suitable. For example, to understand user traffic on a company website, internally recorded site visits and click frequency may

EXHIBIT 2 Data Preparation and Wrangling Stage

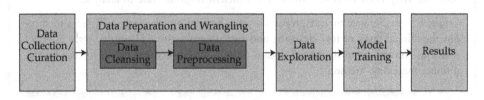

be captured and stored in the internal databases. External data are advantageous when a project requires generic data, such as demographics of a geographic area or traffic data of a public service. Another consideration in using external vendor provided data is that during the cleansing process, underlying trends in the data that are important for particular end-uses may be masked or even lost. This is where alpha is often found; so by simply buying a data-set from a vendor, you may lose your information edge. Of course, application of the data (e.g., merging and combining, putting through different types of models) will be different for everyone who uses it; there are always different ways to extract value.

Once the data are collected, the data preparation and wrangling stage begins. This stage involves two important tasks: cleansing and preprocessing, respectively. Exhibit 2 outlines data preparation and wrangling and defines the two component tasks. These tasks are explained in detail under the structured and unstructured sub-sections because the steps vary by the nature of data.

Data Preparation (Cleansing): This is the initial and most common task in data preparation that is performed on raw data. Data cleansing is the process of examining, identifying, and mitigating errors in raw data. Normally, the raw data are neither sufficiently complete nor sufficiently clean to directly train the ML model. Manually entered data can have incomplete, duplicated, erroneous, or inaccurate values. Automated data (recorded by systems) can have similar problems due to server failures and software bugs.

Data Wrangling (Preprocessing): This task performs transformations and critical processing steps on the cleansed data to make the data ready for ML model training. Raw data most commonly are not present in the appropriate format for model consumption. After the cleansing step, data need to be processed by dealing with outliers, extracting useful variables from existing data points, and scaling the data.

4.1. Structured Data

4.1.1. Data Preparation (Cleansing)
Structured data are organized in a systematic format that is readily searchable and readable by computer operations for processing and analyzing. In structured data, data errors can be in the form of incomplete, invalid, inaccurate, inconsistent, non-uniform, and duplicate data observations. The data cleansing process mainly deals with identifying and mitigating all such errors. Exhibit 3 shows a raw dataset before cleansing. The data have been collected from different sources and are organized in a data matrix (or data table) format. Each row contains observations of each customer of a US-based bank. Each column represents a variable (or feature) corresponding to each customer.

EXHIBIT 3   Raw Data Before Cleansing

ID	Name	Gender	Date of Birth	Salary	Other Income	State	Credit Card
1	Mr. ABC	M	12/5/1970	$50,200	$5,000	VA	Y
2	Ms. XYZ	M	15 Jan, 1975	$60,500	$0	NY	Yes
3	EFG		1/13/1979	$65,000	$1,000	CA	No
4	Ms. MNO	F	1/1/1900	—	—	FL	Don't Know
5	Ms. XYZ	F	15/1/1975	$60,500	$0		Y
6	Mr. GHI	M	9/10/1942	NA	$55,000	TX	N
7	Mr. TUV	M	2/27/1956	$300,000	$50,000	CT	Y
8	Ms. DEF	F	4/4/1980	$55,000	$0	British Columbia	N

The possible errors in a raw dataset include the following:

1. *Incompleteness error* is where the data are not present, resulting in missing data. This can be corrected by investigating alternate data sources. Missing values and NAs (not applicable or not available values) must be either omitted or replaced with "NA" for deletion or substitution with imputed values during the data exploration stage. The most common imputations are mean, median, or mode of the variable or simply assuming zero. In Exhibit 3, rows 4 (ID 3), 5 (ID 4), 6 (ID 5), and 7 (ID 6) are incomplete due to missing values in either Gender, Salary, Other Income, Name (Salutation), and State columns.

2. *Invalidity error* is where the data are outside of a meaningful range, resulting in invalid data. This can be corrected by verifying other administrative data records. In Exhibit 3, row 5 likely contains invalid data as the date of birth is out of the range of the expected human life span.

3. *Inaccuracy error* is where the data are not a measure of true value. This can be rectified with the help of business records and administrators. In Exhibit 3, row 5 is inaccurate (it shows "Don't Know"); in reality, every person either has a credit card or does not.

4. *Inconsistency error* is where the data conflict with the corresponding data points or reality. This contradiction should be eliminated by clarifying with another source. In Exhibit 3, row 3 (ID 2) is likely to be inconsistent as the Name column contains a female title and the Gender column contains male.

5. *Non-uniformity error* is where the data are not present in an identical format. This can be resolved by converting the data points into a preferable standard format. In Exhibit 3, the data under the Date of Birth column is present in various formats. The data under the Salary column may also be non-uniform as the monetary units are ambiguous; the dollar symbol can represent US dollar, Canadian dollar, or others.

6. *Duplication error* is where duplicate observations are present. This can be corrected by removing the duplicate entries. In Exhibit 3, row 6 is a duplicate as the data under Name and Date of Birth columns are identical to the ones in row 3, referring to the same customer.

Exhibit 4 shows the dataset after completion of the cleansing process.

Data cleansing can be expensive and cumbersome because it involves the use of automated, rule-based, and pattern recognition tools coupled with manual human inspection to

EXHIBIT 4   Data After Cleansing

ID	Name	Gender	Date of Birth	Salary	Other Income	State	Credit Card
1	Mr. ABC	M	12/5/1970	USD 50200	USD 5000	VA	Y
2	Ms. XYZ	F	1/15/1975	USD 60500	USD 0	NY	Y
3	Mr. EFG	M	1/13/1979	USD 65000	USD 1000	CA	N
6	Mr. GHI	M	9/10/1942	USD 0	USD 55000	TX	N
7	Mr. TUV	M	2/27/1956	USD 300000	USD 50000	CT	Y
8	Ms. DEF	F	4/4/1980	CAD 55000	CAD 0	British Columbia	N

sequentially check for the aforementioned types of errors row by row and column by column. The process involves a detailed data analysis as an initial step in identifying various errors that are present in the data. In addition to a manual inspection and verification of the data, analysis software, such as SPSS, can be used to understand **metadata** (data that describes and gives information about other data) about the data properties to use as a starting point to investigate any errors in the data. The business value of the project determines the necessary quality of data cleansing and subsequently the amount of resources used in the cleansing process. In case the errors cannot be resolved due to lack of available resources, the data points with errors can simply be omitted depending on the size of the dataset. For instance, if a dataset is large with more than 10,000 rows, removing a few rows (approximately 100) may not have a significant impact on the project. If a dataset is small with less than 1,000 rows, every row might be important and deleting many rows thus harmful to the project.

4.1.2. Data Wrangling (Preprocessing)

To make structured data ready for analyses, the data should be preprocessed. Data preprocessing primarily includes transformations and scaling of the data. These processes are exercised on the cleansed dataset. The following transformations are common in practice:

1. *Extraction:* A new variable can be extracted from the current variable for ease of analyzing and using for training the ML model. In Exhibit 4, the Date of Birth column consists of dates that are not directly suitable for analyses. Thus, an additional variable called "Age" can be extracted by calculating the number of years between the present day and date of birth.
2. *Aggregation:* Two or more variables can be aggregated into one variable to consolidate similar variables. In Exhibit 4, the two forms of income, Salary and Other Income, can be summed into a single variable called Total Income.
3. *Filtration:* The data rows that are not needed for the project must be identified and filtered. In Exhibit 4, row 7 (ID 8) has a non-US state; however, this dataset is for the US-based bank customers where it is required to have a US address.
4. *Selection:* The data columns that are intuitively not needed for the project can be removed. This should not be confused with feature selection, which is explained later. In Exhibit 4, Name and Date of Birth columns are not required for training the ML model. The ID column is sufficient to identify the observations, and the new extracted variable Age replaces the Date of Birth column.

5. *Conversion:* The variables can be of different types: nominal, ordinal, continuous, and categorical. The variables in the dataset must be converted into appropriate types to further process and analyze them correctly. This is critical for ML model training. Before converting, values must be stripped out with prefixes and suffixes, such as currency symbols. In Exhibit 4, Name is nominal, Salary and Income are continuous, Gender and Credit Card are categorical with 2 classes, and State is nominal. In case row 7 is not excluded, the Salary in row 7 must be converted into US dollars. Also, the conversion task applies to adjusting time value of money, time zones, and others when present.

Outliers may be present in the data, and domain knowledge is needed to deal with them. Any outliers that are present must first be identified. The outliers then should be examined and a decision made to either remove or replace them with values imputed using statistical techniques. In Exhibit 4, row 6 (ID 7) is an outlier because the Salary value is far above the upper quartile. Row 5 (ID 6) is also an outlier because the Salary value is far below the lower quartile. However, after the aggregation and formation of a new variable Total Income, as shown in Exhibit 5, row 5 (ID 6), it is no longer an outlier.

In practice, several techniques can be used to detect outliers in the data. Standard deviation can be used to identify outliers in normally distributed data. In general, a data value that is outside of 3 standard deviations from the mean may be considered an outlier. The interquartile range (IQR) can be used to identify outliers in data with any form of distribution. IQR is the difference between the 75th and the 25th percentile values of the data. In general, data values outside of the following are considered as outliers: $+1.5$ x IQR $+ 3^{rd}$ Quartile Upper Bound; and -1.5 x IQR $+ 2^{nd}$ Quartile Lower Bound. Using a multiple of 3.0 (instead of 1.5) times IQR would indicate extreme values.

There are several practical methods for handling outliers. When extreme values and outliers are simply removed from the dataset, it is known as **trimming** (also called truncation). For example, a 5 percent trimmed dataset is one for which the 5 percent highest and the 5 percent lowest values have been removed. When extreme values and outliers are replaced with the maximum (for large value outliers) and minimum (for small value outliers) values of data points that are not outliers, the process is known as **winsorization**.

Scaling is a process of adjusting the range of a feature by shifting and changing the scale of data. Variables, such as age and income, can have a diversity of ranges that result in a heterogeneous training dataset. For better ML model training when using such methods as support vector machines (SVMs) and artificial neural networks (ANNs), all variables should have values in the same range to make the dataset homogeneous. It is important to remove outliers before scaling is performed. Here are two of the most common ways of scaling:

EXHIBIT 5   Data After Applying Transformations

1	ID	Gender	Age	Total Income	State	Credit Card
2	1	M	48	55200	VA	Y
3	2	F	43	60500	NY	Y
4	3	M	39	66000	CA	N
5	6	M	76	55000	TX	N

1. *Normalization* is the process of rescaling numeric variables in the range of [0, 1]. To normalize variable X, the minimum value (X_{min}) is subtracted from each observation (X_i), and then this value is divided by the difference between the maximum and minimum values of X ($X_{max} - X_{min}$) as follows:

$$X_{i \,(normalized)} = \frac{X_i - X_{min}}{X_{max} - X_{min}} \tag{1}$$

2. *Standardization* is the process of both centering and scaling the variables. Centering involves subtracting the mean (μ) of the variable from each observation (X_i) so the new mean is 0. Scaling adjusts the range of the data by dividing the centered values ($X_i - \mu$) by the standard deviation (σ) of feature X. The resultant standardized variable will have an arithmetic mean of 0 and standard deviation of 1.

$$X_{i \,(standardized)} = \frac{X_i - \mu}{\sigma} \tag{2}$$

Normalization is sensitive to outliers, so treatment of outliers is necessary before normalization is performed. Normalization can be used when the distribution of the data is not known. Standardization is relatively less sensitive to outliers as it depends on the mean and standard deviation of the data. However, the data must be normally distributed to use standardization.

EXAMPLE 2   Preparing and Wrangling Structured Data

Paul Wang's analytics team at LendALot Corporation is working to develop its first ML model for classifying prospective borrowers' creditworthiness. Wang has asked one of his data scientists, Lynn Lee, to perform a preliminary assessment of the data cleansing and preprocessing tasks the team will need to perform. As part of this assessment, Lee pulled the following sample of data for manual examination, which she brings to Wang to discuss.

ID	Name	Loan Outcome	Income (USD)	Loan Amount (USD)	Credit Score	Loan Type
1	Mr. Alpha	No Default	34,000	10,000	685	Mortgage
2	Ms. Beta	No Default	-63,050	49,000	770	Student Loan
3	Mr. Gamma	Defaulted	20,565	35,000	730	
4	Ms. Delta	No Default	50,021	unknown	664	Mortgage
5	Mr. Epsilon	Defaulted	100,350	129,000	705	Car Loan
6	Mr. Zeta	No Default	800,000	300,000	800	Boat Loan
6	Mr. Zeta	No Default	800,000	300,000	800	Boat Loan

After sharing a concern that the data should be thoroughly cleansed, Wang makes the following statements:

Statement 1: "Let's keep the ID column and remove the column for Name from the dataset."

Statement 2: "Let's create a new feature, 'Loan Amount as a Percent of Income,' to use as an additional feature."

1. The data shown for Ms. Beta contain what is *best described* as an:
   A. invalidity error.
   B. inaccuracy error.
   C. incompleteness error.

2. The data shown for Mr. Gamma contain what is *best described* as an:
   A. invalidity error.
   B. duplication error.
   C. incompleteness error.

3. The data shown for Ms. Delta contain what is *best described* as an:
   A. invalidity error.
   B. inaccuracy error.
   C. duplication error.

4. The data shown for Mr. Zeta contain what is *best described* as an:
   A. invalidity error.
   B. inaccuracy error.
   C. duplication error.

5. The process mentioned in Wang's first statement is *best described* as:
   A. feature selection.
   B. feature extraction.
   C. feature engineering

6. Wang's second statement is *best described* as:
   A. feature selection.
   B. feature extraction.
   C. feature engineering.

Solution to 1: A is correct. This is an invalidity error because the data are outside of a meaningful range. Income cannot be negative.

Solution to 2: C is correct. This is an incompleteness error as the loan type is missing.

Solution to 3: B is correct. This is an inaccuracy error because LendALot must know how much they have lent to that particular borrower (who eventually repaid the loan as indicated by the loan outcome of no default).

Solution to 4: C is correct. Row 8 duplicates row 7: This is a duplication error.

Solution to 5: A is correct. The process mentioned involves selecting the features to use. The proposal makes sense; with "ID," "Name" is not needed to identify an observation.

Solution to 6: B is correct. The proposed feature is a ratio of two existing features. *Feature extraction* is the process of creating (i.e., extracting) new variables from existing ones in the data.

4.2. Unstructured (Text) Data

Unstructured data are not organized into any systematic format that can be processed by computers directly. They are available in formats meant for human usage rather than computer processing. Unstructured data constitute approximately 80 percent of the total data available today. They can be in the form of text, images, videos, and audio files. Unlike in structured data, preparing and wrangling unstructured data are both more challenging. For analysis and use to train the ML model, the unstructured data must be transformed into structured data. In this section, text data will be used to demonstrate unstructured data preparation and wrangling. The cleansing and preprocessing of text data is called *text processing*. Text processing is essentially cleansing and transforming the unstructured text data into a structured format. Text processing can be divided into two tasks: cleansing and preprocessing. The following content is related to text data in the English language.

4.2.1. Text Preparation (Cleansing)

Raw text data are a sequence of characters and contain other non-useful elements, including html tags, punctuation, and white spaces (including tabs, line breaks, and new lines). It is important to clean the text data before preprocessing. Exhibit 6 shows a sample text from the home page for the hypothetical company Robots Are Us website. The text appears to be clean visually and is designed for human readability.

However, the source text that can be downloaded is not as clean. The raw text contains html tags and formatting elements along with the actual text. Exhibit 7 shows the raw text from the source.

The initial step in text processing is cleansing, which involves basic operations to clean the text by removing unnecessary elements from the raw text. Text operations often use regular expressions. A **regular expression (regex)** is a series that contains characters in a particular order. Regex is used to search for patterns of interest in a given text. For example, a regex "<.*?>" can be used to find all the html tags that are present in the form of <...> in

EXHIBIT 6   Sample Text from Robots Are Us Home Page

EXHIBIT 7   Raw Text from the Source

```
<h1 class="text-left mb-3">Robots Are Us</h1>
<h2> Every home and business shoudl have a robot    </h2>
```

text.[1] GREP (global regular expression print) is a commonly available utility in programming languages for searching patterns using regex. Once a pattern is found, it can be removed or replaced. Additionally, advanced html parsers and packages are available in the popular programming languages, such as R and Python, to deal with this task.

The following steps describe the basic operations in the text cleansing process.

1. *Remove html tags*: Most of the text data are acquired from web pages, and the text inherits html markup tags with the actual content. The initial task is to remove (or strip) the html tags that are not part of the actual text using programming functions or using regular expressions. In Exhibit 7, </h2> is an html tag that can be identified by a regex and be removed. Note that it is not uncommon to keep some generic html tags to maintain certain formatting meaning in the text.

2. *Remove Punctuation*: Most punctuation are not necessary for text analysis and should be removed. However, some punctuation, such as percentage signs, currency symbols, and question marks, may be useful for ML model training. This punctuation should be substituted with such annotations as /percentSign/, /dollarSign/, and /questionMark/ to preserve its grammatical meaning in the text. Such annotations preserve the semantic meaning of important characters in the text for further text processing and analysis stages. It is important to note that periods (dots) in the text need to be processed carefully. There are different circumstances for periods to be present in text— characteristically used for abbreviations, sentence boundaries, and decimal points. The periods and the context in which they are used need to be identified and must be appropriately replaced or removed. In general, periods after abbreviations can be removed, but the periods separating sentences should be replaced by the annotation /endSentence/. Some punctuation, such as hyphens and underscores, can be kept in the text to keep the consecutive words intact as a single term (e.g., e-mail). Regex are often used to remove or replace punctuation.

3. *Remove Numbers*: When numbers (or digits) are present in the text, they should be removed or substituted with an annotation /number/. This helps inform the computer that a number is present, but the actual value of the number itself is not helpful for categorizing/analyzing the text. Such operations are critical for ML model training. Otherwise, the computers will treat each number as a separate word, which may complicate the analyses or add noise. Regex are often used to remove or replace numbers. However, the number and any decimals must be retained where the outputs of interest are the actual values of the number. One such text application is information extraction (IE), where the goal is to extract relevant information from a given text. An IE task could be extracting monetary values from financial reports, where the actual number values are critical.

4. *Remove white spaces*: It is possible to have extra white spaces, tab spaces, and leading and ending spaces in the text. The extra white spaces may be introduced after executing the previously mentioned operations. These should be identified and removed to keep the text intact and clean. Certain functions in programming languages can be used to remove unnecessary white spaces from the text. For example, the text mining package in R offers a *stripwhitespace* function.

---

[1] A regex of the form "<.*?>" will identify all html tags with anything (*) of any length (?) between the brackets (< >).

EXHIBIT 8   Text Cleansing Process Example

Original text from a financial statement as shown on a webpage

CapEx on the normal operations remained stable on historicallylow levels, $800,000 compared to $1.2 million last year. Quarter 3, so far, is 5% sales growth quarter-to-date, and year-to-date, we have a 4% local currency sales development.

Raw text after scraping from the source

<font size = "4"> CapEx on the normal operations remained stable on historically low levels, $800,000 compared to $1.2 million last year. <b/><b/> Quarter 3, so far, is 5% sales growth quarter-to-date, and year-to-date, we have a 4% local currency sales development.</font>

Text after removing html tags

CapEx on the normal operations remained stable on historically low levels, $800,000 compared to $1.2 million last year. Quarter 3, so far, is 5% sales growth quarter-to-date, and year-to-date, we have a 4% local currency sales development.

Text after removing and replacing punctuation

CapEx on the normal operations remained stable on historically low levels /dollarSign/800000 compared to /dollarSign/12 million last year /endSentence/ Quarter 3 so far is 5 /percentSign/ sales growth quarter-to-date and year-to-date we have a 4 /percentSign/ local currency sales development /endSentence/

Text after replacing numbers

CapEx on the normal operations remained stable on historically low levels /dollarSign//number / compared to/dollarSign//number/ million last year /endSentence/ Quarter/number/ so far is /number/ /percentSign/sales growth quarter-to-date and year-to-date we have a /number/ / percentSign/ local currency sales development /endSentence/

Text after removing extra white spaces

CapEx on the normal operations remained stable on historically low levels/dollarSign//number /compared to/dollarSign//number/million last year/endSentence/ Quarter/number/so far is /number//percentSign/sales growth quarter-to-date and year-to-date we have a/number// percentSign/local currency sales development/endSentence/

Exhibit 8 uses a sample financial text to show the transformations occurring after applying each operation of the text cleansing process. The four steps are applied on a mock financial text after scraping from a source. As noted previously, scraping (or web scraping) is a technique to extract raw content from a source, typically web pages. It is important to note that the sequence and choice of cleansing operations does matter. For instance, after removing punctuation, the "1.2 million" becomes "12 million." This is acceptable here since a subsequent operation replaces all numbers with a "/number/" tag. However, if numbers were not replaced with such tags, the punctuation removal operation could affect the data.

4.2.2. Text Wrangling (Preprocessing)

To further understand text processing, tokens and tokenization need to be defined. A **token** is equivalent to a word, and **tokenization** is the process of splitting a given text into separate tokens. In other words, a text is considered to be a collection of tokens. Tokenization can be

EXHIBIT 9   Tokenization of Four Texts

	Cleaned Texts	**Tokens**
Text 1	The man went to the market today	The man went to the market today
Text 2	Market values are increasing	Market values are increasing
Text 3	Increased marketing is needed	Increased marketing is needed
Text 4	There is no market for the product	There is no market for the product

performed at word or character level, but it is most commonly performed at word level. Exhibit 9 shows a sample dataset of four cleansed texts and their word tokens.

Similar to structured data, text data also require normalization. The normalization process in text processing involves the following:

1. *Lowercasing* the alphabet removes distinctions among the same words due to upper and lower cases. This action helps the computers to process the same words appropriately (e.g., "The" and "the").

2. *Stop words* are such commonly used words as "the," "is," and "a." Stop words do not carry a semantic meaning for the purpose of text analyses and ML training. However, depending on the end-use of text processing, for advance text applications it may be critical to keep the stop words in the text in order to understand the context of adjacent words. For ML training purposes, stop words typically are removed to reduce the number of tokens involved in the training set. A predefined list of stop words is available in programming languages to help with this task. In some cases, additional stop words can be added to the list based on the content. For example, the word "exhibit" may occur often in financial filings, which in general is not a stop word but in the context of the filings can be treated as a stop word.

3. *Stemming* is the process of converting inflected forms of a word into its base word (known as stem). Stemming is a rule-based approach, and the results need not necessarily be linguistically sensible. Stems may not be the same as the morphological root of the word. Porter's algorithm is the most popular method for stemming. For example, the stem of the words "analyzed" and "analyzing" is "analyz." Similarly, the British English variant "analysing" would become "analys." Stemming is available in R and Python. The text mining package in R provides a *stemDocument* function that uses this algorithm.

4. *Lemmatization* is the process of converting inflected forms of a word into its morphological root (known as lemma). Lemmatization is an algorithmic approach and depends on the knowledge of the word and language structure. For example, the lemma of the words "analyzed" and "analyzing" is "analyze." Lemmatization is computationally more expensive and advanced.

Stemming or lemmatization will reduce the repetition of words occurring in various forms and maintain the semantic structure of the text data. Stemming is more common than lemmatization in the English language since it is simpler to perform. In text data, data sparseness refers to words that appear very infrequently, resulting in data consisting of many

EXHIBIT 10   Bag-of-Words Representation of Four Texts Before and After Normalization Process

BOW before normalizing

"The"	"man"	"went"	"to"	"the"	"market"
"today"	"Market"	"values"	"are"	"increasing"	"Increased"
"marketing"	"is"	"needed"	"There"	"no"	"for"
"product"					

BOW after removing uppercase letters

"the"	"man"	"went"	"to"	"market"	"today"
"values"	"are"	"increasing"	"increased"	"marketing"	"is"
"needed"	"there"	"no"	"for"	"product"	

BOW after removing stop words

"man"	"went"	"market"	"today"	"values"	"increasing"
"increased"	"marketing"	"needed"	"product"		

BOW after stemming

"man"	"went"	"market"	"today"	"valu"	"increas"	"need"	"product"

unique, low frequency tokens. Both techniques decrease data sparseness by aggregating many sparsely occurring words in relatively less sparse stems or lemmas, thereby aiding in training less complex ML models.

After the cleansed text is normalized, a bag of words is created. **Bag-of-words (BOW)** representation is a basic procedure used to analyze text. It is essentially a collection of a distinct set of tokens from all the texts in a sample dataset. BOW is simply a set of words and does not capture the position or sequence of words present in the text. However, it is memory efficient and easy to handle for text analyses.

Exhibit 10 shows the BOW and transformations occurring in each step of normalization on the cleansed texts from Exhibit 9. Note that the number of words decreases as the normalizing steps are applied, making the resulting BOW smaller and simpler.

The last step of text preprocessing is using the final BOW after normalizing to build a **document term matrix (DTM)**. DTM is a matrix that is similar to a data table for structured data and is widely used for text data. Each row of the matrix belongs to a document (or text file), and each column represents a token (or term). The number of rows of DTM is equal to the number of documents (or text files) in a sample dataset. The number of columns is equal to the number of tokens from the BOW that is built using all the documents in a sample dataset. The cells can contain the counts of the number of times a token is present in each document. The matrix cells can be filled with other values that will be explained in the financial forecasting project section of this chapter; a large dataset is helpful in understanding the concepts. At this point, the unstructured text data are converted to structured data that can be processed further and used to train the ML model. Exhibit 11 shows a DTM constructed from the resultant BOW of the four texts from Exhibit 10.

As seen in Exhibit 10, BOW does not represent the word sequences or positions, which limits its use for some advanced ML training applications. In the example, the word *no* is treated as a single token and has been removed during the normalization because it is a stop word. Consequently, this fails to signify the negative meaning ("no market") of the text

EXHIBIT 11   DTM of Four Texts and Using Normalized BOW Filled with Counts of Occurrence

	man	went	market	today	valu	increas	need	product
Text 1	1	1	1	1	0	0	0	0
Text 2	0	0	1	0	1	1	0	0
Text 3	0	0	1	0	0	1	1	0
Text 4	0	0	1	0	0	0	0	1

EXHIBIT 12   N-Grams and N-Grams BOW

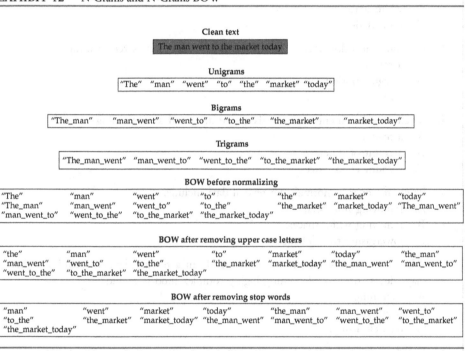

(i.e., Text 4). To overcome such problems, a technique called n-grams can be employed. **N-grams** is a representation of word sequences. The length of a sequence can vary from 1 to *n*. When one word is used, it is a unigram; a two-word sequence is a bigram; and a 3-word sequence is a trigram; and so on. Exhibit 10, for example, shows a unigram (*n* = 1) BOW. The advantage of n-grams is that they can be used in the same way as unigrams to build a BOW. In practice, different n-grams can be combined to form a BOW and eventually be used to build a DTM. Exhibit 12 shows unigrams, bigrams, and trigrams. Exhibit 12 also shows a combined unigram-to-trigram BOW for the particular text. Stemming can be applied on the cleansed text before building n-grams and BOW (not shown in Exhibit 12).

The n-grams implementation will vary the impact of normalization on the BOW. Even after removing isolated stop words, stop words tend to persist when they are attached to their adjacent words. For instance, "to_the" (Exhibit 12) is a single bigram token consisting of stop words and will not be removed by the predetermined list of stop words.

EXAMPLE 3   Unstructured Data Preparation and Wrangling

1. The output produced by preparing and wrangling textual data is best described as a:
   A. data table.
   B. confusion matrix.
   C. document term matrix.

2. In text cleansing, situations in which one may need to add an annotation include the removal of:
   A. html tags.
   B. white spaces.
   C. punctuation.

3. A column of a document term matrix is *best* described as representing:
   A. a token.
   B. a regularization term.
   C. an instance.

4. A cell of a document term matrix is *best* described as containing:
   A. a token.
   B. a count of tokens.
   C. a count of instances.

5. Points to cover in normalizing textual data include:
   A. removing numbers.
   B. removing white spaces.
   C. lowercasing the alphabet.

6. When some words appear very infrequently in a textual dataset, techniques that may address the risk of training highly complex models include:
   A. stemming.
   B. scaling.
   C. data cleansing.

7. Which of the following statements concerning tokenization is *most* accurate?
   A. Tokenization is part of the text cleansing process.
   B. Tokenization is most commonly performed at the character level.
   C. Tokenization is the process of splitting a given text into separate tokens.

Solution to 1: C is correct. The objective of data preparation and wrangling of textual data is to transform the unstructured data into structured data. The output of these processes is a document term matrix that can be read by computers. The document term matrix is similar to a data table for structured data.

Solution to 2: C is correct. Some punctuation, such as percentage signs, currency symbols, and question marks, may be useful for ML model training, so when such punctuation is removed, annotations should be added.

Solution to 3: A is correct. Each column of a document term matrix represents a token from the bag of words that is built using all the documents in a sample dataset.

Solution to 4: B is correct. A cell in a document term matrix contains a count of the number of tokens of the kind indicated in the column heading.

Solution to 5: C is correct. The other choices are related to text cleansing.

Solution to 6: A is correct. Stemming, the process of converting inflected word forms into a base word (or stem), is one technique that can address the problem described.

Solution to 7: C is correct, by definition. The other choices are not true.

5. DATA EXPLORATION OBJECTIVES AND METHODS

Data exploration is a crucial part of big data projects. The prepared data are explored to investigate and comprehend data distributions and relationships. The knowledge that is gained about the data in this stage is used throughout the project. The outcome and quality of exploration strongly affects ML model training results. Domain knowledge plays a vital role in exploratory analysis as this stage should involve cooperation between analysts, model designers, and experts in the particular data domain. Data exploration without domain knowledge can result in ascertaining spurious relationships among the variables in the data that can mislead the analyses. The data exploration stage follows the data preparation stage and leads to the model training stage.

Data exploration involves three important tasks: exploratory data analysis, feature selection, and feature engineering. These three tasks are outlined in Exhibit 13 and are defined and further explained under the structured and unstructured data subsections.

Exploratory data analysis (EDA) is the preliminary step in data exploration. Exploratory graphs, charts, and other visualizations, such as heat maps and word clouds, are designed to summarize and observe data. In practice, many exploratory graphs are made for investigation and can be made swiftly using statistical programming and generic spreadsheet software tools. Data can also be summarized and examined using quantitative methods, such as descriptive statistics and central tendency measures. An important objective of EDA is to serve as a communication medium among project stakeholders, including business users, domain experts, and analysts. Relatively quick and easy exploratory visualizations help stakeholders connect and ensure the prepared data are sensible. Other objectives of EDA include:

- understanding data properties,
- finding patterns and relationships in data,
- inspecting basic questions and hypotheses,

EXHIBIT 13   Data Exploration Stage

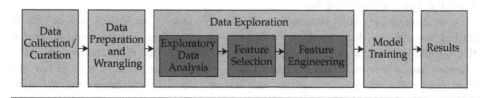

- documenting data distributions and other characteristics, and
- planning modeling strategies for the next steps.

Feature selection is a process whereby only pertinent features from the dataset are selected for ML model training. Selecting fewer features decreases ML model complexity and training time. **Feature engineering** is a process of creating new features by changing or transforming existing features. Model performance heavily depends on feature selection and engineering.

5.1. Structured Data

5.1.1. Exploratory Data Analysis

For structured data, each data table row contains an observation and each column contains a feature. EDA can be performed on a single feature (one-dimension) or on multiple features (multi-dimension). For high-dimension data with many features, EDA can be facilitated by using a dimension reduction technique, such as principal components analysis (PCA). Based on the number of dimensions, the exploratory techniques will vary.

For one-dimensional data, summary statistics, such as mean, median, quartiles, ranges, standard deviations, skewness, and kurtosis, of a feature can be computed. One-dimension visualization summarizes each feature in the dataset. The basic one-dimension exploratory visualizations are as follows:

- Histograms
- Bar charts
- Box plots
- Density plots

Histograms represent equal bins of data and their respective frequencies. They can be used to understand the high-level distribution of the data. Bar charts summarize the frequencies of categorical variables. Box plots show the distribution of continuous data by highlighting the median, quartiles, and outliers of a feature that is normally distributed. Density plots are another effective way to understand the distribution of continuous data. Density plots are smoothed histograms and are commonly laid on top of histograms, as shown in Exhibit 14. This histogram shows a hypothetical annual salary distribution (in £) of entry-level analyst positions at UK banks. The data represent a normal distribution with an approximate mean of £68,500.

For data with two or more dimensions, summary statistics of relationships, such as a correlation matrix, can be calculated. Two- or more-dimensional visualization explores interactions between different features in the dataset. Common methods include scatterplots and line graphs. In multi-dimensional visualization, one-dimensional plots are overlaid to summarize each feature, thus enabling comparison between features. Additionally, attributes (e.g., color, shape, and size) and legends can be used creatively to pack more information about the data into fewer graphs.

For multivariate data, commonly utilized exploratory visualization designs include stacked bar and line charts, multiple box plots, and scatterplots showing multivariate data that use different colors or shapes for each feature. Multiple box plots can be arranged in a single chart, where each individual box plot represents a feature. Such a multi-box plot chart assesses the relationship between each feature (x-axis) in the dataset and the target

EXHIBIT 14   Histogram with Superimposed Density Plot

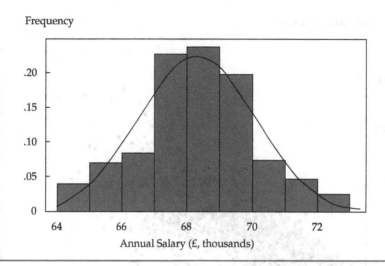

variable of interest (y-axis). The multi-box plot chart in Exhibit 15 represents units of shares purchased versus stock price for a hypothetical stock. The x-axis shows the stock price in increments of $0.125, and the y-axis shows units of shares purchased. The individual box plots indicate the distribution of shares purchased at the different stock prices. When the stock price is $0.25, the median number of shares purchased is the highest; when the stock price is $0.625, the median number of shares purchased is the lowest. However, visually it appears that the number of shares purchased at different stock prices is not significantly different.

EXHIBIT 15   Multiple Box Plots in One Chart

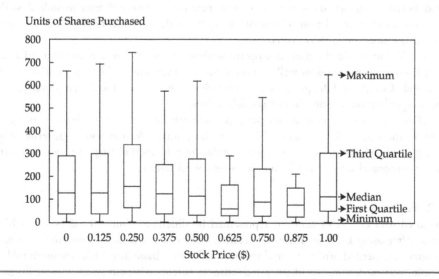

EXHIBIT 16   Scatterplot Showing a Linear Relationship Between Two Features

Annual Salary (thousands)

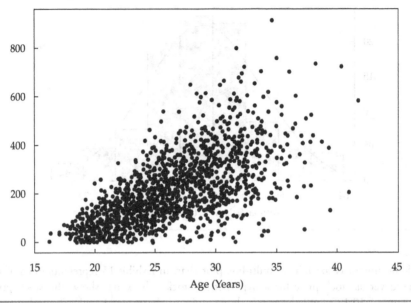

Age (Years)

Two-dimensional charts can summarize and approximately measure relationships between two or more features. An example scatterplot in Exhibit 16 shows the interaction of two hypothetical features: age (x-axis) and annual salary (y-axis). The feature on the y-axis tends to increase as the feature on the x-axis increases. This pattern appears true visually; however, it may not be a statistically significant relationship. A scatterplot provides a starting point where relationships can be examined visually. These potential relationships should be tested further using statistical tests. Common parametric statistical tests include ANOVA, t-test, and Pearson correlation. Common non-parametric statistical tests include chi-square and the Spearman rank-order correlation.

In addition to visualization, descriptive statistics are a good means to summarize data. Central tendency measures as well as minimum and maximum values for continuous data are useful. Counts and frequencies for categorical data are commonly employed to gain insight regarding the distribution of possible values.

EDA is not only useful for revealing possible relationships among features or general trends in the data; it is also beneficial during the feature selection and engineering stages. These possible relationships and trends in the data may be used to suggest new features that, when incorporated into a model, may improve model training.

5.1.2. Feature Selection

Structured data consist of features, represented by different columns of data in a table or matrix. After using EDA to discover relevant patterns in the data, it is essential to identify and remove unneeded, irrelevant, and redundant features. Basic diagnostic testing should also be performed on features to identify redundancy, heteroscedasticity, and multi-collinearity.

The objective of the feature selection process is to assist in identifying significant features that when used in a model retain the important patterns and complexities of the larger dataset while requiring fewer data overall. This last point is important since computing power is not free (i.e., explicit costs and processing time).

Typically, structured data even after the data preparation step can contain features that do not contribute to the accuracy of an ML model or that negatively affect the quality of ML training. The most desirable outcome is a parsimonious model with fewer features that provides the maximum predictive power out of sample.

Feature selection must not be confused with the data preprocessing steps during data preparation. Good feature selection requires an understanding of the data and statistics, and comprehensive EDA must be performed to assist with this step. Data preprocessing needs clarification only from data administrators and basic intuition (e.g., salary vs. income) during data preparation.

Feature selection on structured data is a methodical and iterative process. Statistical measures can be used to assign a score gauging the importance of each feature. The features can then be ranked using this score and either retained or eliminated from the dataset. The statistical methods utilized for this task are usually univariate and consider each feature independently or with regard to the target variable. Methods include chi-square test, correlation coefficients, and information-gain measures (i.e., R-squared values from regression analysis). All of these statistical methods can be combined in a manner that uses each method individually on each feature, automatically performing backward and forward passes over features to improve feature selection. Prebuilt feature selection functions are available in popular programming languages used to build and train ML models.

Dimensionality reduction assists in identifying the features in the data that account for the greatest variance between observations and allows for the processing of a reduced volume of data. Dimensionality reduction may be implemented to reduce a large number of features, which helps reduce the memory needed and speed up learning algorithms. Feature selection is different from dimensionality reduction, but both methods seek to reduce the number of features in the dataset. The dimensionality reduction method creates new combinations of features that are uncorrelated, whereas feature selection includes and excludes features present in the data without altering them.

5.1.3. Feature Engineering

After the appropriate features are selected, feature engineering helps further optimize and improve the features. The success of ML model training depends on how well the data are presented to the model. The feature engineering process attempts to produce good features that describe the structures inherent in the dataset. This process depends on the context of the project, domain of the data, and nature of the problem. Structured data are likely to contain quantities, which can be engineered to better present relevant patterns in the dataset. This action involves engineering an existing feature into a new feature or decomposing it into multiple features.

For continuous data, a new feature may be created—for example, by taking the logarithm of the product of two or more features. As another example, when considering a salary or income feature, it may be important to recognize that different salary brackets impose a different taxation rate. Domain knowledge can be used to decompose an income feature into different tax brackets, resulting in a new feature: "income_above_100k," with possible values 0 and 1. The value 1 under the new feature captures the fact that a subject has an annual salary of more than $100,000. By grouping subjects into income categories, assumptions about income tax can be made and utilized in a model that uses the income tax implications of higher and lower salaries to make financial predictions.

For categorical data, for example, a new feature can be a combination (e.g., sum or product) of two features or a decomposition of one feature into many. If a single categorical feature represents education level with five possible values—high school, associates, bachelor's, master's, and doctorate—then these values can be decomposed into five new features, one for each possible value (e.g., is_highSchool, is_doctorate) filled with 0s (for false) and 1s (for true). The process in which categorical variables are converted into binary form (0 or 1) for machine reading is called **one hot encoding**. It is one of the most common methods for handling categorical features in text data. When date-time is present in the data, such features as "second of the hour," "hour of the day," and "day of the date" can be engineered to capture critical information about temporal data attributes—which are important, for example, in modeling trading algorithms.

Feature engineering techniques systemically alter, decompose, or combine existing features to produce more meaningful features. More meaningful features allow an ML model to train more swiftly and easily. Different feature engineering strategies can lead to the generation of dramatically different results from the same ML model. The impact of feature selection and engineering on ML training is discussed further in the next section.

5.2. Unstructured Data: Text Exploration

5.2.1. Exploratory Data Analysis

Just like with structured data, it is important to gain insight into existing patterns in the unstructured data for further analysis. In this section, text data will be discussed. Text analytics has various applications. The most common applications are text classification, topic modeling, fraud detection, and sentiment analysis. Text classification uses supervised ML approaches to classify texts into different classes. Topic modeling uses unsupervised ML approaches to group the texts in the dataset into topic clusters. Sentiment analysis predicts sentiment (negative, neutral, or positive) of the texts in a dataset using both supervised and unsupervised approaches.

Various statistics are used to explore, summarize, and analyze text data. Text data include a collection of texts (also known as a corpus) that are sequences of tokens. It is useful to perform EDA of text data by computing on the tokens such basic text statistics as **term frequency (TF)**, the ratio of the number of times a given token occurs in all the texts in the dataset to the total number of tokens in the dataset (e.g., word associations, average word and sentence length, and word and syllable counts).

Text statistics reveal patterns in the co-occurrence of words. There are many applications of text analytics, and necessary text statistics vary according to the context of the application. Topic modeling is a text data application in which the words that are most informative are identified by calculating the TF of each word. For example, the word "soccer" can be informative for the topic "sports." The words with high TF values are eliminated as they are likely to be stop words or other common vocabulary words, making the resulting BOW compact and more likely to be relevant to topics within the texts. In sentiment analysis and text classification applications, the chi-square measure of word association can be useful for understanding the significant word appearances in negative and positive sentences in the text or in different documents. The chi-square measure is further

EXHIBIT 17   Word Cloud of Generic Financial Newsfeed Data Sample

explained under feature selection. Such EDA plays a vital role in executing the feature selection step.

Text statistics can be visually comprehended by using the same methods as explained in the structured data section. For example, bar charts can be used to show word counts or frequency. Words clouds are common visualizations when working with text data as they can be made to visualize the most informative words and their TF values. The most commonly occurring words in the dataset can be shown by varying font size, and color is used to add more dimensions, such as frequency and length of words. Exhibit 17 shows a word cloud constructed from a sample dataset of generic financial news wires after text processing. Word cloud building functions and packages are available in several popular programming languages. A detailed demonstration of text data EDA will be presented in Section 7, where we work with actual text data in a financial forecasting project.

5.2.2. Feature Selection

For text data, feature selection involves selecting a subset of the terms or tokens occurring in the dataset. The tokens serve as features for ML model training. Feature selection in text data effectively decreases the size of the vocabulary or BOW. This helps the ML model be more efficient and less complex. Another benefit is to eliminate noisy features from the dataset. Noisy features are tokens that do not contribute to ML model training and actually might detract from the ML model accuracy.

Noisy features are both the most frequent and most sparse (or rare) tokens in the dataset. On one end, noisy features can be stop words that are typically present frequently in all the texts across the dataset. On the other end, noisy features can be sparse terms that are present in only a few text cases. Text classification involves dividing text documents into assigned classes (a class is a category; examples include "relevant" and "irrelevant" text documents or "bearish" and "bullish" sentences). The *frequent* tokens strain the ML model to

EXHIBIT 18   Tokens with Mutual Information (MI) Values for Two Given Text Classes

Text Classes: Sports or Politics

Sports		Politics	
Token	MI Value	Token	MI Value
soccer	0.0781	election	0.0612
cup	0.0525	president	0.0511
match	0.0456	polls	0.0341
play	0.0387	vote	0.0288
game	0.0299	party	0.0202
team	0.0265	candidate	0.0201
win	0.0189	campaign	0.0201

choose a decision boundary among the texts as the terms are present across all the texts, an example of model *underfitting*. The *rare* tokens mislead the ML model into classifying texts containing the rare terms into a specific class, an example of model *overfitting*. Identifying and removing noise features is very critical for text classification applications. The general feature selection methods in text data are as follows:

1. *Frequency* measures can be used for vocabulary pruning to remove noise features by filtering the tokens with very high and low TF values across all the texts. **Document frequency (DF)** is another frequency measure that helps to discard the noise features that carry no specific information about the text class and are present across all texts. The DF of a token is defined as the number of documents (texts) that contain the respective token divided by the total number of documents. It is the simplest feature selection method and often performs well when many thousands of tokens are present.

2. *Chi-square* test can be useful for feature selection in text data. The chi-square test is applied to test the independence of two events: occurrence of the token and occurrence of the class. The test ranks the tokens by their usefulness to each class in text classification problems. Tokens with the highest chi-square test statistic values occur more frequently in texts associated with a particular class and therefore can be selected for use as features for ML model training due to higher discriminatory potential.

3. *Mutual information* (MI) measures how much information is contributed by a token to a class of texts. The **mutual information** value will be equal to 0 if the token's distribution in all text classes is the same. The MI value approaches 1 as the token in any one class tends to occur more often in only that particular class of text. Exhibit 18 shows a simple depiction of some tokens with high MI scores for their corresponding text classes. Note how the tokens (or features) with the highest MI values narrowly relate to their corresponding text class name.

5.2.3. Feature Engineering

As with structured data, feature engineering can greatly improve ML model training and remains a combination of art and science. The following are some techniques for feature engineering, which may overlap with text processing techniques.

1. *Numbers*: In text processing, numbers are converted into a token, such as "/number/." However, numbers can be of different lengths of digits representing different kinds of numbers, so it may be useful to convert different numbers into different tokens. For example, numbers with four digits may indicate years, and numbers with many digits could be an identification number. Four-digit numbers can be replaced with "/number4/," 10-digit numbers with "/number10/," and so forth.

2. *N-grams*: Multi-word patterns that are particularly discriminative can be identified and their connection kept intact. For example, "market" is a common word that can be indicative of many subjects or classes; the words "stock market" are used in a particular context and may be helpful to distinguish general texts from finance-related texts. Here, a bigram would be useful as it treats the two adjacent words as a single token (e.g., stock_market).

3. *Name entity recognition (NER)*: NER is an extensive procedure available as a library or package in many programming languages. The **name entity recognition** algorithm analyzes the individual tokens and their surrounding semantics while referring to its dictionary to tag an object class to the token. Exhibit 19 shows the NER tags of the text "*CFA Institute was formed in 1947 and is headquartered in Virginia.*" Additional object classes are, for example, MONEY, TIME, and PERCENT, which are not present in the example text. The NER tags, when applicable, can be used as features for ML model training for better model performance. NER tags can also help identify critical tokens on which such operations as lowercasing and stemming then can be avoided (e.g., Institute here refers to an organization rather than a verb). Such techniques make the features more discriminative.

4. *Parts of speech (POS)*: Similar to NER, **parts of speech** uses language structure and dictionaries to tag every token in the text with a corresponding part of speech. Some common POS tags are noun, verb, adjective, and proper noun. Exhibit 19 shows the POS tags and descriptions of tags for the example text. POS tags can be used as features for ML model training and to identify the number of tokens that belong to each POS tag. If a given text contains many proper nouns, it means that it may be related to people and organizations and may be a business topic. POS tags can be useful for separating verbs and nouns for text analytics. For example, the word "market" can be a verb when used as "to market ..." or noun when used as "in the market." Differentiating such

EXHIBIT 19   Name Entity Recognition (NER) and Parts of Speech (POS) on Example Text

Token	NER Tag	POS Tag	POS Description
CFA	ORGANIZATION	NNP	Proper noun
Institute	ORGANIZATION	NNP	Proper noun
was		VBD	Verb, past tense
formed		VBN	Verb, past participle
in		IN	Preposition
1947	DATE	CD	Cardinal number
and		CC	Coordinating conjunction
is		VBZ	Verb, 3rd person singular present
headquartered		VBN	Verb, past participle
in		IN	Preposition
Virginia	LOCATION	NNP	Proper noun

tokens can help further clarify the meaning of the text. The use of "market" as a verb could indicate that the text relates to the topic of marketing and might discuss marketing a product or service. The use of "market" as a noun could suggest that the text relates to a physical or stock market and might discuss stock trading. Also for POS tagging, such compound nouns as "CFA Institute" can be treated as a single token. POS tagging can be performed using libraries or packages in programming languages.

In addition, many more creative techniques convey text information in a structured way to the ML training process. The goal of feature engineering is to maintain the semantic essence of the text while simplifying and converting it into structured data for ML.

EXAMPLE 4   Data Exploration

Paul Wang's analytics team at LendALot Corporation has completed its initial data preparation and wrangling related to their creditworthiness classification ML model building efforts. As a next step, Wang has asked one of the team members, Eric Kim, to examine the available structured data sources to see what types of exploratory data analysis might make sense. Kim has been tasked with reporting to the team on high-level patterns and trends in the data and which variables seem interesting. Greater situational awareness about the data can inform the team's decisions regarding model training and whether (and how) to incorporate textual big data in conjunction with the structured data inputs. Use the following sample of columns and rows Kim pulled for manual examination to answer the next questions.

ID	Loan Outcome	Income (USD)	Loan Amount (USD)	Credit Score	Loan Type	Free Responses to "Explain Credit Score" (excerpts from full text)
1	No Default	34,000	10,000	685	Mortgage	I am embarrassed that my score is below 700, but it was due to mitigating circumstances. I have developed a plan to improve my score.
2	No Default	63,050	49,000	770	Student Loan	I have a good credit score and am constantly looking to further improve it...
3	Defaulted	20,565	35,000	730	Student Loan	I think I have great credit. I don't think there are any issues. Having to provide a written response to these questions is kind of annoying...
4	No Default	50,021	10,000	664	Mortgage	I have a decent credit score. I regret not being as responsible in the past but feel I have worked hard to improve my score recently...

ID	Loan Outcome	Income (USD)	Loan Amount (USD)	Credit Score	Loan Type	Free Responses to "Explain Credit Score" (excerpts from full text)
5	Defaulted	100,350	129,000	705	Car Loan	Honestly, my score probably would have been higher if I had worked harder. But it is probably good enough…
6	No Default	800,000	300,000	800	Boat Loan	I have worked hard to maintain a good credit rating. I am very responsible. I maintain a payment schedule and always stick to the payment plan…

1. Evaluate whether data visualization techniques, such as histograms, box plots, and scatterplots, could be relevant to exploratory data analysis.
2. State one visualization technique that could be used in relation to the free responses.
3. Describe how ranking methods can be used to select potentially interesting features to report back to the team.
4. State an example of a bigram from the free response texts that could be used to discriminate among loan outcomes.

Solution to 1: The data provided include structured features (ID, Loan Outcome, Income, Loan Amount, Credit Score) and unstructured data. Histograms, box plots, and scatterplots are relevant visualization methods for structured data features. Histograms and box plots could be used by Kim to see how income, loan amount, and credit score are distributed. Moreover, these visualizations can be performed across all historical borrowing instances in the dataset as well as within the sets of defaulted loans versus non-defaulted loans. Scatterplots of income versus loan amount, income versus credit score, and loan amount versus credit score, both overall and within defaulted and non-defaulted datasets, can shed light on relationships between potentially important continuous variables.

Solution to 2: For the text in the free response field, word clouds offer an appropriate starting point for exploratory analysis. A word cloud can enable a quick glimpse into the most frequently occurring words (i.e., term frequency). While some obvious words (e.g., "credit" and "score") may be valuable, other frequently occurring words (e.g., "worked," "hard," "probably," "embarrassed," "regret," "good," "decent," and "great") might have potential use for creditworthiness prediction.

Solution to 3: Kim can use feature selection methods to rank all features. Since the target variable of interest (loan outcome) is discrete in this case, such techniques as chi-square and information gain would be well suited. These are univariate techniques that can score feature variables individually. In addition to the structured features, these univariate ranking methods can also be applied to word count-related features, such as term frequency and document frequency, that are derived from the text using frequently occurring words. Such frequently occurring words (e.g., "worked" and "hard") can be identified from the word cloud.

Solution to 4: The bigrams "credit_score" and "worked_hard" from the text in the free response section may have potential to discriminate among loan outcomes.

EXAMPLE 5 Textual Feature Representations for ML Model Building

Having completed their exploration of the data, Paul Wang's analytics team at LendALot Corporation recognizes the importance of incorporating features derived from text data in their ML models for classifying creditworthiness. Wang has asked his colleagues, Lynn Lee and Eric Kim, to propose textual feature representations that might be well suited to constructing features for their task. As a starting point, Lee and Kim review the following sample of data:

ID	Loan Outcome	Income (USD)	Loan Amount (USD)	Credit Score	Loan Type	Free Responses to "Explain Credit Score" (excerpts from full text)
1	No Default	34,000	10,000	685	Mortgage	I am embarrassed that my score is below 700, but it was due to mitigating circumstances. I have developed a plan to improve my score.
2	No Default	63,050	49,000	770	Student Loan	I have a good credit score and am constantly looking to further improve it...
3	Defaulted	20,565	35,000	730	Student Loan	I think I have great credit. I don't think there are any issues. Having to provide a written response to these questions is kind of annoying...
4	No Default	50,021	10,000	664	Mortgage	I have a decent credit score. I regret not being as responsible in the past but feel I have worked hard to improve my score recently...
5	Defaulted	100,350	129,000	705	Car Loan	Honestly, my score probably would have been higher if I had worked harder. But it is probably good enough...
6	No Default	800,000	300,000	800	Boat Loan	I have worked hard to maintain a good credit rating. I am very responsible. I maintain a payment schedule and always stick to the payment plan...

Based on the information given, address the following questions.

1. Describe three textual feature representations that Lee and Kim should consider for their text data.
2. Describe a rationale for adopting each of the three textual feature representations identified in Question 1.

Solution to 1: Lee and Kim should consider bag of words (BOW), n-grams, and parts of speech (POS) as key textual feature representations for their text data. Conversely, name entity recognition (NER) might not be as applicable in this context because the data on prospective borrowers does not include any explicit references to people, locations, dates, or organizations.

Solution to 2: All three textual feature representations have the potential to add value.

Bag of words (BOW) is typically applicable in most contexts involving text features derived from languages where token boundaries are explicitly present (e.g., English) or can be inferred through processing (e.g., a different language, such as Spanish). BOW is generally the best starting point for most projects exploring text feature representations.

N-grams, representations of word or token sequences, are also applicable. N-grams can offer invaluable contextual information that can complement and enrich a BOW. In this specific credit-worthiness context, we examine the BOW token "worked." It appears three times (rows 5–7), twice in no-default loan texts and once in a defaulted loan text. This finding suggests that "worked" is being used to refer to the borrower's work ethic and may be a good predictor of credit worthiness. Digging deeper and looking at several trigrams (i.e., three-token sequences) involving "worked," we see that "have_worked_hard" appears in the two no-default loan related texts (referring to borrower accomplishments and plans) and "had_worked_harder" appears in the defaulted loan text (referring to what could have been done). This example illustrates how n-grams can provide richer contextualization capabilities for the creditworthiness prediction ML models.

Parts-of-speech tags can add value because they identify the composition of the texts. For example, POS provides information on whether the prospective borrowers are including many action words (verbs) or descriptors (adjectives) and whether this is being done differently in instances of no-default versus instances of defaulted loans.

6. MODEL TRAINING

Machine learning model training is a systematic, iterative, and recursive process. The number of iterations required to reach optimum results depends on:

- the nature of the problem and input data and
- the level of model performance needed for practical application.

Machine learning models combine multiple principles and operations to provide predictions. As seen in the last two sections, typical ML model building requires data preparation

EXHIBIT 20   Model Training Stage

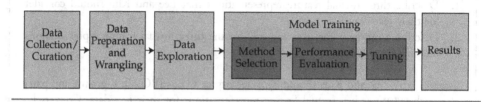

and wrangling (cleansing and preprocessing) and data exploration (exploratory data analysis as well as feature selection and engineering). In addition, domain knowledge related to the nature of the data is required for good model building and training. For instance, knowledge of investment management and securities trading is important when using financial data to train a model for predicting costs of trading stocks. It is crucial for ML engineers and domain experts to work together in building and training robust ML models.

The three tasks of ML model training are method selection, performance evaluation, and tuning. Exhibit 20 outlines model training and its three component tasks. Method selection is the art and science of deciding which ML method(s) to incorporate and is guided by such considerations as the classification task, type of data, and size of data. Performance evaluation entails using an array of complementary techniques and measures to quantify and understand a model's performance. Tuning is the process of undertaking decisions and actions to improve model performance. These steps may be repeated multiple times until the desired level of ML model performance is attained. Although no standard rulebook for training an ML model exists, having a fundamental understanding of domain-specific train-ing data and ML algorithm principles plays a vital role in good model training.

Before training a model, it is important to state the problem, define objectives, identify useful data points, and conceptualize the model. Conceptualization is like a blueprint on a drawing board, a modifiable plan that is necessary to initiate the model training process. Because modeling is an iterative process, many changes and refinements will be made to the model plan as the process evolves.

6.1. Structured and Unstructured Data

The ML model training process for structured and unstructured data is typically the same. Most ML models are intended to train on structured data, so unstructured data in the data preparation stage are processed and organized into a structured format. The systematic proc-essing of unstructured text data so that they can be structured in the form of a data matrix has been previously covered. Similarly, other forms of unstructured data can also be prepared and formed into data matrixes or tables for ML training.

The fundamental idea of ML model training is fitting a system of rules on a training dataset to reveal a pattern in the data. In other words, fitting describes the degree to which (or how well) an ML model can be generalized to new data. A good model fit results in good model performance and can be validated using new data outside of the training dataset (i.e., out-of-sample). Exhibit 21 shows model decision boundaries in three possible model fitting scenarios for a classification task comprising two different classes of data (i.e., circles and triangles). The model on the left is underfit; it does not fit the training data well enough

EXHIBIT 21   Model Fitting Scenarios: Underfit, Overfit, and Good Fit

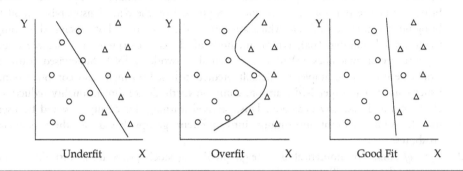

since it results in four misclassification errors (three circles and one triangle). Although the center model that generates the "S"-shaped line has the best accuracy (no errors) on the training data, it is overfit (i.e., fits the training data too well) and thus unlikely to perform well on future test cases. The model on the right (with one classification error, a circle) is a model with good fit (i.e., it fits the training data well but not so well that it cannot be generalized to out-of-sample data).

Model fitting errors are caused by several factors—the main ones being dataset size and number of features in the dataset.

- *Dataset Size*: Small datasets can lead to underfitting of the model since small datasets often are not sufficient to expose patterns in the data. Restricted by a small dataset, an ML model may not recognize important patterns.
- *Number of Features*: A dataset with a small number of features can lead to underfitting, and a dataset with a large number of features can lead to overfitting. As with small dataset size, a small number of features may not carry all the characteristics that explain relationships between the target variable and the features. Conversely, a large number of features can complicate the model and potentially distort patterns in the data due to low degrees of freedom, causing overfitting. Therefore, appropriate feature selection using the types of techniques described earlier (e.g., chi-square, mutual information) is a key factor in minimizing such model overfitting.

Feature engineering tends to prevent underfitting in the training of the model. New features, when engineered properly, can elevate the underlying data points that better explain the interactions of features. Thus, feature engineering can be critical to overcome underfitting. Method-related factors that affect model fitting are explained shortly under tuning.

6.1.1. Method Selection

ML model training is a craft (part art and part science); it has no strict guidelines. Selecting and applying a method or an algorithm is the first step of the training process. Method selection is governed by the following factors:

1. *Supervised or unsupervised learning.* The data for training and testing supervised ML models contain **ground truth**, the known outcome (i.e., target variable) of each

observation in these datasets. Unsupervised ML modeling is relatively challenging because of the absence of ground truth (i.e., no target variable). Supervised models bring a structure that may or may not be supported by the data. Unsupervised models bring no structure beyond that which arises from the given data. For supervised learning (with labeled training data), typical methods of choice are regression, ensemble trees, support vector machines (SVMs), and neural networks (NNs). Supervised learning would be used, for example, for default prediction based on high-yield corporate bond issuer data. For unsupervised learning, common methods are dimensionality reduction, clustering, and anomaly detection. Unsupervised learning, for example, would be used for clustering financial institutions into different groups based on their financial attributes.

2. *Type of data.* For numerical data (e.g., predicting stock prices using historical stock market values), classification and regression tree (CART) methods may be suitable. For text data (for example, predicting the topic of a financial news article by reading the headline of the article), such methods as generalized linear models (GLMs) and SVMs are commonly used. For image data (e.g., identifying objects in a satellite image, such as tanker ships moving in and out of port), NNs and deep learning methods tend to perform better than others. For speech data (e.g., predicting financial sentiment from quarterly earnings' conference call recordings), deep learning methods can offer promising results.

3. *Size of data.* A typical dataset has two basic characteristics: number of instances (i.e., observations) and number of features. The combination of these two characteristics can govern which method is most suitable for model training. For instance, SVMs have been found to work well on "wider" datasets with 10,000 to 100,000 features and with fewer instances. Conversely, NNs often work better on "longer" datasets, where the number of instances is much larger than the number of features.

Once a method is selected, certain method-related decisions (e.g., on hyperparameters) need to be made. These decisions include the number of hidden layers in a neural network and the number of trees in ensemble methods (discussed later in the sub-section on tuning). In practice, datasets can be a combination of numerical and text data. To deal with mixed data, the results from more than one method can be combined. Sometimes, the predictions from one method can be used as predictors (features) by another. For example, unstructured financial text data can be used with logistic regression to classify stock sentiment as either positive or negative. Then, this sentiment classification cam be used as a predictor in a larger model, say CART, that also uses structured financial data as predictors for the purpose of stock selection. Finally, more than one method can be used and the results combined with quantitative or subjective weighing to exploit the advantages of each method.

Before model training begins, in the case of supervised learning the master dataset is split into three subsets used for model training and testing purposes. The first subset, a training set used to train the model, should constitute approximately 60 percent of the master dataset. The second subset, a cross-validation set (or validation set) used to tune and validate the model, should constitute approximately 20 percent of the master dataset. The third subset is a test set for testing the model and uses the remaining data. The data are split using a random sampling technique, such as the k-fold method. A commonly recommended split ratio is 60:20:20, as detailed above; however, the split percentages can vary. For unsupervised learning, no splitting is needed due to the absence of labeled training data.

Class imbalance, where the number of instances for a particular class is significantly larger than for other classes, may be a problem for data used in supervised learning because the ML classification method's objective is to train a high-accuracy model. In a high-yield bond default prediction example, say for corporate issuers in the BB+/Ba1 to B+/B1 credit quality range, issuers who defaulted (positive or "1" class) would be very few compared to issuers who did not default (negative or "0" class). Hence, on such training data, a naive model that simply assumes no corporate issuer will default may achieve good accuracy— albeit with all default cases misclassified. Balancing the training data can help alleviate such problems. In cases of unbalanced data, the "0" class (majority class) can be randomly under-sampled or the "1" class (minority class) randomly oversampled. The random sampling can be done with or without replacement because they both work the same in general probability theory. Exhibit 22 depicts the idea of undersampling of the majority class and oversampling of the minority class. In practice, the choice of whether to undersample or oversample depends on the specific problem context. Advanced techniques can also reproduce synthetic observations from the existing data, and the new observations can be added to the dataset to balance the minority class.

EXHIBIT 22   Undersampling and Oversampling

Undersampling Majority Class ("0" class)

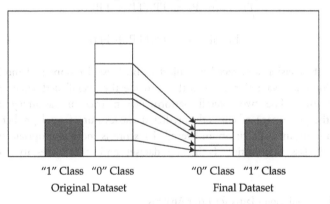

"1" Class   "0" Class   "0" Class   "1" Class
Original Dataset   Final Dataset

Oversampling Minority Class ("1" class)

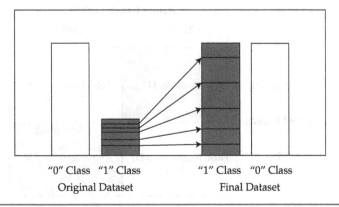

"0" Class   "1" Class   "1" Class   "0" Class
Original Dataset   Final Dataset

6.1.2. Performance Evaluation

It is important to measure the model training performance or goodness of fit for validation of the model. We shall cover several techniques to measure model performance that are well suited specifically for binary classification models.

1. *Error analysis.* For classification problems, error analysis involves computing four basic evaluation metrics: true positive (TP), false positive (FP), true negative (TN), and false negative (FN) metrics. FP is also called a Type I error, and FN is also called a Type II error. Exhibit 23 shows a **confusion matrix**, a grid that is used to summarize values of these four metrics.

   Additional metrics, such as precision and recall, can be computed. Assume in the following explanation that Class "0" is "not defective" and Class "1" is "defective." **Precision** is the ratio of correctly predicted positive classes to all predicted positive classes. Precision is useful in situations where the cost of FP, or Type I error, is high—or example, when an expensive product fails quality inspection (predicted Class "1") and is scrapped, but it is actually perfectly good (actual Class "0"). **Recall** (also known as *sensitivity*) is the ratio of correctly predicted positive classes to all actual positive classes. Recall is useful in situations where the cost of FN or Type II error is high—for example, when an expensive product passes quality inspection (predicted Class "0") and is sent to the valued customer, but it is actually quite defective (actual Class "1"). The formulas for precision and recall are:

$$\text{Precision (P)} = \text{TP}/(\text{TP} + \text{FP}). \tag{3}$$

$$\text{Recall (R)} = \text{TP}/(\text{TP} + \text{FN}). \tag{4}$$

Trading off precision and recall is subject to business decisions and model application. Therefore, additional evaluation metrics that provide the overall performance of the model are generally used. The two overall performance metrics are accuracy and F1 score. **Accuracy** is the percentage of correctly predicted classes out of total predictions. **F1 score** is the harmonic mean of precision and recall. F1 score is more appropriate (than accuracy) when unequal class distribution is in the dataset and it is necessary to measure the

EXHIBIT 23   Confusion Matrix for Error Analysis

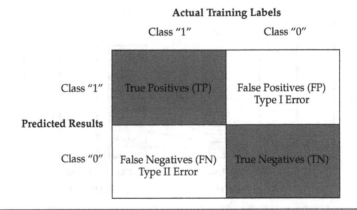

equilibrium of precision and recall. High scores on both of these metrics suggest good model performance. The formulas for accuracy and F1 score are as follows:

$$\text{Accuracy} = (TP + TN)/(TP + FP + TN + FN) \tag{5}$$

$$\text{F1 score} = (2 \times P \times R)/(P + R) \tag{6}$$

Exhibit 24 illustrates computations of model evaluation metrics and performance scores on a sample dataset.

In Exhibit 24, if all "1" classes were predicted correctly (no FPs), the precision would have been equal to 1. If all "0" classes were predicted correctly (no FNs), the recall would have been equal to 1. Thus, the resulting F1 score would have been equal to 1. The precision of 0.75 and recall of 0.60 indicate that the model is better at minimizing FPs than FNs. To find the equilibrium between precision and recall, F1 score is calculated, which is equal to 0.67. The F1 score is closer to the smaller value among both precision and recall, giving the model a more appropriate score rather than just an arithmetic mean. Accuracy, the

EXHIBIT 24   Performance Metrics and Scores Computation

Sample Dataset with Classification Results

Observation	Actual Training Labels	Predicted Results	Classification
1	1	1	TP
2	0	0	TN
3	1	1	TP
4	1	0	FN
5	1	1	TP
6	1	0	FN
7	0	0	TN
8	0	0	TN
9	0	0	TN
10	0	1	FP

Confusion Matrix

		Actual Training Labels	
		Class "1"	Class "0"
Predicted Results	Class "1"	3 (TP)	1 (FP)
	Class "0"	2 (FN)	4 (TN)

Performance Metrics

TP = 3, FP = 1, FN = 2, TN = 4
P = 3 / (3+1) = 0.75
R = 3 / (3+2) = 0.60
F1 Score = (2 × 0.75 × 0.60) / (0.75 + 0.60) = 0.67
Accuracy = (3 + 4) / (3 + 1 + 4 + 2) = 0.70

percentage of correct predictions (for both classes) made by the model, is equal to 0.70. Accuracy would be equal to 1 if all predictions were correct. As the number of "1" and "0" classes is equal in the dataset (i.e., a balanced dataset), accuracy can be considered an appropriate performance measure in this case. If the number of classes in a dataset is unequal; however, then F1 score should be used as the overall performance measure for the model.

2. *Receiver Operating Characteristic (ROC)*. This technique for assessing model performance involves the plot of a curve showing the trade-off between the false positive rate (x-axis) and true positive rate (y-axis) for various cutoff points—for example, for the predicted probability (p) in a logistic regression. The formulas for false positive rate and true positive rate (note that true positive rate is the same as recall) are:

$$\text{False positive rate (FPR)} = \text{FP}/(\text{TN} + \text{FP}) \text{ and} \quad (7)$$

$$\text{True positive rate (TPR)} = \text{TP}/(\text{TP} + \text{FN}) \quad (8)$$

If p from a logistic regression model for a given observation is greater than the cutoff point (or threshold), then the observation is classified as class = 1. Otherwise, the observation will be classified as class = 0.

The shape of the ROC curve provides insight into the model's performance. A more convex curve indicates better model performance. Area under the curve (AUC) is the metric that measures the area under the ROC curve. An AUC close to 1.0 indicates near perfect prediction, while an AUC of 0.5 signifies random guessing. Exhibit 25 displays three ROC curves and indicates their respective AUC values. It is clear from observing the

EXHIBIT 25   ROC Curves and AUCs

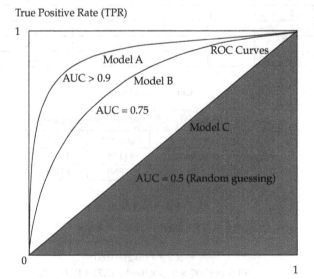

shapes of the ROC curves and their AUCs that Model A—with the most convex ROC curve with AUC of more than 0.9 (or 90 percent)—is the best performing among the three models.

3. *Root Mean Squared Error (RMSE).* This measure is appropriate for continuous data prediction and is mostly used for regression methods. It is a single metric that captures all the prediction errors in the data (n). The root mean squared error is computed by finding the square root of the mean of the squared differences between the actual values and the model's predicted values (error). A small RMSE indicates potentially better model performance. The formula for RMSE is:

$$RMSE = \sqrt{\sum_{i=1}^{n} \frac{(Predicted_i - Actual_i)^2}{n}}. \qquad (9)$$

6.1.3. Tuning

Once the model is evaluated, certain decisions and actions must be taken based on the findings to improve the performance of the model. If the prediction error on the training set is high, the model is underfitting. If the prediction error on the cross-validation (CV) set is significantly higher than on the training set, the model is overfitting. Model fitting has two types of error: bias and variance. Bias error is associated with underfitting, and variance error is associated with overfitting. Bias error is high when a model is overly simplified and does not sufficiently learn from the patterns in the training data. Variance error is high when the model is overly complicated and memorizes the training data so much that it will likely perform poorly on new data. It is not possible to completely eliminate both types of errors. However, both errors can be minimized so the total aggregate error (bias error + variance error) is at a minimum. The bias–variance trade-off is critical to finding an optimum balance where a model neither underfits nor overfits.

1. *Parameters* are critical for a model and are dependent on the training data. Parameters are learned from the training data as part of the training process by an optimization technique. Examples of parameters include coefficients in regression, weights in NN, and support vectors in SVM.

2. *Hyperparameters* are used for estimating model parameters and are not dependent on the training data. Examples of hyperparameters include the regularization term (λ) in supervised models, activation function and number of hidden layers in NN, number of trees and tree depth in ensemble methods, k in k-nearest neighbor classification and k-means clustering, and p-threshold in logistic regression. Hyperparameters are manually set and tuned.

For example, if a researcher is using a logistic regression model to classify sentences from financial statements into positive or negative stock sentiment, the initial cutoff point for the trained model might be a p-threshold of 0.50 (50 percent). Therefore, any sentence for which the model produces a probability >50% is classified as having positive sentiment. The researcher can create a confusion matrix from the classification results (of running the CV dataset) to determine such model performance metrics as accuracy and F1 score. Next, the researcher can vary the logistic regression's p-threshold—say to 0.55 (55 percent), 0.60 (60 percent), or even 0.65 (65 percent)—and then re-run the CV set, create new confusion matrixes from the new classification results, and compare accuracy and F1 scores.

Ultimately, the researcher would select the logistic regression model with a p-threshold value that produces classification results generating the highest accuracy and F1 scores. Note that the process just outlined will be demonstrated in Section 7.

There is no general formula to estimate hyperparameters. Thus, tuning heuristics and such techniques as grid search are used to obtain the optimum values of hyperparameters. **Grid search** is a method of systematically training an ML model by using various combinations of hyperparameter values, cross validating each model, and determining which combination of hyperparameter values ensures the best model performance. The model is trained using different combinations of hyperparameter values until the optimum set of values are found. Optimum values must result in similar performance of the model on training and CV datasets, meaning that the training error and CV error are close. This ensures that the model can be generalized to test data or to new data and thus is less likely to overfit. The plot of training errors for each value of a hyperparameter (i.e., changing model complexity) is called a fitting curve. Fitting curves provide visual insight on the model's performance (for the given hyperparameter and level of model complexity) on the training and CV datasets and are visually helpful to tune hyperparameters. Exhibit 26 shows the bias–variance error trade-off by plotting a generic fitting curve for a regularization hyperparameter (λ).

Slight regularization lightly penalizes model complexity, thereby allowing most or all of the features to be included in the model and thus potentially enabling the model to

EXHIBIT 26   Fitting Curve for Regularization Hyperparameter (λ)

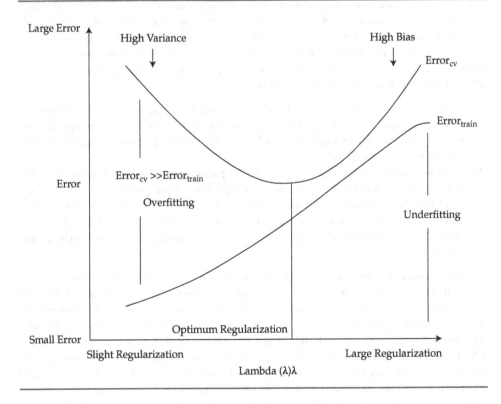

"memorize" the data. Typically with no or slight regularization, the prediction error on the training dataset is small while the prediction error on the CV dataset is significantly larger. This difference in error is variance. High variance error, which typically results from too many features and model complexity, results in model overfitting. When high variance error and low bias error exist, the model performs well on the training dataset but generates many FP and FN errors on the CV dataset; in other words, the model is overfitted and does not generalize to new data well.

Large regularization excessively penalizes model complexity, thereby allowing too few of the features to be included in the model and causing the model to learn less from the data. The model may lack the necessary predictor variables and complexity needed to discern underlying patterns in the data. Typically with large regularization, the prediction errors on the training and CV datasets are both large. Large prediction errors on the training dataset indicate high bias, and high bias error results from model underfitting. When high bias error exists, the model does not perform well on either training or CV datasets because it is typically lacking important predictor variables.

Optimum regularization minimizes both variance and bias errors in a balanced fashion. It penalizes model complexity just enough so that only the most important features are included in the model. This process prevents the model from memorizing the data while enabling the model to learn enough from the data to distinguish important patterns. This results in prediction errors in both training and CV datasets that are similar and also minimal. The range of optimum regularization values can be found heuristically using such techniques as grid search.

If high bias or variance exists after the tuning of hyperparameters, either a larger number of training examples (instances) may be needed or the number of features included in the model may need to be decreased (in the case of high variance) or increased (in the case of high bias). The model then needs to be re-trained and re-tuned using the new training dataset. In the case of a complex model, where a large model is comprised of sub-model(s), ceiling analysis can be performed. **Ceiling analysis** is a systematic process of evaluating different components in the pipeline of model building. It helps to understand what part of the pipeline can potentially improve in performance by further tuning. For example, a stock market prediction model needs historical data from the stock market and perhaps news articles related to the stocks. The sub-model will extract relevant information from the news articles or classify the sentiment of the news articles. The results of the sub-model will feed into the larger model as features. Thus, the performance of the larger model depends on performance of the sub-model(s). Ceiling analysis can help determine which sub-model needs to be tuned to improve the overall accuracy of the larger model.

7. FINANCIAL FORECASTING PROJECT: CLASSIFYING AND PREDICTING SENTIMENT FOR STOCKS

Robo-readers are automated programs used to analyze large quantities of text, including news articles and social media. In the financial services space, robo-readers are being used by investors to examine how views expressed in text relate to future company performance. One important dimension that robo-readers look to analyze is sentiment polarity—which means how positive, negative, or neutral a particular phrase or statement is regarding a "target." For example, in the statement "XYZ Corporation is doing terrific things with its new product innovation," positive sentiment (i.e., the polarity) is being expressed regarding XYZ Corporation (i.e., the target of the sentiment). Such sentiment can provide invaluable predictive power, both alone and when coupled with structured financial data, for predicting stock price movements for individual firms and for portfolios of companies.

To provide a practical application, we use a financial forecasting project to examine how effectively sentiment—expressed in English news articles on LexisNexis (a searchable database of news articles) related to all companies listed on the NASDAQ OMX Helsinki (Finland)—can be classified. To accomplish this task, we followed the text ML model building steps presented in Sections 3 to 6 of this chapter.

7.1. Text Curation, Preparation, and Wrangling

7.1.1. Text Curation
The text data used in this financial forecasting project are a collection of English language sentences from financial and economic news sources. The text data are acquired from the Financial Phrase Bank located on the website Researchgate.net.[2] The compressed folder contains six text files. The first two files are license and readme files. The other four files contain the text data. The data are presented in a text document format (.txt), which can be opened and viewed using any text editor. Note that this is cross-sectional data (not time series data).

A total of 14,780 sentences are in the four files. The sentiment of each sentence has already been labeled with one of three sentiment classes: positive, neutral, or negative. The sentiment classes are provided from an investor's perspective and may be useful for predicting whether a sentence may have a corresponding positive, neutral, or negative influence on the respective company's stock price.

This project uses sentences from two of the text files (Sentences_AllAgree and Sentences_75Agree), labeled as either in the positive or negative sentiment class, for a total of 2,180 sentences. There are 1,457 positive sentiment class sentences and 723 negative sentiment class sentences. A supervised ML model is trained, validated, and tested using these data. The final ML model can be used to predict the sentiment classes of sentences present in similar financial news statements. Exhibit 27 shows a sample of 10 rows of raw text from the Sentences_AllAgree text file. Note the sentiment annotations at the end of each sentence with prefix character "@."

EXHIBIT 27   Ten Sample Sentences and Sentiment from Raw Text File (Sentences_AllAgree.txt)

```
Profit before taxes amounted to EUR 56.5 mn , down from EUR 232.9 mn a year ago .@negative
Profit before taxes decreased by 9 % to EUR 187.8 mn in the first nine months of 2008 , compared to EUR 207.1 mn a year earlier .@negative
Profit before taxes decreased to EUR 31.6 mn from EUR 50.0 mn the year before .@negative
Profit before taxes was EUR 4.0 mn , down from EUR 4.9 mn .@negative
The company 's profit before taxes fell to EUR 21.1 mn in the third quarter of 2008 , compared to EUR 35.8 mn in the corresponding period in 2007 .@negative
In August-October 2010 , the company 's result before taxes totalled EUR 9.6 mn , up from EUR 0.5 mn in the corresponding period in 2009 .@positive
Finnish Bore that is owned by the Rettig family has grown recently through the acquisition of smaller shipping companies .@positive
The plan is estimated to generate some EUR 5 million ( USD 6.5 m ) in cost savings on an annual basis .@positive
Finnish pharmaceuticals company Orion reports profit before taxes of EUR 70.0 mn in the third quarter of 2010 , up from EUR 54.9 mn in the corresponding period in 2009 .@positive
Finnish Sampo Bank , of Danish Danske Bank group , reports profit before taxes of EUR 152.3 mn in 2010 , up from EUR 32.7 mn in 2009 .@positive
```

[2]https://www.researchgate.net/publication/251231364_FinancialPhraseBank-v10.

7.1.2. Text Preparation (Cleansing)

The raw text data (i.e., sentences) are initially organized into a data table. The data table contains two columns: The first column (sentence) is for the text, and the second column (sentiment) is for the corresponding sentiment class. The separator character, which is "@" in this case, is used to split the data into text and sentiment class columns. A collection of text data in any form, including list, matrix, or data table forms, is called a **corpus**. Exhibit 28 shows a sample of 10 sentences from the data table corpus.

The raw text contains punctuation, numbers, and white spaces that may not be necessary for model training. Text cleansing involves removing, or incorporating appropriate substitutions for, potentially extraneous information present in the text. Operations to remove html tags are unnecessary because none are present in the text.

Punctuation: Before stripping out punctuation, percentage and dollar symbols are substituted with word annotations to retain their essence in the financial texts. Such word annotation substitutions convey that percentage and currency-related tokens were involved in the text. As the sentences have already been identified within and extracted from the source text, punctuation helpful for identifying discrete sentences—such as periods, semi-colons, and commas—are removed. Some special characters, such as "+" and "©," are also removed. It is a good practice to implement word annotation substitutions before removing the rest of the punctuation.

Numbers: Numerical values of numbers in the text have no significant utility for sentiment prediction in this project because sentiment primarily depends on the words in a sentence. Here is an example sentence: *"Ragutis, which is based in Lithuania's second-largest city,*

EXHIBIT 28   Ten Sample Rows of the Data Table (Corpus)

Sentence	Sentiment
Profit before taxes amounted to EUR 56.5 mn, down from EUR 232.9 mn a year ago.	negative
Profit before taxes decreased by 9 % to EUR 187.8 mn in the first nine months of 2008, compared to EUR 207.1 mn a year earlier.	negative
Profit before taxes decreased to EUR 31.6 mn from EUR 50.0 mn the year before.	negative
Profit before taxes was EUR 4.0 mn, down from EUR 4.9 mn.	negative
The company's profit before taxes fell to EUR 21.1 mn in the third quarter of 2008, compared to EUR 35.8 mn in the corresponding period in 2007.	negative
In August-October 2010, the company's result before taxes totalled EUR 9.6 mn, up from EUR 0.5 mn in the corresponding period in 2009.	positive
Finnish Bore that is owned by the Rettig family has grown recently through the acquisition of smaller shipping companies.	positive
The plan is estimated to generate some EUR 5 million (USD 6.5 m) in cost savings on an annual basis.	positive
Finnish pharmaceuticals company Orion reports profit before taxes of EUR 70.0 mn in the third quarter of 2010, up from EUR 54.9 mn in the corresponding period in 2009.	positive
Finnish Sampo Bank, of Danish Danske Bank group, reports profit before taxes of EUR 152.3 mn in 2010, up from EUR 32.7 mn in 2009.	positive

EXHIBIT 29   Ten Sample Rows After Cleansing Process

Sentence	Sentiment
Profit before taxes amounted to EUR million down from EUR million a year ago	negative
Profit before taxes decreased by percentSign to EUR million in the first nine months of compared to EUR million a year earlier	negative
Profit before taxes decreased to EUR million from EUR million the year before	negative
Profit before taxes was EUR million down from EUR million	negative
The companys profit before taxes fell to EUR million in the third quarter of compared to EUR million in the corresponding period in	negative
In August October the companys result before taxes totalled EUR million up from EUR million in the corresponding period in	positive
Finnish Bore that is owned by the Rettig family has grown recently through the acquisition of smaller shipping companies	positive
The plan is estimated to generate some EUR million USD million in cost savings on an annual basis	positive
Finnish pharmaceuticals company Orion reports profit before taxes of EUR million in the third quarter of up from EUR million in the corresponding period in	positive
Finnish Sampo Bank of Danish Danske Bank group reports profit before taxes of EUR million in up from EUR million in	positive

Kaunas, boosted its sales last year 22.3 percent to 36.4 million litas." The word "boosted" implies that there was growth in sales, so analysis of this sentiment does not need to rely on interpretation of numerical text data. Sentiment analysis typically does not involve extracting, interpreting, and calculating relevant numbers but instead seeks to understand the context in which the numbers are used. Other commonly occurring numbers are dates and years, which are also not required to predict sentence sentiment. Thus, all numbers present in the text are removed for this financial sentiment project. However, prior to removing numbers, abbreviations representing orders of magnitude, such as million (commonly represented by "m," "mln," or "mn"), billion, or trillion, are replaced with the complete word. Retaining these orders of magnitude-identifying words in the text preserves the original text meaning and can be useful in predicting sentence sentiment.

   Whitespaces: White spaces are present in the raw text. Additional white spaces occur after performing the above operations to remove extraneous characters. The white spaces must be removed to keep the text intact. Exhibit 29 shows the sample text after cleansing. The cleansed text is free of punctuation and numbers, with useful substitutions.

7.1.3. Text Wrangling (Preprocessing)
The cleansed text needs to be normalized using the following normalization procedures:

1. *Lowercasing* of all text to consolidate duplicate words (example, "THE," "The," and "the").
2. *Stop words* are not removed because some stop words (e.g., not, more, very, and few) carry significant meaning in the financial texts that is useful for sentiment prediction. Some stop words, such as articles (a, an, the), may be removed. Nevertheless, to avoid

confusion no words are removed at this point. This issue will be revisited during the data exploration stage, which will carefully examine the text using frequency analysis and find custom stop words (common words) for these particular text data.

3. *Stemming,* the converting of inflected forms of a word into its base word (stem), is performed on the text as it is simple to perform and is appropriate for training an ML model for sentiment prediction.

White spaces are stripped after performing these operations. As part of text normalization, different currency abbreviations, such as EUR and USD, can be converted into a single token, such as "currencysign." As we are dealing with financial domain text, the earlier substitution of dollarsign can be replaced with currencysign as well. This step will remove tokens that are different but redundant in nature while maintaining their meaning. Through careful examination of the text and use of domain knowledge, similar substitutions of redundant tokens can be performed. Exhibit 30 shows how the sample text appears after normalization.

The normalized text is tokenized, resulting in 2,673 unique tokens. Altogether, these unique tokens comprise the BOW of the text corpus. Exhibit 31 shows a sample of 100 tokens from the BOW. This preliminary unigram BOW can be used to construct a document term matrix (DTM) for ML training.

The final DTM for ML model training will be prepared after the data exploration stage. Data exploration may reveal unnecessary tokens or anomalies in the data. Any unnecessary tokens that are not informative must be removed, which will also impact the creation of n-grams. Thus, the final DTM must be made after further analyses and operations, such as exploratory data analysis and feature selection.

EXHIBIT 30   Ten Sample Rows After Normalization Process

Sentence	Sentiment
profit befor tax amount to currencysign million down from currencysign million a year ago	negative
profit befor tax decreas by percentsign to currencysign million in the first nine month of compar to currencysign million a year earlier	negative
profit before tax decreas to currencysign million from currencysign million the year befor	negative
profit befor tax was currencysign million down from currencysign million	negative
the compani profit befor tax fell to currencysign million in the third quarter of compar to currencysign million in the correspond period in	negative
in august octob the compani result befor tax total currencysign million up from currencysign million in the correspond period in	positive
finnish bore that is own by the rettig famili has grown recent through the acquisit of smaller shipping company	positive
the plan is estim to generat some currencysign million currencysign million in cost save on an annual basi	positive
finnish pharmaceut compani orion report profit befor tax of currencysign million in the third quarter of up from currencysign million in the correspond period in	positive
finnish sampo bank of danish danske bank group report profit befor tax of currencysign million in up from currencysign million in	positive

EXHIBIT 31   One Hundred Sample Tokens from Preliminary Unigram BOW

"for"	"foundri"	"quarter"	"shop"	"net"	"share"	"to"
"currencysign"	"nokia"	"same"	"plan"	"year"	"sanyo"	"it"
"move"	"nokian"	"tax"	"earn"	"in"	"expect"	"by"
"percentsign"	"director"	"rose"	"dividend"	"total"	"megafon"	"talentum"
"report"	"as"	"chain"	"number"	"consolid"	"accord"	"compar"
"prior"	"last"	"machin"	"componenta"	"afx"	"doubl"	"higher"
"led"	"from"	"announc"	"a"	"with"	"while"	"g"
"handset"	"pre"	"fourth"	"loss"	"analyst"	"increas"	"said"
"board"	"oper"	"propos"	"repres"	"paid"	"finnish"	"base"
"user"	"retail"	"market"	"is"	"late"	"amount"	"estim"
"the"	"divis"	"of"	"helsinki"	"sale"	"close"	
"million"	"after"	"period"	"team"	"earlier"	"manufactur"	
"zero"	"tyre"	"profit"	"beat"	"third"	"dealer"	
"and"	"will"	"correspond"	"per"	"up"	"subscrib"	
"cloth"	"decemb"	"sepp"	"custom"	"reach"	"teliasonera"	

7.2. Data Exploration

7.2.1. Exploratory Data Analysis

Exploratory data analysis (EDA) performed on text data provides insights on word distribution in the text. Word counts from all the sentences are computed. These word counts can be used to examine outlier tokens—words that are most commonly and least commonly present in the texts. The most frequent word occurrences in all sentences from the dataset are shown in Exhibit 32. These common words will be removed during the feature selection step. Notably, the tokens "million" and "currencysign" occur frequently due to the financial nature of the data.

EXHIBIT 32   Most Frequently Used Tokens in the Corpus

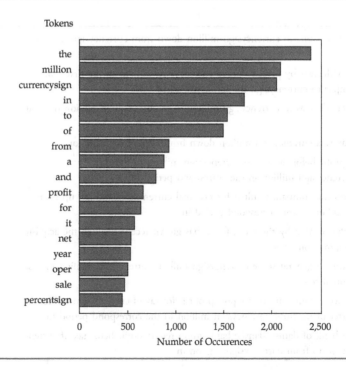

EXHIBIT 33   Most Frequently Used Tokens in Two Sentiment Classes of the Corpus

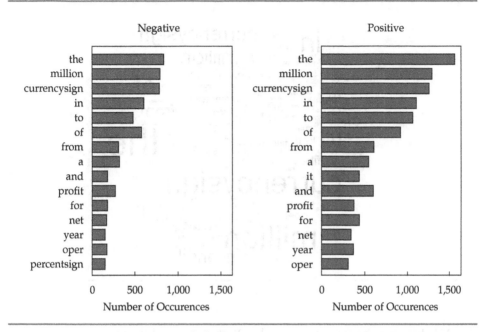

The most frequent word occurrences in the sentences in the negative sentiment and the positive sentiment classes are shown in Exhibit 33. The most commonly occurring words are similar for both sentiment classes, meaning that they are not useful in discriminating between the two sentiment classes. This finding demonstrates the utility of removing the most commonly used tokens from the BOW.

Exhibit 34 shows a histogram of sentence length distribution. **Sentence length** is defined as the number of characters, including spaces, in a sentence. The longest sentence

EXHIBIT 34   Histogram of Sentence Lengths with Mean Sentence Length

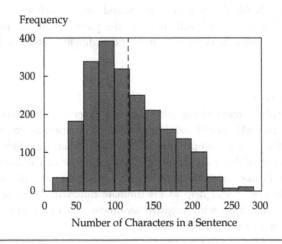

EXHIBIT 35   Word Cloud of Entire Corpus

has 273 characters; the shortest sentence has 26 characters; and the average number of characters is about 120 (indicated by the vertical line). Although this distribution does not have any direct impact on model training, this histogram visually demonstrates the range of sentence lengths and helps identify any extremely long or short sentences. This histogram does not appear unusual, so no outlier sentences need to be removed.

Word clouds are a convenient method of visualizing the text data because they enable rapid comprehension of a large number of tokens and their corresponding weights. Exhibit 35 shows a word cloud for all the sentences in the corpus. The font sizes of the words are proportionate to the number of occurrences of each word in the corpus. Similarly, Exhibit 36 shows the word cloud divided into two halves: one half representing negative sentiment class sentences (upper half); one half representing positive sentiment class sentences (lower half). Notably, some highly discriminative stems and words, such as "decreas" and "down" in the negative half and "increas" and "rose" in the positive half, are present. The feature selection process will eliminate common words and highlight useful words for better model training.

7.2.2. Feature Selection

Exploratory data analysis revealed the most frequent tokens in the texts that could potentially add noise to this ML model training process. In addition to common tokens, many rarely occurring tokens, often proper nouns (i.e., names), are not informative for understanding the sentiment of the sentence. Further analyses must be conducted to decide which words to eliminate. Feature selection for text data involves keeping the useful tokens in the BOW that are informative and help to discriminate different classes of texts—those with positive sentiment and those with negative sentiment. At this point, a total of 44,151 non-unique tokens are in the 2,180 sentences.

EXHIBIT 36 Word Cloud Divided by Two Sub-Groups of the Corpus

Frequency analysis on the processed text data helps in filtering unnecessary tokens (or features) by quantifying how important tokens are in a sentence and in the corpus as a whole. Term frequency (TF) at the corpus level—also known as **collection frequency (CF)**—is the number of times a given word appears in the whole corpus (i.e., collection of sentences) divided by the total number of words in the corpus. Term frequency can be calculated and examined to identify outlier words. Exhibit 37 shows the descriptive statistics of term frequency for the words at the collection level. The statistics of TF range between 0 and 1 because TF values are ratios of total occurrences of a particular word to total number of words in the collection. A sample of words with the highest TF and lowest TF values is also shown to gain insight into what kinds of words occur at these extreme frequencies.

Calculating highest and lowest TFs at the collection level is a general strategy to identify noisy terms. The histogram in Exhibit 37 shows a long tail to the right, which represents common terms that must be removed. The high frequency bars on the left show that there are also many rare terms (e.g., ones appearing only once or twice across the data). Such rare terms do not appear enough to be used as meaningful features and are often removed. The words with the highest TF are mostly stop words that are not useful because they are present in most of the sentences and thus do not contribute to differentiating the sentiment embedded in the text. The words with the lowest TF values are mostly proper nouns or sparse terms that are also not important to the meaning of the text. In this example, after careful examination of words with extreme frequencies, the words with high TF values (>99.5th percentile, 14 words) and low TF values (<30th percentile, 714 words) are removed before forming the final document term matrix (DTM). Exhibit 38 shows the 14 words with the highest TF values (>99.5th percentile) that are the custom stop words for this project.

To construct a DTM for ML training, different TF measures need to be computed to fill in the cells of the DTM. Exhibit 39 displays part of a TF measures table that is computed for the text data before the removal of custom stop words.

EXHIBIT 37   Summary Statistics of TF for Words at the Collection Level, Sample Words with High and Low TF Values, and Histogram of TF Values

Min.	1st Qu.	Median	Mean	3rd Qu.	Max.
2.265e-05	2.265e-05	4.530e-05	3.741e-04	1.585e-04	5.429e-02

word	TF	word	TF
<chr>	<dbl>	<chr>	<dbl>
the	0.05429096	yet	2.264954e-05
million	0.04722430	yihn	2.264954e-05
currencysign	0.04627302	young	2.264954e-05
in	0.03870807	zahariev	2.264954e-05
to	0.03476705	zone	2.264954e-05
of	0.03377047	zoo	2.264954e-05

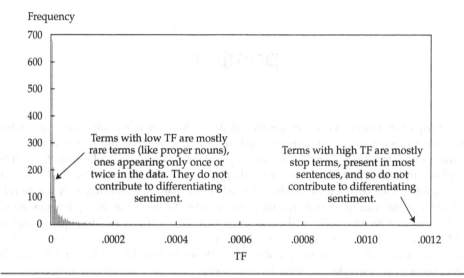

Frequency

Terms with low TF are mostly rare terms (like proper nouns), ones appearing only once or twice in the data. They do not contribute to differentiating sentiment.

Terms with high TF are mostly stop terms, present in most sentences, and so do not contribute to differentiating sentiment.

TF

EXHIBIT 38   Fourteen Custom Stop Words for the Project

"the"	"million"	"currencysign"	"in"	"to"	"of"	"from"
"and"	"profit"	"for"	"it"	"not"	"year"	"a"

EXHIBIT 39   Sample Output of Term Frequency (TF) Measures Table

SentenceNo	TotalWordsInSentence	Word	TotalWordCount	WordCountInSentence	SentenceCountWithWord	TF	DF	IDF	TFIDF
<int>	<int>	<chr>	<int>	<int>	<int>	<dbl>	<dbl>	<dbl>	<dbl>
624	34	a	873	6	687	0.1764706	0.3151376	1.1547459	0.20377868
701	39	the	2397	6	1453	0.1538462	0.6665138	0.4056945	0.06241454
1826	34	a	873	6	687	0.1764706	0.3151376	1.1547459	0.20377868
1963	39	the	2397	6	1453	0.1538462	0.6665138	0.4056945	0.06241454
128	30	of	1491	5	984	0.1666667	0.4513761	0.7954543	0.13257571
223	37	the	2397	5	1453	0.1351351	0.6665138	0.4056945	0.05482358

The columns of the term frequency measures table are as follows:

1. *SentenceNo*: A unique identification number assigned to each sentence in the order they are present in the original dataset. For example, sentence number 701 is a sentence in row 701 from the data table: "*the airlin estim that the cancel of it flight due to the closur of european airspac and the process of recommenc traffic have caus a the compani a loss of currencysign million includ the cost of strand passeng accommod.*"
2. *TotalWordsInSentence*: Count of total number of words present in the sentence. For example, sentence number 701 has a total of 39 words.
3. *Word*: A word token that is present in the corresponding sentence.
4. *TotalWordCount*: Total number of occurrences of the word in the entire corpus or collection. For example, the token "the" occurs 2,397 times in the whole collection of sentences. The following equation can be used to compute TF at the collection level:

$$TF \text{ (Collection Level)} = TotalWordCount/\text{Total number of words in collection} \qquad (10)$$

The TF of the word "the" at the collection level is calculated as $2,397/44,151 = 0.05429096$. Note that this result was seen previously in Exhibit 37.
5. *WordCountInSentence*: Number of times the token is present in the corresponding sentence. For example, token "the" is present six times in sentence number 701.
6. *SentenceCountWithWord*: Number of sentences in which the word is present. For example, the token "the" is present in 1,453 sentences.
7. *TF (Term Frequency) at Sentence Level*: Number of times a word is present in a sentence divided by the total number of words in that sentence. The following equation can be used to compute TF at the sentence level:

$$TF \text{ (Sentence Level)} = WordCountInSentence/TotalWordsInSentence \qquad (11)$$

For example, TF at the sentence level for the word "the" in sentences number 701 and 223 is calculated as $6/39 = 0.1538462$ and $5/37 = 0.1351351$, respectively.
8. *DF (Document Frequency)*: Defined as the number of documents (i.e., sentences) that contain a given word divided by the total number of sentences (here, 2,180). Document frequency is important since words frequently occurring across sentences provide no differentiating information in each sentence. The following equation can be used to compute DF:

$$DF = SentenceCountWithWord/\text{Total number of sentences} \qquad (12)$$

For example, DF of the word "the" is $1,453/2,180 = 0.6665138$; so, 66.7% of the sentences contain the word "the." A high DF indicates high word frequency in the text.
9. *IDF (Inverse Document Frequency)*: A relative measure of how unique a term is across the entire corpus. Its meaning is not directly related to the size of the corpus. The following equation can be used to compute IDF:

$$IDF = \log(1/DF). \qquad (13)$$

For example, IDF of the word "the" is $\log(1/0.6665138) = 0.4056945$. A low IDF indicates high word frequency in the text.

EXHIBIT 40   Sample Output of High TF–IDF Words

SentenceNo	TotalWordsInSentence	Word	TotalWordCount	WordCountInSentence	SentenceCountWithWord	TF	DF	IDF	TFIDF
<int>	<int>	<chr>	<int>	<int>	<int>	<dbl>	<dbl>	<dbl>	<dbl>
28	7	risen	3	1	3	0.1428571	0.0013761468	6.588468	0.9412097
830	7	diminish	2	1	2	0.1428571	0.0009174312	6.993933	0.9991333
1368	9	great	4	1	4	0.1111111	0.0018348624	6.300786	0.7000873
1848	8	injuri	1	1	1	0.1250000	0.0004587156	7.687080	0.9608850
1912	7	cheaper	1	1	1	0.1428571	0.0004587156	7.687080	1.0981543
1952	6	argument	1	1	1	0.1666667	0.0004587156	7.687080	1.2811800

10. *TF–IDF*: To get a complete representation of the value of each word, TF at the *sentence level* is multiplied by the IDF of a word across the entire dataset. Higher TF–IDF values indicate words that appear more frequently within a smaller number of documents. This signifies relatively more unique terms that are important. Conversely, a low TF–IDF value indicates terms that appear in many documents. TF–IDF values can be useful in measuring the key terms across a compilation of documents and can serve as word feature values for training an ML model. The following equation can be used to compute TF–IDF:

$$TF\text{–}IDF = TF \times IDF \tag{14}$$

For example, TF–IDF of the token "of" is calculated as $0.1666667 \times 0.7954543 = 0.13257571$.

Similarly, Exhibit 40 shows high TF–IDF words for the text data before the removal of custom stop words.

TF or TF–IDF values are placed at the intersection of sentences (rows) and terms (columns) of the document term matrix. For this project, TF values are used for the DTM as the texts are sentences rather than paragraphs or other larger bodies of text. TF–IDF values vary by the *number* of documents in the dataset; therefore, the model performance can vary when applied to a dataset with just a few documents. In addition to removing custom stop words and sparse terms, single character letters are also eliminated because they do not add any value to the sentiment significance.

7.2.3. Feature Engineering

N-grams are used as a feature engineering process in this project. Use of n-grams helps to understand the sentiment of a sentence as a whole. As mentioned previously, the objective of this project is to predict sentiment class (positive and negative) from financial texts. Both unigram and bigrams are implemented, and the BOW is created from them. Bigram tokens are helpful for keeping negations intact in the text, which is vital for sentiment prediction. For example, the tokens "not" and "good" or "no" and "longer" can be formed into single tokens, now bigrams, such as "not_good" and "no_longer." These and similar tokens can be useful during ML model training and can improve model performance. Exhibit 41 shows a sample of 100 words from the BOW containing both unigram and bigram tokens after removal of custom stop words, sparse terms, and single characters. Note that the BOW contains such tokens as increas, loss, loss_prior, oper_rose, tax_loss, and sale_increas. Such tokens are informative about the embedded sentiment in the texts and are useful for training an ML model. The corresponding word frequency measures for the document term matrix are computed based on this new BOW.

EXHIBIT 41   One-Hundred Sample Tokens from Final BOW of Entire Corpus

"last"	"last_quarter"	"quarter"	"quarter_componenta"	"componenta"
"componenta_sale"	"sale"	"sale_doubl"	"doubl"	"doubl_same"
"same"	"same_period"	"period"	"period_earlier"	"earlier"
"earlier_while"	"while"	"while_move"	"move"	"move_zero"
"zero"	"zero_pre"	"pre"	"pre_tax"	"tax"
"tax_pre"	"tax_loss"	"loss"	"third"	"third_quarter"
"quarter_sale"	"sale_increas"	"increas"	"increas_by"	"by"
"by_percentsign"	"percentsign"	"percentsign_oper"	"oper"	"oper_by"
"oper_rose"	"rose"	"rose_correspond"	"correspond"	"correspond_period"
"period_repres"	"repres"	"repres_percentsign"	"percentsign_sale"	"oper_total"
"total"	"total_up"	"up"	"up_repres"	"finnish"
"finnish_talentum"	"talentum"	"talentum_report"	"report"	"report_oper"
"oper_increas"	"increas_sale"	"sale_total"	"cloth"	"cloth_retail"
"retail"	"retail_chain"	"chain"	"chain_sepp"	"sepp"
"sepp_ls"	"ls"	"ls_sale"	"consolid"	"consolid_sale"
"incres_percentsign"	"percentsign_reach"	"reach"	"reach_while"	"while_oper"
"oper_amount"	"amount"	"amount_compar"	"compar"	"compar_loss"
"loss_prior"	"prior"	"prior_period"	"foundri"	"foundri_divis"
"divis"	"divis_report"	"report_sale"	"percentsign_correspond"	"period_sale"
"sale_machin"	"machin"	"machin_shop"	"shop"	"shop_divis"

EXAMPLE 6   Calculating and Interpreting Term Frequency Measures

Data scientists Jack and Jill are using financial text data to develop sentiment indicators for forecasting future stock price movements. They have assembled a BOW from the corpus of text being examined and have pulled the following abbreviated term frequency measures tables.

Term Frequency Measures Table 1

SentenceNo	TotalWordsInSentence	Word	TotalWordCount	WordCountInSentence	SentenceCountWithWord
<int>	<int>	<chr>	<int>	<int>	<int>
624	34	a	873	6	687
701	39	the	2397	6	1453
1826	34	a	873	6	687
1963	39	the	2397	6	1453
128	30	of	1491	5	984
223	37	the	2397	5	1453

Term Frequency Measures Table 2

SentenceNo	TotalWordsInSentence	Word	TotalWordCount	WordCountInSentence	SentenceCountWithWord
<int>	<int>	<chr>	<int>	<int>	<int>
28	7	risen	3	1	3
830	7	diminish	2	1	2
1368	9	great	4	1	4
1848	8	injuri	1	1	1
1912	7	cheaper	1	1	1
1952	6	argument	1	1	1

1. Determine and interpret term frequency (TF) at the collection level and at the sentence level for the word (i.e., token) "a" in sentence 1,826 in term frequency measures Table 1 and then for the token "great" in sentence 1,368 in term frequency measures Table 2.
2. Determine and interpret TF–IDF (term frequency–inverse document frequency) for the word "a" in sentence 1,826 in term frequency measures Table 1 and then for the token "great" in sentence 1,368 in term frequency measures Table 2.

Solution to 1: TF at the collection level is calculated using Equation 10:

TF (Collection Level) = TotalWordCount/Total number of words in collection.

For token "a" in sentence 1,826 (Table 1), TF (Collection Level) is 873/44,151 = 0.019773 or 1.977 percent.

For token "great" in sentence 1,368 (Table 2), TF (Collection Level) is 4/44,151 = 0.000091 or 0.009%.

TF at the collection level is an indicator of the frequency, in percentage terms, that a token is used throughout the whole collection of texts (here, 44,151). It is useful for identifying outlier words: Tokens with highest TF values are mostly stop words that do not contribute to differentiating the sentiment embedded in the text (such as "a"), and tokens with lowest TF values are mostly proper nouns or sparse terms that are also not important to the meaning of the text. Conversely, tokens with intermediate TF values potentially carry important information useful for differentiating the sentiment embedded in the text.

TF at the sentence level is calculated using Equation 11:

$$TF \text{ (Sentence Level)} = WordCountInSentence/TotalWordsInSentence.$$

For token "a" in sentence 1,826, TF (Sentence Level) is 6/34 = 0.176471 or 17.647 percent.

For token "great" in sentence 1,368, TF (Sentence Level) is 1/9 = 0.111111 or 11.111 percent.

TF at the sentence level is an indicator of the frequency, in percentage terms, that a token is used in a particular sentence (i.e., instance). Therefore, it is useful for understanding the importance of the specific token in a given sentence.

Solution to 2: To calculate TF–IDF, besides TF at the sentence level, document frequency (DF) and inverse document frequency (IDF) are also required.

DF is the number of documents (i.e., sentences) that contain a given word divided by the total number of sentences in the corpus (here, 2,180). DF is calculated using Equation 12:

$$DF = SentenceCountWithWord/Total \text{ number of sentences.}$$

For token "a" in sentence 1,826, DF is 687/2,180 = 0.315138 or 31.514 percent.
For token "great" in sentence 1,368, DF is 4/2,180 = 0.001835 or 0.184 percent.

Document frequency is important since tokens occurring frequently across sentences (such as "a") provide no differentiating information in each sentence. Tokens occurring less frequently across sentences (such as "great"), however, may provide useful differentiating information.

IDF is a relative measure of how important a term is across the entire corpus (i.e., collection of texts/sentences). IDF is calculated using Equation 13:

$$IDF = \log(1/DF).$$

For token "a" in sentence 1,826, IDF is log(1/0.315138) = 1.154746.
For token "great" in sentence 1,368, IDF is log(1/0.001835) = 6.300786.
Using TF and IDF, TF–IDF can now be calculated using Equation 14:

$$TF\text{–}IDF = TF \times IDF.$$

> For token "a" in sentence 1,826, TF–IDF = 0.176471 × 1.154746 = 0.203779, or 20.378 percent.
> For token "great" in sentence 1,368, TF–IDF = 0.111111 × 6.300786 = 0.700087, or 70.009 percent.
> As TF–IDF combines TF at the *sentence level* with IDF across the entire corpus, it provides a complete representation of the value of each word. A high TF–IDF value indicates the word appears many times within a small number of documents, signifying an important yet unique term within a sentence (such as "great"). A low TF–IDF value indicates tokens that appear in most of the sentences and are not discriminative (such as "a"). TF–IDF values are useful in extracting the key terms in a document for use as features for training an ML model.

7.3. Model Training

The sentiment class labels (positive and negative) constitute the target variable (y) for model training. They are relabeled as 1 (for positive) and 0 (for negative) to enable calculating the performance metrics, such as receiver operating characteristic (ROC) curve and area under the curve (AUC) from the trained model results. The master dataset that has been cleansed and preprocessed is partitioned into three separate sets: 1) training set; 2) cross-validation (CV) set; and 3) test set. These are in the ratio of 60:20:20, respectively (following common practice). For splitting, simple random sampling is applied within levels of the target variable to balance the class distributions within the splits. The final DTM is built using the sentences (rows), which are the instances, and resulting tokens (columns), which are the feature variables, from the BOW of the training dataset. The final BOW consists of unigram and bigram tokens from the sentences in the training corpus only. The DTM is then filled in with resultant TF values of the tokens from the training corpus.

Similarly, the DTMs for the CV set and the test set are built using tokens from the final training BOW for tuning, validating, and testing of the model. To be clear, the final BOW from the training corpus is used for building DTMs across all the splits because the model has been trained on that final BOW. Thus, the columns (think, features) of all three DTMs are the same, but the number of rows varies because a different number of sentences are in each split. The DTMs are filled with resultant term frequency values calculated using sentences in the corpuses of the respective splits—sentences from the CV set corpus and sentences from the test set corpus. Exhibit 42 tabulates the summary of dimensions of the data splits and their uses in the model training process. As mentioned, the columns of DTMs for the splits are the same, equal to the number of unique tokens (i.e., features) from the final training corpus BOW, which is 9,188. Note that this number of unique tokens (9,188) differs from that in the master corpus (11,501) based on the sentences that are included in the training corpus after the random sampling.

7.3.1. Method Selection

Alternative ML methods, including SVM, decision trees, and logistic regression, were examined because these techniques are all considered potentially suitable for this particular task (i.e., supervised learning), type of data (i.e., text), and size of data (i.e., wider data with

EXHIBIT 42   Summary of the Three Data Splits

Corpus	Split %	Number of Sentences	DTM Dimensions	Purpose
Master	100%	2180	2180 × 11501	Used for data exploration
Training	60%	1309	1309 × 9188	Used for ML model training
CV	20%	435	435 × 9188	Used for tuning and validating the trained model
Test	20%	436	436 × 9188	Used for testing the trained, tuned, and validated model

many potential variables). The SVM and logistic regression methods appeared to offer better performance than decision trees. For brevity, we discuss logistic regression in the remainder of the chapter. Logistic regression was used to train the model, using the training corpus DTM containing 1,309 sentences. As a reminder, in this project texts are the sentences and the classifications are positive and negative sentiment classes (labeled 1 and 0, respectively). The tokens are feature variables, and the sentiment class is the target variable. Text data typically contain thousands of tokens. These result in sparse DTMs because each column represents a token feature and the values are mostly zeros (i.e., not all the tokens are present in every text). Logistic regression can deal with such sparse training data because the regression coefficients will be close to zero for tokens that are not present in a significant number of sentences. This allows the model to ignore a large number of minimally useful features. Regularization further helps lower the coefficients when the features rarely occur and do not contribute to the model training.

Logistic regression is applied on the final training DTM for model training. As this method uses maximum likelihood estimation, the output of the logistic model is a probability value ranging from 0 to 1. However, because the target variable is binary, coefficients from the logistic regression model are not directly used to predict the value of the target variable. Rather, a mathematical function uses the logistic regression coefficient (β) to calculate probability (p) of sentences having positive sentiment ($y = 1$).[3] If p for a sentence is 0.90, there is a 90% likelihood that the sentence has positive sentiment. Theoretically, the sentences with p > 0.50 likely have positive sentiment. Because this is not always true in practice, however, it is important to find an ideal threshold value of p. We elaborate on this point in a subsequent example. The threshold value is a cutoff point for p values, and the ideal threshold p value is influenced by the dataset and model training. When the p values (i.e., probability of sentences having positive sentiment) of sentences are above this ideal threshold p value, then the sentences are *highly* likely to have positive sentiment ($y = 1$). The ideal threshold p value is estimated heuristically using performance metrics and ROC curves, as will be demonstrated shortly.

7.3.2. Performance Evaluation and Tuning
The trained ML model is used to predict the sentiments of the sentences in the training and CV DTMs. Exhibit 43 displays the ROC curves for the training (Panel A) and CV

---

[3]This mathematical function is an exponential function of the form: $P(y = 1) = \frac{1}{1+\exp^{-(\beta_0+\beta_1 x_1+\beta_2 x_2+\cdots+\beta_n x_n)}}$ where the βs are the logistic regression coefficients.

(Panel B) data. Remember that the x-axis is false positive rate, FP/(TN + FP), and the y-axis is true positive rate, TP/(TP + FN). As the model is trained using the training DTM, it clearly performs well on the same training data (so there is no concern about underfitting) but does not perform as well on the CV data. This is apparent as the ROC curves are significantly different between the training and CV datasets. The AUC is 96.5 percent on training data and 86.2 percent on CV data. This finding suggests that the model performs comparatively poorly (with a higher rate of error or misclassification) on the CV data when compared to training data. Thus, the implication is that the model is overfitted.

As the model is overfitted, least absolute shrinkage and selection operator (LASSO) regularization is applied to the logistic regression. LASSO regularization penalizes the coefficients of the logistic regression to prevent overfitting of the model. The penalized regression will select the tokens (features) that have statistically significant (i.e., non-zero) coefficients and that contribute to the model fit; LASSO does this while disregarding the other tokens. Exhibit 44 shows the ROC curves for the new model that uses regularized logistic regression. The ROC curves look similar for model performance on both datasets, with an AUC of 95.7 percent on the training dataset (Panel A) and 94.8 percent on the CV dataset (Panel B). These findings suggest that the model performs similarly on both training and CV data and thus indicate a good fitting model (one that is not overfitted).

Regularization along with careful feature selection help to prevent overfitting in logistic regression models. Another model was trained using all token features, including stop words, sparse terms, and single characters, with no regularization. That model showed an AUC of 99.1 percent when applied on the training dataset and an AUC of 89.4 percent when applied on the CV dataset, suggesting that the model is overfitting. As the AUC values in all of the models discussed are not far from 100 percent, these models are clearly not underfitting. In sum, the final ML model for this project uses logistic regression with LASSO regularization.

To further evaluate the model, error analysis is conducted by calculating a confusion matrix using the ML model results from the cross-validation dataset. The threshold p value of 0.5 is used as a cutoff point. When target value p > 0.5, the prediction is assumed to be $y = 1$ (meaning, positive sentiment). Otherwise, the prediction is assumed to be $y = 0$

EXHIBIT 43   ROC Curves of Model Results for Training and CV Data Before Regularization

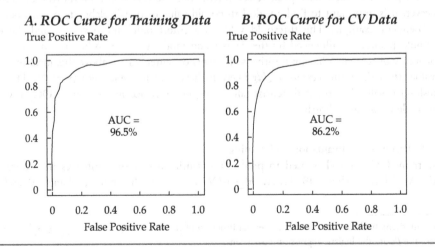

A. ROC Curve for Training Data

True Positive Rate

AUC = 96.5%

False Positive Rate

B. ROC Curve for CV Data

True Positive Rate

AUC = 86.2%

False Positive Rate

EXHIBIT 44   ROC Curves of Model Results for Training and CV Data After Regularization

A. ROC Curve for Training Data

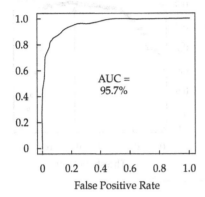

B. ROC Curve for CV Data

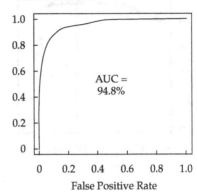

(negative sentiment). A confusion matrix, with performance metrics and overall scores for the model results using the CV data, is shown in Exhibit 45.

The model accuracy is 90 percent with a theoretically suggested (default) threshold p value of 0.5. The CV data are used to tune the threshold value for best model performance. Various p values from 0.01 to 0.99 are systematically evaluated individually, and confusion matrixes and performance metrics are calculated using each of these p values. Based on these metrics, the p value resulting in the highest model accuracy is selected as the ideal threshold p value. However, there are often trade-offs: Minimizing false positives (FPs) comes at a cost of increasing false negatives (FNs), and vice versa. Prioritizing various performance statistics (e.g., precision versus recall) depends on the context and relative consequences of FP and FN on the project applications. In this project, the values of negative sentiment and positive

EXHIBIT 45   Confusion Matrix of Model Results for CV Data with Threshold p Value = 0.50

Confusion Matrix for CV Data with Threshold = 0.5

		Actual Training Labels	
		Class "1"	Class "0"
Predicted Results	Class "1"	284 (TP)	38 (FP)
	Class "0"	7 (FN)	106 (TN)

Performance Metrics

$$TP = 284, FP = 38, FN = 7, TN = 106$$
$$P = 284 \ / \ (284+38) = 0.88$$
$$R = 284 \ / \ (284+7) = 0.98$$
$$F1 \ Score = (2 \times 0.88 \times 0.98) \ / \ (0.88 + 0.98) = 0.93$$
$$Accuracy = (284 + 106) \ / \ (284 + 38 + 106 + 7) = 0.90$$

EXHIBIT 46   Threshold Values Versus Overall Performance Measures

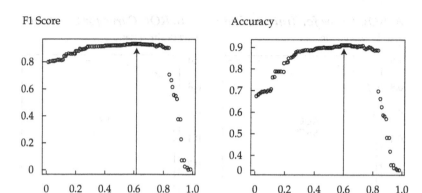

sentiment sentences are assumed to be equal, thus the impacts of FP and FN are also equal. It is common practice to simulate many model results using different threshold p values and to search for maximized accuracy and F1 statistics that minimize these trade-offs. As noted earlier, accuracy and F1 scores are overall performance measures that give equal weight to FP and FN.

Exhibit 46 shows the overall performance measures (i.e., F1 score and accuracy) for various threshold p values. The threshold p value that results in the highest accuracy and F1 score can now be identified. From the charts in Exhibit 45, the ideal threshold p value appears to be around 0.60. To investigate further, a table of performance measures (i.e., precision, recall, F1 score, and accuracy) is generated for a series of threshold p values ranging from 0.45 to 0.75. The table in Exhibit 47 demonstrates that threshold p values between 0.60 and 0.63 result in the highest accuracy and F1 score for the CV dataset. As a result of this analysis, a final threshold p value of 0.60 is selected.

Finally, the confusion matrix using the ideal threshold p value of 0.60 is constructed to observe the performance of the final model. When target value p > 0.60, the prediction is assumed to be $y = 1$ (indicating positive sentiment); otherwise, the prediction is assumed to be $y = 0$ (negative sentiment). The confusion matrix for the CV data is shown in Exhibit 48. It is clear that the model performance metrics have improved in the final model compared to the earliest case when the threshold p value was 0.50. Now, the accuracy and F1 score have both increased by one percentage point to 91 percent and 94 percent, respectively, while precision has increased by two percentage points to 90 percent.

7.4. Results and Interpretation

The final ML model with the appropriate threshold p value has been validated and is now ready for use. The model can be used to predict the sentiment of new sentences from the test data corpus as well as new sentences from similar financial text data sources, such as news wires, earnings call transcripts, and quarterly financial reports. The final model is a collection of penalized regression coefficients for unigram and bigram tokens from the BOW of the training corpus. To use the model to predict the sentiment of new sentences, tokenization

EXHIBIT 47   Performance Measures of the Model for a Series of Threshold Values

Threshold	Precision	Recall	F1	Accuracy
0.45	0.8750000	0.986254296	0.927302100	0.8965517
0.46	0.8827160	0.982817869	0.930081301	0.9011494
0.47	0.8827160	0.982817869	0.930081301	0.9011494
0.48	0.8819876	0.975945017	0.926590538	0.8965517
0.49	0.8819876	0.975945017	0.926590538	0.8965517
0.50	0.8819876	0.975945017	0.926590538	0.8965517
0.51	0.8819876	0.975945017	0.926590538	0.8965517
0.52	0.8819876	0.975945017	0.926590538	0.8965517
0.53	0.8902821	0.975945017	0.931147541	0.9034483
0.54	0.8930818	0.975945017	0.932676519	0.9057471
0.55	0.8930818	0.975945017	0.932676519	0.9057471
0.56	0.8958991	0.975945017	0.934210526	0.9080460
0.57	0.8958991	0.975945017	0.934210526	0.9080460
0.58	0.8958991	9.975945017	0.934210526	0.9080460
0.59	0.9015873	0.975945017	0.937293729	0.9126437
0.60	0.9044586	0.975945017	0.938842975	0.9149425
0.61	0.9044586	0.975945017	0.938842975	0.9149425
0.62	0.9044586	0.975945017	0.938842975	0.9149425
0.63	0.9041534	0.972508591	0.937086093	0.9126437
0.64	0.9041534	0.972508591	0.937086093	0.9126537
0.65	0.9041534	0.972508591	0.937086093	0.9126437
0.66	0.9035370	0.965635739	0.933554817	0.9080460
0.67	0.9035370	0.965635739	0.933554817	0.9080460
0.68	0.9064516	0.965635739	0.935108153	0.9103448
0.69	0.9064516	0.965635739	0.935108153	0.9103448
0.70	0.9061489	0.962199313	0.933333333	0.9080460
0.71	0.9061489	0.962199313	0.933333333	0.9080460
0.72	0.9090909	0.962199313	0.934891486	0.9103448
0.73	0.9090909	0.962199313	0.934891486	0.9103448
0.74	0.9078947	0.948453608	0.927731092	0.9011494
0.75	0.9072848	0.941580756	0.924114671	0.8965517

*The shaded row shows the selected threshold p value (0.60) and the performance metrics for the selected model.

EXHIBIT 48   Confusion Matrix of Model Results for CV Data with Threshold p Value = 0.60

Confusion Matrix for CV Data with Threshold = 0.6

		Actual Training Labels	
		Class "1"	Class "0"
Predicted Results	Class "1"	284 (TP)	30 (FP)
	Class "0"	7 (FN)	114 (TN)

Performance Metrics

TP = 284, FP = 30, FN = 7, TN = 114

P = 284 / (284+30) = 0.90

R = 284 / (284+7) = 0.98

F1 Score = (2 × 0.90 × 0.98) / (0.90 + 0.98) = 0.94

Accuracy = (284 + 114) / (284 + 30 + 114 + 7) = 0.91

and identical cleansing and preprocessing operations must be performed on the new sentences. All the processes performed on the training data must be performed on the new data to which the model will be applied (as was done for the test dataset). The model will use the trained penalized regression coefficients on the term frequency (TF) values of the tokens in the document term matrix (DTM) of the new sentences and will determine the target value (p). The columns of the DTM of the new sentences are the same as those of the training DTM, but the TF values are calculated based on the test corpus. Using the threshold p value of 0.60, the sentiment class for each sentence in the test corpus will be predicted.

The model is now applied on the test data that contains 436 sentences. Note that the test data were not used to train or validate/tune the model and are new to the model. The test data were preprocessed identically to the training and CV data while a part of the master corpus. The model is then applied to the test DTM, and the results are obtained. Exhibit 49 displays 30 sample results from the test corpus. The results table contains cleansed and preprocessed sentences, actual sentiment, target p values from the model, and predicted sentiment. Note that this sample contains three cases of misclassification: the 10th sentence (text), where p = 0.46; the 26th text, where p = 0.77; and the 30th text, where p = 0.71. Therefore, accuracy of this 30-text sample is 27/30 = 90 percent.

EXHIBIT 49   Thirty Sample Results of Test Data

Sentence	Sentiment	p	Predicted Sentiment
exclude non recur item pre tax surg percentsign	1	0.81	1
adp news feb finnish retail kesko oyj hel kesbv said today total sale exclud valu ad tax vat stood at januari down percentsign on yea	0	0.12	0
india trade with russia current stand at four billion dollar grow per cent fiscal	1	0.83	1
refin margin was bbl combar bbl prior	1	0.81	1

Sentence	Sentiment	p	Predicted Sentiment
scania morgan Stanley lift share target on swedish heavi duti truck bus maker scania ab crown euro crown euro	1	0.83	1
deal is like bring save	1	0.83	1
will also strengthen ruukki offshore busi	1	0.83	1
last week finnish metl technolog group announc plan sell more than percent technolog unit further compani strategy goal becom world largest stainless steel maker	1	0.83	1
nest oil board propos dividend full compar with ago	1	0.81	1
pre tax loss total compar loss first quarter	1	0.46	0
pretax total compar loss fourth quarter	1	0.74	1
re use back into pet bottle has also steadili increas rate use strap tape has pick up again after dip pector said previous	1	0.95	1
satama sale would be higher than befor	1	0.83	1
octob finnish wood product technolog supplier raut oyj hel rutav said today swung first nine month versus loss same period earlier	1	0.79	1
ebit total compar loss correspond period	1	0.74	1
finnish consum packag manufactur huhtamaki oyj said swung euro first nine month loss euro same period	1	0.77	1
finnish dental care group oral hammaslaakarit oyj post total euro first nine month versus loss euro same period	1	0.79	1
finnish silicon water manufactur okmet oyj said swung euro first nine month loss euro earlier	1	0.77	1
adp news feb finnish print circuit board pcb maker aspocomp group oyj hel acg said today swung versus loss	1	0.79	1
mn pretax third quarter	1	0.83	1
oper total compar correspond period	1	0.81	1
raut post euro third quarter compar loss euro correspond period	1	0.74	1
russian export duti will active harvest finland sale russia will increas also	1	0.91	1
compani expect sale signific increas	1	0.91	1
compani amount ee which was percentsign more than	1	0.81	1
third quarter fiscal efor swung loss versus correspond period fiscal	0	0.77	1
acando ab acanb ss fell percent kronor lowest close sinc dec	0	0.20	0
compani oper loss total compar	0	0.27	0
last paseng flew airlin down percent	0	0.12	0
loss after financi item total compar correspond period	0	0.71	1

EXHIBIT 50   Confusion Matrix of Model Results for Test Data with Threshold p Value = 0.60

Confusion Matrix for Test Data

		Actual Training Labels	
		Class "1"	Class "0"
Predicted Results	Class "1"	284 (TP)	35 (FP)
	Class "0"	7 (FN)	110 (TN)

Performance Metrics

TP = 284, FP = 35, FN = 7, TN = 110

P = 284 / (284+35) = 0.89

R = 284 / (284+7) = 0.98

F1 Score = (2 × 0.89 × 0.98) / (0.89 + 0.98) = 0.93

Accuracy = (284 + 110) / (284 + 35 + 110 + 7) = 0.90

Exhibit 50 shows the confusion matrix for the test data. Accuracy and F1 score are 90 percent and 93 percent, respectively, while precision and recall are 89 percent and 98 percent, respectively. Therefore, it is apparent that the model performs similarly on the training, CV, and test datasets. These findings suggest that the model is robust and is not overfitting. They also suggest that the model should generalize well out-of-sample and can thus be used to predict the sentiment classes for new sentences from similar financial text data sources. Of course, these new text data must first be subjected to identical tokenization, cleansing, and preprocessing as done for the training dataset.

To recap, this project involves converting unstructured data (i.e., text data from financial data sources) into structured data (i.e., tokens, sentences, and term frequency values) in a document term matrix that is used as input for training, validating, and testing machine learning-based models (here, logistic regression) for predicting classification (here, sentiment classes). Similar models can be built and used in different contexts to understand the sentiment embedded in larger texts. The derived sentiment classification can be useful as a visualization tool to provide insight about the text without reading large documents. These sentiment classifications can also be used as structured input data for larger ML models that have a specific purpose, such as to predict future stock price movements.

EXAMPLE 7   Comparing Performance Metrics for Confusion Matrixes with Different Threshold p Values

In the previous analysis using the cross-validation dataset, performance measures for the sentiment classification ML model were calculated for a wide range (from 0.45 to 0.75) of threshold p values. The threshold value of 0.60 was determined to be the p value that maximizes model accuracy and F1 score; the confusion matrix for this model is shown in Exhibit 48. Use the following confusion matrixes with threshold p values of 0.75 and 0.45, A and B, respectively, to answer the following questions.

Confusion Matrix A
Confusion Matrix for CV, Threshold = 0.75

N = 436		Actual Training Labels	
		Class "1"	Class "0"
Predicted Results	Class "1"	281	28
	Class "0"	17	110

Confusion Matrix B
Confusion Matrix for CV, Threshold = 0.45

N = 436		Actual Training Labels	
		Class "1"	Class "0"
Predicted Results	Class "1"	281	41
	Class "0"	4	110

Performance Metrics

TP = 281, FP = 28, FN = 17, TN = 110
Precision = TP/(TP + FP) = 0.91
Recall = TP/(TP + FN) = 0.94
F1 Score = HMean: Prec. & Recall = 0.93
Accuracy = (TP + TN)/N = 0.90

Performance Metrics

TP = 281, FP = 41, FN = 4, TN = 110
Precision = TP/(TP + FP) = 0.87
Recall = TP/(TP + FN) = 0.99
F1 Score = HMean: Prec. & Recall = 0.93
Accuracy = (TP + TN)/N = 0.90

1. Compare the performance metrics of confusion matrix A (using a threshold p value of 0.75) with the confusion matrix in Exhibit 48 (using a threshold p value of 0.60).
2. Compare the performance metrics of confusion matrix B (using a threshold p value of 0.45) with the confusion matrix in Exhibit 48 (using a threshold p value of 0.60).
3. Contrast the performance metrics of confusion matrixes A and B, and explain the trade-offs implied between them.

Solution to 1: Since confusion matrix A has fewer true positives (TPs) and fewer true negatives (TNs) than the confusion matrix in Exhibit 48 (281 vs. 284 and 110 vs. 114, respectively), confusion matrix A has lower accuracy and a lower F1 score compared to the one in Exhibit 48 (0.90 vs. 0.91 and 0.93 vs. 0.94, respectively). Also, although confusion matrix A has slightly better precision, 0.91 vs. 0.90, due to a few less false positives (FPs), it has significantly lower recall, 0.94 vs. 0.98, due to having many more false negatives (FNs), 17 vs. 7, than the confusion matrix in Exhibit 48. On balance, the ML model using the threshold p value of 0.60 is the superior model for this sentiment classification problem.

Solution to 2: Confusion matrix B has the same number of TPs (281) and TNs (110) as confusion matrix A. Therefore, confusion matrix B also has lower accuracy (0.90) and a lower F1 score (0.93) compared to the one in Exhibit 48. Although confusion matrix B has slightly better recall, 0.99 vs. 0.98, due to fewer FNs, it has somewhat lower precision, 0.87 vs. 0.90, due to having many more FPs, 41 vs. 30, than the confusion matrix in Exhibit 48. Again, it is apparent that the ML model using the threshold p value of 0.60 is the better model in this sentiment classification context.

Solution to 3: The main differences in performance metrics between confusion matrixes A and B are in precision and recall. Confusion matrix A has higher precision, at 0.91 vs. 0.87, but confusion matrix B has higher recall, at 0.99 vs. 0.94. These differences highlight the trade-off between FP (Type I error) and FN (Type II error). Precision is useful when the cost of FP is high, such as when an expensive product that is fine mistakenly fails quality inspection and is scrapped; in this case, FP should be minimized. Recall is useful when the cost of FN is high, such as when an expensive product is defective but mistakenly passes quality inspection and is sent to the customer; in this case, FN should be minimized. In the context of sentiment classification, FP might result in buying a stock for which sentiment is incorrectly classified as positive when it is actually negative. Conversely, FN might result in avoiding (or even shorting) a stock for which the sentiment is incorrectly classified as negative when it is actually positive. The model behind the confusion matrix in Exhibit 48 strikes a balance in the trade-off between precision and recall.

8. SUMMARY

In this chapter, we have discussed the major steps in big data projects involving the development of machine learning (ML) models—namely, those combining textual big data with structured inputs.

- Big data—defined as data with volume, velocity, variety, and potentially lower veracity—has tremendous potential for various fintech applications, including several related to investment management.
- The main steps for traditional ML model building are conceptualization of the problem, data collection, data preparation and wrangling, data exploration, and model training.
- For textual ML model building, the first four steps differ somewhat from those used in the traditional model: Text problem formulation, text curation, text preparation and wrangling, and text exploration are typically necessary.
- For structured data, data preparation and wrangling entail data cleansing and data preprocessing. Data cleansing typically involves resolving incompleteness errors, invalidity errors, inaccuracy errors, inconsistency errors, non-uniformity errors, and duplication errors.
- Preprocessing for structured data typically involves performing the following transformations: extraction, aggregation, filtration, selection, and conversion.
- Preparation and wrangling text (unstructured) data involves a set of text-specific cleansing and preprocessing tasks. Text cleansing typically involves removing the following: html tags, punctuation, most numbers, and white spaces.
- Text preprocessing requires performing normalization that involves the following: lowercasing, removing stop words, stemming, lemmatization, creating bag of words (BOW) and n-grams, and organizing the BOW and n-grams into a document term matrix (DTM).
- Data exploration encompasses exploratory data analysis, feature selection, and feature engineering. Whereas histograms, box plots, and scatterplots are common techniques for exploring structured data, word clouds are an effective way to gain a high-level picture of the composition of textual content. These visualization tools help share knowledge among the team (business subject matter experts, quants, technologists, etc.) to help derive optimal solutions.
- Feature selection methods used for text data include term frequency, document frequency, chi-square test, and a mutual information measure. Feature engineering for text data includes converting numbers into tokens, creating n-grams, and using name entity recognition and parts of speech to engineer new feature variables.
- The model training steps (method selection, performance evaluation, and model tuning) often do not differ much for structured versus unstructured data projects.

- Model selection is governed by the following factors: whether the data project involves labeled data (supervised learning) or unlabeled data (unsupervised learning); the type of data (numerical, continuous, or categorical; text data; image data; speech data; etc.); and the size of the dataset.
- Model performance evaluation involves error analysis using confusion matrixes, determining receiver operating characteristics, and calculating root mean square error.
- To carry out an error analysis for each model, a confusion matrix is created; true positives (TPs), true negatives (TNs), false positives (FPs), and false negatives (FNs) are determined. Then, the following performance metrics are calculated: accuracy, F1 score, precision, and recall. The higher the accuracy and F1 score, the better the model performance.
- To carry out receiver operating characteristic (ROC) analysis, ROC curves and area under the curve (AUC) of various models are calculated and compared. The more convex the ROC curve and the higher the AUC, the better the model performance.
- Model tuning involves managing the trade-off between model bias error, associated with underfitting, and model variance error, associated with overfitting. A fitting curve of in-sample (training sample) error and out-of-sample (cross-validation sample) error on the y-axis versus model complexity on the x-axis is useful for managing the bias vs. variance error trade-off.
- In a real-world big data project involving text data analysis for classifying and predicting sentiment of financial text for particular stocks, the text data are transformed into structured data for populating the DTM, which is then used as the input for the ML algorithm.
- To derive term frequency (TF) at the sentence level and TF–IDF, both of which can be inputs to the DTM, the following frequency measures should be used to create a term frequency measures table: TotalWordsInSentence; TotalWordCount; TermFrequency (Collection Level); WordCountInSentence; SentenceCountWithWord; Document Frequency; and Inverse Document Frequency.

PRACTICE PROBLEMS

The following information relates to Questions 1–15

Aaliyah Schultz is a fixed-income portfolio manager at Aries Investments. Schultz supervises Ameris Steele, a junior analyst.

A few years ago, Schultz developed a proprietary machine learning (ML) model that aims to predict downgrades of publicly-traded firms by bond rating agencies. The model currently relies only on structured financial data collected from different sources. Schultz thinks the model's predictive power may be improved by incorporating sentiment data derived from textual analysis of news articles and Twitter content relating to the subject companies.

Schultz and Steele meet to discuss plans for incorporating the sentiment data into the model. They discuss the differences in the steps between building ML models that use traditional structured data and building ML models that use textual big data. Steele tells Schultz:

Statement 1: The second step in building text-based ML models is text preparation and wrangling, whereas the second step in building ML models using structured data is data collection.

Statement 2: The fourth step in building both types of models encompasses data/text exploration.

Steele expresses concern about using Twitter content in the model, noting that research suggests that as much as 10–15 percent of social media content is from fake accounts. Schultz tells Steele that she understands her concern but thinks the potential for model improvement outweighs the concern.

Steele begins building a model that combines the structured financial data and the sentiment data. She starts with cleansing and wrangling the raw structured financial data. Exhibit 1 presents a small sample of the raw dataset before cleansing: Each row represents data for a particular firm.

EXHIBIT 1   Sample of Raw Structured Data Before Cleansing

ID	Ticker	IPO Date	Industry (NAICS)	EBIT	Interest Expense	Total Debt
1	ABC	4/6/17	44	9.4	0.6	10.1
2	BCD	November 15, 2004	52	5.5	0.4	6.2
3	HIJ	26-Jun-74	54	8.9	1.2	15.8
4	KLM	14-Mar-15	72	5.7	1.5	0.0

After cleansing the data, Steele then preprocesses the dataset. She creates two new variables: an "Age" variable based on the firm's IPO date and an "Interest Coverage Ratio" variable equal to EBIT divided by interest expense. She also deletes the "IPO Date" variable from the dataset. After applying these transformations, Steele scales the financial data using normalization. She notes that over the full sample dataset, the "Interest Expense" variable ranges from a minimum of 0.2 and a maximum of 12.2, with a mean of 1.1 and a standard deviation of 0.4.

Steele and Schultz then discuss how to preprocess the raw text data. Steele tells Schultz that the process can be completed in the following three steps:

Step 1: Cleanse the raw text data.

Step 2: Split the cleansed data into a collection of words for them to be normalized.

Step 3: Normalize the collection of words from Step 2 and create a distinct set of tokens from the normalized words.

With respect to Step 1, Steele tells Schultz:

"I believe I should remove all html tags, punctuation, numbers, and extra white spaces from the data before normalizing them."

After properly cleansing the raw text data, Steele completes Steps 2 and 3. She then performs exploratory data analysis. To assist in feature selection, she wants to create a visualization that shows the most informative words in the dataset based on their term frequency (TF) values. After creating and analyzing the visualization, Steele is concerned that some tokens are likely to be noise features for ML model training; therefore, she wants to remove them.

Steele and Schultz discuss the importance of feature selection and feature engineering in ML model training. Steele tells Schultz:

"Appropriate feature selection is a key factor in minimizing model overfitting, whereas feature engineering tends to prevent model underfitting."

Once satisfied with the final set of features, Steele selects and runs a model on the training set that classifies the text as having positive sentiment (Class "1" or negative sentiment (Class "0"). She then evaluates its performance using error analysis. The resulting confusion matrix is presented in Exhibit 2.

EXHIBIT 2   Confusion Matrix

		Actual Training Results	
		Class "1"	Class "0"
Predicted Results	Class "1"	TP = 182	FP = 52
	Class "0"	FN = 31	TN = 96

1. Which of Steele's statements relating to the steps in building structured data-based and text-based ML models is correct?
   A. Only Statement 1 is correct.
   B. Only Statement 2 is correct.
   C. Statement 1 and Statement 2 are correct.

2. Steele's concern about using Twitter data in the model *best* relates to:
   A. volume.
   B. velocity.
   C. veracity.

3. What type of error appears to be present in the IPO Date column of Exhibit 1?
   A. invalidity error.
   B. inconsistency error.
   C. non-uniformity error.

4. What type of error is most likely present in the last row of data (ID #4) in Exhibit 1?
   A. Inconsistency error
   B. Incompleteness error
   C. Non-uniformity error

5. During the preprocessing of the data in Exhibit 1, what type of data transformation did Steele perform during the data preprocessing step?
   A. Extraction
   B. Conversion
   C. Aggregation

6. Based on Exhibit 1, for the firm with ID #3, Steele should compute the scaled value for the "Interest Expense" variable as:
   A. 0.008.
   B. 0.083.
   C. 0.250.

7. Is Steele's statement regarding Step 1 of the preprocessing of raw text data correct?
   A. Yes.
   B. No, because her suggested treatment of punctuation is incorrect.
   C. No, because her suggested treatment of extra white spaces is incorrect.

8. Steele's Step 2 can be *best* described as:
   A. tokenization.
   B. lemmatization.
   C. standardization.

9. The output created in Steele's Step 3 can be *best* described as a:
   A. bag of words.
   B. set of n-grams.
   C. document term matrix.

10. Given her objective, the visualization that Steele should create in the exploratory data analysis step is a:
    A. scatter plot.
    B. word cloud.
    C. document term matrix.

11. To address her concern in her exploratory data analysis, Steele should focus on those tokens that have:
    A. low chi-square statistics.
    B. low mutual information (ML) values.
    C. very low and very high term frequency (TF) values.

12. Is Steele's statement regarding the relationship between feature selection/feature engineering and model fit correct?
    A. Yes.
    B. No, because she is incorrect with respect to feature selection.
    C. No, because she is incorrect with respect to feature engineering.

13. Based on Exhibit 2, the model's precision metric is *closest* to:
    A. 78 percent.
    B. 81 percent.
    C. 85 percent.

14. Based on Exhibit 2, the model's F1 score is *closest* to:
    A. 77 percent.
    B. 81 percent.
    C. 85 percent.

15. Based on Exhibit 2, the model's accuracy metric is *closest* to:
    A. 77 percent.
    B. 81 percent.
    C. 85 percent.

The following information relates to Questions 16–22

Iesha Azarov is a senior analyst at Ganymede Moon Partners (Ganymede), where he works with junior analyst Pàola Bector. Azarov would like to incorporate machine learning (ML) models into the company's analytical process. Azarov asks Bector to develop ML models for two unstructured stock sentiment datasets, Dataset ABC and Dataset XYZ. Both datasets have been cleaned and preprocessed in preparation for text exploration and model training.

Following an exploratory data analysis that revealed Dataset ABC's most frequent tokens, Bector conducts a collection frequency analysis. Bector then computes TF–IDF (term frequency–inverse document frequency) for several words in the collection and tells Azarov the following:

Statement 1:   IDF is equal to the inverse of the document frequency measure.

Statement 2:   TF at the collection level is multiplied by IDF to calculate TF–IDF.

Statement 3:   TF–IDF values vary by the number of documents in the dataset, and therefore, model performance can vary when applied to a dataset with just a few documents.

Bector notes that Dataset ABC is characterized by the absence of ground truth.

Bector turns his attention to Dataset XYZ, containing 84,000 tokens and 10,000 sentences. Bector chooses an appropriate feature selection method to identify and remove unnecessary tokens from the dataset and then focuses on model training. For performance evaluation purposes, Dataset XYZ is split into a training set, cross-validation (CV) set, and test set. Each of the sentences has already been labeled as either a positive sentiment (Class "1") or a negative sentiment (Class "0") sentence. There is an unequal class distribution between the positive sentiment and negative sentiment sentences in Dataset XYZ. Simple random sampling is applied within levels of the sentiment class labels to balance the class distributions within the splits. Bector's view is that the false positive and false negative evaluation metrics should be given equal weight. Select performance data from the cross-validation set confusion matrices is presented in Exhibit 1:

EXHIBIT 1   Performance Metrics for Dataset XYZ

Confusion Matrix	CV Data (threshold *p*-value)	Performance Metrics			
		Precision	Recall	F1 Score	Accuracy
A	0.50	0.95	0.87	0.91	0.91
B	0.35	0.93	0.90	0.91	0.92
C	0.65	0.86	0.97	0.92	0.91

Azarov and Bector evaluate the Dataset XYZ performance metrics for Confusion Matrices A, B, and C in Exhibit 1. Azarov says, "For Ganymede's purposes, we should be most concerned with the cost of Type I errors."

Azarov requests that Bector apply the ML model to the test dataset for Dataset XYZ, assuming a threshold *p*-value of 0.65. Exhibit 2 contains a sample of results from the test dataset corpus.

EXHIBIT 2   10 Sample Results of Test Data for Dataset XYZ

Sentence #	Actual Sentiment	Target p-Value
1	1	0.75
2	0	0.45
3	1	0.64
4	1	0.81
5	0	0.43
6	1	0.78
7	0	0.59
8	1	0.60
9	0	0.67
10	0	0.54

Bector makes the following remarks regarding model training:

Remark 1: Method selection is governed by such factors as the type of data and the size of data.
Remark 2: In the performance evaluation stage, model fitting errors, such as bias error and variance error, are used to measure goodness of fit.

16. Based on the text exploration method used for Dataset ABC, tokens that potentially carry important information useful for differentiating the sentiment embedded in the text are *most likely* to have values that are:
    A. low.
    B. intermediate.
    C. high.

17. Which of Bector's statements regarding TF, IDF, and TF–IDF is correct?
    A. Statement 1
    B. Statement 2
    C. Statement 3

18. What percentage of Dataset ABC should be allocated to a training subset?
    A. 0 percent
    B. 20 percent
    C. 60 percent

19. Based only on Dataset XYZ's composition and Bector's view regarding false positive and false negative evaluation metrics, which performance measure is *most appropriate*?
    A. Recall
    B. F1 score
    C. Precision

20. Based on Exhibit 1, which confusion matrix demonstrates the *most* favorable value of the performance metric that *best* addresses Azarov's concern?
    A. Confusion Matrix A
    B. Confusion Matrix B
    C. Confusion Matrix C

21. Based on Exhibit 2, the accuracy metric for Dataset XYZ's test set sample is *closest to*:
    A. 0.67.
    B. 0.70.
    C. 0.75.

22. Which of Bector's remarks related to model training is correct?
    A. Only Remark 1
    B. Only Remark 2
    C. Both Remark 1 and Remark 2

The following information relates to Questions 23–31

Bernadette Rivera is a portfolio manager at Voxkor, a private equity company that provides financing to early-stage start-up businesses. Rivera is working with a data analyst, Tim Achler, on a text-based machine-learning (ML) model to enhance Voxkor's predictive ability to identify successful start-ups.

Voxkor currently uses ML models based only on traditional, structured financial data but would like to develop a new ML model that analyzes textual big data gathered from the internet. The model will classify text information into positive or negative sentiment classes for each respective start-up. Rivera wants to confirm her understanding of any differences in the ML model building steps between data analysis projects that use traditional structured data and projects that involve unstructured, text-based data. Rivera makes the following statements:

Statement 1:   Some of the methods used in the exploration step are different for structured and unstructured data, but for both types of data, the step involves feature selection and feature engineering.

Statement 2:   A major difference when developing a text-based ML model is the curation step, which involves cleansing, preprocessing, and converting the data into a structured format usable for model training.

Achler uses a web spidering program to obtain the data for the text-based model. The program extracts raw content from social media webpages, which contains English language sentences and special characters. After curating the text, Achler removes unnecessary elements from the raw text using regular expression software and completes additional text cleansing and preprocessing tasks.

Next, Achler and Rivera discuss remaining text wrangling tasks—specifically, which tokens to include in the document term matrix (DTM). Achler divides unique tokens into three groups; a sample of each group is shown in Exhibit 1.

EXHIBIT 1   Summary of Sample Tokens

Token Group 1	Token Group 2	Token Group 3
"not_increas_market"	"not_increased_market"	"not," "increased," "market"
"currencysign"	"currencysign"	"EUR"
"sale_decreas"	"sale_decreased"	"Sales," "decreased"

The dataset is now ready for the text exploration step. At this point in the process, Rivera wants to better comprehend the collection of unique words. Achler recommends an exploratory data analysis technique that visualizes words by varying their font size proportionately to the number of occurrences of each word in the corpus.

As an additional part of the text exploration step, Achler conducts a term frequency analysis to identify outliers. Achler summarizes the analysis in Exhibit 2.

EXHIBIT 2   Words with Highest and Lowest Frequency Value

Group 1		Group 2	
Word	Frequency	Word	Frequency
the	0.04935	naval	1.0123e-05
and	0.04661	stereotype	1.5185e-05
to	0.04179	till	1.5185e-05
that	0.03577	ribbon	2.0247e-05
in	0.03368	deposit	2.5308e-05

Note: "e-05" represents 10^{-5}.

Achler has the data ready for the model training process. Rivera asks Achler to include start-up failure rates as a feature. Achler notices that the number of start-ups that fail (majority class) is significantly larger than the number of the start-ups that are successful (minority class). Achler is concerned that because of class imbalance, the model will not be able to discriminate between start-ups that fail and start-ups that are successful.

Achler splits the DTM into training, cross-validation, and test datasets. Achler uses a supervised learning approach to train the logistic regression model in predicting sentiment. Applying the receiver operating characteristics (ROC) technique and area under the curve (AUC) metrics, Achler evaluates model performance on both the training and the cross-validation datasets. The trained model performance for three different logistic regressions' threshold p-values is presented in Exhibit 3.

EXHIBIT 3   AUC for Different Threshold p-values

Threshold p-Value	Training Set	Cross-Validation Set
$p = 0.57$	56.7%	57.3%
$p = 0.79$	91.3%	89.7%
$p = 0.84$	98.4%	87.1%

Rivera suggests adjusting the model's hyperparameters to improve performance. Achler runs a grid search that compares the difference between the prediction error on both the training and the cross-validation datasets for various combinations of hyperparameter values. For the current values of hyperparameters, Achler observes that the prediction error on the training dataset is small, whereas the prediction error on the cross-validation dataset is significantly larger.

23. Which of Rivera's statements about differences in ML model building steps is correct?
    A. Only Statement 1
    B. Only Statement 2
    C. Both Statement 1 and Statement 2

24. Based on the source of the data, as part of the data cleansing and wrangling process, Achler *most likely* needs to remove:
    A. html tags and perform scaling.
    B. numbers and perform lemmatization.
    C. white spaces and perform winsorization.

25. Based on Exhibit 1, which token group has *most likely* undergone the text preparation and wrangling process?
    A. Token Group 1
    B. Token Group 2
    C. Token Group 3

26. The visual text representation technique that Achler recommends to Rivera is a:
    A. word cloud.
    B. bag of words.
    C. collection frequency.

27. Based on Exhibit 2, Achler should exclude from further analysis words in:
    A. only Group 1.
    B. only Group 2.
    C. both Group 1 and Group 2.

28. Achler's model training concern related to the model's ability to discriminate could be addressed by randomly:
    A. oversampling the failed start-up data.
    B. oversampling the successful start-up data.
    C. undersampling the successful start-up data.

29. Based on Exhibit 3, which threshold *p*-value indicates the *best* fitting model?
    A. 0.57
    B. 0.79
    C. 0.84

30. Based on Exhibit 3, if Achler wants to improve model performance at the threshold *p*-value of 0.84, he should:
    A. tune the model to lower the AUC.
    B. adjust model parameters to decrease ROC convexity.
    C. apply LASSO regularization to the logistic regression.

31. Based on Achler's grid search analysis, the current model can be characterized as:
    A. underfitted.
    B. having low variance.
    C. exhibiting slight regularization.

CHAPTER 12

USING MULTIFACTOR MODELS

Jerald E. Pinto, PhD, CFA

Eugene L. Podkaminer, CFA

LEARNING OUTCOMES

The candidate should be able to:

- describe arbitrage pricing theory (APT), including its underlying assumptions and its relation to multifactor models;
- define arbitrage opportunity and determine whether an arbitrage opportunity exists;
- calculate the expected return on an asset given an asset's factor sensitivities and the factor risk premiums;
- describe and compare macroeconomic factor models, fundamental factor models, and statistical factor models;
- explain sources of active risk and interpret tracking risk and the information ratio;
- describe uses of multifactor models and interpret the output of analyses based on multifactor models;
- describe the potential benefits for investors in considering multiple risk dimensions when modeling asset returns.

1. INTRODUCTION

As used in investments, a **factor** is a variable or a characteristic with which individual asset returns are correlated. Models using multiple factors are used by asset owners, asset managers, investment consultants, and risk managers for a variety of portfolio construction, portfolio management, risk management, and general analytical purposes. In comparison to single-factor models (typically based on a market risk factor), multifactor models offer increased explanatory power and flexibility. These comparative strengths of multifactor models allow practitioners to

Quantitative Methods for Investment Analysis, Second Edition, by Jerald E. Pinto, PhD, CFA, and Eugene L. Podkaminer, CFA. Copyright © 2020 by CFA Institute.

- build portfolios that replicate or modify in a desired way the characteristics of a particular index;
- establish desired exposures to one or more risk factors, including those that express specific macro expectations (such as views on inflation or economic growth), in portfolios;
- perform granular risk and return attribution on actively managed portfolios;
- understand the comparative risk exposures of equity, fixed-income, and other asset class returns;
- identify active decisions relative to a benchmark and measure the sizing of those decisions; and
- ensure that an investor's aggregate portfolio is meeting active risk and return objectives commensurate with active fees.

Multifactor models have come to dominate investment practice, having demonstrated their value in helping asset managers and asset owners address practical tasks in measuring and controlling risk. We explain and illustrate the various practical uses of multifactor models.

We first describe the modern portfolio theory background of multifactor models. We then describe arbitrage pricing theory and provide a general expression for multifactor models. We subsequently explore the types of multifactor models and certain applications. Lastly, we summarize major points.

2. MULTIFACTOR MODELS AND MODERN PORTFOLIO THEORY

In 1952, Markowitz introduced a framework for constructing portfolios of securities by quantitatively considering each investment in the context of a portfolio rather than in isolation; that framework is widely known today as modern portfolio theory (MPT). Markowitz simplified modeling asset returns using a multivariate normal distribution, which completely defines the distribution of returns in terms of mean returns, return variances, and return correlations. One of the key insights of MPT is that any value of correlation among asset returns of less than one offers the potential for risk reduction by means of diversification.

In 1964, Sharpe introduced the capital asset pricing model (CAPM), a model for the expected return of assets in equilibrium based on a mean–variance foundation. The CAPM and the literature that developed around it has provided investors with useful and influential concepts—such as alpha, beta, and systematic risk—for thinking about investing. The concept of systematic risk, for example, is critical to understanding multifactor models: An investment may be subject to many different types of risks, but they are generally not equally important so far as investment valuation is concerned. Risk that can be avoided by holding an asset in a portfolio, where the risk might be offset by the various risks of other assets, should not be compensated by higher expected return, according to theory. By contrast, investors would expect compensation for bearing an asset's non-diversifiable risk: **systematic risk**. Theory indicates that only systematic risk should be **priced risk**. In the CAPM, an asset's systematic risk is a positive function of its beta, which measures the sensitivity of an asset's return to the market's return. According to the CAPM, differences in mean return are explained by a single factor: market portfolio return. Greater risk with respect to the market factor, represented by higher beta, is expected to be associated with higher return.

The accumulation of evidence from the equity markets during the decades following the CAPM's development have provided clear indications that the CAPM provides an incomplete description of risk and that models incorporating multiple sources of systematic risk more effectively model asset returns. Bodie, Kane, and Marcus (2017) provide an introduction to the empirical evidence. There are, however, various perspectives in practice on how to model risk in the context of multifactor models. We will examine some of these —focusing on macroeconomic factor models and fundamental factor models—in subsequent sections.

3. ARBITRAGE PRICING THEORY

In the 1970s, Ross (1976) developed the arbitrage pricing theory (APT) as an alternative to the CAPM. APT introduced a framework that explains the expected return of an asset (or portfolio) in equilibrium as a linear function of the risk of the asset (or portfolio) with respect to a set of factors capturing systematic risk. Unlike the CAPM, the APT does not indicate the identity or even the number of risk factors. Rather, for any multifactor model assumed to generate returns ("return-generating process"), the theory gives the associated expression for the asset's expected return.

Suppose that K factors are assumed to generate returns. Then the simplest expression for a multifactor model for the return of asset i is given by

$$R_i = a_i + b_{i1}I_1 + b_{i2}I_2 + \ldots + b_{iK}I_K + \varepsilon_i, \tag{1}$$

where

R_i = the return to asset i
a_i = an intercept term
I_k = the return to factor k, $k = 1, 2, \ldots, K$
b_{ik} = the sensitivity of the return on asset i to the return to factor k, $k = 1, 2, \ldots, K$
ε_i = an error term with a zero mean that represents the portion of the return to asset i
      not explained by the factor model

The intercept term a_i is the expected return of asset i given that all the factors take on a value of zero. Equation 1 presents a multifactor return-generating process (a time-series model for returns). In any given period, the model may not account fully for the asset's return, as indicated by the error term. But error is assumed to average to zero. Another common formulation subtracts the risk-free rate from both sides of Equation 1 so that the dependent variable is the return in excess of the risk-free rate and one of the explanatory variables is a factor return in excess of the risk-free rate. (The Carhart model described next is an example.)

Based on Equation 1, the APT provides an expression for the expected return of asset i assuming that financial markets are in equilibrium. The APT is similar to the CAPM, but the APT makes less strong assumptions than the CAPM. The APT makes just three key assumptions:

1. A factor model describes asset returns.
2. With many assets to choose from, investors can form well-diversified portfolios that eliminate asset-specific risk.
3. No arbitrage opportunities exist among well-diversified portfolios.

Arbitrage is a risk-free operation that requires no net investment of money but earns an expected positive net profit. (Note that "arbitrage," or the phrase "risk arbitrage," is also sometimes used in practice to describe investment operations in which significant risk is present). An **arbitrage opportunity** is an opportunity to conduct an arbitrage—an opportunity to earn an expected positive net profit without risk and with no net investment of money.

In the first assumption, the number of factors is not specified. The second assumption allows investors to form portfolios with factor risk but without asset-specific risk. The third assumption is the condition of financial market equilibrium.

Empirical evidence indicates that Assumption 2 is reasonable (Fabozzi, 2008). When a portfolio contains many stocks, the asset-specific or non-systematic risk of individual stocks makes almost no contribution to the variance of portfolio returns.

According to the APT, if these three assumptions hold, the following equation holds:

$$E(R_p) = R_F + \lambda_1 b_{p,1} + \ldots + \lambda_K b_{p,K}, \qquad (2)$$

where

$E(R_p)$ = the expected return to portfolio p
R_F = the risk-free rate
λ_j = the expected reward for bearing the risk of factor j
$b_{p,j}$ = the sensitivity of the portfolio to factor j
K = the number of factors

The APT equation, Equation 2, says that the expected return on any well-diversified portfolio is linearly related to the factor sensitivities of that portfolio. The equation assumes that a risk-free rate exists. If no risk-free asset exists, in place of R_F we write λ_0 to represent the expected return on a risky portfolio with zero sensitivity to all the factors. The number of factors is not specified but must be much lower than the number of assets, a condition fulfilled in practice.

The **factor risk premium** (or **factor price**), λ_j, represents the expected reward for bearing the risk of a portfolio with a sensitivity of 1 to factor j and a sensitivity of 0 to all other factors. The exact interpretation of "expected reward" depends on the multifactor model that is the basis for Equation 2. For example, in the Carhart four-factor model, shown later in Equation 3a and 3b, the risk premium for the market factor is the expected return of the market in excess of the risk-free rate. Then, the factor risk premiums for the other three factors are the mean returns of the specific portfolios held long (e.g., the portfolio of small-cap stocks for the "small minus big" factor) minus the mean return for a related but opposite portfolio (e.g., a portfolio of large-cap stocks, in the case of that factor). A portfolio with a sensitivity of 1 to factor j and a sensitivity of 0 to all other factors is called a **pure factor portfolio** for factor j (or simply the **factor portfolio** for factor j).

For example, suppose we have a portfolio with a sensitivity of 1 with respect to Factor 1 and a sensitivity of 0 to all other factors. Using Equation 2, the expected return on this portfolio is $E_1 = R_F + \lambda_1 \times 1$. If $E_1 = 0.12$ and $R_F = 0.04$, then the risk premium for Factor 1 is

$$0.12 = 0.04 + \lambda_1 \times 1.$$

$$\lambda_1 = 0.12 - 0.04 = 0.08, \text{ or } 8\%$$

EXAMPLE 1   Determining the Parameters in a One-Factor APT Model

Suppose we have three well-diversified portfolios that are each sensitive to the same single factor. Exhibit 1 shows the expected returns and factor sensitivities of these portfolios. Assume that the expected returns reflect a one-year investment horizon. To keep the analysis simple, all investors are assumed to agree upon the expected returns of the three portfolios as shown in the exhibit.

EXHIBIT 1   Sample Portfolios for a One-Factor Model

Portfolio	Expected Return	Factor Sensitivity
A	0.075	0.5
B	0.150	2.0
C	0.070	0.4

We can use these data to determine the parameters of the APT equation. According to Equation 2, for any well-diversified portfolio and assuming a single factor explains returns, we have $E(R_p) = R_F + \lambda_1 b_{p,1}$. The factor sensitivities and expected returns are known; thus there are two unknowns, the parameters R_F and λ_1. Because two points define a straight line, we need to set up only two equations. Selecting Portfolios A and B, we have

$$E(R_A) = 0.075 = R_F + 0.5\lambda_1$$

and

$$E(R_B) = 0.150 = R_F + 2\lambda_1$$

From the equation for Portfolio A, we have $R_F = 0.075 - 0.5\lambda_1$. Substituting this expression for the risk-free rate into the equation for Portfolio B gives

$$0.15 = 0.075 - 0.5\lambda_1 + 2\lambda_1$$

$$0.15 = 0.075 + 1.5\lambda_1$$

So, we have $\lambda_1 = (0.15 - 0.075)/1.5 = 0.05$. Substituting this value for λ_1 back into the equation for the expected return to Portfolio A yields

$$0.075 = R_F + 0.05 \times 0.5$$

$$R_F = 0.05$$

So, the risk-free rate is 0.05 or 5 percent, and the factor premium for the common factor is also 0.05 or 5 percent. The APT equation is

$$E(R_p) = 0.05 + 0.05b_{p,1}$$

From Exhibit 1, Portfolio C has a factor sensitivity of 0.4. Therefore, according to the APT, the expected return of Portfolio C should be

$$E(R_B) = 0.05 + (0.05 \times 0.4) = 0.07$$

which is consistent with the expected return for Portfolio C given in Exhibit 1.

EXAMPLE 2 Checking Whether Portfolio Returns Are Consistent with No Arbitrage

In this example, we examine how to tell whether expected returns and factor sensitivities for a set of well-diversified portfolios may indicate the presence of an arbitrage opportunity. Exhibit 2 provides data on four hypothetical portfolios. The data for Portfolios A, B, and C are repeated from Exhibit 1. Portfolio D is a new portfolio. The factor sensitivities given relate to the one-factor APT model $E(R_p) = 0.05 + 0.05b_{p,1}$ derived in **Example 1**. As in **Example 1**, all investors are assumed to agree upon the expected returns of the portfolios. The question raised by the addition of this new Portfolio D is whether the addition of this portfolio created an arbitrage

EXHIBIT 2   Sample Portfolios for a One-Factor Model

Portfolio	Expected Return	Factor Sensitivity
A	0.0750	0.50
B	0.1500	2.00
C	0.0700	0.40
D	0.0800	0.45
0.5A + 0.5C	0.0725	0.45

opportunity. If a portfolio can be formed from Portfolios A, B, and C that has the same factor sensitivity as Portfolio D but a different expected return, then an arbitrage opportunity exists: Portfolio D would be either undervalued (if it offers a relatively high expected return) or overvalued (if it offers a relatively low expected return).

Exhibit 2 gives data for an equally weighted portfolio of A and C. The expected return and factor sensitivity of this new portfolio are calculated as weighted averages of the expected returns and factor sensitivities of A and C. Expected return is thus $(0.50)(0.0750) + (0.50)(0.07) = 0.0725$, or 7.25 percent. The factor sensitivity is $(0.50)(0.50) + (0.50)(0.40) = 0.45$. Note that the factor sensitivity of 0.45 matches the factor sensitivity of Portfolio D. In this case, the configuration of expected returns in relation to factor risk presents an arbitrage opportunity involving Portfolios A, C, and D. Portfolio D offers, at 8%, an expected return that is too high given its factor sensitivity. According to the assumed APT model, the expected return on Portfolio D should be $E(R_D) = 0.05 + 0.05\beta_{D,1} = 0.05 + (0.05 \times 0.45) = 0.0725$, or 7.25 percent. Portfolio D is undervalued relative to its factor risk. We will buy D (hold it long) in the portfolio that exploits the arbitrage opportunity (the **arbitrage portfolio**). We purchase D using the proceeds from selling short an equally weighted portfolio of A and C with exactly the same 0.45 factor sensitivity as D.

The arbitrage thus involves the following strategy: Invest $10,000 in Portfolio D and fund that investment by selling short an equally weighted portfolio of Portfolios A and C; then close out the investment position at the end of one year (the investment horizon for expected returns). Exhibit 3 demonstrates the arbitrage profits to the arbitrage strategy. The final row of the exhibit shows the net cash flow to the arbitrage portfolio.

EXHIBIT 3 Arbitrage Opportunity within Sample Portfolios

	Initial Cash Flow	Final Cash Flow	Factor Sensitivity
Portfolio D	−$10,000.00	$10,800.00	0.45
Portfolios A and C	$10,000.00	−$10,725.00	−0.45
Sum	$0.00	$75.00	0.00

As Exhibit 3 shows, if we buy $10,000 of Portfolio D and sell $10,000 of an equally weighted portfolio of Portfolios A and C, we have an initial net cash flow of $0. The expected value of our investment in Portfolio D at the end of one year is $10,000(1 + 0.08) = $10,800$. The expected value of our short position in Portfolios A and C at the end of one year is $-$10,000(1.0725) = -$10,725$. So, the combined expected cash flow from our investment position in one year is $75.

What about the risk? Exhibit 3 shows that the factor risk has been eliminated: Purchasing D and selling short an equally weighted portfolio of A and C creates a portfolio with a factor sensitivity of $0.45 - 0.45 = 0$. The portfolios are well-diversified, and we assume any asset-specific risk is negligible.

Because an arbitrage is possible, Portfolios A, C, and D cannot all be consistent with the same equilibrium. If Portfolio D actually had an expected return of 8 percent, investors would bid up its price until the expected return fell and the arbitrage opportunity vanished. Thus, arbitrage restores equilibrium relationships among expected returns.

The Carhart four-factor model, also known as the four-factor model or simply the Carhart model, is a frequently referenced multifactor model in current equity portfolio management practice. Presented in Carhart (1997), it is an extension of the three-factor model developed by Fama and French (1992) to include a momentum factor. According to the model, three groups of stocks tend to have higher returns than those predicted solely by their sensitivity to the market return:

- Small-capitalization stocks
- Low price-to-book stocks, commonly referred to as "value" stocks
- Stocks whose prices have been rising, commonly referred to as "momentum" stocks

On the basis of that evidence, the Carhart model posits the existence of three systematic risk factors beyond the market risk factor. They are named, in the same order as above, the following:

- Small minus big (SMB)
- High minus low (HML)
- Winners minus losers (WML)

Equation 3a is the Carhart model, in which the excess return on the portfolio is explained as a function of the portfolio's sensitivity to a market index (RMRF), a market capitalization factor (SMB), a book-to-market factor (HML), which is essentially the reciprocal of the aforementioned price-to-book ratio, and a momentum factor (WML).

$$R_p - R_F = a_p + b_{p1}\text{RMRF} + b_{p2}\text{SMB} + b_{p3}\text{HML} + b_{p4}\text{WML} + \varepsilon_p \qquad (3a)$$

where

R_p and R_F = the return on the portfolio and the risk-free rate of return, respectively

a_p = "alpha" or return in excess of that expected given the portfolio's level of systematic risk (assuming the four factors capture all systematic risk)

b_p = the sensitivity of the portfolio to the given factor

RMRF = the return on a value-weighted equity index in excess of the one-month T-bill rate

SMB = small minus big, a size (market capitalization) factor; SMB is the average return on three small-cap portfolios minus the average return on three large-cap portfolios

HML = high minus low, the average return on two high book-to-market portfolios minus the average return on two low book-to-market portfolios

WML = winners minus losers, a momentum factor; WML is the return on a portfolio of the past year's winners minus the return on a portfolio of the past year's losers. (Note that WML is an equally weighted average of the stocks with the highest 30% month returns lagged 1 month minus the equally weighted average of the stocks with the lowest 30% 11-month returns lagged 1 month.)

ε_p = an error term that represents the portion of the return to the portfolio, p, not explained by the model

Following Equation 2, the Carhart model can be stated as giving equilibrium expected return as

$$E(R_p) = R_F + b_{p,1}\text{RMRF} + b_{p,2}\text{SMB} + b_{p,3}\text{HML} + b_{p,4}\text{WML} \qquad (3b)$$

because the expected value of alpha is zero.

The Carhart model can be viewed as a multifactor extension of the CAPM that explicitly incorporates drivers of differences in expected returns among assets variables that are viewed as anomalies from a pure CAPM perspective. (The term *anomaly* in this context refers to an observed capital market regularity that is not explained by, or contradicts, a theory of asset pricing.) From the perspective of the CAPM, there are size, value, and momentum anomalies. From the perspective of the Carhart model, however, size, value, and momentum represent systematic risk factors; exposure to them is expected to be compensated in the marketplace in the form of differences in mean return.

Size, value, and momentum are common themes in equity portfolio construction, and all three factors continue to have robust uses in active management risk decomposition and return attribution.

4. MULTIFACTOR MODELS: TYPES

Having introduced the APT, it is appropriate to examine the diversity of multifactor models in current use.

In the following sections, we explain the basic principles of multifactor models and discuss various types of models and their application. We also expand on the APT, which relates the expected return of investments to their risk with respect to a set of factors.

4.1. Factors and Types of Multifactor Models

Many varieties of multifactor models have been proposed and researched. We can categorize most of them into three main groups according to the type of factor used:

- In a **macroeconomic factor model**, the factors are surprises in macroeconomic variables that significantly explain returns. In the example of equities, the factors can be understood as affecting either the expected future cash flows of companies or the interest rate used to discount these cash flows back to the present. Among macroeconomic factors that have been used are interest rates, inflation risk, business cycle risk, and credit spreads.
- In a **fundamental factor model**, the factors are attributes of stocks or companies that are important in explaining cross-sectional differences in stock prices. Among the fundamental factors that have been used are the book-value-to-price ratio, market capitalization, the price-to-earnings ratio, and financial leverage.
- In a **statistical factor model**, statistical methods are applied to historical returns of a group of securities to extract factors that can explain the observed returns of securities in the group. In statistical factor models, the factors are actually portfolios of the securities in the group under study and are therefore defined by portfolio weights. Two major types of factor models are factor analysis models and principal components models. In factor analysis models, the factors are the portfolios of securities that best explain (reproduce)

historical *return covariances*. In principal components models, the factors are portfolios of securities that best explain (reproduce) the historical *return variances*.

A potential advantage of statistical factor models is that they make minimal assumptions. But the interpretation of statistical factors is generally difficult in contrast to macroeconomic and fundamental factors. A statistical factor that is a portfolio with weights that are similar to market index weights might be interpreted as "the market factor," for example. But in general, associating a statistical factor with economic meaning may not be possible. Because understanding statistical factor models requires substantial preparation in quantitative methods, a detailed discussion of statistical factor models is outside the scope of our coverage.

Our discussion concentrates on macroeconomic factor models and fundamental factor models. Industry use has generally favored fundamental and macroeconomic models, perhaps because such models are much more easily interpreted and rely less on data-mining approaches. Nevertheless, statistical factor models have proponents and are also used in practical applications.

4.2. The Structure of Macroeconomic Factor Models

The representation of returns in macroeconomic factor models assumes that the returns to each asset are correlated with only the surprises in some factors related to the aggregate economy, such as inflation or real output. We can define *surprise* in general as the actual value minus predicted (or expected) value. A factor's surprise is the component of the factor's return that was unexpected, and the factor surprises constitute the model's independent variables. This idea contrasts with the representation of independent variables as returns in Equation 2, reflecting the fact that how the independent variables are represented varies across different types of models.

Suppose that K macro factors explain asset returns. Then in a macroeconomic factor model, Equation 4 expresses the return of asset i:

$$R_i = a_i + b_{i1}F_1 + b_{i2}F_2 + \ldots + b_{iK}F_K + \varepsilon_i, \tag{4}$$

where

R_i = the return to asset i

a_i = the expected return to asset i

b_{ik} = the sensitivity of the return on asset i to a surprise in factor k, $k = 1, 2, \ldots, K$

F_k = the surprise in the factor k, $k = 1, 2, \ldots, K$

ε_i = an error term with a zero mean that represents the portion of the return to asset i not explained by the factor model

Surprise in a macroeconomic factor can be illustrated as follows: Suppose we are analyzing monthly returns for stocks. At the beginning of each month, we have a prediction of inflation for the month. The prediction may come from an econometric model or a professional economic forecaster, for example. Suppose our forecast at the beginning of the month is that inflation will be 0.4 percent during the month. At the end of the month, we find that inflation was actually 0.5 percent during the month. During any month,

Actual inflation = Predicted inflation + Surprise inflation.

In this case, actual inflation was 0.5 percent and predicted inflation was 0.4 percent. Therefore, the surprise in inflation was 0.5% − 0.4% = 0.1%.

What is the effect of defining the factors in terms of surprises? Suppose we believe that inflation and gross domestic product (GDP) growth are two factors that carry risk premiums; that is, inflation and GDP represent priced risk. (GDP is a money measure of the goods and services produced within a country's borders.) We do not use the predicted values of these variables because the predicted values should already be reflected in stock prices and thus in their expected returns. The intercept a_i, the expected return to asset i, reflects the effect of the predicted values of the macroeconomic variables on expected stock returns. The surprise in the macroeconomic variables during the month, however, contains new information about the variable. As a result, this model structure analyzes the return to an asset in three components: the asset's expected return, its unexpected return resulting from new information about the factors, and an error term.

Consider a factor model in which the returns to each asset are correlated with two factors. For example, we might assume that the returns for a particular stock are correlated with surprises in inflation rates and surprises in GDP growth. For stock i, the return to the stock can be modeled as

$$R_i = a_i + b_{i1}F_{INFL} + b_{i2}F_{GDP} + \varepsilon_i$$

where

R_i = the return to stock i
a_i = the expected return to stock i
b_{i1} = the sensitivity of the return on stock i to inflation rate surprises
F_{INFL} = the surprise in inflation rates
b_{i2} = the sensitivity of the return on stock i to GDP growth surprises
F_{GDP} = the surprise in GDP growth (assumed to be uncorrelated with F_{INFL})
ε_i = an error term with a zero mean that represents the portion of the return to asset i not explained by the factor model

Consider first how to interpret b_{i1}. The factor model predicts that a 1 percentage point surprise in inflation rates will contribute b_{i1} percentage points to the return to stock i. The slope coefficient b_{i2} has a similar interpretation relative to the GDP growth factor. Thus, slope coefficients are naturally interpreted as the factor sensitivities of the asset. A *factor sensitivity* is a measure of the response of return to each unit of increase in a factor, holding all other factors constant. (Factor sensitivities are sometimes called *factor betas* or *factor loadings*.)

Now consider how to interpret the intercept a_i. Recall that the error term has a mean or average value of zero. If the surprises in both inflation rates and GDP growth are zero, the factor model predicts that the return to asset i will be a_i. Thus, a_i is the expected value of the return to stock i.

Finally, consider the error term, ε_i. The intercept a_i represents the asset's expected return. The term $(b_{i1}F_{INFL} + b_{i2}F_{GDP})$ represents the return resulting from factor surprises, and we have interpreted these as the sources of risk shared with other assets. The term ε_i is the part of return that is unexplained by expected return or the factor surprises. If we have adequately represented the sources of common risk (the factors), then ε_i must represent an asset-specific risk. For a stock, it might represent the return from an unanticipated company-specific event.

The risk premium for the GDP growth factor is typically positive. The risk premium for the inflation factor, however, is typically negative. Thus, an asset with a positive sensitivity to the inflation factor—an asset with returns that tend to be positive in response to unexpectedly high inflation—would have a lower required return than if its inflation sensitivity were negative; an asset with positive sensitivity to inflation would be in demand for its inflation-hedging ability.

This discussion has broader applications. It can be used for various asset classes, including fixed income and commodities. It can also be used in asset allocation, where asset classes can be examined in relation to inflation and GDP growth, as illustrated in the following exhibit. In Exhibit 4, each quadrant reflects a unique mix of inflation and economic growth expectations. Certain asset classes or securities can be expected to perform differently in various inflation and GDP growth regimes and can be plotted in the appropriate quadrant, thus forming a concrete illustration of a two-factor model.

In macroeconomic factor models, the time series of factor surprises are constructed first. Regression analysis is then used to estimate assets' sensitivities to the factors. In practice, estimated sensitivities and intercepts are often acquired from one of the many consulting companies that specialize in factor models. When we have the parameters for the individual assets in a portfolio, we can calculate the portfolio's parameters as a weighted average of the parameters of individual assets. An individual asset's weight in that calculation is the proportion of the total market value of the portfolio that the individual asset represents.

EXHIBIT 4   Growth and Inflation Factor Matrix

	Inflation	
	Low Inflation/Low Growth • Cash • Government bonds	**High Inflation/Low Growth** • Inflation-linked bonds • Commodities • Infrastructure
Growth		
	Low Inflation/High Growth • Equity • Corporate debt	**High Inflation/High Growth** • Real assets (real estate, timberland, farmland, energy)

Note: Entries are assets likely to benefit from the specified combination of growth and inflation.

EXAMPLE 3   Estimating Returns for a Two-Stock Portfolio Given Factor Sensitivities

Suppose that stock returns are affected by two common factors: surprises in inflation and surprises in GDP growth. A portfolio manager is analyzing the returns on a portfolio of two stocks, Manumatic (MANM) and Nextech (NXT). The following equations describe the returns for those stocks, where the factors F_{INFL} and F_{GDP} represent the surprise in inflation and GDP growth, respectively:

$$R_{MANM} = 0.09 - 1F_{INFL} + 1F_{GDP} + \varepsilon_{MANM}$$

$$R_{NXT} = 0.12 + 2F_{INFL} + 4F_{GDP} + \varepsilon_{NXT}$$

One-third of the portfolio is invested in Manumatic stock, and two-thirds is invested in Nextech stock.

1. Formulate an expression for the return on the portfolio.
2. State the expected return on the portfolio.
3. Calculate the return on the portfolio given that the surprises in inflation and GDP growth are 1 percent and 0 percent, respectively, assuming that the error terms for MANM and NXT both equal 0.5 percent.

In evaluating the equations for surprises in inflation and GDP, convert amounts stated in percentage terms to decimal form.

Solution to 1: The portfolio's return is the following weighted average of the returns to the two stocks:

$$R_P = (1/3)(0.09) + (2/3)(0.12) + [(1/3)(-1) + (2/3)(2)]F_{INFL}$$
$$+ [(1/3)(1) + (2/3)(4)]F_{GDP} + (1/3)\varepsilon_{MANM} + (2/3)\varepsilon_{NXT}$$
$$= 0.11 + 1F_{INFL} + 3F_{GDP} + (1/3)\varepsilon_{MANM} + (2/3)\varepsilon_{NXT}$$

Solution to 2: The expected return on the portfolio is 11%, the value of the intercept in the expression obtained in the solution to 1.

Solution to 3:

$$R_P = 0.11 + 1F_{INFL} + 3F_{GDP} + (1/3)\varepsilon_{MANM} + (2/3)\varepsilon_{NXT}$$
$$= 0.11 + 1(0.01) + 3(0) + (1/3)(0.005) + (2/3)(0.005)$$
$$= 0.125, \text{ or } 12.5\%$$

4.3. The Structure of Fundamental Factor Models

We earlier gave the equation of a macroeconomic factor model as

$$R_i = a_i + b_{i1}F_1 + b_{i2}F_2 + \ldots + b_{iK}F_K + \varepsilon_i$$

We can also represent the structure of fundamental factor models with this equation, but we need to interpret the terms differently.

In fundamental factor models, the factors are stated as *returns* rather than return *surprises* in relation to predicted values, so they do not generally have expected values of zero. This approach changes the meaning of the intercept, which is no longer interpreted as the expected return. Note that if the coefficients were not standardized, as described in the following paragraph, the intercept could be interpreted as the risk-free rate because it would be the return to an asset with no factor risk (zero factor betas) and no asset-specific risk (with standardized coefficients, the intercept is not interpreted beyond being an intercept in a regression included so that the expected asset-specific risk equals zero).

Factor sensitivities are also interpreted differently in most fundamental factor models. In fundamental factor models, the factor sensitivities are attributes of the security. An asset's sensitivity to a factor is expressed using a **standardized beta**: the value of the attribute for the asset minus the average value of the attribute across all stocks divided by the standard deviation of the attribute's values across all stocks.

$$b_{ik} = \frac{\text{Value of attribute } k \text{ for asset } i - \text{Average value of attribute } k}{\sigma(\text{Values of attribute } k)} \tag{5}$$

Consider a fundamental model for equities that uses a dividend yield factor. After standardization, a stock with an average dividend yield will have a factor sensitivity of 0; a stock with a dividend yield one standard deviation above the average will have a factor sensitivity of 1; and a stock with a dividend yield one standard deviation below the average will have a factor sensitivity of −1. Suppose, for example, that an investment has a dividend yield of 3.5 percent and that the average dividend yield across all stocks being considered is 2.5 percent. Further, suppose that the standard deviation of dividend yields across all stocks is 2 percent. The investment's sensitivity to dividend yield is (3.5% − 2.5%)/2% = 0.50, or one-half standard deviation above average. The scaling permits all factor sensitivities to be interpreted similarly, despite differences in units of measure and scale in the variables. The exception to this interpretation is factors for binary variables, such as industry membership. A company either participates in an industry or does not. The industry factor is represented by dummy variables: The value of the variable is 1 if the stock belongs to the industry and 0 if it does not.

A second distinction between macroeconomic multifactor models and fundamental factor models is that with the former, we develop the factor (surprise) series first and then estimate the factor sensitivities through regressions. With the latter, we generally specify the factor sensitivities (attributes) first and then estimate the factor returns through regressions.

Financial analysts use fundamental factor models for a variety of purposes, including portfolio performance attribution and risk analysis. (*Performance attribution* consists of return attribution and risk attribution. *Return attribution* is a set of techniques used to identify the sources of the excess return of a portfolio against its benchmark. *Risk attribution* addresses the sources of risk, identifying the sources of portfolio volatility for absolute mandates and the sources of tracking risk for relative mandates.) Fundamental factor models focus on explaining the returns to individual stocks using observable fundamental factors that describe either attributes of the securities themselves or attributes of the securities' issuers. Industry membership, price-to-earnings ratio, book-value-to-price ratio, size, and financial leverage are examples of fundamental factors.

Example 4 discusses a study that examined macroeconomic, fundamental, and statistical factor models.

EXAMPLE 4   Comparing Types of Factor Models

Connor (1995) contrasted a macroeconomic factor model with a fundamental factor model to compare how well the models explain stock returns.

Connor reported the results of applying a macroeconomic factor model to the returns for 779 large-cap US stocks based on monthly data from January 1985 through December 1993. Using five macroeconomic factors, Connor was able to explain approximately 11 percent of the variance of return on these stocks. Exhibit 5 shows his results.

EXHIBIT 5   The Explanatory Power of the Macroeconomic Factors

Factor	Explanatory Power from Using Each Factor Alone	Increase in Explanatory Power from Adding Each Factor to All the Others
Inflation	1.3%	0.0%
Term structure	1.1%	7.7%
Industrial production	0.5%	0.3%
Default premium	2.4%	8.1%
Unemployment	−0.3%	0.1%
All factors (total explanatory power)		10.9%

Notes: The explanatory power of a given model was computed as 1 − [(Average asset −Specific variance of return across stocks)/(Average total variance of return across stocks)]. The variance estimates were corrected for degrees of freedom, so the marginal contribution of a factor to explanatory power can be zero or negative. Explanatory power captures the proportion of the total variance of return that a given model explains for the average stock.

Source: Connor (1995).

Connor also reported a fundamental factor analysis of the same companies. The factor model employed was the BARRA US-E2 model (as of 2019, the current version is E4). Exhibit 6 shows these results. In the exhibit, "variability in markets" represents the stock's volatility, "success" is a price momentum variable, "trade activity" distinguishes stocks by how often their shares trade, and "growth" distinguishes stocks by past and anticipated earnings growth (explanations of variables are from Grinold and Kahn 1994).

As Exhibit 6 shows, the most important fundamental factor is "industries," represented by 55 industry dummy variables. The fundamental factor model explained approximately 43 percent of the variation in stock returns, compared with approximately 11 percent for the macroeconomic factor model. Because "industries" must sum to the market and the market portfolio is not incorporated in the macroeconomic factor model, some advantage to the explanatory power of the fundamental factor may be built into the specific models being compared. Connor's article also does not provide tests of the statistical significance of the various factors in either model; however, Connor's research is strong evidence for the usefulness of

EXHIBIT 6   The Explanatory Power of the Fundamental Factors

Factor	Explanatory Power from Using Each Factor Alone	Increase in Explanatory Power from Adding Each Factor to All the Others
Industries	16.3%	18.0%
Variability in markets	4.3%	0.9%
Success	2.8%	0.8%
Size	1.4%	0.6%
Trade activity	1.4%	0.5%
Growth	3.0%	0.4%
Earnings to price	2.2%	0.6%
Book to price	1.5%	0.6%
Earnings variability	2.5%	0.4%
Financial leverage	0.9%	0.5%
Foreign investment	0.7%	0.4%
Labor intensity	2.2%	0.5%
Dividend yield	2.9%	0.4%
All factors (total explanatory power)		42.6%

Source: Connor (1995).

fundamental factor models. Moreover, this evidence is mirrored by the wide use of those models in the investment community. For example, fundamental factor models are frequently used in portfolio performance attribution. Typically, fundamental factor models employ many more factors than macroeconomic factor models, giving a more detailed picture of the sources of an investment manager's returns.

We cannot conclude from this study, however, that fundamental factor models are inherently superior to macroeconomic factor models. Each major type of model has its uses. The factors in various macroeconomic factor models are individually backed by statistical evidence that they represent systematic risk (i.e., risk that cannot be diversified away). The same may not be true of each factor in a fundamental factor model. For example, a portfolio manager can easily construct a portfolio that excludes a particular industry, so exposure to a particular industry is not systematic risk.

The two types of factors, macroeconomic and fundamental, have different implications for measuring and managing risk, in general. The macroeconomic factor set is parsimonious (five variables in the model studied) and allows a portfolio manager to incorporate economic views into portfolio construction by adjustments to portfolio exposures to macro factors. The fundamental factor set examined by Connor is large (67 variables, including the 55 industry dummy variables); at the expense of greater complexity, it can give a more detailed picture of risk in terms that are easily related to company and security characteristics. Connor found that

> the macroeconomic factor model had no marginal explanatory power when added to the fundamental factor model, implying that the fundamental risk attributes capture all the risk characteristics represented by the macroeconomic factor betas. Because the fundamental factors supply such a detailed description of the characteristics of a stock and its issuer, however, this finding is not necessarily surprising.

We encounter a range of distinct representations of risk in the fundamental models that are currently used in practical applications. Diversity exists in both the identity and exact definition of factors as well as in the underlying functional form and estimation procedures. Despite the diversity, we can place the factors of most fundamental factor models for equities into three broad groups:

- **Company fundamental factors**. These are factors related to the company's internal performance. Examples are factors relating to earnings growth, earnings variability, earnings momentum, and financial leverage.
- **Company share-related factors**. These factors include valuation measures and other factors related to share price or the trading characteristics of the shares. In contrast to the previous category, these factors directly incorporate investors' expectations concerning the company. Examples include price multiples, such as earnings yield, dividend yield, and book to market. Market capitalization falls under this heading. Various models incorporate variables relating to share price momentum, share price volatility, and trading activity that fall in this category.
- **Macroeconomic factors**. Sector or industry membership factors fall under this heading. Various models include such factors as CAPM beta, other similar measures of systematic risk, and yield curve level sensitivity—all of which can be placed in this category.

For global factor models, in particular, a classification of country, industry, and style factors is often used. In that classification, country and industry factors are dummy variables for country and industry membership, respectively. Style factors include those related to earnings, risk, and valuation that define types of securities typical of various styles of investing.

4.4. Fixed-Income Multifactor Models

While the previous discussion focuses on equity applications, similar approaches are equally suited to fixed income. In addition, some of the same broad factor groupings are relevant for bonds.

4.4.1. Macroeconomic Multifactor Models

Macroeconomic models, as discussed earlier, are easily translatable to fixed-income investing. For instance, surprises to economic growth, interest rates, and inflation will impact bond pricing, often mechanically.

Consider a bond factor model in which the returns are correlated with two factors. Following our earlier discussion, returns for bonds are assumed to be correlated with surprises in inflation rates and surprises in GDP growth. The return to *bond i*, R_i, can be modeled as

$$R_i = a_i + b_{i1}F_{INFL} + b_{i2}F_{GDP} + \varepsilon_i$$

where

   R_i = the return to bond i
   a_i = the expected return to bond i
   b_{i1} = the sensitivity of the return on bond i to inflation rate surprises
   F_{INFL} = the surprise in inflation rates
   b_{i2} = the sensitivity of the return on bond i to GDP growth surprises
   F_{GDP} = the surprise in GDP growth (assumed to be uncorrelated with F_{INFL})
   ε_i = an error term with a zero mean that represents the portion of the return to bond i
        not explained by the factor model

4.4.2. Fundamental Multifactor Models

Fundamental factor approaches have been developed to address the unique aspects of fixed income by using, for example, the following categories:

- Duration (ranging from cash to long-dated bonds)
- Credit (ranging from government securities to high yield)
- Currency (ranging from home currency to foreign developed and emerging market currencies)
- Geography (specific developed and emerging markets)

A simplified structure, shown in Exhibit 7, divides the US Barclays Bloomberg Aggregate index, a standard bond benchmark, into sectors, where each has such unique factor exposures as spread or duration. This factor model was developed by Dopfel (2004), and the factors have been chosen to cover three macro sectors plus high yield. The government

EXHIBIT 7   A Simple Fixed-Income Fundamental Framework

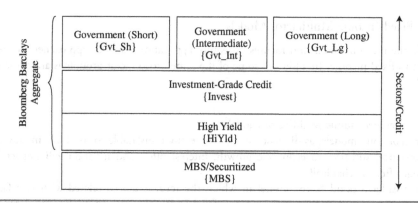

Source: Dopfel (2004).

sector is further broken down into three maturity buckets to help explain duration exposures.

These components can be thought of as both macroeconomic and fundamental. They are macroeconomically oriented because spread, or expected return above similar duration government bonds, is closely related to the growth factor and is sometimes expressed as simply credit spread. Fundamentally, duration can also be thought of as a factor. This simplistic approach can be extended to encompass global fixed-income markets or adapted to a specific country's market:

$$R_i = a_i + b_{i1}F_{Gvt\_Sh} + b_{i2}F_{Gvt\_Int} + b_{i3}F_{Gvt\_Lg} + b_{i4}F_{Invest} + b_{i5}F_{HiYld} + b_{i6}F_{MBS} + \varepsilon_i$$

where

R_i = the return to bond i
a_i = the expected return to bond i
b_{ik} = the sensitivity of the return on bond i to factor k
F_k = factor k, where k represents "Gov't (Short)," "Gov't (Long)," and so on
ε_i = an error term with a zero mean that represents the portion of the return to bond i not explained by the factor model

The historic style factor weights, b_{ik}, are determined by a constrained regression (the constraint being that the total "weights" add up to 100 percent) of the portfolio returns against the listed style factors.

This framework lends itself readily to performance and risk attribution, along with portfolio construction. When evaluating a fixed-income manager, such characteristics as spread, duration, yield, and quality can be incorporated. This type of framework can also be extended to ESG (environmental, social, and governance) considerations as these should be generally unrelated to the basic duration and spread foundation presented. For instance, each box in Exhibit 7 could also contain E, S, and G scores, which after the initial disaggregation of a fixed-income return stream into duration and spread components could be used to model the overall portfolio's aggregate scores. For forward-looking portfolio construction purposes, a desired loading on duration, spread, and ESG scores could be handled with a quantitative objective function.

4.4.3. Risk and Style Multifactor Models

Another category of multifactor approach incorporates risk, or style, factors, several of which can thematically apply across asset classes. Examples of such factors include momentum, value, carry, and volatility. Many of these are similar in construction to those commonly used in equity portfolios. Examples include defining value as real (inflation-adjusted) yield, momentum as the previous 12-month excess return, and carry as the term spread. An illustrative example of risk factor approaches, in this case across asset classes, can be found in Exhibit 8.

Of the three types of multifactor models (macroeconomic, fundamental, and statistical), statistical models can be most easily applied to various asset classes, including fixed income, as no asset-class-specific tuning is required given the minimal required assumption set.

EXHIBIT 8   An Illustration of Factor Approaches across Asset Classes

	Factor/Asset Class	Equity	Credit	Treasury	Commodities	Currency
Macro	Economic Growth	xx	x			
	Rates		x	xx		
	Inflation			x	xx	x
Style	Value	xx	x		x	x
	Size	xx				
	Momentum	xx	xx	xx	xx	xx
	Carry	x	xx	xx	xx	xx
	Low-Volume	xx	x			

Note: Double check marks denote strong alignment between risk factor and asset class; single check marks denote moderate alignment.
Source: Podkaminer (2017).

This is in contrast to macroeconomic and fundamental models, which both require adjustments and repurposing to ensure the frameworks are fit for the specifics of bond investing. **Example 5** shows how expected return could be expressed.

EXAMPLE 5   Calculating Factor-Based Expected Returns at the Portfolio Level

A fixed-income portfolio has the following estimated exposures: 35 percent intermediate government bonds, 40 percent investment-grade credit, 5 percent securitized, and 20 percent high yield. The expected component returns are

Short government bonds: 0.25%
Intermediate government bonds: 1.50%
Long government bonds: 3.00%
Investment-grade credit: 4.25%
MBS/Securitized: 1.75%
High yield: 5.75%
Express the expected return of the portfolio.

Solution Expected return could be expressed as

$$E(R) = 3.46\% = (0.35)(1.50\%) + (0.40)(4.25\%) + (0.05)(1.75\%) + (0.20)(5.75\%).$$

EXAMPLE 6   Reconciling Bond Portfolio Characteristics Using Style Factors

Talia Ayalon is evaluating intermediate duration (between 5 and 7 years) investment-grade fixed-income strategies using the framework presented in Exhibit 7. One of the strategies has the following sector attribution (totaling 100 percent):

Gov't (Short) 2%	Gov't (Intermediate) 4%	Gov't (Long) 14%
Investment-Grade Credit 56%		
MBS/Securitized 6%		
High Yield 18%		

Are these sector exposures consistent with an intermediate duration investment-grade approach? Why or why not?

Suggested answer:

No, the sector exposures are inconsistent with the stated approach for two reasons: 1) The 18 percent exposure to high yield constitutes a significant amount of below investment-grade exposure. A true investment-grade portfolio would, for example, not have exposure to high yield. 2) The loading to longer duration sectors implies a longer-than-intermediate duration for the portfolio.

5. MULTIFACTOR MODELS: SELECTED APPLICATIONS

The following sections present selected applications of multifactor models in investment practice. The applications discussed are return attribution, risk attribution, portfolio construction, and strategic portfolio decisions. We begin by discussing portfolio return attribution and risk attribution, focusing on the analysis of benchmark-relative returns. After discussing performance attribution and risk analysis, we explain the use of multifactor models in creating a portfolio with a desired set of risk exposures.

Additionally, multifactor models can be used for asset allocation purposes. Some large, sophisticated asset owners have chosen to define their asset allocation opportunity sets in terms of macroeconomic or thematic factors and aggregate factor exposures (represented by pure factor portfolios as defined earlier). Many others are examining their traditionally derived asset allocation policies using factor models to map asset class exposure to factor sensitivities. The trend toward factor-based asset allocation has two chief causes: First is the increasing availability of sophisticated factor models (like the BARRA models used in the following examples); second is the more intense focus by asset owners on the many dimensions of risk.

5.1. Factor Models in Return Attribution

Multifactor models can help us understand in detail the sources of a manager's returns relative to a benchmark. For simplicity, in this section we analyze the sources of the returns of a portfolio fully invested in the equities of a single national equity market, which allows us to ignore the roles of country selection, asset allocation, market timing, and currency hedging. The same methodology can, however, be applied across asset classes and geographies.

Analysts often favor fundamental multifactor models in decomposing (separating into basic elements) the sources of returns. In contrast to statistical factor models, fundamental factor models allow the sources of portfolio performance to be described using commonly understood terms. Fundamental factors are also thematically understandable and can be incorporated into simple narratives for clients concerning return or risk attribution.

Also, in contrast to macroeconomic factor models, fundamental models express investment style choices and security characteristics more directly and often in greater detail.

We first need to understand the objectives of active managers. As mentioned previously, managers are commonly evaluated relative to a specified benchmark. Active portfolio managers hold securities in different-from-benchmark weights in an attempt to add value to their portfolios relative to a passive investment approach. Securities held in different-from-benchmark weights reflect portfolio manager expectations that differ from consensus expectations. For an equity manager, those expectations may relate to common factors driving equity returns or to considerations unique to a company. Thus, when we evaluate an active manager, we want to ask such questions as, did the manager have insights that were effectively translated into returns in excess of those that were available from a passive alternative? Analyzing the sources of returns using multifactor models can help answer these questions.

The return on a portfolio, R_p, can be viewed as the sum of the benchmark's return, R_B, and the **active return** (portfolio return minus benchmark return):

$$\text{Active return} = R_p - R_B \tag{6}$$

With the help of a factor model, we can analyze a portfolio manager's active return as the sum of two components. The first component is the product of the portfolio manager's factor tilts (over- or underweights relative to the benchmark factor sensitivities) and the factor returns; we call this component the return from factor tilts. The second component of active return reflects the manager's skill in individual asset selection (ability to overweight securities that outperform the benchmark or underweight securities that underperform the benchmark); we call this component security selection. Equation 7 shows the decomposition of active return into those two components, where k represents the factor or factors represented in the benchmark portfolio:

$$\text{Active return} = \sum_{k=1}^{K} [(\text{Portfolio sensitivity})_k - (\text{Benchmark sensitivity})_k] \\ \times (\text{Factor return})_k + \text{Security selection} \tag{7}$$

In Equation 7, the portfolio's and benchmark's sensitivities to each factor are calculated as of the beginning of the evaluation period.

EXAMPLE 7   Four-Factor Model Active Return Decomposition

As an equity analyst at a pension fund sponsor, Ronald Service uses the Carhart four-factor multifactor model of Equation 3a to evaluate US equity portfolios:

$$R_p - R_F = a_p + b_{p1}\text{RMRF} + b_{p2}\text{SMB} + b_{p3}\text{HML} + b_{p4}\text{WML} + \varepsilon_p.$$

Service's current task is to evaluate the performance of the most recently hired US equity manager. That manager's benchmark is an index representing the performance of the 1,000 largest US stocks by market value. The manager describes himself as a "stock picker" and points to his performance in beating the benchmark as evidence that he is successful. Exhibit 9 presents an analysis based on the Carhart model of the sources of that manager's active return during the year, given an assumed set of factor returns. In Exhibit 9, the entry "A. Return from Factor Tilts = 2.1241%" is the sum of the four numbers above it. The entry "B. Security Selection" gives security selection as equal to –0.05%. "C. Active Return" is found as the sum of these two components: 2.1241% + (–0.05%) = 2.0741%.

EXHIBIT 9   Active Return Decomposition

Factor	Factor Sensitivity			Factor Return (4)	Contribution to Active Return	
	Portfolio (1)	Benchmark (2)	Difference (3) = (1) – (2)		Absolute (3) × (4)	Proportion of Total Active
RMRF	0.95	1.00	–0.05	5.52%	–0.2760%	–13.3%
SMB	–1.05	–1.00	–0.05	–3.35%	0.1675%	8.1%
HML	0.40	0.00	0.40	5.10%	2.0400%	98.4%
WML	0.05	0.03	0.02	9.63%	0.1926%	9.3%
			A. Return from Factor Tilts =		2.1241%	102.4%
			B. Security Selection =		–0.0500%	–2.4%
			C. Active Return (A + B) =		2.0741%	100.0%

From his previous work, Service knows that the returns to growth-style portfolios often have a positive sensitivity to the momentum factor (WML). By contrast, the returns to certain value-style portfolios, in particular those following a contrarian strategy, often have a negative sensitivity to the momentum factor. Using the information given, address the following questions (assume the benchmark chosen for the manager is appropriate):

1. Determine the manager's investment mandate and his actual investment style.
2. Evaluate the sources of the manager's active return for the year.
3. What concerns might Service discuss with the manager as a result of the return decomposition?

Solution to 1: The benchmarks chosen for the manager should reflect the baseline risk characteristics of the manager's investment opportunity set and his mandate. We can ascertain whether the manager's actual style follows the mandate by examining the portfolio's actual factor exposures:

- The sensitivities of the benchmark are consistent with the description in the text. The sensitivity to RMRF of 1 indicates that the assigned benchmark has average market risk, consistent with it being a broad-based index; the negative sensitivity to SMB indicates a large-cap orientation. The mandate might be described as large-cap without a value/growth bias (HML is zero) or a momentum bias (WML is close to zero).
- Stocks with high book-to-market ratios are generally viewed as value stocks. Because the equity manager has a positive sensitivity to HML (0.40), it appears that the manager has a value orientation. The manager is approximately neutral to the momentum factor, so the equity manager is not a momentum investor and probably not a contrarian value investor. In summary, these considerations suggest that the manager has a large-cap value orientation.

Solution to 2: The dominant source of the manager's positive active return was his positive active exposure to the HML factor. The bet contributed approximately 98 percent of the realized active return of about 2.07 percent. The manager's active exposure to the overall market (RMRF) was unprofitable, but his active exposures to small stocks (SMB) and to momentum (WML) were profitable. The magnitudes of the manager's active exposures to RMRF, SMB, and WML were relatively small, however, so the effects of those bets on active return were minor compared with his large and successful bet on HML.

Solution to 3: Although the manager is a self-described stock picker, his active return from security selection in this period was actually negative. His positive active return resulted from the concurrence of a large active bet on HML and a high return to that factor during the period. If the market had favored growth rather than value without the manager doing better in individual security selection, the manager's performance would have been unsatisfactory. Service's conversations with the manager should focus on evidence that he can predict changes in returns to the HML factor and on the manager's stock selection discipline.

5.2. Factor Models in Risk Attribution

Building on the discussion of active returns, this section explores the analysis of active risk. A few key terms are important to the understanding of how factor models are used to build an understanding of a portfolio manager's risk exposures. We will describe them briefly before moving on to the detailed discussion of risk attribution.

Active risk can be represented by the standard deviation of active returns. A traditional term for that standard deviation is **tracking error** (TE). **Tracking risk** is a synonym for tracking error that is often used in the CFA Program curriculum. We will use the abbreviation TE for the concept of active risk and refer to it usually as tracking error:

$$TE = s(R_p - R_B) \tag{8}$$

In Equation 8, $s(R_p - R_B)$ indicates that we take the sample standard deviation (indicated by s) of the time series of differences between the portfolio return, R_p, and the benchmark return, R_B. We should be careful that active return and tracking error are stated on the same time basis. As an approximation assuming returns are serially uncorrelated, to annualize a daily TE based on daily returns, we multiply daily TE by $(250)^{1/2}$ based on 250 trading days in a year. To annualize a monthly TE based on monthly returns, we multiply monthly TE by $(12)^{1/2}$.

As a broad indication of the range for tracking error, in US equity markets a well-executed passive investment strategy can often achieve a tracking error on the order of 0.10% or less per year. A low-risk active or enhanced index investment strategy, which makes tightly controlled use of managers' expectations, often has a tracking error goal of 2% per year. A diversified active large-cap equity strategy that might be benchmarked to the S&P 500 Index would commonly have a tracking error in the range of 2%–6% per year. An aggressive active equity manager might have a tracking error in the range of 6%–10% or more.

Somewhat analogous to the use of the traditional Sharpe measure in evaluating absolute returns, the **information ratio** (IR) is a tool for evaluating mean active returns per unit of active risk. The historical or *ex post* IR is expressed as follows:

$$IR = \frac{\bar{R}_p - \bar{R}_B}{s(R_p - R_B)} \tag{9}$$

In the numerator of Equation 9, $\bar{R}_p$ and $\bar{R}_B$ stand for the sample mean return on the portfolio and the sample mean return on the benchmark, respectively. The equation assumes that the portfolio being evaluated has the same systematic risk as its benchmark. To illustrate the calculation, if a portfolio achieved a mean return of 9 percent during the same period that its benchmark earned a mean return of 7.5 percent and the portfolio's tracking error (the denominator) was 6 percent, we would calculate an information ratio of (9% − 7.5%)/6% = 0.25. Setting guidelines for acceptable active risk or tracking error is one of the methods that some investors use to ensure that the overall risk and style characteristics of their investments are in line with their chosen benchmark.

Note that in addition to focusing exclusively on *active* risk, multifactor models can also be used to decompose and attribute sources of *total* risk. For instance, a multi-asset class multi-strategy long/short fund can be evaluated with an appropriate multifactor model to reveal insights on sources of total risk.

EXAMPLE 8   Creating Active Manager Guidelines

The framework of active return and active risk is appealing to investors who want to manage the risk of investments. The benchmark serves as a known and continuously observable reference standard in relation to which quantitative risk and return objectives may be stated and communicated. For example, a US public employee retirement system invited investment managers to submit proposals to manage a "low-active-risk US large-cap equity fund" that would be subject to the following constraints:

- Shares must be components of the S&P 500.
- The portfolio should have a minimum of 200 issues. At time of purchase, the maximum amount that may be invested in any one issuer is 5 percent of the portfolio at market value or 150 percent of the issuers' weight within the S&P 500, whichever is greater.
- The portfolio must have a minimum information ratio of 0.30 either since inception or over the last seven years.
- The portfolio must also have tracking risk of less than 3% with respect to the S&P 500 either since inception or over the last seven years.

Once a suitable active manager is found and hired, these requirements can be written into the manager's guidelines. The retirement system's individual mandates would be set such that the sum of mandates across managers would equal the desired risk exposures.

Analysts use multifactor models to understand a portfolio manager's risk exposures in detail. By decomposing active risk, the analyst's objective is to measure the portfolio's active exposure along each dimension of risk—in other words, to understand the sources of tracking error. This can even be done at the level of individual holdings. Among the questions analysts will want to answer are the following:

- What active exposures contributed most to the manager's tracking error?
- Was the portfolio manager aware of the nature of his active exposures, and if so, can he articulate a rationale for assuming them?
- Are the portfolio's active risk exposures consistent with the manager's stated investment philosophy?
- Which active bets earned adequate returns for the level of active risk taken?

In addressing these questions, analysts often choose fundamental factor models because they can be used to relate active risk exposures to a manager's portfolio decisions in a fairly direct and intuitive way. In this section, we explain how to decompose or explain a portfolio's active risk using a multifactor model.

We previously addressed the decomposition of active return; now we address the decomposition of active risk. In analyzing risk, it is more convenient to use variances rather than standard deviations because the variances of uncorrelated variables are additive. We refer to the variance of active return as **active risk squared**:

$$\text{Active risk squared} = s^2(R_p - R_B) \tag{10}$$

We can separate a portfolio's active risk squared into two components:

- **Active factor risk** is the contribution to active risk squared resulting from the portfolio's different-from-benchmark exposures relative to factors specified in the risk model.
- **Active specific risk** or **security selection risk** measures the active non-factor or residual risk assumed by the manager. Portfolio managers attempt to provide a positive average return from security selection as compensation for assuming active specific risk.

As we use the terms, "active specific risk" and "active factor risk" refer to variances rather than standard deviations. When applied to an investment in a single asset class, active risk squared has two components:

$$\text{Active risk squared} = \text{Active factor risk} + \text{Active specific risk} \qquad (11)$$

Active factor risk represents the part of active risk squared explained by the portfolio's active factor exposures. Active factor risk can be found indirectly as the risk remaining after active specific risk is deducted from active risk squared. Active specific risk can be expressed as

$$\text{Active specific risk} = \sum_{i=1}^{n} (w_i^a)^2 \sigma_{\varepsilon_i}^2$$

where w_i^a is the ith asset's active weight in the portfolio (that is, the difference between the asset's weight in the portfolio and its weight in the benchmark) and $\sigma_{\varepsilon_i}^2$ is the residual risk of the ith asset (the variance of the ith asset's returns left unexplained by the factors).

The direct procedure for calculating active factor risk is as follows. A portfolio's active factor exposure to a given factor j, b_j^a, is found by weighting each asset's sensitivity to factor j by its active weight and summing the terms: $b_j^a = \sum_{i=1}^{n} w_i^a b_{ji}$. Then active factor risk equals $\sum_{i=1}^{K} \sum_{j=1}^{K} b_i^a b_j^a \text{cov}(F_i, F_j)$.

EXAMPLE 9   A Comparison of Active Risk

Richard Gray is comparing the risk of four US equity managers who share the same benchmark. He uses a fundamental factor model, the BARRA US-E4 model, which incorporates 12 style factors and a set of 60 industry factors. The style factors measure various fundamental aspects of companies and their shares, such as size, liquidity, leverage, and dividend yield. In the model, companies have non-zero exposures to all industries in which the company operates. Exhibit 10 presents Gray's analysis of the active risk squared of the four managers, based on Equation 11 (note that there is a covariance term in active factor risk, reflecting the correlation of industry membership and the risk indexes, which we assume is negligible in this example). In Exhibit 10, the column labeled "Industry" gives the portfolio's active factor risk associated with the industry exposures of its holdings; the "Style Factor" column gives the portfolio's active factor risk associated with the exposures of its holdings to the 12 style factors.

EXHIBIT 10   Active Risk Squared Decomposition

	Active Factor				
Portfolio	Industry	Style Factor	Total Factor	Active Specific	Active Risk Squared
A	12.25	17.15	29.40	19.60	49
B	1.25	13.75	15.00	10.00	25
C	1.25	17.50	18.75	6.25	25
D	0.03	0.47	0.50	0.50	1

Note: Entries are in % squared.

Using the information in Exhibit 10, address the following:

1. Contrast the active risk decomposition of Portfolios A and B.
2. Contrast the active risk decomposition of Portfolios B and C.
3. Characterize the investment approach of Portfolio D.

Solution to 1: Exhibit 11 restates the information in Exhibit 10 to show the proportional contributions of the various sources of active risk. (e.g., Portfolio A's active risk related to industry exposures is 25 percent of active risk squared, calculated as 12.25/49 = 0.25, or 25 percent).

The last column of Exhibit 11 now shows the square root of active risk squared—that is, active risk or tracking error.

EXHIBIT 11   Active Risk Decomposition (restated)

	Active Factor (% of total active)			Active Specific (% of total active)	Active Risk
Portfolio	Industry	Style Factor	Total Factor		
A	25%	35%	60%	40%	7%
B	5%	55%	60%	40%	5%
C	5%	70%	75%	25%	5%
D	3%	47%	50%	50%	1%

Portfolio A has assumed a higher level of active risk than B (7 percent versus 5 percent). Portfolios A and B assumed the same proportions of active factor and active specific risk, but a sharp contrast exists between the two in the types of active factor risk exposure. Portfolio A assumed substantial active industry risk, whereas Portfolio B was approximately industry neutral relative to the benchmark. By contrast, Portfolio B had higher active bets on the style factors representing company and share characteristics.

Solution to 2: Portfolios B and C were similar in their absolute amounts of active risk. Furthermore, both Portfolios B and C were both approximately industry neutral relative to the benchmark. Portfolio C assumed more active factor risk related to the style factors, but B assumed more active specific risk. It is also possible to infer from the greater level of B's active specific risk that B is somewhat less diversified than C.

Solution to 3: Portfolio D appears to be a passively managed portfolio, judging by its negligible level of active risk. Referring to Exhibit 11, Portfolio D's active factor risk of 0.50, equal to 0.707 percent expressed as a standard deviation, indicates that the portfolio's risk exposures very closely match the benchmark.

The discussion of performance attribution and risk analysis has used examples related to common stock portfolios. Multifactor models have also been effectively used in similar roles for portfolios of bonds and other asset classes. For example, such factors as duration and spread can be used to decompose the risk and return of a fixed-income manager.

5.3. Factor Models in Portfolio Construction

Equally as important to the use of multifactor models in analyzing a portfolio's active returns and active risk is the use of such multifactor models in portfolio construction. At this stage of the portfolio management process, multifactor models permit the portfolio manager to make focused bets or to control portfolio risk relative to the benchmark's risk. This greater level of detail in modeling risk that multifactor models afford is useful in both passive and active management.

- *Passive management.* In managing a fund that seeks to track an index with many component securities, portfolio managers may need to select a sample of securities from the index. Analysts can use multifactor models to replicate an index fund's factor exposures, mirroring those of the index tracked.
- *Active management.* Many quantitative investment managers rely on multifactor models in predicting alpha (excess risk-adjusted returns) or relative return (the return on one asset or asset class relative to that of another) as part of a variety of active investment strategies. In constructing portfolios, analysts use multifactor models to establish desired risk profiles.
- *Rules-based active management (alternative indexes).* These strategies routinely tilt toward such factors as size, value, quality, or momentum when constructing portfolios. As such, alternative index approaches aim to capture some systematic exposure traditionally attributed to manager skill, or "alpha," in a transparent, mechanical, rules-based manner at low cost. Alternative index strategies rely heavily on factor models to introduce intentional factor and style biases versus capitalization-weighted indexes.

In the following, we explore some of these uses in more detail. As indicated, an important use of multifactor models is to establish a specific desired risk profile for a portfolio. In the simplest instance, the portfolio manager may want to create a portfolio with sensitivity to a single factor. This particular (pure) factor portfolio would have a sensitivity of 1 for that factor and a sensitivity (or weight) of 0 for all other factors. It is thus a portfolio with exposure to only one risk factor and exactly represents the risk of that factor. As a pure bet on a source of risk, factor portfolios are of interest to a portfolio manager who wants to hedge that risk (offset it) or speculate on it. This simple case can be expanded to multiple factors where a factor replication portfolio can be built based either on an existing target portfolio or on a set of desired exposures. **Example 10** illustrates the use of factor portfolios.

EXAMPLE 10   Factor Portfolios

Analyst Wanda Smithfield has constructed six portfolios for possible use by portfolio managers in her firm. The portfolios are labeled A, B, C, D, E, and F in Exhibit 12. Smithfield adapts a macroeconomic factor model based on research presented in Burmeister, Roll, and Ross (1994). The model includes five factors:

- Confidence risk, based on the yield spread between corporate bonds and government bonds. A positive surprise in the spread suggests that investors are willing to accept a smaller reward for bearing default risk and so that confidence is high.
- Time horizon risk, based on the yield spread between 20-year government bonds and 30-day Treasury bills. A positive surprise indicates increased investor willingness to invest for the long term.
- Inflation risk, measured by the unanticipated change in the inflation rate.
- Business cycle risk, measured by the unexpected change in the level of real business activity.
- Market timing risk, measured as the portion of the return on a broad-based equity index that is unexplained by the first four risk factors.

EXHIBIT 12   Factor Portfolios

Risk Factor	Portfolios					
	A	B	C	D	E	F
Confidence risk	0.50	0.00	1.00	0.00	0.00	0.80
Time horizon risk	1.92	0.00	1.00	1.00	1.00	1.00
Inflation risk	0.00	0.00	1.00	0.00	0.00	−1.05
Business cycle risk	1.00	1.00	0.00	0.00	1.00	0.30
Market timing risk	0.90	0.00	1.00	0.00	0.00	0.75

Note: Entries are factor sensitivities.

1. A portfolio manager wants to place a bet that real business activity will increase.
   A. Determine and justify the portfolio among the six given that would be most useful to the manager.
   B. Would the manager take a long or short position in the portfolio chosen in Part A?

2. A portfolio manager wants to hedge an existing positive (long) exposure to time horizon risk.
   A. Determine and justify the portfolio among the six given that would be most useful to the manager.
   B. What type of position would the manager take in the portfolio chosen in Part A?

Solution to 1A: Portfolio B is the most appropriate choice. Portfolio B is the factor portfolio for business cycle risk because it has a sensitivity of 1 to business cycle risk and a sensitivity of 0 to all other risk factors. Portfolio B is thus efficient for placing a pure bet on an increase in real business activity.

Solution to 1B: The manager would take a long position in Portfolio B to place a bet on an increase in real business activity.

Solution to 2A: Portfolio D is the appropriate choice. Portfolio D is the factor portfolio for time horizon risk because it has a sensitivity of 1 to time horizon risk and a sensitivity of 0 to all other risk factors. Portfolio D is thus efficient for hedging an existing positive exposure to time horizon risk.

Solution to 2B: The manager would take a short position in Portfolio D to hedge the positive exposure to time horizon risk.

5.4. How Factor Considerations Can Be Useful in Strategic Portfolio Decisions

Multifactor models can help investors recognize considerations that are relevant in making various strategic decisions. For example, given a sound model of the systematic risk factors that affect assets' mean returns, the investor can ask, relative to other investors,

- What types of risk do I have a comparative advantage in bearing?
- What types of risk am I at a comparative disadvantage in bearing?

For example, university endowments, because they typically have very long investment horizons, may have a comparative advantage in bearing business cycle risk of traded equities or the liquidity risk associated with many private equity investments. They may tilt their strategic asset allocation or investments within an asset class to capture the associated risk premiums for risks that do not much affect them. However, such investors may be at a comparative disadvantage in bearing inflation risk to the extent that the activities they support have historically been subject to cost increases running above the average rate of inflation.

This is a richer framework than that afforded by the CAPM, according to which all investors optimally should invest in two funds: the market portfolio and a risk-free asset. Practically speaking, a CAPM-oriented investor might hold a money market fund and a portfolio of capitalization-weighted broad market indexes across many asset classes, varying the weights in these two in accordance with risk tolerance. These types of considerations are also relevant to individual investors. An individual investor who depends on income from salary or self-employment is sensitive to business cycle risk, in particular to the effects of recessions. If this investor compared two stocks with the same CAPM beta, given his concern about recessions, he might be very sensitive to receiving an adequate premium for investing in procyclical assets. In contrast, an investor with independent wealth and no job-loss concerns would have a comparative advantage in bearing business cycle risk; his optimal risky asset portfolio might be quite different from that of the investor with job-loss concerns in tilting toward greater-than-average exposure to the business cycle factor, all else being equal. Investors should be aware of which priced risks they face and analyze the extent of their exposure.

A multifactor approach can help investors achieve better-diversified and possibly more-efficient portfolios. For example, the characteristics of a portfolio can be better explained by a combination of SMB, HML, and WML factors in addition to the market factor than by using the market factor alone.

Thus, compared with single-factor models, multifactor models offer a richer context for investors to search for ways to improve portfolio selection.

6. SUMMARY

In our coverage of multifactor models, we have presented concepts, models, and tools that are key ingredients to quantitative portfolio management and are used to both construct portfolios and to attribute sources of risk and return.

- Multifactor models permit a nuanced view of risk that is more granular than the single-factor approach allows.
- Multifactor models describe the return on an asset in terms of the risk of the asset with respect to a set of factors. Such models generally include systematic factors, which explain the average returns of a large number of risky assets. Such factors represent priced risk—risk for which investors require an additional return for bearing.
- The arbitrage pricing theory (APT) describes the expected return on an asset (or portfolio) as a linear function of the risk of the asset with respect to a set of factors. Like the CAPM, the APT describes a financial market equilibrium; however, the APT makes less strong assumptions.
- The major assumptions of the APT are as follows:
  - Asset returns are described by a factor model.
  - With many assets to choose from, asset-specific risk can be eliminated.
  - Assets are priced such that there are no arbitrage opportunities.

- Multifactor models are broadly categorized according to the type of factor used:
  - Macroeconomic factor models
  - Fundamental factor models
  - Statistical factor models

- In *macroeconomic* factor models, the factors are surprises in macroeconomic variables that significantly explain asset class (equity in our examples) returns. Surprise is defined as actual minus forecasted value and has an expected value of zero. The factors can be understood as affecting either the expected future cash flows of companies or the interest rate used to discount these cash flows back to the present and are meant to be uncorrelated.
- In *fundamental* factor models, the factors are attributes of stocks or companies that are important in explaining cross-sectional differences in stock prices. Among the fundamental factors are book-value-to-price ratio, market capitalization, price-to-earnings ratio, and financial leverage.
- In contrast to macroeconomic factor models, in fundamental models the factors are calculated as returns rather than surprises. In fundamental factor models, we generally specify the factor sensitivities (attributes) first and then estimate the factor returns through regressions. In macroeconomic factor models, however, we first develop the factor (surprise) series and then estimate the factor sensitivities through regressions. The factors of most

fundamental factor models may be classified as company fundamental factors, company share-related factors, or macroeconomic factors.

- In *statistical* factor models, statistical methods are applied to a set of historical returns to determine portfolios that explain historical returns in one of two senses. In factor analysis models, the factors are the portfolios that best explain (reproduce) historical return covariances. In principal components models, the factors are portfolios that best explain (reproduce) the historical return variances.
- Multifactor models have applications to return attribution, risk attribution, portfolio construction, and strategic investment decisions.
- A factor portfolio is a portfolio with unit sensitivity to a factor and zero sensitivity to other factors.
- Active return is the return in excess of the return on the benchmark.
- Active risk is the standard deviation of active returns. Active risk is also called tracking error or tracking risk. Active risk squared can be decomposed as the sum of active factor risk and active specific risk.
- The information ratio (IR) is mean active return divided by active risk (tracking error). The IR measures the increment in mean active return per unit of active risk.
- Factor models have uses in constructing portfolios that track market indexes and in alternative index construction.
- Traditionally, the CAPM approach would allocate assets between the risk-free asset and a broadly diversified index fund. Considering multiple sources of systematic risk may allow investors to improve on that result by tilting away from the market portfolio. Generally, investors would gain from accepting above average (below average) exposures to risks that they have a comparative advantage (comparative disadvantage) in bearing.

REFERENCES

Bodie, Zvi, Alex Kane, and Alan J. Marcus. 2017. *Investments*. 11th ed. New York: McGraw-Hill Education.

Burmeister, Edwin, Richard Roll, and Stephen A. Ross. 1994. "A *Practitioner's* Guide to Arbitrage Pricing Theory." In *A Practitioner's Guide to Factor Models*. Charlottesville, VA: Research Foundation of the Institute of Chartered Financial Analysts.

Carhart, Mark M. 1997. "On Persistence in Mutual Fund Performance." *Journal of Finance* 52 (1): 57–82. 10.1111/j.1540-6261.1997.tb03808.x.

Connor, Gregory. 1995. "The Three Types of Factor Models: A Comparison of Their Explanatory Power." *Financial Analysts Journal* 51 (3): 42–46. 10.2469/faj.v51.n3.1904.

Dopfel, Frederick E. 2004. "Fixed-Income Style Analysis and Optimal Manager Structure." *Journal of Fixed Income* 14 (2): 32–43. 10.3905/jfi.2004.439835.

Fabozzi, Frank J. 2008. *Handbook of Finance, Financial Markets and Instruments*. Wiley.

Fama, Eugene F. and Kenneth R. French. 1992. "The Cross-Section of Expected Stock Returns." *Journal of Finance* 47 (2): 427–65. 10.1111/j.1540-6261.1992.tb04398.x.

Grinold, Richard and Ronald N. Kahn. 1994. "Multi-Factor Models for Portfolio Risk." In *A Practitioner's Guide to Factor Models*. Charlottesville, VA: Research Foundation of the Institute of Chartered Financial Analysts.

Podkaminer, Eugene L. 2017. "Smart Beta Is the Gateway Drug to Risk Factor Investing." *Journal of Portfolio Management* 43 (5): 130–34. 10.3905/jpm.2017.43.5.130.

Ross, S. A. 1976. "The Arbitrage Theory of Capital Asset Pricing." *Journal of Economic Theory* 13 (3): 341–60. 10.1016/0022-0531(76)90046-6.

PRACTICE PROBLEMS

1. Compare the assumptions of the arbitrage pricing theory (APT) with those of the capital asset pricing model (CAPM).
2. Last year the return on Harry Company stock was 5 percent. The portion of the return on the stock not explained by a two-factor macroeconomic factor model was 3 percent. Using the data given below, calculate Harry Company stock's expected return.

Macroeconomic Factor Model for Harry Company Stock

Variable	Actual Value (%)	Expected Value (%)	Stock's Factor Sensitivity
Change in interest rate	2.0	0.0	−1.5
Growth in GDP	1.0	4.0	2.0

3. Assume that the following one-factor model describes the expected return for portfolios:

$$E(R_p) = 0.10 + 0.12\beta_{p,1}$$

Also assume that all investors agree on the expected returns and factor sensitivity of the three highly diversified Portfolios A, B, and C given in the following table:

Portfolio	Expected Return	Factor Sensitivity
A	0.20	0.80
B	0.15	1.00
C	0.24	1.20

Assuming the one-factor model is correct and based on the data provided for Portfolios A, B, and C, determine if an arbitrage opportunity exists and explain how it might be exploited.

4. Which type of factor model is most directly applicable to an analysis of the style orientation (for example, growth vs. value) of an active equity investment manager? Justify your answer.

5. Suppose an active equity manager has earned an active return of 110 basis points, of which 80 basis points is the result of security selection ability. Explain the likely source of the remaining 30 basis points of active return.

6. Address the following questions about the information ratio.
   A. What is the information ratio of an index fund that effectively meets its investment objective?
   B. What are the two types of risk an active investment manager can assume in seeking to increase his information ratio?

7. A wealthy investor has no other source of income beyond her investments and that income is expected to reliably meet all her needs. Her investment advisor recommends that she tilt her portfolio to cyclical stocks and high-yield bonds. Explain the advisor's advice in terms of comparative advantage in bearing risk.

The following information relates to Questions 8–13

Carlos Altuve is a manager-of-managers at an investment company that uses quantitative models extensively. Altuve seeks to construct a multi-manager portfolio using some of the funds managed by portfolio managers within the firm. Maya Zapata is assisting him.

Altuve uses arbitrage pricing theory (APT) as a basis for evaluating strategies and managing risks. From his earlier analysis, Zapata knows that Funds A and B in Exhibit 1 are well diversified. He has not previously worked with Fund C and is puzzled by the data because it is inconsistent with APT. He asks Zapata gather additional information on Fund C's holdings and to determine if an arbitrage opportunity exists among these three investment alternatives. Her analysis, using the data in Exhibit 1, confirms that an arbitrage opportunity does exist.

EXHIBIT 1   Expected Returns and Factor Sensitivities (One-Factor Model)

Fund	Expected Return	Factor Sensitivity
A	0.02	0.5
B	0.04	1.5
C	0.03	0.9

Using a two-factor model, Zapata now estimates the three funds' sensitivity to inflation and GDP growth. That information is presented in Exhibit 2. Zapata assumes a zero value for the error terms when working with the selected two-factor model.

EXHIBIT 2   Expected Returns and Factor Sensitivities (Two-Factor Model)

Fund	Expected Return	Factor Sensitivity	
		Inflation	GDP Growth
A	0.02	0.5	1.0
B	0.04	1.6	0.0
C	0.03	1.0	1.1

Altuve asks Zapata to calculate the return for Portfolio AC, composed of a 60 percent allocation to Fund A and 40 percent allocation to Fund C, using the surprises in inflation and GDP growth in Exhibit 3.

EXHIBIT 3   Selected Data on Factors

Factor	Research Staff Forecast	Actual Value
Inflation	2.0%	2.2%
GDP Growth	1.5%	1.0%

Finally, Altuve asks Zapata about the return sensitivities of Portfolios A, B, and C given the information provided in Exhibit 3.

8. Which of the following is *not* a key assumption of APT, which is used by Altuve to evaluate strategies and manage risks?
   A. A factor model describes asset returns.
   B. Asset-specific risk can be eliminated through diversification.
   C. Arbitrage opportunities exist among well-diversified portfolios.

9. The arbitrage opportunity identified by Zapata can be exploited with:
   A. Strategy 1: Buy $50,000 Fund A and $50,000 Fund B; sell short $100,000 Fund C.
   B. Strategy 2: Buy $60,000 Fund A and $40,000 Fund B; sell short $100,000 Fund C.
   C. Strategy 3: Sell short $60,000 of Fund A and $40,000 of Fund B; buy $100,000 Fund

10. The two-factor model Zapata uses is a:
    A. statistical factor model.
    B. fundamental factor model.
    C. macroeconomic factor model.

11. Based on the data in Exhibits 2 and 3, the return for Portfolio AC, given the surprises in inflation and GDP growth, is *closest* to:
    A. 2.02 percent.
    B. 2.40 percent.
    C. 4.98 percent.

12. The surprise in which of the following had the greatest effect on fund returns?
    A. Inflation on Fund B
    B. GDP growth on Fund A
    C. GDP growth on Fund C

13. Based on the data in Exhibit 2, which fund is most sensitive to the combined surprises in inflation and GDP growth in Exhibit 3?
    A. Fund A
    B. Fund B
    C. Fund C

The following information relates to Questions 14–19

Hui Cheung, a portfolio manager, asks her assistant, Ronald Lam, to review the macroeconomic factor model currently in use and to consider a fundamental factor model as an alternative.

The current macroeconomic factor model has four factors:

$$R_i = a_i + b_{i1}F_{GDP} + b_{i2}F_{CAP} + b_{i3}F_{CON} + b_{i4}F_{UNEM} + \varepsilon_i$$

where F_{GDP}, F_{CAP}, F_{CON}, and F_{UNEM} represent unanticipated changes in four factors: gross domestic product, manufacturing capacity utilization, consumer spending, and the rate of unemployment, respectively. Lam assumes the error term is equal to zero when using this model.

Lam estimates the current model using historical monthly returns for three portfolios for the most recent five years. The inputs used in and estimates derived from the macroeconomic factor model are presented in Exhibit 1. The US Treasury bond rate of 2.5 percent is used as a proxy for the risk-free rate of interest.

EXHIBIT 1 Inputs for and Estimates from the Current Macroeconomic Model

Factor	Factor Sensitivities and Intercept Coefficients				Factor Surprise (%)
	Portfolio 1	Portfolio 2	Portfolio 3	Benchmark	
Intercept (%)	2.58	3.20	4.33		
F_{GDP}	0.75	1.00	0.24	0.50	0.8
F_{CAP}	−0.23	0.00	−1.45	−1.00	0.5
F_{CON}	1.23	0.00	0.50	1.10	2.5
F_{UNEM}	−0.14	0.00	−0.05	−0.10	1.0
	Annual Returns, Most Recent Year				
Return (%)	6.00	4.00	5.00	4.50	

Lam uses the macroeconomic model to calculate the tracking error and the mean active return for each portfolio. He presents these statistics in Exhibit 2.

EXHIBIT 2 Macroeconomic Factor Model Tracking Error and Mean Active Return

Portfolio	Tracking Error	Mean Active Return
Portfolio 1	1.50%	1.50%
Portfolio 2	1.30%	−0.50%
Portfolio 3	1.00%	0.50%

Lam considers a fundamental factor model with four factors:

$$R_i = a_j + b_{j1}F_{LIQ} + b_{j2}F_{LEV} + b_{j3}F_{EGR} + b_{j4}F_{VAR} + \varepsilon_j$$

where F_{LIQ}, F_{LEV}, F_{EGR}, and F_{VAR} represent liquidity, financial leverage, earnings growth, and the variability of revenues, respectively.

Lam and Cheung discuss similarities and differences between macroeconomic factor models and fundamental factor models, and Lam offers a comparison of those models to statistical factor models. Lam makes the following statements.

Statement 1. The factors in fundamental factor models are based on attributes of stocks or companies, whereas the factors in macroeconomic factor models are based on surprises in economic variables.

Statement 2. The factor sensitivities are generally determined first in fundamental factor models, whereas the factor sensitivities are estimated last in macroeconomic factor models.

Lam also tells Cheung: "An advantage of statistical factor models is that they make minimal assumptions, and therefore, statistical factor model estimation lends itself to easier interpretation than macroeconomic and fundamental factor models."

Lam tells Cheung that multifactor models can be useful in active portfolio management, but not in passive management. Cheung disagrees; she tells Lam that multifactor models can be useful in both active and passive management.

14. Based on the information in Exhibit 1, the expected return for Portfolio 1 is *closest* to:
    A. 2.58 percent.
    B. 3.42 percent.
    C. 6.00 percent.

15. Based on Exhibit 1, the active risk for Portfolio 2 is explained by surprises in:
    A. GDP.
    B. consumer spending.
    C. all four model factors.

16. Based on Exhibit 2, which portfolio has the best information ratio?
    A. Portfolio 1
    B. Portfolio 2
    C. Portfolio 3

17. Which of Lam's statements regarding macroeconomic factor models and fundamental factor models is correct?
    A. Only Statement 1
    B. Only Statement 2
    C. Both Statements 1 and 2

18. Is Lam's comment regarding statistical factor models correct?
    A. Yes
    B. No, because he is incorrect with respect to interpretation of the models' results
    C. No, because he is incorrect with respect to the models' assumptions

19. Whose statement regarding the use of multifactor models in active and passive portfolio management is correct?
    A. Lam only
    B. Cheung only
    C. Both Lam and Cheung

CHAPTER 13

MEASURING AND MANAGING MARKET RISK

Don M. Chance, PhD, CFA
Michelle McCarthy Beck

LEARNING OUTCOMES

The candidate should be able to:

- explain the use of value at risk (VaR) in measuring portfolio risk;
- compare the parametric (variance–covariance), historical simulation, and Monte Carlo simulation methods for estimating VaR;
- estimate and interpret VaR under the parametric, historical simulation, and Monte Carlo simulation methods;
- describe advantages and limitations of VaR;
- describe extensions of VaR;
- describe sensitivity risk measures and scenario risk measures and compare these measures to VaR;
- demonstrate how equity, fixed-income, and options exposure measures may be used in measuring and managing market risk and volatility risk;
- describe the use of sensitivity risk measures and scenario risk measures;
- describe advantages and limitations of sensitivity risk measures and scenario risk measures;
- explain constraints used in managing market risks, including risk budgeting, position limits, scenario limits, and stop-loss limits;
- explain how risk measures may be used in capital allocation decisions;
- describe risk measures used by banks, asset managers, pension funds, and insurers.

Quantitative Methods for Investment Analysis, Second Edition, by Don M. Chance, PhD, CFA, and Michelle McCarthy Beck. Copyright © 2020 by CFA Institute.

1. INTRODUCTION

This chapter is an introduction to the process of measuring and managing market risk. Market risk is the risk that arises from movements in stock prices, interest rates, exchange rates, and commodity prices. Market risk is distinguished from credit risk, which is the risk of loss from the failure of a counterparty to make a promised payment, and also from a number of other risks that organizations face, such as breakdowns in their operational procedures. In essence, market risk is the risk arising from changes in the markets to which an organization has exposure.

Risk management is the process of identifying and measuring risk and ensuring that the risks being taken are consistent with the desired risks. The process of managing market risk relies heavily on the use of models. A model is a simplified representation of a real world phenomenon. Financial models attempt to capture the important elements that determine prices and sensitivities in financial markets. In doing so, they provide critical information necessary to manage investment risk. For example, investment risk models help a portfolio manager understand how much the value of the portfolio is likely to change given a change in a certain risk factor. They also provide insight into the gains and losses the portfolio might reasonably be expected to experience and the frequency with which large losses might occur.

Effective risk management, though, is much more than just applying financial models. It requires the application of judgment and experience not only to know how to use the models appropriately but also to appreciate the strengths and limitations of the models and to know when to supplement or substitute one model with another model or approach.

Financial markets operate more or less continuously, and new prices are constantly being generated. As a result, there is a large amount of data on market risk and a lot of collective experience dealing with this risk, making market risk one of the easier financial risks to analyze. Still, market risk is not an easy risk to capture. Although a portfolio's exposures can be identified with some certainty, the potential losses that could arise from those exposures are unknown. The data used to estimate potential losses are generated from past prices and rates, not the ones to come. Risk management models allow the experienced risk manager to blend that historical data with their own forward-looking judgment, providing a framework within which to test that judgment.

We first lay a foundation for understanding value at risk, discuss three primary approaches to estimating value at risk, and cover the primary advantages and limitations as well as extensions of value at risk. We then address the sensitivity measures used for equities, fixed-income securities, and options and also cover historical and hypothetical scenario risk measures. Next, we discuss the use of constraints in risk management, such as risk budgeting, position limits, scenario limits, stop-loss limits, and capital allocation as risk management tools. Lastly, we describe various applications and limitations of risk measures as used by different types of market participants and summarize our discussion.

2. UNDERSTANDING VALUE AT RISK

Value at risk (VaR) was developed in the late 1980s, and over the next decade, it emerged as one of the most important risk measures in global financial markets.

2.1. Value at Risk: Formal Definition

Value at risk is the minimum loss that would be expected a certain percentage of the time over a certain period of time given the assumed market conditions. It can be expressed in either currency units or as a percentage of portfolio value. Although this statement is an accurate definition of VaR, it does not provide sufficient clarity to fully comprehend the concept. To better understand what VaR means, let us work with an example. Consider the statement: *The 5% VaR of a portfolio is €2.2 million over a one-day period.* The following three points are important in understanding the concept of VaR:

- VaR can be measured in either currency units (in this example, the euro) or in percentage terms. In this example, if the portfolio value is €400 million, the VaR expressed in percentage terms would be 0.55% (€2.2 million/€400 million = 0.0055).
- VaR is a *minimum* loss. This point cannot be emphasized enough. VaR is often mistakenly assumed to represent *how much one can lose.* If the question is, "how much can one lose?" there is only one answer: *the entire portfolio.* In a €400 million portfolio, assuming no leverage, the most one can lose is €400 million.
- A VaR statement references a time horizon: losses that would be expected to occur over a given period of time. In this example, that period of time is one day. (If VaR is measured on a daily basis, and a typical month has 20–22 business days, then 5% of the days equates to about one day per month.)

These are the explicit elements of a VaR statement: the *frequency* of losses of a given *minimum magnitude* expressed either in *currency* or *percentage* terms. Thus, the VaR statement can be rephrased as follows: A loss of at least €2.2 million would be expected to occur about once every month.

A 5 percent VaR is often expressed as its complement—a 95 percent level of confidence. In this chapter, we will typically refer to the notion as a 5 percent VaR, but we should be mindful that it does imply a 95 percent level of confidence.

Using the example given, it is correct to say any of the following:

- €2.2 million is the minimum loss we would expect 5 percent of the time.
- 5 percent of the time, losses would be at least €2.2 million.
- We would expect a loss of no more than €2.2 million 95 percent of the time.

The last sentence is sometimes mistakenly phrased as "95 percent of the time we would expect to lose less than €2.2 million," but this statement could be taken to mean that 95 percent of the time we would incur losses, although those losses would be less than €2.2 million. In fact, a large percentage of the time we will make money.

Exhibit 1 illustrates the concept of VaR using the 5 percent case. It depicts a probability distribution of returns from a hypothetical portfolio. The distribution chosen is the familiar normal distribution, known sometimes as the bell curve, but that distribution is only one curve that might be used. In fact, there are compelling arguments that the normal distribution is not the right one to use for financial market returns. We discuss these arguments later.

EXHIBIT 1   Illustration of 5 Percent VaR in the Context of a Probability Distribution

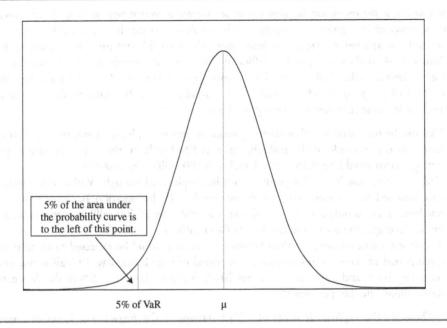

5% of the area under the probability curve is to the left of this point.

5% of VaR   μ

Note that the distribution in Exhibit 1 is centered on the value μ. [The symbol μ (Greek: *mu*) is a common symbol used to represent an expected value.] Near the left tail of the distribution is the notation "5% VaR," indicating that 5 percent of the area under the curve is to the left of the point of the VaR (i.e., the probability of observing a value less than the VaR is 5 percent).

Thus, it is apparent that VaR is simply a point on the probability distribution of profits or returns from a portfolio. Given the characteristics of the normal distribution, a 5 percent VaR is equivalent to the point on the distribution that is 1.65 standard deviations below the expected value. Although the concept of VaR can be easily visualized in this manner, actually measuring the VaR is a challenge.

Before we take on that challenge, however, note that there is no formal requirement that VaR be measured at a 5 percent threshold. It is also common to use a 1 percent threshold (2.33 standard deviations from the expected value), and some investment managers use a one standard deviation movement (equal to a 16 percent VaR)—both assuming a normal distribution. There is no definitive rule for what VaR cutoff should be used. A specification with a higher confidence level will produce a higher VaR. It is up to the decision maker to choose an appropriate level.

VaR and Standard Deviations

The 16 percent VaR relates to a one standard deviation move as follows: In a normal distribution, 50 percent of the outcomes are to the right of the expected value and

50 percent are to the left. A one standard deviation interval implies that 68 percent of the outcomes lie within one standard deviation of the expected value; thus, 34 percent of the outcomes lie one standard deviation to the left of the expected value and 34 percent of the outcomes one standard deviation to the right. Adding the 50 percent of the outcomes that lie to the right of the expected value to the 34 percent of the outcomes that lie one standard deviation below the expected value means that 84 percent of all outcomes lie to the right of the point that is one standard deviation to the left of the expected value. Therefore, 16 percent of all outcomes lie below this point. Thus, a one standard deviation movement is equivalent to a 16 percent VaR (or an 84 percent level of confidence).

Just as there is no formal requirement that VaR be measured at a 5 percent cutoff, there is also no formal requirement that VaR be measured using a daily loss estimate. One could reasonably measure VaR on a weekly, bi-weekly, monthly, quarterly, semiannually, or annual basis. Choosing the VaR threshold and the time horizon are examples of why VaR is not a precise measure but in fact entails considerable judgment.

We should also reiterate that VaR can be expressed as a rate of return or in monetary terms. It is typically easier to process the data necessary to estimate VaR in terms of returns, but VaR is most frequently expressed in terms of profits or losses. This point will become clearer as we work through examples.

EXAMPLE 1   Definition of VaR

1. Given a VaR of $12.5 million at 5 percent for one month, which of the following statements is correct?
    A. There is a 5 percent chance of losing $12.5 million over one month.
    B. There is a 95 percent chance that the expected loss over the next month is less than $12.5 million.
    C. The minimum loss that would be expected to occur over one month 5 percent of the time is $12.5 million.

2. Which of the following statements is **not** correct?
    A. A 1% VaR implies a downward move of 1 percent.
    B. A one standard deviation downward move is equivalent to a 16 percent VaR.
    C. A 5 percent VaR implies a move of 1.65 standard deviations less than the expected value.

Solution to 1: C is correct because it is the only statement that accurately expresses the VaR. A is incorrect because VaR does not give the likelihood of losing a specific amount. B is incorrect because VaR is not an expected loss; rather, it is a minimum loss.

Solution to 2: A is correct. A 1 percent VaR (99 percent confidence) is the point on the distribution 2.33 standard deviations below the expected value. Answers B and C correctly describe a 16 percent and 5 percent VaR, respectively.

To this point, we have given only the conceptual definition of VaR. Defining something is one thing; measuring it can be quite challenging. Such is the case for VaR.

2.2. Estimating VaR

Three methods are typically used to estimate VaR: the parametric (variance–covariance) method, the historical simulation method, and the Monte Carlo simulation method. Each of these will be discussed in turn.

The first step of every VaR calculation, regardless of the VaR method used, is to convert the set of holdings in the portfolio into a set of exposures to **risk factors**, a process called **risk decomposition**. In some instances, this process can be very simple: An equity security can be the risk factor itself. In other instances, the process can be highly complex. For example, a convertible bond issued by a foreign entity has both currency and equity risk factors as well as exposures to multiple points on a yield curve of a given credit quality. Fixed-income instruments and derivatives products often contain distinct risk exposures that require decomposition in order to accurately capture their loss potential.

The second step of VaR estimation requires gathering a data history for each of the risk factors in the VaR model. The three methods use different approaches to specifying these inputs, which will be discussed in the following sections. We will see that the parametric and Monte Carlo methods do not formally require a data history. They require only that the user enter estimates of certain parameters into the computational procedure (expected return, standard deviation, and for some models, skewness and kurtosis). One of the most common sources for estimating parameter inputs for any financial model is historical data, but the user could substitute estimates based on judgement or alternative forecasting models. Indeed, shortly we will override some historical estimates with our own judgement. Nonetheless, the collection of a data history is typically used at least as a starting point in the parametric and Monte Carlo methods, and it is absolutely required for the historical simulation method.

The third step of each method is where the differences between the three VaR methods are most apparent: how each method uses the data to make an estimate of the VaR.

Although most portfolios contain a large number of individual securities and other assets, we will use a two-asset portfolio to illustrate the three VaR methods. Using a limited number of assets permits us to closely observe the essential elements of the VaR estimation procedure without getting mired in the complex mathematics required to accommodate a large number of assets. The objective is to understand the concept of VaR, be aware of how it is estimated, know how it is used, appreciate the benefits of VaR, and be attentive to its limitations. We can achieve these objectives by keeping the portfolio fairly simple.

Our example portfolio has a market value of $150 million and consists of two ETFs— SPDR S&P 500 ETF (SPY), representing the US equity exposure, and SPDR Portfolio Long-Term Corporate Bond ETF (SPLB), representing a corporate bond exposure. We will allocate 80 percent of the portfolio to SPY and 20 percent of the portfolio to SPLB. For the sake of simplicity, the two securities will represent the risk factors and the return history of each ETF will serve as the risk factor history used in the VaR model. We have collected a set of two years of daily total return data, reflecting both capital appreciation and dividends on each ETF. The period used for this historical data set is called the **lookback period**. The question of exactly how much data are required to be a representative data set is a complex

EXHIBIT 2 Statistical Estimates from Daily Return Data, 1 July 2015–28 June 2019

	Daily		Annualized	
	Average Return	Standard Deviation	Average Return	Standard Deviation
SPY	0.047%	0.86%	12.51%	13.64%
SPLB	0.031%	0.49%	8.03%	7.73%

Note: The correlation of SPLB and SPY = –0.0607.

question that is common to all estimation problems in economics and finance. We will discuss some of the issues on this matter later in this chapter.

Exhibit 2 provides statistical summary information based on the two years of daily data in the lookback period, covering the period of 1 July 2015 through 28 June 2019.

SPY produced an annualized average return of about 12.5 percent with a standard deviation of 13.6 percent, significantly different from the long-term historical performance of the S&P 500 Index of approximately 10.5 percent average return and 20 percent standard deviation. SPLB produced an annualized average return of 8 percent with a standard deviation of about 7.7 percent. These numbers compare with an average annual return for long-term corporate bonds of slightly more than 6 percent and a standard deviation of about 8.5 percent (historical data are drawn from Malkiel 2007). Although the average return of SPLB in the last four years was higher than that of the overall long-term corporate bond sector, the standard deviations were similar.

The risk and return parameters for each risk factor in Exhibit 2 illustrate how one might collect historical data. It is necessary, however, to critically assess the data and apply judgment to modify the inputs if the lookback period is not representative of the expected performance of the securities (or risk factors) going forward. Exercising our judgment, and believing that we have no information to suggest that future performance will deviate from the long-run historical performance, we adjust our inputs and use returns of 10.5 percent for SPY and 6 percent for SPLB, with standard deviations of 20 percent for SPY and 8.5 percent for SPLB. These adjustments align the inputs more closely with the long-run historical performance of each sector. In practice, users will want to use estimates they believe are reflective of current expectations, though clearly one user's estimates could differ widely from another's.

Although the returns and standard deviations experienced over the lookback period have been adjusted to more closely align with long-run historical experience, we will use a correlation estimate approximately equal to the observed correlation over our lookback period. We are assuming that the recent historical relationship of equity and fixed-income returns is a reasonable assumption moving forward. To keep the numbers simple, we round the observed correlation of –0.0607 to –0.06.

Exhibit 3 illustrates our input assumptions for the VaR estimations.

EXHIBIT 3 Input Assumptions, 1 July 2015–28 June 2019

		Annualized	
	Allocation	Return	Standard Deviation
SPY	80%	10.5%	20.0%
SPLB	20%	6.0%	8.5%

Note: The correlation of SPLB and SPY = –0.06.

2.2.1. The Parametric Method of VaR Estimation

The **parametric method** of estimating VaR is sometimes referred to as the analytical method and sometimes the variance–covariance method. The parametric method begins, as does each method, with a risk decomposition of the portfolio holdings. It typically assumes that the return distributions for the risk factors in the portfolio are normal. It then uses the expected return and standard deviation of return for each risk factor to estimate the VaR.

Note that we said that this method *typically* uses the normal distribution. Indeed, that is the common case in practice, but there is no formal requirement that the normal distribution be used. The normal distribution conveniently requires only two parameters—the expected value and standard deviation—to encompass everything there is to know about it. If other distributions are used, additional parameters of the distribution, such as skewness and kurtosis, would be required. We will limit the presentation here to the normal distribution, but be aware that other, more accurately representative distributions could be used but would add complexity to the VaR estimation process.

Recall that in defining VaR, we identified a VaR threshold—a point in the left tail of the distribution, typically either the 5 percent left tail, the 1 percent left tail, or a one standard deviation move (16 percent). If the portfolio is characterized by normally distributed returns and the expected value and standard deviation are known, it is a simple matter to identify any point on the distribution. A normal distribution with expected value μ and standard deviation σ can be converted to a standard normal distribution, which is a special case of the normal distribution in which the expected value is zero and the standard deviation is one. A standard normal distribution is also known as a z-distribution. If we have observed a return R from a normal distribution, we can convert to its equivalent z-distribution value by the transformation:

$$z = \frac{R-\mu}{\sigma}.$$

In a standard normal (z) distribution, a 5 percent VaR is 1.65 standard deviations below the expected value of zero. A 1 percent VaR is 2.33 standard deviations below the expected value of zero. A 16 percent VaR is one standard deviation below the expected value of zero. Thus, in our example, for a 5 percent VaR, we wish to know the return that is 1.65 standard deviations to the left of the expected return.

To estimate this VaR, we need the expected return and volatility of the portfolio. The expected return is estimated from the following equation:

$$E(R_p) = w_{SPY}E(R_{SPY}) + w_{SPLB}E(R_{SPLB}) \tag{1}$$

where the expected return of the portfolio, $E(R_p)$, is equal to the portfolio weights of SPY (w_{SPY}) and SPLB (w_{SPLB}) multiplied by the expected return of each asset, $E(R_{SPY})$ and $E(R_{SPLB})$.

The volatility of the portfolio, σ_p, is estimated from the following equation:

$$\sigma_p = \sqrt{w_{SPY}^2\sigma_{SPY}^2 + w_{SPLB}^2\sigma_{SPLB}^2 + 2w_{SPY}w_{SPLB}\rho_{SPY,SPLB}\sigma_{SPY}\sigma_{SPLB}} \tag{2}$$

where σ_{SPY} and σ_{SPLB} are the standard deviations (volatilities) of SPY and SPLB, respectively; $\rho_{SPY,SPLB}$ is the correlation between the returns on SPY and SPLB, respectively; and $\rho_{SPY,SPLB}\sigma_{SPY}\sigma_{SPLB}$ is the covariance between SPY and SPLB.

Recall that we estimated these parameters from the historical data, with some modifications to make them more consistent with long-run values. The formal calculations for our portfolio based on these adjusted estimates are as follows:

$$E(R_p) = 0.8(0.105) + 0.2(0.06) = 0.096000$$

$$\sigma_p = \sqrt{(0.8)^2(0.2)^2 + (0.2)^2(0.085)^2 + 2(0.8)(0.2)(-0.06)(0.2)(0.085)}$$

$$=0.159883$$

Thus, our portfolio, consisting of an 80 percent position in SPY and a 20 percent position in SPLB, is estimated to have an expected return of 9.6 percent and a volatility of approximately 15.99 percent.

But these inputs are based on annual returns. If we want a one-day VaR, we should adjust the expected returns and volatilities to their daily counterparts. Assuming 250 trading days in a year, the expected return is adjusted by dividing by 250 and the standard deviation is adjusted by dividing by the square root of 250. (Note that the variance is converted by dividing by time, 250 days; thus, the standard deviation must be adjusted by using the square root of time, 250 days.) Thus, the daily expected return and volatility are

$$E(R_p) = \frac{0.096}{250} = 0.000384 \tag{3}$$

and

$$\sigma_p = \frac{0.159883}{\sqrt{250}} = 0.010112 \tag{4}$$

It is important to note that we have assumed that the statistical properties of the return distribution are constant across the year. Earlier, we annualized the daily data in Exhibit 2 in order to see how our estimates compared with long-term estimates. We made some modest adjustments to the annualized data and then, in Equations 3 and 4, returned to using daily data. To estimate an annual VaR, we would need to use annual data, but we would need a longer lookback period in order to have sufficient data points.

It is important to note that we cannot estimate a daily VaR and annualize it to arrive at an annual VaR estimate. First, to assume that a daily distribution of returns can be extrapolated to an annual distribution is a bold assumption. Second, annualizing the daily VaR is not the same as adjusting the expected return and the standard deviation to annual numbers and then calculating the annual VaR. The expected return is annualized by multiplying the daily return by 250, and the standard deviation is annualized by multiplying the daily standard deviation by the square root of 250. Thus, we can annualize the data and estimate an annual VaR, but we cannot estimate a daily VaR and annualize it without assuming a zero expected return.

Having calculated the daily expected return and volatility, the parametric VaR is now easily obtained. With the distribution centered at the expected return of 0.0384 percent and a one standard deviation move equal to 0.996 percent, a 5 percent VaR is obtained by identifying the point on the distribution that lies 1.65 standard deviations to the left of the mean. It is now easy to see why parametric VaR is so named: The expected values, standard deviations, and covariances are the *parameters* of the distributions.

The following step-by-step procedure shows how the VaR is derived:

$$\{[E(Rp) - 1.65\sigma_p](-1)\}(\$150,000,000)$$

Step 1: Multiply the portfolio standard deviation by 1.65.

$$0.010112 \times 1.65 = 0.016685$$

Step 2: Subtract the answer obtained in Step 1 from the expected return.

$$0.000384 - 0.016685 = -0.016301$$

Step 3: Because VaR is expressed as an absolute number (despite representing an expected loss), change the sign of the value obtained in Step 2.

$$\text{Change } -0.016301 \text{ to } 0.016301$$

Step 4: Multiply the result in Step 3 by the value of the portfolio.

$$\$150,000,000 \times 0.016301 = \$2,445,150$$

Thus, using the parametric method, our estimate of VaR is $2,445,150, meaning that on 5 percent of trading days the portfolio would be expected to incur a loss of at least $2,445,150. Note that asset managers may stop at Step 3 because at that point the measure is expressed as a percentage of the value of the portfolio, which is the unit this group more commonly uses.

EXAMPLE 2   Parametric VaR

1. The parameters of normal distribution required to estimate parametric VaR are:
   A. expected value and standard deviation.
   B. skewness and kurtosis.
   C. standard deviation and skewness.

2. Assuming a daily expected return of 0.0384 percent and daily standard deviation of 1.0112 percent (as in the example in the text), which of the following is *closest* to the 1 percent VaR for a $150 million portfolio? Express your answer in dollars.
   A. $3.5 million
   B. $2.4 million
   C. $1.4 million

3. Assuming a daily expected return of 0.0384 percent and daily standard deviation of 1.0112 percent (as in the example in the text), the daily 5 percent parametric VaR is $2,445,150. Rounding the VaR to $2.4 million, which of the following values is *closest* to the annual 5 percent parametric VaR? Express your answer in dollars.
   A. $38 million
   B. $25 million
   C. $600 million

Solution to 1: A is correct. The parameters of a normal distribution are the expected value and standard deviation. Skewness, as mentioned in B and C, and kurtosis, as mentioned in B, are characteristics used to describe a *non*-normal distribution.

Solution to 2: A is correct and is obtained as follows:

Step 1: $2.33 \times 0.010112 = 0.023561$
Step 2: $0.000384 - 0.023561 = -0.023177$
Step 3: Convert -0.023177 to 0.023177
Step 4: $0.023177 \times \$150$ million $= \$3,476,550$

B is the estimated VaR at a 5 percent threshold, and C is the estimated VaR using a one standard deviation threshold.

Solution to 3: B is correct. It is found by annualizing the daily return and standard deviation and using these figures in the calculation. The annual return and standard deviation are, respectively, 0.096000 (0.000384×250) and 0.159885 ($0.010112 \times \sqrt{250}$).

Step 1: $0.159885 \times 1.65 = 0.263810$
Step 2: $0.096000 - 0.263810 = -0.167810$
Step 3: Convert -0.167810 to 0.167810
Step 4: $0.167810 \times \$150$ million $= \$25,171,500$

A incorrectly multiplies the daily VaR by the square root of the number of trading days in a year ($\sqrt{250}$), and C incorrectly multiplies the daily VaR by the approximate number of trading days in a year (250). Neither A nor C make the appropriate adjustment to annualize the standard deviation.

To recap, we see that the parametric VaR method generally makes the assumption that the distribution of returns on the risk factors is normal. Under that assumption, all of the information about a normal distribution is contained in the expected value and standard deviation. Therefore, finding the 5 percent VaR requires only that we locate the point in the distribution beyond which 5 percent of the outcomes occur. Although normality is the general assumption of the parametric method, it is not an absolute requirement. Other distributions could be accommodated by incorporating skewness and kurtosis, the third and fourth parameters of the distribution, but that added complexity is not needed to demonstrate the general approach to parametric VaR and is rarely done in practice.

The major advantage of the parametric method is its simplicity and straightforwardness. The assumption of the normal distribution allows us to easily estimate the parameters using historical data, although judgment is required to adjust the parameters when the historical data may be misleading. The parametric method is best used in situations in which one is confident that the normal distribution can be applied as a reasonable approximation of the true distribution and the parameter estimates are reliable or can be turned into reliable estimates by suitable adjustments. It is important to understand that VaR under the parametric method is very sensitive to the parameter estimates, especially the covariances.

One of the major weaknesses of the parametric method is that it can be difficult to use when the investment portfolio contains options. When options are exercised, they pay off linearly with the underlying; however, if never exercised, an option loses 100 percent of its value.

This characteristic leads to a truncated, non-normal distribution that does not lend itself well to the parametric method. But some adjustments can render options more responsive to the parametric method. These adjustments are helpful but not perfect, limiting the usefulness of the parametric method when options are in the portfolio. Additionally, although the expected return and volatility of the underlying fixed income or equity security may be stable over the life of the option, the distribution of the option changes continuously as the value of the underlying, the volatility of the underlying, and the time to expiration all change.

2.2.2. The Historical Simulation Method of VaR Estimation

The **historical simulation method** of VaR uses the *current* portfolio and reprices it using the actual *historical* changes in the key factors experienced during the lookback period. We begin, as with the parametric method, by decomposing the portfolio into risk factors and gathering the historical returns of each risk factor from the chosen lookback period. Unlike the parametric method, however, we do not characterize the distribution using estimates of the mean return, the standard deviation, or the correlations among the risk factors in the portfolio. Instead, we reprice the current portfolio given the returns that occurred on each day of the historical lookback period and sort the results from largest loss to greatest gain. To estimate a one-day VaR at a 5 percent confidence interval, we choose the point on the resulting distribution beyond which 5 percent of the outcomes result in larger losses.

Illustrating this point using a full four years of daily observations would be tedious and consume a great deal of space, so we will condense the process quite a bit and then extrapolate the methodology. Exhibit 4 shows the daily returns on the SPY, the SPLB, and our 80 percent SPY/20 percent SPLB portfolio over the first five days of our historical data set. Please note that fixed weights are assumed for all days. Neither historical simulation nor Monte Carlo simulation is intended to be a replication of sequences of prices. They are intended to create a sample of one-day returns for a portfolio of given weights.

EXHIBIT 4   First Five Days of Historical Returns on the SPY/SPLB Portfolio Using the 1 July 2015–28 June 2019 Data

Day	SPY Return	SPLB Return	Portfolio Return
1	0.80%	−0.53%	0.53%
2	−0.09%	0.45%	0.02%
3	−0.28%	1.47%	0.07%
4	−0.63%	0.28%	0.56%
5	−1.68%	−0.23%	−1.39%

Notes: The Day 1 portfolio return is obtained by multiplying each holding (SPY, SPLB) by its respective weight in the portfolio (80%/20%) and adding the two results together: 0.80(0.008) + 0.20(−0.0053). Although Exhibit 4 shows only five days of returns, we would, of course, use all of the data at our disposal that is reasonably representative of possible future outcomes.

The historical simulation VaR extracts the portfolio return that lies at the appropriate confidence interval along the distribution. Using Excel's "=percentile(x,y)" function, we calculated the following historical simulation VaRs for our sample portfolio:

- 1% VaR (99% confidence) $2,643,196
- 5% VaR (95% confidence) $1,622,272
- 16% VaR (84% confidence) $880,221

Now, it will be interesting to compare this result with the parametric VaR estimates. Exhibit 5 shows the results side-by-side with the parameters used. The historical simulation method does not directly use these parameters but uses the data itself, and these numbers are the parameters implied by the data itself.

The historical simulation VaRs are much smaller, and the differences stem primarily from the adjustments we made to the historical parameters. We adjusted the volatility and the average return estimates of SPY to more closely reflect the historical norms and slightly raised the volatility of SPLB. Recall, in particular, that our factor history for the S&P 500 exhibited abnormally low volatility relative to the long-run experience.

Additionally, our calculations using the historical simulation method were not constrained by the assumption of a normal distribution as was the case with the parametric method. Exhibit 6 is a histogram of the portfolio returns used in the historical simulation results, overlaid with a normal distribution.

As can be seen, the resulting distribution under the historical simulation method is a departure from a normal distribution. This point again highlights the importance of understanding the underlying assumptions of any VaR model.

There is *no single right way* of estimating VaR. Each method provides an estimate of VaR and is highly sensitive to the input parameters, and similar to many estimation models, they will disagree.

Both the parametric and historical simulation methods in their most basic forms have the limitation that, as with most samples, all observations are weighted equally. The historical simulation method can adjust for this problem, however, by using a weighting methodology that gives more weight to more recent observations and less weight to more distant observations.

The primary advantage of the historical simulation method compared with the parametric method is that the historical simulation method estimates VaR based on what actually happened, so it cannot be dismissed as introducing impossible outcomes. Yet, therein also lies the primary weakness of the historical simulation method: There can be no certainty

EXHIBIT 5   Comparison of Historical and Parametric VaR Estimates Using 1 July 2015–28 June 2019 Data

	Historical Simulation Method		Parametric Method	
1% VaR	$2,643,196		$3,476,550	
5% VaR	$1,622,272		$2,445,150	
16% VaR	$880,221		$1,459,200	

	Average Return	Standard Deviation		Average Return	Standard Deviation
SPY	12.51%	13.64%		10.50%	20.00%
SPLB	8.03%	7.73%		6.00%	8.50%
Correlation of SPY and SPLB	−0.061			−0.06	

EXHIBIT 6   Histogram of Historical Portfolio Returns (80% SPY and 20% SPLB) Using 1 July 2015–28 June 2019 Data

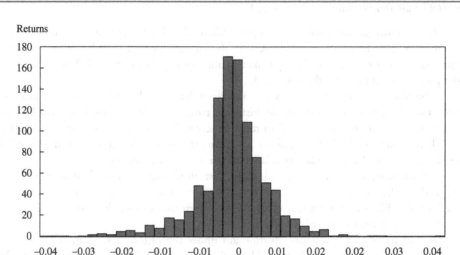

that a historical event will re-occur or that it would occur in the same manner or with the same likelihood as represented by the historical data. If one uses a relatively short historical data set, such as from January 1987 through December 1988 (a period encompassing the "Black Monday" of 19 October 1987, when stock markets around the world collapsed in a very short time), an occurrence of this magnitude might be projected to occur once every two years, surely an overstatement of its probability. Thus, the historical simulation method is best used when the distribution of returns during the lookback period are expected to be representative of the future.

The historical method is capable of handling the adjustment of one time horizon to another; that is, the information derived from daily data can be extrapolated to estimate an annual VaR, provided the distribution can be assumed to be stationary. In other words, one can convert each daily return to an annual return and then estimate the annual VaR. Although using annual data to estimate an annual VaR is always preferred, that would require a much longer lookback period.

We noted earlier that the parametric method is not well suited for options. Because the historical simulation method captures the returns that actually occurred regardless of the type of financial instrument used, it can accommodate options.

EXAMPLE 3   Historical Simulation VaR

1. Which of the following statements about the historical simulation method of estimating VaR is *most* correct?
   A. A 5 percent historical simulation VaR is the value that is 5 percent to the left of the expected value.
   B. A 5 percent historical simulation VaR is the value that is 1.65 standard deviations to the left of the expected value.

     C. A 5 percent historical simulation VaR is the fifth percentile, meaning the point on the distribution beyond which 5 percent of the outcomes result in larger losses.

2. Which of the following is a limitation of the historical simulation method?
    A. The past may not repeat itself.
    B. There is a reliance on the normal distribution.
    C. Estimates of the mean and variance could be biased.

Solution to 1: C is correct. In the historical method, the portfolio returns are arrayed lowest to highest and the observation at the fifth percentile (95 percent of the outcomes are better than this outcome) is the VaR. A is not correct because it draws a point on the distribution relative to the expected value rather than using the 5% of the outcomes that are in the left-most of the distribution. B confuses the parametric and historical methods. In the parametric method, the 5 percent VaR lies 1.65 standard deviations below the mean.

Solution to 2: A is correct. The historical simulation method estimates VaR based on the historical distribution of the risk factors. B is not correct; the historical simulation method does not rely on any particular distribution because it simply uses whatever distribution applied in the past. C is not correct because the historical distribution does not formally estimate the mean and variance.

2.2.3. The Monte Carlo Simulation Method of VaR Estimation

Monte Carlo simulation is a method of estimating VaR in which the user develops his own assumptions about the statistical characteristics of the distribution and uses those characteristics to generate random outcomes that represent hypothetical returns to a portfolio with the specified characteristics. This method is widely used in the sciences to estimate the statistical distribution of scientific phenomena and has many applications in business and finance. For example, a corporation considering the investment of a large amount of capital in a new project with many uncertain variables could simulate the possible values of these variables and thus gain an understanding of the distribution of the possible returns from this investment. Or, complex options can often be priced by simulating outcomes of the underlying, determining the payoffs of the option, and then averaging the option payoffs and discounting that value back to the present. The reference to the famous Mediterranean casino city allegedly came from an observation made by a scientist that the method is similar to tossing dice at a casino.

    Monte Carlo simulation avoids the complexity inherent in the parametric method when the portfolio has a large number of assets. (A large number of assets makes the parameters of the distribution difficult to extract.) There can be many risk factors, and the interactions among these risk factors can be too complex to specify. Moreover, Monte Carlo simulation does not need to be constrained by the assumption of normal distributions. Rather than attempt to determine the expected return and volatility of a combination of multiple statistical processes, one would simply simulate these processes, tabulate the statistical results of the simulations, and thereby gain a measure of the combined effects of these complex component processes on the overall risk.

Monte Carlo simulation requires the generation of random values of the underlying unknowns. In our example, the unknowns are the returns on the two risk factors, represented by the SPY and SPLB ETFs. We can, of course, assume that the statistical properties of the historical returns—their averages, volatilities, and correlation—are appropriate for use in a simulation, or we can modify those values to conform to what we expect to be relevant for the future. For illustrative purposes here, we will simply use the inputs we used in the parametric method.

Recall that we previously assumed for the sake of simplicity that the two securities represent the risk factors. We now decompose the portfolio holdings into these risk factors. First we simulate the returns of these two risk factors, and then we re-price our exposures to the risk factors under the range of simulated returns, recording the results much as we do in the historical simulation method. We then sort the results in order from worst to best. A 5 percent Monte Carlo VaR would simply be the fifth percentile of the simulated values instead of the historical values.

Yet, it is not quite that simple. We must first decide how many random values to generate. There is no industry standard. The more values we use, the more reliable our answers are but the more time-consuming the procedure becomes. In addition, we cannot just simulate values of two random variables without accounting for the correlation between the two. For example, if you spin two roulette wheels, you can assume they are independent of each other in much the same manner as are two uncorrelated assets. But most assets have at least a small degree of correlation. In our example, we used the historical correlation of about –0.06. Monte Carlo simulation must take that relationship into account.

For simplicity, this chapter will not go into detail on either the mathematical techniques that can account for the correlations among risk factor returns or the specific method used to simulate outcomes given average values and volatilities for each risk factor. Both are beyond the scope of this chapter.

For this example, we will use 10,000 simulated returns on SPY and SPLB drawn from a normal distribution. Of course, non-normal distributions can be used—and they commonly are in practice—but we want to keep the illustration simple to facilitate comparisons between methods. Each set of simulated returns combines to produce a sample with the expected returns and volatilities as we specified. In addition, the returns will have the pre-specified correlation of –0.06. Each pair of returns is weighted 80/20 as desired. We generate the 10,000 outcomes, sort them from worst to best, and either select the outcome at the 5th percentile for a 5 percent VaR, the outcome at the 1st percentile for a 1 percent VaR, or the outcome at the 16th percentile if we want to evaluate the impact of a one standard deviation move. Using the parameters specified in our example, the simulation returns a distribution from which we can draw the following VaR numbers:

$$1\% \text{ VaR} = \$3,541,035$$

$$5\% \text{ VaR} = \$2,517,702$$

$$16\% \text{ VaR} = \$1,524,735$$

Note that these results are fairly close to VaR under the parametric VaR method, where the 5 percent VaR was $2,445,150. The slight difference arises from the fact that

Monte Carlo simulation only *samples* from a population with certain parameters while the parametric method *assumes* those parameters. A sample of a distribution will not produce statistics that match the parameters precisely except in extremely large sample sizes, much larger than the 10,000 used here. Exhibit 7 displays a histogram of the simulated returns overlaid with a bell curve representing a normal distribution. Note how the simulated returns appear more normally distributed than do the historical values, as illustrated in Exhibit 6. This is because we explicitly assumed a normal distribution when running the simulation to generate the values in our example.

Although we conveniently assumed a normal distribution, one of the advantages of the Monte Carlo method is that it can accommodate virtually *any* distribution. In fact, the flexibility of the Monte Carlo method to handle more complex distributions is its primary attraction. The Monte Carlo and historical simulation methods are much more capable than the parametric method of accurately incorporating the effects of option positions or bond positions with embedded options.

Similar to the historical simulation method, you can scale daily returns to annual returns and extrapolate an estimate of the annual VaR by running a Monte Carlo simulation on these annual returns.

At one time, calculating VaR using the Monte Carlo simulation method was slow, but with the speed of today's computers, it is relatively easy and fast to simulate extremely complex processes for portfolios with thousands of exposures.

EXHIBIT 7   Monte Carlo Simulated Returns 80/20 Portfolio of SPY and SPLB

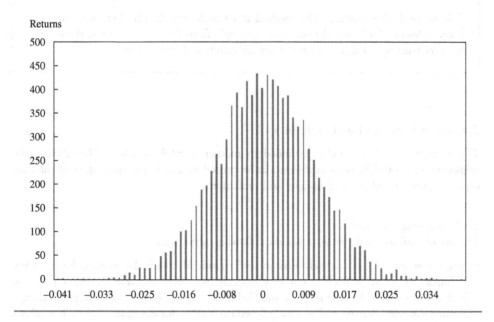

EXAMPLE 4   Monte Carlo Simulation VaR

1. When will the Monte Carlo method of estimating VaR produce virtually the same results as the parametric method?
   A. When the Monte Carlo method assumes a non-normal distribution.
   B. When the Monte Carlo method uses the historical return and distribution parameters.
   C. When the parameters and the distribution used in the parametric method are the same as those used in the Monte Carlo method and the Monte Carlo method uses a sufficiently large sample.

2. Which of the following is an advantage of the Monte Carlo method?
   A. The VaR is easy to calculate with a simple formula.
   B. It is flexible enough to accommodate many types of distributions.
   C. The number of necessary simulations is determined by the parameters.

Solution to 1: C is correct. The Monte Carlo method simulates outcomes using whatever distribution is specified by the user. *If* a normal distribution is used *and* a sufficiently large number of simulations are run, the parameters of the Monte Carlo sample will converge with those used in the parametric method and the overall VaR should be very close to that of the parametric method. A is incorrect because the parametric method is not well-adapted to a non-normal distribution. B is incorrect because neither the Monte Carlo method nor the parametric method focuses on historical outcomes.

Solution to 2: B is correct. The method can handle any distribution. A is incorrect because Monte Carlo simulation is not a simple formula. C is incorrect; there is no industry-wide agreement as to the necessary number of simulations.

2.3. Advantages and Limitations of VaR

The concept of VaR is solidly grounded in modern portfolio analysis. Nonetheless, the implementation of VaR, both in the estimation procedure and in the application of the concept, presents a number of advantages and limitations.

2.3.1. Advantages of VaR
The use of VaR as a risk measure has the following advantages:

- *Simple concept.* VaR is relatively easy to understand. Although the methodology is fairly technical, the concept itself is not very difficult. So, decision makers without technical backgrounds should be able to grasp the likelihood of possible losses that might endanger the organization. Reporting that a daily 5 percent VaR is, for example, €2.2 million allows the user to assess the risk in the context of the capital deployed. If a portfolio is expected to incur losses of a minimum of €2.2 million on 5 percent of the trading days, about once a month, this information is valuable in the context of the size of the portfolio.

- *Easily communicated concept.* VaR captures a considerable amount of information into a single number. If the recipient of the information fully understands the meaning and limitations of VaR, it can be a very significant and practical piece of information.
- *Provides a basis for risk comparison.* VaR can be useful in comparing risks across asset classes, portfolios, and trading units—giving the risk manager a better picture of which constituents are contributing the least and the most to the overall risk. As such, the risk manager can be better informed as he looks for potential hot spots in the organization. This point will be discussed further in a later section.
- *Facilitates capital allocation decisions.* The ability to compare VaR across trading units or portfolio positions provides management with a benchmark that can be used in capital allocation decisions. A proprietary trading firm, for example, can find that its VaR in equity trading is $20 million and its VaR in fixed-income trading is $10 million. If its equity trading portfolio is not expected to take more risk than its fixed-income trading portfolio, then the equity trading activities are taking too much risk or there is too much capital allocated to equity trading. The firm should either make adjustments to realign its VaR or allocate capital in proportion to the relative risks. If a firm is looking to add a position to a portfolio or change the weights of existing portfolio positions, certain extensions of VaR allow the manager to assess the risk of these changes. This topic will be covered in more detail later.
- *Can be used for performance evaluation.* Risk-adjusted performance measurement requires that return or profit be adjusted by the level of risk taken. VaR can serve as the basis for risk adjustment. Without this adjustment, more profitable units could be perceived as more successful; however, when adjusted by VaR, a less profitable unit that poses less risk of loss may be judged more desirable.
- *Reliability can be verified.* VaR is easily capable of being verified, a process known as backtesting. For example, if the daily VaR is $5 million at 5 percent, we would expect that on 5 percent of trading days a loss of at least $5 million would be incurred. To determine whether a VaR estimate is reliable, one can determine over a historical period of time whether losses of at least $5 million were incurred on 5% of trading days, subject to reasonable statistical variation.
- *Widely accepted by regulators.* In the United States, the SEC requires that the risk of derivatives positions be disclosed either in the form of a summary table, by sensitivity analysis (a topic we cover later), or by VaR. Thus, VaRs are frequently found in annual reports of financial firms. Global banking regulators also encourage banks to use VaR. These regulations require or encourage the use of VaR, but they do not prescribe how it should be implemented, which estimation method to use, or the maximum acceptable VaR.

2.3.2. Limitations of VaR

Despite its many advantages, users of VaR must also understand its limitations. The primary limitations of VaR are the following:

- *Subjectivity.* In spite of the apparent scientific objectivity on which it is based, VaR is actually a rather subjective method. As we saw in the descriptions of the three methods of estimating VaR, there are many decisions to make. At the fundamental level, decisions must be made as to the desired VaR cutoff (5 percent, 1 percent, or some other cutoff);

over what time horizon the VaR will be measured; and finally, which estimation method will be used. As we have seen here, for each estimation method, there are numerous other discretionary choices to make about inputs, source of data, and so on.

- *Underestimating the frequency of extreme events.* In particular, use of the normal distribution in the parametric method and sometimes in the Monte Carlo method commonly underestimates the likelihood of extreme events that occur in the left tail of the distribution. In other words, there are often more extreme adverse events, called "left-tail events," than would be expected under a normal distribution. As mentioned previously, there is no particular requirement that one use the normal distribution. The historical simulation method uses whatever distribution the data produce. We chose to illustrate the Monte Carlo method with a normal distribution, and it is virtually always used in the parametric method. Nonetheless, the tendency to favor the normal distribution and other simple and symmetrical distributions often leads to an understatement of the frequency of left-tail events.

- *Failure to take into account liquidity.* If some assets in a portfolio are relatively illiquid, VaR could be understated, even under normal market conditions. Additionally, liquidity squeezes are frequently associated with tail events and major market downturns, thereby exacerbating the risk. Although illiquidity in times of stress is a general problem that affects virtually all of a firm's financial decisions, reliance on VaR in non-normal market conditions will lead the user to underestimate the magnitude of potential losses.

- *Sensitivity to correlation risk.* Correlation risk is the risk that during times of extreme market stress, correlations among all assets tend to rise significantly. Thus, markets that provide a reasonable degree of diversification under normal conditions tend to decline together under stressed market conditions, thereby no longer providing diversification.

- *Vulnerability to trending or volatility regimes.* A portfolio might remain under its VaR limit every day but lose an amount approaching this limit each day. Under such circumstances, the portfolio could accumulate substantial losses without technically breaching the VaR constraint. Also, during periods of low volatility, VaR will appear quite low, underestimating the losses that could occur when the environment returns to a normal level of volatility.

- *Misunderstanding the meaning of VaR.* VaR is not a worst-case scenario. Losses can and will exceed VaR.

- *Oversimplification.* Although we noted that VaR is an easily communicated concept, it can also oversimplify the picture. And although VaR does indeed consolidate a considerable amount of information into a single number, that number should be interpreted with caution and an awareness of the other limitations as well as supported by additional risk measures.

- *Disregard of right-tail events.* VaR focuses so heavily on the left tail (the losses) that the right tail (potential gains) are often ignored. By examining both tails of the distribution, the user can get a better appreciation of the overall risk–reward trade-off, which is often missed by concentrating only on VaR.

These limitations are not unique to VaR; they apply equally to any technique or measure used to quantify the expected rewards and risks of investing.

EXAMPLE 5   Advantages and Limitations of VaR

1. Which of the following is **not** an advantage of VaR?
   A. It is a simple concept to communicate.
   B. There is widespread agreement on how to calculate it.
   C. It can be used to compare risk across portfolios or trading units.

2. Which of the following is a limitation of VaR?
   A. It requires the use of the normal distribution.
   B. The maximum VaR is prescribed by federal securities regulators.
   C. It focuses exclusively on potential losses, without considering potential gains.

Solution to 1: B is correct. There is no consensus on how to calculate VaR. A and C are both advantages of VaR, as we noted that VaR is fairly simple to communicate and it can show the contribution of each unit to the overall VaR.

Solution to 2: C is correct. VaR deals exclusively with left-tail or adverse events. A is wrong because although parametric VaR does generally use the normal distribution, the historical simulation method uses whatever distribution occurred in the past and Monte Carlo simulation uses whatever distribution the user chooses. B is incorrect because regulators do not specify maximum VaRs, although they may encourage and require that the measure be used.

2.4. Extensions of VaR

Clearly no single risk model can answer all of the relevant questions a risk manager may have. As a result, VaR has laid a foundation for a number of variations, each of which provides additional information.

As discussed previously, VaR is a minimum loss and is typically expressed as the minimum loss that can be expected to occur 5 percent of the time. An important and related measure can determine the average loss that would be incurred if the VaR cutoff is exceeded. This measure is sometimes referred to as the **conditional VaR (CVaR)**, although it is not technically a VaR measure. It is the average loss conditional on exceeding the VaR cutoff. So, VaR answers the question, "What is the minimum loss I can expect at a certain confidence?" And CVaR answers the question, "How much can I expect to lose if VaR is exceeded?" CVaR is also sometimes referred to as the **expected tail loss** or **expected shortfall**. CVaR is best derived using the historical simulation and Monte Carlo methods, in which one can observe all of the returns throughout the distribution and calculate the average of the losses beyond the VaR cutoff. The parametric method uses a continuous distribution, so obtaining the average loss beyond the VaR cutoff would require a level of mathematics beyond the scope of this chapter.

Using our earlier example, in the historical simulation method, our sample of 500 historical returns was sorted from lowest to highest and the 5 percent VaR was $1,622,272. With 1,006 returns in the sample, 50 observations (5% of 1,006) lie below the VaR estimate.

The average of these losses is $2,668,389. Thus, when the VaR is exceeded, we would expect an average loss of about $2.7 million.

For the Monte Carlo method, we generated 10,000 random values and obtained a 5 percent VaR of $2,517,705. Given 10,000 random values, 500 observations are in the lowest 5 percent of the VaR distribution. The CVaR using the Monte Carlo method would be the average of the 500 lowest values, which is $4,397,756.

Note that once again, the CVaR derived using the historical simulation method is lower than the CVaR derived using the Monte Carlo method. As explained earlier, this result can largely be attributed to the lower volatility of the S&P 500 component in the historical data series.

Beyond assessing tail loss, a risk manager often wants to know how the portfolio VaR will change if a position size is changed relative to the remaining positions. This effect can be captured by a concept called **incremental VaR (IVaR)**. Using our example, suppose the portfolio manager is contemplating increasing the risk by increasing the investment in SPY to 90 percent of the portfolio. We recalculate the VaR under the proposed allocation, and the incremental VaR is the difference between the "before" and "after" VaR. As an example, using the parametric method, the VaR would be expected to increase from $2,445,150 to $2,752,500; thus, the IVaR for the 5 percent case would be $307,350. Or, the portfolio manager might wish to add a new asset, thereby reducing the exposure to the existing assets. The risk manager would calculate the VaR under the assumption that the change is made, and then the difference between the new VaR and the old VaR is the IVaR. This measure is useful because it reflects the effect of an anticipated change on the VaR. The risk manager could find that the new VaR will be unacceptably high or that it has possibly even decreased.

A related concept is called **marginal VaR (MVaR)**. It is conceptually similar to incremental VaR in that it reflects the effect of an anticipated change in the portfolio, but it uses formulas derived from calculus to reflect the effect of a very small change in the position. Some people interpret MVaR as a change in the VaR for a $1 or 1 percent change in the position, although that is not strictly correct. Nonetheless, this interpretation is a reasonable approximation of the concept behind marginal VaR, which is to reflect the impact of a small change. In a diversified portfolio, marginal VaR may be used to determine the contribution of each asset to the overall VaR; the marginal VaRs for all positions may be proportionately weighted to sum to the total VaR.

Both incremental and marginal VaR address the question of what impact a change in the portfolio holdings might have on the total VaR of the portfolio. Both take into account the potential diversifying effects of various positions or subportfolios, and thus they both can be useful in evaluating the potential effect of a trade before the trade is done.

Another related measure is *ex ante* **tracking error**, also known as **relative VaR**, which is a measure of the degree to which the performance of a given investment portfolio might deviate from its benchmark. It is computed using any of the standard VaR models, described earlier, but the portfolio to which VaR is applied contains the portfolio's holdings *minus* the holdings in the specified benchmark. In other words, the benchmark's holdings, weighted in proportion to the value of the subject portfolio, are entered into the VaR modeling process as short positions. VaR for this measure is typically expressed as a one standard deviation annualized measure. If the portfolio is a perfect match to the benchmark, *ex ante* tracking error will be at or near zero. The more the portfolio differs from the benchmark, the larger the *ex ante* tracking error will be.

EXAMPLE 6   Extensions of VaR

1. Conditional VaR measures the:
    A. VaR over all possible losses.
    B. VaR under normal market conditions.
    C. average loss, given that VaR is exceeded.

2. Which of the following correctly identifies incremental VaR?
    A. The change in VaR from increasing a position in an asset.
    B. The increase in VaR that might occur during extremely volatile markets.
    C. The difference between the asset with the highest VaR and the asset with the second highest VaR.

3. Which of the following statements is correct about marginal VaR?
    A. The marginal VaR is the same as the incremental VaR.
    B. The marginal VaR is the VaR required to meet margin calls.
    C. Marginal VaR estimates the change in VaR for a small change in a given portfolio holding.

Solution to 1: C is correct. Conditional VaR is the average loss conditional on exceeding the VaR. A is not correct because CVaR is not concerned with losses that do not exceed the VaR threshold, and B is incorrect because VaR does not distinguish between normal and non-normal markets.

Solution to 2: A correctly defines incremental VaR. Incremental VaR is the change in VaR from increasing a position in an asset, not a change in VaR from an increase in volatility. B is not correct because incremental volatility reflects the results of intentional changes in exposure, not uncontrollable market volatility. C is not correct because incremental VaR is not the difference in the VaRs of the assets with the greatest and second greatest VaRs.

Solution to 3: C is correct. In A, marginal VaR is a similar concept to incremental VaR in that they both deal with the effect of changes in VaR, but they are not the same concept. B is incorrect because marginal VaR has nothing to do with margin calls.

3. OTHER KEY RISK MEASURES—SENSITIVITY AND SCENARIO MEASURES

Just as no single measure of a person's health gives a complete picture of that person's physical condition, no single risk measure gives a full picture of a portfolio's risk profile. As we saw, although VaR has many advantages, it also has many limitations. Therefore, good risk managers will use a comprehensive set of risk tools. In this section, we will look at two additional classes of risk measures: those based on sensitivity analysis and those based on the use of hypothetical or historical scenarios. The former enable us to estimate how our estimated gains and losses change with changes in the underlying risk factors, whereas the latter are based on situations involving considerable market stress from which we estimate how our portfolio will perform.

3.1. Sensitivity Risk Measures

Equity, fixed-income, and options positions can be characterized by a number of exposure measures that reflect the sensitivities of these positions to movements in underlying risk factors. Sensitivity measures examine how performance responds to a single change in an underlying risk factor. Understanding and measuring how portfolio positions respond to the underlying sources of risk are primary objectives in managing risk.

3.1.1. Equity Exposure Measures

The primary equity exposure measure is the beta. In a simple world, a single market factor drives equity returns. The return on a stock is given by the familiar capital asset pricing model (CAPM):

$$E(R_i) = R_F + \beta_i[E(R_M) - R_F]$$

where $E(R_i)$ is the expected return on the asset or portfolio i, R_F is the risk-free rate, $E(R_m)$ is the expected return on the market portfolio, and β_i is the beta, which is the risk measure. The expression $E(R_m) - R_F$ is the equity risk premium, which is the return investors demand for investing in equities rather than risk-free instruments. It should be apparent from this often-used equation that beta measures the sensitivity of the security's expected return to the equity risk premium. The beta is defined as the covariance of the asset return with the market return divided by the variance of the market return. The broad market beta, which is an average of all individual betas, is 1.0. Assets with betas more (less) than 1 are considered more (less) volatile than the market as a whole. The CAPM has a number of extensions, including multifactor models, and risk measures derived from those models can also provide more nuanced information on equity risk exposures.

3.1.2. Fixed-Income Exposure Measures

The primary sensitivity exposure measures for fixed-income investments are duration and convexity. (Note that credit, a major factor driving non-government fixed-income markets, is covered elsewhere.) **Duration** is sometimes described as the weighted-average time to maturity of a bond, in which the bond is treated as partially maturing on each coupon payment date. Duration is a sensitivity measure. Under the assumption that all interest rates that affect a bond change by the same percentage, the duration is a measure of the sensitivity of the bond price to the interest rate change that characterizes all rates. This single rate can be viewed as the bond's yield, y. Given a bond priced at B and yield change of Δy, the rate of return or percentage price change for the bond is approximately given as follows:

$$\frac{\Delta B}{B} \approx -D\frac{\Delta y}{1+y}$$

where D is the duration. (The $\approx$ sign stands for the phrase "approximately equal" and reflects the fact that the relationship is not exact.) In this expression, it is easy to see that duration does reflect the sensitivity of a bond's price to its yield, although under the restrictive assumption of a single change to all rates. The assumption of a single change to all rates may seem fairly restrictive, but ultimately the assumption is encapsulated by assuming that a single discount rate, the yield, drives the bond price. Duration is considered to be a fairly good sensitivity measure. As previously mentioned, duration is a time measure, the weighted-average maturity of a bond, in which the bond is viewed as maturing progressively as it makes its coupon payments.

The relationship shown here is approximate. The formula is derived under the assumption that the yield change is infinitesimally small, and duration fails to accurately capture bond price movements when yield changes are relatively large. Thus, in the above expression, Δy is for small yield changes. It is not possible, however, to say how small a yield change must be before it is small enough for the expression to hold true. In addition, the expression holds only at any instant in time and only for that instant. Over longer periods, the relationship will be less accurate because of the passage of time and because Δy is likely to be larger. To accommodate longer periods of time and larger yield changes, we can incorporate a second factor called **convexity**, which is denoted C. Convexity describes the sensitivity of a bond's duration to changes in interest rates. Adding convexity to the expression, we obtain the following formula:

$$\frac{\Delta B}{B} \approx -D\frac{\Delta y}{1+y} + \frac{1}{2}C\frac{\Delta y^2}{(1+y)^2}$$

Convexity can play an important role as a risk measure for large yield changes and long holding periods.

Duration and convexity are essential tools in fixed-income risk management. They allow the risk manager to assess the potential losses to a fixed-income portfolio or position under a given change in interest rates.

3.1.3. Options Risk Measures

Derivatives have their own unique exposure measures. Because forwards, futures, and swaps have payoffs that are linear in relation to their underlying, they can often be evaluated using the same exposure measures as their underlying. Options, however, have non-linear payoffs, which result in them having their own family of exposure measures that incorporate this non-linear behavior.

Although options can be very risky instruments in and of themselves, they are a critical tool for effective risk management and are often used to create an exposure to offset an existing risk in the portfolio. The relative riskiness of an option arises from the high degree of leverage embedded in most options. An additional and very important risk can also arise from the sensitivity of an option to the volatility of the underlying security. We will expand on these points in the next few paragraphs.

The most fundamental risk of an option is its sensitivity to the price of the underlying. This sensitivity is called the option's **delta**. Although delta is derived by using mathematics beyond the scope of this chapter, we can provide a simple and reasonably effective definition as follows:

$$\Delta \, (\text{delta}) \approx \frac{\text{Change in value of option}}{\text{Change in value of underlying}}$$

Call option deltas range from a value of 0 to a value of 1, whereas put option deltas range from a value of 0 to a value of −1. A value of 0 means that the option value does not change when the value of the underlying changes, a condition that is never absolutely true but can be roughly true for a very deep out-of-the-money option. A call delta of 1 means that the price of the call option changes in unison with the underlying, a condition that is also never absolutely true but is *approximately* true for very deep in-the-money calls. A put delta of −1 means that the price of the put option changes in unison with the underlying but in the opposite direction, a condition that is also never absolutely true but is *approximately* true for very deep in-the-money puts. As expiration approaches, an in-the-money call (put) delta approaches 1 (−1) and an out-of-the-money call (put) delta approaches 0.

Delta can be used to approximate the new price of an option as the underlying changes. For a call option, we can use the following formula:

$$c + \Delta c \approx c + \Delta_c \Delta S$$

Here, c is the original price of the option and Δc is the change in the price. We approximate the change in the price as the product of the call's delta, Δ_c, and the change in the value of the underlying, ΔS. The same relationship would hold for puts, simply changing the c's to p's.

The delta of an option is somewhat analogous to the duration of a fixed-income security. It is a first-order effect, reflecting the direct change in the value of the option or fixed-income security when the underlying price or yield, respectively, changes. Just as duration captures the effect of only small changes in the yield over a short period of time, delta captures the effect of only small changes in the value of the underlying security over a short period of time. Similar to duration, which has the second-order effect of convexity, we can add a second-order effect for options called **gamma**. Gamma is a measure of how sensitive an option's delta is to a change in the underlying. It is a second-order effect in that it is measuring the sensitivity of the first-order effect, delta. Gamma can be interpreted in several ways. The delta reflects the direct change in the value of the underlying position, whereas gamma reflects the indirect change (i.e., the change in the change). Technically, it reflects the change in the delta, as indicated by the following:

$$\Gamma \text{ (gamma)} \approx \frac{\text{Change in delta}}{\text{Change in value of underlying}}$$

As with convexity, gamma itself is not simple to interpret. For example, a call option might have a delta of 0.6 and a gamma of 0.02. It is not easy to determine whether the gamma is large or small. Using the equation just given, if the value of the underlying increases by 0.10 and the gamma is 0.02, then the delta would increase by 0.002 (0.10 × 0.02), from 0.6 to 0.602. Gammas get larger as the option approaches at-the-money, and they are large when options approach expiration, unless the option is deeply in or out of the money. Gamma reflects the uncertainty of whether the option will expire in or out of the money. When an option is close to expiration and roughly at the money, a small change in the price of the underlying will determine whether the option expires worthless or in the money. The uncertainty associated with this win-or-lose situation over a very short time frame leads to a large gamma.

Using delta and gamma, the new call price is

$$c + \Delta c \approx c + \Delta_c \Delta S + \frac{1}{2}\Gamma_c(\Delta S)^2$$

where Γ_c is the gamma of the call. This equation is similar to the corresponding expression that relates yield changes to bond price changes through duration and convexity. Indeed, as we said, gamma is a second-order effect, like convexity.

A third important sensitivity measure for options is **vega**, and it reflects the effect of volatility. Vega is a first-order effect reflecting the relationship between the option price and the volatility of the underlying. Vega is expressed by the following relationship:

$$\text{Vega} \approx \frac{\text{Change in value of option}}{\text{Change in volatility of underlying}}$$

Most options are very sensitive to the volatility of the underlying security. The effect of changing volatility can have a material impact on the value of the option, even when the value of the underlying is not changing.

Using delta, gamma, and vega, the new value of an option given an old value, a change in the value of the underlying, and a change in the volatility can be estimated as follows:

$$c + \Delta c \approx c + \Delta_c \Delta S + \frac{1}{2}\Gamma_c(\Delta S)^2 + \text{vega}(\Delta \sigma)$$

where $\Delta \sigma$ is the change in volatility.

The expression represents a composite sensitivity relationship for options. It reflects the expected response of an option value to changes in the value and volatility of the underlying, the two primary factors that change in an unpredictable manner and influence the option value. For portfolios that contain options, understanding these relationships and using them to assess the portfolio's response to market movements are essential elements of effective risk management.

These option measures are applicable not only to options but also to portfolios that contain options. For example, the delta of a portfolio consisting of a long position in an S&P 500 ETF and a short position in a call option on the ETF has a delta that is determined by both the ETF and the option. The ETF has a delta of 1; it changes one-for-one with the S&P 500. The option delta, as noted, has a delta between 0 and 1, though technically 0 and −1 because the option position is short. The ETF has no gamma or vega, so the portfolio gamma and vega are determined by the option. The overall deltas, gammas, and vegas are sums of the deltas, gammas, and vegas of the component positions, taking into account the relative amounts of money invested in each position. Risk managers need to know the overall deltas, gammas, vegas, durations, convexities, and betas to get a comprehensive picture of the sensitivity of the entire portfolio to the prices and volatilities of the underlying.

EXAMPLE 7   Sensitivity Risk Measures

1. Which of the following *most* accurately characterizes duration and convexity?
   A. Sensitivity of bond prices to interest rates
   B. First- and second-order effects of yield changes on bond prices
   C. Weighted-average time to maturity based on the coupon payments and principal

2. Which of the following statements about the delta of a call option is **not** correct?
   A. It ranges between 0 and 1.
   B. It precisely captures the change in the call value when the underlying changes.
   C. It approaches 1 for an in-the-money option and 0 for an out-of-the-money option.

3. Which of the following statements about gamma and vega are correct?
   A. Gamma is a second-order effect, and vega is a first-order effect.
   B. Gamma is the effect of volatility, and vega is the effect of changes in volatility.
   C. Gamma is a second-order effect arising from changes in the sensitivity of volatility to the underlying price.

Solution to 1: B is correct. Duration is the first-order effect and convexity the second-order effect of a change in interest rates on the value of a bond. A and C are correct with respect to duration, but not for convexity.

Solution to 2: B is correct. A and C correctly characterize delta, whereas B states that delta is precise, which is incorrect because it gives an approximate relationship.

Solution to 3: A is correct. B is not correct because gamma does not capture the effect of volatility. Vega is the effect of volatility, but it relates to the level and not the change in volatility. C is incorrect because although gamma is a second-order effect on the option value, it is not related to the sensitivity of volatility to the underlying price.

3.2. Scenario Risk Measures

A scenario risk measure estimates the portfolio return that would result from a hypothetical change in markets (a hypothetical scenario) or a repeat of a historical event (a historical scenario). As an example, the risk manager might want to understand how her current portfolio would perform if an event, such as the Black Monday of October 1987, were to reoccur. The factor movements that characterized the historical event would be applied to the factor exposures of the current portfolio. Alternatively, the risk manager may develop a hypothetical scenario to describe a market event that has not occurred in the past but which he or she believes has some probability of occurring in the future. The two elements of scenario risk measures that set them apart from sensitivity risk measures are (1) the use of multiple factor movements used in the scenario measures versus the single factor movements typically used in risk sensitivity measures and (2) the typically larger size of the factor movement used in the scenario measures. Scenario risk measures are related to VaR in that they focus on extreme outcomes, but they are not bound by either recent historical events or assumptions about parameters or probability distributions. **Stress tests**, which apply extreme negative stress to a particular portfolio exposure, are closely related to scenario risk measures. Scenario analysis is an open-ended exercise that could look at positive or negative events, although its most common application is to assess the negative outcomes. Stress tests intentionally focus on extreme negative events to assess the impact of such an event on the portfolio.

The two types of scenario risk measures—historical scenarios and hypothetical scenarios—are discussed in the following sections.

3.2.1. Historical Scenarios

Historical scenarios are scenarios that measure the portfolio return that would result from a repeat of a particular period of financial market history. Historical scenarios used in risk management include such events as the currency crisis of 1997–1998, the market dislocation surrounding the failure of Long-Term Capital Management, the market rout of October 1987, the bursting of the technology bubble in 2001, and the financial crisis of 2008–2009. In order to create a historical scenario, the current set of portfolio holdings is placed into the appropriate valuation models.

Equity positions can often be modeled using their price histories as proxies for their expected behavior, although some practitioners model equities using factor analysis. Valuation models are needed for fixed-income and derivatives products because they have a maturity or an expiration feature that must be accommodated when modeling the portfolio. Historical prices for the fixed-income and derivatives positions currently held in the portfolio may not exist, as in the case of a bond that was issued after the historical period being modeled. Even when historical prices for specific instruments do exist, they may not be relevant to the current characteristics of the instrument. Take the case of a 5-year historical price series for a 10-year bond with 1 year remaining to maturity; the historical price series reflects the price volatility of what used to be a longer bond (e.g., five years ago, the bond had six years remaining to maturity; three years ago, the bond had four years remaining to maturity). The volatility of the bond when it had six years remaining to maturity would be higher than it is today, with only one year remaining to maturity. Using its historical price history would mischaracterize the risk of the current portfolio holding. For this reason, the historical yields, spreads, implied volatilities, prices of the underlying assets in derivatives contracts, and the other input parameters that drive the pricing of these instruments are more important in explaining the risks of these instruments than the price history of the instrument itself.

Some examples may help to show how fixed-income or derivatives valuation models are used in a historical scenario. In the case of a convertible bond, the bond's terms and conditions (e.g., coupon, conversion ratio, maturity) are entered into a convertible bond pricing model. In the case of standard bonds, the terms and conditions of these instruments (e.g., coupon, call features, put features, any amortization or sinking fund features, maturity) are entered into fixed-income pricing models. These modeled fixed-income or derivatives holdings, together with the equity holdings, are then re-priced under the conditions that prevailed during the scenario period—a given set of dates in the past. Changes in interest rates, credit spreads, implied volatility levels, and any asset underlying a derivatives product, as well as the historical price changes in the equity portfolio, would all be reflected in the re-priced portfolio. The value of each position is recorded before and after these changes in order to arrive at the gain or loss that would occur under the chosen scenario. Historical scenario events are specifically chosen to represent extreme market dislocations and often exhibit abnormally high correlations among asset classes. It is most common to run the scenario or stress test as if the total price action movement across the period occurs instantaneously, before any rebalancing or management action is possible. The output of the scenario can include

- the total return of the portfolio;
- for long-only asset managers, the total return of the portfolio relative to its benchmark;
- for pensions, insurers, and others whose liabilities are not already incorporated into the portfolio, the total return of the portfolio relative to the change in liabilities under the scenario; and
- any collateral requirements and other cash needs that will be driven by the changes specified in the scenario.

One variation of the historical scenario approach includes running the scenario over multiple days and incorporating actions that the manager might be expected to take during the period. Instead of assuming the shock is a single instant event, this approach assumes it takes place over a number of days and that on each day the portfolio manager can take such actions as selling assets or rebalancing hedges.

Many risk managers are skeptical of this approach because it produces smaller potential loss measures (by design) and does not answer important questions that have been relevant in real crises, such as, "What if the severe price action happens so quickly that the portfolio manager cannot take remedial actions?" Generally, risk managers prefer that a stress testing exercise be tailored to the *initial outcome of a large shock*, to ensure that the event is survivable by a portfolio that uses leverage, and that there will be no unacceptable counterparty exposures or portfolio concentrations before action can be taken to improve the situation. This method also helps to simulate the possibility that liquidity may be unavailable.

Risk managers seeking to measure the impact of a historical scenario need to ensure all relevant risk factors are included. For instance, foreign equities will need to be decomposed into foreign exchange exposure and equity exposure in the analysis. Stress tests typically take the explicit currency approach, which measures the currency exposure of each foreign equity. Alternatively, the risk manager may use an approach that incorporates implicit currency risks, such as companies that may be registered in one country but have earnings flowing in from other countries, and may hedge some of those revenues back to their base currency.

When the historical simulation fully revalues securities under rate and price changes that occurred during the scenario period, the results should be highly accurate. Sometimes, however, scenarios are applied to risk sensitivities rather than the securities themselves. This approach is a simpler form of analysis, but it should not be used for options or option-embedded securities. Although it may be tempting to use delta and gamma or duration and convexity to estimate the impact of a scenario on options or option-embedded securities, these measures are not suited for handling the kinds of extreme movements analyzed in scenario analysis. Although gamma and convexity are second-order adjustments that work with delta and duration to estimate extreme movements, they are inadequate for scenario analysis.

Even in simpler fixed-income cases in which no options are present, care needs to be taken to ensure the analysis does not oversimplify. Duration sensitivities can be used as the inputs to a scenario analysis for straightforward fixed-income instruments, but these sensitivities need to be mapped to the most relevant sectors, credit curves, and yield curve segments before beginning the analysis. If assets are mapped too broadly, the analysis will miss the important differences that could drive the most meaningful outcomes in a given scenario.

It is also important to pay careful attention to how securities or markets that did not yet exist at the time of the scenario are modeled. If, for instance, an analyst is measuring a current portfolio's sensitivity to a recurrence of the 1987 US stock market crash, the analyst needs to determine how to treat stocks in the portfolio that had an initial public offering after 1987. They may need to be mapped to a relevant index or to a similar company or be decomposed into the relevant statistical factors (such as growth, value, volatility, or momentum) by using a factor model before beginning the analysis. Similarly, because credit default swaps did not come into widespread use until 2002, historical scenarios for dates preceding this time would need to be adapted to appropriately reflect the impact of a repeat of that scenario on these new securities.

3.2.2. Hypothetical Scenarios
Scenarios have a number of benefits. They can reflect the impact of extreme market movements, and they make no specific assumptions regarding normality or correlation. Historical scenarios have the extra benefit of being uncontroversial; no one can claim it is impossible for such events to occur, because they did. One problem with scenario analysis, however, lies in ascribing the probability of a given scenario. Most would agree that it is improbable to assume that the exact historical scenario specified will actually occur in precisely the same way in the future. Another potential problem is that, because it has happened (particularly when it has happened recently), risk managers or portfolio managers are inclined to take precautions that make their portfolios safer for a replay of that historical crisis—and, in the process, make their portfolios more vulnerable to a crisis that has not yet happened.

For that reason, risk managers also use hypothetical scenarios—extreme movements and co-movements in different markets that have not necessarily previously occurred. The scenarios used are somewhat difficult to believe, and it is difficult to assess their probability. Still, they represent the only real method to assess portfolio outcomes under market movements that might be imagined but that have not yet been experienced.

To design an effective hypothetical scenario, it is necessary to identify the portfolio's most significant exposures. Targeting these material exposures and assessing their behavior in various environments is a process called **reverse stress testing**. The risk manager is seeking answers to such questions as the following: What are the top 10 exposures or risk drivers in my portfolio? What would make them risky? What are the top 10 benchmark-relative exposures? Under what scenario would hedges not hedge? Under what scenario would my securities lending activity, ordinarily thought to be riskless, be risky? The ideal use of hypothetical scenarios is, then, not to model every possible future state of every market variable, but rather to target those that are highly significant to the portfolio in order to assess, and potentially address, vulnerabilities.

Reverse stress testing is particularly helpful in estimating potential losses if more than one important exposure is affected in a market crisis, as often happens when participants crowd into the same exposures. Sometimes, apparently unrelated markets experience stress at the same time.

The risk manager might also choose to design a hypothetical geopolitical event, estimating its potential effect on markets and the resulting impact on the portfolio. To develop these scenarios, individuals with varying areas of expertise posit an event—such as an earthquake in Country Y, or Country X invades Country Z, or the banking system implodes in Region A. The group conducting the analysis identifies which markets are most likely to be affected as well as any identifiable secondary effects. The next step is to establish a potential range of movement for the affected markets. The final scenario is intended to meet the standard of "rare, but not impossible." The exercise is unlikely to be truly accurate in the face of the real event, but it will often help to identify unexpected portfolio vulnerabilities and outcomes and to think through counterparty credit and operational considerations that could exacerbate or accelerate the scenario.

Hypothetical scenarios are particularly beneficial in being able to stress correlation parameters. The scenario is not constrained to assume that assets will co-move as they have done in the past, which can help identify dangers that other forms of risk analysis may miss. Scenarios can be designed to highlight that correlations often increase in times of stress. This is often achieved by subjecting markets that typically have little or no correlation with one another to the same or similar movements, thereby simulating a temporarily higher correlation. Scenarios can also be devised to pinpoint times when hedging might work poorly— when assets, such as a bond and the credit default swap used to hedge it, that normally have a high correlation might temporarily decouple and move by different percentages or even in different directions. This often occurs when markets experience a "flight to quality; the swap rate may move down as a result of their relative credit strength, whereas the bond yield might increase given its perceived credit risk.

Once a risk manager has completed a scenario analysis, common questions may be, "What do you do with a scenario analysis? What are the action steps?" If the portfolios are within all other rules and guidelines—their exposures have been kept within desired limits and their VaR or *ex ante* tracking error is within the desired range—scenario analysis provides one final opportunity to assess the potential for negative surprises during a given stress event. The action steps might be to trim back positions that are otherwise within all limits and that appear to present comfortable risk exposures under the current environment but would perform unacceptably during a plausible stress environment. In the case of asset management, where clients have elected to be in a given asset class and the asset manager is constrained by that investment mandate, action steps may include adjusting benchmark-relative risk, disclosing to clients the manager's concerns regarding the risks in the portfolio, or changing counterparty or operational procedures to avoid an unwanted event.

But a caution is in order: A portfolio that has no sensitivity to any stress event is unlikely to earn more than the risk-free rate, or in the case of long-only asset managers, outperform the benchmark index. Stress tests and scenarios analyses are best used in the effort to *understand* a portfolio's risk exposures, not to eliminate them. Effective risk management sets a tolerance range for a stress test or scenario that reflects a higher loss possibility than the investment manager would normally find acceptable. Scenarios should be periodically run again, and action should be taken only if the portfolio exceeds this relatively high tolerance level. It is also important to continually evaluate new threats and new market developments and to periodically refresh the set of scenarios, removing scenarios that are no longer meaningful for the portfolio.

Note also that scenario risk measures and stress tests are best used as the final screen in a series of position constraints that include position size limits, exposure limits, and VaR or *ex ante* tracking error limits. They do not serve well as the initial or primary screen, for reasons that will be discussed shortly.

Parties that use leverage, such as banks and hedge funds, are more likely to use single-factor stress tests rather than multifactor scenario analyses. The focus on a single factor helps in assessing whether a given exposure is likely to impair their capital under a given stress movement; these are pass/fail tests. If capital falls below an acceptable level, it could set off a chain reaction of margin calls, withdrawal of financing, and other actions that threaten the viability of the business.

EXAMPLE 8   Scenario Analysis

1. Which of the following is an example of a reverse stress test?
   A. Identify the top 10 exposures in the portfolio, and then generate a hypothetical stress that could adversely affect all 10 simultaneously.
   B. Find the worst single day's performance that could have occurred for the current portfolio had it been held throughout the past five years.
   C. Find the returns that occurred in all risk factors in the 2008 global financial crisis, reverse the sign on these, and apply them to today's portfolio.

2. Which kind of market participant is *least likely* to use scenario analysis as a pass/fail stress test?
   A. Bank
   B. Long-only asset manager
   C. Hedge fund using leverage

3. What is the *most* accurate approach to scenario analysis for a portfolio that uses options?
   A. Apply the scenario to option delta.
   B. Apply the scenario to option delta + gamma.
   C. Fully reprice the options using the market returns specified under the scenario.

Solution to 1: A is correct. B is not a reverse stress test because reverse stress tests focus more narrowly on trouble spots for a specific portfolio. C would illustrate how the portfolio would have performed in an extremely strong market, quite unlike what occurred in 2008.

Solution to 2: B is correct. Long-only asset managers do not typically use leverage and are thus less likely to become insolvent, making a pass/fail test for solvency less relevant to them. A and C are not correct because parties that use leverage, such as hedge funds and banks, are likely to use stress tests to determine what market movements could impair their capital and lead to insolvency.

Solution to 3: C is correct. Both A and B risk misestimating the actual results of the scenario because both delta and gamma estimate how an option's value might change for a small move in the underlying asset, not the large movements typically used in a scenario analysis.

3.3. Sensitivity and Scenario Risk Measures and VaR

Although both VaR and sensitivity risk measures deal with related concepts, they have their own distinctions. VaR is a measure of losses and the probability of large losses. Sensitivity risk measures capture changes in the value of an asset in response to a change in something else, such as a market index, an interest rate, or an exchange rate; they do not, however, tell us anything about the probability of a given change in value occurring. For example, we could use duration to measure the change in a bond price for an instantaneous 1 bp change in the yield, but duration does not tell us anything about the likelihood of such a change occurring. Similar statements could be made about equities and the various option measures: Betas and deltas do not tell us how likely a change might be in the underlying risk factors, but given a change, they tell us how responsive the asset or derivative would be.

VaR gives us a broader picture of the risk in the sense that it accounts for the probability of losses of certain amounts. In this sense, it incorporates what we know about the probability of movements in the risk factors. Nonetheless, these sensitivity measures are still very useful in that they allow us to take a much more detailed look at the relationships driving the risk. It is one thing to say that a VaR is $2 million for one day at 5 percent. We know what that means. But it is equally important to understand what is driving the risk. Is it coming from high beta stocks, high duration bonds, or high delta options? If we find our VaR unacceptable, we have to know where to look to modify it. If we simply use VaR by itself, we will blindly rely on a single number without understanding what factors are driving the number.

VaR has much in common with scenario risk measures in that both types of measures estimate potential loss. VaR tends to do so using a model for which input parameters are created based on market returns from a particular time in history. Thus, the VaR estimate is vulnerable if correlation relationships and market volatility during the period in question are not representative of the conditions the portfolio may face in the future. VaR does, however, allow a disciplined method for stressing all factors in the portfolio. Scenario analysis allows either the risk assessment to be fully hypothetical or to be linked to a different and more extreme period of history, helping reduce some of the biases imposed by the VaR model. But there is no guarantee that the scenario chosen will be the "right" one to estimate risk for future markets. Moreover, it is particularly difficult to stress all possible risk factors in a hypothetical scenario in a way that does not embed biases similar to those that occur in VaR modeling.

Each of these measures—sensitivity risk measures, scenario risk measures, and VaR— has distinct limitations and distinct benefits. They are best used in combination because no one measure has the answer, but all provide valuable information that can help risk managers understand the portfolio and avoid unwanted outcomes and surprises.

3.3.1. Advantages and Limitations of Sensitivity Risk Measures and Scenario Risk Measures

Before portfolios began using risk measures based on modern portfolio theory, the very first risk measure was position size—the value invested in a given type of asset. Position size is a very effective risk measure for homogeneous, long-only portfolios, particularly for those familiar with the homogenous asset class in question; an experienced person can assess what the loss potential of such a portfolio is just by knowing its size. But position size is less useful for assessing interest rate risk, even less useful for summarizing the risk of a multi-asset class portfolio, and less useful still at assessing net risk in a portfolio that uses hedging instruments, short positions, and liabilities.

Sensitivity measures address some of the shortcomings of position size measures. Duration, for example, addresses the difference between a 1-year note and a 30-year note; it measures the level of interest rate risk. Option delta and duration (for fixed income) help to display net risk in a portfolio that has hedging or short positions with optionality or interest rate risk.

Sensitivities typically do not often distinguish assets by volatility, though. When measured as the sensitivity to a 1 bp or 1 percent move, they do not tell the user which portfolio has greater loss potential any more than position size measures do. A high-yield bond portfolio might have the same sensitivity to a 0.01 percent credit spread movement as an investment-grade portfolio, but they do not have the same risk because the credit spreads of the high-yield portfolio are more likely to move 0.01 percent, or more, than the credit spreads of the investment-grade bonds. Sensitivity measures do not distinguish by standard deviation/volatility or other higher confidence loss measures. Measuring sensitivity to a one standard deviation movement in an asset's price or yield, however, is one way to overcome this shortcoming of sensitivity.

Granularity: Too Much or Too Little?

Sensitivity measures are aggregated in categories or buckets. (A bucket is a risk factor description such as "one- to five-year French sovereign debt.") When a number of fixed-income positions are assigned to the same bucket, the effect is an assumption of perfect correlation across the risks encompassed by that bucket. For the "one- to five-year French sovereign debt" risk factor, a short duration position in four-year French sovereign debt will be assumed to fully offset a long duration position in two-year French sovereign debt. However, this may not be true in the case of a non-parallel interest rate change; these points on the yield curve do not have a correlation coefficient of 1 to one another. The broader the buckets used, the more they can hide this kind of correlation risk; but the narrower the buckets used, the greater the complexity and thus the more difficult to portray portfolios in simple, accessible ways. The width or the narrowness of the risk-factor buckets used to portray sensitivity measures is referred to as granularity.

Scenario analysis and stress testing have well-deserved popularity, and they address many of the shortcomings of VaR described earlier. Sensitivity and scenario risk measures can complement VaR in the following ways:

- They do not need to rely on history. Sensitivity and scenario risk measures can be constructed to test the portfolio's vulnerability to a truly never-before-seen market movement. In this way, they can be free of the volatility and correlation behavior of recent market history, which may simply not be representative of stress conditions. In a scenario analysis, assets that typically have a low correlation with one another can be modeled under an assumption of perfect positive correlation simply by simulating an identical price movement for these assets. Alternatively, they can be modeled under an assumption of perfect negative correlation by simulating identical price movements (i.e., in the opposite direction). A scenario might be designed in which a market that typically exhibits an annual standard deviation of 15 percent moves by 20 percent in a single day.

- Scenarios can be designed to overcome any assumption of normal distributions; the shock used could be the equivalent of 1, 10, or 1,000 standard deviations, at the choice of the analyst—or as provided by an actual moment in history.
- Scenarios can be tailored to expose a portfolio's most concentrated positions to even worse movement than its other exposures, allowing liquidity to be taken into account.

But scenario measures are not without their own limitations:

- Historical scenarios are interesting, and illuminating, but are not going to happen in exactly the same way again, making hypothetical scenarios necessary to truly fill the gaps identified with the other risk measures listed.
- Hypothetical scenarios may incorrectly specify how assets will co-move, they may get the magnitude of movements wrong, and they may incorrectly adjust for the effects of liquidity and concentration.
- Hypothetical scenarios can be very difficult to create and maintain. Getting all factors and their relationships accurately represented in the suite of scenarios is a painstaking and possibly never-ending exercise. Accordingly, it is necessary to draw a line of "reasonableness" at which to curtail the scenario analysis, and by the very act of being curtailed, the scenario might miss the real risk.
- It is very difficult to know how to establish the appropriate limits on a scenario analysis or stress test. Because we are proposing hypothetical movements in markets and risk factors, we cannot use history to assign a probability of such a move occurring. What if rates rise instantaneously 0.50 percent, 1.00 percent, or 3.00 percent? How should the short end of the yield curve move versus the long end? How much should credit spreads of different qualities move? It is difficult to choose.

The more extreme the scenario, and the farther from historical experience, the less likely it is to be found believable or actionable by management of a company or a portfolio. This issue tends to lead scenario constructors to underestimate movement in order to appear credible. As an example, prior to the very large drop in real estate values that prevailed in the United States from 2008 to 2010, no similar nationwide price decline had occurred in history. Risk measurement teams at a number of firms did prepare scenarios that estimated the potential outcome if real estate prices declined meaningfully, but their scenarios in many cases were only half as large as the movements that subsequently occurred. Because these large market movements had never before occurred, there was no historical basis for estimating them, and to do so appeared irresponsible. This is an additional risk of scenario analysis: The need to keep the scenario plausible may lead to it being incorrect.

In sum, scenario analyses and stress tests have the opportunity to correct the failings of probabilistic risk measures, such as VaR and *ex ante* tracking error; however, because the version of the future they suggest may be no more accurate than that used in VaR, they may also fail to predict potential loss accurately.

As we can see, each risk measure has elements that are better than the others, and each has important failings. No one measure is the "solution" to risk management. Each is useful and necessary to answer certain questions but not sufficient to answer all possible questions—or to prevent all forms of unexpected loss. Using the measures in combination, to correct each other's failings, is as close to a solution as we come. Designing constraints by using multiple measures is the key practice used by successful risk managers. Viewing a portfolio through these multiple lenses provides a more solid framework for a risk manager or an investor to exercise judgment and can help reduce conceptual bias in portfolio management.

EXAMPLE 9   Limitations of Risk Measures

1. Which of the following is **not** a limitation of VaR?
   A. It does not adjust for bonds of different durations.
   B. It largely relies on recent historical correlations and volatilities.
   C. It can be inaccurate if the size of positions held is large relative to available liquidity.

2. Which of the following statements about sensitivities is true?
   A. When duration is measured as the sensitivity to a 1 bp change in interest rates, it can be biased by choice of the historical period preceding this measure.
   B. Sensitivity measures are the best way to determine how an option can behave under extreme market movements.
   C. Duration effectively assumes that the correlation between a fixed-income exposure and the risk-free rate is 1, whereas beta takes into account the historical correlation between an equity and its comparison index.

3. Which of the following is **not** a limitation of scenario measures?
   A. It is difficult to ascribe probability to a given scenario.
   B. Scenario measures assume a normal distribution, and market returns are not necessarily normal.
   C. They risk being an infinite task; one cannot possibly measure all of the possible future scenarios.

4. Which measures are based on market returns during a particular historical period?
   A. Hypothetical scenario analysis and duration sensitivity
   B. Historical scenario analysis and VaR
   C. Option delta and vega

Solution to 1: A is correct. Well-executed VaR measures do adjust for bonds of differing duration, and therefore it is not a limitation of VaR. B is incorrect because VaR ordinarily uses some period of recent history as part of the calculation, and this reliance on history is one of its limitations. C is incorrect because VaR can be inaccurate and underestimate risk if portfolio positions are too large relative to the available market liquidity, and this inability to account for the illiquidity of an individual investor's position is an additional limitation of VaR.

Solution to 2: C is correct. Duration assumes that all interest rates that affect a bond change by the same percentage (an effective correlation of 1). A is incorrect because the 1 bp change in rates is applied to current rates, not historical rates. B is incorrect because sensitivity measures are often too small to reveal the most extreme movements for option positions; the larger shocks used in scenario measures are preferable to reveal option characteristics.

Solution to 3: B is correct. Scenario measures do not assume any given distribution, and thus this is not a limitation of scenario analysis. A is incorrect because it is in fact difficult to ascribe probability to many scenarios, and thus this is a limitation of scenario analysis. C is also incorrect because it is in fact impossible to measure all possible future scenarios, and this is a limitation of scenario analysis.

Solution to 4: B is correct. Historical scenarios apply market returns from a particular period to the portfolio, and virtually all VaR methodologies use a historical period to underpin the VaR model (although certain methods may make adjustments if this historical period is seen to be anomalous in some way). A is incorrect because a hypothetical scenario is not based on an actual historical period, and duration sensitivity measures change in value for a given small change in rates, not for a given historical period. C is incorrect because option delta and vega measure how much an option's value will change for a given change in the price of the underlying (delta) or implied volatility (vega), and these are sensitivity measures, not measures based on a particular historical period.

4. USING CONSTRAINTS IN MARKET RISK MANAGEMENT

Designing suitable constraints to be used in market risk management is essential to managing risk effectively. Risk *measurements* in and of themselves cannot be said to be restrictive or unrestrictive: The *limits* placed on the measures drive action. VaR can be measured to a very high confidence level (for example, 99 percent) or to a low level (for example, 84 percent). But placing a loose limit on a 99 percent confidence VaR measure could be less of a constraint than placing a tight limit on an 84 percent confidence measure. It is not the confidence interval that drives conservatism as much as the limit that is placed on it.

If constraints are too tight, they may limit the pursuit of perceived opportunities and shrink returns or profitability to a sub-optimal level. If constraints are too loose, outsized losses can occur, threatening the viability of the portfolio or business. The concept of "restrictive" or "unrestrictive" relates to the risk appetite of the firm or portfolio and the sizes of losses it can tolerate. Unrestrictive limits are typically set far from current risk levels and permit larger losses than restrictive limits. As an example, for a leveraged portfolio in which insolvency could occur if cumulative daily losses exceed $10 million and the portfolio's current two week, 1 percent VaR measure is $3 million, an unrestrictive limit might be one set at $10 million. If the portfolio increased positions and went right up to its limit, a misestimation of VaR could result in insolvency; moreover, the fact that losses are expected to exceed the measure at least 1% of the time could mean disaster. But if the limit were set at $4 million, the portfolio might under-allocate the capital it has to invest and fail to make a high enough return on equity to thrive in a competitive environment.

Before applying constraints, particularly those involving such potential loss measures as VaR or a scenario analysis, it is worth considering how far down in the organizational hierarchy to impose them. If applied exclusively to lower level business units, the firm's aggregate risk exposure fails to take advantage of offsetting risks that may occur at higher levels of the organization. As a result, the overall company may never be able to invest according to its risk tolerance because it is "stopped out" by rules lower in the organization. For example, imagine a bank with five trading desks: It might have an overall VaR tolerance of €10 million and might set each trading desk's limit for its standalone VaR at €2 million, which seems reasonable. If there is anything lower than perfect correlation across these desks' positions, however—and particularly if one desk has a short position that to some degree serves as an offset to another desk's long position—the firm will never be able to use its €10 million risk appetite in full. The cure for this problem is over-allocation, with the caveat that a given desk might need to be cut back to its pro rata share in the event that correlations among trading desks are higher than, or the short positions across the different portfolios are not as offsetting as, the over-allocation assumes. Alternatively, some firms might use marginal VaR for each trading desk, allocating each desk a VaR budget such that the total VaR is the sum of each individual desk's marginal VaR. This approach permits each trading desk to "reinvest" the diversification benefits obtained at the aggregate level.

Among the constraints most often used in risk management are risk budgeting, position limits, scenario limits, and stop-loss limits. As is the case in risk measurement, for which multiple measures work better than any one measure alone does, so it is in risk constraints. No one approach on its own works perfectly; they are most effective in combination.

4.1. Risk Budgeting

In **risk budgeting**, the total risk appetite of the firm or portfolio is agreed on at the highest level of the entity and then allocated to sub-activities. Risk budgeting typically rests on a foundation of VaR or *ex ante* tracking error.

A bank might establish a limit on total economic capital or VaR and describe this limit as its risk appetite. Next, it might allocate this risk appetite among the basic risk types (market, credit, and operational) and different business units, geographies, and activities. It allocates to the business unit and/or risk type by specifying a limit, using its chosen measure, for that given activity. For example, it might allow its European business to use 20 percent of its market risk capital (the portion of its economic capital expected to be used to support market risk taking) and 40 percent of its credit risk capital, whereas its Asian business might have a different limit. It will set these limits based on the expected long-term profitability of the opportunity set and the demonstrated skill of a business at delivering profitable results, taking into consideration shareholders' expectations regarding the activities the bank is engaged in. As an example of potential shareholder expectations, consider a case in which a firm's shareholder disclosure suggests that the firm's predominant market risk-taking activities are in the Asian markets and that less risk-taking activity is in Europe. Shareholders will be surprised if greater losses are incurred from its European business than its Asian business. Market risk capital limits for the European business should be lower than for the Asian business to be consistent with shareholder disclosures.

A pension fund sponsor might begin with its tolerance for how much of a mismatch it is willing to tolerate overall between the total value of assets and its liabilities—its surplus at risk. Surplus at risk can be the starting point for its asset allocation decision making. Once the broad asset allocation is established, usually expressed via a set of benchmarks, the pension fund sponsor might further establish its tolerance for underperformance in a given asset class and allocate that tolerance to the asset managers selected to manage the assets by assigning each an *ex ante* tracking error budget.

A portfolio manager might have an *ex ante* tracking error budget explicitly provided by the client, or if none is provided by the client, it might instead develop a tracking error budget based on her investment philosophy and market practice. Given this budget, she will seek to optimize the portfolio's exposures relative to the benchmark to ensure that the strategies that generate the most tracking error for the portfolio are those for which she expects the greatest reward.

4.2. Position Limits

Risk budgeting follows a clear logic; but as we have noted, VaR-based measures have a number of drawbacks. One of them is that they perform poorly if portfolios are unusually concentrated, particularly with respect to market liquidity.

Position limits are limits on the market value of any given investment, or the notional principal amount for a derivatives contract. They can be expressed in currency units or as a percentage of some other value, such as net assets. Position limits do not take into account duration, volatility, and correlation, as VaR does, but they are excellent controls on overconcentration. Like risk budgeting, position limits need to be used carefully; if every asset type that a portfolio manager could invest in is constrained, he will have no room to succeed in outperforming the benchmark or generating absolute returns, assuming that is the mandate. Position limits should not be overly prescriptive but should address the event risk and single name risk that VaR handles so poorly, such as

- limits per issuer;
- limits per currency or country;
- limits on categories expected to be minimized in a given strategy, such as high-yield credit or emerging market equities;
- limits on gross size of long–short positions or derivatives activity; and
- limits on asset ownership that correspond to market liquidity measures, such as daily average trading volume.

4.3. Scenario Limits

A scenario limit is a limit on the estimated loss for a given scenario, which if exceeded, would require corrective action in the portfolio.

As discussed in Section 3.3, scenarios also address shortcomings of VaR, such as the potential for changes in correlation or for extreme movements that might not be predicted using a normal distribution or the historical lookback period used for the VaR measure. Just producing scenario analysis, however, without having any related action steps is not a very valuable exercise.

The action steps that generally follow a scenario analysis are to examine (1) whether the results are within risk tolerance and, in the case of asset managers, (2) whether the results are well incorporated into investor disclosures. To determine whether results are within the established risk tolerance, a tolerance level for each scenario must be developed. It is better to establish a higher tolerance for potential loss under the most extreme scenarios. If the same limit is applied to all scenarios, even extremely unlikely scenarios (e.g., "interest rates rise 1,000,000 percent"), then the portfolio will simply not be able to take any risk. The risk manager then observes over time whether the portfolio's sensitivity to the scenario is increasing or crosses this high-tolerance bound.

4.4. Stop-Loss Limits

A **stop-loss limit** requires a reduction in the size of a portfolio, or its complete liquidation, when a loss of a particular size occurs in a specified period.

One of the limitations of VaR described in Section 2.3.2 was "trending," in which a portfolio remains under its VaR limit each day but cumulatively loses more than expected. This trending can be managed by imposing and monitoring stop-loss limits in addition to the VaR constraints. In one form of a stop-loss limit, the portfolio's positions are unwound if its losses over a pre-specified period exceed a pre-specified level. (Those levels are typically defined to align with the overall risk tolerance.) As an example, a portfolio might have a 10-day, 1 percent VaR limit of $5 million, but it will be liquidated if its cumulative monthly loss ever exceeds $8 million. The relationship between the stop-loss and the VaR measure can vary depending on management preferences as well as the differing time periods with which the measures are specified.

An alternative approach to a stop-loss limit might instead be to impose a requirement to undertake hedging activity, which may include purchases of protective options, after losses of a given magnitude, with the magnitude of the hedge increasing as losses increase. This approach, called drawdown control or portfolio insurance, is more dynamic and more sophisticated than the simpler stop-loss limit.

4.5. Risk Measures and Capital Allocation

In market risk management, capital allocation is the practice of placing limits on each of a company's activities in order to ensure that the areas in which it expects the greatest reward and has the greatest expertise are given the resources needed to accomplish their goals. Allocating capital wisely ensures that an unproven strategy does not use up all of the firm's risk appetite and, in so doing, deprive the areas most likely to be successful of the capital they need to execute on their strategy.

Economic capital is often used to estimate how much of shareholders' equity could be lost by the portfolio under very unfavorable circumstances. Capital allocation may start with a measurement of economic capital (the amount of capital a firm needs to hold if it is to survive severe losses from the risks in its businesses). The company's actual, physical on-balance-sheet capital must exceed the measure of economic capital, and a minimum level of economic capital must be established to ensure that the company does not take on a risk of loss that will exceed its available capital. The company first establishes its overall risk appetite in economic capital terms, and then it subdivides this appetite among its units. This exercise is similar to risk budgeting, but in the case of corporations, banks, insurers, or hedge funds, it is more likely to be called "capital allocation." Capital allocation is often used in cases in which leverage is used by the portfolio or in which the strategy has meaningful **tail risk**, meaning that losses in extreme events could be far greater than would be expected for a portfolio of assets with a normal distribution. Economic capital is designed to measure how much shareholders' equity could be required to meet tail risk losses. Strategies that have greater-than-expected tail risk include those that sell options, sell insurance, take substantial credit risk, or have unique liquidity or exposure concentration risks. Although risk budgeting more commonly focuses on losses at the one standard deviation level, capital allocation focuses on losses at a very high confidence level in order to capture the magnitude of capital that is placed at risk by the strategy. Capital allocation seeks to understand how much of an investor's scarce resources are, or could be, used by a given portfolio, thereby making it unavailable to other portfolios.

Because a company's capital is a scarce resource and relatively expensive, it should be deployed in activities that have the best chance of earning a superior rate of return. It also should be deployed in a way that investors expect, in activities in which the company has expertise, and in strategies that investors believe the company can successfully execute.

To optimize the use of capital, the "owner" of the capital will typically establish a hurdle rate over a given time horizon; this is often expressed as the expected rate of return per unit of capital allocated. Two potential activities, Portfolio A and Portfolio B, might require different amounts of capital. Portfolio A might require €325,000, and its expected return might be €50,000 per year (15.4 percent). Portfolio B might have a reasonable expectation of earning €100,000 per year, but it might require €1,000,000 in capital (a 10 percent return). If the investor has an annualized hurdle rate of 15%, Portfolio A will exceed the hurdle rate and appear a better user of capital than Portfolio B, even though the absolute income for Portfolio B is higher.

Beyond measuring and limiting economic capital, capital allocation is sometimes used as a broad term for allocating costly resources. In some cases, the costly resource is cash; if, for instance, the portfolio has invested in options and futures trading strategies that require heavy use of margin and overcollateralization, its use of economic capital could be low and available cash may be the constraining factor. For other types of investors, such as banks or insurance companies, the capital required by regulatory bodies could be relatively large; as a result, these capital measures may be the most onerous constraint and thus the basis of capital allocation.

When the current measure of economic capital is a smaller number than the portfolio's cash or regulatory capital needs, it may not be the binding constraint. But when it is higher than other measures, it can become the binding constraint, and the one to which hurdle rates should be applied.

EXAMPLE 10 Creating Constraints with Risk Measures

1. Which of the following is **not** an example of risk budgeting?
   A. Giving a foreign exchange trading desk a VaR limit of $10 million
   B. Allowing a portfolio manager to have an *ex ante* tracking error up to 5 percent in a given portfolio
   C. Reducing the positions in a portfolio after a loss of a 5 percent of capital has occurred in a single month

2. Which statement is true regarding risk budgeting in cases in which marginal VaR is used?
   A. The total risk budget is never equal to the sum of the individual sub-portfolios' risk budgets.
   B. The total risk budget is always equal to the sum of the individual sub-portfolios' risk budgets.

C. If the total risk budget is equal to the sum of the individual sub-portfolios' risk budgets, there is a risk that this approach may cause capital to be underutilized.

Solution to 1: C is correct. This is an example of a stop-loss limit, not risk budgeting. The other choices are both examples of risk budgeting.

Solution to 2: B is correct. When using marginal VaR, the total risk budget will be equal to the sum of the individual risk budgets. Choice A is not correct. C is also incorrect; it would be correct if each sub-portfolio's individual VaR measure, not adjusted for its marginal contribution, were used, which could lead to underutilization of capital.

5. APPLICATIONS OF RISK MEASURES

In this section, we examine the practical applications of risk measures. First, we will look at how different types of market participants use risk measures. An understanding of how various market participants use these measures will help as we move to a discussion of their limitations.

5.1. Market Participants and the Different Risk Measures They Use

Three factors tend to greatly influence the types of risk measures used by different market participants:

• The degree to which the market participant is leveraged and the resulting need to assess minimum capitalization/maximum leverage ratios;
• The mix of risk factors to which their business is exposed (e.g., the degree of equity or fixed-income concentration in their portfolios);
• The accounting or regulatory requirements that govern their reporting.

Market participants who use a high degree of leverage typically need to assess their sensitivity to shocks to ensure that they will remain a going concern under very severe, but foreseeable, stresses. This leads them to focus on potential loss measures with a high confidence interval or to focus on rare events that might occur in a short period of time, such as two weeks. Those who use minimal (or no) leverage, such as long-only asset managers, are interested in shock sensitivity as well, but they are likely less concerned with trying to discern the difference between a 99.99 percent (0.01 percent VaR) worst case and a 99.95 percent (0.05 percent VaR) worst case. Their focus is more likely on avoiding underperformance— for example, failing to keep pace with their market benchmark when markets are doing well. For this reason, they are often more interested in lower confidence intervals—events that are more likely to occur and lead to underperformance for a given strategy. Unleveraged asset managers may also prefer to measure potential underperformance over longer periods of time, such as a quarter or a year, rather than shorter periods.

For portfolios dominated by fixed-income investments, risk managers focus on how sensitive the portfolios are to instantaneous price and yield changes in a variety of categories and typically emphasize duration, credit spread duration, and key rate duration measures. Credit spread duration measures the impact on an instrument's value if credit spreads move while risk-free rates remain unchanged. Key rate duration (sometimes called partial duration) measures the sensitivity of a bond's price to changes in specific maturities on the benchmark yield curve. Risk measurement for fixed-income portfolios is conducted using bond pricing models and by shifting each market rate assumption in the model and aggregating their portfolio's sensitivity to these market rates. Often, these factors are combined into scenarios representing expected central bank policies, inflation expectations, and/or anticipated fiscal policy changes. When portfolios are dominated by equities, risk managers typically categorize the equities by broad country markets, industries, and market capitalization levels. Also, they may additionally regress the returns of their portfolios against fundamental factor histories (such as those for growth, value, momentum, and capitalization size) to understand their exposure to such factors.

Portfolios with full fair value accounting (also called mark-to-market accounting), such as US mutual funds, European UCITS funds, and the held-for-sale portfolios of banks, are very well suited to such risk measures as VaR, economic capital (the amount of capital a firm needs to hold if it is to survive severe losses from the risks in its businesses), duration, and beta—all of which rely on measuring the changes in the fair values of assets. Asset/liability gap models are more meaningful when portfolios are subject to book value accounting in whole or in part.

5.1.1. Banks

Banks need to balance a number of sometimes competing aspects of risk to manage their business and meet the expectations of equity investors/equity analysts, bond investors, credit rating agencies, depositors, and regulatory entities. Some banks apply risk measures differently depending on whether the portfolio being assessed is designated as a "held-to-maturity" portfolio, which requires book value accounting, or a "held-for-sale" or "trading book" portfolio, which requires fair value accounting. Other banks will use fair value measures for all risk assessments regardless of the designation used for accounting purposes. In the following list are some of the factors that banks seek to address through their use of risk tools. In compiling this list, we have assumed that banks may treat measures differently depending on accounting treatment.

- *Liquidity gap:* The extent of any liquidity and asset/liability mismatch. The ability to raise sufficient cash for foreseeable payment needs; a view of the liquidity of assets, as well as the expected repayment date of debt.
- *VaR:* The value at risk for the held-for-sale or trading (fair value) portion of the balance sheet.
- *Leverage:* A leverage ratio is typically computed, sometimes according to a regulatory requirement or to an internally determined measure. Leverage ratios will weight risk assets using a variety of methods and rules and divide this weighted asset figure by equity. The result is that riskier assets will be assigned a greater weighting and less risky assets a lower weighting so that more equity is required to support riskier assets.
- *Sensitivities:* For the held-for-sale portion of their balance sheet, banks measure duration, key rate duration or partial duration, and credit spread duration for interest rate risk positions. Banks will also measure foreign exchange exposure and any equity or commodity

exposures. All these exposure measures will include the delta sensitivities of options with any other exposures to the same underlying asset and will also monitor gamma and vega exposures of options. Gamma and vega exposures can be broken out by term to identify how much of these risks come from long-dated versus short-dated options.

- *Economic capital:* This is measured by blending the company's market, credit, and operational risk measures to estimate the total loss the company could suffer at a very high level of confidence (e.g., 99 percent to 99.99 percent), usually in one year's time. Economic capital measures are applied to the full balance sheet, including both the held-for-sale and held-for-investment portfolios, and include market, credit, and operational risk capital.
- *Scenario analysis:* Stress tests are applied to the full balance sheet and augment economic capital and liquidity; they are used to identify whether capital is sufficient for targeted, strong negative shocks. Outside of stress testing, significant scenario analysis takes places. Scenario analysis is used to examine how the full balance sheet might be affected by different interest rate, inflation, and credit environments, such as unemployment levels for credit card lenders, home price appreciation/depreciation for mortgage lenders, and business cycle stresses for corporate lenders.

It is common for banks to compute risk measures in distinct business units and geographies and then aggregate these measures to the parent company entity.

5.1.2. Asset Managers

Asset managers are not typically regulated with regard to sufficient capital or liquidity; they are more commonly regulated for fair treatment of investors—that disclosures are full and accurate, that marketing is not misleading, that one client is not favored over the other. In some jurisdictions, certain market risk measures may be used to define risk limits for different fund types.

In asset management portfolios, risk management efforts are focused primarily on volatility, probability of loss, or probability of underperforming a benchmark rather than insolvency. A diversified, unleveraged, long-only fund is unlikely to see asset values decline below zero in the absence of a wholesale withdrawal of assets by the firm's clients. Although service costs and other items make insolvency a technical possibility, in practice, insolvency is a much higher threat for leveraged portfolios. Although derivatives use by asset managers can create effective leverage, these positions are often balanced by an amount of cash in the portfolio equal to the notional exposure created by the derivatives mitigating, if not fully eliminating, the impact of leverage.

Asset managers typically measure and view each portfolio separately with respect to its own constraints and limits. However, there are a few exceptions:

- Long-only asset managers: If the adviser has invested its own capital in any of the funds that it manages, these investments may need to be aggregated for the firm to assess its risk exposures across portfolios.
- Hedge funds: A hedge fund manager needs to aggregate the adviser's side-by-side investment in the various funds it advises.
- Funds of funds: Risk measures for these portfolios typically aggregate the risks of the underlying hedge funds to the master fund level.

An asset manager may choose to aggregate exposures across all funds and strategies to determine if there are unusual concentrations in individual securities or counterparties that would make management actions across all portfolios difficult to carry out (e.g., a single portfolio's holdings in a given security may not pose a liquidity risk, but if the firm were to aggregate all of its holdings in that security, it may find that the portfolio fails to meet the desired liquidity target).

It is important when observing risk measures for asset managers to determine whether the measures represent the backward-looking variability of realized returns in the portfolio as it was then constituted or use the current portfolio and measure its potential loss. Backward-looking returns-based measures (typically including standard deviation, *ex post* tracking error, Sharpe ratio, information ratio, and historical beta) have the value of showing the fund's behavior over time and help assess the skill of the manager. Only an analysis of the current holdings, however, will reveal current risk exposures. Measures that use current holdings typically include VaR, *ex ante* tracking error, duration and forward-looking beta, stress tests, and scenario analyses. All risk and performance measures can be conducted on past portfolio holdings or current portfolio holdings; it is important for the user of any measure to determine which ingredients (which set of portfolio holdings, and for market history, what length and smoothing techniques) have been used in order to use it correctly. Assessing the trends in risk exposures, including whether risk has recently risen or if other important changes have taken place in the strategy, can be accomplished by tracking the risk measures through time.

5.1.2.1. Traditional Asset Managers

Asset managers that use little leverage typically find relative risk measures most meaningful and actionable. The decision to invest in a given asset class is normally the client's, not the adviser's. The adviser seeks to outperform the benchmark representative of the asset class. Exceptions include absolute return funds and asset allocation strategies, but even these can be measured relative to a benchmark. For absolute return strategies, the benchmark is typically cash or a cash-like hurdle rate. When cash is the benchmark, VaR and *ex ante* tracking error will be effectively the same if measured using the same holding period and confidence interval. (Cash has no volatility, so adding a cash benchmark into a relative VaR calculation does not affect the calculation because its zero volatility cancels out its impact; thus, the resulting calculation is the same as the VaR of the portfolio.) Asset allocation funds can use an asset allocation index as the benchmark for a relative risk measure, or they can use a custom combination of market benchmarks.

Although banks, insurers, and other market participants favor measuring VaR in currency terms relevant for the institution (e.g., dollars for a US-based insurer, yen for a Japanese bank) and measure duration and similar statistics as the value change for a 1 bp interest rate change, long-only asset managers generally prefer to express VaR in percentage terms and will divide VaR and duration by the net assets of the portfolio being analyzed. (Note that using returns as the fundamental source of data removes the last step in calculating VaR: multiplying by the size of the portfolio.)

A typical sample of risk measures used by asset managers includes the following:

• *Position limits:* Asset managers use position limits as the most frequent form of risk control for the portfolios they manage, particularly in fund offering documents that need to be understandable to a broad range of investors. Position limits include restrictions on country, currency, sector, and asset class. They may measure them in absolute terms or relative to a benchmark, and they are almost always expressed as a percentage of the portfolio's value.

- *Sensitivities:* Asset managers use the full range of sensitivity measures, including option-adjusted duration, key rate duration, and credit spread duration, and they will typically include the delta exposure of options in these measures. Measures can be expressed in absolute terms as well as relative to a benchmark.
- *Beta sensitivity:* Beta is frequently used for equity-only accounts.
- *Liquidity:* Asset managers often look at the liquidity characteristics of the assets in their portfolios. For equity portfolios, it is common to measure what percentage of daily average trading volume the portfolio holds of each equity security and how many days it would take to liquidate a security if the manager did not want it to be too large a portion of trading volume to avoid taking a price concession.
- *Scenario analysis:* Long-only asset managers typically use stress tests or scenario analyses to verify that the risks in the portfolio are as they have been disclosed to investors and to identify any unusual behavior that could arise in stressed markets.
- *Redemption risk:* Open-end fund managers often assess what percentage of the portfolio could be redeemed at peak times and track this behavior across the funds and asset classes they manage.
- *Ex post versus ex ante tracking error:* Limits on *ex ante* tracking error are often used by traditional asset managers as a key risk metric for the portfolios they manage. It provides an estimate of the degree to which the current portfolio could underperform its benchmark. It is worth noting the distinction between *ex post* tracking error and *ex ante* tracking error: Asset managers use *ex post* tracking error to identify sources of performance and manager skill and *ex ante* tracking error to identify whether today's positions could give rise to unexpected potential performance. *Ex post* tracking error measures the historical deviation between portfolio returns and benchmark returns, and thus both the portfolio holdings and market returns are historical in this measure. *Ex ante* tracking error takes today's benchmark-relative position and exposes it to the variability of past markets to estimate what kind of benchmark-relative performance could arise from the current portfolio. *Ex post* tracking error is a useful tool for assessing manager skill and behavior. The day after a large change in portfolio strategy, *ex ante* tracking will immediately reflect the portfolio's new return profile, whereas *ex post* tracking error will not do so until the new strategy has been in place long enough to dominate the data history. (If *ex post* tracking error is computed using 200 days of history, the day after a large strategy change, only 1 of the 200 data points will reflect the current risk positioning.) Some asset managers focus on maintaining *ex ante* tracking error boundaries for the portfolios they manage to monitor and balance the potential performance impact of the active risks they are taking. **Active share** is a measure of that percentage of the portfolio that differs from the benchmark (i.e., a deviation from the benchmark). It is often monitored to help limit tracking error of the portfolio.
- *VaR:* VaR is less commonly used as a risk measure than *ex ante* tracking error by traditional asset managers, but it is used by some—particularly for portfolios that are characterized as "absolute return" strategies for which a given market benchmark may not serve as the portfolio objective.

5.1.2.2. Hedge Funds

Similar to banks, hedge funds that use leverage need to observe sources and uses of cash through time, including when credit lines could be withdrawn, and need to simulate the interplay between market movements, margin calls, and the redemption rights of investors in order to understand worst-case needs for cash. A sample of the typical range of hedge fund market risk measures includes the following:

- *Sensitivities:* All hedge fund strategies will display some form of sensitivity or exposure, so the full range of sensitivity measures are useful for hedge fund risk management.
- *Gross exposure:* Long–short, market neutral, and arbitrage strategies will typically measure long exposure, short exposure, and gross exposure (the sum of the absolute value of long plus short positions) separately. Gross position risk is an important guide to the importance of correlation risk for the portfolio.
- *Leverage:* Leverage measures are common for hedge funds. It is important to understand how the measure is treating derivatives and what elements appear in the numerator versus the denominator because there are many different ways to execute the measure.
- *VaR:* Hedge funds that use VaR measures tend to focus on high confidence intervals (more than 90 percent) and short holding periods, and they rarely use a benchmark-relative measure.
- *Scenarios:* Hedge funds commonly use scenario/stress tests that are well tuned to the specific risks of their strategy—in merger arbitrage strategies, for example, the chance that the merger will not take place.
- *Drawdown:* In the case of the following types of hedge fund strategies, standard deviation and historical beta measures can be particularly misleading when seeking to understand what the more extreme risks can be. This is because the strategies listed frequently display decidedly non-normal return distributions, and when this is true, standard deviation is not a good guide to worst-case outcomes. For the following strategies, any historical standard deviation or historical beta measures should be supplemented by a measure of what has been the **maximum drawdown**, often defined as the worst-returning month or quarter for the portfolio or the worst peak-to-trough decline in a portfolio's returns:
  - Strategies that focus on credit risk taking, such as long–short credit, credit arbitrage, or bankruptcy investing
  - Strategies that focus on events, such as merger arbitrage
  - Strategies that make meaningful investments in non-publicly issued assets or other assets that do not reliably have a daily, independent fair value determination
  - Strategies that invest in illiquid asset classes or take large positions relative to market size in any asset class
  - Strategies that sell options or purchase bonds with embedded options
  - Strategies that are highly reliant on correlation relationships, such as equity market neutral

In addition, it is not uncommon for those investing in hedge funds to look at the returns of the hedge fund during a relevant historical period, such as the 2008 financial crisis.

5.1.3. Pension Funds

A defined benefit pension plan is required to make payments to its pensioners in the future that are typically determined as a function of a retiree's final salary. This differs from a defined contribution plan, in which the plan's sponsor may be required to make contributions currently but is not responsible to ensure that they grow to a particular future amount. To meet the required payouts, defined benefit plans have significant market risk management responsibilities. This section describes the practices of defined benefit pension plans only; all mentions in this section of "pension funds" or "pension plans" refer to defined benefit pensions.

The risk management goal for pension funds is to be sufficiently funded to make future payments to pensioners. The requirements for sufficient funding vary from country to country. Different jurisdictions will have regulations concerning such items as how to compute the present value of pension liabilities (including which interest rates are permitted to be used as a discount rate) and what the sponsor of the pension plan is required to contribute when the assets in the pension fund are lower than the present value of the liabilities. In addition, some jurisdictions impose taxes when surplus—the value of the assets less the value of the liabilities—is withdrawn for other use by the plan sponsor. Although these regional differences will shape the practice of pension plan risk management in different countries, it is typically an exercise in ensuring that the plan is not likely to become significantly under- or overfunded. Overfunding occurs when the funding ratio (the assets divided by the present value of the liabilities) is greater than 100%; underfunding occurs when the funding ratio is under 100%. Overfunding may be cured over time by the plan sponsor not needing to make regular contributions to the plan because the number of employees and their salary levels, which drive the pension benefit, are growing. Underfunding, if not cured by growth in the assets in the fund over a suitable time horizon as permitted by regulation, is cured by the plan sponsor contributing to the fund. The pension plan's actions will also vary depending on its age (whether it is a new or established plan) and whether it is currently meaningfully under- or overfunded. Important market risk measures or methods for pension funds often include the following:

- *Interest rate and curve risk:* The first step of risk measurement for pension funds is the analysis of expected payments to pensioners in the future. The expected future cash flows are grouped by maturity. In the case of an international pension fund that must make future payouts in multiple currencies, they may also be grouped by currency. In cases in which the jurisdiction requires a particular fixed-income instrument or curve be used to provide the discount rate for arriving at the present value of the pension liability (such as corporate bonds in the United States, inflation-linked gilts in the United Kingdom, or government bonds in the Netherlands), the liability cash flows will be expressed as a short position at the relevant points on the curve.
- *Surplus at risk:* This measure is an application of VaR. It is computed by entering the assets in the portfolio into a VaR model as long positions and the pension liabilities as short fixed-income positions. It estimates how much the assets might underperform the liabilities, usually over one year, and pension plan sponsors may vary with respect to how high a level of confidence they choose to use (e.g., 84 percent, 95 percent, 99 percent). If the assets in the portfolio were invested precisely in the same fixed-income instruments to which the liabilities have been apportioned and in the same amounts, it would result in zero surplus at risk. In practice, however, it may be impossible to invest in the sizes required in the particular fixed-income instruments specified in the liability analysis, so the pension will invest in other, non-fixed-income investments, such as equities or real assets. The more volatile the investments in the pension fund and the less well correlated these assets are with the liabilities, the higher the surplus at risk. The pension fund may set a threshold level or limit on surplus at risk; when the pension fund's surplus at risk exceeds this limit, pension staff will change the fund's asset allocation to make the assets in the fund better match the liabilities. This liability-focused form of pension investing is commonly referred to as "liability driven investing."

- *Liability hedging exposures versus return generating exposures:* Although matching liabilities is an important goal of pension fund management, it is not the only goal. Pension staff may separate their investment portfolio into investments designed to match the pension liability versus those meant to generate excess returns. The precise instruments linked to the liability cannot always be directly invested in, so a separate portion of the portfolio may be necessary and should perform the function of earning returns that can minimize the chance of having an over- or underfunded status greater than the pension fund's risk tolerance. The return-generating portion of the portfolio also helps to hedge the potential for future changes in the size of the liability that could be caused by longevity risk or by wage growth that exceeds the forecasts currently used to compute the liability.

5.1.4. Insurers

Insurers in the largest global economies are subject to significant regulation and accounting oversight regarding how they must retain reserves and reflect their liabilities. Regulation may also affect the pricing permitted by product line. It is common for insurers to aggregate risk from underlying business units to arrive at a firm-wide view of risk.

Insurance liabilities vary in their correlation with financial markets. The risk metrics of property and casualty insurance differ significantly from those used for life insurance and annuity products. Property and casualty insurance, including home, auto, corporate liability insurance, and health insurance, are typically not highly correlated with financial asset markets.

Insurers focus on managing a number of forms of insurance risk, for which they may use such tools as reinsurance and geographic dispersion. The market risk management measures in the property and casualty lines of business include the following:

- *Sensitivities and exposures:* Insurers often design an asset allocation for these portfolios and monitor current exposures to remain within the target ranges set forth in the target asset allocation.
- *Economic capital and VaR:* The risk measurement focus for these lines of business is capital at risk and VaR. The premiums earned in these areas are typically set to compensate for the expected payouts (usually defined as a range of possible payouts), so it is only in cases of greater-than-expected payouts that capital is tapped. The risk modeling effort is to estimate what that catastrophic loss amount could be at a given level of probability. Assessment of the risk to economic capital will include the market risks in the portfolio as well as characteristics of the insurance exposures and reinsurance coverage.
- *Scenario analysis:* Insurers use scenario analysis like other market participants that have capital at risk, such as banks and hedge funds. For the property and casualty lines, these scenarios may stress the market risks and the insurance risks in the same scenario.

Insurers do not focus on matching assets with liabilities in their property and casualty lines of business. Investment portfolios are not designed to pay out insurance claims in property and casualty insurance businesses; the premium income is primarily used for that purpose. These investments are designed to achieve a good absolute return within the constraints imposed under regulatory reserve requirements. Riskier assets are discounted relative to safer, fixed-income assets in measuring required reserves.

Life insurance and annuities have stronger ties to the financial markets, even while retaining distinct mortality-based risk profiles. Life liabilities are very long, and the reserves that insurers are required to maintain by insurance regulators are highly dependent on discount rate assumptions. Non-financial inputs include assumptions about mortality and which policyholders will either tap into options in their policy to add coverage at a given level or cancel their policy. Annuities produce returns based on financial assets, with some extra optionality driven by any life insurance elements embedded in the policy. These activities are paired with long-term investment portfolios in a variety of assets that are designed to help the insurer meet future claims.

For life portfolios, market risk measures include the following:

- *Sensitivities:* The exposures of the investment portfolio and the annuity liability are measured and monitored.
- *Asset and liability matching:* The investment portfolio is not designed to be a perfect match to the liabilities, but it is more closely matched to liabilities than is the case in property and casualty insurance.
- *Scenario analysis:* The main focus of risk measurement for the life lines of insurance are measures of potential stress losses based on the differences between the assets in which the insurance company has invested and the liabilities driven by the insurance contracts it has written to its customers. Scenario analyses need to stress both market and non-market sources of cash flow change (in which non-market changes can include changes in longevity).

EXAMPLE 11   Uses of Risk Measures by Market Participants

1. Which type of market participant is *most likely* to consistently express risk measures as a percentage of assets and relative to a benchmark?
   A. Banks
   B. Corporations
   C. Long-only asset managers

2. How does *ex ante* tracking error differ from *ex post* tracking error?
   A. *Ex ante* tracking error takes into account the behavior of options, whereas *ex post* tracking error does not.
   B. *Ex post* tracking error uses a more accurate forecast of future markets than the forecast used for *ex ante* tracking error.
   C. *Ex ante* tracking error uses *current* portfolio holdings exposed to the variability of historical markets, whereas *ex post* tracking error measures the variability of *historical* portfolio holdings in historical markets.

Solution to 1: C is correct. Long-only asset managers most commonly express risk measures in percentage terms and relative to a benchmark, whereas the entities in answers A and B measure risk more commonly in currency units and in absolute terms (not relative to a benchmark). Banks occasionally express risk measures, such as economic capital, as a percentage of assets or other balance sheet measures, but bank risk measures are typically expressed in currency units.

Solution to 2: C is correct. A is incorrect because although *ex post* tracking error accounts for the options that were in the portfolio in the past, *ex ante* tracking error might actually misstate the risk of options if it is computed using the parametric method. B is incorrect because *ex post* tracking error is not aiming to forecast the future; it is only measuring the variability of past results.

6. SUMMARY

This chapter on market risk management models covers various techniques used to manage the risk arising from market fluctuations in prices and rates. The key points are summarized as follows:

- Value at risk (VaR) is the minimum loss in either currency units or as a percentage of portfolio value that would be expected to be incurred a certain percentage of the time over a certain period of time given assumed market conditions.
- VaR requires the decomposition of portfolio performance into risk factors.
- The three methods of estimating VaR are the parametric method, the historical simulation method, and the Monte Carlo simulation method.
- The parametric method of VaR estimation typically provides a VaR estimate from the left tail of a normal distribution, incorporating the expected returns, variances, and covariances of the components of the portfolio.
- The parametric method exploits the simplicity of the normal distribution but provides a poor estimate of VaR when returns are not normally distributed, as might occur when a portfolio contains options.
- The historical simulation method of VaR estimation uses historical return data on the portfolio's current holdings and allocation.
- The historical simulation method has the advantage of incorporating events that actually occurred and does not require the specification of a distribution or the estimation of parameters, but it is only useful to the extent that the future resembles the past.
- The Monte Carlo simulation method of VaR estimation requires the specification of a statistical distribution of returns and the generation of random outcomes from that distribution.
- The Monte Carlo simulation method is extremely flexible but can be complex and time consuming to use.
- There is no single right way to estimate VaR.
- The advantages of VaR include the following: It is a simple concept; it is relatively easy to understand and easily communicated, capturing much information in a single number. It can be useful in comparing risks across asset classes, portfolios, and trading units and, as such, facilitates capital allocation decisions. It can be used for performance evaluation and can be verified by using backtesting. It is widely accepted by regulators.
- The primary limitations of VaR are that it is a subjective measure and highly sensitive to numerous discretionary choices made in the course of computation. It can underestimate the frequency of extreme events. It fails to account for the lack of liquidity and is sensitive to correlation risk. It is vulnerable to trending or volatility regimes and is often misunderstood as a worst-case scenario. It can oversimplify the picture of risk and focuses heavily on the left tail.
- There are numerous variations and extensions of VaR, including conditional VaR (CVaR), incremental VaR (IVaR), and marginal VaR (MVaR), that can provide additional useful information.
- Conditional VaR is the average loss conditional on exceeding the VaR cutoff.
- Incremental VaR measures the change in portfolio VaR as a result of adding or deleting a position from the portfolio or if a position size is changed relative to the remaining positions.

- MVaR measures the change in portfolio VaR given a small change in the portfolio position. In a diversified portfolio, MVaRs can be summed to determine the contribution of each asset to the overall VaR.
- *Ex ante* tracking error measures the degree to which the performance of a given investment portfolio might deviate from its benchmark.
- Sensitivity measures quantify how a security or portfolio will react if a single risk factor changes. Common sensitivity measures are beta for equities; duration and convexity for bonds; and delta, gamma, and vega for options. Sensitivity measures do not indicate which portfolio has greater loss potential.
- Risk managers can use deltas, gammas, vegas, durations, convexities, and betas to get a comprehensive picture of the sensitivity of the entire portfolio.
- Stress tests apply extreme negative stress to a particular portfolio exposure.
- Scenario measures, including stress tests, are risk models that evaluate how a portfolio will perform under certain high-stress market conditions.
- Scenario measures can be based on actual historical scenarios or on hypothetical scenarios.
- Historical scenarios are scenarios that measure the portfolio return that would result from a repeat of a particular period of financial market history.
- Hypothetical scenarios model the impact of extreme movements and co-movements in different markets that have not previously occurred.
- Reverse stress testing is the process of stressing the portfolio's most significant exposures.
- Sensitivity and scenario risk measures can complement VaR. They do not need to rely on history, and scenarios can be designed to overcome an assumption of normal distributions.
- Limitations of scenario measures include the following: Historical scenarios are unlikely to re-occur in exactly the same way. Hypothetical scenarios may incorrectly specify how assets will co-move and thus may get the magnitude of movements wrong. And, it is difficult to establish appropriate limits on a scenario analysis or stress test.
- Constraints are widely used in risk management in the form of risk budgets, position limits, scenario limits, stop-loss limits, and capital allocation.
- Risk budgeting is the allocation of the total risk appetite across sub-portfolios.
- A scenario limit is a limit on the estimated loss for a given scenario, which, if exceeded, would require corrective action in the portfolio.
- A stop-loss limit either requires a reduction in the size of a portfolio or its complete liquidation (when a loss of a particular size occurs in a specified period).
- Position limits are limits on the market value of any given investment.
- Risk measurements and constraints in and of themselves are not restrictive or unrestrictive; it is the limits placed on the measures that drive action.
- The degree of leverage, the mix of risk factors to which the business is exposed, and accounting or regulatory requirements influence the types of risk measures used by different market participants.
- Banks use risk tools to assess the extent of any liquidity and asset/liability mismatch, the probability of losses in their investment portfolios, their overall leverage ratio, interest rate sensitivities, and the risk to economic capital.
- Asset managers' use of risk tools focuses primarily on volatility, probability of loss, or the probability of underperforming a benchmark.
- Pension funds use risk measures to evaluate asset/liability mismatch and surplus at risk.

- Property and casualty insurers use sensitivity and exposure measures to ensure exposures remain within defined asset allocation ranges. They use economic capital and VaR measures to estimate the impairment in the event of a catastrophic loss. They use scenario analysis to stress the market risks and insurance risks simultaneously.
- Life insurers use risk measures to assess the exposures of the investment portfolio and the annuity liability, the extent of any asset/liability mismatch, and the potential stress losses based on the differences between the assets in which they have invested and the liabilities resulting from the insurance contracts they have written.

REFERENCE

Malkiel, Burton. 2007. *A Random Walk Down Wall Street*. New York: W.W. Norton.

PRACTICE PROBLEMS

The following information relates to Questions 1–5.

Randy Gorver, chief risk officer at Eastern Regional Bank, and John Abell, assistant risk officer, are currently conducting a risk assessment of several of the bank's independent investment functions. These reviews include the bank's fixed-income investment portfolio and an equity fund managed by the bank's trust department. Gorver and Abell are also assessing Eastern Regional's overall risk exposure.

Eastern Regional Bank Fixed-Income Investment Portfolio
The bank's proprietary fixed-income portfolio is structured as a barbell portfolio: About half of the portfolio is invested in zero-coupon Treasuries with maturities in the 3- to 5-year range (Portfolio P_1), and the remainder is invested in zero-coupon Treasuries with maturities in the 10- to 15-year range (Portfolio P_2). Georges Montes, the portfolio manager, has discretion to allocate between 40 percent and 60 percent of the assets to each maturity bucket. He must remain fully invested at all times. Exhibit 1 shows details of this portfolio.

EXHIBIT 1   US Treasury Barbell Portfolio

	Maturity	
	P_1	P_2
	3–5 Years	10–15 Years
Average duration	3.30	11.07
Average yield to maturity	1.45%	2.23%
Market value	$50.3 million	$58.7 million

Trust Department's Equity Fund

a. **Use of Options:** The trust department of Eastern Regional Bank manages an equity fund called the Index Plus Fund, with $325 million in assets. This fund's objective is to track the S&P 500 Index price return while producing an income return 1.5 times that of the S&P 500. The bank's chief investment officer (CIO) uses put and call options on S&P 500 stock index futures to adjust the risk exposure of certain client accounts that have an investment in this fund. The portfolio of a 60-year-old widow with a below-average risk tolerance has an investment in this fund, and the CIO has asked his assistant, Janet Ferrell, to propose an options strategy to bring the portfolio's delta to 0.90.

b. **Value at Risk:** The Index Plus Fund has a value at risk (VaR) of $6.5 million at 5 percent for one day. Gorver asks Abell to write a brief summary of the portfolio VaR for the report he is preparing on the fund's risk position.

Combined Bank Risk Exposures

The bank has adopted a new risk policy, which requires forward-looking risk assessments in addition to the measures that look at historical risk characteristics. Management has also become very focused on tail risk since the subprime crisis and is evaluating the bank's capital allocation to certain higher-risk lines of business. Gorver must determine what additional risk metrics to include in his risk reporting to address the new policy. He asks Abell to draft a section of the risk report that will address the risk measures' adequacy for capital allocation decisions.

1. If Montes is expecting a 50 bp increase in yields at all points along the yield curve, which of the following trades is he *most likely* to execute to minimize his risk?
   A. Sell $35 million of P_2 and reinvest the proceeds in three-year bonds
   B. Sell $15 million of P_2 and reinvest the proceeds in three-year bonds
   C. Reduce the duration of P_2 to 10 years and reduce the duration of P_1 to 3 years

2. Which of the following options strategies is Ferrell *most likely* to recommend for the client's portfolio?
   A. Long calls
   B. Short calls
   C. Short puts

3. Which of the following statements regarding the VaR of the Index Plus Fund is correct?
   A. The expected maximum loss for the portfolio is $6.5 million.
   B. Five percent of the time, the portfolio can be expected to experience a loss of at least $6.5 million.
   C. Ninety-five percent of the time, the portfolio can be expected to experience a one-day loss of no more than $6.5 million.

4. To comply with the new bank policy on risk assessment, which of the following is the *best* set of risk measures to add to the chief risk officer's risk reporting?
   A. Conditional VaR, stress test, and scenario analysis
   B. Monte Carlo VaR, incremental VaR, and stress test
   C. Parametric VaR, marginal VaR, and scenario analysis

5. Which of the following statements should *not* be included in Abell's report to manage-
    ment regarding the use of risk measures in capital allocation decisions?
    A. VaR measures capture the increased liquidity risk during stress periods.
    B. Stress tests and scenario analysis can be used to evaluate the effect of outlier events
        on each line of business.
    C. VaR approaches that can accommodate a non-normal distribution are critical to
        understand relative risk across lines of business.

The following information relates to Questions 6–11.

Hiram Life (Hiram), a large multinational insurer located in Canada, has received permission
to increase its ownership in an India-based life insurance company, LICIA, from 26 percent
to 49 percent. Before completing this transaction, Hiram wants to complete a risk assessment
of LICIA's investment portfolio. Judith Hamilton, Hiram's chief financial officer, has been
asked to brief the management committee on investment risk in its India-based insurance
operations.

   LICIA's portfolio, which has a market value of CAD260 million, is currently structured
as shown in Exhibit 1. Despite its more than 1,000 individual holdings, the portfolio is
invested predominantly in India. The Indian government bond market is highly liquid,
but the country's mortgage and infrastructure loan markets, as well as the corporate bond
market, are relatively illiquid. Individual mortgage and corporate bond positions are large
relative to the normal trading volumes in these securities. Given the elevated current and fiscal account deficits, Indian investments are also subject to above-average economic risk.

   Hamilton begins with a summary of the India-based portfolio. Exhibit 1 presents the
current portfolio composition and the risk and return assumptions used to estimate value
at risk (VaR).

EXHIBIT 1   Selected Assumptions for LICIA's Investment Portfolio

	Allocation	Average Daily Return	Daily Standard Deviation
India government securities	50%	0.015%	0.206%
India mortgage/infrastructure loans	25%	0.045%	0.710%
India corporate bonds	15%	0.025%	0.324%
India equity	10%	0.035%	0.996%

   Infrastructure is a rapidly growing asset class with limited return history; the first infrastructure loans were issued just 10 years ago.
   Hamilton's report to the management committee must outline her assumptions and
provide support for the methods she used in her risk assessment. If needed, she will also
make recommendations for rebalancing the portfolio to ensure its risk profile is aligned with
that of Hiram.
   Hamilton develops the assumptions shown in Exhibit 2, which will be used for estimating the portfolio VaR.

EXHIBIT 2   VaR Input Assumptions for Proposed CAD260 Million Portfolio

Method	Average Return Assumption	Standard Deviation Assumption
Monte Carlo simulation	0.026%	0.501%
Parametric approach	0.026%	0.501%
Historical simulation	0.023%	0.490%

Hamilton elects to apply a one-day, 5 percent VaR limit of CAD2 million in her risk assessment of LICIA's portfolio. This limit is consistent with the risk tolerance the committee has specified for the Hiram portfolio.

The markets' volatility during the last 12 months has been significantly higher than the historical norm, with increased frequency of large daily losses, and Hamilton expects the next 12 months to be equally volatile.

She estimates the one-day 5 percent portfolio VaR for LICIA's portfolio using three different approaches:

EXHIBIT 3   VaR Results over a One-Day Period for Proposed Portfolio

Method	5% VaR
Monte Carlo simulation	CAD2,095,565
Parametric approach	CAD2,083,610
Historical simulation	CAD1,938,874

The committee is likely to have questions in a number of key areas—the limitations of the VaR report, potential losses in an extreme adverse event, and the reliability of the VaR numbers if the market continues to exhibit higher-than-normal volatility. Hamilton wants to be certain that she has thoroughly evaluated the risks inherent in the LICIA portfolio and compares them with the risks in Hiram's present portfolio.

Hamilton believes the possibility of a ratings downgrade on Indian sovereign debt is high and not yet fully reflected in securities prices. If the rating is lowered, many of the portfolio's holdings will no longer meet Hiram's minimum ratings requirement. A downgrade's effect is unlikely to be limited to the government bond portfolio. All asset classes can be expected to be affected to some degree. Hamilton plans to include a scenario analysis that reflects this possibility to ensure that management has the broadest possible view of the risk exposures in the India portfolio.

6. Given Hamilton's expectations, which of the following models is *most appropriate* to use in estimating portfolio VaR?
   A. Parametric method
   B. Historical simulation method
   C. Monte Carlo simulation method

7. Which risk measure is Hamilton *most likely* to present when addressing the committee's concerns regarding potential losses in extreme stress events?
   A. Relative VaR
   B. Incremental VaR
   C. Conditional VaR

8. The scenario analysis that Hamilton prepares for the committee is *most likely* a:
   A. stress test.
   B. historical scenario.
   C. hypothetical scenario.

9. The scenario analysis that Hamilton prepares for the committee is a valuable tool to supplement VaR *because* it:
   A. incorporates historical data to evaluate the risk in the tail of the VaR distribution.
   B. enables Hamilton to isolate the risk stemming from a single risk factor—the ratings downgrade.
   C. allows the committee to assess the effect of low liquidity in the event of a ratings downgrade.

10. Using the data in Exhibit 2, the portfolio's annual 1% parametric VaR is *closest* to:
    A. CAD17 million.
    B. CAD31 million.
    C. CAD48 million.

11. What additional risk measures would be most appropriate to add to Hamilton's risk assessment?
    A. Delta
    B. Duration
    C. Tracking error

The following information relates to Questions 12–19.

Tina Ming is a senior portfolio manager at Flusk Pension Fund (Flusk). Flusk's portfolio is composed of fixed-income instruments structured to match Flusk's liabilities. Ming works with Shrikant McKee, Flusk's risk analyst.

Ming and McKee discuss the latest risk report. McKee calculated value at risk (VaR) for the entire portfolio using the historical method and assuming a lookback period of five years and 250 trading days per year. McKee presents VaR measures in Exhibit 1.

EXHIBIT 1   Flusk Portfolio VaR (in $ millions)

Confidence Interval	Daily VaR	Monthly VaR
95%	1.10	5.37

After reading McKee's report, Ming asks why the number of daily VaR breaches over the last year is zero even though the portfolio has accumulated a substantial loss.

Next, Ming requests that McKee perform the following two risk analyses on Flusk's portfolio:

Analysis 1.   Use scenario analysis to evaluate the impact on risk and return of a repeat of the last financial crisis.

Analysis 2.   Estimate over one year, with a 95 percent level of confidence, how much Flusk's assets could underperform its liabilities.

Ming recommends purchasing newly issued emerging market corporate bonds that have embedded options. Prior to buying the bonds, Ming wants McKee to estimate the effect of the purchase on Flusk's VaR. McKee suggests running a stress test using a historical period specific to emerging markets that encompassed an extreme change in credit spreads.

At the conclusion of their conversation, Ming asks the following question about risk management tools: "What are the advantages of VaR compared with other risk measures?"

12.   Based on Exhibit 1, Flusk's portfolio is expected to experience:
   A.   a minimum daily loss of $1.10 million over the next year.
   B.   a loss over one month equal to or exceeding $5.37 million 5 percent of the time.
   C.   an average daily loss of $1.10 million 5 percent of the time during the next 250 trading days.

13.   The number of Flusk's VaR breaches *most likely* resulted from:
   A.   using a standard normal distribution in the VaR model.
   B.   using a 95 percent confidence interval instead of a 99 percent confidence interval.
   C.   lower market volatility during the last year compared with the lookback period.

14.   To perform Analysis 1, McKee should use historical bond:
   A.   prices.
   B.   yields.
   C.   durations.

15.   The limitation of the approach requested for Analysis 1 is that it:
   A.   omits asset correlations.
   B.   precludes incorporating portfolio manager actions.
   C.   assumes no deviation from historical market events.

16.   The estimate requested in Analysis 2 is *best* described as:
   A.   liquidity gap.
   B.   surplus at risk.
   C.   maximum drawdown.

17.   Which measure should McKee use to estimate the effect on Flusk's VaR from Ming's portfolio recommendation?
   A.   Relative VaR
   B.   Incremental VaR
   C.   Conditional VaR

18.   When measuring the portfolio impact of the stress test suggested by McKee, which of the following is *most likely* to produce an accurate result?
   A.   Marginal VaR
   B.   Full revaluation of securities
   C.   The use of sensitivity risk measures

19. The risk management tool referenced in Ming's question:
    A. is widely accepted by regulators.
    B. takes into account asset liquidity.
    C. usually incorporates right-tail events.

The following information relates to questions 20–26.

Carol Kynnersley is the chief risk officer at Investment Management Advisers (IMA). Kynnersley meets with IMA's portfolio management team and investment advisers to discuss the methods used to measure and manage market risk and how risk metrics are presented in client reports.

The three most popular investment funds offered by IMA are the Equity Opportunities, the Diversified Fixed Income, and the Alpha Core Equity. The Equity Opportunities Fund is composed of two exchange-traded funds: a broadly diversified large-cap equity product and one devoted to energy stocks. Kynnersley makes the following statements regarding the risk management policies established for the Equity Opportunities portfolio:

Statement 1. IMA's preferred approach to model value at risk (VaR) is to estimate expected returns, volatilities, and correlations under the assumption of a normal distribution.

Statement 2. In last year's annual client performance report, IMA stated that a hypothetical $6 million Equity Opportunities Fund account had a daily 5 percent VaR of approximately 1.5 percent of portfolio value.

Kynnersley informs the investment advisers that the risk management department recently updated the model for estimating the Equity Opportunities Fund VaR based on the information presented in Exhibit 1.

EXHIBIT 1   Equity Opportunities Fund—VaR Model Input Assumptions

	Large-Cap ETF	Energy ETF	Total Portfolio
Portfolio weight	65.0%	35.0%	100.0%
Expected annual return	12.0%	18.0%	14.1%
Standard deviation	20.0%	40.0%	26.3%
Correlation between ETFs: 0.90			
Number of trading days/year: 250			

For clients interested in fixed-income products, IMA offers the Diversified Fixed-Income Fund. Kynnersley explains that the portfolio's bonds are all subject to interest rate risk. To demonstrate how fixed-income exposure measures can be used to identify and manage interest rate risk, Kynnersley distributes two exhibits featuring three hypothetical Treasury coupon bonds (Exhibit 2) under three interest rate scenarios (Exhibit 3).

EXHIBIT 2   Fixed-Income Risk Measure

Hypothetical Bond	Duration
Bond 1	1.3
Bond 2	3.7
Bond 3	10.2

EXHIBIT 3   Interest Rate Scenarios

Scenario	Interest Rate Environment
Scenario 1	Rates increase 25 bps
Scenario 2	Rates increase 10 bps
Scenario 3	Rates decrease 20 bps

One of the investment advisers comments that a client recently asked about the performance of the Diversified Fixed-Income Fund relative to its benchmark, a broad fixed-income index. Kynnersley informs the adviser as follows:

Statement 3.   The Diversified Fixed-Income Fund manager monitors the historical deviation between portfolio returns and benchmark returns. The fund prospectus stipulates a target deviation from the benchmark of no more than 5 bps.

Kynnersley concludes the meeting by reviewing the constraints IMA imposes on securities included in the Alpha Core Equity Fund. The compliance department conducts daily oversight using numerous risk screens and, when indicated, notifies portfolio managers to make adjustments. Kynnersley makes the following statement:

Statement 4.   It is important that all clients investing in the fund be made aware of IMA's compliance measures. The Alpha Core Equity Fund restricts the exposure of individual securities to 1.75 percent of the total portfolio.

20.   Based on Statement 1, IMA's VaR estimation approach is *best* described as the:
   A.   parametric method.
   B.   historical simulation method.
   C.   Monte Carlo simulation method.

21.   In Statement 2, Kynnersley implies that the portfolio:
   A.   is at risk of losing $4,500 each trading day.
   B.   value is expected to decline by $90,000 or more once in 20 trading days.
   C.   has a 5 percent chance of falling in value by a maximum of $90,000 on a single trading day.

22. Based *only* on Statement 2, the risk measurement approach:
    A. ignores right-tail events in the return distribution.
    B. is similar to the Sharpe ratio because it is backward looking.
    C. provides a relatively accurate risk estimate in both trending and volatile regimes.

23. Based on Exhibit 1, the daily 5 percent VaR estimate is *closest* to:
    A. 1.61 percent.
    B. 2.42 percent.
    C. 2.69 percent.

24. Based *only* on Exhibits 2 and 3, it is *most likely* that under:
    A. Scenario 1, Bond 2 outperforms Bond 1.
    B. Scenario 2, Bond 1 underperforms Bond 3.
    C. Scenario 3, Bond 3 is the best performing security.

25. The risk measure referred to in Statement 3 is:
    A. active share.
    B. beta sensitivity
    C. *ex post* tracking error.

26. In Statement 4, Kynnersley describes a constraint associated with a:
    A. risk budget.
    B. position limit.
    C. stop-loss limit.

CHAPTER 14

BACKTESTING AND SIMULATION

Yin Luo, CPA, PStat, CFA
Sheng Wang

LEARNING OUTCOMES

The candidate should be able to:

- describe objectives in backtesting an investment strategy;
- describe and contrast steps and procedures in backtesting an investment strategy;
- interpret metrics and visuals reported in a backtest of an investment strategy;
- identify problems in a backtest of an investment strategy;
- describe different ways to construct multifactor models;
- compare methods of modeling randomness;
- evaluate and interpret a scenario analysis;
- contrast Monte Carlo and historical simulation;
- explain inputs and decisions in simulation and interpret a simulation; and
- demonstrate the use of sensitivity analysis.

1. INTRODUCTION

This chapter provides an overview of backtesting and simulation of investment strategies. Backtesting and related techniques enable investment practitioners to simulate the performance of investment strategies (especially quantitative strategies) using historical data or data derived from the distributions of historical data, to generate test results, and to analyze risk and return, without investing any real capital in the strategies.

The rise of big data and the increase in computing power have spurred the development and spread of quantitative investing. Almost every major data vendor has available tools that make systematic backtesting and simulation increasingly accessible. Off-the-shelf software

Quantitative Methods for Investment Analysis, Second Edition, by Yin Luo, CPA, PStat, CFA, and Sheng Wang. Copyright © 2020 by CFA Institute.

allows backtesting and simulation of endless combinations of possible investment strategies, formulation of multifactor models, and construction of investable portfolios. Developing quantitative investment strategies may appear relatively straightforward, but in reality, it is not. However, understanding the steps and procedures, the implicit assumptions, the pitfalls, and the interpretation of results in backtesting and simulation is a prerequisite for proper utilization of these tools and successful development and implementation of investment strategies.

In a CFA Institute survey of nearly 250 analysts, portfolio managers, and private wealth managers on quantitative investment techniques, 50 percent of respondents reported that they had conducted backtesting of an investment strategy within the past 12 months of the survey date. This result underscores the importance of backtesting (and other simulation techniques) for investors in practice, and this chapter is a starting point on the journey to building this core professional competency.

2. THE OBJECTIVES OF BACKTESTING

Backtesting is the process that approximates the real-life investment process, using historical data, to assess whether the strategy would have produced desirable results. Backtesting offers investors some comfort as to whether their investment strategies and analytical models would have performed well historically. More importantly, it allows investors to refine and optimize their investment process.

Backtesting has been widely used in the investment community for many years. Although backtesting fits quantitative and systematic investment styles more naturally, it has also been heavily used by fundamental managers. As long as you use any form of stock screening, you may want to first backtest and see whether your selection criteria and process indeed add any incremental excess return.

Notably, not all strategies that have performed well in a backtest will continue to produce excess returns in live investing. Although in theory a model that does not show much predictive power in backtesting could still deliver excess return in the future, such a model is unlikely to be sufficiently convincing for portfolio managers to implement.

Importantly, the implicit assumption in backtesting is that the future will as least somewhat resemble history. Therefore, if we implement our investment strategies that have performed well in backtesting, we may expect similar performance going forward. The reality, however, as we will show, is far more complicated. There are a number of factors—some are under the investment managers' control and some are not—that may completely disrupt our investment process.

3. THE BACKTESTING PROCESS

Backtesting typically follows the steps and procedures of strategy design, historical investment simulation, and analysis of backtesting output. These steps and associated procedures are set out in Exhibit 1. We will explain each of these steps and procedures in detail in the following sections.

EXHIBIT 1   Backtesting Flowchart

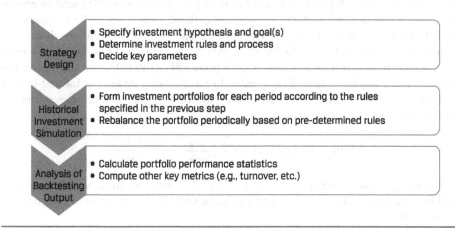

Source: Wolfe Research Luo's QES.

3.1. Strategy Design

The first step in backtesting is to specify the investment hypothesis and goals. For active strategies, the goal is typically to achieve superior risk-adjusted excess returns. However, in many situations, downside risk management is also critical. Furthermore, depending on how the strategies will be deployed—quantitatively or in a fundamental investment process—other considerations, such as portfolio turnover, portfolio concentration, and investment horizon, should also be taken into account.

Common equity investment strategies often use factor-based models. A factor can be broadly considered as any variable that is believed to be useful in ranking stocks (in terms of attractiveness) for investment and in predicting future returns or risks. Value and momentum (which we will discuss later) are two classic examples of factors; factors represent unique sources of risk with sound economic foundations. A factor-based strategy aims to identify significant signals that drive stock prices, with the aim of forming investable portfolios to outperform the market.

As mentioned earlier, although fundamental portfolio managers do not invest solely based on factors, they typically perform some type of stock screening to identify potential investment opportunities. This is especially the case for small-cap and global equity managers, because their investment universes are too large to conduct detailed fundamental analysis on all companies. Most commonly known investment styles can be proxied by factors. For example, the return of most value funds is highly correlated to the performance of valuation factors, such as book-to-market ratio, earnings yield (earnings-to-price ratio), and price-to-sales ratio. Therefore, backtesting such factors is a critical element for managers to improve and refine their investment process.

In this section, we will use a basic value signal and a classic price momentum factor to demonstrate how backtesting can be conducted.

3.1.1. Value

Value investing is based on the concept of buying undervalued stocks whose prices would eventually rise and converge toward their intrinsic values. Academic literature has a long history of documenting the value phenomenon. Early researchers found that stocks with low price-to-earnings ratios (P/Es) or high earnings yield (i.e., the inverse of P/E) tend to provide higher returns. Fama and French (1993) formally outlined value investing by proposing the use of the book-to-market ratio as a way to differentiate value stocks from growth stocks.

In practice, value factors can be based on almost any fundamental performance metrics of a company, such as dividends, earnings, cash flow, EBIT, EBITDA, and sales. Most valuation ratios can also be computed using either historical (called trailing) or forward-looking (i.e., expected future) metrics. In this section, we use a simple metric as our factor—trailing earnings yield:

$$\text{Trailing earnings yield} = \frac{\text{Trailing 12-month EPS}}{\text{Current share price}} \tag{1}$$

Following industry practice, we expect cheap stocks with more attractive valuations (i.e., with higher earnings yields) to outperform expensive stocks (i.e., with lower or even negative earnings yields).

3.1.2. Momentum

Researchers have found a strong price momentum effect in almost all asset classes. Jegadeesh and Titman (1993), in a study of the US market, first documented that stocks that are the winners over the last 12 months tend to outperform past losers over the next 2–12 months. The authors also found there is a short-term reversal effect—that is, stocks with a high price momentum over the last month tend to underperform in the next 2–12 months. As a result, practitioners often define the price momentum factor using the following equation, which focuses on the total return in the past 12 months, excluding the most recent month:

$$\text{Price momentum} = r_{-12:-1} \tag{2}$$

Note that the reason to exclude the most recent month's return is to account for the short-term mean-reversal effect.

3.2. Rolling Window Backtesting

Once a potential investment strategy is designed, the investment manager needs to perform a series of backtests to assess the factor's performance and effectiveness. Some investors argue that the most important test is the "intuition" test: Does the factor make intuitive sense? Is there an underlying economic rationale? A factor can often pass statistical backtesting, but if it does not make sense and a reasonable justification for the factor's efficacy is lacking, then the manager may have fallen into the data-mining trap. The economic intuition test, however, lacks theoretical rigor and can be easily abused. It is often difficult (and subjective) to differentiate what counts as being intuitive and what does not.

Investors, therefore, always need to remind themselves that what appears to be impressive performance from backtesting does not guarantee the same returns in the future.

In a typical backtest, researchers first form their investment hypothesis—for example, stocks with higher earnings yield should earn higher subsequent returns—and then determine their investment rules and processes. Next, they collect the necessary data—in this case, historic earnings yield and return for each stock. In the simplest type of backtest, researchers divide the historical data into two subsamples. The first few years of data, the

EXHIBIT 2   An Example of Rolling Window Backtesting of the Earnings Yield Factor

	2010:12	2011:01	2011:02	2011:03	2011:04	2011:05	2011:06	2011:07	2011:08	2011:09	2011:10	2011:11	2011:12	2012:01	2012:02	2012:03	2012:04	2012:05
11/30/2011									In-Sample (Last 12M EPS/Price)				OOS					
12/31/2011										In-Sample (Last 12M EPS/Price)				OOS				
1/31/2012											In-Sample (Last 12M EPS/Price)				OOS			
2/29/2012												In-Sample (Last 12M EPS/Price)				OOS		
3/31/2012													In-Sample (Last 12M EPS/Price)				OOS	
4/30/2012														In-Sample (Last 12M EPS/Price)				OOS

Source: Wolfe Research Luo's QES.

first subset, is used to train the model (i.e., in-sample/training data). The trained model is then tested using the second subset of data (i.e., out-of-sample/testing data).

In the **rolling window backtesting** methodology, instead of dividing the data into only two samples, researchers typically use a rolling window (or walk-forward) framework, fit/calibrate factors or trade signals based on the rolling window, rebalance the portfolio periodically (i.e., after each period), and then track the performance over time. In this case, backtesting is a proxy for actual investing. As new information arrives, investment managers re-adjust their models and rebalance their stock positions. To avoid overfitting, in the backtesting, the key model methodology should be specified up front. Therefore, at each given point in time, the model is tuned according to its specification. Most backtesting procedures assume monthly model optimization and position rebalancing—that is, researchers repeat the same in-sample training/out-of-sample testing process on the last day of each month. Other common frequencies, such as daily, weekly, and quarterly, are also used in practice by investors. Note that these overlapping periods may not be considered fully independent statistically, and the rolling window methodology may be slow to pick up regime changes.

Exhibit 2 shows a snapshot of such a rolling window backtesting of the value (trailing 12-month earnings yield) factor. Assume that we start our backtesting on 30 November 2011. First, we compute every stock's trailing 12-month earnings yield, using EPS reported in the previous 12 months (i.e., from December 2010 to November 2011), divided by current stock price as of 30 November 2011. We can then form our investment strategy—for example, buying the top 20 percent of stocks with the highest earnings yield and shorting the bottom quintile of companies (the 20 percent of stocks with the lowest earnings yield). The performance of such a strategy can be assessed using returns in the next month, December 2011, which is the out-of-sample (OOS) period. The same process is repeated on 31 December 2011, and so on. In our simple example, we backtest our value strategy from November 2011 to April 2012. We then compute the average monthly return, volatility, Sharpe ratio, and drawdown of our strategy from the test results of the six OOS periods.

If the performance of the investment strategy in the out-of-sample periods is desirable and the strategy meets the economic intuition test, then it is generally considered successful. Otherwise, the strategy is rejected.

3.3. Key Parameters in Backtesting

Before we can perform a backtesting exercise, there are a few key parameters that must be specified, including the investment universe, the specific definition of stock return, the frequency of portfolio rebalancing, and the start and end dates for the backtest.

3.3.1. Investment Universe

First, we need to decide on the investment universe—that is, the universe of stocks in which we can potentially invest. Investment strategy performance can be vastly different between different countries, different sectors, and different contexts (e.g., value versus growth). While academic research typically uses the union of Compustat/Worldscope and CRSP[1] as the research universe, practitioners often use a well-known broad market index, such as the S&P 500 Index, the Russell 3000 Index, or the MSCI World, to define their investment universe. In this chapter, unless it is otherwise specified, we use the Russell 3000 index to represent the US market, the S&P/TSX Composite Index to represent the Canadian market, the MSCI China A Index to represent the Mainland China market, and the S&P Global Broad Market Index (BMI) for markets covering all other countries.

3.3.2. Stock Return

Since the goal of backtesting is to proxy the real investment process, we compute stock returns by taking into account not only capital appreciation but also dividend reinvestment.

As we extend our investment universe from a single country to a global context, multiple complexities arise, such as currency, trading, and regulatory considerations. For example, we need to decide in what currency the return should be computed. The two most frequent choices are either to translate all investment returns into one single currency, typically the home-country currency (e.g., US dollar or euro) or to denominate returns in local currencies. The choice of currency in backtesting often depends on whether portfolio managers prefer to hedge their currency exposures. Managers who do not hedge their foreign exchange risk often choose to backtest using single-currency-denominated returns.

3.3.3. Rebalancing Frequency and Transaction Cost

Academic studies typically use investment returns calculated quarterly or annually, while practitioners mostly use a monthly frequency for their rolling windows for model optimization and portfolio rebalancing. Note that daily or even higher-frequency rebalancing can incur high transaction costs, and the price data will likely be biased by bid–ask spreads, asynchronous trading across different parts of the world, and missing days due to holidays in different countries.

In most standard backtesting, transaction costs are typically not included, because researchers want to first understand the pure alpha from the strategy. More importantly, transaction costs critically depend on the portfolio construction process; therefore, they vary significantly from one portfolio manager to another. For example, the following issues should be accounted for when estimating transaction costs:

- whether the strategy is implemented in a systematic approach or used as a stock screening process;
- whether the portfolio is long only or long/short market neutral;
- the size of the portfolio (i.e., assets under management);
- whether currency is hedged; and
- how trades are executed—via electronic trading, program trading, or single-stock trading.

In sum, transaction costs are critical to whether a strategy is profitable in practice, because many market anomalies simply disappear once costs are included.

---

[1] CRSP (the Center for Research in Security Prices) provides high-quality data and security returns. The CRSP data series of New York Stock Exchange–listed stocks begins on 31 December 1925.

3.3.4. Start and End Date

Everything else being equal, investment managers typically prefer to backtest their investment strategies using as long a history as possible for their model inputs. Using a longer history for asset prices, returns, factors, and so on, provides a larger sample; therefore, the investment manager would have a greater statistical confidence in the backtesting results. Conversely, however, since financial data are likely to be non-stationary with structural breaks, backtested performance using a long data history may not be very relevant looking forward. Our recommendation is to backtest as far back as possible. However, managers may choose to weight recent periods more heavily compared with distant history. Importantly, researchers need to be aware that historical periods may not be relevant for their investment thesis (e.g., past periods of high inflation may be less relevant for a strategy based on a low-inflation environment). Later, in the coverage of scenario analysis, we will discuss how to deal with structural changes and regime shifts.

3.4. Long/Short Hedged Portfolio Approach

The most traditional and widely used method for implementing factor-based portfolios is the hedged portfolio approach, pioneered and formulated by Fama and French (1993). In this approach, after having chosen the factor to be scrutinized and having ranked the investable stock universe by that factor, the analyst divides the universe into groups referred to as quantiles (typically into quintiles or deciles) to form hypothetical portfolios. Stocks are either equally weighted or market capitalization weighted within each quantile. A long/short hedged portfolio is then formed by going long the top quantile (i.e., the one with the best factor scores) and shorting the bottom quantile (i.e., the one with the worst factor scores). The rolling window backtesting framework is then implemented and the portfolio is rebalanced periodically—for example, monthly. The performance of the long/short hedged portfolio is then tracked over time (i.e., for each successive out-of-sample period).

The long/short hedged portfolio is dollar neutral but not necessarily beta neutral. For example, the long portfolio formed using the book-to-market factor typically contains stocks with higher beta than the short portfolio, because cheap stocks are often more volatile than expensive stocks. As a result, the return from such a portfolio is partially due to exposures to the market. Similarly, the portfolio may also have exposures to other common factors. However, as a reasonable and straightforward approximation of the performance of the factor-based strategy, the hedged portfolio approach serves the purpose. We care about not only the average return of the portfolio but also the risk profile (e.g., volatility and downside risk). Therefore, most common performance measurement metrics, such as the Sharpe ratio, the Sortino ratio, and maximum drawdown, can be used to assess the efficacy of our investment strategy.

EXAMPLE 1   Performance of Earnings Yield Factor in the United States and Europe, 1986–2019

Panel A of Exhibit 3 shows the performance of the earnings yield factor in the United States from January 1986 to May 2019. The bars in the chart indicate the monthly

EXHIBIT 3   Earnings Yield Factor, Long/Short Hedged Quintile Portfolio Returns (January 1986–May 2019)

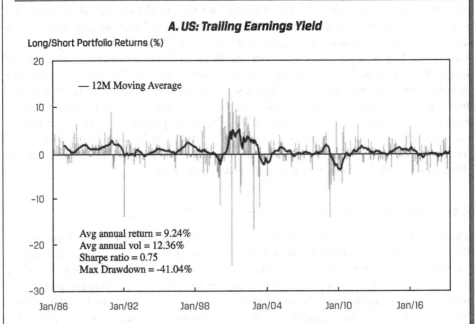

A. US: Trailing Earnings Yield

Long/Short Portfolio Returns (%)

Avg annual return = 9.24%
Avg annual vol = 12.36%
Sharpe ratio = 0.75
Max Drawdown = -41.04%

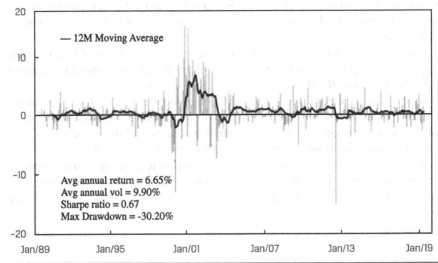

B. Europe: Trailing Earnings Yield

Long/Short Portfolio Returns (%)

Avg annual return = 6.65%
Avg annual vol = 9.90%
Sharpe ratio = 0.67
Max Drawdown = -30.20%

Sources: Bloomberg Finance LLP, FTSE Russell, S&P Capital IQ, Thomson Reuters, Wolfe Research Luo's QES.

portfolio returns generated from buying companies with the highest earnings yields, those in the top quintile, and shorting companies with the lowest/most negative earnings yields, those in the bottom quintile. Stocks in both long and short baskets are equally weighted. Panel B shows the performance of the earnings yield factor in Europe over the same time period.

Describe how the backtest performance of value investing, based on the earnings yield factor, in Europe compares with that in the United States over the period of 1986–2019.

Solution: In the United States, the average annual return from the value investing strategy is about 9.2 percent, with a Sharpe ratio of 0.75, over the backtesting period (January 1986–May 2019). In Europe, the same investment strategy generated a significantly lower (by 250 bps) average annual return, about 6.7 percent, but with significantly lower volatility. Hence, the Sharpe ratio for the European strategy, 0.67, is close to that of the US strategy. In both markets, the maximum drawdown is just over three times the volatility of the strategy.

Therefore, as a long-term value strategy, the earnings yield factor offers slightly better performance in the United States than in Europe.

There are a few drawbacks to this approach. First, the information contained in the middle quantiles is wasted, because only the top and bottom quantiles are used in forming the hedged portfolio. Second, it is implicitly assumed that the relationship between the factor and future stock returns is linear or at least monotonic (they move in the same direction but not necessarily at a constant rate), which may not always be the case. Third, equally weighting all stocks in the long and the short quantiles does not properly take account of each stock's volatility and its correlation with other stocks in the portfolio. Fourth, the hedged portfolio approach requires managers to short stocks. Shorting may not be possible in some markets or may be overly expensive in others, particularly some emerging markets. Notably, transaction costs are not incorporated in the backtesting.

EXAMPLE 2   Performance of Momentum Factor in Mainland China Equity Market, 2004–2019

At first glance, Panel A of Exhibit 4 appears to show that the price momentum factor has produced counterintuitive results in Mainland China's domestic equity market during the July 2004–May 2019 period. Backtesting results indicate that the long/short quintile portfolio that invests in the highest momentum bucket and shorts the lowest momentum bucket of stocks delivered a negative return of about –2.7 percent per annum over the period. However, examining Panel B shows that the payoff pattern is actually an inverse U-shape curve. So, although the highest momentum quintile slightly underperformed the lowest momentum quintile—at 10.3 percent and 11.0 percent, respectively—the middle three quintiles substantially outperformed both of the extreme portfolios. There are a few explanations for why the momentum effect is not apparent in Mainland China equities. One explanation, for example, is that

EXHIBIT 4   Price Momentum Factor, China A-Shares Market

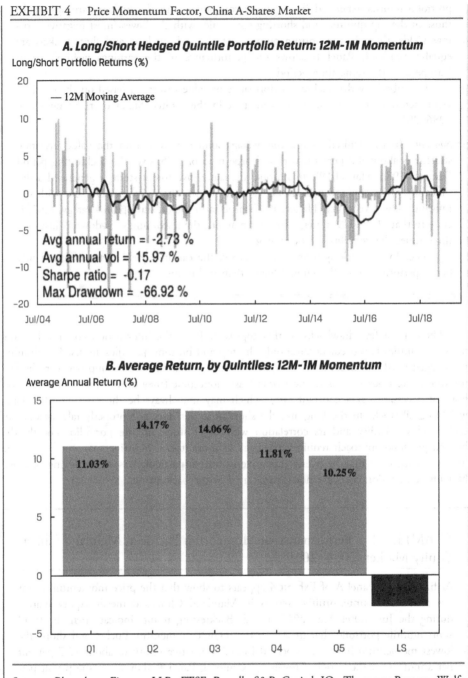

Sources: Bloomberg Finance LLP, FTSE Russell, S&P Capital IQ, Thomson Reuters, Wolfe Research Luo's QES.

the Chinese Mainland equity market consists largely of retail investors (rather than institutional investors) and retail investors tend to overreact to news, which is a behavior that may lead to a mean-reversal effect.

Describe with respect to **Examples 1** and **2** some of the issues with the simple long/short hedged portfolio backtesting approach, and explain why it is important to know your investment universe.

Solution: The long/short hedged portfolio backtesting approach implicitly assumes the pattern between quantile portfolios and future stock returns is at least monotonic. It also uses information from only the highest and lowest quantiles and thus wastes potentially important information in the middle quantiles. As shown in the example of the price momentum factor in the Mainland Chinese equity market, stocks in the middle quintiles produced higher returns than those in both extreme quintiles. Therefore, for this market, the results from the long/short hedged portfolio backtesting approach are not so meaningful. So, although the medium-term price momentum effect is well documented in the United States and in many other markets (e.g., Europe), we observe a very different pattern in China A-shares. The bottom line is that depending on the equity market in which one invests, one cannot assume the same anomaly exists and operates in the same way in all markets.

3.5. Pearson and Spearman Rank IC

The information coefficient (IC) is more commonly used than the hedged portfolio approach by practitioners as the standard metric of a factor's predictive power for future stock returns. Since most quantitative models are linear, the IC approach captures the entire spectrum of stocks. This approach contrasts with the long/short quantile portfolio approach, which focuses only on the top and bottom extremes. Therefore, the IC is generally considered to be the better measure for identifying and assessing factors than the quantile-based hedged portfolio approach.

The **Pearson IC** is the simple correlation coefficient between the factor scores (also known as "factor loadings")—for such factors as earnings yield or momentum for the prior period, denoted by f_{t-1}, for all stocks in the investment universe under consideration—and the current period's stock returns, r_t:

$$\text{Pearson IC} = \text{Correlation}(f_{t-1}, r_t) \tag{3}$$

Because it is a correlation coefficient, the IC's value is always between −100 percent and +100 percent (or −1.0 and +1.0). The higher the average IC, the higher the predictive power of the factor for subsequent returns. In practice, any factor with an average monthly IC of 5–6 percent is already considered very strong in this context. An important caveat for the Pearson IC, however, is that it is sensitive to outliers.

A similar but more robust measure often preferred by practitioners is the **Spearman Rank IC**. The Spearman Rank IC is essentially the Pearson IC between the prior-period ranked factor scores and the ranked current-period returns:

$$\text{Spearman Rank IC} = \text{Correlation}\Big(\text{rank}(f_{t-1}),\text{rank}(r_t)\Big) \qquad (4)$$

Exhibit 5 shows the Pearson IC and Spearman Rank IC for a hypothetical set of nine stocks (A to I) at a point in time (i.e., end of period $t - 1$). As you recall from earlier chapters, the correlation coefficient is the ratio of the covariance of two random variables to the product of their standard deviations. The exhibit shows that the Pearson IC for these stocks is marginally negative, at −0.80 percent (i.e., −0.008), suggesting that the signal did not perform well, and was negatively correlated with the subsequent month's (i.e., period t's) returns. Looking more carefully, however, one can see that the sample factors are generally in line with the subsequent stock returns. The exception is stock I, where the factor predicts the highest return (given that it has the highest score of 1.45), whereas the stock turns out to be the worst performer (−8.50 percent). This example demonstrates that a single outlier can turn what may actually be a good factor into a bad one because of the Pearson IC's sensitivity to outliers.

In contrast, the Spearman Rank IC of 40.0 percent suggests that the factor has strong predictive power for subsequent returns. If three equally weighted portfolios (i.e., tercile portfolios) were constructed, the long basket, which includes stocks I, H, and G (ranked 1, 2, and 3, respectively), would have outperformed the short basket, which includes stocks A, B, and C (ranked 9, 8, and 7, respectively), by 56 bps in absolute return in this period. Therefore, in this case, the Spearman Rank IC is consistent with the long/short portfolio approach, but the Pearson IC is inconsistent.

EXHIBIT 5   Pearson IC and Spearman Rank IC

Stock	Factor Score	Subsequent Return	Factor Score Rank	Return Rank
A	(1.45)	(3.00%)	9	8
B	(1.16)	(0.60%)	8	7
C	(0.60)	(0.50%)	7	6
D	(0.40)	(0.48%)	6	5
E	0.00	1.20%	5	4
F	0.40	3.00%	4	3
G	0.60	3.02%	3	2
H	1.16	3.05%	2	1
I	1.45	(8.50%)	1	9
Mean	0.00	(0.31%)		
Standard Deviation	1.00	3.71%		
Pearson IC		(0.80%)		
Spearman Rank IC				40.00%
Long/Short Tercile Portfolio Return				0.56%

Source: Wolfe Research Luo's QES.

In the same manner as the long/short hedged portfolio approach, the IC is also computed periodically—for example, monthly—in accordance with the rolling window backtesting and portfolio rebalancing methodology described previously. Typically, investment managers are interested not only in the average IC over time but also in the stability or consistency of the IC. Therefore, managers generally compute the risk-adjusted Spearman IC as a primary performance measure:

$$\text{Risk Adjusted IC} = \frac{\text{Mean(IC)}}{\text{Standard Deviation(IC)}} \tag{5}$$

EXAMPLE 3   Contrasting Long/Short Hedged Portfolio and Rank IC Approaches in Backtesting

Exhibit 6 compares the backtesting performance of the earnings yield factor in Europe from January 1989 to May 2019 using two different approaches—long/short hedged quintile portfolio (Panel A) versus Spearman Rank IC (Panel B). In Panel A, the bars indicate monthly returns from the long/short hedged quintile portfolio. In Panel B, the bars show the Spearman Rank IC—that is, the rank correlation between the previous month's factor scores and the current month's stock returns.

The two evaluation approaches paint a broadly similar picture—namely, that cheaper stocks (ones with higher earnings yields or higher ranked factor scores) have outperformed expensive stocks (ones with lower earnings yields or lower ranked factor scores) in this sample period.

Describe the pros and cons of using the Spearman Rank IC versus the long/short hedged portfolio approaches to backtesting.

Solution: The long/short hedged portfolio backtesting approach is more intuitive, since investment managers essentially form paper portfolios and then performance is measured on these hypothetical portfolios. In contrast, the Spearman Rank IC is a measure of the predictive power of a given factor on future stock returns. Importantly, the Rank IC is a correlation, not a portfolio return.

Since the long/short hedged portfolio approach concerns only the top and bottom quantiles of stocks, the middle quantiles are ignored, so information is wasted. In practice, managers typically need to balance risk, return, correlation, transaction costs, trading liquidity, and other issues when they form their portfolios. Since the Rank IC approach captures the predictive power of a given factor via correlation, although it

EXHIBIT 6   Earnings Yield Factor, Performance Comparisons in Europe

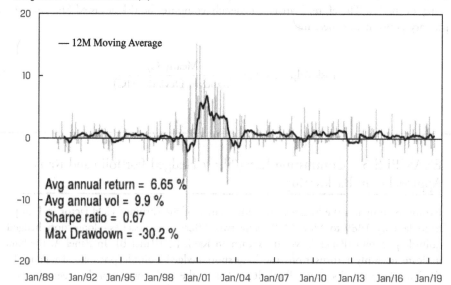

A. Long/Short Hedged Quintile Portfolio: Trailing Earnings Yield

Long/Short Portfolio Returns (%)

— 12M Moving Average

Avg annual return = 6.65 %
Avg annual vol = 9.9 %
Sharpe ratio = 0.67
Max Drawdown = -30.2 %

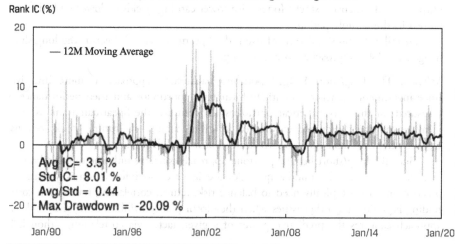

B. Spearman Rank IC: Trailing Earnings Yield

Rank IC (%)

— 12M Moving Average

Avg IC = 3.5 %
Std IC = 8.01 %
Avg/Std = 0.44
Max Drawdown = -20.09 %

Sources: Bloomberg Finance LLP, FTSE Russell, S&P Capital IQ, Thomson Reuters, Wolfe Research Luo's QES.

still assumes a linear relationship between the factor score rank and the future stock return rank, it is generally more consistent with actual performance, regardless of how the investment managers construct their portfolios.

3.6. Univariate Regression

Another common way to assess factor performance with backtesting is by performing a cross-sectional (univariate) regression of the following form:

$$r_t = \beta_{0,t} + \beta_{1,t} f_{t-1} + \varepsilon_t \tag{6}$$

where,

r_t = a vector of stock returns at time t and
f_{t-1} = a vector of stock factor scores at time $t - 1$.

This regression is typically performed monthly and is often referred to as Fama–MacBeth (1973) regression.

The inference centers on whether $\beta_{1,t}$, the fitted factor return, is statistically significant. Note the difference in time subscripts for the factor loading (t) and the factor score ($t - 1$).

In an ordinary least squares (OLS) regression, $\beta_{1,t}$ can be computed as

$$\beta_{1,t} = \frac{\text{cov}(r_t, f_{t-1})}{\text{var}(f_{t-1})} = \frac{\text{corr}(r_t, f_{t-1})\text{std}(r_t)}{\text{std}(f_{t-1})} \tag{7}$$

where

$\text{cov}(r_t, f_{t-1})$ = the covariance between the prior factor score and the current stock return
$\text{var}(f_{t-1})$ = the variance of the factor scores
$\text{corr}(r_t, f_{t-1})$ = the correlation between the prior factor score and the current stock return—that is, the information coefficient
$\text{std}(r_t)$ = the cross-sectional dispersion (i.e., standard deviation) of stock returns, and
$\text{std}(f_{t-1})$ = the cross-sectional dispersion (i.e., standard deviation) of prior factor scores

The dispersions in stock returns and factor scores—that is, respectively, $\text{std}(r_t)$ and $\text{std}(f_{t-1})$—are both positive numbers. Therefore, the regression coefficient, $\beta_{1,t}$, and IC, $\text{corr}(r_t, f_{t-1})$, always have the same sign. As a result, the regression approach typically produces results (i.e., whether the results confirm our hypothesis or whether to accept/reject the strategy) similar to those of the IC method.

3.7. Do Different Backtesting Methodologies Tell the Same Story?

Exhibit 7 compares the performance of eight common stock-selection factors in the United States and Asia excluding Japan during 1989–2019 using two backtesting evaluation methods: average Spearman rank IC (*y*-axis) and long/short hedged quintile portfolio (*x*-axis).

If the factors are arrayed in roughly a straight line, then the two methods yield similar assessments. As shown in Panel A, in the United States, the performance of the eight common stock-selection signals is roughly in line using the two backtesting approaches. In contrast, in Asia ex-Japan (Panel B), we observe some significant deviations. For example, the book-to-market factor appears to be strong using the long/short hedged portfolio approach, with an average annual return of 8.2 percent. Conversely, based on the Spearman rank IC approach, the book-to-market factor has an average IC close to zero, indicating that it is relatively uncorrelated with future stock returns.

This example illustrates that different backtesting evaluation methodologies do not always tell the same (or even a similar) story. There are many reasons why different approaches can deliver vastly different results. For example, if the true relationship between a factor and future

EXHIBIT 7   Long/Short Hedge Portfolio vs. Spearman Rank IC

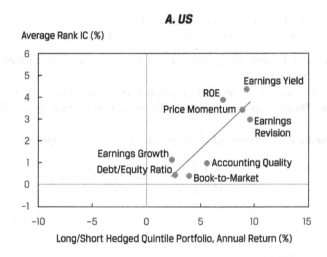

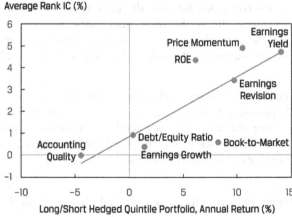

Sources: Bloomberg Finance LLP, FTSE Russell, S&P Capital IQ, Thomson Reuters, Wolfe Research Luo's QES.

stock returns is highly non-linear, then the Spearman rank IC could be close to zero while the long/short quantile portfolio may still have a highly significant return spread.

There is no simple rule of thumb as to which approach should be relied on. Ideally, investment strategies should show promising backtested performance using both methodologies. In practice, however, the choice of backtesting methodology depends on a number of considerations, including

- the researcher's personal preference,
- the intended use of the investment strategy, and
- the portfolio construction technique.

For instance, on the one hand, if an investment manager plans to combine factors into a linear multifactor model and use mean–variance optimization to create investable portfolios, then the Spearman rank IC is typically more aligned with the final portfolio performance. When we combine multiple factors into one model, it is not just about the top and bottom quantiles ranked by each factor. Instead, we are interested in the overall distribution of all factors. Furthermore, if mean–variance optimization is used for portfolio construction, we need to rank all stocks and then balance return, risk, trading costs, and liquidity. Again, rank IC is about the overall relationship between a factor and future stock returns, whereas the long/short hedged portfolio approach focuses exclusively on the two extreme quantiles.

On the other hand, if the investment manager intends to construct long/short quintile portfolios for each factor—which is the standard approach used by many alternative beta funds—then that approach should be used as the primary backtesting evaluation method.

EXAMPLE 4   Choosing the Appropriate Backtesting Methodology

A quantitative equity portfolio manager wants to develop a systematic multifactor stock selection model and use a mean–variance optimization technique to construct her portfolio.

Explain whether the manager should use the long/short hedged quantile portfolio approach or the Spearman rank IC approach as the primary decision criterion for evaluating backtests of her portfolio.

Solution: The investment manager is developing a systematic multifactor model for stock selection and will use mean–variance optimization (MVO) to construct her portfolio. Since she will combine multiple factors into one model, the overall distribution of the factors and the ranking of her stock universe by these factors is crucial. Balancing return, risk, trading costs, and liquidity are also important concerns. For these reasons—and because MVO requires more than just the top and bottom quantiles (ranked by each factor) from the long/short hedged quantile approach—the investment manager should use the Spearman rank IC approach as the primary decision criterion for evaluating backtests of her portfolio.

4. METRICS AND VISUALS USED IN BACKTESTING

In this section, we introduce some of the common metrics and visuals that can assist in interpreting backtesting results and in assessing the effectiveness of a proposed investment strategy.

4.1. Coverage

Not all factors have full coverage in the investment universe. Missing coverage is a practical issue and can be due to a number of reasons—lack of data availability, inapplicability, or outliers. All else equal, managers typically prefer factors with wider coverage.

It is interesting to contrast the price-to-earnings ratio (P/E) with the earnings yield (E/P) factor. The P/E is likely the most commonly used valuation metric among investors; both professionals and retail investors regularly monitor the P/E before making their investment decisions. However, a serious flaw with the P/E is that it cannot be computed if the denominator is zero or negative (i.e., there are no earnings or there are losses), because any such P/E would lack intuitive interpretation. This limitation affects new companies, companies in certain industries (i.e., technology), and companies in distress and turnaround situations, thereby constraining coverage of the P/E metric. Conversely, the earnings yield factor can be computed for any stock, so long as EPS (e.g., positive, zero, or negative) and price data are available.

This difference in coverage between the earnings yield and P/E factors is illustrated in Exhibit 8 for the Russell 3000 from January 1986 to May 2019. Panel A shows P/E coverage averaging about 2,350 stocks, whereas Panel B indicates that the coverage of the earnings yield factor is about 28 percent higher, at nearly 3,000 stocks. Furthermore, there is a significant difference in the average annual return between these factors. Backtesting of portfolios formed by the long/short hedge method using the P/E (Panel C) and earnings yield (Panel D) factors reveals that the average annual return is 35 percent higher for portfolios using the earning yield factor (9.24 percent versus 6.83 percent). This return difference reflects a strong information signal on the short side. That is, shorting stocks with losses (i.e., negative earnings yield) generated substantial incremental return but also added volatility over this period.

EXHIBIT 8   P/E Factor vs. Earnings Yield Factor, United States (1986–2019)

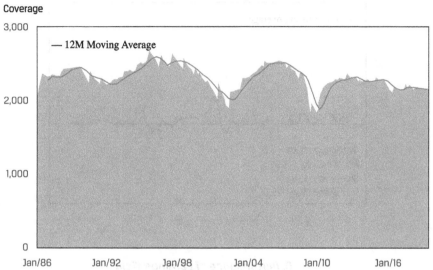

A. Coverage of P/E

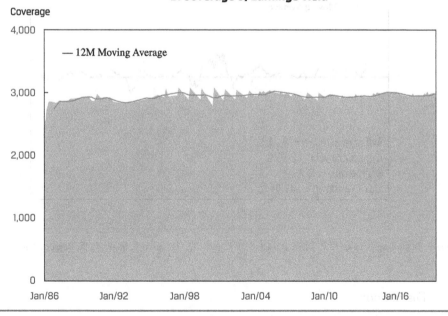

B. Coverage of Earnings Yield

C. Performance of P/E

Long/Short Portfolio Returns (%)

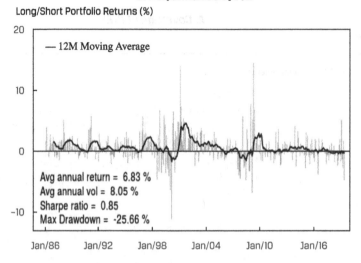

Avg annual return = 6.83 %
Avg annual vol = 8.05 %
Sharpe ratio = 0.85
Max Drawdown = -25.66 %

D. Performance of Earnings Yield

Long/Short Portfolio Returns (%)

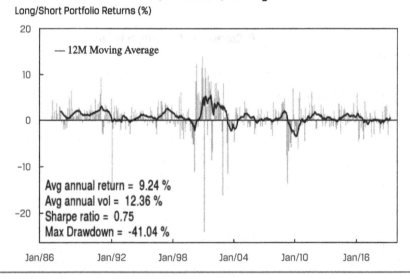

Avg annual return = 9.24 %
Avg annual vol = 12.36 %
Sharpe ratio = 0.75
Max Drawdown = -41.04 %

Sources: Bloomberg Finance LLP, FTSE Russell, S&P Capital IQ, Thomson Reuters, Wolfe Research Luo's QES.

4.2. Distribution

In assessing backtests of multifactor-based models, factor distribution is an important consideration for which two issues need to be addressed. One issue is the factor score distribution. If the distribution of scores is highly skewed with outliers, then the factor scores may need to be transformed. For example, z-score transformation (which re-scales the data into unit standard deviation and centers it with a zero mean) and percentile transformation (which results in a percentile rank factor score) are commonly used in practice. The impact of outliers may be further reduced using winsorization or truncation techniques. Otherwise, combining the skewed factor scores with those of other factors may cause undesirable distortions in the resulting multifactor model. Differences in factor score distributions can be revealed by visual inspection of the probability density function curves of the factors under investigation.

For example, as shown in Panel A of Exhibit 9, compared with a normal distribution (with the same mean and standard deviation), the distribution of raw earnings yield factor scores is clearly skewed to the left, with significant outliers as high as 200 percent or as negative as –

EXHIBIT 9   Distribution of Value and Momentum Factors in the United States, May 2019

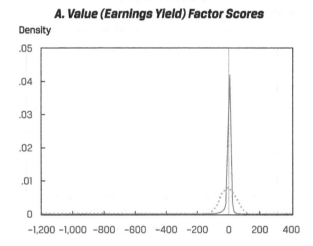

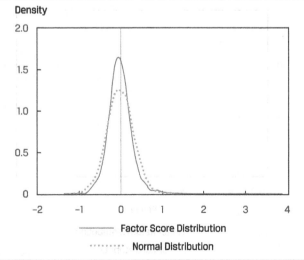

Sources: Bloomberg Finance LLP, FTSE Russell, S&P Capital IQ, Thomson Reuters, Wolfe Research Luo's QES.

1,000 percent. The distribution of price momentum factor scores, however, appears to more closely resemble the normal distribution (see Panel B of Exhibit 9); more precisely, it is reasonably symmetric but has fat tails. Note that the x-axis represents the total return in the past 12 months excluding the most recent month, which ranges from –90 percent to 200 percent.

In addition to factor score distribution, it is even more important to study the distribution of the investment strategy's returns. The traditional assumption of a normal distribution for asset returns is in fact highly unrealistic in most cases. As shown in Panels A and B of

EXHIBIT 10   The Distribution of Factor Returns, United States (1986–2019)

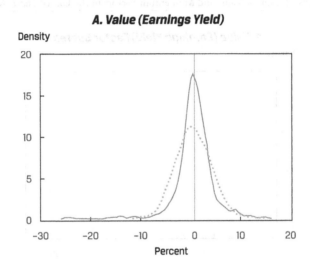

A. Value (Earnings Yield)

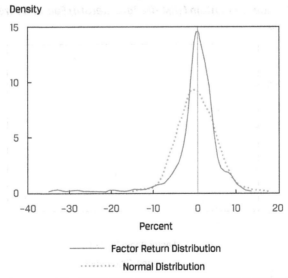

B. Price Momentum (12M–1M Total Return)

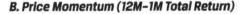

——— Factor Return Distribution

········· Normal Distribution

Sources: Bloomberg Finance LLP, FTSE Russell, S&P Capital IQ, Thomson Reuters, Wolfe Research Luo's QES.

Exhibit 10, the distributions of the classic value and momentum strategy returns, respectively, are clearly non-normal. More problematically, both factor-based strategies tend to suffer from excess kurtosis (i.e., fat tails) and negative skewness. The excess kurtosis implies that these strategies are more likely to generate surprises, meaning extreme returns, whereas the negative skewness suggests that those surprises are more likely to be negative (than positive).

4.3. Performance Decay, Structural Breaks, and Downside Risk

In practice, it is often useful to examine the backtested cumulative performance of an investment strategy over an extended history. For example, the total wealth generated by a long/short hedged quantile portfolio might be calculated, assuming periodic rebalancing (monthly or quarterly). Such performance is often calculated without accounting for transaction costs, because costs depend on the portfolio construction process, which varies from one manager to another. We recommend plotting performance using a logarithmic scale, wherein equal percentage changes are presented as the same vertical distance on the *y*-axis. Using these cumulative performance graphs, one can readily identify potential performance decay, structural breaks, and downside risk in the backtested investment strategies being assessed.

For example, as shown in Panel A of Exhibit 11, the value strategy (i.e., earnings yield factor) has delivered strong performance over the long run (1990–2019), especially in Asia ex-Japan. However, performance has flattened since 2016 in the United States, Europe, and Japan. Significant drawdowns and potential structural breaks can also be observed in late 1990s (i.e., during the tech bubble) and in March–May 2009 (i.e., the risk rally during the global financial crisis) in most regions.

The price momentum factor has also produced significant excess returns during the same time frame (Panel B of Exhibit 11) in the United States, Europe, and Asia ex-Japan. However, the price momentum effect does not appear to exist in Japan. It is also clear that the momentum strategy suffers from more pronounced periodic downside risk (e.g., March–May 2009) than the value strategy does. The performance of the momentum strategy has also been flattening in the United States since 2016.

4.4. Factor Turnover and Decay

One of the most common issues concerning interpretation of backtest results of an investment strategy is related to the strategy's turnover. Low factor turnover is desirable, all else equal, since the higher the factor turnover, the higher the portfolio turnover needed to capture the factor. High transaction costs associated with high turnover factors may make them difficult or unrealistic to implement. The turnover of a factor-based portfolio depends not only on the frequency and magnitude of changes in factor scores over time but also on the portfolio construction process itself.

To isolate the effect of factor changes from portfolio construction, signal autocorrelation (i.e., serial correlation) is commonly used to measure factor turnover. Signal autocorrelation is computed as the correlation between the vector of today's (t) factor scores and the factor scores from the preceding period ($t - 1$):

$$\text{Signal autocorrelation}_t = \text{Correlation}(f_t, f_{t-1}) \tag{8}$$

where f_t is the vector of factor scores as of time t.

EXHIBIT 11   Cumulative Performance of Earnings Yield and Momentum Factors (January 1990–
May 2019)

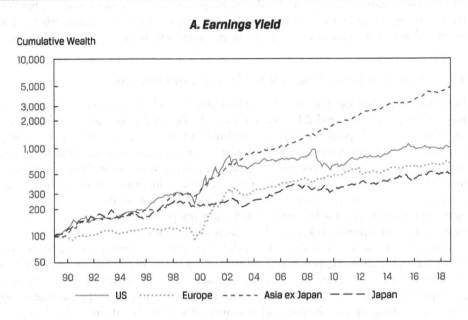

A. Earnings Yield

Cumulative Wealth

——— US   ·········· Europe   – – – – – Asia ex Japan   — — Japan

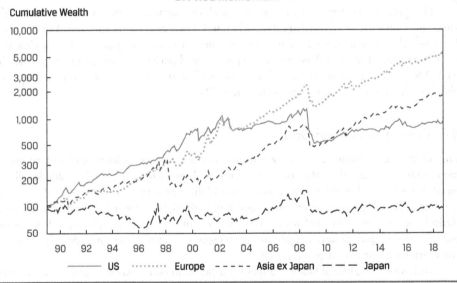

B. Price Momentum

Cumulative Wealth

——— US   ·········· Europe   – – – – – Asia ex Japan   — — Japan

Sources: Bloomberg Finance LLP, FTSE Russell, S&P Capital IQ, Thomson Reuters, Wolfe Research Luo's QES.

The signal autocorrelation is then plotted over time. Assuming the identified factors indeed produce strong excess return, all else being equal, factors with low turnover, indicated by high autocorrelation, are preferred because such factors lead to lower portfolio turnover, lower transactions costs, and, therefore, higher after-cost cumulative performance.

For example, as shown in Panel A of Exhibit 12, the average signal autocorrelation for the earnings yield–based value strategy over the period 1986–2019 is 95 percent. Therefore, because the ranking of stocks based on earnings yield changes very minimally from month to month, the periodic rebalancing of portfolios formed using this factor experience low turnover. Similarly, the average serial correlation for the price momentum factor during that period is about 88 percent (see Panel B of Exhibit 12), slightly lower than for the value factor, meaning portfolios formed using the momentum strategy experience slightly higher turnover.

A concept that is closely related but different from factor turnover (i.e., signal autocorrelation) is information decay, which measures the decline in a factor's predictive power as the forecasting horizon (or backtesting history) is extended. Essentially, information decay is proxied by computing the Spearman rank IC between factor scores in the qth month prior (f_{t-q}) and the current month's stock returns (r_t):

$$\text{Spearman rank IC}_q = \text{Correlation}[\text{rank}(f_{t-q}), \text{rank}(r_t)] \qquad (9)$$

We can then plot the IC decay chart to show how long the predictive power of the factors under investigation tends to last. For example, Panel A of Exhibit 13, shows the information decay profile for the US value strategy (based on the earnings yield factor): The predictive power of the underlying factor remains positive (approximately 3 percent or more) for up to one year. So, the value factor's signal provides strong predictive power, and it decays slowly. In contrast, although the front-month correlation (i.e., IC_1) of the US momentum strategy is only slightly lower than for the value strategy, the predictive power of the momentum strategy decays much faster (Panel B, with a somewhat different y-axis from that in Panel A). In sum, the ideal factor has a high initial IC, a low factor turnover, and a slow factor decay.

5. COMMON PROBLEMS IN BACKTESTING

In this section, we discuss some of the most common mistakes investors make when they conduct backtests. Many quantitative investment managers believe that their models are free from human behavioral biases, but we will show how quantitative strategies can suffer from the same biases as fundamental and other investment styles.

5.1. Survivorship Bias

Ignoring **survivorship bias**, the bias that results when data as of a given date reflects only those entities that have survived to that date, is one of the most obvious but, interestingly, also one of the most common mistakes that investors make when conducting backtests. Although widely covered in the academic literature, relatively few practitioners, whether investing in equities, fixed income, indexes, hedge funds, or other asset classes, bother to quantify the real but significant implications of survivorship bias in their backtesting.

Although it is straightforward to backtest an investment strategy with the companies that are currently in the index (i.e., the survivors), tracking all companies that have ever existed in a correct point-in-time fashion (i.e., the casualties as well as the survivors) is actually not so straightforward. **Point-in-time data** means the exact information that was available to market participants as of a given point in time. Point-in-time data allow analysts to use the most complete data for any given time period, thereby enabling the construction (and backtesting) of the most realistic investment strategies.

EXHIBIT 12   Signal Autocorrelation: Value vs. Price Momentum Strategies, United States (1986–2019)

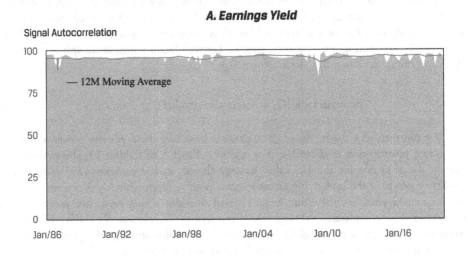

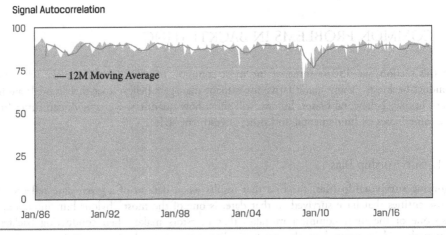

Sources: Bloomberg Finance LLP, FTSE Russell, S&P Capital IQ, Thomson Reuters, Wolfe Research Luo's QES.

Companies continually appear and disappear. A company can disappear (i.e., be delisted) because of many factors, including privatization, acquisition, bankruptcy, and prolonged underperformance. Similarly, new firms appear via entrepreneurship, spin-offs, and carve-outs that go public and are eventually included in the major indexes. As shown in Panel A of Exhibit 14, the number of true point-in-time companies in the US Russell 3000 Index has stayed relatively stable, at around 3,000, over the past 30 years. However, among the 3,000 companies in the index as of 31 December 1985, less than 400 (or roughly 13 percent) have survived as of 31 May 2019. Similarly, the S&P BMI Europe Index, which tracks the broad European market, started with about 720 stocks in 1989 and now comprises around 1,200 companies. Among the 720 stocks in the index at inception, only 142 (or about 20 percent) were still in the index as of May 2019 (Panel B of Exhibit 14).

EXHIBIT 13   Signal Decay: Value vs. Price Momentum Strategies, United States

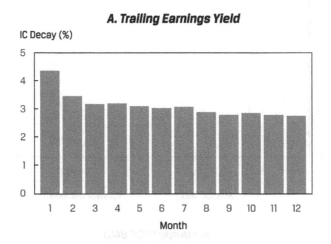

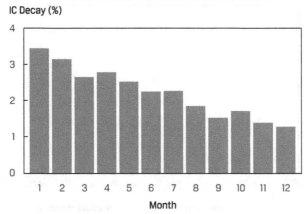

Sources: Bloomberg Finance LLP, FTSE Russell, S&P Capital IQ, Thomson Reuters, Wolfe Research Luo's QES.

Backtesting with only the surviving stocks can create considerable bias and often produces completely incorrect results and conclusions. Unfortunately, tracking companies at each point in time over a long history is not easy, so many practitioners conduct (and data vendors' platforms facilitate) backtesting using the current index constituents. They contend that since you can invest only in the companies that exist today, there is nothing wrong with backtesting strategies on only these firms. However, the problem, as mentioned previously, is that in the past, one could not know which companies would survive in the future, which

EXHIBIT 14   Number of Stocks in Index vs. Survivors

A. US (Russell 3000)

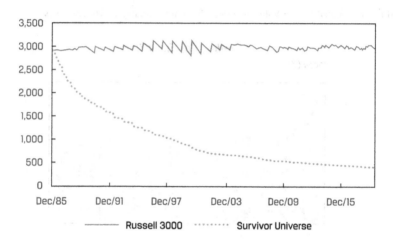

B. Europe (S&P BMI)

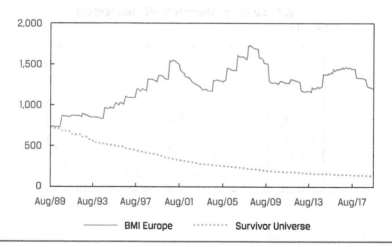

Sources: Bloomberg Finance LLP, FTSE Russell, S&P Capital IQ, Thomson Reuters, Wolfe Research Luo's QES.

companies would disappear, and which companies would be created and become successful enough to be added to the index in the future. In sum, backtesting with just current index constituents is a bad practice that can result in faulty investment conclusions.

The danger in ignoring survivorship bias is illustrated using the low-volatility anomaly, a popular investment strategy that argues that stocks with low volatilities tend to outperform high-volatility stocks in the long term. As shown in Panel A of Exhibit 15—here the portfolio is constructed by going long (shorting) the lowest-volatility (highest-volatility) quintile of stocks—a proper backtesting methodology using the point-in-time Russell 3000 universe finds that low-volatility stocks do indeed very significantly outperform high-volatility stocks over the three decades up to 2019. Importantly, however, if we repeat the backtesting exercise but form the long/short portfolio using only those companies that have survived until the current period, May 2019, then the result is exactly the opposite: The incorrect conclusion now is that high-volatility stocks outperform low-volatility stocks by about $5.5\times$ (see Panel B of Exhibit 15). This example underscores the importance of accounting for survivorship bias in backtesting by using point-in-time index constituent stocks and not just the current survivors.

EXAMPLE 5   Survivorship Bias and the Low-Volatility Anomaly

Explain the rationale behind the big difference in backtesting performance results for the low-volatility anomaly strategy shown in Exhibit 15 using point-in-time data on index constituents versus current data on index constituents.

Solution: These contradictory results are fairly straightforward to explain. The proper backtesting methodology uses point-in-time data and thus includes current survivors as well as all the stocks that have dropped out of the index—because of mergers and acquisitions or perhaps financial distress or bankruptcy—along with their poor performance during prior periods. So, when the past casualties are properly taken into account, the low-volatility quintile easily outperforms the high-volatility quintile of stocks.

The improper backtesting methodology uses just the current companies in the index (i.e., survivors only). These survivors likely included many companies that in the past experienced financial distress, did not go bankrupt, and ultimately became turnaround successes with considerable upside performance. Such companies likely propelled the outperformance of the high-volatility quintile versus the low-volatility quintile in this biased sample.

5.2. Look-Ahead Bias

Another common mistake investors make in backtesting is failing to recognize and account for **look-ahead bias**. This is the bias created by using information that was unknown or unavailable during the time periods over which the backtesting is conducted. Look-ahead bias is likely the most common mistake that practitioners make when performing backtesting. Survivorship bias can be considered a special case of look-ahead bias, because the

EXHIBIT 15   Survivorship Bias and the Low-Volatility Anomaly

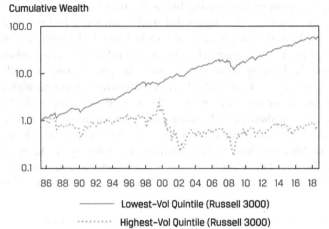

A. Using a Point-in-Time Universe

Cumulative Wealth

——— Lowest–Vol Quintile (Russell 3000)

········ Highest–Vol Quintile (Russell 3000)

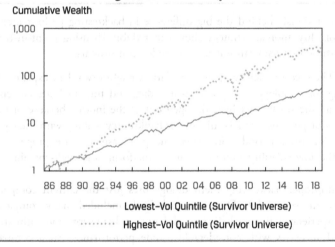

B. Using the Survived Companies

Cumulative Wealth

——— Lowest–Vol Quintile (Survivor Universe)

········ Highest–Vol Quintile (Survivor Universe)

Sources: Bloomberg Finance LLP, FTSE Russell, S&P Capital IQ, Thomson Reuters, Wolfe Research Luo's QES.

question of whether a stock will survive or be added to an index in the future is unknown during the earlier periods over which the backtesting occurs.

Ideally, in backtesting one should use only point-in-time data. Unfortunately, since not all vendor databases provide point-in-time data, there are several issues that must be addressed.

First, analysts must make reporting lag assumptions. For example, we would not have EPS results for the quarter ending 31 December 2018 for all companies on 31 January 2019, since many companies will not yet have reported their earnings. Therefore, analysts typically compensate by adding several months of reporting lag. However, this process can also introduce stale information. Continuing the example, by 31 January 2019, many companies, especially the larger-cap ones, will have reported earnings, but others, especially mid- and small-cap companies, will not have had the chance to report their Q4 2018 earnings. By using the assumption of a reporting lag of three months, we essentially assume that Q4 2018 data are available for all companies on 31 March 2019. In this case, look-ahead bias is significantly reduced. However, because most companies would have reported earnings before 31 March 2019, by using the three-month lag assumption for backtesting done on 31 January and 28 February 2019, we would be using stale financial data; this typically makes backtesting overly conservative.

Instead, using point-in-time data effectively solves this reporting lag problem—no assumption is needed—since we simply use the best information available at any given point in time for our research. In this case, if by 31 January 2019 a company has reported Q4 2018 earnings results, then we would use them; otherwise, we would use Q3 2018 earnings or whatever was available as of 31 January 2019.

A second problem is that companies often re-state their financial statements owing to corrections of accounting errors or changes in accounting policies. Economic data from government agencies are also often being re-stated. Traditional databases keep only the latest numbers or the last re-stated financial statements. By using such databases, an analyst trying to build realistic investment scenarios going back in time would be using information that was not available during the earlier periods of the backtesting. Another form of look-ahead bias arises when data vendors add new companies to their databases. When doing so, they often add several years of historical financial statements into the system. Thus, an analyst backtesting with the current database would be using companies that were not actually in the database during the backtesting period. The consequence of this look-ahead bias is often overly optimistic results.

The third problem stemming from traditional non-point-in-time databases is survivorship bias. As mentioned previously, because of merger and acquisition activities, bankruptcy, delisting, and other forms of corporate actions, corporate stocks are constantly being removed from these databases.

To demonstrate the impact of look-ahead bias and the reporting lag assumption, we conduct monthly backtesting using the earnings yield factor. The benchmark is a proper point-in-time database with the actual EPS data as of each month end, so it is free from look-ahead bias. Next, we perform backtesting using EPS data without any reporting lag; this assumes EPS data become available immediately after the close of the quarter (or any other reporting period), so it suffers from full look-ahead bias. Lastly, we add a series of reporting lags, from one to six months.

As shown in Panel A Exhibit 16, it is clear from the backtesting results of the point-in-time and no-lag scenarios that look-ahead bias inflates the performance of our value factor in the United States by almost 100 percent. The impact of look-ahead bias is evident in all regions. In the United States, Canada, and Japan (Panel B), it appears that a reporting lag of between one and two months produces backtest results that are consistent with those of the proper point-in-time data. Note that using a reporting lag beyond two months introduces stale information and drags performance down significantly. In Europe, the United Kingdom, and Australia and New Zealand, or ANZ (Panel C), a lag assumption of between two and three months appears appropriate, whereas for Asia ex-Japan (AxJ), Latin America (LATAM), and emerging Europe, Middle East, and Africa, or EMEA (Panel D), the point-in-time consistent lag assumption increases to three months. These different lag assumptions reflect the timeliness with which companies in each region report their earnings.

EXHIBIT 16   Look-Ahead Bias: Impact on Backtesting of Reporting Lag Assumptions (1986–2016)

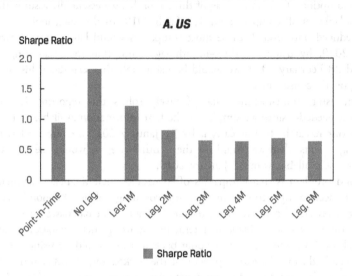

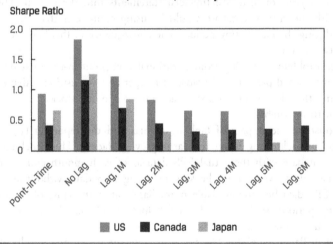

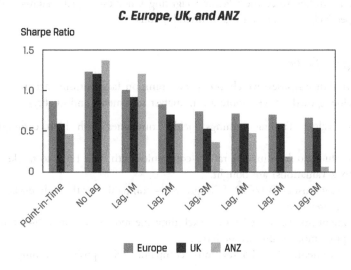

C. Europe, UK, and ANZ

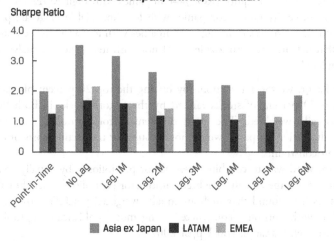

D. Asia ex Japan, LATAM, and EMEA

Sources: Bloomberg Finance LLP, FTSE Russell, S&P Capital IQ, Thomson Reuters, Wolfe Research Luo's QES.

6. BACKTESTING FACTOR ALLOCATION STRATEGIES

Few investment managers use a single signal in their models. In practice, most stock selection models share some common multifactor structure, with a linear combination of factors being the dominant framework. Similarly, many fundamental managers use some form of stock screening, and most such filtering systems use more than one factor. In this section, we use a benchmark factor portfolio, which equally weights factors, and a **risk parity** factor portfolio, which weights factors based on equal risk contribution, to discuss how to combine factor portfolios in a multifactor allocation framework. We focus on the benchmark and risk parity factor portfolios since their factor weighting schemes—equal weights and equal risk weights, respectively—are objective and unambiguous.

6.1. Setting the Scene

For demonstration purposes, we choose a few common factors from each main investment style (i.e., value, growth, price momentum, analyst sentiment, and quality):

1. Defensive value: Trailing earnings yield—companies with high earnings yield are preferred.
2. Cyclical value: Book-to-market ratio—companies with high book-to-market ratios (i.e., cheap stock valuations) are bought.
3. Growth: Consensus FY1/FY0 EPS growth—companies with high expected earnings growth are preferred.
4. Price momentum: 12M total return excluding the most recent month—companies with positive price momentum are preferred.
5. Analyst sentiment: 3M EPS revision—companies with positive earnings revisions are bought.
6. Profitability: Return on equity (ROE)—companies with high ROEs are bought.
7. Leverage: Debt/equity ratio—companies with low financial leverage are preferred.
8. Earnings quality: Non-cash earnings—companies with low accruals are bought. Research suggests that net income with low levels of non-cash items (i.e., accruals) is less likely to be manipulated.

For each factor, we form a portfolio by buying the top 20 percent of stocks and shorting the bottom 20 percent of stocks ranked by the factor. Stocks in both long and short buckets are equally weighted. The eight different factor portfolios are each rebalanced monthly. For illustration purposes, we do not account for transaction costs or other portfolio implementation constraints.

A straightforward way to combine these factor portfolios is by equally weighting them. In this section, we call the equally weighted multifactor portfolio the benchmark (BM) portfolio. Researchers have found that such an equally weighted portfolio either outperforms or performs in line with portfolios constructed using more sophisticated optimization techniques (e.g., DeMiguel, Garlappi, and Uppal 2007).

Risk parity is a popular alternative portfolio construction technique used in the asset allocation space. Risk parity accounts for the volatility of each factor and the correlations of returns among all factors to be combined in the portfolio. The objective is for each factor to make an equal (hence "parity") risk contribution to the overall (or targeted) risk of the portfolio. Thus, a risk parity (RP) multifactor portfolio can be created by equally weighting the risk contribution of each of the eight factors mentioned above.

6.2. Backtesting the Benchmark and Risk Parity Strategies

Backtesting an asset allocation/multifactor strategy is similar to the method introduced earlier but has a few more complications, since the rolling window procedure is implemented twice.

First, we form eight factor portfolios at each given point in time (i.e., monthly) from 1988 until May 2019 using the rolling window procedure discussed previously.

Once the underlying assets (i.e., factor portfolios) are created, we combine them into multifactor portfolios using the two approaches—equally weighting all factors (i.e., benchmark, or BM, allocation) and equally risk weighting all factors (i.e., risk parity, or RP, allocation).

The process for creating the multifactor portfolios requires a second rolling-window procedure, similar to the one presented earlier in Exhibit 2, to avoid look-ahead bias; note that this second rolling window covers the same time span as the first one (i.e., 1988 until May 2019). At each month end, the previous five years of monthly data are used to estimate the variance–covariance matrix for the eight factor portfolios; this is the most important ingredient to form the RP portfolio. Once the covariance matrix is estimated, we can optimize and compute the weights for each of the eight factor portfolios and then form the RP portfolio. Finally, we can compute the returns of the two combination portfolios (BM and RP) during this out-of-sample period using the weights at the end of the previous month and the returns of the eight underlying factors for the current month. This process is repeated every month over the entire horizon of 1988 until May 2019.

We backtested our multifactor strategies using both the equal weighting (benchmark, or BM) scheme and risk parity (RP) scheme for each of the following markets: the United States, Canada, LATAM, Europe, the United Kingdom, emerging EMEA, AxJ, Japan, ANZ, and mainland China. Both multifactor portfolios are rebalanced monthly to maintain equal factor weights or equal factor risk contributions (i.e., risk parity). As noted previously, the key input to the RP allocation is the monthly variance–covariance matrix for the eight underlying factor portfolios derived from the rolling (five-year) window procedure. To be clear, each of the eight factor portfolios is a long/short portfolio. However, our factor allocation strategies to form the BM and RP multifactor portfolios are long only, meaning the weights allocated to each factor portfolio are restricted to be non-negative. Therefore, factor weights for the BM and RP portfolios are positive and add up to 100 percent.

Panel A of Exhibit 17 shows that the weights of the eight factor portfolios in the RP allocation are relatively stable over time (1993–2019) in the United States. Notably, book-to-market and earnings quality factor portfolios receive the largest allocations, whereas ROE and price momentum factor portfolios have the lowest weights. Although the RP portfolio appears to deliver a lower cumulative return than the BM portfolio does (Panel B), Panel C shows that the RP portfolio's volatility is less than half the volatility of the BM portfolio. As a result, the Sharpe ratio of the RP portfolio is nearly twice that of the BM portfolio (Panel D).

EXHIBIT 17   Backtesting Multifactor Strategies: Equally Weighted Benchmark Portfolio versus Risk
Parity Weighted Portfolio

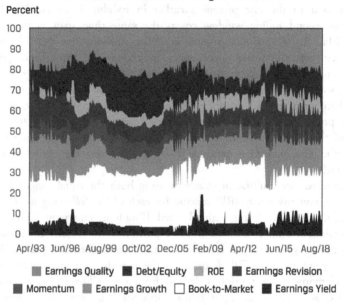

A. RP Portfolio Allocation Weights in the US

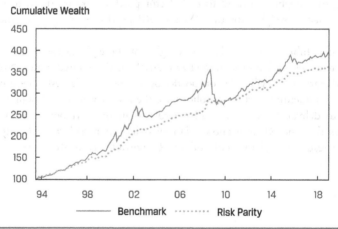

B. Cumulative Return

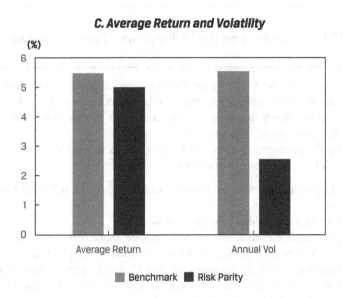

C. Average Return and Volatility

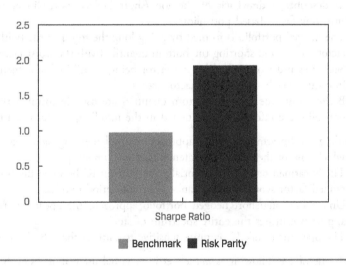

D. Sharpe Ratio

Sources: Bloomberg Finance LLP, FTSE Russell, S&P Capital IQ, Thomson Reuters, Wolfe Research Luo's QES.

EXAMPLE 6   Backtesting the Performance of Factor Allocation Strategies

Sarah Koh heads the team at Newton Research Pte. responsible for assessing clients' equity strategies using backtesting and simulation techniques. SWF Fund, one of Newton's biggest clients, has asked for an assessment of two factor-based allocation strategies it is considering implementing.

During the presentation of her backtesting results to SWF's investment committee, Koh is asked the following questions:

1. Regarding rolling window backtesting, which one of the following statements is *inaccurate*?
   A. The data are divided into just two samples.
   B. The data are divided using a walk-forward framework, where today's out-of-sample data become part of the next period's in-sample data.
   C. Repeated in-sample training and out-of-sample testing allow managers to revise their models and readjust security positions on the basis of the arrival over time of new information.

2. Which describes a drawback of the long/short hedged portfolio approach for implementing factor-based portfolios?
   A. The hedged portfolio is formed by going long the top quantile (with the best factor scores) and shorting the bottom quantile (with the worst factor scores).
   B. Securities must be ranked by the factor being scrutinized and then grouped into quantiles based on their factor scores.
   C. Because only the top and bottom quantiles are used in forming the hedged portfolio, the information contained in the middle quantiles is wasted.

3. Regarding the Spearman rank IC approach to implementing factor-based portfolios, which one of the following statements is *inaccurate*?
   A. The Spearman rank IC is essentially the Pearson IC between the prior-period ranked factor scores and the ranked current-period returns.
   B. Unlike the long/short hedged portfolio approach, the Spearman ranked IC approach captures the entire spectrum of stocks.
   C. The Spearman rank IC is more sensitive to outliers than the Pearson IC is.

4. Which one of the following is *not* a metric or visual used in assessing backtesting of a factor-based investment strategy?
   A. Distribution plots of factor returns
   B. A word cloud of text describing the characteristics of the factor
   C. Signal autocorrelation as a measure of factor decay

5. Point-in-time data are useful for avoiding the following problems that may affect backtesting *except*:
   A. insufficient factor coverage.
   B. survivorship bias.
   C. look-ahead bias.

6. Regarding the use of rolling window backtesting in assessing factor allocation to a risk parity–based strategy, which statement is correct?
   A. The procedure is used once for estimating factor returns over the rolling window.
   B. The procedure is used once for dividing the data into just two samples.
   C. The procedure is used twice, once for estimating factor returns over the rolling window and a second time for estimating the covariance matrix of factor returns (for deriving risk parity weights) over the rolling window.

Solution to 1: A is correct, since the statement is inaccurate. B and C are incorrect, because they accurately describe the rolling window backtesting technique.

Solution to 2: C is correct, since it best describes a drawback of the long/short hedged portfolio approach. A and B are incorrect because they describe the approach itself.

Solution to 3: C is correct, since the statement is inaccurate. A and B are incorrect, because they accurately describe the Spearman rank IC approach to implementing factor-based portfolios.

Solution to 4: B is correct, since a word cloud is not a visual used in assessing backtesting of a factor-based investment strategy. A and C are correct, because they are visuals and metrics, respectively, used to assess backtests of factor-based strategies.

Solution to 5: A is correct, since this choice is wrong. B and C are incorrect, since point-in-time data are useful for avoiding survivorship bias and look-ahead bias in backtesting.

Solution to 6: C is correct, since the procedure must be used a second time for estimating the covariance matrix of factor returns (for deriving risk parity weights) over the rolling window. A and B are incorrect.

7. COMPARING METHODS OF MODELING RANDOMNESS

The backtesting process as described previously preserves the integrity of the time dimension very well. In backtesting, we essentially assume that we can go back in time, develop our investment strategies, and rebalance our portfolios according a prescribed set of rules. Then, we assess the performance of our investment ideas. It is intuitive, because it mimics how investing is done in reality—that is, forming our ideas, testing our strategies, and implementing periodically.

Importantly, however, we implicitly assume that the same pattern is likely to repeat itself over time. Asset allocation decisions, in particular, have traditionally depended heavily on the assumption that asset returns follow a multivariate normal distribution. In reality, however, asset returns often show skewness and excess kurtosis (i.e., fat tails). Therefore, traditional portfolio construction techniques that depend heavily on estimation of the covariance matrix, such as mean–variance optimization and risk parity, may sometimes yield flawed results. Moreover, conventional rolling window backtesting may not fully account for the dynamic nature of financial markets or potentially extreme downside risks (because it cannot account for such dynamic/extreme events that have not yet occurred). We now explore how scenario analysis and simulation can provide a more complete picture of investment strategy performance.

Traditionally, simulation and scenario analysis are used more regularly in asset allocation, risk management, and derivative pricing compared with quantitative equity investing. In the following sections, we describe how such techniques can be implemented by investment managers.

7.1. Factor Portfolios and BM and RP Allocation Strategies

We pick up from the prior discussion, which described the set of eight factor portfolios. To reiterate, for each factor, a portfolio is formed by buying the top 20 percent of stocks and by shorting the bottom 20 percent of stocks ranked by the factor. Stocks in both long and short buckets are equally weighted, and all portfolios are rebalanced monthly. Next, we construct the multifactor portfolios (using these factor portfolios) following the two approaches described earlier—that is, the equally weighted benchmark (BM) and the equally risk weighted risk parity (RP) strategies.

As shown in Exhibit 18 (which uses a logarithm scale on the y-axis), all eight factors have delivered reasonable return performance over the long term (1988–2019). In terms of cumulative return, the earnings revision, earnings yield, and price momentum factors produce the highest returns, and the earnings growth and debt/equity factors lag far behind. The eight factor portfolios appear to share some commonalities. Their returns seem to fall into three clusters: (1) earnings revision, earnings yield, and price momentum; (2) ROE

EXHIBIT 18   Cumulative Return of Eight Factor Portfolios, United States (1988–2019)

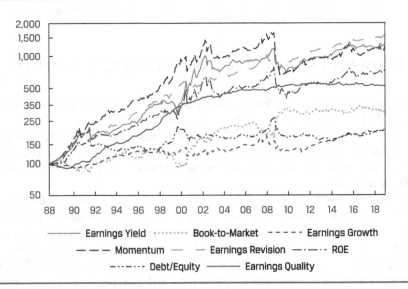

Sources: Bloomberg Finance LLP, FTSE Russell, S&P Capital IQ, Thomson Reuters, Wolfe Research Luo's QES.

and earnings quality; and (3) book-to-market ratio, earnings growth, and debt/equity. They also show significant dispersions at times.

The issue with financial data is that there is only one realization of a time series. Therefore, we must rely heavily on the statistical distribution of asset returns in our modeling. As we will demonstrate, the common assumptions of a multivariate normal distribution and time-series stationarity are often unrealistic, which highlights the importance of using simulation and scenario analysis to supplement the traditional rolling window backtesting.

7.2. Factor Return Statistical Properties

Asset and factor returns often are left skewed and display excess kurtosis, which is characterized by fat tails, as seen in Panel A of Exhibit 19 for the earnings yield factor. Furthermore, the joint distribution of such returns is rarely multivariate normal, so typically the means and variances of these returns and the correlations between them are not sufficient to describe the joint return distribution. In other words, the return data do not line up tightly around a trend line because of fat tails and outliers. For example, as shown in Panel B, the scatterplot for value (earnings yield) and momentum (12M–1M return) shows some significant deviations from a linear fit, especially at the left tails, where a number of outliers are clearly discernible.

7.2.1. Mean, Standard Deviation, Skewness, and Kurtosis

If asset and factor returns are normally distributed, then mean and standard deviation should fully capture the randomness in the data. However, the normality assumption is often not valid in investment data, so skewness and kurtosis, the third and fourth moments of the return distribution, respectively, are needed to properly characterize the distribution. As a reminder, skewness measures symmetry (or lack thereof) of the return distribution. Kurtosis measures fat tails (extreme occurrences or outliers) relative to the normal distribution. For normally distributed data, skewness is zero and kurtosis is three (i.e., excess kurtosis, which is kurtosis minus three, is greater than zero).

Exhibit 20 presents statistics for the return distributions of the eight factor portfolios and the equally weighted BM and RP weighted multifactor portfolios from 1993 to 2019. Six of the eight factor portfolios have negative skewness (the BM portfolio does as well), and all factors and factor allocation portfolios show excess kurtosis (i.e., kurtosis exceeding 3.0. The downside risk (i.e., minimum monthly return) is clearly greater in magnitude than the maximum upside for most factor strategies. The two factor allocation strategy portfolios—BM and RP—both display moderate mean returns (0.5 percent and 0.4 percent per month, respectively) and low standard deviations (1.6 percent and 0.7 percent per month, respectively) compared with the eight underlying factor portfolios, highlighting the diversification benefits from factor allocation decisions.

EXHIBIT 19   Distribution of Selected Factor Returns, United States (1988–2019)

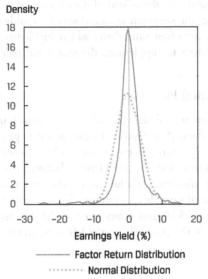

A. Value (Earnings Yield)

—— Factor Return Distribution

········· Normal Distribution

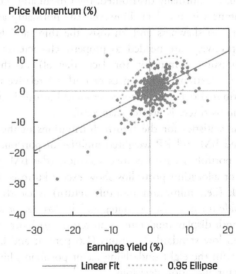

B. Value vs. Momentum (US)

—— Linear Fit   ········· 0.95 Ellipse

Sources: Bloomberg Finance LLP, FTSE Russell, S&P Capital IQ, Thomson Reuters, Wolfe Research Luo's QES.

EXHIBIT 20   Monthly Return Distributions: Factor, BM, and RP Portfolios (1993–2019)

	Earnings Yield	Book-to-Market	Earnings Growth	Momentum	Earnings Revision	ROE	Debt/Equity	Earnings Quality	Benchmark	Risk Parity
Mean	0.7%	0.4%	0.2%	0.6%	0.7%	0.5%	0.1%	0.4%	0.5%	0.4%
Median	0.6%	0.1%	0.4%	0.8%	0.8%	0.6%	0.1%	0.4%	0.5%	0.4%
Maximum	14.5%	28.9%	6.2%	11.7%	9.1%	10.8%	11.9%	5.3%	4.3%	3.7%
Minimum	(24.0%)	(12.1%)	(15.8%)	(32.7%)	(18.7%)	(28.0%)	(17.1%)	(2.6%)	(10.9%)	(2.5%)
Std. Dev	3.8%	3.7%	2.1%	4.6%	2.4%	3.9%	2.5%	1.2%	1.6%	0.7%
Skewness	(1.00)	2.82	(2.46%)	(2.36)	(2.39)	(1.92)	(0.58)	0.41	(2.40)	0.51
Kurtosis	11.06	23.61	17.80	16.56	20.76	14.96	11.55	3.87	17.78	5.37

Sources: Bloomberg Finance LLP, FTSE Russell, S&P Capital IQ, Thomson Reuters, Wolfe Research Luo's QES.

EXAMPLE 7   Risk and Return beyond Normal Distribution

Compare return distributions for the BM and RP strategy multifactor portfolios and explain which investment strategy offers the more attractive statistical properties for risk-averse investors (refer to Exhibit 20 to answer this question).

Solution: The BM and RP portfolios have nearly the same mean monthly returns, at 0.5 percent and 0.4 percent, respectively. Although the maximum returns are not much different, the RP factor allocation strategy has a much smaller minimum return (–2.5 percent) and a significantly lower standard deviation (0.7 percent) compared with those of the BM factor portfolio (–10.9 percent and 1.6 percent, respectively). The RP portfolio is also slightly positively skewed (0.51 percent) and has moderate kurtosis (5.37), in contrast to the negative skew (–2.40 percent) and high kurtosis (17.78) of the BM portfolio.

Since the RP portfolio offers similar returns, less downside risk, lower volatility, and slightly higher probability of positive returns (i.e., positive skew) and is less fat tailed (i.e., moderate kurtosis, meaning lower probability of extreme negative surprises) than the BM portfolio is, the RP portfolio has the more attractive distribution properties for risk-averse investors.

7.2.2. Tail Dependence

The **tail dependence coefficient** is similar to the correlation coefficient but focuses on co-movements (i.e., correlation) in the tails of two random variables. Panel A of Exhibit 21 shows the theoretical bivariate normal distribution between the returns of value and momentum factor portfolios over 1988–2019. The theoretical bivariate normal distribution follows a classic bell-shaped curve. However, plotting the empirical distribution between the value and momentum factor returns reveals something quite different. As shown in Panel B, the

EXHIBIT 21   Distributions for Value and Momentum Portfolios (1988–2019)

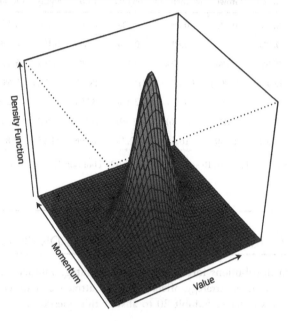

A. Theoretical Bivariate Normal Distribution

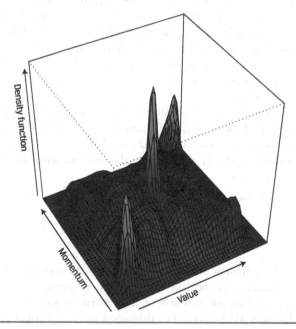

B. Empirical Distribution

Sources: Bloomberg Finance LLP, FTSE Russell, S&P Capital IQ, Thomson Reuters, Wolfe Research Luo's QES.

joint distribution between returns for these two factors is clearly tri-modal, with three distinct peaks (i.e., modes). There is one peak at the center, as would be implied by the bivariate normal distribution. There are also two peaks in the tails, indicating that the probabilities of returns for these two factors move up and down together in the tails. The probabilities in the tails are also much higher than what is implied by the normal distribution. Therefore, this visual (Panel B) confirms that the value and momentum factors have a high, positive tail dependence coefficient.

A consequence of failing to properly account for tail dependence (such as that shown in Panel B of Exhibit 21) is that the actual realized downside risk of our portfolios is often higher than what is suggested by our backtesting. The various tools that will be described shortly are designed to help better understand the risk profiles of our strategies.

7.3. Performance Measurement and Downside Risk

The Sharpe ratio and the Sortino ratio (which replaces standard deviation with target semi-deviation in the denominator) are common measures of investment strategy performance. Since we are discussing non-normal return distributions, the focus here is on the downside risk of investment strategies. Given that (negative) skewness, excess kurtosis, and tail dependence are common distributional characteristics of asset (and factor) returns, investment strategies are typically prone to significantly higher downside risk than what is implied by a normal distribution.

7.3.1. Value at Risk
Value at risk (VaR) for a given portfolio is a money measure of the minimum value of losses expected during a specified time period at a given level of probability. Although it is widely used to characterize downside risk in terms of the size of the left tail of a portfolio's return distribution, VaR is sensitive to assumptions about the distribution's shape (i.e., fat versus normal tails). Another issue with VaR is that it is not sub-additive, meaning that the VaR of a portfolio can be greater than the sum of the individual risks (i.e., VaRs) of each asset in the portfolio.

7.3.2. Conditional VaR
A closely related measure to VaR is **conditional VaR (CVaR)**, which is the weighted average of all loss outcomes in the statistical (i.e., return) distribution that exceed the VaR loss. Thus, CVaR is a more comprehensive measure of tail loss than VaR is. For example, at a preset confidence level denoted α, which typically is set as 1 percent or 5 percent, the CVaR of a return series is the expected value of the return when the return is less than its α-quantile. With a sufficiently large dataset, CVaR is typically estimated as the sample average of all returns that are below the α empirical quantile.

7.3.3. Drawdown Measure
A widely used measure of downside risk is **maximum drawdown**, the worst cumulative loss ever sustained by an asset or portfolio. More specifically, maximum drawdown is the difference between an asset's or a portfolio's maximum cumulative return and its subsequent lowest cumulative return. Maximum drawdown is a preferred way of expressing downside

risk—particularly as associated track records become longer—for investors who believe that observed loss patterns over longer periods of time are the best available proxy for actual exposure. Use of the maximum drawdown measure is particularly common among hedge funds and commodity trading advisers.

EXHIBIT 22   Maximum Drawdown for BM and RP Factor Portfolios (1993–2019)

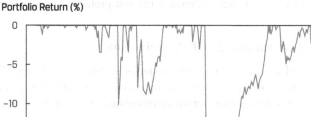

A. Benchmark Factor Portfolio

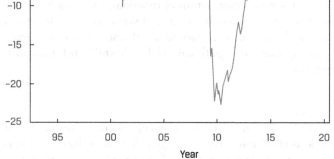

B. Risk Parity Factor Portfolio

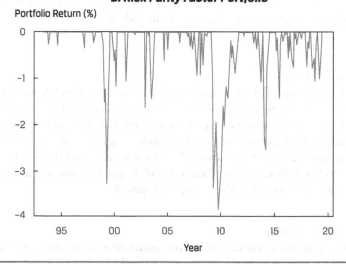

Sources: Bloomberg Finance LLP, FTSE Russell, S&P Capital IQ, Thomson Reuters, Wolfe Research Luo's QES.

EXHIBIT 23   Downside Risk Using Monthly Returns: Factor, BM, and RP Portfolios (1993–2019)

	Earnings Yield	Book-to-Market	Earnings Growth	Momentum	Earnings Revision	ROE	Debt/ Equity	Earnings Quality	Benchmark	Risk Parity
VaR(95%)	(5.9%)	(0.7%)	(3.9%)	(8.4%)	(3.7%)	(6.8%)	(4.0%)	(1.3%)	(2.6%)	(0.7%)
CVaR (95%)	(14.3%)	(11.1%)	(10.9%)	(22.9%)	(12.8%)	(18.7%)	(8.4%)	(1.7%)	(7.9%)	(0.9%)
Max Drawdown	41.0%	35.3%	27.2%	59.7%	23.9%	47.5%	41.8%	8.3%	22.6%	3.8%

Sources: Bloomberg Finance LLP, FTSE Russell, S&P Capital IQ, Thomson Reuters, Wolfe Research Luo's QES.

Panel A of Exhibit 22, presents the drawdown pattern of the benchmark portfolio, which comprises the eight equally weighted factor portfolios from May 1993 to May 2019. Serious drawdowns, of –8 percent to –10 percent, occurred in the early 2000s, but the maximum drawdown for the BM portfolio was more than –20 percent and coincided with the risk rally in March–May 2009, toward the end of the global financial crisis. Note that downside movements of long/short systematic strategies are mostly associated with market rallies instead of market sell-offs, which is exactly the opposite of long-only market portfolios. As shown in Panel B (which has a different *y*-axis range than Panel A does), the magnitude of drawdowns—between –1 percent and –4 percent—for the risk parity portfolio, consisting of the eight equal-risk-weighted factor portfolios, is considerably lower than for the BM portfolio. In fact, the maximum drawdown for the RP portfolio also occurred in the March–May 2009 period and was relatively moderate, at less than –4 percent.

Exhibit 23 compares the various downside risk measures for the eight factor portfolios and the BM and RP portfolios from 1993 to 2019. All three downside risk measures—VaR, CVaR, and maximum drawdown—suggest that the price momentum factor, followed by the ROE factor, has the largest downside risk. The smallest downside risk is observed for the earnings quality factor. As for the factor allocation strategies, the risk parity portfolio shows considerably lower downside risk than any of the eight underlying factors and the benchmark portfolio. This evidence suggests that the RP strategy benefits greatly from risk diversification (in the United States for the period under investigation).

7.4. Methods to Account for Randomness

We now discuss several different approaches to account for randomness in asset returns. We will elaborate on the pros and cons of each method and show the differences.

7.4.1. Rolling Window Backtesting Revisited

So far, we have used the most conventional approach to simulating the past performance of an investment strategy—rolling window backtesting. The rolling window backtesting technique is widely used among practitioners since it is an intuitive approach that mimics a realistic investment process simulated in the past. The implied assumption with rolling window backtesting is that the future environment will resemble the past, which is often not the case.

Investment time-series data are often non-stationary, with periodic structural breaks. As you may recall, a time series is stationary if its mean, variance, and covariance with itself (for a fixed number of periods) are all constant and finite in all periods. Assuming time-series data to be stationary when in reality they are non-stationary will produce biased (or even invalid) backtesting results. Moreover, other investors are also constantly learning from the data and attempting to improve their own investment decision-making processes; consequently, any alpha from a given investment strategy may be eroded over time. Therefore, the rolling window approach may not necessarily be able to fully capture the randomness in financial data.

Lastly, although rolling window backtesting tests the investment strategy using out-of-sample data, researchers can still easily misuse the technique. For example, financial researchers are often tempted to try various modeling techniques, backtest each of them, and then pick the best performing model. In this case, if the backtested performance does not account for the model selection process, then it suffers from model selection bias. This bias is called **data snooping**, the subconscious or conscious manipulation of data in a way that produces a statistically significant result (i.e., a p-value that is sufficiently small or a t-statistic that is sufficiently large to indicate statistical significance). A preferred approach by leading researchers is, briefly put, to specify an acceptable proportion (q-value) of significant results that can be false positives and establish, on the basis of the q-value and ranked p-values, a critical value for the reported p-values; then, only the tests with smaller p-values are accepted as significant. Alternatively, the data snooping problem may be mitigated by setting a much higher hurdle than typical—for example, a t-statistic greater than $3.0\times$—for assessing whether a newly discovered factor is indeed adding incremental value (i.e., is statistically significant).

7.4.2. Cross Validation

Cross validation is a technique heavily used in the machine learning field. As you may remember, in cross validation, researchers partition their data into training data and testing data (i.e., "validation data"). Essentially, a model is first fitted using the training data, and then its performance is assessed using the testing data. To reduce variability, the process is often repeated multiple times. The validation results are combined over the successive rounds of testing to provide a more accurate estimate of the model's predictive performance.

In machine learning, data sampling is often performed by random draws. For example, in the standard k-fold cross-validation procedure, the original sample data are randomly partitioned into k equal-sized subsamples. At each of the k iterations, a single subsample is held out as the validation data for testing the model and the remaining $k - 1$ subsamples are used to train the model. The process is repeated k times, and the k validation results are averaged to produce a single estimation of the model's predictive performance.

Note that the rolling window backtesting method follows a philosophy similar to that of the cross-validation technique, albeit in a deterministic, non-random manner, meaning that past data (from the rolling window) are used to train a model and then the model is used to invest in the next period.

Another way to perform cross validation is to validate the investment strategy using data from different geographic regions. For example, suppose the risk parity strategy is developed and tested initially using factors based on US equities. The same RP modeling framework can be extended to other markets globally. Then, the average performance from the non-US markets can be used to assess whether risk parity is a robust factor allocation strategy.

As shown in Panel A of Exhibit 24, as a risk-based factor allocation technique, the RP strategy does indeed deliver a lower realized volatility (i.e., standard deviation of returns) than does the benchmark (i.e., equal-weighted factor) strategy in all 10 global markets over 1993–2019. Similarly, the RP portfolios also outperform the BM portfolios in terms of Sharpe ratio (see Panel B) in 7 of the 10 global markets.

EXHIBIT 24   Global Cross-Validation, Equally Weighted Benchmark Portfolio vs. Risk Parity Weighted Portfolio (1993–2019)

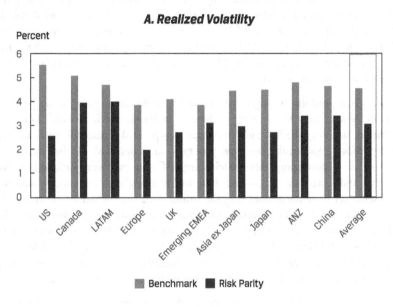

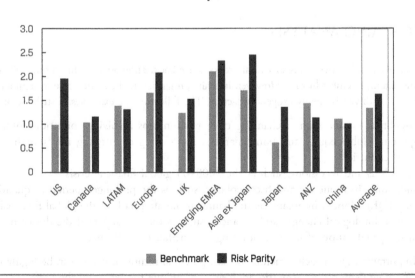

Sources: Bloomberg Finance LLP, FTSE Russell, S&P Capital IQ, Thomson Reuters, Wolfe Research Luo's QES.

EXAMPLE 8   Data Snooping in Investment Management

One of the firm's research analysts has just presented to you and several other portfolio managers her risk factor–based quantitative/systematic investment model for the UK market. She reports the development and backtesting of several different models: The number of factors ranged from 5 to 10, rebalancing periods were monthly and quarterly, and rolling windows were implemented for 5, 15, and 25 years of historical data. She recommends the 10-factor model (with monthly rebalancing) since backtesting of 15 years of data generated the following annualized performance metrics: Sharpe ratio of 3.0 and realized volatility of 1.0%. She also reports a t-statistic of 2.5 and a p-value of 1.3 percent for this model of UK market returns, which were the highest and lowest statistics, respectively, of all the models.

Describe the concerns you should raise around the issue of data snooping for this seemingly very attractive strategy.

Solution: As a portfolio manager, you must be careful in assessing these performance results in light of how the analyst developed and backtested her model. For example, it is critical to know whether backtesting has incorporated transaction costs and trading liquidity. More importantly, however, you need to understand whether data snooping was involved in developing this model/strategy. Given the many variations of models developed and tested by the analyst, it is highly likely that her process suffers from model selection bias. Recommending the model with the highest t-statistic and lowest p-value also points to data snooping. One way to mitigate the problem is to raise the hurdle for an acceptable model to a t-statistic exceeding 3.0 (thereby lowering the p-value). Cross validation of the recommended model's results using the k-fold technique and testing in other global markets are other techniques that can be used to help the portfolio managers better understand the true performance of this model/strategy.

---

8. SCENARIO ANALYSIS

A serious issue in backtesting is structural breaks, since backtesting assumes the future will, at least to some extent, resemble history. However, in reality, financial markets often face structural breaks, which can be driven by many exogenous factors. The following are examples of such factors:

- Geopolitical events, such as changing trade relationships involving countries representing important global equity and bond markets, and exiting or entering major trading blocs by key countries
- Depressions and recessions, such as the 2008–09 global financial crisis
- Major shifts in monetary and fiscal policies, such as the prolonged period of quantitative easing (QE) adopted by major central banks in the aftermath of the global financial crisis
- Major technological changes and advances, such as those that fueled the dot-com bubble and the proliferation of machine learning and artificial intelligence

Importantly, given such structural breaks, potential future outcomes can be highly uncertain. We now demonstrate **scenario analysis**, a technique for exploring the performance and risk of investment strategies in different structural regimes, using two real-world examples:

- *Recession environment.* In the United States, since the start of our risk parity allocation strategy in 1993, the National Bureau of Economic Research (NBER) has recognized two official recessions: March 2001–November 2001 and December 2007–June 2009. These recessions are shown in Panel A of Exhibit 25.
- *High- and low-volatility regimes.* The Chicago Board Options Exchange (CBOE) computes the VIX index, which gauges options-implied volatility on the S&P 500 Index. To transform the VIX into a volatility regime indicator, a five-year moving average is computed. Then, the periods when the VIX is above (below) its five-year moving average

EXHIBIT 25   Macro-Factor Regime Changes

A. Recession Indicator

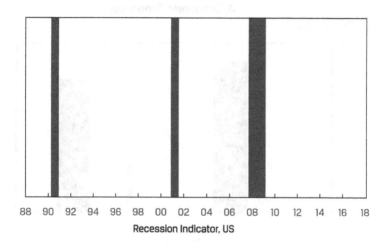

Recession Indicator, US

B. VIX: High- vs. Low-Volatility Regimes

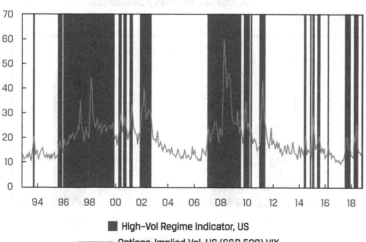

■ High–Vol Regime Indicator, US

——— Options-Implied Vol, US (S&P 500) VIX

Sources: Bloomberg Finance LLP, FTSE Russell, Haver, S&P Capital IQ, Thomson Reuters, Wolfe Research Luo's QES.

are defined as high-volatility (low-volatility) regime periods, as shown in Panel B of Exhibit 25 for 1988–2019.

We can examine the sensitivity of the benchmark and risk parity factor allocation strategies to these two macroeconomic regimes—recession versus non-recession and high volatility versus low volatility. As shown in Panel A of Exhibit 26, in terms of the Sharpe ratio, the RP strategy is quite robust to recession and the BM strategy struggles in recessions. Panel B of Exhibit 26 reveals that the BM strategy's performance is slightly worse in low-volatility

EXHIBIT 26   Sharpe Ratio for BM and RP Portfolios in Different Macro-Scenarios (1993–2019)

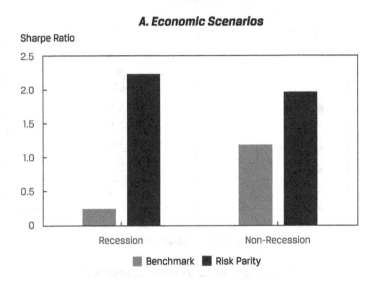

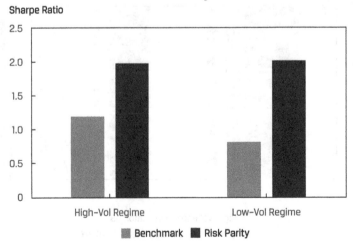

Sources: Bloomberg Finance LLP, FTSE Russell, S&P Capital IQ, Thomson Reuters, Wolfe Research Luo's QES.

regimes than in high-volatility regimes, whereas the RP strategy performs equally well in both volatility environments.

In addition to the Sharpe ratio, a density plot can reveal additional information about the sensitivity of the overall distributions of these investment strategies—for example, during recession versus non-recession periods. As shown in Exhibit 27, the distribution of returns for both the BM and RP strategies is flatter in a non-recession environment, which implies higher standard deviations during these regimes. The BM strategy suffers from negative skewness and excess kurtosis (i.e., fat tails to the left), regardless of the recession regime, but its average return is clearly lower in a recession environment (see Panel A). The RP

EXHIBIT 27   Distribution of Returns for Factor Allocation Strategies: Recession and Non-Recession Regimes

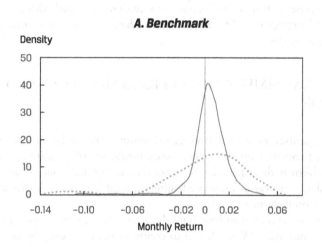

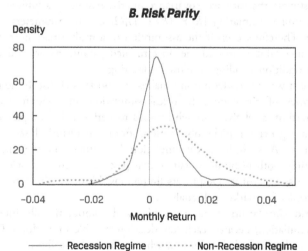

Sources: Bloomberg Finance LLP, FTSE Russell, S&P Capital IQ, Thomson Reuters, Wolfe Research Luo's QES.

strategy has a lower average return in the recession regime, but its volatility is also much lower (see Panel B); as a result, the Sharpe ratio is about the same in the two regimes (which is consistent with Panel A of Exhibit 26).

In the previous analysis, the regimes are pre-defined. However, in practice, we do not know the type of regime into which the economy is heading. Although the details are beyond the scope of this chapter, it warrants mentioning that a Markov regime-switching model can be used to fit historical data and estimate the probabilities of each different regime in the future. Using these probabilities, we can then compute the weighted average expected return and risk profile of our investment strategy.

A closely related concept is **stress testing**—the process that tests how our strategies would perform under some of the most negative (i.e., adverse) combinations of events and scenarios. For example, an evaluation of the potential downside risks for the BM and RP portfolios could be done via stress testing under the following assumed adverse combination of scenarios: a severe and prolonged economic recession combined with a period of sharply elevated financial market volatility, all at a time when investors have crowded into factor-based investing strategies.

9. HISTORICAL SIMULATION VERSUS MONTE CARLO SIMULATION

Given that the distribution of asset (and factor) returns may not be multivariate normal, the question is how to account for skewness/excess kurtosis, volatility clustering, and tail dependence. The problem with historical time-series data is that only one set of realized data is observable, and the critical assumption behind classical time-series analysis, that the data are stationary, is unlikely to be true.

Investment data also tend to have high dimensionality. In the factor allocation case, we have eight factor portfolios ($K = 8$), and to construct the risk parity factor allocation strategy, one must estimate the variance–covariance matrix. Assuming a multivariate normal distribution, this requires estimating $[K \times (K + 1)]/2$, or 36, parameters at each monthly rebalancing date. Therefore, even if the assumption of a multivariate normal distribution is reasonable, the uncertainties around the 36 estimated parameters are still difficult to fully account for in a traditional rolling window backtesting.

Simulation is a way to model non-normal asset (and factor) distributions, and there are basically two types of simulation: historical simulation and Monte Carlo simulation. **Historical simulation** is relatively straightforward to perform: It uses past return data, and a random number generator picks observations from the historical series to simulate an asset's future returns. As such, historical simulation does suffer from the same issue as rolling window backtesting; both techniques assume that past asset returns provide sufficient guidance about future asset returns. Despite its limitations, historical simulation is widely used, particularly by banks for market risk analysis.

Monte Carlo simulation is more complex and computationally intensive compared with historical simulation, because each key decision variable in a Monte Carlo simulation requires an assumed statistical distribution, where a normal distribution is most frequently used as the default. However, as suggested by the previous discussions of non-normality, fat tails, and tail dependence, there is a clear need to incorporate non-normality in modeling. Researchers typically calibrate the parameters of the assumed distributional form (e.g., mean and standard deviation for a univariate normal distribution) using historical return data. The Monte Carlo simulation approach is popular because it is highly flexible and adaptable for solving high-dimensionality problems.

A properly designed simulation analysis is typically implemented by the following steps:

1. Determine the target variable that we want to understand. In investment research, the target variable is often the return on our investment strategy portfolio, $r_{p,t}$ (the return on portfolio p at time t), and we want to investigate its distribution.

2. Specify key drivers and decision variables that directly determine the value of our target variable. In an asset allocation strategy, key drivers/decision variables are the returns of each underlying asset, $r_{i,t}$ (the return on asset i at time t), in the overall portfolio and the weight, $\omega_{i,t}$ (the weight of asset i at time t), allocated to each asset. Once we know the returns and weights of all underlying assets, we can readily compute the return of our asset allocation strategy as $r_{p,t} = \sum_{i=1}^{K}(\omega_{i,t} \times r_{i,t})$.

3. Specify the number of trials (N) to run. Practitioners often choose a sufficiently large number of trials to get a useful distribution profile but not so many repetitions that the simulation exercise may consume too much computing time. In theory, exactly how to determine the appropriate number of iterations is a complex topic (for an example, see Ritter, Schoelles, Quigley, and Klein 2011). In practice, researchers typically choose between 1,000 and 10,000 simulation runs, and the greater the number of trials, the more stable are the predictions of performance and variance of performance.

4. Define the distributional properties of the key drivers and decision variables in Step 2. This is the point where historical and Monte Carlo simulations diverge. In historical simulation, we assume that the distribution pattern of the historical data is sufficient to represent uncertainty in the future. Conversely, in Monte Carlo simulation, we must specify an exact functional form of the underlying statistical distribution for each key driver/decision variable. Note that researchers might specify different distributional functions (e.g., normal, lognormal, binomial) for different variables in a Monte Carlo simulation and thereby account for the impact of correlations and tail dependence in the multivariate distribution.

5. Use a random number generator to draw N random numbers—more specifically, **pseudo-random numbers**, or numbers that look random but are actually deterministic—for each key decision variable. A benefit of using a pseudo-random number generator is that once we fix the seed (the number that specifies the starting point for the pseudo-random number generator), we can re-run the simulation and verify the results; such reproducibility is an important property in scientific research. Note that different programming languages may use different random number generators. Even for the same language (with the same seed), the results may still be different with different versions and on different operating systems. However, the results should be qualitatively similar and thus, in this sense, are reproducible.

6. For each set of simulated drivers/decision variables, compute the value of the target variable. The value of the target variable is then saved for later analysis.

7. Repeat the same process from Steps 5 and 6 until completing the desired number of trials (N).

8. Now we have a set of N values of the target variable. In asset allocation simulations, this is the N likely returns of the investment strategy. The analyst can now calculate the typical performance measurements for the investment strategy, such as mean return, volatility, Sharpe ratio, and the various downside risk metrics. In simulation analysis, analysts

typically focus on the downside risk profiles, so CVaR and maximum drawdown are appropriate.

Historical and Monte Carlo simulation techniques for evaluating an investment strategy will be demonstrated using the risk parity and benchmark strategies (comprising the eight underlying factor portfolios). To evaluate the results of these simulations, the performance of our investment strategies will be measured using the Sharpe ratio, as well as VaR, CVaR, and maximum drawdown metrics.

10. HISTORICAL SIMULATION

In historical simulation, the key assumption is that past performance is a good indicator of future performance. So, to model randomness, the random number generator is used to randomly sample data from the historical return data in order to simulate future returns. First, a decision must be made about whether to sample from the historical returns with replacement or without replacement. Random sampling with replacement, also known as **bootstrapping**, is often used in investment research, because the number of simulations needed is often larger than the size of historical dataset.

Before delving into the details of historical simulation, we first need to understand the difference between historical simulation and the rolling window backtesting technique demonstrated previously. Although both approaches rely on history to understand the future, they address the problem differently. Rolling window backtesting is deterministic. The investment manager constructs his or her investment strategy using historical data at each given point in time and then measures the strategy's performance in the next period. The same process is repeated consecutively from one past period to the next period. Thus, rolling window backtesting is designed to understand what the final outcome, in terms of performance, would have been if the investment manager had followed the specified trading rules (such as long/short hedge, Spearman rank IC, or some other trading algorithm).

Historical simulation (as well as Monte Carlo simulation) is non-deterministic and random (i.e., stochastic) in nature. Researchers randomly draw data from the historical track record—thus, not in a time-ordered sequence (which is another difference from rolling window backtesting). Hence, an important goal of simulation is to verify the investment performance obtained from backtesting. Moreover, simulation accounts for the randomness of the data in a different way from backtesting. As we will show, historical simulation randomly samples (with replacement) from the past record of asset returns, where each set of past monthly returns is equally likely to be selected. In contrast, to perform Monte Carlo simulation, researchers must first fit a multivariate joint probability distribution (e.g., normal or another type of distribution), where the past asset return data are used to calibrate the parameters. Once a particular model is fitted, we can randomly select data from the fitted distribution. Simulation is especially useful in measuring the downside risk of investment strategies, if the data are non-normal and tail dependence is captured properly.

Using the factor allocation strategies (BM and RP) for the eight factor portfolios as an example, a historical simulation can be designed in the following steps:

1. In this case, the target variables are the returns for the benchmark and the risk parity portfolios.
2. The key drivers/decision variables are the returns of the eight underlying factors. Note that for this simulation, the weights allocated to the eight factors are already known. For the BM portfolio, the weight is 1/8 for each factor. As noted earlier, the variance–covariance matrix for the eight factor portfolios is the key input for determining the weights assigned in the current period (May 2019) to each of the eight factor portfolios in the RP portfolio (see Panel A of Exhibit 17).
3. The simulation will be performed for $N = 1,000$ trials.
4. The historical simulation will be implemented using bootstrapped sampling. In this case, we will randomly draw a number from a uniform distribution (so there is equal probability of being selected) between 0 and 1.[2] Once a random number is generated, it can be mapped to a specific historical month. Note that we have a total of 374 months of historical factor return data (April 1988–May 2019). We can map a random number of a specific month by dividing the span of the uniform distribution by the number of months ($1.0/374 = 0.00267$). Therefore, if the random number is between 0 and 0.00267, then the first month is selected. Similarly, if the random number generator picks a number between 0.00267 and 0.00535 ($= 2 \times 0.00267$), then the second month is chosen, and so on.
5. The random number generator will then randomly draw 1,000 numbers from the uniform distribution between 0 and 1, and, as mentioned, sampling of the historical return

EXHIBIT 28   The First Five Randomly Selected Months

Simulation #	Month	Random #	Month #	Earnings Yield	Book-to-Market	Earnings Growth	Momentum
1	9/30/2006	0.59163	222	2.5%	0.3%	(0.8%)	(0.0%)
2	4/30/1998	0.32185	121	0.1%	0.8%	(0.2%)	(0.5%)
3	2/29/2012	0.76485	287	(1.9%)	0.5%	1.7%	1.8%
4	2/29/2016	0.89474	335	2.5%	2.4%	(0.4%)	(1.5%)
5	5/31/2002	0.45431	170	6.3%	(3.3%)	1.8%	2.4%

Simulation #	Month	Random #	Month #	Earnings Revision	ROE	Debt/ Equity	Earnings Quality
1	9/30/2006	0.59163	222	(0.8%)	2.5%	0.5%	(0.5%)
2	4/30/1998	0.32185	121	(0.1%)	(0.1%)	0.3%	1.6%
3	2/29/2012	0.76485	287	1.8%	(0.5%)	(2.1%)	(0.8%)
4	2/29/2016	0.89474	335	(1.5%)	1.2%	(1.2%)	1.3%
5	5/31/2002	0.45431	170	2.4%	6.4%	(0.7%)	(1.2%)

Sources: Bloomberg Finance LLP, FTSE Russell, S&P Capital IQ, Thomson Reuters, Wolfe Research Luo's QES.

---

[2]Technically, the random number generator will draw a random number that equals or is greater than 0 but is less than 1.

data is with replacement. For example, as shown in Exhibit 28, the first five numbers generated are 0.59163, 0.32185, 0.76485, 0.89474, and 0.45431, which are then mapped to Months 222 (September 2006), 121 (April 1998), 287 (February 2012), 335 (February 2016), and 170 (May 2002), respectively. To be clear, months are mapped by dividing the random number by 0.00267, so Month 222 is determined as 0.59163/0.00267, Month 121 is 0.32185/0.00267, and so on.

6. Once a given month is selected, the returns of the corresponding eight factor portfolios are used to represent one possible set of outcomes. Then, using the factor portfolio returns and the prespecified factor weights, we can compute the values of our target variables—the returns of the BM and RP portfolios. For example, the first trial picks the month of September 2006. The return of the benchmark portfolio is the equally weighted average of the eight factor returns, or 0.46 percent (= 0.125 × 2.5% + 0.125 × 0.3% + 0.125 × –0.8% + 0.125 × 0.0% + 0.125 × –0.8% + 0.125 × 2.5% + 0.125 × 0.5% + 0.125 × –0.5%).

To compute the return on the risk parity portfolio, we need the weights allocated to each of the eight factors for the current month (May 2019). As shown in Exhibit 29, for the first trial, September 2006, the weighted average return of the risk parity portfolio is 0.2 percent (actually, 0.17 percent). It should be clear that each trial in the historical simulation assumes the simulated returns of the eight factors follow the same patterns observed in the sampled month—in this case, September 2006.

7. The same simulation process (from Steps 5 to 6) is repeated for 1,000 trials, and then we have a collection of 1,000 simulated returns for the benchmark and risk parity portfolios.
8. Finally, equipped with these 1,000 return scenarios, we can calculate the performance metrics of interest (Sharpe ratio, CVaR, etc.) and plot the distributions of the benchmark and risk parity portfolio returns.

As shown in Panel A of Exhibit 30, the results of the historical simulation (over the 1,000 iterations) suggest that the Sharpe ratios of the BM and RP strategies are largely in line with the rolling window backtesting method demonstrated previously. In particular,

EXHIBIT 29   How to Compute the Return of the Risk Parity Portfolio, Historical Simulation #1

Asset (Factor)	September 2006 Return	May 2019 Weight	Weighted Return
Earnings Yield	2.5%	6.0%	0.2%
Book-to-Market	0.3%	30.3%	0.1%
Earnings Growth	(0.8%)	11.7%	(0.1%)
Momentum	(0.0%)	5.2%	(0.0%)
Earnings Revision	(0.8%)	10.4%	(0.1%)
ROE	2.5%	6.3%	0.2%
Debt/Equity	0.5%	9.6%	0.0%
Earnings Quality	(0.5%)	20.4%	(0.1%)
Risk Parity Portfolio			**0.2%**

Sources: Bloomberg Finance LLP, FTSE Russell, S&P Capital IQ, Thomson Reuters, Wolfe Research Luo's QES.

the RP portfolio outperforms the naive BM portfolio in terms of Sharpe ratio using both methodologies. Similarly, as shown in Panel B, both methodologies indicate that the RP portfolio carries substantially less downside risk, measured by CVaR, than the BM portfolio carries.

In addition to capturing downside risk with a single number (e.g., CVaR), we can also plot the estimated probability distribution of returns for our two investment strategies. Panel A of Exhibit 31, plots the estimated probability distribution of returns for the BM and RP

EXHIBIT 30   Comparing Historical Simulation with Backtesting

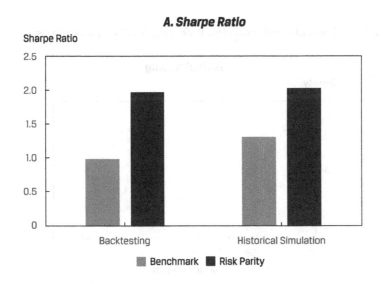

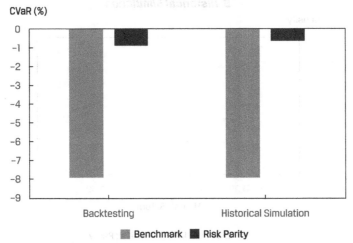

Sources: Bloomberg Finance LLP, FTSE Russell, S&P Capital IQ, Thomson Reuters, Wolfe Research Luo's QES.

portfolios using backtested returns, whereas Panel B shows the estimated return distribution plots using the historical simulated returns. We can observe a broadly similar pattern between them. Both the backtesting and historical simulation approaches suggest that the RP portfolio returns are less volatile and more skewed to the right with lower downside risk (i.e., lower standard deviation and thinner tails) than the BM portfolio returns.

However, an important issue with this historical simulation (and historical simulation generally) is that the path dependency of the time series of factor returns (and asset returns, generally) is not preserved. This deficiency can be addressed with the Monte Carlo simulation method.

EXHIBIT 31   Estimated Distribution Plots: Backtesting and Historical Simulation

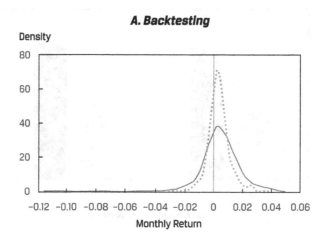

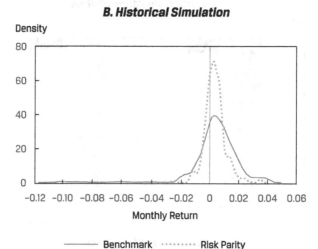

Sources: Bloomberg Finance LLP, FTSE Russell, S&P Capital IQ, Thomson Reuters, Wolfe Research Luo's QES.

11. MONTE CARLO SIMULATION

Monte Carlo simulation follows similar steps as historical simulation but with a few key differences.

First, in historical simulation, each random variable of interest (key driver or decision variable) is randomly drawn from historical data (Step 4 in the prior discussion of historical simulation). In a Monte Carlo simulation, we need to specify a functional form for each decision variable. The exploratory data analysis presented earlier—focusing on moments (i.e., mean, standard deviation, skewness, kurtosis) and tail dependence—can help us understand the empirical distribution of key drivers and decision variables. The usefulness of the Monte Carlo simulation technique critically depends on whether the functional form of the statistical distribution that we specify accurately reflects the true distribution of the underlying data. Because the true distribution of the data is unknown, we need to be aware of the fact that our model, like all models, only provides guidance and will not be perfect.

Second, once we specify the functional form(s) (note that different key drivers/decision variables may have different functional forms), regression and optimization techniques are used to estimate the parameters (i.e., mean, standard deviation, skewness, kurtosis) underlying the statistical distribution. This step is typically called model calibration. Although it may sound difficult, computer programming languages widely used by data scientists (e.g., R, Python, Matlab) can readily fit empirical data to a multivariate normal distribution with a few lines of code. For example, the fMultivar package in the R programming language offers many useful functions to fit data and simulate from multivariate distributions.

When we choose the functional form of the statistical distribution, we need to account for the following considerations:

- The distribution should be able to reasonably describe the key empirical patterns of the underlying data. For example, asset returns typically follow a bell curve pattern (e.g., the value factor returns observed in Exhibit 19); therefore, the normal distribution and Student's *t*-distribution are often used as a first-cut approximation.
- It is equally critical to account for the correlations between multiple key drivers and decision variables. In the case of asset or factor allocation strategies, as shown previously, the returns from multiple factors are clearly correlated; therefore, we need to specify a multivariate distribution rather than modeling each factor or asset on a standalone basis.
- The complexity of the functional form and number of parameters that determine the functional form are equally important. This is the trade-off between model specification error and estimation error. We can specify a highly complex model with many parameters (all of which need to be estimated/calibrated from historical data) that describe the empirical properties of the data well. However, given limited historical data, we may not be able to estimate all the underlying parameters with sufficient precision. Such models tend to have low specification errors, but they suffer from large estimation errors. On the other extreme, overly simplistic models require fewer parameters (therefore, they might have low estimation errors), but they may not fit the data well (because they are mis-specified). You should recognize this phenomenon as the bias–variance trade-off, introduced in earlier chapters on machine learning and big data projects.

For asset or factor allocation strategy simulation, the distribution of asset or factor returns is typically modeled as a multivariate normal distribution—as a first-cut approximation—which captures some of the key properties of the underlying data reasonably well.

More importantly, a multivariate normal distribution can be fully specified with only a few key parameters—the mean, the standard deviation, and the covariance matrix. For K assets, we need to estimate K mean returns, K standard deviations, and $[K \times (K - 1)]/2$ correlations.

However, we have to be aware that the multivariate normal distribution does not fully account for the empirical characteristics of (negative) skewness, excess kurtosis, and tail dependence in the data. We will address these non-normal distribution properties shortly, when we cover sensitivity analysis.

Continuing with the same benchmark and risk parity allocation strategies, we now perform the Monte Carlo simulation using the following steps:

1. The target variables are the returns of the benchmark and the risk parity portfolios.
2. The key drivers/decision variables are the returns of the eight underlying factor portfolios.
3. We will perform the simulation using 1,000 trials (the same as for the historical simulation exercise).
4. We choose the multivariate normal distribution as our initial functional form. We calibrate the model—calculate the eight factor portfolio mean returns, the eight standard deviations, and the 28 elements of the covariance matrix—using the 374 months of historical factor return data (April 1988–May 2019).
5. The calibrated multivariate normal distribution is then used to simulate the future factor returns. The process by which this occurs will be described (roughly) first in the simpler context of one normally distributed random variable and then in the current context of a multivariate normal distribution of eight random variables.

   In the case of one normally distributed (i.e., univariate normal) random variable, the simulation process for future returns can be thought of as follows: First, the random number generator selects a number from the uniform distribution between 0 and 1 (think of this random number as an x-axis coordinate). Next, that number is directly mapped onto the random variable's cumulative probability distribution function (cdf), which also ranges from 0 to 1. Finally, the y coordinate of the point on the cdf curve is used to determine the value of the random variable for that trial. The process of converting a randomly generated uniformly distributed number into a simulated value of a random variable of a desired distribution is known as the **inverse transformation method**. It is depicted in Exhibit 32, where randomly generated values from the uniform distribution (x's) are mapped into a standard normal distribution to determine simulated values (y's) of the random variable.

   It is a remarkable fact that random observations from any distribution can be produced using the uniform random variable with endpoints 0 and 1. To see why this is so, consider the inverse transformation method that converts from the uniform distribution to the standard normal distribution (as in Exhibit 32). Suppose we are interested in obtaining random observations for a random variable y, with cumulative distribution function $F(y)$. Recall that $F(y)$ evaluated at y is a number between 0 and 1. For instance, to produce a random outcome of 2.00 from the standard normal distribution (i.e., a +2 × sigma event), the uniform random number generator must select the number 0.98 (chosen from the range of 0 and 1), since $F(2.00) = 0.98$. Define the inverse function of F—call it $y = F^{-1}(x)$—that transforms the input number 0.98 into the random outcome of 2.00; so, $F^{-1}(0.98) = 2.00$. To generate random observations on variable y, the steps are to generate a uniform random number, x, between 0 and

EXHIBIT 32   Inverse Transformation: From Uniform Distribution to Standard Normal Distribution

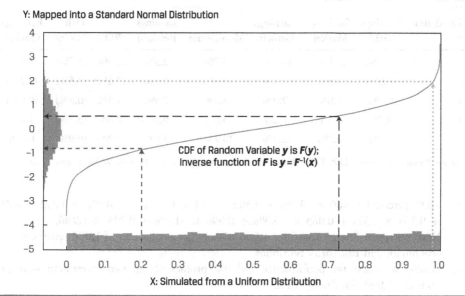

Y: Mapped into a Standard Normal Distribution

CDF of Random Variable **y** is F(**y**);
Inverse function of **F** is **y** = F⁻¹(**x**)

X: Simulated from a Uniform Distribution

Sources: Wolfe Research Luo's QES.

1 using the random number generator and then to evaluate $F^{-1}(x)$ to obtain a random observation of y.

Random observation generation is a field of study in itself, and we have briefly discussed the inverse transformation method here just to illustrate a point. As a generalist, you do not need to address the technical details of converting random numbers into random observations, but you do need to know that random observations from any distribution can be generated using a uniform random variable.

In the context of a multivariate normal distribution with eight random variables, the process is considerably more complex to visualize and explain. Suffice it to say, in this case, eight randomly generated numbers from the uniform distribution are mapped onto a point on the joint cumulative probability distribution function (actually, a high-dimensional cdf space), and this point is used to jointly determine the values of the eight factor returns in this trial.

Exhibit 33 shows the first five simulated sets of returns for the eight underlying factors that result from implementing the inverse transformation method.

6. Once the returns of the eight factor portfolios are simulated, we can compute the values of our target variables—the returns of the two factor allocation portfolios. For example, for the first simulated set of returns, the benchmark portfolio (with equally weighted factor returns) delivers a monthly return of –0.83 percent (= 0.125 × – 3.2% + 0.125 × –3.1% + 0.125 × –0.2% + 0.125 × 0.7% + 0.125 × 2.3% + 0.125 × –3.3% + 0.125 × –1.7% + 0.125 × 1.9%).

Similarly, using the RP allocation factor weights for the current month, May 2019, shown in Exhibit 29, the risk parity portfolio return for this simulated month is

EXHIBIT 33   Monte Carlo Simulation: First Five Simulated Months of Factor Returns Using a Multivariate Normal Distribution

Simulation #	Earnings Yield	Book-to-Market	Earnings Growth	Momentum	Earnings Revision	ROE	Debt/ Equity	Earnings Quality
1	(3.2%)	(3.1%)	(0.2%)	0.7%	2.3%	(3.3%)	(1.7%)	1.9%
2	(0.0%)	3.5%	0.9%	(0.4%)	0.9%	(2.4%)	(3.5%)	(0.2%)
3	0.7%	(1.8%)	2.9%	3.8%	2.5%	1.3%	(0.8%)	(0.0%)
4	9.7%	(0.5%)	1.2%	3.8%	(0.9%)	7.6%	(3.7%)	1.6%
5	1.7%	0.2%	2.9%	(0.2%)	3.0%	0.2%	(0.9%)	0.2%

Sources: Bloomberg Finance LLP, FTSE Russell, S&P Capital IQ, Thomson Reuters, Wolfe Research Luo's QES.

-0.86 percent ($= 0.06 \times -3.2\% + 0.303 \times -3.1\% + 0.117 \times -0.2\% + 0.052 \times 0.7\% + 0.104 \times 2.3\% + 0.063 \times -3.3\% + 0.096 \times -1.7\% + 0.204 \times 1.9\%$).

7. Next, we repeat Steps 5 and 6 for 1,000 trials to get a collection of 1,000 returns for the benchmark and risk parity portfolios.
8. Finally, we assess the performance and risk profiles of our two investment strategies from the 1,000 simulated returns.

EXAMPLE 9   How to Interpret the Results from Historical and Monte Carlo Simulations

Exhibit 34 shows the Sharpe ratios (Panel A) and downside risk measures (CVaRs, Panel B) for the returns of the benchmark and risk parity allocation strategies based on rolling window backtesting, historical simulation, and Monte Carlo simulation of the returns on the eight underlying factor portfolios.

Discuss the similarities and differences among the three approaches for simulated performance of the benchmark and risk parity portfolios.

Solution: Note the backtesting approach provides realistic performance metrics assuming investors have been following the same trading rules throughout the past periods under investigation. The two simulation analyses are complementary to backtesting and deliver additional insights. In particular, they account for the random nature of investment data in different ways. Historical simulation randomly samples (with replacement) from the past record of asset returns, where each set of past monthly returns is equally likely to be selected. Monte Carlo simulation randomly samples from an assumed multivariate joint probability distribution (e.g., normal or another type of distribution), where the past record of asset returns is used to calibrate the parameters of the multivariate distribution. Therefore, these simulation methods are used to independently verify the results from the rolling window backtesting.

As shown in Panel A of Exhibit 34, the Sharpe ratio appears relatively insensitive to the simulation and backtesting methods used, with the RP strategy outperforming the BM strategy by nearly the same margin for each method. In contrast, CVaR seems to be sensitive to how randomness is treated. In particular, the Monte Carlo

EXHIBIT 34   Comparing Backtesting, Historical Simulation, and Monte Carlo Simulation for
the BM and RP Strategies

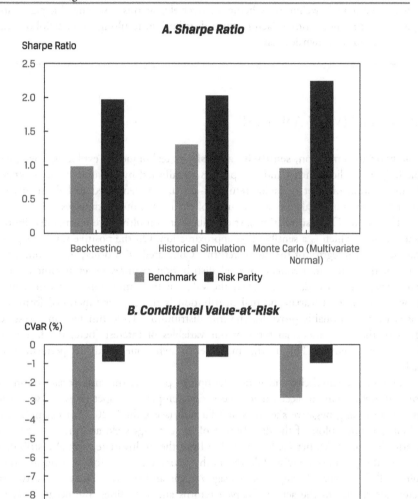

Sources: Bloomberg Finance LLP, FTSE Russell, S&P Capital IQ, Thomson Reuters, Wolfe Research Luo's
QES.

simulation appears to understate the downside risk of the BM strategy compared with
both rolling window backtesting and historical simulation methods (Panel B). Since
the factor returns are negatively skewed with fat tails (i.e., excess kurtosis), the multivariate normal distribution assumption is likely to be underestimating the true

downside risk of the BM strategy. This underestimation of risk appears only for the BM strategy because factor risks and correlations are not properly accounted for in the naive (equal) weighting scheme. Conversely, in this case, the risk parity strategy is robust to a non-normal factor return distribution, resulting in a portfolio with considerably lower downside risk.

12. SENSITIVITY ANALYSIS

In addition to simulation, **sensitivity analysis**—a technique for exploring how a target variable (e.g., portfolio returns) and risk profiles are affected by changes in input variables (e.g., the distribution of asset or factor returns)—can be implemented to help managers further understand the potential risks and returns of their investment strategies.

The Monte Carlo simulation just described fits a multivariate normal distribution to the factor returns, which is a sensible first approximation. On the positive side, this preserves the cross-sectional integrity of the factor returns. Compared with other, more complex distribution functions, the multivariate normal distribution requires fewer parameters to be estimated from historical data. However, the value of the simulation results depends crucially on whether the multivariate normal distribution is the correct functional form or whether it is at least a reasonable proxy for the true distribution. Unfortunately, in investment management, the true functional form of our variables of interest (here, the factor returns) is almost never known. This is the main reason why one needs to perform a sensitivity analysis.

Despite the simplicity and wide adoption in practice, the multivariate normal distribution assumption fails to account for the various empirical properties we observed for factor returns, including negative skewness and fat tails (see Exhibit 20). For example, Panel A of Exhibit 35 shows plots of the distribution of the earnings yield and price momentum factor returns derived by Monte Carlo simulation from the multivariate normal distribution model fitted in the previous exercise. Clearly, both factors appear to follow a normal distribution quite well. However, although the average returns and the volatilities of the two simulated factors are similar to the actual observed returns and volatilities, the negative skewness and fat tails observed empirically (see Panel A of Exhibit 19) now completely disappear.

Furthermore, the correlation between the two factors (see Panel B of Exhibit 35) also appears to be nicely behaved. A 95 percent ellipse circle contains the vast majority of simulated return data, which is somewhat different from the actual observed returns in Panel B of Exhibit 19.

As a robustness test, instead of the multivariate normal distribution used previously, we conduct a sensitivity analysis. We do this by fitting our factor return data to a different distribution, a multivariate skewed Student's t-distribution, and then we repeat the Monte Carlo simulation accordingly. The Student's t-distribution is also symmetric (similar to a normal distribution), but it has fatter tails than a normal distribution. To capture the negative skewness in the factor returns, we use the skewed generalized t-distribution; it is a natural extension of the multivariate normal distribution but has the ability to account for the skewness and the excess kurtosis often observed in factor and asset return data.

EXHIBIT 35   Distribution of Selected Monte Carlo Simulated Factor Returns (Assuming Multivariate Normal Distribution)

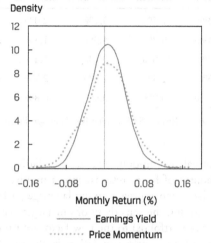

A. Value (Earnings Yield) and Momentum

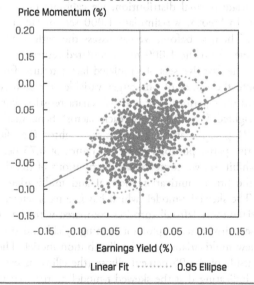

B. Value vs. Momentum

Sources: Bloomberg Finance LLP, FTSE Russell, S&P Capital IQ, Thomson Reuters, Wolfe Research Luo's QES.

The multivariate skewed *t*-distribution is mathematically more complex and requires estimating a larger number of parameters than a normal distribution. Therefore, although the assumption of this distribution may better approximate the statistical properties of asset return data, there is no guarantee that it will deliver more accurate predictions than the

EXHIBIT 36   First Five Simulated Months of Factor Returns Using Multivariate Skewed
t-Distribution

Simulation #	Earnings Yield	Book-to-Market	Earnings Growth	Momentum	Earnings Revision	ROE	Debt/ Equity	Earnings Quality
1	2.0%	0.3%	1.7%	3.1%	2.0%	0.9%	0.2%	(0.5%)
2	1.8%	(1.4%)	0.2%	4.9%	1.8%	2.7%	0.4%	(0.1%)
3	(0.6%)	0.2%	(1.0%)	(0.1%)	0.4%	1.5%	1.6%	0.9%
4	11.2%	2.6%	1.8%	1.5%	2.2%	9.6%	(2.9%)	(1.9%)
5	(3.9%)	(1.3%)	0.9%	0.9%	0.8%	(3.5%)	2.9%	0.2%

Sources: Bloomberg Finance LLP, FTSE Russell, S&P Capital IQ, Thomson Reuters, Wolfe Research Luo's QES.

traditional multivariate normal assumption. Again, it is fairly straightforward to fit our empirical data (i.e., 374 months of factor returns) into a multivariate skewed t-distribution using any of the standard data science programming language packages.

With the goal of determining the sensitivity of our target variables (the returns of the benchmark and the risk parity portfolios) to the new factor return distribution assumption, the procedure for the new Monte Carlo simulation is almost identical to the one performed previously. The only two exceptions are Steps 4 and 5. In Step 4, instead of fitting the data to a multivariate normal distribution, we calibrate our model to a multivariate skewed t-distribution. In Step 5, we simulate 1,000 sets of factor returns from this new distribution function. Then, as before, we can assess the performance and risk profiles of our investment strategies from the 1,000 new simulated returns.

Exhibit 36 shows the first five sets of simulated factor returns from this new model. As previously, we compute the values of our target variables for each set of simulated factor returns and then assess their performance and risk characteristics. For the first set of factor returns, the equal-weighted (i.e., 0.125 for each factor) benchmark portfolio achieves a monthly return of 1.21 percent, and the equal-risk-weighted (i.e., factor weights for May 2019 in Exhibit 29) risk parity portfolio delivers a return of 0.75 percent.

In Panel A of Exhibit 37, we compare the distributions of the simulated earnings yield factor returns from the fitted multivariate normal and multivariate skewed t-distribution models, respectively. The skewed t-model, which has five parameters,[3] shows more negative skewness with potentially more left-tail surprises compared with the other model. Similarly, Panel B illustrates the pairwise scatterplot for earnings yield and price momentum factors simulated from the new multivariate skewed t-distribution model. The new plot appears to have more outliers outside of the 95 percent ellipse (the ellipse is based on the multivariate normal distribution), indicating that the skewed t-model captures fat tails better than a normal distribution does (see Panel B of Exhibit 35).

Turning to the performance and risk profiles of our investment strategies, as shown in Panel A of Exhibit 38, the Sharpe ratio appears insensitive to any of the particular simulation methods used: They all consistently suggest that the risk parity factor allocation strategy outperforms the benchmark strategy. Downside risk (expressed as CVaR), however, appears quite sensitive to the choice of simulation approach for the BM strategy but not very

---

[3]The five parameters in specifying a skewed t-distribution are scale, location, skewness, and two parameters controlling for kurtosis.

EXHIBIT 37   Distribution of Select Simulated Factor Returns (Multivariate Skewed *t*-Distribution)

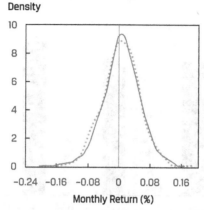

A. Value (Earnings Yield)

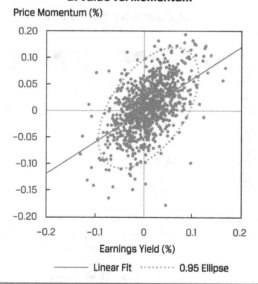

B. Value vs. Momentum

Sources: Bloomberg Finance LLP, FTSE Russell, S&P Capital IQ, Thomson Reuters, Wolfe Research Luo's QES.

sensitive for the RP strategy (Panel B). Focusing on the BM strategy, the CVaR results from historical simulation and rolling window backtesting resemble each other very closely. The CVaR results of the skewed *t*-distribution and multivariate normal Monte Carlo simulations are also very similar: They both underestimate the downside risk of the BM strategy. This finding suggests that additional sensitivity analyses should be run with different functional forms for the factor return distribution.

EXHIBIT 38   Comparing Simulation Methods with Backtesting

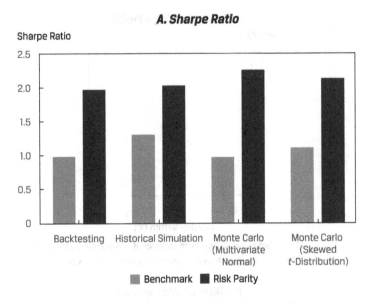

A. Sharpe Ratio

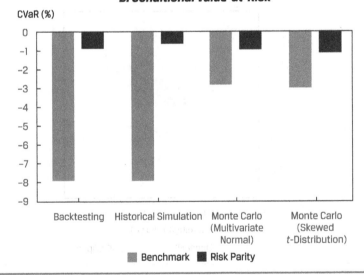

B. Conditional Value-at-Risk

Sources: Bloomberg Finance LLP, FTSE Russell, S&P Capital IQ, Thomson Reuters, Wolfe Research Luo's QES.

Using estimated probability density plots, shown in Panel A of Exhibit 39, it can be seen that the difference between the historical simulation and the two Monte Carlo methods is rather large for the BM strategy. Given the negative skewness and excess kurtosis of the BM strategy's returns, which is apparent from the shape of the historical simulation return distribution, it is not surprising that the two Monte Carlo simulations fail to account for this left-tail risk property. Conversely, since the distribution of the RP strategy's returns is relatively symmetric and without much excess kurtosis, all three simulation methods provide a fairly similar picture (Panel B).

EXHIBIT 39   Estimated Distribution Plots for BM and RP Strategies Using Three Different Simulations

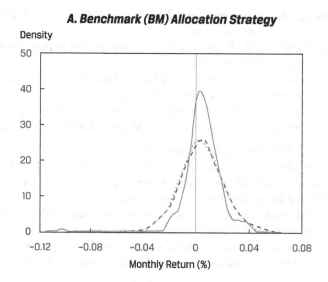

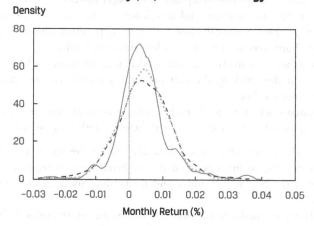

Sources: Bloomberg Finance LLP, FTSE Russell, S&P Capital IQ, Thomson Reuters, Wolfe Research Luo's QES.

EXAMPLE 10   Simulating the Performance of Factor Allocation Strategies

Earlier, Sarah Koh presented her team's backtesting results for the factor-based allocation strategies being considered by an important client, SWF Fund. Now, while presenting the simulation results for these same strategies, SWF Fund's investment
committee asks Koh the following questions:

1. The following are caveats regarding the use of rolling window backtesting in
    assessing investment strategies *except*:
    A. this technique implicitly assumes that the same pattern of past performance is
        likely to repeat itself over time.
    B. this technique may not fully account for the dynamic nature of financial mar-
        kets and potentially extreme downside risks.
    C. this technique is intuitive, because it mimics how investing is done in
        reality—that is, forming ideas, testing strategies, and implementing periodically.

2. Which one of the following statements is *false*?
    A. Volatility clustering is when a period of high volatility is likely to be followed
        by another period of high volatility or when a low-volatility period is likely to
        be followed by another low-volatility period.
    B. The tail dependence coefficient is a type of correlation coefficient that focuses
        on co-movements in the tails of two random variables.
    C. If the distribution of factor returns is non-normal, then just mean and stan-
        dard deviation are needed to capture the randomness in the data.

3. Which of the following situations is *most likely* to involve data snooping?
    A. A researcher specifies an acceptable proportion (q-value) of significant results
        that can be false positives and establishes, on the basis of the q-value and
        ranked p-values, a critical value for reported p-values. She will only accept
        as significant tests with p-values below the critical value.
    B. A researcher tries many different modeling techniques, backtesting each of
        them, and then picking the best performing model without accounting for
        model selection bias.
    C. A researcher sets a relatively high hurdle, a t-statistic greater than $3.0\times$, for
        assessing whether a newly discovered factor is statistically significant.

4. Which of the following situations is *least likely* to involve scenario analysis?
    A. Simulating the performance and risk of investment strategies by first using
        stocks in the Nikkei 225 index and then using stocks in the TOPIX 1000
        index.
    B. Simulating the performance and risk of investment strategies in both "trade
        agreement" and "no-trade-agreement" environments.
    C. Simulating the performance and risk of investment strategies in both high-
        volatility and low-volatility environments.

5. Which one of the following statements concerning historical simulation and Monte Carlo simulation is *false*?
   A. Historical simulation randomly samples (with replacement) from the past record of asset returns, where each set of past monthly returns is equally likely to be selected.
   B. Neither historical simulation nor Monte Carlo simulation makes use of a random number generator.
   C. Monte Carlo simulation randomly samples from an assumed multivariate joint probability distribution where the past record of asset returns is used to calibrate the parameters of the multivariate distribution.

6. Which one of the following statements concerning Monte Carlo simulation is *false*?
   A. When simulating multiple assets (factors) whose returns are correlated, it is crucial to specify a multivariate distribution rather than modeling each asset on a standalone basis.
   B. The inverse transformation method is a process for converting a randomly generated number into a simulated value of a random variable.
   C. The Monte Carlo simulation process is deterministic and non-random in nature.

7. Which of the following situations concerning simulation of a multifactor asset allocation strategy is *most likely* to involve sensitivity analysis?
   A. Changing the specified multivariate distribution assumption from a normal to a skewed t-distribution to better account for skewness and fat tails.
   B. Splitting the rolling window between periods of recession and non-recession.
   C. Splitting the rolling window between periods of high volatility and low volatility.

Solution to 1: C is correct, since it is not a caveat in using rolling window backtesting. A and B are incorrect because they are caveats in the use of this technique.

Solution to 2: C is correct, since statement C is false. A and B are incorrect because those statements are true.

Solution to 3: B is correct, since this situation most likely involves data snooping. A and C are incorrect because these are approaches to avoiding data snooping.

Solution to 4: A is correct, since there is no structural break or different structural regime. B and C are incorrect because they involve structural breaks/different structural regimes and thus represent different scenarios.

Solution to 5: B is correct, since this statement is false. A and C are incorrect because they are true statements about historical and Monte Carlo simulation, respectively.

Solution to 6: C is correct, since this statement is false. A and B are incorrect because they are true statements about Monte Carlo simulation.

Solution to 7: A is correct, since this choice represents sensitivity analysis. B and C are incorrect because these choices represent scenario analysis.

13. SUMMARY

In this chapter, we have discussed on how to perform rolling window backtesting—a widely used technique in the investment industry. Next, we described how to use scenario analysis and simulation along with sensitivity analysis to supplement backtesting, so investors can better account for the randomness in data that may not be fully captured by backtesting.

- The main objective of backtesting is to understand the risk–return trade-off of an investment strategy, by approximating the real-life investment process.
- The basic steps in a rolling window backtesting include specifying the investment hypothesis and goals, determining the rules and processes behind an investment strategy, forming an investment portfolio according to the rules, rebalancing the portfolio periodically, and computing the performance and risk profiles of the strategy.
- In the rolling window backtesting methodology, researchers use a rolling window (or walk-forward) framework, fit/calibrate factors or trade signals based on the rolling window, rebalance the portfolio periodically, and then track the performance over time. Thus, rolling window backtesting is a proxy for actual investing.
- There are two commonly used approaches in backtesting—long/short hedged portfolio and Spearman rank IC. The two approaches often give similar results, but results can be quite different at times. Choosing the right approach depends on the model building and portfolio construction process.
- In assessing backtesting results, in addition to traditional performance measurements (e.g., Sharpe ratio, maximum drawdown), analysts need to take into account data coverage, return distribution, factor efficacy, factor turnover, and decay.
- There are several behavioral issues in backtesting to which analysts need to pay particular attention, including survivorship bias and look-ahead bias.
- Risk parity is a popular portfolio construction technique that takes into account the volatility of each factor (or asset) and the correlations of returns between all factors (or assets) to be combined in the portfolio. The objective is for each factor (or asset) to make an equal (hence "parity") risk contribution to the overall or targeted risk of the portfolio.
- Asset (and factor) returns are often negatively skewed and exhibit excess kurtosis (fat tails) and tail dependence compared with normal distribution. As a result, standard rolling window backtesting may not be able to fully account for the randomness in asset returns, particularly on downside risk.
- Financial data often face structural breaks. Scenario analysis can help investors understand the performance of an investment strategy in different structural regimes.
- Historical simulation is relatively straightforward to perform but shares pros and cons similar to those of rolling window backtesting. For example, a key assumption these methods share is that the distribution pattern from the historical data is sufficient to represent the uncertainty in the future. Bootstrapping (or random draws with replacement) is often used in historical simulation.
- Monte Carlo simulation is a more sophisticated technique than historical simulation is. In Monte Carlo simulation, the most important decision is the choice of functional form of the statistical distribution of decision variables/return drivers. Multivariate normal distribution is often used in investment research, owing to its simplicity. However, a multivariate normal distribution cannot account for negative skewness and fat tails observed in factor and asset returns.

- The Monte Carlo simulation technique makes use of the inverse transformation method—the process of converting a randomly generated uniformly distributed number into a simulated value of a random variable of a desired distribution.
- Sensitivity analysis, a technique for exploring how a target variable and risk profiles are affected by changes in input variables, can further help investors understand the limitations of conventional Monte Carlo simulation (which typically assumes a multivariate normal distribution as a starting point). A multivariate skewed *t*-distribution takes into account skewness and kurtosis but requires estimation of more parameters and thus is more likely to suffer from larger estimation errors.

REFERENCES

DeMiguel, V., L. Garlappi, and R Uppal. 2007. *"Optimal Versus Naïve Diversification: How Inefficient Is the 1/N Portfolio Strategy?"* London Business School Working Paper. http://faculty.london.edu/avmiguel/DeMiguel-Garlappi-Uppal-RFS.pdf.

Fama, E. and K. R French. 1993. "Common Risk Factors in the Returns on Stocks and Bonds." *Journal of Financial Economics* 33 (1): 3–56. 10.1016/0304-405X(93)90023-5.

Fama, E. and J. D MacBeth. 1973. "Risk, Return, and Equilibrium: Empirical Tests." *Journal of Political Economy* 81 (3): 607–36. 10.1086/260061.

Jegadeesh, N. and S Titman. 1993. "Returns to Buying Winners and Selling Losers: Implications for Stock Market Efficiency." *Journal of Finance* 48 (1): 65–91. 10.1111/j.1540-6261.1993.tb04702.x.

Ritter, F. E., M. J. Schoelles, K. S. Quigley, and L. C Klein. 2011. "Determining the Number of Simulation Runs: Treating Simulations as Theories by Not Sampling Their Behavior." In *Human-in-the-Loop Simulations: Methods and Practice*, ed. Rothrock, L. and S Narayanan. 97–116. Berlin: Springer. 10.1007/978-0-85729-883-6_5.

PRACTICE PROBLEMS

The following information relates to Questions 1–8.

Emily Yuen is a senior analyst for a consulting firm that specializes in assessing equity strategies using backtesting and simulation techniques. She is working with an assistant, Cameron Ruckey, to develop multifactor portfolio strategies based on nine factors common to the growth style of investing. To do so, Yuen and Ruckey plan to construct nine separate factor portfolios and then use them to create factor-weighted allocation portfolios.

Yuen tasks Ruckey with specifying the investment universe and determining the availability of appropriate reporting data in vendor databases. Ruckey selects a vendor database that does not provide point-in-time data, then makes adjustments to include point-in-time constituent stocks and assumes a reporting lag of four months.

Next, Yuen and Ruckey run initial backtests by creating a stock portfolio and calculating performance statistics and key metrics for each of the nine factors based on a Spearman rank information coefficient (IC) approach. For backtesting purposes, the factor portfolios are each rebalanced monthly over a 30-year time horizon using a rolling-window procedure.

Yuen and Ruckey consider a variety of metrics to assess the results of the factor portfolio backtests. Yuen asks Ruckey what can be concluded from the data for three of the factor strategies in Exhibit 1:

EXHIBIT 1   Backtest Metrics for Factor Strategies

	Factor 1	Factor 2	Factor 3
Thirty-year average signal autocorrelation	90%	80%	85%
Spearman rank IC: Month 1 (IC_1)	5%	4%	3%
Spearman rank IC decay speed	Fast	Slow	Modest

Yuen and Ruckey then run multifactor model backtests by combining the factor portfolios into two factor-weighted multifactor portfolios: an equally weighted benchmark portfolio (Portfolio A) and a risk parity portfolio (Portfolio B). Ruckey tells Yuen the following:

Statement 1:   A risk parity multifactor model is constructed by equally weighting the risk contribution of each factor.

Statement 2:   The process of creating Portfolios A and B requires a second rolling-window procedure in order to avoid model selection bias.

To gain a more complete picture of the investment strategy performance, Yuen and Ruckey design and then run two simulation methods to generate investment performance data for the underlying factor portfolios, assuming 1,000 simulation trials for each approach:

Approach 1:   Historical simulation
Approach 2:   Monte Carlo simulation

Yuen and Ruckey discuss the differences between the two approaches and then design the simulations, making key decisions at various steps. During the process, Yuen expresses a number of concerns:

Concern 1: Returns from six of the nine factors are clearly correlated.
Concern 2: The distribution of Factor 1 returns exhibits excess kurtosis and negative skewness.
Concern 3: The number of simulations needed for Approach 1 is larger than the size of the historical dataset.

For each approach, Yuen and Ruckey run 1,000 trials to obtain 1,000 returns for Portfolios A and B. To help understand the effect of the skewness and excess kurtosis observed in the Factor 1 returns on the performance of Portfolios A and B, Ruckey suggests simulating an additional 1,000 factor returns using a multivariate skewed Student's t-distribution, then repeating the Approach 2 simulation.

1. Following Ruckey's adjustments to the initial vendor database, backtested returns will most likely be subject to:
    A.   stale data.
    B.   look-ahead bias.
    C.   survivorship bias.

2. Based on Exhibit 1, Ruckey should conclude that:
   A. Factor Strategy 1 portfolios experience the highest turnover.
   B. Factor Strategy 2 provides the strongest predictive power in the long term.
   C. Factor Strategy 3 provides the strongest predictive power in the first month.

3. Which of Ruckey's statements about constructing multifactor portfolios is correct?
   A. Only Statement 1
   B. Only Statement 2
   C. Both Statement 1 and Statement 2

4. Approach 1 differs from Approach 2 in that:
   A. it is deterministic.
   B. a functional form of the statistical distribution for each decision variable needs to be specified.
   C. it assumes that sampling the returns from the actual data provides sufficient guidance about future asset returns.

5. To address Concern 1 when designing Approach 2, Yuen should:
   A. model each factor or asset on a standalone basis.
   B. calculate the 15 covariance matrix elements needed to calibrate the model.
   C. simulate future factor returns using a joint cumulative probability distribution function.

6. Based on Concern 2, the Factor 1 strategy is *most likely* to:
   A. be favored by risk-averse investors.
   B. generate surprises in the form of negative returns.
   C. have return data that line up tightly around a trend line.

7. To address Concern 3 when designing Approach 1, Yuen should:
   A. bootstrap additional returns using a walk-forward framework.
   B. randomly sample from the historical returns with replacement.
   C. choose the multivariate normal distribution as the initial functional form.

8. The process Ruckey suggests to better understand how the performance of Portfolios A and B using Approach 2 is affected by the distribution of Factor 1 returns is *best* described as:
   A. data snooping.
   B. sensitivity analysis.
   C. inverse transformation.

The following information relates to Questions 9–16.

Kata Rom is an equity analyst working for Gimingham Wealth Partners (GWP), a large investment advisory company. Rom meets with Goran Galic, a Canadian private wealth client, to explain investment strategies used by GWP to generate portfolio alpha for its clients.

Rom describes how GWP creates relevant investment strategies and then explains GWP's backtesting process. Rom notes the following:

Statement 1: Using historical data, backtesting approximates a real-life investment process to illustrate the risk–return tradeoff of a particular proposed investment strategy.

Statement 2:   Backtesting is used almost exclusively by quantitative investment managers
               and rarely by fundamental investment managers, who are more concerned
               with information such as forward estimates of company earnings, macroeco-
               nomic factors, and intrinsic values.

Rom states that GWP is recognized in the Canadian investment industry as a value
manager and that it uses traditional value parameters to build and backtest portfolios
designed to outperform benchmarks stipulated in each client's investment policy statement.
Galic, who is 62 years old, decides to allocate C$2 million (representing 10% of his net
worth) to an account with GWP and stipulates that portfolio assets be restricted exclusively
to domestic securities. Rom creates Value Portfolio I for Galic based on value factors analyzed in a series of backtests.

At a subsequent meeting with Galic, Rom explains the long–short hedged portfolio
approach for implementing factor-based portfolios that GWP used to create Value
Portfolio I and the steps involved in the backtesting procedure. One specific step in the process concerns Galic, who states the following:

Statement 3:   I have never sold a stock that I did not own, and I really do not like the
               notion of giving the banks almost all of the income earned on the cash pro-
               ceeds from the stock dispositions. On top of the forgone interest income, I
               think it could be really difficult to avoid high turnover and transaction costs,
               which would also negatively affect my risk-adjusted performance.

In an effort to relieve the concern raised by Galic, Rom suggests using an alternative
backtesting approach to evaluate Value Portfolio I. This method uses the correlation
between the prior-period ranked factor scores and the ranked current-period returns to evaluate the model's effectiveness. The approach generates a measure of the predictive power of
a given factor relative to future stock returns.

Rom explains that the two backtesting approaches discussed so far have a weakness
embedded in them. The approaches generally do not capture the dynamic nature of financial
markets and in particular may not capture extreme downside risk. In an attempt to remedy
this issue, Rom suggests considering different methods of modeling randomness. Rom states
that GWP recently performed a statistical study of value and momentum factors, which
found that both distributions were negatively skewed with fat tails. Additionally, the joint
distribution of the returns for the factors had two peaks in the tails, and the peaks were
higher than that from a normal distribution.

The study also investigated the return distributions of a number of individual value and
momentum factors and found that they were non-normal based on their negative skewness,
excess kurtosis, and tail dependence. Rom indicated that investment strategies based on this
type of data are prone to significantly higher downside risk. Exhibit 1 compares downside
risk measures for three model factors.

EXHIBIT 1   Downside Risk Measures for Model Factors

Risk Measure	Factor 1	Factor 2	Factor 3
Value at risk (VaR) (95%)	(6.49%)	(0.77%)	(2.40%)
Conditional VaR (CVaR) (95%)	(15.73%)	(4.21%)	(3.24%)
Maximum drawdown	35.10%	38.83%	45.98%

Rom explains that many of the examples used so far have incorporated the rolling-window backtesting approach. When comparing GWP's studies with those performed by Fastlane Wealth Managers for the same data and factors, Rom finds that the results are quite different. Rom discovers that Fastlane uses various modeling techniques, backtests each of them, and then picks the best-performing models. This discovery leads Rom to believe that Fastlane's modeling approach may exhibit selection bias.

Finally, after evaluating financial data that has periods of structural breaks, Rom informs Galic that GWP uses a technique commonly referred to as scenario analysis. This technique helps investment managers understand the performance of an investment strategy in different structural regimes. Exhibit 2 compares the performance of two factor allocation strategies under varying macroeconomic conditions.

EXHIBIT 2   Scenario Analysis Using the Sharpe Ratio

Strategy/Regime	High Volatility	Low Volatility	Recession	Non-recession
Strategy I	0.88	0.64	0.20	1.00
Strategy II	1.56	1.60	1.76	1.52

9. Which of Rom's statements concerning backtesting is correct?
   A. Only Statement 1
   B. Only Statement 2
   C. Both Statement 1 and Statement 2

10. The key parameter *most likely* to be incorporated in the analysis of Value Portfolio I is:
   A. monthly rebalancing.
   B. the MSCI World equity index.
   C. hedged returns into domestic currency.

11. In Statement 3, Galic expresses the *most* concern about the backtesting step that involves:
   A. strategy design.
   B. analysis of backtesting output.
   C. historical investment simulation.

12. The alternative approach to evaluate the backtesting of Value Portfolio I suggested by Rom is *most likely*:
   A. the Pearson information coefficient.
   B. the Spearman rank information coefficient.
   C. a cross-sectional regression.

13. Based on the statistical study performed by GWP, the tail dependence coefficient is *most likely*:
   A. low and negative.
   B. high and negative.
   C. high and positive.

14. Based on Exhibit 1, the factor with the smallest downside risk as measured by the weighted average of all losses that exceed a threshold is:
    A. Factor 1.
    B. Factor 2.
    C. Factor 3

15. The approach used by Fastlane Wealth Managers *most likely* incorporates:
    A. risk parity.
    B. data snooping.
    C. cross-validation.

16. Comparing the two strategies in Exhibit 2, the *best* risk-adjusted performance is demonstrated by:
    A. Strategy II in periods of low volatility and recession.
    B. Strategy I in periods of high volatility and non-recession.
    C. Strategy II in periods of high volatility and non-recession.

APPENDICES

APPENDICES

Appendix A
Cumulative Probabilities for a Standard Normal Distribution
$P(Z \leq x) = N(x)$ for $x \geq 0$ or $P(Z \leq z) = N(z)$ for $z \geq 0$

x or z	0	0.01	0.02	0.03	0.04	0.05	0.06	0.07	0.08	0.09
0.00	0.5000	0.5040	0.5080	0.5120	0.5160	0.5199	0.5239	0.5279	0.5319	0.5359
0.10	0.5398	0.5438	0.5478	0.5517	0.5557	0.5596	0.5636	0.5675	0.5714	0.5753
0.20	0.5793	0.5832	0.5871	0.5910	0.5948	0.5987	0.6026	0.6064	0.6103	0.6141
0.30	0.6179	0.6217	0.6255	0.6293	0.6331	0.6368	0.6406	0.6443	0.6480	0.6517
0.40	0.6554	0.6591	0.6628	0.6664	0.6700	0.6736	0.6772	0.6808	0.6844	0.6879
0.50	0.6915	0.6950	0.6985	0.7019	0.7054	0.7088	0.7123	0.7157	0.7190	0.7224
0.60	0.7257	0.7291	0.7324	0.7357	0.7389	0.7422	0.7454	0.7486	0.7517	0.7549
0.70	0.7580	0.7611	0.7642	0.7673	0.7704	0.7734	0.7764	0.7794	0.7823	0.7852
0.80	0.7881	0.7910	0.7939	0.7967	0.7995	0.8023	0.8051	0.8078	0.8106	0.8133
0.90	0.8159	0.8186	0.8212	0.8238	0.8264	0.8289	0.8315	0.8340	0.8365	0.8389
1.00	0.8413	0.8438	0.8461	0.8485	0.8508	0.8531	0.8554	0.8577	0.8599	0.8621
1.10	0.8643	0.8665	0.8686	0.8708	0.8729	0.8749	0.8770	0.8790	0.8810	0.8830
1.20	0.8849	0.8869	0.8888	0.8907	0.8925	0.8944	0.8962	0.8980	0.8997	0.9015
1.30	0.9032	0.9049	0.9066	0.9082	0.9099	0.9115	0.9131	0.9147	0.9162	0.9177
1.40	0.9192	0.9207	0.9222	0.9236	0.9251	0.9265	0.9279	0.9292	0.9306	0.9319
1.50	0.9332	0.9345	0.9357	0.9370	0.9382	0.9394	0.9406	0.9418	0.9429	0.9441
1.60	0.9452	0.9463	0.9474	0.9484	0.9495	0.9505	0.9515	0.9525	0.9535	0.9545
1.70	0.9554	0.9564	0.9573	0.9582	0.9591	0.9599	0.9608	0.9616	0.9625	0.9633
1.80	0.9641	0.9649	0.9656	0.9664	0.9671	0.9678	0.9686	0.9693	0.9699	0.9706
1.90	0.9713	0.9719	0.9726	0.9732	0.9738	0.9744	0.9750	0.9756	0.9761	0.9767
2.00	0.9772	0.9778	0.9783	0.9788	0.9793	0.9798	0.9803	0.9808	0.9812	0.9817
2.10	0.9821	0.9826	0.9830	0.9834	0.9838	0.9842	0.9846	0.9850	0.9854	0.9857
2.20	0.9861	0.9864	0.9868	0.9871	0.9875	0.9878	0.9881	0.9884	0.9887	0.9890
2.30	0.9893	0.9896	0.9898	0.9901	0.9904	0.9906	0.9909	0.9911	0.9913	0.9916
2.40	0.9918	0.9920	0.9922	0.9925	0.9927	0.9929	0.9931	0.9932	0.9934	0.9936
2.50	0.9938	0.9940	0.9941	0.9943	0.9945	0.9946	0.9948	0.9949	0.9951	0.9952
2.60	0.9953	0.9955	0.9956	0.9957	0.9959	0.9960	0.9961	0.9962	0.9963	0.9964
2.70	0.9965	0.9966	0.9967	0.9968	0.9969	0.9970	0.9971	0.9972	0.9973	0.9974
2.80	0.9974	0.9975	0.9976	0.9977	0.9977	0.9978	0.9979	0.9979	0.9980	0.9981
2.90	0.9981	0.9982	0.9982	0.9983	0.9984	0.9984	0.9985	0.9985	0.9986	0.9986
3.00	0.9987	0.9987	0.9987	0.9988	0.9988	0.9989	0.9989	0.9989	0.9990	0.9990
3.10	0.9990	0.9991	0.9991	0.9991	0.9992	0.9992	0.9992	0.9992	0.9993	0.9993
3.20	0.9993	0.9993	0.9994	0.9994	0.9994	0.9994	0.9994	0.9995	0.9995	0.9995
3.30	0.9995	0.9995	0.9995	0.9996	0.9996	0.9996	0.9996	0.9996	0.9996	0.9997
3.40	0.9997	0.9997	0.9997	0.9997	0.9997	0.9997	0.9997	0.9997	0.9997	0.9998
3.50	0.9998	0.9998	0.9998	0.9998	0.9998	0.9998	0.9998	0.9998	0.9998	0.9998
3.60	0.9998	0.9998	0.9999	0.9999	0.9999	0.9999	0.9999	0.9999	0.9999	0.9999
3.70	0.9999	0.9999	0.9999	0.9999	0.9999	0.9999	0.9999	0.9999	0.9999	0.9999
3.80	0.9999	0.9999	0.9999	0.9999	0.9999	0.9999	0.9999	0.9999	0.9999	0.9999
3.90	1.0000	1.0000	1.0000	1.0000	1.0000	1.0000	1.0000	1.0000	1.0000	1.0000
4.00	1.0000	1.0000	1.0000	1.0000	1.0000	1.0000	1.0000	1.0000	1.0000	1.0000

For example, to find the z-value leaving 2.5 percent of the area/probability in the upper tail, find the element 0.9750 in the body of the table. Read 1.90 at the left end of the element's row and 0.06 at the top of the element's column, to give 1.90 + 0.06 = 1.96. *Table generated with Excel.*

Quantitative Methods for Investment Analysis, Second Edition, by Richard A. DeFusco, CFA, Dennis W. McLeavey, CFA, Jerald E. Pinto, CFA, and David E. Runkle, CFA. Copyright © 2004 by CFA Institute.

Appendix A (continued)
Cumulative Probabilities for a Standard Normal Distribution
$P(Z \leq x) = N(x)$ for $x \leq 0$ or $P(Z \leq z) = N(z)$ for $z \leq 0$

x or z	0	0.01	0.02	0.03	0.04	0.05	0.06	0.07	0.08	0.09
0.0	0.5000	0.4960	0.4920	0.4880	0.4840	0.4801	0.4761	0.4721	0.4681	0.4641
−0.10	0.4602	0.4562	0.4522	0.4483	0.4443	0.4404	0.4364	0.4325	0.4286	0.4247
−0.20	0.4207	0.4168	0.4129	0.4090	0.4052	0.4013	0.3974	0.3936	0.3897	0.3859
−0.30	0.3821	0.3783	0.3745	0.3707	0.3669	0.3632	0.3594	0.3557	0.3520	0.3483
−0.40	0.3446	0.3409	0.3372	0.3336	0.3300	0.3264	0.3228	0.3192	0.3156	0.3121
−0.50	0.3085	0.3050	0.3015	0.2981	0.2946	0.2912	0.2877	0.2843	0.2810	0.2776
−0.60	0.2743	0.2709	0.2676	0.2643	0.2611	0.2578	0.2546	0.2514	0.2483	0.2451
−0.70	0.2420	0.2389	0.2358	0.2327	0.2296	0.2266	0.2236	0.2206	0.2177	0.2148
−0.80	0.2119	0.2090	0.2061	0.2033	0.2005	0.1977	0.1949	0.1922	0.1894	0.1867
−0.90	0.1841	0.1814	0.1788	0.1762	0.1736	0.1711	0.1685	0.1660	0.1635	0.1611
−1.00	0.1587	0.1562	0.1539	0.1515	0.1492	0.1469	0.1446	0.1423	0.1401	0.1379
−1.10	0.1357	0.1335	0.1314	0.1292	0.1271	0.1251	0.1230	0.1210	0.1190	0.1170
−1.20	0.1151	0.1131	0.1112	0.1093	0.1075	0.1056	0.1038	0.1020	0.1003	0.0985
−1.30	0.0968	0.0951	0.0934	0.0918	0.0901	0.0885	0.0869	0.0853	0.0838	0.0823
−1.40	0.0808	0.0793	0.0778	0.0764	0.0749	0.0735	0.0721	0.0708	0.0694	0.0681
−1.50	0.0668	0.0655	0.0643	0.0630	0.0618	0.0606	0.0594	0.0582	0.0571	0.0559
−1.60	0.0548	0.0537	0.0526	0.0516	0.0505	0.0495	0.0485	0.0475	0.0465	0.0455
−1.70	0.0446	0.0436	0.0427	0.0418	0.0409	0.0401	0.0392	0.0384	0.0375	0.0367
−1.80	0.0359	0.0351	0.0344	0.0336	0.0329	0.0322	0.0314	0.0307	0.0301	0.0294
−1.90	0.0287	0.0281	0.0274	0.0268	0.0262	0.0256	0.0250	0.0244	0.0239	0.0233
−2.00	0.0228	0.0222	0.0217	0.0212	0.0207	0.0202	0.0197	0.0192	0.0188	0.0183
−2.10	0.0179	0.0174	0.0170	0.0166	0.0162	0.0158	0.0154	0.0150	0.0146	0.0143
−2.20	0.0139	0.0136	0.0132	0.0129	0.0125	0.0122	0.0119	0.0116	0.0113	0.0110
−2.30	0.0107	0.0104	0.0102	0.0099	0.0096	0.0094	0.0091	0.0089	0.0087	0.0084
−2.40	0.0082	0.0080	0.0078	0.0075	0.0073	0.0071	0.0069	0.0068	0.0066	0.0064
−2.50	0.0062	0.0060	0.0059	0.0057	0.0055	0.0054	0.0052	0.0051	0.0049	0.0048
−2.60	0.0047	0.0045	0.0044	0.0043	0.0041	0.0040	0.0039	0.0038	0.0037	0.0036
−2.70	0.0035	0.0034	0.0033	0.0032	0.0031	0.0030	0.0029	0.0028	0.0027	0.0026
−2.80	0.0026	0.0025	0.0024	0.0023	0.0023	0.0022	0.0021	0.0021	0.0020	0.0019
−2.90	0.0019	0.0018	0.0018	0.0017	0.0016	0.0016	0.0015	0.0015	0.0014	0.0014
−3.00	0.0013	0.0013	0.0013	0.0012	0.0012	0.0011	0.0011	0.0011	0.0010	0.0010
−3.10	0.0010	0.0009	0.0009	0.0009	0.0008	0.0008	0.0008	0.0008	0.0007	0.0007
−3.20	0.0007	0.0007	0.0006	0.0006	0.0006	0.0006	0.0006	0.0005	0.0005	0.0005
−3.30	0.0005	0.0005	0.0005	0.0004	0.0004	0.0004	0.0004	0.0004	0.0004	0.0003
−3.40	0.0003	0.0003	0.0003	0.0003	0.0003	0.0003	0.0003	0.0003	0.0003	0.0002
−3.50	0.0002	0.0002	0.0002	0.0002	0.0002	0.0002	0.0002	0.0002	0.0002	0.0002
−3.60	0.0002	0.0002	0.0001	0.0001	0.0001	0.0001	0.0001	0.0001	0.0001	0.0001
−3.70	0.0001	0.0001	0.0001	0.0001	0.0001	0.0001	0.0001	0.0001	0.0001	0.0001
−3.80	0.0001	0.0001	0.0001	0.0001	0.0001	0.0001	0.0001	0.0001	0.0001	0.0001
−3.90	0.0000	0.0000	0.0000	0.0000	0.0000	0.0000	0.0000	0.0000	0.0000	0.0000
−4.00	0.0000	0.0000	0.0000	0.0000	0.0000	0.0000	0.0000	0.0000	0.0000	0.0000

For example, to find the z-value leaving 2.5 percent of the area/probability in the lower tail, find the element 0.0250 in the body of the table. Read −1.90 at the left end of the element's row and 0.06 at the top of the element's column, to give −1.90 − 0.06 = −1.96. *Table generated with Excel.*

Appendix B

Table of the Student's t-Distribution (One-Tailed Probabilities)

DF	p = 0.10	p = 0.05	p = 0.025	p = 0.01	p = 0.005	DF	p = 0.10	p = 0.05	p = 0.025	p = 0.01	p = 0.005
1	3.078	6.314	12.706	31.821	63.657	31	1.309	1.696	2.040	2.453	2.744
2	1.886	2.920	4.303	6.965	9.925	32	1.309	1.694	2.037	2.449	2.738
3	1.638	2.353	3.182	4.541	5.841	33	1.308	1.692	2.035	2.445	2.733
4	1.533	2.132	2.776	3.747	4.604	34	1.307	1.691	2.032	2.441	2.728
5	1.476	2.015	2.571	3.365	4.032	35	1.306	1.690	2.030	2.438	2.724
6	1.440	1.943	2.447	3.143	3.707	36	1.306	1.688	2.028	2.434	2.719
7	1.415	1.895	2.365	2.998	3.499	37	1.305	1.687	2.026	2.431	2.715
8	1.397	1.860	2.306	2.896	3.355	38	1.304	1.686	2.024	2.429	2.712
9	1.383	1.833	2.262	2.821	3.250	39	1.304	1.685	2.023	2.426	2.708
10	1.372	1.812	2.228	2.764	3.169	40	1.303	1.684	2.021	2.423	2.704
11	1.363	1.796	2.201	2.718	3.106	41	1.303	1.683	2.020	2.421	2.701
12	1.356	1.782	2.179	2.681	3.055	42	1.302	1.682	2.018	2.418	2.698
13	1.350	1.771	2.160	2.650	3.012	43	1.302	1.681	2.017	2.416	2.695
14	1.345	1.761	2.145	2.624	2.977	44	1.301	1.680	2.015	2.414	2.692
15	1.341	1.753	2.131	2.602	2.947	45	1.301	1.679	2.014	2.412	2.690
16	1.337	1.746	2.120	2.583	2.921	46	1.300	1.679	2.013	2.410	2.687
17	1.333	1.740	2.110	2.567	2.898	47	1.300	1.678	2.012	2.408	2.685
18	1.330	1.734	2.101	2.552	2.878	48	1.299	1.677	2.011	2.407	2.682
19	1.328	1.729	2.093	2.539	2.861	49	1.299	1.677	2.010	2.405	2.680
20	1.325	1.725	2.086	2.528	2.845	50	1.299	1.676	2.009	2.403	2.678
21	1.323	1.721	2.080	2.518	2.831	60	1.296	1.671	2.000	2.390	2.660
22	1.321	1.717	2.074	2.508	2.819	70	1.294	1.667	1.994	2.381	2.648
23	1.319	1.714	2.069	2.500	2.807	80	1.292	1.664	1.990	2.374	2.639
24	1.318	1.711	2.064	2.492	2.797	90	1.291	1.662	1.987	2.368	2.632
25	1.316	1.708	2.060	2.485	2.787	100	1.290	1.660	1.984	2.364	2.626
26	1.315	1.706	2.056	2.479	2.779	110	1.289	1.659	1.982	2.361	2.621
27	1.314	1.703	2.052	2.473	2.771	120	1.289	1.658	1.980	2.358	2.617
28	1.313	1.701	2.048	2.467	2.763	200	1.286	1.653	1.972	2.345	2.601
29	1.311	1.699	2.045	2.462	2.756	∞	1.282	1.645	1.960	2.326	2.576
30	1.310	1.697	2.042	2.457	2.750						

To find a critical t-value, enter the table with df and a specified value for α, the significance level. For example, with 5 DF, $\alpha = 0.05$ and a one-tailed test, the desired probability in the tail would be $p = 0.05$ and the critical t-value would be $t(5, 0.05) = 2.015$. With $\alpha = 0.05$ and a two-tailed test, the desired probability in each tail would be $p = 0.025 = \alpha/2$, giving $t(0.025) = 2.571$. Table generated using Excel.

Quantitative Methods for Investment Analysis, Second Edition, by Richard A. DeFusco, CFA, Dennis W. McLeavey, CFA, Jerald E. Pinto, CFA, and David E. Runkle, CFA. Copyright © 2004 by CFA Institute.

Appendix C

Values of χ^2 (Degrees of Freedom, Level of Significance)

Degrees of Freedom	Probability in Right Tail								
	0.99	0.975	0.95	0.9	0.1	0.05	0.025	0.01	0.005
1	0.000157	0.000982	0.003932	0.0158	2.706	3.841	5.024	6.635	7.879
2	0.020100	0.050636	0.102586	0.2107	4.605	5.991	7.378	9.210	10.597
3	0.1148	0.2158	0.3518	0.5844	6.251	7.815	9.348	11.345	12.838
4	0.297	0.484	0.711	1.064	7.779	9.488	11.143	13.277	14.860
5	0.554	0.831	1.145	1.610	9.236	11.070	12.832	15.086	16.750
6	0.872	1.237	1.635	2.204	10.645	12.592	14.449	16.812	18.548
7	1.239	1.690	2.167	2.833	12.017	14.067	16.013	18.475	20.278
8	1.647	2.180	2.733	3.490	13.362	15.507	17.535	20.090	21.955
9	2.088	2.700	3.325	4.168	14.684	16.919	19.023	21.666	23.589
10	2.558	3.247	3.940	4.865	15.987	18.307	20.483	23.209	25.188
11	3.053	3.816	4.575	5.578	17.275	19.675	21.920	24.725	26.757
12	3.571	4.404	5.226	6.304	18.549	21.026	23.337	26.217	28.300
13	4.107	5.009	5.892	7.041	19.812	22.362	24.736	27.688	29.819
14	4.660	5.629	6.571	7.790	21.064	23.685	26.119	29.141	31.319
15	5.229	6.262	7.261	8.547	22.307	24.996	27.488	30.578	32.801
16	5.812	6.908	7.962	9.312	23.542	26.296	28.845	32.000	34.267
17	6.408	7.564	8.672	10.085	24.769	27.587	30.191	33.409	35.718
18	7.015	8.231	9.390	10.865	25.989	28.869	31.526	34.805	37.156
19	7.633	8.907	10.117	11.651	27.204	30.144	32.852	36.191	38.582
20	8.260	9.591	10.851	12.443	28.412	31.410	34.170	37.566	39.997
21	8.897	10.283	11.591	13.240	29.615	32.671	35.479	38.932	41.401
22	9.542	10.982	12.338	14.041	30.813	33.924	36.781	40.289	42.796
23	10.196	11.689	13.091	14.848	32.007	35.172	38.076	41.638	44.181
24	10.856	12.401	13.848	15.659	33.196	36.415	39.364	42.980	45.558
25	11.524	13.120	14.611	16.473	34.382	37.652	40.646	44.314	46.928
26	12.198	13.844	15.379	17.292	35.563	38.885	41.923	45.642	48.290
27	12.878	14.573	16.151	18.114	36.741	40.113	43.195	46.963	49.645
28	13.565	15.308	16.928	18.939	37.916	41.337	44.461	48.278	50.994
29	14.256	16.047	17.708	19.768	39.087	42.557	45.722	49.588	52.335
30	14.953	16.791	18.493	20.599	40.256	43.773	46.979	50.892	53.672
50	29.707	32.357	34.764	37.689	63.167	67.505	71.420	76.154	79.490
60	37.485	40.482	43.188	46.459	74.397	79.082	83.298	88.379	91.952
80	53.540	57.153	60.391	64.278	96.578	101.879	106.629	112.329	116.321
100	70.065	74.222	77.929	82.358	118.498	124.342	129.561	135.807	140.170

To have a probability of 0.05 in the right tail when DF = 5, the tabled value is $\chi^2(5, 0.05)$ = 11.070.

Quantitative Methods for Investment Analysis, Second Edition, by Richard A. DeFusco, CFA, Dennis W. McLeavey, CFA, Jerald E. Pinto, CFA, and David E. Runkle, CFA. Copyright © 2004 by CFA Institute.

Appendix D
Table of the F-Distribution

Panel A. Critical values for right-hand tail area equal to 0.05

Numerator: DF$_1$ and Denominator: DF$_2$

DF2 \ DF1	1	2	3	4	5	6	7	8	9	10	11	12	15	20	21	22	23	24	25	30	40	60	120	∞
1	161	200	216	225	230	234	237	239	241	242	243	244	246	248	248	249	249	249	249	250	251	252	253	254
2	18.5	19.0	19.2	19.2	19.3	19.3	19.4	19.4	19.4	19.4	19.4	19.4	19.4	19.4	19.4	19.5	19.5	19.5	19.5	19.5	19.5	19.5	19.5	19.5
3	10.1	9.55	9.28	9.12	9.01	8.94	8.89	8.85	8.81	8.79	8.76	8.74	8.70	8.66	8.65	8.65	8.64	8.64	8.63	8.62	8.59	8.57	8.55	8.53
4	7.71	6.94	6.59	6.39	6.26	6.16	6.09	6.04	6.00	5.96	5.94	5.91	5.86	5.80	5.79	5.79	5.78	5.77	5.77	5.75	5.72	5.69	5.66	5.63
5	6.61	5.79	5.41	5.19	5.05	4.95	4.88	4.82	4.77	4.74	4.70	4.68	4.62	4.56	4.55	4.54	4.53	4.53	4.52	4.50	4.46	4.43	4.40	4.37
6	5.99	5.14	4.76	4.53	4.39	4.28	4.21	4.15	4.10	4.06	4.03	4.00	3.94	3.87	3.86	3.86	3.85	3.84	3.83	3.81	3.77	3.74	3.70	3.67
7	5.59	4.74	4.35	4.12	3.97	3.87	3.79	3.73	3.68	3.64	3.60	3.57	3.51	3.44	3.43	3.43	3.42	3.41	3.40	3.38	3.34	3.30	3.27	3.23
8	5.32	4.46	4.07	3.84	3.69	3.58	3.50	3.44	3.39	3.35	3.31	3.28	3.22	3.15	3.14	3.13	3.12	3.12	3.11	3.08	3.04	3.01	2.97	2.93
9	5.12	4.26	3.86	3.63	3.48	3.37	3.29	3.23	3.18	3.14	3.10	3.07	3.01	2.94	2.93	2.92	2.91	2.90	2.89	2.86	2.83	2.79	2.75	2.71
10	4.96	4.10	3.71	3.48	3.33	3.22	3.14	3.07	3.02	2.98	2.94	2.91	2.85	2.77	2.76	2.75	2.75	2.74	2.73	2.70	2.66	2.62	2.58	2.54
11	4.84	3.98	3.59	3.36	3.20	3.09	3.01	2.95	2.90	2.85	2.82	2.79	2.72	2.65	2.64	2.63	2.62	2.61	2.60	2.57	2.53	2.49	2.45	2.40
12	4.75	3.89	3.49	3.26	3.11	3.00	2.91	2.85	2.80	2.75	2.72	2.69	2.62	2.54	2.53	2.52	2.51	2.51	2.50	2.47	2.43	2.38	2.34	2.30
13	4.67	3.81	3.41	3.18	3.03	2.92	2.83	2.77	2.71	2.67	2.63	2.60	2.53	2.46	2.45	2.44	2.43	2.42	2.41	2.38	2.34	2.30	2.25	2.21
14	4.60	3.74	3.34	3.11	2.96	2.85	2.76	2.70	2.65	2.60	2.57	2.53	2.46	2.39	2.38	2.37	2.36	2.35	2.34	2.31	2.27	2.22	2.18	2.13
15	4.54	3.68	3.29	3.06	2.90	2.79	2.71	2.64	2.59	2.54	2.51	2.48	2.40	2.33	2.32	2.31	2.30	2.29	2.28	2.25	2.20	2.16	2.11	2.07
16	4.49	3.63	3.24	3.01	2.85	2.74	2.66	2.59	2.54	2.49	2.46	2.42	2.35	2.28	2.26	2.25	2.24	2.24	2.23	2.19	2.15	2.11	2.06	2.01
17	4.45	3.59	3.20	2.96	2.81	2.70	2.61	2.55	2.49	2.45	2.41	2.38	2.31	2.23	2.22	2.21	2.20	2.19	2.18	2.15	2.10	2.06	2.01	1.96
18	4.41	3.55	3.16	2.93	2.77	2.66	2.58	2.51	2.46	2.41	2.37	2.34	2.27	2.19	2.18	2.17	2.16	2.15	2.14	2.11	2.06	2.02	1.97	1.92
19	4.38	3.52	3.13	2.90	2.74	2.63	2.54	2.48	2.42	2.38	2.34	2.31	2.23	2.16	2.14	2.13	2.12	2.11	2.11	2.07	2.03	1.98	1.93	1.88
20	4.35	3.49	3.10	2.87	2.71	2.60	2.51	2.45	2.39	2.35	2.31	2.28	2.20	2.12	2.11	2.10	2.09	2.08	2.07	2.04	1.99	1.95	1.90	1.84
21	4.32	3.47	3.07	2.84	2.68	2.57	2.49	2.42	2.37	2.32	2.28	2.25	2.18	2.10	2.08	2.07	2.06	2.05	2.05	2.01	1.96	1.92	1.87	1.81
22	4.30	3.44	3.05	2.82	2.66	2.55	2.46	2.40	2.34	2.30	2.26	2.23	2.15	2.07	2.06	2.05	2.04	2.03	2.02	1.98	1.94	1.89	1.84	1.78
23	4.28	3.42	3.03	2.80	2.64	2.53	2.44	2.37	2.32	2.27	2.24	2.20	2.13	2.05	2.04	2.02	2.01	2.01	2.00	1.96	1.91	1.86	1.81	1.76
24	4.26	3.40	3.01	2.78	2.62	2.51	2.42	2.36	2.30	2.25	2.22	2.18	2.11	2.03	2.01	2.00	1.99	1.98	1.97	1.94	1.89	1.84	1.79	1.73
25	4.24	3.39	2.99	2.76	2.60	2.49	2.40	2.34	2.28	2.24	2.20	2.16	2.09	2.01	2.00	1.98	1.97	1.96	1.96	1.92	1.87	1.82	1.77	1.71
30	4.17	3.32	2.92	2.69	2.53	2.42	2.33	2.27	2.21	2.16	2.13	2.09	2.01	1.93	1.92	1.91	1.90	1.89	1.88	1.84	1.79	1.74	1.68	1.62
40	4.08	3.23	2.84	2.61	2.45	2.34	2.25	2.18	2.12	2.08	2.04	2.00	1.92	1.84	1.83	1.81	1.80	1.79	1.78	1.74	1.69	1.64	1.58	1.51
60	4.00	3.15	2.76	2.53	2.37	2.25	2.17	2.10	2.04	1.99	1.95	1.92	1.84	1.75	1.73	1.72	1.71	1.70	1.69	1.65	1.59	1.53	1.47	1.39
120	3.92	3.07	2.68	2.45	2.29	2.18	2.09	2.02	1.96	1.91	1.87	1.83	1.75	1.66	1.64	1.63	1.62	1.61	1.60	1.55	1.50	1.43	1.35	1.25
Infinity	3.84	3.00	2.60	2.37	2.21	2.10	2.01	1.94	1.88	1.83	1.79	1.75	1.67	1.57	1.56	1.54	1.53	1.52	1.51	1.46	1.39	1.32	1.22	1.00

Panel B. Critical values for right-hand tail area equal to 0.025

Numerator: DF₁ and Denominator: DF₂

DF2 \ DF1:1	2	3	4	5	6	7	8	9	10	11	12	15	20	21	22	23	24	25	30	40	60	120	∞
1	648	799	864	900	922	937	948	957	963	969	973	977	985	993	994	995	996	997	998	1001	1006	1010	1014	1018
2	38.51	39.00	39.17	39.25	39.30	39.33	39.36	39.37	39.39	39.40	39.41	39.41	39.43	39.45	39.45	39.45	39.45	39.46	39.46	39.46	39.47	39.48	39.49	39.50
3	17.44	16.04	15.44	15.10	14.88	14.73	14.62	14.54	14.47	14.42	14.37	14.34	14.25	14.17	14.16	14.14	14.13	14.12	14.12	14.08	14.04	13.99	13.95	13.90
4	12.22	10.65	9.98	9.60	9.36	9.20	9.07	8.98	8.90	8.84	8.79	8.75	8.66	8.56	8.55	8.53	8.52	8.51	8.50	8.46	8.41	8.36	8.31	8.26
5	10.01	8.43	7.76	7.39	7.15	6.98	6.85	6.76	6.68	6.62	6.57	6.52	6.43	6.33	6.31	6.30	6.29	6.28	6.27	6.23	6.18	6.12	6.07	6.02
6	8.81	7.26	6.60	6.23	5.99	5.82	5.70	5.60	5.52	5.46	5.41	5.37	5.27	5.17	5.15	5.14	5.13	5.12	5.11	5.07	5.01	4.96	4.90	4.85
7	8.07	6.54	5.89	5.52	5.29	5.12	4.99	4.90	4.82	4.76	4.71	4.67	4.57	4.47	4.45	4.44	4.43	4.41	4.40	4.36	4.31	4.25	4.20	4.14
8	7.57	6.06	5.42	5.05	4.82	4.65	4.53	4.43	4.36	4.30	4.24	4.20	4.10	4.00	3.98	3.97	3.96	3.95	3.94	3.89	3.84	3.78	3.73	3.67
9	7.21	5.71	5.08	4.72	4.48	4.32	4.20	4.10	4.03	3.96	3.91	3.87	3.77	3.67	3.65	3.64	3.63	3.61	3.60	3.56	3.51	3.45	3.39	3.33
10	6.94	5.46	4.83	4.47	4.24	4.07	3.95	3.85	3.78	3.72	3.66	3.62	3.52	3.42	3.40	3.39	3.38	3.37	3.35	3.31	3.26	3.20	3.14	3.08
11	6.72	5.26	4.63	4.28	4.04	3.88	3.76	3.66	3.59	3.53	3.47	3.43	3.33	3.23	3.21	3.20	3.18	3.17	3.16	3.12	3.06	3.00	2.94	2.88
12	6.55	5.10	4.47	4.12	3.89	3.73	3.61	3.51	3.44	3.37	3.32	3.28	3.18	3.07	3.06	3.04	3.03	3.02	3.01	2.96	2.91	2.85	2.79	2.72
13	6.41	4.97	4.35	4.00	3.77	3.60	3.48	3.39	3.31	3.25	3.20	3.15	3.05	2.95	2.93	2.92	2.91	2.89	2.88	2.84	2.78	2.72	2.66	2.60
14	6.30	4.86	4.24	3.89	3.66	3.50	3.38	3.29	3.21	3.15	3.09	3.05	2.95	2.84	2.83	2.81	2.80	2.79	2.78	2.73	2.67	2.61	2.55	2.49
15	6.20	4.77	4.15	3.80	3.58	3.41	3.29	3.20	3.12	3.06	3.01	2.96	2.86	2.76	2.74	2.73	2.71	2.70	2.69	2.64	2.59	2.52	2.46	2.40
16	6.12	4.69	4.08	3.73	3.50	3.34	3.22	3.12	3.05	2.99	2.93	2.89	2.79	2.68	2.67	2.65	2.64	2.63	2.61	2.57	2.51	2.45	2.38	2.32
17	6.04	4.62	4.01	3.66	3.44	3.28	3.16	3.06	2.98	2.92	2.87	2.82	2.72	2.62	2.60	2.59	2.57	2.56	2.55	2.50	2.44	2.38	2.32	2.25
18	5.98	4.56	3.95	3.61	3.38	3.22	3.10	3.01	2.93	2.87	2.81	2.77	2.67	2.56	2.54	2.53	2.52	2.50	2.49	2.44	2.38	2.32	2.26	2.19
19	5.92	4.51	3.90	3.56	3.33	3.17	3.05	2.96	2.88	2.82	2.76	2.72	2.62	2.51	2.49	2.48	2.46	2.45	2.44	2.39	2.33	2.27	2.20	2.13
20	5.87	4.46	3.86	3.51	3.29	3.13	3.01	2.91	2.84	2.77	2.72	2.68	2.57	2.46	2.45	2.43	2.42	2.41	2.40	2.35	2.29	2.22	2.16	2.09
21	5.83	4.42	3.82	3.48	3.25	3.09	2.97	2.87	2.80	2.73	2.68	2.64	2.53	2.42	2.41	2.39	2.38	2.37	2.36	2.31	2.25	2.18	2.11	2.04
22	5.79	4.38	3.78	3.44	3.22	3.05	2.93	2.84	2.76	2.70	2.65	2.60	2.50	2.39	2.37	2.36	2.34	2.33	2.32	2.27	2.21	2.14	2.08	2.00
23	5.75	4.35	3.75	3.41	3.18	3.02	2.90	2.81	2.73	2.67	2.62	2.57	2.47	2.36	2.34	2.33	2.31	2.30	2.29	2.24	2.18	2.11	2.04	1.97
24	5.72	4.32	3.72	3.38	3.15	2.99	2.87	2.78	2.70	2.64	2.59	2.54	2.44	2.33	2.31	2.30	2.28	2.27	2.26	2.21	2.15	2.08	2.01	1.94
25	5.69	4.29	3.69	3.35	3.13	2.97	2.85	2.75	2.68	2.61	2.56	2.51	2.41	2.30	2.28	2.27	2.26	2.24	2.23	2.18	2.12	2.05	1.98	1.91
30	5.57	4.18	3.59	3.25	3.03	2.87	2.75	2.65	2.57	2.51	2.46	2.41	2.31	2.20	2.18	2.16	2.15	2.14	2.12	2.07	2.01	1.94	1.87	1.79
40	5.42	4.05	3.46	3.13	2.90	2.74	2.62	2.53	2.45	2.39	2.33	2.29	2.18	2.07	2.05	2.03	2.02	2.01	1.99	1.94	1.88	1.80	1.72	1.64
60	5.29	3.93	3.34	3.01	2.79	2.63	2.51	2.41	2.33	2.27	2.22	2.17	2.06	1.94	1.93	1.91	1.90	1.88	1.87	1.82	1.74	1.67	1.58	1.48
120	5.15	3.80	3.23	2.89	2.67	2.52	2.39	2.30	2.22	2.16	2.10	2.05	1.94	1.82	1.81	1.79	1.77	1.76	1.75	1.69	1.61	1.53	1.43	1.31
Infinity	5.02	3.69	3.12	2.79	2.57	2.41	2.29	2.19	2.11	2.05	1.99	1.94	1.83	1.71	1.69	1.67	1.66	1.64	1.63	1.57	1.48	1.39	1.27	1.00

(continued)

Appendix D (continued)
Table of the F-Distribution

Panel C. Critical values for right-hand tail area equal to 0.01

Numerator: DF$_1$, and Denominator: DF$_2$

DF2:\DF1:	1	2	3	4	5	6	7	8	9	10	11	12	15	20	21	22	23	24	25	30	40	60	120	∞
1	4052	5000	5403	5625	5764	5859	5928	5982	6023	6056	6083	6106	6157	6209	6216	6223	6229	6235	6240	6261	6287	6313	6339	6366
2	98.5	99.0	99.2	99.2	99.3	99.3	99.4	99.4	99.4	99.4	99.4	99.4	99.4	99.4	99.5	99.5	99.5	99.5	99.5	99.5	99.5	99.5	99.5	99.5
3	34.1	30.8	29.5	28.7	28.2	27.9	27.7	27.5	27.3	27.2	27.1	27.1	26.9	26.7	26.7	26.6	26.6	26.6	26.6	26.5	26.4	26.3	26.2	26.1
4	21.2	18.0	16.7	16.0	15.5	15.2	15.0	14.8	14.7	14.5	14.5	14.4	14.2	14.0	14.0	14.0	13.9	13.9	13.9	13.8	13.7	13.7	13.6	13.5
5	16.3	13.3	12.1	11.4	11.0	10.7	10.5	10.3	10.2	10.1	10.0	9.89	9.72	9.55	9.53	9.51	9.49	9.47	9.45	9.38	9.29	9.20	9.11	9.02
6	13.7	10.9	9.78	9.15	8.75	8.47	8.26	8.10	7.98	7.87	7.79	7.72	7.56	7.40	7.37	7.35	7.33	7.31	7.30	7.23	7.14	7.06	6.97	6.88
7	12.2	9.55	8.45	7.85	7.46	7.19	6.99	6.84	6.72	6.62	6.54	6.47	6.31	6.16	6.13	6.11	6.09	6.07	6.06	5.99	5.91	5.82	5.74	5.65
8	11.3	8.65	7.59	7.01	6.63	6.37	6.18	6.03	5.91	5.81	5.73	5.67	5.52	5.36	5.34	5.32	5.30	5.28	5.26	5.20	5.12	5.03	4.95	4.86
9	10.6	8.02	6.99	6.42	6.06	5.80	5.61	5.47	5.35	5.26	5.18	5.11	4.96	4.81	4.79	4.77	4.75	4.73	4.71	4.65	4.57	4.48	4.40	4.31
10	10.0	7.56	6.55	5.99	5.64	5.39	5.20	5.06	4.94	4.85	4.77	4.71	4.56	4.41	4.38	4.36	4.34	4.33	4.31	4.25	4.17	4.08	4.00	3.91
11	9.65	7.21	6.22	5.67	5.32	5.07	4.89	4.74	4.63	4.54	4.46	4.40	4.25	4.10	4.08	4.06	4.04	4.02	4.01	3.94	3.86	3.78	3.69	3.60
12	9.33	6.93	5.95	5.41	5.06	4.82	4.64	4.50	4.39	4.30	4.22	4.16	4.01	3.86	3.84	3.82	3.80	3.78	3.76	3.70	3.62	3.54	3.45	3.36
13	9.07	6.70	5.74	5.21	4.86	4.62	4.44	4.30	4.19	4.10	4.02	3.96	3.82	3.66	3.64	3.62	3.60	3.59	3.57	3.51	3.43	3.34	3.25	3.17
14	8.86	6.51	5.56	5.04	4.70	4.46	4.28	4.14	4.03	3.94	3.86	3.80	3.66	3.51	3.48	3.46	3.44	3.43	3.41	3.35	3.27	3.18	3.09	3.00
15	8.68	6.36	5.42	4.89	4.56	4.32	4.14	4.00	3.89	3.80	3.73	3.67	3.52	3.37	3.35	3.33	3.31	3.29	3.28	3.21	3.13	3.05	2.96	2.87
16	8.53	6.23	5.29	4.77	4.44	4.20	4.03	3.89	3.78	3.69	3.62	3.55	3.41	3.26	3.24	3.22	3.20	3.18	3.16	3.10	3.02	2.93	2.84	2.75
17	8.40	6.11	5.19	4.67	4.34	4.10	3.93	3.79	3.68	3.59	3.52	3.46	3.31	3.16	3.14	3.12	3.10	3.08	3.07	3.00	2.92	2.83	2.75	2.65
18	8.29	6.01	5.09	4.58	4.25	4.01	3.84	3.71	3.60	3.51	3.43	3.37	3.23	3.08	3.05	3.03	3.02	3.00	2.98	2.92	2.84	2.75	2.66	2.57
19	8.19	5.93	5.01	4.50	4.17	3.94	3.77	3.63	3.52	3.43	3.36	3.30	3.15	3.00	2.98	2.96	2.94	2.92	2.91	2.84	2.76	2.67	2.58	2.49
20	8.10	5.85	4.94	4.43	4.10	3.87	3.70	3.56	3.46	3.37	3.29	3.23	3.09	2.94	2.92	2.90	2.88	2.86	2.84	2.78	2.69	2.61	2.52	2.42
21	8.02	5.78	4.87	4.37	4.04	3.81	3.64	3.51	3.40	3.31	3.24	3.17	3.03	2.88	2.86	2.84	2.82	2.80	2.79	2.72	2.64	2.55	2.46	2.36
22	7.95	5.72	4.82	4.31	3.99	3.76	3.59	3.45	3.35	3.26	3.18	3.12	2.98	2.83	2.81	2.78	2.77	2.75	2.73	2.67	2.58	2.50	2.40	2.31
23	7.88	5.66	4.76	4.26	3.94	3.71	3.54	3.41	3.30	3.21	3.14	3.07	2.93	2.78	2.76	2.74	2.72	2.70	2.69	2.62	2.54	2.45	2.35	2.26
24	7.82	5.61	4.72	4.22	3.90	3.67	3.50	3.36	3.26	3.17	3.09	3.03	2.89	2.74	2.72	2.70	2.68	2.66	2.64	2.58	2.49	2.40	2.31	2.21
25	7.77	5.57	4.68	4.18	3.86	3.63	3.46	3.32	3.22	3.13	3.06	2.99	2.85	2.70	2.68	2.66	2.64	2.62	2.60	2.53	2.45	2.36	2.27	2.17
30	7.56	5.39	4.51	4.02	3.70	3.47	3.30	3.17	3.07	2.98	2.91	2.84	2.70	2.55	2.53	2.51	2.49	2.47	2.45	2.39	2.30	2.21	2.11	2.01
40	7.31	5.18	4.31	3.83	3.51	3.29	3.12	2.99	2.89	2.80	2.73	2.66	2.52	2.37	2.35	2.33	2.31	2.29	2.27	2.20	2.11	2.02	1.92	1.80
60	7.08	4.98	4.13	3.65	3.34	3.12	2.95	2.82	2.72	2.63	2.56	2.50	2.35	2.20	2.17	2.15	2.13	2.12	2.10	2.03	1.94	1.84	1.73	1.60
120	6.85	4.79	3.95	3.48	3.17	2.96	2.79	2.66	2.56	2.47	2.40	2.34	2.19	2.03	2.01	1.99	1.97	1.95	1.93	1.86	1.76	1.66	1.53	1.38
Infinity	6.63	4.61	3.78	3.32	3.02	2.80	2.64	2.51	2.41	2.32	2.25	2.18	2.04	1.88	1.85	1.83	1.81	1.79	1.77	1.70	1.59	1.47	1.32	1.00

Panel D. Critical values for right-hand tail area equal to 0.005

Numerator: DF_1 and Denominator: DF_2

DF1:	1	2	3	4	5	6	7	8	9	10	11	12	15	20	21	22	23	24	25	30	40	60	120	∞
DF2: 1	16211	20000	21615	22500	23056	23437	23715	23925	24091	24222	24334	24426	24630	24836	24863	24892	24915	24940	24959	25044	25146	25253	25359	25464
2	198.5	199.0	199.2	199.2	199.3	199.3	199.4	199.4	199.4	199.4	199.4	199.4	199.4	199.4	199.4	199.4	199.4	199.4	199.4	199.5	199.5	199.5	199.5	200
3	55.55	49.80	47.47	46.20	45.39	44.84	44.43	44.13	43.88	43.68	43.52	43.39	43.08	42.78	42.73	42.69	42.66	42.62	42.59	42.47	42.31	42.15	41.99	41.83
4	31.33	26.28	24.26	23.15	22.46	21.98	21.62	21.35	21.14	20.97	20.82	20.70	20.44	20.17	20.13	20.09	20.06	20.03	20.00	19.89	19.75	19.61	19.47	19.32
5	22.78	18.31	16.53	15.56	14.94	14.51	14.20	13.96	13.77	13.62	13.49	13.38	13.15	12.90	12.87	12.84	12.81	12.78	12.76	12.66	12.53	12.40	12.27	12.14
6	18.63	14.54	12.92	12.03	11.46	11.07	10.79	10.57	10.39	10.25	10.13	10.03	9.81	9.59	9.56	9.53	9.50	9.47	9.45	9.36	9.24	9.12	9.00	8.88
7	16.24	12.40	10.88	10.05	9.52	9.16	8.89	8.68	8.51	8.38	8.27	8.18	7.97	7.75	7.72	7.69	7.67	7.64	7.62	7.53	7.42	7.31	7.19	7.08
8	14.69	11.04	9.60	8.81	8.30	7.95	7.69	7.50	7.34	7.21	7.10	7.01	6.81	6.61	6.58	6.55	6.53	6.50	6.48	6.40	6.29	6.18	6.06	5.95
9	13.61	10.11	8.72	7.96	7.47	7.13	6.88	6.69	6.54	6.42	6.31	6.23	6.03	5.83	5.80	5.78	5.75	5.73	5.71	5.62	5.52	5.41	5.30	5.19
10	12.83	9.43	8.08	7.34	6.87	6.54	6.30	6.12	5.97	5.85	5.75	5.66	5.47	5.27	5.25	5.22	5.20	5.17	5.15	5.07	4.97	4.86	4.75	4.64
11	12.23	8.91	7.60	6.88	6.42	6.10	5.86	5.68	5.54	5.42	5.32	5.24	5.05	4.86	4.83	4.80	4.78	4.76	4.74	4.65	4.55	4.45	4.34	4.23
12	11.75	8.51	7.23	6.52	6.07	5.76	5.52	5.35	5.20	5.09	4.99	4.91	4.72	4.53	4.50	4.48	4.45	4.43	4.41	4.33	4.23	4.12	4.01	3.90
13	11.37	8.19	6.93	6.23	5.79	5.48	5.25	5.08	4.94	4.82	4.72	4.64	4.46	4.27	4.24	4.22	4.19	4.17	4.15	4.07	3.97	3.87	3.76	3.65
14	11.06	7.92	6.68	6.00	5.56	5.26	5.03	4.86	4.72	4.60	4.51	4.43	4.25	4.06	4.03	4.01	3.98	3.96	3.94	3.86	3.76	3.66	3.55	3.44
15	10.80	7.70	6.48	5.80	5.37	5.07	4.85	4.67	4.54	4.42	4.33	4.25	4.07	3.88	3.86	3.83	3.81	3.79	3.77	3.69	3.59	3.48	3.37	3.26
16	10.58	7.51	6.30	5.64	5.21	4.91	4.69	4.52	4.38	4.27	4.18	4.10	3.92	3.73	3.71	3.68	3.66	3.64	3.62	3.54	3.44	3.33	3.22	3.11
17	10.38	7.35	6.16	5.50	5.07	4.78	4.56	4.39	4.25	4.14	4.05	3.97	3.79	3.61	3.58	3.56	3.53	3.51	3.49	3.41	3.31	3.21	3.10	2.98
18	10.22	7.21	6.03	5.37	4.96	4.66	4.44	4.28	4.14	4.03	3.94	3.86	3.68	3.50	3.47	3.45	3.42	3.40	3.38	3.30	3.20	3.10	2.99	2.87
19	10.07	7.09	5.92	5.27	4.85	4.56	4.34	4.18	4.04	3.93	3.84	3.76	3.59	3.40	3.37	3.35	3.33	3.31	3.29	3.21	3.11	3.00	2.89	2.78
20	9.94	6.99	5.82	5.17	4.76	4.47	4.26	4.09	3.96	3.85	3.76	3.68	3.50	3.32	3.29	3.27	3.24	3.22	3.20	3.12	3.02	2.92	2.81	2.69
21	9.83	6.89	5.73	5.09	4.68	4.39	4.18	4.01	3.88	3.77	3.68	3.60	3.43	3.24	3.22	3.19	3.17	3.15	3.13	3.05	2.95	2.84	2.73	2.61
22	9.73	6.81	5.65	5.02	4.61	4.32	4.11	3.94	3.81	3.70	3.61	3.54	3.36	3.18	3.15	3.12	3.10	3.08	3.06	2.98	2.88	2.77	2.66	2.55
23	9.63	6.73	5.58	4.95	4.54	4.26	4.05	3.88	3.75	3.64	3.55	3.47	3.30	3.12	3.09	3.06	3.04	3.02	3.00	2.92	2.82	2.71	2.60	2.48
24	9.55	6.66	5.52	4.89	4.49	4.20	3.99	3.83	3.69	3.59	3.50	3.42	3.25	3.06	3.04	3.01	2.99	2.97	2.95	2.87	2.77	2.66	2.55	2.43
25	9.48	6.60	5.46	4.84	4.43	4.15	3.94	3.78	3.64	3.54	3.45	3.37	3.20	3.01	2.99	2.96	2.94	2.92	2.90	2.82	2.72	2.61	2.50	2.38
30	9.18	6.35	5.24	4.62	4.23	3.95	3.74	3.58	3.45	3.34	3.25	3.18	3.01	2.82	2.80	2.77	2.75	2.73	2.71	2.63	2.52	2.42	2.30	2.18
40	8.83	6.07	4.98	4.37	3.99	3.71	3.51	3.35	3.22	3.12	3.03	2.95	2.78	2.60	2.57	2.55	2.52	2.50	2.48	2.40	2.30	2.18	2.06	1.93
60	8.49	5.79	4.73	4.14	3.76	3.49	3.29	3.13	3.01	2.90	2.82	2.74	2.57	2.39	2.36	2.33	2.31	2.29	2.27	2.19	2.08	1.96	1.83	1.69
120	8.18	5.54	4.50	3.92	3.55	3.28	3.09	2.93	2.81	2.71	2.62	2.54	2.37	2.19	2.16	2.13	2.11	2.09	2.07	1.98	1.87	1.75	1.61	1.43
Infinity	7.88	5.30	4.28	3.72	3.35	3.09	2.90	2.74	2.62	2.52	2.43	2.36	2.19	2.00	1.97	1.95	1.92	1.90	1.88	1.79	1.67	1.53	1.36	1.00

With 1 degree of freedom (DF) in the numerator and 3 DF in the denominator, the critical F-value is 10.1 for a right-hand tail area equal to 0.05.

Quantitative Methods for Investment Analysis, Second Edition, by Richard A. DeFusco, CFA, Dennis W. McLeavey, CFA, Jerald E. Pinto, CFA, and David E. Runkle, CFA. Copyright © 2004 by CFA Institute.

Appendix E
Critical Values for the Durbin-Watson Statistic ($\alpha = .05$)

n	$K=1$ d_l	d_u	$K=2$ d_l	d_u	$K=3$ d_l	d_u	$K=4$ d_l	d_u	$K=5$ d_l	d_u
15	1.08	1.36	0.95	1.54	0.82	1.75	0.69	1.97	0.56	2.21
16	1.10	1.37	0.98	1.54	0.86	1.73	0.74	1.93	0.62	2.15
17	1.13	1.38	1.02	1.54	0.90	1.71	0.78	1.90	0.67	2.10
18	1.16	1.39	1.05	1.53	0.93	1.69	0.82	1.87	0.71	2.06
19	1.18	1.40	1.08	1.53	0.97	1.68	0.86	1.85	0.75	2.02
20	1.20	1.41	1.10	1.54	1.00	1.68	0.90	1.83	0.79	1.99
21	1.22	1.42	1.13	1.54	1.03	1.67	0.93	1.81	0.83	1.96
22	1.24	1.43	1.15	1.54	1.05	1.66	0.96	1.80	0.86	1.94
23	1.26	1.44	1.17	1.54	1.08	1.66	0.99	1.79	0.90	1.92
24	1.27	1.45	1.19	1.55	1.10	1.66	1.01	1.78	0.93	1.90
25	1.29	1.45	1.21	1.55	1.12	1.66	1.04	1.77	0.95	1.89
26	1.30	1.46	1.22	1.55	1.14	1.65	1.06	1.76	0.98	1.88
27	1.32	1.47	1.24	1.56	1.16	1.65	1.08	1.76	1.01	1.86
28	1.33	1.48	1.26	1.56	1.18	1.65	1.10	1.75	1.03	1.85
29	1.34	1.48	1.27	1.56	1.20	1.65	1.12	1.74	1.05	1.84
30	1.35	1.49	1.28	1.57	1.21	1.65	1.14	1.74	1.07	1.83
31	1.36	1.50	1.30	1.57	1.23	1.65	1.16	1.74	1.09	1.83
32	1.37	1.50	1.31	1.57	1.24	1.65	1.18	1.73	1.11	1.82
33	1.38	1.51	1.32	1.58	1.26	1.65	1.19	1.73	1.13	1.81
34	1.39	1.51	1.33	1.58	1.27	1.65	1.21	1.73	1.15	1.81
35	1.40	1.52	1.34	1.58	1.28	1.65	1.22	1.73	1.16	1.80
36	1.41	1.52	1.35	1.59	1.29	1.65	1.24	1.73	1.18	1.80
37	1.42	1.53	1.36	1.59	1.31	1.66	1.25	1.72	1.19	1.80
38	1.43	1.54	1.37	1.59	1.32	1.66	1.26	1.72	1.21	1.79
39	1.43	1.54	1.38	1.60	1.33	1.66	1.27	1.72	1.22	1.79
40	1.44	1.54	1.39	1.60	1.34	1.66	1.29	1.72	1.23	1.79
45	1.48	1.57	1.43	1.62	1.38	1.67	1.34	1.72	1.29	1.78
50	1.50	1.59	1.46	1.63	1.42	1.67	1.38	1.72	1.34	1.77
55	1.53	1.60	1.49	1.64	1.45	1.68	1.41	1.72	1.38	1.77
60	1.55	1.62	1.51	1.65	1.48	1.69	1.44	1.73	1.41	1.77
65	1.57	1.63	1.54	1.66	1.50	1.70	1.47	1.73	1.44	1.77
70	1.58	1.64	1.55	1.67	1.52	1.70	1.49	1.74	1.46	1.77
75	1.60	1.65	1.57	1.68	1.54	1.71	1.51	1.74	1.49	1.77
80	1.61	1.66	1.59	1.69	1.56	1.72	1.53	1.74	1.51	1.77
85	1.62	1.67	1.60	1.70	1.57	1.72	1.55	1.75	1.52	1.77
90	1.63	1.68	1.61	1.70	1.59	1.73	1.57	1.75	1.54	1.78
95	1.64	1.69	1.62	1.71	1.60	1.73	1.58	1.75	1.56	1.78
100	1.65	1.69	1.63	1.72	1.61	1.74	1.59	1.76	1.57	1.78

Note: K = the number of slope parameters in the model.

Source: From J. Durbin and G. S. Watson, "Testing for Serial Correlation in Least Squares Regression, II." *Biometrika* 38 (1951): 159–178.

GLOSSARY

A priori probability A probability based on logical analysis rather than on observation or personal judgment.

Absolute dispersion The amount of variability present without comparison to any reference point or benchmark.

Absolute frequency The actual number of observations counted for each unique value of the variable (also called raw frequency).

Accuracy The percentage of correctly predicted classes out of total predictions. It is an overall performance metric in classification problems.

Activation function A functional part of a neural network's node that transforms the total net input received into the final output of the node. The activation function operates like a light dimmer switch that decreases or increases the strength of the input.

Active factor risk The contribution to active risk squared resulting from the portfolio's different-than-benchmark exposures relative to factors specified in the risk model.

Active return The return on a portfolio minus the return on the portfolio's benchmark.

Active risk squared The variance of active returns; active risk raised to the second power.

Active risk The standard deviation of active returns.

Active share A measure of how similar a portfolio is to its benchmark. A manager who precisely replicates the benchmark will have an active share of zero; a manager with no holdings in common with the benchmark will have an active share of one.

Active specific risk The contribution to active risk squared resulting from the portfolio's active weights on individual assets as those weights interact with assets' residual risk.

Addition rule for probabilities A principle stating that the probability that A or B occurs (both occur) equals the probability that A occurs, plus the probability that B occurs, minus the probability that both A and B occur.

Adjusted R^2 A measure of goodness-of-fit of a regression that is adjusted for degrees of freedom and hence does not automatically increase when another independent variable is added to a regression.

Agglomerative clustering A bottom-up hierarchical clustering method that begins with each observation being treated as its own cluster. The algorithm finds the two closest clusters, based on some measure of distance (similarity), and combines them into one new larger cluster. This process is repeated iteratively until all observations are clumped into a single large cluster.

Analysis of variance (ANOVA) The analysis of the total variability of a dataset (such as observations on the dependent variable in a regression) into components representing different sources of variation. With reference to regression, ANOVA provides the inputs for an F-test of the significance of the regression as a whole.

Annual percentage rate The cost of borrowing expressed as a yearly rate.

Annuity due An annuity having a first cash flow that is paid immediately.

Annuity A finite set of level sequential cash flows.

Application programming interface (API) A set of well-defined methods of communication between various software components and typically used for accessing external data.

Arbitrage opportunity An opportunity to conduct an arbitrage; an opportunity to earn an expected positive net profit without risk and with no net investment of money.

Arbitrage portfolio   The portfolio that exploits an arbitrage opportunity.

Arbitrage   (1) The simultaneous purchase of an undervalued asset or portfolio and sale of an over-valued but equivalent asset or portfolio in order to obtain a riskless profit on the price differential. Taking advantage of a market inefficiency in a risk-free manner. (2) The condition in a financial market in which equivalent assets or combinations of assets sell for two different prices, creating an opportunity to profit at no risk with no commitment of money. In a well-functioning financial market, few arbitrage opportunities are possible. (3) A risk-free operation that earns an expected positive net profit but requires no net investment of money.

Arithmetic mean   The sum of the observations divided by the number of observations.

Asian call option   A European-style option with a value at maturity equal to the difference between the stock price at maturity and the average stock price during the life of the option, or $0, whichever is greater.

Autocorrelations   The correlations of a time series with its own past values.

Autoregressive model (AR)   A time series regressed on its own past values in which the independent variable is a lagged value of the dependent variable.

Backtesting   The process that approximates the real-life investment process, using historical data, to assess whether an investment strategy would have produced desirable results.

Backward propagation   The process of adjusting weights in a neural network, to reduce total error of the network, by moving backward through the network's layers.

Bag-of-words (BOW)   A collection of a distinct set of tokens from all the texts in a sample dataset. BOW does not capture the position or sequence of words present in the text.

Bar chart   A chart for plotting the frequency distribution of categorical data, where each bar represents a distinct category and each bar's height is proportional to the frequency of the corresponding category. In technical analysis, a bar chart that plots four bits of data for each time interval—the high, low, opening, and closing prices. A vertical line connects the high and low prices. A cross-hatch left indicates the opening price and a cross-hatch right indicates the closing price.

Base error   Model error due to randomness in the data.

Bernoulli random variable   A random variable having the outcomes 0 and 1.

Bernoulli trial   An experiment that can produce one of two outcomes.

Bias error   Describes the degree to which a model fits the training data. Algorithms with erroneous assumptions produce high bias error with poor approximation, causing underfitting and high in-sample error.

Bimodal   A distribution that has two most frequently occurring values.

Binomial model   A model for pricing options in which the underlying price can move to only one of two possible new prices.

Binomial random variable   The number of successes in n Bernoulli trials for which the probability of success is constant for all trials and the trials are independent.

Binomial tree   The graphical representation of a model of asset price dynamics in which, at each period, the asset moves up with probability p or down with probability $(1 - p)$.

Bootstrap aggregating (or bagging)   A technique whereby the original training dataset is used to generate n new training datasets or bags of data. Each new bag of data is generated by random sampling with replacement from the initial training set.

Bootstrapping   Random sampling with replacement; it is often used in investment research since the number of simulations needed is often larger than the size of historical dataset.

Box and whisker plot   A graphic for visualizing the dispersion of data across quartiles. It consists of a "box" with "whiskers" connected to the box.

Breusch–Pagan test   A test for conditional heteroskedasticity in the error term of a regression.

Bubble line chart   A line chart that uses varying-sized bubbles to represent a third dimension of the data. The bubbles are sometimes color-coded to present additional information.

Cash flow additivity principle   The principle that dollar amounts indexed at the same point in time are additive.

Categorical data Values that describe a quality or characteristic of a group of observations and therefore can be used as labels to divide a dataset into groups to summarize and visualize (also called **qualitative data**).

Categorical dependent variables An alternative term for qualitative dependent variables.

Ceiling analysis A systematic process of evaluating different components in the pipeline of model building. It helps to understand what part of the pipeline can potentially improve in performance by further tuning.

Centroid The center of a cluster formed using the k-means clustering algorithm.

Chain rule of forecasting A forecasting process in which the next period's value as predicted by the forecasting equation is substituted into the right-hand side of the equation to give a predicted value two periods ahead.

Chi-square test of independence A statistical test for detecting a potential association between categorical variables.

Classification and regression tree A supervised machine learning technique that can be applied to predict either a categorical target variable, producing a classification tree, or a continuous target variable, producing a regression tree. CART is commonly applied to binary classification or regression.

Cluster A subset of observations from a dataset such that all the observations within the same cluster are deemed "similar."

Clustered bar chart see **grouped bar chart**.

Clustering The sorting of observations into groups (clusters) such that observations in the same cluster are more similar to each other than they are to observations in other clusters.

Coefficient of variation The ratio of a set of observations' standard deviation to the observations' mean value.

Cointegrated Describes two time series that have a long-term financial or economic relationship such that they do not diverge from each other without bound in the long run.

Collection frequency (CF) The number of times a given word appears in the whole corpus (i.e., collection of sentences) divided by the total number of words in the corpus.

Combination A listing in which the order of the listed items does not matter.

Common size statements Financial statements in which all elements (accounts) are stated as a percentage of a key figure, such as revenue for an income statement or total assets for a balance sheet.

Company fundamental factors Factors related to the company's internal performance, such as factors relating to earnings growth, earnings variability, earnings momentum, and financial leverage.

Company share-related factors Valuation measures and other factors related to share price or the trading characteristics of the shares, such as earnings yield, dividend yield, and book-to-market value.

Complements Goods that tend to be used together; technically, two goods whose cross-price elasticity of demand is negative.

Complexity A term referring to the number of features, parameters, or branches in a model and to whether the model is linear or non-linear (non-linear is more complex).

Composite variable A variable that combines two or more variables that are statistically strongly related to each other.

Compounding The process of accumulating interest on interest.

Conditional expected value The expected value of a stated event given that another event has occurred.

Conditional heteroskedasticity Heteroskedasticity in the error variance that is correlated with the values of the independent variable(s) in the regression.

Conditional probability The probability of an event given (conditioned on) another event.

Conditional VaR (CVaR) The weighted average of all loss outcomes in the statistical (i.e., return) distribution that exceed the VaR loss. Thus, CVaR is a more comprehensive measure of tail loss than VaR is. Sometimes referred to as the *expected tail loss* or *expected shortfall*.

Conditional variances The variance of one variable, given the outcome of another.

Confusion matrix A grid used for error analysis in classification problems, it presents values for four evaluation metrics including true positive (TP), false positive (FP), true negative (TN), and false negative (FN).

Consistent With reference to estimators, describes an estimator for which the probability of estimates close to the value of the population parameter increases as sample size increases.

Contingency table A tabular format that displays the frequency distributions of two or more categorical variables simultaneously and is used for finding patterns between the variables. A contingency table for two categorical variables is also known as a two-way table.

Continuous data Data that can be measured and can take on any numerical value in a specified range of values.

Continuous random variable A random variable for which the range of possible outcomes is the real line (all real numbers between $-\infty$ and $+\infty$ or some subset of the real line).

Continuous time Time thought of as advancing in extremely small increments.

Continuously compounded return The natural logarithm of 1 plus the holding period return, or equivalently, the natural logarithm of the ending price over the beginning price.

Convexity A measure of how interest rate sensitivity changes with a change in interest rates.

Corpus A collection of text data in any form, including list, matrix, or data table forms.

Correlation A measure of the linear relationship between two random variables.

Cost averaging The periodic investment of a fixed amount of money.

Covariance matrix A matrix or square array whose entries are covariances; also known as a variance–covariance matrix.

Covariance stationary Describes a time series when its expected value and variance are constant and finite in all periods and when its covariance with itself for a fixed number of periods in the past or future is constant and finite in all periods.

Cross-sectional data A list of the observations of a specific variable from multiple observational units at a given point in time. The observational units can be individuals, groups, companies, trading markets, regions, etc.

Cross-validation A technique for estimating out-of-sample error directly by determining the error in validation samples.

Cumulative absolute frequency Cumulates (i.e., adds up) in a frequency distribution the absolute frequencies as one moves from the first bin to the last bin.

Cumulative distribution function A function giving the probability that a random variable is less than or equal to a specified value.

Cumulative frequency distribution chart A chart that plots either the cumulative absolute frequency or the cumulative relative frequency on the y-axis against the upper limit of the interval and allows one to see the number or the percentage of the observations that lie below a certain value.

Cumulative relative frequency A sequence of partial sums of the relative frequencies in a frequency distribution.

Data mining The practice of determining a model by extensive searching through a dataset for statistically significant patterns. Also called *data snooping*.

Data preparation (cleansing) The process of examining, identifying, and mitigating (i.e., cleansing) errors in raw data.

Data snooping The subconscious or conscious manipulation of data in a way that produces a statistically significant result (i.e., the p-value is sufficiently small or the t-statistic is sufficiently large to indicate statistical significance), such as by running multiple simulations and naively accepting the best result.

Data table see **two-dimensional rectangular array**.

Data wrangling (preprocessing) This task performs transformations and critical processing steps on cleansed data to make the data ready for ML model training (i.e., preprocessing), and includes dealing with outliers, extracting useful variables from existing data points, and scaling the data.

Data A collection of numbers, characters, words, and text—as well as images, audio, and video—in a raw or organized format to represent facts or information.

Deciles Quantiles that divide a distribution into 10 equal parts.

Deep learning Algorithms based on deep neural networks, ones with many hidden layers (more than two), that address highly complex tasks, such as image classification, face recognition, speech recognition, and natural language processing.

Deep neural networks Neural networks with many hidden layers—at least 2 but potentially more than 20—that have proven successful across a wide range of artificial intelligence applications.

Default risk premium An extra return that compensates investors for the possibility that the borrower will fail to make a promised payment at the contracted time and in the contracted amount.

Degree of confidence The probability that a confidence interval includes the unknown population parameter.

Degrees of freedom (df) The number of independent observations used.

Delta The relationship between the option price and the underlying price, which reflects the sensitivity of the price of the option to changes in the price of the underlying. Delta is a good approximation of how an option price will change for a small change in the stock.

Dendrogram A type of tree diagram used for visualizing a hierarchical cluster analysis; it highlights the hierarchical relationships among the clusters.

Dependent variable The variable whose variation about its mean is to be explained by the regression; the left-hand-side variable in a regression equation.

Dependent With reference to events, the property that the probability of one event occurring depends on (is related to) the occurrence of another event.

Descriptive statistics Measures that summarize central tendency and spread variation in the data's distribution.

Diffuse prior The assumption of equal prior probabilities.

Dimension reduction A set of techniques for reducing the number of features in a dataset while retaining variation across observations to preserve the information contained in that variation.

Discount To reduce the value of a future payment in allowance for how far away it is in time; to calculate the present value of some future amount. Also, the amount by which an instrument is priced below its face (par) value.

Discrete data Numerical values that result from a counting process; therefore, practically speaking, the data are limited to a finite number of values.

Discrete random variable A random variable that can take on at most a countable number of possible values.

Discriminant analysis A multivariate classification technique used to discriminate between groups, such as companies that either will or will not become bankrupt during some time frame.

Dispersion The variability of a population or sample of observations around the central tendency.

Divisive clustering A top-down hierarchical clustering method that starts with all observations belonging to a single large cluster. The observations are then divided into two clusters based on some measure of distance (similarity). The algorithm then progressively partitions the intermediate clusters into smaller ones until each cluster contains only one observation.

Document frequency (DF) The number of documents (texts) that contain a particular token divided by the total number of documents. It is the simplest feature selection method and often performs well when many thousands of tokens are present.

Document term matrix (DTM) A matrix where each row belongs to a document (or text file), and each column represents a token (or term). The number of rows is equal to the number of documents (or text files) in a sample text dataset. The number of columns is equal to the number of tokens from the BOW built using all the documents in the sample dataset. The cells typically contain the counts of the number of times a token is present in each document.

Down transition probability The probability that an asset's value moves down in a model of asset price dynamics.

Downside risk Risk of incurring returns below a specified value.

Dummy variable A type of qualitative variable that takes on a value of 1 if a particular condition is true and 0 if that condition is false. Also known as a categorical variable, binary variable or qualitative variable.

Duration A measure of the approximate sensitivity of a security to a change in interest rates (i.e., a measure of interest rate risk).

Dutch Book theorem A result in probability theory stating that inconsistent probabilities create profit opportunities.

Effective annual rate The amount by which a unit of currency will grow in a year with interest on interest included.

Eigenvalue A measure that gives the proportion of total variance in the initial dataset that is explained by each eigenvector.

Eigenvector A vector that defines new mutually uncorrelated composite variables that are linear combinations of the original features.

Empirical probability The probability of an event estimated as a relative frequency of occurrence.

Ensemble learning A technique of combining the predictions from a collection of models to achieve a more accurate prediction.

Ensemble method The method of combining multiple learning algorithms, as in ensemble learning.

Error autocorrelations The autocorrelations of the error term.

Error term The portion of the dependent variable that is not explained by the independent variable(s) in the regression.

Estimate The particular value calculated from sample observations using an estimator.

Estimated parameters With reference to a regression analysis, the estimated values of the population intercept and population slope coefficients in a regression.

Estimation With reference to statistical inference, the subdivision dealing with estimating the value of a population parameter.

Estimator An estimation formula; the formula used to compute the sample mean and other sample statistics are examples of estimators.

European-style options Said of an option contract that can only be exercised on the option's expiration date.

Event Any outcome or specified set of outcomes of a random variable.

Ex ante **tracking error** A measure of the degree to which the performance of a given investment portfolio might be expected to deviate from its benchmark; also known as *relative VaR*.

Excess kurtosis Degree of kurtosis (fatness of tails) relative to the kurtosis of the normal distribution.

Exhaustive Covering or containing all possible outcomes.

Expected shortfall See *conditional VaR*.

Expected tail loss See *conditional VaR*.

Expected value The probability-weighted average of the possible outcomes of a random variable.

Exploratory data analysis (EDA) The preliminary step in data exploration, where graphs, charts, and other visualizations (heat maps and word clouds) as well as quantitative methods (descriptive statistics and central tendency measures) are used to observe and summarize data.

F1 score The harmonic mean of precision and recall. F1 score is a more appropriate overall performance metric (than accuracy) when there is unequal class distribution in the dataset and it is necessary to measure the equilibrium of precision and recall.

Face value The amount of cash payable by a company to the bondholders when the bonds mature; the promised payment at maturity separate from any coupon payment.

Factor portfolio See *pure factor portfolio*.

Factor price The expected return in excess of the risk-free rate for a portfolio with a sensitivity of 1 to one factor and a sensitivity of 0 to all other factors.

Factor risk premium The expected return in excess of the risk-free rate for a portfolio with a sensitivity of 1 to one factor and a sensitivity of 0 to all other factors. Also called *factor price*.

Factor A common or underlying element with which several variables are correlated.

Fat-tailed Describes a distribution that has fatter tails than a normal distribution (also called leptokurtic).

Feature engineering A process of creating new features by changing or transforming existing features.

Feature selection A process whereby only pertinent features from the dataset are selected for model training. Selecting fewer features decreases model complexity and training time.

Features The independent variables (X's) in a labeled dataset.

Financial risk The risk that environmental, social, or governance risk factors will result in significant costs or other losses to a company and its shareholders; the risk arising from a company's obligation to meet required payments under its financing agreements.

First-differencing A transformation that subtracts the value of the time series in period $t - 1$ from its value in period t.

First-order serial correlation Correlation between adjacent observations in a time series.

Fitted parameters With reference to a regression analysis, the estimated values of the population intercept and population slope coefficients in a regression.

Fitting curve A curve which shows in- and out-of-sample error rates (E_{in} and E_{out}) on the y-axis plotted against model complexity on the x-axis.

Forward propagation The process of adjusting weights in a neural network, to reduce total error of the network, by moving forward through the network's layers.

Fractile A value at or below which a stated fraction of the data lies. Also called quantile.

Frequency analysis The process of quantifying how important tokens are in a sentence and in the corpus as a whole. It helps in filtering unnecessary tokens (or features).

Frequency distribution A tabular display of data constructed either by counting the observations of a variable by distinct values or groups or by tallying the values of a numerical variable into a set of numerically ordered bins (also called a one-way table).

Frequency polygon A graph of a frequency distribution obtained by drawing straight lines joining successive points representing the class frequencies.

Fundamental factor models A multifactor model in which the factors are attributes of stocks or companies that are important in explaining cross-sectional differences in stock prices.

Future value (FV) The amount to which a payment or series of payments will grow by a stated future date.

Gamma A measure of how sensitive an option's delta is to a change in the underlying. The change in a given instrument's delta for a given small change in the underlying's value, holding everything else constant.

Generalized least squares A regression estimation technique that addresses heteroskedasticity of the error term.

Generalize When a model retains its explanatory power when predicting out-of-sample (i.e., using new data).

Geometric mean A measure of central tendency computed by taking the nth root of the product of n non-negative values.

Grid search A method of systematically training a model by using various combinations of hyper-parameter values, cross validating each model, and determining which combination of hyper-parameter values ensures the best model performance.

Ground truth The known outcome (i.e., target variable) of each observation in a labelled dataset.

Grouped bar chart A bar chart for showing joint frequencies for two categorical variables (also known as a **clustered bar chart**).

Harmonic mean A type of weighted mean computed as the reciprocal of the arithmetic average of the reciprocals.

Heat map A type of graphic that organizes and summarizes data in a tabular format and represents it using a color spectrum.

Heteroskedastic With reference to the error term of regression, having a variance that differs across observations.

Heteroskedasticity-consistent standard errors   Standard errors of the estimated parameters of a regression that correct for the presence of heteroskedasticity in the regression's error term.

Heteroskedasticity   The property of having a nonconstant variance; refers to an error term with the property that its variance differs across observations.

Hierarchical clustering   An iterative unsupervised learning procedure used for building a hierarchy of clusters.

Histogram   A chart that presents the distribution of numerical data by using the height of a bar or column to represent the absolute frequency of each bin or interval in the distribution.

Historical simulation   A simulation method that uses past return data and a random number generator that picks observations from the historical series to simulate an asset's future returns.

Holdout samples   Data samples that are not used to train a model.

Homoskedasticity   The property of having a constant variance; refers to an error term that is constant across observations.

Hyperparameter   A parameter whose value must be set by the researcher before learning begins.

Hypothesis testing   With reference to statistical inference, the subdivision dealing with the testing of hypotheses about one or more populations.

Hypothesis   With reference to statistical inference, a statement about one or more populations.

Incremental VaR (IVaR)   A measure of the incremental effect of an asset on the VaR of a portfolio by measuring the difference between the portfolio's VaR while including a specified asset and the portfolio's VaR with that asset eliminated.

Independent variable   A variable used to explain the dependent variable in a regression; a right-hand-side variable in a regression equation.

Independent   With reference to events, the property that the occurrence of one event does not affect the probability of another event occurring.

Independently and identically distributed (IID)   With respect to random variables, the property of random variables that are independent of each other but follow the identical probability distribution.

Indexing   An investment strategy in which an investor constructs a portfolio to mirror the performance of a specified index.

Inflation premium   An extra return that compensates investors for expected inflation.

Information gain   A metric which quantifies the amount of information that the feature holds about the response. Information gain can be regarded as a form of non-linear correlation between Y and X.

Information ratio   (IR) Mean active return divided by active risk; or alpha divided by the standard deviation of diversifiable risk.

In-sample forecast errors   The residuals from a fitted time-series model within the sample period used to fit the model.

Interest rate   A rate of return that reflects the relationship between differently dated cash flows; a discount rate.

Intergenerational data mining   A form of data mining that applies information developed by previous researchers using a dataset to guide current research using the same or a related dataset.

Interquartile range   The difference between the third and first quartiles of a dataset.

Interval   With reference to grouped data, a set of values within which an observation falls.

Inverse transformation method   A process for converting a randomly generated uniformly distributed number into a simulated value of a random variable of the desired distribution.

Joint frequencies   The entry in the cells of the contingency table that represent the joining of one variable from a row and the other variable from a column to count observations.

Joint probability function   A function giving the probability of joint occurrences of values of stated random variables.

Joint probability   The probability of the joint occurrence of stated events.

K-fold cross-validation A technique in which data (excluding test sample and fresh data) are shuffled randomly and then are divided into k equal sub-samples, with $k - 1$ samples used as training samples and one sample, the kth, used as a validation sample.

K-means A clustering algorithm that repeatedly partitions observations into a fixed number, k, of non-overlapping clusters.

K-nearest neighbor A supervised learning technique that classifies a new observation by finding similarities ("nearness") between this new observation and the existing data.

kth-order autocorrelation The correlation between observations in a time series separated by k periods.

Kurtosis The statistical measure that indicates the combined weight of the tails of a distribution relative to the rest of the distribution.

Labeled dataset A dataset that contains matched sets of observed inputs or features (Xs) and the associated output or target (Y).

LASSO Least Absolute Shrinkage and Selection Operator is a type of penalized regression which involves minimizing the sum of the absolute values of the regression coefficients. LASSO can also be used for regularization in neural networks.

Learning curve A curve that plots the accuracy rate (= 1 − error rate) in the validation or test samples (i.e., out-of-sample) against the amount of data in the training sample, which is thus useful for describing under- and overfitting as a function of bias and variance errors.

Learning rate A parameter that affects the magnitude of adjustments in the weights in a neural network.

Leptokurtic Describes a distribution that has fatter tails than a normal distribution (also called fat-tailed).

Level of significance The probability of a Type I error in testing a hypothesis.

Likelihood The probability of an observation, given a particular set of conditions.

Line chart A type of graph used to visualize ordered observations. In technical analysis, a plot of price data, typically closing prices, with a line connecting the points.

Linear classifier A binary classifier that makes its classification decision based on a linear combination of the features of each data point.

Linear interpolation The estimation of an unknown value on the basis of two known values that bracket it, using a straight line between the two known values.

Linear regression Regression that models the straight-line relationship between the dependent and independent variables.

Linear trend A trend in which the dependent variable changes at a constant rate with time.

Liquidity premium An extra return that compensates investors for the risk of loss relative to an investment's fair value if the investment needs to be converted to cash quickly.

Logistic regression (logit model) A qualitative-dependent-variable multiple regression model based on the logistic probability distribution.

Log-linear model With reference to time-series models, a model in which the growth rate of the time series as a function of time is constant.

Log-log regression model A regression that expresses the dependent and independent variables as natural logarithms.

Longitudinal data Observations on characteristic(s) of the same observational unit through time.

Look-ahead bias A bias caused by using information that was unavailable on the test date.

Look-ahead bias The bias created by using information that was unknown or unavailable in the time periods over which backtesting is conducted. Survivorship bias is a type of look-ahead bias.

Lookback period The time period used to gather a historical data set.

Lower bound The lowest possible value of an option.

Macroeconomic factor model A multifactor model in which the factors are surprises in macroeconomic variables that significantly explain equity returns.

Macroeconomic factors Factors related to the economy, such as the inflation rate, industrial production, or economic sector membership.

Majority-vote classifier A classifier that assigns to a new data point the predicted label with the most votes (i.e., occurrences).

Marginal frequencies The sums determined by adding joint frequencies across rows or across columns in a contingency table.

Marginal probability The probability of an event *not* conditioned on another event.

Marginal VaR (MVaR) A measure of the effect of a small change in a position size on portfolio VaR.

Market timing Asset allocation in which the investment in the market is increased if one forecasts that the market will outperform T-bills.

Maturity premium An extra return that compensates investors for the increased sensitivity of the market value of debt to a change in market interest rates as maturity is extended.

Maximum drawdown The worst cumulative loss ever sustained by an asset or portfolio. More specifically, maximum drawdown is the difference between an asset's or a portfolio's maximum cumulative return and its subsequent lowest cumulative return.

Mean absolute deviation With reference to a sample, the mean of the absolute values of deviations from the sample mean.

Mean reversion The tendency of a time series to fall when its level is above its mean and rise when its level is below its mean; a mean-reverting time series tends to return to its long-term mean.

Mean–variance analysis An approach to portfolio analysis using expected means, variances, and covariances of asset returns.

Measure of central tendency A quantitative measure that specifies where data are centered.

Measures of location Quantitative measures that describe the location or distribution of data. They include not only measures of central tendency but also other measures, such as percentiles.

Median The value of the middle item of a set of items that has been sorted into ascending or descending order (i.e., the 50th percentile).

Mesokurtic Describes a distribution with kurtosis equal to that of the normal distribution, namely, kurtosis equal to three.

Metadata Data that describes and gives information about other data.

Modal interval With reference to grouped data, the interval containing the greatest number of observations (i.e., highest frequency).

Mode The most frequently occurring value in a distribution.

Model specification With reference to regression, the set of variables included in the regression and the regression equation's functional form.

Monetary policy Actions taken by a nation's central bank to affect aggregate output and prices through changes in bank reserves, reserve requirements, or its target interest rate.

Monte Carlo simulation A technique that converts a randomly generated uniformly distributed number into a simulated value of a random variable of a desired distribution. Each key decision variable in a Monte Carlo simulation requires an assumed statistical distribution; this facilitates incorporating non-normality, fat tails, and tail dependence and solving high-dimensionality problems.

Multicollinearity A regression assumption violation that occurs when two or more independent variables (or combinations of independent variables) are highly but not perfectly correlated with each other.

Multiple linear regression Linear regression involving two or more independent variables.

Multiplication rule for probabilities The rule that the joint probability of events A and B equals the probability of A given B times the probability of B.

Multivariate distribution A probability distribution that specifies the probabilities for a group of related random variables.

Multivariate normal distribution A probability distribution for a group of random variables that is completely defined by the means and variances of the variables plus all the correlations between pairs of the variables.

Mutual information Measures how much information is contributed by a token to a class of texts. MI will be 0 if the token's distribution in all text classes is the same. MI approaches 1 as the token in any one class tends to occur more often in only that particular class of text.

n Factorial For a positive integer n, the product of the first n positive integers; 0 factorial equals 1 by definition. n factorial is written as $n!$.

Name entity recognition An algorithm that analyzes individual tokens and their surrounding semantics while referring to its dictionary to tag an object class to the token.

Negative serial correlation Serial correlation in which a positive error for one observation increases the chance of a negative error for another observation, and vice versa.

Neural networks Highly flexible machine learning algorithms that have been successfully applied to a variety of supervised and unsupervised tasks characterized by non-linearities and interactions among features.

N-grams A representation of word sequences. The length of a sequence varies from 1 to N. When one word is used, it is a unigram; a two-word sequence is a bigram; and a 3-word sequence is a trigram; and so on.

Node Each value on a binomial tree from which successive moves or outcomes branch.

Nominal data Categorical values that are not amenable to being organized in a logical order. An example of nominal data is the classification of publicly listed stocks into sectors.

Nominal risk-free interest rate The sum of the real risk-free interest rate and the inflation premium.

Nonparametric test A test that is not concerned with a parameter, or that makes minimal assumptions about the population from which a sample comes.

Nonstationarity With reference to a random variable, the property of having characteristics, such as mean and variance, that are not constant through time.

n-Period moving average The average of the current and immediately prior $n - 1$ values of a time series.

Numerical data Values that represent measured or counted quantities as a number. Also called **quantitative data.**

Objective probabilities Probabilities that generally do not vary from person to person; includes a priori and objective probabilities.

Observation The value of a specific variable collected at a point in time or over a specified period of time.

One hot encoding The process by which categorical variables are converted into binary form (0 or 1) for machine reading. It is one of the most common methods for handling categorical features in text data.

One-dimensional array The simplest format for representing a collection of data of the same data type.

One-sided hypothesis test A test in which the null hypothesis is rejected only if the evidence indicates that the population parameter is greater than (smaller than) θ_0. The alternative hypothesis also has one side.

One-tailed hypothesis test A test in which the null hypothesis is rejected only if the evidence indicates that the population parameter is greater than (smaller than) θ_0. The alternative hypothesis also has one side.

Opportunity cost The value that investors forgo by choosing a particular course of action; the value of something in its best alternative use.

Ordinal data Categorical values that can be logically ordered or ranked.

Ordinary annuity An annuity with a first cash flow that is paid one period from the present.

Outcome A possible value of a random variable.

Out-of-sample forecast errors The differences between actual and predicted values of time series outside the sample period used to fit the model.

Out-of-sample test A test of a strategy or model using a sample outside the time period on which the strategy or model was developed.

Overfitting When a model fits the training data too well and so does not generalize well to new data.

Paired comparisons test   A statistical test for differences based on paired observations drawn from samples that are dependent on each other.

Paired observations   Observations that are dependent on each other.

Pairs arbitrage trade   A trade in two closely related stocks involving the short sale of one and the purchase of the other.

Panel data   A mix of time-series and cross-sectional data that contains observations through time on characteristics of across multiple observational units.

Parameter   A descriptive measure computed from or used to describe a population of data, conventionally represented by Greek letters.

Parametric method   A method of estimating VaR that uses the historical mean, standard deviation, and correlation of security price movements to estimate the portfolio VaR. Generally assumes a normal distribution but can be adapted to non-normal distributions with the addition of skewness and kurtosis. Sometimes called the *variance–covariance method* or the *analytical method*.

Parametric test   Any test (or procedure) concerned with parameters or whose validity depends on assumptions concerning the population generating the sample.

Partial regression coefficients   The slope coefficients in a multiple regression. Also called *partial slope coefficients*.

Partial slope coefficients   The slope coefficients in a multiple regression. Also called *partial regression coefficients*.

Parts of speech   An algorithm that uses language structure and dictionaries to tag every token in the text with a corresponding part of speech (i.e., noun, verb, adjective, proper noun, etc.).

Pearson IC   The simple correlation coefficient between the factor scores for such factors as earnings yield or momentum.

Penalized regression   A regression that includes a constraint such that the regression coefficients are chosen to minimize the sum of squared residuals *plus* a penalty term that increases in size with the number of included features.

Percentiles   Quantiles that divide a distribution into 100 equal parts that sum to 100.

Permutation   An ordered listing.

Perpetuity   A perpetual annuity, or a set of never-ending level sequential cash flows, with the first cash flow occurring one period from now. A bond that does not mature.

Platykurtic   Describes a distribution that has relatively less weight in the tails than the normal distribution (also called thin-tailed).

Point estimate   A single numerical estimate of an unknown quantity, such as a population parameter.

Point-in-time data   Data consisting of the exact information that was available to market participants as of a given point in time.

Population   All members of a specified group.

Positive serial correlation   Serial correlation in which a positive error for one observation increases the chance of a positive error for another observation; a negative error for one observation increases the chance of a negative error for another observation.

Posterior probability   An updated probability that reflects or comes after new information.

Power of a test   The probability of correctly rejecting the null—that is, rejecting the null hypothesis when it is false.

Precision   In error analysis for classification problems it is ratio of correctly predicted positive classes to all predicted positive classes. Precision is useful in situations where the cost of false positives (FP), or Type I error, is high.

Present value (PV)   The present discounted value of future cash flows: For assets, the present discounted value of the future net cash inflows that the asset is expected to generate; for liabilities, the present discounted value of the future net cash outflows that are expected to be required to settle the liabilities.

Price relative   A ratio of an ending price over a beginning price; it is equal to 1 plus the holding period return on the asset.

Priced risk   Risk for which investors demand compensation for bearing (e.g., equity risk, company-specific factors, macroeconomic factors).

Principal components analysis (PCA)   An unsupervised ML technique used to transform highly correlated features of data into a few main, uncorrelated composite variables.

Principal   The amount of funds originally invested in a project or instrument; the face value to be paid at maturity.

Prior probabilities   Probabilities reflecting beliefs prior to the arrival of new information.

Probability density function   A function with non-negative values such that probability can be described by areas under the curve graphing the function.

Probability distribution   A distribution that specifies the probabilities of a random variable's possible outcomes.

Probability function   A function that specifies the probability that the random variable takes on a specific value.

Probability   A number between 0 and 1 describing the chance that a stated event will occur.

Projection error   The vertical (perpendicular) distance between a data point and a given principal component.

Pruning   A regularization technique used in CART to reduce the size of the classification or regression tree—by pruning, or removing, sections of the tree that provide little classifying power.

Pseudo-random numbers   Numbers that look random but are actually deterministic. A benefit of using a pseudo-random number generator is that once the seed is fixed, the results can be replicated.

Pure factor portfolio   A portfolio with sensitivity of 1 to the factor in question and a sensitivity of 0 to all other factors.

Qualitative data   see **categorical data**.

Qualitative dependent variables   Dummy variables used as dependent variables rather than as independent variables.

Quantile   A value at or below which a stated fraction of the data lies. Also referred to as a fractile.

Quantitative data   see **numerical data**.

Quartiles   Quantiles that divide a distribution into four equal parts.

Quintiles   Quantiles that divide a distribution into five equal parts.

Quoted interest rate   A quoted interest rate that does not account for compounding within the year. Also called *stated annual interest rate*.

Random forest classifier   A collection of a large number of decision trees trained via a bagging method.

Random number generator   An algorithm that produces uniformly distributed random numbers between 0 and 1.

Random number   An observation drawn from a uniform distribution.

Random variable   A quantity whose future outcomes are uncertain.

Random walk   A time series in which the value of the series in one period is the value of the series in the previous period plus an unpredictable random error.

Range   The difference between the maximum and minimum values in a dataset.

Raw data   Data available in their original form as collected.

Readme files   Text files provided with raw data that contain information related to a data file. They are useful for understanding the data and how they can be interpreted correctly.

Real risk-free interest rate   The single-period interest rate for a completely risk-free security if no inflation were expected.

Recall   Also known as *sensitivity*, in error analysis for classification problems it is the ratio of correctly predicted positive classes to all actual positive classes. Recall is useful in situations where the cost of false negatives (FN), or Type II error, is high.

Regime   With reference to a time series, the underlying model generating the times series.

Regression coefficients   The intercept and slope coefficient(s) of a regression.

Regular expression (regex)   A series of texts that contains characters in a particular order. Regex is used to search for patterns of interest in a given text.

Regularization   A term that describes methods for reducing statistical variability in high-dimensional data estimation problems.

Reinforcement learning   Machine learning in which a computer learns from interacting with itself or data generated by the same algorithm.

Relative dispersion   The amount of dispersion relative to a reference value or benchmark.

Relative frequency   The absolute frequency of each unique value of the variable divided by the total number of observations of the variable.

Relative VaR   See *ex ante tracking error.*

Residual autocorrelations   The sample autocorrelations of the residuals.

Reverse stress testing   A risk management approach in which the user identifies key risk exposures in the portfolio and subjects those exposures to extreme market movements.

Risk budgeting   The allocation of an asset owner's total risk appetite among groups or divisions (in the case of a trading organization) or among strategies and managers (in the case of an institutional or individual investor).

Risk decomposition   The process of converting a set of holdings in a portfolio into a set of exposures to risk factors.

Risk factors   Variables or characteristics with which individual asset returns are correlated. Sometimes referred to simply as *factors.*

Risk parity   A portfolio allocation scheme that weights stocks or factors based on an equal risk contribution.

Risk premium   An extra return expected by investors for bearing some specified risk.

Robust standard errors   Standard errors of the estimated parameters of a regression that correct for the presence of heteroskedasticity in the regression's error term.

Robust   The quality of being relatively unaffected by a violation of assumptions.

Rolling window backtesting   A backtesting method that uses a rolling window (or walk-forward) framework, rebalances the portfolio after each period, and then tracks performance over time. As new information arrives each period, the investment manager optimizes (revises and tunes) the model and readjusts stock positions.

Root mean squared error (RMSE)   The square root of the average squared forecast error; used to compare the out-of-sample forecasting performance of forecasting models.

Rule of 72   The principle that the approximate number of years necessary for an investment to double is 72 divided by the stated interest rate.

Safety-first rules   Rules for portfolio selection that focus on the risk that portfolio value will fall below some minimum acceptable level over some time horizon.

Sample correlation coefficient   A standardized measure of how two variables in a sample move together. It is the ratio of the sample covariance to the product of the two variables' standard deviations.

Sample covariance   A measure of how two variables in a sample move together.

Sample excess kurtosis   A sample measure of the degree of a distribution's kurtosis in excess of the normal distribution's kurtosis.

Sample mean   The sum of the sample observations divided by the sample size.

Sample selection bias   Bias introduced by systematically excluding some members of the population according to a particular attribute—for example, the bias introduced when data availability leads to certain observations being excluded from the analysis.

Sample skewness   A sample measure of the degree of asymmetry of a distribution.

Sample standard deviation   The positive square root of the sample variance.

Sample statistic   A quantity computed from or used to describe a sample.

Sample variance   The sum of squared deviations around the mean divided by the degrees of freedom.

Sample   A subset of a population.

Sampling distribution The distribution of all distinct possible values that a statistic can assume when computed from samples of the same size randomly drawn from the same population.

Sampling error The difference between the observed value of a statistic and the quantity it is intended to estimate.

Sampling plan The set of rules used to select a sample.

Sampling The process of obtaining a sample.

Scaling The process of adjusting the range of a feature by shifting and changing the scale of the data. Two of the most common ways of scaling are normalization and standardization.

Scatter plot A type of graph for visualizing the joint variation in two numerical variables. It is a useful tool for displaying and understanding potential relationships between variables.

Scatter plot matrix A tool for organizing scatter plots between pairs of variables, making it easy to inspect all pairwise relationships in one combined visual.

Scenario analysis Analysis that shows the changes in key financial quantities that result from given (economic) events, such as the loss of customers, the loss of a supply source, or a catastrophic event; a risk management technique involving examination of the performance of a portfolio under specified situations. Closely related to stress testing.

Scree plots A plot that shows the proportion of total variance in the data explained by each principal component.

Seasonality A characteristic of a time series in which the data experience regular and predictable periodic changes; for example, fan sales are highest during the summer months.

Security selection risk See *active specific risk.*

Sensitivity analysis A technique for exploring how a target variable (e.g., portfolio returns) and risk profiles are affected by changes in input variables (e.g., the distribution of asset or factor returns).

Sentence length The number of characters, including spaces, in a sentence.

Serially correlated With reference to regression errors, errors that are correlated across observations.

Sharpe ratio The average return in excess of the risk-free rate divided by the standard deviation of return; a measure of the average excess return earned per unit of standard deviation of return.

Shortfall risk The risk that portfolio value will fall below some minimum acceptable level over some time horizon.

Simple interest The interest earned each period on the original investment; interest calculated on the principal only.

Simple random sample A subset of a larger population created in such a way that each element of the population has an equal probability of being selected to the subset.

Simple random sampling The procedure of drawing a sample to satisfy the definition of a simple random sample.

Simulation trial A complete pass through the steps of a simulation.

Skewed Not symmetrical.

Skewness A quantitative measure of skew (lack of symmetry); a synonym of skew. It is computed as the average cubed deviation from the mean standardized by dividing by the standard deviation cubed.

Soft margin classification An adaptation in the support vector machine algorithm which adds a penalty to the objective function for observations in the training set that are misclassified.

Spearman rank correlation coefficient A measure of correlation applied to ranked data.

Spearman rank IC The Pearson IC between the prior-period ranked factor scores and the ranked current-period returns.

Spurious correlation Refers to: 1) correlation between two variables that reflects chance relationships in a particular dataset; 2) correlation induced by a calculation that mixes each of two variables with a third variable; and 3) correlation between two variables arising not from a direct relation between them but from their relation to a third variable.

Stacked bar chart An alternative form for presenting the frequency distribution of two categorical variables, where bars representing the sub-groups are placed on top of each other to form a single bar. Each sub-section is shown in a different color to represent the contribution of each sub-group, and the overall height of the stacked bar represents the marginal frequency for the category.

Standard deviation   The positive square root of the variance; a measure of dispersion in the same units as the original data.

Standard normal distribution   The normal density with mean (μ) equal to 0 and standard deviation (σ) equal to 1.

Standardized beta   With reference to fundamental factor models, the value of the attribute for an asset minus the average value of the attribute across all stocks, divided by the standard deviation of the attribute across all stocks.

Standardizing   A transformation of a variable that involves subtracting the mean and dividing the result by the standard deviation.

Stated annual interest rate   A quoted interest rate that does not account for compounding within the year. Also called *quoted interest rate*.

Statistical factor model   A multifactor model in which statistical methods are applied to a set of historical returns to determine portfolios that best explain either historical return covariances or variances.

Statistically significant   A result indicating that the null hypothesis can be rejected; with reference to an estimated regression coefficient, frequently understood to mean a result indicating that the corresponding population regression coefficient is different from 0.

Statistic   A summary measure of a sample of observations.

Stop-loss limit   Constraint used in risk management that requires a reduction in the size of a portfolio, or its complete liquidation, when a loss of a particular size occurs in a specified period.

Stress testing   A specific type of scenario analysis that estimates losses in rare and extremely unfavorable combinations of events or scenarios.

Structured data   Data that are highly organized in a pre-defined manner, usually with repeating patterns.

Subjective probability   A probability drawing on personal or subjective judgment.

Summation operator   A functional part of a neural network's node that multiplies each input value received by a weight and sums the weighted values to form the total net input, which is then passed to the activation function.

Supervised learning   Machine learning where algorithms infer patterns between a set of inputs (the Xs) and the desired output (Y). The inferred pattern is then used to map a given input set into a predicted output.

Support vector machine   A linear classifier that determines the hyperplane that optimally separates the observations into two sets of data points.

Survivorship bias   The bias resulting from a test design that fails to account for companies that have gone bankrupt, merged, or are otherwise no longer reported in a database.

Systematic risk   Risk that affects the entire market or economy; it cannot be avoided and is inherent in the overall market. Systematic risk is also known as non-diversifiable or market risk.

Systematic sampling   A procedure of selecting every kth member until reaching a sample of the desired size. The sample that results from this procedure should be approximately random.

Tag cloud   see **word cloud**.

Tail dependence coefficient   A correlation coefficient that focuses on co-movements in the tails of two random variables.

Tail risk   The risk that losses in extreme events could be greater than would be expected for a portfolio of assets with a normal distribution.

Target semideviation   A measure of downside risk, calculated as the square root of the average of the squared deviations of observations below the target (also called target downside deviation).

Target   In machine learning, the dependent variable (Y) in a labeled dataset; the company in a merger or acquisition that is being acquired.

Term frequency (TF)   Ratio of the number of times a given token occurs in all the texts in the dataset to the total number of tokens in the dataset.

Test sample A data sample that is used to test a model's ability to predict well on new data.

Thin-tailed Describes a distribution that has relatively less weight in the tails than the normal distribution (also called platykurtic).

Time series A set of observations on a variable's outcomes in different time periods.

Time value of money The principles governing equivalence relationships between cash flows with different dates.

Time-period bias The possibility that when we use a time-series sample, our statistical conclusion may be sensitive to the starting and ending dates of the sample.

Time-series data A sequence of observations for a single observational unit of a specific variable collected over time and at discrete and typically equally spaced intervals of time (such as daily, weekly, monthly, annually, or quarterly).

Token The equivalent of a word (or sometimes a character).

Tokenization The process of splitting a given text into separate tokens. Tokenization can be performed at the word or character level but is most commonly performed at word level.

Total probability rule for expected value A rule explaining the expected value of a random variable in terms of expected values of the random variable conditional on mutually exclusive and exhaustive scenarios.

Total probability rule A rule explaining the unconditional probability of an event in terms of probabilities of the event conditional on mutually exclusive and exhaustive scenarios.

Tracking error The standard deviation of the differences between a portfolio's returns and its benchmark's returns; a synonym of active risk. Also called *tracking risk*.

Tracking risk The standard deviation of the differences between a portfolio's returns and its benchmark's returns; a synonym of active risk. Also called *tracking error*.

Training sample A data sample that is used to train a model.

Tree diagram A diagram with branches emanating from nodes representing either mutually exclusive chance events or mutually exclusive decisions.

Tree-Map Another graphical tool for displaying categorical data. It consists of a set of colored rectangles to represent distinct groups, and the area of each rectangle is proportional to the value of the corresponding group.

Trend A long-term pattern of movement in a particular direction.

Trimmed mean A mean computed after excluding a stated small percentage of the lowest and highest observations.

Trimming Also called truncation, it is the process of removing extreme values and outliers from a dataset.

Trimodal A distribution that has the three most frequently occurring values.

***t*-Test** A hypothesis test using a statistic (*t*-statistic) that follows a *t*-distribution.

Two-dimensional rectangular array A popular form for organizing data for processing by computers or for presenting data visually. It is comprised of columns and rows to hold multiple variables and multiple observations, respectively (also called a **data table**).

Two-tailed hypothesis test A test in which the null hypothesis is rejected in favor of the alternative hypothesis if the evidence indicates that the population parameter is either smaller or larger than a hypothesized value.

Type I error The error of rejecting a true null hypothesis.

Type II error The error of not rejecting a false null hypothesis.

Unconditional heteroskedasticity Heteroskedasticity of the error term that is not correlated with the values of the independent variable(s) in the regression.

Unconditional probability The probability of an event *not* conditioned on another event.

Unimodal A distribution with a single value that is most frequently occurring.

Unit normal distribution see the standard normal distribution.

Unit root A time series that is not covariance stationary is said to have a unit root.

Univariate distribution A distribution that specifies the probabilities for a single random variable.

Unstructured data Data that do not follow any conventionally organized forms.

Unsupervised learning Machine learning that does not make use of labeled data.

Up transition probability The probability that an asset's value moves up.

Validation sample A data sample that is used to validate and tune a model.

Value at risk (VaR) A money measure of the minimum value of losses expected during a specified time period at a given level of probability.

Variable A characteristic or quantity that can be measured, counted, or categorized and that is subject to change (also called a field, an attribute, or a feature).

Variance error Describes how much a model's results change in response to new data from validation and test samples. Unstable models pick up noise and produce high variance error, causing overfitting and high out-of-sample error.

Variance The expected value (the probability-weighted average) of squared deviations from a random variable's expected value.

Vega The change in a given derivative instrument for a given small change in volatility, holding everything else constant. A sensitivity measure for options that reflects the effect of volatility.

Visualization The presentation of data in a pictorial or graphical format for the purpose of increasing understanding and for gaining insights into the data.

Volatility As used in option pricing, the standard deviation of the continuously compounded returns on the underlying asset.

Web spidering (scraping or crawling) programs Programs that extract raw content from a source, typically web pages.

Weighted mean An average in which each observation is weighted by an index of its relative importance.

White-corrected standard errors A synonym for robust standard errors.

Winsorization The process of replacing extreme values and outliers in a dataset with the maximum (for large value outliers) and minimum (for small value outliers) values of data points that are not outliers.

Winsorized mean A mean computed after assigning a stated percentage of the lowest values equal to one specified low value and a stated percentage of the highest values equal to one specified high value.

Word cloud A visual device for representing textual data, which consists of words extracted from a source of textual data. The size of each distinct word is proportional to the frequency with which it appears in the given text (also known as **tag cloud**).

ABOUT THE AUTHORS

Richard A. DeFusco, CFA, is a professor of finance at the University of Nebraska–Lincoln (UNL). He earned his CFA charter in 1999. A member of CFA Society Nebraska, he also serves on committees for CFA Institute. Dr. DeFusco's primary teaching interest is investments, and he coordinates the Cornhusker Fund, UNL's student-managed investment fund. He has published a number of journal articles, primarily in the field of finance. Dr. DeFusco earned his bachelor's degree in management science from the University of Rhode Island and his doctoral degree in finance from the University of Tennessee–Knoxville.

Dennis W. McLeavey, CFA, is Faculty Advisor to the Ram Fund and Professor Emeritus of Finance and or/MS at the University of Rhode Island. Previously, he served as Vice President of Curriculum Development at CFA Institute and co-authored several texts for use in the CFA Program. He earned his CFA charter in 1990 and his Stanford University Certificate in Strategic Decisions and Risk Management in 2012. His research articles have appeared in *Management Science, Journal of Operations Research, Journal of Portfolio Management*, and other journals. He served as chairperson of the CFA Institute Retirement Investment Policy Committee and as a New York Stock Exchange Arbitrator. After studying economics to earn his bachelor's degree at Western University in 1968, he earned a doctorate in production management and industrial engineering and minor in mathematics, from Indiana University in 1972, with the late John F. Muth as his dissertation chair.

Jerald E. Pinto, CFA, was at CFA Institute from 2002 to 2020 first as a visiting scholar, then as Vice President and, subsequently, Director, Curriculum Projects in the Education Division for the CFA and CIPM Programs. Prior to joining CFA Institute, he worked for nearly two decades in the investment and banking industries in New York City, including as a consultant in investment planning. He was an assistant professor at NYU's Stern School from 1992 to 1994, where he taught MBA and undergraduate investments and financial institution management and received a School of Business award for teaching. He was a co-author of *Quantitative Investment Analysis* and *Equity Asset Valuation*, and a co-editor and co-author of chapters of the third edition of Managing Investment Portfolios: A Dynamic Process, and co-editor of *Investments: Principles of Portfolio and Equity Analysis (2011) and Economics for Investment Decision Makers* (2013) (all published by John Wiley & sons). He holds an MBA from Baruch College, a PhD in finance from the Stern School, and is a member of CFA Virginia.

Eugene L. Podkaminer, CFA, is a senior vice president in the capital markets research group at Callan Associates. He is responsible for assisting clients with their strategic investment planning, conducting asset allocation studies, developing optimal investment manager structures, and providing custom research on a variety of investment topics. Prior to joining Callan in 2010, Mr. Podkaminer spent nearly a decade with Barclays Global investors. As a senior strategist in the Client Advisory Group, he advised some of the world's largest and most sophisticated pension plans, non-profits, and sovereign wealth funds in the areas of strategic asset allocation, liability-driven investing, manager structure optimization, and risk budgeting. As Chief Strategist of Barclays' CIO-outsourcing platform, Mr. Podkaminer executed CIO-level functions for corporate pension plans and endowments.

Mr. Podkaminer received a BA in economics from the University of San Francisco and an MBA from Yale University. He is a member of CFA Institute and CFA Society of San Francisco. He is a frequent speaker on investment related topics, and his work on risk factor allocation and alternative indexes has been featured in numerous publications.

David E. Runkle, CFA, is Director of Quantitative Research for Trilogy Global Advisors, LP. He joined Trilogy in 2007 from Piper Jaffray, where he was an Investment Research Manager. Dr. Runkle has been an award-winning professor in finance, accounting, and economics at Brown University and the University of Minnesota, and has served as a research officer at the Federal Reserve Bank of Minneapolis. In addition to holding a PhD in economics from the Massachusetts Institute of Technology, Dr. Runkle has served on the CFA Institute Curriculum Committee and Corporate Disclosure Policy Committee and on the Financial Accounting Standards Advisory Council.

Sanjiv Sabherwal, PhD, is Associate Professor of Finance and Distinguished Teaching Professor at the University of Texas at Arlington, where he teaches graduate and undergraduate courses in international corporate finance, investments, and financial modeling. He has received several teaching awards and was inducted into the Academy of Distinguished Teachers of the university in 2012. He has been working with CFA Institute as a consultant since 2000. He has published several research articles in journals such as the *Journal of Finance, Journal of Financial and Quantitative Analysis, Journal of Banking and Finance, Financial Review, Journal of Investment Management*, and *Decision Sciences*. He holds a B. Tech. in chemical engineering from the Indian Institute of Technology, New Delhi, an MBA from the University of Miami, and a PhD in finance from Georgia Institute of Technology, Atlanta. Prior to his PhD studies, he worked at an international management consulting firm and contributed to projects sponsored by international funding institutions such as the World Bank and the Danish International Development Agency.

CFA Institute

ABOUT THE
CFA PROGRAM

If the subject matter of this book interests you, and you are not already a CFA Charterholder, we hope you will consider registering for the CFA Program and starting progress toward earning the Chartered Financial Analyst designation. The CFA designation is a globally recognized standard of excellence for measuring the competence and integrity of investment professionals. To earn the CFA charter, candidates must successfully complete the CFA Program, a global graduate-level self-study program that combines a broad curriculum with professional conduct requirements as preparation for a career as an investment professional.

Anchored by a practice-based curriculum, the CFA Program body of knowledge reflects the knowledge, skills, and abilities identified by professionals as essential to the investment decision-making process. This body of knowledge maintains its relevance through a regular, extensive survey of practicing CFA charterholders across the globe. The curriculum covers 10 general topic areas, ranging from equity and fixed-income analysis to portfolio management to corporate finance—all with a heavy emphasis on the application of ethics in professional practice. Known for its rigor and breadth, the CFA Program curriculum highlights principles common to every market so that professionals who earn the CFA designation have a thoroughly global investment perspective and a profound understanding of the global marketplace.

www.cfainstitute.org

885

INDEX

Note: An n after a page number indicates a footnote.

A

Absolute dispersion, 109
Absolute frequency, 57, 60, 70
Acceptance region, 282–283
Accuracy, as metric, 555, 556
Activation function, 577
Active return, 696–698
Active risk
  active factor risk, 701n
  active manager guidelines, 699–700
  active risk squared, 700
  active specific risk, 700
  decomposition of, 700–703
  information ratio, 698–699
  tracking error, 698–699
Active share, 759
Addition rule for probabilities, 155–157
Adjusted R^2, 380–381
Agglomerative clustering, 566, 574–575
  co-movement similarity, 570–573
  dendrograms, 567, 568
Aggregation, 548, 606
AlphaGo program, 579
α (alpha), 280–281, 349, 395, 528, 555
Alternative data, 50–51
Alternative hypothesis, 278–279
American options, 209–210, 210n
Analysis of variance (ANOVA)
  bid–ask spread explained, 3868
  definition, 347
  F-tests, 347–350
  population means and, 287n
  regression analysis (see Regression analysis)
  regression sum of squares, 348
  sum of squared errors, 348
Analyst sentiment, 808
Analytical data, 50
Analytical method of VaR estimation, 720–724
ANNs (artificial neural networks), 531, 575–578

Annualizing, volatility estimation, 226–228, 226n
Annual percentage rate (APR), 12n
Annual percentage yield (APY), 12n
Annual value at risk, 721
Annuities
  annuities due, 14, 21–22
  lump sum as, 35–36
  ordinary annuities, 13–15, 20–24, 26
  perpetuities, 14, 24–26
  solving for payment size, 31–36
ANOVA. see Analysis of variance
Anscombe's Quartet, 130–131
Antilogarithm conversion, 370
Application programming interface (API), 603
APR (annual percentage rate), 12n
A priori probability, 150
APY (annual percentage yield), 12n
Arbitrage pricing theory (APT)
  APT definition, 677
  APT equation, 678–679
  arbitrage definition, 678
  arbitrage opportunity, 678, 680–681
  arbitrage portfolio, 681
  factor risk premium, 678
  pairs arbitrage trade, 151
  parameters, 679–680
  pure factor portfolios, 678
ARCH (autoregressive conditional heteroskedasticity), 497–500, 500n, 506
Area under the curve (AUC), 636–637, 656
Arithmetic average. see Sample mean
Arithmetic mean
  of Bernoulli random variables, 207–208
  of binomial random variables, 207–208
  calculating, for P/Es, 100–101
  Chebyshev's inequality, 213
  definition, 85, 207n
  geometric mean and, 96–98
  measures of central tendency, 85–89
  outliers, 88–89
  population mean, 216, 216n

887